Lecture Notes in Computer Science   12804

More information about this subseries at http://www.springer.com/series/7410

Orr Dunkelman · Michael J. Jacobson, Jr. ·
Colin O'Flynn (Eds.)

Selected Areas in Cryptography

27th International Conference
Halifax, NS, Canada (Virtual Event), October 21–23, 2020
Revised Selected Papers

 Springer

Editors
Orr Dunkelman (iD)
University of Haifa
Haifa, Israel

Michael J. Jacobson, Jr. (iD)
University of Calgary
Calgary, AB, Canada

Colin O'Flynn (iD)
Dalhousie University
Halifax, NS, Canada

ISSN 0302-9743 ISSN 1611-3349 (electronic)
Lecture Notes in Computer Science
ISBN 978-3-030-81651-3 ISBN 978-3-030-81652-0 (eBook)
https://doi.org/10.1007/978-3-030-81652-0

LNCS Sublibrary: SL4 – Security and Cryptology

This Springer imprint is published by the registered company Springer Nature Switzerland AG
The registered company address is: Gewerbestrasse 11, 6330 Cham, Switzerland

Preface

For the last 27 years, the Selected Areas in Cryptography (SAC) conference has been the leading Canadian venue for cryptographic research. The conference circulates between different Canadian locations, with the aim to offer an accessible venue for dissemination of cryptographic knowledge and a meeting point for local and international researchers. For SAC 2020, we were hosted by Dalhousie University in Halifax, Nova Scotia, which due to the COVID-19 pandemic had to accommodate us virtually. The conference took place during October 21–23, 2020.

SAC has three regular themes:

- Design and analysis of symmetric key primitives and cryptosystems, including block and stream ciphers, hash functions, MAC algorithms, and authenticated encryption schemes.
- Efficient implementations of symmetric and public key algorithms.
- Mathematical and algorithmic aspects of applied cryptology.

In addition, each year a fourth special theme is selected. For this edition of SAC we chose the following:

- Secure elections and related cryptographic constructions.

A total of 52 submissions were received, out of which the Program Committee selected 27 papers for presentation. It is our pleasure to thank the authors of all the submissions for the high quality of their work. The double-blind review process was thorough (each submission received the attention of at least three reviewers, and at least five for submissions involving a Program Committee member), and used the iChair package by Matthieu Finisaz and Thomas Baigéneres.

To complement the online program, there were two invited talks. The Stafford Taveres Lecture was given by Vanessa Teague who spoke about "What's so hard about Internet voting?". The second invited talk "Trustless groups of unknown order" was given by Benjamin Smith.

Continuing the tradition since SAC 2015, we also had the pleasure of hosting the SAC summer school (S3) 2020. While the special situation led to this school taking place virtually as well and with somewhat more fall-oriented weather, the talks by Antoine Joux and Benjamin Smith about the Mathematics of Cryptography, and by Jeremy Clark and Vanessa Teague about Secure Elections, were a delight. We encourage interested readers to see all recordings of all talks at http://sacworkshop.org/SAC20/sac2020.ca/videos.html.

Finally, we would like to express our sincere gratitude to all the members of the Program Committee, as well as all the external sub-reviewers who helped in selection process, especially given the challenging times.

May 2021

Orr Dunkelman
Michael J. Jacobson, Jr.
Colin O'Flynn

Organization

Program Chairs

Orr Dunkelman	University of Haifa, Israel
Michael J. Jacobson Jr.	University of Calgary, Canada
Colin O'Flynn	Dalhouise University, Canada

Program Committee

Riham AlTawy	University of Victoria, Canada
Diego Aranha	Aarhus University, Denmark
Tomer Ashur	TU Eindhoven, the Netherlands, and KU Leuven, Belgium
Roberto Avanzi	ARM, Germany
Paulo Barreto	University of Washington Tacoma, USA
Josh Benaloh	Microsoft Research, USA
Daniel J. Bernstein	University of Illinois at Chicago, USA, and Ruhr University Bochum, Germany
Jean-François Biasse	University of South Florida, USA
Claude Carlet	Université Paris 8, France, and University of Bergen, Norway
Carlos Cid	Royal Holloway, University of London, UK, and Simula UiB, Norway
Aleksander Essex	Western University, Canada
Maria Eichlseder	Graz University of Technology, Austria
Ryan Henry	University of Calgary, Canada
Howard Heys	Memorial University, Canada
Marcel Keller	CSIRO's Data61, Australia
Yunwen Liu	National University of Defense Technology, China
Subhamoy Maitra	Indian Statistical Institute Kolkata, India
Kalikinkar Mandal	University of New Brunswick, Canada
Atefeh Mashatan	Ryerson University, Canada
Barbara Masucci	University of Salerno, Italy
Abderrahmane Nitaj	University of Caen Normandy, France
Christiane Peters	IBM, Belgium
Christophe Petit	University of Birmingham, UK
Olivier Pereira	Université Catholique de Louvain, Belgium
Elizabeth Quaglia	Royal Holloway, University of London, UK
Francisco Rodríguez-Henríquez	CINVESTAV, Mexico
Eyal Ronen	Tel Aviv University, Israel
Tobias Schneider	NXP Semiconductors, Austria

Nicolas Sendrier	Inria, France
Leonie Simpson	Queensland University of Technology, Australia
Benjamin Smith	Inria and École Polytechnique, Institut Polytechnique de Paris, France
Djiby Sow	Cheikh Anta Diop University, Senegal
Martijn Stam	Simula UiB, Norway
Douglas Stebila	University of Waterloo, Canada
Vanessa Teague	Australian National University and Thinking Cybersecurity, Australia
Yosuke Todo	NTT Secure Platform Laboratories, Japan
Yuntao Wang	Japan Advanced Institute of Science and Technology, Japan
Huapeng Wu	University of Windsor, Canada

Subreviewers

Davide Bellizia	Romy Minko
Olivier Bronchain	Chandrasekhar Mukherjee
Arcangelo Castiglione	Lorenz Panny
Debrup Chakraborty	Souradyuti Paul
Jesús-Javier Chi-Domínguez	Edoardo Persichetti
Hien Thi Thu Chu	Jeroen Pijnenburg
Jack Connor	Raffaele Pizzolante
Thomas Debris-Alazard	Benjamin Pring
Ashley Fraser	Matthieu Rivain
Si Gao	Raghvendra Rohit
Lydia Garms	Arnab Roy
Essam Ghadafi	Dibyendu Roy
Brian Goncalves	Paolo Santini
Péter Kutas	Yu Sasaki
Julien Lavauzelle	Tjerand Silde
Jooyoung Lee	Chunhua Su
Chris Leonardi	Fernando Virdia
Anthony Leverrier	Junwei Wang
Cuauhtemoc Mancillas-López	Charlotte Weitkaemper
Wilfried Meidl	Lennert Wouters
Willi Meier	Mahmoud Yehia

Invited Talks

What's So Hard About Internet Voting?

Vanessa Teague

Abstract. The first papers about electronic voting were written only a year or two after the invention of public key cryptography. It all seemed so simple: some voting codes, a mixnet or two, and we could have private and verifiable remote voting for everyone.

But the more we think about elections as a specific engineering problem, the more subtle problems appear. How do we ensure that people can't sell their votes or be coerced into voting in a particular way? What if the voter's computer sends a different vote from the one the voter wanted? How can independent auditors test for mistakes or manipulation? If the protocol assumes a separation of powers or a distribution of trust, how do we make those independence assumptions true in practice? What if we discover after the election that there was a bug in the maths?

I'll survey the history of good ideas in the literature, and explain why recent examinations of real systems have identified problems that researchers didn't even consider.

We're learning something about democracy and security as we go, but unfortunately we're mostly learning about the fragility of our democratic systems and the limitations of our clever cryptographic solutions.

I'll conclude with some positive developments, including Risk-Limiting Audits and pollsite e-voting systems, and why I think those directions are more promising than paperless Internet voting.

Trustless Groups of Unknown Order

Benjamin Smith

Abstract. Groups of unknown order have cryptographic applications including time-lock puzzles, verifiable delay functions, and accumulators. While a trusted authority might simply choose an RSA group and be done with it, in the trustless setting the problem of generating cryptographically secure unknown-order groups is much more subtle. We will explore this problem, comparing two concrete constructions—class groups of quadratic imaginary fields, and Jacobians of hyperelliptic curves—with a special focus on the surprisingly complicated issues of security levels and appropriate key sizes.

Contents

Side Channel Attacks

Cryptographic Applications

Public-Key Cryptography

Efficient Lattice-Based Polynomial Evaluation and Batch ZK Arguments

Veronika Kuchta[1]([⊠]), Amin Sakzad[2], Ron Steinfeld[2], and Joseph K. Liu[2]

[1] The University of Queensland, Brisbane, Australia
v.kuchta@uq.edu.au
[2] Monash University, Melbourne, Australia

Abstract. In this paper we provide an efficient construction of a lattice-based polynomial argument and a polynomial batch-protocol, where the latter contains the polynomial argument as a building block. Our contribution is motivated by the discrete log based construction (EURO-CRYPT'16), where in our case we employ different techniques to obtain a communication efficient lattice-based scheme. In the zero-knowledge polynomial batch-protocol, we prove the knowledge of an easy relation between two polynomials which also allows batching of several instances of the same relation. Our batch-protocol is applicable to an efficient lattice-based range proof construction which represents a useful application in cryptocurrencies. In contrast to the existing range proof (CRYPTO'19), our proof is more efficient for large number of batched instances.

1 Introduction

Lattice-based cryptography has attracted an immense interest from the cryptographic community in the last years. Lattice problems are supposed to be resistant against quantum attacks and satisfy the worst-case to average-case reductions. Zero-knowledge proofs and arguments are significant building blocks in many cryptographic protocols which are used to provide privacy. Goldwasser et al. [13] introduced the main concept of a zero-knowledge proof. We emphasize that there is a significant difference between zero-knowledge proofs and zero-knowledge arguments, where the former satisfy statistical soundness property, while the latter achieve computational soundness. One of the main advantages of zero-knowledge arguments against zero-knowledge proofs is their low communication complexity as showed in [16]. Because of the increasing interest for post-quantum cryptography, the cryptographic community has been focusing among others also on the post-quantum constructions of zero-knowledge protocols. First such protocol was introduced by Stern [21], where the security of the protocol is based on a post-quantum assumption called hardness of "syndrome decoding". Another approach for zero-knowledge proof constructions was proposed by Lyubashevsky [15,18] and further developed in [19] and is known as the "Fiat-Shamir with Aborts" technique. The main advantage of these protocols is a

© Springer Nature Switzerland AG 2021
O. Dunkelman et al. (Eds.): SAC 2020, LNCS 12804, pp. 3–33, 2021.
https://doi.org/10.1007/978-3-030-81652-0_1

small soundness error with only one repetition. Using lattices for zero-knowledge proofs constructions seems to be a challenging task. While there are efficient zero-knowledge arguments [8] and polynomial evaluation arguments [4,9] in the discrete log setting, a lattice-based analogy of these protocols is a popular but not a trivial research question. Several amortization techniques are proposed and employed in such works like [5,10] to improve the efficiency of zero-knowledge proofs especially for arithmetic circuits with linear communication length [2]. Benhamouda et al. [6] introduced a new challenge space consisting of monomials such that the soundness error of the zero-knowledge proof which is defined over cyclotomic rings $\mathcal{R}_q = \mathbb{Z}_q[X]/(X^n+1)$ could be reduced from $1/2$ to $1/(2n)$. New techniques for zero-knowledge proof constructions were proposed in [11] where an efficient one-shot proof mechanism was provided. Bootle et al. [8] presented an honest-verifier zero-knowledge proof for an arithmetic circuit defined in the discrete log setting. Their protocol improves in complexity compared to [14] by achieving fewer moves. Another contribution in [8] is a subroutine to commit to a polynomial and later reveal its evaluation at any point. They achieve a square root communication complexity which motivated us to our first contribution in this paper. In a later work [9], the authors introduced a framework for simple relations between commitments and a batch protocol which proves multiple copies of the same relation in a single argument. Zero-knowledge proofs have useful applications in cryptocurrencies [20,23]. Batch polynomial proof is used to prove knowledge of multiple instances at once. For instance, range proof often requires to prove that multiple inputs are in a certain interval. In case of cryptocurrencies it proves that the sum of multiple spending inputs is equal to the multiple outputs. Batched range proofs are more efficient than running a simple range proof on different instances. Our new batch proof using the new approach of polynomial evaluation argument as a building block will provide a useful tool for blockchain and cryptocurrency applications.

1.1 Our Contribution

We provide the first construction of a lattice based polynomial evaluation argument and show how to commit to a secret polynomial and later reveal its evaluation at a certain value. Our second contribution is an extension of the first one, where the polynomial evaluation argument is used as a building block. We provide the first lattice-based version of a batch protocol with communication cost overhead of a square root in the number of batched instances.

Our Techniques. The instantiation of the polynomial evaluation protocol in [8] in the lattice setting is not a straightforward task and yields several difficulties which were not an issue in the discrete log setting. The first issue is the choice of a challenge set. In order to guarantee soundness of our polynomial evaluation protocol, which requires the extracted witnesses to be small, we use a challenge space which contains monomials of form X^ω. Committing to a polynomial $f(X) \in \mathcal{R}_q$ of degree $n - 1 = n' \cdot m'$, we embed its coefficients into a matrix $\mathcal{A}$ of size $n' \times m'$. The polynomial $f(X)$ can be represented as the following product: $f(X) = (1, X, \ldots, X^{n'-1}) \cdot \mathcal{A} \cdot (1, X^{n'}, \ldots, X^{(m'-1)n'})^{tr}$. In order to prove the knowledge of this polynomial we need to mask $\mathcal{A}$ using a procedure which we explain here briefly. Since we are using monomials as a challenge, the masking procedure is a highly challenging task. To commit to a vector $\tilde{\mathbf{f}}(X) = (1, X, \ldots, X^{n'-1}) \cdot \tilde{\mathcal{A}}$, where $\tilde{\mathcal{A}}$ is the masked matrix, we need to ensure that $\tilde{\mathbf{f}}(X)$ does not leak any information about the coefficients of $\mathcal{A}$. Our solution is to mask all coefficients $a_{j,i}$ as follows: We sample values $u_{j,i} \leftarrow_{\$} \mathbb{Z}_q, j \in [0, n'-1], i \in [0, m'-1]$ and compute the masked coefficients $\tilde{a}_{j,i} = a_{j,i} - u_{j,i} X^{n'-(2j+1)}$. The last of the matrix is given as $a_{(\cdot,\cdot)}$ is masked by a value $u_{(\cdot,\cdot)}$. The second component is also masked perfectly. In the last case, $x = X^{-1}$ implies $X^{-2} = -1$ and $X^{-3} = X^{-1}$ and the first component is equal to $a_{0,0} + a_{1,0} X^{-1} - u_{1,1} - u_{0,1} X^{-1}$ such that each coefficient $a_{(\cdot,\cdot)}$ is fully masked. After running this experiment for higher n', m' we concluded that the only possible challenge values which fully mask the polynomial coefficients are $\{1, X, X^{-1}\}$. On the one hand the low number of challenges means that to achieve negligible soundness error of our protocol we need to repeat it $\lambda / \log(|\mathcal{CH}|)$ times, where $|\mathcal{CH}|$ is the size of the challenge space. On the other hand we deal with a generalised Vandermonde matrix which is a concatenation of simple Vandermonde matrices of dimension 3, which yields a determinant equal to 6. This determinant represents the relaxation factor of the extracted witness which is relatively small in contrast to the proof in [11]. We commit to each row of $\tilde{\mathcal{A}}$ using a commitment scheme which is defined in [3,7] and is secure under the M-SIS assumption over $\mathcal{R}_q$. We commit to $\tilde{\mathbf{f}}(X) = (1, X, \ldots, X^{n'-1}) \cdot \tilde{\mathcal{A}}$ and evaluate it at the challenge $x = X^{\omega}$. The verifier can check that the evaluation in the challenge is correct. While the protocol in [8] proves evaluation in an integer challenge, we needed to separate the evaluation point of the polynomial from our challenge set. For our polynomial evaluation protocol we come up with the following idea: Let $f(X) = q(X) \cdot (X - v) + w$, where $v \in \mathbb{Z}_q$ is the evaluation point and $f(v) = w \in \mathbb{Z}_q$. It is obvious that while $f(X)$ is a polynomial of degree $n - 1$, the degree of $q(X)$ is $n - 2$. To commit to $f(x)$ and to prove knowledge of an evaluation point v and the corresponding evaluation value w we proceed as follows. We commit to $f(X)$ and $q(X)$ using the polynomial commitment scheme from [8], while commitments to $v, w, (X - v)$ are computed using the classical technique, i.e. we encode v, w into constant coefficients and commit to them.

One of the main challenges in all lattice-based zero-knowledge proofs is the smallness property of extracted values as required by the underlying SIS problem. While in [8] the polynomial $f(X)$ has the following form: $(1, X^{n'}, \ldots, X^{(m'-1)n'}) \cdot \mathcal{A} \cdot (1, X, \ldots, X^{n'-1})^{tr}$. the same representation in the lattice setting would yield problems during the extraction procedure because a commitment to $\tilde{\mathbf{f}}(X) = (1, X^{n'}, \ldots, X^{(m'-1)n'}) \cdot \mathcal{A}$ would break the smallness property of the extracted witness. We fixed the problem by transposing the $m' \times n'$ matrix $\mathcal{A}$ to an $n' \times m'$ matrix $\mathcal{A}^{tr}$, such that the prover commits to $\hat{\mathbf{f}}(X) = (1, X, \ldots, X^{n'-1}) \cdot \mathcal{A}^{tr}$ which is a partial polynomial evaluation at a challenge point X. For the witness extraction procedure we apply a Vandermonde matrix $\mathbf{V}$ to a system of equations $\mathbf{V} \cdot \mathbf{a} = \mathbf{c}$, where $\mathbf{a}$ denotes a row of the matrix $\tilde{\mathcal{A}}$ and $\mathbf{c}$ is a commitment of the corresponding row in the masked matrix $\widetilde{A}$. The inverse of a Vandermonde matrix is small, since the determinant of $\mathbf{V}$ is a product of $(x_j - x_i)$, such that its inverse is small according to Lemma 6 in [12].

Our second contribution is motivated by the polynomial batch protocol from [9]. The main difference to their construction [9] is that our proof is defined over lattices using the modified polynomial argument from our first contribution. We compute a simple relation between two multivariate polynomials $\mathbf{P}$ and $\mathbf{Q}$, where each polynomial is represented by a vector of l_P, l_Q polynomials in multiple variables, respectively. In the construction of the batch polynomial protocol the main challenge is to find a suitable packing procedure to pack several multi-variate polynomial instances into one commitment. The inputs to the polynomials $\mathbf{P}$, $\mathbf{Q}$ are vectors of multivariate polynomials $\mathbf{a}_{j,i} \in \mathbb{Z}_q^{l_a}, \mathbf{b}_{j,i} \in \mathbb{Z}_q^{l_b}$ for all $j \in [0, n' - 1], i \in [0, m' - 1]$. Each of these polynomials is a vector of l_a, l_b monomial coefficients, respectively. It holds $\mathbf{a}_{j,i} = (a_{j,i,1}, \ldots, a_{j,i,l_a})$ and $\mathbf{b}_{j,i} = (b_{j,i,1}, \ldots, b_{j,i,l_b})$. The input vector $\mathbf{a}_j, i$ is private while the vector $\mathbf{b}_{j,i}$ is public to the protocol. Therefore following the idea of the polynomial evaluation protocol we first need to mask $\mathbf{a}_{j,i}$ using the technique from Sect. 3 and obtain the masked vector $\tilde{\mathbf{a}}_{j,i}$. The next challenge of this contribution is to find a suitable technique to commit to the multivariate polynomial $\mathbf{Q}(\mathbf{a}_{j,i}, \mathbf{b}_{j,i})$ over lattices. Our solution is to use a module-SIS-based commitment scheme to commit to the multivariate polynomial vector $\mathbf{Q} = (Q_1, \ldots, Q_{l_Q})$. The dimension of this vector is l_Q and corresponds to the number of batched instances that we want to prove the relation $\mathsf{R}_{\texttt{batch}}$ of. Each of the l_Q vector components $\mathbf{Q}_\iota$, for $\iota \in [l_Q]$ is again a polynomial in $l_a + l_b$ variables. The packing procedure works as follows: Let $n = n' \cdot m' - 1$ and m' be the number of instances we want to pack into one commitment C_i for $i \in [0, n']$. We define each component $\mathbf{Q}_\iota$ of $\mathbf{Q}$ in each of it's $l_a + l_b$ variables, by holding the remaining $l_a + l_b - 1$ variables fixed. Then, we pack polynomials which are defined in the same variable into one ring element. Finally, we obtain a matrix $\mathbf{Q}$ of size $l_Q \times (l_a + l_b)$ of packed m' polynomials. We commit to this matrix using a module-SIS commitment.

1.2   Application

With our solution we achieve a communication-efficient lattice-based polynomial batch protocol which can be applied to an efficient range-proof protocol in post-quantum setting. The latter can be compared to the results in [11,22,23]. For the conversion of our batch polynomial protocol into a range proof we follow the technique from [9]. In the following table we provide a comparison of our range proof application with those in [11,22]. All three constructions are based on the module SIS assumption. The main difference between our construction and the proof in [11] is that a simple repetition of our range proof has a soundness error of $1/3$. Thus, we require up to $\kappa = \mathcal{O}(\lambda/\log(3))$ repetitions to achieve an overall soundness error of $1/(2^\lambda)$, while in [11] the authors provide an one-shot proof to achieve the same soundness error. Compared to [11], we achieve a square-root improvement in the number of batched instances t, while the dependence of n remains linear. We note, that for a higher number of batched instances our proof

Table 1. Important notations for Sect. 3 and 4 (in chronological order)

Notation	Description
$\mathcal{R}_q = \mathbb{Z}_q[X]/(X^n + 1)$	Polynomial ring
q	Prime modulus defining $\mathcal{R}_q$
λ	Security parameter
$n(= n'm' - 1)$	Degree of polynomials in $\mathcal{R}_q$
$f(X) = (X - u)q(X) + w$	A polynomial of degree n in $\mathcal{R}_q$ with coefficients $a_k \in \mathbb{Z}_q$, u the evaluation value and w the evaluated value of $f(u)$
$\mathcal{A} = (a_{j,i})_{j \in [0,n'-1], i \in [0,m'-1]}$	Coefficient matrix of $f(X)$ of dimension $n' \times m'$
$\tilde{\mathcal{A}} = (\tilde{a}_{j,i})_{j \in [0,n'], i \in [0,m'-1]}$	Matrix $\mathcal{A}$ of dimension $(n'+1) \times m'$ after masking
$\mathcal{T} = (t_{j,i})_{j' \in [0,\nu-1], i \in [0,\mu-1]}$	Coefficient matrix of $q(X)$ of dimension $\nu \times \mu$, $\deg(q(X)) = n - 1 = \nu\mu - 1$
$\tilde{\mathcal{T}} = (\tilde{t}_{j',i'})_{j' \in [0,\nu], i' \in [0,\mu-1]}$	Masked coefficient matrix of polynomial $q(X)$
$\mathbf{a}_j, \mathbf{t}_{j'}$	The j-th, j'-th row of the matrix $\mathcal{A}$, $\mathcal{T}$
$\mathbf{r}_{a,j}, \mathbf{r}_{t,j'} \in \mathcal{R}_q^m$	Randomness of $\mathbf{a}_j, \mathbf{t}_{j'}$, respectively
$\mathtt{A}_j, \mathtt{T}_{j'}$	Commitment to the j-th row $\mathbf{a}_j$, j'-th row $\mathbf{t}_{j'}$, respectively
$\hat{f}(X)$	The vector-matrix product defined as: $(1, X, \ldots, X^{n'-1}) \cdot \mathcal{A}$
$\mathfrak{D}_\sigma^n$	n-dimensional discrete Normal distribution with stand. deviation σ
$u_{j,i}, s_{j',i'}$	Masking values used in $\mathcal{A}$, $\mathcal{T}$, respectively
$\tilde{\mathbf{a}}_j$	The j-th row of the matrix $\tilde{\mathcal{A}}$
$\tilde{\mathtt{A}}_j, \tilde{\mathtt{T}}_{j'}$	Commitment to $\tilde{\mathbf{a}}_j, \tilde{\mathbf{t}}_{j'}$, respectively
$\mathbf{u}, \mathbf{s}$	The $(n'+1)$-th, $(\nu+1)$-th row of matrix $\tilde{\mathcal{A}}, \tilde{\mathcal{T}}$, respectively
$\mathbf{r}_u, \mathbf{r}_s$	Randomness to $\mathbf{u}, \mathbf{s}$, respectively
$\mathtt{U}, \mathtt{S}$	Commitment to $\mathbf{u}, \mathbf{s}$ with randomness $\mathbf{r}_u, \mathbf{r}_s$, respectively
$\tilde{\mathbf{r}}_\mathbf{f}, \tilde{\mathbf{r}}_\mathbf{q}$	Polynomials: $\sum_{j=0}^{n'-1} \mathbf{r}_{a,j} X^j + \mathbf{r}_u X^{n'}$, $\sum_{j=0}^{\nu-1} \mathbf{r}_{t,j} X^j + \mathbf{r}_s X^{n'}$, resp.
$\mathtt{R}_{(\cdot)}$	Relation to be proved
ν, μ	Decomposition of $n - 1$. It holds $n - 1 = \nu\mu - 1$
$\mathtt{c}_{(\cdot)}$	Commitment to a certain input $(\cdot)$
$\mathtt{m}_{(\cdot)}$	Masking value of a certain input $(\cdot)$
$\mathcal{CH}, \Delta\mathcal{CH} = |\mathcal{CH} - \mathcal{CH}|$	Set of challenges, set of challenge differences, resp.
β	Euclidean norm of a randomness $\mathbf{r}_{(\cdot)}$
$\mathcal{B}$	Infinity norm of a randomness $\mathbf{r}_{(\cdot)}$
Π_{PolEv}	Polynomial evaluation zero-knowledge protocol
$\xi_{\mathtt{m}_{(\cdot)}}$	Masked responses
$\mathbf{r}_{\xi,\mathtt{m}_{(\cdot)}}$	Randomness to the masked response $\xi_{\mathtt{m}_{(\cdot)}}$
$\mathbf{P}$	Polynomial vector of l_P multiv. polynomials $\{P_{\iota'}\}_{\iota' \in [l_P]}$ of total degree d_P
$\mathbf{Q}$	A Polynomial vector of l_Q polynomials $\{Q_\iota\}_{\iota \in [l_Q]}$ of total degree d_Q
$n = n'm' - 1$	Degree of polynomials in $\mathcal{R}_q$
$\mathbf{a}_{j,i} = (a_{j,i,1}, \ldots, a_{j,i,l_a})$	l_a-variate polynomial input vector to $\mathbf{P}$ and $\mathbf{Q}$, $j \in [0, m'-1]$, $i \in [0, n'-1]$
$\mathbf{b}_{j,i} = (b_{j,i,1}, \ldots, b_{j,i,l_b})$	l_b-variate polynomial input vector to $\mathbf{Q}$, $j \in [0, m'-1]$, $i \in [0, n'-1]$
$\mathbf{Q}(\mathbf{a}_{j,i}, \mathbf{b}_{j,i})$	A vector of $l_Q(l_a + l_b)$-variate polynomials of total degree d_Q
$\mathbf{P}(\mathbf{a}_{j,i})$	A vector of $l_P l_a$-variate polynomials of total degree d_P
$A_\kappa = (a_{j,i,\kappa})_{j \in [0,n'], i \in [0,m'-1]}$	Coefficient matrix of dimension $n' \times m'$ for $\kappa \in [l_a]$
$B_{\kappa'} = (b_{j,i,\kappa'})_{j \in [0,n'], i \in [0,m'-1]}$	Coefficient matrix of dimension $n' \times m'$ for $\kappa' \in [l_b]$
$\tilde{\mathbf{a}}_{j,i} = (\tilde{a}_{j,i,1}, \ldots, \tilde{a}_{j,i,l_a})$	l_a-variate polynomial input vector to $\mathbf{P}$ and $\mathbf{Q}$ after masking A_κ
$l_j(X)$	Lagrange polynomials for all $j \in [0, n']$
$\mathbf{P}_i^*(X)$	Polynomial $\mathbf{P}(\mathbf{a}_{j,i})$ evaluated at X
$\mathcal{P}_i^* = (p_{\nu,\mu})_{\nu \in [0,t_1], \mu \in [0,t_2]}$	Coefficient matrix (as in Sect. 3) of $\mathbf{P}_i^*(X)$ of dimension $t_1 \times t_2$
$\tilde{\mathcal{P}}_i^* = (\tilde{p}_{\mu,\nu})_{\mu \in [0,t_2+1], \nu \in [0,t_2]}$	Masked coefficient matrix $\mathcal{P}_i^*$
$\mathcal{Q}_i^* = (q_{\tilde{\mu},\tilde{\nu}})_{\tilde{\mu} \in [0,\tau_2], \tilde{\nu} \in [0,\tau_1]}$	Coefficient matrix (as in Sect. 3) of $\mathbf{Q}_i^*(X)$ of dimension $\tau_1 \times \tau_2$
$\tilde{\mathcal{Q}}_i^* = (\tilde{q}_{\tilde{\mu},\tilde{\nu}})_{\tilde{\mu} \in [0,\tau_2+1], \tilde{\nu} \in [0,\tau_1]}$	Masked coefficient matrix $\mathcal{Q}_i^*$
${}^{\mathtt{A}}\mathbf{P}_{i,\mu}^*, {}^{\mathtt{A}}\mathbf{Q}_{i,\tilde{\mu}}^*$	Commitment to the μ-th or $\tilde{\mu}$-th row of the matrix $\tilde{\mathcal{P}}_i^*, \tilde{\mathcal{Q}}_i^*$, resp.
$\mathbf{H}_{\chi_i}, \chi_i \in \{\mathbf{P}_i^*, \mathbf{Q}_i^*\}$	Divisor (with rest) of χ_i s.t. $\chi_i = (X - \mathbf{y}) \cdot \mathbf{H}_{\chi_i} + \mathbf{z}$, where $\chi_i(\mathbf{y}) = \mathbf{z}$
$\tilde{\mathcal{H}}_{\chi_i}$	Masked coefficient matrix of $\mathbf{H}_{\chi_i}(X)$ for all $\chi_i \in \{\mathbf{P}_i^*, \mathbf{Q}_i^*\}$
${}^{\mathtt{T}}\mathbf{P}_{i,\mu}^*, {}^{\mathtt{T}}\mathbf{Q}_{i,\tilde{\mu}}^*$	Commitment to the μ-th or $\tilde{\mu}$-th row of the matrix $\tilde{\mathcal{H}}_{\chi_i}$, resp.
${}^{\mathtt{U}}\chi_i, {}^{\mathtt{S}}\chi_i$	Commitment to the last row of $\tilde{\mathcal{P}}_i^*, \tilde{\mathcal{Q}}_i^*$ for $\chi_i \in \{\mathbf{P}_i^*, \mathbf{Q}_i^*\}$

outperforms the proof from [11], while for lower batched instances it performs less than the concurrent proof in [11]. In contrast to [22], our range proof yields a significant improvement of communication costs, since the range proof in [22] is linear in the number of batched instances t and the ring dimension n and quadratic in the logarithm of the range size $N = 2^\ell - 1$, while our proof is only linear in ℓ. We achieve an asymptotic improvement of the proof size (Tables 1 and 2).

Table 2. Comparison of communication costs, with l being the logarithm of range size $N = 2^\ell - 1$ in [23], t - the number of batched instances and κ is the number of repetitions and $\tilde{n}$ - module rank of M-SIS

Protocols	Torres et al. [22]	Esgin et al. [11]	Our work
1 batched instance	$\kappa\tilde{n}n(\ell+1)\log q$	$\mathcal{O}((\tilde{n}+1)n\log q)$	$\mathcal{O}(\kappa(\sqrt{n})\log q)$
t batched instances	$t\tilde{n}n(\ell+1)\log q$	$\mathcal{O}((\tilde{n}+t)n\log q + tn\ell)$	$\mathcal{O}(\kappa(\sqrt{\ell t})n\log q)$

2   Preliminaries

Σ**-Protocols.** A Σ-protocol is an interactive proof system between a prover $\mathcal{P}$ and a verifier $\mathcal{V}$ which is defined for a relation R and for a statement-witness pair $(v, w) \in \mathsf{R}$. We use the definition from [12].

Definition 1 ([12], **Definition** 4). *For relations* R, R' *where* $\mathsf{R} \subseteq \mathsf{R}'$, $(\mathcal{P}, \mathcal{V}$ *is a* Σ*-protocol with completeness error* α, *a challenge space* $\mathcal{CH}$, *public-private inputs* (v, w) *if the following security properties are satisfied:*

Completeness: A transcript between an honest prover and an honest verifier is accepted with probability at least $1 - \alpha$.

$(k + 1)$*-special soundness: There exists an efficient PPT extractor* $\mathcal{E}$ *that computes* w' *satisfying* $(v, w') \in \mathsf{R}'$ *given* $(k + 1)$ *accepting transcripts.*

Special honest-verifier zero-knowledge (SHVZK): There exists an efficient PPT simulator $\mathcal{S}$ *that outputs a transcript given the public input in the language of* R *and a challenge in* $\mathcal{CH}$, *such that this transcript is indistinguishable from an accepting transcript produced by a real run of the protocol.*

Definition 2 ($Module - SIS_{q,n,m,\beta}$, [17]). *Let* $\mathcal{R}$ *be some ring and* $\mathcal{K}$ *some distribution over* $\mathcal{R}_q$. *Given a random matrix* $\mathbf{A} \in \mathcal{R}_q^{n \times m}$ *sampled from* $\mathcal{K}$, *find a non-zero vector* $\mathbf{v} \in \mathcal{R}_q^m$ *such that* $\mathbf{A}\mathbf{v} = 0$ *and* $\|\mathbf{v}\|_2 \leq \beta$.

Definition 3 ($Module - LWE_{q,n,m,\chi}$, [17]). *Let* χ *be a distribution over* $\mathcal{R}_q$, $\mathbf{s} \leftarrow \chi^n$ *be a secret key.* $LWE_{q,\mathbf{s}}$ *distribution is obtained by sampling* $\mathbf{a} \leftarrow \mathcal{R}_q^n$ *and error* $e \leftarrow \chi$ *and outputting* $(\mathbf{a}, \langle \mathbf{a}, \mathbf{s} \rangle + e)$. *The goal is to distinguish between* m *given samples which are either from* $LWE_{q,\mathbf{s}}$ *or from* $\mathcal{U}(\mathcal{R}_q^n, \mathcal{R}_q)$.

Theorem 1 (Rejection Sampling [19]**).** *Let V be a subset of $\mathbb{Z}^n$ in which all elements have norms less than T, and let h be a probability distribution over V. Then, for any constant M, discrete normal distribution $\mathfrak{D}_\sigma$ over $\mathbb{Z}$ with standard deviation σ, there exists a $\sigma = \tilde{\Theta}(T)$, such that the output distribution of the following algorithms A, F are statistically close:*

Algorithm A: (1). $\mathbf{v} \leftarrow_\$ h$. (2). $\mathbf{z} \leftarrow_\$ \mathfrak{D}^n_{\mathbf{v},\sigma}$. (3). *Output* $(\mathbf{z}, \mathbf{v})$ *with probability* $\min\left(\exp\left(\frac{-2\langle \mathbf{z}, \mathbf{v}\rangle + \|\mathbf{v}\|^2}{2\sigma^2}\right), 1\right)$.

Algorithm F: (1). $\mathbf{v} \leftarrow_\$ h$, (2). $\mathbf{z} \leftarrow_\$ \mathfrak{D}^n_\sigma$, (3). *Output* $(\mathbf{z}, \mathbf{v})$ *with prob.* $1/M$. *Moreover, the probability that A outputs something is exponentially close to that of F, i.e. $1/M$.*

Lemma 1 (Adapted from [6]**).** *Let $\mathcal{R} = \mathbb{Z}[X]/(X^n + 1)$ where $n > 1$ is a power of 2 and $0 < i, j < 2n - 1$. Then all the coefficients of $2(X^i - X^j)^{-1} \in \mathcal{R}$ are in $\{-1, 0, 1\}$. This implies that $\|2(X^i - X^j)^{-1}\| \leq \sqrt{n}$.*

Esgin et al. [12] provided a generalization of Lemma 1 stating that for all monomial challenges $x_i = X^{\omega_i}$ for $0 \leq \omega_i \leq 2n - 1$ the following relation holds for the zero-coefficient of the last row of inverse of the Vandermonde matrix:

$$\|2^k a_0\| = \left\|\prod_{i=1}^{k} \frac{2}{x_i - x_0}\right\| = \left\|\prod_{i=1}^{k} 2(X^{\omega_i} - X^{\omega_0})^{-1}\right\| \leq n^{k-1/2} \qquad (1)$$

Lemma 2. *Let $x_i = X^{\omega_i} \in \mathcal{R} = \mathbb{Z}[X]/(X^n + 1)$ for $0 \leq \omega_i \leq 2n - 1$ and $0 \leq i \leq k$. Define the Vandermonde matrix $\mathbf{V}$ of dimension $k + 1$, where i-th row is the vector $(1, x_i, x_i^2, \ldots, x_i^k)$. Then $\mathbf{V}$ is invertible, and for any entry α_j in the last row of $\mathbf{V}^{-1}$, we have $\|2^k \alpha_j\| \leq n^{k-0.5}$.*

Lemma 3 (Lemma 4.4 in [19]**).** *For any $\alpha > 0, \Pr[|z| > \alpha\sigma; z \leftarrow \mathfrak{D}_\sigma] \leq 2\exp\left(-\alpha^2/2\right)$. For any $\alpha > 1, \Pr[\|\mathbf{z}\| > \alpha\sigma\sqrt{m}, \mathbf{z} \leftarrow \mathfrak{D}^m_\sigma] \leq \alpha^m \exp\left(\frac{m(1-\alpha^2)}{2}\right)$.*

In particular: $\Pr[|z| > 12\sigma : z \leftarrow \mathfrak{D}_\sigma] < 2^{-100}$ *and* $\Pr[\|\mathbf{z}\| > 5\sigma : z \leftarrow \mathfrak{D}^n_\sigma] < 2^{-100}$, *if $n \geq 7$.*

Definition 4 (Commitment Scheme). *Let $n = \nu + \nu', m, q, \mathcal{B}$ be positive integers. Let $S_\mathcal{M}$ denote a message space. The relaxed commitment of a message $\mathbf{x} \in S_\mathcal{M}$ is defined as:*

KeyGen: *Create* $(\mathbf{A}_1, \mathbf{A}_2) \in \mathcal{R}^{\nu \times m}_q \times \mathcal{R}^{\nu' \times m}_q$. *Public parameters are created as follows:*

$$\mathbf{A}_1 = [\mathbf{I}_\nu \| \mathbf{A}'_1], \quad where \quad \mathbf{A}'_1 \leftarrow \mathcal{R}^{\nu \times (m-\nu)}_q$$

$$\mathbf{A}_2 = [\mathbf{0}^{\nu' \times \nu} \| \mathbf{I}_{\nu'} \| \mathbf{A}'_2], \quad where \quad \mathbf{A}'_2 \leftarrow \mathcal{R}^{\nu' \times (m-\nu-\nu')}_q$$

Set the commitment key $ck = \mathbf{A} = \begin{bmatrix} \mathbf{A}_1 \\ \mathbf{A}_2 \end{bmatrix}$. This commitment key is used to commit to messages $\mathbf{x} \in \mathcal{R}^{\nu'}_q$.

Com: *To commit to a message* $\mathbf{x} \in \mathcal{R}_q^{\nu'}$, *choose a random polynomial vector* $\mathbf{r} \leftarrow \{-\mathcal{B}, \ldots, \mathcal{B}\}^m$ *and output the commitment* $\mathsf{C} := \mathsf{Com}_{ck}(\mathbf{x}, \mathbf{r}) = \mathbf{A} \cdot \mathbf{r} + \mathbf{x} = \mathbf{A} \cdot \mathbf{r} + \mathsf{enc}(\mathbf{x})$, *where* $\mathsf{enc}(\mathbf{x}) = \begin{bmatrix} \mathbf{0}^\nu \\ \mathbf{x} \end{bmatrix}$.

ROpen: *A valid opening of a commitment* C *is a tuple consisting of* $\mathbf{x} \in \mathcal{R}_q^{\nu'}$, $\mathbf{r} \in \mathcal{R}_q^m$ *and* $d \in \Delta \mathcal{CH}$. *The verifier checks that* $d \cdot \mathsf{C} = \mathbf{A} \cdot \mathbf{r} + d \cdot \mathsf{enc}(\mathbf{x})$, *and that* $\forall\, 1 \leq i \leq k$, *we have that* $\|r_i\|_2 \leq \gamma_{bind}$. *Otherwise return* 0.

Security of this commitment scheme has been proved in [2].

Lemma 4. *If* $\mathsf{M-LWE}_{q,m-\nu-\nu',\nu+\nu',\mathcal{U}(\{-\mathcal{B},\ldots,\mathcal{B}\}^m)}$ *problem is hard than the above commitment scheme is computationally hiding. If* $\mathsf{M-SIS}_{q,\nu+\nu',m,\beta}$ *problem is hard, then our commitment scheme is computationally* γ_{bind}-*binding with respect to the relaxation factor* d.

The binding property of this commitment scheme relies on the hardness of Ring-SIS problem defined in Definition 2 where the number of rows of matrix $\mathbf{A}$ is set to be equal 1. If $\nu + \nu' > 1$, we obtain a commitment scheme whose binding property relies on the hardness of $Module - SIS_{q,\nu+\nu',m,\beta}$ assumption. For the full security proof of Module-SIS commitment scheme, we refer to [17].

3 Lattice-Based Polynomial Zero-Knowledge Argument

We present the first lattice-based version of protocol where we commit to a polynomial and later reveal the evaluation of $f(X)$ at any point $x \in \mathbb{Z}_q$. The commitment scheme Com is a primitive that allows one party to commit to a chosen value while keeping it secret to other parties, then this committed value can be revealed later. We use the commitment scheme from Definition 4.

3.1 Commitments to Polynomials (PolyCom)

Let $f(X) = \sum_{k=0}^{n-1} a_k X^k \in \mathcal{R}_q$, where $a_k \in \mathbb{Z}_q$ for $k = [0, n-1]$ and let $n = m'n' - 1$. Decomposition of this polynomial yields: $f(X) = \sum_{i=0}^{m'-1} \sum_{j=0}^{n'-1} a_{j,i} X^{in'+j}$, $a_{j,i} \in \mathbb{Z}_q$, where the coefficients form the following matrix

$$\mathcal{A} = \begin{pmatrix} a_{0,0} & a_{0,1} & \cdots & a_{0,m'-1} \\ a_{1,0} & a_{1,1} & \cdots & a_{1,m'-1} \\ \vdots & \vdots & \vdots & \vdots \\ a_{n'-1,0} & a_{n'-1,1} & \cdots & a_{n'-1,m'-1} \end{pmatrix}. \tag{2}$$

Let $S_{\mathbf{r}}(\beta) = \{\mathbf{r}_{a,j} \in \mathcal{R}_q^m : \|\mathbf{r}_{a,j}\| \leq \beta, j \in [0, m']\}$ be the randomness space. The commitment to each row $\mathbf{a}_j = (a_{j,0}, \ldots, a_{j,m'-1})$ of $\mathcal{A}$ is given as:

$$\mathbb{A}_j = \mathsf{Com}_{\mathbf{A}}(\mathbf{a}_j, \mathbf{r}_{a,j}) = \mathbf{A}\mathbf{r}_{a,j} + \mathsf{enc}(\mathbf{a}_j) \in \mathcal{R}_q^2, \tag{3}$$

where $\mathsf{enc}(\mathbf{a}_j) = \begin{bmatrix} \mathbf{0}^{n-m'} \\ \mathbf{a}_j \end{bmatrix}$ is a polynomial in $\mathcal{R}_q^2$ and $\mathbf{A} \in \mathcal{R}_q^{2 \times m}$, $\mathbf{r}_{a,j} \leftarrow \mathcal{U}(S_{\mathbf{r}}(\beta))$, for all $0 \le j \le n' - 1$ and $\mathbf{a}_j \in \mathbb{Z}_q^{m'}$ and $\mathbf{0}$ is a $(n - m')$-dimensional zero-vector. We describe the polynomial commitment via the function PolyCom which on input $f, \mathbf{r}_{a,j}$ follows the following computation steps:

$$\hat{\mathbf{f}}(X) = (1, X, \ldots, X^{n'-1}) \cdot \mathcal{A} = \Big(\sum_{j=0}^{n'-1} a_{j,0} X^j, \ldots, \sum_{j=0}^{n'-1} a_{j,m'-1} X^j \Big). \quad (4)$$

The function $\hat{\mathbf{f}}(X)$ can not be sent to the verifier, since it would leak information about the coefficients of f. To avoid any leakage of the secret values, we sample masking values, $u_{j,i} \leftarrow_s \mathfrak{D}_\sigma$. We encode the masking values into monomials for all $i \in [1, m' - 1]$ as follows: $\overline{\mathsf{enc}}(u_{0,i}) = u_{0,i} X^{n'-1}, \overline{\mathsf{enc}}(u_{1,i}) = u_{1,i} X^{n'-3}, \ldots, \overline{\mathsf{enc}}(u_{n'-1,i}) = u_{n'-1,i} X^{1-n'}$ and mask each entry of the coefficient matrix as follows:

$$\tilde{\mathcal{A}} = \begin{pmatrix} a_{0,0} & a_{0,1} - u_{0,1}X^{n'-1} & \cdots & a_{0,m'-1} - u_{0,m'-1}X^{n'-1} \\ a_{1,0} & a_{1,1} - u_{1,1}X^{n'-3} & \cdots & a_{1,m'-1} - u_{1,m'-1}X^{n'-3} \\ \vdots & \vdots & \vdots & \vdots \\ a_{n'-1,0} & a_{n'-1,1} - u_{n'-1,1}X^{1-n'} & \cdots & a_{n'-1,m'-1} - u_{n'-1,m'-1}X^{1-n'} \\ \sum_{j=0}^{n'-1} u_{n'-j-1,1}X^j & \sum_{j=0}^{n'-1} u_{n'-j-1,2}X^j & \cdots & 0 \end{pmatrix} \quad (5)$$

To show correctness we let: $f(X) = (1, X, \ldots, X^{n'-1}) \cdot \tilde{\mathcal{A}} \cdot (1, X^{n'}, \ldots, X^{(m'-1)n'})^{tr}$. We compute $\tilde{\mathbf{f}}(X) = (1, X, \ldots, X^{n'-1}) \cdot \tilde{\mathcal{A}}$. The result is:

$$\begin{pmatrix} a_{0,0} + a_{1,0}X + \ldots + a_{n'-1,0}X^{n'-1} + X^{n'} \sum_{j=0}^{n'-1} u_{n'-j-1,1}X^j, \\ a_{0,1} - u_{0,1}X^{n'-1} + \ldots + (a_{n'-1,1} - u_{n'-1,1}X^{1-n'})X^{n'-1} + X^{n'} \sum_{j=0}^{n'-1} u_{n'-j-1,2}X^j, \\ a_{0,2} - u_{0,2}X^{n'-1} + \ldots + (a_{n'-1,2} - u_{n'-1,2}X^{1-n'})X^{n'-1} + X^{n'} \sum_{j=0}^{n'-1} u_{n'-j-1,3}X^j, \\ \vdots \\ a_{0,m'-2} - u_{0,m'-2}X^{n'-1} + \ldots + X^{n'} \sum_{j=0}^{n'-1} u_{n'-j-1,m'-1}X^j, \\ a_{0,m'-1} - u_{0,m'-1}X^{n'-1} + \ldots + (a_{n'-1,m'-1} - u_{n'-1,m'-1}X^{1-n'})X^{n'-1} \end{pmatrix} \quad (6)$$

It is important to notice that the last component also hides all coefficients by adding the coefficients $u_{i,m'-2}$ to $a_{i,m'-1}$ for $i \in [0, n'-1]$. We reconstruct $f(X)$ by multiplying $\tilde{\mathbf{f}}(X)$ by $(1, X^{n'}, \ldots, X^{(m'-1)n'})^{tr}$ from the right. To improve the readability of the final result, we first provide the results of component-wise multiplication and add up the results in the next step:

(0). $a_{0,0} + a_{1,0}X + \ldots + a_{n'-1,0}X^{n'-1} + X^{n'} \sum_{j=0}^{n'-1} u_{n'-j-1,1}X^j$

$$\vdots$$

$(m'-1)$. $a_{0,m'-1} - u_{0,m'-1}X^{m'n'-1} + \ldots + (a_{n'-1,m'-1} - u_{n'-1,m'-1}X^{1-n'})X^{m'n'-1}$

Finally, we add up the m' results. We need to show that the coefficients $u_i, i \in [1, m'-1]$ will be cancelled out such that the final result yields $f(X)$. This can be followed from a careful decomposition of the above system. To justify that this masking scheme does not reveal the secret coefficients of the polynomials we consider the following observation. When an adversary obtains the term $\tilde{\mathbf{f}}(X)$, she sees the vector (6). Let's have a look at the i-th coordinate of this vector, where $i \in [1, m'-1]$: $a_{0,i} - u_{0,i}X^{n'-1} + (a_{1,i} - u_{1,i}X^{n'-3})X + \ldots + X^{n'}\sum_{j=0}^{n'-1} u_{n'-j-1,i+1}X^j$. It follows that $\mathsf{enc}(u_{0,i})$ can be combined with the coefficient $a_{n'-1,i}$, $\mathsf{enc}(u_{1,i})$ can be combined with coefficient $a_{n'-2,i}$ and so on, such that all polynomial coefficients are perfectly hidden. When an adversary observes the last term $X^{n'}\sum_{j=0}^{n'-1} u_{n'-j-1,i+1}X^j$, she will get monomials $\mathsf{Coef}_0 \cdot X^{n'}, \ldots, \mathsf{Coef}_{n'-1} \cdot X^{2n-1}$, where Coef_j are equal to $u_{(.)}$ and serve as the masking coefficients. The commitments to the rows of $\widetilde{\mathcal{A}}$ are:

$$\widetilde{\mathbb{A}}_j = \mathsf{Com_A}(\tilde{\mathbf{a}}_j, \mathbf{r}_{a,j}) = \mathbf{A}\mathbf{r}_{a,j} + \mathsf{enc}(\tilde{\mathbf{a}}_j), \quad \forall j \in [0, m'-1] \tag{7}$$

where $\tilde{\mathbf{a}}_j$ are the rows of the masked matrix $\widetilde{\mathcal{A}}$. We also commit to the vector $\mathbf{u} = \left(\sum_{j=0}^{n'-1} u_{n'-j-1,1}X^j, \ldots, \sum_{j=0}^{n'-1} u_{n'-j-1,m'-1}X^j, 0 \right)$ by firstly encoding each component $\sum_{j=0}^{n'-1} u_{n'-j-1,i+1}X^j$ into the i-th coefficient c_i of the polynomial $f(X) = \sum_{i=0}^{n-1} c_i X^i$. Let $\mathbf{r}_u \leftarrow S_\mathbf{r}(\beta)$, then holds:

$$\mathbb{U} = \mathsf{Com_A}(\mathbf{u}, \mathbf{r}_u) = \mathbf{A} \cdot \mathbf{r}_u + \mathsf{enc}(\mathbf{u}). \tag{8}$$

Commitment to the vector $\tilde{\mathbf{f}}(X)$ is: $\mathsf{Com_A}\left(\tilde{\mathbf{f}}(X); \tilde{\mathbf{r}}_\mathbf{f}\right) = \sum_{j=0}^{n'-1} X^j \widetilde{\mathbb{A}}_j + \mathbb{U} \cdot X^{n'}$ where $\tilde{\mathbf{r}}_\mathbf{f} = \sum_{j=0}^{n'-1} \mathbf{r}_{a,j}X^j + \mathbf{r}_u X^{n'}$.

Remark 1. Our commitments $\widetilde{\mathbb{A}}_j$ for $j \in [0, n'-1]$, $\mathbb{U}$ satisfy binding and hiding property as showed in [3], Lemma 2.6 and 2.7.

3.2   Polynomial Evaluation Protocol Π_{PEv}

Definition 5. *The relation and the corresponding relaxed relation of the polynomial evaluation protocol are defined as follows:*

$$R_\beta^{\mathsf{PEv}} = \left\{ (v, w, f(X), q(X), \mathbf{r}_v, \mathbf{r}_w), (\mathbf{C}_v, \mathbf{C}_w) : f(X) = q(X)(X-v) + w, f(v) = w, \right.$$
$$\left. \|\mathbf{r}_\iota\| \le \beta, \iota \in \{v, w\} \right\}$$
$$\widehat{R}_\beta^{\mathsf{PEv}} = \left\{ (\hat{v}, \hat{w}, \hat{f}(X), \hat{q}(X), \hat{\mathbf{r}}_v, \hat{\mathbf{r}}_w), (\mathbf{C}_{\hat{v}}, \mathbf{C}_{\hat{w}}) : \hat{f}(X) = \hat{q}(X)(X-\hat{v}) + \hat{w}, f(\hat{v}) = \hat{w}, \right.$$
$$\left. \|\mathbf{r}_\iota\| \le \hat{\beta}, \iota \in \{\hat{v}, \hat{w}\} \right\}.$$

Challenge Space. We define the challenge space $\mathcal{CH}$ being a set of monomials $X^\iota \in \mathcal{R}_q$ for $\iota \in \{-1, 0, 1\}$. Since the protocol does not fit into the usual security definitions of soundness, completeness and zero-knowledge property, similar to [9] we provide these definitions adapted to our protocol.

The protocol consists of four steps **Prover**, **Challenge**, **Response**, **Verification** where the prover runs PolCom algorithm and after receiving a challenge from the verifier, she runs the Resp algorithm. Finally the verifier runs the PolVrfy algorithm. For all $j \in [0, n' - 1], j' \in [0, \nu - 1]$ we set $\mathsf{pc} = \{\{\widetilde{\mathbf{A}}_j\}_j, \{\widetilde{\mathbb{T}}_{j'}\}_{j'}, \mathbb{U}, \mathbb{S}\}, \mathsf{c} = \{\mathsf{C_{m_v}}, \mathsf{C_{m_w}}\}, \mathsf{st}_1 = \{\{\mathbf{r}_{a,j}\}_j, \{\mathbf{r}_{t,j'}\}_{j'}, \mathbf{r}_u, \mathbf{r}_s\}$, $\mathsf{st}_2 = \{\mathbf{r}_v, \mathbf{r}_w\}$ and $\mathsf{re} = \{\mathsf{C_{\tilde{f}}}, \mathsf{C_{\tilde{q}}}, \mathsf{C_{0,\tilde{f}}}, \mathsf{C_{0,\tilde{q}}}, \xi_{\mathsf{m}_v}, \xi_{\mathsf{m}_w}, \mathbf{r}_{\xi,\mathsf{m}_v}, \mathbf{r}_{\xi,\mathsf{m}_w}\}$.

Definition 6 (Completeness). *Our protocol has perfect completeness if for all non-uniform PPT adversaries $\mathfrak{A}$ and completeness error α holds:*

$$Pr\big[(\mathbf{A}, m', n', f(X), q(X), p(X) \leftarrow \mathfrak{A}(1^\lambda), (\mathsf{pc}, \mathsf{st}_1) \leftarrow \mathtt{PolCom}(\mathbf{A}, m', n', f(X), q(X));$$
$$(\mathsf{c}, \mathsf{st}_2) \leftarrow \mathtt{Com}(v, w); \mathsf{re} \leftarrow \mathtt{Resp}(f(X), q(X), x), w \leftarrow \mathtt{PolVrfy}(\mathbf{A}, m', n', \mathsf{pc}, \mathsf{c}, \mathsf{re}, u):$$
$$w = f(v)\big] = 1 - \alpha.$$

Next, we define 3–special soundness which given 3 accepting evaluations for the challenges $x_\ell, \ell \in [1,3]$ but using the same commitments allows to either extract a witness or it breaks the binding property of our commitment scheme.

Definition 7 (3-Special Soundness). *Our protocol is statistically 3-special sound if there exists a PPT algorithm χ that either extracts a valid polynomial $f(X)$ or breaks the binding property of the underlying commitment scheme. For all adversaries $\mathfrak{A}$ and all $L \geq 3$ and $\mathbf{x}_{s,n'} = (1, x_s, \ldots, x_s^{n'}), \bar{\mathbf{r}} = (\mathbf{r}_0, \ldots, \mathbf{r}_{n'-1}, \mathbf{r}_u)$.*

$$Pr\big[\mathbf{A} \leftarrow \mathtt{KeyGen}(1^\lambda), (m', n', \mathsf{pc}, \mathsf{c}, \{x_i, \mathsf{re}_i\}_{i \in [1,L]}) \leftarrow \mathfrak{A}(\mathbf{A}); (\widetilde{\mathcal{A}}, \mathsf{st}_1, \mathsf{st}_2) \leftarrow \chi(\mathbf{A}, m', n', \mathsf{pc}, \mathsf{c},$$
$$\{x_i, \mathsf{re}_i\}_{i \in [1,L]}), w_i \leftarrow \mathtt{PolVrfy}(\mathbf{A}, m', n'\{\mathsf{pc}, \mathsf{c}, \mathsf{re}_i, v_i) : \forall i : w_i = f(v_i) = q(v_i)p(v_i) + w_i$$
$$\vee \exists s : \mathtt{Com_A}(\tilde{\mathbf{f}}(x_s), \tilde{\mathbf{r}}(x_s)) = \mathbf{x}_{s,n'}\mathtt{Com_A}(\widetilde{\mathcal{A}}, \bar{\mathbf{r}}) \wedge \tilde{\mathbf{f}}(x_i) \neq \mathbf{x}_{s,n'} \cdot \widetilde{\mathcal{A}}.\big] \approx 1$$

The next definition states that given any value v and evaluation value x it is possible to simulate the commitments and the evaluation output of PolEv which is distributed as in the real protocol.

Definition 8 (Special Honest Verifier Zero-Knowledge). *Our protocol has special honest verifier zero knowledge if there exists a PPT simulator $\mathcal{S}$ such that for all interactive non-uniform polynomial time adversaries $\mathfrak{A}$ holds:*

$$Pr\big[(\mathbf{A}, m'n', f(X), x) \leftarrow \mathfrak{A}(1^\lambda), (\mathsf{pc}, \mathsf{c}, \mathsf{st}_1, \mathsf{st}_2) \leftarrow \mathtt{PolCom}(\mathbf{A}, m', n', f(X)),$$
$$\mathsf{re} \leftarrow \mathtt{Resp}(\mathsf{st}_1, \mathsf{st}_2, x) : \mathfrak{A}(\mathsf{pc}, \mathsf{c}, \mathsf{re}) = 1\big] \approx Pr\big[\mathbf{A}, m'n', f(X), x \leftarrow \mathfrak{A}(1^\lambda),$$
$$(\mathsf{pc}, \mathsf{c}, \mathsf{re}) \leftarrow \mathcal{S}(\mathbf{A}, m', n', x, f(x)) : \mathfrak{A}(\mathsf{pc}, \mathsf{c}, \mathsf{re}) = 1\big].$$

Construction of Π_{PEv}. The common input to the protocol is given by the public parameter $\mathbf{A} \in \mathcal{R}_q^{2 \times m}$ with $\mathcal{R}_q = \mathbb{Z}_q[X]/(X^n + 1)$. At the beginning the prover commits to a secret value v at which the polynomial $f(X)$ should be evaluated and to the evaluated value w such that $f(v) = w$. We note that a n-degree polynomial $f(X)$ can be represented as follows: $f(X) = q(X) \cdot (X - v) + f(v) = q(X) \cdot (X - v) + w$, where $q(X)$ is a polynomial of degree $n - 2$. We apply the same decomposition technique to this polynomial as we did it for $f(X)$.

Let $q(X) = \sum_{k'=0}^{n-2} t_{k'} X^{k'} = \sum_{i'=0}^{\mu-1} \sum_{j'=0}^{\nu-1} t_{j',i'} X^{i'\nu+j'}$ which can be represented by a matrix T with the corresponding masked matrix $\widetilde{T}$. The commitments to each row of the masked matrix $\widetilde{T}$ are defined as $\{\widetilde{\mathbb{T}}_{j'}\}_{j' \in [0,\nu-1]}$ and $\mathbb{S}$ is the commitment to the last row of the masked matrix $\widetilde{T}$ which is given as $\mathbf{s} = \left(\sum_{j'=0}^{\nu-1} s_{\nu-j'-1,1} X^{j'}, \ldots, \sum_{j'=0}^{\nu-1} s_{\nu-j'-1,\mu-1} X^{j'}, 0 \right)$.

Our protocol contains three moves, where in the first move the prover runs the `PolCom` algorithm to commit to a polynomial $f(X)$, in the second move the verifier sends a challenge $x = X^{\omega}$, and in the last move the prover responds. Finally, verifier runs the `PolVrfy` algorithm to verify $f(x)$. (A more formal description of the protocol is given in Fig. 1.

Common Input: Commitments to the evaluation point $v \in \mathbb{Z}_q$ and to $w = f(v) \in \mathbb{Z}_q$, i.e. $C_v := \mathtt{Com_A}(v, \mathbf{r}_v), C_w := \mathtt{Com_A}(w, \mathbf{r}_w)$ for uniformly random values $\mathbf{r}_v, \mathbf{r}_w \leftarrow_\$ \mathcal{R}_q^m$ which are only known to the prover. These commitments to v, w are computed by encoding the integers into constant polynomials, i.e. $v = vX^0$, $w = wX^0$ and using the commitment scheme from Definition 4.

Prover: The prover runs $\mathtt{PolCom}(n', m', \mathbf{A}, f(X))$ and $\mathtt{PolCom}(\nu, \mu, \mathbf{A}, q(X))$ to commit to the polynomials $f(X) = \sum_{k=0}^{n} a_k X^k \in \mathcal{R}_q$ and $q(X) = \sum_{k'=0}^{n-1} t_{k'} X^{k'} \in \mathcal{R}_q$. Let $f(X), q(X)$ be polynomials with coefficients in $\mathbb{Z}_q$. Let $n = m'n' - 1$ and $n - 1 = \mu\nu - 1$. These polynomials can be encoded into a matrix $\mathcal{A}$ of dimension $n' \times m'$ and into a matrix T of dimension $\nu \times \mu$ as defined in (2). She reconstructs the polynomials $f(X)$ and $q(X)$ using the matrix representation (2) as follows:

$$f(X) = (1, X, \cdots, X^{n'-1}) \cdot \mathcal{A} \cdot (1, X^{n'}, \ldots, X^{(m'-1)n'})^{tr}, \tag{9}$$

$$q(X) = (1, X, \cdots, X^{\nu-1}) \cdot T \cdot (1, X^{\nu}, \ldots, X^{(\mu-1)\nu})^{tr} \tag{10}$$

The prover commits to the polynomial and shows that it evaluates at any point from $\mathcal{R}_q$. Committing to a polynomial is done by computing commitments to each row of $\mathcal{A}$ or T, respectively. She first needs to mask the matrices $\mathcal{A}$ and T, by picking random values $u_{j,i} \leftarrow_\$ \mathbb{Z}_q$, and $s_{j',i'} \leftarrow_\$ \mathbb{Z}_q$ for $i \in [0, m'-1]$, $j \in [0, n'-1]$, $i' \in [0, \mu-1]$, $j' \in [0, \nu-1]$ where $\max |u_{j,i}| \leq \beta$.

Each entry $a_{j,i}$ of $\mathcal{A}$ is masked into $\tilde{a}_{j,i} = a_{j,i} - u_{j,i} X^{n'-(2j+1)}$ of the matrix $\widetilde{\mathcal{A}}$. Similarly, each entry $t_{j',i'}$ of the matrix T is masked into $\tilde{t}_{j',i'} = t_{j',i'} - s_{j',i'} X^{\nu-(2j'+1)}$ of the new matrix $\widetilde{T}$. Similarly, $\widetilde{T}$ is computed as in (5) except that it's dimension is $(\nu + 1) \times \mu$. We denote each entry of $\widetilde{\mathcal{A}}$ and $\widetilde{T}$ by $\tilde{a}_{j,i}$ and $\tilde{t}_{j',i'}$ for $j \in [0, n'-1], i \in [0, m'-1]$ and $j' \in [0, \nu-1], i' \in [0, \mu-1]$, respectively. We add an additional row $\mathbf{u}(X)$ to $\mathcal{A}$ and $\mathbf{s}(X)$ to T where these rows contain the polynomially encoded values of $u_{j,i}$ and $s_{j',i'}$ as it's coordinates, respectively. The vectors $\mathbf{u}(X)$ and $\mathbf{s}(X)$ denote the last rows of $\widetilde{\mathcal{A}}, \widetilde{T}$, respectively: $\mathbf{u}(X) = \left(\sum_{j=0}^{n'-1} u_{n'-j-1,1} X^j, \ldots, \sum_{j=0}^{n'-1} u_{n'-j-1,m'-1} X^j, 0 \right)$ and $\mathbf{s}(X) = \left(\sum_{j'=0}^{\nu-1} s_{\nu-j'-1,1} X^{j'}, \ldots, \sum_{j'=0}^{\nu-1} s_{\nu-j'-1,\mu-1} X^{j'}, 0 \right)$. To ease the notations we omit X in $\mathbf{u}(X), \mathbf{s}(X)$. The prover computes $\widetilde{\mathbb{A}}_j = \mathtt{Com_A}(\tilde{\mathbf{a}}_j, \mathbf{r}_{a,j})$

and $\widetilde{\mathbb{T}}_{j'} = \mathsf{Com}_{\mathbf{A}}(\tilde{\mathbf{t}}_{j'}, \mathbf{r}_{t,j'})$. To commit to the last row of $\widetilde{\mathcal{A}}$ or $\widetilde{\mathcal{T}}$ respectively, the prover picks $\mathbf{r}_u, \mathbf{r}_s \leftarrow_{\$} \mathfrak{D}^{mn}_{12\mathcal{B}\sqrt{mn}}$, where $\|\mathbf{r}_u\|_\infty, \|\mathbf{r}_u\|_\infty \leq \mathcal{B}$, and computes $\mathbb{U} = \mathsf{Com}_{\mathbf{A}}(\mathbf{u}, \mathbf{r}_u), \mathbb{S} = \mathsf{Com}_{\mathbf{A}}(\mathbf{s}, \mathbf{r}_s)$ which is defined as in (8). Additionally, she picks masking elements $\mathbf{m}_v, \mathbf{m}_w \leftarrow_{\$} \mathfrak{D}^n_{12\beta\sqrt{n}}$ for v, w and commits to it $\mathbb{C}_{\mathbf{m}_v} := \mathsf{Com}_{\mathbf{A}}(\mathbf{m}_v; \mathbf{r}_{\mathbf{m}_v}), \mathbb{C}_{\mathbf{m}_w} := \mathsf{Com}_{\mathbf{A}}(\mathbf{m}_w; \mathbf{r}_{\mathbf{m}_w})$, for randomly chosen values $\mathbf{r}_{\mathbf{m}_v}, \mathbf{r}_{\mathbf{m}_w}, \in \mathfrak{D}^{mn}_{12\beta\sqrt{mn}}$.

The prover outputs the commitments $\{\widetilde{\mathbb{A}}_j\}_j, \{\widetilde{\mathbb{T}}_{j'}\}_{j'}, \mathbb{U}, \mathbb{S}, \mathbb{C}_{\mathbf{m}_v}, \mathbb{C}_{\mathbf{m}_w}$ and $\mathsf{st} = (\mathsf{st}_1, \mathsf{st}_2) = \{f(X), q(X), \{\mathbf{r}_{a,j}\}_j, \{\mathbf{r}_{t,j'}\}_{j'}, \mathbf{r}_v, \mathbf{r}_w, \mathbf{r}_{\mathbf{m}_v}, \mathbf{r}_{\mathbf{m}_w}\}$. She sends $\mathsf{pc} = \{\{\widetilde{\mathbb{A}}_j\}_j, \{\widetilde{\mathbb{T}}_{j'}\}_{j'}, \mathbb{U}, \mathbb{S}\}, \mathsf{c} = \{\mathbb{C}_{\mathbf{m}_v}, \mathbb{C}_{\mathbf{m}_w}\}$ to the verifier.

Challenge: The verifier sends a challenge $x = X^\omega \in \mathcal{CH}$ to the prover.

Response: The prover computes $\mathsf{Resp}(\mathsf{st}, x)$ as follows: First determine $\tilde{\mathbf{f}}(x) = (1, x, \dots, x^{n'-1}, x^{n'}) \cdot \widetilde{\mathcal{A}} = \left(\sum_{j=0}^{n'-1} \tilde{a}_{j,0} x^j, \dots, \sum_{j=0}^{n'-1} \tilde{a}_{j,m'-1} x^j\right) + \mathbf{u}(x)$ and $\tilde{\mathbf{q}}(x) = (1, x, \dots, x^{\nu-1}, x^\nu) \cdot \widetilde{\mathcal{T}} = \left(\sum_{j'=0}^{\nu-1} \tilde{t}_{j',0} x^{j'}, \dots, \sum_{j'=0}^{\nu-1} \tilde{t}_{j',\mu-1} x^{j'}\right) + \mathbf{s}(x)$. She commits to $\tilde{\mathbf{f}}(x)$ and $\tilde{\mathbf{q}}(x)$ with randomness $\tilde{\mathbf{r}}_{\mathbf{f}} = \sum_{j=0}^{n'-1} \mathbf{r}_{a,j} x^j + \mathbf{r}_u x^{n'}$, $\tilde{\mathbf{r}}_{\mathbf{q}} = \sum_{j'=0}^{\nu-1} \mathbf{r}_{t,j'} x^{j'} + \mathbf{r}_s x^\nu$ as follows:

$$\widetilde{\mathbb{C}}_{\tilde{\mathbf{f}}} = \mathbf{A} \cdot \left(\sum_{j=0}^{n'-1} \mathbf{r}_{a,j} x^j\right) + \mathsf{enc}\left(\left(\sum_{j=0}^{n'-1} \tilde{a}_{j,0} x^j, \dots, \sum_{j=0}^{n'-1} \tilde{a}_{j,m'-1} x^j\right)\right) + \mathbf{A}\mathbf{r}_u \cdot x^{n'} + \mathsf{enc}(\mathbf{u}) \cdot x^{n'}$$

$$\widetilde{\mathbb{C}}_{\tilde{\mathbf{q}}} = \mathbf{A} \cdot \left(\sum_{j'=0}^{\nu-1} \mathbf{r}_{t,j'} x^{j'}\right) + \mathsf{enc}\left(\left(\sum_{j'=0}^{\nu-1} \tilde{t}_{j',0} x^{j'}, \dots, \sum_{j'=0}^{\nu-1} \tilde{t}_{j',\mu-1} x^{j'}\right)\right) + \mathbf{A}\mathbf{r}_s \cdot x^\nu + \mathsf{enc}(\mathbf{s}) \cdot x^\nu$$

Next, the prover masks the values v, w as follows: $\xi_{\mathbf{m}_v} = \mathbf{m}_v + xv$, $\xi_{\mathbf{m}_w} = \mathbf{m}_w + xw$, and the corresponding randomness: $\mathbf{r}_{\xi,\mathbf{m}_v} = x\mathbf{r}_v + \mathbf{r}_{\mathbf{m}_v}$, $\mathbf{r}_{\xi,\mathbf{m}_w} = x\mathbf{r}_w + \mathbf{r}_{\mathbf{m}_w}$, $\mathbf{r}_\gamma = \tilde{\mathbf{r}}_{\mathbf{f}} - \tilde{\mathbf{r}}_{\mathbf{q}} v - \mathbf{r}_w$. According to Theorem 2, the prover rejects sampled values with probability $\tilde{\rho} = \max_{i \in \{1,2,3\}}(\tilde{\rho}_i)$, where

$$\rho_1 := \frac{\mathfrak{D}^{n'mn}_{12\mathcal{B}\sqrt{n'mn}}(\tilde{\mathbf{r}}_{\mathbf{f}})}{M\mathfrak{D}^{n'mn}_{\{x^j \cdot \mathbf{r}_{a,j}\}_j, 12\mathcal{B}\sqrt{n'mn}}(\tilde{\mathbf{r}}_{\mathbf{f}})}, \quad \rho_2 := \frac{\mathfrak{D}^{\nu mn}_{12\mathcal{B}\sqrt{\nu mn}}(\tilde{\mathbf{r}}_{\mathbf{q}})}{M\mathfrak{D}^{\nu mn}_{\{x^{j'} \cdot \mathbf{r}_{t,j'}\}_{j'}, 12\mathcal{B}\sqrt{\nu mn}}(\tilde{\mathbf{r}}_{\mathbf{q}})},$$

$$\rho_3 := \frac{\mathfrak{D}^{mn}_{12\mathcal{B}\sqrt{3mn}}(\mathbf{r}_{\xi,\mathbf{m}_v}, \mathbf{r}_{\xi,\mathbf{m}_w})}{M\mathfrak{D}^{mn}_{x \cdot \iota, 12\mathcal{B}\sqrt{3mn}}(\mathbf{r}_{\xi,\mathbf{m}_v}, \mathbf{r}_{\xi,\mathbf{m}_w})}$$

for $\iota \in \{\mathbf{r}_v, \mathbf{r}_w\}$. It holds $\|(x^0 \mathbf{r}_{a,0}, \dots, x^{n'} \mathbf{r}_{a,n'-1})\| \leq \mathcal{B}\sqrt{n'mn}$; $\|(x^0 \mathbf{r}_{t,0}, \dots, x^\nu \mathbf{r}_{t,\nu-1})\| \leq \mathcal{B}\sqrt{\nu mn}$ and $n' = \mathcal{O}(\sqrt{n})$. She computes $\mathbb{C}_{0,\tilde{\mathbf{f}}} = \mathsf{Com}_{\mathbf{A}}(\mathbf{0}, \tilde{\mathbf{r}}_{\mathbf{f}}), \mathbb{C}_{0,\tilde{\mathbf{q}}} = \mathsf{Com}_{\mathbf{A}}(\mathbf{0}, \tilde{\mathbf{r}}_{\mathbf{q}})$. She sends $\mathsf{re} = \{\mathbb{C}_{\tilde{\mathbf{f}}}, \mathbb{C}_{\tilde{\mathbf{q}}}, \mathbb{C}_{0,\tilde{\mathbf{f}}}, \mathbb{C}_{0,\tilde{\mathbf{q}}}, \xi_{\mathbf{m}_v}, \xi_{\mathbf{m}_w}, \mathbf{r}_{\xi,\mathbf{m}_v}, \mathbf{r}_{\xi,\mathbf{m}_w}, \mathbf{r}_\gamma\}$ to the verifier.

Verification: The verifier runs $\mathsf{PolyVerify}(\mathbf{A}, m', n', \mathsf{pc}, \mathsf{c}, \mathsf{re}, x)$ and outputs: $\mathsf{Com}_{\mathbf{A}}(\xi_{\mathbf{m}_v}, \mathbf{r}_{\xi,\mathbf{m}_v}) = x\mathbb{C}_v + \mathbb{C}_{\mathbf{m}_v}, \mathsf{Com}_{\mathbf{A}}(\xi_{\mathbf{m}_w}, \mathbf{r}_{\xi,\mathbf{m}_w}) = x\mathbb{C}_w + \mathbb{C}_{\mathbf{m}_w}$. She checks $\max\{\|\mathbf{r}_{\xi,\mathbf{m}_v}\|, \|\mathbf{r}_{\xi,\mathbf{m}_w}\|\} \leq 12\mathcal{B}\sqrt{m'n}$ and:

$$\sum_{j=0}^{n'-1} x^j \widetilde{\mathbb{A}}_j + x^{n'} \mathbb{U} = \mathbb{C}_{\tilde{\mathbf{f}}} = \mathsf{Com}_{\mathbf{A}}(\tilde{\mathbf{f}}(x), \tilde{\mathbf{r}}_{\mathbf{f}}), \quad \sum_{j'=0}^{\nu-1} x^{j'} \widetilde{\mathbb{T}}_{j'} + x^\nu \mathbb{S} = \mathbb{C}_{\tilde{\mathbf{q}}} = \mathsf{Com}_{\mathbf{A}}(\tilde{\mathbf{q}}(x), \tilde{\mathbf{r}}_{\mathbf{q}}),$$

$$\sum_{i=0}^{m'-1} \mathbb{C}_i(\tilde{\mathbf{f}}, \tilde{\mathbf{r}}_{\mathbf{f}}) \cdot x^{n'i} = \sum_{i'=0}^{\mu-1} \mathbb{C}_{i'}(\tilde{\mathbf{q}}, \tilde{\mathbf{r}}_{\mathbf{q}}) \cdot x^{\nu i'} \cdot (x - \mathbb{C}_v) + \mathbb{C}_w - \mathsf{Com}_{\mathbf{A}}(\mathbf{0}, \mathbf{r}_\gamma).$$

Fig. 1. Polynomial evaluation protocol Π_{PEv}

where $C_i(\cdot)$ and $C_{i'}(\cdot)$ denote the i-th or i'-th component of the corresponding commitment vector $\mathtt{Com_A}(\tilde{\mathbf{f}}, \tilde{\mathbf{r}}_{\mathbf{f}})$ and $\mathtt{Com_A}(\tilde{\mathbf{q}}, \tilde{\mathbf{r}}_{\mathbf{q}})$, respectively. Finally, she checks: $\|\tilde{\mathbf{r}}_{\mathbf{f}}\| \leq \mathcal{B}m'\sqrt{n'm}$, $\|\tilde{\mathbf{r}}_{\mathbf{q}}\| \leq \mathcal{B}\mu\sqrt{\nu m}$.

Theorem 2. *The polynomial commitment protocol has completeness, special honest verifier zero-knowledge and 3-special soundness for extracting a breach of the binding property of the commitment scheme, or extracting openings to the polynomials. The binding property relies on the underlying* $\mathtt{M-SIS}_{q,2,m,\beta}$ *assumption, while zero-knowledgeness is guaranteed by the hiding property of our commitment scheme which is given by the hardness of* $\mathtt{M-LWE}_{q,2,m}$ *assumption.*

Proof. To prove the theorem we prove the three properties:

Completeness: It is easy to see that the verification Eqs. (17)–(20) pass the test and that the verifier obtains the evaluation of the committed polynomial $f(X)$ at an evaluation point v. We verified the correctness of Eq. (17) in Sect. 3.1. This implies also correctness of Eq. (18). Both of these equations can verify the Eq. (19). Further, we have to show that $\|\mathbf{u}\|$ and $\|\mathbf{s}\|$ are statistically close to $\mathfrak{D}^{m'-1}_{12\mathcal{B}\sqrt{m'}}$ and $\|x^j \cdot \mathbf{r}_{a,j}\|, \|x^j \cdot \mathbf{r}_{t,j'}\|$ for $j \in [0, n']$ are statistically close to $\mathfrak{D}^{m'n'}_{12\mathcal{B}\sqrt{m'n'}}, \mathfrak{D}^{\mu\nu}_{12\mathcal{B}\sqrt{\mu\nu}}$, respectively. Also $\|\mathbf{r}_{\xi,\iota}\|$ for $\iota \in \{\mathbf{m}_v, \mathbf{m}_w\}$ are statistically close to $\mathfrak{D}_{12\mathcal{B}\sqrt{mn}}$ and $\mathfrak{D}_{12\mathcal{B}\sqrt{n'mn}}$, respectively.

3-Special Soundness: To prove the soundness we provide a reduction to the binding property of our commitment scheme. As explained before, because of the hiding issues we consider a restricted challenge space of 3 different challenges $x \in \mathbb{Z}_q$, x_1, x_2, x_3. These vectors form a generalized Vandermonde matrix

$$\mathbf{V}_{n'+1} = \begin{pmatrix} x_1^i & x_1^{i+1} & x_1^{i+2} \\ x_2^i & x_2^{i+1} & x_2^{i+2} \\ x_3^i & x_3^{i+1} & x_3^{i+2} \end{pmatrix}.$$

Since the columns of this matrix are independent vectors, we can reconstruct any unit vector by taking an appropriate linear combination of these columns. First we rewrite (Sect. 3.2) as:

$$\mathsf{Com}_{\mathbf{A}}(\tilde{\mathbf{f}}(x); \tilde{\mathbf{r}}_f) = \mathbf{A} \cdot \left(\sum_{j=0}^{n'-1} \mathbf{r}_{a,j} x^j + \mathbf{r}_u x^{n'} \right) + \mathsf{enc}(\tilde{\mathbf{f}}(x)) \tag{11}$$

We see that $\tilde{\mathbf{f}}(x) = \sum_{j=0}^{n'-1} x^j \cdot \tilde{\mathbf{a}}_j + \mathbf{u}x^{n'}$. Thus, Eq. (11) is equivalent to:

$$\mathsf{Com}_{\mathbf{A}}(\tilde{\mathbf{f}}(x); \tilde{\mathbf{r}}_f) = \mathbf{A}\left(\sum_{j=0}^{n'-1} \mathbf{r}_{a,j} x^j + \mathbf{r}_u x^{n'} \right) + \mathsf{enc}(\sum_{j=0}^{n'-1} \tilde{\mathbf{a}}_j x^j + \mathbf{u}x^{n'}). \tag{12}$$

Since each $\mathbf{r}_{a,j}, \mathbf{r}_u, \tilde{\mathbf{a}}_j, \mathbf{u}$ for $j \in [0, n' - 1]$ is a m'-dimensional vector, we can extract the openings of any commitments $\widetilde{\mathbb{A}}_j = \mathsf{Com}_{\mathbf{A}}(\tilde{\mathbf{a}}_j; \mathbf{r}_{a,j})$, by computing $2n'$ verification equations in (11) for challenges x_1, x_2, x_3. Then, (12) gives a system of polynomial equations for 3 challenges with $k \in \{1, 2, 3\}$: $\tilde{\mathbf{c}}_k = \mathbf{A}\left(\sum_{j=0}^{n'-1} \mathbf{r}_{a,j} x_k^j + \mathbf{r}_u x_k^{n'}\right) + \sum_{j=0}^{n'-1} \tilde{\mathbf{a}}_j x_k^j + \mathbf{u}x_k$. Next, we take $\mathsf{Com}_{\mathbf{A}}(0, \tilde{\mathbf{r}}_f)$ we compute $\mathbf{c}'_k = \tilde{\mathbf{c}}_k - \mathsf{Com}_{\mathbf{A}}(0, \tilde{\mathbf{r}}_f)$ and get: $\mathbf{c}'_k = \tilde{\mathbf{c}}_k - \mathsf{Com}_{\mathbf{A}}(0, \tilde{\mathbf{r}}_f) = \mathbf{A}\left(\sum_{j=0}^{n'-1} \mathbf{r}_{a,j} x_k^j + \mathbf{r}_u x_k^{n'}\right) + \mathsf{enc}(\sum_{j=0}^{n'-1} \tilde{\mathbf{a}}_j x_k^j + \mathbf{u}x_k^{n'}) - \mathsf{Com}_{\mathbf{A}}(0, \tilde{\mathbf{r}}_f) = \mathsf{enc}(\sum_{j=0}^{n'-1} \tilde{\mathbf{a}}_j x_k^j + \mathbf{u}(x_k)) \in \mathcal{R}_q^2$, where $\mathbf{u}(x_k) = \left(\sum_{j=0}^{n'-1} u_{n'-j-1,1} x_k^j, \ldots, \sum_{j=0}^{n'-1} u_{n'-j-1,m'-1} x_k^j, 0\right)$. Note that $\tilde{a}_{j,i} = a_{j,i} - u_{j,i} x_k^{n'-(2j+1)}$ yielding $\sum_{j=0}^{n'-1} \tilde{a}_{j,i} x_k^j = a_{0,i} - u_{0,i} + \ldots + a_{n'-1,i} x_k^{n'-1} - u_{n'-1} x_k$.

After reshuffling the terms we get $\sum_{j=0}^{n'-1} \tilde{a}_{j,i} x_k^j = \sum_{j=0}^{n'-1} (a_{j,i} - u_{n'-j-1,i}) x_k^j$ and we set $\tilde{a}_{j,i} := a_{j,i} - u_{n'-j-1,i}$. For all $i \in [0, m'-1], j \in [0, n'-1]$ it yields that $(\mathbf{c}'_\iota)^{tr}$ for challenge index $\iota \in \{1, 2, 3\}$ is equal to:

$$
\mathbf{c}'_k = \begin{bmatrix} \tilde{a}_{0,0} \\ \vdots \\ \tilde{a}_{0,m'-1} \end{bmatrix} x_k^0 + \cdots + \begin{bmatrix} \tilde{a}_{n'-1,0} \\ \vdots \\ \tilde{a}_{n'-1,m'-1} \end{bmatrix} x_k^{n'-1} + \begin{bmatrix} \sum_{j=0}^{n'-1} u_{n'-j-1,1} x_k^j \\ \vdots \\ \sum_{j=0}^{n'-1} u_{n'-j-1,m'-1} x_k^j \\ 0 \end{bmatrix} x_k^{n'}
$$

For all $k \in \{1, 2, 3\}$, and $i \in [0, m'-1]$ we write each vector $\mathbf{c}'_{k,i}$ as a linear system of m' equations: $c_{k,i} = \tilde{a}_{0,i} x_k^0 + \ldots + \tilde{a}_{n'-1,i} x_k^{n'-1} + \sum_{j=0}^{n'-1} u_{n'-j-1,k} x_k^{n'+j}$ We obtain 3 blocks B_k, where $k \in \{1, 2, 3\}$ of linear systems where each such system has m' rows and $2n'$ coefficients, i.e. $B_k = [c_{k,0}, \ldots, c_{k,m'-1}]^{tr}$. We reshuffle these 3 blocks as follows: We take the j-th row, i.e. $c_{k,j}$ from each block B_k and collect them into a new block $B^{(j)} = [c_{1,j}, c_{2,j}, c_{3,j}]^{tr}$, such that we get in total m' blocks of linear systems with 3 rows and $2n'$ coefficients. For sake of better visualization, we show the reshuffling process on an example where we collect the 0-th row from each block $\{B_k\}_{k \in \{1,2,3\}}$ into a new block $B^{(0)}$. For all $k \in \{1, 2, 3\}$, we have: $c_{k,0} = \tilde{a}_{0,0} x_k^0 + \ldots + \tilde{a}_{n'-1,0} x_k^{n'-1} + \sum_{j=0}^{n'-1} u_{n'-j-1,1} x_k^{n'+j}$.

In the same manner we compute $B^{(j)}$ for all $j \in [0, n'-1]$, where $B^{(j)}$ can be represented as follows: We define $\mathbf{c}^{(j)} := (c_1^{(j)}, c_2^{(j)}, c_3^{(j)})^{tr}$ being the row from each block $\{B_k\}_k$ and $\tilde{\mathbf{a}}^{(j)} = (\tilde{a}_0^{(j)}, \ldots, \tilde{a}_{n'-1}^{(j)}, u_{n'-1}^{(j)}, \ldots u_0^{(j)})^{tr}$ being the vector of coefficients in each $c_k^{(j)}$. Then, each such system $\mathbf{c}^{(j)}$ can be represented as a product of a challenge matrix $\tilde{\mathbf{V}}_3$ and the vector $\tilde{\mathbf{a}}^{(j)}$. The challenge matrix can be represented by a row-vector consisting of block Vandermonde matrices:

$$
\tilde{\mathbf{V}}_3 = \begin{pmatrix} 1 & x_1^1 & x_1^2 & \cdots & x_1^{(2n'-1)} \\ 1 & x_2^1 & x_2^2 & \cdots & x_2^{(2n'-1)} \\ 1 & x_3^1 & x_3^2 & \cdots & x_3^{(2n'-1)} \end{pmatrix} = \left[\begin{pmatrix} 1 & x_1^1 & x_1^2 \\ 1 & x_2^1 & x_2^2 \\ 1 & x_3^1 & x_3^2 \end{pmatrix} \cdots \begin{pmatrix} x_1^{2n'-3} & x_1^{2n'-2} & x_1^{2n'-1} \\ x_2^{2n'-3} & x_2^{2n'-2} & x_2^{2n'-1} \\ x_3^{2n'-3} & x_3^{2n'-2} & x_3^{2n'-1} \end{pmatrix} \right].
$$

Since our challenge space is restricted to the set of $\mathcal{CH} = \{1, x^1, x^{-1}\}$, then:

$$
\tilde{\mathbf{V}}_3 = \left[\begin{pmatrix} 1 & x^1 & x^2 \\ 1 & x^{-1} & x^{-2} \\ 1 & 1 & 1 \end{pmatrix} \begin{pmatrix} x^3 & x^4 & x^5 \\ x^{-3} & x^{-4} & x^{-5} \\ 1 & 1 & 1 \end{pmatrix} \cdots \begin{pmatrix} x^{2n'-3} & x^{2n'-2} & x^{2n'-1} \\ x^{3-2n'} & x^{2-2n'} & x^{1-2n'} \\ 1 & 1 & 1 \end{pmatrix} \right].
$$

We denote each block of $\tilde{\mathbf{V}}_3$ as $\tilde{\mathbf{V}}_{3,\kappa}$ for $\kappa \in [1, (2n'/3)]$. The determinant of each $\tilde{\mathbf{V}}_{3,\kappa}$ is equal and is calculated to the following value: $2x^{-1} - 2x + x^2 - x^{-2}$ with Euclidean norm equal to 6. We define the inverses of all $\tilde{\mathbf{V}}_{3,\kappa}$ and set it into the following $2n' \times 3$ matrix $(\tilde{\mathbf{V}}_3^{-1})^{tr} = [(\tilde{\mathbf{V}}_{3,1}^{-1}, \tilde{\mathbf{V}}_{3,2}^{-1}, \tilde{\mathbf{V}}_{3,3}^{-1})]^{tr}$. We get m' blocks which can be represented for all $i \in [0, m'-1]$ as the following equation $B^{(i)}$: $\mathbf{c}^{(i)} = \tilde{\mathbf{V}}_3 \cdot \tilde{\mathbf{a}}^{(i)}$. Multiplying each block by $\tilde{\mathbf{V}}_3^{-1}$ from the left extracts the $2n'$ vectors $\tilde{\mathbf{a}}^{(0)}, \ldots, \tilde{\mathbf{a}}^{(n'-1)}$ and $\mathbf{u}_0, \ldots, \mathbf{u}_{n'-1}$.

Similarly, we can extract the randomness $\{\mathbf{r}_{a,j}\}_j$ by setting $\hat{\mathbf{r}} := \sum_{j=0}^{n'-1} \mathbf{r}_{a,j} x^j + \tilde{\mathbf{r}}_u x^{n'}$ using the 3 challenges and the same extraction procedure as described above. We obtain the following system: $\widetilde{B}^{(i)} : \hat{\mathbf{r}}^{(i)} = \widetilde{\mathbf{V}}_3 \cdot \tilde{\mathbf{r}}^{(i)}$ for $i \in \{0, m' - 1\}$ Since we use unbounded commitment scheme, we only need to compute the bound of the extracted randomness. It holds that $\|\hat{\mathbf{r}}^{(i)}\| = \|\widetilde{\mathbf{V}}_3\|\|\tilde{\mathbf{r}}^{(i)}\| \leq 6 \cdot 12\mathcal{B}\sqrt{m'n}$. Since our commitments are binding, each response is computed as it is done by an honest prover in the argument. Therefore, for a bigger number than j challenges, the extracted secrets $\mathbf{r}_{a,j}, \mathbf{r}_u, \tilde{\mathbf{a}}_j, \mathbf{u}, j \in [0, n' - 1]$, yield $\tilde{\mathbf{f}}(x)$.

Similarly we extract the values $\tilde{\mathbf{t}}^{(0)}, \ldots, \tilde{\mathbf{t}}^{(\nu-1)}$ and $\mathbf{s}_0, \ldots, \mathbf{s}_{n'-1}$ (Due to the similarities to the extraction of $\tilde{\mathbf{a}}^{(0)}, \ldots, \tilde{\mathbf{a}}^{(n'-1)}$ and $\mathbf{u}_0, \ldots, \mathbf{u}_{n'-1}$ we omit the details of this extraction procedure). Since the challenge space contains only 3 elements, in order to achieve a negligible soundness error, we need to repeat the protocol $\lambda/log(3)$ times.

Special Honest Verifier Zero-Knowledgeness: To prove the zero-knowledge property of our protocol, we need to show how to simulate an evaluation of the polynomial $f(X)$ at a certain point x, where the evaluation of $f(v) = w$ is given to us and is equal to $w = \tilde{\mathbf{f}}(u) \cdot (1, u^{n'}, \ldots, u^{(m'-1)n'})^t$. To run the simulation, we pick randomly the $m' - 1$ values $\tilde{f}_1(x), \ldots, \tilde{f}_{m'-1}(x) \leftarrow \mathfrak{D}_\sigma^n$ which are components of the vector $\tilde{\mathbf{f}}(x)$ and compute $\tilde{f}_0(x) = w - \sum_{i=1}^{m'-1} \tilde{f}_i(x) \cdot x^{in'}$. We also pick randomly the values $\widetilde{\mathbb{A}}_0, \ldots, \widetilde{\mathbb{A}}_{n'-1} \in \mathcal{R}_q^m$. Then we can compute: $\widetilde{\mathbb{A}}_{n'} = \mathbb{U} = \left(\widetilde{\mathbb{C}}_{\tilde{\mathbf{f}}} - \sum_{j=0}^{n'-1} x^j \widetilde{\mathbb{A}}_j\right) \cdot x^{-n'} = \text{Com}_{\mathbb{A}}\left(\tilde{\mathbf{f}}(x) \cdot x^{-n'}, \tilde{\mathbf{r}}_{\mathbf{f}} \cdot x^{-n'}\right) - \sum_{j=0}^{n'-1} x^{j-1} \widetilde{\mathbb{A}}_j$. If the protocol does not abort, then it holds that the real and the simulated values are indistinguishable under Theorem 1. $\qquad\square$

3.3 Efficiency Analysis

We analyze the efficiency of our protocol Π_{PEv}. The outputs are commitments to the rows $\{\mathbb{A}_j\}_j$ of the masked matrix $\mathcal{A}$ and commitments $\{\mathbb{T}_{j'}\}_{j'}$ of the masked matrix $\mathcal{T}$, commitments $\widetilde{\mathbb{C}}_{\tilde{\mathbf{f}}}, \widetilde{\mathbb{C}}_{\tilde{\mathbf{q}}}$, as well as the commitments $\mathbb{C}_{\xi, \mathbf{m}_v}, \mathbb{C}_{\xi, \mathbf{m}_w}$. The size of these commitments is given as follows: for all $j \in [0, n' - 1], j' \in [0, \nu - 1]$ we have $\|\mathbb{A}_j\| \leq \sqrt{n}\|\mathbb{A}_j\|_\infty \leq \sqrt{n}\log(q)$, $\|\mathbb{T}_{j'}\| \leq \sqrt{n}\|\mathbb{T}_{j'}\|_\infty \leq \sqrt{n}\log(q)$. We get same sizes for the other sent commitments, such that the total cost yields $(2n' + 9)\sqrt{n}\log(q)$. Further outputs are the 2 values $\xi_{\mathbf{m}_v}, \xi_{\mathbf{m}_w}$ of size $\|\xi_{\mathbf{m}_\iota}\| \leq 12\mathcal{B}\sqrt{n}$ for $\iota \in \{v, w\}$, i.e. total bit length $2\log(12\mathcal{B}\sqrt{n})$. Finally the 3 randomness vectors $\mathbf{r}_{\xi, \mathbf{m}_v}, \mathbf{r}_{\xi, \mathbf{m}_w}, \mathbf{r}_\gamma$ of length $\|\mathbf{r}_{\xi, \mathbf{m}_\iota}\| \leq 12\mathcal{B}\sqrt{mn}$ for $\iota \in \{v, w\}$. The total communication cost is $(2n' + 9)\sqrt{n}\log q + 2 \cdot \log(12\mathcal{B}\sqrt{n}) + 3\log(12\mathcal{B}\sqrt{mn})$.

Concrete Parameters. For the instantiation of concrete parameters, we use the results from [19], where the maximum of the columns of public parameter $\mathbf{A}$ is bounded by $\sqrt{n}\log q/\log \delta$, where $\delta = 1.0035$. We balance this security level for LWE using LWE estimator [1] and get the number of integer elements $\hat{m} = \mathcal{O}(n)$ over $\mathbb{Z}$. The length of this short vector is bounded by the following condition: $\beta \geq \min\left(q, 2^{2\sqrt{n\log(q)\log\delta}}\right)$. We know that $\|\mathbf{r}_{a,j}\| \leq \beta$ and $\beta \leq 12\mathcal{B}\sqrt{mn}$. The length of the extracted witness is bounded by $\|(x^0 \cdot \mathbf{r}_0, \ldots x^{n'} \cdot \mathbf{r}_{n'})\| \leq 6 \cdot 12\mathcal{B}\sqrt{mn} = \hat{\beta}$. The length of the non-zero vector in SIS is bounded by

$\hat{\beta} > \min\{q, 2^{2\sqrt{n\log q \log \delta}}\}$. The condition on m needs to satisfy $m = \sqrt{n}\log q/\log \delta$. We assume that $m' = n' = \mathcal{O}(\sqrt{n})$. Then the following estimation holds $\sigma \geq 12\mathcal{B}\sqrt{n'nm}$ is the standard deviations from rejection sampling. The probability from rejection sampling is $(1 - \tilde{\rho})$, where $\tilde{\rho} = \max_{i \in \{1,2,3\}}(\rho_i)$. It holds $\|\tilde{r}_f\|^2 = (\mathcal{B}n\sqrt{mn'})^2 = \mathcal{B}^2 n^3 m$, $\|\tilde{r}_q\|^2 = (\mathcal{B}n\sqrt{m\nu})^2 \approx \mathcal{B}^2 n^2 \nu m$. We pick the parameters so that $\mathcal{B} < \min\left(q, 2^{2\sqrt{n\log(q)\log\delta}}\right)$. In Table 3 we provide four parameter sets. To minimize the soundness error we repeat the protocol 80 times.

Table 3. Sample parameters for Π_{PEv} for $\lambda = 128$

Parameter	Set 1	Set 2	Set 3	Set 4
Commitment modulus q	2^{18}	2^{22}	2^{25}	2^{27}
Ring dimension n	128	256	512	1024
$\hat{m}$	768	768	1024	564
$\log(\hat{\beta})$	17.19	18.19	17.67	18.99
$\mathcal{B}$	65	65	27	40
Proof size	64.64 kB	144 kB	307.14 kB	607.61 kB

4 Batch Polynomial Evaluation

The protocol we present here allows to batch multiple instances into one polynomial and to commit to it. Our construction is based on the polynomial evaluation protocol we introduced in Sect. 3. In this section we discuss how to build such a batch polynomial evaluation zero-knowledge argument from lattices.

4.1 Preliminaries of the Protocol

The prover's witness is given by a vector $\mathbf{a}$, which satisfies some conditions and by an opening of the commitment C that is a commitment to the vector $\mathbf{a}$. To model these relations, we use a polynomial $\mathbf{P}$, s.t. $\mathbf{P}(\mathbf{a}) = 0$, and a polynomial $\mathbf{Q}$ which computes the opening of C. We commit to $\mathbf{Q}$ with randomness $\mathbf{r}$: $C = \text{Com}(\mathbf{Q}(\mathbf{a}); \mathbf{r})$. C is a commitment to the polynomial $\mathbf{Q}$ as introduced in Sect. 3. We also introduce a public vector $\mathbf{b}$ in our polynomial $\mathbf{Q}$. We assume that $\mathbf{P}(\mathbf{a}), \mathbf{Q}(\mathbf{a}, \mathbf{b})$ are vectors of length l_P, l_Q, i.e. $\mathbf{P}(\mathbf{a}) = (\mathbf{P}_1(\mathbf{a}), \ldots, \mathbf{P}_{l_P}(\mathbf{a})), \mathbf{Q}(\mathbf{a}) = (\mathbf{Q}_1(\mathbf{a}, \mathbf{b}), \ldots, \mathbf{Q}_{l_Q}(\mathbf{a}, \mathbf{b}))$ whose components $\mathbf{P}_{i'}(\mathbf{a}), \mathbf{Q}_{j'}(\mathbf{a}, \mathbf{b})$, for $i' \in [1, l_P], j' \in [1, l_Q]$ are $(l_a)-$ or $(l_a + l_b)-$variate polynomials, respectively. We use bold font to indicate vectors, while each of the vector components is a multivariate polynomial and is given in plain font. Let $\mathbf{P}$ and $\mathbf{Q}$ be vectors of polynomials of degree d_P and d_Q, respectively.

Let $d_P = n = m'n' - 1$ be the degree of polynomial $\mathbf{P}$. We provide an argument of knowledge of $\{\mathbf{a}_{j,i}\}_{i \in [0, m'-1], j \in [0, n'-1]} \in \mathbb{Z}_q^{l_a}$ and $\mathbf{r}_j \in \mathcal{R}_q^m$, such that $\mathbf{P}(\mathbf{a}_{j,i}) = 0$. We know that each $\mathbf{a}_{j,i}$ is a vector of l_a monomial coefficients, i.e. $\mathbf{a}_{j,i} = (a_{j,i,1}, \ldots, a_{j,i,l_a})$. We build a matrix for each monomial coefficient $a_\kappa, \kappa \in [l_a]$:

$$A_\kappa = \begin{bmatrix} a_{0,0,\kappa} & a_{0,1,\kappa} & \cdots & a_{0,m'-1,\kappa} \\ \vdots & \vdots & \ddots & \vdots \\ a_{n'-1,0,\kappa} & a_{n'-1,1,\kappa} & \cdots & a_{n'-1,m'-1,\kappa} \end{bmatrix}.$$

The matrix is an encoding of the following polynomial of degree $m'n' - 1$ in X_κ:

$$f(X_\kappa) = \sum_{i=0}^{m'-1} \sum_{j=0}^{n'-1} a_{j,i,\kappa} X_\kappa^{in'+j}. \tag{13}$$

We mask the matrix by adding an additional row $a_{\kappa,u} = (a_{\kappa,u,1}, \ldots, a_{\kappa,u,m'-1})$ at the end of the matrix A_κ, where each masking component $a_{\kappa,u,i}, i \in [1, m'-1]$ is defined as in the previous protocol in Sect. 3. We obtain a masked matrix $\widetilde{A}_\kappa$ having $n' + 1$ rows with indices from 0 to n'. We denote each component of the masked matrix as $\tilde{a}_{\kappa,i,j}$, where $i \in [0, m'-1]$ and $j \in [0, n'-1]$. Similarly we represent $\mathbf{b}_{j,i} \in \mathbb{Z}_q^{l_b}$, i.e. $\mathbf{b}_{j,i} = (b_{j,i,1}, \ldots, b_{j,i,l_b})$. The matrix $B_{\kappa'}$ for each monomial coefficient $b_{\kappa'}, \kappa' \in [l_b]$ is constructed in the same manner as above. This matrix is an encoding of the following polynomial of degree $m'n'$ in $X_{\kappa'}$:

$$f(X_{\kappa'}) = \sum_{i=0}^{m'-1} \sum_{j=0}^{n'-1} b_{\kappa',j,i} X_{\kappa'}^{in'+j}. \tag{14}$$

We take each element from row $i \in [0, m'-1]$ and column $j \in [0, n'-1]$ from matrix $\widetilde{A}_\kappa, \kappa \in [l_a]$ and pack them into the vectors $\tilde{\mathbf{a}}_{j,i} = (\tilde{a}_{j,i,1}, \ldots, \tilde{a}_{j,i,l_a})$, which are vectors of j, i-th coefficients of l_a-variate polynomials, respectively.

4.2 Detailed Protocol

In this section we provide a concrete description of our batch polynomial protocol over lattices. We first define the relations which will be proved by our protocol.

Definition 9. *For positive real bounds β, β' we have the following two relations to be proved:*

$\mathsf{R}_{\mathsf{batch},\beta} = \{\forall j \in [0, n'-1], i \in [0, m'-1] : \mathcal{P}(\{\tilde{\mathbf{a}}_{j,i}\}, \{\mathbf{r}_{a,j}\}, \mathbf{P}, \mathbf{Q}), \mathcal{V}(\{\mathsf{C}_j\}, \{\mathbf{b}_{j,i}\}) :$

$\quad \mathbf{P}(\tilde{\mathbf{a}}_{j,i}) = 0 \wedge \mathsf{C}_j = \mathsf{Com}_\mathbf{A}(\mathbf{Q}(\tilde{\mathbf{a}}_{j,0}, \mathbf{b}_{j,0}), \ldots, \mathbf{Q}(\tilde{\mathbf{a}}_{j,m'-1}, \mathbf{b}_{j,m'-1}); \mathbf{r}_j) \wedge \|\mathbf{r}_j\| \le \beta\}$

$\mathsf{R}'_{\mathsf{batch},\beta'} = \{\forall j \in [0, n'-1], i \in [0, m'-1] : \mathcal{P}(\{6\tilde{\mathbf{a}}_{j,i}\}, \{\mathbf{r}'_{a,j}\}, \mathbf{P}, \mathbf{Q}), \mathcal{V}(\{\mathsf{C}_j\}, \{\mathbf{b}_{j,i}\}) :$

$\quad \mathbf{P}(6\tilde{\mathbf{a}}_{j,i}) = 0 \wedge \mathsf{C}_j = \mathsf{Com}_\mathbf{A}(\mathbf{Q}(6\tilde{\mathbf{a}}_{j,0}, \mathbf{b}_{j,0}), \ldots, \mathbf{Q}(6\tilde{\mathbf{a}}_{j,m'-1}, \mathbf{b}_{j,m'-1}); \mathbf{r}'_j) \wedge \|\mathbf{r}'_j\| \le \beta'\}$

Remark 2. The commitments in this protocol rely on the security of $Module - SIS_{\tilde{n},m,\beta}$, where $\tilde{n}$ denotes the number of rows of the public parameter $\mathbf{A} \in \mathcal{R}_q^{\tilde{n} \times m}$. Note that for the computation of commitments C_i and D_i we have $\tilde{n} = l_Q$ where $j \in [0, n'-1]$ and l_Q, l_a are defined in the protocol below.

Construction. The prover computes a function on the vectors $\tilde{\mathbf{a}}_{j,i}, \mathbf{b}_{j,i}$ yielding a vector $\mathbf{Q}(\tilde{\mathbf{a}}_{j,i}, \mathbf{b}_{j,i})$ of multivariate polynomial of degree l_Q.

$$\mathbf{Q}(\tilde{\mathbf{a}}_{j,i}, \mathbf{b}_{j,i}) = \left(Q_1(\tilde{\mathbf{a}}_{j,i}, \mathbf{b}_{j,i}), \ldots, Q_{l_Q}(\tilde{\mathbf{a}}_{j,i}, \mathbf{b}_{j,i})\right)^{tr}. \tag{15}$$

The prover computes n' commitments knowing the openings to a vector of m' multivariate polynomial vectors $\{\mathbf{Q}(\tilde{\mathbf{a}}_{j,i}, \mathbf{b}_{j,i})\}_{j \in [0,n'-1], i \in [0,m'-1]}$, where each of those m' vectors are defined in (15). Note, that each of these polynomial vectors contains l_Q different $(l_a + l_b)$-variate polynomials in $l_a + l_b$ variables, i.e. for each $i \in [0, m'-1], j \in [0, n'-1]$ and for each $\iota \in [l_Q]$ we have a vector of l_Q multivariate polynomials in $l_a + l_b$ variables of the following form: $Q_\iota(\tilde{\mathbf{a}}_{j,i}, \mathbf{b}_{j,i}) = \sum_{k=0}^{d_Q} K_{\iota,k}\left(\prod_{\substack{\{d_i\}_{i \in [l_a+l_b]} \\ \sum d_i \le k}} X_1^{d_1} \cdots X_{l_a+l_b}^{d_{l_a+l_b}}\right) = Q_{\iota,j,i}(X_1, \ldots, X_{l_a+l_b})$. where $K_{\iota,k}$ is the k-th coefficient in the sum which is equal to a combination of $a_{\iota,j,i}$ from (13) and $b_{\iota,j,i}$ from (14). In order to commit to a m'-dimensional vector of multivariate polynomials, we first redefine each multivariate polynomial into regular polynomials as follows: Let K_{ι,k,d_i} denote the d_ι-th coefficient of $X_k^{d_i}$, i.e. K_{ι,k,d_i} depends on the values $\{X_k\}_{k \in [l_a+l_b], k \ne d_i}$. For $k \in [l_a + l_b]$ and $\iota \in [l_Q]$ we have: $Q_{\iota,j,i}(X_k) = \sum_{d_i=0}^{d_Q} K_{\iota,k,d_i}(x_1, \ldots x_{l_a+l_b}) X_k^{d_i}$. We fix $j \in [0, n'-1]$ and $\iota \in [l_Q]$, and define a vector over the indices $i \in [0, m'-1]$ as $\mathbf{Q}_{\iota,j}(X_k) = \left(Q_{\iota,j,0}(X_k), \ldots, Q_{\iota,j,m'-1}(X_k)\right)^{tr}$ being a vector of m' polynomials in X_k for $\iota \in [l_Q]$. Each of these polynomials is of degree d_Q. The public key is $\mathbf{A} \in \mathcal{R}_q^{l_Q \times m}$ and the randomnesses $\mathbf{r}_j \in \mathcal{R}_q^{m \times (l_a+l_b)}$. Let $n = m'n'-1$. We commit to a matrix in $\mathcal{R}_q^{l_Q \times (l_a+l_b)}$ which has the following form:

$$\mathbf{Q}_j := \begin{pmatrix} \mathbf{Q}_{1,j}(X_1) & \cdots & \mathbf{Q}_{1,j}(X_{l_a+l_b}) \\ \vdots & \ddots & \vdots \\ \mathbf{Q}_{l_Q,j}(X_1) & \cdots & \mathbf{Q}_{l_Q,j}(X_{l_a+l_b}) \end{pmatrix}$$

Its commitment is defined as: $\mathsf{C}_j = \mathsf{Com}_\mathbf{A}\left(\mathbf{Q}(\tilde{\mathbf{a}}_{j,0}, \mathbf{b}_{j,0}), \ldots, \mathbf{Q}(\tilde{\mathbf{a}}_{j,m'-1}, \mathbf{b}_{j,m'-1}); \mathbf{r}_j\right) = \mathsf{Com}_\mathbf{A}(\mathbf{Q}_j, \mathbf{r}_j)$. Public inputs to the protocol are $\{\mathsf{C}_j\}_j, \mathbf{Q}, \mathbf{P}$ and the vectors $\mathbf{b}_{j,i}$. For better understanding of how we commit to m' vectors of multivariate polynomials of degree d_Q, see Example in Appendix A.

Common Reference String Generation: The batch protocol embeds multiple instances of the same polynomial equality into a single polynomial by using Lagrange interpolation technique. In order to recover a single instance, we simply evaluate the polynomial in one of the interpolation points. Let $y_1, \ldots, y_{n'}$ be distinct points in $\mathcal{CH}$ (monomials) and $l_1(X), \ldots, l_{n'}(X)$ be their associated Lagrange polynomials, s.t. $l_j(y_i) = \delta_{j,i}$ and $l_0(X) = \prod_{i=1}^{n'}(X - y_i)$. For $j \in [0, n'-1]$ we have: $l_j(X) = \prod_{\substack{0 \le k \le n-1' \\ n'-1' \ne k}} \frac{X - y_k}{y_j - y_k}$.

Public Input: $\mathbf{P}, \mathbf{Q}, \{\mathbf{b}_{j,i}\}_{i \in [0,m'-1], j \in [0,n'-1]}, \{\mathsf{C}_j\}_{j \in [1,n'-1]}$.

Prover's Witness: $\{\tilde{\mathbf{a}}_{j,i}\}$ and $\{\mathbf{r}_j\}$ for $j \in [0, n'-1], i \in [0, m'-1]$.

Initial Message: The prover picks random values $\mathbf{s}_j \in \mathcal{R}_q^m$ and computes the commitments D_j on $\{\tilde{\mathbf{a}}_{j,i}\}$, where $0 \le j \le n'-1$ and $0 \le i \le m'-1$ and $\tilde{\mathbf{a}}_j = (\tilde{\mathbf{a}}_{j,0}, \ldots, \tilde{\mathbf{a}}_{j,m'-1})$, with $\mathbf{A} \in \mathcal{R}_q^{l_Q \times m}$ as follows: $\mathsf{D}_j := \mathsf{Com}_{\mathbf{A}}(\tilde{\mathbf{a}}_{j,0}, \ldots, \tilde{\mathbf{a}}_{j,m'}; \mathbf{s}_j) = \mathbf{A} \cdot \mathbf{s}_j + \tilde{\mathbf{a}}_j$, for a random vector $\mathbf{s}_j \leftarrow_\$ \mathcal{R}_q^m$. For $j = n'$ we sample a vector $(\tilde{\mathbf{a}}_{n',0}, \ldots, \tilde{\mathbf{a}}_{n',m'-1}) \leftarrow_\$ \mathfrak{D}^{l_Q m' n'}_{12\mathcal{B}\sqrt{l_Q m' n'}}$, which is a blinding vector chosen uniformly at random in the preliminary step, i.e. $\tilde{\mathbf{a}}_{n',i} = (b_{1,u,i}, \ldots, b_{l_a,u,i})$ is the additional masking row on A_κ. The prover computes $\hat{\mathbf{a}}_i = \sum_{j=0}^{n'} \tilde{\mathbf{a}}_{j,i} l_j(X)$ and $\hat{\mathbf{b}}_i = \sum_{j=0}^{n'} \mathbf{b}_{j,i} l_j(X)$. She has to show that $\tilde{\mathbf{a}}_{j,i}, \mathbf{b}_{j,i}$ satisfy polynomial relations presented above. When evaluating these vectors at a point y_i we get $\sum_{j=0}^{n'} \tilde{\mathbf{a}}_{j,i} l_j(y_i) = \tilde{\mathbf{a}}_{i,i}$ and $\sum_{j=0}^{n'} \mathbf{b}_{j,i} l_j(y_i) = \mathbf{b}_{i,i}$, respectively. This yields the single evaluation of $\mathbf{P}(\tilde{\mathbf{a}}_{j,i})$. It holds that: $\mathbf{P}_i^*(X) \cdot \prod_{j=0}^{n'}(X - y_j) = \mathbf{P}(\hat{\mathbf{a}}_i) = \mathbf{P}(\sum_{j=0}^{n'} \tilde{\mathbf{a}}_{j,i} l_j(X))$, where evaluating this equation at y_i yields $\mathbf{P}(\tilde{\mathbf{a}}_{j,j}) = 0$. Thus, the prover computes the polynomial

$$\mathbf{P}(\hat{\mathbf{a}}_j)/l_0(X) = \frac{\mathbf{P}\left(\sum_{j=0}^{n'} \tilde{\mathbf{a}}_{j,i} l_j(X)\right)}{\prod_{j=0}^{n'}(X - y_j)} = \mathbf{P}_i^*(X)$$

of degree $(d_P - 1)n'$ and commits to its coefficients. This can be achieved using polynomial commitment scheme from Sect. 3 but generalized to the case of vector coefficients. We take the polynomials $\{\mathbf{P}_i^*(X)\}_i$ and encode them into matrices $\mathcal{P}_i^*$ of dimension $t_1 \times t_2$, i.e. $d_P n' - n' = t_1 t_2$ as in Sect. 3. To do so, we first write $\mathbf{P}_i^*(X) = \sum_{\mu=0}^{t_2} \sum_{\nu=0}^{t_1} p_{\nu,\mu}^{(i)} X^{\mu d_p + \nu}$ and the corresponding matrix of coefficients: $\mathcal{P}_i^* = \left(p_{\mu,\nu}^{(i)}\right)_{\mu,\nu}$, for all $i \in [0, m'-1]$ and $\mu \in [0, t_2], \nu \in [0, t_1]$. Since $\mathbf{P}_i^*$ is a vector of l_P polynomials in the variable X, i.e. $\mathbf{P}_i^* = (\mathbf{P}_{i,1}^*(X), \ldots, \mathbf{P}_{i,l_P}^*(X))$, each $p_{\nu,\mu}^{(i)}$ denotes a row-vector: $p_{\nu,\mu}^{(i)} = \left(\mathsf{Coef}(\mathbf{P}_{i,1}^*(X)), \ldots \mathsf{Coef}(\mathbf{P}_{i,l_P}^*(X))\right)$. Applying the same masking technique as in Sect. 3 and adding an additional row $t_2 + 1$ with the masking vectors $(\mathbf{u}_{\mathbf{P}^*,1}, \ldots, \mathbf{u}_{\mathbf{P}^*,t_1}, 0)$, where each of these vectors is sampled from $\mathfrak{D}_\sigma^{l_P}$, we obtain a matrix $\widetilde{\mathcal{P}}_i^* = \left(\tilde{p}_{\mu,\nu}^{(i)}\right)_{\mu,\nu} \in \mathbb{Z}_q^{(t_2+2)\times(t_1+1)}$ with masked coefficients $\tilde{p}_{\mu,\nu}$. It holds:

$$\mathbf{P}_i^*(X) = \left(1, X, \cdots, X^{t_2}, X^{t_2+1}\right) \cdot \widetilde{\mathcal{P}}_i^* \cdot \left(1, X, \ldots, X^{t_1}\right)^{tr}, \quad i \in [0, m'-1]. \quad (16)$$

According to the polynomial commitment scheme, the prover commits to each row of the matrix $\widetilde{\mathcal{P}}_i^*$ using randomness $\mathbf{r}_{p_\mu}^{(i)} \in \mathcal{R}_q^m$, for $\mu \in [0, t_2]$ and padding with zeros until n. The commitments to the rows are $\mathbb{A}_{\mathbf{P}_i^*,\mu} = \mathsf{Com}_{\mathbf{A}}(\mathbf{p}_\mu^{(i)}, \mathbf{r}_{p_\mu}^{(i)}) = \mathbf{A} \cdot \mathbf{r}_{p_\mu}^{(i)} + \mathsf{enc}(\mathbf{p}_\mu^{(i)})$, w $\mathbf{p}_\mu^{(i)} = (\tilde{p}_{\mu,0}^{(i)}, \ldots, \tilde{p}_{\mu,t_1}^{(i)})$. The prover has also to prove that $\mathsf{C}_1, \ldots, \mathsf{C}_{n'}$ are commitments to $\mathbf{Q}(\tilde{\mathbf{a}}_{j,i}, \mathbf{b}_{j,i})$. To do so she picks random vectors $\mathbf{c}_0, \ldots, \mathbf{c}_{m'} \in \mathcal{R}_q^{l_Q}$ where each of the vectors is encoded into polynomials in $\mathcal{R}_q$ as follows: Let $\mathbf{c}_i = (c_{i,1}, \ldots, c_{i,l_Q}) \in \mathbb{Z}_q^{l_Q}$ for all $i \in [0, m'-1]$. For $\hat{\mathbf{c}} := (\mathbf{c}_1, \ldots, \mathbf{c}_{m'})$

compute $C_0 = \mathrm{Com}_{\mathbf{A}}(\hat{\mathbf{c}}; \mathbf{r}_c) = \mathbf{A} \cdot \mathbf{r}_c + \mathrm{enc}(\hat{\mathbf{c}})$, while $\mathbf{A} \in \mathcal{R}_q^{l_Q \times m}, \mathbf{r}_c \in \mathcal{R}_q^{m \times (l_a + l_b)}$.
We obtain the following polynomial

$$Q_i^*(X) = \mathbf{c}_i + \frac{\sum_{j=0}^{n'-1} \mathbf{Q}(\tilde{\mathbf{a}}_{j,i}, \mathbf{b}_{j,i}) l_j(X) - \mathbf{Q}(\hat{\mathbf{a}}_i, \hat{\mathbf{b}}_i)}{l_0(X)},$$

which is a vector of univariate polynomials in X. The prover computes a poly-
nomial commitment of $\mathbf{Q}_i^*$ for all $i \in [0, m'-1], \tilde{\mu} \in [0, \tau_2], \tilde{\nu} \in [0, \tau_1]$ as
follows. Let $\mathbf{Q}_i^*(X) = \sum_{\tilde{\mu}=0}^{\tau_2} \sum_{\tilde{\nu}=0}^{\tau_1} q_{\tilde{\nu},\tilde{\mu}}^{(i)} X^{\tilde{\mu} d_{Q^*} + \tilde{\nu}}$ with the corresponding coefficient matrix $\mathcal{Q}_i^* = (q_{\tilde{\mu},\tilde{\nu}}^{(i)})_{\tilde{\mu},\tilde{\nu}}$. Since $\mathbf{Q}_i^*$ is a vector of l_Q polynomials X, i.e.
$\mathbf{Q}_i^* = (\mathbf{Q}_{i,1}^*(X), \ldots, \mathbf{Q}_{i,l_Q}^*(X))$, and $q_{\tilde{\nu},\tilde{\mu}}^{(i)} = (\mathrm{Coef}(\mathbf{Q}_{i,1}^*(X)), \ldots, \mathrm{Coef}(\mathbf{Q}_{i,l_Q}^*(X))$.
The masked matrix (computed as in Sect. 3) is $\tilde{\mathcal{Q}}_i^* = (\tilde{q}_{\tilde{\mu},\tilde{\nu}}^{(i)})_{\tilde{\mu},\tilde{\nu}}$ and has $\tau_2 + 2$ rows
enumerated from 0 to $\tau_2 + 1$, where the last row is a masking vector, randomly
sampled from $\mathfrak{D}_{12\beta\sqrt{\tau_1+1}}^{\tau_1}$ which is padded with 0. According to the polynomial
commitment, the prover commits to each row of $\tilde{\mathcal{Q}}_i^*$ using randomness $\mathbf{r}_{q_{\tilde{\mu}}}^{(i)} \in \mathcal{R}_q^m$,
for $\tilde{\mu} \in [0, \tau_2 + 1]$ and padding with zeros until reaching the desired length n.
The commitments are given as $\mathbb{A}_{\mathbf{Q}_i^*, \tilde{\mu}} = \mathrm{Com}_{\mathbf{A}}(\mathbf{q}_{\tilde{\mu}}, \mathbf{r}_{q_{\tilde{\mu}}}^{(i)}) = \mathbf{A} \cdot \mathbf{r}_{q_{\tilde{\mu}}}^{(i)} + \mathrm{enc}(\mathbf{q}_{\tilde{\mu}}^{(i)})$,
where $\mathbf{q}_{\tilde{\mu}}^{(i)} = (q_{\tilde{\mu},0}^{(i)}, \ldots, q_{\tilde{\mu},\tau_1}^{(i)})$.

The prover runs Π_{PEv} from Sect. 3 on input $\mathbf{P}_i^*, \mathbf{Q}_i^*, u, \mathbf{P}_i^*(u), \mathbf{Q}_i^*(u)$. Let $\chi \in \{\mathbf{P}^*, \mathbf{Q}^*\}, \chi_i \in \{\mathbf{P}_i^*, \mathbf{Q}_i^*\}$ and $i \in [0, m'-1]$. She outputs $\{(\mathbf{msg}_{\chi,1}, \mathbf{st}_{\chi^*})\}_\chi$ s.t.
$\mathbf{msg}_{\chi,1} = \{\mathbf{msg}_{\chi_i,1}\}_i$ and $\mathbf{msg}_{\chi_i,1} = (\mathbb{A}_{\chi_i,\mu}, \mathbb{T}_{\chi_i,\mu}, \mathbb{U}_{\chi_i}, \mathbb{S}_{\chi_i}, \mathbb{C}_{\chi_i,v}, \mathbb{C}_{\chi_i,w})$. For all
$\mu \in [0, t_2 - 1], \tilde{\mu} \in [0, \tau_2 - 1]$ we set $\mathbf{st}_{\mathbf{P}_i^*} = (\mathbf{P}_i^*, \{\mathbf{r}_{p_\mu}^{(i)}\}_\mu), \mathbf{st}_{\mathbf{Q}_i^*} = (\mathbf{Q}_i^*, \{\mathbf{r}_{q_{\tilde{\mu}}}^{(i)}\}_{\tilde{\mu}})$.
Let $\mathbf{st}_\chi = \{\mathbf{st}_{\chi_i}\}_i$. The prover sends $\{\mathbf{D}_j\}_{j \in [0,n']}, \{\mathbf{msg}_{\chi,1}\}_\chi$ to the verifier.

Challenge: Verifier sends the challenge $x \in \mathcal{CH}$.

Response: The prover runs **Response** of Π_{PEv} from Sect. 3 on input $\{\mathbf{st}_{\chi_i^*}\}_{\chi_i}$
as follows. It holds $\mathbf{P}_i^* = (x - \mathbf{y})\mathbf{H}_{\mathbf{P}_i^*} + \mathbf{z}$, where $\mathbf{P}_i^*(\mathbf{y}) = \mathbf{z}$ and $\mathbf{y}$ is a vector in
which the polynomial to be evaluated and $\mathbf{z}$ being the evaluation vector of $\mathbf{P}_i^*$
in $\mathbf{y}$. According to the polynomial evaluation protocol the polynomial $\mathbf{H}_{\mathbf{P}_i^*}$ can
be represented as a coefficient matrix $\mathcal{H}_{\mathbf{P}_i^*} = (h_{j',i'})_{j' \in [0,t_2], i' \in [0,t_1']}$. The corresponding masked matrix of $\mathbf{H}_{\mathbf{P}_i^*}$ is $\tilde{\mathcal{H}}_{\mathbf{P}_i^*} = (\tilde{h}_{j',i'})_{j' \in [0,t_2'+1], i' \in [0,t_1']}$ She computes
$\tilde{\mathbf{f}}_{\mathbf{P}_i^*}(x) = (1, x, \ldots, x^{t_2}, x^{t_2+1}) \cdot \tilde{\mathcal{P}}_i^*$ and $\tilde{\mathbf{h}}_{\mathbf{P}_i^*}(x) = (1, x, \ldots, x^{t_2}, x^{t_2+1}) \cdot \tilde{\mathcal{H}}_{\mathbf{P}_i^*}$ with
corresponding randomness $\tilde{\mathbf{r}}_{\mathbf{f},\mathbf{P}_i^*}(x) = \sum_{\mu=0}^{t_2} \mathbf{r}_{p_\mu}^{(i)} x^\mu$ and $\tilde{\mathbf{r}}_{\mathbf{h},\mathbf{P}_i^*}(x) = \sum_{\mu=0}^{t_2} \mathbf{r}_{h_\mu}^{(i)} x^\mu$
and the commitments:

$$\mathbf{F}_{\mathbf{P}_i^*} := \mathrm{Com}_{\mathbf{A}}(\tilde{\mathbf{f}}_{\mathbf{P}_i^*}(x), \tilde{\mathbf{r}}_{\mathbf{f},\mathbf{P}_i^*}(x)), \quad \mathbf{C}_{\mathbf{P}_i^*,0,\tilde{\mathbf{f}}} := \mathrm{Com}_{\mathbf{A}}(0, \tilde{\mathbf{r}}_{\mathbf{f},\mathbf{P}_i^*}(\mathbf{x})).$$

$$\mathbf{G}_{\mathbf{P}_i^*} := \mathrm{Com}_{\mathbf{A}}(\tilde{\mathbf{h}}_{\mathbf{P}_i^*}(x), \tilde{\mathbf{r}}_{\mathbf{h},\mathbf{P}_i^*}(x)), \quad \mathbf{C}_{\mathbf{P}_i^*,0,\tilde{\mathbf{h}}} := \mathrm{Com}_{\mathbf{A}}(0, \tilde{\mathbf{r}}_{\mathbf{h},\mathbf{P}_i^*}(\mathbf{x})).$$

She computes $\tilde{\mathbf{f}}_{\mathbf{Q}_i^*}(x) = (1, x, \ldots, x^{t_2}, x^{t_2+1}) \cdot \tilde{\mathcal{P}}_i^*$ with $\tilde{\mathbf{r}}_{\mathbf{q},\mathbf{Q}^*}^{(i)}(x) = \sum_{\tilde{\mu}=0}^{\tau_2} \mathbf{r}_{q_{\tilde{\mu}}}^{(i)} x^{\tilde{\mu}}$
and the commitments $\mathbf{F}_{\mathbf{Q}^*}^{(i)}, \mathbf{G}_{\mathbf{Q}^*}^{(i)}$ computed as above. $\forall i \in [0, m'-1], \chi_i \in \{\mathbf{P}_i^*, \mathbf{Q}_i^*\}$:

$$\mathbf{msg}_{\chi_i,2} := (\mathbf{F}_{\chi_i}, \mathbf{G}_{\chi_i}, \mathbf{C}_{\chi_i,0,\tilde{\mathbf{f}}}, \mathbf{C}_{\chi_i,0,\tilde{\mathbf{q}}}, \xi_{\mathbf{m}_v,\chi_i}, \xi_{\mathbf{m}_w,\chi_i}, \mathbf{r}_{\xi,\mathbf{m}_v,\chi_i}, \mathbf{r}_{\xi,\mathbf{m}_w,\chi_i})$$

For all $\chi \in \{\mathbf{P}^*, \mathbf{Q}^*\}$ we set $\mathbf{msg}_{\chi,2} = \{\mathbf{msg}_{\chi_i,2}\}_i$. Additionally, the prover computes $\hat{\mathbf{a}}_i(x) = \sum_{j=0}^{n'} \tilde{\mathbf{a}}_{j,i} l_j(x)$, $\hat{\mathbf{r}}(x) = \sum_{j=0}^{n'} \mathbf{r}_j l_j(x)$, $\hat{\mathbf{s}}(x) = \sum_{j=0}^{n'} \mathbf{s}_j l_j(x)$ and sends $\{\hat{\mathbf{a}}_i\}_i$, $\hat{\mathbf{r}}, \hat{\mathbf{s}}$, $\{\mathbf{msg}_{\chi,2}\}_\chi$ to the verifier. She aborts with probability $\tilde{\rho} = \max\{\rho_1, \rho_2, \rho_3\}$ which depends on the rejection sampling of Π_{PEv}:

$$\rho_1 := \frac{\mathfrak{D}_{12\mathcal{B}\sqrt{t_2mn}}^{t_2mn}(\tilde{\mathbf{r}}_{\mathbf{f},\mathbf{P}_i^*}(x))}{M\mathfrak{D}_{\{x^\mu \cdot \mathbf{r}_\mu\}_\mu),12\mathcal{B}\sqrt{t_2mn}}^{\tau_2mn}(\tilde{\mathbf{r}}_{\mathbf{f},\mathbf{P}_i^*}(x))} \cdot \frac{\mathfrak{D}_{12\mathcal{B}\sqrt{t_2mn}}^{t_2mn}(\tilde{\mathbf{r}}_{\mathbf{q},\mathbf{P}_i^*}(x))}{M\mathfrak{D}_{\{x^\mu \cdot \mathbf{r}_{t,\mu}\}_\mu,12\mathcal{B}\sqrt{t_2mn}}^{t_2mn}(\tilde{\mathbf{r}}_{\mathbf{q},\mathbf{P}_i^*}(x))}$$

$$\rho_2 := \frac{\mathfrak{D}_{12\mathcal{B}\sqrt{\tau_2mn}}^{\tau_2mn}(\tilde{\mathbf{r}}_{\mathbf{f},\mathbf{Q}_i^*}(x))}{M\mathfrak{D}_{\{x^\bar{\mu} \cdot \mathbf{r}_{\bar{\mu}}\}_{\bar{\mu}}),12\mathcal{B}\sqrt{\tau_2mn}}^{\tau_2mn}(\tilde{\mathbf{r}}_{\mathbf{f},\mathbf{Q}_i^*}(x))} \cdot \frac{\mathfrak{D}_{12\mathcal{B}\sqrt{\tau_2mn}}^{\tau_2mn}(\tilde{\mathbf{r}}_{\mathbf{q},\mathbf{Q}_i^*}(x))}{M\mathfrak{D}_{\{x^j \cdot \mathbf{r}_{t,\bar{\mu}}\}_{\bar{\mu}},12\mathcal{B}\sqrt{\tau_2mn}}^{\tau_2mn}(\tilde{\mathbf{r}}_{\mathbf{q},\mathbf{Q}_i^*}(x))}$$

and the rejection sampling of the batch protocol:

$$\rho_3 := \frac{\mathfrak{D}_{12\mathcal{B}\sqrt{t_an'}}^{l_an'}(\hat{\mathbf{r}}_i(x))}{M\mathfrak{D}_{\{l_j(x) \cdot \tilde{\mathbf{r}}_{j,i}\}_{i,j},12\mathcal{B}\sqrt{t_an'}}^{l_an'}(\hat{\mathbf{r}}_i(x))}$$

Verification: The verifier runs verification of the underlying polynomial evaluation protocol from Sect. 3 on input $\{D_j\}_{j\in[0,n']}, \{\mathbf{msg}_{\chi,1}\}_\chi, \{\mathbf{msg}_{\chi,2}\}_\chi$ for all $\chi \in \{\mathbf{P}^*, \mathbf{Q}^*\}$. The verifier also computes a commitment to the m' vectors $\hat{\mathbf{a}}_i$ for $i \in [0, m'-1]$ and compares it with the sum over commitments D_j multiplied by the corresponding Lagrange function $l_j(x)$. The verifier checks each $\hat{\mathbf{a}}_i$ against the commitment D_j by exploiting its homomorphic property, i.e. $\hat{\mathbf{a}} = (\hat{\mathbf{a}}_0, \ldots, \hat{\mathbf{a}}_{m'-1})$ with the randomness $\hat{\mathbf{s}}$: $\mathsf{Com}_A(\hat{\mathbf{a}}; \hat{\mathbf{s}}_i) = \mathbf{A} \cdot \hat{\mathbf{s}}_i + \mathsf{enc}(\hat{\mathbf{a}}) = \sum_{j=0}^{n'} D_{j,i} \cdot l_j(X)$, where $\hat{\mathbf{s}}_i = \sum_{j=0}^{n'} \mathbf{s}_{j,i} l_j(X)$ for all $i \in [0, m'-1]$. After accepting the commitment opening, the verifier returns $\mathbf{P}_i^*$. Then, she computes: $\mathbf{P}_i^*(X) \cdot l_0(X) = \mathbf{P}(\hat{\mathbf{a}}_i)$. Additionally she checks the following equation: $\mathsf{Com}_A(\{\mathbf{Q}_i^*(x)l_0(x) + \mathbf{Q}(\hat{\mathbf{a}}_i, \hat{\mathbf{b}}_i)\}_{i\in[0,m'-1]}, \hat{\mathbf{r}}) = \sum_{j=0}^{m} C_j l_j(x)$.

Theorem 3. *The batch protocol given in Fig. 2 has perfect completeness, perfect special honest-verifier zero-knowledge and 3-special soundness.*

Proof. To prove the theorem we prove the three properties:

Perfect Completeness: It follows from the underlying polynomial evaluation protocol from Sect. 3.

3-Special Soundness: For the same reason as in the Π_{PEv} protocol, the challenge space is restricted to 3 challenges $\{X^{-1}, 1, X\}$ It means that we con obtain 3 accepting transcripts for the same message but different challenges x. Pick 3 challenges x_1, x_2, x_3. Because of linear independence of $l_0(X), \ldots, l_n(X)$, the columns of the following matrix are independent and therefore the matrix itself is invertible. So we can obtain any unit vector $(0, \ldots, 1, \ldots, 0)$ by taking an appropriate linear combination of the Vandermonde matrix

$$\mathbf{L} = \begin{pmatrix} l_0(x_1) & l_1(x_1) & l_2(x_1) \\ l_0(x_2) & l_1(x_2) & l_2(x_2) \\ l_0(x_3) & l_1(x_3) & l_2(x_3) \end{pmatrix}.$$

Prover	Verifier
Inputs: $\forall i \in [0, m'-1], j \in [0, n']$	Inputs: $\forall i \in [0, m'-1], j \in [0, n']$
$(\mathbf{P}, \mathbf{Q}, \{\tilde{\mathbf{a}}_{j,i}, \mathbf{b}_{j,i}\}, \{\mathbf{b}_{j,i}\}_{i,j}, \{l_j(X)\}_j, \{C_j\}_j, \{\tilde{\mathbf{a}}_{j,i}\}_{i,j}, \{\mathbf{r}_j\}_j)$	$(\mathbf{P}, \mathbf{Q}, \{\mathbf{b}_{j,i}\}_{i,j}, \{C_j, l_j(X)\}_j)$

$\forall j \in [0, n'], i \in [0, m'-1]:$
1 : $\mathbf{s}_j \leftarrow_{\$}\mathcal{U}(\mathcal{R}_q^m)$
2 : $D_j := \mathrm{Com}_\mathbf{A}(\tilde{\mathbf{a}}_{j,0}, \ldots, \tilde{\mathbf{a}}_{j,m'-1}; \mathbf{s}_j)$
3 : $\hat{\mathbf{a}}_i = \sum_{j=0}^{n'} \tilde{\mathbf{a}}_{j,i} l_j(X), \hat{\mathbf{b}}_i = \sum_{j=0}^{n'-1} \mathbf{b}_{j,i} l_j(X)$
4 : $\frac{\mathbf{P}(\hat{\mathbf{a}}_j)}{l_0(X)} = \frac{\mathbf{P}\left(\sum_{j=0}^{n'} \tilde{\mathbf{a}}_{j,i} l_j(X)\right)}{\prod_{j=0}^{n'}(X - y_j)} = \mathbf{P}_i^*(X)$
5 : $\mathbf{c}_0, \ldots, \mathbf{c}_{m'-1} \in \mathcal{R}_q^{l_Q} \times \cdots \times \mathcal{R}_q^{l_Q},$
   and $\mathbf{r}_c \in \mathcal{R}_q^{m \times (l_a + l_b)}$
6 : $C_0 = \mathrm{Com}_\mathbf{A}(\mathbf{c}_0, \ldots, \mathbf{c}_{m'-1}; \mathbf{r}_c)$
7 : $\mathbf{Q}_i^*(X) = \mathbf{c}_i + \frac{\sum_{j=0}^{n'} \mathbf{Q}(\tilde{\mathbf{a}}_{j,i}, \mathbf{b}_{j,i}) l_j(X) - \mathbf{Q}(\hat{\mathbf{a}}_i, \hat{\mathbf{b}}_i)}{l_0(X)}$
8 : Run $\mathbf{Prover}(\mathbf{P}_i^*)$ and $\mathbf{Prover}(\mathbf{Q}_i^*)$ of Π_{PEv}
9 : $\forall \chi \in \{\mathbf{P}^*, \mathbf{Q}^*\}, \chi_i \in \{\mathbf{P}_i^*, \mathbf{Q}_i^*\}$ set:
   $\mathbf{msg}_{\chi,1} = \{A_{\chi_i, \mu}, T_{\chi_i, \mu'}, U_{\chi_i}, S_{\chi_i}, C_{\chi_i, v}, C_{\chi_i, w}\}_i$

$\xrightarrow{\{D_j\}_j, \{\mathbf{msg}_{\chi,1}\}_\chi}$

$x \leftarrow_{\$} \mathcal{CH}$

$\xleftarrow{\quad x \quad}$

10 : From $\Pi_{PEv}: \tilde{\mathbf{f}}_{\chi_i}(x), \tilde{\mathbf{h}}_{\chi_i}(x),$
$F_{\chi_i} := \mathrm{Com}_\mathbf{A}(\tilde{\mathbf{f}}_{\chi_i}(x), \tilde{\mathbf{r}}_{f,\chi_i}(x)),$
$G_{\chi_i} := \mathrm{Com}_\mathbf{A}(\tilde{\mathbf{h}}_{\chi_i}(x), \tilde{\mathbf{r}}_{h,\chi_i}(x)),$
$C_{0,\chi_i,\hat{\mathbf{h}}} := \mathrm{Com}_\mathbf{A}(0, \tilde{\mathbf{r}}_{h,\chi_i}(x)),$
$C_{0,\chi_i,\tilde{\mathbf{r}}} := \mathrm{Com}_\mathbf{A}(0, \tilde{\mathbf{r}}_{f,\chi_i}^{(i)}(x))$
11 : Run **Response** of $\Pi_{PEv}(\chi)$ output
   $\mathbf{msg}_{\chi,2} = \{F_{\chi_i}, C_{0,\chi_i}, \xi_{\mathbf{u},\chi_i}, \xi_{\mathbf{w},\chi_i}, \mathbf{r}_{\xi,\mathbf{u},\chi_i}, \mathbf{r}_{\xi,\mathbf{w},\chi_i}\}_i$
12 : $\hat{\mathbf{a}}_i(x) = \sum_{j=0}^{n'} \tilde{\mathbf{a}}_{j,i} l_j(x),$
   $\hat{\mathbf{r}}(x) = \sum_{j=0}^{n'} \mathbf{r}_j l_j(x), \hat{\mathbf{s}}(x) = \sum_{j=0}^{n'} \mathbf{s}_j l_j(x)$
13 : Abort with prob. $1 - \bar{p}$

$\xrightarrow{\{\hat{\mathbf{a}}_i\}_i, \hat{\mathbf{r}}, \hat{\mathbf{s}}, \{\mathbf{msg}_{\chi,2}\}_\chi}$

14 : Run **Verification** of Π_{PEv} on
   $\mathbf{msg}_{\chi,1}, \mathbf{msg}_{\chi,2}$
15 : $\|\hat{\mathbf{r}}\| \leq \sqrt{n'}\beta, \|\hat{\mathbf{s}}\| \leq \sqrt{n'}\beta$
16 : $\mathbf{P}_i^*(X) \cdot l_0(X) = \mathbf{P}(\hat{\mathbf{a}}_i).$
17 : $\mathrm{Com}_\mathbf{A}(\{\mathbf{Q}_i^*(x) l_0(x) + \mathbf{Q}(\hat{\mathbf{a}}_i, \hat{\mathbf{b}}_i)\}_i, \hat{\mathbf{r}})$
   $= \sum_{j=0}^{m'-1} C_j l_j(x)$
18 : $\mathrm{Com}_\mathbf{A}(\hat{\mathbf{a}}_0, \ldots, \hat{\mathbf{a}}_{m'-1}, \hat{\mathbf{s}}) = \sum_{j=0}^{n'} D_j l_j(x)$

Fig. 2. Π_{Batch}-protocol

By multiplying the verification equation in steps 16 and 17 of Π_{Batch} by $\mathbf{L}$ from both sides, we can extract the openings $\tilde{\mathbf{a}}_{j,i}, \hat{\mathbf{r}}_j$ for $j \in [0.n']$. Exploiting the special soundness of the underlying polynomial commitment protocol, we can extract the coefficients of the polynomials $\mathbf{P}_i^*$ and $\mathbf{Q}_i^*$ with their corresponding randomness as showed in the proof of soundness of Theorem 2. Having these results, we can apply them to the equation $\mathbf{P}_i^*(X) \cdot l_0(X) = \mathbf{P}(\hat{\mathbf{a}}_i)$. This equation holds for all 3 challenges $x_\iota, \iota \in \{1, 2, 3\}$, i.e. $\mathbf{P}_i^*(x_\iota) \cdot l_0(x_\iota) = \mathbf{P}(\hat{\mathbf{a}}_i)$. Using the same technique as in the previous proof of polynomial evaluation protocol we can extract the witness. Due to the page limitation we omit the details of this proof and only provide a sketch of it.

Evaluating at an interpolation point y_j yields $\mathbf{P}(\mathbf{a}_{j,i}) = \mathbf{P}_i^*(y_j) l_0(y_j) = 0$. In order to extract $\hat{\mathbf{a}}_i$ for all $i \in [0, m'-1]$, we obtain 3 equations using 3 challenges $x_\iota, \iota \in \{1, 2, 3\}$: $\hat{\mathbf{a}}_i = \sum_{j=0}^{n'} \tilde{\mathbf{a}}_{j,i} l_j(x_\iota) = \tilde{\mathbf{a}}_{0,i} l_0(x_\iota) + \ldots + \tilde{\mathbf{a}}_{n',i} l_{n'}(x_\iota)$. We use the following generalised Vandermonde matrix:

$$\mathbf{V}_3 = \begin{bmatrix} \begin{pmatrix} l_0(x_1)\, l_1(x_1)\, l_2(x_1) \\ l_0(x_2)\, l_1(x_2)\, l_2(x_2) \\ l_0(x_3)\, l_1(x_3)\, l_2(x_3) \end{pmatrix} \cdots \begin{pmatrix} l_{n'-3}(x_1)\, l_{n'-2}(x_1)\, l_{n'-1}(x_1) \\ l_{n'-3}(x_2)\, l_{n'-2}(x_2)\, l_{n'-1}(x_2) \\ l_{n'-3}(x_3)\, l_{n'-2}(x_3)\, l_{n'-1}(x_3) \end{pmatrix} \end{bmatrix}$$

whose determinant is equal to 6, as showed in the previous proof. The, the concatenation there equations of $\hat{\mathbf{a}}_i$ are equivalent to the following product: $\hat{\mathbf{a}}_i = \widetilde{\mathbf{V}}_3 \cdot (\tilde{a}_{0,i} \ldots \tilde{a}_{n',i})^{tr}$. It holds: $6\|l_j(X)\| \le 6\sqrt{n}^{n'}$ Let $\tilde{\mathbf{a}}_i = (\tilde{a}_{0,i}, \ldots, \tilde{a}_{n',i})$. For all $i \in \{0, \ldots, m'-1\}$ the following equation is satisfied: $\hat{\mathbf{a}}_i = \mathbf{L} \cdot \tilde{\mathbf{a}}_i = \widetilde{\mathbf{V}}_{n'+1}^{-1} \cdot \tilde{\mathbf{a}}_i$. Multiplying each $\hat{\mathbf{a}}_i$ by $6\mathbf{L}^{-1}$, where $\mathbf{L}^{-1}$ is equivalent to the Vandermonde matrix, i.e. $\mathbf{L}^{-1} = \widetilde{\mathbf{V}}_3$, we can extract the vectors $6\tilde{\mathbf{a}}_i$, for all $i \in [0, m'-1]$. Since the entries of $\widetilde{\mathbf{V}}_3$ are monomials, it follows, that $\widetilde{\mathbf{V}}_3$ is small as required. Similarly, we can extract $\mathbf{r}_i$ from $\hat{\mathbf{s}}_i = \sum_{j=0}^{n'} \mathbf{s}_{j,i} l_j(X)$ using the 3 challenges $x_\iota, \iota \in \{1,2,3\}$: $\hat{\mathbf{s}}_i = \sum_{j=0}^{n'} \tilde{\mathbf{s}}_{j,i} l_j(x_\iota) = \tilde{\mathbf{s}}_{0,i} l_0(x_\iota) + \ldots + \tilde{\mathbf{s}}_{n',i} l_{n'}(x_\iota)$. For all $i \in \{0, \ldots, m'-1\}$ the following equation holds $\hat{\mathbf{s}}_i = \mathbf{L} \cdot \tilde{\mathbf{s}}_i = \mathbf{V}_3^{-1} \cdot \tilde{\mathbf{s}}_i$. Multiplying each $\hat{\mathbf{s}}_i$ by $6\mathbf{L}^{-1}$, we can extract the vectors $6\tilde{\mathbf{s}}_i$ with the following bound: $6\|\tilde{\mathbf{s}}_i\| \le 6\sqrt{mn}\mathcal{B}$.

Spezial Honest-Verifier-Zero-Knowledge: In order to simulate the protocol, we pick $y_1, \ldots, y_{n'}$ for the prover. We select $\hat{\mathbf{a}}_i \leftarrow_\$ \mathfrak{D}_\sigma^{l_a m'}$, $\hat{\mathbf{r}} \leftarrow_\$ \mathfrak{D}_{\sigma_r}^{mn}$ and $D_0, \ldots, D_{n'} \leftarrow_\$ \mathfrak{D}_{\sigma_D}^n$ and simulate the polynomial commitments as in the SHVZK proof of Theorem 2. By the perfect SHVZK property of polynomial commitment protocol, it follows that the simulation is identical to the real values. $\qquad \square$

4.3 Efficiency Analysis

For the efficiency analysis we consider the dimensions of the matrices which are used in the polynomial commitment subprotocol to $\mathbf{P}^*$ and $\mathbf{Q}^*$, which are t_1, t_2 and τ_1, τ_2, respectively. In the underlying protocols of $\mathbf{P}^*$ and $\mathbf{Q}^*$ we communicate $2t_2 + 9$ and $2\tau_2 + 9$ commitments, 4 vectors bounded by $12\mathcal{B}\sqrt{n}$ and 6 masked randomnesses bounded by $12\mathcal{B}\sqrt{3mn}$ respectively. The communication cost is given by the $2t_2 + 2\tau_2 + 18$ commitments and 10 responses from the underlying protocol as well as the n' commitments $\{D_j\}_{j \in [0, n'-1]}$ and the three elements $\hat{\mathbf{a}}, \hat{\mathbf{r}}, \hat{\mathbf{s}}$ from the batch-protocol, i.e. the total costs are $2\tau_2 + 2t_2 + n' + 28$ communicated elements. Since the degree of $\mathbf{P}_i^*$ is equal to $d_P n' - n'$ and because of the definition of $\mathbf{P}_i^*$ being a vector of l_P different l_a-variate polynomials, we set: $d_P n' - n' \approx l_P m'(t_2 + 1)$. Similarly, we set $d_Q n' - n' \approx l_Q m'(\tau_2 + 1)$. We chose the parameters, so that the communication costs are proportional to the number of batched instances $\sqrt{t}$. Thus, we set $t_2 = \lceil \sqrt{(d_P n')/(l_P m')} \rceil$, which yields $t_1 \approx \sqrt{d_P l_P n'}$ and $\tau_2 = \lceil \sqrt{(d_Q n')/(l_Q m')} \rceil$, which yields $\tau_1 \approx \sqrt{d_Q l_Q n'}$.

We set $n' \approx \sqrt{(l_a/8)t}$ and $m' \approx t/n' = \sqrt{(8t/l_a)}$. The total cost for the batched proof with t batch instances is $\sqrt{(l_a/8)}tn \log q + 2\sqrt{d_P l_P}tn \log q + 2\sqrt{d_Q l_Q}tn \log q + 8\sqrt{m'n'} \log q + 6\sqrt{m'n'} \log(12\mathcal{B}\sqrt{(l_a/8)}m') + 4\sqrt{m'n'} \log(12\mathcal{B}\sqrt{3m'n'})$, where the first term describes the costs for communicated $\{D_j\}_{j \in [0, n']}$. The following three terms describe the costs of the underlying polynomial evaluation protocol for $\mathbf{P}^*, \mathbf{Q}^*$, and the last two terms are costs for the sent values $\hat{\mathbf{a}}, \hat{\mathbf{r}}, \hat{\mathbf{s}}$. The number of batched instances is given for polynomials $\mathbf{P}, \mathbf{Q}$ as $t = m'n'$. We approximate each of the batched instances by t and get a total cost approximation of $\mathcal{O}((\sqrt{(l_a/8)}tn + \sqrt{l_Q})\log q$, where l_Q denotes the module-rank of M-SIS problem. The dominant term in the communication cost is $\mathcal{O}(\sqrt{(l_a/8)}tn\log q)\log q$.

Concrete Parameters. We use the results from [19], where the maximum of public parameter $\mathbf{A}$ is bounded by $\sqrt{n\log q/\log \delta}$, where $\tilde{n}$ is the maximal number of rows of $\mathbf{A}$. From Theorem 1, we have $\|\mathbf{r}_x\| \leq \beta$, where $x \in \{\mathbf{P}^*, \mathbf{Q}^*\}$ with $\beta_x \leq 12\mathcal{B}\sqrt{mn}$ and the extracted witness $\|\mathbf{r}'_x\| \leq 6\beta'$. A condition which we obtain from rejection sampling yields $\sigma_{k_x,1} \geq 6 \cdot 12\mathcal{B}\sqrt{k_x mn}$ and $\sigma_{k_x,2} \geq 6 \cdot 12\mathcal{B}\sqrt{k_x n}$, where $k_x \in \{t_2, \tau_2\}$ and $\beta' < \min\{q, 2^{2\sqrt{n\log q\log \delta}}\}$. We choose $\lambda = 128$, set $\delta = 1.0035$ being the root Hermite factor and set $q \geq \beta'$, and $n \geq 2^8$. We balance this security level for LWE using LWE estimator [1] and get the number of integer elements $\hat{m} = \mathcal{O}(n)$ over $\mathbb{Z}$ The underlying polynomial evaluation protocol needs to be repeated 63 times to achieve a negligible soundness error of 2^{-100}. We provide the results for 4 different sets in Table 4.

Table 4. Batch proof parameters

Parameter	Set 1	Set 2	Set 3	Set 4
Commitment modulus q	2^{20}	2^{17}	2^{24}	2^{28}
Ring dimension n	256	512	256	512
d_P	12	12	12	12
d_Q	16	16	16	16
No. of variab. in P $(= l_P)$	2	2	2	2
No. of variab. in Q $(= l_Q)$	4	4	4	4
$\tilde{m}$	768	1024	564	1536
Batches t	10	10	100	100
$\log(\beta')$	≈ 18.9	≈ 14.68	≈ 23.22	≈ 25.86
$\mathcal{B}$	30	2	128	128
Proof size	244.85 KB	332.77 KB	926.95 KB	1.89 MB

5   Application to Range Proof

In this section we apply the batch protocol to a range proof. First we define the relations to be proved.

$$R_{range} = \{\mathcal{P}(\mathbf{a}, \mathbf{r}), \mathcal{V}(C, \mathbf{b}, \mathbf{P}, \mathbf{Q}) : \mathbf{P}(\mathbf{a}) = 0 \wedge C = \text{Com}_{\mathbf{A}}(\mathbf{Q}(\mathbf{a}, \mathbf{b}), \mathbf{r})\}$$
$$R'_{range} = \{\mathcal{P}(6\mathbf{a}, \mathbf{r}'), \mathcal{V}(C, \mathbf{b}, \mathbf{P}, \mathbf{Q}) : \mathbf{P}(6\mathbf{a}) = 0 \wedge C = \text{Com}_{6\mathbf{A}}(\mathbf{Q}(6\mathbf{a}, \mathbf{b}), \mathbf{r}')\}$$

Protocol. This protocol is run between a prover and a verifier, where the former wants to convince the latter that the committed value is inside a range $[0, 2^\ell - 1]$.

Statement: Let $N = 2^\ell - 1$ be the length of an integer a and C a commitment to this integer.

Witness: Let $a \in \mathbb{Z}_q$ and $\mathbf{r} \in \mathcal{R}_q^m$ be the corresponding randomness used in out commitment $\mathsf{C} = \mathsf{Com}_{\mathbf{A}}(a, \mathbf{r})$. The integer a is encoded into a polynomial in $\mathcal{R}_q$ as follows: Set $a = (a_0, \ldots, a_{\ell-1})$ be the binary representation of a. We zero-pad a to reach the dimension of the ring $\mathcal{R}_q$ and encode a into a polynomial by assigning each bit a_i to a coefficient of $a(X) := \sum_{i=0}^{\ell-1} a_i X^i$.

Parameter Choice: We set $l_a = l_b = \ell$, $d_Q = 2$, $l_P = \ell$, $l_Q = 2$, $d_P = \ell + 1$. Let $\mathbf{a} = (a_0, \ldots, a_{\ell-1})$ and $\mathbf{b} = (1, 2, 2^2, \ldots, 2^{\ell-1})$. Then $\mathbf{P}(\mathbf{a}) = \mathbf{a} \circ (1 - \mathbf{a})$ and $\mathbf{Q}(\mathbf{a}, \mathbf{b}) = \sum_{i=0}^{\ell-1} a_i 2^i$.

5.1 Comparison

In this section we provide a comparison of the efficiency of our range proof with the range proof which is currently used in the lattice-based LRCT.v2 scheme [23] and with the range proof in [11]. The total cost of that range proof is: $\tilde{n}n(l + 1) \log q + \tilde{n}\kappa \log q + \tilde{n}(m - 1)n \log(\sigma_{OR})$, where $\sigma_{OR} = 2^{\gamma+1}\sqrt{\kappa\theta n(m - 1)}$, θ is the number of repetitions of the underlying OR proof in [23] and l is the range length, i.e. we prove that an integer is in the range $[0, 2^\ell - 1]$. Let n denote the dimension of $\mathcal{R}_q$, and $\tilde{n}$ denotes the module rank for M-SIS which is specified to be $\tilde{n} = 2$ in [23]. The dominant term in [23] is $\tilde{n}n(\ell + 1) \log q$ which considers only one batched instance. That means for t instances it grows to $tn\tilde{n}(\ell+1) \log q$, making the proof less efficient than ours.

In [11] the authors achieved asymptotic communications cost of $2(\tilde{n} + t)n \log q + \mathcal{O}(t\ell n)$, where $\tilde{n}$ is the module rank of M-SIS. It is obvious that $tn\tilde{n}(\ell + 1) \log q > 2(\tilde{n} + t)n \log q$, since $\tilde{n} = 2$ in [23], yielding that the result in [11] improves by reducing the result in [23] by a factor $t\ell$. As showed in the previous section, our solution achieves asymptotic costs of $\mathcal{O}(\kappa\sqrt{(l_a/8)t})n \log q$, where l_a stands for the length of integer, i.e. $l_a := \ell$ and κ is the number of repetitions of our protocol to achieve a security level of 2^{128}. We set $\kappa = 63$ and l_Q is the number of rows of public parameter $\mathbf{A}$. In this application to the range proof we assume that $l_Q = 2$, i.e. module rank of M-SIS is 2. It is not obvious for which parameters our protocol outperforms the concurrent one [11]. We will compare our results with those in [11] for integer length of 32 bits with ring dimension $n = 16$ and $q = 32$. In order to see when our construction becomes more advantageous than [11] we set $2(\tilde{n} + t)n \log(q) + tn\ell > 63\sqrt{(\ell/8)t}n \log(q)$ and solve it for t when $n = 16$, $\ell = 32$, $\log(q) = 38$ and $\tilde{n} \geq 92$. It yields $2(92 + t) \cdot 38 + t \cdot 32 > 63 \cdot \sqrt{t32/8} \cdot 38$. After plotting the two functions from both sides of the last unequation we conclude that from number $t \geq 1154$ our scheme outperforms the one in [11].

We conclude that our contribution provides a significant improvement compared to [11,23]. In [11] the authors instantiated their range proof with 10 batched instances and a range width of $N = 2^{64}$. In order to make a fair comparison to our work, it hold $\log N = \ell$ and $q \geq 2^{\ell}$. We adapt these sized to our batch protocol in Table 5 and obtain the following results:

Table 5. Range proof parameters

Parameter	[11]	Our Work	[11]	Our Work	[11]	Our work
Modulus q	2^{38}	2^{33}	2^{64}	2^{64}	2^{64}	2^{64}
Ring dim. n	16	16	8	8	8	8
$\log(N)$	32	32	64	64	64	64
# of batches t	1200	1200	1200	1200	10000	10000
λ	128	128	128	128	128	128
Proof size	≈ 13.85 MB	9.69 MB	≈ 22 MB	18.61 MB	≈ 160 MB	54.57

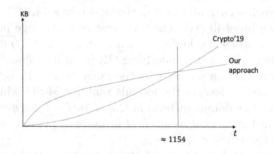

Fig. 3. Comparison graph

We conclude that our approach achieves a significant improvement if the number of batched instances is higher than 1155. Additionally we showed that for a higher number of batched instances we achieve a more significant difference to [11], namely our proof size grows approximately by a square-root factor of t, while the proof size in [11] grows almost linearly. The simplified representation of the two graphs is given in the following graph in Table 5 and (Fig. 3).

A   Example to Batch Technique

Example: We consider the following case of 3-variate polynomials, i.e. $l_a + l_b = 3$ with variables X, Y, Z. Let $l_Q = 2$ and $m' = 2$, i.e. we have 2 elements $\mathbf{Q}(\mathbf{a}_{j,0}, \mathbf{b}_{j,0}), \mathbf{Q}(\mathbf{a}_{j,1}, \mathbf{b}_{j,1})$, where each of them is a vector which contains 2 multivariate polynomials:, i.e.:

$$\mathbf{Q}(\mathbf{a}_{j,0}, \mathbf{b}_{j,0}) = \begin{pmatrix} Q_1(\mathbf{a}_{j,0}, \mathbf{b}_{j,0}) = XYZ^2 + Y^3X^2 + YZ^2 + Y^2XZ^3 \\ Q_2(\mathbf{a}_{j,0}, \mathbf{b}_{j,0}) = XY^3 + X^3Y^2Z^2 + XY^2 + X^2Y^3 \end{pmatrix}$$

$$\mathbf{Q}(\mathbf{a}_{j,1}, \mathbf{b}_{j,1}) = \begin{pmatrix} Q_1(\mathbf{a}_{j,1}, \mathbf{b}_{j,1}) = X^3Y^2 + XZ^2 + XY^3Z + YZ^3 \\ Q_2(\mathbf{a}_{j,1}, \mathbf{b}_{j,1}) = Y^2Z + X^2Z^2 + X^3Y^2Z + XY^2Z^3 \end{pmatrix}$$

In order to construct a commitment $\mathsf{Com}_{\mathbf{A}}(\mathbf{Q}(\mathbf{a}_{j,0}, \mathbf{b}_{j,0}), \mathbf{Q}(\mathbf{a}_{j,1}, \mathbf{b}_{j,1}); \mathbf{r}_j)$ to both vectors $\mathbf{Q}(\mathbf{a}_{j,0}, \mathbf{b}_{j,0})$ and $\mathbf{Q}(\mathbf{a}_{j,1}, \mathbf{b}_{j,1})$ we first define the univariate polynomials $Q_\iota(\mathbf{a}_{j,i}, \mathbf{b}_{j,i}), \iota \in [1, 2], i \in \{0, 1\}$ in each of the variable X, Y, Z:

For $\iota = 1, i = 0$, i.e. $Q_1(\mathbf{a}_{j,0}, \mathbf{b}_{j,0})$ we have: $Q_{j,0,1}(X) = yz^2 + (yz^2 + y^2z^3)X + y^3X^2$, $Q_{j,0,1}(Y) = (xz^2 + z^2)Y + xz^3Y^2 + x^2Y^3$, $Q_{j,0,1}(Z) = y^3x^2 + (xy + y)Z^2 + y^2xZ^3$.

For $\iota = 2, i = 0$, i.e. $Q_2(\mathbf{a}_{j,0}, \mathbf{b}_{j,0})$ we have: $Q_{j,0,2}(X) = (y^2 + y^3)X + y^3X^2 + y^2z^2X^3$, $Q_{j,0,2}(Y) = (x^3z^2 + x)Y^2 + (x + x^2)Y^3$, $Q_{j,0,2}(Z) = xy^3 + xy^2 + x^2y^3 + x^3y^2Z^2$.

For $\iota = 1, i = 1$ i.e. $Q_1(\mathbf{a}_{j,1}, \mathbf{b}_{j,1})$ we have: $Q_{j,1,1}(X) = yz^3 + (y^3z + z^2)X + y^2X^3$, $Q_{j,1,1}(Y) = xz^2 + z^3Y + x^3Y^2 + xzY^3$, $Q_{j,1,1}(Z) = x^3y^2 + xy^3Z + xZ^2 + yZ^3$.

For $\iota = 2, i = 1$, i.e. $Q_2(\mathbf{a}_{j,1}, \mathbf{b}_{j,1})$ we have: $Q_{j,1,2}(X) = y^2z + y^2z^3X + z^2X^2 + y^2zX^3$, $Q_{j,1,2}(Y) = x^2z^2 + (z + x^3z + xz^3)Y^2$, $Q_{j,1,2}(Z) = (y^2 + x^3y^2)Z + x^2Z^2 + xy^2Z^3$.

All lower-case letters x, y, z and their products and sums denote coefficients of variables $X^i, Y^i, Z^i, i \in [0, 3]$. Next, we pack polynomials $Q_{j,i,\iota}$ in a particular variable for $i \in [0, 1], \iota \in [1, 2]$ into one vector, i.e. we define

$$Q_{j,1}(X) = (Q_{j,0,1}(X), Q_{j,1,1}(X)), \quad Q_{j,1}(Y) = (Q_{j,0,1}(Y), Q_{j,1,1}(Y)), \quad Q_{j,1}(Z) = (Q_{j,0,1}(Z), Q_{j,1,1}(Z)),$$
$$Q_{j,2}(X) = (Q_{j,0,2}(X), Q_{j,1,2}(X)), \quad Q_{j,2}(Y) = (Q_{j,0,2}(Y), Q_{j,1,2}(Y)), \quad Q_{j,2}(Z) = (Q_{j,0,2}(Z), Q_{j,1,2}(Z))$$

We pack all these vectors from above into a matrix as follows:

$$\mathbf{Q}_j = \begin{pmatrix} Q_{j,1}(X) & Q_{j,1}(Y) & Q_{j,1}(Z) \\ Q_{j,1}(X) & Q_{j,1}(Y) & Q_{j,1}(Z) \end{pmatrix}$$

Now we can commit to the vectors $\mathbf{Q}(\mathbf{a}_{j,0}, \mathbf{b}_{j,0}), \mathbf{Q}(\mathbf{a}_{j,1}, \mathbf{b}_{j,1})$ which, as we have seen, are now packed into a matrix $\mathbf{Q}_j$, i.e. $\mathsf{Com}_{\mathbf{A}}(\mathbf{Q}(\mathbf{a}_{j,0}, \mathbf{b}_{j,0}), \mathbf{Q}(\mathbf{a}_{j,1}, \mathbf{b}_{j,1}); \mathbf{r}_j) = \mathsf{Com}_{\mathbf{A}}(\mathbf{Q}_j, \mathbf{r}_j)$.

References

1. Albrecht, M.R., Player, R., Scott, S.: On the concrete hardness of learning with errors. J. Math. Cryptol. **9**(3), 169–203 (2015)
2. Baum, C., Damgård, I., Larsen, K.G., Nielsen, M.: How to prove knowledge of small secrets. In: Robshaw, M., Katz, J. (eds.) CRYPTO 2016. LNCS, vol. 9816, pp. 478–498. Springer, Heidelberg (2016). https://doi.org/10.1007/978-3-662-53015-3_17
3. Baum, C., Damgård, I., Lyubashevsky, V., Oechsner, S., Peikert, C.: More efficient commitments from structured lattice assumptions. In: Catalano, D., De Prisco, R. (eds.) SCN 2018. LNCS, vol. 11035, pp. 368–385. Springer, Cham (2018). https://doi.org/10.1007/978-3-319-98113-0_20
4. Bayer, S., Groth, J.: Zero-knowledge argument for polynomial evaluation with application to blacklists. In: Johansson, T., Nguyen, P.Q. (eds.) EUROCRYPT 2013. LNCS, vol. 7881, pp. 646–663. Springer, Heidelberg (2013). https://doi.org/10.1007/978-3-642-38348-9_38
5. Bendlin, R., Damgård, I.: Threshold decryption and zero-knowledge proofs for lattice-based cryptosystems. In: Micciancio, D. (ed.) TCC 2010. LNCS, vol. 5978, pp. 201–218. Springer, Heidelberg (2010). https://doi.org/10.1007/978-3-642-11799-2_13
6. Benhamouda, F., Camenisch, J., Krenn, S., Lyubashevsky, V., Neven, G.: Better zero-knowledge proofs for lattice encryption and their application to group signatures. In: Sarkar, P., Iwata, T. (eds.) ASIACRYPT 2014. LNCS, vol. 8873, pp. 551–572. Springer, Heidelberg (2014). https://doi.org/10.1007/978-3-662-45611-8_29
7. Benhamouda, F., Krenn, S., Lyubashevsky, V., Pietrzak, K.: Efficient zero-knowledge proofs for commitments from learning with errors over rings. In: Pernul, G., Ryan, P.Y.A., Weippl, E. (eds.) ESORICS 2015. LNCS, vol. 9326, pp. 305–325. Springer, Cham (2015). https://doi.org/10.1007/978-3-319-24174-6_16
8. Bootle, J., Cerulli, A., Chaidos, P., Groth, J., Petit, C.: Efficient zero-knowledge arguments for arithmetic circuits in the discrete log setting. In: Fischlin, M., Coron, J.-S. (eds.) EUROCRYPT 2016. LNCS, vol. 9666, pp. 327–357. Springer, Heidelberg (2016). https://doi.org/10.1007/978-3-662-49896-5_12
9. Bootle, J., Groth, J.: Efficient batch zero-knowledge arguments for low degree polynomials. In: Abdalla, M., Dahab, R. (eds.) PKC 2018. LNCS, vol. 10770, pp. 561–588. Springer, Cham (2018). https://doi.org/10.1007/978-3-319-76581-5_19
10. Damgård, I., López-Alt, A.: Zero-knowledge proofs with low amortized communication from lattice assumptions. In: Visconti, I., De Prisco, R. (eds.) SCN 2012. LNCS, vol. 7485, pp. 38–56. Springer, Heidelberg (2012). https://doi.org/10.1007/978-3-642-32928-9_3
11. Esgin, M.F., Steinfeld, R., Liu, J.K., Liu, D.: Lattice-based zero-knowledge proofs: new techniques for shorter and faster constructions and applications (2019). https://eprint.iacr.org/2019/445
12. Esgin, M.F., Steinfeld, R., Sakzad, A., Liu, J.K., Liu, D.: Short lattice-based one-out-of-many proofs and applications to ring signatures. In: Deng, R.H., Gauthier-Umaña, V., Ochoa, M., Yung, M. (eds.) ACNS 2019. LNCS, vol. 11464, pp. 67–88. Springer, Cham (2019). https://doi.org/10.1007/978-3-030-21568-2_4
13. Goldwasser, S., Micali, S., Rackoff, C.: The knowledge complexity of interactive proof-systems (extended abstract). In: Proceedings of the 17th Annual ACM STOC 1985, pp. 291–304. ACM (1985)

14. Groth, J.: Linear algebra with sub-linear zero-knowledge arguments. In: Halevi, S. (ed.) CRYPTO 2009. LNCS, vol. 5677, pp. 192–208. Springer, Heidelberg (2009). https://doi.org/10.1007/978-3-642-03356-8_12
15. Groth, J.: A verifiable secret shuffle of homomorphic encryptions. J. Cryptol. **23**(4), 546–579 (2010). https://doi.org/10.1007/s00145-010-9067-9
16. Kilian, J.: A note on efficient zero-knowledge proofs and arguments (extended abstract). In: ACM Proceedings 1992, pp. 723–732. ACM (1992)
17. Langlois, A., Stehlé, D.: Worst-case to average-case reductions for module lattices. Des. Codes Crypt. **75**(3), 565–599 (2014). https://doi.org/10.1007/s10623-014-9938-4
18. Lyubashevsky, V.: Fiat-Shamir with aborts: applications to lattice and factoring-based signatures. In: Matsui, M. (ed.) ASIACRYPT 2009. LNCS, vol. 5912, pp. 598–616. Springer, Heidelberg (2009). https://doi.org/10.1007/978-3-642-10366-7_35
19. Lyubashevsky, V.: Lattice signatures without trapdoors. In: Pointcheval, D., Johansson, T. (eds.) EUROCRYPT 2012. LNCS, vol. 7237, pp. 738–755. Springer, Heidelberg (2012). https://doi.org/10.1007/978-3-642-29011-4_43
20. Saberhagen, N.V.: Cryptonote v 2.0 (2013)
21. Stern, J.: A new identification scheme based on syndrome decoding. In: Stinson, D.R. (ed.) CRYPTO 1993. LNCS, vol. 773, pp. 13–21. Springer, Heidelberg (1994). https://doi.org/10.1007/3-540-48329-2_2
22. Alberto Torres, W., Kuchta, V., Steinfeld, R., Sakzad, A., Liu, J.K., Cheng, J.: Lattice RingCT V2.0 with multiple input and multiple output wallets. In: Jang-Jaccard, J., Guo, F. (eds.) ACISP 2019. LNCS, vol. 11547, pp. 156–175. Springer, Cham (2019). https://doi.org/10.1007/978-3-030-21548-4_9
23. Alberto Torres, W.A., et al.: Post-quantum one-time linkable ring signature and application to ring confidential transactions in blockchain (lattice RingCT v1.0). In: Susilo, W., Yang, G. (eds.) ACISP 2018. LNCS, vol. 10946, pp. 558–576. Springer, Cham (2018). https://doi.org/10.1007/978-3-319-93638-3_32

FROST: Flexible Round-Optimized Schnorr Threshold Signatures

Chelsea Komlo[1,2] and Ian Goldberg[1(✉)]

[1] University of Waterloo, Waterloo, Canada
iang@uwaterloo.ca
[2] Zcash Foundation, New York, USA

Abstract. Unlike signatures in a single-party setting, threshold signatures require cooperation among a threshold number of signers each holding a share of a common private key. Consequently, generating signatures in a threshold setting imposes overhead due to network rounds among signers, proving costly when secret shares are stored on network-limited devices or when coordination occurs over unreliable networks. In this work, we present FROST, a Flexible Round-Optimized Schnorr Threshold signature scheme that reduces network overhead during signing operations while employing a novel technique to protect against forgery attacks applicable to similar schemes in the literature. FROST improves upon the state of the art in Schnorr threshold signature protocols, as it can safely perform signing operations in a single round without limiting concurrency of signing operations, yet allows for true threshold signing, as only a threshold t out of n possible participants are required for signing operations, such that $t \leq n$. FROST can be used as either a two-round protocol, or optimized to a single-round signing protocol with a pre-processing stage. FROST achieves its efficiency improvements in part by allowing the protocol to abort in the presence of a misbehaving participant (who is then identified and excluded from future operations)—a reasonable model for practical deployment scenarios. We present proofs of security demonstrating that FROST is secure against chosen-message attacks assuming the discrete logarithm problem is hard and the adversary controls fewer participants than the threshold.

Keywords: Secret sharing · Threshold signatures · Schnorr signatures

1 Introduction

Threshold signature schemes are a cryptographic primitive to facilitate joint ownership over a private key by a set of participants, such that a threshold number of participants must cooperate to issue a signature that can be verified by a single public key. Threshold signatures are useful across a range of settings that require a distributed root of trust among a set of equally trusted parties.

Similarly to signing operations in a single-party setting, some implementations of threshold signature schemes require performing signing operations at

ⓒ Springer Nature Switzerland AG 2021
O. Dunkelman et al. (Eds.): SAC 2020, LNCS 12804, pp. 34–65, 2021.
https://doi.org/10.1007/978-3-030-81652-0_2

scale and under heavy load. For example, threshold signatures can be used by a set of signers to authenticate financial transactions in cryptocurrencies [16], or to sign a network consensus produced by a set of trusted authorities [22]. In both of these examples, as the number of signing parties or signing operations increases, the number of communication rounds between participants required to produce the joint signature becomes a performance bottleneck, in addition to the increased load experienced by each signer. This problem is further exacerbated when signers utilize network-limited devices or unreliable networks for transmission, or protocols that wish to allow signers to participate in signing operations asynchronously. As such, optimizing the network overhead of signing operations is highly beneficial to real-world applications of threshold signatures.

Today in the literature, the best threshold signature schemes are those that rely on pairing-based cryptography [6,7], and can perform signing operations in a single round among participants. However, relying on pairing-based signature schemes is undesirable for some implementations in practice, such as those that do not wish to introduce a new cryptographic assumption, or that wish to maintain backwards compatibility with an existing signature scheme such as Schnorr signatures. Surprisingly, today's best non-pairing-based threshold signature constructions that produce Schnorr signatures with unlimited concurrency [14,28] require at least three rounds of communication during signing operations, whereas constructions with fewer network rounds [14] must limit signing concurrency to protect against a forgery attack [10].

In this work, we present FROST, a Flexible Round-Optimized Schnorr Threshold signature scheme[1] that addresses the need for efficient threshold signing operations while improving upon the state of the art to ensure strong security properties *without* limiting the parallelism of signing operations. FROST can be used as either a two-round protocol where signers send and receive two messages in total, or optimized to a (non-broadcast) single-round signing protocol with a pre-processing stage. FROST achieves improved efficiency in the optimistic case that no participant misbehaves. However, in the case where a misbehaving participant contributes malformed values during the protocol, honest parties can identify and exclude the misbehaving participant, and re-run the protocol.

The flexible design of FROST lends itself to supporting a number of practical use cases for threshold signing. Because the preprocessing round can be performed separately from the signing round, signing operations can be performed *asynchronously*; once the preprocessing round is complete, signers only need to receive and eventually reply with a single message to create a signature. Further, while some threshold schemes in the literature require all participants to be active during signing operations [9,14], and refer to the threshold property of the protocol as merely a security property, FROST allows any threshold number of participants to produce valid signatures. Consequently, FROST can support use cases where a subset of participants (or participating devices) can remain offline, a property that is often desirable for security in practice.

Contributions. In this work, we present the following contributions.

---

[1] Signatures generated using the FROST protocol can also be referred to as "FROSTy signatures".

- We review related threshold signature schemes and present a detailed analysis of their performance and designs.
- We present FROST, a Flexible Round-Optimized Schnorr Threshold signature scheme. FROST improves upon the state of the art for Schnorr threshold signatures by defining a signing protocol that can be optimized to a (non-broadcast) single-round operation with a preprocessing stage. Unlike many prior Schnorr threshold schemes, FROST remains secure against known forgery attacks without limiting concurrency of signing operations.
- We present a proof of security and correctness for an interactive two-round variant of FROST, building upon proofs of security for prior related threshold schemes. We then demonstrate how this proof extends to FROST in the single-round setting.

Organization. We present background information in Sect. 2; in Sect. 3 we give an overview of related threshold Schnorr signature constructions. In Sect. 4 we review notation and security assumptions maintained for our work, and we introduce FROST in Sect. 5. In Sect. 6 we give proofs of security and correctness for FROST, and discuss operational considerations in Sect. 7. We conclude in Sect. 8.

2   Background

Let $\mathbb{G}$ be a group of prime order q in which the Decisional Diffie-Hellman problem is hard, and let g be a generator of $\mathbb{G}$. Let H be a cryptographic hash function mapping to $\mathbb{Z}_q^*$. We denote by $x \xleftarrow{\$} S$ that x is uniformly randomly selected from S.

2.1   Threshold Schemes

Cryptographic protocols called (t, n)-*threshold schemes* allow a set of n participants to share a secret s, such that any t out of the n participants are required to cooperate in order to recover s, but any subset of fewer than t participants cannot recover any information about the secret.

Shamir Secret Sharing. Many threshold schemes build upon Shamir secret sharing [27], a (t, n)-threshold scheme that relies on Lagrange interpolation to recover a secret. In Shamir secret sharing, a trusted central dealer distributes a secret s to n participants in such a way that any cooperating subset of t participants can recover the secret. To distribute this secret, the dealer first selects $t - 1$ coefficients $a_1, \ldots, a_{t-1}$ at random, and uses the randomly selected values as coefficients to define a polynomial $f(x) = s + \sum_{i=1}^{t-1} a_i x^i$ of degree $t - 1$ where $f(0) = s$. The secret shares for each participant P_i are subsequently $(i, f(i))$, which the dealer is trusted to distribute honestly to each participant $P_1, \ldots, P_n$. To reconstruct the secret, at least t participants perform Lagrange interpolation to reconstruct the polynomial and thus find the value $s = f(0)$. However, no group of fewer than t participants can reconstruct the secret, as at least t points are required to reconstruct a polynomial of degree $t - 1$.

Verifiable Secret Sharing. Feldman's Verifiable Secret Sharing (VSS) Scheme [11] builds upon Shamir secret sharing, adding a verification step to demonstrate the consistency of a participant's share with a public *commitment* that is assumed to be correctly visible to all participants. To validate that a share is well formed, each participant validates their share using this commitment. If the validation fails, the participant can issue a *complaint* against the dealer, and take actions such as broadcasting this complaint to all other participants. FROST similarly uses this technique as well.

The commitment produced in Feldman's scheme is as follows. As before in Shamir secret sharing, a dealer samples $t - 1$ random values $(a_1, \ldots, a_{t-1})$, and uses these values as coefficients to define a polynomial f of degree $t - 1$ such that $f(0) = s$. However, along with distributing the private share $(i, f(i))$ to each participant P_i, the dealer also distributes the public commitment $C = \langle \phi_0, \ldots, \phi_{t-1} \rangle$, where $\phi_0 = g^s$ and $\phi_j = g^{a_j}$.

Note that in a distributed setting, each participant P_i must be sure to have the same view of C as all other participants. In practice, implementations guarantee consistency of participants' views by using techniques such as posting commitments to a centralized server that is trusted to provide a single view to all participants, or adding another protocol round where participants compare their received commitment values to ensure they are identical.

Threshold Signature Schemes. Threshold signature schemes leverage the (t, n) security properties of threshold schemes, but allow participants to produce signatures over a message using their secret shares such that anyone can validate the integrity of the message, *without* ever reconstructing the secret. In threshold signature schemes, the secret key s is distributed among the n participants, while a single public key Y is used to represent the group. Signatures can be generated by a threshold of t cooperating signers. For our work, we require the resulting signature produced by the threshold signature scheme to be valid under the Schnorr signature scheme [26], which we introduce in Sect. 2.3.

Because threshold signature schemes ensure that no participant (or indeed any group of fewer than t participants) ever learns the secret key s, the generation of s and distribution of shares $s_1, \ldots, s_n$ often require generating shares using a less-trusted method than relying on a central dealer. FROST instead makes use of a Distributed Key Generation (DKG) protocol, which we describe in Sect. 2.2. Similarly, generating Schnorr signatures in a threshold setting requires that the random nonce k be generated in such a way that each participant *contributes to* but *does not know* the resulting k. To perform this task, FROST uses *additive secret sharing*, which we now describe.

Additive Secret Sharing. While Shamir secret sharing and derived constructions require shares to be points on a secret polynomial f where $f(0) = s$, an *additive secret sharing scheme* allows a set of α participants to jointly compute a shared secret s by each participant P_i contributing a value s_i such that the resulting shared secret is $s = \sum_{i=1}^{\alpha} s_i$, the summation of each participant's share. Consequently, additive secret sharing can be performed non-interactively; each participant directly chooses their own s_i. Benaloh and Leichter [4] generalize additive secret sharing to arbitrary monotone access structures, and Cramer, Damgård, and Ishai [8] present a *non-interactive* mechanism, which we use in its simplest case, for participants to locally convert additive shares of the form $s = \sum_i s_i$ to polynomial (Shamir) form, as $\frac{s_i}{\lambda_i}$ are *Shamir* secret shares of the same s, where the λ_i are Lagrange coefficients. In FROST, participants use this technique during signing operations to non-interactively generate a nonce that is Shamir secret shared among all signing participants.

2.2   Distributed Key Generation

Unlike threshold schemes such as Shamir secret sharing that rely on a trusted dealer, Distributed Key Generation (DKG) ensures every participant contributes equally to the generation of the shared secret. At the end of running the protocol, all participants share a joint public key Y, but each participant holds only a share s_i of the corresponding secret s such that no set of participants smaller than the threshold knows s.

Pedersen [23] presents a two-round DKG where each participant acts as the central dealer of Feldman's VSS [11] protocol, resulting in n parallel executions of the protocol. Consequently, this protocol requires two rounds of communication between all participants; after each participant selects a secret x_i, they first broadcast a commitment to x_i to all other participants, and then send all other participants a secret share of x_i.

Gennaro et al. [15] demonstrate a weakness of Pedersen's DKG [23] such that a misbehaving participant can bias the distribution of the resulting shared secret by issuing complaints against a participant *after* seeing the shares issued to them by this participant. To address this issue, the authors propose a three-round protocol, modifying Pedersen's DKG to include an additional "commitment round", such that adversaries are prevented from adaptively disqualifying participants, thereby ensuring the value of the resulting secret is determined before participants reveal their inputs. However, in a later work, Gennaro et al. [14] prove that Pedersen's DKG as originally described [23] is *secure enough* in certain contexts, as the resulting secret is sufficiently random despite the chance for bias from a misbehaving participant adaptively selecting their input after seeing inputs from other participants.

FROST can use either Pedersen's DKG [23] or Gennaro's DKG [15] to generate the shared long-lived secret key among participants during its key generation stage.

2.3   Schnorr Signatures

Often, it is desirable for signatures produced by threshold signing operations to be indistinguishable from signatures produced by a single participant, for reasons of backwards compatibility and to prevent privacy leaks. For our work, we require signatures produced by FROST signing operations to be indistinguishable from Schnorr signatures [26], and thus verifiable using the standard Schnorr verification operation.

A Schnorr signature is generated over a message m (employing a signature format similar to EdDSA [17]) by the following steps:

1. Sample a random nonce $k \xleftarrow{\$} \mathbb{Z}_q$; compute the commitment $R = g^k \in \mathbb{G}$
2. Compute the challenge $c = H(R, Y, m)$
3. Using the secret key s, compute the response $z = k + s \cdot c \in \mathbb{Z}_q$
4. Define the signature over m to be $\sigma = (R, z)$.

Validating the integrity of m using the public key $Y = g^s$ and the signature σ is performed as follows:

1. Parse σ as (R, z); derive $c = H(R, Y, m)$
2. Compute $R' = g^z \cdot Y^{-c}$
3. Output 1 if $R \overset{?}{=} R'$ to indicate success; otherwise, output 0.

Schnorr signatures are simply the standard Σ-protocol proof of knowledge of the discrete logarithm of Y, made non-interactive (and bound to the message m) with the Fiat-Shamir transform.

2.4   Attacks on Parallelized Schnorr Multisignatures

Attack via Wagner's Algorithm. We next describe an attack recently introduced by Drijvers et al. [10] against some two-round Schnorr multisignature schemes in a parallel setting. This attack can be performed when the adversary has control over either choosing the message m to be signed, or the ability to adaptively choose its own individual commitments used to determine the group commitment R after seeing commitments from all other signing parties. In Sect. 5.2 and Sect. 6 we discuss how FROST avoids the attack.

Successfully performing the Drijvers attack[2] requires finding a hash output $c^* = H(R^*, Y, m^*)$ that is the sum of T other hash outputs $c^* = \sum_{j=1}^{T} H(R_j, Y, m_j)$ (where c^* is the challenge, m_j the message, Y the public signing key, and R_j the group's commitment corresponding to a standard Schnorr signature as described in Sect. 2.3). To find T hash outputs that sum to c^*, the adversary can open many (say T number of) parallel simultaneous signing operations, varying in each of the T parallel executions either its individual commitment used to determine R_j or m_j. Drijvers et al. use the k-tree algorithm of Wagner [29] to find such hashes and perform the attack in time $O(\kappa \cdot b \cdot 2^{b/(1+\lg \kappa)})$, where $\kappa = T+1$, and b is the bitlength of the order of the group.

Although this attack was proposed in a multisignature n-out-of-n setting, this attack applies similarly in a threshold t-out-of-n setting for an adversary that controls up to $t - 1$ participants. We note that this attack applies to threshold schemes proposed in the literature, such as the scheme by Gennaro et al. [14].

Drijvers et al. [10] also present a metareduction for the proofs of several Schnorr multisignature schemes that use a generalization of the forking lemma

---

[2] Note that we slightly modify this attack to include the public key Y as an input into H to match the notation used in this paper.

with rewinding, highlighting that the security of this proof technique does not extend to a multi-party setting. Because our proofs of security for FROST (presented in Sect. 6) reduce to the hardness of the discrete logarithm problem for the underlying group, as opposed to the one-more discrete logarithm problem, the metareduction presented by Drijvers et al. [10] does not apply to our proof strategy.

Attack via ROS Solver. Benhamouda et al. [5] recently presented a polynomial-time algorithm that solves the ROS (Random inhomogeneities in a Overdetermined Solvable system of linear equations) problem. As first described by Schnorr [25], the ROS problem challenges an adversary to find an $(\ell + 1) \times \ell$ submatrix of rank ℓ, when given a system of $n \gg \ell$ linear equations modulo q with ℓ unknowns and random constant terms. Benhamouda et al. show how to solve the ROS in expected polynomial time when $\ell > \lg q$. Solving the ROS problem in the setting of Schnorr multisignatures enables an adversary that is allowed to open ℓ simultaneous connections to an honest participant with inputs $m_1, \ldots, m_\ell$ to produce a $(\ell + 1)^{\text{th}}$ signature *without* asking the participant for a signature on $m_{\ell+1}$. The authors demonstrate that threshold schemes using Gennaro et al.'s DKG [15] and multisignature schemes such as two-round MuSig [21] are not secure against their ROS-solving algorithm. However, the authors conclude that (the current version of) FROST is not affected by their ROS-solving algorithm.

3   Related Work

We now review prior threshold schemes with a focus on Schnorr-based designs, and split our review into robust and non-robust schemes. Robust schemes ensure that so long as t participants correctly follow the protocol, the protocol is guaranteed to complete successfully, even if a subset of participants (at most $n - t$) contribute malformed shares. Conversely, designs that are not robust simply abort after detecting any participant misbehaviour.

Robust Threshold Schemes. Stinson and Strobl [28] present a threshold signature scheme producing Schnorr signatures, using the modification of Pedersen's DKG presented by Gennaro et al. [15] to generate both the secret key s during key generation as well as the random nonce k for each signing operation. This construction requires at minimum four rounds for each signing operation (assuming no participant misbehaves): three rounds to perform the DKG to obtain k, and one round to distribute signature shares and compute the group signature. Each round requires participants to send values to every other participant.

Gennaro et al. [14] present a threshold Schnorr signature protocol that uses a modification of Pedersen's DKG [23] to generate both s during key generation and the random nonce k for signing operations. However, their construction requires *all* n signers to participate in signing, while the adversary is allowed to control up to the given threshold number of participants. Recall from Sect. 2.2

that Pedersen's DKG requires two rounds; this construction requires an additional round for signing operations when all participants are equally trusted. Each round requires that all participants send values to all other participants. The authors also discuss an optimization that leverages a *signature aggregator* role, an entity trusted to gather signatures from each participant, perform validation, and publish the resulting signature, a role we also adopt in our work. In their optimized variant, participants can perform Pedersen's DKG to generate multiple k values in a pre-processing stage independently of performing signing operations. In this variant, to compute ℓ signatures, signers first perform two rounds of ℓ parallel executions of Pedersen's DKG, thereby generating ℓ random nonces. The signers can then store these pre-processed values to later perform ℓ single-round signing operations.

Our work builds upon the key generation stage of Gennaro et al. [14]; we use a variant of Pedersen's DKG for key generation with a requirement that in the case of misbehaviour, the protocol aborts and the cause investigated out of band. However, FROST *does not* perform a DKG during signing operations as is done in both of the above schemes, but instead make use of additive secret sharing and share conversion. Consequently, FROST trades off robustness for more efficient signing operations, such that a misbehaving participant can cause the signing operation to abort. However, such a tradeoff is practical to many real-world settings.

Further, because FROST does not provide robustness, FROST is secure so long as the adversary controls fewer than the threshold t participants, an improvement over robust designs, which can at best provide security for $t \leq n/2$ [15].

Non-robust Threshold Schemes. FROST is not unique in trading off favouring increased network efficiency over robustness. Gennaro and Goldfeder [12] present a threshold ECDSA scheme that similarly requires aborting the protocol in the case of participant misbehaviour. Their signing construction uses a two-round DKG to generate the nonce required for the ECDSA signature, leveraging additive-to-multiplicative share conversion. This DKG has been also applied in a Schnorr threshold scheme context to generate the random nonce for more efficient distributed key generation operations [18] in combination with threshold Schnorr signing operations [28]. In later work [13], Gennaro and Goldfeder define an optimization to a single-round ECDSA signing operation with a preprocessing stage, which assumes the protocol will abort in the case of failure or participant misbehaviour. Their end-to-end protocol with identifiable aborts has eight network rounds, six of which require broadcasting to all other signing participants, and two of which require performing pairwise multiplicative-to-additive share conversion protocols. Further, while the protocol can be optimized into a preprocessing phase, the choice of the signing coalition must be determined at the time of preprocessing. FROST defines a more efficient preprocessing phase as secret nonces can be generated in a distributed manner in the preprocessing phase entirely non-interactively. Further, participants can "mix" preprocessed values across different signing coalitions, as FROST requires that the choice for the signing coalition be made only during the signing stage.

Recent work by Damgård et al. [9] define an efficient threshold ECDSA construction that similarly requires aborting in the case of misbehaviour. Their design relies on generating a blinding factor $d + m \cdot e$ such that where d and e are $2t$ secret sharings of zero, such that the entire binding factor evaluates to zero when all signing parties are honest and agree on m. This approach is similar to FROST in that signature shares are bound to the message and to the set of signing parties. However, the security of their scheme requires the majority of participants to be honest, and $n \geq 2t + 1$. Further, their scheme requires all n participants take part in signing operations, where the threshold t is simply a security parameter.

Similarly to FROST, Abidin, Aly, and Mustafa [1] present a design for authentication between devices, and use additive secret sharing to generate the nonce for Schnorr signatures in a threshold setting, a technique also used by FROST. However, the authors do not consider the Drijvers attack and consequently their design is similarly limited to restricted levels of parallelism. Further, their design does not include validity checks for responses submitted by participants when generating signatures and consequently does not detect nor identify misbehaving participants.

FROST improves upon prior work in Schnorr threshold schemes by providing a single-round signing variant with a preprocessing stage that is agnostic to the choice of the signing coalition. Further, the number of signing participants in FROST is required to be simply some $t \leq n$, while remaining secure against the Drijvers attack and misbehaving participants who do not correctly follow the protocol.

4   Preliminaries

Let n be the number of participants in the signature scheme, and t denote the threshold of the secret-sharing scheme. Let i denote the *participant identifier* for participant P_i where $1 \leq i \leq n$. Let s_i be the long-lived secret share for participant P_i. Let Y denote the long-lived public key shared by all participants in the threshold signature scheme, and let $Y_i = g^{s_i}$ be the public key share for the participant P_i. Finally, let m be the message to be signed.

Let α be the number of participants performing a signing operation, where $t \leq \alpha \leq n$. For a set $S = \{p_1, \ldots, p_\alpha\}$ of α participant identifiers in the signing operation, let $\lambda_i = \prod_{j=1, j \neq i}^{\alpha} \frac{p_j}{p_j - p_i}$ denote the ith Lagrange coefficient for interpolating over S. Note that the information to derive these values depends on which α (out of n) participants are selected, and uses only the participant *identifiers*, and not their *shares*.[3]

Security Assumptions. We maintain the following assumptions, which implementations should account for in practice.

- *Message Validation.* We assume every participant checks the validity of the message m to be signed before issuing its signature share.

---

[3] Note that if n is small, the λ_i for every possible S can be precomputed as a performance optimization.

- *Reliable Message Delivery.* We assume messages are sent between participants using a reliable network channel.
- *Participant Identification.* In order to report misbehaving participants, we require that values submitted by participants to be identifiable within the signing group. Implementations can enforce this using a method of participant authentication within the signing group.[4]

5   FROST: Flexible Round-Optimized Schnorr Threshold Signatures

We now present FROST, a Flexible Round-Optimized Schnorr Threshold signature scheme that minimizes the network overhead of producing Schnorr signatures in a threshold setting while allowing for unrestricted parallelism of signing operations and only a threshold number of signing participants.

Efficiency over Robustness. As described in Sect. 3, prior threshold signature constructions [14,28] provide the property of *robustness*. However, in settings where one can expect misbehaving participants to be rare, threshold signing protocols can be relaxed to be more efficient in the "optimistic" case that all participants honestly follow the protocol. In the case that a participant does misbehave, honest participants can identify the misbehaving participant and abort the protocol, and then re-run the protocol after excluding the misbehaving participant. FROST trades off robustness in the protocol for improved round efficiency in this way.

Signature Aggregator Role. We instantiate FROST using a semi-trusted *signature aggregator* role, denoted as $\mathcal{SA}$. Such a role allows for less communication overhead between signers and is often practical in a real-world setting. However, FROST can be instantiated without a signature aggregator; each participant simply performs a broadcast in place of $\mathcal{SA}$ performing coordination.

The signature aggregator role can be performed by *any* participant in the protocol, or even an external party, provided they know the participants' public-key shares Y_i. $\mathcal{SA}$ is trusted to report misbehaving participants and to publish the group's signature at the end of the protocol. If $\mathcal{SA}$ deviates from the protocol, the protocol remains secure against adaptive chosen message attacks, as $\mathcal{SA}$ is not given any more of a privileged view than the adversary we model in our proof of security for FROST in Sect. 6. A malicious $\mathcal{SA}$ does have the power to perform denial-of-service attacks and to falsely report misbehaviour by participants, but *cannot* learn the private key or cause improper messages to be signed. Note this signature aggregator role is also used in prior threshold signature constructions in the literature [14] as an optimization.

---

[4] For example, authentication tokens or TLS certificates could serve to authenticate participants to one another.

FROST KeyGen

Round 1

1. Every participant P_i samples t random values $(a_{i0}, \ldots, a_{i(t-1)})) \xleftarrow{\$} \mathbb{Z}_q$, and uses these values as coefficients to define a degree $t-1$ polynomial $f_i(x) = \sum_{j=0}^{t-1} a_{ij} x^j$.
2. Every P_i computes a proof of knowledge to the corresponding secret a_{i0} by calculating $\sigma_i = (R_i, \mu_i)$, such that $k \xleftarrow{\$} \mathbb{Z}_q$, $R_i = g^k$, $c_i = H(i, \Phi, g^{a_{i0}}, R_i)$, $\mu_i = k + a_{i0} \cdot c_i$, with Φ being a context string to prevent replay attacks.
3. Every participant P_i computes a public commitment $\boldsymbol{C_i} = \langle \phi_{i0}, \ldots, \phi_{i(t-1)} \rangle$, where $\phi_{ij} = g^{a_{ij}}$, $0 \le j \le t-1$
4. Every P_i broadcasts $\boldsymbol{C_i}, \sigma_i$ to all other participants.
5. Upon receiving $\boldsymbol{C_\ell}, \sigma_\ell$ from participants $1 \le \ell \le n, \ell \ne i$, participant P_i verifies $\sigma_\ell = (R_\ell, \mu_\ell)$, aborting on failure, by checking $R_\ell \stackrel{?}{=} g^{\mu_\ell} \cdot \phi_{\ell 0}^{-c_\ell}$, where $c_\ell = H(\ell, \Phi, \phi_{\ell 0}, R_\ell)$.
   Upon success, participants delete $\{\sigma_\ell : 1 \le \ell \le n\}$.

Round 2

1. Each P_i securely sends to each other participant P_ℓ a secret share $(\ell, f_i(\ell))$, deleting f_i and each share afterward except for $(i, f_i(i))$, which they keep for themselves.
2. Each P_i verifies their shares by calculating: $g^{f_\ell(i)} \stackrel{?}{=} \prod_{k=0}^{t-1} \phi_{\ell k}^{i^k \bmod q}$, aborting if the check fails.
3. Each P_i calculates their long-lived private signing share by computing $s_i = \sum_{\ell=1}^{n} f_\ell(i)$, stores s_i securely, and deletes each $f_\ell(i)$.
4. Each P_i calculates their public verification share $Y_i = g^{s_i}$, and the group's public key $Y = \prod_{j=1}^{n} \phi_{j0}$. Any participant can compute the public verification share of any other participant by calculating

$$Y_i = \prod_{j=1}^{n} \prod_{k=0}^{t-1} \phi_{jk}^{i^k \bmod q}.$$

Fig. 1. KeyGen. A distributed key generation (DKG) protocol that builds upon the DKG by Pedersen [23]. Our variant includes a protection against rogue key attacks by requiring each participant to prove knowledge of their secret value commits, and requires aborting on misbehaviour.

5.1 Key Generation

To generate long-lived key shares in our scheme's key generation protocol, FROST builds upon Pedersen's DKG for key generation; we detail these protocol steps in Fig. 1. Note that Pedersen's DKG is simply where each participant executes Feldman's VSS as the dealer in parallel, and derives their secret share as the sum of the shares received from each of the n VSS executions. In addition to the base Pedersen DKG protocol, FROST additionally requires each participant to demonstrate knowledge of their secret a_{i0} by providing other participants with proof in zero knowledge, instantiated as a Schnorr signature, to protect against rogue-key attacks [2] in the setting where $t \geq n/2$.

To begin the key generation protocol, a set of participants must be formed using some out-of-band mechanism decided upon by the implementation. After participating in the Ped-DKG protocol, each participant P_i holds a value (i, s_i) that is their long-lived secret signing share. Participant P_i's public key share $Y_i = g^{s_i}$ is used by other participants to verify the correctness of P_i's signature shares in the following signing phase, while the group public key Y can be used by parties external to the group to verify signatures issued by the group in the future.

View of Commitment Values. As required for *any* multi-party protocol using Feldman's VSS, the key generation stage in FROST similarly requires participants to maintain a consistent view of commitments $C_i, 1 \leq i \leq n$ issued during the execution of Ped-DKG. In this work, we assume participants broadcast the commitment values honestly (e.g., participants do not provide different commitment values to a subset of participants); recall Sect. 2.1 where we described techniques to achieve this guarantee in practice.

Security Tradeoffs. While Gennaro et al. [15] describe the "Stop, Kill, and Rewind" variant of Ped-DKG (where the protocol terminates and is re-run if misbehaviour is detected) as vulnerable to influence by the adversary, we note that in a real-world setting, good security practices typically require that the cause of misbehaviour is investigated once it has been detected; the protocol is not allowed to terminate and re-run continuously until the adversary finds a desirable output. Further, many protocols in practice do not prevent an adversary from aborting and re-executing key agreement at any point in the protocol; adversaries in protocols such as the widely used TLS protocol can skew the distribution of the resulting key simply by re-running the protocol.

However, implementations wishing for a robust DKG can adapt our key generation protocol to the robust construction presented by Gennaro et al. [15]. Note that the efficiency of the DKG for the key generation phase is not extremely critical, because this operation must be done only *once per key generation* for long-lived keys. For the per-signature operations, FROST optimizes the generation of random values *without* utilizing a DKG, as discussed next.

5.2 Threshold Signing with Unrestricted Parallelism

We now introduce the signing protocol for FROST. This operation builds upon known techniques in the literature [1,14] by employing additive secret sharing and share conversion to non-interactively generate the nonce value for each

---

Preprocess$(\pi) \to (i, \langle (D_{ij}, E_{ij}) \rangle_{j=1}^{\pi})$

Each participant $P_i, i \in \{1, \ldots, n\}$ performs this stage prior to signing. Let j be a counter for a specific nonce/commitment share pair, and π be the number of pairs generated at a time, such that π signing operations can be performed before performing another preprocess step.

1. Create an empty list L_i. Then, for $1 \leq j \leq \pi$, perform the following:
   1.a Sample single-use nonces $(d_{ij}, e_{ij}) \xleftarrow{\$} \mathbb{Z}_q^* \times \mathbb{Z}_q^*$
   1.b Derive commitment shares $(D_{ij}, E_{ij}) = (g^{d_{ij}}, g^{e_{ij}})$.
   1.c Append (D_{ij}, E_{ij}) to L_i. Store $((d_{ij}, D_{ij}), (e_{ij}, E_{ij}))$ for later use in signing operations.
2. Publish (i, L_i) to a predetermined location, as specified by the implementation.

Fig. 2. FROST preprocessing protocol

signature. However, signing operations in FROST additionally leverage a binding technique to avoid known forgery attacks without limiting concurrency. We present FROST signing in two parts: a pre-processing phase and a single-round signing phase. However, these stages can be combined for a single two-round protocol if desired.

As a reminder, the attack of Drijvers et al. [10] requires the adversary to either see the victim's T commitment values before selecting their own commitment, or to adaptively choose the message to be signed, so that the adversary can manipulate the resulting challenge c for the set of participants performing a group signing operation. To prevent this attack without limiting concurrency, FROST "binds" each participant's response to a specific message as well as the set of participants and their commitments used for that particular signing operation. In doing so, combining responses over different messages or participant/commitment pairs results in an invalid signature, thwarting attacks such as those of Drijvers et al.

Preprocessing Stage. We present in Fig. 2 a preprocessing stage where participants generate and publish π commitments at a time. In this setting, π determines the number of nonces that are generated and their corresponding commitments that are published in a single preprocess step. Implementations that do not wish to cache commitments can instead use a two-round signing protocol, where participants publish a single commitment to each other in the first round.

Each participant P_i begins by generating a list of *single-use* private nonce pairs and corresponding public commitment shares $\langle ((d_{ij}, D_{ij} = g^{d_{ij}}), (e_{ij}, E_{ij} = g^{e_{ij}})) \rangle_{j=1}^{\pi}$, where j is a counter that identifies the next nonce/commitment share pair available to use for signing. Each P_i then publishes (i, L_i), where L_i is their list of commitment shares $L_i = \langle (D_{ij}, E_{ij}) \rangle_{j=1}^{\pi}$. The location where participants publish these values can depend on the implementation (which we discuss further

---

Sign$(m) \to (m, \sigma)$

Let $\mathcal{SA}$ denote the signature aggregator (who themselves can be one of the signing participants). Let S be the set of $\alpha : t \leq \alpha \leq n$ participants selected for this signing operation, and Y be the group public key. Let $B = \langle (i, D_i, E_i) \rangle_{i \in S}$ denote the ordered list of participant indices corresponding to each participant P_i, s_i be P_i's secret key share, and L_i be the set of commitment values for P_i that were published during the Preprocess stage. Each identifier i is coupled with the commitments (D_i, E_i) published by P_i that will be used for this signing operation. Let H_1, H_2 be hash functions whose outputs are in $\mathbb{Z}_q^*$.

1. $\mathcal{SA}$ begins by fetching the next available commitment for each participant $P_i \in S$ from L_i and constructs B.
2. For each $i \in S$, $\mathcal{SA}$ sends P_i the tuple (m, B).
3. After receiving (m, B), each P_i first validates the message m, and then checks $D_\ell, E_\ell \in \mathbb{G}^*$ for each commitment in B, aborting if either check fails.
4. Each P_i then computes the set of binding values $\rho_\ell = H_1(\ell, m, B), \ell \in S$. Each P_i then derives the group commitment $R = \prod_{\ell \in S} D_\ell \cdot (E_\ell)^{\rho_\ell}$, and the challenge $c = H_2(R, Y, m)$.
5. Each P_i computes their response using their long-lived secret share s_i by computing $z_i = d_i + (e_i \cdot \rho_i) + \lambda_i \cdot s_i \cdot c$, using S to determine λ_i.
6. Each P_i securely deletes $((d_i, D_i), (e_i, E_i))$ from their local storage, and then returns z_i to $\mathcal{SA}$.
7. The signature aggregator $\mathcal{SA}$ performs the following steps:

   7.a Derive $\rho_i = H_1(i, m, B)$ and $R_i = D_{ij} \cdot (E_{ij})^{\rho_i}$ for $i \in S$, and subsequently $R = \prod_{i \in S} R_i$ and $c = H_2(R, Y, m)$.

   7.b Verify the validity of each response by checking $g^{z_i} \overset{?}{=} R_i \cdot Y_i^{c \cdot \lambda_i}$ for each signing share z_i, $i \in S$. If the equality does not hold, identify and report the misbehaving participant, and then abort. Otherwise, continue.

   7.c Compute the group's response $z = \sum z_i$

   7.d Publish $\sigma = (R, z)$ along with m.

Fig. 3. FROST single-round signing protocol

in Sect. 7). The set of (i, L_i) tuples are then stored by any entity that might perform the signature aggregator role during signing.

Signing Protocol. At the beginning of the signing protocol in Fig. 3, $\mathcal{SA}$ selects $\alpha : t \leq \alpha \leq n$ participants (possibly including itself) to participate in the signing. Let S be the set of those α participants. $\mathcal{SA}$ then selects the next available commitment $(D_i, E_i) : i \in S$, which are later used to generate a secret share to a random commitment R for the signing group.[5]

---

[5] Each participant contributes to the group commitment R, which corresponds to the commitment g^k to the nonce k in step 1 of the single-party Schnorr signature scheme in Sect. 2.3.

The resulting secret nonce is $k = \sum_{i \in S} k_i$, where each $k_i = d_i + e_i \cdot \rho_i$ (we next describe how participants calculate ρ_i), and (d_i, e_i) correspond to the $(D_i = g^{d_i}, E_i = g^{e_i})$ values published during the Preprocess stage. Recall from Sect. 2.1 that if the k_i are *additive* shares of k, then the $\frac{k_i}{\lambda_i}$ are *Shamir* shares of k.

After these steps, $\mathcal{SA}$ then creates the set B, where B is the ordered list of tuples $\langle (i, D_i, E_i) \rangle_{i \in S}$. $\mathcal{SA}$ then sends (m, B) to every $P_i, i \in S$.

After receiving (m, B) from $\mathcal{SA}$ to initialize a signing operation, each participant checks that m is a message they are willing to sign. Then, using m and B, all participants derive the "binding values" $\rho_i, i \in S$ such that $\rho_i = H_1(i, m, B)$, where H_1 is a hash function whose outputs are in $\mathbb{Z}_q^*$.

Each participant then computes the commitment R_i for each participant in S by deriving $R_i = D_i \cdot (E_i)^{\rho_i}$. Doing so binds the message, the set of signing participants, and each participant's commitment to each signature share. This binding technique thwarts the attack of Drijvers et al. described in Sect. 2.4 as attackers cannot combine signature shares across disjoint signing operations or permute the set of signers or published commitments for each signer.

The commitment for the set of signers is then simply $R = \prod_{i \in S} R_i$. As in single-party Schnorr signatures, each participant computes the challenge $c = H_2(R, Y, m)$.

Each participant's response z_i to the challenge can be computed using the single-use nonces (d_i, e_i) and the long-term secret shares s_i, converted to additive form:

$$z_i = d_i + (e_i \cdot \rho_i) + \lambda_i \cdot s_i \cdot c$$

$\mathcal{SA}$ finally checks the consistency of each participant's reported z_i with their commitment share (D_i, E_i) and their public key share Y_i. If every participant issued a correct z_i, the group's response is $z = \sum_{i \in S} z_i$, and the group signature on m is $\sigma = (R, z)$. This signature is verifiable to anyone performing a standard Schnorr verification operation with Y as the public key (Sect. 2.3).

Handling Ephemeral Outstanding Shares. Because each nonce and commitment share generated during the preprocessing stage described in Fig. 2 must be used *at most once*, participants should delete these values after using them in a signing operation, as indicated in Step 5 in Fig. 3. An accidentally reused (d_{ij}, e_{ij}) can lead to exposure of the participant's long-term secret s_i.

However, if $\mathcal{SA}$ chooses to re-use a commitment set (D_i, E_i) during the signing protocol, doing so simply results in the participant P_i aborting the protocol, and consequently does not increase the power of $\mathcal{SA}$.

6   Security

We now present proofs of correctness and a high-level overview of our proof of security against chosen-message attacks for FROST. We present our complete proofs of security in Appendix A.

6.1 Correctness

Signatures in FROST are constructed from two polynomials; the first polynomial $F_1(x)$ defines the secret sharing of the private signing key s (such that $Y = g^s$) and the second polynomial $F_2(x)$ defines the secret sharing of the nonce k such that $k = \sum_{i \in S} d_i + e_i \cdot \rho_i$ using the associated public data (m, B) to determine ρ_i. During the key generation phase described in Fig. 1, the first polynomial $F_1(x) = \sum_{j=1}^n f_j(x)$ is generated such that the secret key shares are $s_i = F_1(i)$ and the secret key is $s = F_1(0)$.

During the signature phase (Fig. 3), each of the $\alpha : t \le \alpha \le n$ participants selected for signing use a pair of nonces (d_i, e_i) to define a degree $\alpha - 1$ polynomial $F_2(x)$, interpolating the values $(i, \frac{d_i + e_i \cdot H_1(i, m, B)}{\lambda_i})$, such that $F_2(0) = \sum_{i \in S} d_i + e_i \cdot \rho_i$.

Then let $F_3(x) = F_2(x) + c \cdot F_1(x)$, where $c = H_2(R, Y, m)$. Now z_i equals $d_i + (e_i \cdot \rho_i) + \lambda_i \cdot s_i \cdot c = \lambda_i(F_2(i) + c \cdot F_1(i)) = \lambda_i F_3(i)$, so $z = \sum_{i \in S} z_i$ is simply the Lagrange interpolation of $F_3(0) = (\sum_{i \in S} d_i + e_{ij} \cdot \rho_i) + c \cdot s$. Because $R = g^{\sum_{i \in S} d_i + e_i \cdot \rho_i}$ and $c = H_2(R, Y, m)$, (R, z) is a correct Schnorr signature on m.

6.2 Security Against Chosen Message Attacks

We now present a high-level overview of the proof of security against chosen-message attacks for FROST; our complete proofs are in Appendix A. We begin by summarizing a proof of security for an interactive variant of FROST that we call FROST-Interactive, and then demonstrate how the proof extends to plain FROST.

We employ the generalized forking strategy used by Bellare and Neven [3] to create a reduction to the security of the discrete logarithm problem (DLP) in $\mathbb{G}$. We prove security against the standard notion of existential unforgeability against chosen message attacks (EUF-CMA) by demonstrating that the difficulty to an adversary to forge FROST signatures by performing an adaptively chosen message attack in the random oracle model reduces to the difficulty of computing the discrete logarithm of an arbitrary challenge value ω in the underlying group, so long as the adversary controls fewer than the threshold t participants.

FROST-Interactive. In FROST-Interactive, ρ_i is established using a "one-time" verifiable random function (VRF),[6] as $\rho_i = a_{ij} + (b_{ij} \cdot H_\rho(m, B))$, where (a_{ij}, b_{ij}) are selected and committed to as $(A_{ij} = g^{a_{ij}}, B_{ij} = g^{b_{ij}})$ during the preprocessing stage, along with zero-knowledge proofs of knowledge of (a_{ij}, b_{ij}). To perform a signing operation, participants first generate ρ_i in the first round of the signing protocol using (a_{ij}, b_{ij}), and then publish ρ_i to the signature aggregator, which distributes all $\rho_\ell, \ell \in S$ to all signing participants. These

---

[6] A one-time VRF F_k for key k relaxes the standard properties of a VRF by requiring that $F_k(x)$ be unpredictable to someone who does not know k only when at most one value of $F_k(y)$ has been published by the keyholder (and $y \ne x$). We use the construction $k = (a, b) \in \mathbb{Z}_q^2$ and $F_k(x) = a + b \cdot x$. The public key is $(A = g^a, B = g^b)$.

$\rho_\ell, \ell \in S$ values are then used by all signing participants to compute R in the second round of the signing protocol, which participants use to calculate and publish z_i.

Summary of Proof for EUF-CMA Security for FROST-Interactive. Let n_h be the number of queries made to the random oracle, n_p be the number of allowed preprocess queries, and n_s be the number of allowed signing queries. We assume there exists a forger $\mathcal{F}$ that $(\tau, n_h, n_p, n_s, \epsilon)$-breaks FROST-Interactive, meaning that $\mathcal{F}$ can compute a forgery for a signature generated by FROST-Interactive in time τ with success ϵ, but is limited to making n_h number of random oracle queries, n_p number of preprocess queries, and n_s number of signing queries. We construct an algorithm C that (τ', ϵ')-solves the discrete logarithm problem in $\mathcal{G}$, for an arbitrary challenge value $\omega \in \mathbb{G}$, using as a subroutine a forger $\mathcal{F}$ that can forge FROST signatures.

Without loss of generality, we assume $\mathcal{F}$ controls $t - 1$ participants.

Theorem 1. *If the discrete logarithm problem in $\mathbb{G}$ is (τ', ϵ')-hard, then the FROST-Interactive signature scheme over $\mathbb{G}$ with n signing participants, a threshold of t, and a preprocess batch size of π is $(\tau, n_h, n_p, n_s, \epsilon)$-secure whenever*

$$\epsilon' \leq \frac{\epsilon^2}{2n_h + (\pi + 1)n_p + 1} \quad and$$

$$\tau' = 4\tau + (30\pi n_p + (4t - 2)n_s + (n + t - 1)t + 6) \cdot t_{exp} + O(\pi n_p + n_s + n_h + 1)$$

such that t_{exp} is the time of an exponentiation in $\mathbb{G}$, assuming the number of participants compromised by the adversary is less than the threshold t.

Proof Sketch for FROST-Interactive. We provide our complete proof in Appendix A, but summarize here. We prove Theorem 1 by contradiction.

We begin by embedding the challenge value ω into the group public key Y. The coordinator algorithm C then uses the generalized forking algorithm $GF_{\mathcal{A}}$ to initialize the simulator $\mathcal{A}(Y, \{h_1, \ldots, h_{n_r}\}; \beta)$, providing the group public key Y, outputs for $n_r = 2n_h + (\pi + 1)n_p + 1$ random oracle queries denoted as $\{h_1, \ldots, h_{n_r}\} \xleftarrow{\$} H$, and the random tape β. $\mathcal{A}$ then invokes the forger $\mathcal{F}$, simulating the responses to $\mathcal{F}$'s random oracle queries by providing values selected from $\{h_1, \ldots, h_{n_r}\}$, and also simulates the honest party P_t in the KeyGen, Preprocess, and Sign procedures.

To simulate signing without knowing the secret key corresponding to P_t's own public key Y_t, $\mathcal{A}$ generates the commitment and signature for participant P_t by publishing $(D_{tj} = g^{z_{tj}} \cdot (Y_t)^{-c_j}, E_{tj})$ such that $z_{tj} \xleftarrow{\$} \mathbb{Z}_q$, c_j is the next unused value from the set of random oracle outputs supplied by $GF_{\mathcal{A}}$, and $E_{tj} = g^{e_{tj}}, e_{tj} \xleftarrow{\$} \mathbb{Z}_q^*$. To determine which challenge c_j to return for a particular commitment (D_{ij}, E_{ij}) when simulating a signing operation, $\mathcal{A}$ forks $\mathcal{F}$ to extract its (a_{ij}, b_{ij}) VRF keys from its zero-knowledge proofs during Preprocess for each participant P_ℓ controlled by $\mathcal{F}$, and consequently can directly compute its corresponding ρ_ℓ. Hence, $\mathcal{A}$ can compute R strictly before $\mathcal{F}$ for every signing query, and thus can always correctly program the random oracle for the query $H_2(R, Y, m)$ to return the correct c_j embedded in D_{tj}.

Once $\mathcal{A}$ has returned a valid forgery $\sigma = (R, z)$ and the index J associated to the random oracle query h_J such that $h_J = c$, $GF_\mathcal{A}$ re-executes $\mathcal{A}$ with the same random tape β and public key Y, but with responses to random oracle queries $\{h_1, \ldots, h_{J-1}, h'_J, \ldots, h'_{n_r}\}$, where $\{h'_J, \ldots, h'_{n_r}\} \stackrel{\$}{\leftarrow} H$. Doing so simulates the "forking" of $\mathcal{A}$ at a specific point in its execution, such that all behaviour of $\mathcal{A}$ is identical between executions up to the Jth random oracle query, but different thereafter.

Consequently, given a forger $\mathcal{F}$ that with probability ϵ produces a valid forgery, the probability that $\mathcal{A}$ returns a valid forgery for FROST-Interactive is ϵ, and the probability that $GF_\mathcal{A}$ returns two valid forgeries using the *same commitment* after forking $\mathcal{A}$ is $\frac{\epsilon^2}{n_r}$.

The running time for C to compute the discrete logarithm by procuring two forgeries from FROST-Interactive is four times that for $\mathcal{F}$ (because of the forking of $\mathcal{A}$, which itself forks $\mathcal{F}$), plus the time to compute $(30\pi n_p + (4t - 2)n_s + (n + t - 1)t + 6)$ exponentiations, and $O(\pi n_p + n_s + n_h + 1)$ other minor operations, such as table lookups.

Extension of Proof to FROST. We now heuristically demonstrate how the change from FROST-Interactive to FROST does not open a hole in the proof. The difference between FROST-Interactive and FROST is the replacement of the interactive VRF in FROST-Interactive with a hash function (modelled by a random oracle) to derive ρ_i. This change still achieves the properties required of ρ_i, as deterministic, unpredictable, and bound to (i, m, B). However, the key distinction when generating ρ_i via a VRF versus a hash function is that in FROST-Interactive, the VRF query is part of the signing algorithm, and so each such query uses up a (d_i, e_i) pair; therefore, the adversary can learn only one $\rho_i(m, B)$ value for any given $(i, D_i, E_i) \in B$, and importantly, this allows the simulator $\mathcal{A}$ in the proof to always be able to set $H_2(R, Y, m)$ to the correct c_j value. In plain FROST, the adversary can query the random oracle $\rho_i = H_1(i, m, B)$ polynomially many times, even with the same $(i, D_i, E_i) \in B$. The adversary will be able to produce a forgery if[7] (slightly generalizing the Drijvers attack to arbitrary linear combinations instead of just sums) they can find m^*, r^*, and $\langle m_j, B_j, \gamma_j \rangle_{j=1}^\pi$ such that

$$H_2(R^*, Y, m^*) = \sum_{j=1}^{\pi} \gamma_j \cdot H_2(R_j, Y, m_j) \tag{1}$$

---

[7] This is the main heuristic step; sufficiency ("if") is immediate, but we do not prove necessity ("only if"). That said, the only information the forger has about honest participant P_t's private key s_t is $Y_t = g^{s_t}$ and π pairs $(g^{k_j}, z_j = k_j + s_t \cdot \lambda_t \cdot H_2(R_j, Y, m_j))_{j=1}^\pi$. If the forger can produce a forgery, they must *necessarily* be able to compute a pair $(g^{k^*}, z^* = k^* + s_t \cdot \lambda_t \cdot H_2(R^*, Y, m^*))$. Assuming taking discrete logs is infeasible, writing z^* as a linear combination of the z_j (as polynomials in the unknown s_t) appears to be the forger's only reasonable strategy.

where $R_j = \displaystyle\prod_{(i,D,E)\in B_j} D \cdot E^{H_1(i,m_j,B_j)}$, $\widehat{R_j} = D_{jt} \cdot E_{jt}^{H_1(i,m_j,B_j)}$, $R^* = g^{r^*} \cdot$

$\displaystyle\prod_{j=1}^{\pi} \widehat{R_j}^{\gamma_j}$, each B_j contains the honest party's (t, D_{jt}, E_{jt}), and m^* is not one of the m_j.

Importantly, the key difference between FROST and schemes susceptible to the Drijvers attack is that in FROST, the R^* in the left side of Eq. 1 is itself a function of all the inputs to the hash functions on the right side. Drijvers can use Wagner's generalized birthday attack [29] because the left and right sides of Eq. 1 are independent for schemes vulnerable to their attack, and so Wagner's algorithm can find a collision between a list of possible values on the left (the (m^*, R^*) terms) and a (larger) list of possible values on the right (the (m_j, R_j) terms). In FROST, however, each combination of values on the right *changes* R^*, and so the list of possible values on the left (varying m^*, for example) changes for each such combination, increasing the cost to an attacker from the generalized birthday collision attack to multiple preimage attacks.

As such, we heuristically argue that the difference between generating ρ_i via the one-time VRF in FROST-Interactive and the random oracle in plain FROST has no security consequence.

6.3   Aborting on Misbehaviour

FROST requires participants to abort once they have detected misbehaviour, with the benefit of fewer communication rounds in an honest setting.

If one of the signing participants provides an incorrect signature share, $\mathcal{SA}$ will detect that and abort the protocol, if $\mathcal{SA}$ is itself behaving correctly. The protocol can then be rerun with the misbehaving party removed. If $\mathcal{SA}$ is itself misbehaving, and even if up to $t-1$ participants are corrupted, $\mathcal{SA}$ still cannot produce a valid signature on a message not approved by at least one honest participant.

7   Implementation and Operational Considerations

We have implemented FROST in Rust, using Ristretto over curve25519 [19] for the group operations. Our source code can be found at https://crysp.uwaterloo.ca/software/frost.

We now discuss two topics that may be of interest to implementors.

Publishing Commitments. The preprocessing step for FROST in Sect. 5.2 requires some agreed-upon location for participants to publish their commitments to, such as a commitment server, which is trusted to provide the correct (i.e., valid and unused) commitment shares upon request. If malicious, it could perform a denial-of-service attack, or it could provide stale or malformed commitment values on behalf of honest participants. However, simply having access to the set of a participant's *public* published commitments does not grant any additional powers.

Performing Two-Round FROST Without Central Roles. While the round complexity of FROST can be optimized using central roles such as the signature aggregator, some implementations may wish to remain completely decentralized. In this setting, participants can simply broadcast commitments to each other, and perform signing using a two-round setting (foregoing the preprocessing step) for further simplicity.

8 Conclusion

While threshold signatures provide a unique cryptographic functionality that is applicable across a range of settings, implementations incur network overhead costs when performing signing operations under heavy load. As such, minimizing the number of network rounds required for threshold signing operations has practical benefits for network-limited devices or where signers can go offline but wish to perform a signing operation asynchronously. In this work, we introduce FROST, a flexible Schnorr-based threshold signature scheme that improves upon the state of the art by minimizing the number of network rounds required for signing without limiting the parallelism of signing operations. We present an optimized variant of FROST as a single-round signing protocol with a preprocessing phase, but the protocol can be used in a two-round setting. While FROST requires aborting on misbehaviour, such a tradeoff is often practical in a real-world setting, assuming such cases of misbehaviour are rare. We present proofs of security and correctness for FROST, demonstrating FROST is secure against chosen-message attacks assuming the adversary controls fewer than a threshold number of participants, and the discrete logarithm problem is hard.

Acknowledgments. We thank Douglas Stebila for his discussion on our proof of security and security bounds. We thank Richard Barnes for his discussion on practical constraints and identifying significant optimizations to a prior version of FROST, which our final version of FROST builds upon. We thank Isis Lovecruft for their discussion and parallel implementation of FROST.

We thank colleagues at the Zcash Foundation for discussions on applications of threshold signatures, and Omer Shlomovits and Elichai Turkel for pointing out the case of rogue-key attacks in plain Ped-DKG and the suggestion to use a proof of knowledge for a_{i0} as a prevention mechanism. We acknowledge the helpful description of additive secret sharing and share conversion as a technique to non-interactively generate secrets for Shamir secret-sharing schemes by Lueks [20, §2.5.2].

We thank the Royal Bank of Canada and NSERC grant CRDPJ-534381 for funding this work. This research was undertaken, in part, thanks to funding from the Canada Research Chairs program.

A   Proof of Security

In Sect. 6.2, we presented a high-level overview of the proof of security for FROST-Interactive. We now present the proof in detail.

A.1   Preliminaries

Our proof strategy is to demonstrate that the security of FROST-Interactive reduces to the difficulty of computing the discrete logarithm of an arbitrary challenge value ω. At a high level, ω will be embedded into a public key Y representing a set of participants, such that Y is the output of these participants cooperating to perform the FROST KeyGen protocol. Then, to compute the discrete logarithm of ω, a forger $\mathcal{F}$ will produce two forgeries $(\sigma, \sigma'), \sigma \neq \sigma'$ for the same commitment value R and message m. Using (σ, σ'), the discrete logarithm of ω can subsequently be extracted.

We now describe how we perform this proof strategy in detail, starting by introducing four different algorithms that we use in our proof, and expanding further below.

- $\mathcal{F}$ represents a forger that with probability ϵ and in time t can compute a forgery σ for a public key Y, where Y was generated as part of the FROST KeyGen protocol.
- $\mathcal{A}$ represents a simulator that invokes $\mathcal{F}$ and simulates the necessary inputs/outputs for $\mathcal{F}$ to perform its forgery attack. Specifically, $\mathcal{A}$ simulates honest participants in FROST KeyGen and signing operations, as well as random oracle queries.
- $GF_{\mathcal{A}}$ represents the Generalized Forking Algorithm that establishes a random tape and outputs to random oracle queries, and invokes $\mathcal{A}$ with these values in order to produce two forgeries (σ, σ').
- C represents the coordination algorithm that accepts a challenge value ω and invokes the other algorithms in order to obtain (σ, σ'), which it then uses to compute the discrete logarithm of ω.

Adversary Powers. When performing its forgery attack, we grant $\mathcal{F}$ the role of the signature aggregator $\mathcal{SA}$. Without loss of generality, we assume $\mathcal{F}$ controls $t - 1$ participants, and has full power over how these participants behave, what secret and public values they generate, etc. We also assume the participant P_t is in the signing set S.

We now further describe $GF_{\mathcal{A}}$ and C; note these algorithms remain largely unchanged from their use by Bellare and Neven [3]. We describe the implementation of $\mathcal{A}$ in the proof directly.

Generalized Forking Algorithm and Lemma. We build upon the Generalized Forking Algorithm and Lemma by Bellare and Neven [3], which *simulates* the rewinding of the adversary $\mathcal{A}$, and which we describe next.

Generalized Forking Algorithm. Let n_r be the maximum number of random oracle outputs that $\mathcal{A}$ may need to generate, and let h be the number of possible outputs from the random oracle H.

Algorithm 1. Generalized Forking Algorithm $GF_\mathcal{A}(Y)$

Input A public key Y
Output $(1, h_J, h'_J, \sigma, \sigma')$ if $\mathcal{A}$ produces two forgeries, otherwise $\bot$

1: Instantiate a random tape β and $\{h_1, \ldots, h_{n_r}\} \overset{\$}{\leftarrow} H$
2: (J, σ) or $\bot \leftarrow \mathcal{A}(Y, \{h_1, \ldots, h_{n_r}\}; \beta)$
3: If $\bot$, then return $\bot$. Otherwise, $h'_J, \ldots, h'_{n_r} \overset{\$}{\leftarrow} H$
4: $(J', \sigma') \leftarrow \mathcal{A}(Y, \{h_1, \ldots, h_{J-1}, h'_J, \ldots, h'_{n_r}\}; \beta)$
5: If $J \overset{?}{=} J'$ and $h_J \neq h'_J$ then return $(1, h_J, h'_J, \sigma, \sigma')$. Else, return $\bot$

The adversary $\mathcal{A}$ is an algorithm that accepts as inputs a public key Y, the randomly selected set $h_1, \ldots, h_{n_r}$ of random oracle outputs, and a random tape β. $\mathcal{A}$ outputs an integer J which represents the index corresponding to the random oracle query that can be used to derive c for the forgery $\sigma = (R, z)$, along with σ itself. $GF_\mathcal{A}$ (Algorithm 1) plays the role of setting up these inputs and outputs, and executing $\mathcal{A}$ accordingly.

The execution $GF_\mathcal{A}$ is as follows: first $GF_\mathcal{A}$ instantiates a random tape β, and generates random outputs $h_1, \ldots, h_{n_r}$ which will then be used by $\mathcal{A}$ to simulate the outputs for each random oracle query. $GF_\mathcal{A}$ then executes $\mathcal{A}$ with these inputs as well as a public key Y. $\mathcal{A}$ uses the forger $\mathcal{F}$ as a subroutine to perform its forgery attack, simulating all input and output whenever $\mathcal{F}$ requests a signing operation or random oracle query. Eventually, $\mathcal{F}$ outputs a forgery σ with probability ϵ, which $\mathcal{A}$ returns along with its corresponding index for the random oracle query that can be used to derive c for σ. After $\mathcal{A}$ outputs (J, σ), $GF_\mathcal{A}$ first checks to see if the output is a successful forgery, as indicated by when $J \geq 1$. If so, it continues to the second execution of $\mathcal{A}$.

For the second execution of $\mathcal{A}$, $GF_\mathcal{A}$ will feed in the same random tape β, but will supply a different set of simulated responses for the random oracle H. In order to "fork" $\mathcal{A}$, $GF_\mathcal{A}$ will supply the same responses $h_1, \ldots, h_{J-1}$, but will provide *different* responses for $h_J, \ldots, h_{n_r}$. In doing so, $GF_\mathcal{A}$ simulates forking the adversary at a specific point when performing its attack similar to the proof model by Pointcheval and Stern [24], but without needing to rewind $\mathcal{A}$ to a specific point.

After its second execution, $\mathcal{A}$ will return (J', σ') or $\bot$. If $J' \overset{?}{=} J$ but the output from the random oracle queries is different such that $h_J \neq h'_J$, then $GF_\mathcal{A}$ will output 1 to indicate success along with the two forgeries σ, σ' and the two random oracle queries corresponding to these forgeries (h_J, h'_J). These values can then be used by the coordination algorithm C to determine the discrete logarithm of the challenge value ω (we provide more details on how to perform this operation below).

Generalized Forking Lemma. We will now see how the generalized forking lemma presented by Bellare and Neven [3] determines the probability that $GF_\mathcal{A}$ will return a successful output. Let acc be the accepting probability of $\mathcal{A}$, or

---

Algorithm 2. Algorithm $C(\omega)$

Input A challenge value ω
Output The discrete logarithm of ω, or $\perp$

1: Simulate KeyGen to embed challenge value ω and extract the forger's secret values
   $(Y, (a_{10}, \ldots, a_{(t-1)0})) \leftarrow SimKeyGen(\omega)$
2: $(1, h_J, h'_J, \sigma, \sigma')$ or $\perp \leftarrow GF_A(Y)$
3: If not $\perp$, then ExtractDLog$(\omega, h_J, h'_J, \sigma, \sigma', (a_{10}, \ldots, a_{(t-1)0}))$

---

the probability that $J \geq 1$, and let h be the total number of possible outputs of H. Let e' be the advantage of solving the discrete logarithm problem over some group $\mathbb{G}$. Recall that n_r is the maximum number of random oracle outputs $\mathcal{A}$ may need to generate.

Lemma 1. *Generalized Forking Lemma [3]* Let frk be defined by the following probability:

$$frk = Pr[b = 1 : x \xleftarrow{\$} IG : (b, \sigma, \sigma') \xleftarrow{\$} GF_A(x)]$$

where IG is an input generator for a challenge input x. Then

$$e' \geq frk \geq acc \cdot \left(\frac{acc}{n_r} - \frac{1}{h}\right)$$

Lemma 1 demonstrates the probability e' that running the generalized forking algorithm GF_A will produce two valid forgeries $\sigma = (R, z)$ and $\sigma' = (R', z')$ along with their respective challenge responses from the random oracle (h_J, h'_J) over the same message m and public commitment R, and so enable the extraction of the desired discrete logarithm.

Embedding the Challenge Value During KeyGen. We use a coordination algorithm C described in Algorithm 2 to perform setup for GF_A and to derive the discrete logarithm of the challenge value ω afterward.

Simulating KeyGen. We now describe how C embeds the challenge value ω into the group public key Y during a simulation of the KeyGen phase; Y is in turn fed as input into GF_A. For simplicity of notation, we let $n = t$ (where n is the total number of participants and t is the threshold), and $\mathcal{F}$ controls $t - 1$ participants, and $\mathcal{A}$ simulates the tth (honest) participant to $\mathcal{F}$. The case for general n is similar.

For the first round of the key generation protocol, $\mathcal{A}$ simulates P_t as follows. Let C_i be the set of public commitments $\phi_{i1}, \ldots, \phi_{i(t-1)}$ for participant P_i. To calculate C_t and to distribute shares $f_t(1), \ldots, f_t(t-1)$ to the $t-1$ participants corrupted by $\mathcal{F}$, $\mathcal{A}$ does the following:

1. Randomly generate $\bar{x}_{t1}, \ldots, \bar{x}_{t(t-1)}$ to serve as the secret shares corresponding to $f_t(1), \ldots, f_t(t-1)$

Algorithm 3. Algorithm ExtractDLog($\omega, h_J, h'_J, (\sigma, \sigma'), (a_{10}, \ldots, a_{(t-1)0})$)

Input A challenge value ω, two random oracle responses h_J, h'_J and their corresponding two forgeries (σ, σ'), and secret values $(a_{10}, \ldots, a_{(t-1)0})$
Output The discrete logarithm of ω

1: Parse σ, σ' as $(R, z), (R, z')$, and then compute the discrete logarithm of Y as $\frac{(z'-z)}{(h'_J - h_J)}$.
2: Compute $a_{t0} = dlog(Y) - \sum_{i=1}^{t-1} a_{i0}$
3: Return a_{t0}, which is the discrete logarithm of ω

---

2. Set ϕ_{t0} to be the challenge value ω
3. Calculate $\phi_{t1}, \ldots, \phi_{t(t-1)}$ by performing Lagrange interpolation in the exponent, or $\phi_{tk} = \omega^{\lambda_{k0}} \cdot g^{\sum_{i=1}^{t-1} \lambda_{ki} \cdot \bar{x}_{ti}}$

$\mathcal{A}$ then broadcasts $\boldsymbol{C}_t$ for P_t. For the second round, $\mathcal{A}$ sends $(1, \bar{x}_{t1}), \ldots, (t-1, \bar{x}_{t(t-1)})$ to the participants $P_1, \ldots, P_{t-1}$ corrupted by $\mathcal{F}$. Further, $\mathcal{A}$ simulates the proof of knowledge for a_{t0} by deriving σ as:

$$c_t, z \xleftarrow{\$} \mathbb{Z}_q; \; R = g^z \cdot \omega^{-c_t}; \text{ and } \sigma = (R, z)$$

$\mathcal{A}$ derives the public key for P_t by following the same steps they would use to calculate the public key for their peers (as the discrete log of the challenge value ω is unknown), by deriving $Y_t = \prod_{j=1}^{n} \prod_{k=0}^{t-1} \phi_{jk}^{t^k \bmod q}$.

The participants controlled by $\mathcal{F}$ can derive their private key shares s_i by directly following the KeyGen protocol, then deriving $Y_i = g^{s_i}$. We will see in the proof for FROST-Interactive how $\mathcal{A}$ can still simulate signing for the honest party P_t to $\mathcal{F}$ even without knowing its corresponding private key share. Each party (honest or corrupted by $\mathcal{F}$) can follow the KeyGen protocol to derive the group's long-lived public key, by calculating $Y = \prod_{j=1}^{n} \phi_{j0}$.

In addition, C must obtain $\mathcal{F}$'s secret values $(a_{10}, \ldots, a_{(t-1)0})$ using the extractor for the zero-knowledge proofs that $\mathcal{F}$ generates. C will use these values next in order to convert the discrete logarithm for the group public key Y into the discrete logarithm for the challenge value ω.

Solving Discrete Logarithm of the Challenge. We now describe how two forged signatures (σ, σ') along with the challenge values from the random oracle query (h_J, h'_J) produced as output from $GF_\mathcal{A}$ can be used by C to extract the discrete logarithm of the challenge value ω. We give an overview of the algorithm ExtractDLog in Algorithm 3, which C uses as a subroutine. Note that the advantage e' used later in our proofs denotes the advantage of $C(\omega)$ of solving the discrete logarithm for the challenge value ω.

We can compute $dlog(Y)$, because

$$R = g^z \cdot Y^{-h_J} = g^{z'} \cdot Y^{-h'_J}$$

and since $h_J \neq h'_J$, then

$$dlog(Y) = \frac{(z' - z)}{(h'_J - h_J)}$$

The discrete logarithm corresponding to ω can then be extracted as follows:

$$a_{t0} = dlog(Y) - \sum_{i=1}^{t-1} a_{i0} = dlog(\omega) \tag{2}$$

As discussed in Sect. A.1, all of $\mathcal{F}$'s $a_{i0}, i \neq t$ values are known as these were extracted by $\mathcal{A}$ while performing the key generation protocol. Hence, C can extract a_{t0} using Eq. 2, resulting in learning the discrete log of the challenge value ω.

A.2   Proof of Security for FROST-Interactive

Due to the difficulty of simulating zero-knowledge proofs in parallel, for the purposes of proving the security of FROST, we will first prove security against an *interactive* two-round variant of the FROST signing operation, which we call FROST-Interactive. In Sect. 6.2, we discuss how the security for FROST-Interactive extends to plain FROST.

FROST-Interactive. FROST-Interactive uses the same KeyGen protocol to generate long-lived keys as regular FROST, as further described in Sect. 5.1. We present an overview of the Preprocess step for FROST-Interactive in Fig. 4, and the signing step in Fig. 5.

The distinction between the signing operations for plain FROST and FROST-Interactive is how the binding value ρ_i is generated. Because of the difficulty of simulating non-interactive zero-knowledge proofs of knowledge (NIZKPKs) in a concurrent setting, we instantiate FROST-Interactive using a one-time VRF, from which each participant generates their value ρ_i given the inputs (m, B). We prove this variant to be secure against the standard notion of EUF-CMA security.

Preprocess. The Preprocess phase for FROST-Interactive differs from FROST in two ways. First, participants additionally generate one-time VRF keys (a_{ij}, b_{ij}) and their commitments $(A_{ij} = g^{a_{ij}}, B_{ij} = g^{b_{ij}})$ along with the usual FROST nonce values (d_{ij}, e_{ij}) and their commitments $(D_{ij} = g^{d_{ij}}, E_{ij} = g^{e_{ij}})$ along with a zero-knowledge proof of knowledge for the (a_{ij}, b_{ij}) one-time VRF keys. These keys are later used to generate ρ_i during the signing phase.

We require Preprocess for FROST-Interactive to be performed *serially* so that the simulator can efficiently extract the discrete logarithm of the adversary's non-interactive zero knowledge proof of knowledge of its VRF keys via rewinding. In the setting of plain FROST, the Preprocess step can be performed non-interactively, and thus the requirement of performing this step serially is no longer relevant.

Preprocess(π) $\rightarrow (i, \langle (D_{ij}, E_{ij}, A_{ij}, B_{ij}) \rangle_{j=1}^{\pi})$

Each participant $P_i, i \in \{1, \ldots, n\}$ performs this stage prior to signing. As before, j is a counter for a nonce/commitment pair, and π the number of commitments generated. Let H_3 be a hash function whose input is a sequence of commitment values, and H_4 be one with inputs (i, Φ).

Round 1

1. Create empty list L_i. Then, for $1 \le j \le \pi$, perform the following:

   1.a Generate nonces $d_{ij}, e_{ij}, a_{ij}, b_{ij} \xleftarrow{\$} \mathbb{Z}_q^*$, and derive
   $(D_{ij}, E_{ij}, A_{ij}, B_{ij}) = (g^{d_{ij}}, g^{e_{ij}}, g^{a_{ij}}, g^{b_{ij}})$.

   1.b Generate nonces $k_{aij}, k_{bij} \xleftarrow{\$} \mathbb{Z}_q$, and commitments
   $(R_{aij}, R_{bij}) = (g^{k_{aij}}, g^{k_{bij}})$.

   1.c Let $K_{ij} = (D_{ij}, E_{ij}, A_{ij}, B_{ij}, R_{aij}, R_{bij})$.

   1.d Append $(j, (D_{ij}, E_{ij}, A_{ij}, B_{ij}))$ to L_i, store $((d_{ij}, D_{ij}), (e_{ij}, E_{ij}),$
   $(a_{ij}, A_{ij}), (b_{ij}, B_{ij}))$ for later use in signing operations.

2. Let $K_i = H_3(K_{i1}, \ldots, K_{i\pi})$; send (i, K_i) to all other participants.

Round 2

1. After receiving (ℓ, K_ℓ) from all other participants, generate a zero-knowledge proof of knowledge σ_i for $\langle a_{ij}, b_{ij} \rangle_{j=1}^{\pi}$ by performing:

   1.a Compute $\Phi = H_3(K_1, \ldots, K_n)$ and $c_i = H_4(i, \Phi)$.

   1.b Derive $\mu_{aij} = k_{aij} + a_{ij} \cdot c_i$ and $\mu_{bij} = k_{bij} + b_{ij} \cdot c_i, \forall j \in \{1, \ldots, \pi\}$.

   1.c Set $J_i = \langle \mu_{aij}, \mu_{bij} \rangle_{j=1}^{\pi}$.

2. Send (i, L_i, J_i) to all other participants.

3. After receiving (ℓ, L_ℓ, J_ℓ) from each participant, verify the proofs in J_ℓ using L_ℓ. First, compute $c_\ell = H_4(\ell, \Phi)$. Then, for each $j \in \{1, \ldots, \pi\}$:

   3.a Check that $D_{\ell j}, E_{\ell j}, A_{\ell j}, B_{\ell j} \in \mathbb{G}^*$.

   3.b Derive $R'_{a\ell j} = g^{\mu_{a\ell j}} \cdot (A_{\ell j})^{-c_\ell}$ and $R'_{b\ell j} = g^{\mu_{b\ell j}} \cdot (B_{\ell j})^{-c_\ell}$.

   3.c Let $K'_{\ell j} = (D_{\ell j}, E_{\ell j}, A_{\ell j}, B_{\ell j}, R'_{a\ell j}, R'_{b\ell j})$.

4 Let $K'_\ell = H_3(K'_{\ell 1}, \ldots, K'_{\ell \pi})$. Check $K'_\ell \stackrel{?}{=} K_\ell$, aborting on failure.

5. Abort if any check failed. Otherwise, store (ℓ, L_ℓ) for use in signing operations.

Fig. 4. FROST-interactive two-round preprocessing protocol

Sign. To perform signing, $\mathcal{SA}$ first sends (m, B) to each participant, and each participant responds with $\rho_i = a_{ij} + b_{ij} \cdot H_\rho(m, B)$, where B is derived similarly to in plain FROST via the ordered list of tuples $(i, D_{ij}, E_{ij}), i \in S$. In the second round, $\mathcal{SA}$ then sends each ρ_i to each of the signing participants, who use these values to derive R and then to calculate their own response z_i.

Proof of Security for FROST-Interactive. We now present a proof of EUF-CMA security for FROST-Interactive, demonstrating that an adversary that can

---

Sign(m) → (m, σ)

Round 1

1. $\mathcal{SA}$ selects a set S of t participants for the signing protocol, and the next available commitments for each signing participant ($D_{ij}, E_{ij}, A_{ij}, B_{ij}$), and creates $B = \langle (i, D_{ij}, E_{ij}) \rangle_{i \in S}$. $\mathcal{SA}$ then sends (m, B) to each participant $P_i, i \in S$.
2. After receiving (m, B), each $P_i, i \in S$ first checks that m is a valid message, and validates every tuple ($i, D_{ij}, E_{ij}) \in B$ maps to the next available ($D_{ij}, E_{ij}, A_{ij}, B_{ij}$), aborting if either check fails.
3. Each P_i generates $\rho_i = a_{ij} + b_{ij} \cdot H_\rho(m, B)$, securely deletes ($a_{ij}, A_{ij}$) and ($b_{ij}, B_{ij}$) from their local storage, and returns ρ_i to $\mathcal{SA}$.

Round 2

1. After receiving each ρ_ℓ, $\mathcal{SA}$ then distributes all $\rho_\ell, \ell \in S$ to each signing participant.
2. After receiving the list of ρ_ℓ values, each participant checks the validity of each by verifying ($g^{\rho_\ell} \stackrel{?}{=} A_{\ell j} \cdot B_{\ell j}{}^{H_\rho(m, B)}$).
3. Each P_i then derives $R = \prod_{\ell \in S} D_{\ell j} \cdot E_{\ell j}{}^{\rho_\ell}$, and then $c = H_2(R, Y, m)$.
4. Each P_i computes their response using their long-lived secret share s_i by computing $z_i = d_{ij} + (e_{ij} \cdot \rho_i) + \lambda_i \cdot s_i \cdot c$, using S to determine λ_i.
5. Each P_i securely deletes (d_{ij}, D_{ij}) and (e_{ij}, E_{ij}) from their local storage, and then returns z_i to $\mathcal{SA}$.
6. $\mathcal{SA}$ performs the identical verification, aggregation, and publication of signature shares as in plain FROST.

Fig. 5. FROST-interactive two-round signing protocol

compute forgeries acting against FROST-Interactive can be used to compute the discrete logarithm of an arbitrary challenge value.

Let n_h be the number of queries made to the random oracle, n_p be the number of allowed preprocess queries, and n_s be the number of allowed signing queries.

Theorem 2. *If the discrete logarithm problem in $\mathbb{G}$ is (τ', ϵ')-hard, then the FROST-Interactive signature scheme over $\mathbb{G}$ with n signing participants, a threshold of t, and a preprocess batch size of π is ($\tau, n_h, n_p, n_s, \epsilon$)-secure whenever*

$$\epsilon' \leq \frac{\epsilon^2}{2n_h + (\pi + 1)n_p + 1}$$

and

$$\tau' = 4\tau + (30\pi n_p + (4t - 2)n_s + (n + t - 1)t + 6) \cdot t_{exp} + O(\pi n_p + n_s + n_h + 1)$$

such that t_{exp} is the time of an exponentiation in $\mathbb{G}$, assuming the number of participants compromised by the adversary is less than the threshold t.

Algorithm 4. Algorithm $\mathcal{A}(Y, \{h_1, \ldots, h_{n_r}\}; \beta)$

Input A public key Y and random oracle outputs $\{h_1, \ldots, h_{n_r}\}$
Output An index J and forgery σ, or $\perp$

1: Initialize $ctr = 1, T_\rho = \{\}, T_2 = \{\}, T_3 = \{\}, T_4 = \{\}, J_2 = \{\}, C = \{\}, M = \{\}$
2: Run $\mathcal{F}$ on input Y, answering its queries as follows, until it outputs $(m, \sigma = (R, z))$ or $\perp$.
3: **On simulating $H_\rho(m, B)$:**
4:   If $T_\rho[m, B] = \perp$, set $T_\rho[m, B] = h_{ctr}; ctr = ctr + 1$. Return $T_\rho[m, B]$.
5: **On simulating $H_2(R, Y, m)$:**
6:   If $T_2[m, R] = \perp$, set $T_2[R, Y, m] = h_{ctr}$, $J_2[R, Y, m] = ctr; ctr = ctr + 1$. Return $T_2[R, Y, m]$.
7: **On simulating $H_3(\boldsymbol{X})$:**
8:   If $T_3[\boldsymbol{X}] = \perp$, set $T_3[\boldsymbol{X}] = h_{ctr}; ctr = ctr + 1$. Return $T_3[\boldsymbol{X}]$.
9: **On simulating $H_4(i, \Phi)$:**
10:   If $T_4[i, \Phi] = \perp$, set $T_4[i, \Phi] = h_{ctr}; ctr = ctr + 1$. Return $T_4[i, \Phi]$.
11: **On simulating Preprocess:**
12:   **Round 1:**
13:     For $1 \leq j \leq \pi$, do:
14:       Set $\bar{c}_j = h_{ctr}$, $C[j] = ctr$, $ctr = ctr + 1$, $\bar{z}_{tj} \xleftarrow{\$} \mathbb{Z}_q$, $D_{tj} = g^{\bar{z}_{tj}} \cdot Y_t^{-\bar{c}_j}$.
15:       Follow the protocol honestly to sample (e_{tj}, a_{tj}, b_{tj}) and derive (E_{tj}, A_{tj}, B_{tj}).
16:       Follow the protocol honestly to sample (k_{atj}, k_{btj}) and derive (R_{atj}, R_{btj}).
17:       Derive K_t honestly, publish to $\mathcal{F}$, and wait for all K_ℓ values from $\mathcal{F}$.
18:   **Round 2:**
19:     Derive L_t, Φ, J_t honestly. Send (t, L_t, J_t) to $\mathcal{F}$, and wait to receive the (ℓ, L_ℓ, J_ℓ) tuples from $\mathcal{F}$, following the protocol for validation.
20:     Reprogram $T_3[K_1, \ldots, K_n] = h_{ctr}$; set $ctr = ctr + 1$. Rederive c_t and J_t honestly.
21:     Rewind $\mathcal{F}$ to step 1 in Round 2 of Figure 4, immediately before $\mathcal{F}$ queries H_3 with $(K_1, \ldots, K_n)$.
22:     After allowing $\mathcal{F}$ to proceed after rewinding, use its two sets of outputs to derive the discrete logarithm of each $A_{\ell j}$ and $B_{\ell j}$; store for use in the signing protocol.
23:     Complete the protocol honestly.
24: **On simulating Sign:**
25:   **Round 1:** Input (m, B)
26:     Insert m into M.
27:     Using $(a_{\ell j}, b_{\ell j})$ obtained during Preprocess, derive $\rho_\ell : \ell \in S, \ell \neq t$
28:     Derive $\rho_t = a_{tj} + b_{tj} \cdot H_\rho(m, B)$ and R, following the protocol honestly for validation.
29:     Program $T_2[m, R] = \bar{c}_j$, $J_2[m, R] = C[j]$; return ρ_t.
30:   **Round 2:** Input $(\rho_j, \ldots, \rho_t)$
31:     Let $z_t = \bar{z}_{tj} + (e_{tj} \cdot \rho_t)$; return z_t to $\mathcal{F}$
32: If $\mathcal{F}$ outputs $\perp$, then return $\perp$. Else $\mathcal{F}$ outputs $(m, \sigma = (R, z))$.
33: If $T_2[m, Y, R] = \perp$, set $T_2[m, Y, R] = h_{ctr}$, $J_2[m, Y, R] = ctr$, and $ctr = ctr + 1$.
34: Let $c = T_2[m, Y, R]$. If $R \neq g^z Y^{-c}$ or $m \in M$, then return $\perp$
35: Let $J = J_2[m, Y, R]$. Return $J, \sigma = (R, z)$

Proof. We prove the theorem by contradiction. Assume that $\mathcal{F}$ can $(\tau, n_h, n_p, n_s, \epsilon)$-break the unforgeability property of FROST-Interactive. We will demonstrate that an algorithm C that can (τ', ϵ')-solve the discrete logarithm of an arbitrary challenge value $\omega \in \mathbb{G}$. We first describe the simulator $\mathcal{A}$, which uses $\mathcal{F}$ as a black-box forger.

We now describe how $\mathcal{A}$ simulates FROST-Interactive to $\mathcal{F}$ in Algorithm 4. Recall that $\mathcal{F}$ controls $t-1$ participants, and $\mathcal{A}$ simulates a single honest participant P_t.

Let $n_r = 2n_h + (\pi+1)n_p + 1$ denote the maximum number of random oracle outputs $\mathcal{A}$ may require.

After performing the key generation phase as described in Sect. A.1, $\mathcal{A}$ invokes $\mathcal{F}$ to perform its forgery attack. $\mathcal{A}$ simulates both the responses to the random oracle queries of $\mathcal{F}$ as well as the role of P_t in the Preprocess and Sign algorithms.

Simulating Random Oracle Queries. For each random oracle query to H_ρ, H_2, H_3, and H_4, $\mathcal{A}$ responds by first checking a corresponding associative table (initialized to empty on start) to see if the output has already been determined for that query. If no such output exists, $\mathcal{A}$ sets the output to the next available value from $\{h_1, \ldots, h_{n_r}\}$ supplied by $GF_\mathcal{A}$ upon start, indicated by ctr. After setting the output, $\mathcal{A}$ increments ctr and returns the freshly assigned output. In lieu of the $H_1(i, m, B)$ hash function used in FROST (presented in Sect. 5.2), FROST-Interactive uses an interactive one-time VRF with input $H_\rho(m, B)$ to provide this binding mechanism.

Simulating Preprocess. To perform the Preprocess stage, $\mathcal{A}$ simulates the honest participant P_t, following the protocol honestly with exception of the following steps. When generating D_{tj}, $\mathcal{A}$ first picks $\bar{c}_j$ as the next available h_{ctr} value, and keeps track of which one it used by setting $C[j] = ctr$ in a list C. $\mathcal{A}$ randomly selects $\bar{z}_{tj} \overset{\$}{\leftarrow} \mathbb{Z}_q$, and then derives $D_{tj} = g^{\bar{z}_{tj}} \cdot Y_t^{-\bar{c}_j}$.

$\mathcal{A}$ honestly computes and publishes its proof of knowledge of the (a_{tj}, b_{tj}) values in Round 2. However, during this round, $\mathcal{A}$ itself forks $\mathcal{F}$ in order to extract the discrete logarithms $(a_{\ell j}, b_{\ell j})$ of the commitment values $(A_{\ell j}, B_{\ell j})$ for all of the players P_ℓ controlled by $\mathcal{F}$. $\mathcal{A}$ is able to learn these values by rewinding $\mathcal{F}$ to the point before it makes the query $\Phi = H_3(K_1, \ldots, K_t)$, and programming the random oracle to return a different random output Φ'. Then, when $\mathcal{F}$ republishes $J_i : i \neq t$ for all dishonest parties that $\mathcal{F}$ controls, $\mathcal{A}$ can solve for the discrete log for each commitment.

Simulating Signing. $\mathcal{F}$ initiates the FROST-Interactive signing protocol in the role of $\mathcal{SA}$, sending (m, B) in Round 1. Upon receiving these values, $\mathcal{A}$ is able to compute not only its ρ_t, but also *all of the other ρ_ℓ values for all of the other participants*, because of its knowledge of the $(a_{\ell j}, b_{\ell j})$ that $\mathcal{A}$ obtained during Round 2 of the preprocessing stage. Using these ρ_ℓ values, it can compute the R that will be used in Round 2, and program $H_2(R, Y, m) = \bar{c}_j$. It also saves $C[j]$, the ctr value such that $\bar{c}_k = h_{ctr}$, as $J_2[R, Y, m]$ in a table J_2.

Note that $\mathcal{A}$ is never required to guess which output from the random oracle to program to correctly issue a signature, because $\mathcal{A}$ can always compute R before $\mathcal{F}$ can, and consequently can program the random oracle $H_2(R, Y, m)$ with perfect success. Conversely, a signing request by $\mathcal{A}$ in the simulation for plain Schnorr succeeds only with probability $1/(n_h + n_s + 1)$ [3].

Finding the Discrete Logarithm of the Challenge Input. As described in Sect. A.1, using the two forgeries (σ, σ'), the discrete logarithm of ω can be derived.

Recall that the probability of $\mathcal{F}$ succeeding for one run of $\mathcal{A}$ is simply ϵ, as $\mathcal{A}$ can return the correct challenge for each signing query. Then, using the forking lemma, the probability that the discrete logarithm of ω can be extracted after $\mathcal{A}$ is run twice is at least $\frac{\epsilon^2}{n_r}$ (ignoring the negligible $\frac{\epsilon}{h}$ term, as h—the number of possible hash outputs—is typically at least 2^{256}), and the total time required to extract the discrete logarithm of the challenge value is:

$$\tau' = 4\tau + (30\pi n_p + (4t - 2)n_s + (n + t - 1)t + 6) \cdot t_{exp} + O(\pi n_p + n_s + n_h + 1)$$

The running time for C to compute the discrete logarithm by procuring two forgeries from FROST-Interactive is four times that for $\mathcal{F}$ (because of the forking of $\mathcal{A}$, which itself forks $\mathcal{F}$), plus the time to compute $(30\pi n_p + (4t - 2)n_s + (n + t - 1)t + 6)$ exponentiations:

- In simulating KeyGen, $(t - 1) \cdot t$ to compute C_t, 2 to compute R, and $n \cdot t$ to compute Y_t
- In each of two executions of $\mathcal{A}$:
  - 7 in each of π iterations of Round 1 of simulating Preprocess,
  - 8π to validate each two versions of $t - 1$ J_ℓ lists in Round 2 of simulating Preprocess,
  - $t - 1$ to validate the ρ_ℓ and t to compute R in each simulation of Sign,
  - 2 to compute R to verify the output of $\mathcal{F}$.

and $O(\pi n_p + n_s + n_h + 1)$ other minor operations, such as table lookups.

A.3   Extension of FROST-Interactive to FROST

In this section, we describe the changes we make to FROST-Interactive to remove one round of communication in each of the Preprocess and the Sign phases. We argue in Sect. 6 why our changes do not harm the security of the protocol.

Removal of One-Time Verifiable Random Functions to Generate ρ_i. The primary difference between FROST-Interactive and FROST is that in the former, interactive one-time VRFs are used to generate the ρ_i binding values. In FROST, on the other hand, these values are generated with random oracles (modelling hash functions). Removing the one-time VRFs removes the VRF keys (a_{ij}, b_{ij}) and their commitments (A_{ij}, B_{ij}) from the protocol.

Removal of One Round of the Sign Phase. With the one-time VRFs removed, all participants can compute every other participants' ρ_i values non-interactively, and so the first round of the Sign protocol for FROST-Interactive (where participants exchange their ρ_i values) is no longer necessary for FROST.

Removal of the Proofs of Knowledge of the One-Time VRF Keys and One Round of the Preprocess Phase. As the one-time VRF keys are removed, so are their proofs of knowledge J_i in the Preprocess phase. Removing the J_i then makes the K_i unused, and removing the K_i removes the first round of the Preprocess phase.

References

1. Abidin, A., Aly, A., Mustafa, M.A.: Collaborative authentication using threshold cryptography. In: Emerging Technologies for Authorization and Authentication, pp. 122–137 (2020)
2. Bellare, M., Boldyreva, A., Staddon, J.: Randomness re-use in multi-recipient encryption schemeas. In: Desmedt, Y.G. (ed.) PKC 2003. LNCS, vol. 2567, pp. 85–99. Springer, Heidelberg (2003). https://doi.org/10.1007/3-540-36288-6_7
3. Bellare, M., Neven, G.: Multi-signatures in the plain public-key model and a general forking lemma. In: Proceedings of the 13th ACM Conference on Computer and Communications Security, CCS 2006, pp. 390–399 (2006). https://doi.org/10.1145/1180405.1180453
4. Benaloh, J., Leichter, J.: Generalized secret sharing and monotone functions. In: Goldwasser, S. (ed.) Generalized Secret Sharing and Monotone Functions. LNCS, vol. 403, pp. 27–35. Springer, New York (1990). https://doi.org/10.1007/0-387-34799-2_3
5. Benhamouda, F., Lepoint, T., Orrù, M., Raykova, M.: On the (in)security of ROS. Technical report 2020/945, IACR ePrint (2020). https://eprint.iacr.org/2020/945
6. Boneh, D., Drijvers, M., Neven, G.: Compact multi-signatures for smaller blockchains. In: Peyrin, T., Galbraith, S. (eds.) ASIACRYPT 2018. LNCS, vol. 11273, pp. 435–464. Springer, Cham (2018). https://doi.org/10.1007/978-3-030-03329-3_15
7. Boneh, D., Lynn, B., Shacham, H.: Short signatures from the Weil pairing. J. Cryptol. **17**(4), 297–319 (2004). https://doi.org/10.1007/s00145-004-0314-9
8. Cramer, R., Damgård, I., Ishai, Y.: Share conversion, pseudorandom secret-sharing and applications to secure computation. In: Kilian, J. (ed.) TCC 2005. LNCS, vol. 3378, pp. 342–362. Springer, Heidelberg (2005). https://doi.org/10.1007/978-3-540-30576-7_19
9. Damgård, I., Jakobsen, T.P., Nielsen, J.B., Pagter, J.I., Østergård, M.B.: Fast threshold ECDSA with honest majority. Technical report 2020/501, IACR ePrint (2020). https://eprint.iacr.org/2020/501
10. Drijvers, M., et al.: On the security of two-round multi-signatures. In: 2019 IEEE Symposium on Security and Privacy (SP), pp. 1084–1101 (2019)
11. Feldman, P.: A practical scheme for non-interactive verifiable secret sharing. In: Proceedings of the 28th Annual Symposium on Foundations of Computer Science, SFCS 1987, pp. 427–438 (1987). https://doi.org/10.1109/SFCS.1987.4

12. Gennaro, R., Goldfeder, S.: Fast multiparty threshold ECDSA with fast trustless setup. In: Proceedings of the 2018 ACM SIGSAC Conference on Computer and Communications Security, CCS 2018, pp. 1179–1194 (2018). https://doi.org/10.1145/3243734.3243859
13. Gennaro, R., Goldfeder, S.: One round threshold ECDSA with identifiable abort. Technical report 2020/540, IACR ePrint (2020). https://eprint.iacr.org/2020/540
14. Gennaro, R., Jarecki, S., Krawczyk, H., Rabin, T.: Secure applications of Pedersen's distributed key generation protocol. In: Topics in Cryptology – CT-RSA 2003, pp. 373–390 (2003)
15. Gennaro, R., Jarecki, S., Krawczyk, H., Rabin, T.: Secure distributed key generation for discrete-log based cryptosystems. J. Cryptol. **20**(1), 51–83 (2006). https://doi.org/10.1007/s00145-006-0347-3
16. Goldfeder, S., et al.: Securing Bitcoin wallets via a new DSA/ECDSA threshold signature scheme (2015). http://stevengoldfeder.com/papers/threshold_sigs.pdf. Accessed Dec 2019
17. Josefsson, S., Liusvaara, I.: Edwards-Curve Digital Signature Algorithm (EdDSA), January 2017. https://tools.ietf.org/html/rfc8032
18. KZen Networks: Multi Party Schnorr Signatures (2019). https://github.com/KZen-networks/multi-party-schnorr. Accessed Jan 2020
19. Lovecruft, I., de Valence, H.: The Ristretto Group (2020). https://doc.dalek.rs/curve25519_dalek/
20. Lueks, W.: Security and Privacy via Cryptography – Having your cake and eating it too (2017). https://wouterlueks.nl/assets/docs/thesis_lueks_def.pdf
21. Maxwell, G., Poelstra, A., Seurin, Y., Wuille, P.: Simple Schnorr multi-signatures with applications to Bitcoin. Des. Codes Cryptogr. **87**(9), 2139–2164 (2019). https://doi.org/10.1007/s10623-019-00608-x
22. Mittal, P., Olumofin, F., Troncoso, C., Borisov, N., Goldberg, I.: PIR-Tor: scalable anonymous communication using private information retrieval. In: 20th USENIX Security Symposium, SEC 2011 (2011). http://dl.acm.org/citation.cfm?id=2028067.2028098
23. Pedersen, T.P.: A threshold cryptosystem without a trusted party. In: Davies, D.W. (ed.) EUROCRYPT 1991. LNCS, vol. 547, pp. 522–526. Springer, Heidelberg (1991). https://doi.org/10.1007/3-540-46416-6_47
24. Pointcheval, D., Stern, J.: Security arguments for digital signatures and blind signatures. J. Cryptol. **13**(3), 361–396 (2000). https://doi.org/10.1007/s001450010003
25. Schnorr, C.: Security of blind discrete log signatures against interactive attacks. In: ICICS (2001)
26. Schnorr, C.P.: Efficient identification and signatures for smart cards. In: Brassard, G. (ed.) CRYPTO 1989. LNCS, vol. 435, pp. 239–252. Springer, New York (1990). https://doi.org/10.1007/0-387-34805-0_22
27. Shamir, A.: How to share a secret. Commun. ACM **22**, 612–613 (1979)
28. Stinson, D.R., Strobl, R.: Provably secure distributed Schnorr signatures and a (t, n) threshold scheme for implicit certificates. In: Proceedings of the 6th Australasian Conference on Information Security and Privacy, ACISP 2001, pp. 417–434 (2001). http://dl.acm.org/citation.cfm?id=646038.678297
29. Wagner, D.: A generalized birthday problem. In: Yung, M. (ed.) CRYPTO 2002. LNCS, vol. 2442, pp. 288–304. Springer, Heidelberg (2002). https://doi.org/10.1007/3-540-45708-9_19

Algorithmic Acceleration of B/FV-Like Somewhat Homomorphic Encryption for Compute-Enabled RAM

Jonathan Takeshita[✉], Dayane Reis, Ting Gong, Michael Niemier,
X. Sharon Hu, and Taeho Jung

University of Notre Dame, Notre Dame, IN 46556, USA
{jtakeshi,dreis,tgong,mniemier,shu,tjung}@nd.edu

Abstract. Somewhat Homomorphic Encryption (SHE) allows arbitrary computation with finite multiplicative depths to be performed on encrypted data, but its overhead is high due to memory transfer incurred by large ciphertexts. Recent research has recognized the shortcomings of general-purpose computing for high-performance SHE, and has begun to pioneer the use of hardware-based SHE acceleration with hardware including FPGAs, GPUs, and Compute-Enabled RAM (CE-RAM). CE-RAM is well-suited for SHE, as it is not limited by the separation between memory and processing that bottlenecks other hardware. Further, CE-RAM does not move data between different processing elements. Recent research has shown the high effectiveness of CE-RAM for SHE as compared to highly-optimized CPU and FPGA implementations. However, algorithmic optimization for the implementation on CE-RAM is underexplored. In this work, we examine the effect of existing algorithmic optimizations upon a CE-RAM implementation of the B/FV scheme [19], and further introduce novel optimization techniques for the Full RNS Variant of B/FV [6]. Our experiments show speedups of up to 784x for homomorphic multiplication, 143x for decryption, and 330x for encryption against a CPU implementation. We also compare our approach to similar work in CE-RAM, FPGA, and GPU acceleration, and note general improvement over existing work. In particular, for homomorphic multiplication we see speedups of 506.5x against CE-RAM [34], 66.85x against FPGA [36], and 30.8x against GPU [3] as compared to existing work in hardware acceleration of B/FV.

Keywords: Somewhat Homomorphic Encryption · B/FV scheme ·
Full-RNS variant · Compute-Enabled RAM

1 Introduction

Fully homomorphic encryption (FHE), first presented by Gentry [20], allows arbitrary number of additions and multiplications on ciphertexts. It has wide applications in settings where data privacy is paramount, but the *bootstrapping*

© Springer Nature Switzerland AG 2021
O. Dunkelman et al. (Eds.): SAC 2020, LNCS 12804, pp. 66–89, 2021.
https://doi.org/10.1007/978-3-030-81652-0_3

procedure required to allow an arbitrary number of operations on ciphertexts is highly complex and computationally intensive. Therefore, most active research including this work focuses on improving the efficiency of the underlying Somewhat Homomorphic Encryption (SHE) scheme [6,10,34–36], in which a ciphertext can be operated on arbitrarily up to a certain multiplicative depth. Even without the bootstrapping procedure, SHE schemes lead to high overhead in performing homomorphic operations with ciphertexts due to the large size of the ciphertexts.

Recent research recognizes limitations of traditional general-purpose computing in high-performance realizations of SHE [35,36]. This is due to highly intensive computation involving large amounts of data transfer. Research efforts have thus turned towards special hardware paradigms for accelerating SHE, including Application-Specific Integrated Circuits (ASICs) [29,41], Field-Programmable Gate Arrays (FPGAs) [24,30,35,36], and GPUs [3]. Each of these paradigms has their own strengths and limitations, such as data transfer, memory availability, word size, and cost. While using FPGAs to accelerate SHE has been highly successful, FPGAs are ultimately limited by data transfer (both within the FPGA, and to/from other parts of the system), limits on the amount of on-chip memory, and limited word size. In much previous research, data transfer has been of great significance, with much effort in design and implementation devoted to mitigating the latency of data transfer. The root cause of this need is the inherent separation and bottlenecks between processing and memory present in traditional computing architectures as well as in specialized solutions such as ASICs, FPGAs, and GPUs. Computing paradigms such as Near-Memory Processing (NMP) and Compute-Enabled RAM (CE-RAM) seek to overcome this by reducing or removing the separation of processing and memory. This approach ameliorates the latency induced by data transfer. In addition, CE-RAM also enables a high degree of parallelism by allowing simultaneous operations on data within the same bank of CE-RAM without significant extra overhead. Existing work has shown the efficacy and potential of applying CE-RAM to modern ring-based SHE schemes [34]. Even without the common algorithmic optimizations such as the Number-Theoretic Transform (NTT) and Residue Number System (RNS), utilizing CE-RAM showed speedup as compared to both a CPU environment and related existing work which incorporated the algorithmic optimizations. This showed the viability of using CE-RAM as a hardware accelerator for SHE, and both actual and potential speedups over existing accelerators.

However, algorithmic optimization in the CE-RAM environment is severely underexplored. The efficacy of NTT and RNS has not been explored in CE-RAM, and the algorithmic study of the impact of CE-RAM's support of arbitrary word sizes is unprecedented. In this paper, we present the algorithmic optimization of the SHE implementations with CE-RAM, by applying NTT, RNS, and our novel optimization. We study the Full RNS Variant of Bajard et al. [6] that optimizes the B/FV homomorphic encryption scheme [19], implementing essential SHE operations. There exists another RNS variant of the B/FV scheme formulated by Halevi et al., based on floating-point operations [21], but we choose to study the integer-only variant of Bajard et al. because there is no computational disadvantage to one full-RNS variant over the other [7] and the integer-only variant of Bajard et al. is easier to implement in CE-RAM, as it does not require floating-point computations.

In this work, we realize the RNS and NTT optimizations for the B/FV scheme, along with new optimizations in the CE-RAM implementation. We performed extensive experiments with comparisons to a CPU implementation and a previous CE-RAM implementation. This is the first such work implementing these advanced algorithmic optimizations working within CE-RAM and its limitations. While a myriad of other work applying these optimizations exists [10,35,36], our work differs in that CE-RAM is only friendly to a small class of parameters. The results indicate speedups of up to 784.2x for homomorphic multiplication, compared against a state-of-the-art software library run on a server-grade computer. To the best of our knowledge, this is the best speedup in the literature. Our optimized CE-RAM implementation outperforms other hardware accelerators of B/FV with speedups in homomorphic multiplication of up to 506.5x against existing a CE-RAM implementation, 66.85x against an FPGA implementation, and 30.8x against a GPU implementation.

Summary of Contributions: (1) For the first time, we apply RNS and NTT to the polynomial operations accelerated by CE-RAM and show that such algorithmic optimizations improve homomorphic multiplication by up to 506.5x as compared to an existing CE-RAM implementation. (2) We propose novel algorithmic optimization with new RNS base choices friendly to CE-RAM that allow quicker calculation of modular reduction and some modular multiplications in CE-RAM. This yields additional speedups of approximately up to 1.5x for homomorphic multiplication and 2.9x for encryption/decryption. (3) We present how to continue to support the full-RNS designs and NTT under the new RNS base, overcoming the challenges presented by the limitations of current CE-RAM capabilities.

2   Preliminaries

2.1   Notations

For $x \in \mathbb{R}$, $\lfloor x \rceil$, $\lfloor x \rfloor$ indicate rounding to the nearest integer and rounding down respectively. Also, we use plain lowercase letters (e.g., x, y) to denote scalar values and bold lowercase letters (e.g., $\mathbf{x}, \mathbf{y}$) to denote polynomials. The division-with-rounding (DWR) operation is applied to polynomials as $DWR_{a,b}^c(\mathbf{x}) = ([\lfloor \frac{a}{b} \cdot x_i \rceil]_c)$. We use R to denote a quotient ring of polynomials in the form $\mathbb{Z}[x]/\Phi_M(x)$, where $\Phi(x)$ is the Mth cyclotomic polynomial with M being a power of 2, i.e., its degree N which is $M/2$. R_t is the ring $\mathbb{Z}_t[x]/\Phi(x)$, with coefficients in the set $\mathbb{Z}_t = [\frac{-t}{2}, \frac{t}{2}) \cap \mathbb{Z}$. $|x|_t$ is the ordinary modular reduction defined as $|x|_t = x - \lfloor \frac{x}{t} \rfloor t$, and $[x]_t$ is the centered modular reduction defined as $[x]_t = x - \lfloor \frac{x}{t} \rceil t$. For $\mathbf{x} \in R$, we use $[\mathbf{x}]_t$ to denote an element in R_t which is obtained by applying the centered modular reduction to individual coefficients componentwise. Temporarily, a division may be applied to $\mathbf{x} \in R$ which is performed to every coefficient componentwise. Such a polynomial in $\mathbb{Q}[x]/\Phi(x)$ is immediately mapped to R_t by applying the rounding function to every coefficient.

2.2   The Original B/FV Scheme [19]

Suppose we have $t > 1$ (plaintext modulus) and $q > t$ (ciphertext modulus). The B/FV scheme operates on plaintexts in R_t and ciphertexts in R_q^2. The secret key $\mathbf{s}$ is a randomly chosen element of R with coefficients from a distribution bounded in magnitude by 1 (denoted as 1-bounded distribution). The public key is $(\mathbf{p_0}, \mathbf{p_1}) = ([\mathbf{as} + \mathbf{e}]_q, \mathbf{a})$, where $\mathbf{a}$ is chosen uniformly at random from R_q and $\mathbf{e}$ is also chosen from a 1-bounded distribution. Denote $\Delta = \lfloor \frac{q}{t} \rfloor$.

Encryption: To encrypt $\mathbf{m} \in R_t$, first randomly sample $\mathbf{e_1}, \mathbf{e_2}$ from a 1-bounded distribution and $\mathbf{u}$ uniformly from R_q. Then compute $(\mathbf{c_0}, \mathbf{c_1}) = ([\Delta \mathbf{m} + \mathbf{p_0}\mathbf{u} + \mathbf{e_1}]_q, [\mathbf{p_1}\mathbf{u} + \mathbf{e_2}]_q)$.

Homomorphic Addition/Subtraction: Given ciphertexts $(\mathbf{c_0}, \mathbf{c_1})$, $(\mathbf{c_0'}, \mathbf{c_1'})$, homomorphic addition is calculated by computing $(\mathbf{c_0}^+, \mathbf{c_1}^+) = ([\mathbf{c_0} + \mathbf{c_0'}]_q, [\mathbf{c_1} + \mathbf{c_1'}]_q)$. Subtraction proceeds similarly.

Decryption: To decrypt $(\mathbf{c_0}, \mathbf{c_1})$ under a key $\mathbf{s}$, compute $\mathbf{m} = [\lfloor \frac{t}{q}[\mathbf{c_0} + \mathbf{c_1} \cdot \mathbf{s}]_q \rceil]_t$.

Homomorphic Multiplication: Given ciphertexts $\mathbf{c} = (\mathbf{c_0}, \mathbf{c_1})$, $\mathbf{c'} = (\mathbf{c_0'}, \mathbf{c_1'})$, homomorphic multiplication is computed by first finding $\mathbf{d_0} = [\lfloor \frac{t \cdot \mathbf{c_0} \cdot \mathbf{c_0'}}{q} \rceil]_q$, $\mathbf{d_1} = [\lfloor \frac{t \cdot \mathbf{c_0} \cdot \mathbf{c_1'} + \mathbf{c_1} \cdot \mathbf{c_0'}}{q} \rceil]_q$, $\mathbf{d_2} = [\lfloor \frac{t \cdot \mathbf{c_1} \cdot \mathbf{c_1'}}{q} \rceil]_q$. Then using precomputed relineariza-tion keys $\mathbf{rlk_0}, \mathbf{rlk_1}$ (tuples of T pairs of elements of R_q), write $\mathbf{d_2}$ in base T with $\mathbf{d_2}^{(i)}$ as its ith digit, and return $(\mathbf{d_0'} = [\mathbf{d_0} + \sum_i \mathbf{rlk}[i][0]\mathbf{d_2}^{(i)}]_q, \mathbf{d_1'} = [\mathbf{d_1} + \sum_i \mathbf{rlk}[i][1]\mathbf{d_2}^{(i)}]_q)$.

2.3   The Full-RNS Variant of the B/FV Scheme

RNS: In the B/FV scheme, operations take place on polynomials with large coefficients in $\mathbb{Z}_q$. By the Chinese Remainder Theorem (CRT), if q is a product of k pairwise coprime numbers q_i, $\mathbb{Z}_q$ is isomorphic to the product of the rings $\{\mathbb{Z}_{q_i}\}_i$. A number in $\mathbb{Z}_q$ can then be represented by a k-tuple of numbers in $\{\mathbb{Z}_{q_i}\}_i$, which is denoted as *RNS form*. The ith component of an integer x's RNS form is $|x|_{q_i}$ (or $[x]_{q_i}$ in a centered representation). Because of the isomorphism addition and multiplication on numbers in $\mathbb{Z}_q$ can be performed by performing addition/multiplication componentwise on the RNS form. If each modulus q_i is small enough to fit into a computer word (e.g., 64 bits), then individual opera-tions in an the RNS form become single-precision operations. Also, operations on numbers in RNS form can be parallelized, as each component is independent.

Full-RNS Variant: A Full-RNS variant of an SHE scheme refers to a variant where all operations are performed on the RNS form extended to the poly-nomial rings throughout the entire homomorphic evaluation. Namely, parallel

---

Algorithm 1. Full RNS B/FV Decryption

1: **procedure** $DEC_{RNS}((c_0, c_1), s)$
2:    $x \leftarrow c_0 + (c_1 \cdot s)$
3:    $s^{(t)} \leftarrow | - FastBConv(|\gamma t x|_q, Q, \{t\}) \cdot |q^{-1}|_t|_t,$
4:    $s^{(\gamma)} \leftarrow | - FastBConv(|\gamma t x|_q, Q, \{\gamma\}) \cdot |q^{-1}|_\gamma|_\gamma$
5:    **return** $[(s^{(t)} - [s^{(\gamma)}]_\gamma) \cdot |\gamma^{-1}|_t]_t.$
6: **end procedure**

---

polynomial operations in smaller subrings $\{R_{q_i}\}_i$ are performed instead of an operation in the large ring R_q without reconstructing the polynomials in R_q. This leads to enhanced performance [6,21]. Unlike algorithms only involving addition, subtraction, and multiplication (e.g., homomorphic addition), decryption and homomorphic multiplication require operations not easily performed in RNS form (e.g. division and rounding). The full-RNS variant thus focuses on these algorithms. Let $Q = \{q_0, q_1, \cdots, q_k\}$ and $B = \{b_0, b_1, \cdots, b_\ell\}$ be sets of numbers each relatively coprime with every other element of $Q \cup B$, called *RNS bases*. Let q be the product of the elements of Q. *Fast Base Conversion*, or *FastBConv*, is defined by

$$FastBConv(x, Q, B) = \left\{ \sum_{i=1}^{k} |x_i \cdot \frac{q_i}{q}|_{q_i} \cdot \frac{q}{q_i} \bmod b_i \Big| b_i \in B \right\} \quad (1)$$

The *FastBConv* quickly and approximately converts a number x in RNS form with base Q to one with base B, and it is applied coefficientwise to polynomials. This is used for the operations other than additions and multiplications. It is faster than full CRT reconstruction mainly because the intermediate modular reduction by Q is skipped. As a consequence, the result in base B will be off by some multiple of q, which can be corrected with various efficient methods.

Decryption: The full-RNS variant's decryption is described in Algorithm 1, using a number γ coprime to t (though this is not strictly necessary).

Homomorphic Multiplication: The full-RNS variant's homomorphic multiplication (sans relinearization) is described in Algorithm 2, which gives us $(\tilde{c}_0, \tilde{c}_1, \tilde{c}_2)$ in base Q. In this algorithm, we temporarily extend ciphertexts using *FastBConv* from base Q to $B_{sk} = B \cup \{m_{sk}\}$, to hold the result of a polynomial tensor where coefficients may be as large as nq^2. The next step is relinearization that reduces this ciphertext back to 2 elements. Suppose we are given $(\tilde{c}_0, \tilde{c}_1, \tilde{c}_2)$ as from Algorithm 2. Let $rlk_{RNS}[0], rlk_{RNS}[1]$ be the relinearization keys (precomputed tuples of polynomials in R_q). Define $D_{RNS}(\tilde{c}_2) = (|\tilde{c}_2 \frac{q_1}{q}|_{q_1}, |\tilde{c}_2 \frac{q_2}{q}|_{q_2}, \cdots, |\tilde{c}_2 \frac{q_k}{q}|_{q_k})$. We then perform relinearization by computing: $([\tilde{c}_0 + \langle D_{RNS}(\tilde{c}_2), rlk_{RNS}[0]\rangle]_q, [\tilde{c}_1 + \langle D_{RNS}(\tilde{c}_2), rlk_{RNS}[1]\rangle]_q)$.

This full-RNS variant of Bajard et al. [6] shows a large practical speedup in runtime (up to 20 times faster for decryption, and 4 times faster for multiplication), due in part to faster individual operations on RNS components.

Algorithm 2. Full RNS B/FV Homomorphic Multiplication

1: **procedure** $MULT_{RNS}(\mathbf{c} = (\mathbf{c_0}, \mathbf{c_1}), \mathbf{c'} = (\mathbf{c'_0}, \mathbf{c'_1}))$
2:     Use $FastBConv$ to convert $\mathbf{c}, \mathbf{c'}$ from Q to $B_{sk} \cup \{\tilde{m}\}$. (We now have $\mathbf{c}, \mathbf{c'}$ in $Q \cup B_{sk} \cup \{\tilde{m}\}$.)
3:     Reduce extra multiples of q in the $B_{sk} \cup \tilde{m}$-representation using Small Montgomery Reduction
   [8]. (The intermediate results are now in $Q \cup B_{sk}$.)
4:     Compute the polynomial products $(\tilde{\mathbf{c}_0}, \tilde{\mathbf{c}_1}, \tilde{\mathbf{c}_2}) = (\mathbf{c_0} \cdot \mathbf{c'_0}, \mathbf{c_0} \cdot \mathbf{c'_1} + \mathbf{c_1} \cdot \mathbf{c'_0}, \mathbf{c_1} \cdot \mathbf{c'_1})$ and scale
   by t (in $Q \cup B_{sk}$).
5:     Do a fast floor (using $FastBConv$) from $Q \cup B_{sk}$ to B_{sk}. (This is an approximation of the
   DWR operation.)
6:     Perform a Shenoy and Kumaresan-like reduction from B_{sk} to Q [37].
7:     **return** $(\tilde{\mathbf{c}_0}, \tilde{\mathbf{c}_1}, \tilde{\mathbf{c}_2})$ (in base Q)
8: **end procedure**

2.4 NTT

Naive polynomial multiplication is a $\mathcal{O}(N^2)$ algorithm. Applying the NTT (Appendix C) to polynomials results in transformed polynomials, where coefficientwise multiplication in the new domain corresponds to polynomial multiplication in the original domain. Thus polynomial multiplication can be performed in $\mathcal{O}(N \cdot log(N))$ by transforming polynomials, performing coefficientwise multiplication, and applying the inverse NTT. This is commonly used to expedite polynomial multiplications [10,30,36].

2.5 Compute-Enabled RAM

Compute Enabled RAM (CE-RAM) refers to SRAM storage units with integrated processing elements. The most notable features of CE-RAM are the lack of separation between memory and processing and the massive potential for parallel processing that this allows. In this work, we consider CE-RAM as a SRAM bank at the level of L3 cache. CE-RAM can then be used as coprocessing hardware, performing intensive computations in the CPU's stead, and transferring its data to/from DRAM through the standard memory hierarchy. In the previous work of Reis et al. [34], CE-RAM (referred to as CiM in their paper, but we choose the term CE-RAM to avoid confusion with the analog In-memory Computing) has been utilized as a coprocessing unit, and used to accelerate homomorphic operations of the B/FV scheme. This approach, without algorithmic optimizations of RNS and NTT, is reported to have a significant speedup. Against a CPU implementation with RNS and NTT, a speedup of up to 5.8x for homomorphic multiplication is reported. This work was a first pioneering effort in applying CE-RAM to SHE, and faced several limitations, including a limited choice of ciphertext modulus (only powers of two) and a lack of algorithmic optimizations. Unfortunately, due to the lack of algorithmic optimization, the speedup drops to 1.5x when $N = 2^{14}$ and the ciphertext modulus size $|q|$ is 438 bits [34], which is the largest parameter set among the existing work that we compare against.

3 Novel Optimizations Using Special Moduli

In this section, we discuss choices of RNS bases that are well suited for implementing the Full RNS Variant of the B/FV scheme in CE-RAM [6,19].

3.1 NTT Implementation with CE-RAM

In this work, the NTT algorithm is mapped into a sequence of micro-operations (micro-ops) that can be executed with the CE-RAM hardware described in [34].

The NTT algorithm, shown in Algorithm 7 in Appendix C, takes two inputs: (i) the polynomial coefficients in bit-reverse order, and (ii) the constant Y', which relates to pre-computed twiddle factors of NTT. The polynomial coefficients are initially stored in CE-RAM arrays in a natural manner, therefore the first step for CE-RAM execution of NTT is to implement the bit-reverse (or permutation) step. A sequence of N **MOVE** micro-ops (enabled by the CE-RAM's in-place move buffers, and coordinated by CE-RAM's controller) is used to permute the positions of the coefficients stored in memory. Once the coefficients are in bit-reverse order, execution of the procedure $NTT_p(a)$ can be initiated.

The NTT procedure consists of 3 nested loops. The outermost loop is executed $log(N)$ times with CE-RAM, and it corresponds to NTT stages (i.e., stage $1, 2, ..., log(N)$). Each NTT stage has a number of groups in it, whose execution is controlled by the second (butterfly) loop in Algorithm 7. Inside the butterfly loop, pre-computed twiddle factors are stored in the CE-RAM arrays with parallel **WRITE** micro-ops. Finally, the NTT core consists of modular multiplication between coefficients and the twiddle constants, followed by a subtraction and an addition. In CE-RAM, operations in the NTT core map to **MODMULT**, **SUB**, and **ADD** micro-ops. N micro-ops of each type should be performed (one for each coefficient of the polynomial). Note that CE-RAM can merge the "Butterfly" and "NTT Core" loops, and parallelize the execution of the N micro-ops of each category with the N sets of customized peripherals in a CE-RAM bank.

3.2 Choosing Special Moduli for Optimization

Note that the precise form of the ciphertext modulus q (e.g., whether q is prime, a product of coprime numbers, or a prime power) does not impact the security of the scheme because the RLWE problem is difficult for arbitrary q [6,19,25]. Even before the advent of ring-based SHE, extensive research has been done in the domain of hardware-based RNS systems in searching for moduli that allow for efficient modular reduction and computations [40]. In this work, we present novel optimizations by leveraging existing studies on special moduli, which are specialized for the word sizes of CE-RAM that can be larger than common fixed-size word sizes (e.g., 64 bits). We first find moduli that allow algorithmic optimizations that are especially useful for CE-RAM. In CE-RAM, multiplication is not a basic operation; it is constructed through shifting and addition [34]. We thus consider optimizations that obviate multiplications and replace them with simpler operations. Our strategy is to 1) choose moduli that allow efficient modular reductions, which can accelerate modular polynomial arithmetic as well as the NTT, and 2) choose moduli that allow additional SHE-specific algorithmic optimizations. W investigate two moduli sets for these goals.

Balanced 3-Moduli Set: The first set of moduli we consider is the well-studied set $S_1 = \{q_0, q_1, q_2\} = \{2^g - 1, 2^g, 2^g + 1\}$ [40]. This set has the advantage of being *balanced*, i.e., all elements are equal-sized, and admits easy modular reductions (shown in Sect. 3.3), which can be simplified further within the specific application of SHE. The main disadvantage is that the set is limited to 3 elements, limiting its range and scalability. The set is also limited to representing numbers of approximately $3g$ bits, however with CE-RAM we can choose g to be larger than 64 bits, making this less of a concern. This is mitigated in the CE-RAM because there is no limit in the word size. Further, these moduli produce forms of $|\frac{q_i}{q}|_{q_i}$ that admit extremely efficient computation of the $x \cdot |\frac{q_i}{q}|_{q_i}$, allowing optimization of *FastBConv* as shown in Sect. 3.4.

Mersenne/Fermat-Like Coprimes: Sets of the form $S_2 = \{2^m - 1, 2^m + 1, 2^{2m} + 1, \cdots 2^{2^{f-1}m} + 1, 2^{2^f m} + 1\}$ form a set of coprime moduli [32]. This set of moduli has certain advantages: first, its inverses $|\frac{q_i}{q}|_{q_i}$ are powers of two, allowing the multiplications in *FastBConv* to become bitshifts. Second, all moduli in the set are one separated from a power of two, allowing efficient modular reduction by Algorithms 3 and 4. These combined show that modular multiplication by $|\frac{q_i}{q}|_{q_i}$ in *FastBConv* can be done efficiently with circular bitshifting (Ch. 9, Thm. 9.2.12 [15]). We include relevant lemmas and proofs in the appendix. However, this set is unbalanced, which leads to relative performance disadvantages as shown in the experiments.

3.3   Optimizing Modular Reduction

The moduli in both S_1 and S_2 are powers of two, or unit distance from powers of two. Modular reduction with these moduli can be performed efficiently. In the case of q_1 of S_1, the modulus is a power of two, and reduction is a simple mask. In the other cases, we can extend well-known formulae for efficient modular reduction [15]. In the context of Full-RNS variants of SHE, we perform modular arithmetic by reducing after each operation, and arguments to be reduced are less than the square of the modulus. This obviates the need for iteration or multiplication in modular reduction, so that only simple bit operations and linear-complexity arithmetic are required. This leads us to the optimized Algorithms 3 and 4, which can be used for the moduli in S_1 and S_2. These are applied in all operations in RNS base Q (including NTT).

3.4   Optimizing *FastBConv*

In the frequently used operation *FastBConv*, terms of the form $|x \cdot \frac{q_i}{q}|_{q_i}$ are computed. When using the moduli of S_1, computing this can be done extremely efficiently, with only simple bit-wise operations as shown in Theorems 1 and Lemma 2 (proofs of nontrivial lemmas and theorems are in the appendix.).

Algorithm 3. Fast Modular Reduction - Mersenne (optimized)

```
1: procedure FMR_{-1}(x, 2^g - 1)          ▷ Returns x mod 2^g - 1 for x ∈ [0, (2^g - 1)^2)
2:     y ← x >> g
3:     x ← x&(2^g - 1)
4:     x ← x + y
5:     if x ≥ 2^g - 1 then
6:         x ← x - (2^g - 1)
7:     end if
8:     return x
9: end procedure
```

Algorithm 4. Fast Modular Reduction - Fermat-like (optimized)

```
1: procedure FMR_{+1}(x, 2^g + 1)          ▷ Returns x mod 2^g + 1 for x ∈ [0, (2^g + 1)^2)
2:     y ← x >> g
3:     x ← x&(2^g - 1)
4:     if x ≥ y then
5:         x ← x - y
6:     else
7:         x ← ((2^g + 1) - y) + x
8:     end if
9:     return x
10: end procedure
```

Lemma 1. *For the moduli of S_1, $|\frac{q_0}{q}|_{q_0} = 2^{g-1}$, $|\frac{q_1}{q}|_{q_1} = 2^g - 1$, and $|\frac{q_2}{q}|_{q_2} = 2^{g-1} + 1$.*

Theorem 1. *For the moduli of S_1 with $x \in [0, q_0)$, $|x \cdot \frac{q_0}{q}|_{q_0}$ is $\frac{x}{2}$ when x is even and $2^g - 1 + \frac{x-1}{2}$ when x is odd.*

$|x \cdot \frac{q_0}{q}|_{q_0}$ can be computed efficiently as `(x>>1) + ((x&1) << (g-1))`.

Lemma 2. *For the moduli of S_1 with $x \in [0, q_1)$, $|x \cdot \frac{q_1}{q}|_{q_1} \equiv -x \mod 2^g$.*

$|x \cdot \frac{q_1}{q}|_{q_1}$ can be computed efficiently as `((1 << g) - x) & ((1 << g) - 1)`.

Theorem 2. *For the moduli of S_1 with $x \in [0, q_2)$, $|x \cdot \frac{q_2}{q}|_{q_2}$ is $\frac{x}{2}$ when x is even and $2^{g-1} + \frac{x+1}{2}$ when x is odd.*

$|x \cdot \frac{q_2}{q}|_{q_2}$ can be computed efficiently as `((x+1)>>1) + ((x&1) << (g-1))`.

For the moduli of S_2, the terms $|\frac{q_i}{q}|_{q_i}$ are powers of two, turning the multiplication into shifting, and the modular reductions can again use Algorithms 3 and 4. Alternately, and more efficiently, we can utilize circular bitshifting to perform multiplication and reduction in a single operation, as shown in Algorithms 5 and 6. These optimizations are most useful in systems such as CE-RAM where it is most advantageous to replace multiplications with simple bitwise operations.

3.5 Extended Base

The optimizations presented in Sects. 3.3 and 3.4 are only applicable to operations within base Q. Using more moduli, as when operating in the extended

---

Algorithm 5. Fast Modular Shifting - Mersenne

1: **procedure** $FMS_{-1}(x, y, 2^g - 1)$ ▷ Returns $x \cdot 2^y \mod 2^g + -$
2:      $hi \leftarrow x >> (g - y)$
3:      $lo \leftarrow (x << y) \& ((1 << g) - 1)$
4:      **return** $lo|hi$
5: **end procedure**

Algorithm 6. Fast Modular Shifting - Fermat-like

1: **procedure** $FMS_{+1}(x, y, 2^g + 1)$ ▷ Returns $x \cdot 2^y \mod 2^g + 1$
2:      $hi \leftarrow x >> (g - y)$
3:      $lo \leftarrow (x << y) \& ((1 << g) - 1)$
4:      **if** $lo \geq hi$ **then**
5:          **return** $lo - hi$
6:      **else**
7:          **return** $((1 << g) + 1) - hi + lo$
8:      **end if**
9: **end procedure**

---

base B (as described in Sect. 2.3), presents a challenge - coprime moduli close to a power of two offset by at most one (allowing efficient modular reduction) are already exhausted. We thus choose prime moduli $b_i = 2^g + c$ with $|c| < g$, where $2^g + 1$ is the largest modulus in whichever of S_1 or S_2 being used for Q. This is done so that the largest element of Q and the elements of B are of the same size (number of bits), so that the complexity of multiplication does not increase beyond what is already determined by Q. We further require $b_i \equiv 1 \mod 2N$, to allow for efficient computation of the parameters needed for the NTT (as discussed in Sect. 3.6). No special optimizations such as in Sect. 3.3 and 3.4 are available, so Barrett reduction [9] is utilized for modular reduction for components outside of base Q. Barrett reduction is commonly utilized in other similar research [10,35]. The moduli $m_{sk}, \tilde{m}$ can be chosen as described in [6].

3.6 Finding NTT Parameters

We first discuss applying the NTT for moduli of the form $2^g + 1, 2^g - 1$. NTT with moduli of $2^g + 1$ are known in the literature [1] and are called Fermat Number Transforms (FNT). The twiddle factors will be chosen as 2 or the quadratic residue of 2, in which case they will be the primitive $2g^{th}$ (resp. $4g^{th}$) root of unity. Then when $M \mid 2g$ (resp. $4g$), $2^{2g/M}$ is the Mth root of unity. Similarly, the NTT for $2^g - 1$ (called Mersenne Number Transform MNT) is described in [33], with twiddle factors being 2. In the scenario of RLWE-based homomorphic encryption, $M = 2N$. For moduli of the form 2^g, we are considering a finite field $GF(2)$. NTT twiddle factors over finite fields are largely known. Since $\varphi(2^g) = 2^{g-1}$, we find the primitive root of unity and raise it to $2^{g-1}/M$ to find the Mth root of unity.

As noted in Sect. 3.5, we can choose moduli in the extended base B to be NTT-friendly; with $b_i \equiv 1 \mod 2N$ a $2N^{th}$ primitive root of unity is easily found, which allows efficient computation of NTT parameters (namely the

Table 1. Parameter cases

Case	Moduli	Using our novel optimization?
Case A	$\{2^{146} - 1, 2^{146}, 2^{146} + 1\}$	No
Case B	$\{2^{146} - 1, 2^{146}, 2^{146} + 1\}$	Yes
Case C	$\{2^{220} + 1, 2^{110} + 1, 2^{110} - 1\}$	Yes

twiddle factors Y in Algorithm 7) [27,35]. The moduli $\tilde{m}$ and $m_s k$ can be chosen similarly.

4   Experimental Evaluation

Our optimizations do not change the overall asymptotic complexity of the RNS variant, for the same reason that the variant does not improve the asymptotic complexity [6]. However, they greatly improve the practical efficiency of the CE-RAM implementations, which is shown with our extensive experimental evaluation. We implement primitive operations (modular polynomial arithmetic, NTT, coefficientwise multiplication, and our optimized procedures) in CE-RAM and use those measurements to derive the runtime of relevant homomorphic operations: homomorphic multiplication, addition, and subtraction, along with encryption and decryption. These are compared to a software implementation of B/FV, as well as different research works in hardware acceleration of SHE. Relinearization is considered to be a part of multiplication (i.e., each relinearization is run on a ciphertext with two components, and each multiplication has relinearization as a subroutine). As homomorphic multiplication is the most intensive operation, it is the operation we refer to most when evaluating our work and comparing it to other research.

4.1   CE-RAM Environment and Parameters

We chose a polynomial modulus degree of $N = 2^{14}$ and ciphertext modulus size $|q|$ of at least 438. This choice of parameters provides 128 bits of security [5], matching or exceeding the security afforded by parameters chosen by Roy et al. [36], Reis et al. [34], Al Badawi et al. [3], and HEAX [35]. These parameters also yield a scheme with multiplicative depth of at least 10. We choose the sets $S_{balanced} = \{2^{146} - 1, 2^{146}, 2^{146} + 1\}$ and $S_{unbalanced} = \{2^{220} + 1, 2^{110} + 1, 2^{110} - 1\}$ (i.e., Mersenne/Fermat-like coprimes), and use these sets as the modulus set q. Additional coprime moduli (e.g. the elements of the extended base B) are chosen to be numbers slightly larger than the largest modulus in a set, as discussed in Sect. 3.5. We consider cases A and B to be using $S_{balanced}$ and case C to use $S_{unbalanced}$, with cases B and C additionally utilizing our novel optimizations presented in Sect. 3 (Table 1).

CE-RAM is evaluated following the same methodology reported by Reis et al. [34], i.e., with circuit-level simulations of a CE-RAM bank based on multiple 1 KB CE Static Random-Access Memory Cells (SRAM) arrays. The circuit simulation tools employed are Cadence Encounter (for the CE-RAM controller circuits) [18], and Synopsys HSPICE (for the RAM array and compute-enabled peripherals) [38]. Circuits are based on the 14 nm BSIM-CMG FinFET model [17]. Each CE-RAM array has 8 rows and 1024 columns, consisting of SRAM cells and customized memory peripherals. In our evaluation, we employ a 16 MB CE-RAM, which is built of 16,384 arrays of 8×1024 size (a tiled architecture). CE-RAM performs its operations at the bitline level, which means that the coefficients of 2 polynomials need to be column-aligned for computing in-memory polynomial operations. This condition is ensured by an appropriate mapping of the polynomials to the CE-RAM arrays, i.e., polynomials are always entirely mapped to the same row index across the 16,384 arrays. Through this mapping, two polynomial primitives are performed simultaneously (at the same clock cycle). Because this mapping holds up to 512 bits for coefficients in each row, we can use the spare space to hold coefficients modulo m_{sk} and $\tilde{m}$, avoiding a need for an extra row during calculations with operands in the base $Q \cup B_{sk} \cup \tilde{m}$.

Using circuit simulations, we measure the time for executing each CE-RAM instruction. We then proceed with the mapping of each homomorphic operation into a sequence of CE-RAM instructions. Based on the time measured for each instruction and the mapping of the homomorphic operation to the instructions, we compute the overall time of homomorphic operations in CE-RAM.

We also consider the impact of data transfer in reporting our results, and when comparing to other work, as appropriate. The DDR4 specification gives a peak data transfer rate of 25,600 MB/s, which gives 70 μs seconds per ciphertext transfer from DRAM to CE-RAM (referred to hereafter as the *specified data transfer rate*) In practice, the overhead from data transfer can be significantly less, due to pipelining and interleaving of execution and data transfer. Based on experiments run in our CPU environments, we estimate 21.2 μs seconds per ciphertext (referred to hereafter as the *actual data transfer rate*) transfer from DRAM to CE-RAM. This figure was derived by observing the time difference between operating upon ciphertexts that were/were not resident in cache memory.

4.2 Comparison to CE-RAM Implementation of B/FV

We define the speedup of case X against case Y as $\frac{\text{Run time in case} Y}{\text{Run time in case } X}$.
Full-RNS Variant: To examine the speedup from applying the full-RNS design, we compare our current work with that of Reis et al. [34], as that work used CE-RAM (referred to as CiM) for B/FV but implemented the textbook scheme without the use of any RNS variant. The results for homomorphic multiplication are shown in Table 2. The speedup was found using the actual data transfer time, though the speedup was nearly identical to two decimal places when the specified data transfer time was used. We note that in [34], the ciphertext modulus was chosen to be a power of two, enabling extremely efficient modular reduction with a simple bitmask. Considering this, we conclude that applying RNS alone does not bring much improvement, due to the efficient CE-RAM parameter choices of previous work and the variable word size of CE-RAM.

Table 2. Speedup of Full-RNS CE-RAM (wo/NTT) vs. Existing CE-RAM (wo/RNS, NTT) [34]

Case	Hom. Mult
Case A	1.28×
Case B	**1.90x**
Case C	1.12×

Table 3. Speedup of CE-RAM with NTT v.s. CE-RAM without NTT (w/Full-RNS in both cases)

Case	Operation	Hom. Mult.	Decrypt	Encrypt
Case A	Speedup wo/transfer	396.90x	236.37x	1525.53x
	Imp. w/actual transfer	292.56x	127.91x	554.11x
	Imp. w/spec. transfer	182.22x	82.69x	224.86x
Case B	Speedup w/o transfer	412.59x	315.47x	1085.19x
	Imp. w/actual transfer	265.90x	73.75x	162.63x
	Imp. w/spec. transfer	146.28x	38.89x	55.60x
Case C	Speedup wo/transfer	449.68x	338.39x	1100.51x
	Imp. w/actual transfer	332.32x	109.45x	249.14x
	Imp. w/spec. transfer	207.53x	60.77x	90.09x

NTT: To examine the speedup we get from applying NTT to CE-RAM, we evaluated variants of encryption, decryption and homomorphic multiplication with and without NTT-based polynomial multiplication. These results are shown in Table 3. From this, we see that applying NTT brings a speedup of two orders of magnitude for homomorphic multiplication. Of the optimizations we bring to CE-RAM, NTT is the most effective; this is expected, as the runtime of decryption and homomorphic multiplication in the RNS variant is dominated by polynomial multiplication, which NTT optimizes.

Novel Optimizations: To find the efficacy of our novel optimizations, we examine the speedup for Cases B and C against Case A (Table 4). We note a modest speedup for homomorphic multiplication with Case B, and a larger speedup for other operations. Data transfer dominates the latency in homomorphic addition/subtraction, so the speedup is only notable without data transfer. We conclude the Case B with optimized balanced set is the most effective.

4.3 Comparison to CPU Implementation of B/FV

The software library used for our CPU experiments is the highly optimized Microsoft SEAL homomorphic encryption library [10]. SEAL applies the full-RNS variant and NTT to B/FV. Our tests on CPU are written in C++.

Table 4. Speedup of CE-RAM with novel optimizations v.s. CE-RAM without novel optimizations (not including NTT)

Case	Hom. Mult.	Decrypt	Encrypt	Hom. Add.	Hom. Sub.
Case B, no data trans.	1.49x	2.91x	4.56x	37.08x	35.15x
Case B, actual data trans.	1.49x	2.89x	4.55x	1.01x	1.01
Case B, spec. data trans.	1.49x	2.86x	4.52x	1.00x	1.00
Case C, no data trans.	0.87x	1.72x	2.71x	33.94x	32.32x
Case C, actual data trans.	0.87x	1.72x	2.70x	1.01x	1.01x
Case C, spec. data trans.	0.87x	1.71x	2.69x	1.00x	1.00x

* Overhead of Hom. Mult. dominates the overhead of Hom. Add./Sub. by two orders of magnitude

Table 5. CPU environment specifications

Data	CPU-Server	CPU-Workstation	CPU-Laptop
CPU	AMD EPYC 7451, 2.3 GHz	Intel i7, 3.4 GHz	Intel i5, 2.30 GHz
Level 1 cache size	64 KB(i)/32 KB(d)	32 KB(i)/32 KB(d)	32 KB(i)/32 KB(d)
Level 2 cache size	512 KB	256 KB	256 KB
Level 3 cache size	8 MB	8 MB	3 MB
Memory size	128 GB	8 GB	8 GB
OS	Red hat	Red hat	Ubuntu 18.04 LTS
Sole user?	No	Yes	Yes

For rigorous testing against a wide range of ordinary CPU environments, we evaluate our CE-RAM approach against three different computers (Table 5). We chose these computers to represent a server used in cloud computing (CPU-Server, used for comparison with other research), a research workstation (CPU-Workstation), and an ordinary user's computer (CPU-Laptop). Our CPU experiments use the standard parameters of $N = 2^{14}$, $|q| = 438$, but with moduli limited to computer-supported word size (64 bits). Table 6 shows the speedup that CE-RAM enjoys compared to our CPU environments, using our actually measured data transfer time. Most notably, for homomorphic multiplication, we see speedups of two orders of magnitude. Table 7 shows the number of operations per second that can be computed with CE-RAM using different estimates for data transfer. These are more useful for comparison with related research.

In all three cases we tested, a significant speedup over the CPU environment is seen. For homomorphic multiplication, we see a speedup of two orders of magnitude (up to **784x** faster against CPU-Server). The use of algorithmic optimizations (Case B) shows additional speedup as compared to Case A (no additional optimizations). This is much more pronounced in encryption and decryption, though homomorphic multiplication/addition/subtraction still see some speedup from these optimizations. Encryption and decryption show a more modest speedup, though they still improve upon the CPU environments by two orders of magnitude.

Table 6. Speedup of CE-RAM vs. CPU cases (actual data trans.)

Environment	Case	Hom. Mult.	Hom. Add.	Hom. Sub.	Decrypt	Encrypt
CPU-Server	Case A	579.9x	5.1x	5.2x	75.8x	225.0x
	Case B	**784.2x**	5.1x	5.3x	143.9x	330.3x
	Case C	575.6x	5.1x	5.3x	122.1x	290.2x
CPU-Laptop	Case A	577.5x	5.7x	5.9xx	78.1x	216.3x
	Case B	**781.0x**	5.8x	5.9x	148.3x	317.5x
	Case C	573.2x	5.8x	5.9x	125.9x	279.0x
CPU-Workstation	Case A	406.8x	3.6x	3.8x	52.3x	151.5x
	Case B	**550.1x**	3.6x	3.9x	99.2x	222.4x
	Case C	403.7x	3.6x	3.9x	84.2x	195.4x

Table 7. Operations per second with CE-RAM

Data transfer	Case	Hom. Mult.	Hom. Add.	Hom. Sub.	Decrypt	Encrypt
Actual	Case A	4150	15568	15567	8558	12734
	Case B	**5611**	15740	15740	16248	18694
	Case C	4118	15739	15739	13789	16426
Specified	Case A	2579	4727	4740	4658	5671
	Case B	**3078**	4756	4756	6275	6609
	Case C	2567	4756	4756	5871	6301
Computation only	Case A	5635	1383126	1381215	13421	27636
	Case B	**8719**	51282051	48543689	52074	89685
	Case C	5577	46948357	44642857	33138	53946

The unbalanced moduli set (Case C) does bring some speedups over a balanced set without optimizations (Case A) - for every operation besides homomorphic multiplication, computation time with the unbalanced set improved upon the balanced set without optimizations. However, for homomorphic multiplication the unbalanced set was slower than the balanced set, regardless of whether optimizations were enabled. This is likely due to multiplication's complexity, which increases quadratically with the number of bits in the operands, so that the runtime of parallel operations is now dominated by the size of the largest RNS component. We conclude that despite its interesting mathematical properties, the unbalanced set is less useful for implementing RNS variants in CE-RAM.

4.4 Considering Throughput with Projection

To consider the effects of more parallelism and interleaving and examine possible throughput, assuming two 16 MB banks of CE-RAM allows maximum utilization of data transfer between DRAM and SRAM without failing to write back results as soon as they are available (note that the actual data transfer time is about

Table 8. Speedup of Hom. Mult., Ours vs. Existing [34] CE-RAM

Case	Spec. data trans.	Actual data trans.
Case A	232.8x	374.6x
Case B	**277.8x**	**506.5x**
Case C	231.7x	371.8x

Table 9. Speedup of Hom. Mult. against Roy et al.[36]

Actual data trans.	Spec. data trans.	Computation only
66.85x	36.6x	103.48x

one-eighth the time to compute a B/FV homomorphic multiplication in Case B). Now considering total end-to-end throughput, this approximately doubles the homomorphic multiplications per second CE-RAM can achieve to 11222 in Case B with actual data transfer. While further increasing the number of SRAM banks could further improve throughput, this would require increasing the total SRAM size beyond 32 MB, as well as more sophisticated logic for handling the pipelining. One can also implement the architecture of CE-RAM at the main memory (i.e., DRAM).

4.5 Comparison to Other Hardware Accelerators of B/FV

CE-RAM: Beyond simply improving on a CPU environment, our work also shows speedups over existing work applying CE-RAM to the B/FV scheme [34], as shown in Table 8. With Case B, we see a speedup of up to 506.5x for homomorphic multiplication as compared to the existing CE-RAM implementation. As noted in Sect. 4.2, we only analyze the homomorphic multiplication because it dominates additive operations.

FPGA: The work of Roy et al. [36] constructs an FPGA coprocessor for the B/FV scheme. The closest set of parameters used by Roy et al. was $N = 2^{13}$, $|q| = 360$. We compare our CE-RAM runtime for Case B against Roy et al.'s estimated runtime for homomorphic multiplication in Table 9, and speedups of an order of magnitude (66.85x using the actual data transfer rate) are observed. We note that these are even more impressive when noting that our evaluation uses larger parameters, providing a higher security level.

GPU: Al Badawi et al.'s GPU acceleration of B/FV [2] demonstrates the efficacy of applying the parallelism of GPUs to RNS variants of B/FV. Of the parameters they use, the closest ones to ours are $N = 2^{13}$, $|q| = 360$. All three parameter/optimization cases we tested showed a speedup against the GPU-based acceleration (Table 10), even though our work used a larger and more demanding set of parameters, with a higher level of security. For homomorphic multiplication, we see speedups of up to 30.8x with Case B.

Table 10. Speedup of CE-RAM against B/FV-GPU [2]

Case	Hom. Mult.	Hom. Add	Decrypt	Encrypt
Case A	19.9x	4.1x	2.0x	29.9x
Case B	**30.8x**	153.8x	7.9x	96.9x
Case C	19.7x	140.8x	5.0x	58.3x

5   Related Work

Other works in hardware acceleration of homomorphic encryption consider their hardware as part of a cloud computing system, where clients can outsource encrypted computations to a server that will utilize the hardware to more efficiently carry out the client's desired calculations [35, 36]. Consequently, these works mainly consider homomorphic computations, leaving encryption and decryption to the client. Our work considers more generally the impact that CE-RAM can have on the entire scheme, following the more versatile scenario of [3].

Other hardware solutions for efficient SHE have two types of data transfer that leads to latency. Data must be moved from the ordinary memory hierarchy (i.e. from DRAM) to the special hardware, and once resident in the accelerator it must be moved between storage and processing elements. In contrast, CE-RAM can be directly integrated into a computer's ordinary memory hierarchy as a L3 cache, allowing data to be moved with the ordinary mechanisms for data transfer between the CPU and main memory. Once the data has been moved into CE-RAM, it is instantly available for computation without the need to move data to processing elements. CE-RAM also has the advantage of user-chosen word size. Other implementations (e.g., FPGAs, GPUs, ASICs, and CPUs) have word sizes that are either set or not easily configurable. In contrast, CE-RAM can easily choose word size as convenient for the application.

CE-RAM: Our work is the closest to the line of research seeded by Reis et al. [34], which was the first work pioneering the use of CE-RAM for the acceleration of SHE. We improve upon this work by implementing RNS and NTT optimizations, and choosing RNS moduli systems that allow novel optimizations especially friendly to CE-RAM systems. These optimizations give us an order of magnitude of speedup. We also consider actual data transfer times found in our evaluation, and present all essential functions of the B/FV scheme instead of homomorphic operations only. We further consider a higher level of parallelization (beyond simply within polynomials and RNS representations) by expanding our system to use a 16MB bank, which allows two simultaneous operations.

FPGA: The next most similar work to ours is that of Roy et al. [36], which uses an FPGA as a coprocessor for the more intensive portions of the B/FV encryption scheme. Their work involved careful pipelining and utilized RNS and NTT to accelerate polynomial arithmetic. They report a speedup of 13x as compared to a CPU implementation using an Intel i5 at 1.8 GHz. Existing work in using

CE-RAM has already been shown to improve upon the work of Roy et al., even without RNS or NTT optimizations [34].

HEAX [35] is another FPGA-based coprocessor architecture designed to accelerate the CKKS scheme [11], and it is the current state-of-the-art hardware accelerator. CKKS is similar to but substantially different from B/FV, as the ciphertext moduli in CKKS change with homomorphic multiplications. Despite this difference, we compare our optimized CE-RAM against HEAX since it is the state-of-the-art hardware accelerator with greatest speedups. HEAX reports speedups of two orders of magnitude, as compared to a CPU implementation using Microsoft SEAL. The scenario HEAX considers is multiple CPU-side processes interleaving data transfer to/from the external FPGA, while we consider only a single process using the standard memory hierarchy to transfer data to/from CE-RAM. (This is partially due to the still nascent software tooling available for CE-RAM). One of the main difficulties the HEAX architecture faces is the limited on-chip memory available to the FPGA, forcing the FPGA to rely on off-chip memory. This induces extra cost and latency, though intelligent parallelism mitigates much of this. HEAX reports speedups of up to two orders of magnitude against a CPU implementation running on an Intel Xeon at 1.8 GHz. The parameter set we consider is the same as the most intensive set of HEAX. When compared to a CPU implementation, HEAX achieved a speedup of 174.4x for homomorphic multiplication, which is on the same order of magnitude as our speedups of 748.2x against CPU (with actual data transfer time; our speedup is 430.1x with the specified transfer time). We can conclude that our work brings a similar or slightly better speedup to HEAX, even without any pipelining of data transfer implemented in CE-RAM. Assuming the concurrent operation of two 16 MB CE-RAM banks as discussed in Sect. 4.4, for homomorphic multiplication we may observe a 6.38x speedup using this CE-RAM system as compared to HEAX in theory. For a further comparison to HEAX, we estimated the runtime of CKKS multiplication implemented in CE-RAM. We note that our system design and parameter choices are not optimized for CKKS due to the aforementioned difference. Further, we do not consider the pipelining and interleaving of execution utilized by HEAX, and only consider the end-to-end runtime of a single operation with data transfer to and from CE-RAM. With this consideration, we see a speedup of CE-RAM's CKKS homomorphic mult. of 6.82x (17841 ops/s) without data transfer, 3.19x (8363 ops/s) with the actual data transfer rate, and 1.44x (3755 ops/s) with the specified data transfer rate. Similarly, assuming two 16 MB CE-RAM banks (Sect. 4.4), these speedups may be doubled in theory.

FPGAs have also been utilized as general-purpose cryptographic coprocessors for polynomial ring operations, and as coprocessors specifically designed for acceleration of the YASHE scheme (closely related to B/FV, but proven insecure [4]) [31]. There also exist FPGA-based accelerators of NTRU-based SHE schemes by applying RNS and NTT for polynomial operations. Ozturk et al. construct a FPGA-based accelerator for polynomial arithmetic intended for use in accelerating the LTV scheme [28,30]. Against a CPU implementation, they report speedups of 102x for multiplication and 195x for relinearization. This is in the same order of magnitude with our speedups of 550x as reported in Table 6. Besides being used for scheme-specific operations, FPGAs have also been used to accelerate polynomial and integer arithmetic [12,23] in ways that are generally useful for SHE, and for other applications. Another work [24] using FPGAs with CKKS attempts to decrease the amount of storage needed for NTT operations by computing twiddle factors on-the-fly, saving over 99.8% of the memory that would normally be used to store these. The lessened need for data transfer from this innovation resulted in a 118x speedup against a (less optimized) CPU implementation, and 28x against a similar work using FPGAs. One FPGA-based accelerator for homomorphic multiplication in the LTV scheme [14,28] reported an speedup of 4.42x against a CPU implementation, with the polynomial degree 2^{14} (but only 80 bits of security) and a full API and Linux driver.

GPU: Al Badawi et al. implemented the Full RNS Variant of B/FV on a GPU using CUDA. Much of the innovation in their work comes from choosing the memory layout of polynomial representations and using parallelism to mitigate data transfer. The GPU implementation reports speedups of up to 13.18x for homomorphic multiplication as compared to Microsoft SEAL run on an Intel Xeon operating at 2.4 GHz. Like our work, all essential SHE operations of the B/FV scheme can be run on the accelerator, making this work useful for more general use cases besides cloud-outsourced homomorphic encryption. In contrast, both HEAX and Roy et al. only consider a coprocessor architecture, where the most intensive operations are performed by the FPGA.

ASIC: There has also been some work in using ASICs for SHE [16], but ASICs are not easily reconfigurable, and are thus not as widely used in research despite their great efficiency.

CPU: There exist several high-performance software implementations of homomorphic encryption schemes for use on ordinary CPUs. These libraries include HELib implementing BGV [22], Microsoft SEAL [10] implementing B/FV and CKKS, FV-NFLib and PALISADE implementing the B/FV [13,26] (with PALISADE implementing the floating-point RNS variant of B/FV [21]). While software implementations of homomorphic encryption are becoming mature, hardware acceleration generally outperforms general-purpose computing for homomorphic encryption. GPUs, FPGAs, and CPUs are further limited by hard bounds on machine word size, e.g. 64 bits for modern processors, 27 bits for HEAX (two words are used to store numbers, giving 54 bits), 30 bits for Roy et al. CE-RAM is not limited by a strict upper bound on word size, though it still faces the universal issue of larger numbers requiring asymptotically more computation.

RNS: Special RNS systems are well-studied in electrical engineering for their applications to parallel processing [40]. Many of these systems are not practical for use in CE-RAM due to their complexity, being originally conceived of in the context of FPGAs or other specialized hardware. However, we are able to observe and use some ideas from these works. In particular, we note that moduli near a power of two are amenable to the CE-RAM environment.

6   Conclusion

In this paper, we applied algorithmic optimizations to further accelerate the B/FV SHE scheme in CE-RAM. The optimizations we applied include the NTT, the full RNS variant, and new optimizations for modular reduction and *FastBConv*. We evaluate the effects of applying these optimizations, and compare the benefits of our work with a CPU-based software implementation, as well as with other relevant research efforts. For homomorphic multiplication of B/FV, our approach achieves speedups of up to 784.2x against a CPU server, 506.5x against previous work in CE-RAM [34], 66.85x against an FPGA acceleration [36], and 30.8x against a GPU implementation [3]. Compared to both GPUs and FPGAs, CE-RAM systems are currently at a nascent state with much room of improvement. Nevertheless, CE-RAM SHE realizations show a greater benefit as compared to GPUs and FPGAs.

Acknowledgements. The authors thank Matthew Schoenbauer (University of Notre Dame), Carl Pomerance (Dartmouth College), Kim Laine (Microsoft Research), and M. Sadegh Riazi (UC San Diego) for their insights.

A   Proofs for Novel Optimizations

In this section, we present proofs of correctness for our novel RNS optimizations.

A.1   Proof of Theorem 1

Proof. If x is even, then $x = 2y$, and $x \cdot 2^{g-1} = (2y)2^{g-1} = 2^g y \equiv y \mod 2^g - 1$. If x is odd, then $x = 2y + 1$, and $x2^{g-1} = (2y + 1)2^{g-1} = y2^g + 2^{g-1} \equiv 2^{g-1} + y$ mod $(2^g - 1)$. $\square$

A.2   Proof of Lemma 2

Proof. $x(2^g - 1) = x \cdot 2^g - x \equiv -x \mod 2^g$. $\square$

A.3   Proof of Theorem 2

Proof. If x is even, then $x = 2y$, and $x(2^{g-1} + 1) = (2y)(2^{g-1} + 1) = 2^g y + 2y \equiv -y + 2y \equiv y \mod 2^g + 1$. If x is odd, then $x = 2y + 1$, and $x(2^{g-1} + 1) = (2y + 1)(2^{g-1} + 1) = y2^g + 2y + 2^{g-1} + 1 \equiv -y + 2y + 2^{g-1} + 1 \equiv y + 2^{g-1} + 1$ mod $2^g - 1$. $\square$

B   Proofs for Fermat-like Coprimes

Let the terms q_i be elements of $S_2 = \{2^m - 1, 2^m + 1, 2^{2m} + 1, 2^{4m} + 1, \cdots 2^{2^{f-1}m} + 1, 2^{2^f m} + 1\}$, as in Sect. 3.2. Then the following results hold [32]:

Lemma 3. *For $q_i \in S_2$ with $q_0 = 2^m - 1$, $|\frac{q_0}{q}|_{q_0} = 2^{m-(k-1)}$.*

Proof. Note that $\frac{q}{q_0} = (2^m + 1)(2^{2m})(2^{4m}) \cdots (2^{2^f m})$. Because 2^m is equal to 1 modulo q_0, each of the $f + 1$ terms in this product is equal to two. Thus $|\frac{q}{q_0}|_{q_0} = |2^{f+1}|_{q_0}$. The inverse of this is $|\frac{q_0}{q}|_{q_0} = 2^{m-(f+1)} = 2^{m-(k-1)}$. □

Lemma 4. *For $q_i = 2^{2^i m} + 1$, $i \in [1, k]$, $|\frac{q_i}{q}|_{q_i}$ is $2^{2^{i-1}m - (f-i+2)}$.*

Proof. Note that $\frac{q}{q_i} = (2^{2^i m} - 1)(2^{2^{i+1}m} + 1)(2^{2^{i+2}m} + 1) \cdots (2^{2^f m} + 1)$. We see that $|(2^{2^i m} - 1)|_{q_i} = |(-1) - 1|_{q_i} = |-2|_{q_i}$. For the remaining terms $2^{2^j m} + 1$ (for $j \in [i+1, f]$), we have $|2^{2^j m} + 1|_{q_i} = |(2^{2^{i-1}m})^{2^{j-(i-1)}} + 1|_{q_i} = |(-1)^{2^{j-(i-2)}} + 1|_{q_i}$. Because $j > i$, this is equal to $|1 + 1|_{q_i} = 2$. Combining these, we see that $|\frac{q}{q_i}|_{q_i} = |(-2)2^{f-(i-1)}|_{q_i} = |-2^{f-i+2}|_{q_i}$. Then the inverse term $|\frac{q_i}{q}|_{q_i}$ is $2^{2^{i-1}m-(f-i+2)}$. □

In both of these terms, the exponent of two should always be positive; if this is not the case then too many moduli have been chosen for too small a dynamic range [39].

C   NTT Algorithm

Algorithm 7 gives the algorithm of the Number-Theoretic Transform.

Algorithm 7. Number-Theoretic Transform (NTT) (From [36]).

Input: $a \in \mathbb{Z}_p^n (p \equiv 1 \bmod 2n)$, $Y \in \mathbb{Z}_p^n$ (CE-RAM stores powers of ψ in bit-reverse order, and $Y' = \lfloor Y \cdot 2^w / p \rfloor$).
Output: $\tilde{a} \leftarrow NTT_p(a)$ in bit-reverse order.

```
 1: procedure NTT_p(a)
 2:     for (m = 1; m < n; m = 2m) do
 3:         for (i = 0; i < m; i++) do                ▷ Butterfly Loop
 4:             for (j = i·n/m; j < (2i+1)n/2m; j++) do     ▷ NTT Core
 5:                 v ← MultRed(a_{j+n/m}, y_{m+i}, p)
 6:                 a_{j+n/m} ← a_j − v (mod p)
 7:                 a_j ← a_j + v (mod p)
 8:             end for
 9:         end for
10:     end for
11:     ã ← a
12: end procedure
```

References

1. Agarwal, R., Burrus, C.: Fast convolution using Fermat number transforms with applications to digital filtering. IEEE Trans. Acoust. Speech Signal Process. **22**(2), 87–97 (1974)
2. Al Badawi, A., Veeravalli, B., Mun, C.F., Aung, K.M.M.: High-performance FV somewhat homomorphic encryption on GPUs: an implementation using CUDA. In: IACR CHES, pp. 70–95 (2018)
3. Al Badawi, A.Q.A., Polyakov, Y., Aung, K.M.M., Veeravalli, B., Rohloff, K.: Implementation and performance evaluation of RNS variants of the BFV homomorphic encryption scheme. IEEE TETC (2019)
4. Albrecht, M., Bai, S., Ducas, L.: A subfield lattice attack on overstretched NTRU assumptions. In: Robshaw, M., Katz, J. (eds.) CRYPTO 2016. LNCS, vol. 9814, pp. 153–178. Springer, Heidelberg (2016). https://doi.org/10.1007/978-3-662-53018-4_6
5. Albrecht, M., et al.: Homomorphic encryption security standard. Technical report, HomomorphicEncryption.org, Toronto, Canada (2018)
6. Bajard, J.-C., Eynard, J., Hasan, M.A., Zucca, V.: A full RNS variant of FV like somewhat homomorphic encryption schemes. In: Avanzi, R., Heys, H. (eds.) SAC 2016. LNCS, vol. 10532, pp. 423–442. Springer, Cham (2017). https://doi.org/10.1007/978-3-319-69453-5_23
7. Bajard, J.-C., Eynard, J., Martins, P., Sousa, L., Zucca, V.: Note on the noise growth of the RNS variants of the BFV scheme
8. Bajard, J.-C., Eynard, J., Merkiche, N.: Montgomery reduction within the context of residue number system arithmetic. J. Cryptogr. Eng. **8**(3), 189–200 (2017). https://doi.org/10.1007/s13389-017-0154-9
9. Barrett, P.: Implementing the Rivest Shamir and Adleman public key encryption algorithm on a standard digital signal processor. In: Odlyzko, A.M. (ed.) CRYPTO 1986. LNCS, vol. 263, pp. 311–323. Springer, Heidelberg (1987). https://doi.org/10.1007/3-540-47721-7_24
10. Chen, H., Han, K., Huang, Z., Jalali, A., Laine, K.: Simple encrypted arithmetic library v2. 3.0. Microsoft (2017)
11. Cheon, J.H., Kim, A., Kim, M., Song, Y.: Homomorphic encryption for arithmetic of approximate numbers. In: Takagi, T., Peyrin, T. (eds.) ASIACRYPT 2017. LNCS, vol. 10624, pp. 409–437. Springer, Cham (2017). https://doi.org/10.1007/978-3-319-70694-8_15
12. Cilardo, A., Argenziano, D.: Securing the cloud with reconfigurable computing: an FPGA accelerator for homomorphic encryption. In: 2016 Design, Automation Test in Europe Conference Exhibition (DATE), pp. 1622–1627 (2016)
13. Cousins, D., Rohloff, K., Polyakov, Y., Ryan, G.J.: The PALISADE lattice cryptography library (2015–2020). https://palisade-crypto.org/
14. Cousins, D.B., Rohloff, K., Sumorok, D.: Designing an FPGA-accelerated homomorphic encryption co-processor. IEEE ToETiC **5**(2), 193–206 (2017)
15. Crandall, R., Pomerance, C.B.: Prime Numbers: A Computational Perspective, vol. 182. Springer, New York (2006). https://doi.org/10.1007/978-1-4684-9316-0
16. Doröz, Y., Öztürk, E., Sunar, B.: A million-bit multiplier architecture for fully homomorphic encryption. Microprocess. Microsyst. **38**(8), 766–775 (2014)
17. Duarte, J.P., et al.: BSIM-CMG: standard FinFET compact model for advanced circuit design. In: ESSCIRC, pp. 196–201, September 2015
18. C. D. Environment: Cadence design systems. Inc. (2005). www.cadence.com (2005)

19. Fan, J., Vercauteren, F.: Somewhat practical fully homomorphic encryption. IACR Cryptology ePrint Archive 2012:144 (2012)
20. Gentry, C., et al.: Fully homomorphic encryption using ideal lattices. STOC **9**, 169–178 (2009)
21. Halevi, S., Polyakov, Y., Shoup, V.: An improved RNS variant of the BFV homomorphic encryption scheme. In: Matsui, M. (ed.) CT-RSA 2019. LNCS, vol. 11405, pp. 83–105. Springer, Cham (2019). https://doi.org/10.1007/978-3-030-12612-4_5
22. Halevi, S., Shoup, V.: Bootstrapping for HElib. In: Oswald, E., Fischlin, M. (eds.) EUROCRYPT 2015. LNCS, vol. 9056, pp. 641–670. Springer, Heidelberg (2015). https://doi.org/10.1007/978-3-662-46800-5_25
23. Jayet-Griffon, C., Cornelie, M., Maistri, P., Elbaz-Vincent, P., Leveugle, R.: Polynomial multipliers for fully homomorphic encryption on FPGA. In: 2015 International Conference on ReConFigurable Computing and FPGAs (ReConFig), pp. 1–6 (2015)
24. Kim, S., Lee, K., Cho, W., Nam, Y., Cheon, J.H., Rutenbar, R.A.: Hardware architecture of a number theoretic transform for a bootstrappable RNS-based homomorphic encryption scheme. In: IEEE FCCM, pp. 56–64. IEEE (2020)
25. Langlois, A., Stehlé, D.: Hardness of decision (R) LWE for any modulus. Technical report, Citeseer (2012)
26. Lepoint, T.: FV-NFLlib: library implementing the Fan-Vercauteren homomorphic encryption scheme
27. Longa, P., Naehrig, M.: Speeding up the number theoretic transform for faster ideal lattice-based cryptography. In: Foresti, S., Persiano, G. (eds.) CANS 2016. LNCS, vol. 10052, pp. 124–139. Springer, Cham (2016). https://doi.org/10.1007/978-3-319-48965-0_8
28. López-Alt, A., Tromer, E., Vaikuntanathan, V.: On-the-fly multiparty computation on the cloud via multikey fully homomorphic encryption. In: ACM STOC, pp. 1219–1234 (2012)
29. Oder, T., Güneysu, T., Valencia, F., Khalid, A., O'Neill, M., Regazzoni, F.: Lattice-based cryptography: from reconfigurable hardware to ASIC. In: ISIC, pp. 1–4 (2016)
30. Öztürk, E., Doröz, Y., Sunar, B., Savas, E.: Accelerating somewhat homomorphic evaluation using FPGAS. IACR Cryptology ePrint Archive 2015:294 (2015)
31. Pöppelmann, T., Naehrig, M., Putnam, A., Macias, A.: Accelerating homomorphic evaluation on reconfigurable hardware. In: Güneysu, T., Handschuh, H. (eds.) CHES 2015. LNCS, vol. 9293, pp. 143–163. Springer, Heidelberg (2015). https://doi.org/10.1007/978-3-662-48324-4_8
32. Pourbigharaz, F., Yassine, H.M.: Intermediate signed-digit stage to perform residue to binary transformations based on CRT. In: IEEE ISCAS, vol. 2, pp. 353–356 (1994)
33. Rader, C.M.: Discrete convolutions via Mersenne transforms. IEEE Trans. Comput. **C-21**, 1269–1273 (1972)
34. Reis, D., Takeshita, J., Jung, T., Niemier, M., Hu, X.S.: Computing-in-memory for performance and energy-efficient homomorphic encryption. IEEE Trans. Very Large Scale Integr. (VLSI) Syst. **28**(11), 2300–2313 (2020)
35. Riazi, M.S., Laine, K., Pelton, B., Dai, W.: HEAX: an architecture for computing on encrypted data. In: ACM ASPLOS 2020, pp. 1295–1309 (2020)
36. Roy, S.S., Turan, F., Jarvinen, K., Vercauteren, F., Verbauwhede, I.: FPGA-based high-performance parallel architecture for homomorphic computing on encrypted data. In: 2019 IEEE International Symposium on HPCA, pp. 387–398. IEEE (2019)

37. Shenoy, A., Kumaresan, R.: Fast base extension using a redundant modulus in RNS. IEEE Trans. Comput. **38**(2), 292–297 (1989)
38. Synopsys Inc.: HSPICE. Version O-2018.09-1 (2018)
39. Takeshita, J., Schoenbauer, M., Karl, R., Jung, T.: Enabling faster operations for deeper circuits in full RNS variants of FV-like somewhat homomorphic encryption
40. Wang, W., Swamy, M., Ahmad, M.O., Wang, Y.: A study of the residue-to-binary converters for the three-moduli sets. IEEE ToCS I Fund. Theory Appl. **50**(2), 235–243 (2003)
41. Öztürk, E., Doröz, Y., Savaş, E., Sunar, B.: A custom accelerator for homomorphic encryption applications. IEEE Trans. Comput. **66**(1), 3–16 (2017)

Obfuscating Finite Automata

Steven D. Galbraith[iD] and Lukas Zobernig[(✉)][iD]

Department of Mathematics, The University of Auckland, Auckland, New Zealand
{s.galbraith,lukas.zobernig}@auckland.ac.nz

Abstract. We construct a *virtual black box* and *perfect circuit-hiding* obfuscator for *evasive deterministic finite automata* using a matrix encoding scheme with a limited zero-testing algorithm. We construct the matrix encoding scheme by extending an existing matrix fully homomorphic encryption scheme. Using obfuscated deterministic finite automata we can for example evaluate secret *regular expressions* or disjunctive normal forms on public inputs. In particular, the possibility of evaluating regular expressions solves the open problem of *obfuscated substring matching*.

1 Introduction

There are several constructions of program obfuscation schemes for different evasive functions, such as hyperplane membership [10], boolean conjunctions and pattern matching with wildcards [5–7,9], compute-and-compare programs [18, 24], fuzzy Hamming distance [13], and more [22]. These obfuscation schemes use different security notions such as *virtual black-box* (VBB) obfuscation, *input hiding* obfuscation, *perfect circuit-hiding* obfuscation, and *indistinguishability obfuscation* (iO).

All of the aforementioned obfuscation schemes target specific evasive functions [22]. General obfuscation schemes are less practical. There are candidates for generic iO schemes [14] and VBB branching program obfuscation, but none of them are practical. It seems that by restricting to evasive functions and special purpose obfuscation, it is possible to obtain feasible schemes.

In this work we consider a somewhat more general class of programs, namely *deterministic finite automata* (DFA). The theory of obfuscating a DFA has been considered before by [22]. They give an obfuscator in the random oracle model for a special class of regular expressions for which the symbols are given by point functions. As open problems they ask whether regular languages can be obfuscated and whether there is any non-trivial obfuscation result without using the random oracle model. [20] state that secure obfuscation of DFAs is one of the most challenging problems in the theory of program obfuscation. Note that we cannot simply apply existing circuit obfuscation solutions to the problem of obfuscating DFAs. Unlike a tree-like circuit which we can evaluate on an input by traversing it from the circuit root to one of the leaves, a DFA can cycle back to previous states. Furthermore, a DFA has a variable number of input symbols.

O. Dunkelman et al. (Eds.): SAC 2020, LNCS 12804, pp. 90–114, 2021.
https://doi.org/10.1007/978-3-030-81652-0_4

We give a VBB and perfect circuit-hiding obfuscator for *evasive* DFAs in the standard model. Note that evasive DFAs are more general than other known classes of evasive functions which can be practically obfuscated, such as point functions and conjunctions. It is clear that point functions and conjunctions can be expressed as DFAs, but DFAs can also handle substring matching which is not covered by any previous obfuscation technique.

We will now explain why we do not consider arbitrary DFAs. It is a classical result that certain types of finite automata can be learned from their input/accept/reject behaviour, cf. [3]. We will also give another possible learning strategy for finite automata in Sect. 5.1 if certain information is given. Hence we will only consider those automata which, without loss of generality, reject almost all inputs. We will call such an automaton *evasive*. Any security claims we make are only for an adversary who does not know any accepting input.

Our solution to the problem of DFA obfuscation uses tools that were developed for homomorphic encryption and multilinear maps. These tools are often used to construct indistinguishability obfuscation schemes. Some of the general purpose iO schemes have questionable hardness assumptions or have been broken altogether, see [1, 2, Appendix A]. To prove iO security, the underlying multilinear maps need to come with a hard generalised decisional Diffie-Hellman problem.

For our application, we instead require a different hard computational problem: Distinguishing two related encodings given certain public zero-testing information should be intractable. We will consider only encodings of evasive DFAs for this problem to make sense. Instead of considering iO we will consider virtual black-box obfuscation. Since [4] showed that VBB obfuscation is equivalent to perfect circuit-hiding obfuscation for evasive functions, we indirectly prove that our obfuscator hides all information about the DFA description.

We believe that we have avoided all previous attacks on multilinear maps that exploit the zero-testing parameter, due to our restriction to evasive DFAs and due to our very limited zero-testing information. We discuss this further in Sect. 4.

Finite Automata. Using the matrix fully homomorphic encryption (FHE) schemes by [15, 19] Alice may generate a private key and publish an encrypted secret finite automaton to Bob. A finite automaton is represented by a set of transition matrices, one matrix for each possible input symbol. The transition matrices themselves are $n \times n$ square matrices where n is the number of states of the automaton. The homomorphic properties allow Bob to evaluate the secret finite automaton on an arbitrary input. The result of this evaluation is an encrypted vector which Alice may decrypt using her private key. This can for example be use to evaluate secret *regular expressions* by a remote user while a central server can decide about the result.

[12] consider pattern matching on encrypted streams. For this, they construct a searchable encryption scheme based on public key encryption and bilinear pairings. This approach is sensible when the original data needs to be protected

by encryption. This is different to the situation we consider since we only wish to protect the substring pattern.

[15] state the matching of virus signatures as a possible application of such regular expressions. Consider a security company that analyses computer viruses and distributes virus signatures to their clients. The company wants to protect its intellectual property (the virus signatures). It essentially requires a scheme which allows for the distribution of encrypted virus signatures that the clients can apply to their data. One problem with the setup of [15] is the need for interactivity. In their scheme, Alice uses a matrix FHE scheme to encrypt a virus signature represented by an automaton and sends it to Bob. Bob then applies his input to the hidden automaton which produces an encrypted state vector. If Bob wants to learn whether there indeed is a virus present, he needs to send back an encrypted state vector to Alice. She can then decrypt the encrypted state vector and notify Bob accordingly.

Additionally, the analysis of [15] does not consider an *adaptive attack* in the form of multiple queries with an oracle that reports accept/reject for arbitrary inputs. As mentioned, such an oracle can be used to leak parts or all of the finite automaton description, cf. [3]. In this adaptive setting, we argue that the number of allowed oracle queries needs to be small enough for arbitrary finite automata, or a specific class needs to be used: We propose the class of evasive finite automata.

Our Contribution. We consider obfuscation for deterministic finite automata and in particular restrict to the class of evasive DFAs in light of [3]. DFAs can represent problems such as *regular expressions* and *conjunctions* (also known as *pattern matching with wildcards*).

- We obtain an obfuscator for evasive regular expressions and consequently solve the open problem of *obfuscated substring matching*. Given a plaintext input $s \in \{0,1\}^n$, obfuscated substring matching is the problem of identifying whether s contains a secret substring $x \in \{0,1\}^k$, for $k \leq n \in \mathbb{N}$. We achieve something even more general, as the substring can be given by a regular expression. This gives a complete and non-interactive solution to the virus testing application suggested by [15].
- We obtain an obfuscator for arbitrary evasive conjunctions. A conjunction on Boolean variables $b_1, \ldots, b_k$ is $\chi(b_1, \ldots, b_k) = \bigwedge_{i=1}^{k} c_i$ where each c_i is of the form b_j or $\neg b_j$ for some $1 \leq j \leq k$. Pattern matching with wildcards is an alternative representation of a conjunction. Consider a vector $x \in \{0, 1, \star\}^k$ of length $k \in \mathbb{N}$ where $\star$ is a special *wildcard* symbol. Such an x then corresponds to a conjunction $\chi : \{0,1\}^k \rightarrow \{0,1\}$ which, using Boolean variables $b_1, \ldots, b_k$, can be written as $\chi(b) = \bigwedge_{i=1}^{k} c_i$ where $c_i = \neg b_i$ if $x_i = 0$, $c_i = b_i$ if $x_i = 1$, and $c_i = 1$ if $x_i = \star$. Additionally, we can consider a set of conjunctions to obtain a boolean formula in *disjunctive normal form* $\bigvee_i \bigwedge_j (\neg) b_{ij}$. In conclusion, our DFA obfuscator allows for yet another solution of this problem.

Our Techniques. Consider the matrix FHE scheme by [19] with parameters $q, n \in \mathbb{N}$, and scaling factor $\beta = q/2$. Given a secret matrix $M \in \{0,1\}^{r \times r}$, we encode it to form a matrix C such that $SC = MSG + E$, for another small secret matrix S and small error matrix E. Here G is a so called *gadget matrix* which is used to construct a lattice trapdoor. Given the secret S, we may decode the ciphertext C to recover M. Similarly, we may encrypt a vector $v \in \{0,1\}^r$ to obtain a ciphertext c such that $Sc = \beta v + e$ for a small error vector e. Vector decryption is correct by rounding $\lceil (1/\beta)(Sc \bmod q) \rfloor$ if the error e is bounded by $\|e\|_\infty \leq \beta/2$. The fully homomorphic property then allows us to multiply encoded matrices via $C_1 \odot C_2 := C_1 G^{-1}(C_2)$ which corresponds to an encoding of $M_1 M_2$. We can further apply encoded matrices to encrypted vectors by computing $CG^{-1}(c)$ which corresponds to an encoding of Mv.

Given any DFA with $r \in \mathbb{N}$ states and alphabet Σ, we can obtain *transition matrices* $\{M_\sigma\}_{\sigma \in \Sigma}$ with $M_\sigma \in \{0,1\}^{r \times r}$. These matrices then act on state vectors which for a DFA are simply the canonical basis vectors $e_1, \ldots, e_r$. Without loss of generality, assume that the initial state is given by e_1 and that the accepting state is given by e_r. We will only consider *evasive* DFAs whose shortest accepted input word has a large min-entropy. We will also assume that the DFA matrices are given in a certain *canonical* form which safeguards from leaking states after partial evaluation and intermediate state transitions.

Finally, we encode the DFA matrices $\{M_\sigma\}_{\sigma \in \Sigma}$ to obtain a set of encodings $\{C_\sigma\}_{\sigma \in \Sigma}$, we encrypt the initial state vector e_1 to obtain the ciphertext vector c, and we publish the last row of the HAO15 secret S, call it s_r. The obfuscation of the DFA is then the tuple $(s_r, \{C_\sigma\}_{\sigma \in \Sigma}, c)$. The security of our scheme is based on the security of the HAO15 scheme with the last row of the secret known.

Using the multiplicative property, we may then evaluate the obfuscated DFA on an input word $w \in \Sigma^*$ by first computing an encryption c_w of the state vector of the DFA on input w

$$c_w = \left(\bigodot_{i=|w|}^{1} C_{w_i} \right) G^{-1}(c).$$

This corresponds to evaluating the DFA in the plaintext space by computing $t = (\prod_{i=|w|}^{1} M_{w_i}) e_1$. Finally, to check whether c_w is an encryption of the final state (and thus whether the DFA accepts the input word w), we use the following identity

$$t_r = \left\lceil \frac{s_r \cdot c_w \bmod q}{\beta} \right\rfloor,$$

where $\lceil . \rfloor$ denotes rounding to the nearest integer. This identity implies that knowing the last row s_r of the secret S is sufficient to check whether c_w is an encryption of e_r, in which case $t_r = 1$. If $t_r = 0$, then c_w is an encryption of any of the other possible state vectors $e_1, \ldots, e_{r-1}$. Note that these encryptions are indistinguishable since s_r can only decrypt the last coordinate. All a user can learn is whether or not the final state is the accepting state, there is no other leakage of the structure of the DFA. We will show that this construction preserves functionality as long as the length of the input word is shorter than a certain maximal length which depends on the individual system parameters.

Outline of This Work. Section 2 recalls basic (obfuscation) definitions. Sections 3 and 4 introduce the notion of a matrix graded encoding scheme and exhibits two candidate constructions of matrix (graded) encoding schemes. The hardness of these schemes is based on lattice problems and new computational assumptions. In Sect. 5 we explain how to represent finite automata using *transition matrices* and consider possible ways of learning (partial) information from such a representation. Sections 6 and 7 present the DFA obfuscator, security reductions to VBB and perfect circuit-hiding, and consider some parameters. Additionally, in Appendix C we briefly consider obfuscated DFAs from general matrix graded encoding schemes.

2   Obfuscation Definitions

We are interested in obfuscating a special type of programs, namely ones which either accept or reject almost all inputs. The following definition formalises this situation.

Definition 2.1 (Evasive Program Collection). *Let* $\mathcal{P} = \{\mathcal{P}_n\}_{n \in \mathbb{N}}$ *be a collection of polynomial-size programs such that every* $P \in \mathcal{P}_n$ *is a program* $P : \{0,1\}^n \to \{0,1\}$. *The collection* $\mathcal{P}$ *is called* evasive *if there exists a negligible function* ϵ *such that for every* $n \in \mathbb{N}$ *and for every* $y \in \{0,1\}^n$:

$$\Pr_{P \leftarrow \mathcal{P}_n} [P(y) = 1] \le \epsilon(n).$$

In short, Definition 2.1 means that a random program from an evasive collection $\mathcal{P}$ evaluates to 0 with overwhelming probability. Finally, we call a member $P \in \mathcal{P}_n$ for some $n \in \mathbb{N}$ an *evasive program* or an *evasive function*.

Definition 2.2 (Perfect Circuit-Hiding Obfuscation [4]). *An obfuscator* $\mathcal{O}$ *for a collection of evasive programs* $\mathcal{P}$ *is* perfect circuit-hiding, *if for every PPT adversary* $\mathcal{A}$ *there exists a negligible function* ϵ *such that for every* $n \in \mathbb{N}$, *every balanced predicate* $\varphi : \mathcal{P}_n \to \{0,1\}$, *and every auxilliary input* $\alpha \in \{0,1\}^{poly(n)}$ *to* $\mathcal{A}$:

$$\Pr_{P \leftarrow \mathcal{P}_n} [\mathcal{A}(\alpha, \mathcal{O}(P)) = \varphi(P)] \le \frac{1}{2} + \epsilon(n),$$

where the probability is also over the randomness of $\mathcal{O}$.

[4, Theorem 2.1] showed that for evasive programs perfect circuit-hiding obfuscation is equivalent to *virtual black box* obfuscation.

Definition 2.3 (Distributional Virtual Black-Box Obfuscator with Auxiliary Input). *Let* $\mathcal{P} = \{\mathcal{P}_n\}_{n \in \mathbb{N}}$ *be a family of polynomial-size programs with input size* n *and let* $\mathcal{O}$ *be a PPT algorithm which takes as input a program* $P \in \mathcal{P}$, *a security parameter* $\lambda \in \mathbb{N}$ *and outputs a program* $\mathcal{O}(P)$ *(which itself is* *not necessarily in* $\mathcal{P}$). *Let* $\mathcal{D}$ *be a class of distribution ensembles* $D = \{D_\lambda\}_{\lambda \in \mathbb{N}}$ *that sample* $(P, \alpha) \leftarrow D_\lambda$ *with* $P \in \mathcal{P}$ *and* α *some auxiliary input. The algorithm* $\mathcal{O}$ *is a* VBB *obfuscator for the distribution class* $\mathcal{D}$ *over the program family* $\mathcal{P}$ *if it is functionality preserving, implies polynomial slowdown, and satisfies the following property:*

- *Virtual black-box: For every (non-uniform) polynomial size adversary* $\mathcal{A}$, *there exists a (non-uniform) polynomial size simulator* $\mathcal{S}$ *with oracle access to* P, *such that for every* $D = \{D_\lambda\}_{\lambda \in \mathbb{N}} \in \mathcal{D}$, *and every (non-uniform) polynomial size predicate* $\varphi : \mathcal{P} \to \{0, 1\}$:

$$\left| \Pr_{P \leftarrow D_\lambda, \mathcal{O}, \mathcal{A}} [\mathcal{A}(\mathcal{O}(P), \alpha) = \varphi(P)] - \Pr_{P \leftarrow D_\lambda, \mathcal{S}} [\mathcal{S}^P(|P|, \alpha) = \varphi(P)] \right| \le \epsilon(\lambda)$$

where $\epsilon(\lambda)$ *is a negligible function.*

In simple terms, Definition 2.3 states that a VBB obfuscated program $\mathcal{O}(P)$ does not reveal anything more than would be revealed from having black box access to the program P itself.

A definition that is more convenient to work with for proving security is *distributional indistinguishability*. To make sense of this, we will need the following definition that tells when two distributions are indistinguishable in a computational sense.

Definition 2.4 (Computational Indistinguishability). *We say that two ensembles of random variables* $X = \{X_\lambda\}_{\lambda \in \mathbb{N}}$ *and* $Y = \{Y_\lambda\}_{\lambda \in \mathbb{N}}$ *are computationally indistinguishable and write* $X \overset{c}{\approx} Y$ *if for every (non-uniform) PPT distinguisher* $\mathcal{A}$ *it holds that*

$$|\Pr[\mathcal{A}(X_\lambda) = 1] - \Pr[\mathcal{A}(Y_\lambda) = 1]| \le \epsilon(\lambda)$$

where $\epsilon(\lambda)$ *is some negligible function.*

Definition 2.5 (Distributional Indistinguishability [24]). *An obfuscator* $\mathcal{O}$ *for the distribution class* $\mathcal{D}$ *over a family of programs* $\mathcal{P}$ *satisfies distributional indistinguishability if there exists a (non-uniform) PPT simulator* $\mathcal{S}$ *such that for every distribution ensemble* $D = \{D_\lambda\}_{\lambda \in \mathbb{N}} \in \mathcal{D}$ *the following distributions are computationally indistinguishable*

$$(\mathcal{O}(P), \alpha) \overset{c}{\approx} (\mathcal{S}(|P|), \alpha) \tag{2.1}$$

where $(P, \alpha) \leftarrow D_\lambda$. *Here* α *denotes some auxiliary information.*

Note that the sampling procedure for the left and right side of Eq. (2.1) in Definition 2.5 is slightly different. For both we sample $(P, \alpha) \leftarrow D_\lambda$ and for the left side we simply output $(\mathcal{O}(P), \alpha)$ immediately. On the other hand, for the right side we record $|P|$, discard P and finally output $(\mathcal{S}(|P|), \alpha)$ instead.

Definition 2.6 (Min-Entropy). *The* min-entropy *of a random variable X is defined as*

$$H_\infty(X) = -\log\left(\max_x \Pr[X = x]\right).$$

The (average) conditional min-entropy *of a random variable X conditioned on a correlated variable Y is defined as*

$$H_\infty(X|Y) = -\log\left(\mathop{E}_{y \leftarrow Y}\left[\max_x \Pr[X = x|Y = y]\right]\right).$$

In Definition 2.5 the simulator $\mathcal{S}$ is not given α as an input. Hence, the definition may not be satisfied if the min-entropy of P is small given α. We will consider this only in the context where the min-entropy of P given α is large.

It can be shown that distributional indistinguishability implies VBB security under certain conditions. To see this, we first define the augmentation of a distribution class by a predicate.

Definition 2.7 (Predicate Augmentation [24]). *For a distribution class $\mathcal{D}$, its augmentation under predicates $\text{aug}(\mathcal{D})$ is defined as follows: For any (non-uniform) polynomial-time predicate $\varphi : \{0,1\}^* \rightarrow \{0,1\}$ and any $D = \{D_\lambda\}_{\lambda \in \mathbb{N}} \in \mathcal{D}$, the class $\text{aug}(\mathcal{D})$ indicates the distribution $D' = \{D'_\lambda\}_{\lambda \in \mathbb{N}}$ where D'_λ samples $(P, \alpha) \leftarrow D_\lambda$, computes $\alpha' = (\alpha, \varphi(P))$ and outputs (P, α'). Here α denotes some auxiliary information.*

The following theorem shows that distributional indistinguishability for the larger augmented class $\text{aug}(\mathcal{D})$ implies distributional VBB security for the class $\mathcal{D}$.

Theorem 2.1 (Distributional Indistinguishability Implies VBB [24]). *For any family of programs $\mathcal{P}$ and a distribution class $\mathcal{D}$ over $\mathcal{P}$, if an obfuscator satisfies distributional indistinguishability (Definition 2.5) for the class of distributions $\text{aug}(\mathcal{D})$ then it also satisfies distributional VBB security for the distribution class $\mathcal{D}$ (Definition 2.3).*

Proof. See [9, Lemma 2.2]. □

3   Matrix (Graded) Encoding Schemes

A matrix (graded) encoding scheme allow us to securely encode matrices. We can add and multiply encoded matrices which corresponds to adding and multiplying the underlying plaintext matrices. Finally, a zero-testing primitive should allow us to test whether an encoded matrix is an encoding of the zero matrix.

We will consider the definition of a *matrix (graded) encoding scheme* (similar to [7,8]) first and then remind the reader of possible candidates and give one new specialised construction based on the matrix FHE scheme by [19].

3.1   HAO15

The matrix FHE scheme of [19] is somewhat related to the scheme by [16] we describe in Appendix B. The hardness of both schemes is connected to the hardness of finding *approximate eigenspaces*.

Depending on a security parameter $\lambda \in \mathbb{N}$, fix a modulus q, a lattice dimension n, and a distribution χ over $\mathbb{Z}$. We are working over the ring $R = \mathbb{Z}/q\mathbb{Z}$. Assume the matrices we want to encode are from $\{0,1\}^r$ for some $r \in \mathbb{N}$. Set $\ell = \lceil \log(q) \rceil$, $N = (n+r)\ell$.

Let $g = (2^i)_{i=0,\dots,\ell-1} \in R^\ell$ be the *gadget vector*. Fix $G = g^T \otimes \mathrm{id}_{n+r} \in R^{(n+r) \times N}$, the *gadget matrix*. We may further assume that there exists a randomized algorithm $G^{-1}(v)$ that for an input $v \in R^{n+r}$, samples a vector $v' \leftarrow G^{-1}(v) \in R^N$ such that $Gv' = v$.

Key Generation. For key generation, we sample a secret matrix $S' \leftarrow \chi^{r \times n}$ and set $S = \left(\mathrm{id}_r | -S' \right) \in R^{r \times (n+r)}$. A priori, this matrix FHE scheme does not support zero-testing and since we are not interested in public encryption, we do not need any public parameters here. We will describe the public key when we discuss our solution for a zero-testing primitive.

Matrix Encoding. Given a matrix $M \in \{0,1\}^{r \times r}$, we sample $A' \leftarrow R^{n \times N}$ uniformly and $E \leftarrow \chi^{r \times N}$ and output the encoding

$$C = \begin{pmatrix} S'A' + E \\ A' \end{pmatrix} + \begin{pmatrix} MS \\ 0 \end{pmatrix} G \in R^{(n+r) \times N}.$$

It holds that $SC = MSG + E$.

Vector Encoding. Similarly, given a vector $v \in R^r$, we sample $a \leftarrow R^n$ uniformly and $e \leftarrow \chi^r$ and output the encoding

$$c = \begin{pmatrix} S'a + e \\ a \end{pmatrix} + \begin{pmatrix} v \\ 0 \end{pmatrix} \in R^{n+r}.$$

It holds that $Sc = v + e$.

Vector Encryption. The scheme also supports encryption and decryption of vectors. For this, fix an upper bound b on the $\| \cdot \|_\infty$-norm of vectors that should be possible to encrypt and decrypt and set

$$\beta = \lfloor q/b \rfloor.$$

For example, to encrypt binary secrets we can set $b = 2$. To encrypt a vector v, we will scale it by β such that the $\| \cdot \|_\infty$-norm of the error is bounded by β with high probability. Formally, to encrypt $v \in \{0, \dots, b-1\}^n$, output the encoding c of βv such that $Sc = \beta v + e$. To decrypt c, given the secret S, we compute

$$v = \left\lceil \frac{Sc \mod q}{\beta} \right\rfloor, \tag{3.1}$$

i.e. we round the entries of $(1/\beta)Sc$ to the closest integer.

Homomorphic Operations. Given two encodings C_1, C_2, addition is simply computing $C_1 + C_2$. The encodings can by multiplied by computing $C_1 G^{-1}(C_2)$, denote this by $C_1 \odot C_2$. Applying an encoded matrix C to an encoded vector c is computing $C G^{-1}(c)$.

Zero-Testing. Testing whether a given encoding is an encoding of zero is slightly more complicated because we cannot publish the secret matrix S. For our application, the following construction is sufficient. Let M_f be the $r \times r$ matrix which is zero everywhere except for a single 1 in its lower right corner, i.e. $(M_f)_{r,r} = 1$. Let C_f be the encoding of M_f. Let c be an encrypted vector. We need to test whether $C_f c$ is an encryption of e_r, the r-th canonical basis vector. To test for this, we publish the last row of the secret matrix S, call it $s_r \in R^{n+r}$. Assuming we only ever encrypt canonical basis vectors, the problem is then equivalent to checking whether $\lceil (1/\beta)(s_r \cdot c \mod q) \rfloor$ equals 1, see Eq. (3.1). Equality holds if and only if $C_f c$ is an encryption of a vector that has a 1 in coordinate r, see the proof of Lemma 6.1 for details. This limited construction allows us to use the HAO15 matrix FHE scheme as a matrix encoding scheme.

Error Bounds and Correctness. In the plain HAO15 matrix FHE scheme, to decode an encoded matrix, the error needs to be bounded by $\|E\|_\infty \leq q/8$. In our application, we do not need to decode matrices, but decrypt vectors. To correctly decrypt encrypted vectors, we see from Eq. (3.1) that the error needs to be bounded by $\|e\|_\infty \leq \beta/2 = q/4$. [19] showed that the noise growth is asymmetric and hence computing a polynomial length chain of homomorphic multiplications leads to a noise growth by a multiplicative polynomial factor. Denote with $|\chi|$ the standard deviation of the distribution χ. [15] showed that error produced by the application of κ matrices $(M_i)_{i=1,\dots,\kappa}$ on a vector is bounded by

$$\|e_\kappa\|_\infty \leq |\chi| N \left(1 + \kappa \max_{1 \leq i \leq \kappa} \left\| \prod_{j=\kappa}^{i} M_j \right\|_\infty \right).$$

For our application, we will consider matrices $(M_\sigma)_{\sigma \in \Sigma}$ that describe a DFA. We argue that for such matrices we obtain a large maximal grading $\kappa \sim q/\log(q)$. [15] introduced an *ambiguity measure* that better restricts the error bound for finite automata, depending on their *ambiguity type*. They considered more general NFAs whereas we shall restrict to DFAs only. They showed that DFAs are what they call *unambiguous* and that the error then can be bounded as $\|e_\kappa\|_\infty \leq |\chi|(N\kappa + 1)$. We find that for $\|e_\kappa\|_\infty$ to be bounded by $\beta/2 = q/4$, we require that

$$\kappa \leq \frac{q}{4\sqrt{n}(n+r)\lceil \log(q) \rceil}. \tag{3.2}$$

4   HAO15 Zero-Testing and Computational Assumptions

The original matrix FHE scheme by [19] enjoys CPA security and does not allow for zero-testing. In Sect. 3.1 we constructed a zero-testing primitive. This requires us to introduce an additional hardness assumption if we want to speak about security when using our extended HAO15 scheme as a matrix encoding scheme.

We stress that we do not construct an *absolute* zero-testing primitive which would allow to test whether an arbitrary matrix or vector entry is zero. A zero-testing primitive like this, while very powerful, would potentially reveal much more information about the private key. Instead we construct a primitive that only allows to test entries in the last row of a matrix or the last entry of a vector, respectively. Our construction only reveals partial information about the secret key. Finally, note that we do not consider iO but instead VBB and perfect circuit-hiding obfuscation instead for evasive finite automata. See [1, 2, Appendix A] for a summary of (zeroising) attacks on iO.

Definition 4.1 (DFA Security). *Consider the HAO15 matrix graded encoding scheme with security parameter $\lambda \in \mathbb{N}$ for a matrix dimension $r \in \mathbb{N}$. Let D be a distribution over $\mathcal{M}_r \times \{0,1\}^{poly(\lambda)}$ where $\mathcal{M}_r$ is a family of sequences of matrices $(M_\sigma)_{\sigma \in \Sigma}$ over $\{0,1\}^{r \times r}$.*

Let $((M_\sigma)_{\sigma \in \Sigma}, \alpha) \leftarrow D$ and $(M'_\sigma)_{\sigma \in \Sigma}$ be a sequence of matrices in $\{0,1\}^{r \times r}$ such that $M_\sigma - M'_\sigma$ is all zeroes apart from a single ± 1 in some row but not the last row. Consider, for all $\sigma \in \Sigma$, the HAO15 encodings C_σ of M_σ, C'_σ of M'_σ, and c and c' of the canonical basis vector e_1 as in Sect. 3.1 under a secret key S such that

$$SC_\sigma = M_\sigma SG + E, \; Sc = \beta e_1 + e,$$
$$SC'_\sigma = M'_\sigma SG + E', \; Sc' = \beta e_1 + e',$$

where E, E' and e, e' are error matrices and error vectors, respectively.

We say that HAO15 satisfies DFA security for D if the following two distributions are computationally indistinguishable:

$$(s_r, (C_\sigma)_{\sigma \in \Sigma}, c, \alpha) \stackrel{c}{\approx} (s_r, (C'_\sigma)_{\sigma \in \Sigma}, c', \alpha),$$

where s_r is the last row of the secret key S.

Note that Definition 4.1 is closely related to the definition of IND-CPA security for an asymmetric cipher: The adversary is given a number of encryptions of known messages and needs to distinguish them. In our case, we additionally require that the messages are related and there is some partial knowledge of the secret key revealed.

The sequences of matrices $(M_\sigma)_{\sigma \in \Sigma}$ that we will consider are matrices that encode DFAs such that the min-entropy of the shortest accepting input word conditioned on the auxiliary information α is at least $\lambda(r)$. See Definitions 6.1 and 6.2 for a formal definition of such a distribution.

[19, Theorem 4] states that the plain HAO15 scheme is semantically secure based on a circular security assumption and the hardness of the decisional learning with error problem (DLWE) for parameters n, q, χ. If we did not publish s_r, then their assumption would imply that Definition 4.1 holds for appropriate parameters.

Given s_r we may test whether the last coordinate of an encoded vector is 0 or 1. Hence we need to consider certain safeguards, which are described in detail in Sect. 5.1. We want that for every additional encoded *state vector*, the last coordinate is 0 with overwhelming probability. This is true for the distributions of evasive DFAs that we will consider. Using s_r we can also learn the entries of the last row of the DFA matrices. Hence, we assume that the last row of the encoded matrices always follows a certain structure. This ensures indistinguishability as required by Definition 4.1.

Finally, we conjecture that the knowledge of the last row of the secret does not weaken the security of the HAO15 matrix encoding scheme. The hardness of (D)LWE with *leaky secrets* was studied by [17].

5   Finite Automata and Transition Matrices

Fix a number of states $r \in \mathbb{N}$. Fix an alphabet Σ and for each symbol $\sigma \in \Sigma$, let $M_\sigma \in \{0, 1\}^{r \times r}$ be the *transition matrix* corresponding to σ.

In case of a finite automata M, Σ represents the different input symbols which induce transitions between the r different states, i.e. $(M_\sigma)_{j,i} = 1$ if and only if there is a transition from state i to state j for an input σ. Hence, such an M_σ acts on the i-th canonical basis vector e_i such that $e_j = M_\sigma e_i$. Without loss of generality, let 1 be the initial state (represented by e_1) and let r be the final state (represented by e_r). There is a distinction between *deterministic* and *non-deterministic* finite automata (DFA and NFA, respectively). On the one hand, a DFA has a unique state transition for each state and input. On the other hand, a NFA may transition into multiple states on each input or transition without any input at all. In general, a NFA will not have a unique accepting state.

5.1   General Safeguards

We will now introduce two general safeguards to avoid partial evaluation and leaking intermediate states and state transitions. These safeguards are important for our specific construction based on the HAO15 matrix encoding scheme of Sect. 3.1 as well as the general construction from arbitrary matrix (graded) encoding schemes we will introduce in Appendix C.

State Transitions. Without loss of generality, let $\Sigma = \{\sigma_1, \ldots, \sigma_m\}$ be the set of symbols, for some $m \in \mathbb{N}$. Consider a DFA with $r \in \mathbb{N}$ states and let r be the accepting state. To avoid leaking state transitions, we need to ensure that the matrices representing the DFA have the following structure:

$$M_{\sigma_1} = \begin{pmatrix} * & * \\ 0 & 0 \end{pmatrix}, \ldots, M_{\sigma_{m-1}} = \begin{pmatrix} * & * \\ 0 & 0 \end{pmatrix}, M_{\sigma_m} = \begin{pmatrix} * & \cdots & * & 0 & 0 \\ \vdots & \ddots & \vdots & \vdots & \vdots \\ * & \cdots & * & 0 & 0 \\ 0 & \cdots & 0 & 1 & 1 \end{pmatrix}.$$

We set the last row of the matrices $M_{\sigma_1}, \ldots, M_{\sigma_{m-1}}$ to zero. This means that none of the input symbols $\sigma_1, \ldots, \sigma_{m-1}$ can transition the DFA into the accepting state r. The structure of the matrix M_{σ_m} is chosen such that σ_m is the unique input symbol which can transition the DFA into the accepting state r. We also allow for an arbitrary number of additional inputs of the symbol σ_m sending the state r to itself.

This ensures that an attacker does not learn anything that is not already public knowledge in the system. As mentioned in Sect. 4, this is important for the validity of the security assumption in our application. We require that the last rows of all transition matrices follow the same structure.

Partial Evaluation. We need to make sure that no adversary can distinguish between states after merely partially evaluating the DFA. To see why, consider the following attack strategy.

We can evaluate the obfuscated DFA on progressively longer input words and each time record the encoded state vector. Although we do not learn the state vector itself, using a zero-testing primitive, we can decide when two states are the same for different inputs. Even if we force a fixed input word length (for example by restricting the zero-test to only be possible after evaluating a certain number of input symbols), we can simply prepend each different word by a fixed prefix. Using statistical analysis on the number of encountered states, we can then try to either construct an accepted input directly or at least (partially) learn the *structure* of the underlying DFA.

To remedy this, we need to make sure that nothing can be learned about individual states after (partial) DFA evaluation, apart from whether or not they are accepting states. The key idea is to *erase* all non-accepting states before zero-testing is possible. For this, consider the following matrix

$$M_f = \begin{pmatrix} 0 \cdots 0\,0 \\ \vdots \ddots \vdots \vdots \\ 0 \cdots 0\,0 \\ 0 \cdots 0\,1 \end{pmatrix} \in \{0,1\}^{r \times r}.$$

It holds that for all canonical basis vectors e_i for $i = 1, \ldots, r-1$ we have $M_f e_i = 0$, whereas $M_f e_r = e_r$. Another way to express this is that the matrix M_f maps all state vectors to the zero vector if they are not equal to the final state vector but leaves the final state vector invariant.

6   Obfuscated Finite Automata

We would like to construct an obfuscator for finite automata. Every finite automaton induces a program $P : \Sigma^* \to \{0,1\}$ that outputs 1 for an accepted input sequence and 0 for a rejected one.

Definition 6.1 (Evasive Finite Automata Collection). *Let $\{\mathcal{M}_r\}_{r \in \mathbb{N}}$ be a collection of finite automata such that every automaton in $\mathcal{M}_r$ has r states. The collection is called* evasive *if there exists a negligible function ϵ such that for every $r \in \mathbb{N}$ and for every polynomial-size input $y \in \Sigma^*$:*

$$\Pr_{M \leftarrow \mathcal{M}_r}[M(y) = 1] \leq \epsilon(r).$$

It is important to limit to polynomial size inputs $y \in \Sigma^*$ in Definition 6.1 since otherwise we could let y be the string that contains all possible substrings of a certain length. We need to consider evasive finite automata since the transition matrices of a non-evasive one can be learned from its input/accept/reject behaviour [3]. It is then natural to use Definition 2.2 – perfect circuit-hiding obfuscation – as the security notion for evasive automata. An adversary finds an accepted input with negligible probability and so cannot recover the description of the automata.

Definition 6.2 (DFA Evasive Distribution with Auxiliary Information). *Consider an ensemble $\mathcal{D} = \{D_\lambda\}_{\lambda \in \mathbb{N}}$ of distributions D_λ over $\mathcal{M}_{r(\lambda)} \times \{0,1\}^{poly(\lambda)}$ where $\{\mathcal{M}_{r(\lambda)}\}_{r(\lambda) \in \mathbb{N}}$ is an evasive finite automata collection. We say that $\mathcal{D}$ is* DFA evasive with auxiliary information *if for every $(M, \alpha) \leftarrow D_\lambda$ the min-entropy of the shortest accepted word $w \in \Sigma^*$ of M conditioned on the auxiliary information α is at least λ.*

Examples of DFA Evasive Distributions. We will give two examples for DFA evasive distributions. See Sect. 1 for definitions of substring matching and conjunctions.

– *String Matching.* Consider an alphabet of three symbols $\Sigma = \{0, 1, \perp\}$, where $\perp$ is the unique symbol that may transition the DFA into the accepting state as Sect. 5.1 demands. Consider U_k, the uniform distribution over $\{0, 1\}^k$. Then any string sampled from U_k has min-entropy at least k. Define now $\{\mathcal{M}_r\}_{r \in \mathbb{N}}$ to be the collection of evasive DFAs with $r = k + 2$ states such that a DFA sampled from $\mathcal{M}_r$ matches some string sampled from U_k. Hence $\{\mathcal{M}_r\}_{r \in \mathbb{N}}$ is an evasive DFA collection which has min-entropy at least $\lambda(r) = r - 2 = k$. This collection is efficiently samplable by sampling a random string x from U_k and outputting the DFA matching the word $x \parallel \perp$ (i.e. x concatenated with $\perp$).

– *Conjunctions.* Another example of an evasive DFA collection are conjunctions. We will need to define what it means for a conjunction to be evasive.

Definition 6.3 (Conjunction Evasive Distribution). *Consider an ensemble $\mathcal{D} = \{D_\mu\}_{\mu \in \mathbb{N}}$ of distributions D_μ over $\{0, 1, \star\}^{n(\mu)}$ for some function $n(\mu)$. We say that $\mathcal{D}$ is* conjunction evasive *if the min-entropy of D_μ is at least μ.*

Consider again the alphabet $\Sigma = \{0, 1, \perp\}$ as above. Given a conjunction evasive distribution D_μ for conjunctions of length $n = n(\mu)$, we can define an evasive DFA collection $\mathcal{M}_r$ with $r = n + 2$ states which has min-entropy at least $\lambda(r) = \mu$: Every DFA from this distribution accepts a string y that satisfies the corresponding conjunction from D_μ.

6.1   Obfuscator and Obfuscated Program

For every evasive DFA M with maximal input length κ, there exists a program
$P_M : \Sigma^* \to \{0,1\}$ that computes whether M accepts an input word $w \in \Sigma^*$
(with $|w| \leq \kappa$) and evaluates to 1 in this case, otherwise to 0. Denote by $\mathcal{P}$
the family of all such programs P_M. The obfuscator $\mathcal{O} : \mathcal{P} \to \mathcal{P}'$ takes one
such program $P_M \in \mathcal{P}$ and uses Algorithm 6.1 to output another program in a
different family denoted by $\mathcal{P}'$.

Algorithm 6.1 uses the HAO15 matrix encoding scheme (assume the maximal
grading is κ) to encode the required matrices and vectors. The output is given by
the tuple $(s_r, (C_\sigma)_{\sigma \in \Sigma}, c)$. In this tuple, s_r is the last row of the HAO15 secret S,
$(C_\sigma)_{\sigma \in \Sigma}$ is the sequence of encodings of the state transition matrices $(M_\sigma)_{\sigma \in \Sigma}$,
and c is an encoding of the first canonical basis vector e_1.

We assume that the initial and accepting state of the finite automaton are
given by the state 1 and state r, respectively. We further assume that the DFA
matrices $(M_\sigma)_{\sigma \in \Sigma}$ satisfy the safeguard requirements described in Sect. 5.1. Erasing partial information from the final state using M_f is equivalent to only being
able to test whether the last coordinate of the state vector is 0 or 1. Recall, in
Sect. 3.1, we assumed that our state vectors are always canonical basis vectors.
This is certainly true for any DFA. Hence publishing only s_r is equivalent to
erasing partial state information using M_f.

As the decoding algorithm is a universal algorithm, we will simply denote the
obfuscated program $\mathcal{O}(P_M)$ with the tuple $(s_r, (C_\sigma)_{\sigma \in \Sigma}, c)$. During the execution
of the obfuscated program, Algorithm 6.2 is used to determine whether an input
word $w \in \Sigma^*$ is accepted by the DFA or not.

Algorithm 6.1. Encoding (Obfuscating the finite automaton)

---

procedure ENCODE($(M_\sigma)_{\sigma \in \Sigma}$)
  Run HAO15 matrix encoding scheme key generation and obtain secret key S.
  Compute $(C_\sigma)_{\sigma \in \Sigma}$ by encoding $(M_\sigma)_{\sigma \in \Sigma}$ such that $SC_\sigma = M_\sigma SG + E$ for all
$\sigma \in \Sigma$.
  Compute state vector c by encoding e_1 such that $Sc = \beta e_1 + e$.
  Let s_r be the last row of S.
  return $(s_r, (C_\sigma)_{\sigma \in \Sigma}, c)$
end procedure

6.2   Obfuscated Program Evaluation

We may evaluate the obfuscated automaton on a word $w \in \Sigma^*$ with $|w| \leq \kappa$ as
follows:

1. Compute the encoded vector c_w corresponding to $(\prod_{i=|w|}^{1} M_{w_i})e_1$ using the
   sequence $(C_\sigma)_{\sigma \in \Sigma}$ and the encoded initial state c.

2. The input word w is accepted if c_w is an encryption of the r-th canonical basis vector and thus we simply output $\lceil (1/\beta)(s_r \cdot c_w \mod q) \rfloor$.

Again, Algorithm 6.2 presents an algorithmic description.

Algorithm 6.2. Evaluation (Executing the obfuscated program)

> **procedure** EVALUATE($s_r, (C_\sigma)_{\sigma \in \Sigma}, c; w \in \Sigma^*$)
>> **for all** $i = 1, \ldots, |w|$ **do**
>>> Update the state vector $c = C_{w_i} G^{-1}(c)$.
>> **end for**
>> **return** $\lceil (1/\beta)(s_r \cdot c \mod q) \rfloor$
> **end procedure**

Lemma 6.1 (Correctness). *Consider the algorithms* ENCODE *(Algorithm 6.1) and* EVALUATE *(Algorithm 6.2) (based on the modified HAO15 matrix FHE scheme with maximal grading κ determined by Eq. (3.2)). For every DFA $\mathcal{M}$ represented by $(M_\sigma)_{\sigma \in \Sigma}$, for every*

$$(s_r, (C_\sigma)_{\sigma \in \Sigma}, c) \leftarrow \text{ENCODE}((M_\sigma)_{\sigma \in \Sigma})$$

and for every input $w \in \Sigma^*$ with $|w| < \kappa$ it holds that

$$\text{EVALUATE}(s_r, (C_\sigma)_{\sigma \in \Sigma}, c; w) = P_\mathcal{M}(w).$$

Proof. Recall the modified HAO15 matrix FHE scheme from Sect. 3.1. Given a sequence of transition matrices $(M_\sigma)_{\sigma \in \Sigma}$, the obfuscator produces the tuple $(s_r, (C_\sigma)_{\sigma \in \Sigma}, c)$ such that C_σ is an encoding of M_σ for all $\sigma \in \Sigma$. This means that $SC_\sigma = M_\sigma SG + E$, where S is the HAO15 secret. Further, c is an encoding such that $Sc = \beta e_1 + e$, where e_1 is the first canonical basis vector. Finally, s_r is the last row of the secret S.

The evaluation algorithm computes the final state vector

$$c_w = \left(\bigodot_{i=|w|}^{1} C_{w_i} \right) G^{-1}(c).$$

This corresponds to the following calculation with plaintext information

$$t = \left(\prod_{i=|w|}^{1} M_{w_i} \right) e_1.$$

The automaton accepts the input if $t = e_r$. We see that c_w is an encoding of t such that $Sc_w = \beta t + e$ for some error e. Given only s_r, we have the following equation

$$\begin{pmatrix} 0_{(r-1) \times (n+r)} \\ s_r \end{pmatrix} c_w = \beta \begin{pmatrix} 0_{r-1} \\ t_r \end{pmatrix} + \begin{pmatrix} 0_{r-1} \\ e' \end{pmatrix},$$

where e' is the last coordinate of e. By Eq. (3.2) the error is bounded by $\|e_\kappa\|_\infty \le \beta/2$ if we choose the maximal grading κ such that

$$\kappa = \frac{q}{4\sqrt{n}(n+r)\lceil \log(q) \rceil}.$$

If $|w| < \kappa$, then $|e'| \le \|e\|_\infty < \|e_\kappa\|_\infty \le \beta/2$. Hence, computing $\lceil (1/\beta)(s_r \cdot c_w \mod q) \rfloor$ correctly determines whether c_w is an encryption of the accepting state e_r or not. Correctness follows as required. □

6.3 Security

In this section we analyse the security of our DFA obfuscator using the HAO15 matrix encoding scheme which we introduced in Sect. 3.1.

Note that we make no claim of security once an accepting input is known to an adversary. First and foremost, there is a classical result by [3] that shows that the description of a finite automaton can be learned from oracle access when given accepted and rejected inputs. Second, we need to keep in mind that an actual matrix graded encoding scheme could exhibit non-modelled (and thus unwanted) behaviour, cf. [1,2, Appendix A].

Theorem 6.1. Let $\mathcal{D} = \{D_\lambda\}_{\lambda \in \mathbb{N}}$ be an efficiently samplable DFA evasive distribution with auxiliary information (Definition 6.2). Assume that for every $\lambda \in \mathbb{N}$ it holds that HAO15 with security parameter λ is DFA secure for D_λ (Definition 4.1). Then the obfuscator $\mathcal{O}$ is a VBB obfuscator for $\mathcal{D}$.

Proof. The obfuscator is functionality preserving by Lemma 6.1. It is also clear that the obfuscator causes only a polynomial slowdown when compared to an unobfuscated DFA since the evaluation Algorithm 6.2 runs in time polynomial in all the involved parameters.

By Theorem 2.1 it suffices to show that there exists a (non-uniform) PPT simulator $\mathcal{S}$ such that, for the distribution ensemble $\mathcal{D} = \{D_\lambda\}_{\lambda \in \mathbb{N}}$, it holds that

$$(\mathcal{O}(P), \alpha) \stackrel{c}{\approx} (\mathcal{S}(|P|), \alpha),$$

where $(P, \alpha) \leftarrow D_\lambda$. Recall that D_λ is a distribution over $\{\mathcal{M}_{r(\lambda)}\}_{r(\lambda) \in \mathbb{N}} \times \{0, 1\}^{\text{poly}(\lambda)}$.

We will construct the simulator $\mathcal{S}$: It takes as input $|P|$ and determines the parameter $r \in \mathbb{N}$ and runs Algorithm 6.3.

Denote now with $(s_r, (C_\sigma)_{\sigma \in \Sigma}, c)$ a real instance obtained from obfuscating an evasive DFA given by the transition matrices $(M_\sigma)_{\sigma \in \Sigma}$ sampled from the distribution $\mathcal{M}_{r(\lambda)}$ such that the DFA has min-entropy λ. Similarly, let $(s'_r, (C'_\sigma)_{\sigma \in \Sigma}, c')$ be the output from the simulator $\mathcal{S}$ called on r. This is essentially an obfuscation of a random evasive DFA given by the transition matrices $(M'_\sigma)_{\sigma \in \Sigma}$, again with min-entropy λ. The last rows of M_σ and M'_σ are the same for all $\sigma \in \Sigma$. This follows from our assumption of Sect. 6.1: The input $(M_\sigma)_{\sigma \in \Sigma}$ to Algorithm 6.1 satisfies the safeguards of Sect. 5.1.

Algorithm 6.3. Encoding Simulator

---

procedure SIMULATEENCODE($r \in \mathbb{N}$)

    Sample random DFA $(M'_\sigma)_{\sigma \in \Sigma}$ from $\mathcal{M}_r$, this DFA has min-entropy λ.

    Run HAO15 matrix encoding scheme key generation and obtain secret key S'.

    Compute $(C'_\sigma)_{\sigma \in \Sigma}$ by encoding $(M'_\sigma)_{\sigma \in \Sigma}$ such that $S'C'_\sigma = M'_\sigma S'G + E$ for all $\sigma \in \Sigma$.

    Compute state vector c' by encoding e_1 such that $S'c' = \beta e_1 + e$.

    Let s'_r be the last row of S'.

    return $(s'_r, (C'_\sigma)_{\sigma \in \Sigma}, c')$

end procedure

We will now show, using a sequence of distributions, that $(s_r, (C_\sigma)_{\sigma \in \Sigma}, c, \alpha)$ and $(s'_r, (C'_\sigma)_{\sigma \in \Sigma}, c', \alpha)$ are computationally indistinguishable. The strategy is to start from the real and simulated distributions and remove state transitions one by one from both until we meet in the middle where both encoded DFAs are the same. Hence, we need to consider the matrices $M_\sigma^\Delta = M_\sigma - M'_\sigma$. If an entry of M_σ^Δ is 1, we remove a state transition from M_σ; if an entry is -1, we remove a state transition from M'_σ. This ensures that the min-entropy of the intermediate DFAs can only stay the same or grow, but never shrink. Note that removing state transitions may result in a system that does not accept any inputs, or may not even be an encoding of a DFA.

- Game $(0, 0, 0)$: Here we consider $(s_r, (C_\sigma)_{\sigma \in \Sigma}, c)$, a real instance obtained from the DFA obfuscator $\mathcal{O}$.
- Game $(0, 0, 1)$: Here we consider $(s'_r, (C'_\sigma)_{\sigma \in \Sigma}, c')$, the output of the simulator $\mathcal{S}$.
- Game $(i, j, 0)$ (for $1 \leq i < r, 1 \leq j \leq r$): Start from the real DFA matrices $(M_\sigma)_{\sigma \in \Sigma}$. For all $\sigma \in \Sigma$, do the following:

    Step 1: Replace full columns.   Step 2: Replace partial columns.

    for $1 \leq t < j$ **do**   **for** $1 \leq s \leq i$ **do**

        for $1 \leq s < r$ **do**   **if** $(M_\sigma^\Delta)_{s,j} = 1$ **then**

            if $(M_\sigma^\Delta)_{s,t} = 1$ **then**   Replace $(M_\sigma)_{s,j}$ with 0.

                Replace $(M_\sigma)_{s,t}$ with 0.   **end if**

            end if   **end for**

        end for

    end for

This yields the distribution $(s_r, (C_\sigma^{(i,j,0)})_{\sigma \in \Sigma}, c)$, where $(C_\sigma^{(i,j,0)})_{\sigma \in \Sigma}$ is a randomly chosen encoding of the resulting transition matrices with respect to the fixed secret key S.

- Game $(i, j, 1)$ (for $1 \leq i < r, 1 \leq j \leq r$): Start from the simulated DFA matrices $(M'_\sigma)_{\sigma \in \Sigma}$. For all $\sigma \in \Sigma$, do the following:

Step 1: Replace full columns.

> **for** $1 \leq t < j$ **do**
>> **for** $1 \leq s < r$ **do**
>>> **if** $(M_\sigma^\Delta)_{s,t} = -1$ **then**
>>>> Replace $(M_\sigma')_{s,t}$ with 0.
>>>
>>> **end if**
>>
>> **end for**
>
> **end for**

Step 2: Replace partial columns.

> **for** $1 \leq s \leq i$ **do**
>> **if** $(M_\sigma^\Delta)_{s,j} = -1$ **then**
>>> Replace $(M_\sigma')_{s,j}$ with 0.
>>
>> **end if**
>
> **end for**

This yields the distribution $(s_r', (C_\sigma^{(i,j,1)})_{\sigma \in \Sigma}, c')$, where $(C_\sigma^{(i,j,1)})_{\sigma \in \Sigma}$ is a randomly chosen encoding of the resulting transition matrices with respect to the fixed secret key S'.

For $1 \leq i < r$, $1 \leq j \leq r$, in Game $(i, j, \{0, 1\})$, the min-entropy of the encoded DFA is at least $\lambda(r)$ since we only ever remove state transitions. We have that Game $(i, j, \{0, 1\})$ and Game $(i+1, j, \{0, 1\})$ for $0 \leq i < r-1, 0 \leq j \leq r$ are indistinguishable by the DFA security assumption. We also have that Game $(r - 1, j, \{0, 1\})$ and Game $(1, j + 1, \{0, 1\})$ for $1 \leq j < r$ are indistinguishable by the DFA security assumption. Finally, the two Games $(r - 1, r, 0)$ and $(r - 1, r, 1)$ encode the same DFA under different secret keys S and S' and again are indistinguishable. Hence, by a hybrid argument, it follows that

$$(s_r, (C_\sigma)_{\sigma \in \Sigma}, c, \alpha) \stackrel{c}{\approx} (s_r', (C_\sigma')_{\sigma \in \Sigma}, c', \alpha).$$

We showed that a real obfuscation is computationally indistinguishable from a simulated instance. This completes the proof.

7 Parameters

[15] gave example parameters and runtime analysis for both the matrix FHE schemes of [19] (see Sect. 3.1) and [15]. For a finite automaton with 1024 states, they chose a 42-bit modulus q. Note that such an overstretched modulus is potentially dangerous in the GGHLM19 setting and does not satisfy the claimed security level as was shown by [21]. Nevertheless, the HAO15 scheme is assumed to be secure for these parameters and allows for input words of length up to roughly 140000 symbols.

In our case, we achieve obfuscated evaluation of any evasive DFA with sufficient min-entropy. Since we require zero-testing, we obtain a slightly smaller maximal grading. For HAO15, recall Eq. (3.2) which we can use to compute the maximal grading if we encode DFA matrices. With a zero-testing primitive, the same parameters as above ($n = 1024, r = 1024, q \approx 2^{42}$) yield a maximal input word length of roughly 10^5 symbols. This is already more than enough for the applications that we described in the introduction, such as substring matching or virus testing. Alternatively, we can search for substrings in an input which is longer than the bound κ by running the obfuscated program on overlapping substrings of the original input.

8   Conclusion

We have introduced a new special purpose obfuscator for deterministic finite automata that in particular solves the problem of obfuscated substring matching. We have shown that the obfuscator is VBB secure and perfect circuit-hiding based on a new computational assumption involving the HAO15 FHE matrix scheme.

Open problems include generalisations of substring matching such as securely matching biometric information (for example DNA). This problem seems to be related to obfuscating fuzzy matching with respect to edit distance.

Acknowledgements. We thank the Marsden Fund of the Royal Society of New Zealand for funding this research, and the reviewers for suggestions.

A   Matrix (Graded) Encoding Scheme

In this section we will give a condensed version of a matrix (graded) encoding scheme which describes the essential parts as introduced by [7,8]. A matrix graded encoding scheme consists of the following algorithms:

- *Key Generation.* Given a matrix dimension $n \in \mathbb{N}$, a compatible security parameter $\lambda \in \mathbb{N}$, and a maximal grading $\kappa \in \mathbb{N}$, the key generation algorithm outputs a secret key **sk** and public key **pk**.
- *Matrix Encoding.* Given a matrix $M \in \{0,1\}^{n \times n}$, the encoding algorithm uses the secret key **sk** to output a (possibly *randomised*) encoding C of M.
- *Vector Encoding.* Given a vector $v \in \{0,1\}^n$, the encoding algorithm uses the secret key **sk** to output a (possibly *randomised*) encoding c of v.
- *Zero-testing.* Given an encoded matrix C or vector c, the zero-testing algorithm uses the public key **pk** to decide whether C or c is an encoding of the zero matrix or zero vector, respectively.

There are algorithms that compute the *sum* and *product* operations of two encodings, we will abbreviate them with standard mathematical notation. The homomorphic properties of the encoded matrices should be as follows:

- *Additive.* Given two encodings C_1, C_2 of M_1, M_2, it holds that the encoding of $M_1 + M_2$ equals $C_1 + C_2$ (up to randomisation).
- *Multiplicative.* Given encodings $C_1, C_2, \ldots, C_i$ of $M_1, M_2, \ldots, M_i$, where $i \leq \kappa$, it holds that the encoding of $M_1 M_2 \cdots M_i$ equals $C_1 C_2 \cdots C_i$ (up to randomisation).
- *Applying Matrix to Vector.* Given encodings $C_1, C_2, \ldots, C_i$ of $M_1, M_2, \ldots, M_i$, where $i \leq \kappa - 1$, and an encoded vector c of v, it holds that the encoding of $M_1 M_2 \cdots M_i v$ equals $C_1 C_2 \cdots C_i c$ (up to randomisation).

In the more general definition of [8], there is a grading that we can attach to each encoding. Then it is only possible to add encodings at the same *level* to produce another encoding of the same level. When multiplying elements of different levels, say ℓ_1 and ℓ_2, we produce an encoding of a higher level, for example $\ell_1 + \ell_2$. We should think of the public key **pk** as a collection of individual zero-testing keys $\mathbf{pk} = \{\mathbf{pk}_\ell\}_{\ell \in L}$. Concretely, for a fixed level ℓ, if the public key contains $\mathbf{pk}_\ell \in \mathbf{pk}$ then we may zero-test encodings of level ℓ. The downside is that in all instantiations such a grading implies much larger public keys. We will avoid this at the cost of an additional *circular security* assumption.

B   GGH15

In this section we remind the reader of the matrix graded encoding scheme by [16]. We are working over the ring $R = \mathbb{Z}/q\mathbb{Z}$ for some modulus q. Let $m, n \in \mathbb{N}$ be matrix dimensions.

Matrix Encoding. The key idea is the following: Choose a matrix $A \in R^{n \times m}$, a secret matrix $S \in R^{n \times n}$ with small entries is encoded as a matrix $C \in R^{m \times m}$ with small entries such that

$$AC = SA + E \tag{B.1}$$

for some small error matrix $E \in R^{n \times m}$.

Key Generation. Sampling an encoding C as in Eq. (B.1) generally requires a lattice trapdoor, such as given by [23] for example. In practice, depending on a security parameter $\lambda \in \mathbb{N}$, we fix a modulus q, and matrix dimensions $n, m \in \mathbb{N}$. The private key is then the trapdoor and the public key is the matrix A. The small matrices are sampled from a β-bounded distribution χ. Fix a maximal grading $\kappa \in \mathbb{N}$, then the modulus should satisfy $q > (4m\beta)^\kappa \lambda^{\omega(1)}$ which we require for security and additionally for a κ grading.

Vector Encoding. Similarly, given a secret vector $s \in R^n$ with small entries, we can encode it by sampling a short vector $c \in R^m$ according to $Ac = sA + e$ for some short error vector $e \in R^m$.

Homomorphic Operations. This construction is additively and multiplicatively homomorphic. Take two encodings such that $AC_1 = S_1A + E_1$ and $AC_2 = S_2A + E_2$, then we have

$$A(C_1 + C_2) = (S_1 + S_2)A + E' \tag{B.2}$$

for some small E'. Obviously we can only add a finite number of such encodings before the error grows too big. Similarly, for the multiplication of two encodings we have

$$AC_1C_2 = (S_1A + E_1)C_2 = S_1(S_2A + E_2) + E_1C_2 = S_1S_2A + E' \tag{B.3}$$

for some small E'. Finally, applying an encoded matrix C to a vector c works via the identity

$$ACc = (SA + E)c = S(sA + e) + Ec = SsA + e'. \tag{B.4}$$

Zero-Testing. Given an encoding C of a secret S at *multiplicative level* ℓ such that the error E is bounded by $\|E\|_\infty \leq \beta(2m\beta)^{\ell-1}$, zero-testing is possible. Compute AC and test whether $\|AC\|_\infty \leq \beta(2m\beta)^{\ell-1}$. If $S = 0$ then this test succeeds and if $S \neq 0$ then $\|AC\|_\infty > \beta(2m\beta)^{\ell-1}$ with high probability.

Error Bounds and Correctness. Assuming $\|C\|_\infty, \|S\|_\infty, \|E\|_\infty \leq \beta$ for some threshold β, it is immediately clear from Eq. (B.2) that after adding two encodings, the resulting error is bounded by $\|E'\|_\infty \leq 2\beta$. Similarly, from Eq. (B.3) we see that after multiplying two encodings, the resulting error is bounded by $\|E'\|_\infty \leq 2m\beta^2$ (and also for the secret $S_1 S_2$ and encoding $C_1 C_2$).

We said that the maximal grading of the encoding scheme with our choice of parameters is κ. By induction we find that after multiplying κ encodings, the error is bounded by $\beta(2m\beta)^{\kappa-1}$. Now assume $\|c\|_\infty, \|s\|_\infty, \|e\|_\infty \leq \beta$ for an encoding c of a vector s. Finally, by induction, from Eq. (B.4) we find that after applying a sequence of $\kappa - 1$ matrices to an encoded vector, the resulting error is bounded by $\|e'\|_\infty \leq \beta(2m\beta)^{\kappa-1}$, see also [24].

Security. [11] considered the GGH15 encoding scheme from the viewpoint of obfuscation for *matrix branching programs*. They give rules about the form of the secret matrices S such that security can be reduced to the LWE assumption for lattices. To encode arbitrary matrices M, they give an embedding of M into a larger matrix S that is still compatible with matrix-multiplication. [11] showed that their generalised GGH15 encodings for branching programs are secure under LWE. They are using the stronger graded encoding scheme model which we mentioned in Sect. A that restricts homomorphic interaction between levels. Specifically, in the general GGH15 scheme, they encode a secret S along a *path* (i, j) such that $A_j C = S A_i + E$ for different random matrices A_i, A_j. In the end we only publish the very first A_1 that is required for the final zero-test.

In our setting, we set all those matrices A_i equal to a single matrix A, except for a special *final* matrix M_f which we encode with respect to a different matrix B such that $B C_f = M_f A + E$. We do this because unlike circuits, which can be translated into matrix branching programs of a fixed depth, DFAs usually have loops that connect states to themselves under input of certain symbols. We will keep the matrix A secret and only publish B such that we are forced to apply the final matrix M_f before zero-testing. Hence, we need to assume circular security for the encodings. This also shrinks the size of the public parameters and allows for a much larger number of DFA inputs in our application.

C   General Encoding Schemes

In Sect. 6 we gave a specialised construction based on our extension of the HAO15 matrix FHE scheme (recall Sect. 3.1). In doing so, we were able to give a security reduction from VBB and perfect circuit-hiding to the decisional assumption of Sect. 4. In this section we want to sketch a generic construction for obfuscated evasive DFAs from arbitrary matrix graded encoding schemes. We will refrain from giving a security reduction to a generic assumption. This should rather be investigated on a case-by-case basis.

We will assume that we are given a matrix graded encoding scheme (with maximal grading κ) such as described in Sect. 3. The obfuscator runs the key generation algorithm such that the secret key **sk** allows to encode matrices at and between two subsequent levels. We require that the public key **pk** allows for zero-testing only at the second level.

The obfuscator takes as an input an evasive DFA represented by the transition matrices $(M_\sigma)_{\sigma \in \Sigma}$ and outputs the tuple $(s_r, (C_\sigma)_{\sigma \in \Sigma}, c)$. In the output tuple, c is an encoding of the first canonical basis vector e_1 at the first level and z is an encoding of the r-th canonical basis vector e_r at the second level, $(C_\sigma)_{\sigma \in \Sigma}$ is the sequence of encodings of the state transition matrices $(M_\sigma)_{\sigma \in \Sigma}$ at the first level and C_f is an encoding of the final matrix M_f between the first and second level. We assume that the initial and accepting state of the finite automaton are given by the state 1 and state r, respectively. If necessary, transform the DFA matrices $(M_\sigma)_{\sigma \in \Sigma}$ to satisfy the safeguard requirements described in Sect. 5.1. See Algorithm C.1 for an algorithmic description.

Algorithm C.1. Encoding (Obfuscating the finite automaton)

---

procedure ENCODE($(M_\sigma)_{\sigma \in \Sigma}$)

Run matrix graded encoding scheme key generation and obtain **sk, pk**.

Compute $(C_\sigma)_{\sigma \in \Sigma}$ by encoding $(M_\sigma)_{\sigma \in \Sigma}$ at the first level using **sk** (no zero-testing possible).

Compute C_f by encoding M_f at the second level using **sk** (zero-testing possible).

Compute state vectors c and z by encoding e_1 at the first and e_r at the second level using **sk**, respectively.

return $(\textbf{pk}, (C_\sigma)_{\sigma \in \Sigma}, c, C_f, z)$

end procedure

We may evaluate the obfuscated automaton on a word $w \in \Sigma^*$ with $|w| \leq \kappa$ as follows:

1. Compute the encoded vector c_w corresponding to $(\prod_{i=1}^{|w|} M_{w_i})e_1$ using the sequence $(C_\sigma)_{\sigma \in \Sigma}$ and the encoded initial state c.
2. Evaluate the zero-test using **pk** on $C_f c_w - z$. The word w is accepted by the automaton represented by $(M_\sigma)_{\sigma \in \Sigma}$ if the zero-test succeeds and we output 1 in this case, 0 otherwise.

See Algorithm C.2 for an algorithmic description.

Algorithm C.2. Evaluation (Executing the obfuscated program)

---

   procedure EVALUATE$(s_r, (C_\sigma)_{\sigma \in \Sigma}, c; w \in \Sigma^*)$
      Initialize the state vector $s = c$.
      for all $i = 1, \ldots, |w|$ **do**
         Update the state vector $s = C_{w_i} s$.
      end for
      Evaluate the zero-test using **pk** on $C_f s - z$.
      return 1 **if** the zero-test failed **else** 0
   end procedure

We argue that one should consider VBB or perfect circuit-hiding obfuscation instead of iO for evasive finite automata. One important reason is the possibility of *zeroising attacks*. This class of attacks affects several obfuscation constructions based on graded encoding schemes. The idea is that given an encoding of zero, we get a system of equations over $\mathbb{Z}$ instead of $\mathbb{Z}/q\mathbb{Z}$ that depend not only on small error terms but also on the secret matrices themselves. This seems to be especially problematic for iO schemes which are the prevalent constructions using graded encoding schemes.

References

1. Ananth, P., Jain, A., Naor, M., Sahai, A., Yogev, E.: Universal constructions and robust combiners for indistinguishability obfuscation and witness encryption. In: Robshaw, M., Katz, J. (eds.) CRYPTO 2016. LNCS, vol. 9815, pp. 491–520. Springer, Heidelberg (2016). https://doi.org/10.1007/978-3-662-53008-5_17
2. Ananth, P., Jain, A., Naor, M., Sahai, A., Yogev, E.: Universal obfuscation and witness encryption: boosting correctness and combining security. Cryptology ePrint Archive, report 2016/281 (2016). https://eprint.iacr.org/2016/281
3. Balcázar, J.L., Díaz, J., Gavaldà, R., Watanabe, O.: Algorithms for learning finite automata from queries: a unified view. In: Du, D.Z., Ko, K.I. (eds.) Advances in Algorithms, Languages, and Complexity, pp. 53–72. Springer, Boston (1997). https://doi.org/10.1007/978-1-4613-3394-4_2
4. Barak, B., Bitansky, N., Canetti, R., Kalai, Y.T., Paneth, O., Sahai, A.: Obfuscation for evasive functions. In: Lindell, Y. (ed.) TCC 2014. LNCS, vol. 8349, pp. 26–51. Springer, Heidelberg (2014). https://doi.org/10.1007/978-3-642-54242-8_2
5. Bartusek, J., Lepoint, T., Ma, F., Zhandry, M.: New techniques for obfuscating conjunctions. In: Ishai, Y., Rijmen, V. (eds.) EUROCRYPT 2019. LNCS, vol. 11478, pp. 636–666. Springer, Cham (2019). https://doi.org/10.1007/978-3-030-17659-4_22
6. Bishop, A., Kowalczyk, L., Malkin, T., Pastro, V., Raykova, M., Shi, K.: A simple obfuscation scheme for pattern-matching with wildcards. In: Shacham, H., Boldyreva, A. (eds.) CRYPTO 2018. LNCS, vol. 10993, pp. 731–752. Springer, Cham (2018). https://doi.org/10.1007/978-3-319-96878-0_25
7. Brakerski, Z., Rothblum, G.N.: Obfuscating conjunctions. In: Canetti, R., Garay, J.A. (eds.) CRYPTO 2013. LNCS, vol. 8043, pp. 416–434. Springer, Heidelberg (2013). https://doi.org/10.1007/978-3-642-40084-1_24

8. Brakerski, Z., Rothblum, G.N.: Virtual black-box obfuscation for all circuits via generic graded encoding. In: Lindell, Y. (ed.) TCC 2014. LNCS, vol. 8349, pp. 1–25. Springer, Heidelberg (2014). https://doi.org/10.1007/978-3-642-54242-8_1

9. Brakerski, Z., Vaikuntanathan, V., Wee, H., Wichs, D.: Obfuscating conjunctions under entropic ring LWE. In: ITCS 2016, pp. 147–156. ACM (2016)

10. Canetti, R., Rothblum, G.N., Varia, M.: Obfuscation of hyperplane membership. In: Micciancio, D. (ed.) TCC 2010. LNCS, vol. 5978, pp. 72–89. Springer, Heidelberg (2010). https://doi.org/10.1007/978-3-642-11799-2_5

11. Chen, Y., Vaikuntanathan, V., Wee, H.: GGH15 beyond permutation branching programs: proofs, attacks, and candidates. In: Shacham, H., Boldyreva, A. (eds.) CRYPTO 2018. LNCS, vol. 10992, pp. 577–607. Springer, Cham (2018). https://doi.org/10.1007/978-3-319-96881-0_20

12. Desmoulins, N., Fouque, P.-A., Onete, C., Sanders, O.: Pattern matching on encrypted streams. In: Peyrin, T., Galbraith, S. (eds.) ASIACRYPT 2018. LNCS, vol. 11272, pp. 121–148. Springer, Cham (2018). https://doi.org/10.1007/978-3-030-03326-2_5

13. Galbraith, S.D., Zobernig, L.: Obfuscated fuzzy hamming distance and conjunctions from subset product problems. In: Hofheinz, D., Rosen, A. (eds.) TCC 2019. LNCS, vol. 11891, pp. 81–110. Springer, Cham (2019). https://doi.org/10.1007/978-3-030-36030-6_4

14. Garg, S., Gentry, C., Halevi, S., Raykova, M., Sahai, A., Waters, B.: Candidate indistinguishability obfuscation and functional encryption for all circuits. SIAM J. Comput. 45(3), 882–929 (2016)

15. Genise, N., Gentry, C., Halevi, S., Li, B., Micciancio, D.: Homomorphic encryption for finite automata. In: Galbraith, S.D., Moriai, S. (eds.) ASIACRYPT 2019. LNCS, vol. 11922, pp. 473–502. Springer, Cham (2019). https://doi.org/10.1007/978-3-030-34621-8_17

16. Gentry, C., Gorbunov, S., Halevi, S.: Graph-induced multilinear maps from lattices. In: Dodis, Y., Nielsen, J.B. (eds.) TCC 2015. LNCS, vol. 9015, pp. 498–527. Springer, Heidelberg (2015). https://doi.org/10.1007/978-3-662-46497-7_20

17. Goldwasser, S., Kalai, Y., Peikert, C., Vaikuntanathan, V.: Robustness of the learning with errors assumption. In: Innovations in Computer Science, pp. 230–240 (2010)

18. Goyal, R., Koppula, V., Waters, B.: Lockable obfuscation. In: FOCS 2017, pp. 612–621. IEEE (2017)

19. Hiromasa, R., Abe, M., Okamoto, T.: Packing messages and optimizing bootstrapping in GSW-FHE. In: Katz, J. (ed.) PKC 2015. LNCS, vol. 9020, pp. 699–715. Springer, Heidelberg (2015). https://doi.org/10.1007/978-3-662-46447-2_31

20. Kuzurin, N., Shokurov, A., Varnovsky, N., Zakharov, V.: On the concept of software obfuscation in computer security. In: Garay, J.A., Lenstra, A.K., Mambo, M., Peralta, R. (eds.) ISC 2007. LNCS, vol. 4779, pp. 281–298. Springer, Heidelberg (2007). https://doi.org/10.1007/978-3-540-75496-1_19

21. Lee, C., Wallet, A.: Lattice analysis on MiNTRU problem. Cryptology ePrint Archive, report 2020/230 (2020). https://eprint.iacr.org/2020/230

22. Lynn, B., Prabhakaran, M., Sahai, A.: Positive results and techniques for obfuscation. In: Cachin, C., Camenisch, J.L. (eds.) EUROCRYPT 2004. LNCS, vol. 3027, pp. 20–39. Springer, Heidelberg (2004). https://doi.org/10.1007/978-3-540-24676-3_2

23. Micciancio, D., Peikert, C.: Trapdoors for lattices: simpler, tighter, faster, smaller. In: Pointcheval, D., Johansson, T. (eds.) EUROCRYPT 2012. LNCS, vol. 7237, pp. 700–718. Springer, Heidelberg (2012). https://doi.org/10.1007/978-3-642-29011-4_41
24. Wichs, D., Zirdelis, G.: Obfuscating compute-and-compare programs under LWE. In: FOCS 2017, pp. 600–611. IEEE (2017)

On Index Calculus Algorithms
for Subfield Curves

Steven D. Galbraith[1], Robert Granger[2], Simon-Philipp Merz[3(✉)],
and Christophe Petit[4,5]

[1] Mathematics Department, University of Auckland, Auckland, New Zealand
s.galbraith@auckland.ac.nz
[2] Surrey Centre for Cyber Security, Department of Computer Science,
University of Surrey, Guildford, UK
r.granger@surrey.ac.uk
[3] Information Security Group, Royal Holloway, University of London, Egham, UK
simon-philipp.merz.2018@rhul.ac.uk
[4] Département d'informatique, Université libre de Bruxelles, Brussels, Belgium
christophe.petit@ulb.be
[5] School of Computer Science, University of Birmingham, Birmingham, UK

Abstract. In this paper we further the study of index calculus methods
for solving the elliptic curve discrete logarithm problem (ECDLP). We
focus on the index calculus for subfield curves, also called Koblitz curves,
defined over $\mathbb{F}_q$ with ECDLP in $\mathbb{F}_{q^n}$. Instead of accelerating the solution
of polynomial systems during index calculus as was predominantly done
in previous work, we define factor bases that are invariant under the q-
power Frobenius automorphism of the field $\mathbb{F}_{q^n}$, reducing the number of
polynomial systems that need to be solved. A reduction by a factor of
$1/n$ is the best one could hope for. We show how to choose factor bases to
achieve this, while simultaneously accelerating the linear algebra step of
the index calculus method for Koblitz curves by a factor n^2. Furthermore,
we show how to use the Frobenius endomorphism to improve symmetry
breaking for Koblitz curves. We provide constructions of factor bases
with the desired properties, and we study their impact on the polynomial
system solving costs experimentally.

1 Introduction

Elliptic curve cryptography (ECC) is a classical approach to public-key cryptography based on the algebraic structure of elliptic curves over finite fields. The
use of elliptic curves in cryptography was suggested independently by Koblitz
and Miller in 1985 [17,19]. During the last decades, ECC has become increas-
ingly important because shorter keys yield the same security as in cryptographic
schemes based on discrete logarithms in plain Galois fields or on factorisation
problems. This has allowed to reduce storage and transmission requirements for
various cryptographic applications. Today, ECC is ubiquitous and can for example be found in SSL/TLS which secures the majority of connections in the World
Wide Web (see e.g. [24]).

© Springer Nature Switzerland AG 2021
O. Dunkelman et al. (Eds.): SAC 2020, LNCS 12804, pp. 115–138, 2021.
https://doi.org/10.1007/978-3-030-81652-0_5

Let $\mathbb{F}_{q^n}$ denote the finite field of cardinality q^n, where q is the power of a prime. An elliptic curve is a non-singular algebraic plane curve satisfying an equation of the form

$$E : y^2 + a_1 xy + a_3 y = x^3 + a_2 x^2 + a_4 x + a_6, \quad a_i \in \mathbb{F}_{q^n}$$

and a point at infinity denoted $\mathcal{O}_E$. The set of points $(x,y) \in \mathbb{F}_{q^n}^2$ on an elliptic curve is an abelian group under the "chord and tangent rule", with $\mathcal{O}_E$ being the identity element. For non-negative integers a we define the multiplication by a map as $[a] : E \to E$, $P \mapsto P + P + \cdots + P$ (a times).

The elliptic curve discrete logarithm (ECDLP) is the following computational problem. Given points $P, Q \in E(\mathbb{F}_{q^n})$, find an integer a, if it exists, such that $Q = [a]P$. Many ECC protocols assume that the ECDLP is computationally infeasible for the curves used.

Like any other discrete logarithm problem, ECDLP can be solved using generic algorithms such as Baby-step-Giant-step, Pollard's ρ and their variants [23]. These algorithms can be parallelised efficiently, but have exponential runtime complexity, i.e. roughly square root of the size r of the cyclic subgroup $\langle P \rangle \subset E(\mathbb{F}_{q^n})$. More precisely, Van Oorschot and Wiener showed how to get a heuristic expected running time of $(\sqrt{\pi/2} + o(1))\sqrt{r}$ group operations using "distinguished points" [28]. Therefore, the difficulty of the ECDLP depends, among other things, on the size of r. Moreover, r should be prime to prevent Pohlig-Hellman attacks [22]. To ensure that $\#E(\mathbb{F}_{q^n})$ has a large subgroup of prime order, n is usually chosen to be either 1 or a prime as $\#E(\mathbb{F}_q)$ divides $\#E(\mathbb{F}_{q^n})$.

Index calculus is another approach to solve a discrete logarithm problem by reducing it to a linear algebra problem. Given an elliptic curve, one defines a subset of the curve named the *factor base* and tries to express points of the form $[a_i]P + [b_i]Q$ as a sum of factor base elements. After collecting sufficiently many linearly independent of these so-called *relations*, one can compute the discrete logarithm by solving a system of linear equations.

A *subfield curve*, or *Koblitz curve*, is an elliptic curve defined over a small finite field $\mathbb{F}_q$ which is considered over a large extension field. Put differently, a Koblitz curve is defined using coefficients from $\mathbb{F}_q$ with ECDLP in $E(\mathbb{F}_{q^n})$. Koblitz curves were used in practice because the q-th power Frobenius endomorphism $\pi : E \to E$, $(x,y) \mapsto (x^q, y^q)$ can be used to devise fast point multiplication algorithms via Frobenius expansion [27]. While half of the elliptic curves that were standardised by NIST in the current NIST SP 800-186 draft are Koblitz curves defined over $\mathbb{F}_2$, it is highlighted there that they are now deprecated. It was shown that ECDLP in a Koblitz curve $E(\mathbb{F}_{q^n})$ can be solved at $1/\sqrt{n}$ of the cost compared to a general elliptic curve [30].

The slowest part of index calculus on elliptic curves is the relation collection. Accelerating this step of the algorithm by exploiting the additional structure provided by Koblitz curves compared to general elliptic curves was mentioned as an open problem in the literature [9]. An interesting approach to this question was considered by Gorla and Massierer [12], but it did not lead to a dramatic speed-up. Their idea was to represent the ECDLP instance as a trace zero variety on which index calculus is performed directly. For curves of genus $g > 1$, Gaudry gives one example of a Frobenius invariant factor base and describes how this yields a speed-up [10]. We answer the open question by emulating this idea to the harder case where $g = 1$.

Our Contribution: We describe how the relation collection can be sped up when using factor bases that are carefully chosen with respect to the Frobenius endomorphism acting on Koblitz curves. First, we show how this allows to improve symmetry breaking. Then, we focus on factor bases that are closed under the Frobenius endomorphism. We show that we can reduce such a factor base easily to a smaller one generating the same number of relations. As a consequence, after finding one relation in the larger factor base, one can rewrite them in terms of a reduced factor base consisting of representatives for each Frobenius orbit in the larger factor base. Under certain conditions it is then sufficient to collect $1/n$ as many relations leading to a speed-up of n for the relation collection. Moreover, the dimension of the sparse matrix in the linear algebra step decreases by a factor of $1/n^2$ reducing the cost of the linear algebra step during index calculus by $1/n^2$.

We provide concrete constructions for factor bases with the necessary properties for some classes of elliptic curves and examine experimentally how some of the choices influence the complexity of computations during index calculus.

While Pollard's ρ algorithm remains the fastest method to solve ECDLP instances used in cryptography in practice, this work shows that the performance gap between index calculus and Pollard's ρ is smaller for Koblitz curves. More precisely, the ECDLP in a Koblitz curve $E(\mathbb{F}_{q^n})$ can be solved faster than for general elliptic curves by a factor of $\sqrt{n}$ using Pollard's ρ [30] compared to our speed-up by roughly n.

The paper is organised as follows. Section 2 recalls the index calculus framework, provides details on the current state-of-the-art index calculus methods for ECDLP and references related work. In Sect. 3 we present our improvements for Koblitz curves. This is achieved by choosing factor bases satisfying certain properties with respect to the Frobenius endomorphism. To make these results more concrete, we provide constructions for such factor bases in Sect. 4. In Sect. 5, we display our experimental results before concluding the paper in Sect. 6.

2   Index Calculus

Apart from generic algorithms such as Pollard's ρ, baby-step-giant-step or kangaroo algorithms, one approach to solve discrete logarithm problems (in any cyclic group $\langle P \rangle$) is index calculus. This method tries to reduce the discrete logarithm problem to linear algebra. In this section we recall the index calculus framework to solve discrete logarithms and we recollect how it is applied to elliptic curves in practice.

2.1 Framework of Index Calculus

The basic framework of index calculus is as follows:

1. Define a subset $\mathcal{F}$ of $\langle P \rangle \subset E$, called the factor base.
2. Collect relations:
   (a) Pick random integers a_j and b_j and compute $R = [a_j]P + [b_j]Q$.
   (b) Try to decompose R as a sum of elements of $\mathcal{F}$.
   (c) If the decomposition is successful, call $[a_j]P + [b_j]Q = \sum_{P_i \in \mathcal{F}}[e_{ij}]P_i$ a relation and store both the vector (e_{ij}) as a row of a matrix and the integers (a_j, b_j).
   (d) Repeat the collection of relations until there are $|\mathcal{F}|$ linearly independent ones.
3. Use linear algebra modulo r to compute a non-zero column vector $(\gamma_1, \ldots, \gamma_{|\mathcal{F}|})^T$ in the right kernel of the matrix (e_{ij}) with $1 \le i, j \le |\mathcal{F}|$.
4. Compute the discrete logarithm of Q as $-(\sum_{j=1}^{|\mathcal{F}|} a_j \gamma_j)(\sum_{j=1}^{|\mathcal{F}|} b_j \gamma_j)^{-1} \mod r$, if $\sum_{j=1}^{|\mathcal{F}|} b_j \gamma_j$ is invertible modulo r, otherwise return to Step 2.

The efficiency of the index calculus approach depends on the choice of the factor base $\mathcal{F}$. While it should be possible to write a large proportion of group elements as a sum of elements in $\mathcal{F}$ (to prevent step 2(b) from failing to often), the set $\mathcal{F}$ should not be too large, as we need to collect $\#\mathcal{F}$ relations. Moreover, the decomposition of group elements into a sum of elements in $\mathcal{F}$ should be efficient if it exists.

To tackle these problems, index calculus in elliptic curves requires two crucial ingredients: Semaev's summation polynomials and the Weil restriction of scalars.

One can use the formulae of the group law to decompose a point R into a sum of points of the factor base, $R = P_1 + \cdots + P_k$, if $\mathcal{F}$ has a nice algebraic description. To compute this in practice, Semaev's summation polynomials are used. Our improvements in this paper concern subfield curves and most such curves used in practice are defined over a field of characteristic 2. For simplicity, we therefore recall the results due to Semaev [25] only for this case. However, we want to emphasise that all our improvements presented later in the paper apply to general subfield curves defined over fields of size q.

A subfield curve E with solutions in $\mathbb{F}_{2^n}$ defined over $\mathbb{F}_2$ is specified by an equation

$$E : y^2 + xy = x^3 + ax^2 + 1, \text{ where } a \in \{0, 1\}. \tag{1}$$

Semaev's summation polynomials $\{S_m \in \mathbb{F}_{q^n}[x_1, \ldots, x_m]\}_{m \in \mathbb{N}}$ have the defining property that there is a root at $(X_1, \ldots, X_m) \in \overline{\mathbb{F}}_{q^n}^m$, i.e. $S_m(X_1, \ldots, X_m) = 0$, if and only if there exist $(Y_1, \ldots, Y_m) \in \overline{\mathbb{F}}_{q^n}^m$ such that $(X_i, Y_i) \in E(\overline{\mathbb{F}}_{q^n})$ for all $1 \le i \le m$ and $(X_1, Y_1) + (X_2, Y_2) + \cdots + (X_m, Y_m) = 0$ on the curve.

Theorem 1. *[25] The summation polynomials of E given by Eq. (1) are recursively defined by*

$$S_2(x_1, x_2) := x_1 + x_2,$$

$$S_3(x_1, x_2, x_3) := (x_1 x_2 + x_1 x_3 + + x_2 x_3)^2 + x_1 x_2 x_3 + 1,$$

and for $m \geq 4$ and any k, $1 \leq k \leq m - 3$, the m-th summation polynomial is

$$S_m(x_1, \ldots, x_m) := \mathsf{Res}_X \left(S_{m-k}(x_1, \ldots, x_{m-k-1}, X), \ S_{k+2}(x_{m-k}, \ldots, x_m, X) \right)$$

where Res_X denotes the resultant with respect to X. For $m \geq 2$ the polynomial S_m is symmetric and has degree 2^{m-2} in each variable x_i.

For general elliptic curves defined over fields of even and odd characteristic such formulas exist as well but we omit the details here. For a general formula see Lemma 3.4 of [3].

As a result of trying to decompose points as a sum of factor base elements using Semaev polynomials, we will obtain a system of polynomial equations defined over $\mathbb{F}_{q^n}$. Using Weil restriction of scalars, this can be converted into equations over $\mathbb{F}_q$. The basic idea hereby is to rewrite a polynomial equation over an extension field $\mathbb{F}_{q^n}$ as n polynomial equations over $\mathbb{F}_q$.

Lemma 1. *Let q be a prime power, $n \geq 1$ an integer and fix a vector space basis $\{\theta_1, \ldots, \theta_n\}$ for $\mathbb{F}_{q^n}$ over $\mathbb{F}_q$. Let $f \in \mathbb{F}_{q^n}[x_1, \ldots, x_m]$. There exist unique polynomials $f_k \in \mathbb{F}_q[y_{i,j}]$, $1 \leq i \leq m, 1 \leq j \leq n$, for $1 \leq k \leq n$ such that*

$$f(y_{1,1}\theta_1 + \cdots + y_{1,n}\theta_n, \ldots, y_{m,1}\theta_1 + \cdots + y_{m,m}\theta_n) = \sum_{k=1}^{n} \theta_k f_k(y_{i,j}).$$

If $f(x_1, \ldots, x_m) = 0$ for some $x_1, \ldots, x_m \in \mathbb{F}_{q^n}$ then there exist $y_{i,j} \in \mathbb{F}_q$ such that $x_i = \sum_{j=1}^{\ell} y_{i,j}\theta_j$ and $f_k(y_{i,j}) = 0$ for all $1 \leq k \leq n$.

Now, we are ready to describe the index calculus for elliptic curves in more detail.

2.2 Index Calculus for Elliptic Curves

Semaev was the first one to sketch a framework for index calculus on elliptic curves using the summation polynomials and Weil descent [25], which was fully developed by Gaudry [11] and Diem [3] later.

The approach works as follows: choose an $\mathbb{F}_q$-vector subspace $V = \langle v_1, \ldots, v_{n'} \rangle \subset \mathbb{F}_{q^n}$ of dimension $1 \leq n' \leq n$ and define the factor base to be

$$\mathcal{F} = \{P \in E(\mathbb{F}_{q^n}) : x(P) \in V\}, \tag{2}$$

where $x(P)$ refers to the x-coordinate of a point P.

To collect relations, choose random integers a, b modulo the order of $\langle P \rangle$ and compute the point $R = aP + bQ$ in $\langle P \rangle$. To decompose such a point R as a sum over the factor base, i.e. $R = P_1 + \cdots + P_m$ with $P_i \in \mathcal{F}$, one tries to find roots of the $(m+1)$-th summation polynomials $S_{m+1}(x_1, \ldots, x_m, x(R)) \in \mathbb{F}_{q^n}[x_1, \ldots, x_{m+1}]$ with $x_i \in V$.

To make sure that the P_i in the decomposition lie in the factor base $\mathcal{F}$, one rewrites the summation polynomial using the linear constraints $x_i = v_1 y_{i,1} + v_2 y_{i,2} + \cdots + v_{n'} y_{i,n'}$. This yields a new polynomial in $\mathbb{F}_{q^n}[y_{1,1}, \ldots, y_{m,n'}]$, i.e. in $m \cdot n'$ variables, with $y_{i,j} \in \mathbb{F}_q$. More precisely, we can look at the polynomial as an element f in $\mathbb{F}_{q^n}[y_{1,1}, \ldots, y_{m,n'}]/\langle y_{i,j}^q - y_{i,j} \rangle$, where $\langle y_{i,j}^q - y_{i,j} \rangle$ for $1 \leq i \leq m$ and $1 \leq j \leq n'$ denotes the ideal generated by the field equations.

In order to find solutions to this polynomial f, previous work deemed it most efficient to look at it as a system of polynomials over $\mathbb{F}_q$ and use Gröbner basis methods [14]. That is to apply Weil restriction of scalars to get a system of n polynomials in $\mathbb{F}_q[y_{i,j}], 1 \leq i \leq m, 1 \leq j \leq n$. Namely, let $\{\theta_1, \ldots, \theta_n\}$ be a basis for $\mathbb{F}_{q^n}$ as $\mathbb{F}_q$ vector space. By Lemma 1, we can decompose f as

$$f = f_1 \theta_1 + f_2 \theta_2 + \cdots + f_n \theta_n$$

for some $f_i \in \mathbb{F}_q[y_{1,1}, \ldots, y_{m,n'}]$. Due to the linear independence of $\{\theta_1, \ldots, \theta_n\}$, finding a solution to f is equivalent to solving the polynomial system of n equations

$$f_1 = f_2 = \cdots = f_n = 0$$

in mn' variables. According to [6,16], the best way to solve this system is to compute a Gröbner basis with respect to the graded reverse lexicographical monomial order using Faugère's F4 or F5 algorithm [4,5] and apply the FGLM [7] algorithm to transform the basis into a Gröbner basis with respect to the lexicographical order.

Remark 2. Choosing n' and m is an important decision. In general, one chooses $n'm \approx n$ in order to have as many equations as indeterminates in the polynomial system. This is the natural choice in the sense that it is the smallest value for $n'm$ where one expects to get a solution. In the following, we will assume that $n'm \approx n$.

For a discussion of over- and under-determined systems, we refer to Galbraith and Gaudry [9].

We want to give an estimation of the two most expensive steps of index calculus, the relation collection and the linear algebra steps. To analyse the cost of the relation collection, let $H_1(n, n', m)$ denote the cost of solving one polynomial system with n equations and mn' variables of the above form.

Theorem 3. *Let $n = n' \cdot m + k$, $k \geq 0$. Under the heuristic assumption that a factor base defined by Eq. (2) has size $\#V = q^{n'}$, the cost of the relation collection step during index calculus is approximately*

$$\frac{q^{n'+k}}{2^m} \cdot m! \cdot H_1(n, n', m).$$

Proof. First, we determine the probability that a random point R can be written as a sum of m points from $\mathcal{F}$. Since the group operation on elliptic curves is commutative, if one can write $R = P_1 + \cdots + P_m$ then there are, in general, $m!$ such decompositions. Therefore, we can estimate the number of points that can be represented as sums of m points of our factor base as $\frac{q^{n'm}}{m!}$. Since E has roughly q^n points, we can estimate the probability of a relation naively as $\frac{q^{n'm}}{q^n m!} = (q^k \cdot m!)^{-1}$.

When solving one polynomial system during the relation collection step, we solve for the x-coordinates of points on the curve. Since the factor base $\mathcal{F}$ has some symmetry by negation, there are 2^m choices for the signs for points corresponding to the same m x-coordinates in the polynomial system (2^{m-1} of which are linearly independent). Similarly, we can restrict the computation to half of the targeted points due to negation. Therefore, the probability to find a relation when solving one polynomial system is $\frac{2^m \cdot q^{n'm}}{q^n m!} = \frac{2^m}{q^k \cdot m!}$. Intuitively, solving one polynomial system with respect to the x-coordinates allows to check for 2^m relations of points on the elliptic curve simultaneously.

Hence, we expect to solve $\frac{q^k}{2^m} \cdot m!$ polynomial systems to find a single relation. Assuming roughly the same cost for the solution of all the polynomial systems, $H_1(n, n', m)$, the collection of $q^{n'}$ relations costs $\frac{q^{n'+k}}{2^m} \cdot m! \cdot H_1(n, n', m)$. $\square$

Note that the preceding proof assumes the same cost for solving polynomial systems with and without solutions. This is a simplification and not true in general, e.g. for systems without a solution we might already reach a contradiction earlier in the computation.

To estimate the cost of the linear algebra step, we note that the number of non-zero coefficients for all the points in the factor base per relation is very low, namely at most m. Therefore, it is possible to compute the linear algebra step using sparse linear algebra techniques. Algorithms such as the Wiedemann algorithm [29] allow to find solutions to a matrix of dimension N^2 containing m entries per row in $\mathcal{O}(mN^2)$ multiplications. Let $|\mathcal{F}|$ denote the size of the factor base. As we aim to collect roughly $|\mathcal{F}|$ relations, we get the following theorem.

Theorem 4. *The cost of the linear algebra step is $\mathcal{O}(m \cdot |\mathcal{F}|^2)$.*

Under the heuristic assumption that a factor base as defined by Eq. (2) has size approximately $\#V = q^{n'}$, the cost of the linear algebra step is $\mathcal{O}(m \cdot q^{2n'})$.

In practice, there are various tricks to lower the degree of the polynomial system we need to solve during the decomposition step in the relation collection. For a summary of different approaches we refer to [9]. Amongst ideas like breaking the symmetry, which we will address in the next subsection, there are approaches to introduce additional variables to lower the degree of the polynomial systems. These are sometimes referred to as "the splitting trick" or "unrolling the resultant" [13, 14, 26].

2.3   Breaking Symmetries

As addition on elliptic curves is commutative, the symmetric group acts on solutions $(P_1, \ldots, P_m)$ to the point decomposition problem in the relation search. This leads to an inconvenient $m!$ factor in the complexity statements. To "break symmetry" usually refers to removing this redundancy. One approach is to rewrite the summation polynomial in terms of generators of the ring of invariants under the action of the symmetric group, i.e. the elementary symmetric polynomials, as was done in [6]. With respect to these new variables, the polynomial system arising from the summation polynomial has usually $m!$ fewer solutions and the degrees of the polynomials are potentially lower. Given a solution to this system, one needs to recompute a solution in the original variables. However, this only needs to be done for the successful systems and is relatively fast.

Another idea to mitigate the factor of $m!$ in the success probability during the point decomposition is attributed in [20] to Matsuo. He suggested the use of m disjoint factor bases $\mathcal{F}_i$ of size $q^{n'}$ and forcing P_i to be in different factor bases $\mathcal{F}_i$. While this approach allows to avoid the factor $m!$ in the probability to decompose a point over our factor base (see Theorem 3), the factor base is then a union of m sets of size $q^{n'}$ and thus we need to collect m times as many relations. Consequently, the relation collection step is only accelerated by a factor of $(m-1)!$.

Moreover, the cost of the linear algebra step (see Theorem 4) increases by a factor m^2, although the linear system is a block diagonal matrix and some optimisation may be possible.

3   Index Calculus for Koblitz Curves

In this section we present our main improvements for index calculus methods on Koblitz curves. We start by presenting a new approach for symmetry breaking in Koblitz curves. Then, we show how to exploit Frobenius invariant factor bases to speed up the decomposition of points into factor base elements. We conclude with a brief comparison of performance of the different methods.

3.1   Improved Symmetry Breaking for Koblitz Curves

We present a novel way of symmetry breaking for Koblitz curves that builds on top of Matsuo's idea described in Sect. 2.3, but allows for a full saving of $m!$ in the relation collection step and does not have an increased linear algebra cost by a factor of m^2.

As we mention in the introduction, elliptic curves that are interesting in cryptography have one large cyclic subgroup $\langle P \rangle$ of prime order r containing the ECDLP.

Lemma 2. *Let E be a Koblitz curve defined over $\mathbb{F}_q$ with one large cyclic subgroup $\langle P \rangle$ of prime order r and let $\pi : E(\mathbb{F}_{q^n}) \to E(\mathbb{F}_{q^n})$, $(x, y) \mapsto (x^q, y^q)$ denote the q-th power Frobenius endomorphism. Then there exists some $\lambda \in \mathbb{Z}$, $1 \leq \lambda \leq r - 1$ such that $\pi(Q) = [\lambda]Q$ for all $Q \in \langle P \rangle$.*

Proof. The Frobenius endomorphism preserves the order of points on the curve. Therefore, $\pi(P)$ is another point on the Koblitz curve of order r. Since there is only one large cyclic subgroup of order r, it follows that $\pi(P) \in \langle P \rangle$ and there exists some scalar $1 \leq \lambda \leq r-1$ such that $\pi(P) = [\lambda]P$. As scalar multiplication commutes with the Frobenius map, we have $\pi(Q) = [\lambda]Q$ for all $Q \in \langle P \rangle$.   □

It is known that for any point $P \in E$, the Frobenius endomorphism π satisfies

$$\pi^2(P) \pm [t]\pi(P) + [q]P = \mathcal{O}_E,$$

where t is the trace of the curve E, i.e. the integer satisfying $|E(\mathbb{F}_{q^n})| = q^n + 1 - t$. Therefore, it can be shown that the value λ of the preceding lemma is one of the roots of the quadratic congruence

$$X^2 \pm tX + q \equiv 0 \pmod{r},$$

which makes it efficiently computable.

The key of our method is to choose the vector space defining the factor bases in a specific way. As before, let V be an $\mathbb{F}_q$ vector subspace of $\mathbb{F}_{q^n}$ of dimension n' and let $\mathcal{F} = \{P \in E(\mathbb{F}_{q^n}) : x(P) \in V\}$.

Let V_i be vector spaces that give rise to m pairwise "disjoint" factor bases with $\mathcal{F}_1 = \mathcal{F}$, $\mathcal{F}_2 = \pi(\mathcal{F})$, ..., $\mathcal{F}_m = \pi^{m-1}(\mathcal{F})$. Given a normal basis of $\mathbb{F}_{q^n}$ over $\mathbb{F}_q$, it is easy to construct such V_i. Namely, let $\dim V = n'$ be the desired dimension of V with $n'm \leq n$ and let β be a normal basis element of $\mathbb{F}_{q^n}$ over $\mathbb{F}_q$. We can take the vector space $V_i := \langle \beta^{q^{mj+i}} | j \in \{0 \ldots, n'-1\} \rangle$ to define the factor base $\mathcal{F}_i$ for $i = 1, \ldots, m$.

Given such factor bases one can break symmetry as follows:

1. Decompose points as sums of the form

$$R = P_1 + \cdots + P_m, \quad \text{where} \quad P_i \in \mathcal{F}_i, \tag{3}$$

2. Rewrite the relation as

$$R = P_1' + \lambda P_2' + \cdots + \lambda^{m-1} P_m' \quad \text{where all } P_i' \in \mathcal{F}_1 = \mathcal{F}.$$

The restriction $P_i \in \mathcal{F}_i$ is equivalent to the constraints $x(P_i) \in V_i$ that become linear in the Weil restriction. The first part is therefore just like Matsuo's idea.

The second step is possible as a consequence of Lemma 2 and the relation between the different factor bases $\mathcal{F}_i$: for any $P_i \in \mathcal{F}_i$, $i = 1, \ldots, m$, we can find some $P_i' \in \mathcal{F}_1$ such that $P_i = \pi^{(i-1)}(P_i') = \lambda^{(i-1)}(P_i')$.

The analysis given in the proof of Theorem 3 applies still except for saving the full $m!$ term in the probability of finding a relation. Let $H_2(n, n', m)$ denote the cost of solving the polynomial systems during point decomposition for the described factor bases. We arrive at the following theorem.

Theorem 5. *Let $n = n' \cdot m + k$ and let E be a Koblitz curve with coefficients in $\mathbb{F}_q$ and ECDLP in $E(\mathbb{F}_{q^n})$. The cost of the relation collection for index calculus on E is*

$$\frac{q^{n'+k}}{2m} \cdot H_2(n, n', m).$$

Theorem 4 still applies and the cost of the linear algebra step remains $\mathcal{O}(m \cdot q^{2n'})$, as $|\mathcal{F}_1| = q^{n'}$.

Note that this construction applies to every Koblitz curve. Under the assumption that $H_1 = H_2$, the choice of a factor base as described above allows to reduce the necessary work in the relation collection by a factor $m!$ without inflating the size of the factor base. Therefore, the approach also does not suffer any additional cost in the linear algebra step.

3.2   Frobenius Invariant Factor Bases

In this section, we give another idea to accelerate index calculus for Koblitz curves $E(\mathbb{F}_{q^n})$ defined over $\mathbb{F}_q$ even further. The underlying idea is similar to the one used by Joux and Lercier [15] to solve discrete logarithms in the multiplicative group of extension fields. There, the idea was to use factor bases that are Galois invariant.

Our goal in this section is to show how this can be done for Koblitz curves. We use factor bases closed under Frobenius endomorphisms, i.e. $\pi(\mathcal{F}) = \mathcal{F}$. Once a point has been decomposed, we can rewrite the relation in terms of a smaller factor base consisting of representatives for each Frobenius orbit in the factor base. This allows to reduce the number of linearly independent relations we need to collect by a factor n, accelerating the relation collection accordingly. Simultaneously, the dimension of the matrix in the linear algebra step is reduced, decreasing the cost of this step by n^2.

One can define a unique representative of each Frobenius orbit in an ad-hoc manner to get a factor base $\mathcal{F}'$ of size approximately $|\mathcal{F}|/n$. An immediate consequence of Lemma 2 is that every point $P \in \mathcal{F}$ can be written as $P = \pi^j(P') = \lambda^j P'$ for some $P' \in \mathcal{F}'$ and $j \in \{0, \ldots, n-1\}$.

In the relation collection, one uses the summation polynomials to write $R = P_1 + \cdots + P_m$ where $P_i \in \mathcal{F}$. Then one reduces each relation to one consisting entirely of points in the reduced factor base $\mathcal{F}'$.

However, one Frobenius invariant factor base will in general not be enough to generate n linearly independent relations under the action of the Frobenius endomorphism, as we will show in Lemma 3.

First, we recall some background. Let the degree of the extension n be prime to the characteristic of the field $\mathbb{F}_{q^n}$. The Frobenius map π generates the Galois group $\mathsf{Gal}(\mathbb{F}_{q^n}/\mathbb{F}_q)$ and its characteristic polynomial acting on $\mathbb{F}_{q^n}$, considered as a $\mathbb{F}_q$ vector space, is $x^n - 1$. The polynomial $x^n - 1$ factors over $\mathbb{F}_q$ and a unique $\mathbb{F}_q$ subspace $V_f \subset \mathbb{F}_{q^n}$ corresponds to every $\mathbb{F}_q$-irreducible factor f dividing $x^n - 1$ in $\mathbb{F}_q[x]$. By Schur's Lemma, any Galois invariant subspace of $\mathbb{F}_{q^n}$ is a direct sum of such V_f.

Now, we are ready to show that we do not always get n independent relations under the Frobenius action from a single Galois invariant subspace.

Lemma 3. *Let $\mathcal{F}$ be a Frobenius invariant factor base of dimension n' defined by the polynomial $\ell(X) = \sum_{j=0}^{n'} c_j X^j$ dividing $X^n - 1$ in $\mathbb{F}_q[X]$. Given a decomposition of a point $R = \sum_{i=1}^{m} P_i$ as sum of elements in $\mathcal{F}$, the Frobenius action provides at most n' linearly independent relations.*

Proof. This is an immediate consequence of

$$\pi^{n'} \left(\sum_{i=1}^{m} P_i \right) = \sum_{i=1}^{m} \pi^{n'}(P_i) = \sum_{i=1}^{m} \sum_{j=0}^{n'-1} c_j \pi^j (P_i) = \sum_{j=0}^{n'-1} c_j \pi^j \left(\sum_{i=1}^{m} P_i \right) \quad (4)$$

Even though the order of the Frobenius endomorphism is n, when applying the endomorphism to a relation with respect to a Frobenius invariant vector space one only gets n' independent relations. Let $H_3(n, n', m)$ denote the cost of solving the polynomial systems during point decomposition for the described factor bases.

Theorem 6. *As before, let $n = n' \cdot m + k$ and let E be a Koblitz curve with coefficients in $\mathbb{F}_q$ and ECDLP in $E(\mathbb{F}_{q^n})$.*

Given a single Frobenius invariant factor base $\mathcal{F}$ defined by a Galois invariant vector subspace of $\mathbb{F}_{q^n}$ of size $q^{n'}$ such that applying the Frobenius endomorphism to a relation provides n' linearly independent relations, the cost of relation collection for index calculus on E is

$$\frac{1}{n'} \cdot \frac{q^{n'+k}}{2^m} \cdot m! \cdot H_3(n, n', m)$$

and the cost of the linear algebra step is in $\mathcal{O}(\frac{m}{n^2} \cdot q^{2n'})$.

Proof. As in Theorem 3, the probability that a random point R can be written as a sum of m points of $\mathcal{F}$ is $\frac{2^m}{q^k \cdot m!}$. However, because applying Frobenius yields $n' - 1$ additional relations for free, we only need to find $\frac{1}{n'} q^{n'}$ such relations. Thus, the cost of the relation search becomes $\frac{1}{n'} \cdot \frac{q^{n'+k}}{2^m} \cdot m! \cdot H_3(n, n', m)$.

For the linear algebra step, we can choose a unique representative in each Frobenius orbit of factor base elements and reduce each relation to one consisting only of such representatives as described at the beginning of this section. Hence, Theorem 4 implies that the cost of the linear algebra step is reduced by a factor n^2 to $\mathcal{O}(\frac{m}{n^2} \cdot q^{2n'})$. $\quad \Box$

Note, that the linear dependence in Lemma 3 is a consequence of all the points in the sum having been chosen from the same factor base. To get the full saving of $1/n$ in the relation collection, we combine Matsuo's idea of using m different factor bases for symmetry breaking with Frobenius invariance of the factor bases.

Assume we have m Galois invariant factor bases $\mathcal{F}_i$ such that applying the Frobenius endomorphism to a single relation of the form $R = P_1 + \cdots + P_m$ with $P_i \in \mathcal{F}_i$ yields n linearly independent relations. Then not only do we save the symmetry factor $(m-1)!$, as described by Matsuo, but by the Frobenius action we also get n independent relations instead of n'. Intuitively, the reason for this is that in Eq. (4) the coefficients c_j will be different for each index i.

In each factor base we can choose a unique representative in the Galois orbits, but there are m distinct factor bases so the cost of linear algebra is only reduced by a factor $\left(\frac{n}{m}\right)^2$. Let $H_4(n, n', m)$ be the cost of solving one polynomial system during point decomposition in this case.

Theorem 7. *As before, let $n = n' \cdot m + k$ and let E be a Koblitz curve with coefficients in $\mathbb{F}_q$ and ECDLP in $E(\mathbb{F}_{q^n})$. Given m distinct Frobenius invariant factor bases $\mathcal{F}$ of size $q^{n'}$ such that applying Frobenius to sums of m points from distinct factor bases yields linearly independent relations. Then, the cost of the relation collection for index calculus on E is*

$$\frac{1}{n} \cdot \frac{q^{n'+k}}{2^m} \cdot m \cdot H_4(n, n', m)$$

and the cost of the linear algebra step is in $\mathcal{O}(\frac{m^3}{n^2} \cdot q^{2n'})$.

In Sect. 4, we will discuss some constructions of factor bases that are closed under the Frobenius endomorphism. They have a nice algebraic description, which allows them to be easily substituted for the variables in the summation polynomial to restrict the polynomial system to factor base elements.

Remark 8. Note that the overall speed-up factor to solve an instance of ECDLP is relative to the original cost $R + L$, where R is the cost of the relation collection and L is the cost of the linear algebra prior to the improvements presented in this paper. By reducing the relation collection cost by n and linear algebra cost by n^2, the overall speed-up factor is $n^2(R+L)/(nR+L)$. Depending on the relation between R and L, this expression corresponds to a speed-up between n and n^2.

3.3   Comparison of Different Variants

We summarize the results on the performance of the different variations of the index calculus methods described in this section.

We follow the convention of the previous sections that $n = n'm + k$ and the $(m+1)$-th summation polynomial is used to decompose points during the relation collection. Table 1 summarises the cost of various approaches. The relation collection column shows the number of polynomial systems that need to be solved to collect the required number of relations. Each of these polynomial systems arises from the Weil descent of the $(m+1)$-th summation polynomial with variables restricted to the x-coordinates defining the factor bases (as in Sect. 2.2), has n equations and $n'm$ variables. While our methods clearly reduce

Table 1. Cost of the relation collection and linear algebra steps for different index calculus methods solving ECDLP in $E(\mathbb{F}_{q^n})$

Method	Relation collection	Linear algebra	Reference
General index calculus	$m! \cdot \frac{q^{n'+k}}{2^m} \cdot H_1(n, n', m)$	$\mathcal{O}(m \cdot q^{2n'})$	[3,8,25]
Sym. breaking with m factor bases	$m \cdot \frac{q^{n'+k}}{2^m} \cdot H_1(n, n', m)$	$\mathcal{O}(m^3 \cdot q^{2n'})$	[20]
Sym. breaking for Koblitz curves	$\frac{q^{n'+k}}{2^m} \cdot H_2(n, n', m)$	$\mathcal{O}(m \cdot q^{2n'})$	This paper
One Frobenius inv. factor base from a Galois inv. vector space	$\frac{m!}{n'} \cdot \frac{q^{n'+k}}{2^m} \cdot H_3(n, n', m)$	$\mathcal{O}(\frac{m}{n^2} \cdot q^{2n'})$	This paper
Frobenius inv. and symmetry breaking combined	$\frac{m}{n} \cdot \frac{q^{n'+k}}{2^m} \cdot H_4(n, n', m)$	$\mathcal{O}(\frac{m^3}{n^2} \cdot q^{2n'})$	This paper

both the number of systems to solve and the linear algebra costs, we stress that using different factor bases may a priori lead to polynomial systems that are harder (or easier) to solve using Gröbner basis methods. We study these costs experimentally in Sect. 5. Finally, we note that the lower three methods in Table 1 are only applicable to subfield curves defined over $\mathbb{F}_q$.

We want to emphasise that there have been various improvements and variants of index calculus since the work listed in the references in Table 1. We refer to Section 9 of Galbraith-Gaudry [9] for further references. However, we note that these works were targeting improvements in the complexity of solving polynomial systems arising in index calculus rather than to lower the number of systems that require solving as displayed in Table 1. Depending on the specific construction used to define the Frobenius invariant factor bases, these improvements carry over to the reduced number of polynomial systems that need to be solved.

4 Frobenius Invariant Factor Bases

In the previous section, we have seen how factor bases closed under the Frobenius endomorphism can be used to accelerate both the relation collection and the linear algebra steps when using index calculus to solve ECDLP instances. Therefore, an important problem is to find such factor bases of suitable size. Moreover, we want the factor bases to have a nice algebraic description in order to get polynomial systems that are similarly fast to solve as the ones described in Sect. 2.2.

In this section, we present the construction of such Frobenius invariant factor bases for some classes of elliptic curves. The first construction is a new idea based on linearised polynomials, while the others use Galois invariant subsets of finite fields constructed from isogenies between commutative algebraic groups, as described by Couveignes and Lercier [2].

4.1 Linearised Polynomials

When using $\mathbb{F}_q$-vector subspaces V of $\mathbb{F}_{q^n}$ to define the factor base with respect to the abscissa of points on the curve, a factor base is Frobenius invariant if and only if the vector space V is Galois invariant. In this subsection we want to address this case.

Let $\mathbb{F}_{q^n}$ be an extension field of $\mathbb{F}_q$. A *linearised polynomial* $f \in \mathbb{F}_{q^n}[x]$ is a polynomial for which the exponents of all the constituent monomials are powers of q, e.g.

$$f(x) = \sum_{i=0}^{k} a_i x^{q^i} \text{ , with } a_i \in \mathbb{F}_{q^n}.$$

This class of polynomials has one particular property that makes it interesting for this work: the set of roots of a linearised polynomial is a $\mathbb{F}_q$ vector space and is closed under the q-th power Frobenius map if and only if $a_i \in \mathbb{F}_q$.

As we wrote prior to Lemma 4, the irreducible factors of $x^n - 1$ in $\mathbb{F}_q[x]$ correspond to unique Galois invariant $\mathbb{F}_q$ subspaces $V_f \subset \mathbb{F}_{q^n}$ and every Galois invariant subspace is a direct sum of such V_f. Thus, finding Galois invariant $\mathbb{F}_q$ vector subspaces of $\mathbb{F}_{q^n}$ depends on the factorisation of $x^n - 1$ over $\mathbb{F}_q[x]$.

We use the remainder of this section to demonstrate how to obtain Frobenius invariant factor bases in the case of Koblitz curves defined over characteristic 2 fields, which are the most common ones in practice. However, the method can be generalised easily to fields of odd characteristics.

Lemma 4. *([18], Lemma 7). Let n be an odd prime, let ℓ denote the multiplicative order of 2 modulo n and let $n = s\ell + 1$. The polynomial $x^n - 1$ factors in $\mathbb{F}_2[x]$ as $(x-1)f_1 f_2 \dots f_s$, where the f_i are distinct irreducible polynomials of degree ℓ.*

When defining a factor base using some vector space V corresponding to the polynomial f_i, the size of V depends on the degree ℓ of f_i. Restricting ourselves to Galois invariant vector spaces, means losing the fine control over the size of $\mathcal{F}$, as we will see in the following.

Suppose the order of 2 modulo n is ℓ. Then by Lemma 4 $x^n - 1$ has factors $f_j = \sum_k f_{j,k} x^k$ of degree ℓ. Introducing the linearised polynomial

$$F_j(X) = \sum_k f_{j,k} X^{2^k}$$

we have that $F_j(X) \mid X^{2^n} - X$ and so we can define

$$\mathcal{F} = \{P \in E(\mathbb{F}_{2^n}) : F_j(x(P)) = 0\}.$$

As F_j is a linearised polynomial with coefficients in $\mathbb{F}_q$, its set of roots is Galois invariant and thus we have $\pi(\mathcal{F}) = \mathcal{F}$. Moreover, from the degree of f_j we can estimate the size of $|\mathcal{F}|$ to be approximately 2^ℓ. Note, that one can group several polynomial factors together to get larger sets $\mathcal{F}$ of size $2^{k \cdot \ell + \epsilon}$, where $\epsilon \in \{0, 1\}$ is due to the factor $(x - 1)$ in Lemma 4 and $k \leq s$, $k \in \mathbb{Z}$, is the number of polynomial factors of degree ℓ.

Consequently, using linearised polynomials we cannot get Galois invariant subspaces of arbitrary size. In particular, we do not have any fine control over the size of $\mathcal{F}$ when the order of 2 modulo n is large. However, if the order of 2 modulo n is small, i.e. $\ell \ll n - 1$, which happens for example when $n = 2^l - 1$ is a Mersenne prime, or if ℓ divides the desirable dimension of our factor base, then linearised polynomials allow for a very easy construction of Frobenius invariant factor bases.

If the factor base $\mathcal{F}$ is defined using a linearised polynomial, it is specified by linear constraints in the Weil restriction and thus it is easily deployable in index calculus. In Sect. 5, we compare the complexity of solving polynomial systems arising from index calculus when using Frobenius invariant vector spaces instead of the vector spaces that are commonly used so far to define the factor base.

4.2 Factor Bases from Isogenies Between Algebraic Groups

In this subsection we recall results due to Couveignes and Lercier, who gave a framework on how to construct Galois invariant flags of subsets of $\mathbb{F}_{q^n}$ using isogenies between algebraic groups [2]. First, we recall the basic idea behind their results. Then, we show how their results for two specific algebraic groups, algebraic tori of dimension 1 and elliptic curves, give rise to factor bases for index calculus in elliptic curves using Semaev polynomials.

Let G be a commutative algebraic group defined over the finite field $\mathbb{F}_q$. Moreover, let $T \subset G(\mathbb{F}_q)$ be a non-trivial finite group of $\mathbb{F}_q$-rational points in G of cardinality n. Then, the quotient isogeny $I : G \to H$ of G by T is of degree n.

Given a point $a \in H$ such that the preimage $I^{-1}(a)$ is irreducible over $\mathbb{F}_q$, any point $b \in G(\overline{\mathbb{F}_q})$ with $I(b) = a$ defines a cyclic degree n extension of $\mathbb{F}_q$, i.e. $\mathbb{F}_{q^n} = \mathbb{F}_q(b)$. We refer to (5) for an example of what it means for the set $I^{-1}(a)$ to be irreducible in this context.

Under this identification of $\mathbb{F}_{q^n}$ with $\mathbb{F}_q(b)$, any Galois action permutes elements in $G(\mathbb{F}_{q^n})$ that have the same image under I. In other words, we can identify $T = \ker(I)$ with the Galois group of $\mathbb{F}_{q^n}$ over $\mathbb{F}_q$.

In particular, the elements $b \oplus_G t$ are all Galois conjugates of b for all $t \in T$ as

$$I(b \oplus_G t) = I(b) \oplus_H I(t) = a \oplus_H 0 = a.$$

Conversely, all Galois conjugates of b are obtained this way. Here, $\oplus_G$ and $\oplus_H$ denote the addition in G and H respectively.

Consequently, if there exist formulae to describe the translations $P \to P \oplus_G t$ for $t \in T$ in G, we get an explicit description of the Galois action on $\mathbb{F}_{q^n}$. This can be used to derive descriptions of Galois invariant subsets of $\mathbb{F}_{q^n}$.

During the remainder of this section, we will see that different commutative algebraic groups bring their own contribution to this general construction of

Galois invariant subsets. We show that this can be used to obtain Frobenius invariant factor bases that can be used for index calculus.

Isogenies Between Algebraic Tori. The simplest commutative algebraic groups beyond the ones underlying Kummer and Artin-Schreier theory are algebraic tori of dimension 1. They can be used to obtain Galois invariant sets in $\mathbb{F}_{q^n}$ through the previously described construction by Couveignes and Lercier. First, we will recall the details in this case. Then, we compute the size of the resulting sets and show how this leads to practical Frobenius invariant factor bases for Koblitz curves with ECDLP defined over field extensions $\mathbb{F}_{q^n}/\mathbb{F}_q$ whenever the extension degree n divides $q + 1$.

Let $\mathbb{F}_q$ be a finite field of characteristic different from 2, let $D \in \mathbb{F}_q^*$ and let $\mathbf{G}$ denote the open subset of the projective line $\mathbb{P}^1(\mathbb{F}_q)$ defined by

$$U^2 - DV^2 \neq 0,$$

where $[U, V]$ are the projective coordinates. We associate affine coordinates to points on the projective line using the map $u : \mathbb{P}^1 \to \mathbb{F}_q \cup \{\infty\}$, $[U, V] \mapsto \frac{U}{V}$.

On $\mathbf{G}$ we have a group structure: for $P_1, P_2 \neq 0_\mathbf{G}$, addition is given by

$$u(P_1 \oplus_\mathbf{G} P_2) = \frac{u(P_1)u(P_2) + D}{u(P_1) + u(P_2)} \quad \text{and} \quad u(\ominus_\mathbf{G}) = -u(P_1).$$

The neutral element $0_\mathbf{G}$ is the point with projective coordinates $[1, 0]$ and affine coordinate ∞. Assuming D is not a square in $\mathbb{F}_q$, the group $\mathbf{G}(\mathbb{F}_q)$ is cyclic of order $q + 1$.

Let a be a generator of $\mathbf{G}(\mathbb{F}_q)$ and let $[n] : \mathbf{G} \to \mathbf{G}$ denote the multiplication by n isogeny. Furthermore, let $A(X)$ be the polynomial annihilating the associated affine coordinates of all points in the preimage of a by $[n]$, i.e.

$$A(X) = \prod_{b \in [n]^{-1}(a)} (X - u(b)). \tag{5}$$

Couveignes and Lercier show that this degree n polynomial is irreducible in $\mathbb{F}_q[X]$. Hence, we have $\mathbb{F}_q[X]/A(X) = \mathbb{F}_{q^n}$.

Using the general framework, they show that every $\mathbb{F}_q$-automorphism of $\mathbb{F}_{q^n}$ transforms $\omega := X \mod A(X)$ into a linear rational fraction of ω. This proves that for every integer k such that $0 \leq k < n$, the subset

$$V_k := \left\{ \frac{u_0 + u_1\omega + u_2\omega^2 + \cdots + u_k\omega^k}{v_0 + v_1\omega + v_2\omega^2 + \cdots + v_k\omega^k} \,\middle|\, (u_0, u_1, \ldots, u_k, v_0, v_1, \ldots, v_k) \in \mathbb{F}_q^{2k+2} \right\} \subset \mathbb{F}_{q^n} \tag{6}$$

is Galois invariant.

The results of Couveignes and Lercier give rise to Frobenius invariant factor bases for index calculus on Koblitz curves.

Assume we want to solve the discrete logarithm problem in an elliptic curve $E(\mathbb{F}_{q^n})$ where n divides $q+1$. We can choose some $D \in \mathbb{F}_q^*$ that is not a square in $\mathbb{F}_q$ to define an algebraic torus $\mathbf{G}$ of dimension 1. Then, we find a generator a of $\mathbf{G}(\mathbb{F}_q)$. Using the exponentiation formulae in $\mathbf{G}$, we can compute the polynomial $A(X)$ given in Eq. (5) explicitly. As before, we set $\omega = X \mod A(X)$ and define V_k as in (6).

Lemma 5. *Let $k < n/2$. Then, we have $|V_k| = q^{2k+1}$.*

Proof. Identifying elements of the set V_k given in (6) with vectors in $\mathbb{F}_q^{2k+2}$, we see that elements are counted multiple times if and only if the numerator and denominator are not coprime. Hence we want to count the number of coprime pairs of polynomials of degree $\leq k$ with one polynomial corresponding to the non-zero denominator. Theorem 3 in [1] proves that $\frac{q-1}{q}$ of pairs of polynomials not both of degree 0 are coprime in $\mathbb{F}_q[x]$. Note that this contains those pairs where the polynomial corresponding to the denominator is 0, which we don't want to count. Moreover, being coprime in $\mathbb{F}_q[x]$ is up to multiplication by units of the field $\mathbb{F}_q$, e.g. $\gcd(2x, 2) = 1$ if q is no power of 2. Thus, we need to reduce the count again under orbits of multiplication by the $(q-1)$ units in $\mathbb{F}_q$. Hence, the $q^{2k+2} - q^2$ elements in V_k given by fractions of polynomials not both of degree 0 represent

$$\frac{1}{q-1} \cdot \frac{q-1}{q} \cdot (q^{2k+2} - q^2) = q^{2k+1} - q$$

distinct elements in $\mathbb{F}_{q^n}$. Additionally, we get the q field elements in our set by considering the fractions of degree 0 elements, which finishes the proof.   □

Let $V = V_k$ for some k such that V_k is of the size we desire our factor base to be, which can be computed using the previous lemma. We can define a factor base for index calculus on some curve E by requiring the x-coordinates of factor base elements to be in the set $V \subset \mathbb{F}_{q^n}$, as it was done before in the case of vector spaces, i.e.

$$\mathcal{F} := \{P \in E(\mathbb{F}_{q^n}) : x(P) \in V\}.$$

The Galois invariance of V in $\mathbb{F}_{q^n}/\mathbb{F}_q$ implies the invariance under the q-th power Frobenius of $\mathcal{F}$ in E.

As described in Sect. 2, we use the $(m+1)$-th Semaev summation polynomial and Weil restriction of scalars to solve the decomposition problem during the relation search in the index calculus. However, instead of restricting the variables of the Semaev polynomial to some vector space, we restrict them to V. After substitution of expressions of the form (6) into the Semaev polynomial, we clear the denominator.

The resulting polynomial systems can be solved using the same methods as applied in the case of factor bases arising from vector spaces. While the systems have some additional structure, i.e. they are homogeneous with respect to certain blocks of variables before the Weil descent, they are generally of larger degree. This means it is harder to make a direct comparison of the complexity of solving those systems with the case where factor bases arising from vector spaces are used. We discuss this matter more together with our experimental evidence in Sect. 5.

Isogenies Between Elliptic Curves. Different commutative algebraic groups allow to construct Galois invariant subsets for different classes of finite field extensions. In addition to the construction using algebraic tori, Couveignes and Lercier give an explicit description using ordinary elliptic curves [2]. It allows to write down Galois invariant subsets of field extensions $\mathbb{F}_{q^n}$ of characteristic p, whenever n has a squarefree multiple N such that $N \not\equiv 1 \pmod{p}$ and

$$q + 1 - 2\sqrt{q} < N < q + 1 + 2\sqrt{q}.$$

Their results also give rise to Frobenius invariant factor bases for index calculus for Koblitz curves with ECDLP problem defined in $\mathbb{F}_{q^n}$. Our description of their result follows [2] and we reproduce it here for completeness.

First, we use another elliptic curve H to construct a Galois invariant subset of $\mathbb{F}_{q^n}$. We choose H to have N rational points over $\mathbb{F}_q$ and trace $t = q + 1 - N$. Such a curve can be found using exhaustive search or complex multiplication theory. Note that this precomputation needs to be done only once for any field. The ideal $(\pi - 1) \subset \text{End}(H)$ has a degree n factor $\mathfrak{i}$. Therefore, $\text{End}(H)/\mathfrak{i}$ is cyclic of order n and H contains a cyclic subgroup $T := \ker(\mathfrak{i})$ of order n.

Let $I : H \to F$ be the quotient isogeny with kernel T. As the quotient $F(\mathbb{F}_q)/I(E(\mathbb{F}_q))$ is isomorphic to T and thus cyclic of order n, we can take a generator a of this quotient. As in the case of algebraic tori, the preimage of a under I is an irreducible divisor. Thus, there are n geometric points in the preimage of a that are defined in $\mathbb{F}_{q^n}$ and permuted by Galois action.

Let $B := I^{-1}(a)$ denote the corresponding prime divisor. Then $\mathbb{F}_{q^n}$ is the residue extension of E at B, i.e. the elements of $\mathbb{F}_{q^n}$ can be represented as residues of functions on E at B that do not have a pole at B.

For a function f in $H(\mathbb{F}_q)$, let the degree of f be the number of poles of f counted with multiplicities. We denote the set of functions in $H(\mathbb{F}_q)$ of degree $\leq k$ having no pole at B by $\mathcal{F}_k$ for every $k \geq 0$. Define V_k to be the corresponding set of residues at B in $\mathbb{F}_{q^n}$:

$$V_k := \{f \pmod{B} \mid f \in \mathcal{F}_k\}.$$

As shown in [2], we have $\mathbb{F}_q = V_0 = V_1 \subset V_2 \subset \cdots \subset V_d = \mathbb{F}_{q^n}$ and translations by an element in $T = \ker(\mathfrak{i})$ do not change the number of poles of functions in $H(\mathbb{F}_q)$. Consequently, V_k is invariant under the action of $\text{Gal}(\mathbb{F}_{q^n}/\mathbb{F}_q)$.

As in the case of algebraic tori, these results give rise to a construction of Frobenius invariant factor bases for Koblitz curves. Note that functions in the sets $\mathcal{F}_k$ have at most k poles and thus can be written as a quotient of two homogeneous polynomials of degree $\lceil \frac{k+1}{3} \rceil$ polynomials.

Evaluating $\mathcal{F}_k$ at B gives the values of V_k. As before, we define our factor base for index calculus to be the set of points on the curve containing the ECDLP problem with x-coordinates in V_k.

As conjectured by Couveignes and Lercier [2], other commutative algebraic groups might bring their own contribution to the construction of Galois invariant subsets of $\mathbb{F}_{q^n}$ which give rise to factor bases for index calculus in various classes of Koblitz curves.

5 Experimental Results

We implemented the construction of Frobenius invariant factor bases emerging both from linearised polynomials and from isogenies between algebraic tori. We used this to construct and solve the polynomial systems arising from Weil descent after constraining the variables in Semaev's summation polynomials to these factor bases. All the experiments were executed using the 64-bit version of MAGMA. Gröbner bases were computed using Faugère's F4 algorithm, as implemented in MAGMA.

5.1 Frobenius Invariant Vector Spaces

In the case of factor bases from vector spaces defined by linearised polynomials, we tested our implementation on a Koblitz curve over $\mathbb{F}_{q^n} = \mathbb{F}_{2^{31}}$, using $m = 3$. Since the order of 2 in $\mathbb{Z}_{31}$ is 5, the vector space arising from our construction using linearised polynomials is of dimension 5. More precisely, the vector space is generated by $\{x, x^2, x^4, x^8, x^{16}\}$, where x is a symbolic root of an irreducible polynomial of degree n over the base field $\mathbb{F}_q$. We implemented the index calculus methods of Faugère et al. [8] to compute the polynomial system arising from Weil descent of the $(m + 1)$-th Semaev polynomial, S_4. We timed the set-up of the polynomial system via Weil descent and the solving of the resulting system for different factor bases. We compared our Frobenius invariant factor base to factor bases from randomly chosen vector spaces and "standard" vector spaces, i.e. spanned by $\{1, x, x^2, \ldots, x^k\}$, of the same dimension. Our measurements over 200 runs of the experiments are displayed in Table 2.

As was observed previously, using factor bases from standard vector spaces is faster than from randomly chosen vector spaces [14]. However, the results also show that our Frobenius invariant vector spaces do not behave worse than a randomly chosen one on average. Considering that we would only need to solve $1/n = 1/31$ as many such systems to compute an ECDLP instance when using the Frobenius invariant vector space, the experiments suggest that the full speed-up by a factor n in the relation collection could be (nearly) reached for these parameters.

Table 2. Time in seconds for setting up the polynomial system and the Gröbner basis computation during point decomposition in index calculus for factor bases arising from different vector spaces. Parameters $m = 3$, $p = 2$, $n = 31$ and vector spaces are of dimension 5.

Factor base from vector space	$t_{\text{set-up}}$	t_{Groeb}
Standard	0.19	2.95
Random	0.19	3.15
Frobenius invariant	0.19	3.15

5.2   Factor Bases from Isogenies Between Algebraic Tori

In the case of factor bases arising from isogenies between algebraic tori, our experimental results are less promising and less clear.

The polynomials S_{m+1} are symmetric and have degree 2^{m-1} in each of their variables. Consider sums of the form $\sum_{i=0}^{k} x_i \omega^i$ for some fixed $\omega \in \mathbb{F}_{q^n}$ as one *block of variables*. When substituting vector space constraints into the Semaev polynomial S_{m+1} with one fixed variable, we get an equation containing m blocks of variables.

In the case of fractions of polynomials, we have $2m$ (shorter) blocks of variables. After clearing the denominator, we are left with a homogeneous polynomial in terms of these blocks. The degree of every monomial equals $m \cdot 2^{m-1}$. Therefore, we have more monomials of a large degree compared to the case of vector spaces. However, the blocks of variables are shorter compared to a factor base of the same size from a vector space.

The following example compares the degree of the polynomial systems after Weil descent for vector spaces and the polynomial fractions of (6) in the case $m = 3$.

Example 1. By Lemma 5, the size of a vector space of dimension 3 equals the number of elements of the set (6) for $k = 1$. For $m = 3$ we substitute three blocks of variables into the Semaev polynomial. In the case of vector spaces, blocks containing 3 variables are taken to the $2^{m-1} = 4$-th power. According to the multinomial theorem, the generalisation of the binomial theorem, in characteristic $p = 2$ this only leads to mixed terms containing monomials with at most two variables over the base field from the same block. After reducing modulo the field equations, we are left with polynomials of degree at most $m \cdot 2 = 6$.

In the case of polynomial fractions, each block of variables to the 3-rd and 4-th power also contains monomials with at most two variables. After substituting the variables into S_4 and clearing denominators, the summation polynomial is homogeneous of degree 12 with respect to the blocks of variables. Multiplying out and reducing modulo the field equations, this leads to an upper bound of 9 on the degree of the polynomials after Weil descent. Both values of the degree match the degrees observed in our experiments.

Table 3. Average time of Weil descent and Gröbner basis over 5 instances for parameters $p = q = 2$ and $\log_q(|\mathcal{F}|) = 5$ and $\log_q(|\mathcal{F}|) = 7$ in s using factor bases defined by vector spaces and fractions of the form given in (6).

m=3, $\log_q(|\mathcal{F}|) = 5$				m=3, $\log_q(|\mathcal{F}|) = 7$		
n		$t_{\text{set-up}}$	t_{Groeb}	n	$t_{\text{set-up}}$	t_{Groeb}
17	vector spaces	0.16	5.32	101 vector spaces	3.53	115.05
	fractions	1.43	1390.34	fractions	67.64	701.33
23	vector spaces	0.20	3.94	103 vector spaces	4.02	35.55
	fractions	2.09	1290.14	fractions	76.63	827.00
29	vector spaces	0.23	3.66	107 vector spaces	4.42	43.50
	fractions	2.31	3764.22	fractions	83.00	338.75
31	vector spaces	0.24	3.57	109 vector spaces	4.57	15.85
	fractions	2.48	950.64	fractions	82.70	252.14
37	vector spaces	0.30	6.41	113 vector spaces	5.00	15.26
	fractions	3.18	853.79	fractions	84.88	243.68
41	vector spaces	0.32	6.26	127 vector spaces	5.27	0.91
	fractions	3.34	1130.67	fractions	92.48	235.91
43	vector spaces	0.33	3.03	131 vector spaces	5.46	0.84
	fractions	3.30	972.56	fractions	96.53	237.70

However, the degree of the system alone does not determine the difficulty of the Gröbner basis computation.

We did not find instances fulfilling the requirements for factor bases as defined in (6), i.e. where n divides $q + 1$, that were tractable for experiments. However, we computed and solved the polynomial systems for $p = q = 2$, $m = 3$ and various primes n when using vector spaces of dimension 5 and 7 and polynomial fractions as in (6) for $k = 2$ and $k = 3$. Note that we paired the factor bases of the same size by Lemma 5. The results of our experiments are shown in Table 3. Note that for these parameters the factor bases are *not* Galois invariant and the experiments are merely to observe the computational impact of using factor bases defined by the given fractions instead of vector spaces.

For the chosen parameters it is apparent that both the transformation from Semaev polynomial to binary polynomial system and the computation of Gröbner bases are significantly slower when using the polynomial fractions to express the factor bases. The increased cost does not seem to be justified by needing $1/n$ fewer relations. Moreover, we were not able to run experiments on less underdetermined systems in the case of $\log_q(|\mathcal{F}|) = 7$. This was because the solution of the polynomial systems in the fraction case took either too long or met our memory limit of 1.4 TB. While the factor bases from isogenies between algebraic tori do not seem to give very hopeful results, we want to point out that the algorithm used to solve the polynomial systems did not exploit the homogeneous structure of the polynomial system and therefore speed-ups might be possible.

We leave the research of the combined effects of larger degrees, smaller block sizes and the homogeneous structure on the complexity of solving the polynomial systems for future work. It will be interesting to study the impact in practice for different characteristics and asymptotically.

6   Conclusion

This work presents multiple ideas on how to accelerate index calculus on Koblitz curves using careful choices of factor bases with respect to the q-power Frobenius endomorphism. This allows for better symmetry breaking, and Frobenius invariant factor bases enable us to reduce both the computational effort in the relation collection and the linear algebra step of index calculus.

While a lot of work in the literature has been directed at improving the complexity of solving polynomial systems arising during index calculus, our speed-ups are achieved by reducing the number of such polynomial systems that need to be solved in the first place.

For suitable parameters, we define Frobenius invariant factor bases from Galois invariant vector spaces that can be constructed using linearised polynomials. We can rewrite every relation found in terms of a reduced factor base consisting only of representatives for each Frobenius orbit. As a consequence, we need to find n times fewer relations, which leads to a speed-up by a factor of roughly n in the relation collection and by n^2 during the linear algebra step. Our experimental evidence supports that the polynomial systems arising in this way appear to be roughly as hard to solve as the ones arising from a more standard choice used in index calculus.

For further parameter sets, we construct Frobenius invariant factor bases using the work of Couveignes and Lercier. Yet, the polynomial systems arising in the relation collection in this case were more expensive to solve in our experiments. The experiments suggest that this second approach is less promising.

Given the uncertainties in computing the exact cost of Gröbner basis algorithms, a precise complexity estimate of index calculus methods for Koblitz curves is beyond the scope of this work. Nevertheless, based on previous work such as [21] our improvements do not lead to index calculus algorithms faster than Pollard ρ on instances used in practice. However, this work shows that index calculus on Koblitz curves can be accelerate beyond the $\sqrt{n}$ previously achieved for Pollard ρ compared to the same algorithm on general curves and thus can be used to narrow the gap in performance for Koblitz curves. Moreover, this paper answers an open problem raised in [9] about how the Frobenius endomorphism on Koblitz curves can be exploited to accelerate index calculus.

We hope the new ideas described in this work may be used as another building block for more efficient index calculus based methods to solve ECDLP in theory and practice.

Acknowledgements. We thank Jean-Marc Couveignes and Reynald Lercier for their work on Galois invariant smoothness bases [2] and helpful conversations about the topic. Furthermore, we would like to thank the anonymous reviewers for their helpful comments on the submitted manuscript of this paper. Christophe Petit's work was supported by EPSRC grant EP/S01361X/1. Simon-Philipp Merz was supported by the EPSRC grant EP/P009301/1.

References

1. Benjamin, A.T., Bennett, C.D.: The probability of relatively prime polynomials. Math. Mag. **80**(3), 196–202 (2007)
2. Couveignes, J.-M., Lercier, R.: Galois invariant smoothness basis. In: Algebraic Geometry and Its Applications: Dedicated to Gilles Lachaud on His 60th Birthday, pp. 142–167. World Scientific (2008)
3. Diem, C.: On the discrete logarithm problem in elliptic curves. Compos. Math. **147**(1), 75–104 (2011)
4. Faugère, J.-C.: A new efficient algorithm for computing Gröbner bases (F4). J. Pure Appl. Algebra **139**(1–3), 61–88 (1999)
5. Faugère, J.-C.: A new efficient algorithm for computing Gröbner bases without reduction to zero (F5). In: Proceedings of the 2002 International Symposium on Symbolic and Algebraic Computation, pp. 75–83 (2002)
6. Faugère, J.-C., Gaudry, P., Huot, L., Renault, G.: Using symmetries in the index calculus for elliptic curves discrete logarithm. J. Cryptol. **27**(4), 595–635 (2014)
7. Faugère, J.-C., Gianni, P., Lazard, D., Mora, T.: Efficient computation of zero-dimensional Gröbner bases by change of ordering. J. Symb. Comput. **16**(4), 329–344 (1993)
8. Faugère, J.-C., Perret, L., Petit, C., Renault, G.: Improving the complexity of index calculus algorithms in elliptic curves over binary fields. In: Pointcheval, D., Johansson, T. (eds.) EUROCRYPT 2012. LNCS, vol. 7237, pp. 27–44. Springer, Heidelberg (2012). https://doi.org/10.1007/978-3-642-29011-4_4
9. Galbraith, S.D., Gaudry, P.: Recent progress on the elliptic curve discrete logarithm problem. Des. Codes Crypt. **78**(1), 51–72 (2015). https://doi.org/10.1007/s10623-015-0146-7
10. Gaudry, P.: An algorithm for solving the discrete log problem on hyperelliptic curves. In: Preneel, B. (ed.) EUROCRYPT 2000. LNCS, vol. 1807, pp. 19–34. Springer, Heidelberg (2000). https://doi.org/10.1007/3-540-45539-6_2
11. Gaudry, P.: Index calculus for abelian varieties of small dimension and the elliptic curve discrete logarithm problem. J. Symb. Comput. **44**(12), 1690–1702 (2009)
12. Gorla, E., Massierer, M.: Index calculus in the trace zero variety. Adv. Math. Commun. **9**(4), 515–539 (2015)
13. Huang, M.-D.A., Kosters, M., Yeo, S.L.: Last fall degree, HFE, and Weil descent attacks on ECDLP. In: Gennaro, R., Robshaw, M. (eds.) CRYPTO 2015. Part I, LNCS, vol. 9215, pp. 581–600. Springer, Heidelberg (2015). https://doi.org/10.1007/978-3-662-47989-6_28
14. Huang, Y.-J., Petit, C., Shinohara, N., Takagi, T.: Improvement of Faugère *et al.*'s method to solve ECDLP. In: Sakiyama, K., Terada, M. (eds.) IWSEC 2013. LNCS, vol. 8231, pp. 115–132. Springer, Heidelberg (2013). https://doi.org/10.1007/978-3-642-41383-4_8
15. Joux, A., Lercier, R.: The function field sieve in the medium prime case. In: Vaudenay, S. (ed.) EUROCRYPT 2006. LNCS, vol. 4004, pp. 254–270. Springer, Heidelberg (2006). https://doi.org/10.1007/11761679_16

16. Joux, A., Vitse, V.: Elliptic curve discrete logarithm problem over small degree extension fields. J. Cryptol. **26**(1), 119–143 (2013)
17. Koblitz, N.: Elliptic curve cryptosystems. Math. Comput. **48**(177), 203–209 (1987)
18. Menezes, A., Qu, M.: Analysis of the Weil descent attack of Gaudry, Hess and smart. In: Naccache, D. (ed.) CT-RSA 2001. LNCS, vol. 2020, pp. 308–318. Springer, Heidelberg (1999). https://doi.org/10.1007/3-540-45353-9_23
19. Miller, V.S.: Use of elliptic curves in cryptography. In: Williams, H.C. (ed.) CRYPTO 1985. LNCS, vol. 218, pp. 417–426. Springer, Heidelberg (1986). https://doi.org/10.1007/3-540-39799-X_31
20. Nagao, K.: Decomposition formula of the Jacobian group of plane curve (2013)
21. Petit, C., Quisquater, J.-J.: On polynomial systems arising from a Weil descent. In: Wang, X., Sako, K. (eds.) ASIACRYPT 2012. LNCS, vol. 7658, pp. 451–466. Springer, Heidelberg (2012). https://doi.org/10.1007/978-3-642-34961-4_28
22. Pohlig, S., Hellman, M.: An improved algorithm for computing logarithms over GF(p) and its cryptographic significance (corresp.). IEEE Trans. Inf. Theory **24**(1), 106–110 (1978)
23. Pollard, J.M.: Kangaroos, monopoly and discrete logarithms. J. Cryptol. **13**(4), 437–447 (2000)
24. Rescorla, E., Dierks, T.: The transport layer security (TLS) protocol version 1.3 (2018)
25. Semaev, I.: Summation polynomials and the discrete logarithm problem on elliptic curves. IACR Cryptology ePrint Archive 2004:31 (2004)
26. Semaev, I.: New algorithm for the discrete logarithm problem on elliptic curves. Cryptology ePrint Archive, Report 2015/310 (2015). https://eprint.iacr.org/2015/310
27. Smart, N.P.: Elliptic curve cryptosystems over small fields of odd characteristic. J. Cryptol. **12**(2), 141–151 (1999)
28. Van Oorschot, P.C., Wiener, M.J.: Parallel collision search with cryptanalytic applications. J. Cryptol. **12**(1), 1–28 (1999)
29. Wiedemann, D.: Solving sparse linear equations over finite fields. IEEE Trans. Inf. Theory **32**(1), 54–62 (1986)
30. Wiener, M.J., Zuccherato, R.J.: Faster attacks on elliptic curve cryptosystems. In: Tavares, S., Meijer, H. (eds.) SAC 1998. LNCS, vol. 1556, pp. 190–200. Springer, Heidelberg (1999). https://doi.org/10.1007/3-540-48892-8_15

Symmetric-Key Analysis

Weak-Key Distinguishers for AES

Lorenzo Grassi[1,4(✉)], Gregor Leander[2], Christian Rechberger[1],
Cihangir Tezcan[3], and Friedrich Wiemer[2]

[1] IAIK, Graz University of Technology, Graz, Austria
christian.rechberger@iaik.tugraz.at
[2] Horst Görtz Institute for IT-Security, Ruhr-Universität Bochum,
Bochum, Germany
{gregor.leander,friedrich.wiemer}@rub.de
[3] Informatics Institute, Department of Cyber Security, CyDeS Laboratory,
Middle East Technical University, Ankara, Turkey
cihangir@metu.edu.tr
[4] Digital Security Group, Radboud University, Nijmegen,
Nijmegen, The Netherlands
lgrassi@science.ru.nl

Abstract. In this paper, we analyze the security of AES in the case in which the whitening key is a weak key.

After a systematization of the classes of weak-keys of AES, we perform an extensive analysis of weak-key distinguishers (in the single-key setting) for AES instantiated with the original key-schedule and with the new key-schedule proposed at ToSC/FSE'18. As one of the main results, we show that (almost) all the secret-key distinguishers for round-reduced AES currently present in the literature can be set up for a higher number of rounds of AES if the whitening key is a weak-key.

Using these results as starting point, we describe a property for 9-round AES-128 and 12-round AES-256 in the chosen-key setting with complexity 2^{64} without requiring related keys. These new chosen-key distinguishers – set up by exploiting a variant of the multiple-of-8 property introduced at Eurocrypt'17 – improve all the AES chosen-key distinguishers in the single-key setting.

The entire analysis has been performed using a new framework that we introduce here – called "weak-key subspace trails", which is obtained by combining invariant subspaces (Crypto'11) and subspace trails (FSE'17) into a new, more powerful, attack.

Keywords: AES · Key schedule · Weak-keys · Chosen-key distinguisher

1 Introduction

Block ciphers are certainly among the most important cryptographic primitives. Their design and analysis are well advanced, and with today's knowledge designing a secure block cipher is a problem that is largely considered solved. Especially

© Springer Nature Switzerland AG 2021
O. Dunkelman et al. (Eds.): SAC 2020, LNCS 12804, pp. 141–170, 2021.
https://doi.org/10.1007/978-3-030-81652-0_6

with the AES we have at hand a very well analyzed and studied cipher that, after more than 20 years of investigation still withstands all cryptanalytic attacks.

Clearly, security of symmetric crypto is always security against specific attacks. First of all, the number of available attacks has increased significantly ever since the introduction of differential [2] and linear [29] cryptanalysis in the early 1990. Another important aspect is that the attacker model is regularly changing. With the introduction of statistical attacks, especially linear and differential cryptanalysis, the attacker was suddenly assumed to be able to retrieve, or even choose, large amounts of plaintext/ciphertext pairs. Later, in the related-key setting, the attacker became even more powerful and was assumed to be able to choose not only plaintexts but also ask for the encryption of chosen messages under a key that is related to the unknown secret key. Finally, in the open-key model, the attacker either knows the key or has the ability to choose the key herself. While the practical impact of such models is often debatable, they actually might become meaningful when the block cipher is used as a building block for other primitives, in particular for the construction of hash-functions. Moreover, even if those considerations do not pose practical attacks, they still provide very useful insights and observations that strengthen our understanding of block ciphers in general.

Our work builds upon the above in the sense that we combine previously separate attacks to derive new results on the AES in the secret-/open-key model.

Weak Keys and Key-Schedule

A key is said to be "weak" if, used with a specific cipher, it makes the cipher behave in some undesirable way (namely, if it makes the cipher weaker w.r.t. other keys). The most famous example of weak-keys is given for the DES, which has a few specific keys termed "weak-keys" and "semi-weak-keys" [30]. These are keys that cause the encryption mode of DES to act identically to the decryption mode of DES (albeit potentially that of a different key). Even if weak keys usually represent a very small fraction of the overall key-space, it is desirable for a cipher to have no weak keys. Weak-keys are much more often a problem where the adversary has some control over what keys are used, such as when a block cipher is used in a mode of operation intended to construct a secure cryptographic hash function. For example, in the Davies-Meyer construction or the Miyaguchi-Preneel, one can transform a secure block cipher into a secure compression function. In a hash setting, block cipher security models such as the known-key model (or the chosen-key model) makes sense since in practice the attacker has full access and control over the internal computations.

The presence of a set of weak keys is usually related to the details of the key-schedule, namely the algorithm that takes as input a master key and outputs so-called round keys that are used in each round to mix the current state with the key. While the concrete security of the AES and other well-known ciphers is well studied, it is not clear what properties a good key schedule has to have. Even if there are some general guidelines on what a key schedule should not look like, these guidelines are rather basic and ensure mainly that trivial guess-and-determine or/and meet-in-the-middle attacks or/and structural attacks (e.g. slide-attacks, symmetries, invariant subspace attacks) are not possible.

Our Contribution

Recently, more and more attacks on perfectly good ciphers – that exploit only weak-keys and key schedule weaknesses, e.g. [20] – indicate that the research on key schedule design principles is pressing. For the case in which the r-th round-key k_r is simply defined by the XOR of the whitening key K and a round constant RC_r, that is $k_r = K \oplus RC_r$ (a key-schedule largely used for lightweight ciphers), in [1] authors show that a proper choice of round constants can easily avoid (unwanted) properties related to structural attacks. In this paper, we first analyze *the security of AES instantiated with a weak-key* against secret-key distinguishers, both for the case of the AES key-schedule and for the case of a recent proposed key-schedule based only on permutation of the byte positions [22]. Then, we use these results as starting points in order to construct new chosen-key distinguishers for AES in the single-key model.

Systematization of Knowledge: Weak-Key Subspace Trail Cryptanalysis. First of all, we start by recalling the basic set-up of subspace trail cryptanalysis (see [18,19,28]) and invariant subspace attacks (see [26,27]) in Sect. 2. Our first main focus is to point out the important differences of these two attacks. As we will explain, those concepts are not generalizations of each other but rather orthogonal attack vectors. From this point of view, a natural step is to *fill this gap, by combining both approaches into a new, more powerful, attack.* This is in line with what was done previously with other attacks as mentioned above.

As invariant subspace attacks are weak-key attacks by nature, the new attack originating from the combination of invariant subspace attacks and subspace trail cryptanalysis is a weak-key attack as well. Here, weak-key refers to the fact that the attacks do not work for any key, but rather only for a fraction of all keys (besides the fact that they heavily depend on details of the key-schedule). Consequently, in Sect. 2 we coin the new strategy *weak-key subspace trail cryptanalysis.*

Weak-Key Secret-Key Distinguishers for AES. Previously, invariant subspace attacks were only applied to ciphers with very simple key schedule algorithms. As a result, ciphers where the round keys differed not only by round constants seemed secure against this type of attacks. E.g. up to now, it seemed impossible to apply invariant subspace attacks on the AES.

With our new combination of invariant subspace attacks and subspace trail cryptanalysis, we overcome this inherently difficult problem. As a showcase of the increased possibilities of our attack, and as the most important example anyway, in Sects. 3.2 and 4 we present several new observations on the AES. Using as starting point the invariant subspace found by our algorithm and presented in Sect. 3.2, we show that several secret-key distinguishers for round-reduced AES currently present in the literature (in particular, truncated differential distinguishers) can be set up for a higher number of rounds of AES *if the whitening key is a weak-key*.

In particular, we show that the secret-key distinguisher based on the multiple-of-n property proposed at Eurocrypt 2017 [19] can be extended by one round if the (secret) whitening key is a weak-key. As a concrete application of such result, in Appendix C we present examples of compression collisions for 6- and 7-round AES-256 used in Davies–Meyer, Miyaguchi-Preneel and Matyas-Meyer-Oseas construction.

As a side-result, we analyze the security of an alternative AES key schedule proposed at ToSC'18 [22], which is defined by a permutation of the byte positions only and that aims to provide resistance against *related-key differential attacks*. In Sect. 3.2, we show the importance of adding random constants at every round in order to prevent the weak-key subspace trail attack proposed here.

Chosen-Key Distinguisher for AES. Known-key distinguishers were introduced by Knudsen and Rijmen in [23] for their analysis of AES and a class of Feistel ciphers in order to examine the security of these block ciphers in a model where the adversary knows the key. To succeed, the adversary has to discover some property of the attacked cipher that e.g. holds with a probability higher than for an ideal cipher, or is generally believed to be hard to exhibit generically. The idea of chosen-key distinguishers was popularized in the attack on the full-round AES-256 [3,4] in a related-key setting. This time the adversary is assumed to have a full control over the key. A chosen-key attack was shown on 9-round reduced AES-128 in [13] in the related-key setting, and on 8-round AES-128 in [11] in the single-key setting. Both the known-key and chosen-key distinguishers are collectively known as *open-key distinguishers*.

Building up on our weak-key multiple-of-n results, we are able to construct new chosen-key distinguishers for up to 9-round AES-128 and 12-round AES-256 in the single-key model and based on the multiple-of-n (weak-key) property. This improves all the chosen-key distinguishers for AES in the single-key setting. In particular, in Sect. 5 we exhibit *a chosen-key distinguisher with complexity 2^{64} for 9-round AES-128 in the single-key model*[1], valid for 2^{32} keys. For these results we combine two weak-key subspace trails in an inside-out manner and, instead of a simple truncated differential property at the plaintexts and ciphertexts, we use a variant of the "multiple-of-n" property recently shown for AES in [19].

2   Weak-Key (Invariant) Subspace Trails

2.1   Subspace Trails

Subspace trails have been first defined in [18], and a connection between subspace trails and truncated differential attacks has been studied in details in [28].

---

[1] A 10-round known-key distinguisher for AES has been proposed by Gilbert [14] at Asiacrypt 2014. Echoing [17], in Appendix E we argue why such distinguisher can be considered artificial. Briefly, the property of this distinguisher does not involve *directly* the plaintexts/ciphertexts, but their encryption/decryption after one round.

We recall the definition of a subspace trail next. Our treatment here is however meant to be self-contained. For this, let F denote a round function of a key-alternating block cipher, and let $U \oplus a$ denote a coset of a vector space U. By U^c we denote the complementary subspace of U.

Definition 1 (Subspace Trails). *Let $(U_1, U_2, \ldots, U_{r+1})$ denote a set of $r+1$ subspaces with $\dim(U_i) \leqslant \dim(U_{i+1})$. If for each $i = 1, \ldots, r$ and for each a_i, there exists (unique) $a_{i+1} \in U^c_{i+1}$ such that $F(U_i \oplus a_i) \subseteq U_{i+1} \oplus a_{i+1}$, then $(U_1, U_2, \ldots, U_{r+1})$ is a* subspace trail *of length r for the function F. If all the previous relations hold with equality, the trail is called a* constant-dimensional subspace trail.

One important observation is the following. Consider a key-alternating cipher E_k using F as a round function and where the round keys are xored in between the rounds, that is

$$E(\cdot) = k_r \oplus F(\ldots \oplus F(k_1 \oplus F(k_0 \oplus \cdot)))$$

where k^i is the i-th subkey. In this case, a subspace trail for F will extend to a subspace trail for E_k for any choice of round keys. This is a simple consequence as

$$F(U_i \oplus a_i) \subseteq U_{i+1} \oplus a_{i+1} \text{ implies } F_{k^i}(U_i \oplus a_i) \equiv F(U_i \oplus a_i) \oplus k^i \subseteq U_{i+1} \oplus a'_{i+1}$$

for a suitable $a'_{i+1} = a_{i+1} \oplus k^i$. In other words, the key addition changes only the coset of the subspace U_{i+1}, while it does not affect the subspace itself. Thus, not only do subspace trails work for all keys, they are also completely independent of the key schedule. Here, invariant subspace attacks behave very differently.

2.2   Invariant Subspace Attacks

Invariant subspace attacks, which can be seen as a general way of capturing symmetries, have been first introduced in [26] in an attack on PRINTCipher. Later, those attacks have been applied to several other (lightweight) primitives, e.g. in [27], where a generic tool to detect them has been proposed.

As above, denoting by $F_k(\cdot) = F(\cdot) \oplus k$ the round function of a key-alternating block-cipher, let $U \subset \mathbb{F}_2^n$ be a subspace. Then, U is called an invariant subspace if there exist constants $a, b \in \mathbb{F}_2^n$ such that $F_k(U \oplus a) = U \oplus b$. In order to extend the invariant subspace $U \oplus a_i \mapsto U \oplus a_{i+1}$ to the whole cipher, we need all round keys to be in specific cosets of U namely, $k_i \in U \oplus (a_{i+1} \oplus b_i)$ (where $F(U \oplus a_i) = U \oplus b_i$): $F_k(U \oplus a_i) = F(U \oplus a_i) \oplus k = U \oplus b_i \oplus k = U \oplus a_{i+1}$.

Definition 2 (Invariant Subspace Trail). *Let K_{weak} be a set of weak keys and $k \in K_{weak}$, with $k \equiv (k^0, k^1, \ldots, k^r)$ where k^j is the j-th round key. For each $k \in K_{weak}$, the subspace U generates an* invariant subspace trail *of length r for the function $F_k(\cdot) \equiv F(\cdot) \oplus k$ if for each $i = 1, \ldots, r$ there exists a non-empty set $A_i \subseteq U^c$ for which the following property holds:*

$$\forall a_i \in A_i : \quad \exists a_{i+1} \in A_{i+1} \text{ s.t. } F_{k^i}(U \oplus a_i) \equiv F(U \oplus a_i) \oplus k^i = U \oplus a_{i+1}.$$

2.3 Weak-Key Subspace Trails

When comparing subspace trail and invariant subspace attacks, two obvious but important differences can be observed. First, subspace trails are clearly much more general as they allow different spaces in the domain and co-domain of F. Second, subspace trails are by far more restrictive, as not only one coset of the subspace has to be mapped to one coset of (a potentially different) subspace, but rather all cosets have to be mapped to cosets. For subspace trails, the later fact is the main reason for allowing arbitrary round keys.

The main idea for weak-key subspace trails is to stick to the property of invariant subspace attacks where only few (even just one) cosets of a subspace are mapped to other cosets of a subspace. However, borrowing from subspace trails, we allow those subspaces to be different for each round. As this will again restrict the choice of round keys that will keep this property invariant to a class of weak-keys we call this combination *weak-key subspace trails* (or simply, weak subspace trails). The formal definition is the following.

Definition 3 (Weak-Key Subspace Trails). *Let K_{weak} be a set of keys and $k \in K_{weak}$ with $k \equiv (k^0, k^1, \ldots, k^r)$ where k^j is the j-th round key. Further let $(U_1, U_2, \ldots, U_{r+1})$ denote a set of $r + 1$ subspaces with $\dim(U_i) \leqslant \dim(U_{i+1})$. For each $k \in K_{weak}$, $(U_1, U_2, \ldots, U_{r+1})$ is a* weak-key subspace trail *(WKST) of length r for the function $F_k(\cdot) \equiv F(\cdot) \oplus k$ if for each $i = 1, \ldots, r$ there exists a non-empty set $A_i \subseteq U_i^c$ for which the following property holds:*

$$\forall a_i \in A_i : \quad \exists a_{i+1} \in A_{i+1} \text{ s.t. } F_{k^i}(U_i \oplus a_i) \equiv F(U_i \oplus a_i) \oplus k^i \subseteq U_{i+1} \oplus a_{i+1}.$$

All keys in the set K_{weak} are weak-keys. *If all the previous relations hold with equality, the trail is called a* weak-key constant-dimensional subspace trail.

Usually, the set $A_i \subseteq U_i^c$ reduces to a single element a_i: $A_i \equiv \{a_i\}$. Moreover, we can easily see that Definition 3 is a generalization of both Definitions 1 and 2:

- if K_{weak} is equal to the whole set of keys and if $A_i = U_i^c$, then it corresponds to subspace trails;
- if $U_i = U_{i+1}$ for all i, then it corresponds to invariant subspace trails.

Security Problem. Clearly, a WKST allows greater freedom for an attacker. In comparison to invariant subspace attacks, WKSTs have the potential of being better applicable to block ciphers with non trivial key schedules. At the same time, with respect to subspace trails it is not necessary for WKSTs to hold for all possible keys.

Interestingly, proving resistance against invariant subspace (or more generally invariant sets) in the case of identical round keys (up to the addition of round constants) is well understood, see [1]. However, the situation changes completely when considering WKSTs and/or ciphers with a non-trivial key schedule. In those situations, the analysis of [1] is no longer applicable and we do not have a generic approach to argue the resistance against WKSTs. It follows that the concept of WKSTs opens up many new opportunities and raises many new, probably highly non-trivial questions on how to protect against it.

3 Preliminary – Subspace Trail Properties of the AES

The Advanced Encryption Standard [9] is a *Substitution-Permutation network* that supports key sizes of 128, 192 and 256 bits. The 128-bit plaintext initializes the internal state as a 4×4 matrix of bytes as values in the finite field $\mathbb{F}_{256}$, defined using the irreducible polynomial $x^8 + x^4 + x^3 + x + 1$. Depending on the version of AES, N_r rounds are applied to the state: $N_r = 10$ for AES-128, $N_r = 12$ for AES-192 and $N_r = 14$ for AES-256. One round of AES can be described as $R(x) = K \oplus \text{MC} \circ \text{SR} \circ \text{SB}(x)$, where

- *SubBytes* (SB) – applying the same 8-bit to 8-bit invertible S-Box 16 times in parallel on each byte of the state (it provides non-linearity in the cipher);
- *ShiftRows* (SR) – cyclic shift of each row to the left;
- *MixColumns* (MC) – multiplication of each column by a constant 4×4 invertible matrix M_{MC} (MC and SR provide diffusion in the cipher);
- *AddRoundKey* (ARK) – XORing the state with a 128-bit subkey.

In the first round an additional AddRoundKey operation (using a whitening key) is applied, and in the last round the MixColumns operation is omitted.

Key Schedule AES-128. The key schedule of AES-128 takes the user key and transforms it into 11 subkeys of 128 bits each. The subkey array is denoted by $W[0, \ldots, 43]$, where each word of $W[\cdot]$ consists of 4 bytes and where the first 4 words of $W[\cdot]$ are loaded with the user secret key. The remaining words of $W[\cdot]$ are updated according to the following rule:

$$W[i][j] = \begin{cases} W[i][j-4] \oplus \text{SB}(W[i+1][j-1]) \oplus R[i][j/4] & \text{if } j \bmod 4 = 0 \\ W[i][j-1] \oplus W[i][j-4] & \text{otherwise} \end{cases}$$

where $i = 0, 1, 2, 3$, $j = 4, \ldots, 43$ and $R[\cdot]$ is an array of constants[2]

The Notation used in the Paper. Let x denote a plaintext, a ciphertext, an intermediate state or a key. Then $x_{i,j}$ or $x_{i+4 \times j}$ with $i, j \in \{0, \ldots, 3\}$ denotes the byte in the row i and in the column j. We denote by k^r the key of the r-th round. If only one key is used, then we denote it by k to simplify the notation. Finally, we denote by R one round of AES, while we denote r rounds of AES by R^r. We sometimes use the notation R_K instead of R to highlight the round key K. As last thing, in the paper we often use the term "partial collision" (or "collision") when two texts belong to the same coset of a given subspace X.

---

[2] The round constants are defined in $GF(2^8)[X]$ as $R[0][1] = X$, $R[0][r] = X \cdot R[0][r-1]$ if $r \geq 2$ and $R[i][\cdot] = 0$ if $i \neq 0$. For the following, let $R[r] \equiv R[0][r]$.

3.1 Subspace Trails of AES

In this section, we recall the main concepts of the subspace trails of AES presented in [18]. In the following, we only work with vectors and vector spaces over $\mathbb{F}_{2^8}^{4\times4}$, and we denote by $\{e_{0,0},\dots,e_{3,3}\}$ or $\{e_0,\dots,e_{15}\}$ the unit vectors of $\mathbb{F}_{2^8}^{4\times4}$ (e.g. $e_{i,j}$ or $e_{i+4\times j}$ has a single 1 in row i and column j). We also recall that given a subspace X, the cosets $X\oplus a$ and $X\oplus b$ (where $a\neq b$) are *equal* ($X\oplus a\equiv X\oplus b$) if and only if $a\oplus b\in X$.

Definition 4. *The* column spaces $\mathcal{C}_i$ *are defined as* $\mathcal{C}_i=\langle e_{0,i},e_{1,i},e_{2,i},e_{3,i}\rangle$.

Definition 5. *The* diagonal spaces $\mathcal{D}_i$ *and the* inverse-diagonal spaces $\mathcal{ID}_i$ *are respectively defined as* $\mathcal{D}_i=\mathrm{SR}^{-1}(\mathcal{C}_i)\equiv\langle e_{0,i},e_{1,i+1},e_{2,i+2},e_{3,i+3}\rangle$ *and* $\mathcal{ID}_i=\mathrm{SR}(\mathcal{C}_i)\equiv\langle e_{0,i},e_{1,i-1},e_{2,i-2},e_{3,i-3}\rangle$, *where the indexes are taken modulo 4.*

Definition 6. *The i-th* mixed spaces $\mathcal{M}_i$ *are defined as* $\mathcal{M}_i=\mathrm{MC}(\mathcal{ID}_i)$.

Definition 7. *For* $I\subseteq\{0,1,2,3\}$, *let* $\mathcal{C}_I$, $\mathcal{D}_I$, $\mathcal{ID}_I$ *and* $\mathcal{M}_I$ *be defined as*

$$\mathcal{C}_I=\bigoplus_{i\in I}\mathcal{C}_i,\qquad \mathcal{D}_I=\bigoplus_{i\in I}\mathcal{D}_i,\qquad \mathcal{ID}_I=\bigoplus_{i\in I}\mathcal{ID}_i,\qquad \mathcal{M}_I=\bigoplus_{i\in I}\mathcal{M}_i.$$

For completeness, we briefly describe the subspace trail notation using a more "classical" one. If two texts t^1 and t^2 are equal except for the bytes in the i-th diagonal[3] for each $i\in I$, then they belong in the same coset of $\mathcal{D}_I$. Two texts t^1 and t^2 belong in the same coset of $\mathcal{M}_I$ if the bytes of their difference $\mathrm{MC}^{-1}(t^1\oplus t^2)$ in the i-th anti-diagonal for each $i\notin I$ are equal to zero. Similar considerations hold for the spaces $\mathcal{C}_I$ and $\mathcal{ID}_I$.

Theorem 1 ([18]). *For each I and for each $a\in\mathcal{D}_I^{\perp}$, there exists one and only one $b\in\mathcal{M}_I^{\perp}$ such that $R^2(\mathcal{D}_I\oplus a)=\mathcal{M}_I\oplus b$.*

Observe that if X is a generic subspace, $X\oplus a$ is a coset of X and x and y are two elements of the (same) coset $X\oplus a$, then $x\oplus y\in X$. It follows that:

Lemma 1. *For all* $I\subseteq\{0,1,2,3\}$: $\Pr\left[R^2(x)\oplus R^2(y)\in\mathcal{M}_I\mid x\oplus y\in\mathcal{D}_I\right]=1$.

Finally, for the follow-up, we introduce a generic subspace trail of length 1.

Definition 8. *Given* $I\subseteq\{(0,0),(0,1),\dots,(3,2),(3,3)\}\equiv\{(i,j)\}_{0\leq i,j\leq3}$, *let the subspace* $\mathcal{X}_I$ *be defined as* $\mathcal{X}_I=\langle\{e_{i,j}\}_{(i,j)\in I}\rangle\equiv\left\{\bigoplus_{(i,j)\in I}\alpha_{i,j}\cdot e_{i,j}\mid\forall\alpha_{i,j}\in\mathbb{F}_{2^8}\right\}$.

In other words, $\mathcal{X}_I$ is the set of elements given by linear combinations of $\{e_{i,j}\}_{(i,j)\in I}$, where $e_{i,j}\in\mathbb{F}_{2^8}^{4\times4}$ has a single 1 in row i and column j.

---

[3] The i-th diagonal of a 4×4 matrix A is defined as the elements that lie on row r and column c such that $r-c=i\bmod4$. The i-th anti-diagonal of a 4×4 matrix A is defined as the elements that lie on row r and column c such that $r+c=i\bmod4$.

Theorem 2. *For each* $I \subseteq \{(0,0),(0,1),\ldots,(3,2),(3,3)\} \equiv \{(i,j)\}_{0 \leq i,j \leq 3}$ *and for each* $a \in \mathcal{X}_I^{\perp}$, *there exists one and only one* $b \in \mathcal{Y}_I^{\perp}$ *such that* $R(\mathcal{X}_I \oplus a) = \mathcal{Y}_I \oplus b$, *where* $\mathcal{Y}_I = \mathrm{MC} \circ \mathrm{SR}(\mathcal{X}_I)$.

Proof is given in Appendix A. Such subspace trail cannot be extended on two rounds for any generic $\mathcal{X}_I$, due to the non-linear S-Box operation of the next round (that *can* destroy the linear relations that hold among the bytes).

3.2 (Weak-Key) Invariant Subspace Trail for AES

In this section, we present a subspace $\mathcal{IS}$ which is invariant for a key-less AES round, and a set of weak-keys for AES-128 that allows to set up an invariant subspace trail for 2-round AES-128. Similar results – presented in Appendix B – can be provided for AES-192 and AES-256. Then, we discuss a weakness of an alternative linear key-schedule for AES-128 proposed at ToSC/FSE 2018 [22], based on permutations of the byte positions.

Invariant Subspace $\mathcal{IS}$ for AES. Let the subspace $\mathcal{IS}$ be defined as

$$
\mathcal{IS} := \left\{ \begin{bmatrix} a & b & a & b \\ c & d & c & d \\ e & f & e & f \\ g & h & g & h \end{bmatrix} \middle| \ \forall a,b,c,d,\ldots,h \in \mathbb{F}_{2^8} \right\} \tag{1}
$$

This subspace is invariant under a key-less round $R(\cdot) = \mathrm{MC} \circ \mathrm{SR} \circ \mathrm{SB}(\cdot)$, since

$$
\mathrm{SB}(\mathcal{IS}) = \mathcal{IS} \qquad \mathrm{SR}(\mathcal{IS}) = \mathcal{IS} \qquad \mathrm{MC}(\mathcal{IS}) = \mathcal{IS}.
$$

This subspace – already presented and used in e.g. [7,25] – will be our starting point to set up a weak-key invariant subspace trail for all versions of AES.

Weak-Keys of AES-128 & Invariant Subspace Trail. In the case of the AES key-schedule, under one of the 2^{32} weak-keys in K_{weak}

$$
K_{\mathrm{weak}} := \left\{ \begin{bmatrix} A & A & A & A \\ B & B & B & B \\ C & C & C & C \\ D & D & D & D \end{bmatrix} \middle| \ \forall A,B,C,D \in \mathbb{F}_{2^8} \right\} \tag{2}
$$

the subspace $\mathcal{IS}$ is mapped into a coset of $\mathcal{IS}$ after two complete AES rounds.

In more details, given $k \in K_{\mathrm{weak}}$, let $\hat{k}$ be the corresponding subkey after 2 rounds of the key schedule (where $\hat{k} \notin K_{\mathrm{weak}}$ in general). It follows that

$$
\mathcal{IS} \xrightarrow{R_K^2 \circ \mathrm{ARK}(\cdot)} \mathcal{IS} \oplus \hat{k}
$$

where $R_K(\cdot) \equiv \mathrm{ARK} \circ \mathrm{MC} \circ \mathrm{SR} \circ \mathrm{SB}(\cdot)$, that is $\mathcal{IS}$ *forms a weak invariant subspace of length 2*. In order to prove this result, it is sufficient to note that

1. $K_{\text{weak}} \subseteq \mathcal{IS}$, which implies that $\mathcal{IS} \oplus k = \mathcal{IS}$ for all $k \in K_{\text{weak}}$;
2. the first round key derived from the key-schedule of K_{weak} – denoted by K'_w – is a subset of $\mathcal{IS}$

$$
K'_w \equiv \begin{bmatrix}
\text{SB}(B) \oplus A \oplus R[1] & \text{SB}(B) \oplus R[1] & \text{SB}(B) \oplus A \oplus R[1] & \text{SB}(B) \oplus R[1] \\
\text{SB}(C) \oplus B & \text{SB}(C) & \text{SB}(C) \oplus B & \text{SB}(C) \\
\text{SB}(D) \oplus C & \text{SB}(D) & \text{SB}(D) \oplus C & \text{SB}(D) \\
\text{SB}(A) \oplus D & \text{SB}(A) & \text{SB}(A) \oplus D & \text{SB}(A)
\end{bmatrix}
$$

Key Schedules Based on Permutation of the Byte Positions. The possibility to set up a weak invariant subspace trail depends on the concrete value of the secret key and of the key schedule details. To better understand this point, here we analyze another key-schedule recently proposed at ToSC/FSE 2018 [22] *in the case in which no random round-constant is added.* Such a key-schedule – proposed with the only goal to provide resistance against *related key-differential attacks* – is linear and it is based on permutations of the byte positions: each subkey is the result of a particular permutation applied to the whitening key defined as follows

$$
\begin{pmatrix}
0 & 4 & 8 & 12 \\
1 & 5 & 9 & 13 \\
2 & 6 & 10 & 14 \\
3 & 7 & 11 & 15
\end{pmatrix}
\rightarrow
\begin{pmatrix}
11 & 15 & 3 & 7 \\
12 & 0 & 4 & 8 \\
1 & 5 & 9 & 13 \\
2 & 6 & 10 & 14
\end{pmatrix}
\tag{3}
$$

In the case in which random round-constants are added, an invariant subspace attack that covers an unlimited number of rounds is very unlikely, as showed e.g. in [1] (for the case of other ciphers). Hence, by adding random constants at every round, such key-schedule is perfectly fine and could be a good candidate for future designs. Instead, in the case in which *no random round-constant is added,* then an "infinitely-long" weak invariant subspace can be set up. Indeed, consider the previous subspace $\mathcal{IS}$ defined in Eq. (1) and *assume that the whitening key belongs to such subspace:* It follows that any subkey generated by the previous permutation belongs to this subspace (due to particular symmetries of the permutation).

Adding a (Partial) S-Box Layer. Besides adding random round-constants, another possible way to prevent such invariant subspace attack is by adding non-linear operations in the key-schedule. In [22, Sect. 6], authors propose to *"tweak this design (without increasing the tracking effort) by adding an S-Box layer every round to the entire first row of the key state".* Due to the analysis just proposed and only in the case in which no round-constant is added, this operation does not improve the security against the presented invariant subspace attack. Indeed, note that the invariant subspace $\mathcal{IS}$ is still mapped into itself *even if* an S-Box layer is applied to the entire first row of the key state:

$$\begin{bmatrix} \text{SB}(a) & \text{SB}(b) & \text{SB}(a) & \text{SB}(b) \\ c & d & c & d \\ e & f & e & f \\ g & h & g & h \end{bmatrix} = \begin{bmatrix} a' & b' & a' & b' \\ c & d & c & d \\ e & f & e & f \\ g & h & g & h \end{bmatrix} \in \mathcal{IS}.$$

We emphasize that this problem can be easily fixed by applying such an S-Box layer every round to the entire (e.g.) first column/diagonal. As a result, even in the case in which *no* random round-constant are added, the partial S-Box layer applied every round to the entire first column/diagonal[4] is sufficient by itself to prevent "*infinitely-long*" weak invariant subspace trails based on $\mathcal{IS}$.

Follow-Up Works: Key-Schedule Based on Permutation. After the initial work [22], other key-schedules based only on permutations have been recently proposed at SAC 2018 [12]. Here we focus on the one proposed in [12, Theorem 2], and defined by the following byte-permutation:

$$\begin{pmatrix} 15 & 0 & 2 & 3 & 4 & 11 & 5 & 7 & 6 & 12 & 8 & 10 & 9 & 1 & 13 & 14 \end{pmatrix},$$

which guarantees more security than the AES one w.r.t. related-key differential attacks. W.r.t. the key-schedule proposed in [22] and only in the case in which no random round-constant is added, here an "*infinitely-long*" invariant subspace trail can be set up for a set of 2^8 weak keys only (which corresponds to the case in which all bytes of the whitening key are equal).

4   Weak-Key Secret-Key Distinguishers for AES

As a first application of the invariant subspaces just found, we are going to show that *under the assumption of weak-keys* it is possible to extend the secret-key distinguishers present in the literature to more rounds (note that all the following results are independent of the details of the S-Box and of the MixColumns operation). In the following, we present in detail only the results for AES-128 for the encryption/forward direction (analogous results hold also in the decryption/backward direction). Similar results can be obtained also for AES-192 and AES-256, using the corresponding weak-keys and weak-key invariant subspace trails defined in Appendix B. The results – which have been practically tested using a C/C++ implementation – are summarized in Table 1.

Assumption. *From now on we assume that the secret key is a weak-key (that is, a key in the set K_{weak} as described previously).*

4.1   Subspace Trail Distinguishers

In the case of AES, it is possible to set up subspace trail distinguishers for 3-round AES *independently* of the secret-key, of the details of the S-Box and of the MixColumns matrix (assuming branch number equal to five). It is based on

---

[4] For completeness, we emphasize that the same result holds in the case of the original AES key-schedule without random constants.

Table 1. *Secret-key properties for round-reduced AES.* In the following, we list the properties for round-reduced AES which are independent of the secret key, together with the corresponding number of rounds. "Number of keys" denotes the number of keys (with respect to the total space) for which a particular property holds for up to r rounds. Just for simplicity, we do not add the distinguisher complexity (or equivalently, the probability of the exploited property).

Property	Version of AES	Rounds	Number of keys	Reference
Weak-key Subspace Trail	AES-128/256	3	*All:* $2^{128} / 2^{256}$	folklore
	AES-128/256	4	$2^{32} / 2^{128}$	Section 4.1
	AES-256	6/7/8	$2^{96} / 2^{64} / 2^{32}$	Section 4.1
Multiple-of-n	AES-128/256	5	*All:* $2^{128} / 2^{256}$	[19]
	AES-128/256	6	$2^{32} / 2^{128}$	Section 4.2
	AES-256	7/8/9	$2^{96} / 2^{64} / 2^{32}$	Section 4.2

the fact that $\Pr\left[R^3(x) \oplus R^3(y) \in \mathcal{M}_J \mid x \oplus y \in \mathcal{D}_I\right] = (2^8)^{-4|I|+|I|\cdot|J|}$ as showed in detail in [18], while for a random permutation Π the previous probability is (approximately) equal to

$$\Pr\left[\Pi(x) \oplus \Pi(y) \in \mathcal{M}_J \mid x \oplus y \in \mathcal{D}_I\right] = (2^8)^{-16+4J|}. \qquad (4)$$

In the following, we extend the previous subspace trail distinguisher for up to 4 rounds in the case of weak-keys. Focusing on the case of AES-128, we have just seen that the subspace $\mathcal{IS}$ is mapped into a coset $\mathcal{IS} \oplus a$ after two rounds if the secret key is a weak-key. In other words, given two plaintexts $x, y \in \mathcal{IS}$, then $R^2(x) \oplus R^2(y) \in \mathcal{IS}$ under a weak-key. Since the 1st and the 3rd diagonals of each text in $\mathcal{IS}$ are equal (as well as the 2nd and the 4th ones) and by definition of $\mathcal{D}_I$, note that

$$\Pr\left[z \in \mathcal{D}_I \mid z \in \mathcal{IS}\right] = \begin{cases} 2^{-32} & I \equiv \{0,2\}, \{1,3\} \\ 0 & \text{otherwise} \end{cases} \qquad (5)$$

where we assume that $z \notin \mathcal{D}_L$ for all $L \subseteq \{0,1,2,3\}$ s.t. $|L| < |I| < 4$. This is the starting point for our results, together with the fact that $\Pr\left[z \in \mathcal{D}_{0,2}\right] = \Pr\left[z \in \mathcal{D}_{1,3}\right] = 2^{-64}$ for a generic text z.

Weak-Key Subspace Trail over 4-Round AES-128. Since $R^2(\mathcal{D}_I \oplus a) = \mathcal{M}_I \oplus b$ (that is $\Pr\left[R^2(x) \oplus R^2(y) \in \mathcal{M}_I \mid x \oplus y \in \mathcal{D}_I\right] = 1$), it follows that for an AES permutation and for a weak-key[5]

$$\Pr\left[R^4(x) \oplus R^4(y) \in \mathcal{M}_I \mid x, y \in \mathcal{IS}, k \in K_{\text{weak}}\right] = 2^{-32} \qquad \text{if } I \equiv \{0,2\}, \{1,3\},$$

while for a random permutation Π the probability is equal to 2^{-64} (see Eq. (4)).

This fact can also be re-written using the subspace trail notation.

---

[5] Note that the condition "$x, y \in \mathcal{IS}$" cannot be replaced by the weaker one: "x, y s.t. $x \oplus y \in \mathcal{IS}$". Indeed, if $x, y \in \mathcal{IS}$, then $R^2(x) \oplus R^2(y) \in \mathcal{IS}$ (as showed before), while this is not true – in general – for x, y s.t. $x \oplus y \in \mathcal{IS}$.

Proposition 1. *Consider 2^{64} plaintexts in the subspace $\mathcal{IS}$, and the corresponding ciphertexts after 4-rounds AES-128 encrypted under a weak-key $k \in \mathcal{K}_{weak}$.*

With probability 1, there exist 2^{32} (in 2^{64}) different cosets of $\mathcal{M}_{0,2}$ and there exist 2^{32} (in 2^{64}) different cosets of $\mathcal{M}_{1,3}$ s.t. each one of them contains exactly 2^{32} ciphertexts. For a random permutation, each one of the previous events is satisfied with probability $\binom{2^{64}}{2^{32}} \cdot \prod_{i=0}^{2^{32}-1} \left[\left(2^{-64}\right)^{2^{32}-1} \cdot \left(1 - i \cdot 2^{-64}\right) \right] \approx 2^{-2^{70}}$.

A complete proof of this proposition can be found in Appendix D.1.

4.2   Weak-Key "Multiple-of-n" Property for 5-/6-Round AES-128

At Eurocrypt 2017, Grassi et al. [19] presented the first property on 5-round AES which is independent of the secret key and of the details of the S-Box and of the MixColumns. The result can be summarized as follows: Given $2^{32 \cdot |I|}$ plaintexts in the same coset of a diagonal space $\mathcal{D}_I$, the number of different pairs of ciphertexts that belong to the same coset of $\mathcal{M}_J$ after 5-round AES is always a multiple of 8. The "multiple-of-8" property is related to the "mixture differential" cryptanalysis presented in [16], and recently re-visited in [5].

In the case of a weak-key, we are able to extend the previous result for up to 6-round AES-128. The obtained results – which hold also in the *decryption* direction – are proposed in the following Theorems:

Theorem 3. *Let $\mathcal{IS}$ and $\mathcal{M}_I$ be the subspaces defined as before for a fixed I with $1 \leq |I| \leq 3$. Assume that the whitening key is a weak-key, that is it belongs to the set K_{weak} as defined in Eq. (2). Given 2^{64} plaintexts in $\mathcal{IS}$, the number n of different pairs[6] of ciphertexts $(c^i = R^5(p^i), c^j = R^5(p^j))$ after 5-round AES for $i \neq j$ that belong to the same coset of $\mathcal{M}_I$ (that is $c^i \oplus c^j \in \mathcal{M}_I$) is a multiple of 128, independently of the details of the S-Box and of the MixColumns matrix.*

Proof. First of all, since the invariant subspace $\mathcal{IS}$ is mapped into a coset of $\mathcal{IS}$ after 2-round encryption, and similarly a coset of $\mathcal{M}_I$ is mapped into a coset of $\mathcal{D}_I$ after 2-round decryption, that is

$$\forall k \in K_{weak} : \quad \mathcal{IS} \xrightarrow[\text{prob. 1}]{R^2(\cdot)} \mathcal{IS} \oplus a \xrightarrow{R(\cdot)} \mathcal{D}_I \oplus a' \xrightarrow[\text{prob. 1}]{R^2(\cdot)} \mathcal{M}_I \oplus b'$$

we *focus only on the middle round*, and we prove the following equivalent result: given 2^{64} plaintexts in a coset of $\mathcal{IS}$, the number n of different pairs of ciphertexts (c^i, c^j) for $i \neq j$ that belong to the same coset of $\mathcal{D}_I$ (that is $c^i \oplus c^j \in \mathcal{D}_I$) after 1 round is a multiple of 128. This result can be achieved by observing that, given a pair of texts $t^1, t^2 \in \mathcal{IS} \oplus a$, there exist other pair(s) of texts $s^1, s^2 \in \mathcal{IS} \oplus a$ s.t.

- $R(t^1) \oplus R(t^2) \in \mathcal{D}_I \Leftrightarrow R(s^1) \oplus R(s^2) \in \mathcal{D}_I$;
- the texts s^1, s^2 are given by any different combination of the generating variables of t^1, t^2.

---

[6] Two pairs (s, t) and (t, s) are considered to be equivalent.

By definition of $\mathcal{IS}$, let t^1 and t^2 be as $t^i = a \oplus \bigoplus_{j=0}^{7} x_j^i \cdot (e_j \oplus e_{j+8})$ where $x_j \equiv x_{r+4 \times c}$ denotes the byte in the r-th row and in the c-th & $(c+2)$-th columns. For simplicity, let $t^i \equiv (x_0^i, x_1^i, x_2^i, x_3^i, x_4^i, x_5^i, x_6^i, x_7^i)$.

Case: Different Generating Variables. Consider initially the case in which all the generating variables are different, that is $x_j^1 \neq x_j^2$ for $j = 0, 1, \ldots, 7$. Let S_{t^1, t^2} be the set of pairs of texts $s^1, s^2 \in \mathcal{IS} \oplus a$ defined by swapping some generating variables of t^1 and t^2. More formally, the set S_{t^1, t^2} contains all 128 pairs of texts (s^1, s^2) for all $I \subseteq \{0, 1, 2, 3, 4, 5, 6, 7\}$ where

$$s^1 = a \oplus \bigoplus_{j=0}^{7} \left\{ \left[\left(x_j^1 \cdot \delta_j(I) \right) \oplus \left(x_j^2 \cdot [1 - \delta_j(I)] \right) \right] \cdot \left(e_j \oplus e_{j+8} \right) \right\}$$

$$s^2 = a \oplus \bigoplus_{j=0}^{7} \left\{ \left[\left(x_j^2 \cdot \delta_j(I) \right) \oplus \left(x_j^1 \cdot [1 - \delta_j(I)] \right) \right] \cdot \left(e_j \oplus e_{j+8} \right) \right\}$$

where the pairs (s^1, s^2) and (s^2, s^1) are considered to be equivalent, and where $\delta_x(A)$ is the Dirac measure defined as $\delta_x(A) = \begin{cases} 1 & \text{if } x \in A \\ 0 & \text{if } x \notin A \end{cases}$. By showing that

$$\forall (s^1, s^2) \in S_{t^1, t^2}: \qquad R(t^1) \oplus R(t^2) = R(s^1) \oplus R(s^2), \qquad (6)$$

it follows immediately that $R(t^1) \oplus R(t^2) \in \mathcal{D}_I \Leftrightarrow R(s^1) \oplus R(s^2) \in \mathcal{D}_I$ for each $(s^1, s^2) \in S_{t^1, t^2}$. The equivalence Eq. (6) is due to the facts that *the S-Box operation works independently on each byte and that the XOR-sum is commutative.* Since each set S_{t^1, t^2} has cardinality 128, in the case in which one focuses on the pairs of texts with different generating variables, it follows that the multiple-of-128 property previously defined holds.

Generic Case. In the case in which some variables are equal, e.g. $x_j^1 = x_j^2$ for $j \in J \subseteq \{0, \ldots, 7\}$ with $|J| \geq 1$, the difference $R(t^1) \oplus R(t^2)$ is independent of the value of $x_j^1 = x_j^2$ for each $j \in J$. Thus, the idea is to consider all the different pairs of texts given by swapping one or more variables x_l^1 and x_l^2 for $l = 0, 1, \ldots, 7$, *where x_j for $j \in J$ can take any possible value in $\mathbb{F}_{2^8}$.* Note that in the case in which $0 \leq |J| < 8$ variables are equal, it is possible to identify

$$\underbrace{2^{7-|J|}}_{\text{by swapping different gen. variables}} \times \underbrace{2^{8 \cdot |J|}}_{\text{due to equal gen. variables}} = 2^{7 \cdot (1+|J|)} = 128^{1+|J|}$$

different texts s^1 and s^2 in $\mathcal{IS} \oplus a$ that satisfy the condition $R(t^1) \oplus R(t^2) = R(s^1) \oplus R(s^2)$. More formally, given t^1 and t^2, the set S_{t^1, t^2} contains all $2^{7 \cdot (1+|J|)}$ pairs of texts $(s^1 \oplus a, s^2 \oplus a)$ for all $I \subseteq \{0, 1, 2, 3, 4, 5, 6, 7\} \setminus J$ and for all $\alpha_0, \ldots, \alpha_{|J|} \in \mathbb{F}_{2^8}$ where s^1, s^2 are defined as

$$s^1 = \bigoplus_{j \in \{0,\ldots,7\} \setminus J} \left\{ \left[\left(x_j^1 \cdot \delta_j(I) \right) \oplus \left(x_j^2 \cdot [1 - \delta_j(I)] \right) \right] \cdot \left(e_j \oplus e_{j+8} \right) \right\} \oplus \bigoplus_{j \in J} \alpha_j \cdot \left(e_j \oplus e_{j+8} \right)$$

$$s^2 = \bigoplus_{j \in \{0,\ldots,7\} \setminus J} \left\{ \left[\left(x_j^2 \cdot \delta_j(I) \right) \oplus \left(x_j^1 \cdot [1 - \delta_j(I)] \right) \right] \cdot \left(e_j \oplus e_{j+8} \right) \right\} \oplus \bigoplus_{j \in J} \alpha_j \cdot \left(e_j \oplus e_{j+8} \right)$$

In conclusion, given plaintexts in the same coset of $\mathcal{IS}$, the number of different pairs of ciphertexts that belong to the same coset of $\mathcal{D}_I$ after one round is a multiple of 128. □

Theorem 4. *Let $\mathcal{IS}$, $\mathcal{M}_J$ and $\mathcal{X}_I$ be the subspaces defined as before, for an arbitrary $J \subseteq \{0, 1, 2, 3\}$ and arbitrary $I \subset \{(0,0), (0,1), \ldots, (3,2), (3,3)\} \equiv \{(i,j)\}_{0 \leq i,j \leq 3}$. Assume that the whitening key is a weak-key, i. e. it belongs to the set K_{weak} defined in Eq. (2). Given 2^{64} plaintexts in $\mathcal{IS}$, the following properties hold independently of the details of the S-Box:*

- *5-round AES-128: the number n of different pairs of ciphertexts (c^i, c^j) for $i \neq j$ that belong to the same coset of $\mathcal{X}_I$ is a multiple of 2;*
- *6-round AES-128: the number n of different pairs of ciphertexts (c^i, c^j) for $i \neq j$ that belong to the same coset of $\mathcal{M}_J$ is a multiple of 2.*

The proof of these properties – similar to the one given in [19] and to the one already given – is proposed in details in Appendix D.2.

4.3   Practical Experiments

Most of the previous properties have been practically verified[7]. Here we briefly present the practical results and we compare them with the theoretical ones.

All our distinguishers are based on $\mathcal{IS}$ and their practical verification requires at least 2^{64} reduced-round AES encryptions. For this reason, we performed our experiments on small-scale AES [8], where each word is composed of 4-bit instead of 8 (note that all previous results are independent of the details of the S-Box). This implies that the dimension of $\mathcal{IS}$ reduces to 32 bits from 64.

Practical Results. For Theorem 3 and Theorem 4, we performed 5-round and 6-round encryptions of $\mathcal{IS}$ for more than 100 randomly chosen weak-keys in K_{weak}. We counted the collisions in each of the four inverse diagonals space $\mathcal{ID}$ and observed the multiple-of-128 and multiple-of-2 properties hold for 5-round and 6-round encryptions, respectively. Similar tests have been performed in order to check the multiple-of-2 property on the subspaces $\mathcal{X}_I$ as defined in Definition 8 for each $|I| \leq 4$. Due to increased time and memory complexity, these properties were not verified for $|I| > 4$. The experiment results – also performed in the decryption direction – agree with the theoretical ones summarized in Tables 1 and 2.

---

[7] The source codes of the distinguishers/attacks are publicly available, and they can be found in https://github.com/cihangirtezcan/AES_weak_keys.

Table 2. *AES Chosen-Key Distinguishers.* The computation cost is the cost to generate N-tuples of plaintexts/ciphertexts. "SK" denotes a chosen-key distinguisher in the Single-Key setting, while "RK" denotes a chosen-key distinguisher in the Related-Key setting. We mention that the known-key distinguishers presented in [14] are excluded from this Table due to the arguments reported in Appendix E.

AES	Rounds	Computations	Property	SK	RK	Reference
AES-128	8	2^{24}	Multiple Diff. Trail	✓		[11]
	8	$2^{13.4}$	Multiple Diff. Trail	✓		[21]
	9	2^{55}	Multi-Collision Diff.		✓	[13]
	9	$\mathbf{2^{64}}$	**Multiple-of-n** (2^{32} keys)	✓		Section 5.3
AES-256	9	2^{24}	Multiple Diff. Trail	✓		[11]
	12	$\mathbf{2^{64}}$	**Multiple-of-n** (2^{32} keys)	✓		Appendix B.3
	14 (full)	2^{120}	Multi-Collision Diff.		✓	[4]

5   New Chosen-Key Distinguishers for AES

In this section we present new chosen-key distinguishers for AES in the single-key setting. In particular, as major results, we are able to present *the first candidate 9-round chosen-key distinguisher for AES-128* and *a 12-round candidate chosen-key distinguisher for AES-256, both in the single-key setting*. All the distinguishers that we present are based on the (practically verified) multiple-of-n property proposed in Sect. 4.2.

The goal of an open-key distinguisher is to differentiate between a block cipher E which allows to generate plaintext/ciphertext pairs which exhibit a rare relation, even for a small set of keys or a single key, and an ideal cipher Π that does not have such a property. However, this poses a definitional problem as it was shown already in [6] that any concrete implementable cipher (like the AES) can be trivially distinguished from an ideal cipher. To the best of our knowledge, finding a proper formal definition that captures the intuition behind chosen-key distinguishers has been a challenging task for the last fifteen years and is still an open problem.

We do not attempt to address this formalization challenge here, but proceed in the way that is custom in the literature to describe chosen-key distinguisher: *(1st)* describe the rare property (see Sect. 5.2), *(2nd)* show that it can be efficiently constructed for the block cipher usually using an inside-out approach (see Sect. 5.3 for 9-round AES-128), and *(3rd)* argue or prove in some model that any generic method is less efficient or has low success probability (see Sect. 5.4). Our results are summarized in Table 2: in order to compare the results, note that an attack/distinguisher with *no* key difference is (logically) harder than an attack/distinguisher for which key differences are allowed, since the attacker has less freedom.

As before, in the following we limit ourselves to give all the details for the AES-128 case (analogous result for AES-256 are presented in Appendix B.3).

5.1   Open-Key Distinguishers – State of the Art for AES

Chosen-Key Distinguishers – State of the Art for AES. To the best of our knowledge, the first chosen-key distinguisher for AES in the single-key setting has been proposed in [11]. In there, the chosen-key model asks the adversary to find two plaintexts/ciphertexts pairs and a key such that the two plaintexts are equal in 3 diagonals and the two ciphertexts are equal in 3 anti-diagonals (if the final MixColumns is omitted). Equivalently, using the subspace trail notation, the goal is to find $(p^1, c^1 \equiv R^8(p^1))$ and $(p^2, c^2 \equiv R^8(p^2))$ for $p^1 \neq p^2$ s.t. $p^1 \oplus p^2 \in \mathcal{D}_I$ and $c^1 \oplus c^2 \in \mathcal{M}_J$ for a certain $I, J \subseteq \{0, 1, 2, 3\}$ s.t. $|I| = |J| = 1$. This problem is equivalent to the one proposed in [15,21] in the known-key scenario. In particular, the main (and only) difference is related to the freedom of choosing the key, which allows to reduce the computational cost. For completeness, similar results have been proposed for 9-round AES-256.

The chosen-key model has been popularized some years before by Biryukov et al. [4], since a distinguisher in this model has been extended to a related-key attack on full AES-256. A related distinguisher for 9-round AES-128 has been proposed by Fouque et al. [13]. Both the chosen-key distinguisher proposed in these papers are in the related-key setting. Here we briefly recall them, but we emphasize that we do not consider related-keys in this article. In [4], authors show that it is possible to construct a q-*multicollision* on Davies-Meyer compression function using AES-256 in time $q \cdot 2^{67}$, whereas for an ideal cipher it would require on average $q \cdot 2^{\frac{q-1}{q+1} 128}$ time complexity. A similar approach has been exploited in [13] to set up the first chosen-key distinguisher for 9-round AES-128. Here, the chosen-key model asks the adversary to find a pair of keys (k, k') satisfying $k \oplus k' = \delta$ with a *known (fixed)* difference δ, and a pair of messages $(p^1, c^1 \equiv R^9(p^1))$ and $(p^2, c^2 \equiv R^9(p^2))$ conforming to a partially instantiated differential characteristic in the data part.

Finally, echoing [17], in Appendix E we briefly recall and discuss the 10-round known-key distinguisher for AES proposed by Gilbert [14] at Asiacrypt 2014.

5.2   The "Simultaneous Multiple-of-n" Property

In our distinguisher, the chosen-key model asks the adversary to find a set of 2^{64} (plaintexts, ciphertexts), that is $(p^i, c^i \equiv R^9(p^i))$ for $i = 0, \ldots, 2^{64} - 1$ – where all the plaintexts/ciphertexts are generated by *the same key* – and a key such that the following "*simultaneous multiple-of-n*" property is satisfied:

- for each $J, I \subseteq \{0, 1, 2, 3\}$, the number of different pairs of ciphertexts that belong to the same coset of $\mathcal{M}_J$ and the number of different pairs of plaintexts that belong to the same coset of $\mathcal{D}_I$ are a multiple of $128 = 2^7$;
- for each $J, I \subset \{(0, 0), (0, 1), \ldots, (3, 2), (3, 3)\} \equiv \{(i, j)\}_{0 \leq i, j \leq 3}$, the number of different pairs of ciphertexts that belong to the same coset of $\mathrm{MC}(\mathcal{X}_I)$ and the number of different pairs of plaintexts that belong to the same coset of $\mathcal{X}_J$ are a multiple of 2.

For the follow-up, we emphasize that the subspaces $\mathcal{X}$ (defined as in Definition 8) are independent, in the sense that e.g. the fact that the multiple-of-2 property is satisfied by $\mathcal{X}_I$ and/or $\mathcal{X}_J$ does not imply anything on $\mathcal{X}_{I \cup J}$ and vice-versa. This is due to the fact that given $\mathcal{X}_I$ and $\mathcal{X}_J$, then $\mathcal{X}_I \cup \mathcal{X}_J \subsetneq \mathcal{X}_{I \cup J}$. As a result, any information about the multiple-of-n property on $\mathcal{X}_I, \mathcal{X}_J$ (and so $\mathcal{X}_I \cup \mathcal{X}_J$) is useless to derive information about the multiple-of-n property on $\mathcal{X}_{I \cup J} \setminus (\mathcal{X}_I \cup \mathcal{X}_J)$ (and so on $\mathcal{X}_{I \cup J}$).

5.3   9-Round Chosen-Key Distinguisher for AES-128

To find a set of 2^{64} plaintexts/ciphertexts with the required "simultaneous multiple-of-n" property, the distinguisher exploits the fact that *the required property can be fulfilled by starting in the middle with a suitable set of texts*. In particular, the idea is simply to *choose the key such that the subkey of the 4-th round k^4 belongs the subset K_{weak} defined as in Eq. (2)*. Thus, consider the invariant subspace $\mathcal{IS}$ defined as in Eq. (1), and define the 2^{64} plaintexts as the 4-round decryption of $\mathcal{IS}$ and the corresponding ciphertexts as the 5-round encryption of $\mathcal{IS}$. Due to the secret-key distinguishers just presented, this set satisfies the required "simultaneous multiple-of-n" property.

In more details, due to the assumption on the key (that is, $k^4 \in K_{\text{weak}} \subseteq \mathcal{IS}$), note that the subspace $\mathcal{IS}$ is mapped into a coset of $\mathcal{IS}$ after two rounds of encryption and one round of decryption, that is

$$\forall k^4 \in K_{\text{weak}}: \qquad \mathcal{IS} \oplus \hat{k} \xleftarrow{R^{-1}(\cdot)} \mathcal{IS} \xrightarrow{R^2(\cdot)} \mathcal{IS} \oplus \tilde{k}.$$

Due to the results of Sect. 4.2 and since $k^4 \in K_{\text{weak}}$, the multiple-of-n properties hold with probability 1 on the plaintexts and on the ciphertexts

$$\text{Multiple-of-}n \xleftarrow{R^{-3}(\cdot)} \mathcal{IS} \oplus \hat{k} \xleftarrow{R^{-1}(\cdot)} \mathcal{IS} \xrightarrow{R^2(\cdot)} \mathcal{IS} \oplus \tilde{k} \xrightarrow{R^3(\cdot)} \text{Multiple-of-}n$$

It follows that the required set can be constructed using 2^{64} computations. Moreover, we emphasize that our experiments on the secret-key distinguishers of Sect. 4.2 implies the *practical verification of this distinguisher*. What remains is to give arguments as to why producing that property simultaneously on the plaintext and ciphertext side of an ideal cipher is unlikely to be as efficient.

5.4   Achieving the "Simultaneous Multiple-of-n" Property Generically

In this case, the adversary faces a family of random and independent *ideal ciphers* $\{\Pi(K, \cdot), K \in \{0,1\}^k\}$, where $k = 128, 192, 256$ respectively for the cases AES-128/192/256. His goal is to find a key k and a set of 2^{64} plaintexts/ciphertexts $(p^i, c^i = \Pi(k, p^i))$ s.t. the "simultaneous multiple-of-n" property is satisfied. As we are going to show, *the probability to find a set of 2^{64} plaintexts/ciphertexts pairs (X_i, Y_i) that satisfies the "simultaneous multiple-of-n" property for a random permutation is upper bounded by $2^{-65\,618}$*.

As first thing, we discuss the freedom to choose the key. Since the adversary does not know the details of the ideal cipher Π, he does not have any advantage to choose a particular key instead of another one. For this reason, in the following we limit to consider the case in which the permutation Π is instantiated by a fixed key chosen at random in the set $\{0,1\}^k$ – from now: $\Pi(p^i) := \Pi(k, p^i)$.

Exploiting the same strategy proposed in [14], it is possible to prove that the success probability of any oracle algorithm of overall time complexity upper bounded by 2^{64} is negligible.

Proposition 2. *Given a perfect random permutation Π of $\{0,1\}^{128}$ (e.g. instantiated by an ideal cipher with a fixed key uniformly chosen at random in $\{0,1\}^k$), consider $N = 2^{64}$ oracle queries made by any algorithm $\mathcal{A}$ to the perfect random permutation Π or Π^{-1}. Denote this set of 2^{64} plaintexts/ciphertexts pairs by $(X_i, Y_i = \Pi(X_i))$ for $i = 0, \ldots, 2^{64} - 1$. The probability that $\mathcal{A}$ outputs a set of 2^{64} plaintexts/ciphertexts pairs $(X_i, Y_i)_{i=0,\ldots,2^{64}-1}$ that satisfies the "simultaneous multiple-of-n" property is upper bounded by $2^{-65\,618}$.*

A complete proof of the previous proposition is given in Appendix F.

What happens if the adversary performs more than 2^{64} computations? To answer this question, we first compute the probability that a *random* set of 2^{64} plaintexts/ciphertexts generated by the same key satisfies the "simultaneous multiple-of-n" property. As formally showed in Appendix F, the "simultaneous multiple-of-n" property is satisfied with probability

$$\left[(2^{-1})^{2^{16}-16} \cdot (2^{-7})^{14} \right]^2 = (2^{-65\,618})^2 \simeq 2^{-2^{17}}$$

since *(1st)* there are $\sum_{i=1}^{15} \binom{16}{i} = 2^{16} - 2$ different subspaces $\mathcal{X}_I$ for which the multiple-of-2 property holds, and among them there are 14 subspaces $\mathcal{M}_I$ for which the multiple-of-128 property holds and *(2nd)* the probability that the number of collisions is a multiple of N is $\approx 1/N$.

As a result, given $2^{64} + 2^{12}$ random texts, the player can find a set of 2^{64} texts that satisfy the required property both on the plaintexts and on the ciphertexts, since it is possible to construct $\binom{2^{64}+2^{12}}{2^{64}} \approx \frac{(2^{64})^{2^{12}}}{2^{12}!} \simeq 2^{2^{17.7}}$ different sets of 2^{64} texts (where $n! \simeq (n/e)^n \cdot \sqrt{2\pi n}$). On the other hand, *the cost to identify the right 2^{64} texts among all the others is in general much higher than 2^{64} computations:* Indeed, to have a chance of success higher than 95%, one must consider approximately $3 \cdot 2^{131\,236}$ different sets (note that $1 - (1 - 2^{-131\,236})^{3 \cdot 2^{131\,236}} \simeq 1 - e^{-3} \equiv 0.95$).

Moreover, consider the following. Given a set of random texts, suppose to change one plaintext in order to modify the number of collisions in the subspace $\mathcal{X}_I$ (or/and $\mathcal{D}_I$) for a particular I. As a consequence, all the other numbers of collisions in the subspace $\mathcal{X}_J$ (or/and $\mathcal{D}_J$) for all $J \neq I$ change. Even if it is possible to have control of these numbers, a problem arises since also the numbers of collisions among the ciphertexts in each subspace $\mathcal{M}_K$ and $\mathrm{MC}(\mathcal{X}_K)$ change, and in general it is not possible to predict such change in advance.

For all these reasons, we conjecture that *there is no (efficient) strategy* – that does not involve brute force search – *to fulfill the required "simultaneous multiple-of-n" property* for which the cost is approximately of 2^{64} computations (or lower). The problem to *formally* prove this fact is left for future work.

Remarks. Finally, we highlight that our previous claim/result is not true in general if one considers *only* the multiple-of-n property (for $n \leq 8$) in the subspaces $\mathcal{D}_I$ and $\mathcal{M}_J$, that is, not for the generic subspaces $\mathcal{X}$. For a broader understanding of the role of the invariant subspace in the previous distinguishers, in Appendix G we discuss the (im)possibility to set up an open-key distinguisher using the multiple-of-8 property [19] for more than 8-round AES.

A   Generic Subspace Trail (of Length 1) for AES – Proof

Here we give a complete proof regarding the subspace trail of length 1 set up using the generic subspace $\mathcal{X}$ defined in Sect. 3.1.

Theorem 5. *For each* $I \subseteq \{(0,0),(0,1),\ldots,(3,2),(3,3)\} \equiv \{(i,j)\}_{0 \leq i,j \leq 3}$ *and for each* $a \in \mathcal{X}_I^\perp$, *there exists one and only one* $b \in \mathcal{Y}_I^\perp$ *such that* $R(\mathcal{X}_I \oplus a) = \mathcal{Y}_I \oplus b$, *where* $\mathcal{Y}_I = MC \circ SR(\mathcal{X}_I)$.

Proof. To prove the Theorem, we simply compute $R(\mathcal{X}_I \oplus a)$. Since SubBytes is bijective and operates on each byte independently, its only effect is to change the coset. In other words, it simply changes the coset $\mathcal{X}_I \oplus a$ to $\mathcal{X}_I \oplus a'$, where $a'_{i,j} = SB(a_{i,j})$ for each $i,j = 0,\ldots,3$. ShiftRows simply moves the bytes of $\mathcal{X}_I \oplus a'$ into $SR(\mathcal{X}_I) \oplus b'$, where $b' = SR(a')$. Since MixColumns is a linear operation, it follows that $MC(SR(\mathcal{X}_I) \oplus b') = MC \circ SR(\mathcal{X}_I) \oplus MC(b') = MC \circ SR(\mathcal{X}_I) \oplus b''$. Key addition then changes the coset to $MC \circ SR(\mathcal{X}_I) \oplus b$.   □

B   Weak-Key Invariant Subspace Trails of AES-256

B.1   AES-256 Key-Schedule

In this case, the subkey array is denoted by $W[0,\ldots,59]$, where here the first 8 words of $W[\cdot]$ are loaded with the user secret key. The remaining words of $W[\cdot]$ are updated according to the following rule:

$$W[i][j] = \begin{cases} W[i][j-8] \oplus \text{SB}(W[i+1][j-1]) \oplus R[i][j/8] & \text{if } j \bmod 8 = 0 \\ W[i][j-8] \oplus \text{SB}(W[i][j-1]) & \text{if } j \bmod 8 = 4 \\ W[i][j-1] \oplus W[i][j-8] & \text{otherwise} \end{cases}$$

where $i = 0, 1, 2, 3$, $j = 8, \ldots, 59$ and $R[\cdot]$ is an array of predetermined constants.

B.2   Invariant Subspace – Weak-Keys of AES-256

For the case AES-256, a set of 2^{128} weak-keys is given by

$$K_{\text{weak}} := \left\{ \begin{bmatrix} A^0 & A^1 & A^0 & A^1 & E^0 & E^1 & E^0 & E^1 \\ B^0 & B^1 & B^0 & B^1 & F^0 & F^1 & F^0 & F^1 \\ C^0 & C^1 & C^0 & C^1 & G^0 & G^1 & G^0 & G^1 \\ D^0 & D^1 & D^0 & D^1 & H^0 & H^1 & H^0 & H^1 \end{bmatrix} \middle| \begin{array}{c} \forall A^i, \ldots, H^i \in \mathbb{F}_{2^8} \\ \forall i = 0, 1 \end{array} \right\}$$

Under any of such keys, the subspace $\mathcal{IS}$ is mapped after two complete rounds into a coset of $\mathcal{IS}$, that is $\mathcal{IS} \xrightarrow{R_K^2 \circ \text{ARK}(\cdot)} \mathcal{IS} \oplus \hat{k}$, where $\hat{k}$ is the corresponding subkey after 2 rounds of the key schedule.

For the follow-up, we also present three subspaces of K_{weak} for which it is possible to construct a longer invariant subspace trail:

3-round: working with any of the 2^{96} keys that satisfy $A^0 = A^1, \ldots D^0 = D^1$, the subspace $\mathcal{IS}$ is mapped after three complete rounds into a coset of $\mathcal{IS}$, that is $\mathcal{IS} \xrightarrow{R_K^3 \circ \text{ARK}(\cdot)} \mathcal{IS} \oplus \hat{k}'$ where $\hat{k}'$ is the subkey after 3 rounds.

4-round: working with any of the 2^{64} keys that satisfy $A^0 = A^1, \ldots, H^0 = H^1$, the subspace $\mathcal{IS}$ is mapped after four complete rounds into a coset of $\mathcal{IS}$, that is $\mathcal{IS} \xrightarrow{R_K^4 \circ \text{ARK}(\cdot)} \mathcal{IS} \oplus \hat{k}''$ where $\hat{k}''$ is the subkey after 4 rounds.

5-round: working with any of the 2^{32} keys that satisfy $A^0 = A^1 = B^0 = \ldots = D^0 = D^1 = 0$ and $E^0 = E^1, \ldots \ H^0 = H^1$, the subspace $\mathcal{IS}$ is mapped after five complete rounds into a coset of $\mathcal{IS}$, that is $\mathcal{IS} \xrightarrow{R_K^5 \circ \text{ARK}(\cdot)} \mathcal{IS} \oplus \hat{k}'''$ where $\hat{k}'''$ is the subkey after 5 rounds.

The complete expressions of the subkeys involved for the previous results are given for completeness in the following.

B.3   Chosen-Key Distinguisher for 12-Round AES-256

Working as for AES-128, in order to set up the 12-round distinguisher of AES-256, one exploits the fact that

$$\forall k \in K_{\text{weak}}: \quad \mathcal{IS} \oplus a \xleftarrow{R^{-1}(\cdot)} \mathcal{IS} \xrightarrow{R^5(\cdot)} \mathcal{IS} \oplus b$$

for each key in K_{weak} defined in Appendix B.2 where

$$A^0 = A^1 = B^0 = \ldots = D^0 = D^1 = 0, \quad E^0 = E^1, F^0 = F^1, \ldots, H^0 = H^1.$$

C   Practical Collisions for 7-Round AES-256 Compressing Modes

Many block cipher hashing modes contain XOR of input and output of the cipher. E.g. given an input $x = (x_0, x_1, \ldots, x_n)$, the corresponding hash $H = (H_0 \equiv IV, H_1, \ldots, H_n)$ can be produced using

Table 3. Examples of compression collisions for 6 and 7-round AES-256 used in Matyas-Meyer-Oseas construction where $k_0 \| k_1$ = 62636363 00000000 00000000 00000000 00000000 00000000 00000000 00000000. Last round contains the matrix multiplication but not the final key addition, which does not affect the collisions. These plaintexts are also collisions for Miyaguchi-Preneel mode and pseudo-collisions for Davies-Meyer mode.

Plaintext		Hash (i.e., Plaintext $\oplus$ Ciphertext)	
7-round Collisions			
6407503c0664335f	0664335f0664335f	4a2e96618b438711	284df5028b438711
c2e01a46a0837925	a0837925a0837925		
fa8cca8ad93ff889	98efa9e9d93ff889	79b1f1b3c1415dd7	1bd292d0c1415dd7
02cc0aa7b96b44b3	60af69c4b96b44b3		
6-round Collisions			
b1b602e8d3d5618b	d3d5618bd3d5618b	f85752eeb3488419	9a34318db3488419
d0122734b2714457	b2714457b2714457		
e75dd657853eb534	853eb534853eb534	c99eec4ba84135a3	abfd8f28a84135a3
27f4f3b1459790d2	459790d2459790d2		

- the Davies–Meyer hash function: $H_i = E_{x_i}(H_{i-1}) \oplus H_{i-1}$;
- the Matyas-Meyer-Oseas hash function $H_i = E_{g(H_{i-1})}(x_i) \oplus x_i$;
- the Miyaguchi–Preneel hash function $H_i = E_{g(H_{i-1})}(x_i) \oplus H_{i-1} \oplus x_i$.

In this section, we show how to produce collisions for some of such constructions exploiting our invariant subspace $\mathcal{IS}$. *Since we assume the attacker is able to choose the initial value IV, we propose our results in the compressing mode.*

Using the result proposed in Appendix B.3 and when the first and second round keys (namely, k_1 and k_2) are all zero, it is possible to show that

$$\mathcal{IS} \oplus k_0 \xleftarrow{R^{-1}(\cdot)} \mathcal{IS} \xrightarrow{R^6(\cdot)} \mathcal{IS} \oplus k_6,$$

where k_0 and k_6 are the initial and final round keys.

Since dimension of $\mathcal{IS}$ is 64, we expect to find a collision with (at least) 2^{32} elements in $\mathcal{IS}$. In fact, since one can construct $\binom{2^{32}}{2} = 2^{32} \cdot (2^{32} - 1)/2 \approx 2^{63}$, the probability to find a collision is approximately $1 - (1 - 2^{-64})^{2^{63}} \approx 1 - e^{-1/2} \approx 39.35\%$. We performed two experiments by encrypting 2^{32} elements in $\mathcal{IS}$ in an inside out fashion by choosing the AES-256 key as $[k_0 \| k_1] = $ [62636363 00000000 00000000 00000000 $\|$ 00000000 00000000 00000000 00000000], which makes first and second round keys zero. In our first experiment we used the smaller invariant subspace $\mathcal{IS}'$ of dimension 32 where every column is identical.

As a result, we got a 7-round collision in both cases for the Matyas-Meyer-Oseas or Miyaguchi-Preneel compressing functions constructed with 7-round AES-256, where the attacker choose IV (= H_0) as k_0. Note that since AES-256 block size is 128 bits and key size is 256 bits, a $g(\cdot)$ conversion/padding function is used on the output to make it suitable as the key. A very natural function $g(\cdot) : \mathbb{F}_{2^n} \mapsto \mathbb{F}_{2^{2n}}$ that turns out to be good for our purpose is given by $g(x) = x \| \underbrace{0...0}_{n \text{ bit}} \in \mathbb{F}_{2^{2n}}$, where $\|$ denotes concatenation. Our collisions for 7-round AES-256 hashing modes are provided in Table 3. Moreover, an perhaps a more natural application, these collisions turn into collisions for Davies-Meyer compressing mode where the message block is fixed to $k_0 \| k_1$ and the plaintexts of Table 3 are used as IVs.

To the best of our knowledge, the best known collision attacks on AES compressing modes are the trivial conversion of the Whirlpool attacks of [24]. They turn into 6-round collision attacks on every key length of AES which require 2^{56} time and 2^{32} memory complexity. Our collisions are on 7 rounds and require 2^{32} time and 2^{32} memory complexity where a time-memory tradeoff is also possible. Our attack is also valid for 6 rounds with the same complexities. It may be conceivable that local collision methods from [4] can be adapted to the compression collision setting we consider here. Note however that this approach can not avoid to simultaniously require differences in both the chaining as well as the message input of an AES-256-based compression functions, whereas we only need a difference in one of the two.

D   Proofs of Results Given in Sect. 4

D.1   Proofs of Proposition 1

As showed in Sect. 4.1, a subspace $\mathcal{IS}$ is mapped into a coset of $\mathcal{IS}$ after 2 rounds AES-128 under a weak-key. By definition of $\mathcal{IS} \oplus a$, the first and the third diagonals (resp. the second and the fourth) are equal. This means that:

- there are 2^{32} texts that are equal in the first and the third diagonals, and that differ in the second and in the fourth ones. By definition, these 2^{32} texts belong to the same coset of $\mathcal{D}_{1,3}$. It follows that after 2-round encryption, the 2^{64} texts are divided into 2^{32} different cosets of $\mathcal{D}_{1,3}$;
- equivalently, there are 2^{32} texts that are equal in the second and in the fourth diagonals, and that differ first and the third ones. By definition, these 2^{32} texts belong to the same coset of $\mathcal{D}_{0,2}$. It follows that after 2-round encryption, the 2^{64} texts are divided into 2^{32} different cosets of $\mathcal{D}_{0,2}$.

The result follows immediately from the fact that each coset of $\mathcal{D}_I$ is mapped into a coset of $\mathcal{M}_I$ after 2-round AES encryption – see Theorem 1.

In the case of a random permutation, note that

- there are $\binom{2^{64}}{2^{32}}$ different ways to divide 2^{64} texts in sets of 2^{32} elements;
- for each set, 2^{32} texts are equal on two diagonals with prob. $\left(2^{-64}\right)^{2^{32}-1}$;
- the probability that these two diagonals are different for each set is equal to $\prod_{i=0}^{2^{32}-1} \frac{2^{64}-i}{2^{64}} = \prod_{i=0}^{2^{32}-1} \left(1 - i \cdot 2^{-64}\right)$.

As a result, the probability for the case of a random permutation is given by

$$\binom{2^{64}}{2^{32}} \cdot \prod_{i=0}^{2^{32}-1}\left[\left(2^{-64}\right)^{2^{32}-1} \cdot \overbrace{\left(1 - i \cdot 2^{-64}\right)}^{\le 1}\right] \le \binom{2^{64}}{2^{32}} \cdot \left(2^{-64}\right)^{2^{64}-2^{33}+1}$$

$$\approx \frac{1}{\sqrt{2\pi \cdot (2^{32}-1)}} \cdot \frac{\left(2^{64}\right)^{2^{64}}}{\left(2^{32}\right)^{2^{32}} \cdot \left(2^{64}-2^{32}\right)^{2^{64}-2^{32}}} \cdot \left(2^{-64}\right)^{2^{64}-2^{33}+1}$$

$$\approx \left(2^{32}\right)^{2^{32}} \cdot (1 - 2^{-32})^{2^{64}-2^{32}} \cdot \left(2^{-64}\right)^{2^{64}-2^{33}+1} \approx 2^{-2^{70}}$$

using Stirling's approximation $n! \approx n^n \cdot e^{-n} \cdot \sqrt{2\pi \cdot n}$. $\qquad\square$

D.2   Proofs of Weak-Key "Multiple-of-n" – Theorem 4

As before, since the invariant subspace $\mathcal{IS}$ is mapped into a coset of $\mathcal{IS}$ after 2-round encryption, since a coset of $\mathcal{X}_I$ is mapped into a coset of $\mathcal{Y}_I = SR^{-1} \circ MC^{-1}(\mathcal{X}_I)$ after 1-round decryption (as showed in Theorem 2) and since a coset of $\mathcal{M}_J$ is mapped into a coset of $\mathcal{D}_J$ after 2-round decryption, that is

$$\forall k \in K_{\text{weak}}: \quad \mathcal{IS} \xrightarrow[\text{prob. 1}]{R^2(\cdot)} \mathcal{IS} \oplus a \xrightarrow{R^2(\cdot)} \mathcal{Y}_I \oplus a' \xrightarrow[\text{prob. 1}]{R(\cdot)} \mathcal{X}_I \oplus b'$$

$$\forall k \in K_{\text{weak}}: \quad \mathcal{IS} \xrightarrow[\text{prob. 1}]{R^2(\cdot)} \mathcal{IS} \oplus a \xrightarrow{R^2(\cdot)} \mathcal{D}_J \oplus a' \xrightarrow[\text{prob. 1}]{R^2(\cdot)} \mathcal{M}_J \oplus b'$$

the idea is to prove an equivalent results that involve only the two middle rounds. Given a pair of texts $t^1, t^2 \in \mathcal{IS} \oplus a$, we prove that there exist other pair(s) of texts $s^1, s^2 \in \mathcal{IS} \oplus a$ such that $R^2(t^1) \oplus R^2(t^2) = R^2(s^1) \oplus R^2(s^2)$, where the texts s^1, s^2 are obtained by swapping the diagonals of t^1, t^2. As before, this implies that

$$R^2(t^1) \oplus R^2(t^2) \in \mathcal{X}_I \Leftrightarrow R^2(s^1) \oplus R^2(s^2) \in \mathcal{X}_I;$$
$$R^2(t^1) \oplus R^2(t^2) \in \mathcal{D}_J \Leftrightarrow R^2(s^1) \oplus R^2(s^2) \in \mathcal{D}_J.$$

In order to prove the previous claim, we use the "Super-S-Box" notation [10], where

$$\text{super-SBox}(\cdot) = \text{SB} \circ ARK \circ \text{MC} \circ \text{SB}(\cdot). \tag{7}$$

Case: Different Diagonals. As before, in the case in which the diagonals are different (i. e., $[x_0^1, x_5^1, x_2^1, x_7^1] \neq [x_0^2, x_5^2, x_2^2, x_7^2]$ and $[x_1^1, x_4^1, x_3^1, x_6^1] \neq [x_1^2, x_4^2, x_3^2, x_6^2]$), given t^1 and t^2 defined as

$$SR(t^i) \equiv (\ \underbrace{[x_0^i, x_5^i, x_2^i, x_7^i]}_{\text{1st and 3rd columns}}, \ \underbrace{[x_1^i, x_4^i, x_3^i, x_6^i]}_{\text{2nd and 4th columns}}\ )$$

where $SR(\cdot)$ denotes the ShiftRows operation, then $R^2(t^1) \oplus R^2(t^2) = R^2(s^1) \oplus R^2(s^2)$ if s^1 and s^2 are defined as

$$SR(s^i) \equiv (\underbrace{[x_0^{3-i}, x_5^{3-i}, x_2^{3-i}, x_7^{3-i}]}_{\text{1st and 3rd columns}}, \ \underbrace{[x_1^i, x_4^i, x_3^i, x_6^i]}_{\text{2nd and 4th columns}}\ ).$$

To prove the previous fact, we first recall that 2-round encryption can be rewritten using the "super-SBox" notation $R^2(\cdot) = \text{ARK} \circ \text{MC} \circ \text{SR} \circ$ super-SBox $\circ \text{SR}(\cdot)$. Thus, we are going to prove that

$$\text{super-SBox}(\hat{t}^1) \oplus \text{super-SBox}(\hat{t}^2) = \text{super-SBox}(\hat{s}^1) \oplus \text{super-SBox}(\hat{s}^2) \in \mathcal{W}_I$$

where $\hat{t}^i = \text{SR}(t^i) \in \mathcal{IS} \oplus \text{SR}(a)$ and $\hat{s}^i = \text{SR}(s^i) \in \mathcal{IS} \oplus \text{SR}(a)$ for $i = 1, 2$ (note that $t^i, s^i \in \mathcal{IS} \oplus a$). Note that the first and the third columns of $\hat{t}^i$ and $\hat{s}^i$ are equal, as well as the second and the fourth columns. Similar to the 5-round case, *since the first and the second columns (and so the third and the fourth ones) of $\hat{t}^1$ and $\hat{t}^2$ depend on different and independent variables, since the Super-S-Box works independently on each column and since the XOR-sum is commutative*, it follows the thesis.

Generic Case. What happens if one diagonal is in common for the two texts, e.g. $[x_0^1, x_5^1, x_2^1, x_7^1] = [x_0^2, x_5^2, x_2^2, x_7^2]$ (analogous for $[x_1^1, x_4^1, x_3^1, x_6^1] = [x_1^2, x_4^2, x_3^2, x_6^2]$)? As before, in this case the difference $R^2(t^1) \oplus R^2(t^2)$ is independent of the values of such diagonal. It follows that the pair of texts s^1 and s^2 can be constructed as

$$\text{SR}(s^i) \equiv \big(\underbrace{[x_0^{3-i}, x_5^{3-i}, x_2^{3-i}, x_7^{3-i}]}_{1st \text{ and } 3rd \text{ columns}}, \underbrace{[\alpha_0, \alpha_5, \alpha_2, \alpha_7]}_{2nd \text{ and } 4th \text{ columns}} \big),$$

$$\text{SR}(s^i) \equiv \big(\underbrace{[x_1^i, x_4^i, x_3^i, x_6^i]}_{1st \text{ and } 3rd \text{ columns}}, \underbrace{[\alpha_0, \alpha_5, \alpha_2, \alpha_7]}_{2nd \text{ and } 4th \text{ columns}} \big),$$

where $\alpha_0, \alpha_5, \alpha_2, \alpha_7$ can take any possible values in $\mathbb{F}_{2^8}$. Note that in this case, it is possible to identify $2 \cdot 2^{32} = 2^{33}$ different texts s^1 and s^2 in $\mathcal{IS} \oplus a$ that satisfy the condition $R^2(t^1) \oplus R^2(t^2) = R^2(s^1) \oplus R^2(s^2)$. In conclusion, given plaintexts in the same coset of $\mathcal{IS}$, the number of different pairs of ciphertexts that belong to the same coset of $\mathcal{X}_I$ and/or $\mathcal{D}_J$ after two rounds is always a multiple of 2. $\square$

E   Gilbert's Known-Key Distinguisher for AES

Here, we briefly mention that a 10-round known-key distinguisher for AES has been proposed by Gilbert [14] at Asiacrypt 2014. In such case, the known-key model asks the adversary to find a set of 2^{64} (plaintext, ciphertext) pairs, that is (p^i, c^i) for $i = 0, \ldots, 2^{64} - 1$, and two keys k^0 and k^{10} with the following properties[8]:

1. the partially encrypted texts $\{R_{k^0}(p^i)\}_i$ are uniformly distributed among the cosets of $\mathcal{D}_I$ for each I with $|I| = 3$;
2. the partially decrypted texts $\{R_{k^{10}}^{-1}(c^i)\}_i$ are uniformly distributed among the cosets of $\mathcal{M}_J$ for each J with $|J| = 3$.

---

[8] For this distinguisher, we abuse the notation k^r to denote a key of a certain round r. We emphasize that k^r is not necessarily equal to the secret key.

We emphasize that *such properties are not verified directly by the plaintexts and by the ciphertexts but after one round encryption/decryption*, and they involve keys k^0 and k^{10} that can be different from the subkeys derived from k. The probability that 2^{64} (plaintext, ciphertext) generated by a random permutation satisfy the previous property is $2^{-7\,200}$. Thus, given $2^{64} + 2^8$ plaintexts/ciphertexts, the probability to find among them a subset of 2^{64} pairs of texts with the required properties is close to 1.

A distinguisher based on the Gilbert's technique is different from all the previous distinguishers up to 8 rounds present in the literature. *For all distinguishers up to 8-round (and for the distinguishers proposed in this paper), the property/relation $\mathcal{R}$ – that the N-tuple of (plaintexts, ciphertexts) must satisfy – does not involve any operation of the block cipher E. On the other hand, the previous Gilbert's like distinguishers do not satisfy this requirement, since in such cases the property/relation $\mathcal{R}$ involves and re-uses some operations of E*: indeed, instead of considering properties "directly" on the plaintexts/ciphertexts, the idea is to show the existence of certain keys for which some properties hold after one round encryption/decryption. Moreover, in order to support such a new kind of distinguisher, it is claimed in [14] that *(1st)* it seems technically difficult to use a stronger property than the uniform distribution one to extend an 8-round known-key distinguisher to a 10-round one and *(2nd)* it is impossible to use the same technique in order to extend a distinguisher for more than 2 rounds. Recently, both claims have been disproved in [17], which leads to the conclusion that argumentation given to support such known-key distinguishers could be *artificial*. Hence, the problem to set up a 9 (or more) rounds open-key distinguisher in the single-key setting for AES-128 without exploiting the Gilbert's technique is still open.

F   Proof of Proposition 2

Assume all the pairs (X_i, Y_i) result from queries to Π or Π^{-1}. Consider a (random) set of $2^{64} - 1$ plaintexts/ciphertexts pairs $\{(X_i, Y_i)\}_{i=0,\ldots,2^{64}-2}$ such that there exists (at least) one plaintext/ciphertext pair $(\hat{X}, \hat{Y})$ for which the set $\{(X_i, Y_i)\}_{i=0,\ldots,2^{64}-1}$ satisfies the required multiple-of-n property. By assumption, the player can always find $\hat{X}'$ (resp. $\hat{Y}'$) such that the "simultaneous multiple-of-n" property is satisfied for the plaintexts (resp. for the ciphertexts). However, the oracle's answer $\hat{Y}'$ (resp. $\hat{X}'$) is *uniformly drawn* from $\{0,1\}^{128} \setminus \{Y_1, Y_2, \ldots, Y_{2^{64}-1}\}$ (resp. from $\{0,1\}^{128} \setminus \{X_1, X_2, \ldots, X_{2^{64}-1}\}$). Therefore, *the probability that the answer to the N-th query allows the output of $\mathcal{A}$ to satisfy property $\mathcal{R}$ (i.e. multiple-of-n) is upper bounded by* $(2^{-1})^{2^{16}-16} \cdot (2^{-7})^{14} = 2^{-65\,618} \simeq 2^{-2^{16}}$ since

- there are $\sum_{i=1}^{15} \binom{16}{i} = 2^{16} - 2$ different subspaces $\mathcal{X}_I$ for which the multiple-of-2 property holds, and among them there are 14 subspaces $\mathcal{M}_I$ for which the multiple-of-128 property holds;
- the probability that the number of collisions is a multiple of N is $\approx 1/N$.

In order to prove this second point, we first show that the probabilistic distribution of the number of collisions is a binomial distribution.

Given a set of n pairs of texts, consider the event that m pairs belong to the same coset of a subspace $\mathcal{X}$. As first thing, we show that the probabilistic distribution of number of collisions is simply described by a *binomial distribution*. By definition, a binomial distribution with parameters n and p is the discrete probability distribution of the number of successes in a sequence of n independent yes/no experiments, each of which yields success with probability p. In our case, given n pairs of texts, each of them satisfies or not the above property/requirement with a certain probability. Thus, this model can be described using a binomial distribution, for which the mean μ and the variance σ^2 are respectively given by $\mu = n \cdot p$ and $\sigma^2 = n \cdot p \cdot (1 - p)$.

In our case, the number of pairs is given by $\binom{2^{64}}{2} \simeq 2^{127}$, the probability that a pair of texts belong to the same coset of $\mathcal{X}_I$ is equal to $2^{-8 \cdot (16 - |I|)}$, while it is equal to $2^{-32 \cdot (4 - |J|)}$ for the subspaces $\mathcal{D}_J$ and $\mathcal{M}_J$.

Probability that "the number of collision is even" is (approximately) 1/2 – Case: subspaces $\mathcal{X}_I$. In order to prove the previous result, let X be a binomial distribution $X \sim \mathcal{B}(n, p)$. Combining the facts that

$$\Pr\left[X \text{ even}\right] + \Pr\left[X \text{ odd}\right] = \sum_{k=0}^{n} \binom{n}{k} \cdot p^k \cdot (1-p)^{n-k} = [(1-p) + p]^n = 1$$

$$\Pr\left[X \text{ even}\right] - \Pr\left[X \text{ odd}\right] = \sum_{k=0}^{n} \binom{n}{k} \cdot (-p)^k \cdot (1-p)^{n-k} = [(1-p) - p]^n,$$

it follows that $\Pr\left[X \text{ even}\right] = \frac{1}{2} + \frac{1}{2} \cdot (1 - 2p)^n$. Hence, the probability that the number of collisions is even is given by $\frac{1}{2} + \frac{1}{2} \cdot (1 - 2p)^n$. In our case, since $n \simeq 2^{127}$ and $2^{-120} \leq p \leq 2^{-8}$ (where the prob. 2^{-120} and 2^{-8} correspond resp. to the cases $|I| = 15$ and $|I| = 1$), the previous probability is well approximated by $1/2 + 1/2 \cdot (1 - 2^{-7})^{2^{127}} \approx 1/2$.

Probability that "the number of collision is a multiple of N" is (approximately) $1/N$ – Case: subspaces $\mathcal{M}_J$ and $\mathcal{D}_J$. In order to prove this result, we first approximate the binomial distribution with a normal one. De Moivre-Laplace Theorem claims that the normal distribution is a good approximation of the binomial one *if* the skewness of the binomial distribution – given by $(1 - 2p)/\sqrt{n \cdot p \cdot (1 - p)}$ – is close to zero. In our case, since $n \simeq 2^{127}$ and $2^{-96} \leq p \leq 2^{-32}$ (where the prob. 2^{-96} and 2^{-32} correspond resp. to the cases $|J| = 3$ and $|J| = 1$), it follows that $2^{-47.5} \leq skew \leq 2^{-15.5}$, which means that the normal approximation is sufficiently good. Thus, we approximate the binomial distribution with a normal one $\mathcal{N}(\mu = n \cdot p, \sigma^2 = n \cdot p \cdot (1 - p))$, where the probability density function is given by $\varphi(x) = \frac{1}{\sqrt{2\pi \cdot \sigma^2}} e^{-\frac{(x-\mu)^2}{2\sigma^2}}$.

In order to compute the probability that the multiple-of-N collisions is satisfied, it is sufficient to sum all the probabilities where the number of collisions is a multiple-of-N (for $N \in \mathbb{N}$ and $N \neq 0$), that is

$$\sum_{x \in \mathbb{Z}} \frac{1}{\sqrt{2\pi \cdot \sigma^2}} e^{-\frac{(N \cdot x - \mu)^2}{2\sigma^2}} = \frac{1}{N} \cdot \underbrace{\sum_{x \in \mathbb{Z}} \frac{1}{\sqrt{2\pi \cdot \tilde{\sigma}^2}} e^{-\frac{(x - \tilde{\mu})^2}{2\tilde{\sigma}^2}}}_{=1 \text{ by definition}} = \frac{1}{N}$$

where $\tilde{\mu} = \mu/N$ and $\tilde{\sigma}^2 = \sigma^2/N^2$. □

G On the Difficulty to Set Up "Multiple-of-n" Open-Key Distinguishers *Without* Relying on Weak-Keys

In order to better understand the role of the invariant subspace, and hence the dependence on weak-keys, we briefly discuss the following problem: is it possible to set up a similar distinguisher using the multiple-of-8 property proposed in [19] which holds for any key? We conjecture that this is hard.

Given a coset of a diagonal space $\mathcal{D}_I$, the multiple-of-8 property holds (1) after 5-round encryption and (2) after 3-round decryption. It follows that given a coset of $\mathcal{C}_I$ in the middle, then

$$\forall k: \qquad \textit{Multiple-of-8} \xleftarrow{R^{-4}(\cdot)} \mathcal{C}_I \oplus a \xrightarrow{R^4(\cdot)} \textit{Multiple-of-8},$$

it is possible to achieve a simultaneous multiple-of-8 property on 8 rounds.

Distinguisher on 8 Rounds? First of all, one may ask if this property is strong enough in order to set up a chosen-key distinguisher. Consider the case of an adversary faces a family of random and independent *ideal ciphers* $\{\Pi(K, \cdot), K \in \{0, 1\}^k\}$, where $k = 128, 192, 256$ respectively for the cases AES-128/192/256: his goal is to find a key k and a set of 2^{64} plaintexts/ciphertexts $(p^i, c^i = \Pi(k, p^i))$ s.t. the "simultaneous multiple-of-n" property is satisfied.

Working exactly as in Sect. 5, a random sets of 2^{64} plaintexts/ciphertexts pairs (X_i, Y_i) satisfies the "simultaneous multiple-of-8" property with prob. $(1/8)(2 \cdot 14) = 2^{-84}$ (since (1) the probability that a number is a multiple of 8 is $1/8$, (2) there are 14 different subspaces D_I and 14 different subspaces M_I for $I \subseteq \{0, 1, 2, 3\}$). It follows that given $2^{64} + 2$ random texts, the adversary can construct $\binom{2^{64}+2}{2^{64}} \approx 2^{127}$ different sets of 2^{64} texts. Hence, it seems the simultaneous multiple-of-8 property is not strong enough to set up a chosen-key distinguisher.

Extension to 9 Rounds. Let's assume that the previous 8-round distinguisher is valid. In order to extend it to more rounds, a possibility can be to use a coset of $\mathcal{D}_I \oplus \mathcal{M}_J$ in the middle. Here we show why this solution does not work.

First of all, observe that

$$\mathcal{D}_I \oplus \mathcal{M}_J \oplus a \equiv \bigcup_{b \in \mathcal{D}_I \oplus a} \mathcal{M}_J \oplus b \equiv \bigcup_{b \in \mathcal{M}_J \oplus a} \mathcal{D}_I \oplus b$$

Thus, consider 5-round encryption (similar for the decryption direction). The number of collisions between the pairs of ciphertexts whose corresponding plaintexts are in the same coset of $\mathcal{D}_I$ is a multiple of 8 with prob. 1. However, it is not possible to claim anything about the the pairs of ciphertexts whose corresponding plaintexts are in the same coset of $\mathcal{M}_J$, or for which one plaintext is in $\mathcal{D}_I \oplus a'$ and the other in $\mathcal{M}_J \oplus b'$. As a result, one looses any multiple-of-n property. A similar argumentation works also in the decryption direction.

References

1. Beierle, C., Canteaut, A., Leander, G., Rotella, Y.: Proving resistance against invariant attacks: how to choose the round constants. In: Katz, J., Shacham, H. (eds.) CRYPTO 2017. LNCS, vol. 10402, pp. 647–678. Springer, Cham (2017). https://doi.org/10.1007/978-3-319-63715-0_22
2. Biham, E., Shamir, A.: Differential cryptanalysis of DES-like cryptosystems. In: Menezes, A.J., Vanstone, S.A. (eds.) CRYPTO 1990. LNCS, vol. 537, pp. 2–21. Springer, Heidelberg (1991). https://doi.org/10.1007/3-540-38424-3_1
3. Biryukov, A., Khovratovich, D.: Related-key cryptanalysis of the full AES-192 and AES-256. In: Matsui, M. (ed.) ASIACRYPT 2009. LNCS, vol. 5912, pp. 1–18. Springer, Heidelberg (2009). https://doi.org/10.1007/978-3-642-10366-7_1
4. Biryukov, A., Khovratovich, D., Nikolić, I.: Distinguisher and related-key attack on the full AES-256. In: Halevi, S. (ed.) CRYPTO 2009. LNCS, vol. 5677, pp. 231–249. Springer, Heidelberg (2009). https://doi.org/10.1007/978-3-642-03356-8_14
5. Boura, C., Canteaut, A., Coggia, D.: A general proof framework for recent AES distinguishers. IACR Trans. Symmetric Cryptol. **2019**(1), 170–191 (2019)
6. Canetti, R., Goldreich, O., Halevi, S.: The random oracle methodology, revisited. J. ACM **51**(4), 557–594 (2004)
7. Chaigneau, C., Fuhr, T., Gilbert, H., Jean, J., Reinhard, J.R.: Cryptanalysis of NORX v2.0. IACR Trans. Symmetric Cryptol. **2017**(1), 156–174 (2017)
8. Cid, C., Murphy, S., Robshaw, M.J.B.: Small scale variants of the AES. In: Gilbert, H., Handschuh, H. (eds.) FSE 2005. LNCS, vol. 3557, pp. 145–162. Springer, Heidelberg (2005). https://doi.org/10.1007/11502760_10
9. Daemen, J., Rijmen, V.: The Design of Rijndael: AES - The Advanced Encryption Standard. Information Security and Cryptography, Springer, Heidelberg (2002). https://doi.org/10.1007/978-3-662-04722-4
10. Daemen, J., Rijmen, V.: Understanding two-round differentials in AES. In: De Prisco, R., Yung, M. (eds.) SCN 2006. LNCS, vol. 4116, pp. 78–94. Springer, Heidelberg (2006). https://doi.org/10.1007/11832072_6
11. Derbez, P., Fouque, P.-A., Jean, J.: Faster chosen-key distinguishers on reduced-round AES. In: Galbraith, S., Nandi, M. (eds.) INDOCRYPT 2012. LNCS, vol. 7668, pp. 225–243. Springer, Heidelberg (2012). https://doi.org/10.1007/978-3-642-34931-7_14
12. Derbez, P., Fouque, P., Jean, J., Lambin, B.: Variants of the AES key schedule for better truncated differential bounds. In: Cid, C., Jacobson Jr., M. (eds.) SAC 2018. LNCS, vol. 11349, pp. 27–49 (2018). https://doi.org/10.1007/978-3-030-10970-7_2
13. Fouque, P.-A., Jean, J., Peyrin, T.: Structural evaluation of AES and chosen-key distinguisher of 9-round AES-128. In: Canetti, R., Garay, J.A. (eds.) CRYPTO 2013. LNCS, vol. 8042, pp. 183–203. Springer, Heidelberg (2013). https://doi.org/10.1007/978-3-642-40041-4_11
14. Gilbert, H.: A simplified representation of AES. In: Sarkar, P., Iwata, T. (eds.) ASIACRYPT 2014. LNCS, vol. 8873, pp. 200–222. Springer, Heidelberg (2014). https://doi.org/10.1007/978-3-662-45611-8_11

15. Gilbert, H., Peyrin, T.: Super-Sbox cryptanalysis: improved attacks for AES-like permutations. In: Hong, S., Iwata, T. (eds.) FSE 2010. LNCS, vol. 6147, pp. 365–383. Springer, Heidelberg (2010). https://doi.org/10.1007/978-3-642-13858-4_21

16. Grassi, L.: Mixture differential cryptanalysis: a new approach to distinguishers and attacks on round-reduced AES. IACR Trans. Symmetric Cryptol. **2018**(2), 133–160 (2018)

17. Grassi, L., Rechberger, C.: Revisiting Gilbert's known-key distinguisher. Des. Codes Cryptogr. **88**(7), 1401–1445 (2020)

18. Grassi, L., Rechberger, C., Rønjom, S.: Subspace trail cryptanalysis and its applications to AES. IACR Trans. Symmetric Cryptol. **2016**(2), 192–225 (2016)

19. Grassi, L., Rechberger, C., Rønjom, S.: A new structural-differential property of 5-round AES. In: Coron, J.-S., Nielsen, J.B. (eds.) EUROCRYPT 2017. LNCS, vol. 10211, pp. 289–317. Springer, Cham (2017). https://doi.org/10.1007/978-3-319-56614-6_10

20. Guo, J., Jean, J., Nikolic, I., Qiao, K., Sasaki, Y., Sim, S.: Invariant subspace attack against Midori64 and the resistance criteria for S-box designs. IACR Trans. Symmetric Cryptol. **2016**(1), 33–56 (2016)

21. Jean, J., Naya-Plasencia, M., Peyrin, T.: Multiple limited-birthday distinguishers and applications. In: Lange, T., Lauter, K., Lisoněk, P. (eds.) SAC 2013. LNCS, vol. 8282, pp. 533–550. Springer, Heidelberg (2014). https://doi.org/10.1007/978-3-662-43414-7_27

22. Khoo, K., Lee, E., Peyrin, T., Sim, S.: Human-readable proof of the related-key security of AES-128. IACR Trans. Symmetric Cryptol. **2017**(2), 59–83 (2017)

23. Knudsen, L.R., Rijmen, V.: Known-key distinguishers for some block ciphers. In: Kurosawa, K. (ed.) ASIACRYPT 2007. LNCS, vol. 4833, pp. 315–324. Springer, Heidelberg (2007). https://doi.org/10.1007/978-3-540-76900-2_19

24. Lamberger, M., Mendel, F., Schläffer, M., Rechberger, C., Rijmen, V.: The rebound attack and subspace distinguishers: application to whirlpool. J. Cryptol. **28**(2), 257–296 (2013). https://doi.org/10.1007/s00145-013-9166-5

25. Van Le, T., Sparr, R., Wernsdorf, R., Desmedt, Y.: Complementation-like and cyclic properties of AES round functions. In: Dobbertin, H., Rijmen, V., Sowa, A. (eds.) AES 2004. LNCS, vol. 3373, pp. 128–141. Springer, Heidelberg (2005). https://doi.org/10.1007/11506447_11

26. Leander, G., Abdelraheem, M.A., AlKhzaimi, H., Zenner, E.: A cryptanalysis of PRINTCIPHER: the invariant subspace attack. In: Rogaway, P. (ed.) CRYPTO 2011. LNCS, vol. 6841, pp. 206–221. Springer, Heidelberg (2011). https://doi.org/10.1007/978-3-642-22792-9_12

27. Leander, G., Minaud, B., Rønjom, S.: A generic approach to invariant subspace attacks: cryptanalysis of Robin, iSCREAM and Zorro. In: Oswald, E., Fischlin, M. (eds.) EUROCRYPT 2015. LNCS, vol. 9056, pp. 254–283. Springer, Heidelberg (2015). https://doi.org/10.1007/978-3-662-46800-5_11

28. Leander, G., Tezcan, C., Wiemer, F.: Searching for subspace trails and truncated differentials. IACR Trans. Symmetric Cryptol. **2018**(1), 74–100 (2018)

29. Matsui, M.: Linear cryptanalysis method for DES cipher. In: Helleseth, T. (ed.) EUROCRYPT 1993. LNCS, vol. 765, pp. 386–397. Springer, Heidelberg (1994). https://doi.org/10.1007/3-540-48285-7_33

30. Moore, J.H., Simmons, G.J.: Cycle structure of the DES with weak and semi-weak keys. In: Odlyzko, A.M. (ed.) CRYPTO 1986. LNCS, vol. 263, pp. 9–32. Springer, Heidelberg (1987). https://doi.org/10.1007/3-540-47721-7_2

Algebraic Key-Recovery Attacks on Reduced-Round Xoofff

Tingting Cui[1,2(⊠)] and Lorenzo Grassi[2]

[1] Hangzhou Dianzi University, Hangzhou 310018, China
cuitingting@hdu.edu.cn
[2] Digital Security Group, Radboud University, Nijmegen, The Netherlands
l.grassi@science.ru.nl

Abstract. Farfalle, a permutation-based construction for building a pseudorandom function (PRF), is really versatile. It can be used for message authentication code, stream cipher, key derivation function, authenticated encryption and so on. Farfalle construction relies on a set of permutations and on so-called rolling functions: it can be split into a compression layer followed by a two-step expansion layer.

As one instance of Farfalle, Xoofff is very efficient on a wide range of platforms from low-end devices to high-end processors by combining the narrow permutation Xoodoo and the inherent parallelism of Farfalle. In this paper, we present key-recovery attacks on reduced-round Xoofff. After identifying a weakness in the expanding rolling function, we first propose practical attacks on Xoofff instantiated with 1-/2-round Xoodoo in the expansion layer. We next extend such attack on Xoofff instantiated with 3-/4-round Xoodoo in the expansion layer by making use of Meet-in-the-Middle algebraic attacks and the linearization technique. All attacks proposed here – which are independent of the details of the compression and/or middle layer – have been practically verified (either on the "real" Xoofff or on a toy-version Xoofff with block-size of 96 bits). As a countermeasure, we discuss how to slightly modified the rolling function for free to reduce the number of attackable rounds.

Keywords: Farfalle · Xoofff · Xoodoo · Key-recovery attacks

1 Introduction

Farfalle is an efficiently parallelizable permutation-based construction of a variable input and output length pseudorandom function (PRF) proposed by Bertoni et al. in [2]. It can be seen as the parallelizable counterpart for sponge-based cryptography [4,6] and duplex constructions [5], which are inherently serial. Similar to sponges, Farfalle is built upon a (composite) primitive and modes on top of it. This primitive is a pseudorandom function (PRF) that takes as input a key and a string (or a sequence of strings), and produces an arbitrary-length output. Its construction involves two basic ingredients: a set of permutations of a b-bit state, and a family of so-called rolling functions used to derive distinct b-bit mask

© Springer Nature Switzerland AG 2021
O. Dunkelman et al. (Eds.): SAC 2020, LNCS 12804, pp. 171–197, 2021.
https://doi.org/10.1007/978-3-030-81652-0_7

values from a b-bit secret key. The Farfalle construction consists of a *compression layer* followed by an *expansion layer*. The compression layer produces a single b-bit accumulator value from a tuple of b-bit blocks representing the input data. The expansion layer first (non-linearly) transforms the accumulator value into a b-bit rolling state. Then, it (non-linearly) transforms a tuple of variants of this rolling state – produced by iterating the rolling function – into a tuple of (truncated) b-bit output blocks. Both the compression and expansion layers involve b-bit mask values derived from the key by the key derivation part of the construction.

A first efficient instantiation of the Farfalle construction named Kravatte is specified in [2,3]. The underlying components are a set of 6-round Keccak-p permutations of a $b = 1600$-bit state. In general, Kravatte is very fast on a wide range of platforms, but there are some exceptions due to the large width of the permutation. For this reason, in [8,9] the authors considered instantiating Farfalle with a narrow permutation, yet larger than 256 bits. In there, they propose Xoodoo, a 384-bit permutation with the same width and objectives as Gimli [1].

In this paper, we focus on the deck function Xoofff [8,9], an instance of Farfalle instantiated with Xoodoo. Here we present key-recovery attacks on Xoofff when it is instantiated with round-reduced Xoodoo in the expansion layer (almost all attacks that we are going to present are independent of the details of the compression/middle layer). Roughly speaking, several strategies can be exploited to set up an attack on a Farfalle scheme:

- working both on the inputs and outputs, one strategy aims to recover the key (input and output mask) by exploiting the relation between them (as in every classical cipher);
- working only on the inputs, one strategy aims to find a pair of inputs which "collide" (that is, that have the same value) before the middle compression function with a probability higher than the birthday-bound one;
- finally, working only on the outputs, one strategy aims to exploit the fact that several outputs are generated from the same unknown input (namely, the output of the middle part) to find the output mask (related to the key), and hence break the scheme.

In this paper, we focus on the last attack strategy. Our results are summarized in Table 1.

1.1   State of the Art

To the best of our knowledge, there is only one key-recovery attack [7] on a Farfalle construction published in the literature. It is an attack on the first version of Kravatte, which differs from the current one for the following facts: (1) the expansion rolling function (namely, the function that maps the output of the middle part to the inputs of the expansion part) was linear and (2) the number of rounds in both of the compression and of the expansion part were only 4 instead of 6.

Two out of the three attacks presented in [7] focus only on the expansion part (they are independent of the compression and of the middle phase), and

Table 1. Key-recovery attacks against Xoofff instantiations for several (n_c, n_d, n_e) values. All attacks are independent of the initial rolling function. We recall that this is a known "output-blocks" attack (namely, the attacker only knows the outputs: she cannot choose them – it is not required to know the input). The computational complexity is measured in number of "elementary operations".

Type	Rounds: (n_c, n_d, n_e)	Data (known outputs)	Time (elementary op.)	Memory (bits)	Ref.
MitM	(any, any, 1)	15	$2^{13.5}$	–	Section 3
MitM	(any, any, 2)	73	$2^{18.5}$	2^{12}	Section 4
Linearization + MitM	(any, any, 2)	12	$2^{28.75}$	$2^{19.2}$	Section 5.2
Linearization + MitM	(any, any, 3)	$2^{11.7}$	$2^{54.6}$	$2^{36.4}$	Section 5.3
Linearization + MitM	(any, any, 4)	$2^{28.9}$	$2^{106.2}$	$2^{70.8}$	Section 5.3
Higher-order + Interp.	(any, 4, 4)	$2^{75.2}$	$2^{90.4}$	2^{69}	[14]
Higher-order + Interp.	(any, 6, 2)	$2^{74.2}$	$2^{90.4}$	2^{68}	[14]
Higher-order + Interp.	(any, $r, 9 - r$)	$2^{100.4}$	$2^{106.3}$	$2^{70.8}$	Appendix E

they heavily exploit both the facts that the rolling function is linear and the degree is not high (due to the small number of rounds). Such attacks are the Meet-in-the-Middle (MitM) algebraic attack and the linearization attack:

- in the first case, the idea is to construct a set of equations that describes the final expansion phase. The rolling state and the output masking key are the unknowns of an algebraic system built by forming expressions of the same intermediate state, either by a forward computation from the rolling state, or by a backward computation from the output. The expansion linear mechanism makes it possible to collect enough equations to solve the system by linearization;
- in the second case, the attack exploits the fact that the sequence generated by the linear rolling function (assimilated to a short LFSR state) satisfies a linear recurrence of order far smaller than what is expected from the size of the state.

The third (and last) attack presented in [7] targets both the middle and the expansion part: by exploiting the property of the compression layer, an adversary can construct simple structures of 2^n n-block input values whose images after the compression layer form an affine subspace of dimension n of $\{0,1\}^b$. This fact can be exploited to set up a higher-order differential attack [11]: since a single round of Kravatte has algebraic degree 2, the algebraic degree after r rounds is upper bounded by 2^r. Hence, given a subspace of dimension n, it is possible to cover (with a zero-sum) at most r rounds of the middle/expansion part if $2^r < n$. The final masking key is derived by inverting the last rounds of the expansion layer, exploiting the fact that each round is a permutation.

After these attacks, the designers of Kravatte updated their designs (1) by increasing the number of rounds of the compression and expansion phases and (2) by replacing the rolling function for the expansion phase with a non-linear one. In this way, both the two attacks just recalled can be prevented: e.g., in the first case, the output states of the expanding rolling functions are not related anymore by simple linear relations. This fact has an impact on the complexity of the attacks (and on the number of attackable rounds), since both the degree grows faster and since the attacker cannot collect for free enough algebraic equations that describe the system.

For completeness, we finally mention that a zero-sum distinguisher on the full Xoodoo permutation has been recently presented in [13]. Moreover, the higher-order attack presented in [7] has been re-considered in [14], where the authors apply the same strategy to several schemes including Xoofff.

1.2 Our Contribution

In this paper, we re-consider the Meet-in-the-Middle algebraic attacks presented on the first version of Kravatte to break Xoofff (instantiated with round-reduced Xoodoo in the expansion part).

To prevent the attacks presented in the first version of Kravatte, the designers of Xoofff defined the expanding rolling function via a non-linear function (namely, a NLFSR). Informally, such rolling function has been chosen to guarantee that

1. *the degree and number of monomials in this ANF grows sufficiently* with the number of iterations;
2. it must have the fewest number of fixed points (namely, cycles of length one) and – more generally – short cycles.

In principle, this should prevent possible weaknesses as the ones exploited in the first version of Kravatte. As shown below, this is not completely the case.

Symmetry Property of the State Rolling Function. As our first contribution, we show that a weakness is actually present in the chosen expanding rolling function. Each internal state of Xoofff in $\mathbb{F}_2^{32 \times 4 \times 3}$ can be represented as a cube with 32 layers, where each layer is composed of 4 columns and 3 rows. We denote by S^3 the state obtained by applying three times the (expanding) rolling function on a state S: we found that part of the state S^3 is equal to part of the state S. In other words, for each layer, three columns of S have the same values of three columns in S^3 (hence the existence of a *linear relation* between part of the state S and part of the state S^3). Since several operations in the Xoodoo round function works at the column level, such property partially survives after one round for "free".

Key-Recovery Attacks on Xoofff. As our second contribution, we show how to exploit such fact to set up Meet-in-the-Middle algebraic attacks similar to the one presented in Kravatte [7]. In particular, the idea is to set up algebraic equations that cover the final expansion part of Xoofff, where both the rolling state and the output masking key are the unknowns of such algebraic system. By making use of the linear relations at the inputs of the expansion part (equivalently, at the outputs of the rolling function), we show how to cancel the variables that describe the unknown rolling state S for "free" (similar to what done in the case of a linear rolling function). In order to cover the highest possible number of rounds, we also exploit the low-degree of the χ^{-1} function (namely, the non-linear function) of Xoodoo: w.r.t. the Keccak χ function used in Kravatte (whose inverse has degree 3), the degree of χ^{-1} function used in Xoodoo is only 2. The system of equations is then solved via the linearization approach. As a result, we present an attack on Xoofff in the case in which the final expansion part is composed of 4 out of 6 rounds. All our attacks has been *practically verified*[1].

Countermeasures. Finally, we show a possible way to modify the rolling function so as to prevent the weakness previously described: we emphasize that the proposed modification does not influence the number of operations required to compute Xoofff (namely, the number of XORs and ANDs are unchanged).

Outline. In Sect. 2, the specification of Farfalle construction and Xoofff is briefly introduced. Then in Sect. 3–4, we propose the practical key-recovery attacks on Xoofff with reduced 1-/2-round Xoodoo respectively, while in Sect. 5 we propose MitM algebraic key-recover attacks on Xoofff with reduce 3-/4-round Xoodoo. At last, we discuss a possible way to fix the weakness in the expanding rolling function (for "free") in Sect. 6.

2   Preliminaries

In this section, we briefly recall the description of the permutation-based mode Farfalle and its instantiation Xoofff (based on the permutation Xoodoo). Next, we recall the basic idea of the linearization attack, which we exploit to break Xoofff instantiated with 3-/4-round Xoodoo in the expansion part.

2.1   Farfalle Construction

Farfalle [2] is composed of four permutations p_b, p_c, p_d, p_e of a n-bit block and two rolling functions $roll_c$ and $roll_e$, depicted as in Fig. 1.

We denote the secret key and the message as K and M, respectively. The $(j + 1)$-block output $C = (C^0, C^1, \dots, C^j)$ is produced via the following three steps:

– **Mask derivation:** The secret key K is padded into a n-bit string $K\|10^*$, which is handled by the permutation p_b as input to yield the masks k for the compression layer and $k' = roll_c^{i+2}(k)$ for the expansion layer.

---

[1] The source codes are public available at https://github.com/Tammy-Cui/AttackXoofff.

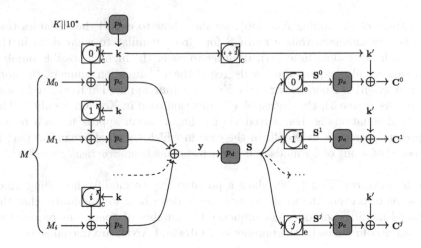

Fig. 1. Farfalle Construction

- **Compression layer:** The message M is divided into a sequence of $i+1$ n-bit blocks (where the last block is padded by 10^*): in the following, we use the notation $M = (M_0, M_1, \ldots, M_i)$ as well. By first applying the permutation p_c on each block $M_i \oplus roll_c^i(k)$, and then by XORing all results together, the message is compressed into an n-bit value y. This step can be summarized as $y = \bigoplus_i (p_c(M_i \oplus roll_c^i(k)))$.
- **Middle layer:** A permutation p_d is then applied to the unknown y: we denote the output by $S = p_d(y)$.
- **Expansion layer:** Finally, a sequence of n-bit data stream $C^j, j = 0, 1, 2, \ldots$ is obtained by consecutively applying the rolling function $roll_e$, the permutation p_d and by XORing the corresponding outputs with the mask k'. These two last steps can be summarized as $C^j = p_e(roll_e^j(S)) \oplus k'$.

2.2 Specification of Xoofff

Before presenting Xoofff, we first recall some useful notations in Table 2 – the concepts of Lane, Plane, State, Sheet and Column are recalled in Fig. 2.

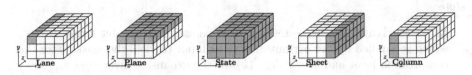

Fig. 2. Toy version of the Xoodoo state (lanes reduced to 8 bits).

Table 2. Notations to describe Xoofff

$A[x, y, z]$	Bit at coordinate (x, y, z) of intermediate state A;
$A[x, y]$ or $A_{x,y}$	Lane (x, y) of intermediate state A;
A_y	Plane y of intermediate state A;
$A_y \lll (t, v)$	Cyclic shift of A_y moving bit in (x, z) to position $(x + t, z + v)$;
$A_{x,y} \lll v$	Cyclic shift of lane $A_{x,y}$ moving bit from x to position $x + v$;
$A_{x,y} \ll v$	Shift of lane $A_{x,y}$ moving bit from x to position $x + v$;
$A_y + A_{y'}$	Bitwise sum (XOR) of planes A_y and $A_{y'}$;
$A_y \cdot A_{y'}$	Bitwise product (AND) of planes A_y and $A_{y'}$;

Algorithm 1: Round function of Xoodoo $(A \leftarrow R_i(A))$

---

1 θ : **for** $0 \le i < 3$ **do**
2 $\quad | \quad P \leftarrow A_0 \oplus A_1 \oplus A_2$;
3 $\quad | \quad E \leftarrow P \lll (1, 5) \oplus P \lll (1, 14)$;
4 $\quad | \quad A_i \leftarrow A_i \oplus E$;
5 ρ_{west} : $A_1 \leftarrow A_1 \lll (1, 0)$ and $A_2 \leftarrow A_2 \lll (0, 11)$;
6 ι : $A_{0,0} \leftarrow A_{0,0} \oplus C_i$; // C_i is a 32-bit constant.
7 χ : **for** $0 \le i < 3$ **do**
8 $\quad | \quad A_y \leftarrow A_y \oplus (A_{y+1} \oplus 1) \cdot A_{y+2}$;
9 ρ_{east} : $A_1 \leftarrow A_1 \lll (0, 1)$ and $A_2 \leftarrow A_2 \lll (2, 8)$;

Xoofff [8,9] is a doubly-extendable cryptographic keyed function by applying the Farfalle construction on two rolling functions $roll_{X_c}$ and $roll_{X_e}$ and permutation Xoodoo as follows:

- $p_b = p_c = p_d = p_e = Xoodoo$;
- $roll_c = roll_{X_c}$ and $roll_e = roll_{X_e}$.

The rolling function $roll_{X_e}$ is a Non-linear Feedback Shift Register (NLFSR), and updates a state A in the following way:

$$A_{0,0} \leftarrow A_{0,1} \cdot A_{0,2} \oplus (A_{0,0} \lll 5) \oplus (A_{0,1} \lll 13) + 0x00000007, \quad B \leftarrow A_0 \lll (3, 0),$$
$$A_0 \leftarrow A_1, \qquad A_1 \leftarrow A_2, \qquad A_2 \leftarrow B.$$

The permutation Xoodoo has totally 6 rounds. Each round is composed of 5 steps: mixing layer θ, a west shifting ρ_{west}, the addition of round constants ι, non-linear layer χ (where $\chi(\cdot) = \chi^{-1}(\cdot)$) and an east shifting ρ_{east}. The round function R_i is specified in Algorithm 1.

2.3   Linearization Attack

Linearization [10] is a well-known technique to solve multivariate polynomial systems of equations. Given a system of polynomial equations, the idea is to turn it into a system of linear equations by adding new variables that replace all the monomials of the system whose degree is strictly greater than 1. This linear system of equations can be solved using linear algebra if there are enough equations to make the linearized system overdetermined, typically at least on the same order as the number of variables after linearization.

The most straightforward way to linearize algebraic expressions in n unknowns of degree limited by d is just by introducing a new variable for every monomial. By a simple computation, the set of monomials considered has cardinality

$$S(n, d) := \sum_{i=1}^{d} \binom{n}{i}. \tag{1}$$

Given $x \leq S(n, d)$ monomials, the costs of the attack are approximately given by:[2]

- computational cost of $\mathcal{O}(x^\omega)$ operations (for $2 < \omega \leq 3$);
- memory cost of $\mathcal{O}(x^2)$ to store x linear equations each one in x variables.

3   Distinguisher and Attack on Xoofff (1-Round Xoodoo)

In the following, we use the notation S^i to denote the state at the output of the i-th expanding rolling function (where S^0 corresponds to S, which is the state after the middle layer). Moreover, we use the notation S_θ^i and S_χ^i to denote the state S^i after θ and χ respectively.

3.1   Symmetry Property of the State Rolling Function

The state rolling function is defined via the following NLFSR: for all $i \geq 0$

$$S^i[z] = \begin{bmatrix} S^i[0,2,z] & S^i[1,2,z] & S^i[2,2,z] & S^i[3,2,z] \\ S^i[0,1,z] & S^i[1,1,z] & S^i[2,1,z] & S^i[3,1,z] \\ S^i[0,0,z] & S^i[1,0,z] & S^i[2,0,z] & S^i[3,0,z] \end{bmatrix}$$

then

$$S^{i+1}[z] = \begin{bmatrix} S^i[1,0,z] & S^i[2,0,z] & S^i[3,0,z] & S^{i+1}[3,2,z] \\ S^i[0,2,z] & S^i[1,2,z] & S^i[2,2,z] & S^i[3,2,z] \\ S^i[0,1,z] & S^i[1,1,z] & S^i[2,1,z] & S^i[3,1,z] \end{bmatrix}$$

for a particular $S^{i+1}[3, 2, z]$ (see "Specification" for more details).

This particular NLFSR produces a strong connection between S^i and S^{i+3}, namely three sheets of S^i are equal to three sheets of S^{i+3}. In particular, the x-th sheet of S^{i+3} is equal to the $(x + 1)$-th sheet of S^{i+3} for $x \in \{0, 1, 2\}$.

---

[2] Note that solving a system of $x \geq 1$ linear equations in x variables corresponds to compute the inverse of a $x \times x$ matrix. Hence, inverting such matrix costs $\mathcal{O}(x^\omega)$ operations for $2 < \omega \leq 3$ (e.g., using the fast Gaussian Elimination algorithm [12] which costs $\mathcal{O}(x^3)$), while the memory cost to store such matrix is proportional to $\mathcal{O}(x^2)$.

$$S^{i+3}[z] = \begin{bmatrix} S^i[1,2,z] & S^i[2,2,z] & S^i[3,2,z] & S^{i+3}[3,2,z] \\ S^i[1,1,z] & S^i[2,1,z] & S^i[3,1,z] & S^{i+3}[3,1,z] \\ S^i[1,0,z] & S^i[2,0,z] & S^i[3,0,z] & S^{i+3}[3,0,z] \end{bmatrix}$$

Since the steps χ and θ work at the column level, this relation can be used to set up a distinguisher, which will be later exploited for key-recovery attacks. In the following, we will usually omit the variable z so as to simplify the equations/text.

3.2 Secret-Key Distinguisher (1-round Xoodoo)

By a simple computation, it is possible to observe that – for each z – the property just presented partially survives after the linear part of the round:[3]

$$\rho_{west} \circ \theta(S^i) = \begin{bmatrix} \star & \star & S^i_\theta[2,2] & S^i_\theta[3,2] \\ S^i_\theta[3,1] & \star & \star & S^i_\theta[2,1] \\ \star & \star & S^i_\theta[2,0] & S^i_\theta[3,0] \end{bmatrix}$$

if and only if

$$\rho_{west} \circ \theta(S^{i+3}) = \begin{bmatrix} \star & S^i_\theta[2,2] & S^i_\theta[3,2] & \star \\ \star & \star & S^i_\theta[2,1] & S^i_\theta[3,1] \\ \star & S^i_\theta[2,0] & S^i_\theta[3,0] & \star \end{bmatrix} .$$

Note that the last column of $\rho_{west} \circ \theta(S^i)$ is equal to the third column of $\rho_{west} \circ \theta(S^{i+3})$. In the case of $\iota[2,\cdot] = \iota[3,\cdot]$, this fact can be exploited to set up a longer distinguisher (indeed, χ maps the same input columns to the same output columns). Since $\iota[x,y,z] = 0$ for each $(x,y) \neq (0,0)$ and since an entire sheet at the input of χ is given, it follows that:

$$S^i_\chi[3,2] = S^{i+3}_\chi[2,2] \text{ and } S^i_\chi[3,1] = S^{i+3}_\chi[2,1] \text{ and } S^i_\chi[3,0] = S^{i+3}_\chi[2,0]; \quad (2)$$

and

$$S^i_\theta[2,2] = S^{i+3}_\theta[1,2] \text{ and } S^i_\theta[2,0] = S^{i+3}_\theta[1,0] \text{ and } S^i_\theta[0,1] = S^{i+3}_\theta[3,1]. \quad (3)$$

These equalities will be the starting point for our key-recovery attacks.

3.3 Attack on Xoofff Instantiated with 1-round Xoodoo in the Expansion Part

As shown in Sect. 2, one round of Xoodoo is defined as: $R_K(\cdot) = k \oplus \rho_{east} \circ \chi \circ \iota \circ \rho_{west} \circ \theta(\cdot)$. Since ρ_{east} is linear, we swap it with the final mask-addition and we remove it: in the following, the final round will be defined as $R'_k(\cdot) = k' \oplus \chi \circ \iota \circ \rho_{west} \circ \theta(\cdot)$.

---

[3] Here we emphasize the relation between $\rho_{west} \circ \theta(S^i)$ and $\rho_{west} \circ \theta(S^{i+3})$ by highlighting the components of $\rho_{west} \circ \theta(S^i)$ that are also in $\rho_{west} \circ \theta(S^{i+3})$. We use the symbol "$\star$" to denote all other components.

Algorithm 2: *Key-Recovery Attack on Xoofff (1-round Xoodoo)*

Data: 6 consecutive known output blocks $C^0, C^1, ..., C^5$

Result: final mask k' (assuming final ρ_{east} is omitted)

// In the following, we omit the variable z to simplify the equations.

1 **for** *each* $z = 0, ..., 31$ **do**

2   **for** *each* $k'[x, y] \in \{0, 1\}$ *where* $x \in \{1, 2\}$ *and* $y \in \{0, 1, 2\}$ *(2^6 possibilities)* **do**

3   **for** *each* $i = 0, 1, 2$ **do**

4   **if** $\left(\chi^{-1}(C^i \oplus k')\right)[2, 2] \neq \left(\chi^{-1}(C^{i+3} \oplus k')\right)[1, 2]$ **then**

5 | break; (test the next – partially – guessed mask)

6   **if** $\left(\chi^{-1}(C^i \oplus k')\right)[2, 0] \neq \left(\chi^{-1}(C^{i+3} \oplus k')\right)[1, 0]$ **then**

7 | break; (test the next – partially – guessed mask)

8   Once $k'[x, y]$ for $x \in \{1, 2\}$ and $y \in \{0, 1, 2\}$ are found:

9    $k'[3, 0] = C^0[3, 0] \oplus C^3[2, 0] \oplus k'[2, 0]$;

10   $k'[3, 1] = C^0[3, 1] \oplus C^3[2, 1] \oplus k'[2, 1]$;

11   $k'[3, 2] = C^0[3, 2] \oplus C^3[2, 2] \oplus k'[2, 2]$;

12   **for** *each* $k'[0, y] \in \{0, 1\}$ *where* $y \in \{0, 1, 2\}$ *(2^3 possibilities)* **do**

13   **for** *each* $i = 0, 1, 2$ **do**

14   **if** $\left(\chi^{-1}(C^i \oplus k')\right)[0, 1] \neq \left(\chi^{-1}(C^{i+3} \oplus k')\right)[3, 1]$ **then**

15 | break; (test the next – partially – guessed mask)

16 **return** k'

The idea of the attack is to partially guess the mask k' and exploit the relations among the bits of $\rho_{west} \circ \theta(S^i)$ and of $\rho_{west} \circ \theta(S^{i+3})$ to filter wrongly guessed key bits:

$$(S^i, S^{i+3}) \xrightarrow{\iota \circ \rho_{west} \circ \theta(\cdot)} \text{distinguisher} \xleftarrow[\text{mask-guessing}]{\chi(\cdot) = \chi^{-1}(\cdot)} (C^i, C^{i+3}).$$

In a similar way, the attack can be mounted by exploiting the relations among the bits of $\chi \circ \iota \circ \rho_{west} \circ \theta(S^i)$ and the ones of $\chi \circ \iota \circ \rho_{west} \circ \theta(S^{i+3})$.

In more detail, for each z, it is possible to set up 32 (independent) systems of 12 equations in 12 variables (namely, the bits of the mask k') of the form

$$\left(\chi^{-1}(C^i \oplus k')\right)[2, 2] = \left(\chi^{-1}(C^{i+3} \oplus k')\right)[1, 2] \tag{4}$$

$$\left(\chi^{-1}(C^i \oplus k')\right)[2, 0] = \left(\chi^{-1}(C^{i+3} \oplus k')\right)[1, 0] \tag{5}$$

$$\left(\chi^{-1}(C^i \oplus k')\right)[0, 1] = \left(\chi^{-1}(C^{i+3} \oplus k')\right)[3, 1] \tag{6}$$

by exploiting the distinguisher presented in Eq. (3), and of the form:

$$\forall j \in \{0, 1, 2\}: \quad C^i[3, j] \oplus k'[3, j] = C^{i+3}[2, j] \oplus k'[2, j] \tag{7}$$

by exploiting the distinguisher presented in Eq. (2).

Table 3. Practical results for Xoofff instantiated by 1-round Xoodoo in the expansion part: relation between the number of blocks used for the attack and the success rate of recovering 12 bits of the mask k' for a single fixed z.

#blocks	Success rate	#blocks	Success rate
6	13.4%	11	94.8%
7	44.1%	12	97.4%
8	70.0%	13	99%
9	80.7%	14	99.3%
10	91.5%	15	99.6%

In order to speed up the attack, we propose to work as follows

1. exploiting Eq. (4)–(5) (equivalently, working on the columns involving $S_\theta^i[2,0], S_\theta^i[2,2]$), find 6 bits of the mask (namely, $k'(1,\cdot), k'(2,\cdot)$);
2. given $k'(2,\cdot)$, note that $k'(3,\cdot)$ is also given by Eq. (7);
3. exploiting Eq. (6), find the last 3 bits of the mask $k'(0,\cdot)$.

The computational cost is so approximated by

$$32 \cdot \left[\underbrace{2^6 \cdot (1 + 1/2 + 1/4 + 1/8 + 1/16 + 1/32)}_{\text{find } k'(\cdot,1), k'(\cdot,2)} + \underbrace{2^3 \cdot ((1 + 1/2 + 1/4))}_{\text{find } k'(\cdot,0)} \right] \approx 2^{12.2}$$

elementary operations, where note that (1) we work independently on each z (32 in total), (2) in order to filter n bits of the mask, we need to check them against (at least) n equations and (3) when testing one candidate of the mask, the probability that it passes the test is 0.5. The required data of the attack is given by 6 output blocks (in order to set up the necessary equations).

3.4 Experimental Results

We practically implemented Algorithm 2 with 1000 repeated experiments. The results between the number of blocks and success rates to recover 12-bit mask $k'[x,y,z]$, $x = 0,1,2,3$, $y = 0,1,2$ for each z are in Table 3 (note that if we use N output blocks, then we can build $N - 3$ text pairs (S^i, S^{i+3})). To recover all 384-bit mask, we need to repeat the same recover-mask process on all 32 possible z. In practice, by 1000 repeated experiments, the success rates to recover the whole mask are 61.8%, 76.6% and 87.3% with 13, 14 and 15 blocks respectively. Hence, more output blocks (than what we predicted before) are actually necessary to find the full mask with a high probability.

Gap Between Theoretical and Practical Results. To explain the previous result, note that the following: Checking if $\left(\chi^{-1}(C^i \oplus k')\right)[2,2]$ is equal or not to $\left(\chi^{-1}(C^{i+3} \oplus k')\right)[1,2]$ is equivalently to check if

$$(C^i[0,2] \oplus k'[0,2]) \oplus (C^i[2,2] \oplus k'[2,2]) \oplus (C^i[1,2] \oplus k'[1,2]) \cdot (C^i[0,2] \oplus k'[0,2]) \neq$$
$$(C^{i+3}[0,1] \oplus k'[0,1]) \oplus (C^{i+3}[2,1] \oplus k'[2,1]) \oplus (C^{i+3}[1,1] \oplus k'[1,1]) \cdot (C^{i+3}[0,1] \oplus k'[0,1]).$$

It is not hard to check that the bits $k'[2,2]$ and $k'[2,1]$ appear only via their difference (that is, $k'[2,2] \oplus k'[2,1]$): as a result, it is only possible to identify their sum, but not the exact value of $k'[2,2]$ and of $k'[2,1]$. In a similar way, when checking $\left(\chi^{-1}(C^i \oplus k')\right)[2,0] \neq \left(\chi^{-1}(C^{i+3} \oplus k')\right)[1,0]$, it is only possible to identify the difference $k'[0,2] \oplus k'[0,1]$. At the same time, one can identify $k'[0,2]$ and $k'[0,1]$ using the first condition and $k'[2,2]$ and $k'[2,1]$ using the second one. As shown below, this allows to recover the full mask, but a bigger number of output blocks is necessary.

About the Success Probability. In order to explain the success probabilities of the attack found before, we first present some practical observations.

Note that according to the χ operation (remember $\chi = \chi^{-1}$), there are 2^4 cases of $(x_0, x_1, x_2, x'_0, x'_1, x'_2)$ s.t. $\chi(x_0, x_1, x_2) = (y_0, y_1, y_2)$ and $\chi(x'_0, x'_1, x'_2) = (y'_0, y'_1, y'_2)$ where $y_0 = y'_0$ and $y_2 = y'_2$. We therefore introduce the sets $\mathcal{X}_0$ and $\mathcal{X}_1$:

$$\mathcal{X}_0 = \{(x_0, x_1, x_2, x'_0, x'_1, x'_2) \in \mathbb{F}_2^6 \mid [\chi(x_0, x_1, x_2)](0) = [\chi(x'_0, x'_1, x'_2)](0)$$
$$\& \; [\chi(x_0, x_1, x_2)](2) = [\chi(x'_0, x'_1, x'_2)](2)\}.$$
$$\mathcal{X}_1 = \{(x_0, x_1, x_2, x'_0, x'_1, x'_2) \in \mathbb{F}_2^6 \mid [\chi(x_0, x_1, x_2)](1) = [\chi(x'_0, x'_1, x'_2)](1)\}.$$

where $[x](i)$ denotes the i-th bit of $x \in \mathbb{F}_2^3$ and where (only for our goal) the pairs $((x_0, x_1, x_2), (x'_0, x'_1, x'_2))$ and $((x'_0, x'_1, x'_2), (x_0, x_1, x_2))$ are *not* considered to be equivalent.

By practical tests, we found the following:

- The sets A and B are defined as follows: $A = \{(a_0, a_1, a_2) \in (\mathbb{F}_2^6)^3 \mid \forall i = 0, 1, 2 : a_i \in \mathcal{X}_0\}$ and set $B = \{(a_0, a_1, a_2) \in (\mathbb{F}_2^6)^3 \mid \exists \; c = (c_0, c_1, c_2, c_3, c_4, c_5) \in \mathbb{F}_2^6 \setminus \{0\} \text{ s.t. } \forall i = 0, 1, 2 : a_i \in \mathcal{X}_0 \text{ and } a_i \oplus c \in \mathcal{X}_0\}$. The cardinalities of A and B are

$$|A| = 4096 \quad \text{and} \quad |B| = 2656 \quad \rightarrow \quad \frac{|B|}{|A|} \approx 0.648. \tag{8}$$

- The sets A' and B' are defined as follows: $A' = \{(a_0, a_1, a_2) \in (\mathbb{F}_2^6)^3 \mid \forall i = 0, 1, 2 : a_i \in \mathcal{X}_1\}$ and set $B' = \{(a_0, a_1, a_2) \in (\mathbb{F}_2^6)^3 \mid \exists \; c = (0, 0, 0, c_0, c_1, c_2) \in \mathbb{F}_2^6 \setminus \{0\} \text{ s.t. } \forall i = 0, 1, 2 : a_i \in \mathcal{X}_1 \text{ and } a_i \oplus c \in \mathcal{X}_1\}$. The cardinalities of A' and B' are

$$|A'| = 32^3 \quad \text{and} \quad |B'| = 22\,016 \quad \rightarrow \quad \frac{|B'|}{|A'|} \approx 0.672. \tag{9}$$

These two results allow us to explain what happens in practice. In the first step of the attack, the goal is to recover the 6-bit mask $k'[x, y]$ (where $x = 1, 2$ and $y = 0, 1, 2$) for each z. Note that all $x^i = (x_0^i, x_1^i, x_2^i, x_0'^i, x_1'^i, x_2'^i)$ must belong to A under right mask, where $x_y^i = C^i[2, y] \oplus k'[2, y]$ and where $x_y'^i = C^{i+3}[1, y] \oplus k'[1, y]$ for $i \in \{0, 1, 2\}$. If there still exists a wrong mask such that $x^i \in \mathcal{X}_0$ for each $i \in \{0, 1, 2\}$ holds under the same blocks, then $\{x^0, x^1, x^2\} \in B$.

Hence, according to Eq. (8), the success rate to recover the right 6-bit mask is $1 - 64.8\% = 35.2\%$ (in theory). In practice, the success rate is about 35.8% with 1000 experiments.

In the third step, the goal is to recover the last 3-bit mask $k'[0, y]$, $y = 0, 1, 2$ for each z. Until now, 3-bit mask $k'[3, y]$ are known. Similar to what happens in the first step and according to Eq. (9), all wrong masks are filtered with probability $1 - 67.2\% = 32.8\%$ (in theory). In practice, the success rate is about 37.5% with 1000 experiments.

It follows that the success probabilities for each step of the attack are:

- for each z: using $6 + m$ output blocks, the probability of success is $1 - (1 - 0.352)^{m+1}$ in the first step; once the 6 bits of the key are found in step 1 (hence, also the 3 bits of the key are found in step 2 as well with prob. 1), the probability of success of the last step is equal to $1 - (1 - 0.328)^{m+1}$. This means that the overall probability to find the full key for each z fixed is $[1 - (1 - 0.352)^{m+1}] \cdot [1 - (1 - 0.328)^{m+1}] \approx 1 - 0.648^{m+1} - 0.672^{m+1} + 0.435^{2m+2} \approx 1 - 2 \cdot 0.66^{m+1}$;
- since all layers z are independent, the overall probability of the attack using $6 + m$ output blocks is $[1 - 2 \cdot 0.66^{m+1}]^{32}$.

Thus, using $m + 6$ outputs blocks, the probability of success is higher than $prob$ if $m \geq \log_{0.66}\left(\frac{1 - prob^{1/32}}{2}\right) - 1$ output blocks. E.g., for a theoretical probability of success of 85%, then 19 output blocks are necessary. By practical tests, it turned out that less data (namely, 15 output blocks) is sufficient since – as we saw before – the practical probabilities are a bit higher than the corresponding theoretical values.

Assuming 15 output blocks are sufficient (that is, $\approx 2.5\text{x}$ more data that the theoretical value given in the previous section), it follows that also the computational cost is higher than what we expected by a factor of 2.5.

4 Distinguisher and Attack on Xoofff Instantiated with 2-round Xoodoo in the Expansion Part

4.1 First Secret-Key Distinguisher

As we have seen in Eq. (2), both due to the weakness in the NLFSR and due to the choice of the round constants, after one complete round (that is, including ρ_{east}), the following relation between $R(S^i)$ and $R(S^{i+3})$ occurs

$$R(S^i) = \begin{bmatrix} \star & S_\chi^i[3,2] & \star & \star \\ \star & \star & \star & S_\chi^i[3,1] \\ \star & \star & \star & S_\chi^i[3,0] \end{bmatrix} \Leftrightarrow R(S^{i+3}) = \begin{bmatrix} S_\chi^i[3,2] & \star & \star & \star \\ \star & \star & S_\chi^i[3,1] & \star \\ \star & \star & S_\chi^i[3,0] & \star \end{bmatrix}.$$

After applying θ, we get the following situation:

$$\theta \circ R(S^i) = \begin{bmatrix} \star \star \star & & \star & \\ \star \star \star & S_\chi^i[3,1] \oplus \Delta & & \\ \star \star \star & S_\chi^i[3,0] \oplus \Delta & & \end{bmatrix} \Leftrightarrow \theta \circ R(S^{i+3}) = \begin{bmatrix} \star \star & & \star & & \star \\ \star \star & S_\chi^i[3,1] \oplus \Delta' & \star & \\ \star \star & S_\chi^i[3,0] \oplus \Delta' & \star & \end{bmatrix}.$$

for certain unknowns $\Delta, \Delta' \in \mathbb{F}_2^{32}$. Indeed, θ adds to each bit on the x-th sheet a given value that depends only on bits in the $(x-1)$-th sheet. Based on this, a distinguisher can be easily set up:

$$\theta \circ R(S^i)[3,1] \oplus \theta \circ R(S^i)[3,0] = \theta \circ R(S^{i+3})[2,1] \oplus \theta \circ R(S^{i+3})[2,0],$$

which modifies as follows when applying the rotation over the west:

$$\rho_{west} \circ \theta \circ R(S^i)[0,1] \oplus \rho_{west} \circ \theta \circ R(S^i)[3,0]$$
$$= \rho_{west} \circ \theta \circ R(S^{i+3})[3,1] \oplus \rho_{west} \circ \theta \circ R(S^{i+3})[2,0]. \tag{10}$$

4.2   Second Secret-Key Distinguisher

Our second distinguisher is based on the "parity". Hence, we first introduce the notion of "parity" and then analyze how it passes through the several operations.

Definition 1 (Parity). *Let $X \in \mathbb{F}^{4 \times 3 \times 32}$ be a state of Xoodoo. For each $0 \leq x \leq 3$ and for each $0 \leq y \leq 2$, we define the parity of X – denoted by $\mathfrak{p}(X[x,y])$ or simply $\mathfrak{p}[x,y]$ – as*

$$\mathfrak{p}[x,y] = \bigoplus_z X[x,y,z].$$

Lemma 1. *Given $t = \theta(s)$:*

$$\begin{bmatrix} t[0,2,z] & t[1,2,z] & t[2,2,z] & t[3,2,z] \\ t[0,1,z] & t[1,1,z] & t[2,1,z] & t[3,1,z] \\ t[0,0,z] & t[1,0,z] & t[2,0,z] & t[3,0,z] \end{bmatrix} = \theta \left(\begin{bmatrix} s[0,2,z] & s[1,2,z] & s[2,2,z] & s[3,2,z] \\ s[0,1,z] & s[1,1,z] & s[2,1,z] & s[3,1,z] \\ s[0,0,z] & s[1,0,z] & s[2,0,z] & s[3,0,z] \end{bmatrix} \right),$$

for each z, then the parity of $t[x,y]$ is equal to the parity of $s[x,y]$:

$$\forall x \in \{0,1,2,3\}, y \in \{0,1,2\} : \qquad \mathfrak{p}(s[x,y]) = \mathfrak{p}(t[x,y]).$$

Proof. Let $ss[x,z] := s[x-1,2,z] \oplus s[x-1,1,z] \oplus s[x-1,0,z]$, then

$$t[x,y,z] = s[x,y,z] \oplus ss[x,z-5] \oplus ss[x,z-14].$$

Since $\bigoplus_z ss[x,z-5] = \bigoplus_z ss[x,z-14]$, then the parity of $t[x,y]$ is equal to the parity of $s[x,y]$: $\mathfrak{p}(s[x,y]) = \mathfrak{p}(t[x,y])$. □

In the following, we analyse how it evolves through a round of Xoodoo.

Lemma 2. *Given $z = \chi(s)$ and $z' = \chi(s')$ where $s, s' \in \mathbb{F}^{3 \times 32}$ s.t.*

- *there exist $i, j \in \{0,1,2\}$ where $i \neq j$ s.t. for each z: $s[i,z] = s'[i,z]$ and $s[j,z] = s'[j,z]$ (that is, the bits in two sheets of s and s' are equal);*
- *parity is equal: $\mathfrak{p}(s[x]) = \mathfrak{p}(s'[x])$ for each x;*

then $\mathfrak{p}(z[l]) = \mathfrak{p}(z'[l])$ where $l \in \{0,1,2\} \setminus \{i,j\}$.

Proof. Since for each z, the i-th and the j-th bits are equal for s and s', then the χ function is "linear" in the l-th bit. The result follows immediately. □

Distinguisher. Given these properties, we can set up another distinguisher, by re-considering the output of the first round. By applying θ and ρ_{west}, for each z we get:

$$\rho_{west} \circ \theta \circ R(S^i) = \begin{bmatrix} \star & \mathsf{p}^i[1,2] \, \star & \star \\ \mathsf{p}^i[0,1] & \star & \star \, \mathsf{p}^i[3,1] \\ \star & \star & \star \, \mathsf{p}^i[3,0] \end{bmatrix}$$

if and only if

$$\rho_{west} \circ \theta \circ R(S^{i+3}) = \begin{bmatrix} \mathsf{p}^i[1,2] \, \star & \star & \star \\ \star & \star \, \mathsf{p}^i[3,1] & \mathsf{p}^i[0,1] \\ \star & \star \, \mathsf{p}^i[3,0] & \star \end{bmatrix} .$$

Hence, the following distinguisher holds:

$$\bigoplus_{z=0}^{31} \rho_{west} \circ \theta \circ R(S^i)[1,2,z] = \bigoplus_{z=0}^{31} \rho_{west} \circ \theta \circ R(S^{i+3})[0,2,z]. \qquad (11)$$

4.3 Attack on Xoofff Instantiated with 2-round Xoodoo in the Expansion Part

As before, we use the distinguisher as the starting point for a mask-recovery attack:

$$(S^i, S^{i+3}) \xrightarrow{\iota \circ \rho_{west} \theta \circ R(\cdot)} \text{distinguisher} \xleftarrow[\text{mask-guessing}]{\chi(\cdot) = \chi^{-1}(\cdot)} (C^i, C^{i+3})$$

In order to minimize the overall cost of the attack, we propose to set up it in the way described in detail as follows:

Step 1. In the first step, the attacker finds $9 \cdot 32 = 288$ bits of the mask (that is, $k'[x,y,z]$ for each z, y and for $x = 0,2,3$) by exploiting the distinguisher presented in Eq. (10). This corresponds to set up a system of equations of the form

$$\left(\chi^{-1}(C^i \oplus k')\right)[0,1] \oplus \left(\chi^{-1}(C^i \oplus k')\right)[3,0]$$
$$= \left(\chi^{-1}(C^{i+3} \oplus k')\right)[3,1] \oplus \left(\chi^{-1}(C^{i+3} \oplus k')\right)[2,0].$$

Hence, for each z, it is sufficient to guess 9 bits of the mask, and filter all wrongly guessed mask using the previous equality. The cost of this step is approximated by $32 \cdot 2^9 \cdot (1 + 1/2 + \ldots + 2^{-8}) \approx 2^{15}$ elementary operations, and 18 known output blocks.

Algorithm 3: *Key-Recovery Attack on Xoofff (2-round Xoodoo)*

Data: 73 consecutive known output blocks $C^0, C^1, ..., C^{72}$

Result: final mask k' (assuming final ρ_{east} is omitted)

1 STEP 1: find 288 bits of $k'[x, y, z]$:

2 **for** *each* $z = 0, 1, ..., 31$ **do**

3   **for** *each* $k'[x, y, z]$ *for each* $y = 0, 2$ *and* $x = 0, 2, 3$ *(2^{12} possibilities for each z)* **do**

4   **for** *each* $i = 0, 1, ..., 17$ **do**

5   **if** $\left(\chi^{-1}(C^i \oplus k')\right)[0, 1] \oplus \left(\chi^{-1}(C^i \oplus k')\right)[3, 0] \neq$ $\left(\chi^{-1}(C^{i+3} \oplus k')\right)[3, 1] \oplus \left(\chi^{-1}(C^{i+3} \oplus k')\right)[2, 0]$ **then**

6   break; (test the next – partially – guessed mask)

7 STEP 2: once $k'[x, y, z]$ for each z, y and $x = 0, 2, 3$ are found, find 64 bits of the mask $k'[1, y, z]$ for each $z = 0, ..., 31$ and for $y = 0, 1$:

8 **for** *each* $i = 0, 1, ..., 68$ **do**

9   Set up the following system of linear equations:

$$\bigoplus_{z=0}^{31} \left[\left(\chi^{-1}(C^i \oplus k')\right)[1, 2, z] \oplus \left(\chi^{-1}(C^{i+1} \oplus k')\right)[1, 2, z]\right] =$$
$$\bigoplus_{z=0}^{31} \left[\left(\chi^{-1}(C^{i+3} \oplus k')\right)[0, 2, z] \oplus \left(\chi^{-1}(C^{i+4} \oplus k')\right)[0, 2, z]\right] \tag{12}$$

     and solve it (via e.g. Gaussian Elimination);

10 STEP 3: to find the last 32 bits of the mask $k'[2, 1, z]$ where $z = 0, ..., 31$, decrypt a complete round and set up a system of linear equations of the form $R^{-1}(C^i \oplus k')[1, 2, z] = R^{-1}(C^{i+3} \oplus k')[0, 2, z]$ (remember that χ is linear given ≥ 2 bits of the mask for each column).

11 **return** k'

Step 2. In order to find 64 more bits of the mask (namely, $k'[1, y, z]$ for each z and for each $y = 0, 2$), one possibility is to exploit the distinguisher presented in Eq. (11). This allows to set up a system of equations of the form

$$\bigoplus_z [(C^i[1, 0, z] \oplus k'[1, 0, z]) \oplus (C^i[1, 1, z] \oplus k'[1, 1, z]) \cdot (C^i[1, 0, z] \oplus k'[1, 0, z]) \oplus$$
$$\oplus (C^i[1, 2, z] \oplus k'[1, 2, z])] = \bigoplus_z [(C^{i+3}[0, 2, z] \oplus k'[0, 2, z]) \oplus (C^{i+3}[0, 0, z] \oplus k'[0, 0, z]) \oplus$$
$$\oplus (C^{i+3}[0, 1, z] \oplus k'[0, 1, z]) \cdot (C^{i+3}[0, 0, z] \oplus k'[0, 0, z])]$$

where the r.h.s. is given.

Each one of these quadratic equations involves 96 bits of the mask. Instead of brute forcing all 2^{96} possible combinations of k', the idea is to set up a system of linear equations starting from these quadratic equations. To achieve this, note that the coefficients of all quadratic monomials (in the masks) are always equal to 1. Hence, it is sufficient to sum over two different output blocks to eliminate all quadratic monomials, getting equations of degree 1 of the form in Eq. (12).

This means that $n + 4$ output (consecutive) blocks are necessary to construct n equations.

Since the coefficients of the monomials that define the linear equations are not independent, it is possible that more than a single solution exists (equivalently, that the matrix corresponding to the linear system of equations is not invertible). As we show in detail in Appendix A, the probability that such 64 equations (which corresponds to 68 output blocks) are linearly independent is approximately 0.29, and at least 61 of them are linearly independent with probability (higher than) 0.89. Hence, by slightly increasing the number of output blocks, it seems possible to find 3 more linearly independent equations with a high probability. By practical tests we found that using 68, 70, 73 output (consecutive) blocks, the probability of success (to find 64 linearly independent equations) is resp. 29.7%, 75.9% and 96.6%.

Step 3. The final step consists of finding the 32 bits of the mask $k[1, 1, z]$. In order to do this, the idea to set up a system of linear equations based on the fact that

$$R^{-1}(C^i \oplus k')[1, 2, z] = R^{-1}(C^{i+3} \oplus k')[0, 2, z]$$

which corresponds to the distinguisher given in Eq. (3).

Note that, since the attacker knows at least two bits of each column of the mask, χ^{-1} reduces to a linear operation. The cost of this step would be approximately $\mathcal{O}(32^3) = \mathcal{O}(2^{15})$ elementary operations.

Summary. The attack requires ≈ 73 known output blocks, and the cost is approximately given by $2^{15} + 2^{18} + 2^{15} = 5 \cdot 2^{16} \approx 2^{18.3}$ elementary operations.

4.4   Experimental Results

We practically implement our 2-round attack. Totally, 73 output blocks are needed to get a success probability of finding the correct key greater than 85%. The practical verification works as expected, with the only exception of the first step.

Step 1 (in Theory). As for the case of the attack on 1-round, note that checking if $\left(\chi^{-1}(C^i \oplus k')\right)[0, 1] \oplus \left(\chi^{-1}(C^i \oplus k')\right)[3, 0]$ is equal or not to $\left(\chi^{-1}(C^{i+3} \oplus k')\right)[3, 1] \oplus \left(\chi^{-1}(C^{i+3} \oplus k')\right)[2, 0]$ corresponds of checking

$$(C^i[0, 2] \oplus k'[0, 2]) \oplus (C^i[0, 1] \oplus k'[0, 1]) \oplus (C^i[0, 2] \oplus k'[0, 2]) \cdot (C^i[0, 0] \oplus k'[0, 0]) \oplus$$
$$\oplus (C^i[3, 0] \oplus k'[3, 0]) \oplus C^i[3, 1] \oplus (C^i[3, 2] \oplus k'[3, 2]) \cdot (C^i[3, 1] \oplus k'[3, 1]) \oplus$$
$$\oplus (C^{i+3}[3, 2] \oplus k'[3, 2]) \oplus C^{i+3}[3, 1] \oplus (C^{i+3}[3, 2] \oplus k'[0, 2]) \cdot (C^{i+3}[3, 0] \oplus k'[3, 0]) \oplus$$
$$\oplus (C^{i+3}[2, 0] \oplus k'[2, 0]) \oplus (C^{i+3}[2, 1] \oplus k'[2, 1]) \oplus (C^{i+3}[2, 2] \oplus k'[0, 2]) \cdot (C^{i+3}[2, 1] \oplus k'[2, 1]).$$

As before, it is possible to note that the bits $k'[0, 1]$ and $k'[2, 0]$ appear only via their difference: $k'[0, 1] \oplus k'[2, 0]$. Hence, it is never possible to find all the

288 bits as expected, but only $288 - 32 = 256$. The probability of finding such 256 bits is obviously related to the number of output blocks: by practical tests, such probability is approximately 81% given 17 output blocks, which becomes resp. 94% and 98% using 18 and 19 output blocks.

Step 1 (in Practice): Parity. How to find the last 32 bits before moving to the next step? The idea is to use the parity, that is the fact that

$$\bigoplus_{z=0}^{31} \rho_{west} \circ \theta \circ R(S^i)[3,1,z] = \bigoplus_{z=0}^{31} \rho_{west} \circ \theta \circ R(S^{i+3})[2,1,z].$$

Due to the argument presented before, we expect that 40 output blocks are largely sufficient to find the 32 remaining bits of the key. This is what we also found in practice, where the prob. of success is 28%, 96%, 100% using resp. 35, 40, 45 output blocks. As a result, the computational cost (including this step) increases to $2^{18.3} + 32^3 = 2^{18.5}$ operations.

5   Linearization MitM Attack on Xoofff (Instantiated with 3-/4-round Xoodoo in the Expansion Part)

As the final main result, we present a competitive linearization attack on Xoofff when Xoodoo is reduced to 3-/4-round in the expansion part. This attack is similar to the one already proposed on Kravatte in [7]. Roughly speaking, the goal of the attack is to set up a system of linear equations that describe the analyzed scheme (by adding new variables that replace all the monomials of the system whose degree is strictly greater than 1): by solving such system of equations, the attacker is able to recover the mask k'. The cost of the attack is obviously related to the number of equations and the number of monomials/variables that composed such equations. For more details, we refer to the detailed description of the attack presented in Sect. 2.3.

Our linearization attack exploits both the low-degree of χ^{-1} and the symmetry of the rolling function presented before. Compared to the linearization attack on Kravatte presented in [7], we point out some important differences:

- since the rolling function of Xoodoo is non-linear, it is *not* possible to set up a linearization attack from the output of the middle part in the forward direction as in the first version Kravatte: at the same time, we can cover one round for free by exploiting the weakness in the NLFSR;
- one more round in the decryption direction can be covered exploiting the lower degree of χ^{-1} of Xoodoo w.r.t. the one of Keccak.

5.1   Idea of the MitM Linearization Attack

The attack proceeds as the ones already presented:

$$(S^i, S^{i+3}) \xrightarrow{R(\cdot)} \text{distinguisher} \xleftarrow[\text{mask-recovery}]{k' \oplus R^{-r}(\cdot)} (C^i, C^{i+3})$$

for $r \geq 1$, where:

- the exploited distinguisher is the one given in Eq. (2) which provides 96 bits of information for each pair of known output blocks (C^i, C^{i+3}) (1 more bit of information can be derived by exploiting the parity);
- the mask-recovery part is performed via linearization.

Hence, in the following we limit ourselves to estimate the cost of the attacks by estimating the number of variables.

5.2 Attacks on Xoofff Instantiated with 2-round Xoodoo in the Expansion Part

For simplicity, we start with the case in which the expansion part is instantiated by 2-round Xoodoo. In this case, the key-recovery part covers only 1 round. Since one backward round has degree 2 and using Eq. (1), it follows that the number of mask-bits monomials (hence, variables) of degree at most 2 is at most $S(384, 2) = \sum_{i=1}^{2} \binom{384}{i} \approx 2^{16.2}$. This number is actually only an upper bound of the real number of variables. Indeed, it would assume that all combinations of degree 2 of the mask-bits are possible. However, this is actually not the case due to the definition of the χ function. Indeed, through the backward computation, new monomials are only created in χ^{-1} layers through the multiplicative combination of input sum of monomials. Since χ^{-1} operates on three input bits only (i.e., one column), the actual number of monomials that one has to face is given by

$$\underbrace{384}_{\text{monomials of degree 1}} + \underbrace{128 \cdot \binom{3}{2}}_{\text{monomials of degree 2}} = 768.$$

Since N known output blocks provides $96 \cdot (N-3) = 96N - 288$ bits of information (namely, equations), it follows that one needs approximately $\lceil \frac{768+288}{96} \rceil = 11$ known output blocks, a computational cost of approximately $\mathcal{O}(768^3) = 2^{28.75}$ elementary operations and a memory cost of $\mathcal{O}(768^2) = 2^{19.2}$ bits.

5.3 Attacks on Xoofff Instantiated with 3-/4-round Xoodoo in the Expansion Part

Considering attacks on more rounds Xoodoo, note that the trick just exploited in the attack on 2-round Xoodoo does not apply anymore, since the input bits of the internal χ^{-1} layers have undergone linear diffusion. As a result, the number of monomials cannot be restricted in the same manner. At the same time, the degree limitation still applies: if $\mathfrak{N}$ monomials can be used to describe the polynomial expressions of all bits before the χ^{-1} layer, the number of monomials that appear in the output bits of this layer is upper-bounded by $S(\mathfrak{N}, r)$ for $r - 1$ rounds.

3-round. By using the previous considerations, it follows that the number of mask-bits monomials (hence, variables) is given by

$$S(768, 2) = \sum_{i=1}^{2} \binom{768}{i} \approx 2^{18.2}.$$

Using the previous argumentation, it follows that

- the data cost is approximately of $\left\lceil \frac{2^{18.2}+288}{96} \right\rceil = 2^{11.7}$ known output blocks;
- the computational cost is approximately given by $\mathcal{O}\left((2^{18.2})^3\right) \approx 2^{54.6}$ elementary operations;
- the memory cost is approximately given by $\mathcal{O}\left((2^{18.2})^2\right) \approx 2^{36.4}$ bits.

4-round. By using the previous considerations, it follows that the number of mask-bits monomials (hence, variables) is given by

$$S(2^{18.2}, 2) = \sum_{i=1}^{2} \binom{2^{18.2}}{i} \approx 2^{35.4}.$$

Using the previous argumentation, it follows that

- the data cost is approximately of $\left\lceil \frac{2^{35.4}+288}{96} \right\rceil = 2^{28.9}$ known output blocks;
- the computational cost is approximately given by $\mathcal{O}\left((2^{35.4})^3\right) \approx 2^{106.2}$ elementary operations;
- the memory cost is approximately given by $\mathcal{O}\left((2^{35.4})^2\right) \approx 2^{70.8}$ bits.

5.4 Experiment Results

We implemented the practical attack on 2-/3-round toy-version Xoofff, in which the state lane is reduced to 8 bits (instead of 32 bits) and the rolling function is slight modified accordingly. The full specification is given in Appendix B.

Practical Attack – 2-round Xoodoo. According to Eq. (1), there are $96+96 = 192$ different monomials in the attack so that $N = 11$ output blocks $(8 \times 3 \times (N-3) = 192)$ are needed in theory. The theoretical number of monomials matches with the practical one, while we found that 12 (instead of 11) output blocks are necessary to recover the right mask. Hence, the theoretical and practical results are almost consistent.

Practical Attack – 3-round Xoodoo. In theory, according to Eq. (1), there are $S(192, 2) = \sum_{i=1}^{2} \binom{192}{i} = 18\,080 \approx 2^{14.2}$ mask-bits monomials (variables) so that $N \approx 757$ output blocks are needed (since $8 \times 3 \times (N-3) \geq 18\,080$). As for the case of 2-round, this theoretical result matches the practical one, where we used 757 output blocks (resulting in $(757-3) \times 3 \times 8 = 18\,096$ equations and $17\,952$ different monomials) to successfully recover the right mask.

6   Summary and Possible Countermeasures

In this paper, we presented new key-recovery attacks on Xoofff instantiated with a round-reduced Xoodoo permutation in the expansion part (up to 4 rounds). The Meet-in-the-Middle and the linearization attacks that we presented are independent of the details of the compression and middle layers.

As we have seen, the starting point of our attacks is a new symmetry property of the rolling function presented in Sect. 3. In this final section we discuss possible countermeasures to reduce the number of attackable rounds.

Countermeasures. Several ways may be (in principle) possible to achieve the goal of reducing the number of attackable rounds for the attacks presented in this paper, including e.g. *changing the layout of the expanding rolling function*, changing the round constants, adding a final mask-schedule and so on.

As we show in Appendix D, the second strategy is useless (for completeness, in Appendix C we present an attack on Xoofff instantiated by a Xoodoo permutation in the expansion part in which no round constant is added: such attack is independent of the number of rounds of Xoodoo). The third one can be based either on a permutation of the key bits (this would increase the number of variables in the first step of the linearization attack) or it could involve a more complex linear/non-linear function. Since the goal is to set up an efficient scheme, we do not take in consideration this option.

Modification of the State Rolling Function. Probably, the simplest way to "prevent" the attack is by changing the state Rolling function. Among several possibilities, we propose the following: given S^i as in Eq. (3.1), then S^{i+1} is defined as:

$$S^{i+1}[z] = \begin{bmatrix} S^i[1,2,z] & S^i[2,2,z] & S^i[3,2,z] & S^{i+1}[3,2,z] \\ S^i[0,2,z] & S^i[0,1,z] & S^i[1,1,z] & S^i[2,1,z] \\ S^i[1,0,z] & S^i[2,0,z] & S^i[3,0,z] & S^i[3,1,z] \end{bmatrix}$$

where $S^{i+1}[3,2,z] = S^i[1,0,z] \cdot S^i[2,0,z] \oplus (S^i[0,0,z] \lll 5) \oplus (S^i[1,0,z] \lll 13) \oplus \text{0x00000007}$ is defined as before.

The crucial point is that the elements are shifted inside the plane in two different directions (left for the first and the third planes, right for the second one). This prevents the fact that certain columns in $S^i[z]$ appears with prob. 1 in $S^{i+j}[z]$ for any $j \geq 1$. As a result, the attacks presented here work on 1 round less.

Acknowledgment. The symmetry property of the state rolling function presented in Sect. 3.1 has been found by Joan Daemen. Authors thank him for his suggestion to exploit such symmetry property as a possible starting point for key-recovery attacks on the expansion part of Xoofff. Authors also thank Reviewers for their valuable comments, and Kalikinkar Mandal for shepherding this final version of the paper. Lorenzo Grassi and Tingting Cui are supported by the European Research Council under the ERC advanced grant agreement under grant ERC-2017-ADG Nr. 788980 ESCADA. Besides that, Tingting Cui is also supported by NSFC Projects (No. 61902100).

A   Attack on Xoofff (2-round Xoodoo): Details for Step 2

Here we provide more details regarding the second step of the attack presented in Sect. 4.3.

In such a step, the attacker sets up a system of linear equations in 64 variables. Since the coefficients of the corresponding matrix are (in general) not independent, it is possible that the matrix is not invertible. Hence, more equations are in general necessary so as to have a good probability to find 64 independent linear equations. By practical tests we found that using 68, 70 and 73 output (consecutive) blocks, the probability of success (to find 64 linearly independent equations) is resp. 29.7%, 75.9% and 96.6%.

Here we analyze these probabilities from a theoretical point of view.

Lemma 3. *If n-bit vectors $\mathbf{a}_0, \mathbf{a}_1, \ldots, \mathbf{a}_{s-1}$ are linearly independent ($s < n$), then the probability that another random n-bit vector $\mathbf{a}_s$ is linearly independent with such s vectors is $\frac{2^n - 2^s + 1}{2^n} \approx 1 - 2^{s-n}$.*

Proof. The space $\mathcal{S}$ spanned by $\mathbf{a}_0, \mathbf{a}_1, \ldots, \mathbf{a}_{s-1}$ involves $2^s - 1$ (non-null) vectors. As long as $\mathbf{a}_s$ does not belong to $\mathcal{S}$, $\mathbf{a}_0, \mathbf{a}_1, \ldots, \mathbf{a}_s$ are linear independent. Thus, $\mathbf{a}_s$ has $2^n - 2^s + 1$ possible values, which means the probability is $\frac{2^n - 2^s + 1}{2^n}$.   □

In order to compute $Prob(\mathbf{a}_0, \mathbf{a}_1, \ldots, \mathbf{a}_{63}$ linearly independent), we can use the law of total probability. Let $\{B_n\}_n$ be a finite or countably infinite partition of a sample space. By the law of total probability: $Prob(A) = \sum_{B_n} Prob(A \mid B_n) \cdot Prob(B_n)$. For each $x \geq 1$, it follows that:

$$Prob(\mathbf{a}_0, \mathbf{a}_1, \ldots, \mathbf{a}_x \text{ linearly independent})$$
$$= Prob(\mathbf{a}_0, \mathbf{a}_1, \ldots, \mathbf{a}_x \text{ linearly independent} \mid \mathbf{a}_0, \mathbf{a}_1, \ldots, \mathbf{a}_{x-1} \text{ linearly independent})$$
$$\times Prob(\mathbf{a}_0, \mathbf{a}_1, \ldots, \mathbf{a}_{x-1} \text{ linearly independent})$$

where note that

$$Prob(\mathbf{a}_0, \mathbf{a}_1, \ldots, \mathbf{a}_x \text{ linearly independent} \mid \mathbf{a}_0, \mathbf{a}_1, \ldots, \mathbf{a}_{x-1} \text{ linearly dependent}) = 0.$$

Working iteratively, it follows that $Prob(\mathbf{a}_0, \mathbf{a}_1, \ldots, \mathbf{a}_{63}$ linearly independent) is equal to

$$\frac{2^{64} - 1}{2^{64}} \cdot \frac{2^{64} - 3}{2^{64}} \cdot \ldots \cdot \frac{2^{63} + 1}{2^{64}} \approx \frac{1}{2} \cdot \frac{3}{4} \cdot \frac{7}{8} \cdot \frac{15}{16} \cdot \ldots \cdot \frac{2^{64} - 1}{2^{64}} \approx 0.29.$$

This result matches the practical probability we found in our experiments.

It follows that, given 64 equations (which corresponds to 68 output blocks), at least 61 of them are linearly independent with probability (higher than) $\frac{15}{16} \cdot \ldots \cdot \frac{2^{64} - 1}{2^{64}} \approx 88.5\%$. Also this theoretical result matches the one found in our practical tests.

B   Specification of Toy-Version Xoofff

In this section, we specify the toy-version Xoofff, which is used to verify the linearization MitM attacks on Xoofff with reduced 3-/4-round Xoodoo. The round function of such toy-version Xoodoo is given in Algorithm 4. Meanwhile, the rolling function $roll_{X_e}$ of the toy-version Xoofff updates a state A in the following way:

$$A_{0,0} \leftarrow A_{0,1} \cdot A_{0,2} \oplus (A_{0,0} \lll 3) \oplus (A_{0,1} \lll 5) \oplus \texttt{0x00000007}, \quad B \leftarrow A_0 \lll (3,0),$$
$$A_0 \leftarrow A_1, \qquad\qquad A_1 \leftarrow A_2, \qquad\qquad A_2 \leftarrow B.$$

Algorithm 4: Round function of toy-version Xoodoo $(A \leftarrow R_i(A))$

---

1 θ : **for** $0 \leq i < 3$ **do**
2 $\quad\lfloor \quad A_i \leftarrow A_i \oplus [(A_0 \oplus A_1 \oplus A_2) \lll (1,3)] \oplus [(A_0 \oplus A_1 \oplus A_2) \lll (1,6)]$;
3 ρ_{west} : $A_1 \leftarrow A_1 \lll (1,0)$ and $A_2 \leftarrow A_2 \lll (0,5)$;
4 ι : $A_{0,0} \leftarrow A_{0,0} \oplus C_i$; // C_i **is an 8-bit constant as same as the lsb 8-bit constant used in original Xoodoo.**
5 χ : **for** $0 \leq i < 3$ **do**
6 $\quad\lfloor \quad A_y \leftarrow A_y \oplus (A_{y+1} \oplus 1) \cdot A_{y+2}$;
7 ρ_{east} : $A_1 \leftarrow A_1 \lll (0,1)$ and $A_2 \leftarrow A_2 \lll (2,4)$;

C   Attack on Full-Round Xoofff without Constants

In this section, we propose an attack on the expansion part of Xoofff where no round constant is present in the round function. Such attack – that can potentially cover any number of rounds – is based on the following property:

Lemma 4. *Consider two states S^1 and S^2 that satisfy the property $S^1[x, y, z] = S^2[x - 1, y, z]$ for all $0 \leq x < 4$, $0 \leq y < 3$ and $0 \leq z < 32$. After one-round Xoodoo without ι operation, the output C^1 and C^2 still satisfy the property $C^1[x, y, z] = C^2[x - 1, y, z]$.*

Proof. By working as in the previous sections, note that:

$$\begin{bmatrix} C^1[0,2] & C[1,2] & C[2,2] & C[3,2] \\ C^1[0,1] & C[1,1] & C[2,1] & C[3,1] \\ C^1[0,0] & C[1,0] & C[2,0] & C[3,0] \end{bmatrix} = \rho_{east} \circ \chi \circ \rho_{west} \circ \theta \left(\begin{bmatrix} S^1[0,2] & S[1,2] & S[2,2] & S[3,2] \\ S^1[0,1] & S[1,1] & S[2,1] & S[3,1] \\ S^1[0,0] & S[1,0] & S[2,0] & S[3,0] \end{bmatrix} \right)$$

$$\begin{bmatrix} C[1,2] & C[2,2] & C[3,2] & C^2[3,2] \\ C[1,1] & C[2,1] & C[3,1] & C^2[3,1] \\ C[1,0] & C[2,0] & C[3,0] & C^2[3,0] \end{bmatrix} = \rho_{east} \circ \chi \circ \rho_{west} \circ \theta \left(\begin{bmatrix} S[1,2] & S[2,2] & S[3,2] & S^2[3,2] \\ S[1,1] & S[2,1] & S[3,1] & S^2[3,1] \\ S[1,0] & S[2,0] & S[3,0] & S^2[3,0] \end{bmatrix} \right).$$

The result follows immediately. $\square$

Due to the relation between the output of the rolling functions S^i and S^{i+3}:

$$S^{i+3} = \begin{bmatrix} S^i[1,2] & S^i[2,2] & S^i[3,2] & S^{i+3}[3,2] \\ S^i[1,1] & S^i[2,1] & S^i[3,1] & S^{i+3}[3,1] \\ S^i[1,0] & S^i[2,0] & S^i[3,0] & S^{i+3}[3,0] \end{bmatrix}.$$

the probability of the event $S^{i+3}[3,y,z] = S^i[0,y,z]$ for $y = 0,1,2$ and for each z is equal to 2^{-96}. Hence, given approximately $3 \cdot 2^{96}$ output blocks, the probability that there exists S^i and S^{i+3} that satisfy the previous property is $1 - (1 - 2^{-96})^{3 \cdot 2^{96}} \approx 1 - e^{-3} \approx 95\%$: as a result, it is possible to break the scheme.

D   Different Constant Addition (Equivalently, ι) Operation

One of the weakness exploited to set up the attack is the fact that for each z

$$\rho_{west} \circ \theta(S^i) = \begin{bmatrix} \star \star \star & S^i_{\rho_{west}}[3,2] \\ \star \star \star & S^i_{\rho_{west}}[2,1] \\ \star \star \star & S^i_{\rho_{west}}[3,0] \end{bmatrix} \text{ iff } \rho_{west} \circ \theta(S^{i+3}) = \begin{bmatrix} \star \star & S^i_{\rho_{west}}[3,2] & \star \\ \star \star & S^i_{\rho_{west}}[2,1] & \star \\ \star \star & S^i_{\rho_{west}}[3,0] & \star \end{bmatrix}$$

implies

$$\chi \circ \iota \circ \rho_{west} \circ \theta(S^i) = \begin{bmatrix} \star \star \star & S^i_{\chi}[3,2] \\ \star \star \star & S^i_{\chi}[3,1] \\ \star \star \star & S^i_{\chi}[3,0] \end{bmatrix} \text{ iff } \chi \circ \iota \circ \rho_{west} \circ \theta(S^{i+3}) = \begin{bmatrix} \star \star & S^i_{\chi}[3,2] & \star \\ \star \star & S^i_{\chi}[3,1] & \star \\ \star \star & S^i_{\chi}[3,0] & \star \end{bmatrix}$$

since $\iota[x,y,z] = 0$ for each $(x,y) \neq (0,0)$.

What happens if $\iota[x,y,z] \neq 0$? Could this change (by itself) prevent the attack? As shown below, this is not the case.

Indeed, note that

$$\chi \circ \iota \circ \rho_{west} \circ \theta(S^i)[3,2] = \left(S^i_{\rho_{west}}[3,2] \oplus S^i_{\rho_{west}}[3,0] \oplus S^i_{\rho_{west}}[3,1] \cdot S^i_{\rho_{west}}[3,0] \right)$$
$$\oplus \left(\iota[3,2] \oplus \iota[3,0] \oplus \iota[3,1] \cdot \iota[3,0] \right) \oplus \left(S^i_{\rho_{west}}[3,0] \cdot \iota[3,1] \oplus S^i_{\rho_{west}}[3,1] \cdot \iota[3,0] \right)$$

$$\chi \circ \iota \circ \rho_{west} \circ \theta(S^i)[3,1] = \left(S^i_{\rho_{west}}[3,1] \oplus S^i_{\rho_{west}}[3,2] \oplus S^i_{\rho_{west}}[3,2] \cdot S^i_{\rho_{west}}[3,0] \right)$$
$$\oplus \left(\iota[3,1] \oplus \iota[3,2] \oplus \iota[3,2] \cdot \iota[3,0] \right) \oplus \left(S^i_{\rho_{west}}[3,2] \cdot \iota[3,0] \oplus S^i_{\rho_{west}}[3,0] \cdot \iota[3,2] \right)$$

$$\chi \circ \iota \circ \rho_{west} \circ \theta(S^i)[3,0] = \left(S^i_{\rho_{west}}[3,1] \oplus S^i_{\rho_{west}}[3,0] \oplus S^i_{\rho_{west}}[3,2] \cdot S^i_{\rho_{west}}[3,1] \right)$$
$$\oplus \left(\iota[3,1] \oplus \iota[3,0] \oplus \iota[3,2] \cdot \iota[3,2] \right) \oplus \left(S^i_{\rho_{west}}[3,2] \cdot \iota[3,1] \oplus S^i_{\rho_{west}}[3,1] \cdot \iota[3,2] \right)$$

if and only if

$$\chi \circ \iota \circ \rho_{west} \circ \theta(S^{i+3})[2,2] = \left(S^i_{\rho_{west}}[3,2] \oplus S^i_{\rho_{west}}[3,0] \oplus S^i_{\rho_{west}}[3,1] \cdot S^i_{\rho_{west}}[3,0] \right)$$

$$\oplus \left(\iota[2,2] \oplus \iota[2,0] \oplus \iota[2,1] \cdot \iota[2,0] \right) \oplus \left(S^i_{\rho_{west}}[3,0] \cdot \iota[2,1] \oplus S^i_{\rho_{west}}[3,1] \cdot \iota[2,0] \right)$$

$$\chi \circ \iota \circ \rho_{west} \circ \theta(S^{i+3})[2,1] = \left(S^i_{\rho_{west}}[3,1] \oplus S^i_{\rho_{west}}[3,2] \oplus S^i_{\rho_{west}}[3,2] \cdot S^i_{\rho_{west}}[3,0] \right)$$

$$\oplus \left(\iota[2,1] \oplus \iota[2,2] \oplus \iota[2,2] \cdot \iota[2,0] \right) \oplus \left(S^i_{\rho_{west}}[3,2] \cdot \iota[2,0] \oplus S^i_{\rho_{west}}[3,0] \cdot \iota[2,2] \right)$$

$$\chi \circ \iota \circ \rho_{west} \circ \theta(S^{i+3})[2,0] = \left(S^i_{\rho_{west}}[3,1] \oplus S^i_{\rho_{west}}[3,0] \oplus S^i_{\rho_{west}}[3,2] \cdot S^i_{\rho_{west}}[3,1] \right)$$

$$\oplus \left(\iota[2,1] \oplus \iota[2,0] \oplus \iota[2,2] \cdot \iota[2,2] \right) \oplus \left(S^i_{\rho_{west}}[3,2] \cdot \iota[2,1] \oplus S^i_{\rho_{west}}[3,1] \cdot \iota[2,2] \right)$$

Hence, since ι is public and known, these 6 output bits depend only on 3 bits. It follows that a distinguisher can still be set up. E.g., by considering

$$\chi \circ \iota \circ \rho_{west} \circ \theta(S^i)[3,2] \oplus \chi \circ \iota \circ \rho_{west} \circ \theta(S^{i+3})[2,2]$$
$$\chi \circ \iota \circ \rho_{west} \circ \theta(S^i)[3,1] \oplus \chi \circ \iota \circ \rho_{west} \circ \theta(S^{i+3})[2,1]$$
$$\chi \circ \iota \circ \rho_{west} \circ \theta(S^i)[3,0] \oplus \chi \circ \iota \circ \rho_{west} \circ \theta(S^{i+3})[2,0]$$

one can get a system of three *linear* equations in $S^i_{\rho_{west}}[3,2], S^i_{\rho_{west}}[3,1]$, $S^i_{\rho_{west}}[3,0]$. Once these 3 values are given, it is sufficient to check them against e.g. the 3 equalities that define $\chi \circ \iota \circ \rho_{west} \circ \theta(S^i)[3,2], \chi \circ \iota \circ \rho_{west} \circ \theta(S^i)[3,1], \chi \circ \iota \circ \rho_{west} \circ \theta(S^i)[3,0]$.

In conclusion, changing the round constants cannot prevent the attacks described before.

E   Higher-Order Differential on Xoofff

Given a function $f : \mathbb{F}_2^n \to \mathbb{F}_2^n$ of algebraic degree d, consider a subspace $\mathcal{V} \subseteq \mathbb{F}_2^n$ of dimension greater than d (that is, $\dim(\mathcal{V}) \geq d+1$). For each affine subspace $\mathcal{V} \oplus v$, it is possible to show that

$$\bigoplus_{x \in \mathcal{V} \oplus v} f(x) = 0.$$

This is the property used in a higher-order differential attack [11].

The attack that we are going to present resembles the one already presented in [7]. Since $\deg(\chi) = 2$, the degree after r rounds of Xoodoo is upper bounded by 2^r: since the complexity of the attack cannot be greater than 2^{128}, we can cover at most 6 rounds using the zero-sum property. Hence:

- we construct a subspace of dimension $2^6 + 1 = 65$;
- we exploit the zero-sum to find the key.

E.1   Idea of the Attack

Constructing the Subspace $\mathcal{V}$. In order to construct the subspace $\mathcal{V}$, we just re-use the same strategy proposed in [7, Sect. 4.1]. Given an n-block padded message $M = (m_0, ..., m_{n-1})$, let $Acc(M)$ be the associated accumulator value $\bigoplus_i p_c(m_i \oplus k_i^{in})$. Let $M^0 = (m_0^0, ..., m_{n-1}^0)$ and $M^j = (m_0^1, ..., m_{n-1}^1)$ denote an arbitrary pair of padded messages such that $m_l^0 \neq m_l^1$ for all l. We define the following structure of 2^n n-block messages:

$$\mathcal{V} \oplus v = Acc(M^0) \oplus \langle \delta_0, ..., \delta_n \rangle$$

where for each i:

$$\delta_i = p_c(m_i^0 \oplus k_i^{in}) \oplus p_c(m_i^1 \oplus k_i^{in}).$$

As showed in [7, Sect. 4.1], δ_i are linearly independent with overwhelming probability if $n \ll b = 384$ (independently of $p_c(\cdot)$).

Finding the Key. Given $\mathcal{V}$, the strategy of the attack is to construct a system of equations that describe the last r rounds (where the final mask k' is the variable) and solve it:

$$\mathcal{V} \oplus v \xrightarrow{R^6(\cdot)} \text{zero-sum} \xleftarrow[\text{mask-recovery}]{k' \oplus R^{-r}(\cdot)} \text{corresponding output blocks } \{C^i\}_i$$

Note that the same output mask k' is used in each output block: hence, the number of variables is independent of the number of considered output blocks. In order to solve the system, the idea is to use the linearization technique described before.

E.2   Cost of the Attack

In order to set up the attack, we just re-use the results presented in Sect. 5. In a linearization attack on 3-round Xoodoo, the number of variables in the system is upper bounded by $2^{35.4}$. Hence:

- at least, $2^{35.4} \cdot 2^{65}$ pairs of input/output blocks are necessary to construct the system of equations to solve, for a total cost of $2^{35.4} \cdot 2^{65} \cdot 2 = 2^{100.4}$ input/output blocks;
- the cost to construct the system of equations is given by $2^{100.4}$ XORs;
- the cost to solve the system of equations is given by $\mathcal{O}\left((2^{35.4})^3\right) = 2^{106.2}$ operations and a memory cost of $\mathcal{O}\left((2^{35.4})^2\right) = 2^{70.8}$ bits.

Hence, the overall cost of the attack is approximately given by $2^{100.4} + 2^{106.2} \approx 2^{106.3}$ operations.

References

1. Bernstein, D.J., et al.: GIMLI?: a cross-platform permutation. In: Fischer, W., Homma, N. (eds.) CHES 2017. LNCS, vol. 10529, pp. 299–320. Springer, Cham (2017). https://doi.org/10.1007/978-3-319-66787-4_15
2. Bertoni, G., Daemen, J., Hoffert, S., Peeters, M., Assche, G.V., Keer, R.V.: Farfalle: parallel permutation-based cryptography. IACR Trans. Symmetric Cryptol. **2017**(4), 1–38 (2017)
3. Bertoni, G., Daemen, J., Hoffert, S., Peeters, M., Assche, G.V., Keer, R.V.: The authenticated encryption schemes Kravatte-SANE and Kravatte-SANSE. Cryptology ePrint Archive, Report 2018/1012 (2018). https://eprint.iacr.org/2018/1012
4. Bertoni, G., Daemen, J., Peeters, M., Van Assche, G.: On the indifferentiability of the sponge construction. In: Smart, N. (ed.) EUROCRYPT 2008. LNCS, vol. 4965, pp. 181–197. Springer, Heidelberg (2008). https://doi.org/10.1007/978-3-540-78967-3_11
5. Bertoni, G., Daemen, J., Peeters, M., Van Assche, G.: Duplexing the sponge: single-pass authenticated encryption and other applications. In: Miri, A., Vaudenay, S. (eds.) SAC 2011. LNCS, vol. 7118, pp. 320–337. Springer, Heidelberg (2012). https://doi.org/10.1007/978-3-642-28496-0_19
6. Bertoni, G., Daemen, J., Peeters, M., Van Assche, G.: Keccak. In: Johansson, T., Nguyen, P.Q. (eds.) EUROCRYPT 2013. LNCS, vol. 7881, pp. 313–314. Springer, Heidelberg (2013). https://doi.org/10.1007/978-3-642-38348-9_19
7. Chaigneau, C., et al.: Key-recovery attacks on full Kravatte. IACR Trans. Symmetric Cryptol. **2018**(1), 5–28 (2018)
8. Daemen, J., Hoffert, S., Assche, G.V., Keer, R.V.: The design of Xoodoo and Xoofff. IACR Trans. Symmetric Cryptol. **2018**(4), 1–38 (2018)
9. Daemen, J., Hoffert, S., Peeters, M., Assche, G.V., Keer, R.V.: Xoodoo cookbook. Cryptology ePrint Archive, Report 2018/767 (2018)
10. Kipnis, A., Shamir, A.: Cryptanalysis of the HFE public key cryptosystem by relinearization. In: Wiener, M. (ed.) CRYPTO 1999. LNCS, vol. 1666, pp. 19–30. Springer, Heidelberg (1999). https://doi.org/10.1007/3-540-48405-1_2
11. Knudsen, L.R.: Truncated and higher order differentials. In: Preneel, B. (ed.) FSE 1994. LNCS, vol. 1008, pp. 196–211. Springer, Heidelberg (1995). https://doi.org/10.1007/3-540-60590-8_16
12. Koç, Ç.K., Arachchige, S.N.: A fast algorithm for gaussian elimination over GF(2) and its implementation on the GAPP. J. Parallel Distrib. Comput. **13**(1), 118–122 (1991)
13. Liu, F., Isobe, T., Meier, W., Yang, Z.: Algebraic Attacks on Round-Reduced Keccak/Xoodoo. Cryptology ePrint Archive, Report 2020/346 (2020). https://eprint.iacr.org/2020/346
14. Zhou, H., Zong, R., Dong, X., Jia, K., Meier, W.: Interpolation Attacks on Round-Reduced Elephant, Kravatte and Xoofff. Cryptology ePrint Archive, Report 2020/781 (2020). https://eprint.iacr.org/2020/781

Improved (Related-key) Differential Cryptanalysis on GIFT

Fulei Ji[1,2], Wentao Zhang[1,2(✉)], Chunning Zhou[1,2], and Tianyou Ding[1,2]

[1] State Key Laboratory of Information Security, Institute of Information Engineering, Chinese Academy of Sciences, Beijing, China
{jifulei,zhangwentao,zhouchunning,dingtianyou}@iie.ac.cn
[2] School of Cyber Security, University of Chinese Academy of Sciences, Beijing, China

Abstract. In this paper, we reevaluate the security of GIFT against differential cryptanalysis under both single-key scenario and related-key scenario. Firstly, we apply Matsui's algorithm to search related-key differential trails of GIFT. We add three constraints to limit the search space and search the optimal related-key differential trails on the limited search space. We obtain related-key differential trails of GIFT-64/128 for up to 15/14 rounds, which are the best results on related-key differential trails of GIFT so far. Secondly, we propose an automatic algorithm to increase the probability of the related-key boomerang distinguisher of GIFT by searching the clustering of the related-key differential trails utilized in the boomerang distinguisher. We find a 20-round related-key boomerang distinguisher of GIFT-64 with probability $2^{-58.557}$. The 25-round related-key rectangle attack on GIFT-64 is constructed based on it. This is the longest attack on GIFT-64. We also find a 19-round related-key boomerang distinguisher of GIFT-128 with probability $2^{-109.626}$. We propose a 23-round related-key rectangle attack on GIFT-128 utilizing the 19-round distinguisher, which is the longest related-key attack on GIFT-128. The 24-round related-key rectangle attack on GIFT-64 and 22-round related-key boomerang attack on GIFT-128 are also presented. Thirdly, we search the clustering of the single-key differential trails. We increase the probability of a 20-round single-key differential distinguisher of GIFT-128 from $2^{-121.415}$ to $2^{-120.245}$. The time complexity of the 26-round single-key differential attack on GIFT-128 is improved from $2^{124.415}$ to $2^{123.245}$.

Keywords: GIFT · Related-key differential trail · Single-key differential trail · Clustering effect · Matsui's algorithm · Boomerang attack · Rectangle attack

1 Introduction

GIFT is a lightweight Substitution-Permutation-Network block cipher proposed by Banik *et al.* at CHES'17 [7]. GIFT has two versions named GIFT-64 and

© Springer Nature Switzerland AG 2021
O. Dunkelman et al. (Eds.): SAC 2020, LNCS 12804, pp. 198–228, 2021.
https://doi.org/10.1007/978-3-030-81652-0_8

GIFT-128, whose block sizes are 64 and 128 bits respectively and round numbers are 28 and 40 respectively. The key length of GIFT-64 and GIFT-128 are both 128 bits. As the inheritor of PRESENT [16], GIFT achieves improvements over PRESENT in both security and efficiency. GIFT is the underlying block cipher of the lightweight authenticated encryption schemes GIFT-COFB [1], HYENA [2], SUNDAE-GIFT [3], LOTUS-AEAD and LOCUS-AEAD [4], which are all the round 2 candidates of the NIST lightweight crypto standardization process [5].

Differential cryptanalysis [13] is one of the most fundamental methods for cryptanalysis of block ciphers. The most important step of differential cryptanalysis is to find differential trails with high probabilities. *Boomerang attack* [31] and *rectangle attack* [11,23] are extensions of differential cryptanalysis. *Related-key boomerang attack* [12,24] is a combination of boomerang attack and related-key differential cryptanalysis [10].

In recent years, the resistance of GIFT against (related-key) differential cryptanalysis have been extensively studied. **In single-key scenario**, Zhou *et al.* [35] succeed in searching the optimal differential trails of GIFT-64 for up to 14 rounds. Ji *et al.* [22] found the optimal differential trails of GIFT-128 for up to 19 rounds. Li *et al.* [25] obtained a 20-round differential trail of GIFT-128 and presented a 26-round attack on GIFT-128. **In related-key scenario**, the designers [7] gave lower bounds of the probabilities of the optimal related-key differential trails of GIFT-64/GIFT-128 for up to 12/9 rounds. Liu and Sasaki [27] searched related-key differential trails of GIFT-64 for up to 21 rounds. They succeed in attacking 21-round GIFT-128 with a 19-round related-key boomerang distinguisher and 23-round GIFT-64 with a 20-round related-key boomerang distinguisher. In [18], Chen *et al.* constructed a 20-round related-key boomerang distinguisher of GIFT-64 with probability $Pr = 2^{-50}$. Based on this 20-round distinguisher, a 23-round related-key rectangle attack was proposed in [18] and a 24-round related-key rectangle attack was proposed by Zhao *et al.* in [34]. According to the analysis in [32], the probability of the 20-round distinguisher should be corrected to $Pr = 2^{-68}$. The 23-round and 24-round attack are invalid since $Pr < 2^{-64}$ [11]. The detailed proof process is demonstrated in Appendix C.

Matsui's algorithm [28] is a branch-and-bound depth-first automatic search algorithm proposed by Matsui to search optimal single-key differential and linear trails of DES. Some improvements of Matsui's algorithm have been presented and applied to DESL, FEAL, NOEKEON and SPONGENT [6,8,22,29]. In [22], Ji *et al.* applied three methods to speed up the search process of Matsui's algorithm. The improved Matsui's algorithm given in [22] is easy to implement and performs well in searching the optimal single-key differential trails of GIFT.

In this paper, we focus on the following two issues. **Firstly**, the lower bounds of the probabilities of the optimal related-key differential trails of GIFT found in [7,27] are loose. We hope to find related-key differential trails of GIFT with higher probabilities. We apply Matsui's algorithm to search related-key differential trails of GIFT. **Secondly**, both the probability of the single-key differential distinguisher and the related-key boomerang distinguisher can be improved by considering the clustering of the differential trails. The definitions of *the clustering of an R-round single-key differential trail* and *the clustering of the related-key* *differential trails utilized in an R-round related-key boomerang distinguisher* are presented in Definition 4 and Definition 5. We study how to find the clustering of the single-key differential trails and the related-key differential trails utilized in the related-key boomerang distinguisher.

Our Contributions

1 **We apply Matsui's algorithm to search related-key differential trails of GIFT.** We search related-key differential trails of GIFT according to the following three steps:
   - Firstly, apply the speeding-up methods in [22] to speed up the search process.
   - Secondly, add three constraints to limit the search space.
   - Finally, search the optimal related-key differential trails on the limited search space.

The adjusted Matsui's algorithm devoted to searching related-key differential trails of GIFT is shown in Algorithm 1.
   - We succeed in finding related-key differential trails of GIFT-64/128 for up to 15/14 rounds. The results are summarized in Table 1.

Table 1. The weight[a] of the *R*-round related-key differential trails of GIFT

	GIFT-64				GIFT-128	
R	[7]	[18]	[27]	Section 3	[7]	Section 3
5	1.415			1.415	7.000	6.830
6	5.000			4.000	11.000	10.830
7	6.415			6.000	20.000	15.830
8	10.000			8.000	25.000	22.830
9	16.000	14.000	13.415	13.415	31.000	30.000
10	22.000			20.415		37.000
11	27.000		28.830	26.000		44.000
12				31.000		56.000
13			39.000	37.000		65.830
14				42.830		77.830
15			50.000	48.000		

[a]The *weight* is the negative logarithm of the *probability* to base 2.

   - As we can see from Table 1, compared with the known results in [7, 18, 27], **the related-key differential trails of GIFT we find are the best results so far.** For GIFT-128, we find related-key differential trails for up to 14 round, while the previous results up to 9 rounds. For both GIFT-64 and GIFT-128, our results provide tighter lower bounds for the probabilities of the optimal related-key trails.

In [27], the authors presented a 9-round related-key differential trail *l* of GIFT-128 with weight 29.830. Through our verification, we find that *l* cannot be reproduced. It is because that the round key difference of *l* cannot be generated from the master key difference.

2 **We propose an automatic search algorithm to search the clustering of the related-key differential trails utilized in the related-key boomerang distinguisher.** The new algorithm is presented as Algorithm 2. The target cipher E of the related-key boomerang distinguisher is decomposed as $E_1 \circ E_m \circ E_0$.

   – **For GIFT-64**, we increase the probability of a 20-round related-key boomerang distinguisher from $2^{-67.660}$ to $2^{-58.557}$. The clustering of the 10-round related-key differential trail utilized in E_0 consists of 5728 trails. The clustering of the 9-round related-key differential trail utilized in E_1 consists of 312 trails.

   The 25-round and 24-round related-key rectangle attacks are achieved taking advantage of the 20-round distinguisher. **This is the longest attack on GIFT-64 so far**, while the previous longest attack is the 23-round related-key boomerang attack proposed in [27].

   – **For GIFT-128**, we increase the probability of a 19-round related-key boomerang distinguisher from $2^{-120.00}$ to $2^{-109.626}$. The clustering of the 9-round related-key differential trail utilized in E_0 contains 3952 trails. The clustering of the 9-round related-key differential trail utilized in E_1 contains 2944 trails.

   Applying the 19-round distinguisher, we propose a 23-round related-key rectangle attack and a 22-round related-key boomerang attack. **This is the longest related-key attack on GIFT-128**, while the previous longest related-key attack is the 21-round related-key boomerang attack proposed in [27].

3 **We apply Matsui's algorithm to search the clustering of the single-key differential trails.**

   – We increase the probability of a 20-round single-key differential distinguisher of GIFT-128 from $2^{-121.415}$ to $2^{-120.245}$. The clustering of the 20-round single-key differential trail is composed by four trails. We improve the time complexity of the 26-round differential attack on GIFT-128 constructed in [25] from $2^{124.415}$ to $2^{123.245}$.

The cryptanalytic results are summarized in Table 2.

Organization. The paper is organized as follows. In Sect. 2, we give a brief description of GIFT, the speeding-up methods on Matsui's algorithm and the related-key boomerang and rectangle attack. The definitions and notations adopted throughout the paper are also presented in Sect. 2. In Sect. 3, we introduce how to apply Matsui's algorithm in related-key scenario. Section 4 declares how to search the clustering of the single-key/related-key differential trails. Section 5 and Sect. 6 provide the details of the 25/24-round attacks on GIFT-64 and the 26/23-round attacks on GIFT-128 respectively. The details of the 22-round attack on GIFT-128 are presented in Appendix B. Sect. 7 is the conclusion and future work.

Table 2. Summary of the cryptanalytic results on GIFT

GIFT-64

Rounds	Approach	Setting	Time	Data	Memory	Ref.
20	DC	SK	$2^{112.68}$	2^{62}	2^{112}	[17]
21	DC	SK	$2^{107.61}$	2^{64}	2^{96}	[17]
23	Boomerang	RK	$2^{126.6}$	$2^{63.3}$	-	[27]
24	Rectangle	RK	$2^{106.00}$	$2^{63.78}$	$2^{64.10}$	Section 5.2
25	Rectangle	RK	$2^{120.92}$	$2^{63.78}$	$2^{64.10}$	Section 5.1

GIFT-128

Rounds	Approach	Setting	Time	Data	Memory	Ref.
21	Boomerang	RK	$2^{126.6}$	$2^{126.6}$	-	[27]
22	Boomerang	RK	$2^{112.63}$	$2^{112.63}$	2^{52}	Appendix B
23	Rectangle	RK	$2^{126.89}$	$2^{121.31}$	$2^{121.63}$	Section 6.2
23	DC	SK	2^{120}	2^{120}	2^{86}	[36]
26	DC	SK	$2^{124.415}$	$2^{124.415}$	2^{109}	[25]
26	DC	SK	$2^{123.245}$	$2^{123.245}$	2^{109}	Section 6.1

2 Preliminaries

2.1 Description of GIFT

Let n be the block size of GIFT. The master key is $iniK := k_7||k_6|| \cdots ||k_0$, in which $|iniK| = 128$, $|k_i| = 16$. Each round of GIFT consists of three steps: SubCells, PermBits, and AddRoundKey.

Table 3. The specifications of the S-box GS in GIFT

x	0	1	2	3	4	5	6	7	8	9	a	b	c	d	e	f
$GS(x)$	1	a	4	c	6	f	3	9	2	d	b	7	5	0	8	e

1 SubCells. The S-box GS is applied to every nibble of the cipher state. The specifications of GS is given in Table 3.
2 PermBits. Update the cipher state by a linear bit permutation $P(\cdot)$ as $b_{P(i)} \leftarrow b_i, \forall i \in \{0, \cdots, n-1\}$.
3 AddRoundKey. An $n/2$-bit round key RK is extracted from the key state. It is further partitioned into two s-bit words $RK := U||V = u_{s-1} \cdots u_0||v_{s-1} \cdots v_0$, $s = n/4$.
For GIFT-64, RK is XORed to the state as $b_{4i+1} \leftarrow b_{4i+1} \oplus u_i$, $b_{4i} \leftarrow b_{4i} \oplus v_i, \forall i \in \{0, \cdots, 15\}$. For GIFT-128, RK is XORed to the state as $b_{4i+2} \leftarrow b_{4i+2} \oplus u_i$, $b_{4i+1} \leftarrow b_{4i+1} \oplus v_i, \forall i \in \{0, \cdots, 31\}$.
For both versions, a single bit "1" and a 6-bit constant C are XORed into the internal state at positions $n-1$, 23, 19, 15, 11, 7 and 3 respectively.

Key Schedule. For GIFT-64, $RK = U||V = k_1||k_0$. For GIFT-128, $RK = U||V = k_5||k_4||k_1||k_0$. For both versions, the key state is updated as

$$k_7||k_6||\cdots||k_1||k_0 \leftarrow k_1 \ggg 2||k_0 \ggg 12||\cdots||k_3||k_2,$$

where $\ggg i$ is an i-bit right rotation within a 16-bit word.

We refer readers to [7] for more details of GIFT.

2.2 Definitions and Notations

Definition 1 ([20]). *The weight of a difference propagation* (a', b') is the negative of the binary logarithm of the difference propagation probability over the transformation h, *i.e.*,

$$w_r(a', b') = -log_2^{Pr^h(a',b')}. \tag{1}$$

a' is the input difference and b' is the output difference.

Definition 2 ([19]). Let φ be an invertible function from $\mathbb{F}_2^m$ to $\mathbb{F}_2^m$, and $\Delta_0, \nabla_0 \in \mathbb{F}_2^m$. The *boomerang connectivity table* (BCT) of φ is defined by a $2^m \times 2^m$ table, in which the entry for (Δ_0, ∇_0) is computed by:

$$\text{BCT}(\Delta_0, \nabla_0) = \sharp\{x \in \{0,1\}^n | \varphi^{-1}(\varphi(x) \oplus \nabla_0) \oplus \varphi^{-1}(\varphi(x \oplus \Delta_0) \oplus \nabla_0) = \Delta_0\}. \tag{2}$$

Definition 3 ([32]). Let φ be an invertible function from $\mathbb{F}_2^m$ to $\mathbb{F}_2^m$, and $\Delta_0, \Delta_1, \nabla_0, \nabla_1 \in \mathbb{F}_2^m$. The *boomerang difference table* (BDT) of φ is a three-dimensional table, in which the entry for $(\Delta_0, \Delta_1, \nabla_0)$ is computed by:

$$\text{BDT}(\Delta_0, \Delta_1, \nabla_0) = \sharp\{x \in \{0,1\}^n | \varphi^{-1}(\varphi(x) \oplus \nabla_0) \oplus \varphi^{-1}(\varphi(x \oplus \Delta_0) \oplus \nabla_0) = \Delta_0,$$
$$\varphi(x) \oplus \varphi(x \oplus \Delta_0) = \Delta_1\}. \tag{3}$$

The iBDT, as a variant of BDT, is evaluated by:

$$\text{iBDT}(\nabla_0, \nabla_1, \Delta_0) = \sharp\{x \in \{0,1\}^n | \varphi(\varphi^{-1}(x) \oplus \Delta_0) \oplus \varphi(\varphi^{-1}(x \oplus \nabla_0) \oplus \Delta_0) = \nabla_0,$$
$$\varphi^{-1}(x) \oplus \varphi^{-1}(x \oplus \nabla_0) = \nabla_1\}. \tag{4}$$

The notations used in this paper are defined as follows:

$S(\cdot), P(\cdot), K(\cdot)$	:	SubCells operation, PermBits operation, AddRoundKey operation
n	:	the block size of cipher E
k	:	the master key size of cipher E
2ns	:	the number of the S-boxes in $S(\cdot)$; 2ns $= n/4$ for GIFT
MKD	:	the master key difference
X_i, Y_i	:	the input and the output of $S(\cdot)$ in round i
Z_i	:	the output of $P(\cdot)$ in round i
K_i	:	the round key of round i
$\Delta X_i, \Delta Y_i, \Delta Z_i, \Delta K_i$	:	the differential value of X_i, Y_i, Z_i and K_i
$W(l)$	:	the weight of the differential trail l
$W(\Delta X_i, \Delta Y_i)$	:	the weight of $\Delta X_i \xrightarrow{S(\cdot)} \Delta Y_i$ in round i
$B_R := min[\Sigma_{i=1}^{R} W(\Delta X_i, \Delta Y_i)]$	:	the weight of the R-round optimal differential trail
Bc_R	:	the upper bound of B_R
bw	:	the value of Bc_R minus B_R; $Bc_R = B_R + bw$
DDT	:	the *difference distribution table* of the S-box
LAT	:	the *linear approximation table* of the S-box
$E := E_1 \circ E_m \circ E_0$	:	the target cipher of the boomerang or rectangle distinguisher
$E' := E_f \circ E \circ E_b$	:	the target cipher of the boomerang or rectangle attack
E_b	:	the extension cipher added at the start of E
E_f	:	the extension cipher added at the end of E
r_b, r_f	:	the number of active bits in the input difference of E_b and the output difference of E_f
m_b, m_f	:	the number of key bits needed to be guessed in E_b and E_f

2.3   Three Methods to Speed up Matsui's Algorithm

Matsui's algorithm [28] works by induction on the number of rounds and derives the R-round optimal weight B_R from the knowledge of all i-round optimal weight B_i ($1 \le i < R$). The program requires an initial value for B_R, which is represented as Bc_R. It works correctly for any Bc_R as long as $Bc_R \ge B_R$. In [22], Ji *et al.* applied three methods to improve the efficiency of Matsui's algorithm. The three speeding-up methods are named (1) *Reconstructing DDT and LAT According to Weight*, (2) *Executing Linear Layer Operations in Minimal Cost* and (3) *Merging Two 4-bit S-boxes into One 8-bit S-box*.

Speeding-up method-1 contributes to pruning unsatisfiable candidates quickly. The authors reconstructed the DDT to sort the input and output differences according to their weights. **Speeding-up method-2 and method-3** contribute to reducing the cost of executing linear layer operations. The authors merged 2ns 4-bit S-boxes into ns 8-bit new S-boxes. The new linear table is

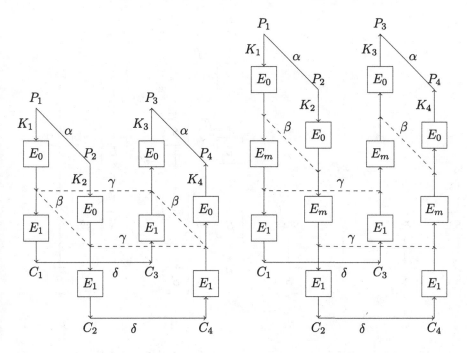

Fig. 1. The boomerang distinguisher   **Fig. 2.** The sandwich distinguisher

constructed according to the output differences of each S-box. The SSE instructions are applied to reduce the cost of linear layer operations.

The improved Matsui's algorithm for GIFT is demonstrated as Algorithm 3 in Appendix A. We refer readers to [22] for more details of the speeding-up methods.

2.4   Related-key Boomerang Attack and Rectangle Attack

Basic Related-key Boomerang Attack and Rectangle Attack. *Related-key boomerang attack* is an adaptive chosen-plaintext/ciphertext attack. As is shown in Fig. 1, the adversary can split the target cipher E into two sub-ciphers E_0 and E_1, i.e., $E = E_1 \circ E_0$. Assume that there are a differential trail $\alpha \to \beta$ under the key difference ΔK over E_0 with probability p and a differential trail $\gamma \to \delta$ under the key difference ∇K over E_1 with probability q. Once K_1 is known, the other three keys are determined: $K_2 = K_1 \oplus \Delta K$, $K_3 = K_1 \oplus \nabla K$, $K_4 = K_2 \oplus \nabla K$. Given $P_1 \oplus P_2 = \alpha$ and $K_1 \oplus K_2 = \Delta K$, the probability that we obtain two plaintexts satisfying $P_3 \oplus P_4 = \alpha$ through the boomerang distinguisher is:

$$p^2 q^2 = Pr[E^{-1}(E(x, K_1) \oplus \delta, K_3) \oplus E^{-1}(E(x \oplus \alpha, K_2) \oplus \delta, K_4) = \alpha] \quad (5)$$

If (P_1, P_2, P_3, P_4) can pass the boomerang distinguisher, then it is called a *right quartet*.

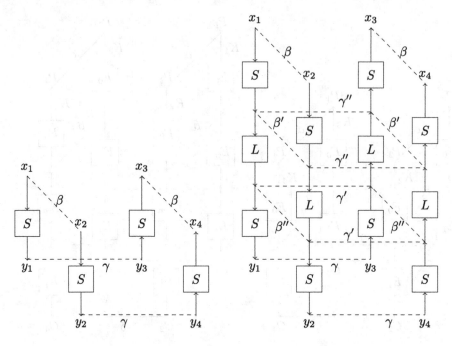

Fig. 3. A 1-round E_m **Fig. 4.** A 2-round E_m

For a random permutation, given $P_1 \oplus P_2 = \alpha$ and $K_1 \oplus K_2 = \Delta K$, the probability that two random plaintexts satisfying $P_3 \oplus P_4 = \alpha$ is 2^{-n}. Therefore, only if $pq > 2^{-n/2}$ can we count more right quartets than random noise through the related-key boomerang distinguisher.

   Related-key rectangle attack is a chosen-plaintext attack, which is a further development of the related-key boomerang attack. In Fig. 1, given $P_1 \oplus P_2 = \alpha$ and $P_3 \oplus P_4 = \alpha$ under K_1, K_2, K_3, K_4, the probability that the corresponding ciphertexts C_1, C_2, C_3, C_4 meets $C_1 \oplus C_3 = \delta$ and $C_2 \oplus C_4 = \delta$ (or $C_1 \oplus C_4 = \delta$ and $C_2 \oplus C_3 = \delta$) is $2^{-n}p^2q^2$. If (P_1, P_2, P_3, P_4) can pass the rectangle distinguisher under (K_1, K_2, K_3, K_4), then it is called a *right quartet*. For a random permutation, we get a right quartet with probability 2^{-2n} in the rectangle attack. Thus, only if $pq > 2^{-n/2}$ can we count more right quartets than random noise.

Boomerang Switch. The interaction between the two differential trails over E_0 and E_1 is utilized to improve the boomerang and rectangle attack [14,15], which is called *the boomerang switch* [15]. The idea of the boomerang switch is to minimize the overall complexity of the distinguisher by optimizing the transition between E_0 and E_1. In [21], a new framework named *sandwich attack* was proposed. As is shown in Fig. 2, the sandwich attack decomposes the target cipher E as $E_1 \circ E_m \circ E_0$. The propagation of the boomerang switch is captured by the propagation of E_m.

For the fixed β and γ, the probability that a quartet can pass E_m is denoted as:

$$r := Pr[E_m^{-1}(E_m(x, K_1) \oplus \gamma, K_3) \oplus E_m^{-1}(E_m(x \oplus \beta, K_2) \oplus \gamma, K_4) = \beta] \quad (6)$$

Thus, the probability that we obtain a right quartet through the sandwich distinguisher (*i.e.*, the boomerang distinguisher with boomerang switch) is $p^2 q^2 r$.

The value of r can be evaluated by the boomerang connectivity table [19] or the boomerang difference table [32] at the S-box level. Let $\beta[2ns]|| \cdots ||\beta[1] := \beta$ and $\gamma[2ns]||\cdots||\gamma[1] := \gamma$. Let S and L be the non-linear and linear layer operations of E, $\beta' = S(\beta)$, $\beta'' = L(\beta')$, $\gamma' = S^{-1}(\gamma)$ and $\gamma'' = L^{-1}(\gamma')$. For a 1-round E_m, the propagation of β and γ is illustrated in Fig. 3. Then we have

$$r = 2^{-n} \Sigma_{1 \leq i \leq 2ns} \mathrm{BCT}(\beta[i], \gamma[i]).$$

For a 2-round E_m, the propagation of β and γ is illustrated in Fig. 4. Then we have

$$r = 2^{-2n} \Sigma_{1 \leq i \leq 2ns} (\mathrm{BDT}(\beta[i], \beta'[i], \gamma''[i]) \times \mathrm{iBDT}(\gamma[i], \gamma'[i], \beta''[i])).$$

For a related-key boomerang distinguisher, if there are multiple trails $\alpha \xrightarrow{E_0} \beta_i$ and $\gamma_j \xrightarrow{E_1} \delta$ ($\beta_i \neq \gamma_j$) under fixed α, ΔK, δ and ∇K, the probability of obtaining a right quartet can be increased to:

$$\hat{p}^2 \hat{q}^2 := \Sigma_{i,j} p_i^2 q_j^2 r_{ij}, \quad (7)$$

in which $p_i = Pr(\alpha \xrightarrow{E_0} \beta_i)$, $q_j = Pr(\gamma_j \xrightarrow{E_1} \delta)$ and $r_{ij} = Pr(\beta_i \xrightarrow{E_m} \gamma_j)$.

A new key-recovery model for the related-key boomerang and rectangle attack against block ciphers with linear key schedules was constructed by Zhao *et al.* in [33,34]. This new model is a modification of Liu *et al.*'s model [26]. In this paper, we utilize the model proposed by Zhao *et al.* to perform the key-recovery attack against GIFT.

3   Searching Related-key Differential Trails

3.1   Applying Matsui's Algorithm in Related-key Scenario

Our objective is to find related-key differential trails with high probabilities. We apply Matsui's algorithm to search related-key differential trails of GIFT. Firstly, we apply the speeding-up methods introduced in Sect. 2.3 to improve the search process. Secondly, we add three constraints to limit the search space. Finally, we search the optimal related-key differential trails on the limited search space. **The adjusted Matsui's algorithm aiming at searching optimal related-key differential trails of GIFT on limited search space is demonstrated in Algorithm 1.**

Algorithm 1. The Adjusted Matsui's Algorithm of Searching Optimal Related-key Differential Trails for GIFT on Limited Search Space

---

Require: R (≥ 3); $B_0 = 0, B_1, B_2, \cdots, B_{R-1}$; Bc_R; iniKeyDiff [4 937 152]; ns $:= n/8$

Ensure: $B_R = Bc_R$; the R-round related-key differential trails with minimal weight

1: **for** each iniKeyDiff $[v]$ **do**
2:   gen roundkey $\Delta K_i, 1 \leq i \leq R$
3:   **for** $fr = 1$ to R **do**
4:     $\Delta X_{fr} \leftarrow 0, \Delta Y_{fr} \leftarrow 0,$
       $w_{fr} \leftarrow 0$
5:     **if** $fr = R$ **then**
6:       $\Delta Y_{fr-1} \leftarrow P^{-1}(\Delta K_{fr-1})$
7:       call Round-i-In
8:     **else**
9:       $\Delta X_{fr+1} \leftarrow \Delta K_{fr}$
10:      call Round-i
11:    **end if**
12: **end for**
13: **end for**

14: **Procedure** Round-$i, 2 \leq i \leq R -1$:
15: **for** each ΔY_i **do**
16:   $w_i \leftarrow W(\Delta X_i, \Delta Y_i)$
17:   **if** $B_{R-i} + B_{fr-1} + \Sigma_{j=fr}^i w_j$
       $\geq Bc_R$ **then**
18:     break
19:   **else**
20:     $\Delta X_{i+1} \leftarrow P(\Delta Y_i) \oplus \Delta K_i$
21:     call Round-$(i+1)$
22:   **end if**
23: **end for**

24: **Procedure** Round-R:

25: $w_R \leftarrow min_{\Delta Y_R} W(\Delta X_R, \Delta Y_R)$
26: **if** $B_{fr-1} + \Sigma_{j=fr}^R w_j \leq Bc_R$ **then**
27:   **if** $fr = 1$ **then**
28:     $Bc_R = \Sigma_{j=1}^R w_j$
29:   **else**
30:     $\Delta Y_{fr-1} \leftarrow P^{-1}(\Delta K_{fr-1})$
31:     call Round-i-In
32:   **end if**
33: **end if**
34: return to the upper procedure

35: **Procedure** Round-i-In, $2 \leq i \leq R - 1$:
36: **for** each ΔX_i **do**
37:   $w_i \leftarrow W(\Delta X_i, \Delta Y_i)$
38:   **if** $B_{i-1} + \Sigma_{j=i}^R w_j \geq Bc_R$ **then**
39:     break
40:   **else**
41:     $\Delta Y_{i-1} \leftarrow P^{-1}(\Delta X_i \oplus \Delta K_{i-1})$
42:     call Round-$(i-1)$-In
43:   **end if**
44: **end for**

45: **Procedure** Round-1-In:
46: $w_1 \leftarrow min_{\Delta X_R} W(\Delta X_R, \Delta Y_R)$
47: **if** $\Sigma_{j=1}^R w_j \leq Bc_R$ **then**
48:   $Bc_R = \Sigma_{j=1}^R w_j$
49: **end if**
50: return to the upper procedure

Let R be the round number of E. Let $\Delta iniK := \Delta k_7 || \cdots || \Delta k_0$ be the master key difference and ΔK_i be the round key difference in round i. **We utilize the following three constraints to limit the search space:**

1 Restricting the input difference of round fr to zero and traverse fr from 1 to R.

It has been declared in [29] that the number of candidates in the first two rounds of Matsui's algorithm is the dominant factor of the search complexity. In Algorithm 3, the number of candidates ΔY_1 in Procedure Round-1 depends on the value of $Bc_R - B_{R-1}$. Algorithm 1 starts from Procedure Round-fr with only one candidate $\Delta Y_{fr} = 0$. Since $\Delta Y_{fr} = 0$, we can determine the input difference of round $i + 1$ which is ΔK_i and the output difference of round $i - 1$ which is ΔK_{i-1}.

Therefore, the complexity of Matsui's algorithm in related-key scenario is improved benefitting from constraint-1.

2 **Restricting the number of the active bits in the master key difference.**
The key schedule of GIFT is a linear transformation. The value of ΔK_i are determined by $\Delta iniK$. The input difference of $S(\cdot)$ in round i is $\Delta X_i = P(\Delta Y_{i-1}) \oplus \Delta K_{i-1}$. The related-key differential trails with small weight will not contain too many active S-boxes in $S(\cdot)$. Thus, there should not be too many active bits in ΔK_i $(1 \leq i \leq R)$. The details of constraint-2 are as follows.
- Restricting the number of the active bits in $\Delta iniK$ to no more than four when $R < 11$.
- Restricting the number of the active bits in $\Delta iniK$ to no more than three when $R \geq 11$.
- Restricting the four active bit positions to belong to four different Δk_j $(0 \leq j \leq 7)$ if the number of the active bits is four.

The total number of the candidate $\Delta iniK$ is $C_{128}^1 + C_{128}^2 + C_{128}^3 + C_7^4 \cdot (C_{16}^1)^4 = 4\,937\,152$.

3 **Restricting the number of the active S-boxes in round i $(1 \leq i \leq R)$ to no more than five when $R \geq 11$.**

3.2 Results on Related-Key Differential Trails of GIFT

Applying Algorithm 1, **we find related-key differential trails of GIFT-64/128 for up to 15/14 rounds.** The results are summarized in Table 1. Table 10 in Appendix D presents a 15-round related-key differential trail of GIFT-64 and a 14-round related-key differential trail of GIFT-128 found by Algorithm 1.

Compared to the previous results in [7,18,27], the optimal related-key differential trails found by Algorithm 1 on the limited search space are the best results known so far. We find related-key differential trails of GIFT-128 for up to 14 rounds, while the previous results up to 9 rounds. We provide tighter lower bounds for the probabilities of the optimal related-key trails of both GIFT-64 and GIFT-128. It indicates that the three constraints we choose perform well in limiting the search space while preserving the related-key differential trails with high probabilities.

4   Increasing the Probability of the Distinguisher Utilizing Clustering Effect

Both the probability of the single-key differential distinguisher and the related-key boomerang distinguisher can be increased by searching the clustering of the differential trails. Next, we give the definitions of **the clustering of an R-round single-key differential trail** and **the clustering of the related-key differential trails utilized in an R-round boomerang distinguisher** and explain how to search the clustering.

4.1   Single-key Scenario

Definition 4. *The clustering of an R-round single-key differential trail* is defined as:

$$\mathcal{C}(R, \eta_{in}, \eta_{out}, Bc_R) := \{\text{all } R\text{-round single-key differential trails } l^i \mid$$
$$W(l^i) \leq Bc_R, \Delta X_1 = \eta_{in}, P(\Delta Y_R) = \eta_{out}\}. \tag{8}$$

In fact, for an R-round single-key differential trail $\mathcal{L}$ with fixed input difference η_{in} and output difference η_{out}, the clustering of $\mathcal{L}$ is composed by all the differential trails whose input difference is η_{in} and output difference is η_{out}, *i.e.*, $\mathcal{C}(R, \eta_{in}, \eta_{out}, \infty)$. It will take immeasurable time to determine all the trails in $\mathcal{C}(R, \eta_{in}, \eta_{out}, \infty)$. Therefore, we only search all the trails with weight no more than Bc_R. The choice of Bc_R is heuristic.

We call Algorithm 3 to search $\mathcal{C}(R, \eta_{in}, \eta_{out}, Bc_R)$. The greater the value of Bc_R, the more trails can we find, while the longer the search time is required.

4.2   Related-key Scenario

Definition 5. *The clustering of the related-key differential trails utilized in an R -round related-key boomerang distinguisher* is defined as:

$$\mathcal{C}(R_0, R_1, R_m, \alpha, \Delta iniK_0, Bc_{R_0}, \delta, \Delta iniK_1, Bc_{R_1}) := \{\text{all combinations of } (l_0^i, l_1^j) \mid$$
$$l_0^i \in \mathcal{C}_I(R_0, \alpha, \Delta iniK_0, Bc_{R_0}), l_1^j \in \mathcal{C}_O(R_1, \delta, \Delta iniK_1, Bc_{R_1})\}, \tag{9}$$

in which

$$\mathcal{C}_I(R_0, \alpha, \Delta iniK_0, Bc_{R_0}) := \{\text{all } R_0\text{-round related-key differential trails } l_0^i \mid$$
$$W(l_0^i) \leq Bc_{R_0}, \Delta X_1 = \alpha, \text{MKD} = \Delta iniK_0\}, \tag{10}$$

$$\mathcal{C}_O(R_1, \delta, \Delta iniK_1, Bc_{R_1}) := \{\text{all } R_1\text{-round related-key differential trails } l_1^j \mid$$
$$W(l_1^j) \leq Bc_{R_1}, K(\Delta Z_{R_1}) = \delta, \text{MKD} = \Delta iniK_1\}, \tag{11}$$

and $R = R_0 + R_m + R_1$.

Algorithm 2. The Algorithm of Increasing the Probability of the Related-key Boomerang Distinguisher for GIFT

Require: R_0, R_1, R_m; bw ; ns $:= n/8$
Ensure: $\hat{p}^2\hat{q}^2 \leftarrow max\{\hat{p_i}^2\hat{q_j}^2\}$; α_i, $\Delta iniK_0^i$; δ_j, $\Delta iniK_1^j$

1: *Phase 1: Search all the related-key differential trails with minimal weight*
2: call Alg.1 to search all the R_0-round related-key trails with minimal weight on the limited search space for E_0
3: $B_{R_0} \leftarrow$ the minimal weight of R_0-round trails
4: $l_0^1, \cdots, l_0^a \leftarrow$ all the R_0-round trails with weight B_{R_0}
5: **for** each l_0^i, $1 \leq i \leq a$ **do**
6:     $\alpha_i \leftarrow \Delta X_1$, $\Delta iniK_0^i \leftarrow$ the master key difference
7: **end for**
8: call Alg.1 to search all the R_1-round related-key trails with minimal weight on the limited search space for E_1
9: $B_{R_1} \leftarrow$ the minimal weight of R_1-round trails
10: $l_1^1, \cdots, l_1^b \leftarrow$ all the R_1-round trails with weight B_{R_1}
11: **for** each l_1^j, $1 \leq j \leq b$ **do**
12:     $\delta_j \leftarrow K \circ P(\Delta Y_{R_1})$, $\Delta iniK_1^j \leftarrow$ the master key difference
13: **end for**

14: *Phase 2: Search all the clustering*
15: **for** each l_0^i, $1 \leq i \leq a$ **do**
16:     call Alg.1 to search $C_I(R_0, \alpha_i, \Delta iniK_0^i, B_{R_0} + bw)$ /* see Eq.10 for definition */
17:     $l_0^{i1}, \cdots, l_0^{i_d} \leftarrow$ all the trails in $C_I(R_0, \alpha_i, \Delta iniK_0^i, B_{R_0} + bw)$
18:     **for** each $l_0^{i_u}$, $1 \leq u \leq d$ **do**
19:         $\beta^{i_u} \leftarrow K \circ P(\Delta Y_{R_0})$, $B_{R_0}^{i_u} \leftarrow W(l_0^{i_u})$
20:     **end for**
21: **end for**
22: **for** each l_1^j, $1 \leq j \leq b$ **do**
23:     call Alg.1 to search $C_O(R_1, \delta_j, \Delta iniK_1^j, B_{R_1} + bw)$ /* see Eq.11 for definition */
24:     $l_1^{j1}, \cdots, l_1^{j_e} \leftarrow$ all the trails in $C_O(R_1, \delta_j, \Delta iniK_1^j, B_{R_1} + bw)$
25:     **for** each $l_1^{j_v}$, $1 \leq v \leq e$ **do**
26:         $\gamma^{j_v} \leftarrow P^{-1} \circ K^{-1}(\Delta X_1)$, $B_{R_1}^{j_v} \leftarrow W(l_1^{j_v})$
27:     **end for**
28: **end for**

29: *Phase 3: Determine the boomerang distinguisher with highest probability*
30: **for** each l_0^i $(1 \leq i \leq a)$ and l_1^j $(1 \leq j \leq b)$ **do**
31:     $\hat{p_i}^2\hat{q_j}^2 \leftarrow \sum_{u,v} 2^{-2B_{R_0}^{i_u}} \cdot 2^{-2B_{R_1}^{j_v}} \cdot \text{Middle}(\beta^{i_u}, \gamma^{j_v}, R_m)$
32: **end for**
33: $\hat{p}^2\hat{q}^2 \leftarrow max_{i,j}\{\hat{p_i}^2\hat{q_j}^2\}$

34: **Function** Middle(β, γ, R_m):
35: calculate Pr_{E_m} by the BCT, if $R_m = 1$
36: calculate Pr_{E_m} by the BDT and the iBDT, if $R_m = 2$
37: **return** Pr_{E_m}

In fact, the clustering of an R_0-round related-key differential trail $\mathcal{L}$ with fixed input difference α and master key difference $\Delta iniK_0$ contains all the related-key differential trails with arbitrary weight, *i.e.*, $\mathcal{C}_I(R_0, \alpha, \Delta iniK_0, \infty)$. It will take immeasurable time to determine all the trails in $\mathcal{C}_I(R_0, \alpha, \Delta iniK_0, \infty)$. Therefore, we only search all the trails with weight no more than Bc_{R_0}. The choice of Bc_{R_0} is heuristic. The modification above also applies to $\mathcal{C}_O(R_1, \delta, \Delta iniK_1, \infty)$.

To construct an R-round related-key boomerang distinguisher $\mathcal{D}$ for the target cipher $E = E_1 \circ E_m \circ E_0$, we firstly determine the round number $R_0/R_m/R_1$ for $E_0/E_m/E_1$ satisfying $R = R_0 + R_m + R_1$. The general way to determine the probability of the distinguisher $\mathcal{D}$ is:

1 Choose an R_0-round trail l_0 for E_0; Get the input difference α, the output difference β and the master key difference $\Delta iniK_0$.
2 Choose an R_1-round trail l_1 for E_1; Get the input difference γ, the output difference δ and the master key difference $\Delta iniK_1$.
3 Apply the BCT to calculate $Pr(\beta \to \gamma)$ if $R_m = 1$; Apply the BDT and the iBDT to calculate $Pr(\beta \to \gamma)$ if $R_m = 2$.

For a distinguisher $\mathcal{D}$ with fixed α and δ, there could be mulitiple values of β and γ. To increase the probability of $\mathcal{D}$, we hope to find as more combinations of (β, γ) as we can. We propose Algorithm 2 to search $\mathcal{C}(\mathcal{D})$, *i.e.*,

$$C(R_0, R_1, R_m, \alpha, \Delta iniK_0, Bc_{R_0}, \delta, \Delta iniK_1, Bc_{R_1})$$

and calculate the probability of $\mathcal{D}$ by traversing all combinations of (l_0^i, l_1^j) in $\mathcal{C}(\mathcal{D})$. The greater the value of Bc_{R_0} and Bc_{R_1}, the more trails can we find.

Explanations on Algorithm 2

1 Different choices of α (or δ) will lead to different amounts and values of β (or γ).

Therefore, in *Phase 1* of Algorithm 2, we first determine all the choices of α and δ.
2 For GIFT, we find the fact that for fixed $S(\alpha)$ of E_0 and fixed $S^{-1} \circ P^{-1} \circ K^{-1}(\delta)$ of E_1, the choices of α and δ will not influence the value of $\hat{p}^2\hat{q}^2$.

Therefore, in the search process of GIFT, we only care about the value of $S(\alpha)$ (*i.e.*, ΔY_1 of E_0) and the value of $S^{-1} \circ P^{-1} \circ K^{-1}(\delta)$ (*i.e.*, ΔX_{R_1} of E_1).
3 For fixed l_0^i and l_1^j ($1 \le i \le a, 1 \le j \le b$), we get $\mathcal{C}_I(R_0, \alpha_i, \Delta iniK_0^i, B_{R_0} + bw)$ and $\mathcal{C}_O(R_1, \delta_j, \Delta iniK_1^j, B_{R_1} + bw)$ through *Phase 2*. In *Phase 3*, we traverse all combinations of $(l_0^{i_u}, l_1^{j_v})$, in which

$$l_0^{i_u} \in \mathcal{C}_I(R_0, \alpha_i, \Delta iniK_0^i, B_{R_0} + bw), \quad l_1^{j_v} \in \mathcal{C}_O(R_1, \delta_j, \Delta iniK_1^j, B_{R_1} + bw),$$

to calculate

$$\hat{p_i}^2 \hat{q_j}^2 \leftarrow \sum_{u,v} 2^{-2B_{R_0}^{i_u}} \cdot 2^{-2B_{R_1}^{j_v}} \cdot \text{Middle}(\beta^{i_u}, \gamma^{j_v}, R_m).$$

For each $l_0^{i_u}$ and $l_1^{j_v}$, the value of β^{i_u} and γ^{j_v} are determined. The incompatibility between β^{i_u} and γ^{j_v} can be captured by the BCT or the BDT.

4 **The value of α and δ should be carefully determined to keep the value of r_b, m_b, r_f and m_f appropriate.** The probability of the distinguisher is the main factor affecting the complexity of the key-recovery attack. Nevertheless the value of r_b, m_b, r_f and m_f can also affect the complexity, which is influenced by the value of α and δ.

Therefore, once we get the value of $max_{i,j}\{\hat{p}_i^2\hat{q}_j^2\}$, α_i and δ_j from Algorithm 2, we should carefully adjust the value of α_i and δ_j to reduce the complexity of the attack.

5 Attacks on GIFT-64

5.1 Related-key Rectangle Attack on 25-Round GIFT-64

Determining the Related-key Rectangle Distinguisher. We utilize a 20-round related-key rectangle distinguisher to attack the 25-round GIFT-64. Choose $R_0 = 10$ for E_0, $R_1 = 9$ for E_1, $R_m = 1$ for E_m. Set $bw = 4$. Apply Algorithm 2 to search the probability of the 20-round distinguisher.

In *Phase 1* of Algorithm 2, we find sixteen 10-round trails with weight 20.415 for E_0, marked as $l_0^1, \cdots, l_0^{16}$. We find eight 9-round trails with weight 13.415 for E_1, marked as $l_1^1, \cdots, l_1^8$. The details of $l_0^1, \cdots, l_0^{16}$ and $l_1^1, \cdots, l_1^8$ are listed in Table 13 and Table 14 in Appendix D.

In *Phase 3*, we determine the maximum value of $\hat{p}_i^2\hat{q}_j^2$, which is $\hat{p}_5^2\hat{q}_8^2 = 2^{-58.557}$. We choose the value of α and δ according to $S(\alpha_5) = 0x0000000000001000$ and $S^{-1} \circ P^{-1} \circ K^{-1}(\delta_8) = 0x0000200000000000$. Finally, we obtain a 20-round related-key rectangle distinguisher with probability $2^{-n}\hat{p}^2\hat{q}^2 = 2^{-64} \cdot 2^{-58.557}$. The specifications of the 20-round related-key rectangle distinguisher of GIFT-64 are shown in Table 4. There are 5728 trails in $\mathcal{C}_I(R_0, \alpha, \Delta iniK_0, Bc_{R_0})$ and 312 trails in $\mathcal{C}_O(R_1, \delta, \Delta iniK_1, Bc_{R_1})$.

Table 4. The specifications of 20-round related-key rectangle distinguisher of GIFT-64

$R_0 = 10, R_m = 1, R_1 = 9; Bc_{R_0} = 24.415, Bc_{R_1} = 17.415; \hat{p}^2\hat{q}^2 = 2^{-58.557}$	
	α	$\Delta iniK_0$
E_0	00 00 00 00 00 00 a0 00	0004 0000 0000 0800 0000 0000 0000 0010
	δ	$\Delta iniK_1$
E_1	04 00 00 00 01 20 10 00	2000 0000 0000 0000 0800 0000 0200 0800

We construct the 25-round key-recovery model for GIFT-64, which is shown in Table 5, by appending two rounds at the end of the 20-round distinguisher and appending three rounds at the beginning of the distinguisher.

Data Collection. Since there is no whitening key XORed to the plaintext, we collect data in ΔZ_1. There are 44 unknown bits in ΔZ_1 marked as "?", affecting 12 S-boxes in round 1 and three S-boxes in round 2. Thus, $r_b = 44$ and the

Table 5. The 25-round key-recovery model of the related-key rectangle attack for GIFT-64

input	???? ???? ???? ???? ???? ???? ???? ???? ???? ???? ???? ???? ???? ???? ???? ????
ΔY_1	??0? 1??0 01?? ?0?? 1?0? ?1?0 0??? ?0?? ??0? ??0? 0??? ?0?? ??0? ??0? 0??? ?0??
ΔZ_1	???? ???? ???? ???? 0000 0000 0000 0000 11?? ???? ???? ???? ???? 11?? ???? ????
ΔX_2	???? ???? ???? ???? 0000 0000 0000 0000 11?? ???? ???? ???? ???? 11?? ???? ????
ΔY_2	0?01 00?0 000? ?000 0000 0000 0000 0000 0100 00?0 000? ?000 ?000 0100 00?0 000?
ΔZ_2	???? 0000 ?1?? 0000 0000 0000 0000 0000 0001 0000 0000 0000 0000 0000 0000 ?1??
ΔX_3	???? 0000 ?1?? 0000 0000 0000 0000 0000 0000 0000 0000 0000 0000 0000 0000 ?1??
ΔY_3	1000 0000 0010 0000 0000 0000 0000 0000 0000 0000 0000 0000 0000 0000 0000 0010
ΔZ_3	0000 0000 0000 0000 0000 0000 0000 0000 0000 0000 0000 0010 1010 0000 0000 0000
$\Delta X_4\ (\alpha)$	0000 0000 0000 0000 0000 0000 0000 0000 0000 0000 0000 0000 1010 0000 0000 0000
:	....
$\Delta X_{24}\ (\delta)$	0000 0100 0000 0000 0000 0000 0000 0000 0000 0001 0010 0000 0001 0000 0000 0000
ΔY_{24}	0000 ???1 0000 0000 0000 0000 0000 0000 0000 ???? ???? 0000 ???? 0000 0000 0000
ΔZ_{24}	00?0 0000 00?? 0?00 0001 0000 ?00? 00?0 ?000 0000 ??00 000? 0?00 0000 0??0 ?000
ΔX_{25}	00?0 0000 00?? 0?00 0001 0000 ?00? 00?0 ?010 0000 ??00 000? 0?00 0000 0??0 ?000
ΔY_{25}	???? 0000 ???? ???? ???? 0000 ???? ???? ???? 0000 ???? ???? ???? 0000 ???? ????
ΔZ_{25}	??0? ??0? ??0? ??0? ??0? ??0? ??0? ??0? 0??? 0??? 0??? 0??? ?0?? ?0?? ?0?? ?0??
output	??0? ??0? ??0? ??0? ??0? ??0? ??0? ??0? 0??? 0??? 0??? 0??? ?0?? ?0?? ?0?? ?0??

number of key bits needed to be guessed in E_b is $m_b = 2 \times (12 + 3) = 30$. Similarly, we have $r_f = 48$ and $m_f = 2 \times (12 + 4) = 32$ in E_f. We utilize the key-recovery model proposed by Zhao $et\ al.$ in [33] to perform the rectangle key-recovery attack.

1 Construct $y = \sqrt{s} \cdot 2^{n/2 - r_b}/\hat{p}\hat{q}$ structures of 2^{r_b} plaintexts each. s is the expected number of right quartets. Each structure takes all the possible values of the r_b active bits while the other $n - r_b$ bits are fixed to some constant.

2 For each structure, query the 2^{r_b} plaintexts by the encryption oracle under K_1, K_2, K_3 and K_4 where K_1 is the secret key, $K_2 = K_1 \oplus \Delta K$, $K_3 = K_1 \oplus \nabla K$ and $K_4 = K_1 \oplus \Delta K \oplus \nabla K$. Obtain four plaintext-ciphertext sets denoted by L_1, L_2, L_3 and L_4. Insert L_2 and L_4 into hash tables H_1 and H_2 indexed by the r_b bits of the plaintexts.

3 Guess the m_b bits subkey involved in E_b, then:

  (a) Initialize a list of 2^{m_f} counters, each of which corresponds to a m_f bits subkey guess.

  (b) For each structure, partially encrypt plaintext $P_1 \in L_1$ to the position of α by the guessed subkeys, and partially decrypt it to the plaintext P_2 after XORing the known difference α. Then we look up H_1 to find the plaintext-ciphertext indexed by the r_b bits. Do the same operations with P_3 and P_4. We get two sets:

$$S_1 = \{(P_1, C_1, P_2, C_2) : (P_1, C_1) \in L_1, (P_2, C_2) \in L_2, E_{b_{K_1}}(P_1) \oplus E_{b_{K_2}}(P_2) = \alpha\},$$

$$S_2 = \{(P_3, C_3, P_4, C_4) : (P_3, C_3) \in L_3, (P_4, C_4) \in L_4, E_{b_{K_3}}(P_3) \oplus E_{b_{K_4}}(P_4) = \alpha\}.$$

  (c) The size of S_1 and S_2 are both $M = y \cdot 2^{r_b}$. Insert S_1 into a hash table H_3 indexed by the $n - r_f$ bits of C_1 and the $n - r_f$ bits of C_2 in which the output difference of E_f are all "0". For each element of S_2, we find the corresponding (P_1, C_1, P_2, C_2) satisfying $C_1 \oplus C_3 = 0$ and $C_2 \oplus C_4 = 0$ in the $n - r_f$ bits. In total, we obtain $M^2 \cdot 2^{-2(n-r_f)}$ quartets.

(d) We use all the quartets obtained in step (c) to recover the subkeys involved in E_f. This step is a guess and filter procedure. We denote the time complexity in this step as ε.

(e) Select the top $2^{m_f - h}$ hits in the counter to be the candidates which delivers a h bits or higher advantage.

(f) Exhaustively search the remaining $k - m_b - m_f$ unknown key bits in the master key.

Key Recovery. Choose the expected number of right quartets s to be 2, then we have $y = 2^{17.78}$ and $M = y \cdot 2^{r_b} = 2^{61.78}$. Make use of all the $M^2 \cdot 2^{-2(n-r_f)} = 2^{91.56}$ quartets obtained in step 3(c) to recover the subkeys involved in E_f.

The following are the details of the guess and filter procedure in step 3(d), which are similar to the process used in [34]. $\Delta X_i[u, \cdots, v]$ represents the uth bit, $\cdots$, the vth bit of ΔX_i.

d.1 $\Delta Y_{25}[63, 62, 61, 60]$ can be computed by the cipertext pair (C_1, C_3) and $\Delta X_{25}[63, 62, 61, 60]$ is known. We guess the 2^2 possible values of the involved key bits in this S-box and partially decrypt the cipertexts (C_1, C_3) and (C_2, C_4). Then check whether $\Delta X_{25}[63, 62, 60]$ is 0 or not. If yes, we keep the guessed key and the quartet, otherwise discard it. There are about $2^{91.56} \cdot 2^2 \cdot 2^{-6} = 2^{87.56}$ remaining quartets associated with the guessed 2-bit keys, i.e. for each of the 2^2 candidate values of the 2-bit involved keys, there are $2^{85.56}$ quartets remain.

d.2 Carry out a similar process to all the active S-boxes in round 25. There are about $2^{87.56} \cdot 2^{(2-4) \times 4} \cdot 2^{(2-6) \times 6} \cdot 2^{(2-8)} = 2^{87.56-38} = 2^{49.56}$ remaining quartets associated with the guessed keys.

d.3 Partially decrypt all the remaining quartets with the obtained key bits in steps 1 and 2. $\Delta Y_{24}[59, 58, 57, 56]$ can be calculated from the end of the distinguisher. Guess the 2^2 possible values of the key bits involved in this S-box. For each guess, only $2^{49.56} \cdot 2^{2-8} = 2^{43.56}$ quartets remain. Carry out a similar process to all the active S-boxes in round 24, there are about $2^{43.56} \cdot 2^{(2-8) \times 3} = 2^{25.56}$ quartets remain.

d.4 Utilize the remaining quartets to count the $m_f = 32$ key bits. The two right quartets will all vote for the right key. The $2^{25.56}$ random quartets will vote for a random key with probability $2^{25.56-m_f} = 2^{-6.44}$.

d.5 Choose $h = 22$. Select the top $2^{m_f - h}$ hits in the counter to be the candidates. Exhaustively search the remaining $128 - m_b - m_f$ unknown key bits in the master key.

Complexity. The **data complexity** is $4M = 4y \cdot 2^{r_b} = 2^{63.78}$ chosen plaintexts. We need $4M$ encryptions in step 2. $2^{m_b} \cdot 3M = 2^{93.36}$ looking-up-table operations are needed in step 3(b) and 3(c). We need $2^{m_b} \cdot M^2 \cdot 2^{-2(n-r_f)} \cdot 4 \cdot 2^2/25 = 2^{120.92}$

encryptions and $2^{k-h} = 2^{106}$ encryptions to recover the master key. So the **time complexity** is bounded by $2^{120.92}$. The **memory complexity** is bounded by the size of sets H_1, H_2, H_3, S_1 and S_2, which is $5M = 2^{64.10}$.

Success Probability. According to the success probability calculation method of differential attacks proposed in [30], for both boomerang and rectangle attack, the success probability is

$$P_r = \Phi(\frac{\sqrt{sS_N} - \Phi^{-1}(1 - 2^{-h})}{\sqrt{S_N + 1}}), \qquad (12)$$

in which $S_N = \hat{p}^2 \hat{q}^2 / 2^{-n}$ is the signal-to-noise ratio.

The success probability of the 25-round attack on GIFT-64 is 74.00%.

5.2   Related-key Rectangle Attack on 24-Round GIFT-64

Determining the Related-key Rectangle Distinguisher. We choose the same 20-round related-key rectangle distinguisher as in Sect. 5.1. We append two rounds at the end of the distinguisher and two rounds at the beginning of the distinguisher. The details of the 24-round key-recovery model are shown in Table 5. The input difference of the 24-round model equals to

$\Delta Z_2 =$ "????0000?1??0000000000000000000000001000000000000000000000000?1??".

Data Collection and Key Recovery. To prepare the plaintexts, we collect data in ΔZ_2 of Table 5. There are ten unknown bits in ΔZ_2 marked as "?", affecting three S-boxes in round 2. Thus, $r_b = 10$ and the number of key bits needed to be guessed in E_b is $m_b = 2 \times 3 = 6$. Similarly, $r_f = 48$ and $m_f = 2 \times (12 + 4) = 32$ in E_f. The following data collection and key recovery process are similar to the process of the 25-round attack in Sect. 5.1.

Construct $y = \sqrt{s} \cdot 2^{n/2 - r_b} / \hat{p}\hat{q}$ structures of 2^{r_b} plaintexts each. For each structure, query the 2^{r_b} plaintexts by the encryption oracle under K_1, K_2, K_3 and K_4. There are about $M^2 \cdot 2^{-2(n-r_f)}$ quartets left after executing step 3(c). Choosing $s = 2$, we have $y = 2^{51.78}$, $M = y \cdot 2^{r_b} = 2^{61.78}$ and $M^2 \cdot 2^{-2(n-r_f)} = 2^{91.56}$. After the key guessing and filtering process, there are about $M^2 \cdot 2^{-2(n-r_f)} \cdot 2^{-66} = 2^{25.56}$ remaining quartets. Choose $h = 22$ and select the top $2^{m_f - h}$ hits in the counter to be the candidates. Exhaustively search the remaining $128 - m_b - m_f$ unknown key bits in the master key.

Complexity and Success Probability. The **data complexity** is $4M = 2^{63.78}$ chosen plaintexts. We need $2^{m_b} \cdot 3M = 2^{69.36}$ looking-up-table operations in step 3(b) and 3(c). We need $2^{m_b} \cdot M^2 \cdot 2^{-2(n-r_f)} \cdot 4 \cdot 2^2 / 24 = 2^{96.98}$ encryptions and $2^{k-h} = 2^{106}$ encryptions to recover the master key. So the **time complexity** is bounded by 2^{106}. The **memory complexity** is bounded by $5M = 2^{64.10}$. The success probability is 74.00% according to Eq. 12.

6   Attacks on GIFT-128

6.1   Single-Key Differential Attack on 26-Round GIFT-128

In [25], Li *et al.* found a 20-round differential trail l^0 of GIFT-128 with probability $p = 2^{-121.415}$. The propagation of l^0 is shown in Table 12 of Appendix D. The 26-round differential attack was obtained by extending four rounds backward and two rounds forward. The data complexity is $2^3/p = 2^{124.415}$. The time complexity is bounded by the data complexity. The memory complexity is the cost of the key filter counter, which is 2^{109}.

Next, we search the clustering of l^0. According to Definition 4, we choose $Bc_{20} = 124$,

$$\eta_{in} = \Delta X_1 = 0x0000000000000000000000000000000a0,$$
$$\eta_{out} = P(\Delta Y_{20}) = 0x0000000004001000020000000010040000. \tag{13}$$

Then call Algorithm 3 to search $\mathcal{C}(20, \Delta X_1, P(\Delta Y_{20}), Bc_{20})$. We find four trails: l^0 with weight 121.415, l^2 and l^3 with weight 122.415 and l^4 with weight 123.415. The probability of the 20-round single-key distinguisher that satisfies Eq. 13 is increased to $\hat{p} = 2^{-120.245}$. The details of $l^i (0 \le i < 4)$ are demonstrated in Table 12.

Hence, the data complexity of the 26-round differential attack on GIFT-128 is reduced to $2^3/\hat{p} = 2^{123.245}$. The time complexity is reduced to $2^{123.245}$ as well. The cost of the key filter counter does not change.

6.2   Related-Key Rectangle Attack on 23-Round GIFT-128

Determining the Related-Key Rectangle Distinguisher. We utilize a 19-round related-key rectangle distinguisher to attack the 23-round GIFT-128. Set $R_0 = 9$ for E_0, $R_1 = 9$ for E_1, $R_m = 1$ for E_m and $bw = 3$. Apply Algorithm 2 to search the probability of the 19-round distinguisher.

In *Phase 1* of Algorithm 2, we find two 9-round trails with weight 30.000 for E_0, marked as l_0^1, l_0^2. We find two 9-round trails with weight 30.000 for E_1, marked as l_1^1, l_1^2. The details of l_0^1, l_0^2 and l_1^1, l_1^2 are listed in Table 15 and Table 16 of Appendix D.

In *Phase 3* of Algorithm 2, we determine $\hat{p_1}^2\hat{q_1}^2 = 2^{-110.987}$, $\hat{p_2}^2\hat{q_1}^2 = 2^{-112.908}$, $\hat{p_1}^2\hat{q_2}^2 = 2^{-107.626}$ and $\hat{p_2}^2\hat{q_2}^2 = 2^{-109.913}$. We select l_0^1 and l_1^2 to make up the 19-round distinguisher. Since

$$S^{-1} \circ P^{-1} \circ K^{-1}(\delta_2) = 0x00000000000000000050000000200000,$$

if we choose $P^{-1} \circ K^{-1}(\delta_2) = 0x000000000000000000f0000000*00000$ (*= 5 or 6), then $r_f = 80$ and the complexity of the key filtering procedure will be too large. As a compromise, we choose $P^{-1} \circ K^{-1}(\delta_2) = 0x00000000000000000020000000600000$ which leads to $\hat{p}^2\hat{q}^2 = 2^{-107.626+2} = 2^{-109.626}$. In Table 11 of Appendix D, we show two examples of l_0^1 and l_1^2.

Finally, we obtain a 19-round related-key rectangle distinguisher with probability $2^{-n}\hat{p}^2\hat{q}^2 = 2^{-128} \cdot 2^{-109.626}$. The specifications of the 19-round distinguisher are shown in Table 6. There are 3952 trails in $\mathcal{C}_I(R_0, \alpha, \Delta iniK_0, Bc_{R_0})$ and 2944 trails in $\mathcal{C}_O(R_1, \delta, \Delta iniK_1, Bc_{R_1})$.

Table 6. The specifications of the 19-round related-key rectangle distinguisher of GIFT-128

$R_0 = 9, R_m = 1, R_1 = 9; Bc_{R_0} = 33.000, Bc_{R_1} = 33.000; \hat{p}^2\hat{q}^2 = 2^{-109.626}$	
E_0	α	$\Delta iniK_0$
	00000000000000a00000000060000000	8000 0000 0000 0000 0000 0000 0002 0000
E_1	δ	$\Delta iniK_1$
	00200000000000000000004000002020	0000 0000 0000 0000 0002 0000 0002 0000

We construct the 23-round key-recovery model for GIFT-128, which is shown in Table 7, by appending two rounds at the end of the 19-round distinguisher and two rounds at the beginning of the distinguisher.

Data Collection and Key Recovery. To prepare the plaintexts, we collect data in ΔZ_1 of Table 7. There are nine unknown bits in ΔZ_1 marked as "?", affecting three S-boxes in round 1. Thus, $r_b = 9$ and the number of key bits needed to be guessed in E_b is $m_b = 2 \times 3 = 6$. We have $r_f = 52$ and $m_f = 2 \times (13 + 4) = 34$ in E_f. The following data collection and key recovery process are similar to the process of the 25-round attack in Sect. 5.1.

Construct $y = \sqrt{s} \cdot 2^{n/2-r_b}/\hat{p}\hat{q}$ structures of 2^{r_b} plaintexts each. For each structure, query the 2^{r_b} plaintexts by the encryption oracle under K_1, K_2, K_3 and K_4. There are about $M^2 \cdot 2^{-2(n-r_f)}$ quartets left after executing step 3(c). Choosing $s = 2$, we have $y = 2^{110.31}$, $M = y \cdot 2^{r_b} = 2^{119.31}$ and $M^2 \cdot 2^{-2(n-r_f)} = 2^{86.62}$. After the key guessing and filtering process, there are about $M^2 \cdot 2^{-2(n-r_f)} \cdot 2^{-(48+24)} = 2^{14.62}$ remaining quartets. The two right quartets will all vote for the right key. The $2^{14.62}$ random quartets will vote for a random key with probability $2^{14.62-m_f} = 2^{-19.38}$. Choose $h = 22$ and select the top 2^{m_f-h} hits in the counter to be the candidates. Exhaustively search the remaining $128 - m_b - m_f$ unknown key bits in the master key.

Complexity and Success Probability. The **data complexity** is $4M = 2^{121.31}$ chosen plaintexts. We need $2^{m_b} \cdot 3M = 2^{126.89}$ looking-up-table operations in step 3(b) and 3(c). We need $2^{m_b} \cdot M^2 \cdot 2^{-2(n-r_f)} \cdot 4 \cdot 2^2/23 = 2^{92.10}$ encryptions and $2^{k-h} = 2^{106}$ encryptions to recover the master key. So the **time complexity** is bounded by $2^{126.89}$. The **memory complexity** is bounded by $5M = 2^{121.63}$. The success probability is 92.01% according to Eq. 12.

The related-key boomerang attack on 22-round GIFT-128 is demonstrated in Appendix B.

Table 7. The 23-round key-recovery model of the related-key rectangle attack for GIFT-128

input	0000 0000 0000 0000 11?? ???? ???? ???? ???? ???? ???? ???? 0000 0000 0000 0000 0000 0000 0000 0000 0000 0000 0000 0000 0000 0000 0000 11?? 0000 0000 0000 0000
ΔY_1	0000 0000 0000 0000 0100 00?0 000? 1000 ?100 0??0 00?? ?00? 0000 0000 0000 0000 0000 0000 0000 0000 0000 0000 0000 0000 0000 0000 0000 0100 0000 0000 0000 0000
ΔZ_1	0000 11?? ?1?? 0000 0000 0000 0000 0000 0000 0000 0000 0000 0000 0000 0100 0000 0000 0000 0000 0000 0000 0000 0000 0000 0000 0000 ???? 0000 0000 0000 0000 0000
ΔX_2	0000 11?? ?1?? 0000 0000 0000 0000 0000 0000 0000 0000 0000 0000 0000 0000 0000 0000 0000 0000 0000 0000 0000 0000 0000 0000 0000 ???? 0000 0000 0000 0000 0000
ΔY_2	0000 0100 0010 0000 0000 0000 0000 0000 0000 0000 0000 0000 0000 0000 0000 0000 0000 0000 0000 0000 0000 0000 0000 0000 0000 0000 1000 0000 0000 0000 0000 0000
ΔZ_2	0000 0000 0000 0000 0000 0000 0000 0000 0000 0000 0000 0000 0000 0000 1000 0000 0000 0000 0000 0000 0000 0000 0000 0000 0110 0000 0000 0000 0000 0000 0000 0000
$\Delta X_3\ (\alpha)$	0000 0000 0000 0000 0000 0000 0000 0000 0000 0000 0000 0000 0000 0000 1010 0000 0000 0000 0000 0000 0000 0000 0000 0000 0110 0000 0000 0000 0000 0000 0000 0000
:	....
$\Delta X_{22}\ (\delta)$	0000 0000 0010 0000 0000 0000 0000 0000 0000 0000 0000 0000 0000 0000 0000 0000 0000 0000 0000 0000 0000 0000 0100 0000 0000 0000 0000 0000 0010 0000 0010 0000
ΔY_{22}	0000 0000 ???? 0000 0000 0000 0000 0000 0000 0000 0000 0000 0000 0000 0000 0000 0000 0000 0000 0000 0000 0000 ???1 0000 0000 0000 0000 0000 ???? 0000 ???? 0000
ΔZ_{22}	000? 0000 0000 0000 0000 0001 0000 0?0? ?000 0000 0000 0000 0000 ?000 0000 ?0?0 0?00 0000 0000 0000 0000 0?00 0000 0?0? 00?0 0000 0000 0000 0000 00?0 0000 ?0?0
ΔX_{23}	000? 0000 0010 0000 0000 0001 0000 0?0? ?000 0000 0000 0000 0000 ?000 0000 ?0?0 0?00 0000 0000 0000 0000 0?00 0000 0?0? 00?0 0000 0000 0000 0000 00?0 0000 ?0?0
ΔY_{23}	???? 0000 ???? 0000 0000 ???? 0000 ???? ???? 0000 0000 0000 0000 ???? 0000 ???? ???? 0000 0000 0000 0000 ???? 0000 ???? ???? 0000 0000 0000 0000 ???? 0000 ????
ΔZ_{23}	0?0? ?0?0 0?00 ?0?0 0?00 ?0?0 0?00 ?0?0 ?0?0 0?0? 00?0 0?0? 00?0 0?0? 00?0 0?0? 0?0? ?0?0 000? ?0?0 000? ?0?0 000? ?0?0 ?0?0 0?0? ?000 0?0? ?000 0?0? ?000 0?0?
output	0?0? ?0?0 0?00 ?0?0 0?00 ?0?0 0?00 ?0?0 ?0?0 0?0? 00?0 0?0? 00?0 0?0? 00?0 0?0? 0?0? ?0?0 000? ?0?0 000? ?0?0 000? ?0?0 ?0?0 0?0? ?000 0?0? ?000 0?0? ?000 0?0?

7 Conclusion and Future Work

In this paper, we carry out a further research on the resistance of GIFT against single-key and related-key differential cryptanalysis. We succeed in finding related-key differential trails of GIFT-64/128 for up to 15/14 rounds. We find the longest related-key differential trails for GIFT-128 and provide tighter lower bounds for the probabilities of the optimal related-key trails for both GIFT-64 and GIFT-128.

We find a 20-round related-key boomerang distinguisher of GIFT-64 with probability $2^{-58.557}$ and construct a 25-round related-key rectangle attack, which is the longest attack on GIFT-64. We obtain a 19-round related-key boomerang distinguisher of GIFT-128 with probability $2^{-109.626}$ and propose a 23-round related-key rectangle attack, which is the longest related-key attack on GIFT-128. The probability of the 20-round single-key differential distinguisher of GIFT-128 is also increased from $2^{-121.415}$ to $2^{-120.245}$. We improve the time complexity of the 26-round differential attack on GIFT-128 from $2^{124.415}$ to $2^{123.245}$.

Among the 32 candidates of the NIST lightweight crypto standardization process, there are four candidates which are based on GIFT: GIFT-COFB, HYENA, SUNDAE-GIFT, LOTUS-AEAD and LOCUS-AEAD. In the next work, we will study the security of these four lightweight authenticated encryption schemes against single-key/related-key differential cryptanalysis. Besides, We will try to apply Algorithm 1 and Algorithm 2 to other SPN ciphers with linear key schedule, for example, SKINNY [9].

Acknowledgements. We would like to thank the anonymous reviewers for their helpful comments. This work is supported by the Natural Science Foundation of China (61379138).

A   Improved Matsui's Algorithm for GIFT

The improved Matsui's algorithm for GIFT proposed in [22] is demonstrated in Algorithm 3. There are ten different weights of the difference propagations for the new 8-bit S-box in GIFT, wich are denoted by the new table:

WeightTable[10] = {6.000, 5.000, 4.415, 4.000, 3.415, 3.000, 2.830, 2.000, 1.415, 0.000}.

To implement speeding-up method-1, the output differences of each S-box are classified according to the corresponding weights and one new table is constructed as follows:

Algorithm 3. Improved Matsui's Algorithm for GIFT

Require: R (≥ 3); $B_1, B_2, \cdots, B_{R-1}$; Bc_R; WeightTable[10]; ns := $n/8$
Ensure: $B_R = Bc_R$; the optimal single-key differential trails of R-round

1: **Generate Tables :**
2: DDTwY[SboxN][WeightN][OutN]

3: **Function** Sbox-1(t, w_1):
4: **for** $j = 9$ to 0 **do**
5:    $\alpha \leftarrow w_1 + \text{WeightTable}[j]$
6:    **if** $[\alpha, B_{R-1}] \geq Bc_R$ **then**
7:      break
8:    **else**
9:      **for each** DDTwY[t][j][r] **do**
10:       $\Delta Y_1^t \leftarrow$ DDTwY[t][j][r]
11:       /* ΔY_1^t is the tth byte of ΔY_1 */
12:       **if** $t < $ ns **then**
13:         call Sbox-1$(t + 1, \alpha)$
14:       **else**
15:         $w_1 \leftarrow \alpha$
16:         call Round-2
17:       **end if**
18:      **end for**
19:    **end if**
20: **end for**

21: **Procedure** Round-1:
22: $w_1 \leftarrow 0, \Delta Y_1 \leftarrow 0, t \leftarrow 1$
23: call Sbox-1(t, w_1)

24: **Procedure** Round-$i, 2 \leq i \leq R - 1$:
25: $\Delta X_i \leftarrow P(\Delta Y_{i-1})$
26: **for each** ΔY_i **do**
27:    $w_i \leftarrow W(\Delta X_i, \Delta Y_i)$
28:    **if** $B_{R-i} + \Sigma_{j=1}^i w_j \geq Bc_R$ **then**
29:      break
30:    **else**
31:      call Round-$(i + 1)$
32:    **end if**
33: **end for**

34: **Procedure** Round-R:
35: $\Delta X_R \leftarrow P(\Delta Y_{R-1})$
36: $w_R \leftarrow min_{\Delta Y_R} W(\Delta X_R, \Delta Y_R)$
37: **if** $\Sigma_{j=1}^R w_j \leq Bc_R$ **then**
38:    $Bc_R = \Sigma_{j=1}^R w_j$
39: **end if**
40: return to the upper procedure

- **DDTwY[SboxN][WeightN][OutN]**
  DDTwY$[t][j][r]$ represents the rth output difference of the tth S-box with weight WeightTable$[j]$.
  SboxN represents the index of the S-box. It ranges from 1 to ns. WeightN represents the index of the weights. It ranges from 0 to 9. OutN represents the index of the output difference. It ranges from 0 to 255.

B   Related-key Boomerang Attack on 22-round GIFT-128

B.1   Determining the Related-key Boomerang Distinguisher

We choose the same 19-round related-key rectangle distinguisher as in Sect. 6.2. We append two rounds at the end of the distinguisher and one round at the beginning of the distinguisher. The details of the 22-round key-recovery model are shown in Table 7. The input difference of the 22-round model equals to $\Delta Z_2 = 0x00000000000000080000000006000000000$.

B.2   Data Collection

We collect data of the value of *output* in Table 7. There are 52 unknown bits in *output* marked as "?", affecting 13 S-boxes in round 23 and four S-boxes in round 22. Thus, $r_f = \mathbf{52}$ and the number of key bits needed to be guessed in E_f is $m_f = \mathbf{34}$. We utilize the key-recovery model proposed by Zhao *et al.* in [33] to perform the boomerang key-recovery attack:

1. Choose $y = s/(2^{r_f} \cdot \hat{p}^2 \hat{q}^2)$ structures of 2^{r_f} ciphertexts each. s is the expected number of right quartets. Each structure takes all the possible values for the r_f active bits while the other $n - r_f$ bits are fixed to some constant.
2. For each structure, we obtain the plaintext P_1 for each ciphertext C_1 by calling the decryption oracle under K_1. Compute P_2 by $P_2 = P_1 \oplus \alpha$ and obtain the ciphertext C_2 by $E_{K_2}(P_2)$. Here we gain a set:

$$L_1 = \{(P_1, C_1, P_2, C_2) : P_1 = E_{K_1}^{-1}(C_1), P_2 = P_1 \oplus \alpha, C_2 = E_{K_2}(P_2)\}.$$

   Construct the set L_2 under K_3 and K_4 in a similar way:

$$L_2 = \{(P_3, C_3, P_4, C_4) : P_3 = E_{K_3}^{-1}(C_3), P_4 = P_3 \oplus \alpha, C_4 = E_{K_4}(P_4)\}.$$

3. Insert L_1 into a hash table H_1 indexed by the $n - r_f$ bits of C_2. For each element of L_2, find the corresponding (P_1, C_1, P_2, C_2) colliding in the $n - r_f$ bits. We gain a total of $y \cdot 2^{2r_f - (n - r_f)} = y \cdot 2^{3r_f - n}$ quartets.
4. The process that recovers the subkeys involved in E_f is the same as the one in the related-key rectangle attack in Sect. 5.1, The complexity of this step is denoted as ε.
5. Select the top $2^{m_f - h}$ hits in the counter to be the candidates which delivers a h bits or higher advantage. Exhaustively search the remaining $k - m_f$ unknown key bits in the master key.

B.3   Key Recovery

Choose the expected number of right quartets s to be 2, then we have $y = s/(2^{r_f} \cdot \hat{p}^2 \hat{q}^2) = 2^{58.63}$ and $y \cdot 2^{r_f} = 2^{110.63}$. Make use of all the $y \cdot 2^{3r_f - n} = 2^{86.63}$ quartets obtained in step 3 to recover the subkeys involved in E_f. The key recovery process are similar to the process of the 25-round attack in Sect. 5.1. There are about $2^{86.63} \cdot 2^{-(48+24)} = 2^{14.63}$ quartets remain after the key guessing and filtering procedure. Choose $h = 22$ and select the top $2^{m_f - h}$ hits in the counter to be the candidates. Exhaustively search the remaining $128 - m_f$ unknown key bits in the key.

B.4   Complexity and Success Probability

The **data complexity** is $4y \cdot 2^{r_f} = 2^{112.63}$ adapted chosen ciphertexts and plain-texts. We need $4y \cdot 2^{r_f}$ chosen ciphertexts and plaintexts and $y \cdot 2^{r_f}$ looking-up-table operations to construct quartets. $y \cdot 2^{3r_f - n} \cdot \varepsilon = 2^{86.63} \cdot 4 \cdot 2^2 / 22$ encryptions are needed in the key recovery process. Thus, the **time complexity** is bounded by $4y \cdot 2^{r_f} = 2^{112.63}$. The **memory complexity** is the size of each structure and the size of the key counter, which is bounded by $2^{r_f} = 2^{52}$. The success probability is 92.01% according to Eq. 12.

C   Analyzing the Probability of the 19-round Distinguisher Proposed in [18]

The propagation of the 2-round boomerang switch E_m is illustrated in Fig. 4. The details of E_m in the 19-round related-key rectangle distinguisher for GIFT-64 proposed in [18] is shown in Table 8. The authors calculated the value of r as 1 according to the BCT. The probability of the rectangle distinguisher is $2^{-n} \cdot \hat{p}^2 \hat{q}^2 r = 2^{-64} \cdot 2^{-50}$. It should be noted that at the time the authors write the paper [18], the BDT technology has not been proposed yet.

Table 8. The propagation of E_m of the 19-round related-key rectangle distinguisher for GIFT-64 in [18]

rounds		E_0		E_1
10	β	01 00 00 00 01 02 02 00		
	β'	08 00 00 00 06 0a 06 00	γ''	00 00 09 06 00 00 00 85
11	β''	00 a2 00 00 80 20 00 44	γ'	00 00 05 0c 0a 00 00 00
			γ	00 00 08 02 01 00 00 00

^{1} $\beta' = S(\beta)$, $\beta'' = K \circ P(\beta')$, $\gamma' = S^{-1}(\gamma)$, $\gamma'' = P^{-1} \circ K^{-1}(\gamma')$.

It has been proved in [32] that when $R_m = 2$, the probability of E_m should be evaluated by the BDT and the iBDT, which is

$$r = 2^{-2n} \Sigma_{1 \le i \le 2ns}(\text{BDT}(\beta[i], \beta'[i], \gamma''[i]) \times \text{iBDT}(\gamma[i], \gamma'[i], \beta''[i])).$$

Meanwhile,

$$\text{BDT}(\beta[i], \beta'[i], \gamma''[i]) = \text{DDT}(\beta[i], \beta'[i]), \text{ if } \gamma''[i] = 0;$$
$$\text{iBDT}(\gamma[i], \gamma'[i], \beta''[i]) = \text{DDT}(\gamma[i], \gamma'[i]), \text{ if } \beta''[i] = 0;$$

$\beta[2ns]||\cdots||\beta[1] := \beta$, $\gamma[2ns]||\cdots||\gamma[1] := \gamma$. We correct the value of r according to the data in Table 8:

$$r = 2^{-2n} \Sigma_{1 \le i \le 16}(\text{BDT}(\beta[i], \beta'[i], \gamma''[i]) \times \text{iBDT}(\gamma[i], \gamma'[i], \beta''[i]))$$
$$= 2^{-2n} \Sigma_{1 \le i \le 16}(\text{DDT}(\beta[i], \beta'[i]) \times \text{DDT}(\gamma[i], \gamma'[i]))$$
$$= 2^{-18}.$$

The value of the DDT is shown in Table 9. As a result, the probability of the rectangle distinguisher in [18] is $2^{-n} \cdot p^2 q^2 r = 2^{-64} \cdot 2^{-68}$.

It has been introduced in Sect. 2.4 that only if $p^2 q^2 r > 2^{-n}$ can we count more right quartets than random noise through the related-key rectangle distinguisher. For GIFT-64, the distinguisher should satisfy $p^2 q^2 r > 2^{-64}$. Therefore, the 23-round related-key rectangle attack proposed in [18] and the 24-round related-key rectangle attack proposed in [34] are invalid.

Table 9. Differential Distribution Table (DDT) of GIFT S-box

Δ_o

Δ_i	0	1	2	3	4	5	6	7	8	9	a	b	c	d	e	f
0	16															
1						2	2		2	2	2	2	2			2
2						4	4			2	2			2	2	
3						2	2		2			2	2	2	2	2
4				2		4		6		2			2			
5			2			2			2				2	2	2	4
6			4	6				2			2			2		
7			2			2			2	2	2	4	2			
8				4				4				4				4
9		2		2			2	2	2		2			2	2	
a		4					4			2	2			2	2	
b		2		2			2	2	2	2			2		2	
c			4		4			2		2			2		2	
d		2	2		4					2	2			2		2
e		4			4				2	2			2	2		
f		2	2		4				2		2				2	2

D   (Related-key) Differential Trails

Table 10. Two related-key differential trails of GIFT-64 and GIFT-128

For l_0, MKD = 0000 0000 0000 0000 0000 0000 8002 0000, weight = 48.000
For l_1, MKD = 0000 0000 0002 0000 0002 0000 0000 0000, weight = 77.830

r	l_0: a 15-round trail of GIFT-64 ΔX_r	w_r	l_1: a 14-round trail of GIFT-128 ΔX_r	w_r
1	0600000000600000	4.000	0000c00112000000000000000000c0000	12.000
2	0000000000000000	0.000	0c60000000000000000000000000c00000	7.000
3	0000000000000000	0.000	00000000000000a00000000060000000	4.000
4	0000000000000000	0.000	00010000000000000000000000000000	3.000
5	0000000000000000	0.000	c0000000000000000000000000000000	2.000
6	2020000000000000	4.000	00000000000000000000000000000000	0.000
7	5000000050000000	6.000	20000000000000000000000000000000	2.000
8	0000202000000000	5.000	60000000200000000000000000000000	4.000
9	0000000005000a00	5.000	00000000202000000000000000000000	6.000
10	0000200100000000	5.000	0000000000a00000000000000a00000	4.000
11	0c00060000000000	4.000	00300010000000000000000000000000	6.000
12	2200000000000000	5.000	11200000000000000440000000000000	12.415
13	6000000090000000	5.000	0000000000003000d0009000e0000000	10.000
14	0000000000100000	3.000	00000040000000000000000000080800	5.415
15	0000008000000000	2.000	01002002000000010400002002000010	
16	0100000000000200			

Table 11. Two 9-round related-key differential trails of GIFT-128

For l_0^1, MKD = 8000 0000 0000 0000 0000 0000 0002 0000.
For l_1^2, MKD = 0000 0000 0000 0000 0002 0000 0002 0000.

r	l_0^1 : a 9-round trail with weight 30.000 ΔX_r	w_r	l_1^2 : a 9-round trail with weight 31.000 ΔX_r	w_r
1	0000000000000a00000000060000000	4.0	0c600000000000000000000000100000	7.0
2	00010000000000000000000000000000	3.0	00000000000000a00000000060000000	4.0
3	c0000000000000000000000000000000	2.0	00010000000000000000000000000000	3.0
4	00000000000000000000000000000000	0.0	c0000000000000000000000000000000	2.0
5	20000000000000000000000000000000	2.0	00000000000000000000000000000000	0.0
6	60000000200000000000000000000000	4.0	20000000000000000000000000000000	2.0
7	00000000202000000000000000000000	5.0	60000000200000000000000000000000	4.0
8	0010000000a0000000000000000000000	5.0	00000000202000000000000000000000	4.0
9	00300000800000000000000000000000	5.0	00000000000000000050000000200000	5.0
10	00200000802000000010000000000000		00200000000000000000004000002020	

Table 12. Four 20-round single-key differential trails with weight w_{sum} of GIFT-128

$l^0 : u = 8, v = 8, w_9 = 4.0, w_{14} = 4.0, w_{sum} = 121.415.$
$l^1 : u = 9, v = 8, w_9 = 5.0, w_{14} = 4.0, w_{sum} = 122.415.$
$l^2 : u = 8, v = 9, w_9 = 4.0, w_{14} = 5.0, w_{sum} = 122.415.$
$l^3 : u = 9, v = 9, w_9 = 5.0, w_{14} = 5.0, w_{sum} = 123.415.$

r								ΔX_r									w_r
1	00	00	00	00	00	00	00	00	00	00	00	00	00	00	00	a0	2.000
2	00	00	00	01	00	00	00	00	00	00	00	00	00	00	00	00	3.000
3	08	00	00	00	00	00	00	00	00	00	00	00	00	00	00	00	2.000
4	20	00	00	00	10	00	00	00	00	00	00	00	00	00	00	00	5.000
5	40	40	00	00	20	20	00	00	00	00	00	00	00	00	00	00	8.000
6	50	50	00	00	00	00	00	00	50	50	00	00	00	00	00	00	11.000
7	00	00	00	00	00	00	00	00	00	00	00	00	a0	00	a0	00	4.000
8	00	00	00	00	00	00	00	00	00	00	00	11	00	00	00	00	6.000
9	00	00	0u	00	00	00	08	00	00	00	00	00	00	00	00	00	w_9
10	02	02	00	00	01	01	00	00	00	00	00	00	00	00	00	00	10.000
11	00	00	00	00	50	50	00	00	00	00	00	00	50	50	00	00	12.000
12	00	00	00	00	00	00	00	00	00	00	00	00	00	a0	00	a0	4.000
13	00	00	00	11	00	00	00	00	00	00	00	00	00	00	00	00	6.000
14	0v	00	00	00	08	00	00	00	00	00	00	00	00	00	00	00	w_{14}
15	20	20	00	00	10	10	00	00	00	00	00	00	00	00	00	00	10.000
16	50	50	00	00	00	00	00	00	50	50	00	00	00	00	00	00	12.000
17	00	00	00	00	a0	00	a0	00	00	00	00	00	00	00	00	00	4.000
18	00	00	00	00	00	00	00	00	00	11	00	00	00	00	00	00	6.000
19	00	00	00	00	00	00	c0	00	00	00	60	00	00	00	00	00	4.000
20	00	04	00	00	00	00	02	00	00	00	00	00	00	00	00	00	3.415
21	00	00	00	00	40	01	00	00	20	00	00	00	10	04	00	00	

Table 13. Sixteen 10-round related-key differential trails of E_0 with weight 20.415 of GIFT-64

i	ΔY_1 of l_0^i	MKD of l_0^i
1	00 00 00 00 00 00 00 01	0008 0000 0000 8000 0000 0000 0000 0001
2	00 00 00 00 00 01 00 00	0080 0000 0000 4000 0000 0000 0000 0002
3	00 00 00 01 00 00 00 00	0800 0000 0000 2000 0000 0000 0000 0004
4	00 01 00 00 00 00 00 00	8000 0000 0000 1000 0000 0000 0000 0008
5	00 00 00 00 00 00 10 00	0004 0000 0000 0800 0000 0000 0000 0010
6	00 00 00 00 10 00 00 00	0040 0000 0000 0400 0000 0000 0000 0020
7	00 00 10 00 00 00 00 00	0400 0000 0000 0200 0000 0000 0000 0040
8	10 00 00 00 00 00 00 00	4000 0000 0000 0100 0000 0000 0000 0080
9	00 00 00 00 00 00 08 02	0040 0004 0000 0000 0000 0000 0000 0000
10	00 00 00 00 00 00 80 20	0080 0008 0000 0000 0000 0000 0000 0000
11	00 00 00 00 08 02 00 00	0400 0040 0000 0000 0000 0000 0000 0000
12	00 00 00 00 80 20 00 00	0800 0080 0000 0000 0000 0000 0000 0000
13	00 00 08 02 00 00 00 00	4000 0400 0000 0000 0000 0000 0000 0000
14	00 00 80 20 00 00 00 00	8000 0800 0000 0000 0000 0000 0000 0000
15	08 02 00 00 00 00 00 00	0004 4000 0000 0000 0000 0000 0000 0000
16	80 20 00 00 00 00 00 00	0008 8000 0000 0000 0000 0000 0000 0000

Table 14. Eight 9-round related-key differential trails of E_1 with weight 13.415 of GIFT-64

j	ΔX_9 of l_1^j	MKD of l_1^j
1	00 00 00 00 00 00 00 02	0004 0000 0000 0000 0040 0000 0004 0010
2	00 00 00 00 00 02 00 00	0040 0000 0000 0000 0004 0000 0008 0020
3	00 00 00 02 00 00 00 00	0400 0000 0000 0000 4000 0000 0010 0040
4	00 02 00 00 00 00 00 00	4000 0000 0000 0000 0400 0000 0020 0080
5	20 00 00 00 00 00 00 00	0002 0000 0000 0000 0080 0000 0040 0100
6	00 00 00 00 00 00 20 00	0020 0000 0000 0000 0008 0000 0080 0200
7	00 00 00 00 20 00 00 00	0200 0000 0000 0000 8000 0000 0100 0400
8	00 00 20 00 00 00 00 00	2000 0000 0000 0000 0800 0000 0200 0800

Table 15. Two 9-round related-key differential trails of E_0 with weight 30.000 of GIFT-128

i	ΔY_1 of l_0^i	MKD of l_0^i
1	00000000000000010000000020000000	80000000000000000000000020000000
2	04200000000000000000000000800000	00000000000000000002000000020000

Table 16. Two 9-round related-key differential trails of E_1 with weight 30.000 of GIFT-128

j	ΔX_9 of l_1^j	MKD of l_1^j
1	00300000800000000000000000000000	80000000000000000000000020000000
2	00000000000000000050000000200000	00000000000000000002000000020000

References

1. The specification of GIFT-COFB. https://csrc.nist.gov/CSRC/media/Projects/lightweight-cryptography/documents/round-2/spec-doc-rnd2/gift-cofb-spec-round2.pdf. Accessed 29 Mar 2019
2. The specification of HYENA. https://csrc.nist.gov/CSRC/media/Projects/lightweight-cryptography/documents/round-2/spec-doc-rnd2/hyena-spec-round2.pdf. Accessed 29 Mar 2019
3. The specification of SUNDAE-GIFT. https://csrc.nist.gov/CSRC/media/Projects/lightweight-cryptography/documents/round-2/spec-doc-rnd2/SUNDAE-GIFT-spec-round2.pdf. Accessed 29 Mar 2019
4. The specification of LOTUS-AEAD and LOCUS-AEAD. https://csrc.nist.gov/CSRC/media/Projects/lightweight-cryptography/documents/round-2/spec-doc-rnd2/lotus-locus-spec-round2.pdf. Accessed 27 Sept 2019
5. NIST Homepage: the round 2 candidates of the NIST lightweight crypto standardization process. https://csrc.nist.gov/projects/lightweight-cryptography/round-2-candidates. Accessed 15 July 2020
6. Aoki, K., Kobayashi, K., Moriai, S.: Best differential characteristic search of FEAL. In: Biham, E. (ed.) FSE 1997. LNCS, vol. 1267, pp. 41–53. Springer, Heidelberg (1997). https://doi.org/10.1007/BFb0052333

7. Banik, S., Pandey, S.K., Peyrin, T., Sasaki, Yu., Sim, S.M., Todo, Y.: GIFT: a small present. In: Fischer, W., Homma, N. (eds.) CHES 2017. LNCS, vol. 10529, pp. 321–345. Springer, Cham (2017). https://doi.org/10.1007/978-3-319-66787-4_16

8. Bao, Z., Zhang, W., Lin, D.: Speeding up the search algorithm for the best differential and best linear trails. In: Lin, D., Yung, M., Zhou, J. (eds.) Inscrypt 2014. LNCS, vol. 8957, pp. 259–285. Springer, Cham (2015). https://doi.org/10.1007/978-3-319-16745-9_15

9. Beierle, C., et al.: The SKINNY family of block ciphers and its low-latency variant MANTIS. In: Robshaw, M., Katz, J. (eds.) CRYPTO 2016. LNCS, vol. 9815, pp. 123–153. Springer, Heidelberg (2016). https://doi.org/10.1007/978-3-662-53008-5_5

10. Biham, E.: New types of cryptanalytic attacks using related keys. J. Cryptol. 7(4), 229–246 (1994). https://doi.org/10.1007/BF00203965

11. Biham, E., Dunkelman, O., Keller, N.: The rectangle attack — rectangling the serpent. In: Pfitzmann, B. (ed.) EUROCRYPT 2001. LNCS, vol. 2045, pp. 340–357. Springer, Heidelberg (2001). https://doi.org/10.1007/3-540-44987-6_21

12. Biham, E., Dunkelman, O., Keller, N.: Related-key boomerang and rectangle attacks. In: Cramer, R. (ed.) EUROCRYPT 2005. LNCS, vol. 3494, pp. 507–525. Springer, Heidelberg (2005). https://doi.org/10.1007/11426639_30

13. Biham, E., Shamir, A.: Differential cryptanalysis of DES-like cryptosystems. In: Menezes, A.J., Vanstone, S.A. (eds.) CRYPTO 1990. LNCS, vol. 537, pp. 2–21. Springer, Heidelberg (1991). https://doi.org/10.1007/3-540-38424-3_1

14. Biryukov, A., De Cannière, C., Dellkrantz, G.: Cryptanalysis of SAFER++. In: Boneh, D. (ed.) CRYPTO 2003. LNCS, vol. 2729, pp. 195–211. Springer, Heidelberg (2003). https://doi.org/10.1007/978-3-540-45146-4_12

15. Biryukov, A., Khovratovich, D.: Related-key cryptanalysis of the full AES-192 and AES-256. In: Matsui, M. (ed.) ASIACRYPT 2009. LNCS, vol. 5912, pp. 1–18. Springer, Heidelberg (2009). https://doi.org/10.1007/978-3-642-10366-7_1

16. Bogdanov, A., et al.: PRESENT: an ultra-lightweight block cipher. In: Paillier, P., Verbauwhede, I. (eds.) CHES 2007. LNCS, vol. 4727, pp. 450–466. Springer, Heidelberg (2007). https://doi.org/10.1007/978-3-540-74735-2_31

17. Chen, H., Zong, R., Dong, X.: Improved differential attacks on GIFT-64. In: Zhou, J., Luo, X., Shen, Q., Xu, Z. (eds.) ICICS 2019. LNCS, vol. 11999, pp. 447–462. Springer, Cham (2020). https://doi.org/10.1007/978-3-030-41579-2_26

18. Chen, L., Wang, G., Zhang, G.: MILP-based related-key rectangle attack and its application to GIFT, Khudra, MIBS. Comput. J. 62(12), 1805–1821 (2019). https://doi.org/10.1093/comjnl/bxz076

19. Cid, C., Huang, T., Peyrin, T., Sasaki, Yu., Song, L.: Boomerang connectivity table: a new cryptanalysis tool. In: Nielsen, J.B., Rijmen, V. (eds.) EUROCRYPT 2018. LNCS, vol. 10821, pp. 683–714. Springer, Cham (2018). https://doi.org/10.1007/978-3-319-78375-8_22

20. Daemen, J., Rijmen, V.: The Design of Rijndael: AES - The Advanced Encryption Standard. Information Security and Cryptography. Springer, Heidelberg (2002), https://doi.org/10.1007/978-3-662-04722-4

21. Dunkelman, O., Keller, N., Shamir, A.: A practical-time related-key attack on the KASUMI cryptosystem used in GSM and 3G telephony. In: Rabin, T. (ed.) CRYPTO 2010. LNCS, vol. 6223, pp. 393–410. Springer, Heidelberg (2010). https://doi.org/10.1007/978-3-642-14623-7_21

22. Ji, F., Zhang, W., Ding, T.: Improving Matsui's search algorithm for the best differential/linear trails and its applications for DES, DESL and GIFT. IACR Cryptol. ePrint Arch. 2019, 1190 (2019). https://eprint.iacr.org/2019/1190

23. Kelsey, J., Kohno, T., Schneier, B.: Amplified boomerang attacks against reduced-round MARS and serpent. In: Goos, G., Hartmanis, J., van Leeuwen, J., Schneier, B. (eds.) FSE 2000. LNCS, vol. 1978, pp. 75–93. Springer, Heidelberg (2001). https://doi.org/10.1007/3-540-44706-7_6

24. Kim, J., Kim, G., Hong, S., Lee, S., Hong, D.: The related-key rectangle attack – application to SHACAL-1. In: Wang, H., Pieprzyk, J., Varadharajan, V. (eds.) ACISP 2004. LNCS, vol. 3108, pp. 123–136. Springer, Heidelberg (2004). https://doi.org/10.1007/978-3-540-27800-9_11

25. Li, L., Wu, W., Zheng, Y., Zhang, L.: The relationship between the construction and solution of the MILP models and applications. IACR Cryptology ePrint Archive 2019, 49 (2019). https://eprint.iacr.org/2019/049

26. Liu, G., Ghosh, M., Song, L.: Security analysis of SKINNY under related-tweakey settings (long paper). IACR Trans. Symmetric Cryptol. **2017**(3), 37–72 (2017). https://doi.org/10.13154/tosc.v2017.i3.37-72

27. Liu, Y., Sasaki, Yu.: Related-key boomerang attacks on GIFT with automated trail search including BCT effect. In: Jang-Jaccard, J., Guo, F. (eds.) ACISP 2019. LNCS, vol. 11547, pp. 555–572. Springer, Cham (2019). https://doi.org/10.1007/978-3-030-21548-4_30

28. Matsui, M.: On correlation between the order of S-boxes and the strength of DES. In: De Santis, A. (ed.) EUROCRYPT 1994. LNCS, vol. 950, pp. 366–375. Springer, Heidelberg (1995). https://doi.org/10.1007/BFb0053451

29. Ohta, K., Moriai, S., Aoki, K.: Improving the search algorithm for the best linear expression. In: Coppersmith, D. (ed.) CRYPTO 1995. LNCS, vol. 963, pp. 157–170. Springer, Heidelberg (1995). https://doi.org/10.1007/3-540-44750-4_13

30. Selçuk, A.A.: On probability of success in linear and differential cryptanalysis. J. Cryptol. **21**(1), 131–147 (2008). https://doi.org/10.1007/s00145-007-9013-7

31. Wagner, D.: The boomerang attack. In: Knudsen, L. (ed.) FSE 1999. LNCS, vol. 1636, pp. 156–170. Springer, Heidelberg (1999). https://doi.org/10.1007/3-540-48519-8_12

32. Wang, H., Peyrin, T.: Boomerang switch in multiple rounds. Application to AES variants and Deoxys. IACR Trans. Symmetric Cryptol. **2019**(1), 142–169 (2019). https://doi.org/10.13154/tosc.v2019.i1.142-169

33. Zhao, B., Dong, X., Jia, K.: New related-tweakey boomerang and rectangle attacks on Deoxys-BC including BDT effect. IACR Trans. Symmetric Cryptol. **2019**(3), 121–151 (2019). https://doi.org/10.13154/tosc.v2019.i3.121-151

34. Zhao, B., Dong, X., Meier, W., Jia, K., Wang, G.: Generalized related-key rectangle attacks on block ciphers with linear key schedule: applications to SKINNY and GIFT. Designs Codes Cryptogr. **88**(6), 1103–1126 (2020). https://doi.org/10.1007/s10623-020-00730-1

35. Zhou, C., Zhang, W., Ding, T., Xiang, Z.: Improving the MILP-based security evaluation algorithm against differential/linear cryptanalysis using a divide-and-conquer approach. IACR Trans. Symmetric Cryptol. **2019**(4), 438–469 (2019). https://doi.org/10.13154/tosc.v2019.i4.438-469

36. Zhu, B., Dong, X., Yu, H.: MILP-based differential attack on round-reduced GIFT. In: Matsui, M. (ed.) CT-RSA 2019. LNCS, vol. 11405, pp. 372–390. Springer, Cham (2019). https://doi.org/10.1007/978-3-030-12612-4_19

Boolean Polynomials, BDDs and CRHS Equations - Connecting the Dots with CryptaPath

John Petter Indrøy, Nicolas Costes, and Håvard Raddum$^{(\boxtimes)}$

Simula UiB, Bergen, Norway
haavardr@simula.no

Abstract. When new symmetric-key ciphers and hash functions are proposed they are expected to document resilience against a number of known attacks. Good, easy to use tools may help designers in this process and give improved cryptanalysis. In this paper we introduce CryptaPath, a tool for doing algebraic cryptanalysis which utilizes Compressed Right-Hand Side (CRHS) equations to attack SPN ciphers and sponge constructions. It requires no previous knowledge of CRHS equations to be used, only a reference implementation of a primitive.

The connections between CRHS equations, binary decision diagrams and Boolean polynomials have not been described earlier in literature. A comprehensive treatment of these relationships is made before we explain how CryptaPath works. We then describe the process of solving CRHS equation systems while introducing a new operation, dropping variables.

Keywords: Algebraic cryptanalysis · Binary decision diagram · Equation system · Block cipher · Tool · Open source

1 Introduction

It is not enough to simply propose a new design for symmetric ciphers. Alongside the design, there must be design rationale and security evaluation which describe how this design is resistant against attacks. This can be quite a laborious task, even if one includes only the most common attacks. As attack vectors are becoming more and more complex, experience and good intuition is important while designing the cipher. We therefore recognize the need of some sort of tool for assisting researchers designing a new symmetric primitive, which allows for automated analysis, enabling efficient testing of alternatives and leading to informed decisions. Ideally, this tool would cover all the most common attack techniques. That would be a large undertaking, and this ambition needs to be divided into several projects.

Fortunately, this is also recognized by other researchers, and an automated tool to use with linear and differential cryptanalysis has already been published: CryptaGraph [16]. We wish to add to this contribution by proposing a tool for algebraic cryptanalysis. There are many algebraic attacks, like Gröbner base

© Springer Nature Switzerland AG 2021
O. Dunkelman et al. (Eds.): SAC 2020, LNCS 12804, pp. 229–251, 2021.
https://doi.org/10.1007/978-3-030-81652-0_9

computations, SAT-solving and interpolation attacks. We decided to go for Compressed Right-Hand Sides (CRHS) due to their compact representation of a set of binary vectors and the promising results for solving non-linear equation systems in [19,24,32]. Our tool is named CryptaPath, as we have drawn inspiration from CryptaGraph. The name is not the only similarity; with only small adjustments a reference implementation made for CryptaPath can be used with CryptaGraph and vice versa. A difference from CryptaGraph is that our tool also extends to sponge constructions.

Algebraic Cryptanalysis. The first step of an algebraic attack is to convert the primitive into a system of equations. Next, we try to solve this system. If the complexity of solving such a system is lower than the complexity of the brute force attack, the cipher is considered broken.

When designing new ciphers, the focus is often on defending against linear and differential attacks. This was also the case for PURE, a variant of the KN cipher [23]. The KN cipher is provably secure against differential cryptanalysis. PURE was broken by an interpolation attack in [23]. In [22], a combined attack using differential paths and an (minimally modified) of-the-shelf SAT solver was able to generate full collisions for the hash functions MD4 and MD5. Last year, a successful Gröbner basis attack against Jarvis and Friday was presented [2]. This goes to show that algebraic cryptanalysis can be efficient on symmetric primitives.

There are various ways to model a cipher as a system of equations, and subsequently attack the cipher via trying to solve the system:

- *SAT solving* first converts the cipher into a Boolean formula, and then tries to find values to the arguments such that the formula evaluate to true [22,31].
- A *Gröbner basis* is a particular kind of generating set of an ideal in a polynomial ring. Finding a Gröbner basis is the crux of this attack. Well-known Gröbner basis finding algorithms are F4 [10] and F5 [11].
- *Compressed Right-Hand Sides* equations models the cipher as a system of linear equations with multiple right-hand sides. The hard problem here is to identify only the few right-hand side vectors which yield a consistent system of linear equations [24,27].

The solution to any of these systems of equations will contain the secret values we are looking for, i.e. the secret key of a symmetric cipher, or a pre-image for a hash function.

Existing Research Tools. Our work focuses extensively on the correspondence between polynomials in the Boolean polynomial ring and binary decision diagrams (BDD). PolyBoRi [4] is an existing framework that has the exact same focus. However, PolyBoRi's way to represent polynomials using BDDs differs from ours. While PolyBoRi associates one monomial with every path in the BDD, we associate paths with the assignment of values to the variables themselves. This difference will become clear in Sect. 2.2.

There exist many tools for BDD manipulation [8,12,14,21,30], the most utilized one probably being CUDD [30]. Unfortunately, none of them suits our needs. We decided to make our own implementation of CRHS equations using Rust. Rust is fast and memory-efficient, with memory-safe and thread-safe guarantees and many classes of bugs being eliminated at compile time.

1.1 Our Contribution

We propose a new tool called CryptaPath for assisted algebraic cryptanalysis using the CRHS representation. CryptaPath allows for algebraic analysis of any symmetric primitive that can be described as an SPN structure, such as most block ciphers, and sponge constructions. Running this tool on an SPN block cipher takes a single plaintext – ciphertext pair, converts it into a system of CRHS equations, and then tries to solve the system. If successful, it will return all solutions to the system, including all keys transforming the given plaintext into the given ciphertext. In the case of a sponge-based hash function, the tool will take in a hash digest, and try to find a matching pre-image. The researcher is only required to provide a reference implementation for CryptaPath to work, but may choose to dive deeper under the hood of the analysis if desired.

The caveat is the amount of memory required to launch a successful attack. For this reason, we have included the possibility of fixing bits in the key or pre-image. This allows CryptaPath to solve systems in practice. The number of rounds in the primitive is also a parameter which is possible to vary.

This tool builds on theory developed over several decades. CHRS equations can be described as a unification of MRHS equations [25] and BDDs. Earlier work describes how CRHS equation systems can be solved, but a thorough explanation of the relationships between Boolean polynomials in algebraic normal form, BDDs and CRHS equations has not been made before. We address this gap in literature in Sect. 2.

In addition, we have included a novel operation to the toolbox of CRHS: *dropping variables*. Dropping of variables is a technique which allows the solver to reduce the size of the system, and thus to save space. This operation comes with its own caveat, see Sect. 4.2 for details.

Finally, the source code of CryptaPath is available at https://github.com/Simula-UiB/CryptaPath.

2 Preliminaries

Algebraic attacks are attacks where a cipher is represented as a system of equations and one tries to break the cipher by solving the system. While it is well known that the general MQ-problem is NP-hard [13], it is less known how to argue convincingly that a system of equations representing one particular cipher specification *must* be hard to solve. If the equation system is represented as Boolean polynomials in algebraic normal form (ANF) one may try to estimate the minimal degree a Gröbner base solver will reach before producing linear forms, and then give a lower bound on the attack complexity based on that. However, there can always be other ways of representing the equations, giving systems that are easier to solve. In this paper we use the CRHS representation, and start by explaining the correspondence between binary decision diagrams and multivariate polynomials in the Boolean polynomial ring $\mathbb{F}_2[x_0, \ldots, x_{n-1}]/(x_0^2 + x_0, \ldots, x_{n-1}^2 + x_{n-1})$.

2.1   Binary Decision Diagrams and Boolean Functions

A *Binary Decision Diagram* (BDD) is an efficient way to represent and evaluate Boolean functions [5]. Boolean functions have numerous use cases, with examples found in computer assisted design [6], network analysis [17], formal verification [6], artificial intelligence, risk assessment [15], cryptology [24,27], and more.

A BDD is a rooted, directed acyclical graph (DAG), with labeled nodes. There are two kinds of nodes, *decision nodes* and *terminal nodes*. A terminal node is labeled either with the value 0 or 1, while each decision node N is labeled by a Boolean variable x_i. A decision node has two children, often called the *low child* and the *high child*. The edge from decision node N to its low (high) child represents an assignment of the associated Boolean variable x_i to 0 (1). These edges are drawn as dashed (solid) lines in all figures.

To construct a BDD representing a given Boolean function $f(x_0, \ldots, x_{n-1})$, we start with the root node and associate f to it. Choose a variable from f, say x_0, as the decision variable, or label, for the root node and create its low and high child. Associate $f(0, x_1, \ldots, x_{n-1})$ with the low child and $f(1, x_1, \ldots, x_{n-1})$ with the high child. Continue recursively from each of the children by deciding on the next variable, then creating more decision nodes associated with polynomials made from partial assignments to f. If several nodes get associated to the same polynomial they will be merged into one. In the end the last variable gets fixed, so the only two nodes created at the bottom will be the terminal nodes 0 and 1.

Conversely, to find the ANF of the Boolean function associated to a given BDD we start with the terminal nodes 0 and 1 and find the ANFs associated to the nodes by going upwards in the BDD. Assume a decision node N decides on variable x_i and that the ANFs corresponding to its low and high children have already been computed as g_0 and g_1, respectively. By the theory of Shannon expansion [29], the ANF of N will then be $x_i g_1 + (x_i + 1) g_0$. Recursively computing ANFs for the nodes in the BDD this way will eventually compute the ANF f associated with the root node. This f will be the ANF of the Boolean function associated with the BDD.

Figure 1 shows a small example of a BDD with the ANFs associated to each node. The ANF associated to the root node is the Boolean function associated with the complete BDD.

Following a path from the root node through the BDD can therefore be viewed as assigning values to the arguments of a Boolean function, and the value of the function for those assignments is given by the terminal node in which the path ends. Each variable x_i can only occur once on any path of the BDD. Every decision node has two children, so all possible assignments are present as paths.

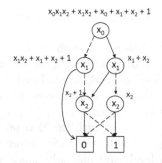

$x_0 x_1 x_2 + x_1 x_2 + x_0 + x_1 + x_2 + 1$

$x_1 x_2 + x_1 + x_2 + 1$

$x_1 + x_2$

$x_2 + 1$

x_2

$f(x_0, x_1, x_2) = x_0 x_1 x_2 + x_1 x_2 + x_0 + x_1 + x_2 + 1$

x_0	x_1	x_2	$f(x_0, x_1, x_2)$
0	0	0	1
0	0	1	0
0	1	0	0
0	1	1	0
1	0	0	0
1	0	1	1
1	1	0	1
1	1	1	0

(a) (RO)BDD, with associated (sub-) Boolean functions.

(b) ANF and truth table

Fig. 1. Example of BDD, ANF and the truth table for a Boolean function. Dashed lines represent 0-assignments, solid lines represent 1-assignments.

The BDD therefore encodes the complete truth table of a Boolean function associated with the BDD. If we encounter the Boolean variables in the same order for each path in the BDD, we say that the BDD is *ordered*. The size of the BDD (i.e., its number of nodes) may be sensitive to the order we choose for the variables. Finding the optimal order of variables is an NP-hard problem [3]. Because a BDD utilizes a DAG, evaluating the Boolean function can be done very efficiently: in n steps or less, where n is the number of variables of the Boolean function.

Size wise, truth tables, Karnaugh maps and other classical representations of Boolean functions grow exponentially with the number of variables involved. There exist more practical approaches where its size is dependent on the Boolean function it represents, and where sub-exponential growth is possible. BDDs fall into this category.

Another desirable property of BDDs, is that a BDD can be reduced to a canonical representation, i.e. for every function there exists a unique BDD representing it, up to the ordering of variables, which has a minimal number of nodes. A BDD in this state is called *reduced* (see [5, Sec. 4.2]).

BDDs may also be understood as a compressed representation of sets or relations, where operations are executed directly on this compressed representation. This view is closer to how we use and understand BDDs in terms of CRHS equations.

2.2 Compressed Right-Hand Sides and Boolean Equations

We use reduced ordered BDDs (ROBDDs) as the fundamental building block of Compressed Right-Hand Side equations. As they are, ROBDDs are too strict in its definition for us to use them the way we would like. We will therefore redefine some of the rules regarding ROBDDs, and call them Compressed Right-Hand Side equations. The changes we make consists of one minor generalization, and two major changes to the definition of ROBDDs, "transforming" them into CRHS equations:

First, we divide the ordered BDD into levels where each level has nodes of only the same Boolean variable. This allows us to generalize the notation slightly, by associating the decision variable with a level instead of individual nodes. Second, we have only one terminal node, the 1-terminal node, instead of both. This means that we no longer associate the Boolean function $f(x_0, \ldots, x_{n-1})$ with the root node. Instead, the root node is now associated with the Booelan *equation* $f(x_0, \ldots, x_{n-1}) = 1$. Third, and more significantly, we allow *linear combinations* of variables to be associated with a level, and not only single variables. We also allow the same variable to be associated with multiple levels, or more generally, we do not require the linear combinations of the levels to be linearly independent. This means that where standard ROBDDs have as many levels as variables, CRHS equations may have both more or fewer variables than levels.

As the CRHS equation is an evolution from the ROBDD, we base the definition of CRHS equations on ROBDDs:

Definition 1. *A CRHS equation is a reduced, ordered BDD with a single terminal node and linear combinations of variables associated to each level. The set of linear combinations is referred to as the* left-hand side *of the CRHS equation, and the paths of the DAG as the equation's* right-hand sides. *A CRHS equation represents the Boolean equation* $f(x_0, \ldots, x_{n-1}) = 1$, *where* f *is the Boolean function corresponding to the BDD.*

Having linear combinations instead of single variables still allows us to use Shannon expansion to compute the ANF of the individual nodes in the CRHS equation, and therefore also for the ANF of the Boolean equation the CRHS equation represents. However, since CRHS equations allow linear combinations to be associated with the levels, it can be even more effective, in terms of nodes, in compressing a polynomial than a standard BDD. Figure 2a shows the CRHS equation made from the same BDD as in Fig. 1a, but where the levels now are associated with some linear combinations. The linear combinations have been randomly chosen for the sake of demonstrating a concrete example. In Fig. 2b the Boolean equation is written out in ANF.

While we have only 6 nodes in the CRHS equation, the ANF contains 46 terms. The BDD representing the same ANF with single variables will contain 18 nodes. In general it is easy to construct CRHS equations where the number of terms in the associated ANF is exponential in the number of nodes in the DAG.

We think of the linear combinations as the left-hand sides of a set of linear equations and all the paths compressed in the DAG as the set of right-hand sides. Choosing a path through the DAG in a CRHS equation, as seen in Fig. 3a, is then the same as fixing a right-hand side vector for the set of linear combinations in the equation's left-hand side (Fig. 3b). This system of linear equations can than be solved using standard linear algebra.

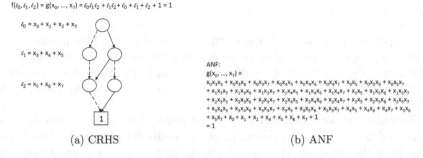

$$f(\ell_0, \ell_1, \ell_2) = g(x_0, ..., x_7) = \ell_0\ell_1\ell_2 + \ell_1\ell_2 + \ell_0 + \ell_1 + \ell_2 + 1 = 1$$

$\ell_0 = x_0 + x_1 + x_2 + x_3$

$\ell_1 = x_3 + x_4 + x_5$

$\ell_2 = x_5 + x_6 + x_7$

ANF:
$g(x_0, ..., x_7) =$
$x_0x_3x_5 + x_0x_3x_6 + x_0x_3x_7 + x_0x_4x_5 + x_0x_4x_6 + x_0x_4x_7 + x_0x_5 + x_0x_5x_6 + x_0x_5x_7$
$+ x_1x_3x_5 + x_1x_3x_6 + x_1x_3x_7 + x_1x_4x_5 + x_1x_4x_6 + x_1x_4x_7 + x_1x_5 + x_1x_5x_6 + x_1x_5x_7$
$+ x_2x_3x_5 + x_2x_3x_6 + x_2x_3x_7 + x_2x_4x_5 + x_2x_4x_6 + x_2x_4x_7 + x_2x_5 + x_2x_5x_6 + x_2x_5x_7$
$+ x_3x_4x_5 + x_3x_4x_6 + x_3x_4x_7 + x_3x_5 + x_3x_5x_6 + x_3x_5x_7 + x_4x_5 + x_4x_6 + x_4x_7 + x_5x_6$
$+ x_5x_7 + x_0 + x_1 + x_2 + x_4 + x_5 + x_6 + x_7 + 1$
$= 1$

(a) CRHS   (b) ANF

Fig. 2. Example of a CRHS equation and its corresponding ANF.

Definition 2. *The solution set of a CRHS equation is the union of the solution sets of all linear equation systems given by the left-hand side and the CRHS equation's right-hand sides.*

This solution set of a CRHS equation is precisely the assignments for which the Boolean function associated with the equation's DAG evaluates to 1.

$\ell_0 = x_0 + x_1 + x_2 + x_3$

$\ell_1 = x_3 + x_4 + x_5$

$\ell_2 = x_5 + x_6 + x_7$

$$
\begin{aligned}
\ell_0 &= x_0 + x_1 + x_2 + x_3 &&= 1 \\
\ell_1 &= \quad\; x_3 + x_4 + x_5 &&= 0 \\
\ell_2 &= \qquad\quad x_5 + x_6 + x_7 &&= 1
\end{aligned}
$$

(a) Choosing a path (blue) through a CRHS   (b) ... assigns a right-hand side to the system
equation...   of linear equations

Fig. 3. Example of CRHS equation and one associated linear system.

While we normally ignore the underlying Boolean polynomials associated with the nodes, including the ANF associated with the root, they are useful for showing that operations available to a BDD can be done on CRHS equations without changing the solution set of the equation.

2.3 Basic Operations on CRHS Equations

Traditionally, there have been two operations on BDDs relevant for CRHS equations: Reduction of a BDD [5] and the swapping of the variables of two adjacent levels of a BDD [26]. With the transition from Multiple Right Hand Sides equations [25] to CRHS equations, two more operations were introduced [27, 28]:

adding the linear combination of one level onto the level below, and level extraction. Both of these operations are a natural consequence of the introduction of linear dependencies among the linear combinations of the CRHS equation. Combined with swapping, they allow for an adapted version of Gaussian elimination to be performed on the linear combinations of the levels. How these operations are used together will be covered in Sect. 4. Here we will briefly describe the operations, for full details see [26,27].

The *reduction algorithm* merges together nodes that have the same Boolean polynomial associated with them. They can easily be identified, since if two nodes have the same low child and high child, they must represent the same Boolean polynomial. The DAG of a CRHS equation can end up in an unreduced state when any of the other operations is performed.

Level extraction can be applied in the special case when the "linear combination" l associated with a level is just a constant $b \in \{0,1\}$. In that case all outgoing edges from the nodes on the level assigning the value $(b + 1)$ give an inconsistency and should be deleted. When only b-edges remain as outgoing edges, it can be shown using Shannon expansion that the polynomial associated with a node on the b-level is equal to the polynomial associated with its remaining child. We can therefore merge the parent and child node. Since all nodes on the level can be merged this way, the whole level is effectively removed, and the number of levels in the CRHS equation decreases by 1.

The *swap operation* is an algorithm which swaps the linear combinations of two adjacent levels, taking care to rearrange the nodes and edges in such a way that the underlying ANF of the root node is preserved. In other words, doing a swap operation does not change the solution set of a CRHS equation.

Adding two levels in a CRHS equation is akin to the matrix operation of adding one row onto another. The first row stays the same, while the second row becomes the sum of the two. However, where any row in a matrix may be added to any other row, adding two levels in a CRHS equation requires the two levels to be adjacent. The procedure adds the linear combination of the top level to the one below it, and modifies edges and nodes in the process. As with the swap operation, the add operation is designed to preserve the underlying Boolean polynomial, so the solution set of a CRHS equation is not changed after an add operation.

One may use the swap operation to achieve both the adjacency and the ordering requirements as needed. In particular, one can use the swap and add operations to produce any linear combination in the span of the linear combinations for the levels, and make it appear on any desired level in a CRHS equation.

Swapping, adding and level extraction may leave the DAG in an unreduced state and it is therefore recommended to run the reduction algorithm afterwards. Swapping and adding levels can increase or decrease the number of nodes on the affected levels. This is entirely deterministic when the levels are known, and the processes are described in [26–28]. Level extraction will always decrease the number of nodes.

3   Modelling Cryptographic Primitives as System of CRHS Equations

Any cryptographic primitive can be modelled as a system of non-linear equations, where any secret material is represented by variables. In this section we first briefly recall how block ciphers designed as substitution-permutation networks (SPN) are built, before explaining how a system of CRHS equations representing an SPN cipher can be constructed. It is straight forward to adapt this description to other types of ciphers or hash functions, as long as the non-linearity comes from S-boxes or other mappings that operate independently on blocks consisting of relatively few bits.

3.1   The Structure of SPN Block Ciphers

SPN block ciphers are constructed by iterating a round function a number of times. Each round consists of the application of a non-linear transformation of the cipher state followed by an affine transformation and the xor addition of a round key. An SPN cipher starts with the addition of a whitening key to the plaintext, before iterating the round function r times. The output of the last round is the ciphertext. We refer to the block of bits at any point during the encryption procedure as the *cipher state*.

The non-linear layer is typically made by dividing the cipher state into blocks of b bits each, and substituting each block with the value given by a fixed b-bit S-box.

The affine transformation in a round can be constructed in many different ways, with various trade-offs. However, any affine transformation can be thought of as a linear transformation of the cipher state, followed by the addition of a constant. The linear transformation can always be realised as the multiplication of the cipher state with a fixed matrix over $GF(2)$. The only thing we care about in this paper is that each bit in the cipher state after the affine transformation is just a linear combination of the bits at the input, with the possible addition of a constant 1-bit.

An SPN cipher with r rounds needs $r + 1$ round keys, denoted as $K^0, K^1, \ldots, K^r$. The whitening key is K^0 and K^i is used in round i for $i = 1, \ldots, r$. The cipher has a master key K of κ bits, and all round keys are derived from K in a deterministic way. The computation of K^i from K can be linear or non-linear. If the key schedule is linear, each bit in K^i is again just a linear combination of the κ bits in K. If the key schedule is non-linear, the non-linear part in computing K^i typically uses the same S-box as used in the rest of the cipher.

3.2   Variables

We introduce the following set of variables to model an encryption $C = E_K(P)$ of an SPN cipher of block size n and key size κ:

- $K = k_0, k_1, \ldots, k_{\kappa-1}$, the bits of the unknown user-selected key
- $P = p_0, p_1, \ldots, p_{n-1}$, the bits of the plaintext
- $C = c_0, c_1, \ldots, c_{n-1}$, the bits of the ciphertext
- $a_0, a_1, \ldots, a_{m-1}$, bits in the cipher state at the output of the S-box layer in rounds $1, \ldots, r-1$

For most ciphers $m = n(r-1)$, but if the S-box layer is incomplete, like for LowMC, $m = s(r-1)$ where s is the number of bits passing through S-boxes in each round. If the key schedule is linear these are all the variables that are needed. If the key schedule is non-linear we introduce auxiliary a_i-variables at the output of the non-linear transformations of the key schedule as well. See Fig. 4 for an illustration of the setup of variables.

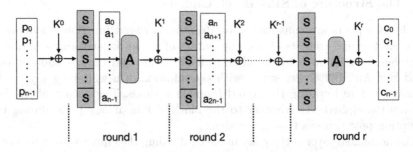

Fig. 4. Variables in a general SPN cipher. The round keys K^i depend on $k_0, \ldots, k_{\kappa-1}$.

The introduction of variables can be done in different ways. The important point is that each bit in the cipher state at the input and output of the non-linear transformations can be expressed as a linear combination of the variables we have introduced. Note that it is not necessary to introduce new variables at the output of the S-boxes in the last round, since these bits can be expressed as linear combinations of the bits in K^r and the known ciphertext.

3.3 Constructing CRHS Equations and the Complete System

We construct the complete system representing the cipher by making one CRHS equation for each S-box instance appearing during the encryption process. For a b-bit S-box, let $l_0, \ldots, l_{b-1}$ represent the input to the S-box and $l_b, \ldots, l_{2b-1}$ the output. We then build a CRHS equation with $2b$ levels associated with $l_0, \ldots, l_{2b-1}$. The CRHS equation will be constructed such that its associated polynomial $f(l_0, \ldots, l_{2b-1})$ evaluates to 1 for all values where $l_0, \ldots, l_{b-1}$ and $l_b, \ldots, l_{2b-1}$ is a matching input/output pair of the S-box, and 0 otherwise.

We now explain how to construct such an CRHS equation, using the 3-bit S-box from LowMC [1] as an example. First, assign the b linear combinations in the cipher state at the input of the S-box to the top b levels. Create a complete binary tree from the top node and down to level $b - 1$. Each path in this tree will correspond to the first $b - 1$ bits of a particular input value. See Fig. 5 for the resulting structure when $b = 3$.

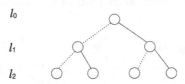

Fig. 5. The three highest levels of the CRHS equation representing the LowMC S-box. The input to the S-box is (l_2, l_1, l_0) with l_0 as least significant bit.

Second, construct a complete tree from the bottom node and upwards to level b. Assign the linear combinations in the cipher state at the output of the S-box to the b lowest levels. From each node on level b down to the bottom node there is now a unique path, representing an output value of the S-box. See Fig. 6 for the 3-bit S-box example.

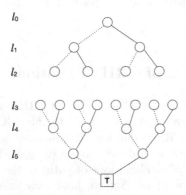

Fig. 6. All nodes and levels of the CHRS equation representing a 3-bit S-box. The output of the S-box is (l_5, l_4, l_3) with l_3 as the least significant bit.

Finally, connect nodes on level $b - 1$ to level b according to the look-up table defining the S-box. All complete paths in the CRHS equation will represent all correct input/output values of the S-box. See Fig. 7 for the complete CRHS equation representing the 3-bit S-box used in LowMC [1].

We construct one CRHS equation for each application of the S-box in the cipher. The complete set of equations makes up the CRHS equation system representing the cipher.

Recall that each path in a CRHS equation gives a right-hand side to a system of $2b$ linear equations. To solve the equation system representing the cipher, we need to find one path in each CRHS equation such that the combined system of linear equations from all CRHS equations is consistent. For a fixed plaintext/ciphertext pair we only need to solve this system to find the values of all variables, in particular finding the variables representing the unknown key. We proceed to explain the techniques used in CryptaPath for solving a CRHS equation system.

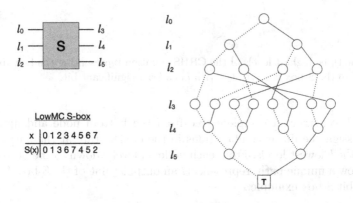

Fig. 7. The CRHS equation representing the LowMC S-box.

4   Solving a System of CRHS Equations

A system of CRHS equations (SOC) is the set of CRHS equations which models one instance of a primitive. The *solution set* to the SOC is the intersection of the solution sets of each CRHS equation, the challenge is to find this set.

The solution set of the SOC is dependent on the paths in its CRHS equations. Collectively, the number of combinations of paths in the SOC is exponential in the number of CRHS equations. Yet we have only one associated system of linear combinations, namely the set of all linear combinations from the CHRS equations. Only a few selections of the paths will yield a consistent linear equation system when assigned to the associated linear combinations, resulting in a solution to the SOC. We call these paths *consistent* and identifying these paths will allow us to calculate the values of all the variables, including any key or pre-image variables. We see that the solution set of the SOC is given by all the consistent paths. *Solving a system of CRHS equation* is therefore a matter of identifying the consistent paths of the SOC, and removing the inconsistent ones.

4.1   Finding the Solution

Allowing arbitrary linear combinations to be associated with levels may give rise to linear dependencies in the set of linear combinations in a CRHS equation.

For a well-defined cipher, a single CRHS equation in the initial system will not have any dependencies among its linear combinations as it would imply a non-invertible linear transformation in the cipher. We therefore need to join multiple CRHS equations to give rise to linear dependencies.

Joining two CRHS equations E_1 and E_2 is a straightforward and memory efficient operation to execute. We simply replace E_1's terminal node with E_2's top node. The resulting CRHS equation contains one fewer node than the combined total of E_1 and E_2. It also contains all possible concatenations of paths from E_1 with paths from E_2, thus preserving the space of possible right-hand side vectors. This operation allows us to easily string together some, or all, CRHS equations into fewer, or even only one, CRHS equation(s).

Identifying linear dependencies in a SOC is straightforward. We extract the set of all linear combinations from all the CHRS equations in the SOC into one matrix, and use normal linear algebra to identify linear combinations that are linearly dependent. We keep track of where the linear combinations come from, and can use this information to decide which CRHS equations to join, and in what order. After joining, the resulting CRHS equation contains dependencies among its linear combinations. We then use linear absorption to remove the linear dependencies.

Linear absorption [28] is the process of resolving one linear dependency from the SOC. Resolving one linear dependency will remove all paths that give right-hand sides in the associated linear system (see Fig. 3) that are inconsistent with this particular dependency. The idea is simple: Adding the relevant levels onto each other, as defined by the linear dependency, will result in a level whose "linear combination" is the constant 0. Since this level now has a constant value, we can remove the level using level extraction. Linear absorption is therefore the repeated applications of swap and add, ending in a level extraction. Figure 8 shows a simple example of linear absorption.

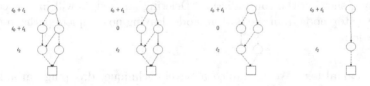

(a) Initial CRHS equation (b) After add operation, creating 0-level (c) Level extraction, part 1: remove 1-edges (d) Level extraction, part 2: remove the level

Fig. 8. Linear Absorption

Solving the SOC is an iterative process: when there are no linear dependencies in any of the existing CRHS equations, join some CRHS equations together that give rise to some linear dependencies. Then use linear absorption to remove all these dependencies. In the end, when all CRHS equations have been joined together and all linear dependencies have been absorbed, we are left with only a single CRHS equation, containing only consistent paths. Any of these paths will give us a consistent system of linear equations that can be solved.

4.2 Supporting Techniques

We have now seen the core techniques required in order to solve a SOC. However, we also have two techniques which may aid in this process: the extraction and injection of linear equations, and the dropping of variables.

Extracting and Injecting Linear Equations. Extracting a linear combination is similar to level absorption. If at any given point all outgoing edges from all nodes on a level with linear combination l_i are 0 (or 1), we know that the linear equation $l_i = 0$ (or $l_i = 1$) must be true. This information is useful in two ways. First, we may use this information to eliminate one variable from the system, by choosing to eliminate any one variable x_j that appears in l_i. This is done by simply adding l_i (or $l_i + 1$) to any linear combination in the system that contains the variable x_j. Note that here we mean "add" in the simple sense of just xoring l_i (or $l_i + 1$) onto any other linear combination without modifying the BDD at all, not the add operation as described in Sect. 2.3.

Second, for the level where we extracted this information, we will get 0 as the linear combination for that particular level. This level should then be removed in the same way as for level extraction. We note that the linear equation $l_i = 0$ (or $l_i = 1$) may be needed after all linear dependencies have been absorbed. It should therefore be stored, so that it can be added back into the final consistent linear system in the end.

We can similarly inject a constraint where we do not know the actual value in order to make a guess. If the guess is wrong the system will have no solutions. A system with no solutions is identified when a 0-level with only outgoing 1-edges appears, showing the contradiction. Deleting all 1-edges will in this case disconnect the top node from the bottom node, leaving no complete paths in the CHRS equation.

Dropping Variables. We introduce a novel technique, dropping variables, which has not been described before. Dropping a variable means to completely remove a variable from the SOC. This should therefore only be used on auxiliary variables, whose values we do not really care about, and not on variables representing the key of a cipher or a pre-image of a hash value.

We can remove any variable x_v from the SOC as follows: First, find all CRHS equations that have linear combinations containing x_v, and join them together. Now x_v only exists in the joined CRHS equation. Second, pick one level where x_v occurs, and use the add and swap operations to add this level to all other levels where x_v occurs. Now x_v only exists in the linear combination of one single level. This level is then moved, using the swap operation, to the lowest level, just above the terminal node. Finally, all incoming edges to the level with x_v are redirected directly to the bottom node and the x_v-level is completely removed, eliminating the last instance of x_v from the system.

Dropping a variable does not disturb the solution space of the variables we care about. This fact can be seen as follows: The consistent path that goes through the level is still valid, since the linear combination containing the single instance of x_v can not be part of any dependency. Assume that a consistent path will fix all other variables in the linear combination of the removed x_v-level. This path will then simply determine the value of x_v, but as x_v does not appear elsewhere in the system no inconsistencies can arise. Note, however, that we will never learn the actual value of dropped variables when solving the remaining system.

The benefit of dropping is that the SOC will contain fewer variables, and the CRHS equation may be simplified after removing a level and reducing. The cost of dropping is the number of add and swap operations that must be performed, possibly increasing the number of nodes. Note also that dropping variables does not resolve any linear dependencies and does not bring us closer to a solution in that sense. It just simplifies the system by eliminating a variable. In practice, variable dropping should only be done when a particular variable is already only contained in a single CRHS equation and the involved levels are already close to the bottom.

4.3   Complexity

We now turn to the complexity of the procedures described above. Absorbing one linear dependency is linear in the number of levels, and the number of dependencies must be less than the number of levels. Hence solving a system is at most quadratic in the number of levels, and the time complexity therefore mostly depends on the number of nodes the levels contain. Solving a non-linear equation system over $GF(2)$ is NP-complete in general and solving systems representing ciphers is still hard. For a cipher to be secure, the number of nodes in the SOC must increase significantly during an attempted solving of the SOC. We will see that all our operations are running in linear time in the number of nodes, and that it is not the run time that is crucial, but rather the memory consumption due to the increase in the number of nodes. We will therefore use the total number of nodes seen during solving as the measure of complexity.

Complexity of the Operations. Running the reduction on a CRHS equation is linear in its number of nodes and will only affect memory by removing nodes, so this operation has no cost in terms of memory. Adding and swapping levels are local operations, in the sense that only two levels are involved, and it only affects the number of nodes on the lower level. Nodes on the lower level may be removed and added, and in the worst case the number of nodes may end up being double that of the upper level.

Linear absorption of one linear dependency in a CRHS equation makes use of repeated applications of the swapping and adding operations, but each level is only involved once. The number of nodes can increase or decrease after resolving a dependency, and in the worst case the number of nodes in the CRHS equation may double when resolving a single linear dependency. This leads to the memory complexity for solving a SOC being potentially exponential in the number of initial dependencies.

As dropping a variable means moving the level to the bottom of the CRHS equation before being removed, repeated use of the swap algorithm may be needed. As with linear absorption, this is linear in terms of affected levels, but may in the worst case double the number of nodes. Finally, the level extraction and extracting linear equations (if any exist) are very quick to do and can only reduce the number of nodes.

Order of Operations Influences Effective Complexity. In [24] it is pointed out that the process of solving a SOC can be summed up as three processes.

1. Joining CRHS equations.
2. Absorbing all linear dependencies.
3. Selecting a path from the remaining consistent paths and solving the linear system.

Of these three processes, absorbing dependencies is the hard one. As noted above, the number of nodes on a level may become the double of the number of nodes on the level above when performing the add and swap operations. That in turn means the number of add and swap operations, and the order of executing said operations are the driving factors in the growth of the memory complexity. Solving a system of CRHS equations will see a growth of memory complexity until a "tipping point" is reached, the point from where the memory usage will decrease towards a solution. Therefore, the order in which the dependencies are absorbed should be considered when solving a SOC, in an attempt to minimize the number of nodes at this tipping point.

Finding the best order for absorbing linear dependencies, and in turn the best order to join CRHS equations, is still an open research question.

5   CryptaPath

CryptaPath is a tool both for those who only want to perform an algebraic cryptanalytical attack on a primitive, and for those who wish to do research on CRHS equations. Only needing a reference implementation of a primitive to begin an attack ensures accessibility for those coming from other areas than algebraic cryptanalysis. For those who wish to go further, ways to specialize the solving algorithm are provided. Finally, being open source means that anyone can adapt the tool, changing it to their needs. An overview of how CryptaPath is organized and used is given in Appendix A.

5.1   Example Usage and Results

The simplest way of using CryptaPath is for example by giving the following command:

```
./cryptagraph cipher -c skinny64128 -r 4
```

This command will:

- Generate a random plaintext p and random key K for an instance of Skinny reduced to 4 rounds with 64-bit block and 128-bit key.
- Use this instance to encrypt p to a ciphertext c with K.
- Discard K.
- Create a SOC and fix the appropriate values of the variables corresponding to p and c.
- Run the default solver to remove all the dependencies in the system.
- Get the solution(s) from the solved SOC.
- Validate that the solution(s) correctly encrypt p to c, and output them.

Additional CLI parameters are available such as providing a known plaintext/ciphertext pair or providing a partially known key.

In Table 1 we present several results of instances of round-reduced ciphers we were able to break using CryptaPath, with both time and the memory complexity given as number of nodes. We present both the maximal number of rounds without guessing any bits that we were able to solve as well as some larger instances that we were able to solve with several known key bits. In Table 2 we give some results on finding pre-images for a few variants of the Keccak hash function. The experiments were run on a laptop with an i7-4720HQ CPU @ 2.60 GHz processor and 16 GB of RAM, which limit the maximum complexity to $\approx 2^{28}$ nodes for this particular hardware.

A few remarks on the numbers and the instances in Table 1: Cryptanalytic results using only one single plaintext/ciphertext pair is not very common, so for some of the ciphers there is little to compare against. In [24] both DES and a small version of AES, $SR^*(r, 2, 2, 4)$, are attacked with a similar approach as in this paper. For DES, 6 rounds can be broken with a dedicated strategy and using 6 chosen plaintexts, while with a single plaintext/ciphertext pair only 4 rounds can be attacked. The complexities are lower than in our case, showing that solving strategy plays a role. DES with a single plaintext/ciphertext pair is also attacked algebraically in [7], where the authors break 6 rounds after guessing more than 20 bits of the key.

Table 1. Results on block ciphers (runtimes in min:sec.milliseconds)

Cipher	Number of rounds attacked	Number of known bits	Runtime	# nodes
DES	3 of 16	0/56	0:0.143	$2^{14.644}$
DES	4 of 16	10/56	7:31.102	$2^{26.899}$
LOWMC 64-1-80	19 of 164	0/80	14:17.784	$2^{26.528}$
LOWMC 64-1-80	27 of 164	26/80	9:28.118	$2^{26.199}$
LOWMC 128-31-80	1 of 12	0/80	0:0.849	$2^{17.741}$
LOWMC 128-31-80	2 of 12	68/80	14:34.702	$2^{26.845}$
LOWMC 256-1-256	24 of 458	0/256	11:24.846	$2^{26.540}$
LOWMC 256-1-256	45 of 458	65/256	9:42.992	$2^{26.228}$
PRESENT 80	2 of 31	7/80	10:0.642	$2^{27.004}$
PRESENT 80	2 of 31	8/80	1:18.747	$2^{24.480}$
PRINCE	2 of 12	0/128	0:5.865	$2^{19.831}$
PRINCE	4 of 12	87/128	5:31.046	$2^{26.153}$
PRINCE-CORE	4 of 12	21/64	0:13.592	$2^{22.298}$
SKINNY 64-128	4 of 36	0/128	0:0.437	$2^{14.975}$
SKINNY 64-128	5 of 36	70/128	14:1.398	$2^{27.120}$
SKINNY 128-128	3 of 40	0/128	0:0.444	$2^{15.285}$
SKINNY 128-128	4 of 40	32/128	16:29.616	$2^{27.247}$
SKINNY 128-128	4 of 40	34/128	3:46.160	$2^{25.825}$
SR* 2-2-8	1	0/32	0:0.108	$2^{15.298}$
SR* 2-2-8	2	12/32	0:0.705	$2^{18.060}$
SR* 2-2-8	3	12/32	6:4.170	$2^{26.743}$
SR* 2-2-8	4	23/32	0:8.904	$2^{21.128}$
SR* 4-4-4	1	0/64	0:0.074	$2^{12.053}$
SR* 4-4-4	2	25/64	0:25.430	$2^{22.970}$
SR* 4-4-4	3	46/64	2:52.634	$2^{25.479}$

Table 2. Results on Keccak variants (runtimes in min:sec.milliseconds) *39 fixed variables in first message block, and 32 in the second.

Rounds	Rate	Capacity	Message-length	Hash-length	Number of known bits	Runtime	# nodes
1	240	160	240	80	0/240	0:9.411	$2^{12.21}$
2	40	160	80	80	(39 + 32)/80*	5:33.516	$2^{25.64}$
2	80	120	80	80	49/80	2:20.401	$2^{24.37}$

6   Conclusions and Further Work

There are two purposes of this paper. The first is to have a thorough explanation of the connection between CRHS equations and Boolean equations represented as ANF polynomials, since this has not been described earlier. The second purpose is to advertise an easy to use tool for doing algebraic cryptanalysis.

CRHS equations give a memory efficient representation of a Boolean equation in several variables. Many Boolean polynomials that are too big to be represented in ANF in practice can still be represented as CRHS equations. The size of a CRHS equation does not depend so much on the degree of its associated Boolean polynomial, but rather on how much "regularity" there is in its paths. The theory for solving CRHS equation systems is now better understood, and with CryptaPath it has been compiled into a library that is available for anyone to use and adapt to their own needs. The optimal solving strategy is cipher dependent, and CryptaPath provides API's to experiment with various strategies.

Another goal of CryptaPath is to provide a user interface for doing algebraic cryptanalysis of a particular cipher, without needing knowledge of how CRHS equations are constructed, and without needing to know how solving systems of CRHS equations work. This is inspired from the tool CryptaGraph, which has an equally simple interface for applying a search for differential or linear characteristics.

Further Work: In a longer perspective, we hope there will be more tools for analysing symmetric key primitives, that can be applied by only giving a reference implementation of the cipher in question. Right now it is not possible to simply copy the Rust source code of the ciphers in CryptaGraph's portfolio and apply them to CryptaPath, due to small differences in the Rust traits used by the two tools. For that reason, a standardized way of coding reference implementations needs to be agreed upon.

In our current work we have focused on attacks recovering the secret key in SPN ciphers or finding pre-images for hash functions. There are several directions further research can take for applying CRHS equations on other problems. In [18] CRHS equations are applied on the cipher GOST [9], which uses addition modulo 2^n for including round keys. Checking whether CRHS equations gives a good model for attacking ARX ciphers in general is one avenue to explore. Another topic for further work is applying CRHS equations on a search for the best linear hull or differential in a cipher. This is a hard problem in general and involves keeping a large number of partial solutions in memory at the same time, exactly the feature that a CRHS equation is suitable for.

Last, it is possible to generalize a BDD to a p-ary decision diagram, having p edges out of each node for $p > 2$. To keep the compactness of the CRHS equation p can not be too large. Apart from ciphers (like MiMC) that are defined over $\mathbb{F}_p$ where p is large, we are only aware of the hash function Troika [20] that uses a non-binary field at its base. Troika is defined over $\mathbb{F}_3$ and could be attacked using CRHS equations containing ternary decision diagrams. In contrast, SAT-solvers are inherently binary and can not be adapted as easily to solve problems defined over non-binary fields.

A   Overview of the Code and Usage of CryptaPath

The code base of CryptaPath is broken into two parts:

> The Crush library which provides an implementation of the CRHS equations and System of CRHS equations along with several APIs for the operations that one can be performed on them (swap, add, absorb, drop and more). An interface (a Rust trait) to construct solvers, with default implementation for several methods is also provided.
>
> the CryptaPath tool uses the Crush library. The tool itself is composed of a simple command line interface (CLI), a set of generic methods for building specifications for a SOC from an implementation of a cipher, and several example ciphers that we implemented for analysis. It also provides a generic solver, built from the interface of the Crush library.

We decided to make this separation from the belief that the usage of CRHS equations can be explored outside of cryptanalysis, and in that case the Crush library as a standalone will be sufficient. However, when used in the case of cryptanalysis, the main obstacle to usage for researchers would be to generate the SOC for every cipher and variant they want to analyze. The goal of CryptaPath is to simplify this task. By specifying an implementation that respects the provided interface, the tool will generate the SOC from the Rust source code.

While we provide several implementations of primitives (reduced versions of AES, LowMC, Skinny, Prince, Present, DES and Keccak) we encourage users to add their own if they want to analyze it. To facilitate any future implementation job we are providing several helper functions making it possible to run an implementation against test vectors to ensure its correctness. As already mentioned, we provide a general good solving algorithm which will work out of the box for any SPN cipher or sponge construction implemented in Rust. As a user gets familiar with the tool, tailor made solvers can be created and tested.

A.1   Usage

Simple usage of the tool can be made by using the provided CLI. A user can generate a SOC for any of the primitives implemented in CryptaPath for any number of rounds and run the solver on it. The user can provide a specific plaintext/ciphertext pair and solve for the key. The user may also fix arbitrary bits of the key to see how much easier solving becomes with a partially guessed key. If no plaintext/ciphertext pair is provided CryptaPath will generate a random plaintext and a random key respecting any fixed bits, and compute the corresponding ciphertext at runtime. Any solution found will be validated by encrypting the plaintext and ensuring the result matches the ciphertext. The system of CRHS equations can be output in the form of a .bdd file for studying and fed back into CryptaPath later.

As specified earlier, it is possible and encouraged to add new ciphers into CryptaPath. We provide for that purpose a `Cipher` trait which a reference implementation has to follow. Existing ciphers can be used as examples on how to make an implementation.

We provide two similar solvers which we believe to be a good general fit for all algorithms. The main difference between them is the use of the drop operation which as noted earlier can either increase or decrease the complexity.

In the case of the solver which uses dropping of variables we consider variables that can be dropped without any joining of CRHS equations, and compare the cost of dropping them against the cost of absorbing the cheapest dependency found. The cost of resolving a dependency or dropping a variable is estimated by summing up the number of nodes in the levels that have to be swapped or added to resolve it. There are a lot of heuristics which can be explored to improve the solving, and in particular we expect a tailor made solver to outperform ours when targeting a specific algorithm. A new solver can be implemented using the traits we provide with a minimal amount of code to rewrite.

A specific part of the solver which we encourage users to tweak is the `feedback` function. This function is called by the solver every time it completes an operation on the system and is used to provide feedback to the user. Its role is to allow for gathering data from the SOC during the solving process. Our default implementation prints several metrics on the terminal window such as the number of individual CRHS equations left in the system, the maximal number of node reached and the number of absorbed dependencies.

References

1. Albrecht, M.R., Rechberger, C., Schneider, T., Tiessen, T., Zohner, M.: Ciphers for MPC and FHE. In: Oswald, E., Fischlin, M. (eds.) EUROCRYPT 2015. LNCS, vol. 9056, pp. 430–454. Springer, Heidelberg (2015). https://doi.org/10.1007/978-3-662-46800-5_17
2. Albrecht, M.R., et al.: Algebraic cryptanalysis of STARK-friendly designs: application to MARVELLOus and MiMC. In: Galbraith, S.D., Moriai, S. (eds.) ASIACRYPT 2019. LNCS, vol. 11923, pp. 371–397. Springer, Cham (2019). https://doi.org/10.1007/978-3-030-34618-8_13
3. Bollig, B.: On the complexity of some ordering problems. In: Csuhaj-Varjú, E., Dietzfelbinger, M., Ésik, Z. (eds.) MFCS 2014. LNCS, vol. 8635, pp. 118–129. Springer, Heidelberg (2014). https://doi.org/10.1007/978-3-662-44465-8_11
4. Brickenstein, M., Dreyer, A.: POLYBORI: a framework for gröbner-basis computations with Boolean polynomials. J. Symbol. Comput. 44(9), 1326–1345 (2009). Effective Methods in Algebraic Geometry
5. Bryant, R.E.: Graph-based algorithms for Boolean function manipulation. IEEE Trans. Comput. 100(8), 677–691 (1986)
6. Bryant, R.E.: Symbolic Boolean manipulation with ordered binary-decision diagrams. ACM Comput. Surv. (CSUR) 24(3), 293–318 (1992)

7. Courtois, N.T., Bard, G.V.: Algebraic cryptanalysis of the data encryption standard. In: Galbraith, S.D. (ed.) Cryptography and Coding 2007. LNCS, vol. 4887, pp. 152–169. Springer, Heidelberg (2007). https://doi.org/10.1007/978-3-540-77272-9_10

8. van Dijk, T.: Sylvan (2019). https://github.com/utwente-fmt/sylvan

9. Dolmatov, V.: GOST 28147-89: Encryption, Decryption, and Message Authentication Code (MAC) Algorithms, March 2010. https://tools.ietf.org/rfc/rfc5830.txt

10. Faugère, J.C.: A new efficient algorithm for computing gröbner bases (F4). J. Pure Appl. Algebra **139**, 61–88 (1999)

11. Faugère, J.C.: A new efficient algorithm for computing gröbner bases without reduction to zero (F5). In: ISSAC 2002 (2002)

12. Filippidis, I.: dd (2020). https://github.com/tulip-control/dd

13. Garey, M.R., Johnson, D.S.: A guide to the theory of NP-completeness. Computers and intractability, pp. 641–650 (1979)

14. Gossen, F., Murtovi, A., Linden, J., Steffen, B.: Add-lib 2.0.0 beta (2018). https://add-lib.scce.info

15. Groth, K., Wang, C., Mosleh, A.: Hybrid causal methodology and software platform for probabilistic risk assessment and safety monitoring of socio-technical systems. Reliab. Eng. Syst. Safety **95**(12), 1276–1285 (2010)

16. Hall-Andersen, M., Vejre, P.S.: Generating graphs packed with paths estimation of linear approximations and differentials. IACR Trans. Symmetric Cryptol. **2018**(3), 265–289 (2018)

17. Kawahara, J., Sonoda, K., Inoue, T., Kasahara, S.: Efficient construction of binary decision diagrams for network reliability with imperfect vertices. Reliab. Eng. Syst. Safety **188**, 142–154 (2019)

18. Kazymyrov, O., Oliynykov, R., Raddum, H.: Influence of addition modulo 2^n on algebraic attacks. Cryptogr. Commun. **8**(2), 277–289 (2016)

19. Krause, M.: BDD-based cryptanalysis of keystream generators. In: Knudsen, L.R. (ed.) EUROCRYPT 2002. LNCS, vol. 2332, pp. 222–237. Springer, Heidelberg (2002). https://doi.org/10.1007/3-540-46035-7_15

20. Kölbl, S., Tischhauser, E., Derbez, P., Bogdanov, A.: Troika: a ternary cryptographic hash function. Designs Codes Cryptogr. **88**(1), 91–117 (2020)

21. Lind-Nielsen, J., Cohen, H., Gorogiannis, N.: Buddy (2014). https://sourceforge.net/projects/buddy/

22. Mironov, I., Zhang, L.: Applications of SAT solvers to cryptanalysis of hash functions. In: Biere, A., Gomes, C.P. (eds.) SAT 2006. LNCS, vol. 4121, pp. 102–115. Springer, Heidelberg (2006). https://doi.org/10.1007/11814948_13

23. Nyberg, K., knudsen, L.R.: Provable security against a differential attack. J. Cryptol. **8**(1), 27–37 (1995). https://doi.org/10.1007/BF00204800

24. Raddum, H., Kazymyrov, O.: Algebraic attacks using binary decision diagrams. In: Ors, B., Preneel, B. (eds.) BalkanCryptSec 2014. LNCS, vol. 9024, pp. 40–54. Springer, Cham (2015). https://doi.org/10.1007/978-3-319-21356-9_4

25. Raddum, H., Semaev, I.: Solving multiple right hand sides linear equations. Designs Codes Cryptogr. **49**(1), 147–160 (2008). https://doi.org/10.1007/s10623-008-9180-z

26. Rudell, R.: Dynamic variable ordering for ordered binary decision diagrams. In: Proceedings of 1993 International Conference on Computer Aided Design (ICCAD), pp. 42–47. IEEE (1993)

27. Schilling, T.E., Raddum, H.: Analysis of trivium using compressed right hand side equations. In: Kim, H. (ed.) ICISC 2011. LNCS, vol. 7259, pp. 18–32. Springer, Heidelberg (2012). https://doi.org/10.1007/978-3-642-31912-9_2

28. Schilling, T.E., Raddum, H.: Solving compressed right hand side equation systems with linear absorption. In: Helleseth, T., Jedwab, J. (eds.) SETA 2012. LNCS, vol. 7280, pp. 291–302. Springer, Heidelberg (2012). https://doi.org/10.1007/978-3-642-30615-0_27

29. Shannon, C.E.: A symbolic analysis of relay and switching circuits. Electr. Eng. **57**(12), 713–723 (1938)

30. Somenzi, F.: CUDD: CU decision diagram package release 3.0.0. https://github.com/ivmai/cudd

31. Soos, M., Nohl, K., Castelluccia, C.: Extending SAT solvers to cryptographic problems. In: Kullmann, O. (ed.) SAT 2009. LNCS, vol. 5584, pp. 244–257. Springer, Heidelberg (2009). https://doi.org/10.1007/978-3-642-02777-2_24

32. Stegemann, D.: Extended BDD-based cryptanalysis of keystream generators. In: Adams, C., Miri, A., Wiener, M. (eds.) SAC 2007. LNCS, vol. 4876, pp. 17–35. Springer, Heidelberg (2007). https://doi.org/10.1007/978-3-540-77360-3_2

Boolean Ring Cryptographic Equation Solving

Sean Murphy[1(✉)], Maura Paterson[2], and Christine Swart[3]

[1] Royal Holloway, University of London, London, UK
s.murphy@rhul.ac.uk
[2] Birkbeck, University of London, London, UK
[3] University of Cape Town, Cape Town, South Africa

Abstract. This paper considers multivariate polynomial equation systems over GF(2) that have a small number of solutions. This paper gives a new method EGHAM2 for solving such systems of equations that uses the properties of the Boolean quotient ring to potentially reduce memory and time complexity relative to existing XL-type or Gröbner basis algorithms applied in this setting. This paper also establishes a direct connection between solving such a multivariate polynomial equation system over GF(2), an MQ problem, and an instance of the LPN problem.

Keywords: MQ problem · XL algorithm · Gröbner basis · Boolean ring · LPN problem

1 Introduction

This paper considers the MQ problem of solving a multivariate nonlinear polynomial equation system over the finite field GF(2), which is an NP-hard problem [24]. The MQ problem arises in cryptology in the algebraic cryptanalysis of symmetric primitives [12,17,33] and in the analysis of asymmetric schemes based explicitly on this problem [14,27,31], an area known as *multivariate cryptography*. In particular, there has been much research on multivariate cryptography, such as [1,4–6,8,11,15,16,18–22,25,26,32]. More recently, a number of multivariate cryptographic schemes have been submitted to the ongoing NIST Post-Quantum Cryptography Standardisation process [30], and the multivariate signature schemes Rainbow and GeMSS have been selected as a Finalist and an Alternate in this NIST Post-Quantum process.

The contribution of this paper is to develop a method, the EGHAM2 process, for solving multivariate nonlinear polynomial systems that is specifically adapted for an underlying field of GF(2). For such polynomial systems over GF(2) with small numbers of solutions, the EGHAM2 process should generally have smaller memory and time complexity than existing XL-type and Gröbner basis algorithms. Furthermore, in equation systems over GF(2) where existing XL-type and Gröbner basis algorithms are used to produce multivariate polynomials over GF(2) which factorise, the EGHAM2 process potentially produces many linear expressions which

© Springer Nature Switzerland AG 2021
O. Dunkelman et al. (Eds.): SAC 2020, LNCS 12804, pp. 252–272, 2021.
https://doi.org/10.1007/978-3-030-81652-0_10

hold with approximate probability $\frac{3}{4}$, so establishing a connection between solving such an equation system over $GF(2)$ and the *Learning Parity with Noise* or LPN problem [7].

2   Cryptographic Equation Systems and the Boolean Ring

We consider the problem of finding a solution to the equation system

$$f_1 = \cdots = f_m = 0, \tag{1}$$

where $f_1, \ldots, f_m$ are (without loss of generality) homogeneous polynomials in the multivariate polynomial ring $GF(2)[x_0, \ldots, x_n]$. We assume the homogeneous system has a small number of solutions, and that they lie in $GF(2)^{n+1}$. In general, it is also the case that $m \geq n+1$. Such assumptions might reasonably be expected to hold true for systems of equations arising from cryptographic applications where a unique nonzero solution corresponds (for example) to a key that has been used for encryption.

Any element of $GF(2)$ is fixed by the Frobenius automorphism that sends an element x to x^2. Any point $(x_0, \ldots, x_n) \in GF(2)^{n+1}$ that is a solution to (1) is therefore also a solution to the (inhomogeneous) polynomial equations $x_i^2 + x_i = 0$ (for $i = 0, \ldots, n$). These are frequently referred to as the *field equations*, and a standard approach is to seek a solution to the (inhomogeneous) equation system

$$f_1 = \cdots = f_m = x_0^2 + x_0 = \cdots = x_n^2 + x_n = 0. \tag{2}$$

We consider an alternative approach to appending the field equations to the original equation system $f_1 = \cdots = f_m = 0$ in the polynomial ring $GF(2)[x_0, \ldots, x_n]$. Instead, we work in the *Boolean ring* of Definition 1 arising as the quotient ring specified by the ideal generated by these field polynomials.

Definition 1. The *Boolean ring* is the multivariate quotient ring

$$\mathcal{B} = \frac{GF(2)[x_0, \ldots, x_n]}{\langle x_0^2 + x_0, \ldots, x_n^2 + x_n \rangle}.$$

The canonical ring homomorphism $\Gamma \colon GF(2)[x_0, \ldots, x_n] \to \mathcal{B}$ or *Boolean mapping* Γ is given by

$$f \mapsto f + \langle x_0^2 + x_0, \ldots, x_n^2 + x_n \rangle.$$

$\square$

The Boolean ring $\mathcal{B}$ is a principal ideal domain with $z^2 = z$ for all $z \in \mathcal{B}$ [2]. For notational convenience we set $z_i = \Gamma(x_i)$ (for $i = 0, \ldots, n$), and we generally write $g = \Gamma(f)$ for the image of a homogeneous polynomial f and in particular $K = \Gamma(L)$ for the image of a homogeneous linear polynomial L and so on. Thus the Boolean ring $\mathcal{B}$ is a vector space of dimension 2^{n+1} over $GF(2)$, with the set of all squarefree monomials in the $z_0, z_1, \ldots, z_n$ (including 1) forming a basis. We also let $\mathcal{B}_r$ denote the subspace of $\mathcal{B}$ generated by all such basis monomials of degree at most r. We note that any element of the Boolean ring $\mathcal{B}$ arising as the Boolean image of a homogeneous polynomial has constant term 0.

The Boolean mapping Γ can be applied to each of the polynomials in the equation system $f_1 = \ldots = f_m = 0$ over GF(2) given by (1) to obtain an equation system in the Boolean ring $\mathcal{B}$ given by

$$\Gamma(f_1) = \cdots = \Gamma(f_m) = 0. \tag{3}$$

Thus equation system (3) can be expressed as $g_1 = \cdots = g_m = 0$ with $g_i = \Gamma(f_i)$. In any case, any element $(x_0, \ldots, x_n) \in \mathrm{GF}(2)^{n+1}$ that is a solution to (1) gives a solution $(z_0, \ldots, z_n) \in \mathcal{B}$ to (3) and vice versa. Our approach in this paper is to seek solutions to the GF(2) system (1) by finding solutions to the corresponding equivalent Boolean system (3).

3   The XL and EGHAM Processes

Many of the proposed approaches for addressing the MQ problem are variants of approaches based on computing Gröbner bases [10], and one such approach is the XL algorithm and its variants [11,15,34]. In particular, a geometrically invariant XL approach is considered by [28,29]. We develop these geometric ideas by giving an improved cryptographic equation solving algorithm (EGHAM2) when the underlying field is GF(2). This improvement is obtained by considering the equation system in the Boolean ring $\mathcal{B}$ rather than in the original polynomial ring $\mathrm{GF}(2)[x_0, \ldots, x_n]$.

3.1   XL-Type Algorithms

For our purposes, the approach of the XL algorithm (and variants) can be described in the following way. A homogeneous equation system of degree D is produced from the original equation system $f_1 = \ldots = f_m = 0$ by multiplying the original polynomials $f_1, \ldots, f_m$ by appropriate monomials. Any such resulting polynomial can be represented as a (row) vector of coefficients with respect to a specified basis of monomials of degree D. The vectors corresponding to a basis for the vector space of all such resulting polynomials give a matrix with these vectors as rows known as the *Macaulay matrix*. By considering an appropriate monomial ordering (corresponding to a Macaulay column ordering), Gaussian elimination can be used efficiently to find (if it exists) a bivariate polynomial in two specified variables in the span of this new system of degree D. If such a bivariate polynomial can be found, then it can be potentially factorised into linear factors, one of which gives information about the solution. Such information essentially allows us to remove one variable from the equation system and so on. If no such bivariate polynomial can be found, the process can be repeated by increasing the degree D. The XL algorithm is summarised in Fig. 1. A similar description can also be given for Gröbner basis algorithms under an appropriate monomial ordering.

1. Consider the system of degree $D \geq 2$ homogeneous polynomials obtained by multiplying each polynomial f_i by the possible monomials of appropriate degree. The resulting system can be expressed in terms of the *Macaulay matrix* $M_{d,m}$ whose columns correspond to the degree D monomials in $GF(2)[x_0, \ldots, x_n]$ and whose rows correspond to the degree D polynomials in the system. Entries in a given row are the coefficients of the various monomials in the corresponding polynomial.
2. Seek a linear combination of these degree D polynomials that involves only two variables. This can be done by selecting an appropriate ordering for the columns of $M_{d,m}$ then performing Gaussian elimination.
3. Such a homogeneous polynomial in two variables can be factored into linear factors using one of the standard factoring algorithms for univariate polynomials.
4. An appropriate linear factor of this two variable polynomial essentially determines the value of one of the coordinates in the solution. By substituting this value into the original system of equations we can reduce the number of variables by one.
5. By repeating the above steps we hope to find the value of all the coordinates, and hence recover the full solution.

Fig. 1. The XL algorithm

In addition to the number m of polynomials and the number $n' = n + 1$ of variables of the original system, the complexity of the XL algorithm clearly depends fundamentally on the degree D required to find a such a bivariate polynomial. Furthermore, not all of the linear factors of the bivariate polynomial give information about any possible solutions. Determining which linear factors of this bivariate polynomial give information about any possible solutions to the system is a potential further complicating issue in assessing the complexity of the XL algorithm.

3.2 The EGHAM Process

The basic XL algorithm is not geometrically invariant as a simple linear change of co-ordinates can greatly change the complexity. This motivated the development of geometrically invariant forms of the XL algorithm [28,29]. The EGHAM (Even Geometric Heuristic Algorithmic Method) process [29] is such a geometrically invariant XL-type algorithm specially designed for equation systems where the underlying field has characteristic 2. The fundamental concept of the EGHAM process is the geometrically invariant generalisation of the homogeneous bivariate polynomial to the Rank-2 Product Polynomial, which is given in its GF(2) formulation in Definition 2. The property of a Rank-2 Product Polynomial giving rise to this terminology is then given in Lemma 1 (proved in [28]). The development of such an approach then yields the $\mathcal{LS}$-Criterion [29] of Definition 3.

Definition 2. *A Rank-2 Product Polynomial* of degree D is a homogeneous polynomial of the form $\prod_{i=1}^{D}(\theta_i' L' + \theta_i'' L'') \in GF(2)[x_0, ..., x_n]$, where L' and L'' are homogeneous linear polynomials over $GF(2)$ and θ_i' and θ_i'' are constants in some extension field of $GF(2)$. □

Lemma 1. The matrix C_f of formal partial derivatives of a Rank-2 Product Polynomial f has rank at most 2.   □

Definition 3. Let $W_D \subset \mathrm{GF}(2)[x_0, \ldots, x_n]$ denote the space of homogeneous polynomials of degree D over $\mathrm{GF}(2)$. A homogeneous polynomial $f \in W_D$ (for $D > 0$) satisfies the $\mathcal{LS}$-*Criterion* if f is an element of

- either the $\mathcal{L}^2\mathcal{S}$ subspace $\left\langle x_i x_j \mathbf{x}^2 \,\middle|\, \mathbf{x} \in W_{\frac{1}{2}(D-2)} \right\rangle$ when D is even
- or the $\mathcal{L}^1\mathcal{S}$ subspace $\left\langle x_i \mathbf{x}^2 \,\middle|\, \mathbf{x} \in W_{\frac{1}{2}(D-1)} \right\rangle$ when D is odd.   □

In particular, Lemma 2 (proved in [29]) shows that the $\mathcal{LS}$-Criterion categorises the Rank-2 Product Polynomials. Example 1 then illustrates Lemma 2 with a Rank-2 Product polynomial that satisfies the $\mathcal{LS}$-Criterion.

Lemma 2. A Rank-2 Product Polynomial satisfies the $\mathcal{LS}$-Criterion.   □

Example 1. We consider the homogenous polynomial f of degree 4 in the polynomial ring $\mathrm{GF}(2)[x_0, x_1, x_2]$ given by

$$f = x_0^4 + x_0 x_1^3 + x_0 x_1^2 x_2 + x_1^3 x_2 + x_0 x_1 x_2^2 + x_1^2 x_2^2 + x_0 x_2^3 + x_1 x_2^3$$
$$= L'L''(L' + \omega L'')(L' + \omega^2 L''),$$

where $L' = x_0 + x_1$, $L'' = x_0 + x_2$ and ω is a root of $y^2 + y + 1 = 0$ over $\mathrm{GF}(2)$. The product form for f shows that f is a Rank-2 Product Polynomial and the monomials of f show that f satisfies the $\mathcal{LS}$-Criterion. Furthermore, the partial derivatives matrix C_f is given with respect to the lexicographic monomial ordering $(x_0^3, x_0^2 x_1, x_0^2 x_2, x_0 x_1^2, x_0 x_1 x_2, x_0 x_2^2, x_1^3, x_1^2 x_2, x_1 x_2^2, x_2^3)$ by

$$C_f = \begin{pmatrix} 0 & 0 & 0 & 0 & 0 & 0 & 1 & 1 & 1 & 1 \\ 0 & 0 & 1 & 0 & 1 & 0 & 1 & 0 & 1 \\ 0 & 0 & 1 & 0 & 1 & 1 & 0 & 1 & 0 \end{pmatrix}.$$

This partial derivatives matrix C_f of f has rank 2 over $\mathrm{GF}(2)$.   □

Lemma 2 gives rise to the EGHAM process of [29], which we now outline. The $\mathcal{L}^2\mathcal{S}$ subspace or the $\mathcal{L}^1\mathcal{S}$ subspace have dimension in general far smaller than the subspace generated by the homogeneous degree D polynomials under consideration. Thus taking the intersection of this subspace generated by these polynomials with the $\mathcal{L}^2\mathcal{S}$ subspace or the $\mathcal{L}^1\mathcal{S}$ subspace allows us to use the $\mathcal{LS}$-Criterion as a highly efficient filter to vastly reduce the number of polynomials under consideration. Suppose therefore (without loss of generality) that $f_1, \ldots, f_m$ are the homogeneous polynomials of degree D in an XL-type process obtained after filtering using the $\mathcal{LS}$-Criterion and that $f_1, \ldots, f_m$ form a basis for this resulting subspace. We can associate an appropriate partial derivatives matrix C_{f_i} with each polynomial f_i ($i = 1, \ldots, m$), so any polynomial $\sum_{i=1}^m \lambda_i f_i$ in the span of $f_1, \ldots, f_m$ has corresponding partial derivatives matrix $\sum_{i=1}^m \lambda_i C_{f_i}$. Lemma 1 shows that a Rank-2 Product Polynomial in the span of

1. Consider the system of degree $D \geq 2$ homogeneous polynomials obtained by multiplying each polynomial f_i by the possible monomials of appropriate degree.
2. Apply the $\mathcal{LS}$-Criterion, restricting attention to either the $\mathcal{L}^2\mathcal{S}$ or $\mathcal{L}^1\mathcal{S}$ subspace as required, thus reducing the dimension of the problem.
3. Find a Rank-2 Product Polynomial in the $\mathcal{L}^2\mathcal{S}$ or $\mathcal{L}^1\mathcal{S}$ subspace. The approach suggested in [29] requires the solution of a system of cubic equations.
4. The Rank-2 Product Polynomial can be factored, and the appropriate substitution then reduces the number of variables by one.
5. This process is repeated until the desired solution is found.

Fig. 2. A summary of the EGHAM process

$f_1, \ldots, f_m$ has corresponding partial derivatives matrix of rank 2, that is to say we would require all 3×3 subdeterminants of $\sum_{i=1}^{m} \lambda_i C_{f_i}$ to be 0. This gives rise to a cubic equation system in $\lambda_1, \ldots, \lambda_m$ whose solutions correspond to Rank-2 Product Polynomials and hence potentially to information about the solution to the original equation system.

The EGHAM process is summarised in Fig. 2, and there are polynomial systems for which the EGHAM process works with a far lower degree of D than is required by XL or standard Gröbner basis algorithms [29]. However, having to solve a cubic system in $\lambda_1, \ldots, \lambda_m$ is not ideal, and this is one of the issues that we seek to address with the EGHAM2 process.

3.3   A Boolean View of the EGHAM process

We now consider how various aspects of the EGHAM process are affected when we move to working directly in the Boolean ring $\mathcal{B}$. In particular, we consider those polynomials whose Boolean image has degree at most 2, giving the $\mathcal{Q}$-Criterion of Definition 4. Lemma 3 then shows that Rank-2 Product Polynomials satisfy this $\mathcal{Q}$-Criterion.

Definition 4. A homogeneous polynomial $f \in W_D$ $(D > 0)$ of degree D satisfies the *Quadratic Criterion* or $\mathcal{Q}$-Criterion if $g = \Gamma(f) \in \mathcal{B}_2$, that is to say the image of f under the Boolean mapping Γ is quadratic or linear or 0.   □

Lemma 3. The image of a Rank-2 Product Polynomial under the Boolean mapping Γ is either a linear Boolean element or is a quadratic Boolean element of the form $K'K'' + K' + K''$ for linear Boolean elements K' and K''. Thus a Rank-2 Product Polynomial satisfies the $\mathcal{Q}$-Criterion.

Proof. Let $f \in \mathrm{GF}(2)[x_0, \ldots, x_n]$ be a Rank-2 Product Polynomial of degree $D \geq 2$ whose factorisation over an extension of $\mathrm{GF}(2)$ is $f = \prod_{i=1}^{D}(\theta_i' L' + \theta_i'' L'')$ for some homogeneous linear polynomials L' and L'' over $\mathrm{GF}(2)$, so f can be expressed as

$$f = L'^D + \sum_{i=1}^{D-1} c_i L'^i L''^{D-i} + L''^D$$

1. Given a set of homogeneous polynomials over GF(2), obtain the corresponding image set of Boolean elements in $\mathcal{B}$ by using the Boolean mapping Γ.
2. From this set of Boolean elements of $\mathcal{B}$, find elements in the span satisfying the $\mathcal{Q}$-Criterion. Such a reduced set of quadratic Boolean equations can be found by taking the intersection of the original Boolean elements with $\mathcal{B}_2$.
3. Find elements in the span of this reduced set of quadratic Boolean elements satisfying the $\mathcal{R}_2$-Criterion by using the Kernel Method or otherwise. Hence find Boolean linear expressions which hold with probability approximately $\frac{3}{4}$.
4. Express these probabilistic Boolean linear expressions as a Learning Parity with Noise (LPN) Problem
   (a) Attempt to solve this LPN problem using the BKW algorithm or otherwise.
   (b) If there are not sufficient Boolean linear expressions to solve this LPN problem, then the original equation system can be expanded by multiplying elements by monomials and the process repeated.

Fig. 3. Overview of the EGHAM2 process

with $c_1, \ldots c_{D-1} \in GF(2)$. The Boolean image of f is therefore given by

$$g = \Gamma(f) = \Gamma(L')^D + \sum_{i=1}^{D-1} c_i \Gamma(L')^i \Gamma(L'')^{D-i} + \Gamma(L'')^D$$
$$= K' + (c_1 + \ldots + c_{D-1})K'K'' + K'',$$

where $K' = \Gamma(L')$ and $K'' = \Gamma(L'')$ are linear Boolean elements. Thus $g = K' + K''$ if $c_1 + \ldots + c_{D-1} = 0$ and $g = K' + K'K'' + K''$ if $c_1 + \ldots + c_{D-1} = 1$. In either case, the image of a Rank-2 Product Polynomial f under Γ has degree at most 2 and so f satisfies the $\mathcal{Q}$-Criterion.   □

Example 2. The homogeneous Rank-2 Product Polynomial of Example 1 given by $f = x_0^4 + x_0 x_1^3 + x_0 x_1^2 x_2 + x_1^3 x_2 + x_0 x_1 x_2^2 + x_1^2 x_2^2 + x_0 x_2^3 + x_1 x_2^3$ satisfies the $\mathcal{LS}$-Criterion. The image

$$g = \Gamma(f) = z_0 + z_0 z_1 + z_0 z_2 + z_1 z_2$$

of f in the Boolean ring $\mathcal{B}$ consists only of linear and quadratic terms, so f satisfies the $\mathcal{Q}$-Criterion.   □

The $\mathcal{Q}$-Criterion gives a further highly restrictive condition for a Rank-2 Product Polynomial in the Boolean case. For example, $x_0^3 x_1^4 x_2^5$ satisfies the $\mathcal{LS}$-Criterion, but its image $\Gamma(x_0^3 x_1^4 x_2^5) = z_0 z_1 z_2$ under Γ does not satisfy the $\mathcal{Q}$-Criterion. This suggests that a development of the EGHAM process directly focussed on the Boolean ring $\mathcal{B}$ and the $\mathcal{Q}$-Criterion offers the potential for substantial performance improvements in identifying Rank-2 Product Polynomials.

4   A Boolean EGHAM process: EGHAM2

We now give a version of the EGHAM process that is adapted to the Boolean ring $\mathcal{B}$ based on the ideas of Sect. 3.3, and we term the resulting Boolean process the EGHAM2 (Even Geometric Heuristic Algorithmic Method for GF(2)) process. We give a high-level view of this EGHAM2 process in Fig. 3, and we discuss issues relating to this EGHAM2 process in this Section. However, we note as motivation for this process that the Q-Criterion generally gives a very much smaller set of quadratic elements than the original set of Boolean elements, which is obviously much simpler and more efficient to handle. We also note that the EGHAM2 process generates probabilistic linear expressions for the solution, so developing a direct relationship between the MQ problem and the LPN problem.

4.1 The Kernel of the Boolean Mapping

The ideal $\langle x_0^2 + x_0, \ldots, x_n^2 + x_n \rangle$ generated by the field equations is by definition the kernel of the Boolean mapping Γ, and so $\ker(\Gamma)$ plays a critical role in the development of the EGHAM2 process. In particular, this Boolean mapping $\ker(\Gamma)$ allows us to extend the ideas of Sect. 3 to certain polynomials that are not Rank-2 Product Polynomials.

The ideas underlying the use of this kernel can be illustrated by considering the polynomial $f_0 = x_i^2 x_j + x_j^2 x_k = x_j(x_i^2 + x_j x_k)$. The polynomial f_0 factorises, but is not itself a Rank-2 Product Polynomial. We do observe however that $\Gamma(f_0) = z_i z_j + z_j z_k = z_j(z_i + z_k)$ is a quadratic element which does factorise. Such a quadratic element factorisation occurs as f_0 differs from a Rank-2 Product Polynomial by an element of $\ker(\Gamma)$. In this case we have $x_j x_k^2 + x_j^2 x_k \in \ker(\Gamma)$, which gives

$$f_0 + (x_j x_k^2 + x_j^2 x_k) = x_i^2 x_j + x_j x_k^2 = x_j(x_i + x_k)^2,$$

so $f_0 + (x_j x_k^2 + x_j^2 x_k)$ is a Rank-2 Product Polynomial satisfying

$$g_0 = \Gamma(f_0) = \Gamma\left(f_0 + (x_j x_k^2 + x_j^2 x_k)\right) = z_j(z_i + z_k).$$

For this example, the application of the Boolean mapping Γ has shown us that the ideal generated by f_0 and the elements of $\ker(\Gamma)$ does contain a Rank-2 Product Polynomial, and has allowed us to find its image.

Applying the Boolean mapping Γ to a single polynomial gives an image that essentially gives us information about its "most useful" preimage, and the same notion can be extended to systems of polynomials. Adding polynomials in the Boolean mapping kernel $\ker(\Gamma)$ to the polynomials defining the set of equations we wish to solve does not affect the solutions over GF(2). However, adding such "kernel polynomials" can significantly lower the smallest degree D for which the EGHAM process succeeds. All polynomials obtained in this way have the same images under Γ, and so a process based on the resulting Boolean equation system, such as the EGHAM2 process, works for the lowest degree D that succeeds for any of these possible preimages of this system. This idea is illustrated by the following Examples which consider two polynomial equation systems that have the same image under Γ. Example 3 gives a homogeneous cubic polynomial equation system that yields a direct factorisation, so potentially giving a solution to the equation system, only using these cubic polynomials, whilst Example 4 gives a similar polynomial equation system that does not give such a factorisation using cubic polynomials. However, Example 5 shows that the Boolean image of these polynomial equation systems yields a factorisation in both cases.

Example 3. We consider twelve homogenous polynomials $f_1, \ldots, f_{12}$ of degree 3 in the polynomial ring $\mathrm{GF}(2)[x_0, x_1, x_2, x_3, x_4, x_5]$ given by

```
001 003 005 011 013 014 024 034 113 122 124 133 134 144 223 234 235 255 333 335 344 345 355 445 555
002 005 011 012 013 014 022 025 033 034 044 045 112 114 115 133 144 145 222 223 224 235 244 245 255 335 345 444 445
001 002 003 004 005 011 023 034 044 045 055 111 112 113 114 115 123 125 134 145 222 223 224 233 244 245 255 335 555
003 011 012 015 025 044 111 113 114 115 124 125 133 134 145 224 233 234 235 244 245 255 333 345 455 555
000 001 003 015 024 025 045 112 122 124 134 135 233 235 255 333 334 355 455 555
000 001 002 003 005 014 022 023 024 025 044 045 055 112 114 123 144 223 224 234 245 333 334 335 344 345 355 455 555
002 003 004 013 014 022 024 025 033 034 035 044 055 113 114 115 122 124 125 133 135 145 223 224 225 345 355 445 555
001 002 003 005 012 013 023 034 035 045 055 111 114 125 135 225 233 234 244 245 255 334 335 345 355 444 445 455
001 003 005 011 012 013 014 015 022 023 034 045 112 115 124 125 133 135 145 155 222 223 225 234 235 333 334 355 444 455
001 004 011 012 013 015 022 023 025 033 111 115 123 134 144 145 155 225 234 235 333 334 344 355 444 445 555
000 001 003 004 005 011 013 022 023 024 033 035 045 113 115 123 145 222 223 234 244 245 333 334 335 344
000 001 002 004 005 011 013 014 015 033 044 111 112 122 123 124 125 133 134 144 224 225 233 244 245 333 334 335 344 355 555
```

The notation abc denotes the monomial $x_a x_b x_c$ and addition signs are omitted, so for example 000 011 123 would denote the polynomial $x_0^3 + x_0 x_1^2 + x_1 x_2 x_3$, and each line gives a single polynomial. The equation system $f_1 = \ldots = f_{12} = 0$ has the unique nonzero solution $x^* = (1, 1, 0, 0, 1, 0)$. To find this solution using the EGHAM process we apply the $\mathcal{LS}$-Criterion, when we obtain the single polynomial

$$x_0^3 + x_0^2 x_2 + x_0^2 x_3 + x_0 x_1^2 + x_0 x_3^2 + x_0 x_5^2 + x_1^2 x_2 + x_1^2 x_3 + x_2 x_3^2 + x_2 x_5^2 + x_3^3 + x_3 x_5^2$$

in the span of the above system. This $\mathcal{LS}$-Criterion polynomial factorises as

$$(x_0 + x_2 + x_3)(x_0 + x_1 + x_3 + x_5)^2,$$

which shows that this polynomial is a Rank-2 Product polynomial. At least one of these linear factors evaluated at the solution is 0, and so an appropriate substitution can remove one of the variables from the system to give a simpler polynomial equation system. □

Example 4. We consider twelve homogenous polynomials $f_1', \ldots, f_{12}'$ of degree 3 in the polynomial ring $\mathrm{GF}(2)[x_0, x_1, x_2, x_3, x_4, x_5]$ given by

```
001 003 005 011 013 014 024 034 115 122 124 134 144 155 223 225 234 235 333 334 345 455 555
001 012 013 014 025 033 034 044 045 055 112 113 114 115 144 145 222 223 225 235 245 335 345 444 455
004 005 022 023 033 034 044 045 055 111 112 115 123 125 133 134 144 145 222 223 233 245 255 355 555
001 005 012 015 025 033 044 055 111 112 114 122 124 125 134 145 155 233 234 235 245 255 333 334 335 344 345 355 445 555
000 002 003 011 015 022 024 025 045 113 114 115 124 133 134 135 144 155 224 225 233 235 244 333 335 344 445 555
000 001 004 014 023 024 025 033 045 114 122 123 144 223 224 245 255 333 334 344 345 455 555
004 013 014 024 025 034 035 044 055 113 114 122 124 125 133 135 145 155 224 225 233 345 355 445 555
003 005 011 012 013 022 023 034 035 045 055 111 114 125 135 224 225 233 234 245 255 334 335 345 355 444
001 003 005 011 012 013 014 015 022 023 034 045 112 113 124 125 135 145 222 223 225 234 235 244 333 344 355 444 445
001 002 005 011 012 013 015 023 025 033 044 045 055 111 112 114 115 122 123 134 145 155 224 225 234 235 244 333 335 444 455 555
000 002 003 004 005 013 023 024 033 035 045 114 115 123 133 144 145 222 223 234 244 245 333 335
000 001 002 003 004 005 011 013 014 015 044 111 113 114 123 124 125 134 223 245 255 333 334 344 555
```

The equation system $f_1' = \ldots = f_{12}' = 0$ has the unique nonzero solution $(1, 1, 0, 0, 1, 0)$, as in Example 3. Applying the $\mathcal{LS}$-Criterion to this equation system gives the single polynomial

$$x_0^3 + x_0^2 x_2 + x_0^2 x_5 + x_0 x_1^2 + x_1^2 x_2 + x_1^2 x_3 + x_1^2 x_4 + x_1^2 x_5$$
$$+ x_1 x_4^2 + x_1 x_5^2 + x_2^2 x_3 + x_2^2 x_5 + x_3^3 + x_3 x_5^2 + x_4^2 x_5 + x_4 x_5^2.$$

in the span of the above system. This polynomial is absolutely irreducible over $GF(2)$ and so is not a Rank-2 Product polynomial. This means that there is no degree three polynomial in the ideal generated by these polynomials that is a Rank-2 Product polynomial. We therefore have to generate a higher degree system from this cubic system for the EGHAM process to succeed. □

Example 5. Both of the polynomial systems of Example 3 and 4 are homogeneous cubic systems of 12 polynomials in 6 variables. However, these two systems have a common image under the Boolean mapping Γ given by the following Boolean element system

```
013 014 024 034 03  05  124 12  134 14  234 235 23  25  345 34  3   45  5
012 013 014 01  025 034 03  045 04  05  12  13  145 15  235 23  245 25  2   345 35  45  4
023 02  034 03  045 123 125 12  134 13  145 14  15  1   245 25  2   35  5
012 015 01  025 03  04  124 125 134 145 14  15  1   234 235 23  245 25  345 3   45  5
015 01  024 025 03  045 0   124 134 135 235 23  25  34  35  3   45  5
014 01  023 024 025 03  045 04  0   123 12  234 23  245 24  345 3   45  5
013 014 024 025 034 035 05  124 125 12  135 145 14  15  23  24  25  345 35  45  5
012 013 01  023 02  034 035 03  045 125 135 14  1   234 23  245 24  345 34  4
012 013 014 015 023 02  034 03  045 05  124 125 12  135 13  145 234 235 23  24  25  2   34  35  3   45  4
012 013 015 023 025 02  03  04  123 134 145 14  1   234 235 25  35  3   45  4   5
013 023 024 02  035 045 04  05  0   123 13  145 15  234 23  245 24  2   35  3
013 014 015 02  03  05  0   123 124 125 134 13  14  1   23  245 25  3   5
```

If we apply the $\mathcal{Q}$-Criterion to this common image of the polynomial systems of Example 3 and 4 we obtain the Boolean element

$$z_0 z_1 + z_0 z_2 + z_0 z_5 + z_0 + z_1 z_2 + z_1 z_3 + z_2 z_3 + z_2 z_5 + z_3 z_5 + z_3$$

in the span of the above Boolean elements, which factorises to give

$$(z_0 + z_2 + z_3)(z_0 + z_1 + z_3 + z_5).$$

This Boolean factorisation is the image under the Boolean mapping Γ of the factorisation of Example 3. □

The fundamental point made by these Examples is that formally mapping polynomials in the polynomial ring over $GF(2)$ to elements of the Boolean ring $\mathcal{B}$ allows us to find potentially useful "Boolean factorisations" in the span of a polynomial system that are not generally found by an EGHAM process in the polynomial ring. We can use such a Boolean factorisation to give trial substitutions of variables for solving the original polynomial system

4.2   The $\mathcal{R}_2$-Criterion for a Quadratic Boolean Element

The application of the $\mathcal{Q}$-Criterion leads us to find quadratic elements of the Boolean ring. However, we can associate a quadratic element of the Boolean ring $\mathcal{B}_2$ with a matrix essentially given by its partial derivatives, namely the ∂-matrix of Definition 5, a symmetric $(n+1) \times (n+1)$ matrix over $GF(2)$. Our analysis of Rank-2 Product Polynomials proceeds by considering such ∂-matrices for quadratic Boolean elements arising in the span of the image of the polynomial equation system under the Boolean mapping Γ. In particular, we consider the $\mathcal{R}_2$-Criterion of Definition 6, as the subsequent Lemma 4 indicates how to use this $\mathcal{R}_2$-Criterion to locate images of Rank-2 Product Polynomials.

Definition 5. A quadratic element $g = \sum_{i=1}^{n} \sum_{j=0}^{i-1} a_{ij} z_i z_j + \sum_{i=1}^{n} a_{ii} z_i + a \in \mathcal{B}_2$ has symmetric $(n+1) \times (n+1)$ ∂-matrix ∂g given by $(\partial g)_{ij} = (\partial g)_{ji} = a_{ij}$ for $j < i$ with 0-diagonal $(\partial g)_{ii} = 0$. $\square$

Definition 6. A quadratic Boolean element $g \in \mathcal{B}_2$ satisfies the $\mathcal{R}_2$-*Criterion* if the ∂-matrix ∂g of g has rank at most 2. $\square$

Lemma 4. A Rank-2 Product Polynomial f has an image $g = \Gamma(f)$ under the Boolean mapping Γ which satisfies the $\mathcal{R}_2$-Criterion. $\square$

Proof. If $g = \Gamma(f) \in \mathcal{B}_1$ then $\partial g = \partial \Gamma(f) = 0$. Lemma 3 shows that the remaining possibility for a Rank-2 Product Polynomial f is that

$$g = \Gamma(f) = K'K'' + K' + K''$$

for images $K' = \sum_{i=0}^{n} b'_i z_i$ and $K'' = \sum_{j=0}^{n} b''_j z_j$ of two homogeneous linear polynomials. In this case we have

$$g = K'K'' + K' + K'' = \sum_{i=1}^{n} \sum_{j=0}^{i-1} (b'_i b''_j + b''_i b'_j) z_i z_j + \sum_{i=0}^{n} (b'_i b''_i + b'_i + b''_i) z_i.$$

with the corresponding ∂-matrix ∂g given by $(\partial g)_{ij} = b'_i b''_j + b''_i b'_j$ for $i \neq j$ and $(\partial g)_{ii} = 0$. If we let $b' = (b'_0, \ldots, b'_n)^T$ and $b'' = (b''_0, \ldots, b''_n)^T$ be the column vectors of coefficients of K' and K'', then the ∂-matrix of g is given by

$$\partial g = b' b''^T + b'' b'^T.$$

The ∂-matrix ∂g of g is the sum of two matrices $b' b''^T$ and $b'' b'^T$ of rank 1, so has rank at most 2. Thus g satisfies the $\mathcal{R}_2$-Criterion. $\square$

Example 6. Example 2 shows that $g = z_0 + z_0 z_1 + z_0 z_2 + z_1 z_2$ is the Boolean image of $f = x_0^4 + x_0 x_1^3 + x_0 x_1^2 x_2 + x_1^3 x_2 + x_0 x_1 x_2^2 + x_1^2 x_2^2 + x_0 x_2^3 + x_1 x_2^3$ of Example 1. This Boolean quadratic element g has ∂-matrix

$$\partial g = \begin{pmatrix} 0 & 1 & 1 \\ 1 & 0 & 1 \\ 1 & 1 & 0 \end{pmatrix},$$

a matrix of rank 2 over GF(2). Thus $g = \Gamma(f)$, the Boolean image of the Rank-2 Product Polynomial f, satisfies the $\mathcal{R}_2$-Criterion.

4.3 Finding Quadratic Elements Satisfying the $\mathcal{R}_2$-Criterion

Suppose that $g_1, \ldots, g_m \in \mathcal{B}_2$ are quadratic Boolean elements, such as might be obtained by applying the $\mathcal{Q}$-Criterion to some larger original polynomial equation system, where we assume that there are significantly more resulting quadratic Boolean elements than variables, so $m \gg n$. We consider how to find an element $g = \sum_{i=1}^{m} \lambda_i g_i$ in their span satisfying the $\mathcal{R}_2$-Criterion. The *Kernel Method* [13, 23] is a method to find a matrix of low rank within the span of a set of matrices. We can use this Kernel Method to attempt to find a quadratic Boolean element $g = \sum_{i=1}^{m} \lambda_i g_i$ satisfying the $\mathcal{R}_2$-Criterion in the span of $g_1, \ldots, g_m$ by finding a $(n+1) \times (n+1)$ matrix in the span of the corresponding ∂-matrices $\partial g_1, \ldots, \partial g_m$ such that

$$\partial g = \sum_{i=1}^{m} \lambda_i \, \partial g_i \quad \text{has rank 2.}$$

A randomly chosen column vector v_1 of dimension $n+1$ lies in the kernel $\ker(\partial g)$ of a matrix ∂g of rank 2 with probability $\frac{1}{4}$, and so

$$v_1^T \left(\sum_{j=1}^{m} \lambda_j \partial g_j \right) = \sum_{j=1}^{m} \lambda_j \left(v_1^T \, \partial g_j \right) = 0 \quad \text{with probability } \tfrac{1}{4}.$$

Any coefficient vector $(\lambda_1, \ldots, \lambda_m)$ satisfying $\sum_{j=1}^{m} \lambda_j \left(v_1^T \, \partial g_j \right) = 0$ lies in the (left) kernel of the $m \times (n+1)$ matrix

$$\Lambda^{(v_1)} = \begin{pmatrix} v_1^T \, \partial g_1 \\ \vdots \\ v_1^T \, \partial g_m \end{pmatrix}.$$

However, $\ker\left(\Lambda^{(v_1)}\right)$ is typically a subspace of large dimension as $m \gg n$, so whilst $\sum_{j=1}^{m} \lambda_j \, \partial g_j$ is not generally a matrix of rank 2 or less for $(\lambda_1, \ldots, \lambda_m)$ in the kernel of $\Lambda^{(v_1)}$, this kernel typically gives rise to many matrices $\sum_{j=1}^{m} \lambda_j \, \partial g_j$ that are of rank 2 or less. We can repeat this process for l further randomly chosen vectors $v_2, \ldots, v_l$ and determine $\ker\left(\Lambda^{(v_1)}\right) \cap \ldots \cap \ker\left(\Lambda^{(v_l)}\right)$. Thus we can determine coefficient vectors $(\lambda_1, \ldots, \lambda_m)$ that could potentially give rise to a matrix $\sum_{j=1}^{m} \lambda_j \, \partial g_j$ of rank 2 or less by determining the (left) kernel of an $m \times l(n+1)$ matrix, that is to say by solving

$$(\lambda_1, \ldots, \lambda_m) \left(\Lambda^{(v_1)} \Big| \ldots \Big| \Lambda^{(v_l)} \right) = (\lambda_1, \ldots, \lambda_m) \left(\begin{array}{c|c|c} v_1^T \partial g_1 & \cdots & v_l^T \partial g_1 \\ \hline \vdots & \ddots & \vdots \\ \hline v_1^T \partial g_m & \cdots & v_l^T \partial g_m \end{array} \right) = 0.$$

In summary, the Kernel Method can be used to find $(\lambda_1, \ldots, \lambda_m)$ such that the matrix $\partial g = \sum_{i=1}^{m} \lambda_i \partial g_i$ is a candidate to be a matrix of rank 2, corresponding to quadratic Boolean element $g = \sum_{i=1}^{m} \lambda_i g_i$ satisfying the $\mathcal{R}_2$-Criterion. We note that we can generate the matrices $\partial g_1, \ldots, \partial g_m$ by an echelon-like process, so they are themselves likely to be matrices of low rank, meaning that we are likely to find matrices of the form $\sum_{i=1}^{m} \lambda_i \partial g_i$ of rank 2. Furthermore, we choose l such that the required kernel, corresponding to possible candidates

$(\lambda_1, \ldots, \lambda_m)$, is not too large. Example 8 of Sect. 4.7 contains a brief discussion about a process for determining l, and we note that an appropriate size for l can easily be determined empirically. By repeating this process, the Kernel Method potentially allows us to generate many such quadratic Boolean elements $g = \sum_{i=1}^m \lambda_i g_i$ in the span of $g_1, \ldots, g_m$ satisfying the $\mathcal{R}_2$-Criterion.

4.4   Probabilistic Linear Expressions

Lemma 4 shows that the $\mathcal{R}_2$-Criterion provides a useful filter for determining whether a polynomial is a Rank-2 Product Polynomial. It is possible for the images of other polynomials which are not Rank-2 Product Polynomials to satisfy the $\mathcal{R}_2$-Criterion, for example $x_0^2 + x_1 x_2$ has image $\Gamma(x_0^2 + x_1 x_2) = z_0 + z_1 z_2$ with ∂-matrix of rank 2. This issue arises as the ∂-matrix depends only on the quadratic coefficients. However, Lemma 5 gives a decomposition for quadratic elements satisfying the $\mathcal{R}_2$-Criterion, which yields probabilistic Boolean linear expressions.

Lemma 5. Suppose that a nontrivial quadratic element $g \in \mathcal{B}_2$ (with constant term 0) satisfies the $\mathcal{R}_2$-Criterion, then there exist homogeneous linear elements $K, K', K'' \in \mathcal{B}_1$ such that $g = K'K'' + K$. If g takes the value 0 and K is not identically 0, then K takes the value 0 with probability approximately $\frac{3}{4}$.   □

Proof. A nontrivial ∂-matrix cannot have rank 1 as it is symmetric. Thus suppose that b'^T and b''^T are two linearly independent rows of the ∂-matrix ∂g, so b'^T and b''^T form a basis for the rowspace of ∂g and $\partial g = b' b''^T + b'' b'^T$ as ∂g is symmetric. If we define the linear elements $K' = \sum_{i=0}^n b_i' z_i$ and $K'' = \sum_{i=0}^n b_i'' z_i$, then clearly $\partial g = \partial(K'K'')$, and so g and $K'K''$ can differ only in their linear terms. Thus we can write $g = K'K'' + K$ for some linear Boolean element $K \in \mathcal{B}_1$. Furthermore, if $g = K'K'' + K$ takes the value 0 and K is not identically 0, then $(K, K', K'') \in \{(0,0,0), (0,0,1), (0,1,0), (1,1,1)\}$, and in three out of the four cases K takes the value 0. As we exclude the trivial $z = 0$ solution, then K takes the value 0 with probability $\frac{3}{4} - 2^{-n} \approx \frac{3}{4}$.   □

Lemma 5 indicates how to use the ∂-matrix ∂g of a Boolean element g satisfying the $\mathcal{R}_2$-Criterion to find probabilistic linear Boolean expressions. If $\partial g \neq 0$, then ∂g is a matrix of rank 2 over $\mathrm{GF}(2)$, so has two linearly independent rows, corresponding to the distinct linear Boolean elements K' and K''. We note that any third distinct nonzero row of ∂g corresponds to the linear Boolean element $K' + K''$. If we then construct the three linear Boolean elements

$$L = g + K'K'', \quad L' = g + K'(K' + K'') \quad \text{and} \quad L'' = g + K''(K' + K''),$$

then Lemma 5 shows that L, L' and L'' take the value 0 with probability $\frac{3}{4}$ if they are not identically 0, though we note that L, L' and L'' are correlated random variables. We also note that $L + L' + L''$ takes the value 0 with approximate probability $\frac{1}{4}$.

Example 7. Consider the quadratic Boolean element

$$g = z_0 + z_0 z_1 + z_2 + z_1 z_2 + z_0 z_3 + z_1 z_3 + z_2 z_3 + z_0 z_4 + z_2 z_4 + z_3 z_4 + z_1 z_5 + z_3 z_5 + z_4 z_5$$

with six variables, which has ∂-matrix over $\mathrm{GF}(2)$ given by

$$\partial g = \begin{pmatrix} 0\,1\,0\,1\,1\,0 \\ 1\,0\,1\,1\,0\,1 \\ 0\,1\,0\,1\,1\,0 \\ 1\,1\,1\,0\,1\,1 \\ 1\,0\,1\,1\,0\,1 \\ 0\,1\,0\,1\,1\,0 \end{pmatrix}$$

of rank 2, so g satisfies the $\mathcal{R}_2$-Criterion. The first and second rows of ∂g correspond to the linear Boolean elements $K' = z_1 + z_3 + z_4$ and $K'' = z_0 + z_2 + z_3 + z_5$, so we obtain (corresponding to fourth row) $K' + K'' = z_0 + z_1 + z_2 + z_4 + z_5$. Thus we can obtain the three linear Boolean elements

$$L = g + (z_1 + z_3 + z_4)(z_0 + z_2 + z_3 + z_5) = z_0 + z_2 + z_3,$$
$$L' = g + (z_1 + z_3 + z_4)(z_0 + z_1 + z_2 + z_4 + z_5) = z_0 + z_1 + z_2 + z_4$$
$$\text{and } L'' = g + (z_0 + z_2 + z_3 + z_5)(z_0 + z_1 + z_2 + z_4 + z_5) = z_5$$

The Boolean element g takes the value 0 on 31 of the 63 nonzero points. On these 31 nonzero 0-points for g, the linear Boolean elements

$$L = z_0 + z_2 + z_3, \quad L' = z_0 + z_1 + z_2 + z_4 \quad \text{and} \quad L'' = z_5$$

each take the value 0 for 23 of these 31 0-points of g, that is to say with approximate probability $\frac{3}{4}$ as stated in Lemma 5. Furthermore, all other nontrivial linear Boolean elements take the value 0 for 15 of the 31 nonzero 0-points of g, apart from $L + L' + L'' = z_1 + z_3 + z_4 + z_5$ which takes the value 0 for 7 of the 31 nonzero 0-points of g. $\square$

4.5   Boolean Ring Equation Solving as an LPN Problem

We now discuss how to use the Boolean image of a homogeneous polynomial equation system to construct a *Learning Parity with Noise* or LPN problem [7], a standard and fundamental cryptographic problem.

We consider a system of quadratic Boolean elements $g_1 = 0, \ldots, g_{m'} = 0$, where $g_1, \ldots, g_{m'}$ satisfy the $\mathcal{R}_2$-Criterion and are obtained by considering the Boolean image under Γ of some original homogeneous polynomial equation system $f_1 = \ldots = f_m = 0$ with a single (for simplicity) nonzero solution z^*. We note that any such derived linear Boolean elements can be used to make a substitution to simplify the original equation system, and so we only consider quadratic Boolean elements without loss of generality. The ideas of Sect. 4.3 show that we can potentially find m_0 linear Boolean elements $L_1, \ldots, L_{m_0}$ each taking the value 0 at z^* with approximate probability $\frac{3}{4}$. If we regard $L_1, \ldots, L_{m_0}$

as (column) vectors of coefficients, then we can write such probabilistic linear expressions as

$$0 = L_j^T z^* + \epsilon_j, \quad \text{where } \mathbf{P}(\epsilon_j = 0) \approx \tfrac{3}{4} \text{ and } \mathbf{P}(\epsilon_j = 1) \approx \tfrac{1}{4} \quad [j = 1, \ldots, m_0],$$

where $\epsilon_1, \ldots, \epsilon_{m_0}$ are independent and identically distributed random variables on GF(2). For the $m_0 \times n$ matrix $C = \left(K_1^T | \ldots | K_{m_0}^T \right)^T$ over GF(2) and error vector $\epsilon = (\epsilon_1, \ldots, \epsilon_{m_0})^T$, we can write the probabilistic linear Boolean expressions in matrix form as the *statistical linear model*

$$0 = Cz^* + \epsilon.$$

The problem of determining z^* in the above probabilistic expression is an instance of the LPN problem, and so we can potentially use the BKW algorithm to address this LPN problem [7]. The BKW algorithm is essentially a form of Gaussian elimination in which the number of row additions is minimised is order to constrain the growth of the error rate, and we examine its use in this case. Without loss of generality, we assume that $n = ab$ and that $m_0 > 2^b$ and partition the matrix C as

$$C = (C_1 | C_2 | \ldots | C_a),$$

that is to say into $(m_0 \times b)$ submatrices $C_1, \ldots, C_a$. We then find distinct pairs j', j'' such the corresponding rows $C_{1j'}^T$ and $C_{1j''}^T$ of rows of C_1 are identical, so $C_{1j'}^T = C_{1j''}^T$. We can therefore construct a row vector

$$C_{j'}^T + C_{j''}^T = \left(0 \,\middle|\, C_{2j'}^T + C_{2j''}^T \,\middle|\, \ldots \,\middle|\, C_{aj'}^T + C_{aj''}^T \right)$$

in which the first b components are all 0. By constructing m_1 such vectors, we can obtain an $m_1 \times n$ matrix

$$C^{(1)} = \left(0 \,\middle|\, C_2^{(1)} \,\middle|\, \ldots \,\middle|\, C_a^{(1)} \right),$$

in which the left-most b columns are 0, giving the statistical linear model

$$0 = C^{(1)} z^* + \epsilon^{(1)},$$

in which a component $\epsilon_j^{(1)}$ of the new error $\epsilon^{(1)}$ is the sum of two of the components of the previous error vector ϵ. Thus $\mathbf{P}(\epsilon_j^{(1)} = 0) \approx \tfrac{3}{4}\tfrac{3}{4} + \tfrac{1}{4}\tfrac{1}{4} = \tfrac{5}{8}$ and $\mathbf{P}(\epsilon_j^{(1)} = 1) \approx \tfrac{3}{8}$. By iterating the process, we can obtain an $m_{a-1} \times n$ matrix

$$C^{(a-1)} = \left(0 \,\middle|\, \ldots \,\middle|\, 0 \,\middle|\, C_a^{(a-1)} \right),$$

in which the left $(a-1)b$ columns are 0, giving the statistical linear model

$$0 = C^{(a-1)} z^* + \epsilon^{(a-1)} = C_a^{(a-1)} z_{(a)}^* + \epsilon^{(a-1)}$$

where $z_{(a)}^* = (z_{(a-1)b+1}^*, \ldots, z_{ab}^*)^T$ is a vector of the final b components of z^*. In this case, a component $\epsilon_j^{(a-1)}$ of this new error is the sum of 2^{a-1} components of the original error, so these components are usually pairwise independent with $\mathbf{P}\left(\epsilon_j^{(a-1)} = 0\right) \approx \frac{1}{2}(1 + 2^{-a})$ and $\mathbf{P}\left(\epsilon_j^{(a-1)} = 1\right) \approx \frac{1}{2}(1 - 2^{-a})$. If this distribution is sufficiently non-uniform, then we can accurately determine $z_{(a)}^*$ and so reduce the problem to an $(n - b)$-dimensional problem and so on.

4.6   Required Degree for the EGHAM2 Process to Succeed

A major determination of the complexity of the EGHAM2 process is the degree D of the underlying polynomial system, and in particular the minimal degree D required for the EGHAM2 process to complete without generating new polynomials of higher degree.

The degree D to which the original equation systems need to be extended for the comparable XL or Gröbner Basis algorithms to give a solution is considered by [1,3]. Loosely speaking, these papers taken together argue that for most sets of m homogeneous polynomials of degree d, the minimal value of D' for which the coefficient of $y^{D'}$ is negative in the expansions of the expressions

$$\frac{(1+y)^{n'}}{(1+y^d)^m} \text{ for Grobner Basis } \mathrm{F}_5 \text{ and } \frac{(1+y)^{n'}}{(1+y^d)^m} - \frac{1+y}{1-y} \text{ for XL,}$$

where $n' = n + 1$ is the number of variables, gives the required degree D. The EGHAM2 process though requires a degree for which a Rank-2 Product Polynomial can be found. We observe that the set of Rank-2 Product Polynomials contains subspaces of $\mathcal{B}$ of dimension $n + 1$, for example $\langle x_0 x_i | i = 0, \ldots, n \rangle$. This suggests that the degree D required for the EGHAM2 process would in general be bounded by the degree D required for the XL algorithm for the same system.

4.7   An Example of the EGHAM2 Process

We illustrate the EGHAM2 process in Example 8, where we discuss a multivariate quadratic system over GF(2). Whilst this system is relatively small (it could easily be solved by exhaustive search), it does demonstrate the advantages of the EGHAM2 process in comparison with an XL or Gröbner basis approach for such a multivariate GF(2)-system. Furthermore, we discuss we can use the Boolean image of the system to generate an LPN instance and how to use the BKW algorithm to solve this LPN instance.

Example 8. We consider as example with $m = 63$ randomly generated homogeneous quadratic equations in $n' = 20$ variables over GF(2). There are 210 homogeneous monomials of degree 2, so each such polynomial consists of about 105 homogeneous quadratic terms. In this case, the "XL-polynomial" of Sect. 4.6 expands as

$$\frac{(1+y)^{20}}{(1+y^2)^{63}} - \frac{1+y}{1-y} = 19y + 145y^2 - 120y^3 + \ldots,$$

so indicating that it should be possible to obtain cancellation with by generating cubic homogeneous polynomials from these 63 polynomial equations in 20 variables. However, there is generally no bivariate polynomial in the span of the resulting 1323 (1260 cubic and 63 quadratic) generated cubic polynomials, so an XL or a Gröbner basis approach would typically require the generation of quartic polynomials.

The EGHAM2 process by contrast can solve this quadratic equation system with 63 quadratic polynomial equation systems in 20 variables whilst only generating cubic polynomials and not using any quartic polynomials. In a typical instance, the 1323 generated cubic polynomials contained 183 polynomials satisfying the Q-Criterion, that is to say polynomials whose image under the Boolean mapping Γ is a quadratic Boolean element.

Given such cubic polynomials with quadratic Boolean images, the EGHAM2 approach uses the Kernel Method to find ∂-matrices of rank 2 in the span of the ∂-matrices arising from the 183 polynomials satisfying the Q-Criterion. This approach proceeds by determining the (left) kernel of the $m \times l(n+1)$ matrix $\left(\Lambda^{(v_1)}\big|\ldots\big|\Lambda^{(v_l)}\right)$, and the usual dimension of this kernel is given for various values of l below.

l	1	2	3	4	5	6	7	8	9	10	11	12	13
Kernel Dimension	164	146	129	113	98	84	71	59	48	38	29	21	14

We make in passing the following observation for the dimension of this kernel as l increases. We originally considered 183 polynomials, we can technically regard the kernel dimension for $l = 0$ corresponding to a "183×0" matrix with kernel of dimension 183. The kernel dimension for $l = 1$ is 164, which is $n = 19$ less than 183. The kernel dimension for $l = 2$ is 146, which is 18 less than 146 and so on. For this example, we use the above values to choose $l = 13$ generally giving rise to a 14-dimensional kernel for the 183×260 matrix $\left(\Lambda^{(v_1)}\big|\ldots\big|\Lambda^{(v_{13})}\right)$.

We used 500 iterations of Kernel Method with $l = 13$, that is to say we generated 500 matrices of the above form $\left(\Lambda^{(v_1)}\big|\ldots\big|\Lambda^{(v_{13})}\right)$, to find ∂-matrices of rank 2, that is to say quadratic Boolean elements satisfying the $\mathcal{R}_2$-Criterion. No linear Boolean elements were found, and each quadratic Boolean element found satisfying the $\mathcal{R}_2$-Criterion can in practice be used to give three probabilistic linear expressions for the solution. These iterations of the Kernel method gave $m_0 = 1905$ linear Boolean expressions each taking the value 0 (with the true z^*) with probability approximately $\frac{3}{4}$. Thus we can obtain the statistical linear model $0 = Cz^* + \epsilon$ over GF(2) with $m_0 \times n'$ or 1905×20 matrix C and $\mathbf{P}(\epsilon_i = 0) \approx \frac{3}{4}$, so giving an instance of the LPN Problem.

This instance of the LPN problem can be solved by implementing the BKW algorithm by taking $a = 2$ and $b = 10$, that is to say by dividing $C = (C_1|C_2)$ into two $m_0 \times b$ or 1905×10 submatrices C_1 and C_2. As $m_0 > 2^b$, the BKW algorithm reduces the left half of the columns to 0 to give a $m_1 \times b$ matrix $C_{(2)}^{(a-1)}$, where $m_1 = 1037$ in this case. Thus the BKW algorithm gives a 10-dimensional statistical linear model $0 = C_2^{(1)} z_{(2)}^* + \epsilon^{(1)}$ over GF(2), where $z_{(2)}^*$ is the "right half" of solution z^* and $\mathbf{P}\left(\epsilon^{(1)} = 0\right) \approx \frac{5}{8}$.

The true value of $z^*_{(a)}$ can then be identified by evaluating the $2^b - 1 = 2^{10} - 1$ counters

$$S_{z'} = m_1 - \text{Wt} \left(C^{(1)}_{(2)} z' \right) = 1037 - \text{Wt} \left(C^{(1)}_{(2)} z' \right)$$

for $z' \neq 0$ giving the number of 0-components of the vector $C^{(1)}_2 z$ of dimension $m_1 = 1037$. The distribution of these counts when $z' = z^*_{(a)}$ takes the correct value and $z' \neq z^*_{(a)}$ takes an incorrect value are given by

$$S_z \sim \text{Bin}(1037, \tfrac{5}{8}) \approx \text{N}(648.1, 15.6^2) \quad [z = z^*_{(a)}]$$
$$\text{and } S_z \sim \text{Bin}(1037, \tfrac{1}{2}) \approx \text{N}(518.5, 16.1^2) \quad [z \neq z^*_{(a)}].$$

In essence, we can identify the true value of $z^*_{(a)}$ if a realisation of $\text{N}(648.1, 15.6^2)$ distribution exceeds the maximum of 1023 realisations of a $\text{N}(518.5, 16.1^2)$ distribution. More generally, an accurate probability for identifying the partial true solution can be determined by techniques using order statistics, as discussed in a cryptographic context by [9]. In this case, the partial true solution immediately identifies itself with an $S_{z'}$-count of 652 compared with the next highest $S_{z'}$-count of 567. Making the appropriate substitutions then gives a polynomial equation system with 63 quadratic polynomial equations in 10 variables. which is a fully linearised system that can be solved directly. Thus the system of 63 quadratic polynomial equations in 20 variables can be solved by the EGHAM2 process using only cubic monomials and basic linear algebra. □

5 Conclusions

We have outlined a new method, the EGHAM2 process, specifically designed for analysing polynomial systems over $\text{GF}(2)$ that have a small number of solutions. This method is expected to be more efficient that the comparable XL or Gröbner Basis methods for the following reasons.

- The EGHAM2 process is geometrically invariant, whereas the comparable XL or Gröbner basis algorithms are in general not geometrically invariant.
- The degree D required by the EGHAM2 process for the extended polynomial system should be bounded by the degree required by the XL or Gröbner Basis algorithms.
- The processing required by the EGHAM2 algorithm should be more straightforward as it is focussed on a much smaller quadratic system. The EGHAM2 algorithm also avoids the possible complexities involved in testing trial roots of high degree polynomials generated by XL or Gröbner Basis algorithms.

Furthermore, the EGHAM2 process establishes a direct natural connection between solving a multivariate polynomial equation system over $\text{GF}(2)$, an instance of an MQ problem, and solving an instance of an LPN problem.

Acknowledgements. We would like to thank the anonymous referees for their helpful comments.

References

1. Ars, G., Faugère, J.-C., Imai, H., Kawazoe, M., Sugita, M.: Comparison between XL and Gröbner basis algorithms. In: Lee, P.J. (ed.) ASIACRYPT 2004. LNCS, vol. 3329, pp. 338–353. Springer, Heidelberg (2004). https://doi.org/10.1007/978-3-540-30539-2_24
2. Atiyah, M., MacDonald, I.: Introduction to Commutative Algebra. Westview Press, Boulder (1994)
3. Bardet, M., Faugère, J., Salvy, B.: Complexity of Gröbner basis computation for semi-regular overdetermined sequences over GF(2) with solutions in GF(2). Technical report, INRIA research report 5049 (2003). http://www-polsys.lip6.fr/~jcf/Papers/RR-5049.pdf
4. Bardet, M., Faugère, J., Salvy, B.: On the complexity of Gröbner basis computation of semi-regular overdetermined algebraic equations. In: International Conference on Polynomial System Solving - ICPSS, pp. 71–75 (2004). http://www-polsys.lip6.fr/~jcf/Papers/43BF.pdf
5. Bettale, L., Faugère, J.C., Peret, L.: Cryptanalysis of HFE, multi-HFE and variants for odd and even characteristic. Des. Codes Crypt. **69**, 1–52 (2013). https://doi.org/10.1007/s10623-012-9617-2
6. Billet, O., Ding, J.: Overview of cryptanalysis techniques in multivariate public key cryptography. In: Sala, M., Sakata, S., Mora, T., Traverso, C., Perret, L. (eds.) Gröbener Bases, Coding, and Cryptography, pp. 263–283. Springer, Heidelberg (2009). https://doi.org/10.1007/978-3-540-93806-4_15
7. Blum, A., Kalai, A., Wasserman, H.: Noise-tolerant learning, the parity problem, and the statistical query model. J. ACM **50**, 506–519 (2003)
8. Bouillaguet, C., Fouque, P.-A., Macario-Rat, G.: Practical key-recovery for all possible parameters of SFLASH. In: Lee, D.H., Wang, X. (eds.) ASIACRYPT 2011. LNCS, vol. 7073, pp. 667–685. Springer, Heidelberg (2011). https://doi.org/10.1007/978-3-642-25385-0_36
9. Bricout, R., Murphy, S., Paterson, K., van der Merwe, T.: Analysing and exploiting the Mantin biases in RC4. Des. Codes Crypt. **84**, 743–770 (2018). https://doi.org/10.1007/s10623-017-0355-3
10. Buchberger, B.: Ein Algorithmus zum Auffinden der Basiselemente des Restklassenringes nach einem nulldimensionalen Polynomideal (An algorithm for finding the basis elements in the residue class ring modulo a zero dimensional polynomial ideal). Ph.D. thesis, Mathematical Institute, University of Innsbruck, Austria (1965). English translation in J. Symb. Comput. Spec. Issue Log. Math. Comput. Sci. Interact. **41**(3–4), 475–511 (2006)
11. Buchmann, J., Ding, J., Mohamed, M., Mohamed, W.: MutantXL: solving multivariate polynomial equations for cryptanalysis. In: Handschuh, H., Lucks, S., Preneel, B., Rogaway, P. (eds.) Symmetric Cryptography. Dagstuhl Seminar Proceedings, vol. 09031 (2009)
12. Courtois, N.T.: Higher order correlation attacks, XL algorithm and cryptanalysis of Toyocrypt. In: Lee, P.J., Lim, C.H. (eds.) ICISC 2002. LNCS, vol. 2587, pp. 182–199. Springer, Heidelberg (2003). https://doi.org/10.1007/3-540-36552-4_13
13. Goubin, L., Courtois, N.T.: Cryptanalysis of the TTM cryptosystem. In: Okamoto, T. (ed.) ASIACRYPT 2000. LNCS, vol. 1976, pp. 44–57. Springer, Heidelberg (2000). https://doi.org/10.1007/3-540-44448-3_4
14. Courtois, N., Goubin, L., Patarin, J.: SFLASHv3, a fast asymmetric signature scheme. IACR Cryptology ePrint Archive 2003/211 (2003). http://eprint.iacr.org/2003/211

15. Courtois, N., Klimov, A., Patarin, J., Shamir, A.: Efficient algorithms for solving overdefined systems of multivariate polynomial equations. In: Preneel, B. (ed.) EUROCRYPT 2000. LNCS, vol. 1807, pp. 392–407. Springer, Heidelberg (2000). https://doi.org/10.1007/3-540-45539-6_27
16. Courtois, N.T., Patarin, J.: About the XL algorithm over $GF(2)$. In: Joye, M. (ed.) CT-RSA 2003. LNCS, vol. 2612, pp. 141–157. Springer, Heidelberg (2003). https://doi.org/10.1007/3-540-36563-X_10
17. Courtois, N.T., Pieprzyk, J.: Cryptanalysis of block ciphers with overdefined systems of equations. In: Zheng, Y. (ed.) ASIACRYPT 2002. LNCS, vol. 2501, pp. 267–287. Springer, Heidelberg (2002). https://doi.org/10.1007/3-540-36178-2_17
18. Diem, C.: The XL-algorithm and a conjecture from commutative algebra. In: Lee, P.J. (ed.) ASIACRYPT 2004. LNCS, vol. 3329, pp. 323–337. Springer, Heidelberg (2004). https://doi.org/10.1007/978-3-540-30539-2_23
19. Ding, J., Yang, B.Y.: Multivariate public key cryptography. In: Bernstein, D.J., Buchmann, J., Dahmen, E. (eds.) Post-Quantum Cryptography, pp. 193–241. Springer, Heidelberg (2009). https://doi.org/10.1007/978-3-540-88702-7_6
20. Faugère, J.C.: A new efficient algorithm for computing GröBner bases without reduction to zero (F5). In: Proceedings of the 2002 International Symposium on Symbolic and Algebraic Computation, ISSAC 2002, pp. 75–83. ACM (2002)
21. Faugère, J.-C., Gligoroski, D., Perret, L., Samardjiska, S., Thomae, E.: A polynomial-time key-recovery attack on MQQ cryptosystems. In: Katz, J. (ed.) PKC 2015. LNCS, vol. 9020, pp. 150–174. Springer, Heidelberg (2015). https://doi.org/10.1007/978-3-662-46447-2_7
22. Faugère, J.-C., Joux, A.: Algebraic cryptanalysis of hidden field equation (HFE) cryptosystems using Gröbner bases. In: Boneh, D. (ed.) CRYPTO 2003. LNCS, vol. 2729, pp. 44–60. Springer, Heidelberg (2003). https://doi.org/10.1007/978-3-540-45146-4_3
23. Faugère, J.-C., Levy-dit-Vehel, F., Perret, L.: Cryptanalysis of MinRank. In: Wagner, D. (ed.) CRYPTO 2008. LNCS, vol. 5157, pp. 280–296. Springer, Heidelberg (2008). https://doi.org/10.1007/978-3-540-85174-5_16
24. Fraenkel, A., Yesha, Y.: Complexity of solving algebraic equations. Inf. Process. Lett. **10**, 178–179 (1980)
25. Kipnis, A., Shamir, A.: Cryptanalysis of the oil and vinegar signature scheme. In: Krawczyk, H. (ed.) CRYPTO 1998. LNCS, vol. 1462, pp. 257–266. Springer, Heidelberg (1998). https://doi.org/10.1007/BFb0055733
26. Kipnis, A., Shamir, A.: Cryptanalysis of the HFE public key cryptosystem by relinearization. In: Wiener, M. (ed.) CRYPTO 1999. LNCS, vol. 1666, pp. 19–30. Springer, Heidelberg (1999). https://doi.org/10.1007/3-540-48405-1_2
27. Matsumoto, T., Imai, H.: Public quadratic polynomial-tuples for efficient signature-verification and message-encryption. In: Barstow, D., et al. (eds.) EUROCRYPT 1988. LNCS, vol. 330, pp. 419–453. Springer, Heidelberg (1988). https://doi.org/10.1007/3-540-45961-8_39
28. Murphy, S., Paterson, M.: A geometric view of cryptographic equation solving. J. Math. Cryptol. **2**(1), 63–107 (2008)
29. Murphy, S., Paterson, M.B.: Geometric ideas for cryptographic equation solving in even characteristic. In: Parker, M.G. (ed.) IMACC 2009. LNCS, vol. 5921, pp. 202–221. Springer, Heidelberg (2009). https://doi.org/10.1007/978-3-642-10868-6_12
30. National Institute of Science and Technology (NIST): Post-quantum cryptographic standardization process. Technical report (2017). https://csrc.nist.gov/projects/post-quantum-cryptography

31. Patarin, J.: Hidden fields equations (HFE) and isomorphisms of polynomials (IP): two new families of asymmetric algorithms. In: Maurer, U. (ed.) EUROCRYPT 1996. LNCS, vol. 1070, pp. 33–48. Springer, Heidelberg (1996). https://doi.org/10.1007/3-540-68339-9_4

32. Patarin, J.: Cryptanalysis of the Matsumoto and Imai public key scheme of Eurocrypt'98. Des. Codes Crypt. **20**, 175–209 (2000). https://doi.org/10.1023/A:1008341625464

33. Sugita, M., Kawazoe, M., Perret, L., Imai, H.: Algebraic cryptanalysis of 58-round SHA-1. In: Biryukov, A. (ed.) FSE 2007. LNCS, vol. 4593, pp. 349–365. Springer, Heidelberg (2007). https://doi.org/10.1007/978-3-540-74619-5_22

34. Yang, B.-Y., Chen, J.-M.: All in the XL family: theory and practice. In: Park, C., Chee, S. (eds.) ICISC 2004. LNCS, vol. 3506, pp. 67–86. Springer, Heidelberg (2005). https://doi.org/10.1007/11496618_7

Interpolation Cryptanalysis
of Unbalanced Feistel Networks
with Low Degree Round Functions

Arnab Roy[1]([⊠]), Elena Andreeva[4], and Jan Ferdinand Sauer[2,3]

[1] Alpen-Adria Universität Klagenfurt, Klagenfurt, Austria
arnab.roy@aau.at
[2] KU Leuven, Leuven, Belgium
[3] KIT, Karlsruhe, Germany
ferdinand.sauer@posteo.de
[4] TU Wien, Vienna, Austria
elena.andreeva@tuwien.ac.at

Abstract. In recent years a new type of block ciphers and hash functions over a (large) field, such as MiMC and GMiMC, have been designed. Their security, particularly over a prime field, is mainly determined by algebraic cryptanalysis techniques, such as Gröbner basis and interpolation attacks. In SAC 2019, Li and Preneel presented low memory interpolation attack against the MiMC and Feistel-MiMC designs.

In this work we answer the open question posed in their work and show that low memory interpolation attacks can be extended to unbalanced Feistel networks (UFN) with low degree functions, and in particular to the GMiMC design. Our attack applies to UFNs with expanding and contracting round functions keyed either via identical (univariate) or distinct round keys (multivariate). Since interpolation attacks do not necessarily yield the best possible attacks over a binary extension field, we focus our analysis on prime fields $\mathbb{F}_p$.

Our next contribution is to develop an improved technique for a more efficient key recovery against UFNs with expanding round function. We show that the final key recovery step can be reduced not only to the gcd but also to the root finding problem. Despite its higher theoretical complexity, we show that our approach has a particularly interesting application on Sponge hash functions based on UFNs, such as GMiMCHash.

We illustrate for the first time how our root finding technique can be used to find *collision*, *second preimage* and *preimage* attacks on (reduced round) members of the GMiMCHash family. In addition, we support our theoretical analysis with small-scale experimental results.

1 Introduction

In recent years we have seen the advent of novel symmetric cryptographic primitives that aim to facilitate efficiency optimizations for higher level Multi-Party

© Springer Nature Switzerland AG 2021
O. Dunkelman et al. (Eds.): SAC 2020, LNCS 12804, pp. 273–300, 2021.
https://doi.org/10.1007/978-3-030-81652-0_11

Computation (MPC), Zero-Knowledge (ZK) proofs, or Fully Homomorphic Encryption (FHE) protocols. Examples of such primitives are the LowMC [5] block cipher, MiMC [4], GMiMC [2,3], Starkard and Poseidon [12], MARVELlous [6,7] families of primitives, Kreyvium [10], FLIP [17], and Rasta [11] stream ciphers.

The main design goals of these novel primitives are to reduce the number of multiplications in the (arithmetic) circuit and/or to reduce the multiplicative depth of the circuit corresponding to the underlying block cipher or hash function. These objectives often mean that the primitives must be designed over one (possibly large) finite field and more generally, require thorough rethinking of the way traditional block ciphers (and hash functions) are designed and cryptanalyzed. A recent effort in that direction was the public STARK-Friendly hash challenge [18] which aimed at the evaluation and developing better understanding of the security of the ZK-friendly hash function families Feistel-MiMC, GMiMC, Starkard and Poseidon, and MARVELlous.

The MiMC and Feistel-MiMC (over $\mathbb{F}_p$) family of block ciphers and hash functions are the first ZKP-friendly dedicated symmetric designs. The MiMC block cipher introduced a novel approach towards designing an ZK/MPC-friendly primitive. Unlike previously existing designs, MiMC iterates a low-degree function sufficiently many times to achieve the target security. Both Feistel-MiMC and GMiMC rely on the Feistel iterative structure which builds a permutation from a low degree polynomial round function(s).

The first third party cryptanalysis on the MiMC construction has been conducted by Li and Preneel [15]. Their main idea of retrieving a key dependent coefficient of interpolating polynomial stems from [20]. Li and Preneel apply algebraic cryptanalysis based on Lagrange interpolation with low memory complexity against MiMC. In essence, their attack boils down to finding a key recovery "shortcut" by reconstructing and evaluating the second highest coefficient in the cipher polynomial representation. In their work the authors left the *open question* whether a similar attack approach applies to the GMiMC design. The main reason behind this question we speculate is – it is not obvious how to extend the algebraic analysis in [15] to generalized Feistel networks. Our technical contribution in this article starts with the analytical results that solve this problem.

GMiMC or Generalized MiMC family is an extension of the Feistel-MiMC family and uses generalized Feistel structures with $t > 2$ branches. GMiMC is proposed for *both* balanced and unbalanced Feistel networks. In particular, two unbalanced Feistel networks (UFN) are investigated: with expanding round function (ERF); and with contracting round function (CRF). For both ZKSNARK and MPC applications, the UFN with ERF was found to be more efficient compared to balanced Feistel networks. The GMiMC designers also use a fixed-key GMiMC permutation in a Sponge hashing mode to construct the hash function GMiMCHash. Since the general design principle in GMiMC family relies on a Feistel network with a low degree round function, in this work we focus on the (interpolation) cryptanalysis of UFN with low degree round function over $\mathbb{F}_p$.

1.1   Related Work

The MiMC and GMiMC constructions use an APN function to instantiate the round function in the Feistel network. Traditional differential cryptanalysis techniques are ineffective against those designs [2,4]. The design rationale and cryptanalysis of these constructions thus, heavily relies on the *algebraic analysis* of the keyed permutation. Known algebraic cryptanalysis is mainly based on Gröbner basis, interpolation, greatest common divisor (GCD), and higher-order differential analysis. We point out that higher-order differential analysis exploits simply the degree of a keyed function over a field.

In CRYPTO 2020, a higher order differential cryptanalysis against the full (round) GMiMC permutation was proposed [8]. More specifically, the authors showed a zero-sum distinguisher against the GMiMC fixed-key permutation. Yet, they do not provide a collision on the full GMiMCHash using this distinguisher, and to the best of our knowledge no result on finding collision using such distinguisher exists to date. A collision on the reduced round GMiMCHash was given via (algebraic) differential analysis of UFNs. Compared to this our analysis is based on purely algebraic techniques such as polynomial interpolation, GCD computation and root finding.

Bonnetain showed an attack [9] on the Feistel-MiMC and GMiMC n-bit key block ciphers with complexity $2^{n/2}$. The attack followed due to a key schedule weakness and is comparable with the slide attack.

Our Results

In this article we analyze UFN constructions over $\mathbb{F}_p$, and their concrete GMiMC instantiation. More specifically, we focus on the interpolation cryptanalysis of UFNs with low degree round functions. Thereafter, we apply our analysis to the GMiMC block cipher over $\mathbb{F}_p$. We further use these ideas to cryptanalyze GMiMCHash ERF and CRF instances.

- We exhibit a low memory interpolation attack on UFNs with both contracting and expanding round functions. Then, we apply our analysis to GMiMC$_{\mathrm{erf}}$ and GMiMC$_{\mathrm{crf}}$ which are UFNs instantiated with the APN function $x \mapsto x^3$. This answers the open question of Li and Preneel [15] – *how to extend the low memory interpolation attack against GMiMC*. The main idea starts with an extension of their low memory (LM) interpolation analysis. Namely, we first construct the key-dependent coefficient of the interpolation polynomial and then recover the coefficient with constant memory. To extend Li and Preneel's attack to our setting we also need to first fix all but one input to a UFN, such that for both ERF and CRF UFNs we can obtain key-dependent polynomial terms with algebraic degree as low as possible. While the method bears similarity with the main idea of [15], we show that a more in-depth analysis (Sect. 3.2) is required to extend the low memory interpolation attacks for UFNs with $t > 2$ branches compared to the two branch FN used to construct Feistel-MiMC. We present a new attack (in Sect. 5.4) which demonstrates how the multiple output branches in UFN$_{\mathrm{erf}}$ can be combined to improve the complexity of the low memory interpolation attack.

- We show how root finding algorithms for polynomials over finite fields can be used instead of the GCD technique. For the target (MPC and ZKP) applications of $GMiMC_{erf}$ and $GMiMC_{crf}$ block ciphers and hash functions this method has roughly the same complexity as the GCD one. This is due to the fact that for these applications the size of the prime field is bounded.
- Another important contribution of this work is that we show for the first time how the interpolation analysis together with the root finding technique can be utilized to attack a *hash function* constructed with UFNs of low degree round function in a Sponge hashing mode, such as the $GMiMC_{erf}$ and $GMiMC_{crf}$ hash functions. Using this technique we mount collision, second preimage and preimage attacks (in section Sect. 7) against these hash functions.
- As a proof-of-concept we apply our cryptanalysis against a few small-scale instantiations of $GMiMC_{erf}$ and $GMiMC_{crf}$ block ciphers and provide the experimental results in Tables 2 and 3.

  For second preimage, preimage and for collision attacks against GMiMCHash we provide small-scale experiments, the results of which are presented in Tables 5 and 6 and Figs. 4 and 5.

2   Preliminaries

$\mathbb{F}_p$ denotes the finite field where p is prime. Let k_i denote the rounds keys, while round constants are denoted by c_i for $i \geqslant 0$. We denote the tuple of all subkeys by $K = (k_0, \ldots, k_{r-1})$. When working with fix but unknown key we denote it by $\bar{k}_i$ or $\bar{K}$. The monic polynomial $f(x) = \sum_{j=0}^{d-1} a_j x^j + x^d$ with degree d is used to define the round function in a UFN. We denote the output of $f(x)$ in round i by σ_i. $(x_0, \ldots, x_{t-1}) \in \mathbb{F}_p^t$ is the plaintext or input to a UFN with t (> 2) branches. $P_j^{(i)}$ denotes the polynomial corresponding to branch j after the i-th round, and $P_j^{(0)} = x_j$ for $0 \leqslant j < t$. For the inputs analyzed in Sect. 3 and because $f(x)$ is monic, we have $P_j^{(i)} = x^{d^y} + q(K)x^{d^y-1} + \ldots$ where y depends on r and t. We call the polynomial $q(K)$ in the key K the "second highest coefficient". We illustrate one-round UFNs with ERF and CRF in Fig. 1.

2.1   Background

We will consider UFNs with the above polynomial round function $f(x)$. The round function UFN_{erf} is defined as $\sigma_i = f(P_0^{(i)} + k_i + c_i)$ where $i \geqslant 0$ and $P_j^{(i)} = x_j$ for $i = 0$, $0 \leqslant j < t$. Each round is viewed as a mapping

$$(P_0^{(i+1)}, \ldots, P_{t-1}^{(i+1)}) \leftarrow (P_1^{(i)} + \sigma_i, \ldots, P_{t-1}^{(i)} + \sigma_i, P_0^{(i)}) \quad (1)$$

in $\mathbb{F}_p^t$.

The round function of an UFN_{crf} is defined as $\sigma_i = f(\sum_{j=1}^{t-1} P_j^{(i)} + k_i + c_i)$. Each round of UFN_{crf} is a mapping defined as

$$(P_0^{(i+1)}, \ldots, P_{t-1}^{(i+1)}) \leftarrow (P_1^{(i)}, \ldots, P_{t-1}^{(i)}, P_0^{(i)} + \sigma_i) \quad (2)$$

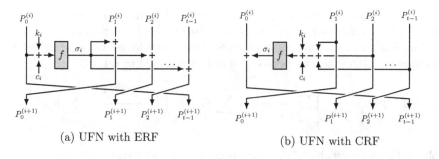

(a) UFN with ERF   (b) UFN with CRF

Fig. 1. One round UFN with ERF (left) and CRF (right)

We will use the notations $\text{UFN}_{\text{erf}}[p, r, t]$ and $\text{UFN}_{\text{crf}}[p, r, t]$ to indicate the number of rounds r and number of branches t for UFNs over $\mathbb{F}_p$.

GMiMC uses the monomial round function $f(x) := x^3$. Typically, GMiMC is defined for primes of size 128 bit or more for their target MPC or ZK applications. The key scheduling in the GMiMC proposal is defined as $k_i = k$ for $i \geqslant 0$ and $k \in \mathbb{F}_p$. However, following the recent attack [9] against GMiMC$_{\text{erf}}$, certain types of GMiMC$_{\text{crf}}$, and Feistel-MiMC, the round key scheduling is updated [16]. The new key schedule defines $k_i := (i + 1)k$ for $i \geqslant 0$. To the best of our knowledge this thwarts the attack of [9]. Using the new key schedule, the round function for GMiMC$_{\text{erf}}$ is defined as $\sigma_i = (P_0^{(i)} + (i + 1)k_i + c_i)^3$, and for GMiMC$_{\text{crf}}$ it is defined as $\sigma_i = (\sum_{j=1}^{t-1} P_j^{(i)} + (i + 1)k_i + c_i)^3$.

We will also use the notations GMiMC$_{\text{erf}}[p, r, t]$ and GMiMC$_{\text{crf}}[p, r, t]$ to indicate the number of rounds and number of branches when necessary or GMiMC.

2.2 Low Memory Interpolation

The interpolation attack [13] on block ciphers was introduced by Jakobsen and Knudsen in 1997. In this attack, the output of a block cipher E_k is viewed as a polynomial in the input of the cipher. The adversary first estimates the degree d of the polynomial and then gathers at least $(d + 1)$ pairs of plaintext and ciphertext. This allows reconstruction of E_k without the knowledge of k. The time complexity for reconstructing the polynomial corresponding to E_k is $\mathcal{O}(d \log d)$ [19] and the space complexity is $\mathcal{O}(d)$.

For polynomials of large degree, the amount of required memory can make interpolation impractical. If the involvement of subkeys in a specific coefficient of the polynomial is "well-understood", a partial recovery of the polynomial can be sufficient to recover the key or reconstruct a decryption oracle. In [15], for example, the reconstruction of only a single coefficient allows the recovery of two subkeys.

This lowers the space complexity to $\mathcal{O}(1)$, meaning that the memory constraints are not an issue with this form of low memory interpolation. One such enabling technique is *choosing* the polynomials' evaluation points. Concretely, when interpolating $f : \mathbb{F}_p \to \mathbb{F}_p$, points $(x_j, y_j) = (\alpha^j, f(\alpha^j))$ are used, where

$\alpha \in \mathbb{F}_p$ is a primitive element. The y_j are retrieved in an online manner, i.e. "on the fly". This removes the need to store a list of $(d+1)$ coordinates.

The low memory interpolation algorithm is developed by rearranging the equation for Lagrange interpolation, which is revisited in Eq. (3).

$$L(x) = \sum_{j=0}^{d} y_j \prod_{\substack{0 \le i \le d \\ i \ne j}} \frac{x - x_i}{x_j - x_i} = \sum_{j=0}^{d} f(\alpha^j) \prod_{\substack{0 \le i \le d \\ i \ne j}} \frac{x - \alpha^i}{\alpha^j - \alpha^i} = \sum_{j=0}^{d} b_j x^j \quad (3)$$

Solving for the coefficient b_{d-1}, the authors of [15] arrive at

$$b_{d-1} = \sum_{j=0}^{d} f(\alpha^j) \frac{\beta_j}{\gamma_j}, \quad \gamma_j = \prod_{\substack{0 \le i \le d \\ i \ne j}} (\alpha^j - \alpha^i), \quad \beta_j = \alpha^j - \sum_{i=0}^{d} \alpha^i \quad (4)$$

The recursive form of $\gamma_{j+1} = \gamma_j \cdot \alpha^d \cdot \alpha^j - \alpha^{-1} / \alpha^j - \alpha^d$ allows its iterative construction. Low memory interpolation can now be achieved by iteratively constructing the summands of Eq. (4). Only current values of variables α^j, β_j, γ_j, and the partial result are stored across iterations, resulting in space requirements of $\mathcal{O}(1)$. Despite the improvements on space complexity, interpolation of even one coefficient amounts to time complexity $\mathcal{O}(d \log d)$.

3   Analysis of Output Polynomials

In this section we will first analyze common properties of the output of Unbalanced Feistel Networks (UFNs) when seen as polynomials of the input and key variable(s). We take output branch j of a $\text{UFN}_{\text{erf}}[p, r, t]$ where the key $K = (k_0, \ldots, k_{r-1})$ values are regarded as indeterminates. Given inputs of the form $(x_0, x_1, \ldots, x_{t-1})$, output branch j can be interpreted as a multivariate polynomial in $\mathbb{F}_p[x_0, \ldots, x_{t-1}, k_0, \ldots, k_{r-1}]$.

Fixing all but one of the input variables to an arbitrary constant will give a polynomial $\mathbb{F}_p[x, k_0, \ldots, k_{r-1}]$ corresponding to any output branch.

3.1   ERF Analysis

We analyze the output polynomials corresponding to different branches after r rounds of a UFN_{erf}. For simplicity we start with the analysis for $\text{UFN}_{\text{erf}}[p, r, 3]$. To give a clear idea of the analysis throughout this section, we progressively generalize it. The first generalization is for the number of rounds r in Proposition 1 and then for t branches in Proposition 2. We simplify the analysis by combining actual round key k_i' and round constant c_i i.e. , $k_i := k_i' + c_i$. Furthermore, we assume $\deg(f) \ge 3$.

Proposition 1. *Given an input of the form (b, b, x) to the $\text{UFN}_{\text{erf}}[p, r, 3]$, after $r \ge 4$ rounds, the output polynomials $P_0^{(r)}, P_1^{(r)}, P_2^{(r)} \in \mathbb{F}_p[x, k_0, \ldots, k_{r-1}]$ for the 3 branches have the following properties:*

1. $deg(P_0^{(r)}) = deg(P_1^{(r)}) = d^{r-2}$ *and* $deg(P_2) = d^{r-3}$
2. $coeff(P_0^{(r)}, x^{d^{r-2}}) = coeff(P_1^{(r)}, x^{d^{r-2}}) = 1$
3. $coeff(P_0^{(r)}, x^{d^{r-2}-1}) = coeff(P_1^{(r)}, x^{d^{r-2}-1}) = d^{r-3}(a_{d-1} + d\beta)$
   where $\beta = f(b + k_0) + f(b + f(b + k_0) + k_1) + k_2 = \sigma_0 + \sigma_1 + k_2$.

Proof. The proof is detailed in Appendix A.1.

We further generalize the result for t branches in the following proposition:

Proposition 2. *Given an input of the form* $(b, \ldots, b, x)$ *to the* $\text{UFN}_{\text{erf}}[p, r, t]$, *let* $r > t \geqslant 3$, *then after* r *rounds, the output polynomials* $P_0^{(r)}, P_1^{(r)}, \ldots, P_{t-1}^{(r)} \in \mathbb{F}_p[x, k_0, \ldots, k_{r-1}]$ *have the following properties:*

1. $deg(P_0^{(r)}) = \ldots = deg(P_{t-2}^{(r)}) = d^{r-(t-1)}$ *and* $deg(P_{t-1}^{(r)}) = d^{r-t}$
2. $coeff(P_0^{(r)}, x^{d^{r-(t-1)}}) = \ldots = coeff(P_{t2}^{(r)}, x^{d^{r-(t-1)}}) = 1$
3. $coeff(P_0^{(r)}, x^{d^{r-(t-1)}-1}) = \ldots = coeff(P_{t-2}^{(r)}, x^{d^{r-(t-1)}-1}) = d^{r-t-1}(a_{d-1} + d\beta)$
   where $\beta = \sum_{i=0}^{t-2} \sigma_i + k_{t-1}$.

Proof. The proof is detailed in Appendix A.2.

Corollary 1. *From Proposition 2 we summarize and can further conclude*

1. $deg(P_t^{(r)}) = deg(P_1^{(r-1)}) = d^{r-t}$
2. $coeff(P_t^{(r)}, x^{d^{r-t}-1}) = coeff(P_1^{(r-1)}, x^{d^{r-t}-1}) = d^{r-t-1}(a_{d-1} + d\beta)$

Corollary 1 gives us the algebraic expression of the coefficient of the second highest degree term in the output polynomial $P_{t-1}^{(r)}$. In the remainder of this article, we will informally refer to this coefficient as the "second highest coefficient." Lastly, we generalize the result for the position of the indeterminate x.

Proposition 3. *Given an input of the form* $(b, \ldots, b, x, b, \ldots, b)$ *to the* $\text{UFN}_{\text{erf}}[p, r, t]$, *where the position of* x *is* $\ell \in \{0, \ldots, t-1\}$, *after* $r > \ell$ *rounds, the output polynomials* $P_0^{(r)}, P_1^{(r)}, \ldots, P_{t-1}^{(r)} \in \mathbb{F}_p[x, k_0, \ldots, k_{r-1}]$ *have the following properties:*

1. $deg(P_0^{(r)}) = \ldots = deg(P_{t-2}^{(r)}) = d^{r-\ell}$ *and* $deg(P_{t-1}^{(r)}) = d^{r-\ell-1}$
2. $coeff(P_0^{(r)}, x^{d^{r-\ell}}) = \ldots = coeff(P_{t-2}^{(r)}, x^{d^{r-\ell}}) = 1$
3. $coeff(P_0^{(r)}, x^{d^{r-\ell}-1}) = \ldots = coeff(P_{t-2}^{(r)}, x^{d^{r-\ell}-1}) = d^{r-\ell-1}(a_{d-1} + d\beta)$
   where $\beta = \sum_{i=0}^{\ell-1} \sigma_i + k_\ell$

Proof. Using the same argumentation as in the proof of Proposition 2, we observe that $deg(\sigma_i) = 0$ for $i < \ell$. In the ℓ-th round, using the same expansion as in the proof of Proposition 2, we have the following expanded form for σ_ℓ:

$$\sigma_\ell = f(x + \sigma_0 + \cdots + \sigma_{\ell-1} + k_\ell)$$
$$= f(x + \beta)$$
$$= x^d + (a_{d-1} + d\beta)x^{d-1} + \cdots + a_0$$

Now we can make an induction over r much in the same way as in Proposition 1.

Corollary 2. *Let σ_i be the output of the round function in round i of a UFN$_{\text{erf}}[p, r, t]$ with input of the form $(b, \ldots, b, x, b, \ldots, b)$, where indeterminate x is at position ℓ, and $d \geqslant 3$. From the proof of Proposition 3 we have*

$$deg(\sigma_i) = \begin{cases} 0, & 0 \leqslant i < \ell \\ d^{i-\ell+1}, & \ell \leqslant i < r \end{cases}$$

Note that generally, the output polynomials in Proposition 3 are of higher degree than those in Proposition 2, unless $\ell = t - 1$, in which case Proposition 2 and Proposition 3 coincide.

3.2   CRF Analysis

For the UFN$_{\text{crf}}[p, r, t]$ we also analyze the degree and coefficients of the highest and second highest term in all the output polynomials, which are described in the following propositions. As in Sect. 3.1, we simplify the analysis by combining actual round key k'_i and round constant c_i to $k_i := k'_i + c_i$. Recall that for a UFN$_{\text{crf}}$, we use $f(\sum_{i=1}^{t-1} x_i + k_i + c_i)$ as round function in round i on inputs $(x_0, \ldots, x_{t-1})$.

Proposition 4. *Given an input of the form $(x, b, \ldots, b)$ to the UFN$_{\text{crf}}[p, r, t]$ with $t \geqslant 3$ branches, after $r \geqslant 2$ rounds, the rightmost output polynomial $P_{t-1}^{(r)} \in \mathbb{F}_p[x, k_0, \ldots, k_{r-1}]$ has the following properties:*

1. $deg(P_{t-1}^{(r)}) = d^{r-1}$
2. $coeff(P_{t-1}^{(r)}, x^{d^{r-1}}) = 1,$
3. $coeff(P_{t-1}^{(r)}, x^{d^{r-1}-1}) = d^{r-1}(a_{d-1} + d\beta)$
   where $\beta = (t-2)b + f((t-1)b + k_0) + k_1$

Proof. The proof is given in Appendix A.3

Corollary 3. *From Proposition 4 we can conclude for $r \geqslant t$*

1. $deg(P_0^{(r)}) = deg(P_{t-1}^{(r-(t-1))}) = d^{r-t}$
2. $coeff(P_0^{(r)}, x^{d^{r-t}-1}) = coeff(P_{t-1}^{(r-(t-1))}, x^{d^{r-t}-1}) = d^{r-t-1}(a_{d-1} + d\beta)$

Corollary 3 gives us the algebraic expression of the coefficient of the second highest degree term in the output polynomial $P_0^{(r)}$. In the remainder of this article, we will informally refer to this coefficient as the "second highest coefficient."

The insight of Proposition 4 allows the algebraic expression of the second highest coefficient in indeterminates k_i, i.e. a polynomial in $\mathbb{F}_p[k_0, k_1]$.

4 Low Memory Interpolation Cryptanalysis of UFNs

Using the results from Sect. 3 we will analyze UFN_{erf} and UFN_{crf} with uniformly randomly fixed but unknown key $\bar{k} \in \mathbb{F}_p^s$ ($s \geqslant 1$), resulting in round keys $(\bar{k}_0, \ldots, \bar{k}_{r-1})$. When the key values are known the output polynomials developed in Sects. 3.1 and 3.2, specifically in Corollaries 1 and 3, are elements of $\mathbb{F}_p[x]$ (not of $\mathbb{F}_p[x, k_0, \ldots, k_{r-1}]$).

Since the interpolation of a single coefficient requires low memory, as outlined in Sect. 2.2, we can recover the second highest coefficient to mount a low memory attack on UFN_{erf} and UFN_{crf}.

4.1 Analysis Outline

The general idea of the cryptanalysis can be described in the following steps:

S1. Obtain the algebraic expression of the second highest coefficient $Q(K)$ of the output polynomial corresponding to the branch with the lowest algebraic degree. For UFN_{erf} and UFN_{crf} these are rightmost branch and leftmost branch respectively (Detailed analysis of UFN_{erf} and UFN_{crf} are in Sect. 5.1 and Sect. 6 respectively).

S2. Find value z of second highest coefficient of $E_{\bar{K}}$ of the same branch as in step 1 by applying the low memory interpolation (used in [15]) technique (Detailed in Sect. 5.2).

S3. Recover the key by evaluating relation $Q(K) = z$ by solving for K. Some of the key recovering techniques may require multiple equations $Q_i(K) = z_i$ (Sects. 5.3 and Sect. 6).

ROUND KEYS. We explore two scenarios *single key* and *multiple keys*. In single key, $k_i = g(k)$, where g is a *linear*[1] function (and degree one) over $\mathbb{F}_p$ and k can have values from $\mathbb{F}_p$. For single round keys, we use two different techniques: a novel *root finding* technique and the *gcd* technique (previously used by [15]).

In Sect. 5.4, we show that the complexity of the key recovery can be further improved for UFN_{erf} by combining the output branch polynomials. We call this technique *branch subtraction*. Table 1 gives an overview of the complexities.

In the multiple key scenario, the round keys are derived from $k = (k_0, k_1) \in \mathbb{F}_p^2$. In GMiMC, the round key $k_i = k_{i \pmod 2}$, where $j \in \{0, \ldots, r-1\}$. The analysis for this multiple key scenario is provided in Sect. 5.5.

5 Cryptanalysis of UFN_{erf}

5.1 Algebraic Expression of Second Highest Coefficient

We consider the output polynomial when all but one branch of the inputs have fixed values. By arranging the terms as in Propositions 1–3, the polynomial has

---

[1] A low degree non-linear function can also be applied. However, the degree of this function will have an effect on the complexity since the time complexity of finding $Q(k)$ depends on the degree.

the form $x^{d^r} + Q(K)x^{d^r-1} + \cdots + cx^0$, where $Q(K)$ depends on the number of rounds r, the number of branches t, and the position ℓ of indeterminate x in the UFNs input. The coefficient $Q(K)$ is a polynomial that we refer as "second highest coefficient." This coefficient is computable by applying the results from Sect. 3, as described below.

In a UFN$_{\mathrm{erf}}[p, r, t]$, the polynomial representing the rightmost output branch has the lowest degree, as shown in Proposition 2. For this polynomial, the coefficient of the second highest degree term has form $Q(K) = d^{r-t-1}(a_{d-1}+d\beta)$, with $\beta = \sum_{i=0}^{t-2} \sigma_i + k_{t-1}$. Algorithm 1 describes the method to obtain the polynomial $Q(K)$, representing the second highest coefficient.

Complexity (of S1). In the single key case, the computation of $Q(K)$ requires multiplications of polynomials over $\mathbb{F}_p$. More specifically, it requires at most $\mathcal{O}(\log D)$ multiplications of two polynomials with degree at most D. The multiplication of two polynomials of degree at most D over $\mathbb{F}_p$ requires $\mathsf{M}(D) := 63.43D \log D \log \log D + \mathcal{O}(D \log D)$ field operations [22, Thm. 8.23]. To simplify the expressions we define $\mathsf{M}'(D) = \mathcal{O}(\log D)\,\mathsf{M}(D)$. Hence, this step has complexity

$$\mathsf{M}'(d^{t-1}) = \mathcal{O}\left(\log d^{t-1}\right)\mathsf{M}(d^{t-1}).$$

Space complexity is $\mathcal{O}\left(d^{t-1}\right)$ since only one polynomial of degree at most d^{t-1} has to be stored at any given time. Note that this space complexity is not due to the interpolation part of the attack.

5.2 Value of Second Highest Coefficient

As outlined at the beginning of Sect. 4, the second step of the analysis consists of recovering the value of the second highest coefficient of the rightmost output polynomial branch of the UFN$_{\mathrm{erf}}$. For this step we use the low memory interpolation of [15] described in Sect. 2.2.

In general, inputs of form α^j are required, where $\alpha \in \mathbb{F}_p$ is a primitive element, $0 \leqslant j \leqslant D$, and D is the degree of the underlying polynomial that is to be interpolated. In the current analysis this means using inputs of the form $x_j = (b, \ldots, b, \alpha^j)$, in accordance with Proposition 2. The evaluation points y_j for the interpolation are the values of the rightmost output branch.

Complexity (of S2). The time complexity of finding the value of the second highest coefficient using the low memory interpolation method of [15] is $\mathsf{I}_{lm}(D) := \mathcal{O}(D \log(D))$ for polynomials of degree D. Its memory complexity is in $\mathcal{O}(1)$, and data complexity is $D+1$. For UFN$_{\mathrm{erf}}$, we have $D = d^{r-t}$, resulting in time complexity $\mathcal{O}((r-t)d^{r-t} \log d)$. The approach requires $d^{r-t}+1$ pairs of plaintext and ciphertext and uses $\mathcal{O}(1)$ space. Better time and data complexities can be achieved by combining branches, as described in Sect. 5.4.

Algorithm 1: Second highest coefficient of rightmost branch in $UFN_{erf}[p, r, t]$ on input $(b, \ldots, b, x)$.

Input: r, t, f, branch constant b, round constants $c_0, \ldots, c_{t-1}$
Output: polynomial $Q(K)$ for second highest coefficient of rightmost branch

1 $s := 0$
2 **for** $i \in (0, \ldots, t-2)$ **do**
3 $\quad \sigma_i := f(s + b + c_i + k_i)$
4 $\quad s := s + \sigma_i$
5 $\beta := s + k_{t-1} + c_{t-1}$
6 **return** $d^{r-t-1}(a_{d-1} + d\beta)$

5.3 Key Recovery with a Single Key

First, we consider the case of single key e.g., $k_i = (i+1) \cdot k$ for $i \geqslant 0$ and k is the master key that can take any value in $\mathbb{F}_p$. We find the polynomial representing the second highest coefficient and the value of the second highest coefficient as described in the previous two sections. For finding the value of the secret key two different techniques can be employed: Finding the gcd, or finding roots.

FINDING THE GCD. This technique was introduced in [1] and also used in [15] to analyze two-branch Feistel networks. We first select two different constants b, b' for input to the UFN_{erf}. We obtain two polynomials $Q(k)$ and $Q'(k)$ as described in Algorithm 1 using b and b' respectively. Next, we interpolate the values of the second highest coefficient say z, z' with as described in Sect. 5.2, twice: The correct key is found from $\gcd(Q(k) - z, Q'(k) - z')$ with high probability.

Complexity of GCD. Finding the gcd of two polynomials of degree at most D over $\mathbb{F}_p$ has time complexity $G(D) := \mathcal{O}(D \log^2 D)$ [22, Cor. 11.9]. For $UFN_{erf}s$, we have $D = d^{t-1}$. Hence the key recovery using the gcd method has time complexity $\mathcal{O}(t^2 d^{(t-1)} \log^2 d)$ and space complexity $\mathcal{O}(d^{t-1})$.

FINDING ROOTS. By construction of $Q(k)$ it satisfies $Q(\bar{k}) - z = 0$, i.e., correct key $\bar{k}$ is a root of above equation $Q(k) - z$. Exhaustively trying the generally very short list of key candidates [14] on one additional pair of plaintext and ciphertext identifies the correct key.

Complexity of Root Finding. Finding all roots without multiplicity of a polynomial with degree D over $\mathbb{F}_p$ has time complexity $R(D) := \mathcal{O}(M(D) \log D \log(Dp))$ [22, Cor. 14.16]. Checking at most D key candidates for a polynomial of degree D has time complexity $\mathcal{O}(D)$. For UFN_{erf}, we have $D = d^{t-1}$. Hence the key recovery using the root finding method has time complexity $\mathcal{O}(M(d^{t-1}) \log d^{t-1} \log(d^{t-1}p))$ and data complexity of $\mathcal{O}(1)$.

FINDING ROOTS VERSUS GCD. Asymptotically, the complexity of the root finding method is worse than using the gcd method. However, for our target constructions, i.e., GMiMC block ciphers and hash functions that are aimed for practical applications, the complexities are roughly the same, since the field's size $\log p \leqslant 2^8$. More importantly, the root finding method can also be used to find collisions when $\mathrm{UFN_{erf}}$ (with a fixed key) is used in sponge mode to construct a hash function, as described in Sect. 7.

5.4 Complexity Improvements via Branch Subtraction

When analyzing a $\mathrm{UFN_{erf}}[p, r, t]$ $E_{\bar{K}}$ with $\bar{K} = (\bar{k}_0, \ldots, \bar{k}_{r-1})$, improvements on the complexities discussed above are possible. From Corollary 2 we have $\deg(\sigma_i) = d^{i-\ell-1}$ for $i \geqslant \ell$ for input of the form $(b, \ldots, b, x, b, \ldots, b)$, where $b \in \mathbb{F}_p$ is a constant and indeterminate x is at position ℓ. After round i, by construction of $\mathrm{UFN_{erf}}$, σ_i has been added to all branches except the rightmost one. As has been used extensively in the proofs of Propositions 1–3, the degree of the output polynomial of any branch is dominated by the largest σ_i. Thus, somehow removing one or more of the highest σ_i from an output branch reduces the degree of the corresponding polynomial. A lower degree in turn allows interpolation with reduced time and data complexity. Since we're using the low memory technique of [15], space complexity cannot be lowered further.

As an example for this effect, consider the output branches $P_0^{(5)}(x), \ldots,$ $P_3^{(5)}(x)$ in Fig. 2. We set $P'(x) := P_1^{(5)}(x) - P_0^{(5)}(x) = \sigma_1 - \sigma_2$. While $\deg(P'(x)) = 0$, crucially $\min_i(\deg(P_i^{(5)}(x))) = \deg(P_3^{(5)}(x)) = \deg(\sigma_3) = d$. This elimination of high degree σ_i is the basic idea behind branch subtraction.

We represent the output of a $\mathrm{UFN_{erf}}[p, r, t]$ E_K with input $(x_0, \ldots, x_{t-1})$ as a vector $\boldsymbol{o}$ using the following matrix notation. Intuitively, the matrix A permutes the inputs like the last operation in any one round of a $\mathrm{UFN_{erf}}$. The matrix B accumulates the necessary σ_i, following the definition of a $\mathrm{UFN_{erf}}$.

$$\boldsymbol{o} := A^r \cdot \boldsymbol{x} + \underbrace{(B_{r\bmod t}| \overbrace{B| \ldots |B}^{\lfloor \frac{r}{t} \rfloor \text{ times}})}_{r \text{ columns}} \cdot \boldsymbol{\sigma} \tag{5}$$

where

$$A = \begin{pmatrix} - e_2 - \\ - e_3 - \\ \vdots \\ - e_t - \\ - e_1 - \end{pmatrix}, \quad \boldsymbol{x} = \begin{pmatrix} x_0 \\ x_1 \\ \vdots \\ x_{t-1} \end{pmatrix}, \quad B = \begin{pmatrix} 0 & & 1 \\ 0 & & \\ & \ddots & \\ 1 & & 0 \end{pmatrix}, \quad \boldsymbol{\sigma} = \begin{pmatrix} \sigma_0 \\ \sigma_1 \\ \vdots \\ \sigma_{r-1} \end{pmatrix}$$

and $B_{r \bmod t}$ are the right $r \bmod t$ columns of B. Summarizing the dimensions, we have $A, B \in \mathbb{F}_p^{t \times t}$, $\boldsymbol{x} \in \mathbb{F}_p^t$, and $\boldsymbol{\sigma} \in \mathbb{F}_p^r$.

Note that Eq. (5) is not recursive. Increasing r to $r + 1$ leads to different dimensions in the composite matrix on the right hand side as well as in $\boldsymbol{\sigma}$. Note also that the output branches $\boldsymbol{o}$ are nonlinear in variable x despite the seemingly linear representation above, since the σ_i are nonlinear for $i \geqslant \ell$.

As an example, we consider a $\mathrm{UFN}_{\mathrm{erf}}[p, 5, 4]$ with inputs (b, b, b, x) like in Fig. 2. In this instance, we have the following:

$$
o = \begin{pmatrix} 0\,1\,0\,0 \\ 0\,0\,1\,0 \\ 0\,0\,0\,1 \\ 1\,0\,0\,0 \end{pmatrix}^5 \cdot \begin{pmatrix} b \\ b \\ b \\ x \end{pmatrix} + \begin{pmatrix} 1\,0\,1\,1\,1 \\ 1\,1\,0\,1\,1 \\ 1\,1\,1\,0\,1 \\ 0\,1\,1\,1\,0 \end{pmatrix} \cdot \begin{pmatrix} \sigma_0 \\ \sigma_1 \\ \sigma_2 \\ \sigma_3 \\ \sigma_4 \end{pmatrix} = \begin{pmatrix} b \\ b \\ x \\ b \end{pmatrix} + \begin{pmatrix} \sigma_0 + \sigma_2 + \sigma_3 + \sigma_4 \\ \sigma_0 + \sigma_1 + \sigma_3 + \sigma_4 \\ \sigma_0 + \sigma_1 + \sigma_2 + \sigma_4 \\ \sigma_1 + \sigma_2 + \sigma_3 \end{pmatrix}
$$

Thus, o is an alternative representation of $P_0^{(5)}(x), \ldots, P_3^{(5)}(x)$, concluding the example.

Given this representation of the output branches o of E_K, we can apply some linear algebra in the following way: First, we observe the inverse of matrix B.

$$
B^{-1} = \frac{1}{t-1} \begin{pmatrix} 2-t & & & 1 \\ & 2-t & & \\ & & \ddots & \\ 1 & & & 2-t \end{pmatrix}
$$

Multiplying the vector of output branches o by B^{-1} limits occurrence of any σ_i in any one component of o to exactly once. This corresponds to every σ_i occurring on only one "combined output branch".

$$
B^{-1} \cdot o = B^{-1} \cdot A^r \cdot x + (\underbrace{I_{r \bmod t} | \overbrace{I_t | \ldots | I_t}^{\lfloor \frac{r}{t} \rfloor \text{ times}}}_{r \text{ columns}}) \cdot \sigma \tag{6}
$$

where $I_t \in \mathbb{F}_p^{t \times t}$ is the identity matrix and $I_{r \bmod t}$ are the right $r \bmod t$ columns of I_t.

From Eq. (6) in combination with Corollary 2 we can derive

$$
\deg(\mathsf{first\_component}(B^{-1} \cdot o)) \tag{7}
$$
$$
= \deg(\sigma_{r-t} + \sigma_{r-2t} + \cdots + B^{-1} A^r x) = \deg(\sigma_{r-t})
$$
$$
= d^{r-2t+2}
$$

for $\ell = t - 1$.

Complexity Improvements. Using the polynomial $\mathsf{first\_component}(B^{-1} \cdot o)$ of Eq. 7 instead of the rightmost branch in the analysis of Sects. 5.1–5.3 lowers the complexities involved. Step 1 and 3 are unaffected by branch subtraction since the complexities do not depend on the number of rounds r. For S2, the computational complexity is $l_{lm}(d^{r-2t+2})$ as opposed to $l_{lm}(d^{r-t})$.

Data complexity with branch subtraction is $d^{r-2t+2} + 1$ as opposed to $d^{r-t} + 1$ without. Space complexity stays $\mathcal{O}(1)$ since the same low memory algorithm for recovery is being used. A summary of all the complexities with and without branch subtraction can be found in Sect. 5.6.

In order to achieve these improvements, B^{-1} needs to be applied to the output branches o. Since we only need the first component of vector $B^{-1} \cdot o$, we can limit ourselves to one product between two vectors of length r, where each of the components has degree at most d^{r-t+1}. The time complexity for r many multiplications of two polynomials of degree at most d^{r-t+1} is $r\mathsf{M}(d^{r-t+1})$.

5.5   Key Recovery with Multiple Keys

Our target case for multiple keys always reduces to keys $(k_0, k_1) \in \mathbb{F}_p^2$, i.e. keys k_i for $i \geqslant 2$ do not influence the analysis, we interpret round keys k_i as derived from k_0 and k_1.

We consider the round key scheduling $k_i = (i+1) \times k_{i \pmod 2}$ for $i \geqslant 0$. As opposed to the variant where the same key is added in every round, the methods from Sect. 5.3 building on Proposition 2 are not directly applicable. Instead, we use the results of Proposition 3. Furthermore, we use multiple instances of the equation $Q_i(K) = z_i$ for different constants b_i for $i \in \{0, 1, 2\}$. This is an adaptation of the approach used in [15] where the authors analyzed balanced Feistel networks.

In Proposition 3, let $\ell = 1$, which corresponds to inputs of the form $(b_i, x, b_i, \ldots, b_i)$. Then, the second highest coefficient of the rightmost branch of E_K is of the form $Q_i(K) = d^{r-2}(a_{d-1} + d\beta_i)$ where $\beta_i = \sigma_0 + k_1 = f(b_i + k_0) + k_1$. Thus, we have $Q_i(K) \in \mathbb{F}_p[k_0, k_1] \subsetneq \mathbb{F}_p[K]$.

We combine the three equations $Q_i(K) = z_i$ in the following manner: By solving for β_i we have

$$\begin{aligned}
\beta_0 &= f(b_0 + k_0) + k_1 = \frac{z_0}{d^{r-1}} - \frac{a_{d-1}}{d} \\
\beta_1 &= f(b_1 + k_0) + k_1 = \frac{z_1}{d^{r-1}} - \frac{a_{d-1}}{d} \\
\beta_2 &= f(b_2 + k_0) + k_1 = \frac{z_2}{d^{r-1}} - \frac{a_{d-1}}{d}
\end{aligned} \tag{8}$$

For $0 \leqslant i, j \leqslant 2$ we get, through subtracting and rearranging,

$$\Delta_{(i,j)} := f(b_i + k_0) - f(b_j + k_0) - \frac{z_i - z_j}{d^{r-1}} = 0 \tag{9}$$

As in Sect. 5.3, it holds by the factor theorem that $(k_0 - \bar{k}_0)$ is a factor of $\Delta_{(i,j)}$ due to the construction of $Q_i(K)$. $\bar{k}_0$ can be found by computing the gcd $(\Delta_{(0,1)}, \Delta_{(0,2)})$. Substituting k_0 with $\bar{k}_0$ in any of Eq. (8) yields $\bar{k}_1$.

$$\bar{k}_1 = \frac{z_0}{d^{r-1}} - \frac{a_{d-1}}{d} - f(b_0 + \bar{k}_0) \tag{10}$$

Complexity (of S1 and S2). Computing the algebraic form of the second highest coefficient can be done in constant time and space. For the complexities of recovering the value of the second highest coefficient, we refer to Sect. 5.2, restating the computational complexity of $\mathsf{I}_{lm}(d^{r-1})$ here. Data complexity is $3d^{r-1} + 3$.

Complexity (of S3). Computing the gcd of polynomials of degree D has computational complexity $\mathsf{G}(D) = \mathcal{O}\left(D\log^2 D\right)$, as discussed in Sect. 5.3. Since, $D = d$, the complexity for recovering $\bar{k}_0$ is $\mathsf{G}(d)$. Once, we recover k_0, the k_1 can be found by using one of the Eq. (8).

5.6 Summary of Complexities

In the sections above, a few approaches for key recovery are proposed. In the case of a single key $\bar{k}$, i.e. $K = (\bar{k}, \ldots, \bar{k})$, we pointed out a novel method using root finding and applied an existing method using the gcd. The time and data complexities of the different approaches are summarized in Table 1. Furthermore, the sections describing the approaches are pointed out. Since the algebraic degree of the round function d is assumed to be small, space complexities are omitted in this overview. In most cases, the interpolation step dominates the computational as well as data complexity.

Table 1. Complexities of low memory interpolation cryptanalysis for $\mathsf{UFN}_{\mathsf{erf}}[p, r, t]$ for $r > 2t$ and $\mathsf{UFN}_{\mathsf{crf}}[p, r, t]$ for $r > t$. The branch subtraction technique of Sect. 5.4 is denoted by "bs".$\mathsf{M}, \mathsf{M}', \mathsf{I}_{lm}, \mathsf{G}$ and R are defined in Sect. 5.2 and Sect. 5.1.

Primitive	Strategy	Time		Data	Section
ERF	root	$\mathsf{M}'(d^{t-1}) + \mathsf{I}_{lm}(d^{r-t}) + \mathsf{R}(d^{t-1})$		$\mathcal{O}\left(d^{r-t}\right)$	5.3
	gcd	$\mathsf{M}'(d^{t-1}) + \mathsf{I}_{lm}(d^{r-t}) + \mathsf{G}(d^{t-1})$		$\mathcal{O}\left(d^{r-t}\right)$	5.3
	root (bs)	$\mathsf{M}'(d^{t-1}) + \mathsf{I}_{lm}(d^{r-2t+2}) + \mathsf{R}(d^{t-1})$		$\mathcal{O}\left(d^{r-2t+2}\right)$	5.3, 5.4
	gcd (bs)	$r\mathsf{M}(d^{r-t+1}) + \mathsf{I}_{lm}(d^{r-2t+2}) + \mathsf{G}(d^{t-1})$		$\mathcal{O}\left(d^{r-2t+2}\right)$	5.3, 5.4
	multikey	$\mathsf{I}_{lm}(d^{r-1}) + \mathsf{G}(d)$		$\mathcal{O}\left(d^{r-1}\right)$	5.5
CRF	root	$\mathsf{I}_{lm}(d^{r-t}) + \mathsf{R}(d)$		$\mathcal{O}\left(d^{r-t}\right)$	6
	gcd	$\mathsf{I}_{lm}(d^{r-t}) + \mathsf{G}(d)$		$\mathcal{O}\left(d^{r-t}\right)$	6
	multikey	$\mathsf{I}_{lm}(d^{r-1}) + \mathsf{G}(d)$		$\mathcal{O}\left(d^{r-t}\right)$	6

5.7 Experimental Verification

We have validated our analysis by running small scale experiments. The UFN instances use randomized key, round constants, and coefficients for the round function. Since our analysis considers monic round functions, the highest coefficient of the round function is always 1. The fixed parameters of our experiments are $q = 99999989, r = 17, t = 4$. The round function is of degree 3. We use both proposed methods of key recovery, namely root finding and the gcd method, and apply the branch subtraction technique of Sect. 5.4. Given above parameters, the degree of the combined output polynomial for $\mathsf{UFN}_{\mathsf{erf}}$ is 3^{11}.

It is interesting to observe the average number of roots: Although up to $3^{4-1}+1 = 10$ roots could occur in theory, our experiments show that in practice, this number is significantly lower, with an average of only 1.89 roots.

Table 2. Observed average running times in milliseconds for key recovery of UFN$_{erf}[p, 17, 4]$ using root finding and the gcd method. The degree of the interpolated polynomial was 3^{11}. ($n = 100$)

	root	gcd
Algebraic coefficient	0.08950	0.10453
Coefficient value	1 468.50751	3 132.21874
Key recovery	0.80580	0.03565
Total	1 469.40283	3 132.35892

Our experiments are implemented in python using sagemath [21]. All random values were generated using python's built in "random" module. Measurements were taken on a machine with a standard Intel Core i5-6300U CPU and 7.22 GiB of RAM. Each experiment was run $n = 100$ times. A summary of the observed average running times can be found in Table 2. We note that the discrepancy of about factor 2 between the two applied methods comes from the fact that the gcd method requires interpolating two polynomials. For the root finding method, only one polynomial is required.

6   Cryptanalysis of UFN$_{crf}$

We now analyze UFNs in the CRF variant according to the steps outlined in Sect. 4. Since the analysis is extremely similar to the ERF variant, covered in section Sect. 5, we only point out significant differences. Notably, recovering the value of the second highest coefficient as well as key recovery with only one round key $\bar{k}$, i. e. $\bar{K} = (\bar{k}, \ldots, \bar{k})$ are not reiterated herein.

ALGEBRAIC EXPRESSION OF SECOND HIGHEST COEFFICIENT. In a UFN$_{crf}[p, r, t]$, the polynomial representing the leftmost output branch has the lowest degree, as shown in Proposition 4. For this branch, the second highest coefficient $Q(K)$ has form $d^{r-t-1}(a_{d-1} + d\beta)$, with $\beta = (t-2)b + f((t-1)b + k_0) + k_1$, as shown in Corollary 3. This coefficient is simpler than that of a UFN$_{erf}$, as it depends only on k_0 and k_1. Consequently, computing $Q(K)$ is simpler, as described in Algorithm 2.

Algorithm 2: Second highest coefficient of leftmost branch in UFN$_{crf}[p, r, t]$ on input $(x, b, \ldots, b)$.

Input: r, t, f, branch constant b, round constants c_0, c_1
Output: polynomial $q(K)$ for second highest coefficient of leftmost branch
1 $\beta := f((t-1)b + k_0 + c_0) + (t-2)b + k_1 + c_1$
2 **return** $d^{r-t-1}(a_{d-1} + d\beta)$

Complexity (of S1). Calculating the algebraic form of the second highest coefficient requires only addition and multiplication of scalars. Thus, the complexity is $\mathcal{O}(1)$.

VALUE OF SECOND HIGHEST COEFFICIENT. We recover the second highest coefficient of the *leftmost* branch for UFN$_{crf}$. Consequently, evaluation points y_j for the interpolation are the values of the leftmost output branch. Inputs of the form $x_j = (\alpha^j, b, \ldots, b)$ are used for the low memory interpolation, where $\alpha \in \mathbb{F}_p$ is a primitive element as before. These changes allow application of Corollary 3.

Complexity (of S2). The complexities do not change from those of UFN$_{erf}$ in Sect. 5.2, i.e., it remains $\mathsf{l}_{lm}(d^{r-t})$.

Complexity (of S3). This is the final key recovery step. For the case of single key, the complexity of this step using GCD technique is $\mathsf{G}(d)$ and using root finding technique is $\mathsf{R}(d)$.

KEY RECOVERY IN THE GENERAL CASE. We now consider UFN$_{crf}$ $E_{\bar{K}}$ with general $\bar{K}$, starting with the bivariate case. That is, $\bar{K} = (\bar{k}_0, \ldots, \bar{k}_{r-1})$ where $\bar{k}_i$ is derived from $\bar{k}_0$ and $\bar{k}_1$. Like in Sect. 5.5, we consider the round key scheduling $k_i = (i+1) \times k_{i \pmod 2}$ for $i \geqslant 0$. The algebraic form of the second highest coefficient is $Q_i(K) = d^{r-1}(a_{d-1} + d\beta_i)$ where $\beta_i = (t-2)b_i + f((t-1)b_i + k_0) + k_1$, as shown in Proposition 4.

Combining the three equations $Q_i(K) = z_i$ works the same way as in Sect. 5.5. Due to the different form of β_i, the equations change slightly: By solving for β_i we have

$$\beta_i = (t-2)b_i + f((t-1)b_i + k_0) + k_1 = \frac{z_i}{d^r} - \frac{a_{d-1}}{d} \tag{11}$$

For $2 \geqslant i, j \geqslant 0$ we get, through subtracting and rearranging,

$$\Delta_{(i,j)} := f((t-1)b_i + k_0) - f((t-1)b_j + k_0) + (t-2)(b_i - b_j) + \frac{z_i - z_j}{d^r} = 0 \tag{12}$$

Now, as in Sect. 5.3, we recover $\bar{k}_0$ by finding $\gcd\left(\Delta_{(0,1)}, \Delta_{(0,2)}\right)$. Then $\bar{k}_1$ can be found using one of the Eq. (11).

Complexity (of S1-S3). Although the form of $q(k)$ and β are slightly different from those in UFN$_{erf}$, the steps are fundamentally the same as for the ERF variant. Thus, the complexities don't differ from those in Sect. 5.5. We summarize the complexities of the different key recovery approaches for UFN$_{crf}$ in Table 1.

Experimental Verification. Just as for UFN$_{erf}$ in Sect. 5.7, we performed small scale experiments for UFN$_{crf}$ with the same number of rounds $r = 17$ and branches $t = 4$. Because the branch subtraction technique of Sect. 5.4 does not apply to UFN$_{crf}$, the degree of the polynomial that is to be interpolated is 3^{13}. Running times of the experiments can be found in Table 3. We note that for the root finding technique, the average length of the key candidate list was 2.1, extremely similar to those of the experiments on UFN$_{erf}$ of Sect. 5.7.

Table 3. Observed average running times in milliseconds for key recovery of $\text{UFN}_{\text{crf}}[p, 17, 4]$ using root finding and the gcd method. The degree of the interpolated polynomial was 3^{13}. $(n = 100)$

	root	gcd
Algebraic coefficient	0.03036	0.04744
Coefficient value	11 832.86184	23 482.13424
Key recovery	0.48999	0.02876
Total	11 833.38219	23 482.21044

7   Cryptanalysis of UFN Based Sponge Hash

Either of the UFNs may be used in a Sponge mode to construct a hash function over $\mathbb{F}_p$. The permutation thereof is instantiated with a fixed key UFN. An example of such hash function is recently proposed GMiMCHash [2]. Here we will describe how the root finding technique can be used to find collision in such hash function. We will assume that the rate in Sponge mode is $r = \log_2 p$ (bits) and the hash value also has the same size. An input message to the hash function $\in \mathbb{F}_p^s$ for $s \geqslant 1$ and consists of message block that are elements of $\mathbb{F}_p$.

PREIMAGE AND SECOND PREIMAGE ATTACK. Let us consider a message $M' = (m'_0, m'_1) \in \mathbb{F}_p^2$ of size $2r$ bits. It is clear that the UFN must have branch size r bits. Suppose, f denotes the permutation instantiated with a fixed key UFN and the rightmost output branch corresponds to the rate in Sponge mode. We find a second preimage M in the following way

1. Choose arbitrary message block $m_0 \in \mathbb{F}_p$. Suppose, h_t ($\in \mathbb{F}_p$) denotes the first r bits (and the rightmost output branch) of $f(m_0)$ and h_i for $i = 2, \ldots t$ denote the outputs corresponding to the $t - 1$ branches of the UFN. Let h be the hash value of the message $M' = (m'_0, m'_1)$.
2. Compute the polynomial $P(x)$ corresponding to the first output branch of the UFN for the input $h_1, h_2, \ldots, h_t + x$. Note that $P(x)$ is the polynomial corresponding to the hash value of (m_0, x).
3. Find the roots of $P(x) - h$.

Note that any root of $P(x) - h$ gives a second preimage attack.

Instead of choosing h as hash value of a message if we choose it arbitrarily then the above attack gives a *preimage* attack on the hash function.

Complexity. The complexity of finding all roots (without multiplicities) is of a polynomial of degree D over $\mathbb{F}_p$ is $\mathsf{R}(D)$. For UFN_{erf} the degree of the polynomial $P(x)$ after r rounds is d^{r-t}. Hence, the the complexity of the root finding step is $\mathsf{R}(d^{r-t})$.

COLLISION ATTACK. Choose two message blocks $m_0, m'_0 \in \mathbb{F}_p$. Then, a collision attack on the hash function is described as following

1. Compute the polynomial $P(x)$ representing the hash value of a message of the form (m_0, x) and $P'(x)$ corresponding to the hash value of the message (m'_0, x).
2. Compute the roots of $Q(x) := P(x) - P'(x)$.

The complexity of the collision attack is same as the complexity of the preimage or second preimage attacks. The degree of the polynomial Q is d^{r-t-1}.

INCREASING THE RATE. If the rate is increased to $2r$ then the attacks apply similarly. For preimage and second preimage attack we choose the message $M = ((m'_{00}, m'_{01}), (m'_{10}, m'_{11}))$ where each $m_{ij} \in \mathbb{F}_p$. The polynomial is constructed for $((m_{00}, m_{01}), (m_{10}, x))$. The collision attack also applies analogously as for rate r. The hash output is in $\mathbb{F}_p$. The complexities remains the same since the degree of the does not change.

We point out that the number of rounds for the UFN$_{\text{erf}}$ given in the GMiMC proposal is not explicitly justified by analyzing the security of the hash function.

7.1 Experimental Verification

We evaluate our results from Sect. 7 by running small scale experiments. We regarded GMiMC$_{\text{erf}}[p, r, t]$ permutation with $p = 99999989$, $3 \leqslant r \leqslant 7$, $3 \leqslant t \leqslant 6$ with $k = 0$ to instantiate the hash function for two different sets of experiments: Finding second preimages and finding collisions. The round constants were randomly chosen and fixed. For each combination of (r, t) in the given intervals, 100 experiments were performed. The messages were re-randomized for every experiment. The experiments were implemented in python using sagemath. To generate the random values, pythons "random" module was used. All the measurements were taken on a machine with a standard Intel Core i5-6300U CPU and 7.22 GiB of RAM.

For the experiments on second preimages, across all 2000 experiments, we observed a total of 751 iterations where no second preimage was found. We consider these experiments to have failed. This puts the estimated success probability of finding at least one preimage to 62.5%. Of secondary interest is the average number of second preimages found given that the attack was successful, i.e. at least one second preimage was found. Over all the 1249 successful experiments, an average of 1.55 s preimages were observed per experiment.

For the experiments on collisions, no collision could be found in 712 of the 2000 experiments. We consider these experiments to have failed. The success probability is thus 64.4%. Of secondary interest is the average number of collisions found in the successful experiments, i.e. at least one collision was found. In 1288 successful experiments, an average of 1.57 collisions were observed per experiment. The failure rates of 37.6% and 35.6% respectively are supported by the fact that for our parameters (p and degree of the underlying polynomial), $\approx 36.8\%$ of the polynomials do not have a root [14]. We elaborate on this in Appendix D.

Table 5 and 6 in Appendix C summarize running times of our experiments on second preimages and collisions. In Fig. 4 in Appendix C, the number of second preimages found in our experiments is plotted. Similarly, Fig. 5 in Appendix C visualizes the number of collisions found.

8   Attacks on Reduced Round GMiMC

The GMiMC family has two members that are based on UFN: GMiMC$_{erf}$ and GMiMC$_{crf}$. The round function used in both variants is $f(x) = x^3$, i.e., $d = 3$. Due to target applications we can also assume that field size is bounded e.g. $\log_2 p \leqslant 256$. For some specific sizes of the field and number of branches in the UFNs, we show the number of rounds of GMiMC block cipher and hash functions that can be attacked in Table 4. Our analysis of the GMiMCHash instances does not contradict their security claims in the GMiMC proposal [2] (in terms of number of secure rounds).

Table 4. Number of attacked rounds for specific GMiMC instances of GMiMC block ciphers and hash functions. For hash function the arity denotes the ratio of no. of branches used for hash output and total number of branches(t) in UFN.

Primitive	Type	$\log_2 p$	Security	t/Arity	Rounds	Time	Data	Attack type
GMiMC$_{erf}$	BC	128	128	4	60	2^{92}	2^{54}	KR
GMiMC$_{erf}$	Permutation	61	128	12	102	2^{48}	–	ZS [8]
GMiMC$_{erf}$	Permutation	125	256	14	206	2^{125}	–	ZS [8]
GMiMC$_{crf}$		256	256	4	100	2^{159}	2^{96}	KR
GMiMC$_{erf}$Hash	Hash	254	127	1:4	60	2^{119}	–	Coll
GMiMC$_{erf}$Hash	Hash	61	128	4:12	52	2^{83}	–	Coll [8]

Recently, in [8] a collision attack on GMiMCHash-256 was proposed for a field $\mathbb{F}_q$ with $q = 2^{125} + 266 \times 2^{64} + 1$ and $t = 14$. This means the hash output is $\mathbb{F}_q^2$. However, our described method is designed for a hash output in $\mathbb{F}_p$. Since the choice of hash outputs over a field in the two cases are incomparable, a direct comparison of our collision attack with the collision attack in [8] (in terms of complexity or number of rounds attacked) is not meaningful. For the attacks on GMiMC block ciphers, we provide key recovery attack on (reduced) 60-round GMiMC$_{erf}$ over a prime field of size 128 bits. On the other hand a zero-sum(ZS) distinguisher on the full GMiMC(ERF) permutation (with fixed key) over $\mathbb{F}_q$ with $\log q = 125$ is proposed in [8].

A   Proofs

A.1   Proof of Proposition 1

Proof. Suppose that Proposition 1 holds for fix r. Applying one more round $r+1$ yields the following, according to Eq. (1):

$$\sigma_r = f(P_0^{(r)} + k_r)$$
$$(P_0^{(r+1)}, P_1^{(r+1)}, P_2^{(r+1)}) = (P_1^{(r)} + \sigma_r, P_2^{(r)} + \sigma_r, P_0^{(r)})$$

Developing σ_r by the binomial theorem we get the following:

$$\sigma_r = (P_0^{(r)} + k_r)^d + \sum_{i=0}^{d-1} a_i (P_0^{(r)} + k_r)^i$$

$$= (x^{d^{r-2}} + d^{r-3}(a_{d-1} + d\beta)x^{d^{r-2}-1} + \cdots + a_0 + k_r)^d + \sum_{i=0}^{d-1} a_i (P_0^{(r)} + k_r)^i$$

$$= (x^{d^{r-2}})^d + d \cdot d^{r-3}(a_{d-1} + d\beta)x^{d^{r-2}-1}(x^{d^{r-2}})^{d-1} + \cdots + (d^{r-3}(a_{d-1} + d\beta)x^{d^{r-2}-1})^d$$

$$+ \cdots + a_0^d + \cdots + k_r^d + \sum_{i=0}^{d-1} a_i (P_0^{(r)} + k_r)^i$$

$$= x^{d^{r-1}} + d^{r-2}(a_{d-1} + d\beta)x^{d^{r-1}-1} + \cdots + a_0$$

By the assumption of the induction, $\deg(P_2^{(r)}) \leqslant \deg(P_1^{(r)}) \leqslant d^{r-2}$. Thus the degree of σ_r dominates, which leads us to the proofs first conclusions.

$$\deg(P_0^{(r+1)}) = \deg(P_1^{(r+1)}) = \deg(\sigma_r) = x^{d^{r-1}}$$

$$\mathsf{coeff}(P_0^{(r+1)}, x^{d^{r-1}}) = \mathsf{coeff}(P_1^{(r+1)}, x^{d^{r-1}}) = \mathsf{coeff}(\sigma_r, x^{d^{r-1}}) = 1$$

Since, by assumption, $d \geqslant 3$ and $r \geqslant 4$, it holds that $d^{r-1} - 1 > d^{r-2}$. The coefficients of the second highest term in $P_0^{(r+1)}$ and $P_1^{(r+1)}$ are thus solely contributed by σ_r. This leads us to the proofs last conclusion.

$$\mathsf{coeff}(P_0^{(r+1)}, x^{d^{r-1}-1}) = \mathsf{coeff}(P_1^{(r+1)}, x^{d^{r-1}-1}) = \mathsf{coeff}(\sigma_r, x^{d^{r-1}-1}) = d^{r-2}(a_{d-1} + d\beta)$$

A.2   Proof of Proposition 2

Proof. Because of the position of the variable x, $(t-1)$ many "swappings" of branches need to be performed before x becomes part of the input to a round function. Each round of the UFN performs exactly one such swap. Thus, we observe that x does not contribute to σ_i for the first $(t-2)$ rounds, i.e. $\deg(\sigma_i) = 0$ for $i < t - 1$. In the $(t-1)$-st round, we have the following:

$$\sigma_{t-1} = f(x + \sigma_0 + \cdots + \sigma_{t-2} + k_{t-1})$$
$$= f(x + \beta)$$

$$= (x + \beta)^d + a_{d-1}(x + \beta)^{d-1} + \sum_{i=0}^{d-2} a_i (x + \beta)^i$$

$$= x^d + d\beta x^{d-1} + \cdots + d\beta^{d-1}x + \beta^d$$
$$+ a_{d-1}x^{d-1} + a_{d-1}(d-1)\beta x^{d-2} + \cdots + a_{d-1}(d-1)\beta^{d-2}x + a_{d-1}\beta^{d-1}$$

$$+ \sum_{i=0}^{d-2} a_i (x + \beta)^i$$

$$= x^d + (a_{d-1} + d\beta)x^{d-1} + \cdots + a_0$$

Now, we can use induction over r much in the same way as in Proposition 1.

A.3 Proof of Proposition 4

Proof. After 1 round, we have

$$\sigma_0 = f(\sum_{j=1}^{t-1} b + k_0) = f((t-1)b + k_0)$$

$$(P_0^{(1)}, \ldots, P_{t-2}^{(1)}, P_{t-1}^{(1)}) = (b, \ldots, b, x + \sigma_0)$$

After 2 rounds, we have

$$\sigma_1 = f(\sum_{j=1}^{t-2} b + x + \sigma_0 + k_1) = f(x + \beta)$$

$$(P_0^{(2)}, \ldots, P_{t-2}^{(2)}, P_{t-1}^{(2)}) = (b, \ldots, x + \sigma_0, b + \sigma_1)$$

Expanding σ_1 by the binomial theorem yields the following:

$$\sigma_1 = f(x + \beta)$$

$$= (x + \beta)^d + a_{d-1}(x + \beta)^{d-1} + \sum_{i=0}^{d-2} a_i(x + \beta)^i$$

$$= x^d + d\beta x^{d-1} + \cdots + \beta^d$$

$$+ a_{d-1}x^{d-1} + a_{d-1}(d-1)\beta x^{d-2} + \cdots + a_{d-1}\beta^{d-1} + \sum_{i=0}^{d-2} a_i(x + \beta)^i$$

$$= x^d + (a_{d-1} + d\beta)x^{d-1} + \cdots + a_0$$

After expanding σ_1, an induction over r like in Proposition 1 finishes the proof.

B   Reduced Round Instances of UFN$_{\text{erf}}$ and UFN$_{\text{crf}}$

We depict the progression of an input (b, b, b, x) through 5 rounds of UFN$_{\text{erf}}$ with 4 branches in Fig. 2. In Fig. 3, we show the progression of an input variable through 4 rounds of UFN$_{\text{erf}}$ with 3 branches and variable input in the rightmost branch as well as UFN$_{\text{crf}}$ with 3 branches and variable input in the leftmost branch.

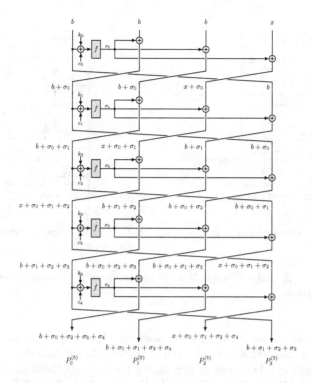

Fig. 2. Example of summands being added in a UFN$_{\text{erf}}$

C   Plots and runtime summaries for GMiMCHash Experiments

In Table 5 and 6 we summarize the running times for the experiments from Sect. 7.1 for $5 \leqslant r \leqslant 7$ and $3 \leqslant t \leqslant 6$. The running times for reconstruction of the polynomial and root finding are reported alongside the total running times.

In Fig. 4, the number of second preimages found in our experiments is plotted. Similarly, Fig. 5 visualizes the number of collisions found. In the subfigures, different numbers of branches t are depicted. Each subfigure shows, for different

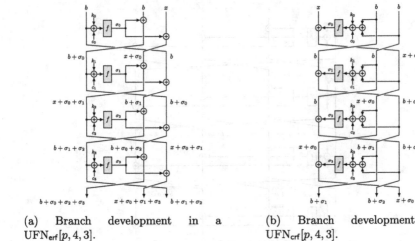

(a) Branch development in a
$UFN_{erf}[p, 4, 3]$.

(b) Branch development in a
$UFN_{crf}[p, 4, 3]$.

Fig. 3. $UFN_{erf}[4, 3]$ and $UFN_{crf}[4, 3]$ with rightmost and leftmost branch input as variable respectively.

numbers of rounds r on the x-axis, the number of additional preimages or collisions on the y-axis found over the 100 randomized experiments. For example, when regarding $t = 3$ branches in Fig. 4a, for the GMiMCHash instance instantiated with $GMiMC_{erf}$ with $r = 6$ rounds, there were 14 of our 100 experiments in which we found 2 preimages, and 9 in which we found 3 preimages. A red bar signifies that no preimage (or no collision for Fig. 5) was found, while the green bars indicate at least one second preimage (or collision, respectively) found, i.e. a successful attack.

D   Roots of Random Polynomials over a Finite Field

In order to validate our failure rate of Sect. 7.1, we calculate the probability that a random polynomial of degree d has no roots in a specific finite field. A formula t_d for the number of polynomials of degree d over finite field $\mathbb{F}_q$ that have no root in $\mathbb{F}_q$ is given in lemma 1 in [14] and reproduced in Eq. (13).

$$t_d = \sum_{i=0}^{d}(-1)^i \binom{q}{i} q^{d-i} \tag{13}$$

The total number of polynomials of degree d over $\mathbb{F}_q$ is q^d. Our parameters are $q = 99999989$ and $d = 3^i$ with $3 \leqslant i \leqslant 7$. This results in a probability of a random polynomial not having any root in $\mathbb{F}_q$ of $t_d/q^d \approx 36.8\%$ for any i in the given interval.

Table 5. Observed average running times in milliseconds for finding second preimages of GMiMCHash using GMiMC$_{\mathrm{erf}}[p, r, t]$. ($n = 100$ per column)

	$r = 5$	$r = 6$	$r = 7$
construct poly	0.0003	0.0003	0.0003
root finding	0.0005	0.0005	0.0004
total	0.0008	0.0009	0.0008

(a) $t = 3$

	$r = 5$	$r = 6$	$r = 7$
construct poly	0.0019	0.0019	0.0019
root finding	0.0026	0.0029	0.0032
total	0.0046	0.0049	0.0052

(b) $t = 4$

	$r = 5$	$r = 6$	$r = 7$
construct poly	0.0233	0.0235	0.0229
root finding	0.0263	0.0267	0.0268
total	0.0498	0.0503	0.0498

(c) $t = 5$

	$r = 5$	$r = 6$	$r = 7$
construct poly	0.2966	0.2940	0.2954
root finding	0.3018	0.3016	0.3025
total	0.5999	0.5971	0.5996

(d) $t = 6$

Table 6. Observed average running times in milliseconds for collision finding of GMiMCHash using GMiMC$_{\mathrm{erf}}[p, r, t]$. ($n = 100$ per column)

	$r = 5$	$r = 6$	$r = 7$
construct poly	0.0006	0.0006	0.0006
root finding	0.0004	0.0004	0.0004
total	0.0010	0.0010	0.0010

(a) $t = 3$

	$r = 5$	$r = 6$	$r = 7$
construct poly	0.0037	0.0037	0.0042
root finding	0.0028	0.0030	0.0038
total	0.0065	0.0067	0.0080

(a) $t = 4$

	$r = 5$	$r = 6$	$r = 7$
construct poly	0.0458	0.0457	0.0458
root finding	0.0275	0.0280	0.0269
total	0.0733	0.0738	0.0728

(a) $t = 5$

	$r = 5$	$r = 6$	$r = 7$
construct poly	0.6015	0.6012	0.6801
root finding	0.3116	0.3063	0.3536
total	0.9131	0.9075	1.0338

(a) $t = 6$

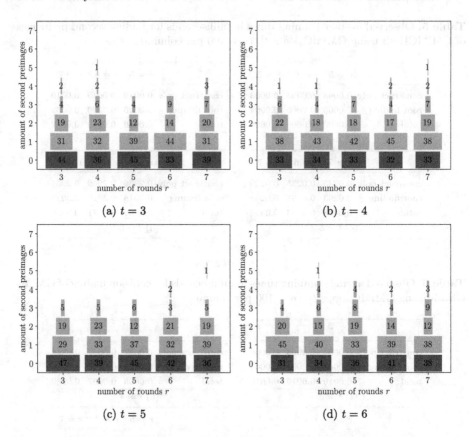

Fig. 4. Number of second preimages found for various numbers of rounds with GMiM-CHash using $GMiMC_{erf}[p, r, t]$. ($n = 100$ per given (r, t))

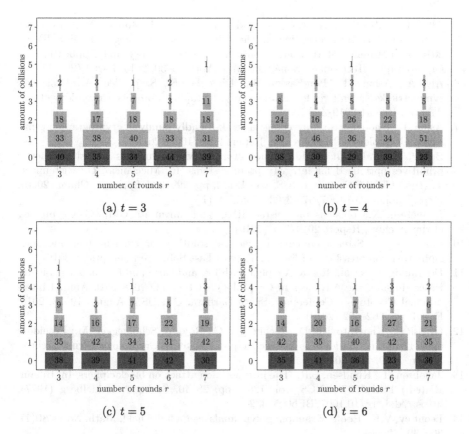

Fig. 5. Number of collisions found for various numbers of rounds with GMiMCHash using $\text{GMiMC}_{\text{erf}}[p, r, t]$. ($n = 100$ per given (r, t))

References

1. Albrecht, M., Grassi, L., Rechberger, C., Roy, A., Tiessen, T.: MiMC: efficient encryption and cryptographic hashing with minimal multiplicative complexity. In: Cheon, J.H., Takagi, T. (eds.) ASIACRYPT 2016. LNCS, vol. 10031, pp. 191–219. Springer, Heidelberg (2016). https://doi.org/10.1007/978-3-662-53887-6_7
2. Albrecht, M.R., et al.: Feistel structures for MPC, and more. In: Proceedings of the Computer Security - ESORICS 2019–24th European Symposium on Research in Computer Security, Luxembourg, 23–27 September 2019, Part II, pp. 151–171 (2019)
3. Albrecht, M.R., et al.: Feistel structures for MPC, and more. Cryptology ePrint Archive, Report 2019/397 (2019)
4. Albrecht, M.R., Grassi, L., Rechberger, C., Roy, A., Tiessen, T.: Mimc: efficient encryption and cryptographic hashing with minimal multiplicative complexity. In: Proceedings of the Advances in Cryptology - ASIACRYPT 2016–22nd International Conference on the Theory and Application of Cryptology and Information Security, Hanoi, Vietnam, 4–8 December 2016, Part I (2016)

5. Albrecht, M.R., Rechberger, C., Schneider, T., Tiessen, T., Zohner. M.: Ciphers for MPC and FHE. In: Proceedings of the Advances in Cryptology - EUROCRYPT 2015–34th Annual International Conference on the Theory and Applications of Cryptographic Techniques, Sofia, Bulgaria, April 26–30, 2015, Part I (2015)

6. Aly, A., Ashur, T., Ben-Sasson, E., Dhooghe, S., Szepieniec, A.: Design of symmetric-key primitives for advanced cryptographic protocols. Cryptology ePrint Archive, Report 2019/426 (2019)

7. Ashur,T., Dhooghe, S.: Marvellous: a stark-friendly family of cryptographic primitives. Cryptology ePrint Archive, Report 2018/1098 (2018)

8. Beyne, T., et al.: Out of oddity – new cryptanalytic techniques against symmetric primitives optimized for integrity proof systems. In: Micciancio, D., Ristenpart, T. (eds.) CRYPTO 2020. LNCS, vol. 12172, pp. 299–328. Springer, Cham (2020). https://doi.org/10.1007/978-3-030-56877-1_11

9. Bonnetain. X.:Collisions on Feistel-MiMC and univariate GMiMC. Cryptology ePrint Archive, Report 2019/951 (2019)

10. Canteaut, A.: Stream ciphers: a practical solution for efficient homomorphic-ciphertext compression. In: Peyrin, T. (ed.) Fast Software Encryption (2016)

11. Dobraunig. C., et al.: Rasta: A cipher with low anddepth and few ands per bit. In: Proceedings of the Advances in Cryptology - CRYPTO 2018–38th Annual International Cryptology Conference, Santa Barbara, CA, USA, August 19–23, 2018, Part I, pp. 662–692 (2018)

12. Grassi, L., Khovratovich, D., Rechberger, C., Roy, A., Schofnegger, M.: Poseidon: anew hash function for zero-knowledge proof systems. Cryptology ePrint Archive, Report 2019/458 (2019)

13. Jakobsen, T., Knudsen, L.R.: The interpolation attack on block ciphers. In: Biham, E. (ed.) FSE 1997. LNCS, vol. 1267, pp. 28–40. Springer, Heidelberg (1997). https://doi.org/10.1007/BFb0052332

14. Leont'ev, V.K.: Roots of random polynomials over a finite field. Math. Notes **80**(1), 300–304 (2006)

15. Li, C., Preneel, B.: Improved interpolation attacks on cryptographic primitives of low algebraic degree. Cryptology ePrint Archive, Report 2019/812 (2019)

16. Grassi, A.R.L., Rechberger, C.: Gmimcs new key schedule. Personal communication, 8 (2019)

17. Méaux, P., Journault, A., Standaert, F.X., Carlet, C.: Towards stream ciphers for efficient the with low-noise ciphertexts. Cryptology ePrint Archive, Report 2016/254 (2016)

18. Starkware: STARK-Friendly Hash Challenge. Website, 8 (2019). https://starkware. co/hash-challenge/

19. Stoss, H.-J.: The complexity of evaluating interpolation polynomials. Theor. Comput. Sci. **41**, 319–323 (1985)

20. Sun, B., Qu, L., Li, C.: New cryptanalysis of block ciphers with low algebraic degree. In: Dunkelman, O. (ed.) FSE 2009. LNCS, vol. 5665, pp. 180–192. Springer, Heidelberg (2009). https://doi.org/10.1007/978-3-642-03317-9_11

21. The Sage Developers: SageMath, the Sage Mathematics Software System (Version x.y.z), YYYY. https://www.sagemath.org

22. Zur, V., Joachim, G., Gerhard, T.: Modern Computer Algebra. Cambridge University Press, Cambridge (2013)

Unintended Features of APIs: Cryptanalysis of Incremental HMAC

Gal Benmocha[✉], Eli Biham[✉], and Stav Perle[✉]

Computer Science Department, Technion – Israel Institute of Technology, Haifa,
Israel
{gal.benmocha,biham,stavp}@cs.technion.ac.il

Abstract. Many cryptographic APIs provide extra functionality that
was not intended by the designers. In this paper we discuss such an
unintended functionality in the API of HMAC, and study the security
implications of it's use by applications.

HMAC authenticates a single message at a time with a single authentication tag. However, most HMAC implementations do not complain
when extra data is added to the stream after that tag is computed, nor
they undo the side effects of the tag computation. Think of it as an API
of a new authentication primitive, that provides tags to prefixes, rather
than just to the full message. We call such primitives Incremental MACs
(IncMACs). IncMACs may be used by applications to efficiently authenticate long messages, broken into fragments, which need their own individual authentication tag for performing an early abort or to retransmit
only bad fragments, while each tag (strongly) authenticates the message
prefix so far, and the last tag fully authenticates the full message.

It appears that some applications (e.g., Siemens S7 protocol) use
the standard HMAC API to provide an incremental MAC, allowing to
identify transmission errors as soon as the first error occurs, while also
directly authenticating the full message. We discuss two common implementations, used by cryptographic libraries and programs, whose APIs
do not forbid using them incrementally, continuing with extra data after
computing the tag. The most common one, which Siemens uses, uses a
naive implementation (as natively coded from the RFCs). The other is
the implementation of the OpenSSL library.

We discuss these implementations, and show that they are not as
secure as HMAC. Moreover, some of them may even be highly insecure
when used incrementally, where in the particular case of OpenSSL it is
possible to instantly find collisions and multi-collisions, which are also
colliding under any key. We also discuss the fine details of the definition
of IncMACs, and propose secure versions of such a primitive.

1 Introduction

It is well known that attackers are keen to use oversights of designers of security
systems. In particular, they like to use features that designers did not intend
to make accessible. This state is a security threat since in many cases when

© Springer Nature Switzerland AG 2021
O. Dunkelman et al. (Eds.): SAC 2020, LNCS 12804, pp. 301–325, 2021.
https://doi.org/10.1007/978-3-030-81652-0_12

naive implementers incorrectly use features in a wrong way, attackers may be able to build their attacks on top of these naive mistakes. Such attacks may be specially attractive when the attackers can use oversights in a standard crypto-graphic API, where application developers call an API function in a situation that the designers did not foresee, and did not check for errors but which may be attractive for the calling application.

In this paper we show that most HMAC implementations have oversights that may be used by application developers. In particular, most HMAC imple-mentations allow to call further API functions after a digest is computed, though the designers of HMAC considered that the digest calculation is the last activity in the HMAC computation. We also show that usage of this oversight may be a security catastrophe, and discuss several such cases. The most common HMAC implementation, when used incrementally, such as by Siemens in their S7 proto-col of their industrial control systems, is not as secure as HMAC. Another one, used in OpenSSL, is highly insecure when used incrementally. It has an instant attack for finding key-independent collisions (collisions that hold for any key). We also discuss forgery, key-recovery and other attacks.

1.1   Authentication of Fragmented Messages

In networks communication, messages are typically fragmented, and each frag-ment is sent separately. If authentication of a full message is needed, the authen-tication tag is computed by a Message Authentication Code (MAC) on the full message, and appended to the end of the message. The problem is that only after the entire message is received the receiver can verify that the message has not been modified. Moreover, the receiver has no clue which of the fragments cause the authentication error, thus the whole message should be retransmitted. If the receiver had the ability to verify authenticity of a fragment immediately after receiving it, he could have performed an early abort, saving reception of many further fragments and much resources needed to keep and process them, or request to retransmit only the non-matching fragments. Therefore, most network protocols authenticate each fragment individually (e.g., IPSec [12]).

Some protocol designers prefer incremental authentication of the fragments (authentication of each fragment in context of the prefix of the message received so far). Since there is no standard for incremental authentication of fragmented messages, developers that need such functionality design their own mode or prim-itive based on existing implementations. In many cases, it performs an incorrect usage of existing MAC primitives (such as HMAC [3]) by calling their API in an unintended way. It results with an unexpected behavior of the MAC code. An example that uses the HMAC code applies HMAC on the first fragment (using init, update, and then finalize). It then calls update with the next fragment (without an extra init, while the context still depends on the prior fragment) and then another finalize to fetch the next digest. As the designers of HMAC (like the designers of hash functions) did not anticipate that a second fragment is to be added after finalize, various implementations give different (unexpected) results in this case. Unless well planed in advance by the programmer, using such a primitive based on misuse of the API of HMAC is typically a bad solution, as we show later.

1.2   IncMACs (Incremental MACs)

In this paper we discuss incremental authentication and the security and efficiency of its implementations. For this purpose, we define IncMACs (Incremental MACs). They are similar to MACs, but with incremental authentication tags. I.e., for a message M divided to t fragments $M = (M_1, ..., M_t)$, there is an authentication tag for authenticating each prefix $M_1||...||M_i$ (the fragment M_i, $i \in \{1, ..., t\}$ together with all prior fragments). The security requirements on these many tags should be similar to those of the single tag of MACs, i.e., each tag should authenticate the full prefix. In some cases, e.g., when transferring records of a database, it is also advantageous to authenticate the division of the message to fragments. We call such a primitive a Fragment-Protecting IncMAC (FP-IncMAC).

We emphasis that it is crucial that each tag authenticates the whole prefix, rather than only the last fragment. One may claim that once each packet is authenticated, the list of tags authenticates the full message. This is true when the protocol that uses the MAC includes a session number and a sequence number in each fragment. But once the MAC is used incrementally as a single primitive, these extra additions are not there. Instead, unless we require each tag to authenticate the whole prefix, it may be the case that an attacker would be able to combine tags from different messages together in a way that will not be identified – and this would be potentially possible just because there is no requirement that strongly connects a tag to the whole prefix. It is therefore that the each tag must always authenticates the full prefix, and thus there is no reason to remember prior tags once a successor is received. Usage of IncMAC primitives provides a strong sense of authentication of the message, transmitted as many fragments. Unlike in common authentication of fragmented messages where each fragment is authenticated independently, IncMACs ensure that any authentication tag authenticates the message prefix. Therefore, no attacks based on replacing individual fragments are possible, independently of any (bad) choice of session IDs.

1.3   The Common (Native) API of Hash Functions and HMAC

Consider how a native implementation of a Merkle-Damgård hash function [7] is typically implemented (and described in the RFCs), starting with MD4 [21], through MD5 [22] to SHA-1 [15] and SHA-2 [16]. Basically, 44 The API includes three functions: init, update and finalize that use a context record with their internal data. The context typically includes the number of bits hashed so far, a chaining value, and a block-sized array that is used to keep partial blocks between calls to update. The init function initializes the context record with zero bits so far and the standard IV. The update function accepts the context record and a byte string and calls the compression function on each block of the

```
initialize{
    initialize empty b-bit buffer;
    streamSize = 0;
    intermediateValue = IV;
}

update(data){
    prepend the content stored in the buffer to the data and
        divide it into b-bit blocks;
    if the last block is not complete, store it in the buffer;
    for each block B:
        intermediateValue = compress(intermediateValue, B);
    streamSize += dataSize;
}

finalize{
    append to the content stored in the buffer a single '1' bit;
    append c '0' bits; \\ c is the smallest non negative number
        such that bufferSize + 1 + c + d is a multiple of b;
    append streamSize as a d-bit big-endian integer;
    divide it into b-bit blocks;
    for each block B:
        intermediateValue = compress(intermediateValue, B);
    return intermediateValue;
}
```

Listing 1.1. Pseudocode of a Naive Merkle-Damgård Hash Function Implementation

input. If a partial block remains at the end, it is kept in the context record, and is processed along with the next input in the next call to update. The finalize function adds the padding to the partial block in the context (sometimes requires an additional block) and compresses the padded block(s). The output of the last compression function is the output of the hash function. A pseudocode of this structure is given in Listing 1.1. A typical implementation of this structure is given in Listing 1.2.[1]

Since finalize is intended to be called last, implementations can arbitrarily choose whether they modify the context state or not during it's calculation, i.e., whether finalize adds the padding directly into the partial block kept in the context, and updates the final intermediate value into the chaining value of the context, or work on a local copy without affecting the context. As a matter of fact, most implementations chose the former case, as done in the RFCs [21], i.e., finalize writes over the context. We call this strategy the *Naive* hash implementation. This strategy is very reasonable as once finalize is called no further calls to update or finalize should be made. But if such calls are made anyway, there is a difference in the behaviour of both strategies.

The API of HMAC also includes the same three functions: init, update and finalize. The init function initializes a context record, which includes two hash contexts that serve for the inner stream and the outer stream, and mixes the key into them. The update function accepts the context record and a byte string, and calls to the hash update of the inner stream. The finalize function make two calls to the hash finalize. The first call operates on the inner stream, and the second on the outer stream. In between, update is called on the outer with the digest of the inner. The digest value of the outer stream is returned as the HMAC output tag.

---

[1] For simplicity, this implementation assumes that the inputs of the update function are always in multiples of full bytes.

```
ctx :
      buffer [b/8]
      bufferSize :  int
      streamSize :  int
      intermediateValue [n/8]
initialize {
      buffer  =  {};
      bufferSize  =  streamSize  =  0;
      intermediateValue  =  IV;
}
update (data) {
   index  =  0;
   while (index  <  data.length) {
      if (bufferSize  +  data.length−index  <  b/8) {
         buffer.append (data[index ,... , data.length − 1]);
         bufferSize  +=  data.length−index;
         index  =  data.length;
      }  else  {
         buffer.append (data[index ,... , b/8− bufferSize − 1]);
         intermediateValue  =  compress (intermediateValue ,  buffer);
         index  +=  b/8− bufferSize;
         buffer  =  {};
         bufferSize  =  0;
      }
   }
   streamSize  +=  data.length ∗8;
}
finalize {
   buffer.append (0x80);
   if (bufferSize+1  >  (b−d)/8) {
      for (int  i =0;  i  <  b/8− bufferSize −1;  i++) {
         buffer.append (0);
      }
      intermediateValue  =  compress (intermediateValue ,  buffer);
      buffer  =  {};
      bufferSize  =  0;
   }
   for (int  i =0;  i  <  (b−d)/8− bufferSize −1;  i++)  {
      buffer.append (0);
   }
   length  =  toBigEndian (streamSize ,  d);
   buffer.append (length);
   intermediateValue  =  compress (intermediateValue ,  buffer);
   buffer  =  {};
   bufferSize  =  0;
   return  intermediateValue;
}
```

Listing 1.2. Naive Merkle-Damgård Hash Function Implementation

1.4 HMAC-Based IncMAC Variants

We present three implementations of HMAC whose API does not raise an error when used as IncMACs, i.e., it is possible to call update and finalize after an earlier finalize. The implementations differs form each other only in the finalize function.

We call the first the *Naive* implementation, as it is just the common simple code, which is also common in the reference implementations and RFCs. This implementation is used by Siemens as IncMAC in their S7 protocol (e.g., while downloading a control program to a PLC).[2] Listing 1.3 shows an example code of such a Naive HMAC implementation. In this implementation, the init function initializes a context record that includes two hash contexts that serve for the inner stream and the outer stream. In this implementation, when finalize is called, two calls to the underlying hash finalize are made, both modify the content state. The first call operates on the inner stream. It pads the data of the inner stream and computes the hash value of the inner stream. Then, the HMAC updates the outer stream with the digest value of the inner stream. The second

---
[2] In their P3 protocol, e.g., between TIA V15 and PLC S7-1500 with firmware v1.8 [6].

```
ctx:
    innerStream:  ctx  of  hash
    outerStrean:  ctx  of  hash

initialize(key){
    while(key.len  <  b/8){
        key.append(0);
    }
    innerStream.initialize();
    outerStream.initialize();
    innerStream.update(key⊕ipad);
    outerStream.update(key⊕opad);
}

update(data){
    innerStream.update(data);
}

finalize{
    inner = innerStream.finalize();
    outerStream.update(inner);
    outer = outerStream.finalize();
    return outer;
}
```

Listing 1.3. Naive HMAC Implementation

```
finalize{
    outerStreamCopy = outerStream.copy();

    inner = innerStream.finalize();
    outerStreamCopy.update(inner);
    outer = outerStreamCopy.finalize();
    return outer;
}
```

Listing 1.4. The Finalize Function of the NIPO HMAC Implementation

call to the hash finalize function operates on the outer stream. Similarly to the inner stream, it pads the data and computes the hash value. The digest value of the outer stream is returned as the HMAC output.

The second implementation protects the outer stream of HMAC, so we call it the *NIPO* (Naive Inner Patched Outer) implementation. The implementation of the OpenSSL library [18] is an example for a NIPO implementation. This implementation protects the outer stream by saving a local copy of the outer content, and works on the local copy during the finalize function. Therefore, each call to finalize uses the correct intermediate value (that follows the key) in the outer stream. This extra protection that seems to make the implementation closer to a real HMAC on the full message so far (and thus seems more secure than the Naive HMAC implementation) is actually much less secure. Listing 1.4 shows a code of the finalize function of the NIPO HMAC implementation.

A third implementation that protects both hash streams of HMAC is used by Python [19]. We call it the *PIPO* (Patched Inner Patched Outer) implementation. This implementation MACs the fragment prefix but not its division to fragments. Unlike the previous two, it computes standard HMAC on the prefixes. In this implementation, the inner and the outer streams are copied during finalize, and further processing is made on the local copy. Listing 1.5 shows a code of the finalize function of the PIPO HMAC implementation.

```
finalize{
    innerStreamCopy = innerStream.copy();
    outerStreamCopy = outerStream.copy();

    inner = innerStreamCopy.finalize();
    outerStreamCopy.update(inner);
    outer = outerStreamCopy.finalize();
    return outer;
}
```

Listing 1.5. The Finalize Function of the PIPO HMAC Implementation

1.5 Related Work

The paper [10] shows that many security vulnerabilities were caused by software developers making mistakes, and argues that security professionals are responsible to create developer-friendly APIs. In addition, it focuses on the usability of cryptographic APIs, and proposes several principles for constructing usable and secure cryptographic APIs. The paper [9] demonstrates that SSL certificate validation is broken in many security applications and libraries due to badly designed APIs of SSL implementations.

Bellare, Goldreich, and Goldwasser defined the concept of incremental cryptography [4,5] as algorithms that allow to efficiently modify their outputs according to modifications in the input message. For example, given a message that is digitally signed. If this input message is slightly modified, an incremental algorithm provides an efficient way to get the new digital signature (without the full computation time of the digital signature of the modified message). Modification of a message includes replacing one block by another, insert a new block or delete an existing block. This definition is different than IncMACs because its purpose is to efficiently update the output (in time proportional to the change made in the underlying message). IncMACs' goal is to supply a secure and efficient algorithms to authenticate incremental prefixes of the same message.

An idea similar to IncMACs was proposed in [1]. It was noted that existing MAC primitives does not allow incremental calls, and some of the difficulties in allowing this kind of usage were mentioned. However, no concrete solution was suggested for this problem. A concrete proposal, but to a related problem, was suggested by Gennaro [8]. While we are interested in incremental symmetric authentication of fragmented messages, he is interested in incremental (public-key) signatures, with the non-repudiation property. He calls the fragmented messages by the term streams. He suggests protocols that provide digital signatures on streams more efficiently than signing each fragment individually, while still being able to provide a usable signature for every received prefix, even if communication hangs at the middle of a message.

1.6 Our Results

We concentrate on three implementations of HMAC-based IncMAC variants. The underlying issue behind all our analysis is that the security proof of HMAC does not hold once HMAC is used incrementally, as it's assumptions hold only on the first fragment. Once a second fragment is processed, the assumptions become invalid, and cannot be cured. We show that the Naive implementation as used as IncMAC by Siemens in their S7 protocol is vulnerable to collision, key recovery, message extension and forgery attacks whose complexity is significantly lower than prior attacks and lower than expected from such primitives. The NIPO implementation (the implementation of the OpenSSL library [18]), which seems to be better protected, is actually even less secure. Collisions can easily be found in a negligible time, which collide under all keys. It is also vulnerable to forgery attacks with negligible time and data complexities.

Table 1. Complexity of attacks against HMAC and HMAC-based IncMACs

Attack	Primitive	Source or Section	Complexity*			Success Prob.
			Data	Compressions	Lookups	
Collision (Single key)	HMAC (non-inc.)	-	$2^{n/2}$ KM	-	$2^{n/2}$	50%
	NIPO HMAC	2.2	0	0	0	100%
	Ideal MAC	-	$2^{n/2}$ KM	-	$2^{n/2}$	50%
Collision (Key independent)	HMAC (non-inc.)	-	No such attack algorithm			
	NIPO HMAC	2.2	0	0	0	100%
	Ideal MAC	-	$2^n \cdot 2^{|K|}$	-	$2^n \cdot 2^{|K|}$	100%
Multi-collision (Single key)	HMAC (non-inc.)	-	$2^{n/2} \log c$ ACM	-	$2^{n/2} \log c$	50%
	NIPO HMAC	2.3, 2.4	0	0	0	100%
	Ideal MAC	-	$(2^n)^{c-1/c}$ KM	-	$(2^n)^{c-1/c}$	50%
Multi-collision (Key independent)	HMAC (non-inc.)	-	No such attack algorithm			
	NIPO HMAC	2.3, 2.4	0	0	0	100%
	Ideal MAC	-	No such attack algorithm			
Key-recovery	HMAC (non-inc.)	Ex. Sea	1 KM	$\min(4 \cdot 2^{|K|}, 2 \cdot 2^{2n})$	-	100%
	HMAC (non-inc.)	[3]	$2^{n/2}$ KM	$2 \cdot 2^n$	$2^{n/2}$	50%
	Naive HMAC	4.1	1 KM	$4 \cdot 2^n$	-	100%
	Ideal MAC	-	$\lceil |K|/n \rceil$	$2^{|K|}$	-	100%
Forgery	HMAC (non-inc.)	[3]	$2^{n/2}$ ACM	-	$2^{n/2}$	50%
	HMAC (non-inc.)	[13]	$2^{n/2}$ ACM	-	$2^{n/2}$	50%
	Naive HMAC	4.4	$2^{n/2}$ CM	$2^{n/2}$	$2^{n/2}$	50%
	NIPO HMAC	3.1	**2 CM**	0	0	100%
	NIPO HMAC	3.2	$2^{n/2}$ CM	-	$2^{n/2}$	50%
	NIPO HMAC	3.3	$2^{n/2}$ KM	-	$2^{n/2}$	50%
	Ideal MAC	-	$\lceil |K|/n \rceil$	$2^{|K|}$	-	100%
Message extension	Naive HMAC	4.2	1 KM	2^n	-	100%
	Naive HMAC	4.3	$2^{n/2}$ KM	$2^{n/2}$	$2^{n/2}$	50%
	Ideal MAC	-	$\lceil |K|/n \rceil$	$2^{|K|}$	-	100%

* '-' marks 0 complexity (compressions or table lookups).

Table 1 summarizes our results compared to previously published attacks. For each attack, the data complexity is the number of required messages, where each message may consist of a small number of fragments (up to three in our case). The suffixes stand for the type of the data, where KM stands for known messages, CM for chosen messages and ACM for adaptive chosen messages. Notice that in some cases zero messages are required. These attacks are key independent and the same pairs of messages are collisions under any key. The time complexity is the number of calls that the attacker calls to the compression function plus the number of table lookups that the attacker performs to insert or fetch messages.

1.7   Notations

Throughout this paper we use the notations listed in Table 2.

Table 2. Notations

Notation	Description
b	is the length of a message block in bits (typically 512 or 1024)
n	is the length of the output of the hash function or MAC in bits
d	is the number of padding bits assigned for length information (typically 64 or 128 bits)
$\|x\|$	is the length of the bit string x
$x\|\|y$	is the concatenation of two bit strings x and y
0^s	is the concatenation of s zeros
K	is a b-bit MAC secret key
	Shorter keys are padded to b bits by 0's ($K \leftarrow K\|\|0^{b-\|K\|}$)
$H(x)$	is the application of a hash function H on a bit string x
$H^*(h, x, l)$	is the application of a hash function H on a bit string x, with the initial value being h (instead of the standard IV), and with the length in the padding being l (instead of $\|x\|$)
$H^*(h, x, \cdot)$	is $H^*(h, x, l)$ when the length l is easily extractable from the context
$pad(x, l)$	is the string $1\|\|0^c\|\|l$, where $c = b - 1 - (\|x\| + 1 + d - 1 \mod b)$, and where l is represented as a d-bit big-endian integer
v_i	The inner intermediate chaining value after the ith fragment
u_i	The outer intermediate chaining value after the ith fragment

1.8   Structure of the Paper

This paper is organized as follows: Sect. 2 presents key-independent collision attacks against the NIPO HMAC implementation, and Sect. 3 describes forgery attacks against this implementation. Section 4 discusses the most common implementation of HMAC—the Naive HMAC implementation, while Sect. 5 does the same for the PIPO HMAC implementation. Section 6 presents Secure IncMAC constructions and discusses their security. Section 7 summarizes this paper.

2   Key-Independent Collision Attacks on the OpenSSL Implementation (NIPO)

The implementation of HMAC in OpenSSL follows the NIPO implementation. The NIPO implementation protects the outer stream by working on a local copy of the content during the finalize function. Therefore, the outer stream always contains only a single tag value from the inner stream, which ensures that any collision in any chaining value of the inner stream results in a collision in the outer stream at the same location, i.e., a collision of the final authentication

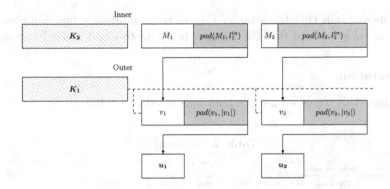

Fig. 1. The inner and outer streams in the HMAC NIPO implementation

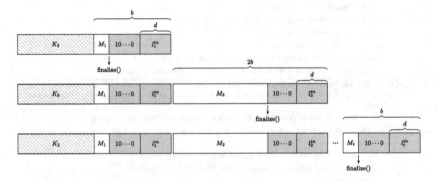

Fig. 2. The padded inner stream of the HMAC NIPO implementation

tag. In this section we present our basic techniques which shows how mixed calls to update/finalize affect the inner stream of NIPO and lead to collisions. Such collisions are then also collisions in the outer stream.

In the NIPO HMAC implementation, when we ask for the authentication tags of a message M fragmented to t fragments $M = (M_1, ..., M_t)$, we receive the incremental outputs that are used to authenticate the prefixes of M which are calculated as follows:

$$v_1 = H(K \oplus ipad \| M_1)$$
$$v_i = H^*(v_{i-1}, M_i, l_i^{in}), \qquad i \geq 2 \text{ where } l_i^{in} = |K| + \sum_{j=1}^{i} |M_j|$$
$$u_i = H(K \oplus opad \| v_i), \qquad i \geq 1$$
$$\text{IncMAC}_K(M_1, .., M_i) = u_i.$$

In this implementation the context of the outer stream remains the same in any call to finalize. Figure 1 demonstrates the inner and outer streams in this implementation. The broken line represent this fixed context. Notice that the outer stream always contains only a single tag value from the inner stream after the key.

2.1   The Padded Inner Stream of NIPO

Consider a long message broken into a number of fragments at the locations of finalize calls. I.e., the first fragment of the message is the concatenated inputs to the calls to update before the first finalize. Any other fragment is the concatenated inputs to all update calls between two consecutive calls to finalize.

As a simple example, lets consider a message consisting of two fragments that are hashed in the following sequence. After init, the first fragment serves as the input to the first update, after which a finalize is called. The digest of the inner stream after this call to finalize is the correct keyed hash value of the first fragment, since this sequence is a legal sequence of calling the API. Consider now that another update is called on the context with a second fragment, after which another finalize is called. Since the first finalize modified the context of the inner stream, padding is added in the padded stream between the two message fragments, where this padding also affect the final result. We define the padded stream of the inner stream of NIPO to be $K \oplus ipad$ (denoted by K_2) followed by the message fragments with the padding added by calling finalize. I.e, the padded stream is K_2 followed by the message with a padding after each of the message fragments. Figure 2 shows this padded inner stream that is passed as inputs to the compression function, and how the padded inner stream evolves when new fragments are added. Each row consists of K_2 followed by the first fragment on the left side, then padding, then the next fragment and its padding, and so on, repeatedly till the end of the message. The key is marked with stripes, the parts with white background mark the fragments of the message, and parts with gray background mark the padding added by the calls to finalize.

Notice that in such fragmented messages:

1. The padded inner stream contains a padding after every fragment. As a result, unlike in pure HMAC, the digest is calculated on a stream that mixes the message and many intermediate paddings rather than only a message and a single padding at the end.
2. Each padding contains the length of the key and message so far (i.e., the sum of the lengths of the key and the fragments, not including the lengths of the paddings). As a result, this length is not the actual length of the stream. Even worse, the number of blocks of the padded stream is not a function of the length any more.

These properties are not welcome. But they are not security threats on their own. The question posed is whether we can use these properties for creating valid attacks. Or in other words, can we find collisions between digests reached from calling finalize with different message fragments? Or maybe we can even devise some other attacks that give unexpected properties that MAC functions should not have? We answer these questions in the next subsections.

2.1.1   Every Message Has Many Possible Authentication Tags

We may expect that each message should have a unique authentication tag, that may serve to uniquely identify the content. However, as we show here, the tag

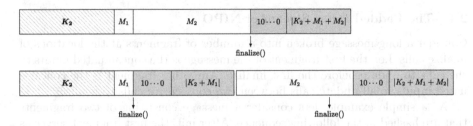

Fig. 3. Two different fragmentations of a message which result with different authentication tags in the NIPO HMAC implementation

depends on the fragmentation: Every message can be fragmented after every bit. Therefore, a message of length n, has $n - 1$ potential fragmentation points, with 2^{n-1} possible fragmentations. Each of these fragmentations results with a different padded inner stream, and thus a different (last) authentication tag.

As a simple example, lets consider a message $M = M_1 \| M_2$. The message M, when not fragmented, is padded with a single '1' bit, followed by (zero or more) zeros and the length of the data (including the key) at the end of the message to create its padded stream. When it is fragmented to two fragments M_1 and M_2, there are two padding, one after M_1 and another after M_2. Figure 3 demonstrates these fragmentations and their padding (the parts with gray background marks the end of fragments). Clearly, the final digests of the two cases are different.

2.1.2   The Merkle-Damgård Proof Does Not Hold

The Merkle-Damgård construction is proven to be collision-resistant if underlying compression function is collision-resistant. This proof[3] serves as the cornerstone of the trust in this construction. We show here that this proof is invalid in the IncMAC case.

The security proof of the Merkle-Damgård construction relies on the following two assumptions that do not hold in our case (M_{pad} is the padded stream of a message M):

1. M is a prefix of M_{pad}.
2. if $|M^1| = |M^2|$ then $|M^1_{pad}| = |M^2_{pad}|$.

In our case, Assumption 1 does not hold because fragmenting a message M results in a padding being added to the padded stream after each fragment. Therefore, the message is not a prefix of the padded stream.

In addition, Assumption 2 does not hold: Same message lengths (as written at the end of the padding) do not ensure that the padded messages have the same lengths. The Merkle-Damgård proof uses the length to ensure that padded messages with different numbers of blocks have different last blocks. This property does not hold in our case because the same message can be fragmented differently with different intermediate paddings, and thus different block-content and

---

[3] An early version of this proof is given in [14].

Padded Inner Stream of M^1

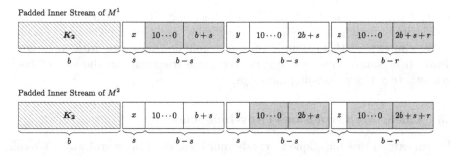

Padded Inner Stream of M^2

Fig. 4. The padded inner stream of colliding messages in the NIPO implementation

different number of total blocks, while still leaving the final padding (in the last block) unchanged.

2.2 Collisions (Key-Independent)

For a collision attack we find two different messages that result in the same padded inner stream under the same key. We actually describe an even stronger attack that finds collisions that collide under any key, and with most underlying hash primitives (conditioned on having the same block length and same padding). The trick of our collision attack is to include the intermediate padding of the first fragment of one message as a part of a fragment of the other message, and vice versa, thus ensuring that both padded streams are equal.

For example, let x, y be two bit-strings of the same length s (modulo b), and let z be some arbitrary string of length r. The following two messages lead to the same padded stream:

1. M^1 is a message fragmented to two fragments: the first is x, and the second is $y||pad(y, |K| + |x| + |y|)||z$.
2. M^2 is also a message fragmented to two fragments: the first is $x||pad(x, |K| + |x|)||y$, and the second is z.

Figure 4 illustrates this collision. The key is marked with stripes. Parts with white background mark fragments of the message itself, and parts with gray background mark the paddings added by the calls to finalize. The messages are different, and the paddings of the first fragment of each message are included as part of the other message. As can easily be seen, these messages result in the same padded inner stream for any key K_2 and x, y, and z for which $|x| = |y|$. Thus, the outputs of $H(K_2||\ldots)$ on these fragmented messages collide. Because the outer stream processes only the colliding value from the inner stream (i.e., only $H(K_2||\ldots)$), any collision in the inner stream results in a collision in the outer stream. Therefore, the authentication tag of these fragmented messages also collide. It can be viewed as shifting of the location of the padding in the padded stream between two possible locations.

Notice that there is no need for the full message to be known for this technique to work. In particular, there is no need to know the key K in order to calculate

$pad(y, |K|+|x|+|y|)$ and $pad(x, |K|+|x|)$, since only the key length matters. The complexity of finding such collisions is negligible, and they are key independent.

We can extend this example to longer colliding messages with more fragments. In a simple case, we append the same fragments to the end of both messages to get new colliding messages.

2.3   Linear Multi-collisions (Key-Independent)

We can extend this technique to create multi-collisions in several ways. We call the first of those *linear multi-collisions*. It shifts the location of the padding in the padded stream between more than two locations. Technically, the message contains several locations in the message that fit to become a valid padding of the message prefix till that location.

2.4   Exponential Multi-collisions (Key-Independent)

Linear multi-collisions are not the most efficient to make k-collisions for large k's. Instead of preparing k locations for setting the paddings and breaking the message to fragments at a single such location, it is possible to make the choice many times in a single message. Moreover, the choice can be made independently for any pair of locations. Therefore, the number of choices become exponential with the length of the message.

Exponential multi-collisions are formed in a similar way to the multi-collisions of [11]. Given t pairs of fragmented sequences $(S^{i,1}, S^{i,2})$ that lead to a collision with any initial value (as in Subsect. 2.2), we create 2^t different messages with the same digest by concatenating any combination of t sequences, where the ith sequence is arbitrarily chosen from $S^{i,1}$ or $S^{i,2}$. As $S^{1,1}$ and $S^{1,2}$ collide, then the chaining values after this sequence are equal. Therefore, also $S^{2,1}$ and $S^{2,2}$ that follow them collide and so on, leading to multi-collision of all the 2^t messages. Figure 5 illustrates exponential multi-collisions. As in the case of collisions, since the length is included in the paddings of the fragments of the sequences, then the length is also included in the partner fragments as part of the message.

With this construction, it is possible to create 2^t-collisions with $2t$-block messages. These multi-collisions are key-independent, and hold for any key. Moreover, the attacker has no need to know the key, or ask the victim to authenticate with the unknown key, in order to find the multi-collisions. All he needs, for example, in case of 8-collision, is to copy the key-independent multi-collisions from Table 3. We stress that these collisions hold to all MD-based Inc-HMAC with 512-bit blocks, as the details of the compression functions are not affecting the collisions.

3   Forgery Attacks Against NIPO HMAC Implementation

In this section we describe attacks against the NIPO and HMAC implementation.

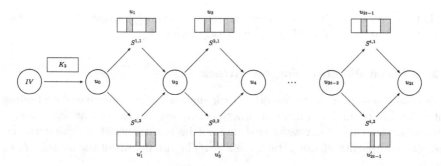

Fig. 5. Exponential multi-collisions

Table 3. Key-independent 8-collisions of Inc-HMAC-SHA-1 and Inc-HMAC-SHA-256

Fragments 1–2	Fragments 3–4	Fragments 5–6
$1 - 110^{446}0^{52}0100000000011$	$1 - 110^{446}0^{52}0110000000111$	$1 - 110^{446}0^{52}1000000001011$
$1 - 110^{446}0^{52}0100000000011$	$1 - 110^{446}0^{52}0110000000111$	$110^{446}0^{52}0110000001011 - 1$
$1 - 110^{446}0^{52}0100000000011$	$110^{446}0^{52}0100000000111 - 1$	$1 - 110^{446}0^{52}1000000001011$
$1 - 110^{446}0^{52}0100000000011$	$110^{446}0^{52}0100000000111 - 1$	$110^{446}0^{52}0110000001011 - 1$
$110^{446}0^{52}0010000000011 - 1$	$1 - 110^{446}0^{52}0110000000111$	$1 - 110^{446}0^{52}1000000001011$
$110^{446}0^{52}0010000000011 - 1$	$1 - 110^{446}0^{52}0110000000111$	$110^{446}0^{52}0110000001011 - 1$
$110^{446}0^{52}0010000000011 - 1$	$110^{446}0^{52}0100000000111 - 1$	$1 - 110^{446}0^{52}1000000001011$
$110^{446}0^{52}0010000000011 - 1$	$110^{446}0^{52}0100000000111 - 1$	$110^{446}0^{52}0110000001011 - 1$

Each row contains one message, each message has six fragments. Content is in binary.

3.1 A Simple Forgery Attack

A forgery attack can easily be performed given a pair of colliding messages, e.g., those mentioned in Subsect. 2.2. Given such a collision, the attacker asks for the authentication tags of the first member of this message pair. Since the second tags of these messages are equal, the attacker only needs to request the tag of the first fragment to forge the authentication tags of the second message. The data and the time complexity of this attack are negligible (computing tags of two messages with a total of three fragments). The full details of the attack are as follows:

1. Choose two bit strings x and y of the same length (modulo b), and any bit string z.
2. Ask for the authentication tags of the message $M = (M_1, M_2)$ fragmented to two fragments, where $M_1 = x$ and $M_2 = y||pad(y, |K| + |x| + |y|)||z$. Let the authentication tags be u_1, u_2.
3. Ask for the authentication tag of the single-fragment message

$$M_1' = x||pad(x, |K| + |x|)||y.$$

Let the authentication tag be u_1'.

4. Let M' be a two-fragment message $M' = (M_1', M_2')$ where $M_2' = z$. The authentication tags of M' are the already known u_1' and $u_2' = u_2$.

3.2 Chosen Plaintext Forgery Attack

This attack is similar to the forgery attack against HMAC, and based on finding collisions in the underlying hash function. In this attack, the attacker forges authentication tags of massages that had not been authenticated. The data and the time complexity of this attack are $2^{n/2}$. The full details of the attack are as follows:

1. Ask for the authentication tags of $2^{n/2}$ messages M^i fragmented to three fragments $M^i = (M_1^i, M_2, M_3^i)$ each, where the first fragment is of fixed length, and the second fragment is identical in all messages. Let the three authentication tags of a message M^i be u_1^i, u_2^i, u_3^i.
2. If there exist i and j such that $u_1^i = u_1^j$ and $u_2^i = u_2^j$, conclude that $v_1^i = v_1^j$.
3. The authentication tags of the three-fragment message $M' = (M_1', M_2', M_3')$, where $M_1' = M_1^i$, $M_2' = M_2$ and $M_3' = M_3^j$ are u_1^i, u_2^i, u_3^j.

3.3 Known Plaintext Forgery Attack

The attack of Subsect. 3.2 is a chosen plaintext attack because it validates that the collision occurs in the inner stream. This attack can be converted into a known plaintext attack, without this validation at the cost of a reduced success rate. The data and the time complexity of this attack are $2^{n/2}$.

4 Cryptanalysis of the Naive HMAC Implementation

In this section we discuss the most common HMAC implementation, to which we call the Naive HMAC implementation. This Naive implementation is the most common in libraries and applications, since it is based on the versions listed in the RFCs. This implementation is used by **Siemens** controllers and control software to incrementally authenticate fragmented messages. It optimizes the memory usage in finalize without any specific means to allow further calls to update afterwards. It uses the Naive hash implementation when it calls the hash function, without any trial to protect against incremental calls.

In the Naive HMAC implementation, the authentication tags of a message M fragmented to t fragments $M = (M_1, ..., M_t)$ are calculated as follows:

$$v_1 = H(K \oplus ipad \| M_1)$$
$$v_i = H^*(v_{i-1}, M_i, l_i^{in}), \qquad i \geq 2 \text{ where } l_i^{in} = |K| + \sum_{j=1}^{i} |M_j|$$
$$u_1 = H(K \oplus opad \| v_1)$$
$$u_i = H^*(u_{i-1}, v_i, l_i^{out}), \qquad i \geq 2 \text{ where } l_i^{out} = |K| + \sum_{j=1}^{i} |v_j|$$
$$\text{IncMAC}_K(M_1, .., M_i) = u_i.$$

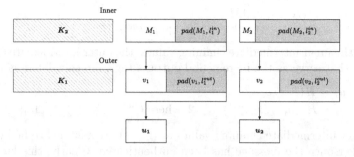

Fig. 6. The inner and outer streams in the HMAC naive implementation

Recall that v_i and u_i are the chaining values of the inner and outer streams after the i'th fragment, respectively. The weaknesses described in Sect. 2.1 cause the inner stream and the outer stream to overwrite their states during every call to finalize. Figure 6 shows the padded streams of a Naive HMAC implementation. The first row shows the padded inner stream, and the second shows the padded outer stream. The arrows represent the chaining values and they point to where they are used. Notice that the outer padded stream contains many fragments, one for each message fragment.

In the following subsections, we present various attacks against the Naive HMAC implementation when used with multiple fragments. Unlike in the case of NIPO, in Naive implementations a collision in the inner stream does not force a collision in the outer stream, because the intermediate digests of the inner stream are mixed as fragments in the outer stream. So more complex algorithms are required to attack the Naive implementation.

4.1 Key Recovery Attack

There are two known key recovery attacks against (standard) HMAC. Exhaustive search allows the attacker to find the key itself,[4] given a single authentication tag of a message, in $\min(4 \cdot 2^{|K|}, 2 \cdot 2^{2n})$ time complexity. The other attack [3] is based on finding collisions in the underlying hash function. In this attack, the attacker finds the intermediate values after compressing $K \oplus ipad$ and $K \oplus opad$ denoted by c^{in} and c^{out}, whose knowledge is equivalent to recovering the key. The data complexity of this attack is $2^{n/2}$ MACed messages, and the time complexity is 2^n.

In our case, where each message is fragmented and each fragment has a tag, we can improve over this attack. When the attacker asks for the authentication tags of a message M fragmented to t fragments $M = (M_1, ..., M_t)$, he receives the incremental outputs computed on the prefixes of M. In the Naive HMAC implementation the inner intermediate chaining values v_i are calculated as follows:

---

[4] Or an equivalent key with the same chaining value.

$$v_1 = H(K \oplus ipad || M_1)$$
$$v_i = H^*(v_{i-1}, M_i, l_i^{in}), \ i \geq 2 \text{ where } l_i^{in} = |K| + \sum_{j=1}^{i} |M_j|.$$

Based on the inner intermediate chaining values, the outer intermediate chaining values u_i, that serve as the incremental outputs tags, are calculated as follows:

$$u_1 = H(K \oplus opad || v_1)$$
$$u_i = H^*(u_{i-1}, v_i, l_i^{out}), \ i \geq 2 \text{ where } l_i^{out} = |K| + \sum_{j=1}^{i} |v_j|.$$

These outer intermediate chaining values u_i ($i \geq 1$) are assumed to be known to the attacker once the message has been authenticated. Clearly, this knowledge may be very helpful to the attacker.

In this attack, the attacker asks for the authentication tags of a single message, fragmented to three fragments, and finds c^{in} and c^{out}, the intermediate values after compressing $K \oplus ipad$ and $K \oplus opad$. These intermediate values are equivalent to the key for the purpose of forging messages. The data complexity of this attack is negligible and the time complexity is 2^n. The full details of the attack are as follows:

1. Ask for the three authentication tags of a message M fragmented to three fragments $M = (M_1, M_2, M_3)$. Let u_1, u_2, u_3 be the tags.
2. Find v_2: For every n-bit string $\alpha \in \{0,1\}^n$:
   (a) Calculate the value of $H^*(u_1, \alpha, \cdot)$.
   (b) If $H^*(u_1, \alpha, \cdot) = u_2$:
       i. Calculate the value of $H^*(u_2, H^*(\alpha, M_3, \cdot), \cdot)$.
       ii. If $H^*(u_2, H^*(\alpha, M_3, \cdot), \cdot) = u_3$, conclude that $v_2 = \alpha$.
3. Find c^{in}: For every n-bit string $\alpha \in \{0,1\}^n$:
   (a) Calculate the value of $H^*(H^*(\alpha, M_1, \cdot), M_2, \cdot)$.
   (b) If $H^*(H^*(\alpha, M_1, \cdot), M_2, \cdot) = v_2$, conclude that $c^{in} = \alpha$.
4. Find c^{out}: For every n-bit string $\alpha \in \{0,1\}^n$:
   (a) Calculate the value of $H^*(\alpha, H^*(c^{in}, M_1, \cdot), \cdot)$.
   (b) If $H^*(\alpha, H^*(c^{in}, M_1, \cdot), \cdot) = u_1$, conclude that $c^{out} = \alpha$.

4.2 A Simple Message Extension Attack

If the attacker had known some intermediate chaining variable v_i ($i \geq 2$) in the inner stream of a message $M = (M_1, ..., M_i)$, he could have easily forged an authentication tag of the message extended by any single fragment M'_{i+1} to $M' = (M_1, ..., M_i, M'_{i+1})$, by calculating the values:

$$v'_{i+1} = H^*(v_i, M'_{i+1}, l_{i+1}^{in'}) \text{ where } l_{i+1}^{in'} = l_i^{in} + |M'_{i+1}|$$
$$u'_{i+1} = H^*(u_i, v'_{i+1}, l_{i+1}^{out'}) \text{ where } l_{i+1}^{out'} = l_i^{out} + |v'_{i+1}|.$$

Then, the attacker could extend this prefix by more fragments. It is therefore that only the knowledge of v_i stands between the attacker and his ability to forge messages. Let's show how the attacker can perform this missing step.

In this attack, the attacker asks for the authentication tags of a single message, fragmented to three fragments, and finds the second intermediate chaining value v_2 in the inner stream. The data complexity of this attack is negligible and the time complexity of is 2^n. The full details of the attack are as follows:

1. Ask for the three authentication tags of a message M fragmented to three fragments $M = (M_1, M_2, M_3)$. Let u_1, u_2, u_3 be the tags.
2. Find v_2: For every n-bit string $\alpha \in \{0,1\}^n$:
   (a) Calculate the value of $H^*(u_1, \alpha, \cdot)$.
   (b) If $H^*(u_1, \alpha, \cdot) = u_2$:
      i. Calculate the value of $H^*(u_2, H^*(\alpha, M_3, \cdot), \cdot)$.
      ii. If $H^*(u_2, H^*(\alpha, M_3, \cdot), \cdot) = u_3$, conclude that $v_2 = \alpha$ and that $v_3 = H^*(\alpha, M_3, \cdot)$
3. Let M' be a message fragmented to four fragments $M' = (M_1, M_2, M_3, M_4')$ (where M_4' can be any fragment). The authentication tags of M' are $u_1, u_2,$ u_3, u_4'. The tag u_4' of M_4' can be forged by computing: $v_4' = H^*(v_3, M_4', \cdot)$ and $u_4' = H^*(u_3, v_4', \cdot)$.

4.3   A More Efficient Message Extension Attack

In this attack the attacker asks for authentication tags of $2^{n/2}$ messages fragmented to three fragments each, where the first fragment is identical in all messages, and the second fragment is different in all messages. The first intermediate chaining values in the outer stream u_1 of all of these messages are identical. The rest is then performed by applying the Birthday Paradox, which allows the attacker to find the second intermediate chaining value in the inner stream of some message. The data and the time complexity of this attack are $2^{n/2}$. The full details of the attack are as follows:

1. Ask for an authentication tags of $2^{n/2}$ messages M^i fragmented to three fragments each $M^i = (M_1, M_2^i, M_3^i)$, where the first fragment is identical in all messages, and the second fragment is different in all messages. Let the three authentication tags of a message M^i be u_1, u_2^i, u_3^i.
2. Do forever (in practice about $2^{n/2}$ times):
   (a) Choose random n-bit string $\alpha \in \{0,1\}^n$.
   (b) Calculate the value of $H^*(u_1, \alpha, \cdot)$.
   (c) If there exists i such that $H^*(u_1, \alpha, \cdot) = u_2^i$:
      i. Calculate the value of $H^*(u_2^i, H^*(\alpha, M_3^i, \cdot), \cdot)$.
      ii. If $H^*(u_2^i, H^*(\alpha, M_3^i, \cdot), \cdot) = u_3^i$, conclude that $v_2^i = \alpha$ and that $v_3^i = H^*(\alpha, M_3^i, \cdot)$.
      iii. Go to Step 3.
3. Let M' be a message fragmented to four fragments $M' = (M_1, M_2^i, M_3^i, M_4')$ (where M_4' can be any fragment). The authentication tags of M' are $u_1, u_2^i,$ u_3^i, u_4'. The tag u_4' of M_4' can be forged by computing: $v_4' = H^*(v_3^i, M_4', \cdot)$ and $u_4' = H^*(u_3^i, v_4', \cdot)$.

4.4   Forgery Attack

Two similar versions of adaptive chosen forgery attack against HMAC, which is based on finding collisions in the underlying hash function, were presented in [3,13]. In this attack, the attacker forges authentication tags of messages that had not been authenticated. The data and the time complexity of this attack are $2^{n/2}$.

We show another authentication forgery attack, which is based on the technique of Subsect. 2.2. This technique creates pairs of messages fragmented to two fragments each, where every pair of messages has the same value of the second inner intermediate chaining value. In this attack the attacker creates $2^{n/2}$ such pairs, and asks for the authentication tags of the first member of each of these message-pairs, resulting with $2^{n/2}$ outputs. Similarly to the attack of Sect. 4.3, the attacker finds the second intermediate chaining value of the inner stream of some first member message. Recall that the second inner intermediate chaining value is identical in both members of the same pair. Now if the attacker knows the authentication tag of the first fragment of the second member, and thus he can forge an authentication tag of the entire message. The data and the time complexity of this attack are $2^{n/2}$. The full details of the attack are as follows:

1. Choose two bit strings x and y of the same length (modulo b).
2. For $1 \le i \le 2^{n/2}$:
    (a) Choose two bit strings z^i and M_3^i.
    (b) Create a message $M^i = (M_1^i, M_2^i, M_3^i)$ fragmented to three fragments, where $M_1^i = x$ and $M_2^i = y||pad(y, |K| + |x| + |y|)||z^i$.
3. Ask for the authentication tags of the messages M^i. Let the three authentication tags of the message M^i be u_1, u_2^i, u_3^i.
4. Ask for the authentication tag of the single-fragment message $x||pad(x, |K| + |x|)||y$. Let the authentication tag be u_1'.
5. Do forever (in practice about $2^{n/2}$ times):
    (a) Choose a random n-bit string $\alpha \in \{0,1\}^n$.
    (b) Calculate the value of $H^*(u_1, \alpha, \cdot)$.
    (c) If there exists i such that $H^*(u_1, \alpha, \cdot) = u_2^i$:
        i. Calculate the value of $H^*(u_2^i, H^*(\alpha, M_3^i, \cdot), \cdot)$.
        ii. If $H^*(u_2^i, H^*(\alpha, M_3^i, \cdot), \cdot) = u_3^i$, conclude that $v_2^i = \alpha$.
6. Let M' be a message fragmented to two fragments $M' = (M_1', M_2')$ where $M_1' = x||pad(x, |K| + |x|)||y$ and $M_2' = z^i$. The authentication tags of M' are the already known u_1', and $u_2' = H^*(u_1', v_2^i, \cdot)$.

5   The PIPO HMAC Implementation

The PIPO (Patched Inner Patched Outer) HMAC implementation is identical to the naive and NIPO ones, except for the finalize function. In this implementation, the inner and the outer streams are copied during finalize, and further processing is made on the local copy. Listing 1.5 shows a code of the finalize function of the PIPO HMAC implementation.

In the PIPO HMAC implementation, when we ask for the authentication tags of a message M fragmented to t fragments $M = (M_1, ..., M_t)$, we receive the incremental outputs that are used to authenticate the prefixes of M. These tags are calculated as follows:

$$v_i = H(K \oplus ipad||M_1||...||M_i)$$
$$u_i = H(K \oplus opad||v_i)$$
$$IncMAC_K(M_1, .., M_i) = u_i.$$

This implementation is used in the Python programing language. In the Python implementation of hash functions, calling finalize does not add the padding to the inner stream—the state of the hash is copied and the padding is only added to the copy. In addition, in the finalize function of HMAC, the outer stream is copied. This is equivalent to copying and using the copies of both inner and outer streams. Therefore, the Python implementation of HMAC is equivalent to the PIPO HMAC implementation.

Note that in this implementation, mixed calls to update/finalize produce correct HMAC values for every prefix of the input. Therefore, the security of PIPO as an IncMAC seems equivalent to the security of HMAC on the same prefixes (the security of HMAC was proven in [2,3]). Indeed any attack on HMAC is also an attack on PIPO, and any chosen plaintext (or adaptive) attack on PIPO is easily convertible to an attack on HMAC (by replacing the request for authentication tags for several fragments of a single message by requests for the HMAC tags for each fragment prefix). The complexity in this latter reduction may increase by a small factor (the maximal number of fragments in a message). However, some chosen plaintext attacks on HMAC may be converted to known plaintext attacks. This is caused by the fact that in PIPO a multiple-fragment message corresponds to several messages in the HMAC case, which have common prefixes. So there exist known plaintext attacks against PIPO that have no corresponding known plaintext attacks against HMAC.[5]

6 Secure IncMACs

Incremental MACs are of a special interest to those that wish to transmit a message that contains many fragments, and wish to be able to authenticate the message both at the packet level and at the application level. The network driver may authenticate each packet as a fragment, linking it directly to it's predecessor fragments, without the extra need for handling a session number and a packet counter typically used to protect against replay and other attacks. Each of these fragments has it's own digest, that also authenticates all the message prefix. At the same time, the application may receive only the last digest, which is useful for it to authenticate the full message, without the need to compute a second MAC instance on the same message, and send a redundant MAC value over the communication channel.

For example, transmission of a long file may be protected by an IncMAC, where the drivers at both side compute and check the digests of the fragments.

---

[5] Applications using the context copy method of HMAC implementations are mostly also vulnerable to such known plaintext attacks.

The drivers then send only the last digest to the application, which can save it along the message on the disk, enabling to verify the file without an extra computation of another MAC instance. Alternatively, a database of many records (or tables) is transmitted, where each record is sent in a separate fragment. The drivers check authenticity of each fragment, while the application receives the fragments and the last digest. The application is able to verify by the single digest that the full message is correct. When using an FP-IncMAC, the application may even know that the division to records is correct, without needing to receive a separate digest to each record.

Notice that in the latter case it may also be desirable to authenticate the division to fragments, rather than just the full message. This additional feature is easy to support, as many IncMAC implementations do it any way, we call them FP-IncMACs. But for those that do not (e.g., PIPO) we propose how to add this feature.

6.1 PIPO and LAPIPO

As mentioned earlier, PIPO is a secure IncMAC. The only drawback is that some potential attacks might use the copying of the state during finalize to gain some factor in the complexity. This issue that also occurs when HMAC is used by the applications with a state copy operation. If an FP-IncMAC is wished for, based on a PIPO, we propose the LAPIPO FP-IncMAC construction. The extension technique is generic and can be used over any secure IncMAC. Also notice that it eliminates the potential issues mentioned for PIPO.

The LAPIPO (Length Added PIPO) construction uses the PIPO implementation with the addition of the fragment length after each fragment. This length is typically added by a call to the update function at the beginning of LAPIPO's finalize, rather than by modifying the PIPO API. It can be done by a direct call to update by the application, or by a dedicated module that provides an LAPIPO API and calls the PIPO API with this extra addition. Listing 1.6 contains an example code of LAPIPO. The difference from PIPO is that the fragment length is added at the end of every fragment, and the length written in the PIPO paddings is the total length of the message prefix and the size of the added lengths (in order to allow to implement LAPIPO using a standard PIPO). We can consider it as a length-added (postfix free) message in which after each fragment the length of the fragment is added. This length-added message is then MACed by PIPO. Figure 7 illustrates the inner stream of LAPIPO (the values marked with dots are the fragments lengths added at the end of every fragment). The addition of the fragment length distinguishes between the same message with different fragmentations, while in the PIPO implementation, an authentication tag is independent of the message fragmentation.

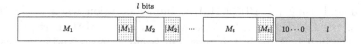

Fig. 7. The padded inner stream of LAPIPO

```
ctx:
      PIPO_ctx:  ctx  of  PIPO
      previousLength :  int

initialize (key){
      PIPO_ctx . initialize (key );
      previousLength  =  0;
}

update (data){
      PIPO_ctx . update (data );
}

finalize (){
      fragmentLength  =  PIPO_ctx . innerStream . streamSize  −
                        previousLength ;
      PIPO_ctx . update (toBigEndian (fragmentLength , d ));
      previousLength  =  PIPO_ctx . innerStream . streamSize ;
      PIPO_ctx . finalize ();
}
```

Listing 1.6. LAPIPO Implementation

7 Summary

This paper discusses unintended features of HMAC APIs. It shows that commonly used HMAC APIs allow calling the update function after the finalize function, which causes unintended features that expose these APIs to a number of vulnerabilities. Moreover, some applications use these unintended features for incremental authentication. It focuses on two implementations of HMAC: NIPO and Naive HMAC, and describe several attacks against them, such as key independent collision and multi-collision attacks, that are one of the strongest attacks possible, as the same collisions hold for any key, and even for other HMACs with other underlying hash functions. Other attacks include forgery, message extension and key recovery attacks.

An extreme example is the OpenSSL library, which implements HMAC using the NIPO implementation. Though the OpenSSL documentation states that hash functions should not be used incrementally, it does not state it regarding HMAC. It is unclear to us why OpenSSL uses the NIPO implementation, i.e., why the outer stream's state is copied in OpenSSL's implemenation to a local variable, while the inner stream's state is not. But this exact decision makes this implementation vulnerable to a number of highly efficient attacks, including key-independent collision and multi-collision attacks, with complexity 0, whose same collisions collide under any key and even when using other underlying hash function.[6]

The paper also discusses two other HMAC implementations, called PIPO and LAPIPO. The former is used as the implementation of Python. Both are secure.

---

[6] Note that this decision does not affect SSL/TLS, as far as we know, as the SSL/TLS protocol [20] does not use HMAC incrementally.

We recommend using the PIPO HMAC implementation when an IncMAC is required, or the LAPIPO construction when an FP-IncMAC is required. Their security is the best possible in the known message scenario, and is equivalent to the security of HMAC in all other scenarios.

We informed Siemens about their non-standard use of HMAC and of our attacks in 2019, and as far as we understand from their response, they made changes to their authentications in their latest product versions. In parallel, we also informed OpenSSL, who had recently opened a discussion on whether they should protect against it [17]. Apparently, they have an agreement to correct their code, and they are already working on correcting it in their EVP_MAC APIs.

Acknowledgements. This research was partially supported by the Technion Hiroshi Fujiwara cyber security research center and the Israel national cyber directorate.

References

1. Austein, R.: [cryptech tech] incremental digest outputs. https://lists.cryptech.is/archives/tech/2014-November/001008.html. Accessed Nov 2014
2. Bellare, M.: New proofs for NMAC and HMAC security without collision resistance. J. Cryptol. **28**(4), 844–878 (2015)
3. Bellare, M., Canetti, R., Krawczyk, H.: Keying hash functions for message authentication. In: Koblitz, N. (ed.) CRYPTO 1996. LNCS, vol. 1109, pp. 1–15. Springer, Heidelberg (1996). https://doi.org/10.1007/3-540-68697-5_1
4. Bellare, M., Goldréich, O., Goldwasser, S.: Incremental cryptography: the case of hashing and signing. In: Desmedt, Y.G. (ed.) CRYPTO 1994. LNCS, vol. 839, pp. 216–233. Springer, Heidelberg (1994). https://doi.org/10.1007/3-540-48658-5_22
5. Bellare, M., Goldreich, O., Goldwasser, S.: Incremental cryptography and application to virus protection. In Proceedings of the 27th Annual ACM Symposium on the Theory of Computing, pp. 45–56. ACM Press (1995)
6. Biham, E., Bitan, S., Carmel, A., Dankner, A., Malin, J., Wool, A.: Rogue7: Rogue engineering-station Attacks On S7 Simatic PLCs, Black Hat, USA (2019)
7. Damgård, I.B.: A design principle for hash functions. In: Brassard, G. (ed.) CRYPTO 1989. LNCS, vol. 435, pp. 416–427. Springer, New York (1990). https://doi.org/10.1007/0-387-34805-0_39
8. Gennaro, R., Rohatgi, P.: How to sign digital streams. In: Kaliski, B.S. (ed.) CRYPTO 1997. LNCS, vol. 1294, pp. 180–197. Springer, Heidelberg (1997). https://doi.org/10.1007/BFb0052235
9. Georgiev, M., Iyengar, S., Jana, S., Anubhai, R., Boneh, D., Shmatikov,V.: The most dangerous code in the world: validating SSL certificates in non-browser software. In: The ACM Conference on Computer and Communications Security (CCS 2012), Raleigh, NC, USA, October 16–18 2012, pp. 38–49 (2012)
10. Green, M., Smith, M.: Developers are not the enemy: the need for usable security APIS. IEEE Secur. Privacy **14**(5), 40–46 (2016)
11. Joux, A.: multicollisions in iterated hash functions. application to cascaded constructions. In: Franklin, M. (ed.) CRYPTO 2004. LNCS, vol. 3152, pp. 306–316. Springer, Heidelberg (2004). https://doi.org/10.1007/978-3-540-28628-8_19
12. Kent, S.: Rfc 4301 - security architecture for the internet protocol (2005). https://tools.ietf.org/html/rfc4301

13. Kim, J., Biryukov, A., Preneel, B., Hong, S.: On the security of HMAC and NMAC based on HAVAL, MD4, MD5, SHA-0 and SHA-1 (Extended Abstract). In: De Prisco, R., Yung, M. (eds.) SCN 2006. LNCS, vol. 4116, pp. 242–256. Springer, Heidelberg (2006). https://doi.org/10.1007/11832072_17

14. Merkle. R.C.: Secrecy, Authentication, and Public Key Systems. UMI Research Press, Ann Arbor (1979)

15. National Bureau of Standards and Technologies: Secure Hash Standard. Federal Information Processing Standards, Publication FIPS-180-1 (1995)

16. National Bureau of Standards and Technologies: Secure Hash Standard. Federal Information Processing Standards, Publication FIPS-180-4 (2001)

17. OpenSSL: Incorrect usage of the HMAC APIs. #13210. https://github.com/openssl/openssl/issues/13210

18. OpenSSL: Openssl website. https://www.openssl.org

19. Python.org. Python website. https://www.python.org

20. Rescorla. E.: RTC 8446 - the transport layer security (TLS) protocol version 1.3 (2018). https://tools.ietf.org/html/rfc8446

21. Rivest, R.: Rfc 3120 - the MD4 message-digest algorithm (1992). https://tools.ietf.org/html/rfc1320

22. Rivest, R.L.: The MD5 message-digest algorithm. RFC **1321**, 1–21 (1992)

Quantum Cryptanalysis

Low-Gate Quantum Golden
Collision Finding

Samuel Jaques[1] and André Schrottenloher[2(✉)]

[1] Department of Materials, University of Oxford, Oxford, UK
samuel.jaques@materials.ox.ac.uk
[2] Inria, Paris, France
andre.schrottenloher@inria.fr

Abstract. The golden collision problem asks us to find a single, special collision among the outputs of a pseudorandom function. This generalizes meet-in-the-middle problems, and is thus applicable in many contexts, such as cryptanalysis of the NIST post-quantum candidate SIKE.

The main quantum algorithms for this problem are memory-intensive, and the costs of quantum memory may be very high. The quantum circuit model implies a linear cost for random access, which annihilates the exponential advantage of the previous quantum collision-finding algorithms over Grover's algorithm or classical van Oorschot-Wiener.

Assuming that quantum memory is costly to access but free to maintain, we provide new quantum algorithms for the golden collision problem with high memory requirements but low gate costs. Under the assumption of a two-dimensional connectivity layout, we provide better quantum parallelization methods for generic and golden collision finding. This lowers the quantum security of the golden collision and meet-in-the-middle problems, including SIKE.

Keywords: Quantum cryptanalysis · Golden collision search · Quantum walks · SIKE

1 Introduction

Quantum computers have a significant advantage in attacking some widely-used public-key cryptosytems. In light of the continuing progress on quantum architectures, the National Institute of Standards and Technology (NIST) launched a standardization process for new primitives [29], which is still ongoing.

The new cryptosytems proposed rely on generic problems that are believed to be hard for quantum computers. That is, contrary to the discrete logarithm problem in abelian groups, or to the factorization of integers, they should not admit polynomial-time quantum algorithms. However, an exponential algorithm could be relevant if the non-asymptotic cost is low enough, so these attacks still require careful analysis.

In this paper, we study quantum algorithms for the *golden collision search* problem. In the context of the NIST call, these algorithms can be applied in a

© Springer Nature Switzerland AG 2021
O. Dunkelman et al. (Eds.): SAC 2020, LNCS 12804, pp. 329–359, 2021.
https://doi.org/10.1007/978-3-030-81652-0_13

generic key-recovery of the NIST candidate SIKE (non-commutative supersingular isogeny-based key encapsulation) [2,15,20]. They can also be used in some lattice attacks [3].

Golden Collision Search. We have access to a function $h : X \to X$ that has collisions, *i.e.* pairs of inputs with the same output value. Collisions happen randomly, but (at most) one of them is *golden* and we wish to retrieve it.

Classically, the most time-efficient method is to retrieve a whole lookup table for h, sort by output value and look at all collisions. However, this incurs a massive cost in random-access memory. A study with limited memory was done in [2]. The authors concluded that the most efficient method was van Oorschot-Wiener's distinguished point technique [30]. In the context of SIKE, they noticed that the proposed parameters offered even more security when accounting for memory limits.

Quantum Circuits. In this work, we study quantum algorithms written in the *quantum circuit model*, which abstracts out the physical architecture. The computation is a sequence of basic *quantum gates* applied to a pool of *qubits*, *i.e.* two-level quantum systems. The time complexity in this model is thought of as the number of operations applied, that is, the number of quantum gates.

The best quantum algorithm for golden collision search is Ambainis' algorithm [4], with time $\widetilde{\mathcal{O}}(N^{2/3})$ if $|X| = N$, matching a query lower bound of $\mathcal{O}(N^{2/3})$ [1]. However, it suffers from a heavy use of *quantum random access* to massive amounts of quantum memory, and does not fare well under depth constraints.

In this paper, we dismiss quantum RAM and use only the *baseline* circuit model, as in [22]. We consider that a memory access to R qubit registers requires $\Theta(R)$ quantum gates. With this restriction, we design new quantum algorithms for golden collision search.

Metrics. We consider the two metrics of *gate count* (G) and *depth-width* product (DW) emphasized in [22]. The first one assumes that the *identity gate* costs 0, meaning we can leave as many qubits idle for as long as we want. This happens *e.g.* if the decoherence time of individual qubits, when no gates are applied, can be prolonged to arbitrary lengths at a fixed cost. The second one considers instead that the identity gate costs 1. This happens *e.g.* if error-correction must be performed at each time step, on all qubits. In addition, since we consider quantum circuits at a large scale, we account for locality constraints with a model of a two-dimensional grid with nearest-neighbour interactions only.

Contributions. We first optimize for the *gate count* in Sect. 3. We rewrite van Oorschot-Wiener collision search as a random walk so that we can obtain a quantum analogue in the MNRS *quantum walk* framework. If h is a single gate evaluated in time 1, our algorithm gives a G-cost of $\widetilde{\mathcal{O}}(N^{6/7})$. Next, we give another algorithm that searches for *distinguished points* with Grover's search. These two methods achieve the exact same complexity.

In Sect. 4, we give a parallel version of our prefix-based walk, and a parallel multi-Grover search algorithm that improves over [8]. This gives the G-cost and DW-cost of our algorithms under depth constraints, improving on the counts of [22].

NIST defined five security levels relative to the hardness of breaking symmetric cryptographic schemes, possibly with some depth limitation. Three of these levels compare to a Grover search, which is well-understood. Two of them compare to a *collision search* (this time, not golden). We extend our study of SIKE parameters to these two security levels. For this purpose, we analyze the collision search algorithm of [14], which gives the lowest gate count and depth-width product when memory accesses are of linear cost. In Sect. 5, we provide its best parallelization to date. Finally, in Sect. 6, we show that the SIKE parameters have lower quantum security than claimed in [22], but they still meet the NIST security levels claimed in [20].

2 Preliminaries

2.1 Computational Model

For classical computers, we imagine a parallel random access machine with a shared memory. Costs are in RAM operations, with access to the memory having unit cost.

We write quantum algorithms in the *quantum circuit model* [28]. In order to give meaningful cost estimates of quantum circuits, we use the memory peripheral model of [22]. We model the quantum computer as a peripheral of a classical parallel random access machine, which acts on the quantum computer using the Clifford+T gate set. We define two cost metrics:

- The G-cost of an algorithm is the number of gates, each of which costs one RAM operation to the classical controller. Here, we assume that error correction is *passive*, meaning that once a qubit is in a particular state, we incur no cost to maintain that state indefinitely.
- The DW-cost is the depth-width product of the circuit. Here, error correction is *active*. At each time step, the classical controller must act on each qubit of the circuit, even if the qubit was idle at this point.

Connectivity. The standard quantum circuit model assumes no connectivity restriction on the qubits. Two-qubit gates can be applied on any pair of qubits without overhead. In Sect. 3 we do not refer to the connectivity, but in Sect. 4, this layout plays a role, so we consider the two following alternatives: a 2-dimensional grid with nearest-neighbor connectivity (*local*) or no restriction (*nonlocal*). It is shown in [8] that the nonlocal case can be emulated by any network, with a multiplicative overhead that is the time to sort the network.

Quantum Memory Models. Many quantum algorithms use the "qRAM" model, in which the access *in superposition* to the elements in memory is a cheap operation. But the cost of qRAM is unclear at the moment[1]. This model

---

[1] See [6,17] for the "bucket-brigade" architecture, which still requires $\Theta(R)$ gates for a memory access to R bits of memory.

can be restricted to *quantum-accessible classical memory* (QRACM, see [24, Section 2]), while the best time complexities for golden collision search [4, 32] require QRAQM, that is, the memory accessed contains quantum states.

Both QRAQM and QRACM can be constructed in the quantum circuit model with Clifford+T gates. The caveat is that, for R bits of memory, both will require $\Theta(R)$ gates for each memory access. QRAQM will necessarily require R qubits, while QRACM could sequentially simulate the access with poly(R) qubits, and R classical memory. In this work we use only the standard quantum circuit model, so each memory access incurs this large gate cost. In other words, we assume a world in which quantum circuits are scalable, but qRAM is not cheap.

2.2   Problem Description

We focus on the golden collision problem (Problem 2.1), although it is possible to go back and forth to *element distinctness* and *claw-finding*.

Problem 2.1 (Golden collision finding). Let $h : X \to X$ be a random function and $g : X \times X \to \{0, 1\}$ be a *check*. The function h has collisions: pairs $x, y \in X$ such that $h(x) = h(y)$. The function g takes a collision as input, and outputs 1 for a certain set of $\mathcal{O}(1)$ collisions, which we call the *golden collisions*. Given access to h and g, find a golden collision.

In many instances there will be a unique golden collision. If h is not pseudo-random, we pick a random function $f : X \to X$ and assume that $f \circ h$ is pseudo-random. In practice, this holds if h does not have a serious restriction on its outputs.

Problem 2.2 (Element distinctness). Given $h : \{0, 1\}^n \to \{0, 1\}^n$, determine if h is a permutation or not.

This reduces to golden collision search by composing with a random function; the check function is to apply just h and check for the true collision.

Problem 2.3 (Claw-finding). Given $f : \{0, 1\}^n \to \{0, 1\}^m$ and $g : \{0, 1\}^n \to \{0, 1\}^m$, where we assume $m \geq 2n$, find a *claw*: a pair x, y such that $f(x) = g(y)$.

If we construct a random function from $\{0, 1\}^m$ to $\{0, 1\} \times \{0, 1\}^n$, then we can act on $\{0, 1\} \times \{0, 1\}^n$ with f and g by sending $(0, x)$ to $f(x)$ and $(1, x)$ to $g(x)$. The claw becomes a golden collision for the concatenation of these two functions, where we check collisions by checking if they are caused because $f(x) = g(y)$ or by our random function.

Notations. We define $N = 2^n$, the size of the domain and range of h. We let H denote the cost of evaluating h and G the cost of g. In cases where we need to distinguish between the gates, depth, or width of evaluating h, we will use subscripts of G, D, and W, respectively. The memory size is denoted R. Memory is typically counted in n-bit registers that represent inputs or outputs of h.

2.3   Previous Works

We assume that h and g can be evaluated in $\mathsf{poly}(n)$ time. Classically, the query complexity is $\Theta(N)$, since one must at least query every element to find the golden collision. One algorithm to achieve this is to construct a table for all $x, h(x)$, sort the table by the value of $h(x)$, and check each collision. The most prominent practical algorithm for golden collision finding is due to van Oorschot and Wiener [30]. Their method is simple and parallelizes perfectly. With R elements of memory, it requires $\mathcal{O}(N^{3/2}/R^{1/2})$ operations, which is asymptotically optimal for $R = N$.

Buhrman *et al.* [13] give a quantum algorithm in time $\widetilde{\mathcal{O}}(N^{3/4})$ and $\mathcal{O}(N^{1/2})$ memory for claw-finding and element distinctness. This algorithm uses Grover search as a subroutine, and can be recovered by the optimization program of [27]. Ambainis [4] gives a quantum walk algorithm with $\widetilde{\mathcal{O}}(N^{2/3})$ quantum time, with a query complexity of $\mathcal{O}(N^{2/3})$, which is optimal [1]. Tani provided a claw-finding version [32].

However, Buhrman *et al.*'s, Ambainis' and Tani's algorithms require respectively $\mathcal{O}(N^{1/2})$ and $\mathcal{O}(N^{2/3})$ qubits with cheap quantum random access. If random access to a memory of size R requires $\Theta(R)$ gates, then the *gate complexity* of these algorithms is actually $\widetilde{\mathcal{O}}(N^{4/3})$, although they can be reparameterized to reach $\widetilde{\mathcal{O}}(N)$. Grover search over all pairs also costs $\widetilde{\mathcal{O}}(N)$ gates. A careful analysis shows that, if evaluating the function h costs H gates, Tani's algorithm only provides a $\mathcal{O}(\sqrt{\mathsf{H}})$ advantage over Grover's algorithm [22].

Another approach based on a distributed computing model achieves a very good time-memory tradeoff of $TM = \widetilde{\mathcal{O}}(N)$ [8]. However, this is the wall-clock time of a distributed algorithm, and the gate cost remains $\widetilde{\mathcal{O}}(N)$ at each point of the tradeoff curve. There are also locality issues; achieving this tradeoff requires a *nonlocal* connectivity model or a network that can sort itself in poly-logarithmic time.

The distributed algorithm for multi-target preimage search given in [7] can also be reframed for golden collision search, in which case it becomes a variant of [8] based on iterating a random function and computing "chain-ends" (instead of using a parallel RAM emulation unitary). But it is also inherently parallel and does not reach a smaller gate cost than $\widetilde{\mathcal{O}}(N)$.

Improvements for Specific Quantum Oracles. In this paper, we will consider generic algorithms, and we make no assumption on the function h. In the case of SIKE, Biasse and Pring [10] remarked that a trade-off in quantum search, between the number of iterates and the number of isogenies evaluated, was available. In short, a quantum search with $\mathcal{O}(2^{n/2})$ iterates, each evaluating n isogenies, can be brought down to a cost of $\mathcal{O}(2^{n/2}\sqrt{n}\log_2 n)$ isogeny computations. Thus an advantage similar to Tani's algorithm can be obtained via this modified quantum search.

Random Collision Search. When $h : X \rightarrow X$ is a random function, a collision can be found in classical time $\mathcal{O}(N^{1/2})$. Brassard *et al.* [12] give a quantum algorithm with time $\widetilde{\mathcal{O}}(N^{1/3})$, using a QRACM of size $\mathcal{O}(N^{1/3})$. In the quantum circuit model, the lowest gate-count to date is obtained with the algorithm of [14]. The algorithm has a gate complexity of $\mathcal{O}(N^{2/5})$ with $\mathcal{O}(N^{1/5})$ *classical memory without random access*, and makes a total of $\mathcal{O}(N^{1/5})$ accesses to the memory.

Quantum Search. Let X be an unstructured search space containing a subset G of good elements. In classical brute-force search, we are given an algorithm Sample_X to sample uniformly at random from X and a function $f : X \mapsto \{0,1\}$ such that $f(x) = 1$ if and only if $x \in G$. Then there exists an algorithm Sample_G that samples uniformly from G, which consists in sampling and testing $\mathcal{O}\left(\frac{|X|}{|G|}\right)$ times, until an element of G is found. *Quantum search* uses analogous building blocks and gives a quadratic speedup. Grover's algorithm [19] is the special case of $X = \{0,1\}^n$, which is generalized by Amplitude Amplification [11].

Theorem 2.1 (Adapted from [11], Theorem 2). *Let* $\mathsf{QSample}_X$ *be a quantum circuit that, on input* $|0\rangle$*, produces the uniform superposition over* X:
$\mathsf{QSample}_X |0\rangle = \frac{1}{\sqrt{|X|}} \sum_{x \in X} |x\rangle$. *Let* O_f *be a circuit that computes* $O_f |x\rangle = (-1)^{f(x)} |x\rangle$. *Then there exists a quantum circuit* $\mathsf{QSample}_G$ *that, on input* $|0\rangle$*, produces* $\frac{1}{\sqrt{|G|}} \sum_{x \in G} |x\rangle$. *It contains* $\mathcal{O}\left(\sqrt{\frac{|X|}{|G|}}\right)$ *calls to* $\mathsf{QSample}_X$ *and* O_f.

Thus, we can describe any quantum search (hereinafter a "Grover search") by describing how we compute f and sample from X in superposition.

3   Golden Collision Finding with Random Walks

In this section we define the Magniez, Nayak, Roland, Santha (MNRS [26]) *quantum walk* framework by analogy with classical random walks. We describe Ambainis' algorithm and review van Oorschot-Wiener's golden collision search as a random walk. While this is a needlessly complicated way to describe the classical algorithm, it allows us to quickly introduce a new quantum "iteration-based" walk giving our best G-cost, thanks to the MNRS framework. Next, we give an alternative "prefix-based" walk that reaches the same gate complexity.

3.1   Random Walk Search

A simple, memory-limited search for collisions is to enumerate R random elements of X in a list, sorted by $h(x)$. We find all collisions of h in the list and we check whether any collision is golden. If we do not find any, we delete a random element from the list and replace it with a new random element of X.

To view this as a random walk on a graph, we let the vertices V be the set of all subsets of X of size R. The insertion-and-deletion process moves from one vertex to another. Two vertices are adjacent if and only if they differ in exactly one element. Such a graph is known as a *Johnson graph*, denoted $J(X, R)$.

In general, let $G = (V, E)$ be an undirected, connected, regular graph. We suppose there is some subset of *marked* vertices M, and our task is to output any vertex $x \in M$. We assume we have circuits to perform the following tasks:

Set-up: Returns a random vertex v.
Update: Given a vertex v, returns a random vertex adjacent to v.
Check: Given a vertex v, returns 1 if v is marked and 0 otherwise.

In practice we assume that the random selection is actually performed via a random selection of a bitstring, and a map from bitstrings to the relevant components of the graph; this ensures that the circuits work equally for classically selecting elements at random or for constructing quantum superpositions.

Magniez *et al.* present a unified framework to solve such tasks [26]. The cost depends on several factors:

- The costs S, U, C of the set-up, update, and check circuits, respectively.
- The fraction of marked vertices, $\epsilon := \frac{|M|}{|V|}$.
- The spectral gap of G, denoted δ, equal to the difference between the largest and second-largest eigenvalues of the normalized adjacency matrix of G.

In this paper we only consider Johnson graphs. For a graph $J(X, R)$, S is the cost of initializing a random subset of R elements of X, and U is the cost of replacing one element in such a subset. In all of our applications, it is easiest to keep a single flag bit or counter for the entire list to indicate when it is marked. We update this flag with every update step when we insert and delete elements, and for the check step we simply look at the flag bit.

If we start from a random vertex and take only a few random steps, then the vertex we reach is highly dependent on our starting vertex. For regular graphs, if we take *enough* random steps we reach a uniformly random vertex. The minimum number of steps for this to happen is the *mixing time*, which is the inverse of the spectral gap. For Johnson graphs, it takes R random insertions and deletions to transform one subset of R elements into a new, uniformly random subset. Thus, the mixing time is $\mathcal{O}(R)$ and the spectral gap is $\Omega(1/R)$.

Classical Random Walk. In a classical random walk, we begin by initializing a random vertex with the set-up circuit. We then repeat the following: We take $\mathcal{O}(\frac{1}{\delta})$ random steps in the graph using the update circuit. We then check if the current vertex is marked using the check circuit; if it is marked, we output it and stop, otherwise we repeat the random steps-and-check process. Since $\mathcal{O}(\frac{1}{\delta})$ is the mixing time of the graph, taking this many random steps turns the current vertex into a uniformly random one, which has a ϵ chance of being marked. Thus, the total cost is

$$\mathcal{O}\left(S + \frac{1}{\epsilon}\left(\frac{1}{\delta}U + C\right)\right). \tag{1}$$

Quantum Random Walk. The quantum walk is analogous to the classical case in the same way that Grover search is analogous to a brute force search. The cost of the quantum random walk is

$$\tilde{\mathcal{O}}\left(\mathsf{S} + \frac{1}{\sqrt{\epsilon}}\left(\frac{1}{\sqrt{\delta}}\mathsf{U} + \mathsf{C}\right)\right). \tag{2}$$

If we use the Tolerant Recursive Amplitude Amplification technique from MNRS, possibly using a qubit as control, we can find a marked vertex in $\mathcal{O}(1/\sqrt{\epsilon})$ iterations when ϵ is only a lower bound on the fraction of marked vertices.

In Eq. 1, the factor of $\frac{1}{\delta}$ appears because we need that many steps to create a uniformly random vertex. For Johnson graphs, this means we need R insertions and deletions to create a new random list. In the quantum algorithm, Eq. 2 seems to imply that we can replace all the elements in an R-element list with only $\sqrt{R}$ insertions and deletions. This is not an accurate description of the quantum walk; to properly describe the algorithm we need to use the graph formalism, but we refer to [26] for full details.

All quantum algorithms in this paper will be quantum walks or quantum walks used as checking oracles in a Grover search. Thus, we will simply describe the graph, the setup, update, and refer to Eq. 2. We omit describing the checking subroutine, because in all cases it will simply check if a counter is non-zero or if a flag is 1. The MNRS framework ensures the existence of a corresponding quantum walk and the soundness of our complexity analyses.

To efficiently represent sets for a random walk, a classical computer can use any sorted list structure that enables efficient insertion, deletion and search. For a quantum data structure, we use the Johnson vertex data structure from [22]. In both cases, we can store extra data with each element in the set. This will be necessary for several algorithms.

3.2   Ambainis' Algorithm

Ambainis' element distinctness algorithm [4] performs a random walk and is a query-optimal algorithm for Problem 2.1.

Graph. Ambainis' algorithm uses the Johnson graph $J(X, R)$, where subsets of X are stored as lists of tuples $(x, h(x))$ sorted by $h(x)$, with a a global counter indicating the total number of golden collisions in the current set.

Update. A random step will delete a random element from the set, select a new random element $x \in X$, and insert $(x, h(x))$ into the new list. It must also check if $h(x) = h(y)$ for any y in the list; for all such y, we increment the global counter if the collision is golden. We do the same check for the deleted element, and decrement the counter for any collisions we find.

It costs $\mathsf{H} + \log R$ to compute a new element and insert it into the list, plus the cost to check for golden collisions. The average number of collisions with a new element will be $\frac{R-1}{N}$, since we assume h is a random function. If it costs G to check if a collision is golden, then the total update cost is, on average, $\mathsf{U} = \mathcal{O}(\mathsf{H} + \log R + \frac{R-1}{N}\mathsf{G})$.

Setup. The setup step consists of R insertions into a sorted list, incrementing the counter for any golden collisions we find. This will cost $S = \mathcal{O}((H + \log R)R)$.

Marked Vertices. A vertex will be marked if it contains both the elements x_g and y_g which form the golden collision. The fraction of such vertices will be $\epsilon = \frac{R(R-1)}{N(N-1)} \approx \frac{R^2}{N^2}$.

Classical Variant. Substituting the previous values into Eq. 1, we obtain

$$\mathcal{O}\left(\underbrace{R(H + \log R)}_{S} + \underbrace{\frac{N^2}{R^2}}_{1/\epsilon}\left(\underbrace{\frac{R}{1/\delta}}_{1/\delta}\underbrace{\left(H + \log R + \frac{R-1}{N}G \right) + \underbrace{1}_{C}}_{U} \right) \right). \tag{3}$$

Assuming G is not much more expensive than H, the optimal occurs when $R = \frac{N^2}{R-1}$, and we conclude that $R = N$ is best, with a cost of roughly $\mathcal{O}(NH)$.

Quantum Variant. Assuming *cheap QRAQM*, the setup, update and checking costs are the same as classically (There are subtle issues ensuring that each subroutine is reversible and constant-time, but we ignore those for now). Equation 2 gives the following complexity:

$$\widetilde{\mathcal{O}}\left(\underbrace{R(H + \log R)}_{S} + \underbrace{\sqrt{\frac{N^2}{R^2}}}_{1/\sqrt{\epsilon}}\left(\underbrace{\sqrt{R}}_{1/\sqrt{\delta}}\underbrace{\left(H + \log R + \frac{R-1}{N}G \right) + \underbrace{1}_{C}}_{U} \right) \right). \tag{4}$$

We optimize this by taking $R = N^{2/3}$, for a total cost of $\widetilde{\mathcal{O}}(N^{2/3})$.

Costing Memory. We need a constant number of memory accesses to insert into the list and to retrieve the collisions in the list to check if they are golden. If each costs $\Theta(R)$ gates, this changes the total cost to

$$\widetilde{\mathcal{O}}\left(\underbrace{R(H + R)}_{S} + \underbrace{\sqrt{\frac{N^2}{R^2}}}_{1/\sqrt{\epsilon}}\left(\underbrace{\sqrt{R}}_{1/\sqrt{\delta}}\underbrace{\left(H + R + \frac{R-1}{N}G \right) + \underbrace{1}_{C}}_{U} \right) \right). \tag{5}$$

Here, the optimal occurs when $R = H$, for a total cost roughly $\mathcal{O}(N\sqrt{H})$. Previous work [22] noticed that Grover's algorithm has gate cost of $\mathcal{O}(NH)$, so Tani's algorithm [32] and Ambainis' algorithm [4] provide, in gate cost, an advantage of $\sqrt{H}$ over Grover's algorithm. This suggests that we should push more of the costs into the function h if we want to beat Grover's algorithm.

3.3   Iteration-Based Walk

Here we present van Oorschot-Wiener's golden collision search as a random walk on a Johnson graph, which is equivalent to the original description. This allows us to easily extend to the quantum version, one of our main results, by simply taking square roots of the relevant terms.

The central idea of [30] is to "lift" the function h via *distinguished points*. We select a random subset X_D of size $|X_D| = \theta N$ for some $\theta < 1$, and denote such points as "distinguished". In practice we choose bitstrings with a fixed prefix. From the random function $h : \{0,1\}^n \to \{0,1\}^n$ we construct a random function $h_D : \{0,1\}^n \to X_D$ such that the collisions of h map to collisions of h_D.

To construct h_D, we iterate h. Since h is a pseudo-random function, there is some probability that $h(x) \in X_D$ for every x. We expect to require $1/\theta$ iterations of h before the output is in X_D. Thus, we pick some u greater than $1/\theta$ and define the following function: $h_D(x) = h^m(x)$, where m is the largest $m \le u$ such that $h^m(x) \in X_D$; if such an m does not exist, we pick a random $y \in X_D$ and set $h_D(x) = y$. If we choose u as a large multiple of $1/\theta$, we expect the case where we do not reach a distinguished point to be exceedingly rare (see Sect. A in the Appendix). For now, we will simply say that $u \approx 1/\theta$.

Graph. The graph is the same as Ambainis' algorithm, $J(X, R)$. However, each element in the list is stored as $(x, h_D(x), u_x)$, where u_x is such that $h_D(x) = h^{u_x}(x)$. We will not detect all golden collisions, so we use a global flag rather than a counter to track whether the list contains a golden collision. Section A in the Appendix explains how this can be done in a history-independent way.

Update. To insert a new element, we select a random x from X and iterate $h^i(x)$ until either $i \ge u$ or $h^i(x)$ is distinguished. We then write $(x, h^{u_x}(x), u_x)$ into the list, where u_x is the maximum i we found.

To check for the golden collision, we look for all y such that $h_D(y) = h_D(x)$. This implies there is some n, m such that $h^n(x) = h^m(y)$. We want to find this collision and check if it is golden. Assume without loss of generality that $u_x \ge u_y$. Then we set $x' = h^{u_x - u_y}(x)$, repeatedly apply h to x' and y and compare the results. As soon as they are equal, we check if this is the golden collision, and update the flag bit if it is. We then delete one of the previous elements from the list, and do the same check for golden collisions, setting the flag to 0 if the deleted element was part of the golden collision.

It costs $u\mathsf{H} = \mathcal{O}(\mathsf{H}/\theta)$ to compute $h_D(x)$ for a random insertion of x, and it classically costs $\log R$ to insert that element. To maintain the flag indicating if the list contains a trail that leads to the golden collision, we must locate where the underlying collision of h occurs, which takes $u\mathsf{H}$ steps for each collision. The average number of collisions is $(R-1)u^2/N = \mathcal{O}(R/N\theta^2)$, because there are u points on the trail leading to the newly-inserted point, and for each of the $R-1$ existing elements in the list, its value under h has a u/N chance of ending up in the trail of the new point.

Thus, the update cost becomes $\mathsf{U} = \mathcal{O}\left(\frac{\mathsf{H}}{\theta} + \log R + \frac{R}{N\theta^2}\frac{\mathsf{H}}{\theta} + \frac{R}{N\theta^2}\mathsf{G}\right)$. From here on we assume that $\mathsf{G} \ll u\mathsf{H}$, so we ignore the last term.

Setup. The setup is just R sequential insertions, maintaining the flag bit, which costs $\mathsf{S} = \mathcal{O}(R(\mathsf{H}n + \log R))$.

Marked Vertices. Section B in the Appendix gives a detailed analysis of the number of marked elements. Roughly speaking, every random function will produce some number of points ("predecessors") z such that $h^k(z) = x_g$ or $h^k(z) = y_g$ for some k. For a vertex to be marked, we must select at least one predecessor for each half of the golden collision among the R random starting points. More predecessors means a higher chance of finding the golden collision, but selecting a random function that gives many predecessors to the golden collision is unlikely.

To find a large number of predecessors, we can select a random function h' and precompose $h \circ h'$ and perform the search on this new function. This acts like a new random function, but preserves the golden collision. Lemma B.2 shows that for a fixed t, the probability that a random function will give at least t predecessors to both halves of the golden collision is $\Theta(1/t)$. From here on, we assume that the golden collision has at least t predecessors, and we will simply repeat the walk with new functions until it works, which will be $\Theta(t)$ times.

Given such a well-behaved function, each random element has a roughly t/N chance of being a predecessor of one half of the golden collision. We need predecessors of both halves, and there are R vertices, so there are $\Omega(\frac{R^2t^2}{N^2})$ marked vertices (Theorem B.1).

Analysis. Assume $\log R \ll \frac{H}{\epsilon}$, and that H/θ dominates G, then the cost of a single walk, by Eq. 1, is:

$$\mathcal{O}\left(\underbrace{R\Big(Hn + \log R\Big)}_{S} + \underbrace{\frac{N^2}{R^2t^2}}_{1/\epsilon}\Big(\underbrace{R}_{1/\delta}\big(\underbrace{\tfrac{H}{\theta} + \log R + \tfrac{(R-1)n^2}{N}\tfrac{H}{\theta}}_{U}\big) + \underbrace{1}_{C}\big)\right) \quad (6)$$

$$= \mathcal{O}\left(\frac{RH}{\theta} + \frac{N^2}{Rt^2\theta}H + \frac{N}{t^2\theta^3}H\right). \quad (7)$$

We expect to repeat the walk $\Theta(t)$ times with different random functions before we select one that gives the golden collision sufficiently long trails. Thus, the total cost is

$$\mathcal{O}\left(\frac{tRH}{\theta} + \frac{N^2}{Rt\theta}H + \frac{N}{t\theta^3}H\right). \quad (8)$$

The right two terms are largest, so we optimize those first. The optimal will occur when the two sides are equal: $\frac{N^2}{Rt\theta} = \frac{N}{t\theta^3}$, which implies $\theta = \sqrt{R/N}$. The remaining terms balance when $t = \frac{N}{R}$, giving a cost of $\mathcal{O}(HN^{3/2}/R^{1/2})$, so long as $R \leq N$. This recaptures van Oorschot and Wiener's result, including their heuristic value of the number of function repetitions.

3.4   Quantum Iteration-Based Walk

As with Ambainis' algorithm, we compute the cost in the quantum case by making the following changes: • the cost to access memory is now $\mathcal{O}(R)$, • the $1/\epsilon$ and $1/\delta$ terms in Eq. 1 get square root speed-ups, as in Eq. 2, • the update subroutine must be reversible and constant-time (Sect. A in the Appendix gives the details of this change), • we perform a Grover search for random functions, and thus only need to repeat the walk $\mathcal{O}(\sqrt{t})$ times.

We will find that the optimal parameters would put $t \geq 1/\theta^2$, which invalidates our arguments from before. If x_g has t predecessors, with high probability we can still expect $\Omega(1/\theta^2)$ predecessors p such that $h^k(p) = x_g$ for $k \leq 1/\theta$ (Theorem B.2). Thus, the fraction of marked vertices will still be $\epsilon = \Omega(\frac{R^2}{N^2\theta^4})$.

This gives a total cost of

$$\tilde{\mathcal{O}}\left(t^{\frac{1}{2}} \left(\underbrace{\frac{RH}{\theta}}_{S} + \underbrace{\frac{N\theta^2}{R}}_{1/\sqrt{\epsilon}} \left(\underbrace{R^{\frac{1}{2}}}_{1/\sqrt{\delta}} \underbrace{\left(\frac{H}{\theta} + R + \frac{(R-1)H}{N\theta^3} \right)}_{U} + \underbrace{1}_{C} \right) \right) \right) \tag{9}$$

The cost increases with t so we want to take $t = 1/\theta^2$, the minimum before the fraction of marked vertices increases. Optimizing the rest gives $\theta = H/R$, $R = N^{2/7}H^{4/7}$, and a total gate cost of $\boxed{\tilde{\mathcal{O}}\left(N^{6/7}H^{5/7} \right)}$.

3.5   Prefix-Based Walk

In this alternative quantum walk, we use a slightly altered definition of distinguished points: X_D becomes the set of inputs x such that $h(x)$ has a given prefix. Either both halves of the golden collision are distinguished, which happens with probability θ, or none is. By choosing different prefixes, we can easily change the definition of X_D, and after $\frac{1}{\theta}$ trials, or $\frac{1}{\sqrt{\theta}}$ quantum search iterates, we expect the golden collision to be distinguished.

Graph. The graph becomes $J(X_D, R)$. Elements are stored as tuples $(x, h(x))$, sorted by $h(x)$. The list has a global counter of the number of golden collisions.

Update. To insert a new element $(x, h(x))$, we need to sample randomly from X_D. We use Grover's algorithm for a partial pre-image search on h to find x such that $h(x)$ has the correct prefix. Once we find a random element, we check for the golden collision with existing elements and increment the counter, as in Ambainis' algorithm. We do the same procedure when we delete a random element. Since the fraction of distinguished points is θ, the update cost is $\frac{H}{\sqrt{\theta}}+R$.[2]

Marked Vertices. A vertex is marked if it contains both halves of the golden collision, chosen among the θN distinguished points. With a wrong prefix, no vertices are marked. With the right prefix, vertices are marked with probability $R^2/(\theta^2 N^2)$.

---

[2] The quantum search in the update unitary cannot be exact, because the exact size of X_D is not known at runtime. The error depends on the difference between $|X_D|$ and θN for the actual good choice of distinguished points. A "hybrid" argument, as in [4], shows that this has no consequence on the walk.

Analysis. With the correct prefix, we find a marked vertex with $\frac{N\theta}{R}$ iterations; with an incorrect prefix, we will never find a marked vertex. Thus, we use the walk as a checking unitary in a Grover search for the correct prefix. From Eq. 2, each walk has a cost of

$$\tilde{\mathcal{O}}\left(\underbrace{R\frac{H}{\sqrt{\theta}} + R\log R}_{S} + \underbrace{\frac{N\theta}{R}}_{1/\sqrt{\epsilon}} \underbrace{\left(\sqrt{R}\underbrace{\left(\frac{H}{\sqrt{\theta}} + R\right)}_{U} + \underbrace{1}_{C}\right)}_{1/\sqrt{\delta}} \right). \qquad (10)$$

Optimizing R and θ gives $R = H/\sqrt{\theta}$. The walk is sound if $N\theta/R \geq 1$ i.e. $N\theta^{3/2} \geq H$ i.e. $\theta \geq (H/N)^{2/3}$. Since there are $1/\theta$ possible prefixes, the Grover search must iterate $1/\sqrt{\theta}$ times. The total gate cost, with the Grover search, is:

$$\tilde{\mathcal{O}}\left(\frac{1}{\sqrt{\theta}}\left(\frac{H^2}{\theta} + \underbrace{N\theta^{3/4}\sqrt{H}}_{\text{Walk}} \right) \right) = \tilde{\mathcal{O}}\left(H^2\theta^{-3/2} + N\theta^{1/4}\sqrt{H} \right). \qquad (11)$$

The minimal gate complexity with this method is reached when $H^2\theta^{-3/2} = N\theta^{1/4}\sqrt{H}$ i.e. $\theta = N^{-4/7}H^{6/7}$. At this point we obtain a total gate cost of $\tilde{\mathcal{O}}(N\theta^{1/4}\sqrt{H}) = \tilde{\mathcal{O}}(N^{6/7}H^{5/7})$ and corresponding memory $R = N^{2/7}H^{4/7}$, the same result as in Sect. 3.3.

Classically, the iteration is appealing because the probability of a collision between two trails is much higher than the probability of a collision between two randomly chosen distinguished points. In contrast, a quantum computer can find preimages of distinguished points faster using Grover search, but cannot iterate a function faster than a classical computer. This advantage and disadvantage cancel out, which is why both methods fall on the same complexity.

4 Parallelization

The algorithms of Sect. 3 optimize only the *gate cost* and benefit from leaving most of the qubits idle for most of the time. Trying to reduce the depth may or may not increase the gate complexity. For example, the depth of the memory access circuit can be brought down easily to $\mathcal{O}(\log R)$. In contrast, reducing the depth of a Grover search by a factor $\sqrt{P}$ multiplies its gate cost by $\sqrt{P}$.

In this section we optimize the gate count under a depth limit. We find that prefix-based walks can maintain an advantage in gate cost over Grover's algorithm. However, by combining prefix methods with the Multi-Grover algorithm of [8], we provide a much better approach to parallelization under very short depth limits. Even with local connectivity in a two-dimensional mesh, this approach can parallelize to depths as low as $\mathcal{O}(N^{1/2})$ without increasing gate cost over $\mathcal{O}(N)$, and to depths as low as $O(N^{1/4})$ with gate cost $\mathcal{O}(N^{3/2}/D)$. We do not analyze parallel iteration-based walks.

In our computational model, we can apply gates freely to as many qubits as we wish, but it is helpful to think of many *parallel processors* that can act on the circuit all at once. We represent this with a parameter P.

There is always a naive strategy of splitting the search space. Each processor would search a disjoint subset of possible inputs; however, since we want a collision, we need to ensure each *pair* of inputs is assigned to one processor. Thus, with P processors, each one must search a space of size $N/P^{1/2}$. We would like to find better methods, if possible.

4.1   Prefix-Based Walk

We consider the algorithm of Sect. 3.5. The setup step can be perfectly parallelized. We do not parallelize the iterations of the walk nor the overall search for prefixes, but instead use our computing power to accelerate the update step. The depth to find an element with a good prefix can be reduced to $\mathsf{H}_D/(\sqrt{\theta}\sqrt{P})$ by parallelizing the Grover search, as long as we have $P \leq R$ and $P \leq \frac{1}{\theta}$. This increases the total gate cost to

$$\widetilde{\mathcal{O}}\left(\ \underbrace{\frac{1}{\sqrt{\theta}}}_{} \Big(\underbrace{\frac{R\mathsf{H}_G}{\sqrt{\theta}} + \mathsf{S}_G}_{\mathsf{S}} + \underbrace{\frac{N\theta}{R}}_{1/\sqrt{\epsilon}} \Big(\underbrace{\sqrt{R}}_{1/\sqrt{\delta}} \Big(\underbrace{\frac{\mathsf{H}_G\sqrt{P}}{\sqrt{\theta}} + R}_{\mathsf{U}} \Big) + \underbrace{1}_{\mathsf{C}} \Big) \Big) \ \right) \qquad (12)$$

where S_G is the gate cost of sorting each vertex, which will depend on the connectivity. Optimizing the gate cost gives $R = \frac{\mathsf{H}_G\sqrt{P}}{\sqrt{\theta}}$. The constraint $P \leq R$ turns into $\sqrt{P} \leq \mathsf{H}_G/\sqrt{\theta}$ which is implied by the condition $P\theta \leq 1$. Even in the local case, where we have $\mathsf{S}_G = R\sqrt{R}$, we find that $\frac{R\mathsf{H}_G}{\sqrt{\theta}}$ dominates the setup cost. By writing an equality between the setup and the walk, we get $\frac{R\mathsf{H}_G}{\sqrt{\theta}} = N\theta\sqrt{R}$. By replacing R in this equation we find $\theta = N^{-4/7}\mathsf{H}_G^{6/7}P^{1/7}$. This gives $R = \mathsf{H}_G^{4/7}N^{2/7}P^{3/7}$. The total gate cost becomes $\boxed{\widetilde{\mathcal{O}}(N^{6/7}\mathsf{H}_G^{5/7}P^{2/7})}$.

The total depth depends on our assumption about locality, because sorting the vertex in the set-up and inserting into the vertex during an update will both depend on the architecture. For both, the depth will be $\mathcal{O}(\log R)$ in a non-local setting but $\mathcal{O}(R^{1/2})$ in the local setting. If we denote this depth as S_D, the total depth of each walk is

$$\widetilde{\mathcal{O}}\left(\frac{\mathsf{H}_D}{\sqrt{\theta}} + \mathsf{S}_D + \frac{N\theta}{R}\sqrt{R}\left(\frac{\mathsf{H}_D}{\sqrt{\theta}\sqrt{P}} + \mathsf{S}_D \right) \right). \qquad (13)$$

As long as $\mathsf{H}_D/\sqrt{\theta P} \geq \mathsf{S}_D$, the depth does not depend on locality; finding distinguished points takes longer than insertion or sorting. We can parallelize up to $\frac{1}{\sqrt{\theta}\sqrt{P}} = \mathsf{S}_D$ which gives $P = \widetilde{\mathcal{O}}(N^{1/2})$ in the non-local setting and $P = \widetilde{\mathcal{O}}(N^{2/11})$ in the local setting.

Beyond this maximum parallelization of the distinguished point search, we can parallelize the search over possible prefixes. In this case the search for the correct prefix is like a normal Grover search, where the oracle is a maximally-parallelized random walk. We can parallelize this way up to $1/\theta$ processors; beyond this, we split the search space.

Table 1. Asymptotic parameters for prefix-based random walks. For readability, H and $\mathcal{O}$ notations are omitted. The line "Any" describes a tradeoff for any $D \leq N^{6/7}$, until $D = N^{1/2}$ in the non-local case and $D = N^{8/11}$ in the local case. "Inner" parallelism is inside a walk. "Outer" parallelism is in the outer Grover iterations. "Memory" is the width of a single walk.

Locality constraint	Depth limit	G-cost	Memory	Parallelism		DW-cost
				Inner	Outer	
Any	$D = N^{\frac{6}{7}}$	$N^{\frac{6}{7}}$	$N^{\frac{2}{7}}$	1	1	$N^{\frac{8}{7}}$
	$N^* \leq D \leq N^{\frac{6}{7}}$	$N^{\frac{6}{5}}D^{-\frac{2}{5}}$	$N^{\frac{4}{5}}D^{-\frac{3}{5}}$	$N^{\frac{6}{5}}D^{-\frac{7}{5}}$	1	$N^{\frac{4}{5}}D^{\frac{2}{5}}$
Non-local	$D = N^{\frac{1}{2}}$	N	$N^{\frac{1}{2}}$	$N^{\frac{1}{2}}$	1	N
	$N^{\frac{1}{4}} \leq D \leq N^{\frac{1}{2}}$	$N^{\frac{3}{2}}D^{-1}$	$N^{\frac{1}{2}}$	$N^{\frac{1}{2}}$	ND^{-2}	$N^{\frac{3}{2}}D^{-1}$
	$D \leq N^{\frac{1}{4}}$	$N^2 D^{-3}$	D^2	D^2	D^2	$N^2 D^{-3}$
2-dim. neighbors	$D = N^{\frac{8}{11}}$	$N^{\frac{10}{11}}$	$N^{\frac{4}{11}}$	$N^{\frac{2}{11}}$	1	$N^{\frac{12}{11}}$
	$N^{\frac{5}{11}} \leq D \leq N^{\frac{8}{11}}$	$N^{\frac{18}{11}}D^{-1}$	$N^{\frac{4}{11}}$	$N^{\frac{2}{11}}$	$N^{\frac{16}{11}}D^{-2}$	$N^{\frac{20}{11}}D^{-1}$
	$D \leq N^{\frac{5}{11}}$	$N^2 D^{-\frac{9}{5}}$	$D^{\frac{4}{5}}$	$D^{\frac{2}{5}}$	$D^{\frac{6}{5}}$	$N^2 D^{-\frac{7}{5}}$

Grover's algorithm under a depth limit D will cost $\mathcal{O}(N^2/D)$ gates. Table 1 shows that prefix-based walks are exponentially cheaper than Grover's algorithm, even under restrictive depth limits, though the factor is small.

4.2   Multi-grover Search

For even shorter depth constraints, our next algorithm is a prefix-based adaptation of [8]. As in the prefix-based random walk of Sect. 3.5, we choose an arbitrary prefix and define distinguished points X_D to be those x where $h(x)$ has the fixed prefix. We wrap the entire algorithm in a Grover search for the correct prefix, which will require $\mathcal{O}(1/\sqrt{\theta})$ iterations.

For each prefix, we run a Grover search over lists of distinguished points. To construct each list, we use each one of the P processors to separately run a Grover search for x such that $h(x)$ is a distinguished point. This has cost $\mathcal{O}(H_G/\sqrt{\theta})$ per processor, so the total gate count is $\mathcal{O}(H_G P/\sqrt{\theta})$.

The Grover search will produce a random list of P points out of the $N\theta$ distinguished ones, so for the good prefix choice, the probability of containing the golden collision is at least $\frac{\binom{P}{2}(N\theta)^{P-2}}{(N\theta)^P} = \Omega\left(\frac{P^2}{N^2\theta^2}\right)$.

The Grover search on prefixes requires $\mathcal{O}(1/\sqrt{\theta})$ iterations, leading to a total cost of

$$\mathcal{O}\left(\frac{1}{\theta^{1/2}}\frac{N\theta}{P}\left(\frac{H_G P}{\theta^{1/2}} + S_G\right)\right) = \mathcal{O}\left(NH_G + \frac{N\theta^{1/2}S_G}{P}\right) \qquad (14)$$

The sorting cost S_G is the interesting factor. If S_G/P is small, then the $\mathcal{O}(NH_G)$ term will be the greatest and lead to a near-perfect parallelization.

Table 2. Prefix-based Multi-Grover on a local architecture limited to a depth D. The three different parallelization strategies are described in the text.

Parallelization	Depth limits	G-cost	Total hardware	Depth	DW-cost
DP search	$N^{\frac{1}{2}} \leq D$	N	ND^{-1}	D	N
Prefix search	$N^{\frac{1}{4}} \leq D \leq N^{\frac{1}{2}}$	$N^{\frac{3}{2}}D^{-1}$	$N^{\frac{3}{2}}D^{-2}$	D	$N^{\frac{3}{2}}D^{-1}$
Split search space	$D \leq N^{\frac{1}{4}}$	$N^2 D^{-3}$	$N^2 D^{-4}$	D	$N^2 D^{-3}$

This is the original result of [8]. Our improvement is that when S_G/P is large, we can adjust θ to compensate. For example, on a two-dimensional mesh, $S_G = \mathcal{O}(P^{3/2})$. In this case we set $\theta = \mathsf{H}_D^2/P$. The depth to construct each list is $\mathcal{O}(\mathsf{H}_D/\theta^{1/2})$ and we denote the depth to sort as S_D, so the total depth is

$$\mathcal{O}\left(\frac{N\theta^{1/2}}{P}\left(\frac{\mathsf{H}_D}{\theta^{1/2}} + S_D\right)\right) = \mathcal{O}\left(\frac{N\mathsf{H}_D}{P} + \frac{N\theta^{1/2}S_D}{P}\right). \tag{15}$$

In the two-dimensional mesh, $S_D = \mathcal{O}(P^{1/2})$, so we find a total depth of $\mathcal{O}(N\mathsf{H}_D/P)$. Thus, this algorithm parallelizes perfectly, even accounting for locality. The maximum parallelization this method can achieve is $P = \mathcal{O}(N^{1/2})$. At this point, each list contains *all* the distinguished points, so the walk provides no advantage. To reach lower depths, we first parallelize the search over prefixes, which can reach a depth of $O(N^{1/4})$. Below this, we split the search space. Table 2 summarizes these results. If we have some architecture where $S_D = o(P^{1/2})$, we can choose $\theta = P/N$ and the asymptotic depth is $\mathcal{O}(N\mathsf{H}_D/P)$ even for large P.

5   Quantum (Parallel) Collision Search

In this section, we study the algorithm of [14] which, in the baseline quantum circuit model, is the only one that achieves a lower gate count than classical for the collision search problem. Here, our goal is to output any collision from a random function $h : \{0,1\}^n \to \{0,1\}^n$ with many expected collisions. We improve the parallelization given in [14] in order to achieve the best gate counts under a depth restriction. This will help us compare our golden collision search algorithms to some NIST security levels.

Algorithm. The algorithm of [14] uses the same definition of distinguished points as in our prefix-based walk. It runs in two phases: first, Grover's algorithm finds M distinguished points. These elements are stored in a *classical* memory with *sequential access*. Second, we search a distinguished point colliding with the memory. Sampling from distinguished points is done with Grover search. Testing membership in the memory is done with a sequential circuit. The gate complexity is: $\mathcal{O}\left(M\frac{\mathsf{H}_G}{\sqrt{\theta}} + \sqrt{\frac{N\theta}{M}}\left(\frac{\mathsf{H}_G}{\sqrt{\theta}} + M\right)\right)$ and the gate count is optimal when $\mathsf{H}_G/\sqrt{\theta} = M$ and $M^2 = M\sqrt{N\theta/M}$ *i.e.* $\theta = M^3/N$ and $M = \mathsf{H}_G^{2/5}N^{1/5}$. Then we have a gate count of $\mathcal{O}(\mathsf{H}_G^{4/5}N^{2/5})$ [14].

Parallelized Algorithm. The authors of [14] considered the first phase to be distributed on many quantum processors, the distinguished points stored in a single classical memory, and the second phase as a distributed Grover search. Using the methods of [8] does better, similar to our Multi-Grover golden collision search. Each processor has a local classical memory of size M/P, where it stores its distinguished points. We do a Grover search over lists of P elements, so in each iteration each processor finds a new distinguished point. To test these new values of h for a collision in the stored data, we use the quantum parallel RAM emulation unitary of [8, Theorem 5]. It emulates in total gate count S_G (and depth S_D) P parallel calls to a RAM of size P. With each call we compare against the *first* distinguished point stored by each processor, then the second, etc. Assuming $P \leq M$, the gate count and depth become:

$$\mathcal{O}\left(M \frac{H_G}{\sqrt{\theta}} + \sqrt{\frac{N\theta}{MP}} \left(P \frac{H_G}{\sqrt{\theta}} + \frac{M}{P} S_G \right) \right) \text{ and } \mathcal{O}\left(\frac{M}{P} \frac{H_D}{\sqrt{\theta}} + \sqrt{\frac{N\theta}{MP}} \left(\frac{H_D}{\sqrt{\theta}} + \frac{M}{P} S_D \right) \right)$$

We set $\frac{H_G}{\sqrt{\theta}} = \frac{M}{P^2} S_G$ and $\theta = M^3/(NP)$. We obtain a gate count of $\frac{M^2}{P^2} S_G = H_G^{4/5} N^{2/5} S_G^{1/5}$, where S_G is a function of P. hence $S_G^{2/5} \leq H_G^{2/5} N^{1/5}$. The parallelization from [14] occurs in the worst-case scenario $S_G = P^2$.

Depth Optimization. Assuming $H_G = H_D = H$, on a local 2-dimensional grid, $S_G = P^{3/2}$, $S_D = P^{1/2}$ and the depth is $H_G^{4/5} N^{2/5} P^{-7/10}$. If we optimize the gate count for a given depth D, we get $P = H_G^{8/7} N^{4/7} D^{-10/7}$ and a gate count: $DP = \mathcal{O}(H_G^{8/7} N^{4/7} D^{-3/7})$ which is valid as long as $P \leq N^{1/3} H_G^{2/3}$ i.e. $N^{1/6} H_G^{1/3} \leq D$.

Further Parallelization. When $D = N^{1/6} H^{1/3}$, there are $P = N^{1/3} H^{2/3}$ processors which independently search for distinguished points. These points are sorted and a collision is expected to occur. The sorting step of depth $\sqrt{P}$ is balanced with the search step, and the gate count is $\widetilde{\mathcal{O}}(\sqrt{N}H)$. We reach depths below $\widetilde{\mathcal{O}}(N^{1/6})$ by doing this independently in parallel. We set θ such that $H\theta^{-1/2} = D$ i.e. $\theta = H^2 D^{-2}$. We set $P = D^2$. We now have chunks of processors that look for distinguished points (one per processor), sort themselves and look whether a collision has occurred. The probability to get a collision for a chunk is $\frac{D^2}{\theta N}$, thus we need $\frac{\theta N}{D^2} = \frac{H^2 N}{D^4}$ chunks. The total gate count is: $\widetilde{\mathcal{O}}\left(\frac{H^2 N}{D^4} D \right) = \widetilde{\mathcal{O}}\left(\frac{H^2 N}{D^3} \right)$.

6 Security of SIKE

Supersingular Isogeny Key Encapsulation (SIKE) [20] is a candidate post-quantum key encapsulation based on isogenies of elliptic curves. So far its security is based on the hardness of generic meet-in-the-middle attacks. SIKE is

Table 3. Security thresholds from NIST. AES key search figures are from [21]. For AES key search, the width is approximately equal to max(13, DW − Maxdepth). The cost of evaluating SHA-3 is taken from [5].

Metric	Maxdepth	AES key search			SHA collisions			
		Security level			Security level			
		1	3	5	2		4	
					Cost	Width	Cost	Width
G-cost	∞	83	116	148	122	12	184	17
	2^{96}	83	126	191	134	50	221	143
	2^{64}	93	157	222	148	96	268	221
	2^{40}	117	181	246	187	158	340	317
DW-cost	∞	87	119	152	134	12	201	17
	2^{96}	87	130	194	145	50	239	143
	2^{64}	97	161	225	159	96	285	221
	2^{40}	121	185	249	198	158	357	317
Classical		143	207	272	146	–	210	–

parameterized by the bit-length of a public prime parameter p (so SIKE-434 uses a 434-bit prime). The meet-in-the-middle attack must search a space of size $\mathcal{O}(p^{1/4})$. Thus, replacing N with $p^{1/4}$ in our algorithms gives the performance against SIKE.

NIST defined security levels relatively to quantum generic attacks on symmetric primitives. Levels 1, 3, and 5 are defined relatively to an exhaustive key search on the AES block cipher. NIST used gate counts from [18], but we use improved numbers from [21]. They are given in Table 3. Levels 2 and 4 are based on searching for collisions for the SHA family of hash functions. We use the collision search of [14] and the results of Sect. 5. Table 3 shows the resulting costs when applied to SHA3 under NIST's depth restrictions. SIKE-434, SIKE-503, SIKE-610, and SIKE-751 target NIST's security levels 1, 2, 3, and 5, respectively.

NIST restricts the total circuit depth available by a parameter "Maxdepth". Quantum search algorithms parallelize very poorly so a depth limit forces enormous hardware requirements.

Security Estimates. Because of the depth restriction, we focus on the parallel prefix-based walk and parallel Multi-Grover. Overall our results are likely to underestimate the real cost by constant or poly-logarithmic factors. For example, the depth of a 2-dimensional mesh sorting network of R elements is not exactly $R^{1/2}$, but likely closer to $3R^{1/2}$ [23]. We also need estimates of the cost of H, and we use those from [22]. Table 4 shows the costs to attack various SIKE

Table 4. Costs of quantum attacks on SIKE. A non-local Multi-Grover attack would have the same cost at all depth limits presented, equal to the values in the first row. The best value for a given metric and depth constraint is in **bold**. We give a comparison with [22] (Grover, Tani and vOW's algorithms) and [10] (improved oracle in Grover search), though neither of these account for locality. Code to produce these estimates available at https://project.inria.fr/quasymodo/golden-collision-costs-tar/.

		Local prefix-based walk				Local multi-grover				Previous [10,22]	
Metric	Depth	SIKE p bitlength				SIKE p bitlength				SIKE p length	
		434	503	610	751	434	503	610	751	434	610
G	∞	**109**	**124**	**147**	**178**	130	148	175	211	124 [22]	169 [22]
	2^{96}	**110**	**134**	184	**255**	130	148	**182**	**255**	143 [22]	200 [22]
	2^{64}	**145**	**181**	235	**307**	154	189	243	314	**145** [22]	**189** [22]
	2^{40}	**184**	**219**	**274**	**345**	186	221	275	346		
DW	∞	150	170	202	243	130	**148**	175	**211**	**126** [10]	**170** [10]
	2^{96}	149	170	223	294	**131**	**158**	**192**	**265**	157 [22]	248 [22]
	2^{64}	174	209	264	336	163	**198**	**252**	**322**	145 [22]	289 [22]
	2^{40}	205	241	296	367	**187**	**222**	**276**	**346**		
Width	∞	51	57	65	76	10	10	10	11	10 [10]	10 [10]
	2^{96}	53	74	127	199	35	63	96	170	62 [22]	115 [22]
	2^{64}	110	146	200	272	99	134	188	258	91 [22]	136 [22]
	2^{40}	166	201	256	328	147	182	236	306		

parameters[3] under different depth restrictions, and shows by how many bits the attacks exceed the cost thresholds for the NIST security levels. The attacks are parallelized only as much as necessary, using the methods from Sect. 4. Overall, we find that our attacks lower the quantum security of SIKE compared to the results of [22], but not enough to reduce the claimed security levels.

The asymptotically improved gate cost of the prefix-based walk is barely noticeable because of the depth restrictions. There is a stark difference between the gate cost and the depth×width cost, but only with unrestricted depth. Multi-Grover outperforms the prefix-based walk in nearly all contexts, even in gate cost, because of its parallelization.

On a non-local architecture, the Multi-Grover algorithm parallelizes almost perfectly. The lowest gate costs in Table 4 would apply at all maximum depth values, complicating the security analysis: SIKE-610 would not reach level 3 security in G-cost under a depth limit of 2^{40}, but would reach level 3 at higher

---

[3] At the moment, we have not tried to combine our results with the technique of [10], which can reduce the oracle's footprint in the case of SIKE. We reckon that their tradeoff will bring a small improvement of the numbers in Table 4, both for quantum walks and Multi-Grover.

depth limits or in DW-cost; SIKE-751 would only reach level 5 security with a depth limit of 2^{96}. Thus, the security level of SIKE depends on one's assumptions about plausible physical layouts of quantum computers. However, the margins are relatively close, and more pessimistic evaluations of the quantum costs of isogeny computations (the factor H) could easily bring SIKE-610 and SIKE-751 back to their claimed security levels, even with a non-local architecture.

7   Conclusion

In this paper, we gave new algorithms for *golden collision* search in the quantum circuit model. We improved the gate counts and depth-width products over previous algorithms when cheap "qRAM" operations are not available. In this model, the NIST candidate SIKE offers less security than claimed in [22], but still more than the initial levels given in [20].

Using two different techniques, we arrived at a gate complexity of $\widetilde{O}(N^{6/7})$ for golden collision search. The corresponding memory used is $N^{2/7}$. Interestingly, our algorithms actually achieve the same tradeoff between gate count T and quantum memory R as the previous result of Ambainis [4]: $T^2 \times R = N^2$. On the positive side, this shows that qRAM is not necessary if we use less than $N^{2/7}$ memory.

Acknowledgments. A.S. would like to thank André Chailloux and María Naya-Plasencia for helpful discussions. This project has received funding from the European Research Council (ERC) under the European Union's Horizon 2020 research and innovation programme (grant agreement no. 714294 - acronym QUASYModo). S.J. was supported by the University of Oxford Clarendon fund, and would like to thank Christophe Petit and Richard Meister for helpful comments. Both authors would like to thank Steven Galbraith for helpful comments.

A   Quantum Circuits for Iterations

This section details the quantum circuits used in the quantum iteration-based walk of Sect. 3.4. The MNRS framework describes the circuit for a quantum random walk, given circuits for the set-up, update, and check subroutines. Beacuse the set-up can done with sequential insertion steps (which are part of the update), and the check step only considers a single cunter or flag, the main analysis is the update step. We use the Johnson vertex data structure from [22]. This is sufficient to describe the steps for the prefix-based walk, but the iteration-based walk is more complicated.

The update will need to do the following:

1. Select a new point in superposition, and iterate the function h until it finds a distinguished point.
2. Find any collisions of the new distinguished point in the existing list.
3. Retrace the trails of any distinguished point collisions to find the underlying collisions of h.

A.1   Iterating the Function

Given a randomly selected point x, we define the *trail* of x to be the sequence $(x, h(x), h^2(x), \ldots, h^{n_x}(x))$, where $h^{n_x}(x)$ is distinguished. The goal of this sub-circuit is to map states $|x\rangle$ to $|x\rangle |h^{n_x}(x)\rangle |n_x\rangle$. Unlike classical distinguished-point finding, the quantum circuit cannot stop when it reaches a distinguished point. Rather, we must preselect a fixed number of iterations which will almost certainly reach a distinguished point.

The length of trails is geometrically distributed [30], with a mean equal to $1/\theta$ if the fraction of distinguished points is θ. Using n iterations, the proportion of trails with length greater than $n = c/\theta$ is approximately e^{-c} [30].

Pebbling. Since h is by definition non-injective, it cannot be applied in-place, so we will need a pebbling strategy (see *e.g.* [7,9,25]). We can choose a simple strategy with $2\sqrt{u}$ qubit registers that we will call "baby-step giant-step". We assume u is a perfect square for ease of description. One iteration of h is a "baby step", and a "giant step" is $\sqrt{u}$ iterations. To compute a giant step, we compute $\sqrt{u}$ sequential baby steps with no uncomputation, then uncompute all but the last. Thus, it takes $2\sqrt{u}$ iterations and $\sqrt{u} + 1$ registers to take one giant step.

It takes $\sqrt{u}$ giant steps to reach $h^u(x)$, and we will keep each giant step until the end before uncomputing. Thus, the total cost is $4u$ sequential iterations of h, and we need $2\sqrt{u}$ registers.

Output. To output the last distinguished point that h reaches, we have a list of k potential distinguished points, all initialized to $|0\rangle$. At every iteration of h, we perform two operations, controlled on whether the new output is distinguished. The first operation cycles the elements in the list: the ith element is moved to location $i + 1 \mod k$. Then the output is copied to the first element in the list.

As long as the iterations reach less thank k distinguished points in *total*, this will put the last distinguished point at the front of the list, where we can copy it out. If there are more than k points reached, the copy operation, consisting of CNOT gates, will produce the bitwise XOR of the new and old distinguished points in the list. This will not cause issues in the random walk, but it is highly unlikely to detect a collision. Thus, we can regard this as reducing the number of marked vertices. By Markov's inequality the probability of more than k points is at most $\frac{c}{k}$, and even smaller if we assume a binomial distribution of the number of distinguished points in a trail.

Error Analysis. Errors occur if a trail finds zero or too many distinguished points. F The only points we need to operate correctly are those leading to the golden collision. Starting from a vertex that would be marked if we had a perfect iteration circuit, it contains two elements that lead to the golden collision (see Sect. B). If either element produces an incorrect iteration output, the circuit will incorrectly conclude that the vertex is not marked[4]. Suppose that some number of points t will produce trails that meet at the golden collision. In the worst case, the probabilities of failure for each point are dependent (say, some point on the trail just before the golden collision causes the error). Then there will be a probability of roughly p that the entire algorithm fails, and a probability roughly $1 - p$ that it works exactly as expected. In this case, we will need to repeat the walk with another random function.

For $p \in \Omega(1)$, such imperfections add only an $\mathcal{O}(1)$ cost to the entire algorithm. Thus, based on the previous analyses, we can choose u to be a small, constant multiple of $1/\theta$, and choose k to be a constant as well.

Locality. The iteration can be done locally in many ways. For our baby-step giant-step pebbling, we can arrange the memory into two loops so that the giant steps are stored in one loop and baby steps in the other. We can then sequentially and locally compute all the baby steps, and ensure that the final register is close to the starting register. Then we can copy the output – which is a giant step – into the loop for giant steps. Then we cyclically shift all the giant steps, which is again local. These loops do not change the time complexity at all, are easy to create in a two-dimensional nearest-neighbour architecture.

Thus, our algorithms retain their gate complexity in a two-dimensional nearest-neighbour architecture, and have a time complexity asymptotically equal to their gate complexity in this model.

A.2   Finding Collisions

According to the optimizations in Sect. 3.4, the average number of collisions per inserted point is $\frac{(R-1)u^2}{N}$ and we choose $R \approx u \approx N^{2/7}$; thus, we have a vanishing expected number of collisions.

This makes our collision-finding circuit simple. We can slightly modify the search circuit on a Johnson vertex [22]. That search circuit assumes a single match to the search string, and so it uses a tree of CNOT gates to copy out the result. With multiple matches, it would return the XOR of all matches. To fix this, we use a constant number t of parallel trees, ordered from 1 to t, and add a flag bit to every node.

Our circuit will first fan out the search string to all data in the Johnson vertex, copy out any that match to the leaf layer of the first tree, and flip the flag bit on all matches. Then it will copy the elements up in a tree; however, it will use the flag bit to control the copying. When copying from two adjacent elements in tree i, one can be identified as the "first" element (perhaps by physical arrangement). If both flag bits are 1, we copy the second element to the first tree where the flag bit for that node is 0, then copy the first element to the higher layer. In any other case, we CNOT each node to its parent. The root nodes of all the trees will be in some designated location, and we can process them from there.

---

[4] If both produce incorrect outputs we may find the marked vertex if they produce the same incorrect value, but the probability of this is vanishingly small.

Such a circuit with t trees will correctly copy out any number of collisions up to t. If there are more collisions, it will miss some: they will not be copied out to another tree, and so they will be lost.

A.3   Finding Underlying Collisions

Here we describe how to detect, given two elements (x, n_x) and (y, n_y) with $h^{n_x}(x) = h^{n_y}(y)$, whether they reach the golden collision.

We initialize a new register r_n containing n, the maximum path length from the iteration step. We then iterate h simultaneously for x and y, using the same pebbling strategy as before. We make one small change: At each step we compare r_n to n_x and n_y. If $r_n \leq n_x$, then we apply h to the current x output, and otherwise we just copy the current x output. We do the same for y. This ensures that at the ith step, both trails are $n - i$ steps away from the common distinguished point, so they will reach the collision at the same time.

After each iteration, we apply the circuit to test if a collision is golden, controlled on whether the current output values for x and y are equal. If the collision is golden, we flip an output bit.

A.4   Detecting Marked Vertices

After the circuit in Sect. A.2, we have a newly-inserted point x, its output $h^{n_x}(x)$ and n_x, as well as (up to) t candidate collisions $y_1, \ldots, y_t$ and their associated numbers n_{y_i}. Our goal is to decide whether the vertex is now marked.

A naive search for the golden collision among each candidate collision will introduce a history dependence. For example, if we insert the golden collision with no extraneous collisions, we will detect it and flip a flag for the vertex. If we then insert more than t predecessors of one half of the golden collision, then we might remove the other half of the golden collision but not detect it, because it might not appear in the list of t candidate collisions.

To avoid this, we modify the circuit based on the number of candidate collisions. If there is exactly one candidate collision, we check for a golden collision with the new point and the candidate collision. If there are are more than two candidate collisions then we do not do any check at all. If it has exactly two candidate collisions, we check for the golden collision between the two candidate collisions (*i.e.* those already in the list).

Theorem A.1 ensures the marked vertices will be precisely those with *exactly* one predecessor from each half of the golden collision. In Sect. B we find that this has negligible impact on the cost; the probability of choosing a predecessor of the golden collision is so small that there are only a tiny handful of vertices which have more than 2 predecessors, and so we can safely ignore them.

Theorem A.1. *Using the circuit above with $t \geq 3$ ensures that a vertex is marked if and only if it contains exactly 1 predecessor for each half of the golden collision.*

Proof. Suppose every vertex is correctly marked in this way. We will show that one update maintains this property.

If the vertex has no predecessors of the golden collision, then a newly inserted element will not create a collision, and the vertex will not become marked.

If the vertex has exactly one predecessor of the golden collision, then it will not be marked. If a newly inserted element forms a collision with this predecessor, then we run the golden collision detection circuit. If the new point is a predecessor of the same half, the vertex remains unmarked; if it is a predecessor of the other half, the new vertex becomes marked.

If the vertex has two predecessors of one half of the golden collision, then when a new element is inserted that collides with these, we run a circuit that only checks for a golden collision among the existing two predecessors. It will not find the golden collision, so it will not flip the "marked" flag for the vertex, so the vertex remains unmarked. This is correct, since the updated vertex will have more than 1 predecessor for one half of the golden collision.

If the vertex has exactly 1 predecessor for each half, it starts marked. When a new element is inserted, we run a circuit that looks for the golden collision among the existing collisions. This circuit will find a collision, and flip the "marked" flag, which un-marks the vertex. The vertex now contains 2 predecessors for one half of the golden collision, so this is correct.

The vertex has more than two predecessors of the golden collision if and only if the circuit detects more than two collisions. In this case, the vertex will not be marked, and we will not run either detection circuit, so it remains unmarked. □

Multiple Golden Collisions. If there are multiple golden collisions, the previous method functions almost correctly. If a vertex contains more than one golden collision, there may be some history dependence if one is a predecessor of the other. We can regard this as an imperfect update. The error is at most ϵ^2, and since we only iterate $1/\sqrt{\epsilon\delta}$ walk steps, this causes no problems.

Errors in Random Walks. We will encounter two types of error for the update procedure U. In Sect. 3.4, we have false negatives: the update will sometimes incorrectly miss a marked vertex, but it will never incorrectly identify an unmarked vertex as marked. Furthermore, these errors are not history-dependent. Thus, we can redefine the underlying set of marked vertices to be precisely the vertices that are correctly identified. This switches our perspective from an imperfect circuit on a perfect graph, to a perfect circuit for an imperfect graph.

If the fraction of marked vertices changes from ϵ to ϵ', then the total runtime changes from

$$\mathcal{O}\left(S + \frac{1}{\sqrt{\epsilon}}\left(\frac{1}{\sqrt{\delta}}U + C\right)\right) \text{ to } \mathcal{O}\left(S + \frac{1}{\sqrt{\epsilon'}}\left(\frac{1}{\sqrt{\delta}}U + C\right)\right) \qquad (16)$$

and thus the change in cost is at most a factor of $\mathcal{O}(\sqrt{\epsilon/\epsilon'})$. This means any $\Omega(1)$ reduction in the fraction of marked vertices will incur only a $\mathcal{O}(1)$ increase in the cost of the walk.

In Sect. 3.5, the update contains a Grover search, which is not exact. This means the actual update circuit U' is close to U, but with some error amplitude, independent of the vertex. This error can be exponentially reduced with more Grover iterations so that after an exponential number of updates, the total error amplitude (and the probability of success of the algorithm) remains constant.

B   Probability Analysis

The analysis of van Oorschot and Wiener [30] rests on several heuristic assumptions and numerical evidence for those assumptions. Since we analyze their algorithm as a random walk, these heuristics do not help our analysis. Thus, we must explicitly prove several results about random functions for our algorithm (see [16] for other standard results).

We define the set of predecessors of x as $\mathcal{P}_x = \{y \in X \,|\, h^n(y) = x, n \geq 0\}$.

We then let $P_x = |\mathcal{P}_x|$. Our goal is to provide distributions of both the number of predecessors, the total height of the tree of predecessors, and the joint distribution among both halves of a particular collision.

Lemma B.1. *The probability that a random function $h : X \rightarrow X$ is chosen such that $P_x = t$ is given by*

$$\Pr[P_x = t] = \frac{t^{t-1}}{e^t t!} \left(1 + \mathcal{O}(\tfrac{1}{N})\right) \tag{17}$$

for $t = o(N)$. In particular, $\Pr[P_x \geq t] = \Theta(1/\sqrt{t})$.

Proof. We count the number of such functions. To form x's predecessors, we select $t - 1$ elements out of the $N - 1$ elements which are not x. These form a tree with x as the root. There are t^{t-2} undirected trees (Cayley's formula), which then uniquely defines a direction for each edge to put x at the root. Then the remaining $N - t$ points must map only to themselves. There are $(N - t)^{N-t}$ ways to do this. Then we have N choices for the value of $h(x)$. There are N^N random functions total, giving a probability of

$$\frac{\binom{N-1}{t-1} t^{t-2} N (N-t)^{N-t}}{N^N} = \frac{t^{t-1}}{t!} \frac{N!}{N^N} \frac{(N-t)^{N-t}}{(N-t)!}. \tag{18}$$

Stirling's formula, applied to terms with N, gives an approximation of

$$\frac{t^{t-1} e^{-t}}{t!} \sqrt{\frac{N}{N-t}} \left(1 + \mathcal{O}(\tfrac{1}{N})\right). \tag{19}$$

Since $\frac{N}{N-t} = 1 + \frac{t}{N-t} = 1 + \mathcal{O}(1/N)$, we get the first result. For the second, we use Stirling's approximation again to show that $\Pr[P_x = t] \sim \frac{1}{\sqrt{2\pi t^3}}$. An integral approximation gives the asymptotics. $\qquad\square$

Lemma B.2. *Fix $x, y \in X$. Let h be a random function under the restriction that $h(x) = h(y)$. Then for $t, s = o(N)$,*

$$\Pr[P_x = t, P_y = s] = \frac{t^{t-1} s^{s-1}}{e^t t! e^s s!} \left(1 + \mathcal{O}(\tfrac{1}{N})\right) \tag{20}$$

and the probability that x and y both have at least t predecessors is $\Theta(1/t)$.

Proof. First, x and y can only have the same set of predecessors if they are in the same cycle, but they cannot be in the same cycle because $h(x) = h(y)$. Thus either their sets of predecessors are disjoint, or x is a predecessor of y (meaning $h(x)$ is a predecessor of y). We assume $s \geq t$ without loss of generality, meaning y cannot be a predecessor of x.

When the sets of predecessors are disjoint, we select $t - 1$ elements to be predecessors of x from the $N - 2$ elements that are neither x nor y, then $s - 1$ elements out of the remainder to be predecessors of y. Then we map the remaining elements to themselves, then pick one of the $N - t - s$ elements that are not predecessors of x or y to be the element $h(x)$. The probablity of such a function is

$$\frac{\binom{N-2}{t-1} t^{t-2} \binom{N-t-1}{s-1} s^{s-2} (N-t-s)^{N-t-s}(N-t-s)}{N^{N-1}}. \tag{21}$$

This can be simplified and then approximated to

$$\frac{t^{t-1}}{t!} \frac{s^{s-1}}{s!} \frac{N!}{N^N} \frac{(N-t-s)^{N-t-s}}{(N-t-s)!} \frac{N-t-s}{N-1} = \frac{t^{t-1}}{e^t t!} \frac{s^{s-1}}{e^s s!} (1 + \mathcal{O}(\tfrac{1}{N})). \tag{22}$$

Our goal is now to show that the remaining term, where x is a predecessor of y, is of order $\mathcal{O}(1/N)$.

If x is a predecessor of y, we choose $s - 2$ predecessors of y (one will be x), and of those, we choose $t - 1$ to be predecessors of x. Then we form a tree behind x, then we form a tree of the remaining $s - t$ elements. Then we must attach the two trees: There are $s - t$ choices for where to attach x, i.e., $s - t$ choices for $h(x)$. This forces $h(y)$ to a specific value. From there, the remaining $N - s$ non-predecessor elements map to themselves. The probability of this type of function is

$$\frac{\binom{N-2}{s-2}\binom{s-2}{t-1} t^{t-2}(s-t)^{s-t-2}(s-t)(N-s)^{N-s}}{N^{N-1}}. \tag{23}$$

This can be simplified to

$$\frac{t^{t-1}}{t!} \frac{(s-t)^{s-t}}{(s-t)!} \frac{N!}{N^N} \frac{(N-s)^{N-s}}{(N-s)!} \frac{1}{N-1} \tag{24}$$

which, up to errors of order $\mathcal{O}(1/N)$, equals

$$\frac{1}{N} \left(\frac{t^{t-1}}{e^t t!} \frac{(s-t)^{s-t}}{e^{s-t}(s-t)!} \right) \tag{25}$$

which fits within the error term of Eq. 22, since $s - t \leq s$.   □

Lemma B.3. *Let n_x be the height of the predecessors of x: the largest integer such that there is some $p \in X$ with $h^{n_x}(p) = x$. Define n_y similarly. Suppose x has t predecessors and y has s predecessors. For $c > 0$, the probability that $n_x > c\sqrt{2\pi t}$ or $n_y > c\sqrt{2\pi s}$ is at most*

$$\frac{2(\pi - 3)}{3(c-1)^2}\left(1 + \mathcal{O}(\tfrac{s}{N})\right). \tag{26}$$

Proof. We can assume that x and y have disjoint trees of predecessors; the case where one is a predecessor of the other fits in the $\mathcal{O}(\frac{s}{N})$ error term.

By [31], the height of a random tree on t vertices has expected value $\sqrt{2\pi t}$ with variance $\frac{2\pi(\pi-3)t}{3}$. Chebyshev's equality implies that the probability that $n_x > c\sqrt{2\pi t}$ is at most $\frac{\pi-3}{3(c-1)^2}$, and this is the same probability that $n_y > c\sqrt{2\pi s}$. The union bound gives the main term of the result.

If x is part of a cycle, then n_x is infinite. This can only occur if $h(x)$ is a predecessor of x, which occurs with probability t/N, hence the error term, which also accounts for infinite n_y. □

We now conclude how many vertices will be marked, assuming that x and y have predecessors with small height. A vertex is marked if and only if it contains exactly one predecessor of x and one predecessor of y.

Theorem B.1. *Let h be a function such that $h(x) = h(y)$, x has t predecessors and the largest trail leading to x has $n_x \leq u$ points, y has s predecessors and the largest trail leading to y has $n_y \leq u$ points. Then the fraction of marked vertices in the graph defined in Sect. 3.3 (with u iterations of h for each point) is*

$$\Theta\left(\frac{R^2 ts}{N^2}\right). \tag{27}$$

Proof. Define the u-predecessors of x by

$$\mathcal{P}_u(x) = \{p \in X \,|\, h^m(p) = x, u \geq m \geq 0\}. \tag{28}$$

A vertex is defined by R random distinct points from X. It will be marked if and only if it contains exactly one point from $\mathcal{P}_u(x)$ and exactly one from $\mathcal{P}_u(y)$. Since $n_x, n_y \leq u$, the sizes of these sets are t and s. This acts as a multinomial distribution, and thus the probability of one element from each set is

$$\binom{R}{2}\frac{t}{N}\frac{s}{N}\left(1 - \frac{t+s}{N}\right)^{R-2} = \Theta\left(\frac{R^2 ts}{N^2}\right). \tag{29}$$

□

This covers the case where h has given the golden collision few predecessors, but we may also wish to analyze functions that give more predecessors. We expect this to increase the odds of detecting the golden collision, since there will probably be more close predecessors, even though the height of the predecessors will be large. However, it is sufficient for us to prove that, with high probability, increasing the height will not decrease the number of close predecessors.

Lemma B.4. *Let h be a random function such that x has t predecessors, for $t \geq \frac{u^2}{c2\pi}$. Then the probability that x has at least $\frac{u^2}{c2\pi}$ predecessors of length at most u is at least $\frac{\pi-3}{3(c-1)^2}$.*

Proof. Consider a subset of t elements of X, and consider the subset of random functions such that these t elements are the predecessors of x. If we choose a random subset of m of these predecessors and form these elements into a tree, then regardless of the shape of this tree, there are exactly the same number of ways to attach the remaining $t - m$ elements to form a larger tree. To see this, once we select the m *labelled* elements and arrange them into a tree, we can view them as m isolated points to which we attach disjoint trees formed from the remaining $t-m$ points. Each unique tree structure for the m points produces a valid and unique tree for all t points, and any such tree with the m selected points forming a subtree can be constructed in this way.

Thus, among trees where these m elements form a connected subtree rooted at x, the number of trees where these particular m elements form any particular tree shape is the same as any other tree shape.

Take any function h with a tree of t predecessors of x. Choose any m-element subset of these elements that form a connected tree rooted at x, with m such that $c\sqrt{2\pi m} = u$. By [31], the probability of this tree having height greater than u is at most

$$\frac{(\pi - 3)}{3(c - 1)^2}. \tag{30}$$

If these elements have a height less than this, then they are all at most u-predecessors of x. Since this reasoning would work for any set of t predecessors, this gives the result. □

Lemma B.4 is somewhat conservative, since the number of close predecessors may grow as the tree size increases. This remains an interesting open question.

This gives us the result we need for the fraction of marked vertices in a function that we know gives many predecessors to the golden collision.

Theorem B.2. *Suppose h is a random function such that x has at least t predecessors and y has at least s predecessors. Then with probability at least $\frac{2(\pi-3)}{2(c-1)^2}\left(1 + \mathcal{O}(\frac{s}{N})\right)$ the fraction of marked vertices, when iterating h at least u times, is*

$$\Omega\left(\frac{R^2 \min\{u^2, t\}\min\{u^2, s\}}{N^2}\right) \tag{31}$$

Proof. Suppose h is such that x has exactly $k_x \geq t$ predecessors. If $k_x \leq u^2$, then by Lemma B.3, with the probability given, all k_x predecessors will be at a distance of at most u. Thus, every predecessor is sufficient and we have a $k_x/N \geq t/N$ probability of choosing such an element.

If $k_x > u^2$, i.e., $k_x = \frac{u^2}{c2\pi}$ for some c, then by Lemma B.4, with at least the same probability, we have at least $\frac{u^2}{c2\pi}$ predecessors of distance at most u, and hence we have a probability of $\frac{u^2}{c2\pi}$ of choosing such an element.

This also holds for y. The result follows by the same logic as Theorem B.1. Since the number of predecessors was arbitrary in this reasoning, this holds for any random function where x and y have at least t and s predecessors.   □

Our only remaining issue is ensuring that the predecessors leading to x and y are detected. If we retain the last distinguished point, we will only detect them if we reach a distinguished point after the golden collision. This is a property of the function h; if the next distinguished point is too far, then *all* predecessors of x and y will fail to detect the collision.

Thus, suppose that we iterate h for $u_1 + u_2$ times. We choose u_1 to optimize the bounds in the previous theorems, assuming that after roughly u_1 steps we reach the golden collision. We choose u_2 to reach a distinguished point.

Each iteration after the golden collision has a θ chance of being a distinguished point. Thus, the probability of missing a distinguished point is $(1 - \theta)^{u_2} < e^{-\theta u_2}$, so $u_2 = \Omega(1/\theta)$ gives a constant probability that a particular function will reach a distinguished point within n_2 steps after the golden collision.

Ultimately, this leads to our main theorem:

Theorem B.3. *Let $1 \leq t$ be in $\mathcal{O}(1/\theta)$. Then with probability $\Omega(\frac{1}{t})$, the fraction of marked vertices is $\Omega(\frac{R^2 \min\{u^4, t^2\}}{N^2})$.*

Proof. From Lemma B.1, the probability is $\Theta(\frac{1}{t})$ that both halves of the golden collision will have at least t predecessors. Theorem B.2 shows that a constant proportion of these functions will have at least $\Omega(\frac{R^2 \min\{u^4, t^2\}}{N^2})$ marked vertices.   □

References

1. Aaronson, S., Shi, Y.: Quantum lower bounds for the collision and the element distinctness problems. J. ACM **51**(4), 595–605 (2004)
2. Adj, G., Cervantes-Vázquez, D., Chi-Domínguez, J.J., Menezes, A., Rodríguez-Henríquez, F.: On the cost of computing isogenies between supersingular elliptic curves. In: Cid, C., Jacobson, M. (eds.) SAC 2018. LNCS, vol. 11349, pp. 322–343. Springer, Cham (2018). https://doi.org/10.1007/978-3-030-10970-7_15
3. Albrecht, M., Player, R., Scott, S.: On the concrete hardness of learning with errors. J. Math. Cryptol. **9**(3), 169–203 (2015)
4. Ambainis, A.: Quantum walk algorithm for element distinctness. SIAM J. Comput. **37**, 210–239 (2007)
5. Amy, M., Di Matteo, O., Gheorghiu, V., Mosca, M., Parent, A., Schanck, J.: Estimating the cost of generic quantum pre-image attacks on SHA-2 and SHA-3. In: Avanzi, R., Heys, H. (eds.) SAC 2016. LNCS, vol. 10532, pp. 317–337. Springer, Cham (2017). https://doi.org/10.1007/978-3-319-69453-5_18
6. Arunachalam, S., Gheorghiu, V., Jochym-O'Connor, T., Mosca, M., Srinivasan, P.V.: On the robustness of bucket brigade quantum ram. New J. Phys. **17**(12), 123010 (2015)

7. Banegas, G., Bernstein, D.J.: Low-communication parallel quantum multi-target preimage search. In: Adams, C., Camenisch, J. (eds.) SAC 2017. LNCS, vol. 10719, pp. 325–335. Springer, Cham (2018). https://doi.org/10.1007/978-3-319-72565-9_16

8. Beals, R., et al.: Efficient distributed quantum computing. In: Proceedings Royal Society London A: Mathematical, Physical and Engineering Sciences, vol. 469 (2013)

9. Bennett, C.H.: Time/space trade-offs for reversible computation. SIAM J. Comput. **18**(4), 766–776 (1989)

10. Biasse, J.F., Pring, B.: A framework for reducing the overhead of the quantum oracle for use with Grover's algorithm with applications to cryptanalysis of SIKE. J. Math. Cryptol. **15**(1), 143–156 (2019)

11. Brassard, G., Hoyer, P., Mosca, M., Tapp, A.: Quantum amplitude amplification and estimation. Contemp. Math. **305**, 53–74 (2002)

12. Brassard, G., HØyer, P., Tapp, A.: Quantum cryptanalysis of hash and claw-free functions. In: Lucchesi, C.L., Moura, A.V. (eds.) LATIN 1998. LNCS, vol. 1380, pp. 163–169. Springer, Heidelberg (1998). https://doi.org/10.1007/BFb0054319

13. Buhrman, H., et al.: Quantum algorithms for element distinctness. SIAM J. Comput. **34**(6), 1324–1330 (2005)

14. Chailloux, A., Naya-Plasencia, M., Schrottenloher, A.: An efficient quantum collision search algorithm and implications on symmetric cryptography. In: Takagi, T., Peyrin, T. (eds.) ASIACRYPT 2017. LNCS, vol. 10625, pp. 211–240. Springer, Cham (2017). https://doi.org/10.1007/978-3-319-70697-9_8

15. Costello, C., Longa, P., Naehrig, M., Renes, J., Virdia, F.: Improved classical cryptanalysis of SIKE in practice. In: Kiayias, A., Kohlweiss, M., Wallden, P., Zikas, V. (eds.) PKC 2020. LNCS, vol. 12111, pp. 505–534. Springer, Cham (2020). https://doi.org/10.1007/978-3-030-45388-6_18

16. Flajolet, P., Odlyzko, A.M.: Random mapping statistics. In: Quisquater, J.-J., Vandewalle, J. (eds.) EUROCRYPT 1989. LNCS, vol. 434, pp. 329–354. Springer, Heidelberg (1990). https://doi.org/10.1007/3-540-46885-4_34

17. Giovannetti, V., Lloyd, S., Maccone, L.: Architectures for a quantum random access memory. Phys. Rev. A. **78**(5), 052310 (2008)

18. Grassl, M., Langenberg, B., Roetteler, M., Steinwandt, R.: Applying Grover's algorithm to AES: quantum resource estimates. In: Takagi, T. (ed.) PQCrypto 2016. LNCS, vol. 9606, pp. 29–43. Springer, Cham (2016). https://doi.org/10.1007/978-3-319-29360-8_3

19. Grover, L.K.: A fast quantum mechanical algorithm for database search. In: Proceedings of the Twenty-Eighth Annual ACM Symposium on the Theory of Computing 1996, pp. 212–219. ACM (1996)

20. Jao, D., et al.: Supersingular isogeny key encapsulation. Submission to NIST postquantum project, November 2017. https://sike.org/#nist-submission

21. Jaques, S., Naehrig, M., Roetteler, M., Virdia, F.: Implementing Grover oracles for quantum key search on AES and LowMC. In: Canteaut, A., Ishai, Y. (eds.) EUROCRYPT 2020. LNCS, vol. 12106, pp. 280–310. Springer, Cham (2020). https://doi.org/10.1007/978-3-030-45724-2_10

22. Jaques, S., Schanck, J.M.: Quantum cryptanalysis in the RAM model: claw-finding attacks on SIKE. In: Boldyreva, A., Micciancio, D. (eds.) CRYPTO 2019. LNCS, vol. 11692, pp. 32–61. Springer, Cham (2019). https://doi.org/10.1007/978-3-030-26948-7_2

23. Kunde, M.: Lower bounds for sorting on mesh-connected architectures. Acta Inf. **24**(2), 121–130 (1987)

24. Kuperberg, G.: Another subexponential-time quantum algorithm for the dihedral hidden subgroup problem. In: TQC 2013. LIPIcs, vol. 22, pp. 20–34 (2013)
25. Levin, R.Y., Sherman, A.T.: A note on Bennett's time-space tradeoff for reversible computation. SIAM J. Comput. **19**(4), 673–677 (1990)
26. Magniez, F., Nayak, A., Roland, J., Santha, M.: Search via quantum walk. SIAM J. Comput. **40**, 142–164 (2011)
27. Naya-Plasencia, M., Schrottenloher, A.: Optimal merging in quantum k-xor and k-sum algorithms. In: Canteaut, A., Ishai, Y. (eds.) EUROCRYPT 2020. LNCS, vol. 12106, pp. 311–340. Springer, Cham (2020). https://doi.org/10.1007/978-3-030-45724-2_11
28. Nielsen, M.A., Chuang, I.: Quantum computation and quantum information. AAPT (2002)
29. NIST: Submission requirements and evaluation criteria for the post-quantum cryptography standardization process (2016). https://csrc.nist.gov/CSRC/media/Projects/Post-Quantum-Cryptography/documents/call-for-proposals-final-dec-2016.pdf
30. van Oorschot, P., Wiener, M.: Parallel collision search with cryptanalytic applications. J. Cryptol. **12**(1), 1–28 (1999)
31. Rényi, A., Szekeres, G.: On the height of trees. J. Aust. Math. Soc. **7**(4), 497–507 (1967)
32. Tani, S.: An improved claw finding algorithm using quantum walk. In: Kučera, L., Kučera, A. (eds.) MFCS 2007. LNCS, vol. 4708, pp. 536–547. Springer, Heidelberg (2007). https://doi.org/10.1007/978-3-540-74456-6_48

Improvements to Quantum Search Techniques for Block-Ciphers, with Applications to AES

James H. Davenport[1] and Benjamin Pring[2(✉)]

[1] Department of Computer Science, University of Bath, Bath, UK
masjhd@bath.ac.uk
[2] Department of Mathematics and Statistics, University of South Florida,
Tampa, USA

Abstract. In this paper we demonstrate that the overheads (ancillae qubits/time/number of gates) involved with implementing quantum oracles for a generic key-recovery attack against block-ciphers using quantum search techniques can be reduced.

In particular, if we require $r \geq 1$ plaintext-ciphertext pairs to uniquely identify a user's key, then using Grover's quantum search algorithm for cryptanalysis of block-ciphers as in [2,3,9,13,18] would require a quantum circuit which requires effort (either Time × Space product or number of quantum gates) proportional to r. We demonstrate how we can reduce this by a fine-grained approach to quantum amplitude amplification [6,17] and design of the required quantum oracles.

We furthermore demonstrate that this effort can be reduced to $< r$ with respect to cryptanalysis of AES-128/192/256 and provide full quantum resource estimations for AES-128/192/256 with our methods, and code in the Q# quantum programming language that extends the work of [13].

Keywords: Quantum search · Quantum cryptanalysis · AES · Block ciphers

1 Introduction

The security of the Advanced Encryption Standard [23] (AES) relative to quantum search techniques is both of independent interest with respect to examining how we can best optimise quantum circuits and as a benchmark against which the security of entries to the NIST Post Quantum Cryptography (PQC) standardisation process [24,25] are currently judged.

Grover's quantum search algorithm [10] (see Theorem 3) is currently thought by the cryptographic community to be the optimal method of attacking the

---

Author list in alphabetical order; see https://www.ams.org/profession/leaders/culture/CultureStatement04.pdf.

Scripts and Q# code available: https://github.com/public-ket/reduced-aes.

O. Dunkelman et al. (Eds.): SAC 2020, LNCS 12804, pp. 360–384, 2021.
https://doi.org/10.1007/978-3-030-81652-0_14

full-round AES [2,4,9,13,18,25]. As well as an important problem in cryptanalysis, AES can also act as a benchmark for new techniques in algorithm design.

1.1 The Key-Search Problem for Block-Ciphers

It is common knowledge that for any block-cipher with an encryption function $E : \{0,1\}^k \times \{0,1\}^n \longrightarrow \{0,1\}^n$ (where $\{0,1\}^k$ is the key-space and n is the block-size), possession of a sufficient number of plaintext-ciphertext pairs is enough to recover the user's key by exhaustive search methods. Formally, these plaintext-ciphertext pairs are the set

$$\Big\{ (P_1, C_1), \ldots, (P_r, C_r) \in \{0,1\}^n \times \{0,1\}^n \ : \ E(K, P_i) = C_i \Big\} \qquad (1)$$

for some unknown user's key $K \in \{0,1\}^k$. To immediately specialise this to AES, we have that $n = 128$ and there exist three security levels for AES parameterised by $k \in \{128, 192, 256\}$—we will respectively refer to these varieties as AES$-k$. Recovering a user's key can be accomplished by exhaustive search methods by modelling the problem by a special boolean function $\chi : \{0,1\}^k \longrightarrow \{0,1\}$

$$\chi(K) = \begin{cases} 1 & \text{if } \big(E(K, P_1) \overset{?}{=} C_1\big) \wedge \cdots \wedge \big(E(K, P_r) \overset{?}{=} C_r\big) \\ 0 & \text{otherwise} \end{cases} \qquad (2)$$

so that we can simply evaluate χ upon elements of the domain $\{0,1\}^k$ until we find the unique element (the user's key) that we are searching for. It is essential that r is large enough, as otherwise this may not uniquely specify the key—for a thorough treatment of this see Section 2.2 of [13], but intuitively it is useful to consider that the problem guarantees there is one $K \in \{0,1\}^k$ that was used to generate the plaintext-ciphertext pairs and that $E(\cdot , P_i) : \{0,1\}^k \longrightarrow \{0,1\}^n$ (the encryption function with a fixed choice of plaintext P_i) is expected to act a pseudorandom function. This last fact implies that we expect there to be $(2^k - 1) \cdot 2^{-rn} \approx 2^{k-rn}$ keys which encrypt any r plaintexts to a fixed choice of r ciphertexts, hence we must chose r such that the chance of obtaining such a spurious key is negligible if we are performing a search via solely evaluating χ.

For AES-128 and AES-192 this implies that we must have $r = 2$ and for AES-256 we must have $r = 3$. These can be reduced to $r = 1$ for AES-128 and $r = 2$ for AES-256, if we are content with being able to correctly identify the user's key with probability $\frac{1}{e} \approx 0.37$ (see Section 2.3 of [13]).

Whilst a classical exhaustive search for the user's key would require on average $O(2^k)$ classical evaluations of $\chi : \{0,1\}^k \longrightarrow \{0,1\}$, Grover's quantum search algorithm [10] gives us that if we implement $\chi : \{0,1\}^k \longrightarrow \{0,1\}$ as a quantum circuit then we need only execute this quantum circuit $O(2^{k/2})$ times and perform a quantum measurement to obtain the user's key with high probability. This quantum circuit is referred to as a *quantum oracle* and has a non-trivial cost to implement [2,9,13,18] and (as with a classical $\chi : \{0,1\}^k \longrightarrow \{0,1\}$) can be constructed out of r quantum circuits which each evaluate AES-k.

No matter the cost of these modular components, the total circuit-size for both the classical and quantum search approach if we just exploit χ is then dependent upon r. However, a different classical strategy is possible if we allow for a slightly modified classical search routine—we test whether an element $x \in \{0,1\}^k$ satisfies $\chi(x) = 1$ if and only if it has first passed a test whether $\gamma(x) = 1$ where $\gamma : \{0,1\}^k \longrightarrow \{0,1\}$ is such that $\gamma(x) \mapsto \left(E(K, P_1) \overset{?}{=} C_1\right)$. This is easily implemented as a classical search procedure, requiring a circuit large enough only to implement the encryption circuit $E : \{0,1\}^k \times \{0,1\}^n \longrightarrow \{0,1\}^n$ if we compute $E(x, P_{i+1})$ if and only if $E(x, P_i)$ was equal to C_i.

Whilst such a classical strategy means we still require on the order of $O(2^k)$ calls to γ (any element $x \in \{0,1\}^k$ may be the user's key), this technique allows us to reduce the number of calls of χ and so reduce the overall cost to implement the search procedure. Such a strategy requires a classical control mechanism which is unavailable in quantum circuitry (which must be reversible). However, the same strategy can be exploited by the *Search with Two Oracles* [17] (STO) approach to quantum search, which relies upon the fact that we have a well-defined relationship of subsets $\chi^{-1}(1) \subseteq \gamma^{-1}(1) \subseteq \{0,1\}^k$ and provides similar computational gains over Grover's quantum search algorithm [10] as the above classical strategy provides compared to brute-force classical search.

Our focus in this paper is in fitting the block-cipher search problem to take advantage of the Search with Two Oracles methodology, ensuring that we use specially designed quantum circuits (quantum oracles) that evaluate the functions $\gamma, \chi : \{0,1\}^k \longrightarrow \{0,1\}$, which allow us to make strictly positive gains in both the Space-Time product and Gate count for performing quantum search.

Our results can be viewed as a quantum analog of classical techniques for cryptanalysis of block-ciphers in [12]—our goal in this paper is to demonstrate that we require far fewer qubits than previously thought to attack AES and that many attacks in literature [2,3,9,13,18] have been overestimating the resources required to attack block-ciphers via quantum search as they have concentrated on the design of individual quantum circuits rather than algorithmic improvements.

1.2 Outline of This Paper

In Sect. 2 we review basic facts concerning quantum computation, quantum search and the AES. In Sect. 3 we examine how the *Search with Two Oracles* [17] (STO) technique can be used to improve upon generic Grover-based attacks on generic block-ciphers. In Sect. 4 we examine what further gains we can make when we consider attacks on AES, providing explicit quantum circuits and resource estimates for this scenario. In Sect. 5 we give our conclusions.

1.3 Contributions

In this paper we make the following contributions

- We examine Algorithm 3 of [17] applied to cryptanalysis of AES, which suggests underclocking inner nestings of amplitude amplification is beneficial.

- We examine how we can avoid unnecessary computation in designing a quantum oracle for breaking AES in conjunction with these techniques.
- We provide a full quantum resource estimation of the resources required to attack AES-128/192/256 with our methods using new circuits written in the Q# quantum programming language, extending the work of [13].

2 Background

2.1 Quantum Computation and Quantum Algorithms

Quantum states consisting of k-qubits can be modelled as vectors $|\psi\rangle \in \mathbb{C}^{2^k}$ and quantum algorithms as unitary matrices $U \in \mathbb{C}^{2^k \times 2^k}$ (a matrix $U \in \mathbb{C}^{2^k \times 2^k}$ is unitary iff $UU^\dagger = U^\dagger U = I$, where $\dagger$ is the conjugate-transpose operator). In the *computational basis* $\{|x\rangle : x \in \{0,1\}^k\}$, a k-qubit quantum state can be written (with $\alpha_x \in \mathbb{C}$)

$$|\psi\rangle = \sum_{x \in \{0,1\}^k} \alpha_x |x\rangle \qquad \text{where} \qquad \sum_{x \in \{0,1\}^k} |\alpha_x|^2 = 1 \qquad (3)$$

and measurement of an k-qubit quantum state in the computational basis will result in a bitstring $x \in \{0,1\}^k$ with probability $|\alpha_x|^2$. Notation-wise, the application of quantum algorithms to quantum states will follow the matrix-interpretation so that $\mathcal{B}\mathcal{A}|\psi\rangle$ denotes we apply the quantum algorithm $\mathcal{A}$ to the quantum state $|\psi\rangle$ to compute $\mathcal{A}|\psi\rangle$ and then apply the quantum algorithm $\mathcal{B}$ to the state $\mathcal{A}|\psi\rangle$.

Quantum algorithms therefore consist of methods which increase the magnitude of amplitudes associated with useful information. These quantum algorithms may be approximated to a high degree of accuracy (or exactly synthesised, assuming noise-free quantum computation) by constructing them out of *quantum gates* which act upon small numbers of qubits (just as classical algorithms are constructed out of bitwise operations). Many algorithms also use *ancillae qubits* for working memory—these may either be *clean* (they begin and end in the state $|0 \ldots 0\rangle$) or *dirty* (they begin and end in the same unknown state).

The Clifford+T gate set is a universal quantum gate set [22], in that it is both finite and we can approximate any quantum algorithm up to an arbitrary degree of accuracy by using only gates from this set. It consists of a union of a set which generates the Clifford group on n-qubits, typically taken to be $\{H, S, \wedge_1(X)\}$ (the Hadamard, Phase and controlled-NOT gates) and $\{T\}$, a singleton set containing the T-gate. This separation of gate sets is of potential real-world importance as T-gates are conjectured [7] to require resources on the order of a magnitude more than those than the Clifford gate set to implement. We define our Clifford gate set as $\{X, Z, H, S, \wedge_1(X)\}$—the X (NOT) gate, the Z gate, the Hadamard gate, the phase gate and Controlled-NOT (CNOT) gate. We also count measurements as a resource that can be used to implement quantum circuits as in [13], but do not use them in our algorithmic design.

The actions of the S and T-gates will be unimportant for the purposes of this paper, but we have that (for $x \in \{0,1\}$) $X|x\rangle \mapsto |x \oplus 1\rangle$, that $Z|x\rangle \mapsto (-1)^x |x\rangle$ and that the Hadamard gate maps $H|x\rangle \mapsto \frac{1}{\sqrt{2}}|0\rangle + \frac{(-1)^x}{\sqrt{2}}|1\rangle$.

The generalised $\wedge_t(X)$ gate (the t-Controlled-NOT) for $t \geq 1$ has the action

$$\wedge_t(X)|x_1 \ldots x_t\rangle|x_{t+1}\rangle \mapsto |x_1 \ldots x_t\rangle|x_{t+1} \oplus x_1 \wedge \cdots \wedge x_t\rangle \tag{4}$$

where $x_i \in \{0,1\}$. We use a design [19] that has both a quantum circuit-depth and circuit-size of $O(t)$ quantum gates if we have $O(t)$ dirty ancillae qubits. A summary of costs for all quantum circuits we use can be found in Appendix C.

The *quantum oracle* is an important quantum subroutine in many quantum search algorithms and its cost is our main concern in this paper.

Definition 1 (Quantum phase oracle). *The quantum oracle $\mathcal{O}_\chi$ defined by the boolean function $\chi : \{0,1\}^k \longrightarrow \{0,1\}$ is a quantum algorithm defined the following action on the computational basis states $\{|x\rangle : x \in \{0,1\}^k\}$*

$$\mathcal{O}_\chi|x\rangle \mapsto \begin{cases} -|x\rangle & \text{if } \chi(x) = 1 \\ |x\rangle & \text{otherwise.} \end{cases} \tag{5}$$

One method of implementing a quantum oracle is to construct it out of *quantum evaluations* for $\chi : \{0,1\}^k \longrightarrow \{0,1\}$ and single-qubit gates.

Definition 2 (Quantum evaluation). *Let $f : \{0,1\}^k \longrightarrow \{0,1\}^m$ be any function. The unitary $\mathcal{E}_f$ is a quantum evaluation of f if it implements the mapping of $k + w + m$ computational basis states (for $x \in \{0,1\}^k$)*

$$\mathcal{E}_f|x\rangle|0^w\rangle|0^m\rangle \mapsto |g(x)\rangle|f(x)\rangle. \tag{6}$$

where $g(x) \in \{0,1\}^{k+w}$ is the end-state of all qubits not in the output register.

Quantum evaluations can naively be constructed via using the quantum gate set $\{X, \wedge_1(X), \wedge_2(X)\}$ (the X, CNOT and Toffoli gates), which allow us to implement the corresponding universal boolean gate set $\{\neg, \oplus, \wedge\}$ in a reversible manner (as quantum algorithms correspond to unitary matrices, each operation must possess a corresponding adjoint unless naive measurement is involved).

To implement the quantum phase oracle $\mathcal{O}_\chi$ defined by $\chi : \{0,1\}^k \longrightarrow \{0,1\}$, we simply require a quantum evaluation $\mathcal{E}_\chi$ and the use of a single Z gate. We simply compute a quantum evaluation $\mathcal{E}_\chi$, use the Z gate on the register holding $|\chi(x)\rangle$ and execute the adjoint $\mathcal{E}_\chi^\dagger$ to obtain the action of the quantum oracle $\mathcal{O}_\chi$ as given in (5), illustrated in (7) which is identical to (6) if we factor out $|0^w\rangle$.

$$|x\rangle|0^w\rangle|0\rangle \xrightarrow{\mathcal{E}_\chi} |g(x)\rangle|\chi(x)\rangle \xrightarrow{Z} (-1)^{\chi(x)}|g(x)\rangle|\chi(x)\rangle \xrightarrow{\mathcal{E}_\chi^\dagger} (-1)^{\chi(x)}|x\rangle|0^w\rangle \tag{7}$$

Cost Metrics. We will be interested in the metrics of quantum circuit-depth (number timesteps taken, where Clifford+T gates may be executed in parallel), quantum circuit-size (number of Clifford+T gates executed) and quantum circuit-width (the maximum number of quantum bits used). In terms of assigning a cost to the quantum algorithm for purposes of cryptography, we will be interested in two metrics—the G-metric, which is the quantum circuit-size of the algorithm and the DW-metric, which is the product of the Depth $\times$ Width of the quantum circuit, a metric designed to capture the cost of quantum error-correction on idle qubits. For details on these metrics we refer the reader to [14].

Cost Notation. We will use the notation D_A, S_A, W_A to represent the quantum circuit-depth, quantum circuit-size and quantum circuit-width required to implement an arbitrary quantum algorithm (or gate) A. We will usually discuss the cost in terms of serial operations and use the notation C_A when we can freely substitute C (Cost) for either D (Depth) or S (Size) in the entire cost equation.

As an example, we have that $C_{O_\chi} = C_{\mathcal{E}_\chi} + C_{\mathcal{E}_\chi^\dagger} + C_Z$ to implement the quantum oracle O_χ via quantum evaluations $\mathcal{E}_\chi$ as described above and in (7).

2.2 Quantum Search via Amplitude Amplification

Definition 3 (Success probability of a quantum algorithm). *Let A be an arbitrary quantum algorithm acting upon n qubits. We say A has a success probability of $a \in [0,1]$ relative to $\chi : \{0,1\}^k \longrightarrow \{0,1\}$ if measurement of the state $A|*\rangle 0^k$ results in an $x \in \{0,1\}^k$ such that $\chi(x) = 1$ with probability a.*

Quantum amplitude amplification is a quantum subroutine that exploits the success probability of a given quantum algorithm A relative to a boolean function $\chi : \{0,1\}^k \longrightarrow \{0,1\}$ and can be used to increase this success probability by performing an iterative loop where the quantum algorithm A (and $A^\dagger$) interact with a *quantum oracles* (see Definition 1) O_χ defined by $\chi : \{0,1\}^k \longrightarrow \{0,1\}$.

Theorem 1 (Quantum amplitude amplification [6]). *Let A be any quantum algorithm (with adjoint $A^\dagger$) which has a success probability of $a \in [0,1]$ relative to the boolean function $\chi : \{0,1\}^k \longrightarrow \{0,1\}$. Then there exists a quantum algorithm $Q(A, O_\chi, t) = \left(A^\dagger O_{\bar{k}} A O_\chi\right)^t A$ that succeeds with probability*

$$a(k) = \sin^2\left((2t+1) \cdot \arcsin\sqrt{a}\right) \tag{8}$$

relative to $\chi : \{0,1\}^k \longrightarrow \{0,1\}$, where $O_{\bar{k}}$ is the quantum oracle defined by the boolean function $\bar{k} : \{0,1\}^k \longrightarrow \{0,1\}$ where $\bar{k}(x) = 1$ iff $x \neq 0^k$.

Amplitude amplification costs $C_{Q(A,O_\chi,t)} = t \cdot \left(C_{O_\chi} + C_{O_{\bar{k}}} + C_A + C_{A^\dagger}\right) + C_A$.

Theorem 2 (Optimal number of amplitude amplification iterations [5]). *Let the success probability of A relative to $\chi : \{0,1\}^k \longrightarrow \{0,1\}$ be $a \in [0,1]$.*

The quantum algorithm $Q(A, O_\chi, t)$ where $t = \left\lfloor \frac{\pi}{4 \cdot \arcsin\sqrt{a}} \right\rfloor$ has a success probability of at least $\max\{1-a, a\}$.

A simple application of Theorem 1 and Theorem 2 is *Grover's algorithm* [10].

Theorem 3 (Grover's algorithm [10]**).** *Let* $\chi : \{0,1\}^k \longrightarrow \{0,1\}$ *and the quantity* $M = |\chi^{-1}(1)|$ *be known. Then an element* $x \in \{0,1\}^k$ *with the property that* $\chi(x) = 1$ *can be found with probability* $\geq \{1 - \frac{M}{2^k}, \frac{M}{2^k}\}$ *and a cost*

$$\leq \frac{\pi}{4}\sqrt{\frac{2^k}{M}} \cdot (2 \cdot C_{H^{\otimes k}} + C_{\mathcal{O}_\chi} + C_{\mathcal{O}_{\bar{k}}}) + C_{H^{\otimes k}}. \tag{9}$$

PROOF: We use Theorem 1 with $\mathcal{A} = H^{\otimes k}$. As

$$H^{\otimes k}|*\rangle 0^k \mapsto \frac{1}{2^{k/2}} \sum_{x \in \{0,1\}^k} |x\rangle \tag{10}$$

we have a probability of success of $a = M \cdot \left(\frac{1}{2^{k/2}}\right)^2 = \frac{M}{2^k}$ relative to χ.

Applying Lemma 2 (using $x \leq \arcsin x$)then gives us that we require a total

of $t = \left\lfloor \frac{\pi}{4\arcsin\sqrt{\frac{M}{2^k}}} \right\rfloor \leq \frac{\pi}{4} \cdot \sqrt{\frac{2^k}{M}}$ iterations of $H^{\otimes k}\mathcal{O}_{\bar{k}}H^{\otimes k}\mathcal{O}_\chi$ and one of $H^{\otimes k}$. □

As $H^{\otimes k}$ is simply the application of k H gates in parallel, we have that the quantum circuit-depth is $D_{H^{\otimes k}} = 1$, whilst the quantum circuit-size is $S_{H^{\otimes k}} = k$. Implementing $\mathcal{O}_{\bar{k}}$ requires $D_{\mathcal{O}_{\bar{k}}} = D_{\wedge_{k-1}(X)} + 2D_X = D_{\wedge_{k-1}(X)} + 2$ and $S_{\mathcal{O}_{\bar{k}}} = S_{\wedge_{k-1}(X)} + 2(k \cdot S_X + S_H) = S_{\wedge_{k-1}(X)} + 2k + 2$.

As the cost $C_{\mathcal{O}_\chi}$ (either quantum circuit-depth or quantum circuit-size) of $\mathcal{O}_\chi$ is usually $\tilde{O}(n^d)$ for $d > 1$, the cost of the quantum oracle $\mathcal{O}_\chi$ usually dominates the cost $(2 \cdot C_{H^{\otimes k}} + C_{\mathcal{O}_\chi} + C_{\mathcal{O}_{\bar{k}}})$ of each *Grover iteration* in cost Eq. (9).

However, in quantum amplitude amplification we may choose a different, more expensive quantum algorithm for $\mathcal{A}$ which yields a better cost-to-success probability ratio than a choice of $\mathcal{A} = H^{\otimes k}$. We follow this strategy to lower the overall cost of the quantum search procedure compared to simply using Grover's algorithm. This is a technique suggested by Kimmel et al. [17] in the *Search with Two Oracles* (STO) method, which exploits *two* quantum oracles—one of which is relatively cheap to implement $\mathcal{O}_\gamma$ which marks both the M items we are searching for as well as a number of false-positives and one of which is expensive $\mathcal{O}_\chi$ to implement but exactly identifies the M items we search for.

The number of queries we require will remain on the order of $O\left(\sqrt{\frac{2^k}{M}}\right)$, *but relative to the cheaper oracle* $\mathcal{O}_\gamma$. The expensive oracle $\mathcal{O}_\chi$ is the same one we would use in Grover's algorithm and it will still be called, but the overall cost of the entire search procedure will be on the order of $O\left(\sqrt{\frac{2^k}{M}} \cdot C_{\mathcal{O}_\gamma}\right)$ instead of the cost $O\left(\sqrt{\frac{2^k}{M}} \cdot C_{\mathcal{O}_\chi}\right)$ that a naive use of Grover's algorithm would imply. Critically, this approach will have a positive impact on all metrics if we design $\mathcal{O}_\gamma$ and $\mathcal{O}_\chi$ such that we balance their costs with the number of false-positives.

2.3 Cryptanalysis of Blockciphers via Search and the AES

Block-ciphers are built out of keyed-pseudorandom permutations of the form $E : \{0,1\}^k \times \{0,1\}^n \longrightarrow \{0,1\}^n$ where n is the size of the *message-space* and k

is the size of the *key-space*. Given any $K \in \{0,1\}^k$, this defines a pseudorandom permutation $E_K : \{0,1\}^n \longrightarrow \{0,1\}^n$ that can be used in various modes of operation [15]. In order for these modes of operation to be secure in the cryptographic sense for a security parameter $\lambda \in \mathbb{N}$, it is necessary (though not sufficient) that for any valid choice of $K \in \{0,1\}^k$ we have that if an unknown $K \in \{0,1\}^k$ produces the pair $(P,C) \in \{0,1\}^n \times \{0,1\}^n$ such that $E_K(P) = C$ then it requires at least 2^λ operations to recover the unknown key K.

If we have r unique plaintext-ciphertext pairs $\{(P_1,C_1),\ldots,(P_r,C_r)\}$ where $P_i, C_i \in \{0,1\}^n$ and $E(K,P_i) = C_i$ for some unknown and fixed $K \in \{0,1\}^k$, the boolean search indicator function $\chi : \{0,1\}^k \longrightarrow \{0,1\}$ for K can be defined

$$\chi(x) \mapsto \left(E(x,P_1) \stackrel{?}{=} C_r\right) \wedge \cdots \wedge \left(E(x,P_r) \stackrel{?}{=} C_r\right). \tag{11}$$

For a fixed and unknown key $K \in \{0,1\}^k$, a single plaintext-ciphertext pair $(P,C) \in \{0,1\}^n \times \{0,1\}^n$ such that $E_K(P) = C$ may not uniquely determine K with high probability. The required number (r) of plaintext-ciphertext pairs to uniquely specify the key is the cipher's known-plaintext unicity distance [21].

For intuitive purposes, we have if we take a random element $x \in \{0,1\}^k$ then the probability that it satisfies each of the $r \cdot n$ binary constraints (r checks whether $E_K(P_i) == C_i$) is 2^{-rn}. As we are guaranteed a single $K \in \{0,1\}^k$ that satisfies this condition, we expect $(2^k - 1) \cdot 2^{-rn} \approx 2^{k-rn}$ other keys that satisfy these r plaintext-ciphertext pairs. We therefore need $r > \frac{k}{n}$ to ensure (with high probability) that there are no other spurious keys in the search-space.

Recent work [14,16,18] determines this is $r = 2$ for $k = 128, 192$ and $r = 3$ for $k = 256$. The Advanced Encryption Standard [23] (AES) is one of the most commonly used block-ciphers today [11] and has been standardised for the cases of $\lambda = 128, 192, 256$. We refer to these as AES-k (where $k \in \{128, 192, 256\}$) or simply AES if we discuss the general algorithm. It consists of a series of mostly similar rounds of substitutions and permutations on an internal state register which begins as the plaintext $P \in \{0,1\}^n$ and ends in the ciphertext $C \in \{0,1\}^n$. Definition 4 captures both the full AES-k for $k \in \{128, 192, 256\}$ which respectively run for $N = 10, 12, 14$ rounds and the reduced-round version.

Definition 4 (Reduced-round AES). *Let $k \in \{128, 192, 256\}$ and $N \in \mathbb{N}$. We use the notation $AES_{k,N} : \{0,1\}^k \times \{0,1\}^{128} \longrightarrow \{0,1\}^{128}$ to denote the function defined by a circuit that implements N rounds of AES-k. The canonical full-round implementations of AES-k are $AES_{128,10}$, $AES_{192,12}$ and $AES_{256,14}$.*

This circuit takes a key $K \in \{0,1\}^k$ and a plaintext $P \in \{0,1\}^{128}$ and outputs a ciphertext $C \in \{0,1\}^{128}$ via the following procedure, where for $X \in \{0,1\}^{8w}$ where $w \in \mathbb{N}$ and $i = 0,\ldots, w-1$ we have that $X[i]$ indicates the ith byte of X and $X[i:j]$ for $i < j$ indicates bytes i to j (including byte j) of X.

1. *Set the state $B := P \in \{0,1\}^{128}$ (16 bytes), the plaintext to be encrypted.*
2. *KeyExpansion: $K \in \{0,1\}^k$ ($k/8$ bytes) is expanded to K_E ($16(N+1)$ bytes)*
3. *AddRoundKey: $B := B \oplus K_E[0:7]$*
4. *For rounds $i = 1,\ldots, N-1$:*

1. *SubBytes*   : *An S-box (an 8-bit permutation) is applied bytewise to B.*
2. *ShiftRows*   : *The byte indices of B are swapped via a fixed permutation.*
3. *MixColumns* : *An invertible linear transformation is applied to each block of 4 bytes $B[4j : 4j + 3]$ for $j = 0, 1, 2, 3$.*
4. *AddRoundKey:* $B := B \oplus K_E[8i : 8i + 7]$
5. *For round N:*
   1. *SubBytes*   : *An S-box (an 8-bit permutation) is bytewise to B.*
   2. *ShiftRows*   : *The byte indices of B are swapped via a fixed permutation.*
   3. *AddRoundKey:* $B := B \oplus K_E[8 : 8i + 7]$
6. *Output the ciphertext $C := B \in \{0, 1\}^{128}$ (16 bytes).*

For AES, the MixColumns stage is linear map on over $\mathbb{F}_2^{32 \times 32}$ and can be implemented as a quantum circuit via $\wedge_1(X)$ gates. As the ShiftRows stage is a fixed permutation, it can be implemented via relabelling the qubits [9]. The Key-Expansion stage and the SubBytes stages involve S-boxes. In classical circuits, S-boxes can be implemented via a look-up table but this is impractical on a quantum computer—a common strategy is to implement the S-box as a function. The S-box requires the use of T-gates (an expensive quantum resource) to implement and so (as in [4]) the number of S-boxes required by an attack can be taken to be a measure of the complexity.

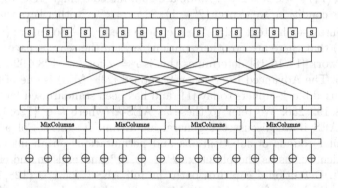

Fig. 1. The structure of an AES round for rounds $1, \ldots, N - 1$ where the 16 bytes of the internal state are represented by individual rectangles and time is represented by moving down the diagram. The SubBytes round is represented by the application of S-boxes (squares labelled by S), the ShiftRows operation is a bytewise permutation and represented by the relabelling of bytes, the MixColumn operation is represented by the labelled 4-byte operation. The AddRound operation is represented by $\oplus$ and represents we are XORing the relevant bytes from a register holding the correct portion of the expanded key. Round N is almost identical, but for the exclusion of the MixColumns operation.

3 Exploiting the Search with Two Oracles Technique

In this section we consider the Search with Two Oracles [17] (STO) technique and how we can exploit it in the context of attacking generic block-ciphers.

Definition 5 (The Search with Two Oracles (STO) problem [17]**).** *Let the quantum oracles $\mathcal{O}_\chi$ and $\mathcal{O}_\gamma$ be defined by $\chi, \gamma : \{0,1\}^k \longrightarrow \{0,1\}$ where we have $\chi^{-1}(1) \subseteq \gamma^{-1}(1) \subseteq \{0,1\}^k$. We denote $M = |\chi^{-1}(1)|$ and $S = |\gamma^{-1}(1)|$. The STO problem is to find an element $x \in \{0,1\}^k$ such that $\chi(x) = 1$.*

The *Search with Two Oracles* problem as given in Definition 5 is a natural extension of the unstructured search problem that Grover's algorithm [17] solves (where we only possess the quantum oracle $\mathcal{O}_\chi$ and knowledge of $M = |\chi^{-1}(1)|$).

Grover's algorithm can be considered a quantum analog of a classical brute-force search, where we exhaustively sample $x \in \{0,1\}^k$ until we find an element where $\chi(x) = 1$. If the quantum and classical oracles are of the same complexity, then this classical analog has an expected cost of $O\left(\frac{2^k}{M} \cdot C_{\mathcal{O}_\chi}\right)$ whilst Grover's algorithm has $O\left(\sqrt{\frac{2^k}{M}} \cdot C_{\mathcal{O}_\chi}\right)$. The STO method also has a classical analog.

If we consider the classical case where $\chi : \{0,1\}^k \longrightarrow \{0,1\}$ is expensive to implement and $\gamma : \{0,1\}^k \longrightarrow \{0,1\}$ is relatively cheap, then we can do better if we use a filtering or sieving technique, whereby we exhaustively sample elements $x \in \{0,1\}^k$, compute $\gamma(x)$ and then test whether $\chi(x) = 1$ if and only if $\gamma(x) = 1$. The complexity is therefore $O\left(\frac{2^k}{M} \cdot C_{\mathcal{O}_\gamma} + \frac{S}{M} \cdot C_{\mathcal{O}_\chi}\right)$ as we still need to make $O\left(\frac{2^k}{M}\right)$ samples of elements $x \in \{0,1\}^k$ to find an element that satisfies $\chi(x) = 1$, but can expect $\frac{S}{2^k}$ of these elements to pass the test $\gamma(x) = 1$. We have substituted making expensive tests with χ for making cheap tests with γ.

The simple quantum analog of the above is the *Search with Two Oracles* technique [17] where we first define an initial algorithm using quantum amplitude amplification (see Theorem 1) with the cheap quantum oracle $\mathcal{O}_\gamma$ and the quantum algorithm chosen to be $\mathcal{A} := H^{\otimes k}$ (the Hadamard transform on k-qubits—see proof of Theorem 3) to increase the probability of measuring an element such that $\gamma(x) = 1$ from $\frac{1}{2^k}$ to approximately 1. We call this algorithm $\mathcal{B}$ and note that its cost (see Theorems 1 and 2) will be on the order of $C_\mathcal{B} \approx \frac{\pi}{4}\sqrt{\frac{2^k}{S}} \cdot C_{\mathcal{O}_\gamma}$.

As $\chi^{-1}(1) \subseteq \gamma^{-1}(1)$, we therefore have that the probability of executing $\mathcal{B}$ and measuring an element such that $\chi(x) = 1$ is $\frac{M}{S}$ and can therefore use quantum amplitude amplification in conjunction with the expensive quantum oracle $\mathcal{O}_\chi$ to create a new quantum algorithm $\mathcal{D}$ that produces an element $x \in \{0,1\}^k$ such that $\chi(x) = 1$ with probability ≈ 1. Using Theorems 1 and 2 again, we have that

$$C_\mathcal{D} \approx \frac{\pi}{4} \cdot \sqrt{\frac{S}{M}} \cdot (C_{\mathcal{O}_\chi} + 2 \cdot C_\mathcal{B}) = \frac{\pi}{4} \cdot \sqrt{\frac{S}{M}} \cdot C_{\mathcal{O}_\chi} + \frac{\pi^2}{8} \cdot \sqrt{\frac{2^k}{M}} \cdot C_{\mathcal{O}_\gamma} \quad (12)$$

in terms of calls to the quantum oracles $\mathcal{O}_\gamma$ and $\mathcal{O}_\chi$.

This is identical to the quantum filtering techniques in [4]—the total number of queries has remained asymptotically $O\left(\sqrt{\frac{2^k}{M}}\right)$, but they have been shifted from calls to the quantum oracle $\mathcal{O}_\chi$ to calls to the oracle $\mathcal{O}_\gamma$. Kimmel et al. [17] additionally provide a "hybrid" method that interpolates between Grover's algorithm and the above method which is slightly more efficient, in that it reduces the constant $\frac{\pi^2}{8} \approx 1.233$ term in front of $C_{\mathcal{O}_\gamma}$ to a value closer to $\frac{\pi}{4} \approx 0.785$. The idea is that we can reduce the number of amplitude amplification iterations in the algorithm $\mathcal{B}$ if we compensate by increasing the number of amplitude amplification iterations in the outer algorithm $\mathcal{D}$. This approach is also noted in [1] (Lemma 9) and could additionally be used to improve the results of [4], which rely upon a large number of nested applications of amplitude amplification.

Theorem 4 (A STO solution (adapted from Algorithm 3 of [17])).
Let $\chi, \gamma : \{0,1\}^k \longrightarrow \{0,1\}$ *be such that* $\chi^{-1}(x) \subseteq \gamma^{-1}(1) \subseteq \{0,1\}^k$ *and the quantities* $M = |\gamma^{-1}(1)|$ *and* $S = |\gamma^{-1}(1)|$ *are exactly known.*
Let $0 \leq t \leq \left\lfloor \frac{\pi}{4}\sqrt{\frac{2^k}{S}} \right\rfloor$ *be an integer and* $b(t) = \sin^2\left((2t+1) \cdot \arcsin\sqrt{\frac{S}{2^k}}\right)$.
Then the quantum algorithm $\mathcal{C}(t) = \mathcal{Q}\left(\mathcal{B}(t), \mathcal{O}_\chi, \left\lfloor \frac{S}{b(t) \cdot M} \right\rfloor\right)$ *where we define* $\mathcal{B}(t) = \mathcal{Q}(H^{\otimes k}, \mathcal{O}_\gamma, t)$ *(using the notation for quantum amplitude amplification in Theorem 1) has a success probability relative to* χ *of at least* $1 - \frac{M}{S}$.
The cost of $\mathcal{C}(t)$ *in terms of oracle calls is* $\leq \frac{\pi}{4} \cdot \sqrt{\frac{S}{b(t) \cdot M}} \cdot \left(C_{\mathcal{O}_\chi} + 2 \cdot t \cdot C_{\mathcal{O}_\gamma}\right)$.

PROOF: We define an initial quantum algorithm $\mathcal{B}(t)$ to be an instance of amplitude amplification (see Theorem 1) using the choice of $\mathcal{A} = H^{\otimes k}$ (the Hadamard transform on k-qubits—see proof of Theorem 3) and the quantum oracle $\mathcal{O}_\gamma$. The algorithm $\mathcal{B}(t)$ therefore has a cost of

$$C_{\mathcal{B}(t)} = t \cdot \left(C_{\mathcal{O}_\gamma} + C_{\mathcal{O}_k}\right) + \left(2t+1\right) \cdot C_{H^{\otimes k}} \approx t \cdot C_{\mathcal{O}_\gamma} \qquad (13)$$

and has a success probability relative to γ of $b(t) = \sin^2\left((2t+1) \cdot \arcsin(\sqrt{\frac{S}{2^k}})\right)$ and a success probability relative to χ of $\frac{b(t) \cdot M}{S}$ as we have a probability of $b(t)$ of measuring one of the S items that satisfy $\gamma(x) = 1$ and each of these has a probability of $\frac{M}{S}$ of satisfying $\chi(x) = 1$.

We can therefore define a quantum algorithm $\mathcal{C}(t)$ via amplitude amplification that uses $\mathcal{B}(t)$ as our initial quantum algorithm and the quantum oracle $\mathcal{O}_\chi$ to boost the probability of measuring an element $x \in \{0,1\}^k$ that satisfies $\chi(x) = 1$ from $\frac{b(t) \cdot M}{S}$ to at least $1 - \frac{b(t) \cdot M}{S} \geq 1 - \frac{M}{S}$ by Theorem 2. We denote this algorithm $\mathcal{C}(t)$, as it is parameterised by the t used in $\mathcal{B}(t)$. The cost of $\mathcal{C}(t)$ is exactly

$$C_{\mathcal{C}(t)} = \left\lfloor \frac{\pi}{4}\sqrt{\frac{S}{b(t) \cdot M}} \right\rfloor \cdot (C_{\mathcal{O}_\chi} + C_{\mathcal{O}_k}) + (2 \cdot \left\lfloor \frac{\pi}{4}\sqrt{\frac{S}{b(t) \cdot M}} \right\rfloor + 1) \cdot C_{\mathcal{B}(t)} \quad (14)$$

which in terms of oracle calls is

$$\leq \frac{\pi}{4} \cdot \sqrt{\frac{S}{b(t) \cdot M}} \cdot \left(C_{\mathcal{O}_\chi} + 2 \cdot t \cdot C_{\mathcal{O}_\gamma}\right). \qquad (15)$$

$\square$

To see the use of using Theorem 4 compared to the first STO approach described in Sect. 3, it helps to view the cost using a small angle approximation $\sin x \approx x$, which gives us the cost

$$C_{C(t)} \leq \frac{\pi}{4}\sqrt{\frac{2^k}{M}}\frac{1}{2t+1} \cdot C_{\mathcal{O}_\chi} + \frac{\pi}{4}\sqrt{\frac{2^k}{M}}\frac{2t}{2t+1} \cdot C_{\mathcal{O}_\gamma} \tag{16}$$

which approximates the cost of the algorithm for $t \ll \frac{\pi}{4}\sqrt{\frac{2^k}{S}}$ and demonstrates the overall behaviour as we vary the parameter t—the cost contribution of $C_{\mathcal{O}_\gamma}$ remains approximately static whilst the cost contribution of C_χ decreases. As we have seen from Eq. (12), when $t \approx \frac{\pi}{4}\sqrt{\frac{N}{S}}$, we have a constant of $\frac{\pi^2}{8}$ in front of the $C_{\mathcal{O}_\gamma}$ term and we know that when $t = 0$ that the algorithm is simply Grover's algorithm. Theorem 4 and the discussion around it is simply a rephrasing of the results from [17] in language designed to provide intuition.

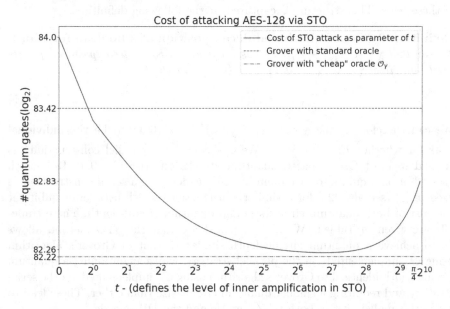

Fig. 2. The cost of attacking AES-128 using our methods, where our algorithm is parameterised by the choice of an integer $t \in \mathbb{Z}_{\geq 0}$ such that $0 \leq t \leq \frac{\pi}{4} \cdot 2^{10}$. The red dashed line on the bottom denotes a theoretical lower-bound for the cost of the search procedure, where we only count calls to the cheap oracle $\mathcal{O}_\gamma$.

Theorem 4 deals with the case where we have perfect knowledge of the value $S = |\gamma^{-1}(1)|$ and $M = |\chi^{-1}(1)|$. The success probability of Theorem 4 will change if we cannot reliably predict the *ratios* $\frac{M}{S}$ and $\frac{S}{2^k}$. For the block-cipher key recovery problem (see Sect. 2.3 and Eq. (11)) we have that $M = 1$ with near certainty if we choose r (the number of plaintext-ciphertext pairs) to be large enough. This is based upon the assumption that if we choose a random key

$x \in \{0,1\}^k$ then each bit of an encrypted n-bit plaintext has an equal chance of being 0 or 1. The value of $S = |\gamma^{-1}(1)|$ is dependent upon exactly how we choose to define $\gamma : \{0,1\}^k \longrightarrow \{0,1\}$. We will design γ such that $\gamma(x) = 1$ iff l specific bytes of the encrypted plaintext match the ciphertext. Crucially, this means that we only have to compute these l specific bytes of the encryption.

3.1   Oracle Design Patterns for Attacking Block-Ciphers with STO

We first consider how the quantum oracle $\mathcal{O}_\chi$ (the expensive oracle) can be constructed. We recall the discussion in Sect. 2.3 and Eq. (11)—to ensure that $M = |\chi^{-1}(1)| = 1$, we wish to choose r large enough so that the key is uniquely specified (with high probability) by testing whether the condition $\chi(x) = \left(E(x, P_1) \overset{?}{=} C_1\right) \wedge \cdots \wedge \left(E(x, P_r) \overset{?}{=} C_r\right)$ holds for a key $x \in \{0,1\}^k$. Each of these form an individual test and we must construct a quantum oracle that implements both these individual tests and which outputs the logical AND of these tests. This structure is captured by the following definition.

Definition 6 (Constraint-based decomposition of a boolean function). *We say that $\chi : \{0,1\}^k \longrightarrow \{0,1\}$ has a constraint-based decomposition if there exist nontrivial $\chi_1, \ldots, \chi_r : \{0,1\}^k \longrightarrow \{0,1\}$ such that*

$$\chi(x) = \chi_1(x) \wedge \cdots \wedge \chi_r(x). \tag{17}$$

We can therefore define $\chi_1, \ldots, \chi_r : \{0,1\}^k \longrightarrow \{0,1\}$ to be the individual tests for whether $E(x, P_i) \overset{?}{=} C_i$. We can consider a parallel construction (as is used in most Grover-based quantum attacks on AES [3,4,9,13,18]) which uses additional qubits to save quantum circuit-depth or a serial construction as used in [2] (see also [26] for a similar construction) which uses fewer qubits at the cost of both quantum circuit-size and quantum circuit-depth. These trade-offs are given in Table 1. We later demonstrate that the STO method allows us to achieve a quantum circuit-depth similar to that of Grover's algorithm using $\mathcal{O}_\chi$ implemented via the parallel strategy, whilst maintaining a quantum circuit-width identical to Grover's algorithm using $\mathcal{O}_\chi$ implemented via the serial strategy and requiring a smaller quantum circuit-size than either. These lead to a strictly smaller cost in both the G-metric and the DW-metric.

Table 1. Costs for several design patterns for implementation of $\mathcal{O}_\chi$.

Metric	Parallel strategy	Serial strategy
Size	$\sum_{i=1}^{r} (S_{\mathcal{E}_{\chi_i}} + S_{\mathcal{E}_{\chi_i}^\dagger}) +$ $2k(r-1) \cdot S_{\wedge_1(X)} + S_{\wedge_{r-1}(Z)}$	$2\sum_{i=1}^{r-1} (S_{\mathcal{E}_{\chi_i}} + S_{\mathcal{E}_{\chi_i}^\dagger}) + S_{\mathcal{E}_{\chi_r}} + S_{\mathcal{E}_{\chi_r}^\dagger} + S_{\wedge_{r-1}(Z)}$
Depth	$\max\{D_{\mathcal{E}_{\chi_i}} + D_{\mathcal{E}_{\chi_i}^\dagger}\}_{i=1}^{r} +$ $2\lceil \log_2 r \rceil \cdot D_{\wedge_1(X)} + D_{\wedge_{r-1}(Z)}$	$2\sum_{i=1}^{r-1} (D_{\mathcal{E}_{\chi_i}} + D_{\mathcal{E}_{\chi_i}^\dagger}) + D_{\mathcal{E}_{\chi_r}} + D_{\mathcal{E}_{\chi_r}^\dagger} + D_{\wedge_{r-1}(Z)}$
idth	$\max\{\sum_{i=1}^{r} W_{\mathcal{E}_{\chi_i}}, \sum_{i=1}^{r} W_{\mathcal{E}_{\chi_i}^\dagger}\}$	$\max\{W_{\mathcal{E}_{\chi_1}}, \ldots, W_{\mathcal{E}_{\chi_r}}, W_{\mathcal{E}_{\chi_1}^\dagger}, \ldots, W_{\mathcal{E}_{\chi_r}^\dagger}\} + r - 1$

Theorem 5 (The cost of $\mathcal{O}_\chi$ for constraint-based $\chi : \{0,1\}^k \longrightarrow \{0,1\}$).
Let the boolean function $\chi : \{0,1\}^k \longrightarrow \{0,1\}$ possess a non-trivial constraint-based decomposition $\chi_1,\ldots,\chi_r : \{0,1\}^k \longrightarrow \{0,1\}$ and $\mathcal{E}_{\chi_1},\ldots,\mathcal{E}_{\chi_r}$ be quantum evaluations (see Definition (2)) for $\chi_1,\ldots,\chi_r$. Then $\mathcal{O}_\chi$ requires the resources

PROOF: **Parallel Strategy.** In this scenario (which first appears in [9]), the register $|x\rangle$ (where $x \in \{0,1\}^k$) is copied to $r-1$ other registers. This can be implemented using $\wedge_1(X)$ gates for a circuit-size of $(r-1) \cdot S_{\wedge_1(X)}$ and a circuit-depth of $\lceil \log_2 r \rceil \cdot D_{\wedge_1(X)}$ steps.

The quantum evaluations $\mathcal{E}_{\chi_1},\ldots,\mathcal{E}_{\chi_r}$ are then executed in parallel, leaving the computational basis state in the form $|x\rangle|*\rangle g_1(x)|*\rangle\chi_1(x)\ldots|*\rangle g_r(x)$ $|*\rangle\chi_r(x)$. A single $\wedge_{r-1}(Z)$ gate can then be applied to the r qubits holding $|*\rangle\chi_1(x)\ldots|*\rangle\chi_r(x)$, with one of them being the target. By the action of $\wedge_{r-1}(Z)$, the conditional phase inversion is performed if and only if $\chi_1(x) = \cdots = \chi_r(x) = 1$.

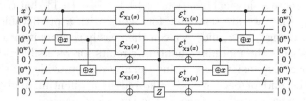

Fig. 3. A parallel design pattern for $\mathcal{O}_\chi$, where $\chi(x) = \chi_1(x) \wedge \cdots \wedge \chi_3(x)$.

After this is performed, the ancilla qubits are restored to their original state by executing $\mathcal{E}_{\chi_1}^\dagger,\ldots,\mathcal{E}_{\chi_r}^\dagger$ and the copies of the state $|x\rangle$ removed.

Serial Strategy. This design was first studied with respect to AES-128 in [2] and a similar pattern used in [26]. For $i = 1,\ldots,r-1$ we compute $|\chi_i(x)\rangle$ via the quantum evaluation $\mathcal{E}_{\chi_i}$, copy the result to a clean qubit and then execute $\mathcal{E}_{\chi_i}^\dagger$ to ensure the ancilla qubits are clean. We can then execute $\mathcal{E}_{\chi_r}$ and will be left with $|*\rangle x|*\rangle g_r(x)|*\rangle\chi_1(x)\ldots|*\rangle\chi_{r-1}(x)|*\rangle\chi_r(x)$, so can apply a single $\wedge_{r-1}(Z)$ gate to the final r qubits to implement the conditional phase inversion.

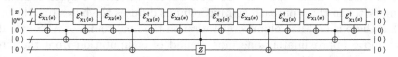

Fig. 4. A serial design pattern for $\mathcal{O}_\chi$ where $\chi(x) = \chi_1(x) \wedge \cdots \wedge \chi_3(x)$.

We then must restore the computational basis state to $|x\rangle|0\ldots0\rangle$, which requires executing adjoint $\mathcal{E}_{\chi_r}^\dagger$ and then uncomputing the stored values of $|\chi_i(x)\rangle$ in the same way they were originally computed. $\square$

We will later choose the serial oracle design to implement our expensive oracle $\mathcal{O}_\chi$, as we wish to conserve qubits and the additional circuit-size/circuit-depth will be negated by use of the STO methodology. We could use the parallel oracle as our expensive oracle, but there is essentially no benefit to this in terms of quantum circuit-depth and circuit-size whilst it requires additional qubits to implement.

4 New Quantum Circuits and Resource Estimates for AES

In this section we consider the cost of attacking the Advanced Encryption Standard with our methods. As we are instantiating the methods described in Sect. 3 with a concrete example, it is natural that there is more structure to be exploited—we demonstrate how to exploit this structure by offering modified circuits which allow us to reduce the cost of $\mathcal{O}_\gamma$ (the cheap oracle) for use with the Search with Two Oracles methods described in Sect. 3. The expensive oracle $\mathcal{O}_\chi$ will remain a serial-oracle design pattern as described in Sect. 3.1 that tests whether all r encrypted plaintexts exactly match the r ciphertexts.

4.1 Refinements to the Quantum Oracle $\mathcal{O}_\gamma$ Specific to AES

Our goal is to create a classical function $\gamma : \{0,1\}^k \longrightarrow \{0,1\}$ that correctly identifies the unique key we are searching for, along with a predictable number of false-positives. Using γ as a guide, we can then easily convert it into a reversible circuit if we possess the modular quantum circuits for reversible S-boxes, Mix-Columns and KeyExpansion steps, using the approach provided in [13], whereby the state at the end of each round is stored in a quantum register and the KeyExpansion is computed in-place on the key-space register.

We can define $\gamma : \{0,1\}^k \longrightarrow \{0,1\}$ by the function which takes a fixed plaintext, computes the encryption of this plaintext under the key $x \in \{0,1\}^k$ and compares if j bytes of the encrypted plaintext are equal to j bytes of the ciphertext, meaning we compare $l = 8j$ bits of the encrypted plaintext with the known ciphertext. As the state consists of 16 bytes and these are operated on at an individual level by S-boxes and AddRoundKey operations at the byte level and by MixColumns operations in sequences of 4 bytes (words), this means that we can select the j output bytes we are interested in and simply compute the gates required in the circuit to output these bytes and need not compute gates solely involved with outputting the $16 - j$ bytes we are not checking.

As the MixColumns operation acts on words (a word is 4 bytes), this is the limiting factor in this approach as MixColumns diffuses the bytes together. The fact that there is no MixColumns operation on the final round of AES will allow us to remove approximately one more round of computation from the circuit than we could otherwise and where the MixColumns operation is only required to output a single byte (as opposed to the usual four) we can vastly reduce the cost of implementing these specific MixColumns operations.

This strategy is more intuitively demonstrated if we consider the final three rounds of a classical circuit for AES in Fig. 5, which is simply three versions of Fig. 1 stacked together, with the MixColumns operations removed for the final round. Specifically, we if choose $j = 4$ bytes so that they correspond to the output of a single MixColumns operations in round $N - 1$ then we need only compute 4 S-boxes in round N of AES which lead out of this MixColumns operation and 4 S-boxes which lead into this MixColumns operation. This means that we need only execute 8 out of the 32 S-boxes in the final two rounds of AES.

There are further savings to be made as each of the MixColumns operations in round $N-2$ takes in four bytes and outputs one byte. This means that we can reduce the cost of implementing these specific MixColumns operations.

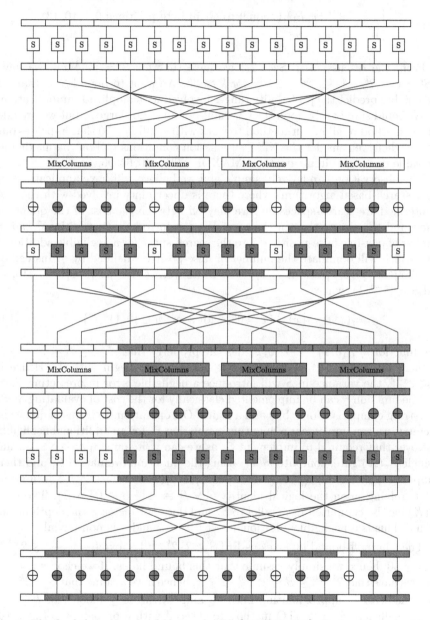

Fig. 5. The final three rounds of N-round AES-$\{128, 192, 256\}$. Each rectangular block represents a byte whilst each $\oplus$ represents the application of AddRoundKey to that specific byte (with the round key being computed off-diagram). Operations we need not compute to compute 4 chosen bytes are in gray.

4.2   On the Probability of Success and Introducing False-Positives

The function $\gamma : \{0,1\}^k \longrightarrow \{0,1\}$ is defined by

$$\gamma(x) \mapsto \begin{cases} 1 & \text{if } E(x, P_1) \text{ is equal to } C_1 \text{ in byte positions } 0,7,10,13 \\ 0 & \text{otherwise.} \end{cases} \tag{18}$$

From the discussion in Sect. 2.3 we have that for $S = |\gamma^{-1}(x)|$, we have $\mathbb{E}[S] = 1 + (2^k - 1) \cdot 2^{-32} \approx 2^{k-32}$ for $k \gg 32$. We want to bound S so that we can reliably predict the probability ranges involved with amplitude amplification.

We could simply rely upon the Chernoff-bound [8] for large k, but we provide a novel method to allow our method to work with small $k \geq 50$ that improves our results when we consider the NIST submission conditions [25] on the maximum allowable quantum circuit-depth of MAXDEPTH= $40, 64, 96$.

The observation is relatively simple and we believe will have applications in other search-based algorithms where there is uncertainty involved with the size of intermediate search-spaces and we play off between the cost of the quantum oracle and the size of the search-space. We can introduce an additional *known* number of possible false-positives into the search-space for a negligible additional cost, which will dominate the number of false-positives defined by γ. Instead of $\gamma : \{0,1\}^k \longrightarrow \{0,1\}$ and $S = |\gamma^{-1}(1)|$ as above, we use $\hat{\gamma} : \{0,1\}^k \longrightarrow \{0,1\}$ and $\hat{S} = |\hat{\gamma}^{-1}(1)|$ where

$$\hat{\gamma}(x) \mapsto \gamma(x) \vee \left(x = 0^r \| y \text{ for some } y \in \{0,1\}^{k-r}\right) \tag{19}$$

The function $\hat{\gamma} : \{0,1\}^k \longrightarrow \{0,1\}$ has the property that $2^{k-r} \leq \hat{S} \leq 2^{k-r} + S$ as there are exactly 2^{k-r} elements $x \in \{0,1\}^k$ that begin with 0^r. Hence if $S \ll 2^{k-r}$, the variance in S will introduce a negligible error in predicting $\hat{S}$.

The function $\hat{\gamma}$ can be implemented classically for the cost of evaluating $\gamma(x)$, a bitstring comparison on r bits and a logical OR operation. In terms of quantum circuitry, we can implement a quantum evaluation $\mathcal{E}_{\hat{\gamma}}$ for an additional negligible cost over that required to implement $\mathcal{E}_\gamma$ as we can write out $|x_1 \wedge \cdots \wedge x_r\rangle$ using a single $\wedge_r(X)$ gate, compute $|\gamma(x)\rangle$ using the quantum evaluation $\mathcal{E}_\gamma$ and then compute $|*\rangle\hat{\gamma}(x) = |*\rangle\gamma(x) \oplus \left(\bar{x}_1 \wedge \cdots \wedge \bar{x}_r\right) \oplus \left(\gamma(x) \wedge \bar{x}_1 \wedge \cdots \wedge \bar{x}_r\right)$ in a clean qubit, relying upon the logical identity $A \vee B \equiv A \oplus B \oplus \left(A \wedge B\right)$. The gate $\wedge_r(X)$ can be computed in parallel to $\mathcal{E}_\gamma$ and does not increase the depth of the circuit. This is a negligible additional cost if $r \ll k$ and γ is non-trivial.

The Chernoff-bound [8] gives us $\Pr\left(S \geq 2 \cdot 2^{k-32}\right) \leq \exp\left(-\frac{2^{k-32}}{3}\right) \leq 2^{-100}$ for $k \geq 50$, hence we simply assume that this bound holds. If we choose $r = 20$, then we have that $2^{k-20} \leq \hat{S} \leq 2^{k-20} + 2^{k-31}$, hence if we assume that $\hat{S} = 2^{k-20}$, then the error in approximating both $\frac{\hat{S}}{2^k}$ and $\frac{1}{\hat{S}}$ will be ≤ 0.0005 for $k \geq 50$. This is sufficient for the STO method to succeed with a probability of at least $1 - 2^{-20} \geq 99.9999\%$ for $k \geq 50$, which is sufficient for our purposes.

4.3 On the Level of Inner Amplification

With our assumptions that $M = 1$ and $\hat{S} = 2^{k-20}$ and a search space of size $N = 2^k$ we recall that the cost Eq. (12) for using the STO technique (see Theorem 4) can be tuned given the parameter $0 \leq t \leq \left\lfloor \dfrac{\pi}{4 \arcsin \sqrt{\frac{2^{k-20}}{2^k}}} \right\rfloor \leq \frac{\pi}{4} \cdot 2^{10}$. The original STO algorithm (see Algorithm 3 of [17]) uses gives the optimal value of t (assuming *exact* amplitude amplification [6], which is used as they assume perfect knowledge of $|\gamma^{-1}(1)|$) via solving the sum $\tan\left(\phi + \sqrt{\frac{S}{N}}\right) = \phi + \frac{C_{O_X}}{C_{O_\gamma}}\sqrt{\frac{S}{N}}$. This is rather unwieldy and we rely upon a computational approach, noting that the cost equation for STO (Eq. (12)) is convex on the range we are interested in (if we relax the floor functions). We can therefore use standard 1-dimensional minimisation techniques, but given that $0 \leq t \leq 2^{10}$, we can easily find an optimal value of t via brute force search.

4.4 Reducing the Cost of Partial MixColumns

As first noted in [9], the MixColumns operation acting on each word of 4 bytes can be viewed an invertible linear map over $\mathbb{F}_2^{32 \times 32}$ and hence be implemented in-place on the input qubits via using $\wedge_1(X)$ gates to implement an LUP decomposition of this linear map. The paper [13] offers a version of the design of [20] requiring 1108 $\wedge_1(X)$ gates (277 gates per word) with a depth of 111 (known as IP standing as it acts in-place) and a low-depth version of this same primitive (known as OOP as it acts out-of-place) via computing the output of the Mix-Columns operation out-of-place on clean qubits, using 1248 $\wedge_1(X)$ gates (312 $\wedge_1(X)$ gates each word) with a depth of 22.

We were able to implement the MixColumns operations in round $N - 2$ of our circuit (see Fig. 5) which consists of a linear map $\mathbb{F}_2^{8 \times 32}$ applied to each word by viewing each of the 8 output wires per word as a linear sum over $\mathbb{F}_2[x_1, \ldots, x_{32}]$, where variables represent input wires. In this way, we identified a unique variable (input wire) that occurs in each sum (output wire) and used these 8 input wires as our output wires (which simply requires a logical relabelling of these qubits). The other variables in these sums were then be added to these output wires via $\wedge_1(X)$ gates and after hand optimising these circuits we obtained that the MixColumns operation in round $N - 2$ could be implemented using just 152 $\wedge_1(X)$ gates (38 $\wedge_1(X)$ gates per word) with a depth of 6.

4.5   Quantum Resource Estimates via Q#

We used the Microsoft quantum programming language Q# to implement our circuits, basing them on those made available by the authors of [9] which includes basic circuits such as MixColumns, S-boxes and functions to implement rounds of AES, as well as utilities to perform quantum resource estimations. In particular, we designed a new MixColumns operation following the principles in Sect. 4.4 and created three new rounds—Antepenultimate, Penultimate and FinalRound to implement the reduction of the circuit. We tested our circuits using random inputs with the Q# Toffoli simulator against the reference implementation for both the full circuit and MixColumns component. Our quantum resource estimations were averaged over 20 cost simulations of each component. We provide the oracle costs we computed in Table 5 (see Appendix C) (Table 2).

Table 2. Our techniques applied to cryptanalysis of AES-128/192/256.

Source	G-cost	DW-cost	#Depth	#Qubits	#Success%
AES-128 [13] ($r = 1$)	$2^{82.42}$	$2^{85.81}$	$2^{75.11}$	1665	$\frac{1}{e} \approx 0.37$
AES-128 [13] ($r = 2$)	$2^{83.42}$	$2^{86.81}$	$2^{75.11}$	3329	≈ 1
AES-128 (This paper)	$2^{82.25}$	$2^{85.75}$	$2^{75.05}$	1667	≈ 1
AES-192 [13] ($r = 2$)	$2^{115.58}$	$2^{119.14}$	$2^{107.19}$	3969	≈ 1
AES-192 (This paper)	$2^{114.44}$	$2^{118.04}$	$2^{107.08}$	1987	≈ 1
AES-256 [13] ($r = 2$)	$2^{147.88}$	$2^{151.54}$	$2^{139.37}$	4609	$\frac{1}{e} \approx 0.37$
AES-256 [13] ($r = 3$)	$2^{148.47}$	$2^{152.11}$	$2^{139.36}$	6913	≈ 1
AES-256 (This paper)	$2^{146.77}$	$2^{150.42}$	$2^{139.38}$	2307	≈ 1

A natural question is how these results impact upon the NIST security levels with respect to the MAXDEPTH parameter (a maximum allowable quantum circuit depth for any quantum algorithm used in cryptanalysis of NIST submissions). The MAXDEPTH parameter can be taken to be MAXDEPTH $= 2^{40}, 2^{64}$ or 2^{96} and previous work [13] has made significant work in reducing this over the initial guidelines. Our techniques can also be used in this scenario, but unless multiple plaintext-ciphertext pairs are involved (which only occurs in the MAXDEPTH $= 2^{96}$ scenario for applying Grover to AES) we do not see a significant reduction, though we have strict gains in all cases, as can be seen in Table 3 below.

Table 3. The effect of our techniques on the MAXDEPTH cryptanalysis scenario. As [13] notes, the NIST estimates did not take into the special-case of AES-128 with MAXDEPTH $= 2^{96}$ and we have substituted the original result of [9].

NIST Security level	Source	G-cost for MAXDEPTH ($\log_2$)		
		2^{40}	2^{64}	2^{96}
1 AES-128	[9,25]	130.0	106.0	87.5
	[13]	117.1	93.1	83.4
	This paper	116.9	92.9	82.3
3 AES-192	[25]	193.0	169.0	137.0
	[13]	181.1	157.1	126.1
	This paper	180.9	156.9	125.0
5 AES-256	[25]	258.0	234.0	202.0
	[13]	245.5	221.5	190.5
	This paper	245.3	221.3	189.3

5 Conclusions

We have demonstrated that there is no advantage in using the parallel quantum oracle construction compared to the serial quantum oracle construction for the well-known Grover-based attack on block-ciphers. Our techniques have shown that it is a strictly advantageous technique for use with cryptanalysis of AES, as we use fewer qubits and have lower costs in the G-cost and DW-cost models. Our message is that the known plaintext-unicity distance (the number r of plaintext-ciphertexts pairs we use) of the block-cipher need not affect the cost of the quantum search procedure, that we may only require as many qubits as are required to implement one quantum circuit evaluation of a block-cipher and that small gains can be made outside of the black-box model via designing reduced quantum circuits for specific block-ciphers that only test whether a small number of bits of the encrypted plaintext match the ciphertext.

Our improvements in using the serial oracle design with the STO technique are generic in the black-box model and should be considered in any quantum resource estimation of a block-cipher where Grover is used. Future improvements on the modular quantum circuit components of AES (such as KeyExpansion, MixColumns or the design of the S-box) or design principles for a single quantum circuit that implements AES will further improve upon our concrete estimates, much as they would for a simple Grover-based attack with a parallel oracle.

Qubits are expected to be an expensive resource, no matter how they are implemented, and techniques such as these demonstrate that quantum cryptanalysis may be slightly cheaper than previously thought. We stress that our results impact upon the *concrete cost* of attacking AES via quantum search techniques but do not impact upon the *query complexity*, hence assuming that AES-k requires $\frac{\pi}{4} \cdot 2^{k/2}$ quantum gates to break remains the safest option for choosing cryptographic parameters.

Acknowledgements. The authors kindly thank the reviewers for their constructive feedback and for pointing out the resource estimation bug in Q# (see Appendix A). Benjamin Pring was funded during the development of this research by EPRSC grant EP/M50645X/1, National Science Foundation grant 183980, NIST grant 60NANB17D184, a Seed grant of the Florida Center for Cybersecurity and a USF proposal enhancement grant. An early version of these results were first announced at the International Workshop on Coding and Cryptography 2019. The authors would like to thank Orr Dunkelman for providing a reference to [12].

A   Code and Disclaimer

A reviewer kindly pointed out to the authors that there was a bug in the Q# quantum resource estimator[1] which resulted in outputting a quantum circuit depth and width for which there is no guarantee that both can be simultaneously realised. This has subsequently been fixed, but there are other issues[2] which may affect the quantum resource estimation routines. Our Q# quantum resource estimates agree with our theoretical gains and our code[3] can easily be checked and run at a later date to confirm these results hold. The unit tests—and thus the correctness of the modified quantum circuits for AES we constructed—are unaffected. In order to produce a version of our results that is invariant with respect to Q#, we perform an abstract quantum resource estimation in terms of quantum circuits which implement S-boxes as suggested in [4] and a quantum evaluation for an AES circuit that simply requires double the number of S-boxes as a classical circuit for AES to capture the fact that the circuit must be reversible (Table 4).

Table 4. Abstract circuit-statistics to compare our attack with a Grover-based approach costed in number of quantum circuits for S-boxes. All values are given in $\log_2$ and we assume 40 ancilla qubits per S-box as in [4].

	S-box count	S-box depth	Width
AES-128 Grover ($r = 2$)	73.3	68.0	12.0
AES-128 (ours)	72.1	68.0	11.0
AES-192 Grover ($r = 2$)	105.5	100.2	12.2
AES-192 (ours)	104.3	100.2	11.2
AES-256 Grover ($r = 3$)	138.3	132.5	12.9
AES-256 (ours)	136.6	132.5	11.3

---

[1] See https://github.com/microsoft/qsharp-runtime/issues/192.
[2] See https://github.com/microsoft/qsharp-runtime/issues/419.
[3] Available at: https://github.com/public-ket/reduced-aes.

B   Error Bounds for Amplitude Amplification

The following theorem is simply a computational method of checking error-bounds with regards to amplitude amplification and is derived in a similar manner to the results from [5], which assumes the initial success probability of $\mathcal{A}$ relative to $\chi : \{0,1\}^k \longrightarrow \{0,1\}$ is known exactly. The case where $a = a_- = a_+$ is exactly the result from [5]. We use these results in our scripts.

Theorem 6 (Error bounds for amplitude amplification (adapted from [5])). *Let $\mathcal{A}$ have a success probability of $a \in [a_-, a_+]$ relative to $\chi : \{0,1\}^k \longrightarrow \{0,1\}$.*
Let $t = \left\lfloor \frac{\pi}{4 \cdot \arcsin \sqrt{a}} \right\rfloor$ for any $a \in [a_-, a_+]$, then if

$$\arcsin \sqrt{a_+} + (2t+1) \cdot (\arcsin \sqrt{a_+} - \arcsin \sqrt{a_-}) \leq \frac{\pi}{2} \quad (20)$$

then $\mathcal{Q}(\mathcal{A}, \mathcal{O}_\chi, t)$ succeeds relative to $\chi : \{0,1\}^k \longrightarrow \{0,1\}$ with probability

$$\geq \cos^2 \left((\arcsin \sqrt{a_+} + (2t+1) \cdot (\arcsin \sqrt{a_+} - \arcsin \sqrt{a_-})) \right). \quad (21)$$

PROOF: In the following, $\theta_+ = \arcsin \sqrt{a_+}$, $\theta_- = \arcsin \sqrt{a_-}$ and $\theta_a = \arcsin \sqrt{a}$. Let $\hat{t} = \frac{\pi}{4\theta_a} - \frac{1}{2}$ and $t = \lfloor \hat{t} \rfloor = \left\lfloor \frac{\pi}{4\theta_a} \right\rfloor$. By choice of k we have that

$$\left| (2\hat{t} + 1)\theta_a - (2t+1)\theta_a \right| \leq \theta_+ \quad (22)$$

and furthermore we know that for $\theta_- \leq \theta \leq \theta_+$

$$\left| (2t+1)\theta_a - (2t+1)\theta \right| \leq (2t+1)(\theta_+ - \theta_-). \quad (23)$$

Noting that $(2\hat{t} + 1)\theta_a = \frac{\pi}{2}$ and applying the triangle inequality then gives us

$$0 \leq \left| \frac{\pi}{2} - (2t+1)\theta) \right| \leq \theta_+ + (2t+1)(\theta_+ - \theta_-) \leq \frac{\pi}{2} \quad (24)$$

hence we can apply sine to this inequality to obtain

$$0 \leq \sin^2 \left(\frac{\pi}{2} - (2t+1)\theta) \right) \leq \sin^2 \left(\theta_+ + (2t+1)(\theta_+ - \theta_-) \right) \leq 1 \quad (25)$$

Finally, we reverse the inequality, add 1 to each component and use the facts $\sin(\frac{\pi}{2} - x) = \cos(x)$ and $1 - \sin^2(x) = \cos^2(x)$ to obtain

$$1 \geq \sin^2 \left((2t+1)\theta) \right) \geq \cos^2 \left(\theta_+ + (2t+1)(\theta_+ - \theta_-) \right) \geq 0 \quad (26)$$

The result follows as $\sin^2 \left((2t+1)\theta) \right)$ is the probability of success of for the amplitude amplification procedure $\mathcal{Q}(\mathcal{A}, \mathcal{O}_\chi, t)$ where $t = \lfloor \frac{\pi}{4\theta_a} \rfloor$.   □

When $a \in [a_-, a_+]$ and $(2t+1) \cdot \arcsin \sqrt{a_+} \leq \frac{\pi}{2}$ can use the simple bound

$$\sin^2 \left((2t+1) \cdot \arcsin \sqrt{a_-} \right) \leq \sin^2 \left((2t+1) \cdot \arcsin \sqrt{a} \right) \leq \sin^2 \left((2t+1) \cdot \arcsin \sqrt{a_+} \right) \quad (27)$$

C   Oracle Costs

We highlight the difference in costs briefly for the case of AES-256, for which our cheap quantum oracle which compares only 32 bits of the ciphertext requires ≈ 200 fewer qubits and 0.91 of the gates as does the standard implementation of the oracle designed by [13] for use with Grover's algorithm. This is to be expected, as we theoretically save just under 1.5 rounds of computation and for AES-256, which has 14 rounds, we have that $\frac{12.5}{14} \approx 0.89$. The serial oracle, on the other hand is approximately $\frac{5}{3}$ the cost of the Grover oracle designed to use $r = 3$ plaintext-ciphertext pairs, which again agrees with the additional cost born by using the serial oracle instead of the parallel approach.

Table 5. A comparison of the original oracles from [13] for use with Grover's algorithm and the cheap/expensive variants we use in this paper that are based upon the code from [13] with our modified circuits. For comparative purposes, we created a serial oracle from the quantum AES evaluation circuits of [13].

Oracle type/MixColumns	r/bits compared	# $\wedge_1 (X)$	#1qCliff	#T	#M	T-depth	Full depth	Width
AES-128 (IP) [13]	1/128	292313	84428	54908	13727	121	2816	1665
AES-128 (OOP) [13]	1/128	294863	84488	54908	13727	121	2086	2817
AES-128 (IP) (this paper)	1/32	255195	73597	47996	12255	121	2656	1466
AES-128 (OOP) (this paper)	1/32	257254	73655	47996	12255	121	2079	2394
AES-128 (IP) [13]	2/256	585051	169184	109820	27455	121	2815	3329
AES-128 (OOP) [13]	2/256	589643	168288	109820	27455	121	2096	5633
AES-128 (IP) (serial [13])	2/256	876637	252156	164728	41182	363	8434	1667
AES-128 (OOP) (serial [13])	2/256	884202	252167	164728	41182	361	6231	2819
Oracle type/MixColumns	r/bits compared	# $\wedge_1 (X)$	#1qCliff	#T	#M	T-depth	Full depth	Width
AES-192 (IP) [13]	1/128	329697	94316	61436	15359	120	2978	1985
AES-192 (OOP) [13]	1/128	332665	94092	61436	15359	120	1879	3393
AES-192 (IP) (this paper)	1/32	292649	83624	54524	13887	114	2716	1786
AES-192 (OOP) (this paper)	1/32	295230	83606	54524	13887	114	1825	2970
AES-192 (IP) [13]	2/256	659727	188520	122876	30719	120	2981	3969
AES-192 (OOP) [13]	2/256	665899	188544	122876	30719	120	1890	6785
AES-192 (IP) (serial [13])	2/256	988939	282120	184312	46078	360	8783	1987
AES-192 (OOP) (serial [13])	2/256	998188	282139	184312	46078	360	5614	2295
Oracle type/MixColumns	r/bits compared	# $\wedge_1 (X)$	#1qCliff	#T	#M	T-depth	Full depth	Width
AES-256 (IP) [13]	1/128	404139	116286	75580	18895	126	3353	2305
AES-256 (OOP) [13]	1/128	407667	116062	75580	18895	126	1951	3969
AES-256 (IP) (this paper)	1/32	366912	105236	68668	17423	126	3118	2106
AES-256 (OOP) (this paper)	1/32	370090	105292	68668	17423	126	1923	3546
AES-256 (IP) [13])	3/384	1212905	347766	226748	56687	126	3347	6913
AES-256 (OOP) [13]	3/384	1223087	346290	226748	56687	126	1956	11905
AES-256 (IP) serial [13])	3/384	2019323	578562	377908	94477	610	16386	2309
AES-256 (OOP) serial [13])	3/384	2037796	578183	377908	94477	608	9440	3973

References

1. Aaronson, S., Ambainis, A.: Quantum search of spatial regions. In: 44th Annual IEEE Symposium on Foundations of Computer Science Proceedings, pp. 200–209. IEEE (2003)
2. Almazrooie, M., Samsudin, A., Abdullah, R., Mutter, K.N.: Quantum reversible circuit of AES-128. Quantum Inf. Process. **17**(5), 1–30 (2018). https://doi.org/10.1007/s11128-018-1864-3
3. Anand, R., Maitra, A., Mukhopadhyay, S.: Grover on SIMON. arXiv:2004.10686 (2020)
4. Bonnetain, X., Naya-Plasencia, M., Schrottenloher, A.: Quantum security analysis of AES. IACR Trans. Symmetric Cryptol. **2**, 55–93 (2019)
5. Boyer, M., Brassard, G., Høyer, P., Tapp, A.: Tight bounds on quantum searching. arXiv:quant-ph/9605034 (1996)
6. Brassard, G., Hoyer, P., Mosca, M., Tapp, A.: Quantum amplitude amplification and estimation. Contemp. Math. **305**, 53–74 (2002)
7. Fowler, A.G., Mariantoni, M., Martinis, J.M., Cleland, A.N.: Surface codes: towards practical large-scale quantum computation. Phys. Rev. A. **86**(3), 032324 (2012)
8. Goemans, M.: 18.310 lecture notes, February 2015. http://math.mit.edu/goemans/18310S15/chernoff-notes.pdf
9. Grassl, M., Langenberg, B., Roetteler, M., Steinwandt, R.: Applying Grover's algorithm to AES: quantum resource estimates. In: Takagi, T. (ed.) PQCrypto 2016. LNCS, vol. 9606, pp. 29–43. Springer, Cham (2016). https://doi.org/10.1007/978-3-319-29360-8_3
10. Grover, L.K.: A fast quantum mechanical algorithm for database search. In: Proceedings of the 28th Annual ACM Symposium on Theory of Computing, pp. 212–219. ACM (1996)
11. Helme, S.: Top 1 million analysis - March 2020 (2020). https://scotthelme.co.uk/top-1-million-analysis-march-2020/
12. Huang, J.L., Lai, X.J.: What is the effective key length for a block cipher: an attack on every practical block cipher. Sci. China Inf. Sci. **57**(7), 1–11 (2014). https://doi.org/10.1007/s11432-014-5096-6
13. Jaques, S., Naehrig, M., Roetteler, M., Virdia, F.: Implementing Grover oracles for quantum key search on AES and LowMC. In: Canteaut, A., Ishai, Y. (eds.) EUROCRYPT 2020. LNCS, vol. 12106, pp. 280–310. Springer, Cham (2020). https://doi.org/10.1007/978-3-030-45724-2_10
14. Jaques, S., Schanck, J.M.: Quantum cryptanalysis in the RAM model: claw-finding attacks on SIKE. In: Boldyreva, A., Micciancio, D. (eds.) CRYPTO 2019. LNCS, vol. 11692, pp. 32–61. Springer, Cham (2019). https://doi.org/10.1007/978-3-030-26948-7_2
15. Katz, J., Lindell, Y.: Introduction to Modern Cryptography. CRC Press, Cambridge (2014)
16. Kim, P., Han, D., Jeong, K.C.: Time-space complexity of quantum search algorithms in symmetric cryptanalysis: applying to AES and SHA-2. Quantum Inf. Process. **17**(12), 339 (2018)
17. Kimmel, S., Yen-Yu Lin, C., Han-Hsuan, L.: Oracles with costs. In: 10th Conference on the Theory of Quantum Computation, Communication and Cryptography. TQC 2015, Brussels, Belgium, vol. 44 (2015)

18. Langenberg, B., Pham, H., Steinwandt, R.: Reducing the cost of implementing AES as a quantum circuit. Cryptology ePrint Archive, Report 2019/854 (2019). https://eprint.iacr.org/2019/854
19. Maslov, D.: Advantages of using relative-phase Toffoli gates with an application to multiple control Toffoli optimization. Phys. Rev. A **93**(2), 022311 (2016)
20. Maximov, A.: AES mixcolumn with 92 XOR gates. IACR Cryptol. ePrint Arch. **2019**, 833 (2019)
21. Menezes, A.J., Katz, J., van Oorschot, P.C., Vanstone, S.A.: Handbook of applied cryptography (1996)
22. Nielsen, M.A., Chuang, I.L.: Quantum Computation and Quantum Information. Cambridge University Press, Cambridge (2010)
23. NIST: 197: Advanced encryption standard (AES). Federal Information Processing Standards Publication, vol. 197, no. 441, p. 0311 (2001)
24. NIST: NIST project for Post-Quantum Cryptography Standardization (2016). https://csrc.nist.gov/Projects/Post-Quantum-Cryptography. Accessed 07 Oct 2018
25. NIST: Submission requirements and evaluation criteria for the post-quantum cryptography standardization process (2016)
26. Schwabe, P., Westerbaan, B.: Solving binary $\mathcal{MQ}$ with Grover's algorithm. In: Carlet, C., Hasan, M.A., Saraswat, V. (eds.) SPACE 2016. LNCS, vol. 10076, pp. 303–322. Springer, Cham (2016). https://doi.org/10.1007/978-3-319-49445-6_17

Post-Quantum Constructions

Not Enough LESS: An Improved Algorithm for Solving Code Equivalence Problems over $\mathbb{F}_q$

Ward Beullens[(✉)]

imec-COSIC, KU Leuven, Leuven, Belgium
ward.beullens@esat.kuleuven.be

Abstract. Recently, a new code based signature scheme, called LESS, was proposed with three concrete instantiations, each aiming to provide 128 bits of classical security [3]. Two instantiations (LESS-I and LESS-II) are based on the conjectured hardness of the linear code equivalence problem, while a third instantiation, LESS-III, is based on the conjectured hardness of the permutation code equivalence problem for weakly self-dual codes. We give an improved algorithm for solving both these problems over sufficiently large finite fields. Our implementation breaks LESS-I and LESS-III in approximately 25 s and 2 s respectively on an Intel i5-8400H CPU. Since the field size for LESS-II is relatively small ($\mathbb{F}_7$) our algorithm does not improve on existing methods. Nonetheless, we estimate that LESS-II can be broken with approximately 2^{44} row operations.

Keywords: Permutation code equivalence problem · Linear code equivalence problem · Code-based cryptography · Post-quantum cryptography

1 Introduction

Two q-ary linear codes $\mathcal{C}_1$ and $\mathcal{C}_2$ of length n and dimension k are called permutation equivalent if there exists a permutation $\pi \in S_n$ such that $\pi(\mathcal{C}_1) = \mathcal{C}_2$. Similarly, if there exists a monomial permutation $\mu \in M_n = (\mathbb{F}_q^\times)^n \rtimes S_n$ such that $\mu(\mathcal{C}_1) = \mathcal{C}_2$ the codes are said to be linearly equivalent (a monomial permutation acts on vectors in $\mathbb{F}_q^n$ by permuting the entries and also multiplying each entry with a unit of $\mathbb{F}_q$). The problem of finding $\pi \in S_n$ (or $\mu \in M_n$) given equivalent $\mathcal{C}_1$ and $\mathcal{C}_2$ is called the permutation equivalence problem (or linear equivalence problem respectively)[1].

---

[1] There also exists a more general notion of equivalence called semi-linear equivalence. Our methods generalize to semi-linear equivalences, but since this is not relevant for the security of LESS, we do not elaborate on this.

This work was supported by CyberSecurity Research Flanders with reference number VR20192203 and the Research Council KU Leuven grants C14/18/067 and STG/17.019. Ward Beullens is funded by FWO SB fellowship 1S95620N.

O. Dunkelman et al. (Eds.): SAC 2020, LNCS 12804, pp. 387–403, 2021.
https://doi.org/10.1007/978-3-030-81652-0_15

Definition 1 (Permutation Code Equivalence Problem). *Given generator matrices of two permutation equivalent codes $\mathcal{C}_1$ and $\mathcal{C}_2$, find a permutation $\pi \in S_n$ such that $\mathcal{C}_2 = \pi(\mathcal{C}_1)$.*

Definition 2 (Linear Code Equivalence Problem). *Given generator matrices of two linearly equivalent codes $\mathcal{C}_1$ and $\mathcal{C}_2$, find a monomial permutation $\mu \in M_n$ such that $\mathcal{C}_2 = \mu(\mathcal{C}_1)$.*

The hardness of the permutation equivalence problem is relevant for the security of the McEliece and Girault post-quantum cryptosystems [7,10]. More recently, Biasse, Micheli, Persichetti, and Santini proposed a new code-based signature scheme whose security only relies on the hardness of the linear code equivalence problem or permutation code equivalence problem. The public key consists of generator matrices for two equivalent codes $\mathcal{C}_1$ and $\mathcal{C}_2$, and a signature is a zero-knowledge proof of knowledge of an equivalence $\mu \in M_n$ (or $\pi \in S_n$) such that $\mu(\mathcal{C}_1) = \mathcal{C}_2$ (or $\pi(\mathcal{C}_1) = \mathcal{C}_2$ respectively). In the case of permutation equivalence, the codes $\mathcal{C}_1$ and $\mathcal{C}_2$ are chosen to be weakly self-dual, because otherwise π can be recovered in polynomial time [12]. Table 1 shows the proposed parameter sets for LESS, aiming for 128 bits of security.

Table 1. Proposed parameter sets for the LESS signature scheme.

Parameter set	n	k	p	Equivalence
LESS-I	54	27	53	Linear
LESS-II	106	45	7	Linear
LESS-III	60	25	31	Permutation

1.1 Previous Work

We will briefly go over some of the algorithms that have been proposed for the permutation and linear code equivalence problems below. The state of the art for the permutation code equivalence problem is that random instances can be solved in polynomial time with the Support Splitting Algorithm (SSA), but that instances with codes that have large hulls require a runtime that is exponential in the dimension of the hull. Weakly self-dual codes (these are codes $\mathcal{C}$ such that $\mathcal{C} \subset \mathcal{C}^{\perp}$) have hulls of maximal dimension $\dim(\mathcal{H}(\mathcal{C})) = \dim(\mathcal{C})$ and are believed to be the hardest instances of the permutation equivalence problem. The state of the art for the linear code equivalence problem is that instances over $\mathbb{F}_q$ with $q \leq 4$ can be solved in polynomial time with the SSA algorithm via a reduction to the permutation equivalence problem, but for $q > 4$ this reduction results in codes with a large hull, which means the SSA algorithm is not efficient. Hence, the linear code equivalence problem is conjectured to be hard on average for $q > 4$ [13].

Leon's Algorithm. Leon's algorithm [9] for finding linear and permutation equivalences relies on the observation that applying a permutation or a monomial permutation does not change the hamming weight of a codeword. Therefore, if we compute the sets X_1 and X_2 of all the minimal-weight codewords of C_1 and C_2 respectively, then it must be that $X_2 = \pi(X_1)$ or $X_2 = \mu(X_1)$ in the case of permutation equivalence or linear equivalence respectively. Leon gives an algorithm to compute a $\mu \in M_n$ that satisfies $X_2 = \mu(X_1)$ with a time complexity that is polynomial in $|X_1|$. Usually, the sets X_1 and X_2 have "enough structure", such that if μ satisfies $X_2 = \mu(X_1)$, then also $C_2 = \mu(C_1)$ with non-negligible probability. If this is not the case, then one can also consider larger sets X_1' and X_2' that contain all the codewords in C_1 and C_2 respectively whose weight is one more than the minimal weight. Since the sets X_1 and X_2 are usually small, the complexity of the algorithm is dominated by the complexity of computing X_1 and X_2.

Feulner gives an algorithm that computes a canonical representative of an equivalence class of codes. The complexity of this algorithm is close to that of Leon's algorithm [6].

Support Splitting Algorithm. The Support Splitting Slgorithm (SSA) of Sendrier [12] defines the concept of a signature. A signature is a property of a position in a code that is invariant for permutations. More precicely, it is a function S that takes a code C and a position $i \in \{1, \cdots, n\}$ as input and outputs an element of an output space P, such that for any permutation $\pi \in S_n$ we have

$$S(C, i) = S(\pi(C), \pi(i)).$$

We say that a signature is totally discriminant for C if $i \neq j$ implies that $S(C, i) \neq S(C, j)$. If a signature S is efficiently computable and totally discriminant for a code C_1, then one can easily solve the permutation equivalence problem by computing $S(C_1, i)$ and $S(C_2, i)$ for all $i \in \{1, \cdots, n\}$ and comparing the outputs. Even if the signature is not totally discriminant, a sufficiently discriminant signature can still be used to solve the permutation equivalence Problem by iteratively refining the signature.

The SSA uses the concept of the hull of a code to construct an efficiently computable signature. The hull of a code C is the intersection of the code with its dual: $\mathcal{H}(C) = C \cap C^\perp$. This concept is very useful in the context of the permutation equivalence problem because taking the hull commutes with applying a permutation[2]

$$\mathcal{H}(\pi(C)) = \pi(C) \cap \pi(C)^\perp = \pi(C \cap C^\perp) = \pi(\mathcal{H}(C)).$$

---

[2] This is not the case for monomial permutations: $\mathcal{H}(\mu(C))$ is not necessarily equal to $\mu(\mathcal{H}(C))$ for $\mu \in M_n$. This is why the SSA can not be directly applied to find linear equivalences.

The SSA defines a signature as $\mathcal{S}(C, i) := W(\mathcal{H}(C_i))$, where C_i is the code C punctured at position i, and $W(\mathcal{C})$ denotes the weight enumerator polynomial of the code $\mathcal{C}$. While this signature is typically not fully discriminant, it is still discriminant enough to efficiently solve the permutation equivalence Problem for random matrices. However, a limitation of the SSA algorithm is that computing the enumerator of the hull is not efficient when the hull of $\mathcal{C}$ is large. For random codes this is not a problem because typically the hull is small.

Algebraic Approach. The code equivalence problems can be solved algebraically, by expressing the condition $\pi(\mathcal{C}_1) = \mathcal{C}_2$ or $\mu(\mathcal{C}_1) = \mathcal{C}_2$ as a system of polynomial equations, and trying to solve this system with Gröbner basis methods [11]. Similar to the SSA algorithm, this solves the permutation code equivalence problem for random instances in polynomial time, but the complexity is exponential in the dimension of the hull. The approach also works for the linear code equivalence problem, but it is only efficient for $q \leq 4$.

1.2 Our Contributions

In this paper, we propose an improvement on Leon's algorithm for code equivalence that works best over sufficiently large finite fields. If $\mathbf{x} \in \mathcal{C}_1$ and $\mathbf{y} = \pi(\mathbf{x}) \in \mathcal{C}_2$, then the multiset of entries of $\mathbf{x}$ matches the multiset of entries of $\mathbf{y}$. Our algorithm is based on the observation that if the size of the finite field is large enough then the implication also holds in the other direction with large probability: If $\mathbf{x} \in \mathcal{C}_1$ and $\mathbf{y} \in \mathcal{C}_2$ are low-weight codewords with the same multiset of entries, then with large probability $\pi(\mathbf{x}) = \mathbf{y}$. Our algorithm does a collision search to find a small number of such pairs $(\mathbf{x}, \mathbf{y} = \pi(\mathbf{x}))$, from which one can easily recover π. We also give a generalization of this idea that works for the linear equivalence problem.

We implemented our algorithm and used it to break the LESS signature scheme. In the LESS-I and LESS-III parameter sets the finite field is large enough for our algorithm to improve on Leons's algorithm. We show that we can recover a LESS-I or LESS-III secret key in only 25 s or 2 s respectively. We estimate that recovering the secret key is also possible in practice with Leon's algorithm, but it would be significantly more costly. LESS-II works over $\mathbb{F}_7$, which is too small for our algorithm to improve on Leon's algorithm: We estimate that our algorithm requires approximately $2^{50.4}$ row operations, while Leon's algorithm would take only $2^{43.9}$ row operations.

2 Preliminaries

2.1 Notation

For a q-ary linear code $\mathcal{C}$ of length n and dimension k we say a matrix $\mathbf{G} \in \mathbb{F}_q^{k \times n}$ is a generator matrix for $\mathcal{C}$ if $\mathcal{C} = \langle \mathbf{G} \rangle$, where $\langle \mathbf{G} \rangle$ denotes the span of the rows of $\mathbf{G}$. Similarly, we say that a matrix $\mathbf{H} \in \mathbb{F}_q^{(n-k) \times n}$ is a parity check matrix for

$\mathcal{C}$ if $\mathcal{C}^{\perp} = \langle H \rangle$, where $\mathcal{C}^{\perp} = \{ \mathbf{x} \in \mathbb{F}_q^n \mid \mathbf{x} \cdot \mathbf{y} = 0 \, \forall \mathbf{y} \in \mathcal{C} \}$ is the dual code of $\mathcal{C}$. For a vector $\mathbf{x} \in \mathbb{F}_q^n$ we denote by $\mathrm{Supp}(\mathbf{x})$ the set of indices of the nonzero entries in $\mathbf{x}$, i.e. $\mathrm{Supp}(\mathbf{x}) = \{ i \mid x_i \neq 0 \}$. We define the support $\mathrm{Supp}(\mathcal{C})$ of a code $\mathcal{C}$ to be the union of the supports of the codewords in $\mathcal{C}$. We let $wt(\mathbf{x}) = |\mathrm{Supp}(\mathbf{x})|$ be the *Hamming weight* of $\mathbf{x}$. We denote by $B_n(w)$ the *Hamming ball* with radius w, i.e. the set of vectors in $\mathbf{x} \in \mathbb{F}_q^n$ with $wt(x) \leq w$. For a permutation $\pi \in S_n$ and a vector $\mathbf{x}$ of length n, we write $\pi(\mathbf{x})$ for the vector obtained by permuting the entries of $\mathbf{x}$ with the permutation π, that is we have $(\pi(\mathbf{x}))_i = \mathbf{x}_{\pi(i)}$ for all $i \in \{1, \cdots, n\}$. For a monomial permutation $\mu = (\nu, \pi) \in M_n = (\mathbb{F}_q^{\times})^n \rtimes S_n$ and a vector $\mathbf{x} \in \mathbb{F}_q^n$, we write $\mu(\mathbf{x})$ to denote the vector obtained by applying μ to the entries of $\mathbf{x}$. Concretely, we have $(\mu(x))_i = \nu_i \cdot \mathbf{x}_{\pi(i)}$ for all $i \in \{1, \cdots, n\}$. For a code $\mathcal{C}$ and $\pi \in S_n$ (or $\mu \in M_n$), we denote by $\pi(\mathcal{C})$ (or $\mu(\mathcal{C})$) the code that consist of permutations (or monomial permutations respectively) of codewords in $\mathcal{C}$.

2.2   Information Set Decoding

The algorithms in this paper will make use of information set decoding to find sparse vectors in q-ary linear codes. In particular, we will use the Lee-Brickell algorithm with parameter $p = 2$. To find low-weight codewords in a code $\mathcal{C} = \langle M \rangle$ the algorithm repeatedly computes the echelon form of M with respect to a random choice of k pivot columns. Then, the algorithm inspects all the linear combinations of $p = 2$ rows of the matrix. Given the echelon form of the matrix, we are guaranteed that all these linear combinations have weight at most $n - k + 2$, but if we are lucky enough we will find codewords that are even more sparse. We repeat this until a sufficiently sparse codeword is found.

Complexity of the Algorithm. The complexity of the algorithm depends on the length n and the dimension k of the code, target weight w, and whether we want to find a single codeword, all the codewords, or a large number N of codewords. First, suppose there is a distinguished codeword $\mathbf{x} \in \mathcal{C}$ with weight w that we want to find. For a random choice of pivot columns, the Lee-Brickell algorithm will output $\mathbf{x}$ if the support of $\mathbf{x}$ intersects the set of pivot columns (also known as the information set) in exactly 2 positions. The probability that this happens is

$$P_{\infty}(n, k, w) := \frac{\binom{n-k}{w-2} \binom{k}{2}}{\binom{n}{w}}.$$

Therefore, since the cost of each iteration is k^2 row operations for the Gaussian elimination and $\binom{k}{2} q$ row operations to iterate over all the linear combinations of 2 rows (up to multiplication by a constant), the algorithm will find $\mathbf{x}$ after approximately

$$C_{\infty}(n, k, w) = \left(k^2 + \binom{k}{2} q \right) P(n, k, w)^{-1} = O\left(\frac{q\binom{n}{w}}{\binom{n-k}{w-2}} \right)$$

row operations. Heuristically, for random codes we expect the support of the different codewords to behave as if they are "independent", so if there exist $(q-1)N$ codewords of weight w (i.e. N different codewords up to multiplication by a scalar), then we expect the probability that one iteration of the Lee-Brickell algorithm succeeds to be

$$P_1(n, k, w) = 1 - (1 - P_\infty(n, k, w))^N.$$

Thus, if N is small enough, we have $P_1(n, k, w) \approx NP_\infty(n, k, w)$, and the complexity of finding is a single weight-w codeword is $C_1(n, k, w) \approx C_\infty(n, k, w)/N$.

Finally, if the goal is to find L out of the N distinct weight-w codewords (up to multiplication by a scalar), the cost of finding the first codeword is $C_1 = C_\infty(n, k, w)/N$, the cost of finding the second codeword is $C_\infty(n, k, w)/(N-1)$, the cost of finding the third codeword is $C_\infty(n, k, w)/(N-2)$ and so on. Summing up these costs, we get that the cost of finding L distinct codewords is

$$C_L(n, k, w) \approx C_\infty(n, k, w) \cdot \left(\sum_{i=0}^{L-1} \frac{1}{N-i} \right).$$

Therefore, if $L << N$, we can estimate $C_L \approx C_\infty L/N$, and if the goal is to find all the codewords, we get $C_N \approx C_\infty \ln(N)$, where $\ln$ denotes the natural logarithm, because $\sum_{i=1}^{N} 1/i \approx \ln(N)$.

3   New Algorithm for Permutation Equivalences over $\mathbb{F}_q$

In this section, we introduce an algorithm for the permutation equivalence Problem over sufficiently large fields $\mathbb{F}_q$ (which is the case of the LESS-III parameter set). The complexity of the algorithm is independent of the size of the hull of the equivalent codes. Therefore, our algorithm can be used to find equivalences when the hull is so large that using the SSA algorithm becomes infeasible. The complexity of the algorithm is better than Leon's algorithm when the size of the finite field is sufficiently large.

Main Idea. Leon's algorithm computes the sets $X_1 = C_1 \cap B_n(w_{min})$ and $X_2 = C_2 \cap B_n(w_{min})$, where w_{min} is the minimal weight of codewords in C_1 and solves the Code equivalence problem by looking for $\pi \in S_n$ such that $\pi(X_1) = X_2$. The bottleneck of Leon's algorithm is computing $X_1 = C_1 \cap B_n(w_{min})$ and $X_2 = C_2 \cap B_n(w_{min})$, so if we want to improve the complexity of the attack we need to avoid computing all of X_1 and X_2. An easy observation is that permuting a codeword $\mathbf{x}$ does not only preserve its Hamming weight, but also the multiset of entries of $\mathbf{x}$. Therefore, if there is an element $\mathbf{x} \in X_1$ with a unique multiset, then one can immediately see to which vector $\mathbf{y} = \pi(\mathbf{x}) \in X_2$ it gets mapped. For example, if X_1 contains the vector

$$\mathbf{x} = (0\,4\,0\,0\,7\,4\,0\,0\,0\,14),$$

and if X_2 contains the vector

$$\mathbf{y} = (0\ 4\ 7\ 0\ 0\ 14\ 0\ 4\ 0\ 0)\,,$$

then assuming there are no other vectors in X_1 and X_2 with the same multiset of entries, we know that $\pi(\mathbf{x}) = \mathbf{y}$. In particular we know that $\pi(5) = 3$, $\pi(10) = 6$ and $\pi(2), \pi(6) \in \{2,8\}$.

Instead of computing all of X_1 and X_2, our algorithm will search for a small number of such pairs $(\mathbf{x}, \mathbf{y} = \pi(\mathbf{x}))$, which will give enough information to determine π. This approach will not work if $\mathbb{F}_q$ is too small, because then X_1 will contain a lot of vectors with the same multiset of entries. (E.g. in the case $q = 2$, all the vectors with the same weight have the same multiset of entries.)

If we compute only $\Theta(\sqrt{|X_1|\log n})$ elements of X_1 and X_2, then we expect to find $\Theta(\log n)$ pairs $(\mathbf{x}, \mathbf{y} = \pi(\mathbf{x}))$, which suffices to recover π. This speeds up the procedure by a factor $\Theta(\sqrt{|X_1|/\log n})$, which is only a small factor. We can improve this further by considering larger sets $X_1' = \mathcal{C}_1 \cap B_n(w)$ and $X_2' = \mathcal{C}_2 \cap B_n(w)$ for a weight w that is not minimal. In the most favorable case where the multisets of the vectors in X_i' are still unique for $w = n - k + 1$, then we can sample from X_1' and X_2' in polynomial time using Gaussian elimination, and we get an algorithm that runs in time $\tilde{O}\left(\sqrt{\binom{n}{k-1}}\right)$, where $\tilde{O}$ is the usual big-O notation but ignoring polynomial factors.

Description of the Algorithm. The algorithm works as follows:

1. Let w be maximal subject to $\frac{n!}{(n-w)!}q^{-n+k} < \frac{1}{4\log n}$ and $w \le n - k + 1$.
2. Repeatedly use information set decoding to generate a list L that contains $\sqrt{|B_n(w)| \cdot q^{-n+k-1} \cdot 2\log n}$ pairs of the form $(\mathbf{x}, \mathsf{lex}(\mathbf{x}))$, where $\mathbf{x} \in \mathcal{C}_1 \cap B_n(w)$ and where $\mathsf{lex}(\mathbf{x})$ is the lexicographically first element of the set $\{\pi(\alpha\mathbf{x})|\pi \in S_n, \alpha \in \mathbb{F}_q^\times\}$.
3. Initialize an empty list P and repeatedly use information set decoding to generate $\mathbf{y} \in \mathcal{C}_2 \cap B_n(w)$. If there is a pair $(\mathbf{x}, \mathsf{lex}(\mathbf{x}))$ in L such that $\mathsf{lex}(\mathbf{x}) = \mathsf{lex}(\mathbf{y})$, then append $(\mathbf{x}, \mathbf{y})$ to P. Continue until P has $2\log(n)$ elements.
4. Use a backtracking algorithm to iterate over all permutations π that satisfy $\langle\pi(\mathbf{x})\rangle = \langle\mathbf{y}\rangle$ for all $(\mathbf{x}, \mathbf{y}) \in P$ until a permutation is found that satisfies $\pi(\mathcal{C}_1) = \mathcal{C}_2$.

Heuristic Analysis of the Algorithm. Heuristically, we expect that for $\mathbf{x} \in \mathcal{C}_1 \cap B_n(w)$ the probability that there exists $\mathbf{x}' \in \mathcal{C}_1 \cap B_n(w)$ such that $\langle\mathbf{x}'\rangle \ne \langle\mathbf{x}\rangle$ and $\mathsf{lex}(\mathbf{x}) = \mathsf{lex}(\mathbf{x}')$ to be bounded by $\frac{n!}{(n-w)!}q^{-n+k}$, because there are at most $\frac{n!}{(n-w)!}$ values of $\mathbf{x}'$ (up to multiplication by a unit) for which $\mathsf{lex}(\mathbf{x}') = \mathsf{lex}(\mathbf{x})$, (namely all the permutations $\mathbf{x}$), and each of these vectors is expected to be in $\mathcal{C}_1$ with probability $q^{-(n-k)}$. In step 1 of the algorithm we choose w such that the probability estimate that $\mathbf{x}$ is part of such a collision in lex is at most $1/(4\log n)$.

We have $\mathsf{lex}(\mathcal{C}_1 \cap B_n(w)) = \mathsf{lex}(\mathcal{C}_2 \cap B_n(w))$ and heuristically the size of this set is close to $|\mathcal{C}_1 \cap B_n(w)|/(q-1) \approx |B_n(w)|/q^{n-k+1}$ since lex is almost $(q-1)$-to-one. Therefore, it takes roughly $|B_n(w)|2\log n/q^{n-k+1}|L|$ iterations of step 3 until $2\log n$ pairs $(\mathbf{x}, \mathbf{y})$ with $\mathsf{lex}(\mathbf{x}) = \mathsf{lex}(y)$ are found. We chose the list size $|L| = \sqrt{|B_n(w)|2\log n/q^{n-k+1}}$ so that the work in step 2 and step 3 is balanced.

The last part of the algorithm assumes that for each pair $(\mathbf{x}, \mathbf{y})$ found in step 3 we have $\langle \pi(\mathbf{x}) \rangle = \langle \mathbf{y} \rangle$. This can only fail with probability bounded by $1/4\log n$, because this implies that $\pi(\mathbf{x})$ and $\mathbf{y} \in \mathcal{C}_2 \cap B_n(w)$ form a collision for lex. Summing over all the $2\log n$ pairs we get that the probability that $\langle \pi(\mathbf{x}) \rangle = \langle \mathbf{y} \rangle$ holds for all the pairs in P is at least $1/2$. If this is the case then there are typically very few permutations σ (most of the time only one) that satisfy $\langle \sigma(\mathbf{x}) \rangle = \langle \mathbf{y} \rangle$ and the true code equivalence π must be one of them.

The complexity of the attack is dominated by the cost of the ISD algorithm to find $|L|$ weight-w codewords in $\mathcal{C}_1$ and $\mathcal{C}_2$ in step 2 and 3, which is

$$2 \cdot C_{|L|}(n, k, w)$$

In our implementation we have used the Lee-Brickell algrithm [8] with $p = 2$ to instantiate the ISD oracle[3]. In this case, the number of row-operations used by the ISD algorithm can be approximated (see Sect. 2.2) as

$$2 \cdot C_{|L|}(n, k, w) \approx C_\infty \frac{|L|}{|\mathcal{C}_1 \cap B_n(w)|/(q-1)} = O\left(\frac{\binom{n}{w}\sqrt{\log n}}{\binom{n-k}{w-2} \cdot \sqrt{|B_n(w)|q^{-n+k}}} \right).$$

The Algorithm in Practice. An implementation of our algorithm in C, as well as a python script to estimate the complexity of our attack is made publicly available at

www.github.com/WardBeullens/LESS_Attack.

We used this implementation to break the LESS-III parameter set. The public key of a LESS-III signature consist of two permutation equivalent codes $\mathcal{C}_1$ and $\mathcal{C}_2$ of length $n = 60$ and dimension $k = 25$ over $\mathbb{F}_{31}$. The codes are chosen to be weakly self-dual. From experiments, we see that the weakly self-dual property does not seem to affect the complexity or the success rate of our attack.

For these parameters, the maximal value of w that satisfies $\frac{n!}{(n-w)!}q^{-n+k} < \frac{1}{4\log n}$ is $w = 30$, so we use the Lee-Brickell algorithm to find codewords in $\mathcal{C}_1$ and $\mathcal{C}_2$ with Hamming weight at most 30. The list size is $\sqrt{|B_n(w)| \cdot q^{-n+k-1} \cdot 2\log n}$,

---

[3] One can also use more advanced ISD algorithms such as Stern's algorithm [14], but since we will be working with relatively large finite fields we found that this does not offer a big speedup. To simplify the analysis and the implementation we have chosen for the Lee-Brickell algorithm.

which is close to 25000. With these parameter choices, the algorithm runs in about 2 s on a laptop with an Intel i5-8400H CPU at 2.50 GHz. The rate at which pairs are found closely matched the heuristic analysis of the previous section: The analysis suggests that we should have to do approximately $2^{14.7}$ Gaussian eliminations, while the average number of Gaussian eliminations measured in our experiments is $2^{14.6}$. However, we find that the heuristic lower bound of $1/2$ for the success probability is not tight: The algorithm terminates successfully in all of the executions. This is because in our heuristic analysis we used $n!/(n-w)!$ as an upper bound for the number of permutations of a vector $\mathbf{x}$ of weight w. This upper bound is only achieved if all the entries of $\mathbf{x}$ are distinct. For a random vector $\mathbf{x}$ the number of permutations is much smaller, which explains why the observed probability of a bad collision is much lower than our heuristic upper bound.

Remark 1. If we use the algorithm for longer codes the list L will quickly be so large that it would be very costly to store the entire list in memory. To avoid this we can define 2 functions F_1 and F_2 that take a random seed as input, run an ISD algorithm to find a weight w codeword $\mathbf{x}$ in $\mathcal{C}_1$ or $\mathcal{C}_2$ respectively and output $\mathsf{lex}(\mathbf{x})$. Then we can use a memoryless claw-finding algorithm such as the Van Oorschot-Wiener algorithm [16] to find inputs a, b such that $F_1(a) = F_2(b)$. This makes the memory complexity of the algorithm polynomial, at essentially no cost in time complexity. Since memory is not an issue for attacking the LESS parameters we did not implement this approach.

Comparison with Leon's Algorithm and New Parameters for LESS. We expect recovering a LESS-III secret key with Leon's algorithm would require $2^{24.5}$ iterations of the Lee-Brickell algorithm, significantly more than the $2^{14.6}$ iterations that our algorithm requires. Figure 1 shows how the complexity of our attack and Leon's attack scales with increasing code length n. The left graph shows the situation where the field size q and the dimension k increases linearly with the code length, while the graph on the right shows the case where $q = 31$ is fixed. In both cases, our algorithm outperforms Leon's algorithm, but since our algorithm can exploit the large field size, the gap is larger in the first case. The sawtooth-like behavior of the complexity of Leon's algorithm is related to the number of vectors of minimal weight, which oscillates up and down. We see that in order to achieve 128 bits of security (i.e. an attack needs 2^{128} row operations) we can use a q-ary code of length $n = 280$, dimension $k = 117$ and $q = 149$. Alternatively, if we keep $q = 31$ fixed, we could use a code of length $n = 305$ and dimension $k = 127$. This would result in an average signature size of 18.8 KB or 21.1 KB respectively. This is almost a factor 5 larger than the current signature size of 3.8 KB[4]. The public key size would increase from 0.53 KB[5] to 16.8 KB or 13.8 KB for the $q = 149$ or $q = 31$ parameter set respectively, an increase of more than a factor 25. The fact that our algorithm performs better in comparison to Leon's algorithm for larger finite fields is illustrated in Fig. 2, where we plot the complexity of both algorithms for $n = 250$, $k = 104$ and for various field sizes.

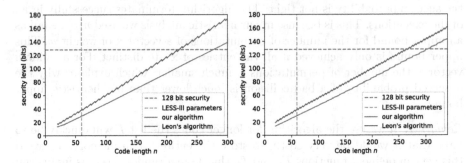

Fig. 1. Complexity of Leon's algorithm and our algorithm for finding permutation equivalences in function of the code Length. In the left graph the field size scales linearly with the code length, in the right graph the field size $q = 31$ is fixed. In both cases the rate of the code is fixed at $k/n = 5/12$.

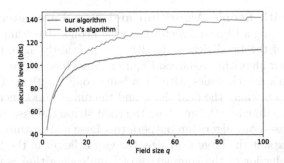

Fig. 2. Complexity of Leon's algorithm and our algorithm for finding permutation equivalences in function of the finite field size for random linear codes of length $n = 250$ and dimension $k = 104$.

---

[4] The LESS paper claims 7.8 KB. but 4 KB of the signature consists of commitments that can be recomputed by the verifier, so this does not need to be included in the signature size.

[5] The LESS paper claims 0.9 KB public keys, but the generator matrix can be put in normal form, which reduces the size from $k \times n$ field elements to $k \times (n - k)$ field elements.

4   New Algorithm for Linear Equivalences over $\mathbb{F}_q$

In this section, we generalize the algorithm from the previous section to the linear equivalence Problem. The main obstacle we need to overcome is that it does not seem possible given sparse vectors $\mathbf{x} \in \mathcal{C}_1$ and $\mathbf{y} \in \mathcal{C}_2$ to verify if $\mu(\mathbf{x}) = \mathbf{y}$, where $\mu \in M_n$ is the monomial transformation such that $\mu(\mathcal{C}_1) = \mathcal{C}_2$. In the permutation equivalence setting, we could guess that if the multiset of entries of $\mathbf{x}$ equals the multiset of entries of $\mathbf{y}$ then $\pi(\mathbf{x}) = \mathbf{y}$. If the size of the finite field was large enough, then this was correct with large probability. This strategy does not work in the linear equivalence setting, because monomial permutations do not preserve the multiset of entries. In fact, monomial transformations do not preserve anything beyond the hamming weight of a vector, because for any two codewords $\mathbf{x}$ and $\mathbf{y}$ with the same weight there exists $\mu \in M_n$ such that $\mu(\mathbf{x}) = \mathbf{y}$.

Main Idea. To overcome this problem, be will replace sparse vectors by 2-dimensional subspaces with small support. Let

$$X_1(w) = \{V \subset \mathcal{C}_1 \mid \dim(V) = 2 \text{ and } |\text{Supp}(V)| \leq w\}$$

be the set of 2 dimensional linear subspaces of $\mathcal{C}_1$ with support of size at most w and similarly we let $X_2(w)$ be the set of 2-spaces in $\mathcal{C}_2$ with support of size w. If $\mu \in M_n$ is a monomial permutation such that $\mu(\mathcal{C}_1) = \mathcal{C}_2$, then for all $V \in X_1(w)$ we have $\mu(V) \in X_2$. Analogously with the algorithm from the previous section, we will sample 2-spaces from $X_1(w)$ and from $X_2(w)$ in the hope of finding spaces $V \in X_1(w)$ and $U \in X_2(w)$ such that $\mu(V) = W$. Then, after finding $\Omega(\log(n))$ such pairs we expect to be able to recover the equivalence μ. To detect if $\mu(V) = W$ we define $\text{lex}(V)$ to be the lexicographically first basis of a 2-space in the M_n-orbit of V. Clearly, if $\mu(V) = W$, then the M_n-orbits of V and W will be the same and hence $\text{lex}(V) = \text{lex}(W)$. Moreover, since the dimension of V and W is only 2, it is feasible to compute $\text{lex}(V)$ and $\text{lex}(W)$ efficiently.

Computing lex(V). To compute $\text{lex}(V)$ we can simply consider all the bases $\mathbf{x}, \mathbf{y}$ that generate V (there are $(q^2 - 1)(q^2 - q)$ of them) and for each of them find the monomial transformation μ such that $\mu(\mathbf{x}), \mu(\mathbf{y})$ comes first lexicographically, and then take the permuted basis that comes first out of these $(q^2 - 1)(q^2 - q)$ options. Given a basis $\mathbf{x}, \mathbf{y}$, finding the lexicographically first value of $\mu(\mathbf{x}), \mu(\mathbf{y})$ is relatively straightforward: First make sure that $\mu(\mathbf{x})$ is minimal, and then use the remaining degrees of freedom to minimize $\mu(\mathbf{y})$. The minimal $\mu(\mathbf{x})$ consists of $n - wt(\mathbf{x})$ zeroes followed by $wt(\mathbf{x})$ ones, which is achieved by multiplying the non-zero entries of $\mathbf{x}$ (and the corresponding entries of $\mathbf{y}$) by their inverse and permuting $\mathbf{x}$ such that all the ones are in the back. The remaining degrees of freedom of μ can be used to make the first $n - wt(\mathbf{x})$ entries of $\mu(\mathbf{y})$ consist of a number of zeros followed by a number of ones and to sort the remaining entries of $\mu(y)$ in ascending order.

A basis $\mathbf{x}, \mathbf{y}$ for V can only lead to the lexicographicallt first $\mu(\mathbf{x}), \mu(\mathbf{y})$ if the hamming weight of $\mathbf{x}$ is minimal among all the vectors in V. Therefore, we only need to consider bases $\mathbf{x}, \mathbf{y}$ where the hamming weight of $\mathbf{x}$ is minimal. When the first basis vector is fixed, choosing the second basis vector and minimizing the basis, can be on average done with a constant number row operations, so the average cost of the algorithm is $q + 1 + O(N) = O(q)$ row operations, where the $q + 1$ operations stem from finding the minimal weigth vectors in V, and N is the number of such vectors.

Example 1. The following is an example what $\mathsf{lex}(V)$ could look like:

$$V = \left\langle \begin{pmatrix} 19 & 3 & 21 & 36 & 17 & 44 & 0 & 47 & 34 & 19 & 48 & 3 & 0 & 47 & 0 & 38 & 27 & 8 & 49 & 18 & 8 & 0 & 0 & 31 & 26 & 52 & 7 & 30 & 37 & 47 \\ 35 & 24 & 13 & 0 & 50 & 40 & 0 & 52 & 6 & 19 & 37 & 28 & 0 & 13 & 0 & 49 & 34 & 20 & 24 & 30 & 24 & 45 & 0 & 39 & 42 & 0 & 18 & 17 & 28 & 36 \end{pmatrix} \right\rangle$$

$$\mathsf{lex}(V) = \begin{pmatrix} 0 & 0 & 0 & 0 & 0 & 0 & 1 & 1 & 1 & 1 & 1 & 1 & 1 & 1 & 1 & 1 & 1 & 1 & 1 & 1 & 1 & 1 & 1 & 1 & 1 & 1 & 1 & 1 & 1 & 1 \\ 0 & 0 & 0 & 0 & 1 & 1 & 0 & 0 & 1 & 1 & 2 & 3 & 4 & 5 & 9 & 9 & 11 & 13 & 15 & 19 & 20 & 21 & 23 & 27 & 32 & 33 & 34 & 36 & 37 & 39 \end{pmatrix}$$

Description of the Algorithm.

The algorithm works as follows:

1. Let w be maximal subject to $\frac{n!}{(n-w)!} q^{w-1+2k-2n} < \frac{1}{4 \log n}$ and $w \le n - k + 2$.
2. Repeatedly use information set decoding to generate a lists L that contains $\sqrt{\binom{n}{w}} \cdot q^{2(-n+k+w-2)} \cdot 2 \log n$ pairs of the form $(V, \mathsf{lex}(V))$, where $V \in X_1(w)$.
3. Initialize an empty list P and repeatedly use information set decoding to generate $W \in X_2$. If there is a pair $(V, \mathsf{lex}(V))$ in L such that $\mathsf{lex}(V) = \mathsf{lex}(W)$, then append (V, W) to P. Continue until P has $2 \log(n)$ elements.
4. Use a backtracking algorithm to iterate over all monomial permutations μ that satisfy $\mu(V) = W$ for all $(V, W) \in P$ until a monomial permutation is found that satisfies $\mu(C_1) = C_2$.

Heuristic Analysis of the Algorithm.

The heuristic analysis of this algorithm is very similar to that of our permutation equivalence algorithm. This time the size of a M_2-orbit of a 2-space V with $|\mathsf{Supp}(V)| \le w$ is bounded by $\frac{n!}{(n-w)!}(q-1)^{w-1}$ and a random 2-space has probability of $\frac{(q^k-1)(q^k-q)}{(q^n-1)(q^n-q)} \approx q^{2(k-n)}$ of being a subspace of C_1. So as long as we pick w such that $\frac{n!}{(n-w)!} q^{w-1+2k-2n} < \frac{1}{4 \log n}$ we expect the probability that one of (V, W) the pairs that we found are such that $\mathsf{lex}(V) = \mathsf{lex}(W)$ but $\mu(V) \ne W$ is bounded by $1/2$. The size of $X_1(w)$ and $|X_2(w)|$ is expected to be at most $\binom{n}{w} \frac{(q^w-1)(q^w-q)}{(q^2-1)(q^2-q)} q^{-2(n-k)} \approx \binom{n}{w} q^{2(w-2-n+k)}$, because for each of the $\binom{n}{w}$ supports S of size w, there are $\frac{(q^w-1)(q^w-q)}{(q^2-1)(q^2-q)}$ 2-spaces whose support is included in S, and we expect one out $q^2(n-k)$ of them to lie in C_1. Therefore, if we set the list size to $\sqrt{\binom{n}{w}} \cdot q^{2(-n+k+w-2)} \cdot 2 \log n$ then we expect the third step of the algorithm to terminate after roughly $|L|$ iterations. (We are counting the subspaces V with

$|\mathrm{Supp}(V)| < w$ multiple times, so $X_1(w)$ is slightly smaller than our estimate. This is not a problem, because it means that the third step will terminate slightly sooner than our analysis suggests.)

The complexity of the algorithm consists of the ISD effort to sample $|L|$ elements from $X_1(w)$ and $X_2(w)$ respectively, and the costs of computing lex. We have to compute lex an expected number of $2|L|$ times; once for each of the 2-spaces in the list L and once for each 2-space found in step 3. Since the number of row operations per lex is $O(q)$, the total cost of computing lex is $O(q|L|)$. To sample the 2-spaces we use asn adaptation of the Lee-Brickell algorithm: We repeatedly put a generator matrix of C_1 in echelon form with respect to a random choice of pivot columns, and then we look at the span of any 2 out of k rows of the new matrix. Given the echelon form of the matrix, the support of these 2-spaces has size at most $n - k + 2$, and if we are lucky the size of the support will be smaller than or equal to w. The complexity of this algorithm is very similar to that of the standard Lee-Brickell algorithm for finding codewords (see Sect. 2.2).

For a 2-space $V \in X_1(w)$, the Lee-Brickell algorithm will find V if the random choice of pivots intersects $\mathrm{Supp}(V)$ in 2 positions, which happens with probability $P_\infty(n, k, w) = \binom{n-k}{w-2}\binom{k}{2}/\binom{n}{w}$. The cost per iteration is $O(k^2 + \binom{k}{2}) = O(k^2)$ row operations for the Gaussian elimination and for enumerating the 2-spaces, so the expected number of row operations until we find $|L|$ elements in $X_1(w)$ and $X_2(w)$ is

$$ O\left(\frac{k^2 \binom{n}{w}|L|}{\binom{n-k}{w-2}\binom{k}{2}|X_1(w)|} \right) \approx O\left(\frac{\sqrt{\binom{n}{w}} \cdot \log n}{\binom{n-k}{w-2}} q^{-w+2+n-k} \right). $$

4.1   The Algorithm in Practice

We have implemented the algorithm and applied it to the LESS-I parameter set. The public key of a LESS-I signature consist of two linearly equivalent codes C_1 and C_2 chosen uniformly at random of length $n = 54$ and dimension $k = 27$ over $\mathbb{F}_{53}$. The largest value of w satisfying $\frac{n!}{(n-w)!} q^{w-1+2k-2n} < \frac{1}{4 \log n}$ is $w = 28$, so we use the Lee-Brickell algorithm to generate $\sqrt{\binom{n}{w}} \cdot q^{2(-n+k+w-2)} \cdot 2 \log n$ subspaces of C_1 and C_2 with support of size at most 28, which comes down to approximately 2800000 subspaces of each code. From our implementation we see that this takes on average about $2^{20.6}$ Gaussian eliminations, which matches the heuristic analysis of the previous section very well. The attack takes in total about $2^{30.9}$ row operations, which amounts to about 25 s on a laptop with an Intel i5-8400H CPU at 2.50 GHz. Approximately 12 s are spent computing the spaces V, the remaining time is spent computing $\mathrm{lex}(V)$.

Remark 2. Similar to the Permutation equivalence case, it is possible to use a memoryless collision search algorithm to remove the large memory cost of the attack at essentially no runtime cost.

Comparison with Leon's Algorithm and New Parameters for LESS.
We expect Leon's algorithm (using the Lee-Brickell algorithm to instantiate the ISD oracle) to require $2^{38.3}$ row operations, which is significantly more than the $2^{30.9}$ operations that our algorithm requires. Figure 3 shows the complexity of our algorithm and Leon's algorithm for increasing code length. If the size of the finite field increases linearly with the code length, then the gap between our algorithm and Leon's algorithm increases exponentially. In contrast, if the field size is fixed, then Leon's algorithm will eventually outperform our algorithm. Figure 4 shows that our algorithm exploits the large field size so well, that in some regimes increasing the field size hurts security. Therefore, when picking parameters for LESS, it is best not to pick a field size that is too big. To achieve 128 bits of security against our algorithm and Leon's algorithm one could use linearly equivalent codes of length 250 and dimension 125 over $\mathbb{F}_{53}$. This results in a signature size of 28.4 KB, more than 3 times the original LESS-I signature size of 8.4 KB. The public key size would be 11.4 KB, more than 22 times the original public key size of 0.5 KB. We found that for the LESS-II parameter set, the finite field $\mathbb{F}_7$ is too small for our algoritm to improve over Leon's algoritm, which we estimate would take about 2^{44} row operations.

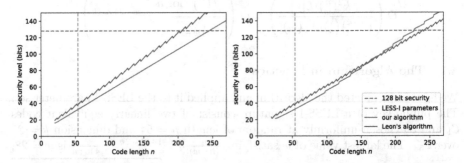

Fig. 3. Complexity of Leon's algorithm and our algorithm for finding linear equivalences in function of the code Length. In the left graph the field size scales linearly with the code length, in the right graph the field size $q = 53$ is fixed. In both cases the rate of the code is fixed at $k/n = 1/2$.

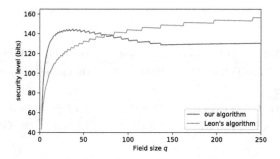

Fig. 4. Estimated complexity of Leon's algorithm and our algorithm for finding linear equivalences in function of the finite field size for random weakly self-dual codes of length $n = 250$ and dimension $k = 125$.

5   Conclusion

We have introduced a new algorithm for finding permutation equivalences and linear equivalences between codes that improves upon Leon's algorithm for sufficiently large field sizes. Leon's algorithm requires computing the set of all the codewords of minimal length, in contrast, to find permutation equivalences our algorithm only requires to compute a small (square root) fraction of the codewords that have a certain (non-minimal) weight. To find linear equivalences we compute a small fraction of the 2-dimensional subspaces of the code with small (but not minimal) support. We implement the algorithm and use it to break the recently proposed LESS system. We show that the LESS-I and LESS-III parameter sets can be broken in only 25 s and 2 s respectively. We propose larger parameters that resist our attack and Leon's original attack that come at the cost of at least a factor 3 increase in signature size and a factor 22 increase in key size. We compare the new parameters of LESS to some other code-based signature schemes in Table 2. Despite the significant increase in signature size and key size, LESS still has smaller signatures than other zero-knowledge based signatures in the Hamming metric, such as Stern's protocol [15], Veron's protocol [17] and the CVE scheme [4]. For example, we estimate that with some straightforward optimizations, the Fiat-Shamir transformed version of CVE identification protocol has a signature size of 38 KB at 128 bits of security. However, the smaller signature size of LESS comes at the cost of larger public keys. Compared to cRVDC [2], a recent zero-knowledge-based proposal using the rank metric, the signature size of LESS is very similar, but the LESS public keys are much larger. Compared to the Durandal scheme [1], LESS has a similar public key size, but larger signatures. Finally, compared to WAVE [5] LESS has much smaller public keys, but also much larger signatures.

Table 2. Comparison of the new LESS parameters with some other code-based signature schemes.

	CVE [15]	cRVDC [2]	Durandal [1]	Wave [5]	LESS-I	LESS-III
Metric	Hamming	Rank	Rank	Hamming	Hamming	
type	FS	FS	FS w/ abort	Trapdoor	FS	
Public key	104 B	152 B	15 KB	3.2 MB	11 KB	17 KB
signature	38 KB	22 KB	4.0 KB	1.6 KB	28 KB	19 KB

References

1. Aragon, N., Blazy, O., Gaborit, P., Hauteville, A., Zémor, G.: Durandal: a rank metric based signature scheme. In: Ishai, Y., Rijmen, V. (eds.) EUROCRYPT 2019. Part III LNCS, vol. 11478, pp. 728–758. Springer, Cham (2019). https://doi.org/10.1007/978-3-030-17659-4_25
2. Bellini, E., Caullery, F., Gaborit, P., Manzano, M., Mateu. V.: Improved veron identification and signature schemes in the rank metric. In:2019 IEEE International Symposium on Information Theory (ISIT), pp. 1872–1876. IEEE (2019)
3. Biasse, J.-F., Micheli, G., Persichetti, E., Santini, P.: LESS is more: code-based signatures without syndromes. Cryptology ePrint Archive, Report 2020/594 (2020). https://eprint.iacr.org/2020/594
4. Cayrel, P.-L., Véron, P., El Yousfi Alaoui, S.M.: A zero-knowledge identification scheme based on the q-ary syndrome decoding problem. In: Biryukov, A., Gong, G., Stinson, D.R. (eds.) SAC 2010. LNCS, vol. 6544, pp. 171–186. Springer, Heidelberg (2011). https://doi.org/10.1007/978-3-642-19574-7_12
5. Debris-Alazard, T., Sendrier, N., Tillich, J.-P.: Wave: a new family of trapdoor one-way preimage sampleable functions based on codes. In: Galbraith, S.D., Moriai, S. (eds.) ASIACRYPT 2019. Part I LNCS, vol. 11921, pp. 21–51. Springer, Cham (2019). https://doi.org/10.1007/978-3-030-34578-5_2
6. Feulner, T.: The automorphism groups of linear codes and canonical representatives of their semilinear isometry classes. Adv. Math. Comm. **3**(4), 363–383 (2009)
7. Girault, M.: A (non-practical) three-pass identification protocol using coding theory. In: Seberry, J., Pieprzyk, J. (eds.) AUSCRYPT 1990. LNCS, vol. 453, pp. 265–272. Springer, Heidelberg (1990). https://doi.org/10.1007/BFb0030367
8. Lee, P.J., Brickell, E.F.: An observation on the security of McEliece's public-key cryptosystem. In: Barstow, D., et al. (ed.) EUROCRYPT 1988. LNCS, vol. 330, pp. 275–280. Springer, Heidelberg (1988). https://doi.org/10.1007/3-540-45961-8_25
9. Leon, J.: Computing automorphism groups of error-correcting codes. IEEE Trans. Inf. Theory **28**(3), 496–511 (1982)
10. McEliece, R.J.: A public-key cryptosystem based on algebraic coding theory. Jet Propulsion Laboratory DSN Progress Report, pp. 42–44 (1978)
11. Saeed, M.A.: Algebraic approach for code equivalence. PhD thesis, Normandie Université; University of Khartoum (2017)
12. Sendrier, N.: Finding the permutation between equivalent linear codes: the support splitting algorithm. IEEE Trans. Inf. Theory **46**(4), 1193–1203 (2000)

13. Sendrier, N., Simos, D.E.: The hardness of code equivalence over $\mathbb{F}_q$ and Its application to code-based cryptography. In: Gaborit, P. (ed.) PQCrypto 2013. LNCS, vol. 7932, pp. 203–216. Springer, Heidelberg (2013). https://doi.org/10.1007/978-3-642-38616-9_14

14. Stern, J.: A method for finding codewords of small weight. In: Cohen, G., Wolfmann, J. (eds.) Coding Theory 1988. LNCS, vol. 388, pp. 106–113. Springer, Heidelberg (1989). https://doi.org/10.1007/BFb0019850

15. Stern, J.: A new identification scheme based on syndrome decoding. In: Stinson, D.R. (ed.) CRYPTO 1993. LNCS, vol. 773, pp. 13–21. Springer, Heidelberg (1994). https://doi.org/10.1007/3-540-48329-2_2

16. van Oorschot, P.C., Wiener, M.J.: Parallel collision search with cryptanalytic applications. J. Cryptol. **12**(1), 1–28 (1999)

17. Pascal, V.: Improved identification schemes based on error-correcting codes. Appl. Algebra Eng. Commun. Comput. **8**(1), 57–69 (1997)

Towards Post-Quantum Security for Signal's X3DH Handshake

Jacqueline Brendel[1]([✉]), Marc Fischlin[2], Felix Günther[3], Christian Janson[2], and Douglas Stebila[4]

[1] CISPA Helmholtz Center for Information Security, Saarbrücken, Germany
mail@jbrendel-info.de
[2] Cryptoplexity, Technische Universität Darmstadt, Darmstadt, Germany
{marc.fischlin,christian.janson}@cryptoplexity.de
[3] Department of Computer Science, ETH Zürich, Zürich, Switzerland
mail@felixguenther.info
[4] University of Waterloo, Waterloo, Canada
dstebila@uwaterloo.ca

Abstract. Modern key exchange protocols are usually based on the Diffie–Hellman (DH) primitive. The beauty of this primitive, among other things, is its potential reusage of key shares: DH shares can be either used a single time or in multiple runs. Since DH-based protocols are insecure against quantum adversaries, alternative solutions have to be found when moving to the post-quantum setting. However, most post-quantum candidates, including schemes based on lattices and even supersingular isogeny DH, are not known to be secure under key reuse. In particular, this means that they cannot be necessarily deployed as an immediate DH substitute in protocols.

In this paper, we introduce the notion of a *split key encapsulation mechanism* (split KEM) to translate the desired key-reusability of a DH-based protocol to a KEM-based flow. We provide the relevant security notions of split KEMs and show how the formalism lends itself to lifting Signal's X3DH handshake to the post-quantum KEM setting without additional message flows.

Although the proposed framework conceptually solves the raised issues, instantiating it securely from post-quantum assumptions proved to be non-trivial. We give passively secure instantiations from (R)LWE, yet overcoming the above-mentioned insecurities under key reuse in the presence of active adversaries remains an open problem. Approaching one-sided key reuse, we provide a split KEM instantiation that allows such reuse based on the KEM introduced by Kiltz (PKC 2007), which may serve as a post-quantum blueprint if the underlying hardness assumption (gap hashed Diffie–Hellman) holds for the commutative group action of CSIDH (Asiacrypt 2018).

The intention of this paper hence is to raise awareness of the challenges arising when moving to KEM-based key exchange protocols with key-reusability, and to propose split KEMs as a specific target for instantiation in future research.

© Springer Nature Switzerland AG 2021
O. Dunkelman et al. (Eds.): SAC 2020, LNCS 12804, pp. 404–430, 2021.
https://doi.org/10.1007/978-3-030-81652-0_16

Keywords: Post-quantum · Key encapsulation mechanisms · Key exchange · Signal protocol · X3DH

1 Introduction

The core Diffie–Hellman protocol [21]—Alice sends g^x, Bob sends g^y, and both compute g^{xy} as shared secret—is a beautiful and versatile cryptographic primitive, plays a central role in modern key exchange protocols, and appears in many variants. For example, a key share (x, g^x) can be *ephemeral* (meaning used only once) or *static* (meaning reused multiple times). Furthermore, the same share can be used in role-symmetric ways, i.e., as both initiator and responder of key exchange sessions and the same message flow can give rise to different authenticated key exchange (AKE) protocols (e.g., HMQV [50], CMQV [75], NAXOS [54]). The security of DH-based constructions can in turn be based on many cryptographic assumptions over the group, ranging from simple passive assumptions like computational (CDH) or decisional (DDH) Diffie–Hellman, to interactive assumptions like GapDH [63], oracle DH (ODH) [1], or PRF-ODH [11,43].

Indeed, modern real-world cryptographic protocols employ the Diffie–Hellman key exchange protocol in ways that often rely on many aspects of this versatility. Table 1 shows key exchange patterns from various Internet protocols that employ a "signed ephemeral Diffie–Hellman" approach. In TLS 1.2 [20], the server sends the initial ephemeral public key, and the client responds, while in TLS 1.3 [69], the roles are reversed to reduce the number of round trips: the client sends the initial ephemeral public key, and the server responds. In both cases the security proofs [30,43] rely on interactive DH assumptions (variants of PRF-ODH) because of how the session key is used in the protocol prior to the session being fully authenticated.

In implicitly authenticated key exchange, static key pairs are used to derive shared secrets that can only be computed by the intended parties; having a peer who successfully computes the shared secret implicitly authenticates that peer, in contrast to the explicit authentication provided by checking a signature computed by one's peer. Implicitly authenticated key exchange protocols have long been of academic interest (e.g., [17,50,77]), and have recently started to be used in real-world protocols, such as the original handshake design of Google's QUIC protocol [57,68] or the Signal protocol [14,72], as well as OPTLS [52] which is the conceptual foundation of the TLS 1.3 handshake (cf. Table 2). In these designs, (semi-)static DH keys enable low-latency, zero round-trip time connections. The Signal protocol even focuses on *asynchronous* communication, enabling parties to initiate a connection despite their peer being offline.

Moving to Post-quantum Solutions. Unfortunately, DH-based protocols are not secure against quantum adversaries, so key exchange protocols need to transition to post-quantum designs. The NIST Post Quantum Cryptography Standardization process [61] is currently in the second round for identifying quantum-resistant primitives. Furthermore, experimental deployment of post-quantum

Table 1. Signed DH key exchange patterns of selected Internet protocols.

Protocol	Core message flow	Session key	Security
SSHv2 [78] (signed eph. DH)	$\xrightarrow{\quad \text{hello} \quad}$ $\xleftarrow{\quad \text{hello} \quad}$ $\xrightarrow{\quad epk_A \quad}$ $\xleftarrow{\ epk_B, lpk_B, \text{sig}\ }$	$DH(epk_A, epk_B)$	DDH [6]
TLS 1.2 [20] (signed eph. DH)	$\xrightarrow{\quad \text{hello} \quad}$ $\xleftarrow{epk_B, \text{cert}[lpk_B], \text{sig}}$ $\xrightarrow{\quad epk_A \quad}$	$DH(epk_A, epk_B)$	snPRF-ODH [43]
TLS 1.3 [69] (signed eph. DH)	$\xrightarrow{\ \text{hello}, epk_A\ }$ $\xleftarrow{epk_B, \text{cert}[lpk_B], \text{sig}}$	$DH(epk_A, epk_B)$	snPRF-ODH [30]

With epk_X and lpk_X we denote the ephemeral resp. long-term key of a party, hello is the protocol initiator's message, sig a signature under the long-term key, and cert$[lpk_X]$ the long-term key and certificate of party X.

algorithms in key exchange protocols has already taken place, e.g., by Google, Cloudflare, and the Open Quantum Safe project [18,53,55,56,73].

While key exchange protocols are a crucial building block for many applications, the NIST standardization process did not explicitly ask for key exchange, but for the conceptually simpler notions of key encapsulation mechanisms (KEMs) [16,71]. A KEM allows encapsulation of a symmetric key under a public key within a ciphertext, such that the symmetric key can be decapsulated only when knowing the corresponding secret key. Security-wise, the ciphertext hides the encapsulated symmetric key indistinguishably from a random string. The proposals to the NIST standardization process mostly follow the approach to first provide a (weakly secure) public-key encryption scheme and then use well-known transforms such as the Fujisaki–Okamoto transform [36,37,41] to achieve a strongly-secure KEM with respect to active adversaries.

In principle, KEMs can directly be used to build and analyze key exchange protocols, and allow to capture (implicitly authenticated) Diffie–Hellman flows (e.g., in the static Diffie–Hellman handshake of TLS 1.2 [51]). The naive approach hence would be to simply replace every DH combination in a key exchange protocol with a KEM. However, whereas DH shares can be freely reused by both parties, particularly allowing static-static combinations (as used, e.g., in Signal [72]), the KEM concept restricts reuse to one side, namely the decapsulator. This in turn limits the possible message flows and contributions of ephemeral randomness that standard KEMs can capture, hindering a direct translation of DH-type protocols to KEM-based designs, and leading to the question:

Can we capture post-quantum KEM designs in a way that enables flexible key reuse and support efficient message flows similar to the widely-used Diffie–Hellman-based designs?

Table 2. Implicitly authenticated DH key exchange patterns of selected Internet protocols. (color table online)

Protocol	Core message flow	Session key	Security
TLS 1.2 [20] (implicit-auth. static DH + explicit-auth. MAC)	hello $\longrightarrow$ $\longleftarrow$ cert$[lpk_B]$, mac epk_A, mac $\longrightarrow$	$\mathrm{DH}(epk_A, lpk_B)$	mnPRF-ODH [51]
OPTLS [52] (implicit-auth. static/eph. DH + explicit-auth. MAC)	hello, epk_A $\longrightarrow$ epk_B, cert$[lpk_B]$, mac $\longleftarrow$	$\mathrm{DH}(epk_A, epk_B)\|$ $\mathrm{DH}(epk_A, lpk_B)$	GapDH, DDH [52] (ROM)
Signal [72] (X3DH: triple DH handshake + opt. eph./eph.)	hello $\dashrightarrow$ $lpk_B, sspk_B, epk_B^{\dagger}$ $\dashleftarrow$ lpk_A, epk_A $\longrightarrow$	$\mathrm{DH}(lpk_A, sspk_B)\|$ $\mathrm{DH}(epk_A, lpk_B)\|$ $\mathrm{DH}(epk_A, sspk_B)\|$ $\mathrm{DH}(epk_A, epk_B)^{\dagger}$	mmPRF-ODH, smPRF-ODH, smPRF-ODH, snPRF-ODH† [14]
QUIC [68,57] (original handshake)	hello, epk_A $\longrightarrow$ $sspk_B$ $\longleftarrow$	$\mathrm{DH}(epk_A, lpk_B)\|$ $\mathrm{DH}(epk_A, sspk_B)$	GapDH [34] (ROM)

With epk_X and lpk_X we denote the ephemeral resp. long-term key of a party (the latter might be known to a peer in advance), hello is the protocol initiator's message, mac a message authentication code under a derived key, and cert$[lpk_X]$ the long-term key and certificate of party X. Dashed arrows in the Signal key exchange indicate obtaining the "prekey bundle" from the Signal server, blue values marked with † are optional.

1.1 Our Contributions

In this paper, we work towards a structure for achieving the key-reusability of Diffie–Hellman-based key exchanges in the KEM setting by introducing the notion of **split KEMs** in Sect. 4.1. In split KEMs, encapsulation of a shared secret takes as input not only the public key of the decapsulator but also a (potentially static) secret key of the encapsulator. Similarly, decapsulation of a ciphertext takes as input not only the decapsulator's secret key, but also the encapsulator public key corresponding to the secret key used in encapsulation.

In Sect. 4.2, we illustrate how split KEMs enable the smooth transfer of popular DH-based key exchanges such as **Signal's** X3DH to the (post-quantum) KEM setting. Especially in the case of the Signal protocol, the complex and asynchronous initial key agreement (X3DH, short for "Extended Triple

Diffie–Hellman") has been abstracted away as an idealized primitive in works on secure messaging with and without post-quantum security considerations (cf., e.g., the work by Alwen, Coretti, and Dodis [2] which is amenable to post-quantum security).

In Sect. 4.3, we transfer the commonly-used security notion for KEMs of indistinguishability of encapsulated keys from random to the split KEM setting. For this we introduce the notion of lr-IND-CCA **security** that is parametrized by $l \in \{n, s, m\}$ and $r \in \{n, m\}$ which will indicate how often the adversary is allowed to query the "left" decapsulation oracle or the "right" encapsulation oracle. (Here, n means no query is allowed, s means a single query is allowed, and m means (polynomially) many queries are allowed.) This **novel fine-grained security notion** allows not only to distinguish between passive and active attacks, but also captures key reuse on either the decapsulator's or the encapsulator's side or on both sides.

As for **realizing the split KEM** notion, we show in Sect. 4.4 that plain (R)LWE-based KEMs do non-trivially match the split KEM structure and maintain security in this formalization. However, known key reuse attacks against (R)LWE-based KEMs prohibit such an instantiation from being secure against active adversaries. We furthermore give an instantiation of an actively-secure split KEM achieving mn-IND-CCA security based on the KEM introduced by Kiltz [48]. While not being a post-quantum secure split KEM per se, the design and hardness assumptions may be replicable in the CSIDH setting (cf. the following discussion in Sect. 1.2). Unfortunately, we have so far been unable to successfully develop an instantiation in the strongest mm-IND-CCA setting from a post-quantum assumption. We identify this as an important challenge for future work.

1.2   Related Work

Related work for our split KEM notion includes approaches towards post-quantum security of concrete protocols, notions for key reuse and the possibility of key reuse in various post-quantum settings, as well as foundational extensions to the definitional framework of KEMs.

Post-quantum Protocols. Post-quantum secure protocol variants based on KEMs have been proposed for TLS 1.3 [70] and WireGuard [42]. These protocols, unlike Signal, allow (multiple) round trips and therefore do not experience the same problem we discuss in this paper. For Signal, Alwen, Coretti, and Dodis [2] give a first variant of Signal's double-ratchet that is amenable to post-quantum secure KEMs, however exclude the crucial initial key agreement. Duits [33] explores transitioning Signal to the post-quantum setting; the suggested replacement of DH with Supersingular Isogeny Diffie–Hellman (SIDH) [19,44] however is not secure under the required key reuse, as we discuss next.

Key Reuse with **LWE** *and SIDH.* There are a number of attacks on lattice-based key exchange schemes when keys are reused [5,22,24–26,35,40,59,62,67].

There exist proposals to enable secure key reuse in (R)LWE-based schemes [23, 39], however, these proposals only seem to at most guard against specific attacks at a time, while still being vulnerable to other attacks. All LWE-based KEMs in Rounds 2 and 3 of the NIST process rely on the Fujisaki–Okamoto transform to achieve IND-CCA security which provides safe key reuse for one party, but comes at the cost of requiring the other party to fully disclose the secret key behind their encapsulation.

Similarly, for key exchange based on SIDH [44] there are attacks when keys are reused [38]; the SIKE NIST submission uses the FO transformation to provide security under key reuse. Azarderakhsh, Jao, and Leonardi [3] proposed k-SIDH for static-static key exchange, where each party has k static keys, and the final shared secret is computed from all k^2 combinations. Security of k-SIDH relies on an additional unproven assumption that the key exchange method be "irreducible", but the best attacks currently known are exponential in k [28]. For k-SIDH at the 128-bit security, each party would need to send $k \approx 100$ public keys and compute $k^2 \approx 10,000$ SIDH computations, making it extremely expensive. A more efficient variant of k-SIDH by Jao and Urbanik [74] was found by Basso et al. [4] to have poorer scaling than the original. There have been several additional attempts which are either inconclusive [7] or insecure [28,29,47].

Static-Static Key Agreement via CSIDH. Castryck et al. [12] introduce a scheme based on supersingular isogenies named CSIDH that supports key reuse without the need for additional transforms. Unlike the previously mentioned supersingular isogeny-based schemes building on [44], CSIDH is considering the hardness of finding isogenies between isogenous supersingular elliptic curves over a *prime* field $\mathbb{F}_p$. While this yields a commutative group action, enabling truly DH-like non-interactive key agreement, the concrete parameter selection for CSIDH has been called into doubt [8,65] and the decisional Diffie–Hellman problem has been challenged for settings related to CSIDH [13] (although not affecting CSIDH itself). De Kock [49] and Kawashima et al. [46] recently considered a translation of the gap Diffie–Hellman assumption [63] to the CSIDH setting as the underlying assumption to construct interactive, tightly post-quantum secure key exchange protocols. So far, the intractability of this and other *interactive* hardness assumptions needed for full-fledged key exchange (cf. Tables 1 and 2) however is unknown for CSIDH.

PRF-ODH. The PRF-ODH assumption is a variant of the oracle-DH assumption [1] which enables to argue pseudorandomness of PRF outputs when keyed with related, reused DH values. It is a natural assumption in DH-based key exchanges and was introduced by Jager et al. in their analysis of TLS 1.2 [43]. Since then it has been used in the analyses of many real-world key exchange protocols, including TLS 1.3 [30,31] and Signal [14,15]. Brendel et al. [11] conducted a systematic study, including the presentation of a unified definition of the various flavors of the PRF-ODH assumption that had been employed in the previous literature. We adopt their unified approach in our definition of Ir-IND-CCA security for split KEMs.

Post-quantum KEMs and KEM Variants. Strongly-secure (IND-CCA) KEMs can be obtained generically through transforming post-quantum secure public-key encryption [36,41]. These transforms, however, do not allow to reuse the encapsulator's secret randomness. Xue et al. [76] introduce the notion of *double-key* KEMs. Here, encapsulation and decapsulation take two public, resp. secret, keys as input belonging to the *same* party, while split KEM encapsulation and decapsulation take one public and one secret input from *each* party, enabling static-static key reuse. The notion of *merged* KEMs [32] aims to optimize bandwidth for public ratchets in the Signal protocol; our work and the notion of split KEMs instead is concerned with the initial key agreement with contributions from both parties. In their notion of *multi-recipient* KEMs, Katsumata et al. [45] also decompose the encapsulation process, though without allowing a secret input of the sender to enter encapsulation as in our split KEM notion.

2   Preliminaries

We begin by briefly introducing the notation we require throughout this paper. Since our main concept builds upon the notion of KEMs, we subsequently review their basic syntax and security notions. We note that we define security with respect to *quantum* polynomial time (QPT) algorithms instead of probabilistic polynomial time (PPT) as this work is motivated by the existence of adversaries with access to local quantum computing power. We note that all problems that can be solved by PPT algorithms can also be solved by QPT algorithms, whereas the reverse is not true (e.g., computing discrete logarithms in special groups or factorization of large composite numbers).

2.1   Notation

For an algorithm A we write $y \leftarrow \mathsf{A}(\cdot)$, resp. $y \xleftarrow{\$} \mathsf{A}(\cdot)$, for deterministically, resp. probabilistically, running A on given inputs and assigning the output to y. We say that an algorithm A is *efficient* if it runs in QPT in the security parameter denoted by λ. By $\mathcal{A}^{\mathcal{O}}$ we express that the adversary denoted by $\mathcal{A}$ is given access to oracle $\mathcal{O}$. Finally, we use $\bot$ as a special symbol to denote rejection or an error, and we assume that $\bot \notin \{0,1\}^*$.

2.2   Key Encapsulation Mechanisms

Definition 1. *A key encapsulation mechanism* KEM *with associated public key space* $\mathcal{PK}$, *secret key space* $\mathcal{SK}$, *ciphertext space* $\mathcal{C}$, *and key space* $\mathcal{K}$ *is a tuple of algorithms* KEM = (KGen, Encaps, Decaps) *defined as follows.*

Key generation KGen: *Takes as input the security parameter* λ *and outputs a public-secret key pair in* $\mathcal{PK} \times \mathcal{SK}$, *i.e.,* $(pk, sk) \xleftarrow{\$} \mathsf{KGen}(1^\lambda)$.

Encapsulation Encaps: *Takes as input a public key* pk *and outputs a ciphertext* $c \in \mathcal{C}$ *and the encapsulated key* $K \in \mathcal{K}$, *i.e.,* $(c, K) \xleftarrow{\$} \mathsf{Encaps}(pk)$.

$\mathcal{G}_{\mathsf{KEM},\mathcal{A}}^{\mathsf{indcpa}}(\lambda):$	$\mathcal{G}_{\mathsf{KEM},\mathcal{A}}^{\mathsf{indcca}}(\lambda):$	$\mathcal{O}_{\mathsf{Decaps}}(c):$
1 $(pk, sk) \xleftarrow{\$} \mathsf{KGen}(1^\lambda)$	1 $(pk, sk) \xleftarrow{\$} \mathsf{KGen}(1^\lambda)$	7 **if** $c = c^*$
2 $(c^*, K_0^*) \xleftarrow{\$} \mathsf{Encaps}(pk)$	2 $(c^*, K_0^*) \xleftarrow{\$} \mathsf{Encaps}(pk)$	8 **return** $\perp$
3 $K_1^* \xleftarrow{\$} \mathcal{K}$	3 $K_1^* \xleftarrow{\$} \mathcal{K}$	9 **else**
4 $b \xleftarrow{\$} \{0,1\}$	4 $b \xleftarrow{\$} \{0,1\}$	10 **return** $\mathsf{Decaps}(sk, c)$
5 $b' \xleftarrow{\$} \mathcal{A}(pk, c^*, K_b^*)$	5 $b' \xleftarrow{\$} \mathcal{A}^{\mathcal{O}_{\mathsf{Decaps}}}(pk, c^*, K_b^*)$	
6 **return** $[\![b' = b]\!]$	6 **return** $[\![b' = b]\!]$	

Fig. 1. IND-CPA and IND-CCA security games for KEM = (KGen, Encaps, Decaps) with key space $\mathcal{K}$.

Decapsulation Decaps: *Takes as input a ciphertext c and secret key sk and outputs* $K' \in \mathcal{K} \cup \{\perp\}$, *where* $\perp$ *indicates an error, i.e.,* $K' \leftarrow \mathsf{Decaps}(sk, c)$.

We say that a KEM KEM = (KGen, Encaps, Decaps) *is* ϵ*-correct if*

$$\Pr_{(pk,sk) \xleftarrow{\$} \mathsf{KGen}(1^\lambda), (c,K) \xleftarrow{\$} \mathsf{Encaps}(pk)} \left[K' \neq K \mid K' \leftarrow \mathsf{Decaps}(sk, c) \right] \leq \epsilon.$$

We call KEM *(perfectly) correct if* $\epsilon = 0$.

KEM Security. The security of key encapsulation mechanisms can be formulated in terms of indistinguishability as well as in terms of one-wayness. We recap *indistinguishability* (of encapsulated keys), defined under either passive (*chosen-plaintext*, IND-CPA) or active (*chosen-ciphertext*, IND-CCA) attacks. The notion of one-wayness captures the (non-)recoverability of the encapsulated key from the ciphertext. In this paper we focus on the notion of indistinguishability but note that all security notions may be transferred to the one-wayness setting.

Definition 2. *Let* KEM *be a KEM with key space* $\mathcal{K}$. *We say that* KEM *is* IND-CPA-*secure, resp.* IND-CCA-*secure, if for every QPT adversary* $\mathcal{A}$ *the advantage function for winning the game* $\mathcal{G}_{\mathsf{KEM},\mathcal{A}}^{\mathsf{indatk}}$ *(with* atk = cpa, *resp.* atk = cca*) from Fig. 1, defined as*

$$\mathsf{Adv}_{\mathsf{KEM},\mathcal{A}}^{\mathsf{indatk}}(\lambda) := \left| \Pr\left[\mathcal{G}_{\mathsf{KEM},\mathcal{A}}^{\mathsf{indatk}}(\lambda) = 1 \right] - \frac{1}{2} \right|,$$

is negligible in the security parameter λ.

3 Instantiating Signal's X3DH Key Exchange with KEMs

In this section, we illustrate the challenges arising when translating DH-based key exchange protocols to the KEM setting following the example of Signal's X3DH initial key exchange design [72] for secure messaging. We will see that simply replacing DH operations with KEM encapsulations results in additional message flows and altered ephemeral/static share combinations for deriving keying material of the involved parties.

While purely ephemeral DH-based key exchanges generally map well to KEMs, many protocol designs further include DH-based combinations of static or semi-static keys with (semi-)static or ephemeral keys, most importantly for implicit authentication (as in Signal [72] or the Noise framework [66]). However, KEMs allow only for restricted key reuse (namely only on the decapsulator's side) and are hence limited in their support of static key share combinations.

3.1   X3DH: The Initial Key Agreement in Signal

X3DH [60] is part of the Signal secure messaging protocol [72] and establishes the initial keys. We limit the following discussion to this initial key exchange. For further information on the remaining cryptographic building blocks of the Signal protocol, especially on the ratcheting stages following X3DH, we refer the interested reader to, e.g., the analyses of Cohn-Gordon et al. [14] and Alwen et al. [2].

In Fig. 2 we give an illustration of X3DH, where Alice wishes to establish a shared key with Bob. The session setup in Signal involves three parties, namely the communicating parties Alice and Bob, plus a central server S. This is due to the fact that Signal aims to provide secure messaging in an *asynchronous* setting, i.e., chats can be initiated and encrypted messages can be exchanged even if not *all* communication partners are online. For this, all users need to register their long-lived identity key and further cryptographic key material with the central server S. In more detail, every user U provides the server S with the public keys of the following key pairs:

- a long-lived static identity key pair (lpk_U, lsk_U),
- a medium-lived semi-static (signed) prekey pair $(sspk_U, sssk_U)$, and
- n ephemeral prekey pairs $(eppk_U^1, epsk_U^1), \ldots, (eppk_U^n, epsk_U^n)$.

When Alice wants to initiate a chat with Bob, she simply requests the necessary information and cryptographic key material of Bob (the so-called "prekey bundle") from the central server S. From this she then derives an initial shared secret that secures her first message(s) to Bob. Once Bob comes online again and receives the first message from Alice (via the server), he requests Alice's cryptographic key material from the server S to be able to derive the same initial key to decrypt Alice's message.

More formally, Alice initiates a session with Bob by first pinging the server S and requesting Bob's public key material: the static identity key lpk_B, the semi-static prekey $sspk_B$, as well as (optionally, if available) a single ephemeral (one-time) prekey $eppk_B$. Alice then generates an ephemeral key pair (epk_A, esk_A) of her own and derives the master secret ms as

$$ \mathsf{ms} \leftarrow sspk_B^{lsk_A} \| lpk_B^{esk_A} \| sspk_B^{esk_A} \| eppk_B^{esk_A}, $$

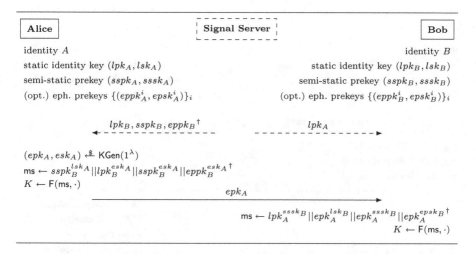

Fig. 2. Signal's X3DH key exchange. Interaction with the Signal server is dashed, the optional ephemeral prekey (combination) is depicted in blue marked with †. (Color figure online)

where the last DH value $eppk_B^{esk_A}$ is only present if Alice has received one of Bob's ephemeral prekeys $eppk_B$ from the server. More on this below in Remark 1.

Alice then derives the initial key K from the master secret via a pseudo-random function F keyed with ms and can then use this key to encrypt her first message to Bob. Finally, Alice sends her ephemeral public key epk_A to Bob (alongside identifiers for, e.g., Bob's semi-static and ephemeral prekeys that she received from the server). Once Bob comes online he will receive this message and can then request Alice's static identity key lpk_A from the server. Analogously to Alice he can then compute the master secret ms and thus the final initial key K that decrypts Alice's first encrypted message to him.

Remark 1 (Exhaustion of ephemeral prekeys). Note that each of the n stored ephemeral prekeys is only handed out once by the server, i.e., in case Charlie wishes to also initiate a session with Bob, he will receive an ephemeral prekey of Bob that is different from the one Alice received. However, if many users initiate a session with Bob while he is offline, it may be the case that the stored ephemeral prekeys on the server are exhausted. Hence, the initial shared secret is only derived from the static identity key lpk_B and the semi-static prekey $sspk_B$.

3.2   A KEM-based X3DH Variant

Considering preparations for a post-quantum secure messaging design, one may ask if any candidate of NIST's post-quantum cryptography process can be used smoothly in the above setting. Unfortunately this is not the case. As mentioned before, replacing the Diffie–Hellman operations in Signal's X3DH protocol with KEMs causes difficulties, as we illustrate in Fig. 3 and discuss in the following.

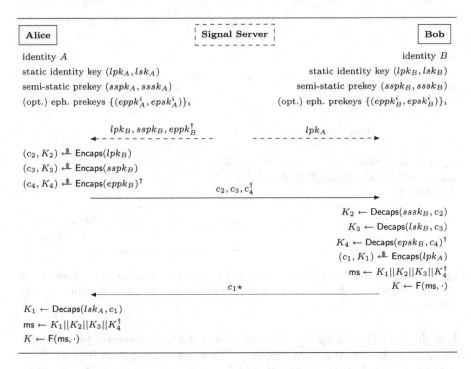

Fig. 3. Signal's X3DH key exchange with KEMs replacing the DH operations. Interaction with the Signal server is dashed, the optional ephemeral prekey (combination) is depicted in blue marked with †. The last flow (in red marked with ⋆), necessary for the key share combination involving Alice's long-term key, breaks the asynchronicity of X3DH. (Color figure online)

As before, when Alice initiates a session with Bob, she requests and receives Bob's static identity key lpk_B, his semi-static prekey $sspk_B$, as well as a single ephemeral prekey $eppk_B$ (if available) from the server. Alice then separately encapsulates key material under each of these keys and sends the resulting ciphertexts to Bob, establishing three shared keys K_1, K_2, and K_3 (if available).

Yet, in order to fully transfer X3DH to the KEM setting, these three keys are not enough: they constitute, in order, the KEM analogues of the DH secrets $\mathsf{DH}(lpk_B, epk_A)$, $\mathsf{DH}(sspk_B, epk_A)$, and $\mathsf{DH}(eppk_B, epk_A)$, where Alice's ephemeral contribution via epk_A is replaced by (differing) randomness inputs on Alice's side to the encapsulation algorithm. What is missing to complete the master secret computation—and thus key derivation—in the same fashion as in X3DH is the analogue of the DH combination of Alice's static identity key and Bob's semi-static key, i.e., $\mathsf{DH}(sspk_B, lpk_A)$.

KEMs, however, do not provide for a *non-ephemeral* contribution of the encapsulating party to the Encaps algorithm. In the KEM-based X3DH variant, Bob can thus at most encapsulate under Alice's static identity key lpk_A, which introduces an additional message flow (depicted in red in Fig. 3). This however eradicates a key feature of instant messaging: asynchronicity, i.e., the ability to send encrypted messages even if the receiving party is offline.[1]

4 Split Key Encapsulation Mechanisms

To tackle the above mentioned issues of KEMs in a DH-based protocol, we introduce a new primitive called *split key encapsulation mechanism*, or split KEM, for short. Split KEMs enable a more fine-grained notion of key encapsulation mechanisms, where the encapsulation procedure is divided up into key generation and a subsequent shared-key computation step. As it turns out, the passively-secure (IND-CPA) versions of many proposals for KEMs submitted to the NIST Post-Quantum Cryptography Standardization process [61], especially those based on lattices, seem to naturally fit into the split KEM format: their encapsulation procedure can be split into a key generation and a shared-key computation part.

4.1 Definition of Split KEMs

Intuitively, a split KEM is a KEM in which *both* parties can contribute to the encapsulation, with either one-time or (semi-)static keys. The key generation on the encapsulator's side (that does implicitly take place in many KEMs) is decoupled from the encapsulation algorithm, thus allowing key reuse similar to the DH setting. Figure 4 shows the communication flow when using a split KEM to establish a shared secret.

Notation. Let enc denote the encapsulating party (in the following referred to as the *encapsulator*) and similarly, dec denotes the decapsulating party (or *decapsulator*). Let $\mathcal{PK}_{enc}$ and $\mathcal{SK}_{enc}$ be the public and secret key space of the encapsulator, and $\mathcal{PK}_{dec}$ and $\mathcal{SK}_{dec}$ analogously for the decapsulator (if irrelevant, or clear from the context, we will in the following omit the explicit mention of these key spaces). Let $\mathcal{C}$ be the ciphertext space and $\mathcal{K}$ the key space.

Definition 3. *A split KEM sKEM consists of four algorithms* $\mathsf{KGen}_{dec}, \mathsf{KGen}_{enc}, \mathsf{sEncaps}, and \mathsf{sDecaps}, where \mathsf{KGen}_{enc} and \mathsf{sEncaps} are executed by the encapsulator, and \mathsf{KGen}_{dec} and \mathsf{sDecaps} by the decapsulator.*

– *split **KEM key generation** for decapsulator and encapsulator, respectively:* $(D, d) \xleftarrow{\$} \mathsf{KGen}_{dec}(1^\lambda)$ *and* $(E, e) \xleftarrow{\$} \mathsf{KGen}_{enc}(1^\lambda)$ *are probabilistic algorithms that output a key pair, consisting of a public key (denoted by capital letters) and a secret key (denoted by lowercase letters) in* $\mathcal{PK}_{dec} \times \mathcal{SK}_{dec}$ *and* $\mathcal{PK}_{enc} \times \mathcal{SK}_{enc}$, *respectively.*

---

[1] Note that it is in general not possible for Bob to precompute and store ciphertext(s) on the server alongside his public keys to avoid the additional message flow since Bob may not know in advance which user wishes to establish a secure chat with him.

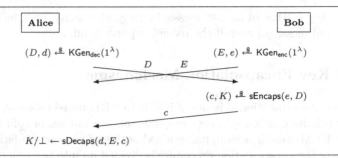

Fig. 4. Communication flow of a split KEM sKEM = (KGen$_{\text{dec}}$, KGen$_{\text{enc}}$, sEncaps, sDecaps), where Alice is the decapsulator and Bob the encapsulator.

- **split KEM encapsulation:** $(c, K) \xleftarrow{\$} \text{sEncaps}(e, D)$ *is a probabilistic algorithm executed by the encapsulator* enc. *It takes as input* $e \in \mathcal{SK}_{\text{enc}}$, *the secret key of the encapsulator, and* $D \in \mathcal{PK}_{\text{dec}}$, *the public key of the decapsulator. Algorithm* sEncaps *then outputs the shared secret* $K \in \mathcal{K}$ *along with its encapsulation* $c \in \mathcal{C}$. *It is common to simply refer to the encapsulation* c *of* K *as* ciphertext.
- **split KEM decapsulation:** $K/\bot \leftarrow \text{sDecaps}(d, E, c)$ *is a deterministic algorithm executed by the decapsulator* dec. *On input a ciphertext* c, *the decapsulator's secret key* d, *and encapsulator's public key* E, *it outputs either the decapsulation* K *of* c *or* $\bot$, *if the operation fails.*

We say that a split key encapsulation sKEM = (KGen$_{\text{dec}}$, KGen$_{\text{enc}}$, sEncaps, sDecaps) *is* ϵ-correct *if*

$$\Pr_{(D,d) \xleftarrow{\$} \text{KGen}_{\text{dec}}, (E,e) \xleftarrow{\$} \text{KGen}_{\text{enc}}, (c,K) \xleftarrow{\$} \text{sEncaps}(e,D)} \left[K' \neq K \mid K' \leftarrow \text{sDecaps}(d,E,c) \right] \leq \epsilon.$$

We call sKEM *(perfectly) correct if* $\epsilon = 0$.

Symmetric Split KEMs. In some supersingular-isogeny-based KEMs the specification of the key generation algorithm depends on the role of the generating party (cf., e.g., the NIST Round 2 candidate SIKE [19]). In these schemes, Alice and Bob generate public points in different subgroups of the curve during key generation, i.e., KGen$_{\text{dec}} \neq$ KGen$_{\text{enc}}$. However, there are also many natural examples (e.g., DH- or LWE-based KEMs), where the key generation algorithms for the encapsulator and the decapsulator do not differ. This allows generated key pairs to be used as input for both the encapsulation and decapsulation algorithms, i.e., across roles. In order to capture these special types of split KEMs, we introduce the notion of a *symmetric* split KEM.

Definition 4 (Symmetric Split KEM). *We call a split KEM* sKEM = $(\mathsf{KGen_{dec}}, \mathsf{KGen_{enc}}, \mathsf{sEncaps}, \mathsf{sDecaps})$ *symmetric if* $\mathsf{KGen_{dec}} = \mathsf{KGen_{enc}}$ *and the same key pair of a party is reused in both roles. In particular, this means that* $\mathcal{PK_{dec}} = \mathcal{PK_{enc}}$ *and* $\mathcal{SK_{dec}} = \mathcal{SK_{enc}}$. *For sake of simplicity, in this case we will often simply refer to the key generation algorithm as* KGen *instead of* $\mathsf{KGen_{dec}}$ *and* $\mathsf{KGen_{enc}}$, *respectively.*

We say that sKEM = $(\mathsf{KGen}, \mathsf{sEncaps}, \mathsf{sDecaps})$ *is ϵ-correct if both*

$$\Pr_{(D,d),(E,e) \xleftarrow{\$} \mathsf{KGen}(1^\lambda),(c,K) \xleftarrow{\$} \mathsf{sEncaps}(e,D)} \left[K' \neq K \mid K' \leftarrow \mathsf{sDecaps}(d,E,c) \right] \leq \epsilon$$

and

$$\Pr_{(D,d),(E,e) \xleftarrow{\$} \mathsf{KGen}(1^\lambda),(c,K) \xleftarrow{\$} \mathsf{sEncaps}(d,E)} \left[K' \neq K \mid K' \leftarrow \mathsf{sDecaps}(e,D,c) \right] \leq \epsilon.$$

Again, as before, a symmetric split KEM is called (perfectly) *correct if $\epsilon = 0$.*

We stress that it is not necessary to move to the symmetric split KEM setting if the key generation algorithms are the same for the encapsulator and decapsulator, but resulting key pair is only ever reused for a fixed role. However, the symmetric split KEM setting is predestined for protocols like Signal's X3DH with KEMs. There, the long-term identity keys are used in both roles, either as the initiating party (the encapsulator) or the responder (the decapsulator).

4.2   X3DH with Split KEMs

We briefly show that using the split KEM formalism could solve the aforementioned problems when switching from the DH to the KEM setting. Figure 5 illustrates the flow between Alice and Bob using only split KEMs. On the one hand, the formalization of split KEMs may now allow both parties to reuse key pairs and have them both contribute to the encapsulation operation(s). Furthermore, regarding the issue of having to encapsulate without knowing the corresponding public key, the split KEM formalism gets rid of the additional message flow from Bob to Alice, thereby effectively regaining the asynchronicity of the secure messaging application.

4.3   Security of Split KEMs

When translating the security definitions from the KEM setting (cf. Sect. 2.2) to split KEMs, we need to address that encapsulation now contains a secret-key input e and the potential reuse of keys. We arrive at fine-grained security notions that we term lr-IND-CCA (cf. Figure 6), which are parametrized by $\mathsf{l} \in \{\mathsf{n}, \mathsf{s}, \mathsf{m}\}$ and $\mathsf{r} \in \{\mathsf{n}, \mathsf{m}\}$. Here, $\mathsf{l} \in \{\mathsf{n}, \mathsf{s}, \mathsf{m}\}$ indicates whether the adversary is allowed to make no ($\mathsf{l} = \mathsf{n}$), a single ($\mathsf{l} = \mathsf{s}$), or polynomially many ($\mathsf{l} = \mathsf{m}$) queries to the *decapsulation* oracle $\mathcal{O}_{\mathsf{sDecaps}}$. Analogously, $\mathsf{r} \in \{\mathsf{n}, \mathsf{m}\}$ indicates the number of queries the adversary is allowed to make to the *encapsulation* oracle $\mathcal{O}_{\mathsf{sEncaps}}$. The case that $\mathsf{r} = \mathsf{s}$ is excluded since the adversary cannot make the encapsulator encapsulate only once more under the secret key e used for challenge generation. The key pair of the encapsulator is used either solely for the challenge generation or polynomially many times. More formally:

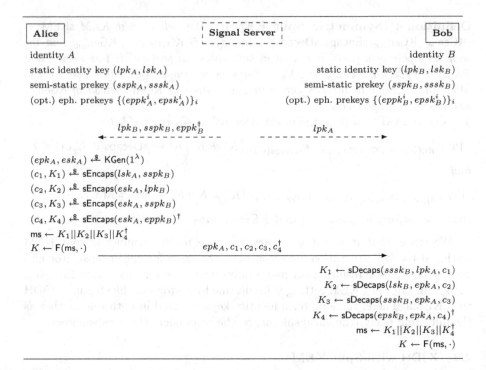

Fig. 5. Split KEM flow for the KEM-based version of Signal's X3DH handshake. Interaction with the Signal server is dashed, the optional ephemeral prekey (combination) is depicted in blue marked with †. (Color figure online)

Definition 5. *Let* sKEM = (KGen$_{dec}$, KGen$_{enc}$, sEncaps, sDecaps) *be a split KEM with key space* $\mathcal{K}$. *Let* l ∈ {n, s, m} *and* r ∈ {n, m}. *We say* sKEM *provides* lr-*indistinguishability under chosen-ciphertext attacks, or for short,* sKEM *is* lr-*IND-CCA-secure, if for every QPT adversary* $\mathcal{A}$ *the advantage* $\mathsf{Adv}_{\mathsf{sKEM},\mathcal{A}}^{\mathsf{lr\text{-}indcca}}(\lambda)$ *in winning the game* $\mathcal{G}_{\mathsf{sKEM},\mathcal{A}}^{\mathsf{lr\text{-}indcca}}(\lambda)$ *as depicted in Fig. 6 defined as*

$$\mathsf{Adv}_{\mathsf{sKEM},\mathcal{A}}^{\mathsf{lr\text{-}indcca}}(\lambda) := \left| \Pr\left[\mathcal{G}_{\mathsf{sKEM},\mathcal{A}}^{\mathsf{lr\text{-}indcca}}(\lambda) = 1 \right] - \frac{1}{2} \right|$$

is negligible in the security parameter λ.

At this point, a couple of remarks are in order to motivate the definition:

Remark 2. One may wonder, why, in contrast to the regular KEM setting, the adversary $\mathcal{A}$ is given access to an encapsulating oracle $\mathcal{O}_{\mathsf{sEncaps}}$. This oracle must be provided to the adversary since in the split KEM setting, the encapsulation algorithm sEncaps not only takes as input the public key D of the decapsulating party, but also its own secret key e. As elaborated in the next remark, in some settings $\mathcal{A}$ must however be able to learn encapsulations sEncaps(e, D') for public keys D' of its own choosing. As this operation cannot be executed by $\mathcal{A}$ itself due to the secret-key input e, an encapsulation oracle will be provided in these cases.

$\mathcal{G}_{\mathsf{sKEM},\mathcal{A}}^{\mathsf{lr\text{-}indcca}}(\lambda):$

1 $n_l, n_r \leftarrow 0$
2 $(D, d) \xleftarrow{\$} \mathsf{KGen}_{\mathsf{dec}}(1^\lambda)$
3 $(E, e) \xleftarrow{\$} \mathsf{KGen}_{\mathsf{enc}}(1^\lambda)$
4 $(c^\star, K_0^\star) \xleftarrow{\$} \mathsf{sEncaps}(e, D)$
5 $K_1^\star \xleftarrow{\$} \mathcal{K}$
6 $b \xleftarrow{\$} \{0, 1\}$
7 $b' \xleftarrow{\$} \mathcal{A}^{\mathcal{O}_{\mathsf{sDecaps}}, \mathcal{O}_{\mathsf{sEncaps}}}(D, E, c^\star, K_b^\star)$
8 **return** $[\![b' = b]\!]$

$\mathcal{O}_{\mathsf{sDecaps}}(E', c):$

9 **if** $n_l \geq l$
10   **return** $\perp$
11 $n_l = n_l + 1$
12 **if** $(E', c) = (E, c^\star)$
13   **return** $\perp$
14 $K \leftarrow \mathsf{sDecaps}(d, E', c)$
15 **return** K

$\mathcal{O}_{\mathsf{sEncaps}}(D'):$

16 **if** $n_r \geq r$
17   **return** $\perp$
18 $n_r = n_r + 1$
19 $(c, K) \xleftarrow{\$} \mathsf{sEncaps}(e, D')$
20 **if** $(D', c) = (D, c^\star)$
21   **return** $\perp$
22 **else**
23   **return** (c, K)

$\mathcal{G}_{\mathsf{sKEM},\mathcal{A}}^{\mathsf{mm\text{-}sym\text{-}indcca}}(\lambda):$

1 $(D, d) \xleftarrow{\$} \mathsf{KGen}(1^\lambda)$
2 $(E, e) \xleftarrow{\$} \mathsf{KGen}(1^\lambda)$
3 $(c^\star, K_0^\star) \xleftarrow{\$} \mathsf{sEncaps}(e, D)$
4 $K_1^\star \xleftarrow{\$} \mathcal{K}$
5 $b \xleftarrow{\$} \{0, 1\}$
6 $b' \xleftarrow{\$} \mathcal{A}^{\left[\mathcal{O}_{\mathsf{sDecaps}}^{sk}, \mathcal{O}_{\mathsf{sEncaps}}^{sk}\right]_{sk \in \{d, e\}}}(D, E, c^\star, K_b^\star)$
7 **return** $[\![b' = b]\!]$

$\mathcal{O}_{\mathsf{sEncaps}}^{sk}(pk):$

12 $(c, K) \xleftarrow{\$} \mathsf{sEncaps}(sk, pk)$
13 **if** $(pk, c) = (D, c^\star)$
14   **return** $\perp$
15 **else**
16   **return** (c, K)

$\mathcal{O}_{\mathsf{sDecaps}}^{sk}(pk, c):$

8 **if** $(sk = d \wedge (pk, c) = (E, c^\star))$
      $\vee \ (sk = e \wedge (pk, c) = (D, c^\star))$
9   **return** $\perp$
10 **else**
11   **return** $\mathsf{sDecaps}(sk, pk, c)$

Fig. 6. Top: lr-IND-CCA security of split KEMs, where $l, r \in \{n, s, m\}$. Note that we only consider $lr \in \{nn, sn, mn, sm, mm\}$ to be relevant in our setting (see Remark 3). Bottom: Definition of mm-sym-IND-CCA security of symmetric split KEMs, where the key pairs (D, d) and (E, e) are reused across roles. In numerical evaluations for l and r we naturally define $n = 0, s = 1$, and $m = \infty$.

Remark 3. We next discuss the six flavors $lr \in \{nn, sn, sm, mn, nm, mm\}$. In the following, let (D, d) and (E, e) be the respective decapsulating and encapsulating key pairs used for generating the challenge ciphertext $c^\star$ and real encapsulated key $K_0^\star$ in the lr-IND-CCA game.

– $lr = nn$: The notion of nn-IND-CCA security corresponds to the IND-CPA case in the classical setting, where the adversary is only able to learn the public keys and challenge ciphertext and key, but remains passive. Furthermore, $\mathcal{A}$ is passive and may thus not learn decapsulations of ciphertexts $c' \neq c^\star$.
– $lr = sn$: The notion of sn-IND-CCA captures that an active adversary may alter the challenge ciphertext $c^\star$ on the transit from the encapsulator to the decapsulator in a setting where no keys are reused. Thus, $\mathcal{A}$ is allowed to learn a single decapsulation $\mathsf{sDecaps}(d, E', c)$ for $(E', c) \neq (E, c^\star)$.
– $lr = sm$: The notion of sm-IND-CCA is similar to the notion of sn-IND-CCA, but here the encapsulator's key pair (E, e) is reused across multiple encapsulations. Therefore, in addition to the single query to $\mathcal{O}_{\mathsf{sDecaps}}$, $\mathcal{A}$ may now also learn multiple encapsulations $\mathsf{sEncaps}(e, D')$.

- lr = mn: The notion of mn-IND-CCA security corresponds to a reuse of the key material (D, d) on the decapsulator's side in the presence of an active adversary. Hence, the adversary is able to learn multiple decapsulations sDecaps(d, E', c) for $(E', c) \neq (E, c^*)$.
- lr = nm: The notion of nm-IND-CCA security corresponds to a reuse of the key material (E, e) on the encapsulator's side in the presence of an active adversary. Hence, the adversary is able to learn multiple encapsulations sEncaps(e, D') for $(D', c) \neq (D, c^*)$. Having l = n encodes that the adversary however cannot obtain the decapsulation of any different ciphertext $c' \neq c^*$ under D (e.g., due to c^* being authentically transmitted to the decapsulator).
- lr = mm: Finally, this notion mm-IND-CCA corresponds to reuse of keys (D, d) and (E, e) on both the decapsulator's and encapsulator's side (in fixed roles). This entails that the adversary can learn multiple related decapsulations and encapsulations.

We note the similarity to the lrPRF-ODH assumption formalization introduced in [11]. This assumption captures security of DH-based key exchanges in the presence of active adversaries in different reuse scenarios.

Security of Symmetric Split KEMs. In the following, we also provide the indistinguishability-based security notion for symmetric split KEMs. Since symmetric split KEMs inherently model key reuse across roles, we only consider the notion of mm-sym-IND-CCA to be relevant in practical settings and therefore do not define lr-sym-IND-CCA in its full generality.[2]

Definition 6. *Let* sKEM = (KGen, sEncaps, sDecaps) *be a symmetric split KEM with key space* $\mathcal{K}$*. We say* sKEM *provides symmetric mm-indistinguishability under* chosen-ciphertext attacks, *in short* sKEM *is* mm-sym-IND-CCA-*secure, if for every QPT adversary* $\mathcal{A}$ *the advantage* $\mathsf{Adv}_{\mathsf{sKEM},\mathcal{A}}^{\mathsf{mm\text{-}sym\text{-}indcca}}$ *in winning the game* $\mathcal{G}_{\mathsf{sKEM},\mathcal{A}}^{\mathsf{mm\text{-}sym\text{-}indcca}}(\lambda)$ *as depicted in Fig. 6 defined as*

$$\mathsf{Adv}_{\mathsf{sKEM},\mathcal{A}}^{\mathsf{mm\text{-}sym\text{-}indcca}}(\lambda) := \left| \Pr\left[\mathcal{G}_{\mathsf{sKEM},\mathcal{A}}^{\mathsf{mm\text{-}sym\text{-}indcca}}(\lambda) = 1 \right] - \frac{1}{2} \right|$$

is negligible in the security parameter λ.

Remark 4. One may wonder whether it is possible to turn every secure symmetric split KEM into a split KEM, and vice versa. It is easy to see that every mm-sym-IND-CCA secure symmetric split KEM is also mm-IND-CCA secure in the sense of non-symmetric split KEMs. The key generation algorithm is simply executed in fixed decapsulator and encapsulator roles and the reduction is straightforward by directly embedding the mm-sym-IND-CCA challenge into the mm-IND-CCA game and relaying the oracle queries and answers to the respective oracles. For the other direction,

---

[2] Note that the symmetric split KEM setting implies key reuse, obsoleting lr = nm. We further consider the notions lr ∈ {sn, mn, sm, nm} to be artificial as these notions encode that only some parties reuse keys across roles while other do not.

KGen'(1^λ):	sEncaps'$(sk = (d, e), pk' = (D', E'))$:
1 $(D, d) \xleftarrow{\$} \mathsf{KGen}_{dec}(1^\lambda)$	6 $(c, K) \xleftarrow{\$} \mathsf{sEncaps}(e, D')$
2 $(E, e) \xleftarrow{\$} \mathsf{KGen}_{enc}(1^\lambda)$	7 **return** (c, K)
3 $pk \leftarrow (D, E)$	sDecaps'$(sk' = (d', e'), pk = (D, E), c)$:
4 $sk \leftarrow (d, e)$	8 $K \leftarrow \mathsf{sDecaps}(d', E, c)$
5 **return** (pk, sk)	9 **return** K

Fig. 7. Transform of mm-IND-CCA-secure split KEM sKEM = $(\mathsf{KGen}_{dec}, \mathsf{KGen}_{enc}, \mathsf{sEncaps}, \mathsf{sDecaps})$ to mm-sym-IND-CCA-secure symmetric split KEM sKEM' = $(\mathsf{KGen}', \mathsf{sEncaps}', \mathsf{sDecaps}')$.

let sKEM = $(\mathsf{KGen}_{dec}, \mathsf{KGen}_{enc}, \mathsf{sEncaps}, \mathsf{sDecaps})$ be an mm-IND-CCA-secure split KEM. Then sKEM' = $(\mathsf{KGen}', \mathsf{sEncaps}', \mathsf{sDecaps}')$ as defined in Fig. 7 is a mm-sym-IND-CCA-secure symmetric split KEM. Again, this can be shown by a simple reduction, where the mm-IND-CCA reduction embeds its challenge $(D, E, c^\star, k^\star)$ in the following manner:

- The mm-sym-IND-CCA adversary $\mathcal{A}$ expects as input $(pk, pk', c^\star, K^\star)$, where pk and pk' are outputs of KGen' and thus are of the form $pk = (pk_{dec}, pk_{enc})$ and $pk' = (pk'_{dec}, pk'_{enc})$.
- $\mathcal{B}$ now sets $pk_{dec} \leftarrow D$ and $pk'_{enc} \leftarrow E$. It generates the remaining key components itself via the respective key generation algorithm.
- Oracle queries concerning d and e of $\mathcal{A}$ can simply be relayed to $\mathcal{B}$'s respective oracles. The other oracles, $\mathcal{B}$ can answer itself due to the knowledge of the secret keys.
- At some point, $\mathcal{A}$ will output its guess b' and $\mathcal{B}$ can output the same guess.

4.4 Instantiations of Split KEMs

We now turn to giving instantiations of secure split KEMs. Let us start by showing that plain lattice-based KEMs secure under the *(Ring-)Learning with Errors* assumption (R)LWE naturally fit the split KEM flow and maintain their security against passive adversaries in this setting.

nn-IND-CCA Security from (R)LWE. Figure 8 illustrates a generic (R)LWE-based key exchange viewed as a split KEM. Encapsulation on Bob's side is split into the generation of Bob's key pair as well as the final encapsulation of the shared key via the computation of an approximate shared secret and so-called *reconciliation information*, which constitutes the ciphertext. As mentioned before, these constructions are not secure against active attacks and/or key reuse in the "standard" KEM setting, and thus they naturally shouldn't achieve security above nn-IND-CCA in their split KEM formalization. We reduce the nn-IND-CCA to what is commonly referred to as the DDH-*like problem* (DDHℓ), which we state for LWE in the following. Note that the hardness of decision (R)LWE implies hardness of the DDH-like problem (cf., e.g., [10,58]).

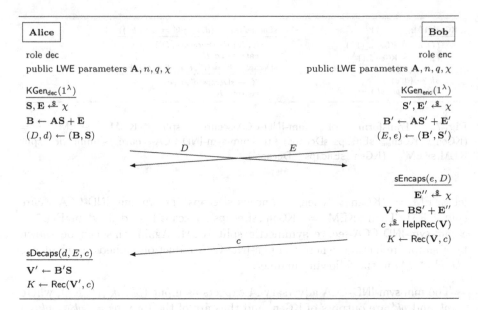

Fig. 8. Instantiation of split KEM flow with plain LWE as, e.g., in [9,27,58,64] with LWE parameters n, q, χ and fixed, public $\mathbf{A}$. The functions HelpRec and Rec aid computation of the shared secret K from the approximate shared secrets $\mathbf{V}, \mathbf{V}'$ and vary among different (R)LWE-based schemes.

Definition 7 (DDHℓ Problem). *Let $\mathbf{A}, n, q, \chi$ be LWE parameters. Given reconciliation information c, the decision Diffie–Hellman-like problem (DDHℓ) for $\mathbf{A}, q, n, \chi$ is to distinguish $(\mathbf{B}, \mathbf{B}', c, K)$ from $(\mathbf{B}, \mathbf{B}', c, K')$, where*

- $\mathbf{S}, \mathbf{S}', \mathbf{E}, \mathbf{E}', \mathbf{E}'' \xleftarrow{\$} \chi$,
- $\mathbf{B} \leftarrow \mathbf{AS} + \mathbf{E}$, *and* $\mathbf{B}' \leftarrow \mathbf{AS}' + \mathbf{E}'$,
- $\mathbf{V} \leftarrow \mathbf{BS}' + \mathbf{E}''$, *and* $c \xleftarrow{\$} \mathsf{HelpRec}(\mathbf{V})$,
- $K \leftarrow \mathsf{Rec}(\mathbf{V}, c)$ *and* $K' \xleftarrow{\$} \mathcal{K}$ *is a random element in the key space.*

For an algorithm $\mathcal{A}$ we define the distinguishing advantage to be

$$\mathsf{Adv}^{\mathsf{DDH}\ell}_{(\mathbf{A}, n, q, \chi), \mathcal{A}}(\lambda) := \big| \Pr[\mathcal{A}(\mathbf{B}, \mathbf{B}', c, K) = 1] - \Pr[\mathcal{A}(\mathbf{B}, \mathbf{B}', c, K') = 1] \big|,$$

and say DDHℓ is hard if $\mathsf{Adv}^{\mathsf{DDH}\ell}_{(\mathbf{A}, n, q, \chi), \mathcal{A}}$ is negligible in the security parameter λ.

Theorem 1. *Let $\mathsf{sKEM} = (\mathsf{KGen}_{\mathsf{dec}}, \mathsf{KGen}_{\mathsf{enc}}, \mathsf{sEncaps}, \mathsf{sDecaps})$ be a split KEM with key space $\mathcal{K}$ as in Fig. 8 for secure LWE parameters $\mathbf{A}, n, q, \chi$. Then for any QPT adversary $\mathcal{A}$ sKEM is nn-IND-CCA secure, assuming the hardness of the DDHℓ problem for $\mathbf{A}, n, q, \chi$.*

Proof. By straightforward reduction. We show that if there exists an efficient adversary $\mathcal{A}$ against the nn-IND-CCA security of sKEM, then this immediately implies an efficient solver $\mathcal{B}$ for the DDHℓ problem over the same parameter set

$\mathsf{KGen}_{\mathsf{dec}}(1^\lambda):$	$\mathsf{KGen}_{\mathsf{enc}}(1^\lambda):$	$\mathsf{sEncaps}(e, D = (X, Y)):$	$\mathsf{sDecaps}(d, E, c):$
1 $x, y \overset{\$}{\leftarrow} \mathbb{Z}_p^*$	7 $e \overset{\$}{\leftarrow} \mathbb{Z}_p^*$	10 $t \leftarrow \mathsf{G}(g^e)$	14 $t' \leftarrow \mathsf{G}(E)$
2 $X \leftarrow g^x$	8 $E \leftarrow g^e$	11 $c \leftarrow (X^t Y)^e$	15 if $E^{xt'+y} \neq c$
3 $Y \leftarrow g^y$	9 return (E, e)	12 $K \leftarrow \mathsf{H}(X^e)$	16 return $\perp$
4 $D \leftarrow (X, Y)$		13 return (c, K)	17 else
5 $d \leftarrow (x, y)$			18 $K \leftarrow \mathsf{H}(E^x)$
6 return (D, d)			19 return K

Fig. 9. Instantiation of mn-IND-CCA-secure split KEM from the KEM by Kiltz [48]. Here, $\mathsf{G} \colon \mathbb{G} \to \mathbb{Z}_p$ is a target collision resistant function defined over a cyclic group $\mathbb{G} = \langle g \rangle$ of prime order p. Furthermore, $\mathsf{H} \colon \mathbb{G} \to \{0,1\}^\lambda$ is a random hash function such that the gap hashed Diffie–Hellman assumption GapHDH is intractable in the security parameter λ wrt. $(\mathbb{G}, g, p, \mathsf{H})$.

$\mathbf{A}, n, q, \chi$. $\mathcal{B}$ receives as input a tuple $(\mathbf{B}, \mathbf{B}', c, K_b^*)$, where $\mathbf{B}, \mathbf{B}', c$ are computed as $\mathbf{B} \leftarrow \mathbf{AS} + \mathbf{E}$, $\mathbf{B}' \leftarrow \mathbf{AS}' + \mathbf{E}'$ and $c \overset{\$}{\leftarrow} \mathsf{HelpRec}(\mathbf{V})$, where $\mathbf{V} \leftarrow \mathbf{BS}' + \mathbf{E}''$a nd $\mathbf{S}, \mathbf{S}', \mathbf{E}, \mathbf{E}', \mathbf{E}'' \overset{\$}{\leftarrow} \chi$. Depending on the internal DDHℓ challenge bit $b \overset{\$}{\leftarrow} \{0,1\}$, K_b^* is either $\mathsf{Rec}(\mathbf{V}, c)$ (for $b = 0$) or a random key from the key space $\mathcal{K}$ (for $b = 1$). $\mathcal{B}$ then runs $\mathcal{A}$ on input $(\mathbf{B}, \mathbf{B}', c, K_b^*)$, i.e., $D \leftarrow B, E \leftarrow B', c^* \leftarrow c$, and K_b^*. Note that in the nn-IND-CCA case, $\mathcal{A}$ has no access to $\mathcal{O}_{\mathsf{sEncaps}}$ and $\mathcal{O}_{\mathsf{sDecaps}}$, i.e., $\mathcal{B}$ must not simulate any oracle queries. At some point, $\mathcal{A}$ will then output a guess bit b', and $\mathcal{B}$ will output the same bit. If $\mathcal{A}$ is successful in the nn-IND-CCA game it has successfully distinguished whether K_b^* is the decapsulation of c or a random key, analogous to the DDHℓ challenge. $\square$

mn-IND-CCA Security from GapHDH. For a non-trivial mn-IND-CCA secure instantiation of a split KEM we rephrase the IND-CCA secure KEM by Kiltz [48] based on the intractability of the gap hashed-DH assumption (GapHDH) as a split KEM. Informally, the GapHDH assumption says that an adversary cannot distinguish the two distributions $(g^x, g^y, \mathsf{H}(g^{xy}))$ and (g^x, g^y, R) for random exponents x, y, and random bit string R from the range of the hash function R, even when given a DDH oracle which on input (g^a, g^b, g^c) determines whether $g^c = g^{ab}$ or not.

Recall that the split KEM notion exploits that some encapsulation algorithms of KEMs perform an implicit key generation before computing the ciphertext and the encapsulated shared key. Thus, Fig. 9 is the same as the original KEM in [48], but with the key generation of the encapsulator made explicit in $\mathsf{KGen}_{\mathsf{enc}}$. Obviously, this KEM is not post-quantum secure. However, if we postulate the hardness of gap hashed-DH in the CSIDH setting, post-quantum security is achieved.[3]

Theorem 2. Let $(\mathbb{G}, g, p, \mathsf{H})$, where $\mathbb{G} = \langle g \rangle$ is a cyclic group of prime order p and $\mathsf{H} \colon \mathbb{G} \to \{0,1\}^\lambda$ is a random hash function, chosen such that GapHDH is

---

[3] Recently, de Kock [49] and Kawashima et al. [46] used a translation of the conceptually related gap Diffie–Hellman (GapDH [63]) assumption to the CSIDH setting to construct interactive, post-quantum secure key exchange protocols with tight security.

intractable in the security parameter λ. Furthermore, let $\mathsf{G}\colon \mathbb{G} \to \mathbb{Z}_p$ *be a target collision resistant function. Then* $\mathsf{sKEM} = (\mathsf{KGen}_{\mathsf{dec}}, \mathsf{KGen}_{\mathsf{enc}}, \mathsf{sEncaps}, \mathsf{sDecaps})$ *as defined in Fig. 9 is an* mn-IND-CCA *secure split KEM.*

Proof Sketch. The proof works analogous to the proof given in [48]. We suppose there exists an efficient adversary $\mathcal{A}$ against the mn-IND-CCA security of sKEM (cf. Figure 9) and show that this immediately implies an efficient adversary $\mathcal{B}$ against GapHDH. The reduction $\mathcal{B}$ gets as input a GapHDH challenge of the form (g^x, g^y, Z) and shall decide whether Z equals $\mathsf{H}(g^{xy})$ or a random bit string in $\{0,1\}^\lambda$. $\mathcal{B}$ samples $w \xleftarrow{\$} \mathbb{Z}_p^*$ and computes $t^\star \leftarrow \mathsf{G}(g^y)$ for the target collision resistant function G specified by sKEM.

$\mathcal{B}$ initiates $\mathcal{A}$ on input $(D \leftarrow (g^x, Y), E \leftarrow g^y, c^\star, Z)$, where $c^\star \leftarrow g^{yw}$ and $Y \leftarrow (g^x)^{-t^\star} g^w$. $\mathcal{A}$ may then query the decapsulation oracle $\mathcal{O}_{\mathsf{sDecaps}}$ multiple times on public encapsulator keys E' and ciphertexts c of its choice. The reduction simulates $\mathcal{O}_{\mathsf{sDecaps}}$ analogously to the decapsulation oracle in the IND-CCA proof in [48]. $\mathcal{B}$ rejects pairs (E', c) that are equal to $(E, c^\star)$. Otherwise it checks consistency of the ciphertexts corresponding to Line 15 of the decapsulation process by querying its DDH oracle on $(g^{xt}Y, E', c)$, where $t \leftarrow \mathsf{G}(E')$.

Case 1: If $t = t^\star$ but $E' \neq E$: $\mathcal{B}$ has found a collision in G (contradicting G's security) and aborts.

Case 2: If $t \neq t^\star$, $\mathcal{B}$ can compute the decapsulation K as $\mathsf{H}\left(\left(\frac{c}{E'^w}\right)^{(t-t^\star)^{-1}}\right)$ and return K to $\mathcal{A}$.

At some point $\mathcal{A}$ will output a guess b' whether $Z = \mathsf{H}(g^{xy})$ or random and $\mathcal{B}$ will output the same bit. $\qquad\square$

5   Conclusion

We have seen that split KEMs could be a way to capture DH-style key exchange flows with post-quantum security through enabling both parties to contribute to the KEM encapsulation. The starting point for this discussion and the need for a split-KEM–like notion stemmed from the fact that key exchange protocols based on DH must eventually be transitioned to post-quantum secure alternatives, which are given in the form of KEMs. For "simple" protocols, that only combine two ephemeral DH key pairs at a time, this should not pose too much of an issue. For specialized usages, such as 0-RTT modes based on DH or intricate patterns with many different DH combinations as in the initial key agreement of Signal, involving static keys, we have seen that standard KEMs are often inadequate.

   We thus introduced the notion of split key encapsulation mechanisms. However, a major challenge remains, when it comes to showing that known KEMs fulfill the split KEM notion with reuse of keys on both sides: while, e.g., many passively-secure lattice-based KEMs are a prime example of the structure of split KEMs (since their encapsulation can be divided up into key generation and key agreement on the encapsulator's side), we know that these are not secure when keys are reused. A promising candidate are constructions that replace the DH operations by CSIDH [12]. However, to achieve full-fledged key exchange security, interactive hardness assumptions such as the gap (hashed) DH assumption, strong DH assumption, or PRF-ODH are needed. We see it as an open problem to define these assumptions in the CSIDH setting and establish their intractability. Only answers to these questions can truly establish CSIDH as a viable building block for key exchange protocols.

Finally, it remains an open question to develop post-quantum solutions that support static-static key exchange, or that can accommodate reversed message flows; in other words, it is an open question to develop strongly-secure post-quantum constructions that have the same flexibility as Diffie–Hellman-based primitives. We believe the notion of split KEMs to be an adequate starting point to this exploration.

Acknowledgements. We thank Håkon Jacobsen for helpful discussions in the early phase of this work.

Marc Fischlin and Christian Janson have been (partially) funded by the Deutsche Forschungsgemeinschaft (DFG) – SFB 1119 – 236615297. Felix Günther has been supported in part by Research Fellowship grant GU 1859/1-1 of the German Research Foundation (DFG) and National Science Foundation (NSF) grants CNS-1526801 and CNS-1717640. Douglas Stebila has been supported in part by Natural Sciences and Engineering Research Council (NSERC) of Canada Discovery grant RGPIN-2016-05146 and a NSERC Discovery Accelerator Supplement.

References

1. Abdalla, M., Bellare, M., Rogaway, P.: The oracle Diffie-Hellman assumptions and an analysis of DHIES. In: Naccache, D. (ed.) CT-RSA 2001. LNCS, vol. 2020, pp. 143–158. Springer, Heidelberg (2001). https://doi.org/10.1007/3-540-45353-9_12
2. Alwen, J., Coretti, S., Dodis, Y.: The double ratchet: security notions, proofs, and modularization for the signal protocol. In: Ishai, Y., Rijmen, V. (eds.) EUROCRYPT 2019, Part I. LNCS, vol. 11476, pp. 129–158. Springer, Cham (2019). https://doi.org/10.1007/978-3-030-17653-2_5
3. Azarderakhsh, R., Jao, D., Leonardi, C.: Post-quantum static-static key agreement using multiple protocol instances. In: Adams, C., Camenisch, J. (eds.) SAC 2017. LNCS, vol. 10719, pp. 45–63. Springer, Cham (2018). https://doi.org/10.1007/978-3-319-72565-9_3
4. Basso, A., Kutas, P., Merz, S.-P., Petit, C., Weitkämper, C.: On adaptive attacks against Jao-Urbanik's isogeny-based protocol. In: Nitaj, A., Youssef, A. (eds.) AFRICACRYPT 2020. LNCS, vol. 12174, pp. 195–213. Springer, Cham (2020). https://doi.org/10.1007/978-3-030-51938-4_10
5. Bauer, A., Gilbert, H., Renault, G., Rossi, M.: Assessment of the key-reuse resilience of NewHope. In: Matsui, M. (ed.) CT-RSA 2019. LNCS, vol. 11405, pp. 272–292. Springer, Cham (2019). https://doi.org/10.1007/978-3-030-12612-4_14
6. Bergsma, F., Dowling, B., Kohlar, F., Schwenk, J., Stebila, D.: Multi-ciphersuite security of the Secure Shell (SSH) protocol. In: Ahn, G.J., Yung, M., Li, N. (eds.) ACM CCS 2014, pp. 369–381. ACM Press, November 2014
7. Boneh, D., et al.: Multiparty non-interactive key exchange and more from isogenies on elliptic curves. J. Math. Cryptol. 14(1), 5–14 (2020). https://www.degruyter.com/view/journals/jmc/14/1/article-p5.xml

8. Bonnetain, X., Schrottenloher, A.: Quantum security analysis of CSIDH. In: Canteaut, A., Ishai, Y. (eds.) EUROCRYPT 2020, Part II. LNCS, vol. 12106, pp. 493–522. Springer, Cham (2020). https://doi.org/10.1007/978-3-030-45724-2_17

9. Bos, J.W., et al.: Frodo: take off the ring! Practical, quantum-secure key exchange from LWE. In: Weippl, E.R., Katzenbeisser, S., Kruegel, C., Myers, A.C., Halevi, S. (eds.) ACM CCS 2016, pp. 1006–1018. ACM Press, October 2016

10. Bos, J.W., Costello, C., Naehrig, M., Stebila, D.: Post-quantum key exchange for the TLS protocol from the ring learning with errors problem. In: 2015 IEEE Symposium on Security and Privacy, pp. 553–570. IEEE Computer Society Press, May 2015

11. Brendel, J., Fischlin, M., Günther, F., Janson, C.: PRF-ODH: relations, instantiations, and impossibility results. In: Katz, J., Shacham, H. (eds.) CRYPTO 2017, Part III. LNCS, vol. 10403, pp. 651–681. Springer, Cham (2017). https://doi.org/10.1007/978-3-319-63697-9_22

12. Castryck, W., Lange, T., Martindale, C., Panny, L., Renes, J.: CSIDH: an efficient post-quantum commutative group action. In: Peyrin, T., Galbraith, S. (eds.) ASIACRYPT 2018, Part III. LNCS, vol. 11274, pp. 395–427. Springer, Cham (2018). https://doi.org/10.1007/978-3-030-03332-3_15

13. Castryck, W., Sotáková, J., Vercauteren, F.: Breaking the decisional Diffie-Hellman problem for class group actions using genus theory. In: Micciancio, D., Ristenpart, T. (eds.) CRYPTO 2020, Part II. LNCS, vol. 12171, pp. 92–120. Springer, Cham (2020). https://doi.org/10.1007/978-3-030-56880-1_4

14. Cohn-Gordon, K., Cremers, C.J.F., Dowling, B., Garratt, L., Stebila, D.: A formal security analysis of the signal messaging protocol. In: IEEE European Symposium on Security and Privacy, EuroS&P 2017, pp. 451–466 (2017)

15. Cohn-Gordon, K., Cremers, C.J.F., Dowling, B., Garratt, L., Stebila, D.: A formal security analysis of key establishment in the Signal messaging protocol. J. Cryptol. **33**, 1914–1983 (2020)

16. Cramer, R., Shoup, V.: Design and analysis of practical public-key encryption schemes secure against adaptive chosen ciphertext attack. SIAM J. Comput. **33**(1), 167–226 (2004)

17. Cremers, C., Feltz, M.: Beyond eCK: perfect forward secrecy under actor compromise and ephemeral-key reveal. In: Foresti, S., Yung, M., Martinelli, F. (eds.) ESORICS 2012. LNCS, vol. 7459, pp. 734–751. Springer, Heidelberg (2012). https://doi.org/10.1007/978-3-642-33167-1_42

18. Crockett, E., Paquin, C., Stebila, D.: Prototyping post-quantum and hybrid key exchange and authentication in TLS and SSH. In: NIST 2nd Post-Quantum Cryptography Standardization Conference 2019, August 2019

19. David Jao, R.A., et al.: Supersingular isogeny key encapsulation, April 2019. https://sike.org/

20. Dierks, T., Rescorla, E.: The Transport Layer Security (TLS) Protocol Version 1.2. RFC 5246 (Proposed Standard), August 2008. https://www.rfc-editor.org/rfc/rfc5246.txt

21. Diffie, W., Hellman, M.E.: New directions in cryptography. IEEE Trans. Inf. Theory **22**(6), 644–654 (1976)

22. Ding, J., Alsayigh, S., Saraswathy, R.V., Fluhrer, S., Lin, X.: Leakage of signal function with reused keys in RLWE key exchange. In: 2017 IEEE International Conference on Communications (ICC), pp. 1–6 (2017)

23. Ding, J., Branco, P., Schmitt, K.: Key exchange and authenticated key exchange with reusable keys based on RLWE assumption. Cryptology ePrint Archive, Report 2019/665 (2019). https://eprint.iacr.org/2019/665

24. Ding, J., Cheng, C., Qin, Y.: A simple key reuse attack on LWE and ring LWE encryption schemes as key encapsulation mechanisms (KEMs). Cryptology ePrint Archive, Report 2019/271 (2019). https://eprint.iacr.org/2019/271

25. Ding, J., Deaton, J., Schmidt, K., Vishakha, Zhang, Z.: A simple and practical key reuse attack on NTRU cryptosystem. Cryptology ePrint Archive, Report 2019/1022 (2019). https://eprint.iacr.org/2019/1022

26. Ding, J., Fluhrer, S., Rv, S.: Complete attack on RLWE key exchange with reused keys, without signal leakage. In: Susilo, W., Yang, G. (eds.) ACISP 2018. LNCS, vol. 10946, pp. 467–486. Springer, Cham (2018). https://doi.org/10.1007/978-3-319-93638-3_27

27. Ding, J., Xie, X., Lin, X.: A simple provably secure key exchange scheme based on the learning with errors problem. Cryptology ePrint Archive, Report 2012/688 (2012). http://eprint.iacr.org/2012/688

28. Dobson, S., Galbraith, S.D., LeGrow, J., Ti, Y.B., Zobernig, L.: An adaptive attack on 2-SIDH. Cryptology ePrint Archive, Report 2019/890 (2019). https://eprint.iacr.org/2019/890

29. Dobson, S., Li, T., Zobernig, L.: A note on a static SIDH protocol. Cryptology ePrint Archive, Report 2019/1244 (2019). https://eprint.iacr.org/2019/1244

30. Dowling, B., Fischlin, M., Günther, F., Stebila, D.: A cryptographic analysis of the TLS 1.3 handshake protocol candidates. In: Ray, I., Li, N., Kruegel, C. (eds.) ACM CCS 2015, pp. 1197–1210. ACM Press, October 2015

31. Dowling, B., Fischlin, M., Günther, F., Stebila, D.: A cryptographic analysis of the TLS 1.3 handshake protocol. J. Cryptol. (2020)

32. Drucker, N., Gueron, S.: Continuous key agreement with reduced bandwidth. In: Dolev, S., Hendler, D., Lodha, S., Yung, M. (eds.) CSCML 2019. LNCS, vol. 11527, pp. 33–46. Springer, Cham (2019). https://doi.org/10.1007/978-3-030-20951-3_3

33. Duits, I.: The post-quantum signal protocol: secure chat in a quantum world. Master's thesis, University of Twente, February 2019. http://essay.utwente.nl/77239/

34. Fischlin, M., Günther, F.: Multi-stage key exchange and the case of Google's QUIC protocol. In: Ahn, G.J., Yung, M., Li, N. (eds.) ACM CCS 2014, pp. 1193–1204. ACM Press, November 2014

35. Fluhrer, S.: Cryptanalysis of ring-LWE based key exchange with key share reuse. Cryptology ePrint Archive, Report 2016/085 (2016). http://eprint.iacr.org/2016/085

36. Fujisaki, E., Okamoto, T.: Secure integration of asymmetric and symmetric encryption schemes. In: Wiener, M. (ed.) CRYPTO 1999. LNCS, vol. 1666, pp. 537–554. Springer, Heidelberg (1999). https://doi.org/10.1007/3-540-48405-1_34

37. Fujisaki, E., Okamoto, T.: Secure integration of asymmetric and symmetric encryption schemes. J. Cryptol. 26(1), 80–101 (2013)

38. Galbraith, S.D., Petit, C., Shani, B., Ti, Y.B.: On the security of supersingular isogeny cryptosystems. In: Cheon, J.H., Takagi, T. (eds.) ASIACRYPT 2016, Part I. LNCS, vol. 10031, pp. 63–91. Springer, Heidelberg (2016). https://doi.org/10.1007/978-3-662-53887-6_3

39. Gao, X., Ding, J., Li, L., Liu, J.: Practical randomized RLWE-based key exchange against signal leakage attack. IEEE Trans. Comput. 67(11), 1584–1593 (2018)

40. Greuet, A., Montoya, S., Renault, G.: Attack on LAC key exchange in misuse situation. Cryptology ePrint Archive, Report 2020/063 (2020). https://eprint.iacr.org/2020/063

41. Hofheinz, D., Hövelmanns, K., Kiltz, E.: A modular analysis of the Fujisaki-Okamoto transformation. In: Kalai, Y., Reyzin, L. (eds.) TCC 2017, Part I. LNCS, vol. 10677, pp. 341–371. Springer, Cham (2017). https://doi.org/10.1007/978-3-319-70500-2_12

42. Hülsing, A., Ning, K.C., Schwabe, P., Weber, F., Zimmermann, P.R.: Post-quantum wireguard. Cryptology ePrint Archive, Report 2020/379 (2020). https://eprint.iacr.org/2020/379

43. Jager, T., Kohlar, F., Schäge, S., Schwenk, J.: On the security of TLS-DHE in the standard model. In: Safavi-Naini, R., Canetti, R. (eds.) CRYPTO 2012. LNCS, vol. 7417, pp. 273–293. Springer, Heidelberg (2012). https://doi.org/10.1007/978-3-642-32009-5_17

44. Jao, D., De Feo, L.: Towards quantum-resistant cryptosystems from supersingular elliptic curve isogenies. In: Yang, B.-Y. (ed.) PQCrypto 2011. LNCS, vol. 7071, pp. 19–34. Springer, Heidelberg (2011). https://doi.org/10.1007/978-3-642-25405-5_2

45. Katsumata, S., Kwiatkowski, K., Pintore, F., Prest, T.: Scalable ciphertext compression techniques for post-quantum KEMs and their applications. In: ASIACRYPT 2020 (2020, to appear). Available as Cryptology ePrint Archive, Report 2020/1107. https://eprint.iacr.org/2020/1107

46. Kawashima, T., Takashima, K., Aikawa, Y., Takagi, T.: An efficient authenticated key exchange from random self-reducibility on CSIDH. Cryptology ePrint Archive, Report 2020/1178 (2020). https://eprint.iacr.org/2020/1178

47. Kayacan, S.: A note on the static-static key agreement protocol from supersingular isogenies. Cryptology ePrint Archive, Report 2019/815 (2019). https://eprint.iacr.org/2019/815

48. Kiltz, E.: Chosen-ciphertext secure key-encapsulation based on gap hashed Diffie-Hellman. In: Okamoto, T., Wang, X. (eds.) PKC 2007. LNCS, vol. 4450, pp. 282–297. Springer, Heidelberg (2007). https://doi.org/10.1007/978-3-540-71677-8_19

49. de Kock, B., Gjøsteen, K., Veroni, M.: Practical isogeny-based key-exchange with optimal tightness. In: SAC 2020 (2020, to appear). Available as Cryptology ePrint Archive, Report 2020/1165. https://eprint.iacr.org/2020/1165

50. Krawczyk, H.: HMQV: a high-performance secure Diffie-Hellman protocol. In: Shoup, V. (ed.) CRYPTO 2005. LNCS, vol. 3621, pp. 546–566. Springer, Heidelberg (2005). https://doi.org/10.1007/11535218_33

51. Krawczyk, H., Paterson, K.G., Wee, H.: On the security of the TLS protocol: a systematic analysis. In: Canetti, R., Garay, J.A. (eds.) CRYPTO 2013, Part I. LNCS, vol. 8042, pp. 429–448. Springer, Heidelberg (2013). https://doi.org/10.1007/978-3-642-40041-4_24

52. Krawczyk, H., Wee, H.: The OPTLS protocol and TLS 1.3. In: 2016 IEEE European Symposium on Security and Privacy, EuroS&P 2016, pp. 81–96. IEEE, Saarbrücken, 21–24 March 2016

53. Kwiatkowski, K., Valenta, L.: The TLS Post-Quantum Experiment. The Cloudflare Blog, October 2019. https://blog.cloudflare.com/the-tls-post-quantum-experiment/

54. LaMacchia, B., Lauter, K., Mityagin, A.: Stronger security of authenticated key exchange. In: Susilo, W., Liu, J.K., Mu, Y. (eds.) ProvSec 2007. LNCS, vol. 4784, pp. 1–16. Springer, Heidelberg (2007). https://doi.org/10.1007/978-3-540-75670-5_1

55. Langley, A.: CECPQ1 results. Imperial Violet, Blog, November 2016. https://www.imperialviolet.org/2016/11/28/cecpq1.html

56. Langley, A.: CECPQ2. Imperial Violet, Blog, December 2018. https://www.imperialviolet.org/2018/12/12/cecpq2.html

57. Langley, A., Chang, W.T.: QUIC Crypto, December 2016. https://docs.google. com/document/d/1g5nIXAIkN_Y-7XJW5K45IblHd_L2f5LTaDUDwvZ5L6g/. Revision 06 Dec 2016

58. Lindner, R., Peikert, C.: Better key sizes (and attacks) for LWE-based encryption. In: Kiayias, A. (ed.) CT-RSA 2011. LNCS, vol. 6558, pp. 319–339. Springer, Heidelberg (2011). https://doi.org/10.1007/978-3-642-19074-2_21

59. Liu, C., Zheng, Z., Zou, G.: Key reuse attack on NewHope key exchange protocol. In: Lee, K. (ed.) ICISC 2018. LNCS, vol. 11396, pp. 163–176. Springer, Cham (2019). https://doi.org/10.1007/978-3-030-12146-4_11

60. Marlinspike, M., Perrin, T.: The X3DH key agreement protocol, November 2016. https://signal.org/docs/specifications/x3dh/

61. National Institute of Standards and Technology (NIST): Post-quantum cryptography, 19 August 2015. https://csrc.nist.gov/projects/post-quantum-cryptography

62. Okada, S., Wang, Y., Takagi, T.: Improving key mismatch attack on NewHope with fewer queries. In: Liu, J.K., Cui, H. (eds.) ACISP 2020. LNCS, vol. 12248, pp. 505–524. Springer, Cham (2020). https://doi.org/10.1007/978-3-030-55304-3_26

63. Okamoto, T., Pointcheval, D.: The gap-problems: a new class of problems for the security of cryptographic schemes. In: Kim, K. (ed.) PKC 2001. LNCS, vol. 1992, pp. 104–118. Springer, Heidelberg (2001). https://doi.org/10.1007/3-540-44586-2_8

64. Peikert, C.: Lattice cryptography for the internet. In: Mosca, M. (ed.) PQCrypto 2014. LNCS, vol. 8772, pp. 197–219. Springer, Cham (2014). https://doi.org/10.1007/978-3-319-11659-4_12

65. Peikert, C.: He Gives C-Sieves on the CSIDH. In: Canteaut, A., Ishai, Y. (eds.) EUROCRYPT 2020, Part II. LNCS, vol. 12106, pp. 463–492. Springer, Cham (2020). https://doi.org/10.1007/978-3-030-45724-2_16

66. Perrin, T.: The Noise protocol framework. https://noiseprotocol.org/

67. Qin, Y., Cheng, C., Ding, J.: A complete and optimized key mismatch attack on NIST candidate NewHope. In: Sako, K., Schneider, S., Ryan, P.Y.A. (eds.) ESORICS 2019, Part II. LNCS, vol. 11736, pp. 504–520. Springer, Cham (2019). https://doi.org/10.1007/978-3-030-29962-0_24

68. QUIC, a multiplexed stream transport over UDP. https://www.chromium.org/quic

69. Rescorla, E.: The Transport Layer Security (TLS) Protocol Version 1.3. RFC 8446 (Proposed Standard), August 2018. https://www.rfc-editor.org/rfc/rfc8446.txt

70. Schwabe, P., Stebila, D., Wiggers, T.: Post-quantum TLS without handshake signatures. Cryptology ePrint Archive, Report 2020/534 (2020). https://eprint.iacr.org/2020/534

71. Shoup, V.: A Proposal for an ISO Standard for Public Key Encryption (version 2.1), December 2001. https://www.shoup.net/papers/iso-2_1.pdf

72. Signal protocol: Technical documentation. https://whispersystems.org/docs/

73. Stebila, D., Mosca, M.: Post-quantum key exchange for the internet and the open quantum safe project. In: Avanzi, R., Heys, H. (eds.) SAC 2016. LNCS, vol. 10532, pp. 14–37. Springer, Cham (2017). https://doi.org/10.1007/978-3-319-69453-5_2

74. Urbanik, D., Jao, D.: New techniques for SIDH-based NIKE. J. Math. Cryptol. **14**(1), 120–128 (2020). https://www.degruyter.com/view/journals/jmc/14/1/article-p120.xml

75. Ustaoglu, B.: Obtaining a secure and efficient key agreement protocol from (H)MQV and NAXOS. Des. Codes Crypt. **46**(3), 329–342 (2008)

76. Xue, H., Lu, X., Li, B., Liang, B., He, J.: Understanding and constructing AKE via double-key key encapsulation mechanism. In: Peyrin, T., Galbraith, S. (eds.) ASIACRYPT 2018, Part II. LNCS, vol. 11273, pp. 158–189. Springer, Cham (2018). https://doi.org/10.1007/978-3-030-03329-3_6

77. Yao, A.C.C., Zhao, Y.: OAKE: a new family of implicitly authenticated Diffie-Hellman protocols. In: Sadeghi, A.R., Gligor, V.D., Yung, M. (eds.) ACM CCS 2013, pp. 1113–1128. ACM Press, November 2013

78. Ylonen, T., Lonvick, C.: The Secure Shell (SSH) Transport Layer Protocol. RFC 4253 (Proposed Standard), January 2005. https://www.rfc-editor.org/rfc/rfc4253.txt

Trapdoor DDH Groups from Pairings and Isogenies

Péter Kutas[1], Christophe Petit[1,2], and Javier Silva[3(✉)]

[1] University of Birmingham, Birmingham, UK
p.kutas@bham.ac.uk
[2] Université libre de Bruxelles, Brussels, Belgium
christophe.petit@ulb.be
[3] Universitat Pompeu Fabra, Barcelona, Spain
javier.silva@upf.edu

Abstract. Trapdoor DDH groups are an appealing cryptographic primitive introduced by Dent–Galbraith (ANTS 2006), where DDH instances are hard to solve unless provided with additional information (i.e., a trapdoor). In this paper, we introduce a new trapdoor DDH group construction using pairings and isogenies of supersingular elliptic curves, and present two instantiations of it. The construction solves all shortcomings of previous constructions as identified by Seurin (RSA 2013). We also present partial attacks on a previous construction due to Dent–Galbraith, and we provide a formal security definition of the related notion of "trapdoor pairings".

Keywords: Elliptic curve cryptography · Pairings · Isogenies · Trapdoor DDH

1 Introduction

The hardness of computing discrete logarithms and related problems (including the computational and decisional Diffie–Hellman problems in various groups) has supported the security of numerous cryptographic protocols for more than 40 years. While the decisional Diffie–Hellman (DDH) problem can be solved by solving a discrete logarithm problem, the converse is not known to be true. There are instances of groups equipped with bilinear pairings, where the discrete logarithm problem is believed to be hard but the decisional Diffie–Hellman problem can be solved efficiently.

Trapdoor DDH groups are a cryptographic primitive introduced by Dent–Galbraith in 2006 [17]. Formally, a trapdoor DDH group involves *two* descriptions of a single group. With either description of the group, the usual group operations, including inversion, can be computed efficiently, and solving the discrete logarithm problem and computational Diffie–Hellman problem must be hard. Crucially, the *decisional* Diffie–Hellman problem must also be hard to solve when provided only with the first description of the group, and easy with

© Springer Nature Switzerland AG 2021
O. Dunkelman et al. (Eds.): SAC 2020, LNCS 12804, pp. 431–450, 2021.
https://doi.org/10.1007/978-3-030-81652-0_17

the second description. The second description can then be used as a trapdoor in a cryptographic protocol, conferring to its owner the power to solve DDH instances.

To the best of our knowledge, there are only two constructions of trapdoor DDH groups in the literature. Dent–Galbraith [17] use supersingular elliptic curves with equations $y^2 = x^3 + x$ defined over RSA rings $\mathbb{Z}_N$. Another construction by Dent–Galbraith was broken in [31]. Seurin [35] uses the group of quadratic residues modulo N^2 where again N is an RSA modulus.

Two more constructions based on the RSA and factoring assumptions are provided by Seurin [35], but these are *static* trapdoor DDH group constructions, where the trapdoor can only solve DDH challenges involving a fixed pair of group elements g, g^x.

Trapdoor DDH groups have been used by Dent–Galbraith to build an identification scheme [17], and by Prabhakaran–Xue to build statistically hiding sets [34]. Seurin further constructs convertible undeniable signature schemes with delegatable verification from *static* trapdoor DDH groups [35]. In his paper, Seurin identifies several features that existing constructions (including his) are lacking, and which could be key to enable "powerful applications of trapdoor DDH groups" [35, Section 1.4].

Our Contributions. We provide a new construction of trapdoor DDH groups which has all the features identified by Seurin. Our construction uses a *random* supersingular curve with a large prime as the group order, and an isogeny between this curve and a curve with a known distortion map as a trapdoor. Security relies on the hardness of solving the Decisional Diffie–Hellman problem on a random supersingular elliptic curve, and the hardness of solving the Computational Diffie–Hellman problem when the trapdoor is known. Interestingly, hardness of DDH implies both hardness of the discrete logarithm problem on the curve and hardness of computing an isogeny between a random supersingular curve and a "special" one, with a known distortion map.[1] Our construction solves all open problems of Seurin [35]: the group has public and prime order, hashing onto the group is efficient, and the trapdoor DDH solver always outputs the correct result.

We also provide attacks on the parameters suggested by Dent–Galbraith in their remaining construction, when used in specific applications. We explain how to increase the parameters or modify the scheme to thwart the attack. While these counter-measures defeat both our attacks and previous attacks, we argue that choosing secure parameters for this construction remains a delicate task.

As an additional contribution, we formally define a notion of *trapdoor pairings* which was only implicit in the work of Dent–Galbraith. A trapdoor pairing construction immediately leads to a trapdoor DDH construction, and our new trapdoor DDH groups are in fact trapdoor pairings. However by using trapdoor pairings we are able to improve the efficiency of an identification protocol

---

[1] We stress that DDH is easy for a supersingular curve with a known distortion map, but finding a distortion map on a random curve is believed to be a hard problem [18,33]. See also Sect. 2.1.

provided in [17] as an application, while relying on a seemingly weaker computational assumption.

Other Constructions Based on Pairings and Isogenies. Pairings and isogeny problems have both considerable applications in cryptography, and since they are both built on elliptic curves, combining them to construct further protocols is a natural idea.

The first work in that direction is due to Koshiba and Takashima [27]. They provided a framework and security definitions for cryptographic protocols involving pairings and isogenies, called *isogenous pairing groups*. They also present key-policy attribute-based encryption schemes based on their framework. We remark that our trapdoor DDH construction does not entirely fit in Koshiba and Takashima's framework: in our construction the pairing is "hidden" and hard to evaluate, whereas in their framework the pairing can be publicly evaluated. Besides, the framework implicitly uses an asymmetric pairing $e : \mathbb{G}_1 \times \mathbb{G}_2 \to \mathbb{G}_T$ with $\mathbb{G}_1 \neq \mathbb{G}_2$, while we use a symmetric pairing. Finally, we remark that their framework seems to be built with the publicly computable Weil pairing in mind (the Weil pairing is degenerate when $\mathbb{G}_1 = \mathbb{G}_2$), and our construction uses a modified Weil pairing instead.

More recently, De Feo, Masson, Petit and Sanso have constructed a Verifiable Delay Function (VDF) that also uses both pairings and isogenies [15]. Similar ideas have been used to build a Delay Encryption scheme [4]. As in our new trapdoor DDH group, the VDF and Delay Encryption use an isogeny from a "special" supersingular elliptic curve to another "random" curve, and a pairing on the image curve. These constructions crucially differ from ours as their isogeny is not secret and it is of extremely large degree (and of course VDFs, Delay Encryption schemes and Trapdoor DDH groups are different primitives). The pairing used is also the Weil pairing, so it cannot be used to solve DDH instances.

Additionally, the patent [28] presents various trapdoor DDH constructions. The first few are based on the ideas of Dent and Galbraith [17], but the last one actually uses a secret isogeny to produce a trapdoor DDH mechanism. The high-level idea is similar to ours, in particular using an isogeny as the trapdoor information used to compute a pairing. However, they do not provide details on a concrete instantiation, or formal security and efficiency analyses.

Outline. The remaining of this paper is organized as follows. In Sect. 2 we provide preliminary background on elliptic curves, computational assumptions, trapdoor DDH groups, and previous constructions. In Sect. 3 we describe our new trapdoor DDH group and we introduce the definition of trapdoor pairing, which the new construction satisfies, and briefly discuss applications. In Sect. 4, we describe two concrete instantiations of our construction. We also analyze security and suggest concrete parameters. We describe our attacks on Dent–Galbraith's first construction in Sect. 5, and we conclude the paper in Sect. 6.

2   Preliminaries

For a detailed exposition of the mathematics of elliptic curves, see [36].

2.1   Computational Assumptions

We first recall the definitions of the discrete logarithm, the decisional and computational Diffie–Hellmann problems. In the following, we consider groups written with multiplicative notation.

Let $\mathbb{G}$ be a group. The discrete logarithm problem (DLP) is the following: Given $g, h \in \mathbb{G}$, find x (if one exists) such that $g^x = h$. In the computational Diffie–Hellmann problem (CDH) one is given a tuple $(g, g^a, g^b) \in \mathbb{G}^3$ and has to compute g^{ab}. In the decisional Diffie–Hellmann problem the input is a quadruple $(g, g^a, g^b, z) \in \mathbb{G}^4$ and one has to decide whether $z = g^{ab}$. We call a tuple of the form (g, g^a, g^b, g^{ab}) a DDH tuple.

We also define computational problems related to isogenies between elliptic curves.

Definition 1. *Let E_1 and E_2 be two uniformly random supersingular elliptic curves defined over a finite field $\mathbb{F}_q$. Let ℓ be a prime number and e be a positive integer. The* isogeny problem *is to compute an isogeny ϕ between E_1 and E_2 of degree ℓ^e.*

Remark 1. As usually ℓ^e is large, one also asks for an efficient representation of the isogeny, i.e., as a composition of low degree isogenies (and not as a pair of rational functions).

Definition 2. *Let E be a uniformly random supersingular elliptic curve defined over a finite field $\mathbb{F}_q$. The* endomorphism ring problem *asks for a set of endomorphisms of E which generate the endomorphism ring as an abelian group.*

We briefly discuss these computational problems in the context of supersingular elliptic curves.

Discrete Logarithm Problem. Menezes-Okamoto-Vanstone [30] proposed the following method (referred to as MOV reduction) for reducing the discrete logarithm problem on elliptic curves to the discrete logarithm problem on finite fields. Let E be an elliptic curve defined over a finite field $\mathbb{F}_q$ and let P be a point of order n. Let Q be a point from the subgroup generated by P. In order to find x such that $Q = xP$ the idea is to find the smallest integer k (called the embedding degree) for which $E[n] \subseteq E(\mathbb{F}_{q^k})$ and to use the Weil pairing on E to reduce the elliptic curve discrete logarithm instance to a discrete logarithm instance on $\mathbb{F}_{q^k}$. For general elliptic curves, this reduction does not run in polynomial time as k may be too large. However, for supersingular curves it can be proven that $k \leq 6$ and the reduction does run in polynomial time [30]. This means that for supersingular curves there exist subexponential algorithms for solving the discrete logarithm problem.

Isogeny and Endomorphism Ring Computation Problems. For curves over $\mathbb{F}_{p^2}$, the only known algorithms for the isogeny problem run in exponential time, even with the use of a quantum computer. The running time of the best known algorithm is $\tilde{O}(d^{\frac{1}{2}})$ (see [19]) where d is the degree of the desired isogeny. For supersingular curves defined over $\mathbb{F}_p$, there is a quantum algorithm that runs in time $L_p(1/2)$ [2] (for ordinary curves there is an $L_p(1/2)$ algorithm in [6] but the best classical algorithm [16] is still exponential. The computational hardness of these problems has been exploited in various protocols [5,13–15,21]. The complexity of the problem does not change if one of the two curves is fixed.

The endomorphism computation problem is closely related to the isogeny problem, as shown in [18,33]. Computing distortion maps (non-scalar endomorphisms) seems to be as hard as the endomorphism ring problem as a small number of endomorphisms will in general generate the full endomorphism ring, unless they satisfy some exceptional conditions. More precisely, one can use a variant of Schoof's point counting algorithm as in Kohel [26, Theorem 81] to compute the Gram matrix associated to a set of maps, and deduce an abstract representation of the endomorphism ring as a $\mathbb{Z}$-basis of elements of $B_{p,\infty}$ (the quaternion algebra ramified at p and at infinity).

While the endomorphism ring computation problem is believed to be hard for random curves, the problem is actually easy for some "special" curves such as the curve $y^2 = x^3 + x$, or more generally any curve defined over $\mathbb{F}_p$ with a small degree non-scalar endomorphism. We note that in [22], an algorithm to produce distortion maps of elliptic curves is given. However, it uses the CM method, which is efficient only for small discriminants. The supersingular curves constructed this way are therefore exactly the "special" curves above. Note that by taking a random isogeny walk we have a negligible probability that the final curve is a special one.

Decisional Diffie–Hellmann Problem. On special curves, and more generally when we know a distortion map for a curve, we can build a pairing for which $e(P, P) \neq 1$. In such cases we can solve the DDH problem on the curve using the observation that $A = aP$, $B = bP$, $Z = abP$ for some a, b if and only if $e(A, B) = e(Z, P)$.

It is somewhat folklore belief that the Decisional Diffie–Hellman problem is easy for all supersingular curves (see e.g. [37, Theorem 6]), however we stress that this is only known to hold when provided with a distortion map for the curve. Without this distortion map, the Weil pairing is useless to solve the DDH problem on a curve since $e(P, xP) = 1$ for any x, and DDH remains a plausible hard problem. As discussed above, computing a distortion map for a uniformly random curve is also believed to be hard.

Computational Diffie–Hellman Problem. While a pairing and distortion maps together can help to solve the Decisional Diffie–Hellman problem on a curve, the Computational Diffie–Hellman problem remains a plausible hard problem in this context. When DDH is easy, the assumption that CDH is hard has been called the gap Diffie–Hellman assumption in the cryptography literature [3].

2.2   Trapdoor DDH Groups

Trapdoor DDH groups were first introduced by Dent–Galbraith [17]. Intuitively, trapdoor DDH groups are a cryptographic construction in which knowledge of the trapdoor gives its owner the ability to solve DDH instances which are otherwise intractable. Formal definitions have appeared in Dent–Galbraith [17], Seurin [35] and Prabhakaran–Xue [34], with different security requirements in all papers. Here we recall the definition provided in [35].

We denote by $\mathsf{DDH}_{\mathbb{G}}$ the set of DDH tuples of a group $\mathbb{G}$. We shorten deterministic polynomial time to DPT and probabilistic polynomial time to PPT. We say that a function $f(\lambda)$ is negligible, and write $f(\lambda) \approx 0$, if for any positive polynomial $p(\lambda)$ there exists an integer $N > 0$ such that for all $\lambda > N$ we have $f(\lambda) < \frac{1}{p(\lambda)}$. We denote the order of $g \in \mathbb{G}$ by $|g|$.

Definition 3. *A trapdoor DDH group is a pair of algorithms* (Gen, Solve) *with the following properties. The trapdoor DDH group generator algorithm* Gen *is a PPT algorithm which takes as input a security parameter* 1^λ *and outputs a tuple* $(\mathbb{G}, P, \tau)$ *where* $\mathbb{G}$ *is a group,* $P \in \mathbb{G}$ *is a group element of order* $2^{\Theta(\lambda)}$, *and* τ *is a trapdoor, such that:*

(i) *Hardness of DDH without the trapdoor: the DDH problem is hard for the group generator* Gen' *which outputs only* $(\mathbb{G}, P)$.
(ii) *Hardness of CDH with the trapdoor: the CDH problem is hard for* Gen.

Solve *is a DPT algorithm which takes as input* $(\mathbb{G}, P, \tau)$ *and a tuple* $(X, Y, Z, T) \in \mathbb{G}^4$, *either accepts (outputs 1) or rejects (outputs 0), and satisfies the following:*

(iii) *Completeness: for all* $(\mathbb{G}, P, \tau)$ *possibly output by* Gen, Solve *always accepts if* $(X, Y, Z, T) \in \mathsf{DDH}_{\mathbb{G}}$.
(iv) *Soundness: for any PPT adversary A, we have that:*

$$\Pr\left[\begin{array}{cc} (\mathbb{G}, P, \tau) \leftarrow \mathsf{Gen}(1^\lambda); (X, Y, Z) \leftarrow \langle P \rangle^3; & 1 \leftarrow \mathsf{Solve}(\mathbb{G}, P, \tau; X, Y, Z, T) \\ T \leftarrow A(\mathbb{G}, P; X, Y, Z) & \wedge (X, Y, Z, T) \notin \mathsf{DDH}_{\mathbb{G}} \end{array} \right] \approx 0.$$

We say that the trapdoor DDH group has perfect soundness when Solve *always rejects on input a non-DH tuple* (X, Y, Z, T), *i.e. the above probability is zero.*

The definitions of Seurin and Dent–Galbraith are almost identical, except that the hardness of CDH with the trapdoor is not required explicitly in the definition of Dent–Galbraith. Nevertheless, their constructions satisfy this property. Prabhakaran–Xue additionally impose a Strong RSA assumption and a Diffie–Hellman Knowledge of Exponent assumption on the trapdoor DDH group [34]. These extra assumptions seem plausible for the specific construction of Dent–Galbraith [17] and needed for their application, but they also seem to restrict the range of possible constructions. For example, the Strong RSA assumption does not hold in a group of known order. Obtaining a trapdoor DDH group of known order is actually among the open problems left by Seurin, and in particular the Strong RSA assumption does not hold for our new construction in Sect. 3.

2.3   Previous Constructions

We briefly sketch previous constructions of trapdoor DDH groups. The first one is the most relevant one for this paper.

Dent–Galbraith's "Hidden Pairing" Construction [17]. Choose p_1, p_2 two large primes congruent to 3 mod 4, such that there are large primes $r_i \mid p_i + 1$. Let $N := p_1 p_2$ and let E be an elliptic curve defined by the equation $y^2 = x^3 + x$ over the ring $\mathbb{Z}_N$. Note that the curve is supersingular, with a well-known distortion map $\phi : E \to E : (x, y) \to (-x, \iota y)$ where $\iota^2 = -1$. The number of points of E over $\mathbb{Z}_N$ is $(p_1 + 1)(p_2 + 1)$. Let P be a point of order $r_1 r_2$ and $\mathbb{G}$ be the group generated by P. The key observation is that a quadruple (P, aP, bP, Z) in $E(\mathbb{Z}_N)$ is a valid DDH tuple if and only if it reduces to a valid DDH tuple in $E(\mathbb{F}_{p_1})$ and $E(\mathbb{F}_{p_2})$. The DDH trapdoor in this construction is the factorization of N: given p_1 and p_2 one can solve the DDH problem using the modified Weil pairing described in Sect. 2.1, since a distortion map on E is known. On the other hand, it seems that without the factorization of N the DDH problem on $E(\mathbb{Z}_N)$ is hard. In Sect. 5, we will show that in certain contexts, factorization is easier, forcing an increase of the parameters

Dent–Galbraith's Second Construction [17]. A second construction was proposed in Dent–Galbraith's paper, based on Frey's idea of disguising an elliptic curve with a Weil descent. However, this construction was subsequently broken in [31].

Seurin's Construction Based on Composite Residuosity [35]. Choose two safe primes p_1 and p_2, namely $p_1 = 2p_1' + 1$ and $p_2 = 2p_2' + 1$ where p_1', p_2' are prime. The group $\mathbb{G}$ is the group of quadratic residues modulo N^2, where $N = p_1 p_2$. The trapdoor is the factorization of N. The group $\mathbb{G}$ is cyclic of order $N p_1' p_2'$. Let g be a generator of $\mathbb{G}$. Given $y \in \mathbb{G}$, the *partial* discrete logarithm problem asks for the discrete logarithm of y modulo N (and not modulo $N p_1' p_2'$). As shown by Paillier [32], one can solve *partial* discrete logarithms in $\mathbb{G}$ given the factorization of N, hence one can also solve Diffie–Hellman problems. On the other hand, the security of the construction is based on the hardness of the CDH problem in $\mathbb{G}$ given the factorization of N, as well as on the DDH and partial CDH problems in $\mathbb{G}$ [35].

Seurin [35] also introduced the definition of a *static* trapdoor DDH scheme where the trapdoor can only be used to solve the DDH problems involving a specific pair of elements $(g, g^x) \in \mathbb{G}^2$.

Seurin's Static Trapdoor DDH Construction Based on the RSA Problem [35]. Let p_1, p_2, N be the same as in the previous construction. Let J_N denote the subgroup of $\mathbb{Z}_N$ consisting of those elements whose Jacobi symbol is 1. This is a cyclic group of order $m = (p_1 - 1)(p_2 - 1)/2$. Let g be a generator of J_N. Generate a random $x \in [0; m - 1]$. The trapdoor is $(m, 1/x \bmod m)$, or equivalently, x and the factorization of N. Using the trapdoor one can recognize DDH instances of the form (g, g^x, g^y, g^z) where g and g^x are fixed beforehand. Indeed, (g, g^x, g^y, g^z)

is a DDH tuple if ond only if $(g^z)^{1/x} = g^y$. However, without the knowledge of the trapdoor, this is RSA inversion which seems to be a hard problem.

Seurin's Static Trapdoor DDH Construction Based on Signed Quadratic Residues. Let $N = p_1 p_2$, where p_1 and p_2 are safe primes congruent to 3 modulo 4. Let $J_N^+ = J_N/\{1, -1\}$. The group J_N^+ is cyclic of order $m = (p_1 - 1)(p_2 - 1)/4$ and let g be a generator of J_N^+. Let $x \in [0; m - 1]$. The trapdoor is $t := 2x \pm m$ (note that the computation of m is equivalent to factoring N). Then an instance (g, g^x, g^y, g^z) is a DDH tuple if and only if $(g^y)^t = (g^z)^2$ as squaring in J_N^+ is injective.

2.4   Seurin's Open Problems

In his "open problems" Section [35, Section 1.4], Seurin highlighs some short-comings of previous trapdoor DDH constructions:

> *"Two key features of trapdoor DDH groups are perfect soundness (the property that the algorithm for solving the DDH problem with the trapdoor perfectly distinguishes DH tuples from non-DH tuples), and the possibility to securely hash into the group [...]. However, none of the two candidates for TDDH groups (the hidden pairing-based proposal of [17], and [Seurin's construction]) fulfills both requirements. We think that providing a plausible candidate possessing both properties is the key to enable powerful applications of TDDH groups.*
>
> *A related open problem is whether there exists a plausible construction of a trapdoor DDH group with publicly known (ideally prime) order, since they are usually simpler to use in cryptography."*

In Sect. 5 we will highlight further issues with Dent–Galbraith's construction, namely attacks on the parameters suggested, in the context of some applications. Interestingly, our new trapdoor DDH group construction will both avoid these issues and solve all of Seurin's open problems.

3   New Trapdoor DDH Groups from Pairings and Isogenies

In this section, we first describe our new trapdoor DDH construction. We then provide our new security definition of "trapdoor pairing" satisfied by both our construction and Dent–Galbraith's one.

3.1   Our Construction

As is widely known, a *non-degenerate symmetric* pairing $e : \mathbb{G} \times \mathbb{G} \to \mathbb{G}_t$ can be used to solve a DDH instance $(P, aP, bP, T) \in \mathbb{G}^4$ by checking whether

$$e(P, T) = e(aP, bP).$$

Let us now consider an elliptic curve E and the Weil pairing $e : E[m] \times E[m] \to \mu_m$, where $\mu_m \subset \mathbb{F}_{p^k}^*$ is the group of m-th roots of unity. The Weil pairing is degenerate, meaning that $e(P, P) = 1$, and so by itself it is not useful to solve DDH problems. This has been solved by using a distortion map, that is, an endomorphism $\phi : E \to E$ such that $\phi(P) \notin \langle P \rangle$. We then define a new pairing as

$$\hat{e}(P, Q) = e(P, \phi(Q)),$$

which is used instead of the Weil pairing.

The key observation of our new construction is that the ability to compute a non-degenerate symmetric pairing relies on the knowledge of a distortion map. Moreover for a random supersingular elliptic curve obtaining this map is a hard problem, and so it constitutes a suitable trapdoor for a trapdoor pairing group.

More precisely, the Gen algorithm works as follows. Assume that we have a curve E_0 with a known distortion map $\phi : E_0 \to E_0$. We choose an isogeny $\varphi : E_0 \to E$ to perform a walk in the isogeny graph. We assume that we can efficiently perform a walk such that the output curve is essentially uniform. In Sect. 4 we will discuss the specifics for each instantiations, and ensure that the walks are indeed efficient and random enough.

The public group G is given by the curve E and the trapdoor information τ is some representation of the isogeny φ. The Solve algorithm has access to the trapdoor, and thus can evaluate the pairing $\hat{e} : E \times E \to \mu_q \subset \mathbb{F}_{p^k}$ defined as

$$\hat{e}(P, Q) = e(\hat{\varphi}(P), \phi(\hat{\varphi}(Q))),$$

where e is the Weil pairing on E_0, and use this to solve DDH instances on E.

3.2 Trapdoor Pairings

In our new construction, the trapdoor does not only allow to solve DDH instances, but also the ability to evaluate a non-degenerate symmetric pairing. We now formalize this property with a new definition.

We first identify a computational problem that is harder than DDH and better captures the power of being able to compute a pairing. Essentially, given group elements, a pairing allows a multiplication of their discrete logarithms. This translates into solving decisional problems which consist of checking a quadratic equation in the exponent. Note that although the corresponding computational problems remain hard, they are easy if we allow the output to be in the target group of the pairing. In particular, we consider the following computational problem.

Definition 4. *Let G be a group and $P \in G$, and let $e : G \times G \to G_T$ be a pairing. We call the* Target Computational Diffie–Hellman (Target CDH) *problem the problem consisting on, given G, P, aP, bP for uniformly random a, b, computing*

$$g, g^{ab} \in G_T,$$

where $g \neq 1$ must be output before[2] receiving aP, bP.

Note that a symmetric non-degenerate pairing can be used to solve the Target CDH problem by computing $g = e(P, P)$ and $g^{ab} = e(aP, bP)$. This implies that both Dent–Galbraith's first construction and our new construction are not only trapdoor DDH groups, but also trapdoor pairings.

Breaking the Target CDH problem implies breaking the DDH problem in $\mathbb{G}$, so the Target CDH problem is at least as hard as the DDH problem, but nevertheless it is still easy given an efficiently computable pairing.

We now formalize the idea of trapdoor pairings by mimicking the previous trapdoor DDH definition, but replacing the requirement that DDH should be solvable with the trapdoor with our harder problem.

Definition 5. *A trapdoor Target CDH group is a pair of algorithms* (Gen, Solve) *with the following properties. The trapdoor pairing group generator algorithm* Gen *is a PPT algorithm which takes as input a security parameter 1^λ and outputs a tuple $(\mathbb{G}, \mathbb{G}_T, P, \tau)$ where $\mathbb{G}$ and $\mathbb{G}_T$ are the descriptions of two group, $P \in \mathbb{G}$ is a group element of order $2^{\Theta(\lambda)}$, and τ is a trapdoor information, such that:*

(i) *Hardness of DDH without the trapdoor: the DDH problem is hard for the group generator* Gen' *which outputs only $(\mathbb{G}, \mathbb{G}_T, P)$, both in $\mathbb{G}$ and $\mathbb{G}_T$.*
(ii) *Hardness of CDH with the trapdoor: the CDH problem is hard for* Gen, *both in $\mathbb{G}$ and $\mathbb{G}_T$.*

Solve *is a DPT algorithm which takes as input $(\mathbb{G}, \mathbb{G}_T, P, \tau)$ and a tuple $(X, Y) \in \mathbb{G}^2$, and outputs $(g, u) \in \mathbb{G}_T^2$, and satisfies the following:*

(iii) *Completeness: for all $(\mathbb{G}, \mathbb{G}_T, P, \tau)$ possibly output by* Gen, *and if $X = aP, Y = bP$,* Solve *always outputs $(g, u) \in \mathbb{G}_T^2$ such that $u = g^{ab}$.*
(iv) *Soundness: for any PPT adversary A, the we have that*

$$\Pr\left[\begin{array}{l} (\mathbb{G}, \mathbb{G}_T, P, \tau) \leftarrow \mathsf{Gen}(1^\lambda); (aP, bP) \leftarrow \langle P \rangle^2; \\ (g, u) \leftarrow \mathsf{Solve}(\mathbb{G}, \mathbb{G}_T, P, \tau; aP, bP) \end{array} : u \neq g^{ab} \right] \approx 0.$$

We say that trapdoor Target CDH group has perfect soundness when the above probability is zero.

An alternative, perhaps more natural definition could require the Target CDH problem to be hard without the trapdoor, as opposed to the DDH problem in Definition 4. We chose to require hardness of DDH (implying hardness of Target CDH) so that trapdoor pairings are naturally trapdoor DDH groups as well. The only difference between them lies in the power provided by the trapdoor: a DDH solver in Definition 3, and a stronger Target CDH solver in Definition 4.

---

[2] The reason for asking for g is that, since the pairing will not be available to all parties, it is not immediate to produce a canonical generator of $\mathbb{G}_T$ from the generator of $\mathbb{G}$. We ask for it in advance so that it does not depend on aP, bP.

3.3 Security of Our New Construction

We now prove that our new construction is a trapdoor pairing in the above sense (hence it is also a trapdoor DDH group).

Theorem 1. *Suppose that the distribution of the curve E output by algorithm* Gen *is statistically equivalent to the uniform distribution. Then, if the DDH problem in E is hard, and the CDH problem in E is hard given the trapdoor, the construction above is a secure trapdoor pairing group.*

Proof. It is clear from the discussion above that the Target CDH problem can be solved efficiently when the trapdoor is known, and by assumption the CDH problem is hard.

Without the trapdoor, solving DDH in $\mathbb{G}$ is exactly the DDH problem on the curve E. While E is not a uniformly random curve, it is the output of a random walk, which is close to uniformly random so that the two problems are equivalent.

We now argue that the DDH and CDH assumptions of Theorem 1 are plausible. First, the DDH has been widely studied and used in the literature, and is believed to hold when a symmetric pairing is not available, and as discussed in Sect. 2.1, the DDH problem is easy for supersingular curves only when a distortion map is known.

We remark that constructing a curve with a distortion map is easy: one can choose a special curve, or do a random walk from one of these special curves as in our trapdoor pairing construction. On the other hand given a randomly chosen supersingular curve, computing a distortion map appears to be a difficult problem, as discussed in Sect. 2.1. Conversely, given the endomorphism ring of a curve E, one can also compute an isogeny between E_0 and E (see [18, 33]), and any such isogeny can be used as a trapdoor in our scheme.

While DDH is easy on E with the trapdoor, the CDH problem still appears to be hard on E. Indeed this is formalized by the so-called Gap-CDH assumption in pairing-based cryptography. Moreover, given the trapdoor the CDH problems on the curves E_0 and E are equivalent, as we can use a trapdoor $\varphi : E_0 \to E$ to send a CDH instance (P, aP, bP) in E_0 to $(\varphi(P), \varphi(aP), \varphi(bP))$. Note that scalar multiplication commutes with any isogeny, so this is a CDH instance on E.

The assumption that the output of the group generation algorithm is close to uniformly random will be discussed for the particular instantiations of the algorithm, in Sect. 4, as the argument is different in each case.

3.4 Applications

We considered two applications of our construction, and more generally of trapdoor pairings. We briefly discuss these applications here and refer to the full version for details.

First, we build an identification scheme that improves on a previous construction by Dent–Galbraith [17] that was based on trapdoor DDH groups. The protocol by Dent–Galbraith has to be iterated several times in order to achieve soundness, while our protocol allows for arbitrarily long challenges. Our improved construction highlights how using a trapdoor pairing in place of a general trapdoor DDH group leads to a more efficient scheme.

We also discuss ElGamal voting and similar protocols, and warn against the use of random supersingular curves in such protocols. Indeed, we show how a construction similar to ours could then be used as a backdoor to break anonymity in these contexts.

4   Two Concrete Instantiations

In [35, Section 2.4], Seurin requests the following useful features for a trapdoor DDH group:

- The group order can be publicly revealed.
- The group order is a prime number.
- There is an efficient hashing algorithm into the group.

We note that no previous construction has achieved these properties at the same time. In particular, all of them use composite-order groups.

We consider two instantiations of our idea, one using curves over $\mathbb{F}_{p^2}$, and another using curves over $\mathbb{F}_p$. The first one satisfies the first property, and either the second or the third, but not both simultaneously. The second instantiation achieves the three properties at the same time.

4.1   Curves over $\mathbb{F}_{p^2}$

We start by stating a simple result that ensures that our isogenies will be defined over $\mathbb{F}_{p^2}$, and we will not need to move to extension fields.

Lemma 1. *Let $p \geq 3$ be a prime, and let E be a supersingular elliptic curve such that $\#E(\mathbb{F}_{p^2}) = (p+1)^2$. Then the 2-isogenies from E are $\mathbb{F}_{p^2}$-rational.*

Proof. Since E has $(p+1)^2$ points over $\mathbb{F}_{p^2}$, we have that $E(\mathbb{F}_{p^2})$ is isomorphic to $\mathbb{Z}_{p+1} \times \mathbb{Z}_{p+1}$ [11, Theorem 54]. Since p is an odd prime, we have that $2 \mid (p+1)$, and so $\mathbb{Z}_{p+1} \times \mathbb{Z}_{p+1}$ contains a copy of $\mathbb{Z}_2 \times \mathbb{Z}_2$, which is necessarily the 2-torsion of the curve. Thus the 2-torsion is $\mathbb{F}_{p^2}$-rational, and so are the 2-isogenies.   □

We also recall a result that ensures that the output of an isogeny random walk has an almost-uniform distribution.

Theorem 2 ([21], **Theorem 1**). *Let p be a prime number, let N_p be the number of vertices in the supersingular isogeny graph, and let j_0 be a supersingular invariant in characteristic p. Let j be the final j-invariant reached by a random walk of degree $n = \ell^e$ from j_0. Then for every j-invariant $\tilde{j}$ we have*

$$\left| \Pr[j = \tilde{j}] - \frac{1}{N_p} \right| < \left(\frac{2\sqrt{\ell}}{\ell+1} \right)^e .$$

By taking $e > 2(1 + \epsilon) \log_\ell p$, it is easy to see that the right-hand side in the equation above is smaller than $2/p^{1+\epsilon}$, for any $\epsilon > 0$, so the output distribution of the random walk is close to uniform (the statistical distance is negligible).

Let p be a prime such that $p = 3 \bmod 4$ and $p+1 = qf$, where q is also prime and f is a small cofactor. We consider the curve $E_0 : y^2 = x^3 + x$ over $\mathbb{F}_{p^2}$. This curve is in the conditions of Lemma 1 above, has j-invariant $j = 1728$, and its endomorphism ring is known (see e.g. [33]).

To generate the trapdoor DDH group, we take a random walk $\varphi : E_0 \to E$ composed of 2-isogenies, long enough to ensure that the output curve E is statistically uniform in the graph. Since isogenies preserve the supersingular property and the number of points, any curve that we reach from E_0 through 2-isogenies is also in the conditions of the lemma, and therefore every step of the walk is defined over $\mathbb{F}_{p^2}$.

At this point, we have two options:

- We consider $E(\mathbb{F}_{p^2})$ as the trapdoor group. The group order is $(p+1)^2$, and is public, and we can efficiently hash into the group using standard techniques [23], but the group is not of prime order. In fact, the group is not even cyclic.
- We consider a subgroup of $E(\mathbb{F}_{p^2})$ of order q as the trapdoor group. It is easy to find a point of order $p+1$ in $E(\mathbb{F}_{p^2})$ and multiply it by f to obtain a point of order q, which is close in size to p. In this case, the group order is public and prime, but there is no obvious way to securely hash into the group.

Algorithm 1 Trapdoor group generation (curves over $\mathbb{F}_{p^2}$)

Require: security parameter λ.
Ensure: group description $(\mathbb{G}, P)$, trapdoor φ.
1: Choose primes $p, q = \Theta(2^\lambda)$ such that $p = 3 \bmod 4$ and $p + 1 = qf$ for small f.
2: Define the curve $E_0 : y^2 = x^3 + x$ over $\mathbb{F}_{p^2}$.
3: Take a random walk $\varphi : E_0 \to E$ of length $2 \log p$ composed of 2-isogenies.
4: Choose a point $Q \in E(\mathbb{F}_{p^2})$ of order $p + 1$. Set $P = fQ$.
5: Output $(\langle P \rangle, P, \varphi)$.

The hardness of computing a distortion map then relies on the hardness of computing an isogeny between a fixed curve and a random curve over $\mathbb{F}_{p^2}$, for which only exponential-time attacks are known, as discussed in Sect. 2.1. This justifies the assumptions of Theorem 1.

4.2 Curves over $\mathbb{F}_p$

We now present an alternative instantiation that uses curves over $\mathbb{F}_p$. In the previous section, we have seen an instantiation that uses a prime-order group which we cannot efficiently hash into. The reason is that $E(\mathbb{F}_{p^2})$ does not have a unique subgroup of order q, so the trapdoor group must be specified though a generator. With this description, there is no obvious way to hash into the group without knowing the discrete logarithm of the hash, which is undesirable for security. To solve this, we want to find a group in which we can canonically identify a subgroup of order q.

To do so, we work over $\mathbb{F}_p$ instead of $\mathbb{F}_{p^2}$, taking an approach similar to CSIDH [5]. We choose a prime $p = 3 \bmod 4$ such that $p + 1 = 4\ell_1 \ldots \ell_n q$, for a large prime q, and we consider again the curve $E_0 : y^2 = x^3 + x$, now over $\mathbb{F}_p$.

The idea is again to take a random walk in the isogeny graph, using only $\mathbb{F}_p$-rational isogenies.

Lemma 2. $E(\mathbb{F}_p)$ *has a unique subgroup of order* q.

Proof. $E(\mathbb{F}_p)$ has $p+1$ points. Since $q \mid (p+1)$ but $q^2 \nmid (p+1)$, we have that there is a subgroup of order q in $E(\mathbb{F}_p)$, but the $\mathbb{F}_p$-rational curve does not contain the whole q-torsion. Then $E(\mathbb{F}_p)$ contains only one subgroup $\mathbb{G}$ of order q. $\square$

We will use this unique subgroup $\mathbb{G}$ as the trapdoor DDH group. Note that the embedding degree of the pairing is the smallest integer k such that $\#\mathbb{G} \mid (p^k - 1)$, so in this case we have $k = 2$. Hashing into this group is now easy. We make it explicit in the following result.

Lemma 3. *There is an efficient algorithm to hash into* $\mathbb{G}$.

Proof. Given a string, we hash it into $\mathbb{F}_p$. We interpret the result as the x-coordinate of a point in $E(\mathbb{F}_p)$. Note that a uniformly random element of $\mathbb{F}_p$ will correspond to a point in the curve with probability roughly $1/2$. If that is not the case, we increase the x-coordinate until it corresponds to a point P. Then we compute $\frac{p+1}{q}P$, landing into the unique subgroup of order q. Note that $\frac{p+1}{q}$ is coprime to q, so given a uniformly random $P \in E(\mathbb{F}_p)$, we have that $\frac{p+1}{q}P$ is a uniformly random point in $\mathbb{G}$. $\square$

It only remains to specify how to move through the graph using only $\mathbb{F}_p$-rational isogenies. Note that the same argument used in Lemma 2 for q works for any ℓ_i, so $E(\mathbb{F}_p)$ contains only one subgroup of order ℓ_i for each $i = 1, \ldots, n$. We make use of the following result (see [12, Section 15] for a proof).

Lemma 4. *Let* $\ell \geq 3, p \geq 5$ *be different prime numbers, such that* $\left(\frac{D}{\ell}\right) = 1$, *where* $D = t^2 - 4p$, *and* t *is the trace of Frobenius. Let* E *be a supersingular elliptic curve. Then* $\#E(\mathbb{F}_p) = p + 1$ *and there are two* ℓ-*isogenies from* E *that are* $\mathbb{F}_p$-*rational. Moreover, these correspond to:*

- *The unique subgroup* H *of order* ℓ *of* $E(\mathbb{F}_p)$.
- *The unique subgroup* $\tilde{H}$ *of order* ℓ *of* $\tilde{E}(\mathbb{F}_p)$, *where* $\tilde{E}$ *is the quadratic twist of* E.

Then, the random walk consists of choosing exponents $e_1, \ldots, e_n \in [-B, B]$. An exponent corresponds to $|e_i|$ steps in which we use the isogeny with kernel H

or $\tilde{H}$, respectively, depending on whether the sign of e_i is positive or negative. The distribution of the output of the random walk depends on the structure of the class group of $\mathrm{End}_p(E_0)$. Although for certain parameters it has been computed [1], in general we make the heuristic assumption that, for B and n large enough, the random walk reaches any point in the graph with roughly the same probability.[3]

Algorithm 2 Trapdoor group generation (curves over $\mathbb{F}_p$)

Require: security parameter λ.
Ensure: group description $(\mathbb{G}, P)$, trapdoor φ.
1: Choose primes $p, q = \Theta(2^\lambda)$ such that $p = 3 \bmod 4$, and small odd primes $\ell_1, \ldots, \ell_n$ and integers $e_1, \ldots, e_n$ such that $p + 1 = 4\ell_1 \ldots \ell_n q$, and $\prod_n \ell_i > 2\sqrt{p}$.
2: Define the curve $E_0 : y^2 = x^3 + x$ over $\mathbb{F}_p$.
3: Take a random walk $\varphi : E_0 \to E$ composed of e_i isogenies of degree ℓ_i, for each $i = 1, \ldots, n$.
4: Let $\mathbb{G}$ be the unique subgroup of $E(\mathbb{F}_p)$ of order q, and let P be a generator.
5: Output $(\mathbb{G}, P, \varphi)$.

In a similar way to the case above, the distortion map is protected by the hardness of computing an isogeny between curves over $\mathbb{F}_p$. We note that there is a quantum subexponential algorithm for this problem [2]. However, our construction depends on the discrete logarithm assumption, which is broken in the quantum setting anyway, so we focus on classical security.

4.3 Parameter Choices

Let λ be the security parameter. There are two main ways to break the security of the constructions: recovering the trapdoor or solving the discrete logarithm problem. The first approach amounts to finding a non-scalar endomorphism on E or an isogeny to E_0. Recall that for supersingular elliptic curves, the best known classical algorithm [19] has complexity $\tilde{O}(p^{\frac{1}{2}})$.

As for the discrete logarithm problem, one can apply the MOV reduction [30] to reduce any discrete logarithm problem over either E_0 or E to a discrete logarithm problem over $\mathbb{F}_{p^k}$, where $k = 3$ in the first construction and $k = 2$ in the second. Note that the reduction from E is only available if the trapdoor is known, but nevertheless we do not want a party that knows the trapdoor to be able to solve CDH. The best algorithm for computing discrete logarithms in finite fields of large characteristic is the number field sieve and its variants [24, 25], which have complexity $L_n(1/3)$, where in this case $n = p^k$. On the other hand, the best algorithms for solving the discrete logarithm directly in the curve are the generic ones, with complexity $\tilde{O}(q^{1/2})$. One should therefore choose $\log p = \Omega(\lambda^3)$ to avoid these attacks.

---

[3] In CSIDH [5], the authors suggest $B = 5$ and $n = 74$ for a prime p of length 512 bits.

- For the construction over $\mathbb{F}_{p^2}$, recall that $p+1 = qf$ for a small cofactor f, so $\log p \approx \log q$. Thus, the trapdoor group $\mathbb{G}$ is formed by $\Theta(2^{\lambda^3})$ $\mathbb{F}_{p^2}$-elements.
- For the construction over $\mathbb{F}_p$, we have that $p+1 = 4\ell_1 \ldots \ell_n q$, and we require that $\prod_i \ell_i > 2\sqrt{p}$, so roughly $\log p \approx 2\log q$. Therefore, our trapdoor group is again formed by $\Theta(2^{\lambda^3})$ elements over $\mathbb{F}_p$.

The trapdoor is easy to store, as a d-isogeny requires $\log d = O(\log p)$ bits.

4.4   Comparison with Previous Constructions

Dent–Galbraith's Construction. Since the trapdoor is the factorization of N, which in turn can be obtained from the factorization of $r_1 r_2$, as explained in Sect. 5, we need to ensure that this is hard. We must therefore choose $\log(r_1 r_2) = \Omega(\lambda^3)$ to prevent the number field sieve, and since we require $r_i < \sqrt{p_i}$, we need at least $N = p_1 p_2 = \Omega((r_1 r_2)^2)$. We refer to Sect. 5 for a discussion of the case $r_1 = r_2$ and potential further attack developments.

Seurin's Construction. This one also relies on the factoring $N = p_1 p_2$, so we must ensure $\log N = \Omega(\lambda^3)$. Then the trapdoor DDH group is of order $Np_1'p_2' \approx N^2$.

We note that our new construction is asymptotically comparable to the previous proposals in terms of efficiency, while satisfying a stronger definition than Seurin's construction and some desirable properties missing in previous constructions. Also, choosing parameters is more straightforward than in Dent–Galbraith's construction, as the new construction is in a prime-order group, hence we do not need to account for potential factorization attacks, as those described described in the next section.

5   Partial Attacks on Dent–Galbraith's Construction

Dent–Galbraith's hidden pairing construction uses pairings on elliptic curves defined over RSA rings. As already pointed out in [20], selecting parameters for such constructions may be tricky. We now demonstrate this by showing attacks on the construction when the group order is revealed. Note that Dent–Galbraith suggest to reveal this information in some applications, for example to allow delegation of the pairing computation.

5.1   Case $r_1 r_2$ Known and Small, $r_1 \neq r_2$

We first give a simple attack on the parameters suggested by Dent–Galbraith ($p_i \approx 2^{512}$ and $r_i \approx 2^{160}$) for their construction. Let p_1, p_2, r_1, r_2 as in Dent–Galbraith's construction, and assume that $r_1 \neq r_2$ (this condition is not explicitly required in their paper, but it is implied by their later statement that P has order $r_1 r_2$). With $r_i \approx 2^{160}$ the product $r_1 r_2$ can be easily factored with current techniques, so we can assume knowledge of r_1 and r_2. We can then apply a technique from [20, Section 4] to factor N. Namely, we apply x-only addition and doubling formulae to compute the x-coordinate of $[r_1]P$. This leads to the point at infinity modulo p_1 but not modulo p_2, hence a factor of N can be recovered as in the elliptic curve factorization method [29].

To defeat this attack one can choose parameters such that r_1 and r_2 cannot be computed from their product $r_1 r_2$, and make sure other attacks are not feasible. One condition stated in [17] is that $r_i < \sqrt{p_i}$, so the attack requires to at least double the size of p_1 and p_2.

An a priori plausible alternative way to defeat the attack is to enforce $r_1 = r_2$. In this case $E(\mathbb{Z}_N)$ is the direct product of two cyclic groups of order $p_i + 1$ and similarly $\mathbb{G}$ is the direct product of two cyclic groups of order r. With this configuration, multiplying any point in $\mathbb{G}$ by r gives ∞ modulo both p_1 and p_2, hence no factor is recovered. We now consider this case more thoroughly.

5.2   Case $r_1 = r_2$ a Known Prime

The setting for a known $r := r_1 = r_2$ was in fact already studied in [20], and the best attack presented there has a complexity $O(N^{1/4}/r)$. Taking p_1 and p_2 with 512 bits and r with 160 bits leads to a cost of 2^{96} for this attack, which seems impractical today.

However, we now present an alternative attack in this setting, using Coppersmith's techniques for finding small integer roots of bivariate polynomials [7] and its generalizations by Coron [8–10].[4] In order to factor N, we only need to find x and y such that $N = (rx - 1)(ry - 1)$, i.e., we are looking for roots of the bivariate polynomial $p(x, y) = 1 - N - rx - ry + r^2 xy$. For the parameters above there is a root (x_0, y_0) such that $|x_0| \leq 2^{352}$ and $|y_0| \leq 2^{352}$. We will use the following result.

Theorem 3 ([7], **Corollary 2**). *Let $p(x, y) \in \mathbb{Z}[x, y]$ be a bivariate irreducible polynomial of maximum degree δ in each variable. Let X, Y be upper bounds on the desired integer solution (x_0, y_0) and let $W = \max_{i,j} \{|p_{ij}| X^i Y^j\}$. If $XY < W^{2/(3\delta)}$, then in time polynomial in $(\log W, 2^\delta)$ one can find an integer solution (x_0, y_0) to the equation $p(x, y) = 0$ such that $|x_0| \leq X$, $|y_0| \leq Y$.*

An easy calculation shows that we cannot apply Theorem 3 directly here: indeed our polynomial p has degree 1 in each variable, and we have $XY \approx 2^{704}$ and $W^{2/3} \approx N^{2/3} \approx 2^{683}$. However, we can still apply the theorem by guessing a few bits of both x and y and iterating Coron's algorithm. Specifically, we set $x := 2^{12} x' + c_1$ and $y := 2^{12} y' + c_2$ where $0 \leq c_i \leq 2^{12}$ and we try to find a solution for each admissible pair (c_1, c_2). With this approach we now have bounds $X = Y = 2^{340}$ on x' and y', and we still have $W^{2/3} \approx N^{2/3} \approx 2^{683}$. As there are 2^{12} choices for each of the c_i, we only need to run the algorithm from [9] at most 2^{24} times to find p_1 and p_2.

---

[4] This attack can be readily extended when $r_1 \neq r_2$, but in that case the attack from the previous section will be simpler.

One way to defeat this attack in practice is to increase the number of guesses needed; we now estimate the parameters needed to guarantee that this is bigger than 2^{80}. Assume r is a k bit integer and the p_i are $k + \ell$ bit primes, where k and ℓ are positive integers. Then XY is a 2ℓ bit integer and the number of bits of $W^{2/3}$ is $\frac{4}{3}(k + \ell)$. In order to achieve the desired security we need that $2\ell - 80 > \frac{4}{3}(k + \ell)$ or $\ell > 2k + 120$. When r has $k = 160$ bits, we need p_i with at least $\ell + k > 600$ bits, hence N should have at least 1200 bits.

6   Conclusion and Further Work

In this paper, we presented a new trapdoor DDH group construction based on supersingular elliptic curves and pairings. We also gave partial attacks on a previous trapdoor DDH group construction, and we provided a formal security definition for a related but more powerful primitive called "trapdoor pairing" (which our new construction also satisfies). Our new construction has a number of interesting properties; in particular it has all the properties identified by Seurin in his "open problems" Section [35, Section 1.4] as crucial for applications.

Although trapdoor DDH groups were introduced in 2006, the number of applications of it has been so far quite limited. Seurin [35] identified some limitations of all the previous constructions (included their own), and hoped that solving these would allow for more meaningful applications. Our new construction satisfies all the properties required by Seurin, yet no obvious application seems to arise. The notions of trapdoor DDH groups and trapdoor pairings seem to fit quite naturally with the idea of a distinguished party, which would use the trapdoor to perform some operation that is only allowed to them. This suggests that trapdoor DDH groups might be useful in constructing schemes where there is an authority figure. For example, in group signatures, members of the group can sign messages anonymously on behalf of the group. There is a group manager that can trace the signer, but cannot produce forgeries. In this setting, a manager with a trapdoor could identify a signer by noticing a DDH tuple involving the user's public key, message and signature. At the same time, hardness of DDH for the rest of the parties would keep the signatures anonymous for them. We leave the development of such a scheme to further work.

Acknowledgements. We thank Jens Groth, Steven Galbraith and Frederik Vercauteren for discussions related to this work. In particular, some of our applications were suggested by Jens Groth. We also thank the anonymous reviewers. Work by the first and second author was supported by an EPSRC New Investigator grant (EP/S01361X/1). The third author was supported by a PhD grant from the Spanish government, co-financed by the ESF (Ayudas para contratos predoctorales para la formación de doctores 2016). This work was partially done while the third author visited the University of Birmingham.

References

1. Beullens, W., Kleinjung, T., Vercauteren, F.: CSI-FiSh: efficient isogeny based signatures through class group computations. In: Galbraith, S.D., Moriai, S. (eds.) ASIACRYPT 2019. LNCS, vol. 11921, pp. 227–247. Springer, Cham (2019). https://doi.org/10.1007/978-3-030-34578-5_9
2. Biasse, J.-F., Jao, D., Sankar, A.: A quantum algorithm for computing isogenies between supersingular elliptic curves. In: Meier, W., Mukhopadhyay, D. (eds.) INDOCRYPT 2014. LNCS, vol. 8885, pp. 428–442. Springer, Cham (2014). https://doi.org/10.1007/978-3-319-13039-2_25
3. Blake, I.F., Seroussi, G., Smart, N.P.: Advances in Elliptic Curve Cryptography, vol. 317. Cambridge University Press, Cambridge (2005)
4. Burdges, J., De Feo, L.: Delay encryption (2020)
5. Castryck, W., Lange, T., Martindale, C., Panny, L., Renes, J.: CSIDH: an efficient post-quantum commutative group action. In: Peyrin, T., Galbraith, S. (eds.) ASIACRYPT 2018. LNCS, vol. 11274, pp. 395–427. Springer, Cham (2018). https://doi.org/10.1007/978-3-030-03332-3_15
6. Childs, A., Jao, D., Soukharev, V.: Constructing elliptic curve isogenies in quantum subexponential time. J. Math. Cryptol. 8(1), 1–29 (2014)
7. Coppersmith, D.: Small solutions to polynomial equations, and low exponent RSA vulnerabilities. J. Cryptol. 10(4), 233–260 (1997)
8. Coron, J.-S.: Finding small roots of bivariate integer polynomial equations revisited. In: Cachin, C., Camenisch, J.L. (eds.) EUROCRYPT 2004. LNCS, vol. 3027, pp. 492–505. Springer, Heidelberg (2004). https://doi.org/10.1007/978-3-540-24676-3_29
9. Coron, J.-S.: Finding small roots of bivariate integer polynomial equations: a direct approach. In: Menezes, A. (ed.) CRYPTO 2007. LNCS, vol. 4622, pp. 379–394. Springer, Heidelberg (2007). https://doi.org/10.1007/978-3-540-74143-5_21
10. Coron, J.-S., Kirichenko, A., Tibouchi, M.: A note on the bivariate Coppersmith theorem. J. Cryptol. 26, 246–250 (2013)
11. De Feo, L.: Mathematics of isogeny-based cryptography. arXiv preprint arXiv:1711.04062 (2017)
12. De Feo, L.: Isogeny graphs in cryptography (2019)
13. De Feo, L., Galbraith, S.D.: SeaSign: compact isogeny signatures from class group actions. Technical report, IACR Cryptology ePrint Archive (2018)
14. De Feo, L., Jao, D., Plût, J.: Towards quantum-resistant cryptosystems from supersingular elliptic curve isogenies. J. Math. Cryptol. 8(3), 209–247 (2014)
15. De Feo, L., Masson, S., Petit, C., Sanso, A.: Verifiable delay functions from supersingular isogenies and pairings. Technical report, Cryptology ePrint Archive, Report 2019/166 (2019)
16. Delfs, C., Galbraith, S.D.: Computing isogenies between supersingular elliptic curves over $\mathbb{F}_p$. Designs, Codes Crypt. 78(2), 425–440 (2016)
17. Dent, A.W., Galbraith, S.D.: Hidden pairings and trapdoor DDH groups. In: Hess, F., Pauli, S., Pohst, M. (eds.) ANTS 2006. LNCS, vol. 4076, pp. 436–451. Springer, Heidelberg (2006). https://doi.org/10.1007/11792086_31
18. Eisenträger, K., Hallgren, S., Lauter, K., Morrison, T., Petit, C.: Supersingular isogeny graphs and endomorphism rings: reductions and solutions. In: Nielsen, J.B., Rijmen, V. (eds.) EUROCRYPT 2018. LNCS, vol. 10822, pp. 329–368. Springer, Cham (2018). https://doi.org/10.1007/978-3-319-78372-7_11

19. Galbraith, S.D.: Constructing isogenies between elliptic curves over finite fields. LMS J. Comput. Math. **2**, 118–138 (1999)

20. Galbraith, S.D., McKee, J.F.: Pairings on elliptic curves over finite commutative rings. In: Smart, N.P. (ed.) Cryptography and Coding 2005. LNCS, vol. 3796, pp. 392–409. Springer, Heidelberg (2005). https://doi.org/10.1007/11586821_26

21. Galbraith, S.D., Petit, C., Silva, J.: Identification protocols and signature schemes based on supersingular isogeny problems. In: Takagi, T., Peyrin, T. (eds.) ASIACRYPT 2017. LNCS, vol. 10624, pp. 3–33. Springer, Cham (2017). https://doi.org/10.1007/978-3-319-70694-8_1

22. Galbraith, S.D., Rotger, V.: Easy decision Diffie-Hellman groups. LMS J. Comput. Math. **7**, 201–218 (2004)

23. Icart, T.: How to hash into elliptic curves. In: Halevi, S. (ed.) CRYPTO 2009. LNCS, vol. 5677, pp. 303–316. Springer, Heidelberg (2009). https://doi.org/10.1007/978-3-642-03356-8_18

24. Joux, A., Lercier, R., Smart, N., Vercauteren, F.: The number field sieve in the medium prime case. In: Dwork, C. (ed.) CRYPTO 2006. LNCS, vol. 4117, pp. 326–344. Springer, Heidelberg (2006). https://doi.org/10.1007/11818175_19

25. Kim, T., Barbulescu, R.: Extended tower number field sieve: a new complexity for the medium prime case. In: Robshaw, M., Katz, J. (eds.) CRYPTO 2016. LNCS, vol. 9814, pp. 543–571. Springer, Heidelberg (2016). https://doi.org/10.1007/978-3-662-53018-4_20

26. Kohel, D.R.: Endomorphism rings of elliptic curves over finite fields. Ph.D. thesis, University of California, Berkeley (1996)

27. Koshiba, T., Takashima, K.: Pairing cryptography meets isogeny: a new framework of isogenous pairing groups. IACR Cryptology ePrint Archive 2016, 1138 (2016)

28. Lauter, K.E., Charles, D., Mityagin, A.: Trapdoor pairings, May 15 2012. US Patent 8,180,047 (2012)

29. Lenstra Jr., H.W.: Factoring integers with elliptic curves. Ann. Math. 649–673 (1987)

30. Menezes, A.J., Okamoto, T., Vanstone, S.A.: Reducing elliptic curve logarithms to logarithms in a finite field. IEEE Trans. Inf. Theory **39**(5), 1639–1646 (1993)

31. Morales, D.J.M.: An attack on disguised elliptic curves. J. Math. Cryptol. **2**(1), 1–8 (2008)

32. Paillier, P.: Public-key cryptosystems based on composite degree residuosity classes. In: Stern, J. (ed.) EUROCRYPT 1999. LNCS, vol. 1592, pp. 223–238. Springer, Heidelberg (1999). https://doi.org/10.1007/3-540-48910-X_16

33. Petit, C., Lauter, K.E.: Hard and easy problems for supersingular isogeny graphs. IACR Cryptology ePrint Archive 2017, 962 (2017)

34. Prabhakaran, M., Xue, R.: Statistically hiding sets. In: Fischlin, M. (ed.) CT-RSA 2009. LNCS, vol. 5473, pp. 100–116. Springer, Heidelberg (2009). https://doi.org/10.1007/978-3-642-00862-7_7

35. Seurin, Y.: New constructions and applications of trapdoor DDH groups. In: Kurosawa, K., Hanaoka, G. (eds.) PKC 2013. LNCS, vol. 7778, pp. 443–460. Springer, Heidelberg (2013). https://doi.org/10.1007/978-3-642-36362-7_27

36. Silverman, J.H.: The Arithmetic of Elliptic Curves. GTM, vol. 106. Springer, New York (2009). https://doi.org/10.1007/978-0-387-09494-6

37. Verheul, E.R.: Evidence that XTR is more secure than supersingular elliptic curve cryptosystems. J. Cryptol. **17**(4), 277–296 (2004)

Practical Isogeny-Based Key-Exchange with Optimal Tightness

Bor de Kock⑩, Kristian Gjøsteen⑩, and Mattia Veroni(✉)⑩

NTNU – Norwegian University of Science and Technology, Trondheim, Norway
{bor.dekock,kristian.gjosteen,mattia.veroni}@ntnu.no

Abstract. We exploit the Diffie-Hellman-like structure of CSIDH to build a quantum-resistant authenticated key-exchange algorithm. Our security proof has optimal tightness, which means that the protocol is efficient even when instantiated with theoretically-sound security parameters. Compared to previous isogeny-based authenticated key-exchange protocols, our scheme is extremely simple, its security relies only on the underlying CSIDH-problem and it has optimal communication complexity for CSIDH-based protocols. Our security proof relies heavily on the re-randomizability of CSIDH-like problems and carries on in the ROM.

Keywords: Post-quantum · Isogenies · Key-exchange · Provable-security · Tightness · Re-randomization

1 Introduction

Authenticated key-exchange protocols allow two parties to collaborate in order to create a shared secret key, providing each of them with some assurance on the identity of the partner. Authentication can be achieved in two ways: *implicitly*, if it follows from the algebraic properties of the scheme, or *explicitly*, by receiving a confirmation that the interlocutor has actually computed the key. The latter implies the use of a second mechanism, like a signature scheme, a KEM or a MAC. Even if explicit authentication might seem a stronger and preferable feature, in the real world it does not add much to the security of the protocol. First of all, it does not guarantee that the partner holds the shared key for all the time between the key confirmation and the use of the key. Moreover, the generation of signatures or the use of KEMs and MACs produces evidence of participation to a key-exchange, while implicit authentication does not. Finally, the schemes relying on implicit authentication typically require less computations and message exchanges compared to those involving an explicit authentication mechanism, with a significant profit in computational cost and communication efficiency.

The security proof limits the advantage of an adversary in breaking the scheme to the probability of solving some mathematical hard problem. Deploying a cryptographic algorithm should always be done in a *theoretically sound* way: the size of the concrete parameters must be large enough to guarantee the

© Springer Nature Switzerland AG 2021
O. Dunkelman et al. (Eds.): SAC 2020, LNCS 12804, pp. 451–479, 2021.
https://doi.org/10.1007/978-3-030-81652-0_18

required λ bits of security. If on one hand any security proof asymptotically guarantees the desired security level, on the other hand we want to use the smallest parameters possible, in order to obtain the most efficient implementation under the given security constraints. It is therefore extremely relevant to measure the so-called *tightness* of the proof by computing its security loss $L(\lambda)$, which should be as small as possible. The parameters on which we focus are, in particular, the number of users running the protocol and the number of sessions per user; both quantities are approximated to 2^{16} for small-scale and 2^{32} for large-scale applications. Note that, nowadays, security proofs [JKSS12,KPW13,BFK+14] for a widely deployed protocol such as TLS have a quadratic loss in the number of sessions, fact that is not taken into account for the implementation.

In 2019 Cohn-Gordon et al. [CCG+19] developed a key-exchange protocol with an nearly (but optimally) tight security proof. In particular, the security loss is linear in the number of users and constant in the number of sessions per user. The security is based on the Strong-DH assumption defined over cyclic groups of prime order. The re-randomization of Diffie-Hellman problems plays a fundamental role in achieving the optimal tightness of the proof, and thus it is a feature that we cannot disregard. The tightness and practicality of these scheme raise an interesting question: is it possible to adapt the protocol (together with its security proof) in order to make it quantum-safe?

In 1997, Peter Shor [Sho97] published a quantum algorithm for integer factorization and one for computing discrete logarithms, both running in polynomial time. As soon as a large-scale quantum computer will become available, the information security based on primitives like the RSA cryptosystem and the Diffie-Hellman key-exchange will be breached. In order to address this quantum threat, many researchers have focused their attention on post-quantum cryptography. The goal is to find new cryptographic primitives which can be implemented on classical computers, still guaranteeing security against both classical and quantum adversaries. In 2016, NIST announced a world-wide competition for new post-quantum standards in public-key encryption and digital signature algorithms. 69 submissions were accepted in the first round, 26 made it to the second step, and 7 finalists were announced on July 22, 2020.

Supersingular-Isogeny based Diffie-Hellman (SIDH) [JD11] is a promising candidate in the search for post-quantum cryptographic protocols. Key-exchange protocols based on isogenies are unique in the sense that they provide key-sizes roughly similar to those of pre-quantum alternatives, but they are also known for being more complex (algebraically) compared to some of the post-quantum alternatives. An example of a scheme that is based on SIDH is SIKE [JAC+19], which is one of the 26 candidates in the second round of NIST's 2016 competition for post-quantum cryptographic protocols. Even if SIKE is not among the finalists announced in July 2020, NIST has shown high interest on isogeny-based cryptography, encouraging further research on this field [AASA+]. Although SIDH-based schemes have been around for a few years now, there are still open questions about the security behind them. In particular, random self-reducibility of SIDH problems seems very hard to achieve.

A different isogeny-based scheme is CSIDH [CLM+18]: introduced in 2018, it offers a much more flexible and adaptable algebraic structure. In our paper, we obtain an optimally tight security proof for a CSIDH-based key-exchange protocol, making use of random self-reducibility. This kind of re-randomization plays a fundamental role in the tight proofs of, for instance, the classical Diffie-Hellman key-exchange, as well as in more modern schemes.

The protocol we introduce is, to our knowledge, the best proven-secure result for isogeny-based key-exchange protocols. The proofs presented here draw on the proofs from Cohn-Gordon et al. [CCG+19], but with changes to the re-randomization strategy, since re-randomization in the isogeny case is different from the one in the cyclic group case. Both efficiency and tightness are a significant improvement over the state of the art, and can lead to the deployment of schemes with more efficient parameter choices obtaining high security at computational costs which are as low as possible.

1.1 Our Contributions

In Sect. 3.2 we adapt protocol Π by Cohn-Gordon et al. [CCG+19] to the isogeny setting, obtaining the first implicitly authenticated CSIDH-like protocol with weak forward secrecy, under only the Strong-CSIDH assumption. This is the first scheme with a security proof (moreover with optimal tightness) in the same setting as CSIDH. The protocol requires each user to perform 4 ideal-class evaluations, and its security proof, shown in Appendix B, has a tightness loss which is linear in the number of sessions performed by a single user.

The adaptation we perform is, however, not entirely straightforward. In the new setting we have only one operation, namely the multiplication of ideal classes, while in the original protocol re-randomization is achieved via two operations (addition and multiplication of exponents). This leads to a different re-randomization technique which relies one the random self-reducibility of the computational CSIDH problem shown in Sect. 4.1.

We obtain a significant improvement over the state of the art of isogeny-based key-exchange protocols. Compared to one of the latest scheme, from "Strongly Secure Authenticated Key Exchange from Supersingular Isogenies" [XXW+19], we obtain better efficiency and tightness. Moreover, unlike this latter scheme, our protocol does not require any authentication mechanism. This allows us to rely on the same class (and a smaller number) of hardness assumptions, and to avoid the use of signatures, which are tricky and expensive [DG19] to produce in the isogeny setting. Compared to the CSIDH protocol, which lacks a security proof and for which authentication seems hard to achieve, our Π-SIDE protocol has implicit authentication at the cost of a few more ideal-class evaluations. As shown in Sect. 6, our Π-SIDE protocol is competitive with other post-quantum candidates, once instantiated with theoretically-sound parameters.

A few days after the publication of our paper, the same protocol appeared in the work by Kawashima et al. [KTAT20]. The results have been obtained independently and there was not collaboration between the two groups of authors.

1.2 Related Work

In the last years, a lot of research has been conducted on SIDH-based schemes. For example, Galbraith [Gal18] has shown how to adapt generic constructions to the SIDH setting, and he introduced two new SIDH-AKE protocols. Similar results were achieved by Longa [Lon18], except for the introduction of the two new schemes. Assuming a straightforward adaptation, a few other protocols have a non-quadratic tightness loss. For example KEA+ [LM06] has a linear loss in the number of participants multiplied by the number of sessions, assuming the hardness of the Gap-DH problem. Although, it does not achieve wPFS and takes $O(t \log t)$ time only when instantiated on pairing-friendly curves.

In their recent paper, Xu et al. [XXW+19] propose SIAKE$_2$ and SIAKE$_3$, a two-pass and a three-pass AKE respectively. SIAKE$_2$, whose security relies on the decisional SIDH assumption, has a rather convoluted construction: they design a strong One-Way CPA secure PKE scheme, which is then turned into a One-Way CCA KEM through the modified FO-transform and finally used as a building block for the AKE scheme. The three-pass AKE SIAKE$_3$ is obtained by modifying the previously designed KEM, once a new assumption (the 1-Oracle SI-DH, an analogue of the Oracle Diffie-Hellman assumption in which only one query is allowed) is made. Compared to this scheme, our result is simpler and it has a tighter security proof, smaller communication complexity and improved overall efficiency. Finally, we remark that it is also possible to look at CSIDH-based key-exchange from a non-interactive viewpoint, as it has been recently done by Brendel et al. [BFG+19].

2 Preliminaries

In this section, we first recall the definition of tightness for security reductions. Then we provide the reader with key-concepts and results which are indispensable to understand the constructions of SIDH and CSIDH. Good references regarding elliptic curves and isogenies are Silverman [HS09], Washington [Was08] and De Feo [Feo17]; the original papers introducing SIDH and CSIDH are Jao-De Feo [JD11] and Castryck et al. [CLM+18], respectively.

2.1 Tight Reductions

When comparing schemes, one should always consider protocols once they have been instantiated with theoretically-sound parameters, which guarantee the desired level of security. These parameters (such as the bit-length of the prime defining a base field or the key size) strongly depend on the security proof correlated with the protocol. A security proof usually consists of

- a security model, in which we describe an adversary by listing a set of queries that it can make (and therefore specifying what it is allowed to do);
- a sequence of games leading to a *reduction*, in which an adversary $\mathcal{A}$ against the protocol is turned into a solver $\mathcal{B}$ for an allegedly hard problem.

The "quality" of a reduction can be measured by computing its security loss: if t_A and ϵ_A are the running time and the success probability of A respectively, and t_B and ϵ_B respectively are the running time and the success probability of B, then we define the *security loss* L as

$$\frac{t_A}{\epsilon_A} = L \, \frac{t_B}{\epsilon_B}. \tag{1}$$

If L is constant, then we say that the reduction is *tight*. Having a tight proof is as relevant as building an efficient protocol, because this leads to deploy the smallest possible parameters when concretely instantiating a protocol.

In some cases, however, it is impossible to obtain a tight reduction. In a *simple scheme* the adversary is run only once, in opposition to other protocols which use the Forking Lemma in order to run multiple copies of the adversary. A linear loss in the number of participants to the protocol is unavoidable for simple schemes, while applying the Forking Lemma leads to a non-tight proof. We therefore focus on *optimal tightness* whenever tightness is unachievable: the L in Eq. (1) turns out to be not constant, but one proves that it is impossible to decrease it. We rely on the same strategies adopted in the paper by Cohn-Gordon et al. [CCG+19] to prove the lower bound on the tightness loss, applying their variant of the meta-reduction techniques by Bader et al. [BJLS16].

Many available schemes, which are currently taken into account for standardization processes, have quite non-tight security reductions. Let μ be the number of users running the protocol and let k be the number of sessions per user. HMQV [Kra05], a classically secure protocol in the random-oracle model under the CDH assumption, has security loss $O\left(\mu^2 k^2\right)$. If we consider a generic signed KEM approach, we get a $O\left(\mu^2 k^2\right)$ loss in addition to the signature scheme loss. In many cases, parameters are chosen in a non theoretically-sound way, while tightness loss should always be considered when comparing protocols.

2.2   Elliptic Curves, Isogenies and Endomorphism Rings

Let $\mathbb{F}_p$ be a finite field for a large prime p and let E be an elliptic curve over $\mathbb{F}_p$. We say that E is *supersingular* if and only if it has order $\#E(\mathbb{F}_p) = p + 1$. Consider the isomorphisms of elliptic curves, i.e. all the invertible algebraic maps. Any two elliptic curves over the algebraic closure $\overline{\mathbb{F}}_p$ are *isomorphic* if and only if they have the same j-invariant. Thus we can use isomorphisms to define an equivalence relation between elliptic curves and identify an equivalence class by the j-invariant of the curves in the class.

Let E_1 and E_2 be two elliptic curves defined over $\mathbb{F}_p$, and let $0_{E_1}, 0_{E_2}$ denote their respective points at infinity. An *isogeny* from E_1 to E_2 is a morphism $\phi : E_1 \rightarrow E_2$ such that $\phi(0_{E_1}) = 0_{E_2}$. For any isogeny $\phi : E_1 \rightarrow E_2$ there exists a *dual isogeny* $\hat{\phi} : E_2 \rightarrow E_1$ such that $\hat{\phi} \circ \phi = [deg(\phi)]_{E_1}$ and $\phi \circ \hat{\phi} = [deg(\phi)]_{E_2}$. An isogeny is essentially determined by its kernel: given a finite subgroup $G \subset E(\overline{\mathbb{F}}_p)$, there exist a unique (up to isomorphisms) elliptic curve $E_2 \simeq E_1/G$ and a separable isogeny $\phi : E_1 \rightarrow E_2$ such that $ker(\phi) = G$. The isogeny ϕ has *degree*

ℓ equal to the cardinality of its kernel, and we call it an ℓ-isogeny. Given the kernel of an isogeny, we can exploit Vélu's formulae [Vél71] to compute the isogeny ϕ together with the codomain curve E_2 in $O(\ell \, log(p)^2)$ bit operations. This is the best approach when ℓ is small enough and p is shorter than a few thousand bits. Any separable isogeny defined over $\mathbb{F}_p$ can be written as the composition of isogenies of prime degrees.

An *endomorphism* is an isogeny from E to itself; the set of endomorphisms of E, together with the zero map and equipped with pointwise addition and composition, forms the *endomorphism ring* $End(E)$. We denote by $End_p(E)$ the ring of endomorphisms defined over $\mathbb{F}_p$. For ordinary curves $End_p(E) = End(E)$, while for supersingular curves $End_p(E) \subset End(E)$. In particular, $End(E)$ is an order in a quaternion algebra, whilst $End_p(E)$ is an order in the imaginary quadratic field $\mathbb{Q}(\sqrt{p})$. A classical result by Deuring [Deu41] reveals that $End(E)$ is a maximal order in $B_{p,\infty}$, the quaternion algebra ramified at p and at ∞.

2.3 The Ideal Class Group Action

We hereafter provide the reader with the basic definitions and known results regarding ideal class group action. In particular, this section gravitates around a recurring sentence in isogeny-based cryptography:

> "The ideal class group of an imaginary quadratic order $\mathcal{O}$ acts freely via isogenies on the set of elliptic curves with $End_p(E) \simeq \mathcal{O}$."

We will then focus on the computational aspects, essential to understand CSIDH.

Algebraic Foundations. An *algebra* A is a vector space over a field $\mathbb{K}$ equipped with a bilinear operation. If the bilinear operation is associative, then we say that A is an associative algebra. Given a unitary ring R, a left R-*module* $_R M$ consists of an abelian group $(M, +)$ and a scalar multiplication $R \times_R M \longrightarrow_R M$ which satisfies left/right distributivity, associativity and neutrality of ring's unit. Let R be an integral domain (a commutative unitary ring without zero-divisors) and let $\mathbb{K}$ be its field of fractions; a left R-module $_R M$ is a *lattice* in the vector space V over $\mathbb{K}$ if $_R M$ is finitely generated, R-torsion free and an R-submodule of V. An *order* is a subring $\mathcal{O}$ of a ring A such that 1) A is a finite dimensional algebra over $\mathbb{Q}$, 2) $\mathcal{O}$ spans A over $\mathbb{Q}$ (i.e. $\mathbb{Q}\mathcal{O} = A$), 3) $\mathcal{O}$ is an integer lattice in A.

The Ideal Class Group. Let $\mathbb{K}$ be a finite extension of $\mathbb{Q}$ of degree 2, which is called a *quadratic number field*, and let $\mathcal{O} \subseteq \mathbb{K}$ be an order. The *norm* of an $\mathcal{O}$-ideal $\mathfrak{a} \subseteq \mathcal{O}$ is defined as $N(\mathfrak{a}) = |\mathcal{O}/\mathfrak{a}|$, which is equal to $gcd(\{N(\alpha) \mid \alpha \in \mathfrak{a}\})$. Norms are multiplicative: $N(\mathfrak{ab}) = N(\mathfrak{a}) N(\mathfrak{b})$. A *fractional ideal* of $\mathcal{O}$ is an $\mathcal{O}$-submodule of $\mathbb{K}$ of the form $\alpha \mathfrak{a}$, where $\alpha \in \mathbb{K}^*$ and $\mathfrak{a}$ is an $\mathcal{O}$-ideal. Fractional ideals can be multiplied and conjugated in the obvious way, and the norm extends multiplicatively to fractional ideals. A fractional $\mathcal{O}$-ideal is *invertible* if there exists a fractional $\mathcal{O}$-ideal $\mathfrak{b}$ such that $\mathfrak{ab} = \mathcal{O}$. If such $\mathfrak{b}$ exists, we denote $\mathfrak{a}^{-1} = \mathfrak{b}$. All the principal fractional ideals $\alpha \mathcal{O}$ where $\alpha \in \mathbb{K}^*$ are invertible.

The *ideal class group* of $\mathcal{O}$, defined as $cl(\mathcal{O}) := I(\mathcal{O})/P(\mathcal{O})$, is the quotient of the set of invertible fractional ideals $I(\mathcal{O})$ by the set of principal invertible fractional ideals $P(\mathcal{O})$. For any $M \in \mathbb{Z} \setminus \{0\}$, every ideal class $[\mathfrak{a}]$ has an integral representative of norm coprime to M. There is a unique *maximal order* of $\mathbb{K}$ with respect to inclusion, which is called the *ring of integers* and is denoted by $\mathcal{O}_\mathbb{K}$. The *conductor* of $\mathcal{O}$ in $\mathcal{O}_\mathbb{K}$ is the index $f = [\mathcal{O}_\mathbb{K}/\mathcal{O}]$. Every $\mathcal{O}$-ideal of norm coprime to the conductor is invertible and factors uniquely into prime ideals.

The Class Group Action. Let $\mathcal{E}\ell\ell_p(\mathcal{O})$ be the set of supersingular elliptic curves over $\mathbb{F}_p$ with $End_p(E)$ isomorphic to an order $\mathcal{O}$ in an imaginary quadratic field and let $E \in \mathcal{E}\ell\ell_p(\mathcal{O})$. Given an $\mathcal{O}$-ideal $\mathfrak{a}$, we define the *action* of $\mathfrak{a}$ on E as follows:

1. we consider all the endomorphisms α in $\mathfrak{a}$,
2. we compute the $\mathfrak{a}$-torsion subgroup $E[\mathfrak{a}] = \cap_{\alpha \in \mathfrak{a}} ker(\alpha) = \{P \in E(\overline{\mathbb{F}}_p) : \alpha P = 0_E \ \forall \alpha \in \mathfrak{a}\}$,
3. we compute the isogeny $\phi_\mathfrak{a} : E \to E_\mathfrak{a} \simeq E/E[\mathfrak{a}]$.

It is common practice to denote the action of $\mathfrak{a}$ on E by $\mathfrak{a} * E$.

A fundamental result in isogeny-based protocols is the *Deuring correspondence* between the set of maximal orders in $B_{p,\infty}$ and the set of elliptic curves: fixing a supersingular elliptic curve E_0, every ℓ-isogeny $\alpha : E_0 \to E$ corresponds to an ideal $\mathfrak{a}$ of norm ℓ, and vice-versa. Since $E_\mathfrak{a}$ is determined (up to isomorphism) by the ideal class of $\mathfrak{a}$, finding different representatives of an ideal class corresponds to finding different isogenies between two fixed curves.

We can rewrite any ideal $\mathfrak{a}$ of $\mathcal{O}$ as the product of $\mathcal{O}$-ideals $\mathfrak{a} = (\pi_p \mathcal{O})^r \mathfrak{a}_s$, where π_p is the p-th Frobenius endomorphism and $\mathfrak{a}_s \not\subseteq \pi_p \mathcal{O}$. This defines an elliptic curve $\mathfrak{a} * E$ and an isogeny $\phi_\mathfrak{a} : E \longrightarrow \mathfrak{a} * E$ of degree $N(\mathfrak{a})$ as follows:

- the separable part of $\phi_\mathfrak{a}$ has kernel $\cap_{\alpha \in \mathfrak{a}_s} ker(\alpha)$;
- the purely inseparable part consists of r iterations of Frobenius.

The isogeny $\phi_\mathfrak{a}$ and the codomain $\mathfrak{a} * E$ are both defined over $\mathbb{F}_p$ and are unique up to $\mathbb{F}_p$-isomorphism. Directly from this construction it is clear that multiplying ideals and composing isogenies are equivalent operations.

Let $\mathcal{E}\ell\ell_p(\mathcal{O}, \pi)$ be the set of elliptic curves defined over $\mathbb{F}_p$ whose endomorphism ring is isomorphic to $\mathcal{O}$ such that the Frobenius endomorphism π_p corresponds to π. As explained by Castryck et al. [CLM+18], we get the following fundamental result:

Theorem 1. *Let $\mathcal{O}$ be an order in an imaginary quadratic field and $\pi \in \mathcal{O}$ such that $\mathcal{E}\ell\ell_p(\mathcal{O}, \pi)$ is non-empty. Then the ideal class group $cl(\mathcal{O})$ acts freely and transitively on the set $\mathcal{E}\ell\ell_p(\mathcal{O}, \pi)$ via the map*

$$cl(\mathcal{O}) \times \mathcal{E}\ell\ell_p(\mathcal{O}, \pi) \longrightarrow \mathcal{E}\ell\ell_p(\mathcal{O}, \pi)$$
$$([\mathfrak{a}], E) \longrightarrow [\mathfrak{a}] * E.$$

From now on, we drop the class notation "$[\mathfrak{a}]$" in favor of a simpler "$\mathfrak{a}$" by considering any integral representative in the class.

The Structure of the Class Group. The class group $cl(\mathcal{O})$ is a finite abelian group whose cardinality is asymptotically $\#cl(\mathcal{O}) \sim \sqrt{|\Delta|}$. As argued by CSIDH's authors [CLM+18], computing the exact structure of the class group requires a lot of computational effort. The best known algorithm (by Hafner and McCurley [HM89]) for computing the structure of the class group is subexponential in Δ, which is typically very large for CSIDH (about the size of p). Therefore, the authors opt for heuristics which allow to find a very good approximation.

We are interested in the primes for which there exist distinct prime ideals $\mathfrak{l}, \bar{\mathfrak{l}}$ of $\mathcal{O}$ such that $\ell\mathcal{O} = \mathfrak{l}\bar{\mathfrak{l}}$. If ℓ is such a prime, we say that it splits in $\mathcal{O}$; ℓ is called an *Elkies prime* in the point-counting setting. The ideal $\mathfrak{l}$ is generated as $(\ell, \pi - \lambda)$, where $\lambda \in \mathbb{Z}/\ell\mathbb{Z}$ is an eigenvalue of π_p on the ℓ-torsion, and its conjugate is $\bar{\mathfrak{l}} = (\ell, \pi - \pi/\lambda)$, where p/λ is any integral representative of that quotient modulo ℓ. The prime ℓ splits in $\mathcal{O}$ if and only if Δ is a non-zero square modulo ℓ. The CSIDH protocol is carefully designed such that a long list of primes (74 in the 512-bit implementation) are Elkies primes.

Computing the Group Action. According to the heuristics assumed in CSIDH, any element of the group can be represented as the product of small primes ideals. We can compute $\mathfrak{l} * E$, the action of a prime ideal $\mathfrak{l} = (\ell, \pi - \lambda)$ on E, in three different ways:

(a) by using the modular polynomials [Sut13]:
   1. find $\mathbb{F}_p$-rational roots of the modular polynomial $\Phi_l(X, j(E))$, which are the j-invariants of the two possible codomains;
   2. compute the kernel polynomials $\chi(x) \in \mathbb{F}_p[x]$ for the corresponding isogenies;
   3. determine which of the options is the correct one by checking if $\pi_p(x, y) = [\lambda](x, y)$ modulo $\chi(x)$ over the curve;
(b) by using the division polynomials [Was08, XI.3]:
   1. factor the ℓ-th division polynomial $\psi_l(E)$ over $\mathbb{F}_p$;
   2. match the irreducible factors with the right Frobenius eigenvalues;
   3. use Kohel's formulae to compute the codomain;
(c) by using Vélu's formulae:
   1. find a basis of the ℓ-torsion points and compute the eigenspaces of π_p;
   2. apply Vélu's formulae to a basis point of the correct eigenspace to compute the codomain.

In CSIDH, the authors opt for the last method, which is the fastest when the necessary extension fields (in which the basis points lie) are small.

When $\lambda = 1$, the curve has a rational point defined over the base field $\mathbb{F}_p$. If we also have that $p/\lambda = -1$, then the other eigenspace of Frobenius endomorphism modulo ℓ is defined over $\mathbb{F}_{p^2}$, so both codomains can be easily computed using Vélu's formulae over the base field, switching from a curve to its quadratic twist if necessary. The parameters of the implementation are decided such that $p \equiv -1 \pmod{\ell}$ for many different primes ℓ: in this case, $\lambda = 1$ automatically implies that $p/\lambda = -1$.

3   Isogeny-Based Key-Exchange Protocols

Isogeny-based cryptography is a class of allegedly quantum-resistant schemes resulting from NIST's competition. Two of the most peculiar features that distinguish them from the other candidates are the use of shorter keys and the deployment of more sophisticated algebraic structures. In this section, we first provide an overview of CSIDH (pronounced "seaside") [CLM+18], a key-exchange protocol which does not take part in NIST's competition but is extremely interesting and promising. Then, we introduce our new protocol Π-SIDE (pronounced "pieside"), a translation if the protocol Π [CCG+19] in the CSIDH setting.

3.1   CSIDH

What follows is an outline of the CSIDH protocol, whose underlying algebraic structures are briefly explained in Sect. 2.3. We dwell in particular on the aspects which are relevant to our results.

Parameters. Fix a large prime $p = 4 \cdot \ell_1 \cdot \ell_2 \cdots \ell_n - 1$ where ℓ_i are small distinct odd primes. p is designed such that $p \equiv 3 \pmod 4$, in order to

- easily write down supersingular elliptic curves over $\mathbb{F}_p$;
- make use of the Montgomery form of elliptic curves in the implementation.

The starting curve for each execution of the protocol is the supersingular elliptic curve in Montgomery form $E_0 : y^2 = x^3 + x$ over $\mathbb{F}_p$. In this case the characteristic equation of the Frobenius endomorphism is $\pi_p^2 = -p$, which implies that the $\mathbb{F}_p$-rational endomorphism ring $End_p(E_0)$ is an order in the imaginary quadratic field $\mathbb{Q}(\sqrt{-p})$; in particular, $End_p(E_0) = \mathbb{Z}[\pi]$. The resulting ℓ_i-isogeny graph is a disjoint union of cycles. Moreover, since $\pi^2 - 1 \equiv 0 \pmod{\ell_i}$ for each $i = 1, \ldots, n$, the ideals $\ell_i \mathcal{O}$ split as $\ell_i \mathcal{O} = \mathfrak{l}_i \bar{\mathfrak{l}}_i = (\ell_i, \pi - 1)(\ell_i, \pi + 1)$ (so all the ℓ_i are Elkies primes). Furthermore, the kernel of $\phi_{\mathfrak{l}_i}$ is the subgroup generated by a point P of order ℓ_i which lies in the kernel of $\pi - 1$. Analogously, the kernel of $\phi_{\bar{\mathfrak{l}}_i}$ is generated by a point Q of order ℓ_i that is defined over $\mathbb{F}_{p^2}$ but not in $\mathbb{F}_p$ and such that $\pi(Q) = -Q$.

Sampling Ideals and Computing Their Action. Although we want to sample uniformly at random from the ideal class group $cl(\mathcal{O})$, it is preferable not to compute its exact structure because of the large size of the discriminant Δ. By heuristically assuming that

- the ideals $\mathfrak{l}_i$ do not have very small order,
- the ideals $\mathfrak{l}_i$ are evenly distributed in the class group,

two ideals $\mathfrak{l}_1^{e_1} \mathfrak{l}_2^{e_2} \cdots \mathfrak{l}_n^{e_n}$ for small e_i will rarely lie in the same class. The e_i are sampled from a short range $\{-m, \ldots m\}$ for some integer m such that $2m + 1 \geq \sqrt[n]{\#cl(\mathcal{O})}$. Since the prime ideals $\mathfrak{l}_i$ are fixed, we represent any ideal $\prod_i \mathfrak{l}_i^{e_i}$ (which will be the user's secret key) as a vector $(e_1, e_2, \ldots, e_n) \in [-m, m]^n$.

Since $\pi^2 \equiv -p \equiv 1 \pmod{\ell_i}$, the eigenvalues of all ℓ_i-torsion subgroups are $+1$ and -1. This allows us to efficiently compute the action of $\mathfrak{l}_i$ by using method 3 in Sect. 2.3.

Representing and Validating $\mathbb{F}_p$-Isomorphism Classes. The SIDH protocol misses a key-validation mechanism, and countermeasures are expensive. We recall how the authors of CSIDH solve the problem for their protocol. First of all, they provide a result [CLM+18, Proposition 8]) which states that, for the chosen p and supersingular elliptic curve, the Montgomery coefficient uniquely represents the class of elliptic curves resulting from the evaluation of an ideal. Secondly, to prove that an elliptic curve is supersingular (and thus $\#E(\mathbb{F}_p) = p + 1$), it is enough to find a point $Q \in E$ whose order is a divisor of $p + 1$ greater than $4\sqrt{p}$ (by Hasse's theorem, we have only one multiple of that divisor in the interval $[p+1-2\sqrt{p}, p+1+2\sqrt{p}]$, which must be the group order by Lagrange's theorem). They therefore provide an algorithm which takes a point at random and computes its order. With high probability (increasing with ℓ_i), this will tell in only one step if the curve is supersingular or not. If x-only Montgomery arithmetic is used, a random point P is obtained by randomly picking $x \in \mathbb{F}_p$, and there is no need to differentiate points in $\mathbb{F}_p$ and in $\mathbb{F}_{p^2}$ (in the second case, the point will correspond to an $\mathbb{F}_p$-rational point in the quadratic twist, which is supersingular if and only if the original curve is supersingular).

The CSIDH Protocol. We first describe how to perform the Setup and the key generation, then we schematise the simple structure of key-exchange protocol.

Setup. In this phase we set up the global parameters of the key-exchange protocol. In particular, we fix:

- n distinct odd primes ℓ_i, corresponding to n isogeny-degrees;
- a large prime $p = 4 \cdot \ell_1 \cdot \ell_2 \cdots \ell_n - 1$;
- the supersingular elliptic curve $E_0 : y^2 = x^3 + x$ over $\mathbb{F}_p$ with endomorphism ring $\mathcal{O} = \mathbb{Z}[\pi]$.

Key Generation. The *private key* is an n-tuple $(e_1, \ldots, e_n)$ of integers, randomly sampled from a range $\{-m, \ldots, m\}$ such that $2m + 1 \geq \sqrt[n]{\#cl(\mathcal{O})}$, representing the ideal class $\mathfrak{a} = \mathfrak{l}_1^{e_1} \mathfrak{l}_2^{e_2} \ldots \mathfrak{l}_n^{e_n} \in cl(\mathcal{O})$. The *public key* is the Montgomery coefficient $A \in \mathbb{F}_p$ of the elliptic curve $\mathfrak{a} * E_0 : y^2 = x^3 + Ax^2 + x$, obtained by applying the action of $\mathfrak{a}$ to the curve E_0.

Algorithm 2: CSIDH, the non-interactive key-exchange protocol.

Alice	**Bob**
$ssk_A : \mathfrak{a} \in cl(\mathcal{O})$	$ssk_B : \mathfrak{b} \in cl(\mathcal{O})$
$spk_A : E_A = \mathfrak{a} * E_0$	$spk_B : E_B = \mathfrak{b} * E_0$

retrieve E_B and check its supersingularity;

$$K_A = \mathfrak{a} * E_B$$

retrieve E_A and check its supersingularity;

$$K_B = \mathfrak{b} * E_A$$

$$K_A = \mathfrak{a}\mathfrak{b} * E_0 = K_B$$

3.2 Our Protocol: Π-SIDE

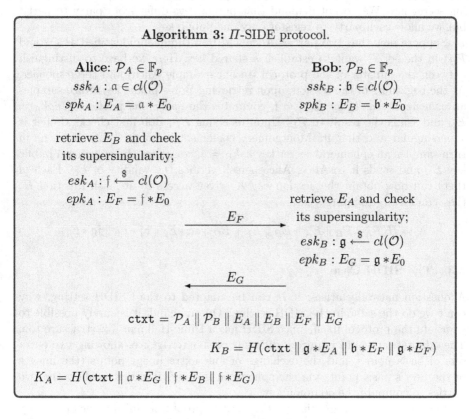

Algorithm 3: Π-SIDE protocol.

Alice: $\mathcal{P}_A \in \mathbb{F}_p$

$ssk_A : \mathfrak{a} \in cl(\mathcal{O})$

$spk_A : E_A = \mathfrak{a} * E_0$

Bob: $\mathcal{P}_B \in \mathbb{F}_p$

$ssk_B : \mathfrak{b} \in cl(\mathcal{O})$

$spk_B : E_B = \mathfrak{b} * E_0$

retrieve E_B and check its supersingularity;

$esk_A : \mathfrak{f} \xleftarrow{\$} cl(\mathcal{O})$

$epk_A : E_F = \mathfrak{f} * E_0$

$\xrightarrow{\quad E_F \quad}$

retrieve E_A and check its supersingularity;

$esk_B : \mathfrak{g} \xleftarrow{\$} cl(\mathcal{O})$

$epk_B : E_G = \mathfrak{g} * E_0$

$\xleftarrow{\quad E_G \quad}$

$$\mathtt{ctxt} = \mathcal{P}_A \,\|\, \mathcal{P}_B \,\|\, E_A \,\|\, E_B \,\|\, E_F \,\|\, E_G$$

$$K_B = H(\mathtt{ctxt} \,\|\, \mathfrak{g} * E_A \,\|\, \mathfrak{b} * E_F \,\|\, \mathfrak{g} * E_F)$$

$$K_A = H(\mathtt{ctxt} \,\|\, \mathfrak{a} * E_G \,\|\, \mathfrak{f} * E_B \,\|\, \mathfrak{f} * E_G)$$

Just like in CSIDH, we fix a large prime $p = 4 \cdot \ell_1 \cdot \ell_2 \cdots \ell_n - 1$ for odd and distinct primes ℓ_i. Then we consider the supersingular elliptic curve E_0 :

$y^2 = x^3 + x$ defined over $\mathbb{F}_p$, with endomorphism ring $\mathcal{O} = \mathbb{Z}[\pi]$. We recall that a key-pair $(\mathfrak{a}, E_A)$ can be correctly (with heuristic assumptions) formed as follows:

1. for $i = 1, 2, \ldots, n$, sample the exponent $a_i \xleftarrow{\$} \{-m, \ldots m\}$, where m is the smallest integer such that $2m + 1 \geq \sqrt[n]{\#cl(\mathcal{O})}$;
2. construct the fractional ideal $\mathfrak{a} = \mathfrak{l}_1^{a_1} \cdot \mathfrak{l}_2^{a_2} \cdots \mathfrak{l}_n^{a_n}$. The ideal class $\mathfrak{a}$ will play the role of secret key;
3. evaluate the action of the ideal class $\mathfrak{a}$ on the elliptic curve E_0, obtaining the curve $E_A = \mathfrak{a} * E_0$; E_A is the Montgomery curve defined by the equation $y^2 = x^3 + Ax^2 + x$ over $\mathbb{F}_p$ and it will be the public part of the key pair.

The implementation-oriented reader should always remember that each elliptic curve should be represented using its Montgomery coefficient. For the sake of notation we will refer to the curve instead.

Let $\mathcal{P}$ be the set of participants to the key-exchange protocol. We assume that each party in $\mathcal{P}$ holds a *static secret key ssk* and a *static public key spk*, the latter registered at a certificate authority $\mathcal{CA}$. The certificate authority, upon registering a public key, does not require a proof of knowledge on the corresponding secret key. We do not demand that public keys differ from party to party, but we allow each party to register only one public key.

Suppose now that two parties Alice and Bob (uniquely identified as $\mathcal{P}_A$ and $\mathcal{P}_B$) in the set $\mathcal{P}$ want to establish a shared key. Here we have to distinguish between the initiator of the protocol (in our example Alice) and the responder. At the beginning of the session, upon retrieving Bob's public key, Alice samples an *ephemeral secret key* $esk_A = \mathfrak{f}$, computes the *ephemeral public key* $epk_A = E_F$ and sends the result to $\mathcal{P}_B$. Upon receiving E_F, Bob first checks that it is supersingular and that its Montgomery coefficient is not in $\{\pm 2\}$; if so, he in turn samples an ephemeral secret key $esk_B = \mathfrak{g}$, computes the ephemeral public key E_G and sends it to Alice. Alice herself verifies the validity of E_G. Each of them can now obtain the *session key* K: given access to an hash function H, they can locally compute

$$K = H(\mathcal{P}_A \parallel \mathcal{P}_B \parallel E_A \parallel E_B \parallel E_F \parallel E_G \parallel \mathfrak{a}\mathfrak{g} * E_0 \parallel \mathfrak{b}\mathfrak{f} * E_0 \parallel \mathfrak{f}\mathfrak{g} * E_0).$$

3.3 The SIDH Case

A question naturally arises: if Π can be adapted to the CSIDH setting, why can't we do the same in the SIDH setting? On one hand, it is surely possible to translate the protocol itself, since SIDH has a Diffie-Hellman-like structure too. The adaptation would require a different parameter choice, allowing two extra sets of basis points, and the exchange of four extra image points (the images of the peer's basis points via the ephemeral isogeny) in order to allow the two parties to compute the common key.

On the other hand, in this case the security proof wouldn't hit the optimality bound in the tightness loss. As it will be clarified in the next section, a property that plays a fundamental role in this sense is the random self-reducibility of the computational problem. In the next section we provide a formal proof of this feature in the CSIDH case. At our knowledge, there exists no evidence that SIDH shares this property, and it is rather unlikely to find a way to prove it.

4   Random Self-reducibility

According to a fundamental definition by Blum and Micali, later rephrased by Naor [NR97], a problem f is *random self-reducible* if solving it at any given instance x can be reduced in polynomial time to the solution of f at one or more random instances y_i. In order to achieve random self-reducibility, there are two conditions that have to be satisfied:

- the generation of the random instances $y_1, \ldots y_n$ has to be performed non-adaptively;
- the instances $y_1, \ldots y_n$ must be uniformly distributed.

Random self-reducible problems are extremely relevant for cryptographic purposes. First of all, they are used in *worst-case to average-case reductions*: a worst-case instance of the problem can be used to generate a set of random instances, so that solving f on the random instances allows us to solve f at the worst-case instance in polynomial time. In the early '80s, Goldwasser and Micali exploited random self-reducibility of mathematical problems to construct cryptographic algorithms for probabilistic encryption [GM82] and pseudorandom generation [BM82]. Even more, if the group G and its generator g are properly chosen, the random self-reducibility of the discrete logarithm problem guarantees passive security of the plain Diffie-Hellman key-exchange protocol.

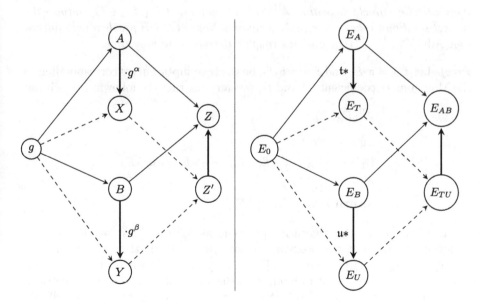

Fig. 1. Rerandomization graphs for Computational Diffie-Hellman and Computational-CSIDH problems.

4.1 Random Self-reducibility on CSIDH

It is folklore that the key-recovery problem in CSIDH is random self-reducible, while SIDH-based problems are not. De Feo and Galbraith [DG19] provide a short proof of random self-reducibility of CSIDH; hereafter, we prove this property more verbosely, in a fashion that resembles the classical proof of re-randomizability for the Computational Diffie-Hellman problem. A fundamental role is played by the commutative action of $cl(\mathcal{O})$ on the set of elliptic curves with endomorphism ring isomorphic to $\mathcal{O}$. The presence of a commutative action is a very strong element of resemblance with the Diffie-Hellman protocol.

Let us now prove random self-reducibility of the Computational CSIDH problem, from which we can deduce the same property for the Gap and the Strong variants. Let $\mathbb{G}$ be the set of elliptic curves defined over $\mathbb{F}_p$.

Problem 1 (Computational-CSIDH problem). *Given n distinct odd primes ℓ_i and a large prime $p = 4 \cdot \ell_1 \cdot \ell_2 \cdots \ell_n - 1$, let $E_0 \in \mathbb{G}$ be the supersingular elliptic curve in Montgomery form $y^2 = x^3 + x$. Given two valid CSIDH public keys $A, B \in \mathbb{F}_p$, where A is the Montgomery coefficient of the elliptic curve $E_A = \mathfrak{a} * E_0$ and B is the one of $E_B = \mathfrak{b} * E_0$, find the Montgomery coefficient $Z \in \mathbb{F}_p$ of the elliptic curve $E_{A,B} = \mathfrak{a}\mathfrak{b} * E_0$.*

Theorem 2. *The computational-CSIDH problem is random self-reducible. In other words, given any two random elliptic curves $E_T = \mathfrak{t}*E_0$ and $E_U = \mathfrak{u}*E_0$, for any algorithm $\mathcal{B}$ which solves the computational-CSIDH problem with advantage*

$$\mathrm{Adv}_{\mathbb{G}}^{\mathrm{Comp-CSIDH}}(\mathcal{B}) = \mathrm{Prob}\big[\, \mathcal{B}(E_T, E_U) = Z' \mid E_T \xleftarrow{\$} \mathbb{G}, E_U \xleftarrow{\$} \mathbb{G}\big]$$

there exists an oracle algorithm $\mathcal{A}^{\mathcal{B}}$ that, for any input $E_A, E_B \in \mathbb{G}$, outputs the correct solution to the corresponding computational-CSIDH problem with advantage $\mathrm{Adv}_{\mathbb{G}}^{\mathrm{Comp-CSIDH}}(\mathcal{B})$, and has roughly the same running time.

Proof. Let $E_A = \mathfrak{a}*E_0$ and $E_B = \mathfrak{b}*E_0$ be the two elliptic curves corresponding to the Montgomery coefficients A and B; we can construct the following algorithm:

$$\mathcal{A}^{\mathcal{B}}(E_A, E_B)$$

$\mathfrak{t}, \mathfrak{u} \xleftarrow{\$} cl(\mathcal{O})$

$E_T \leftarrow \mathfrak{t}*E_A = \mathfrak{t}' *E_0, \ E_U \leftarrow \mathfrak{u}*E_B = \mathfrak{u}' *E_0$

$Z' \leftarrow \mathcal{B}(E_T, E_U)$

return Z of $[\mathfrak{t}^{-1}\mathfrak{u}^{-1}] *E_{Z'}$

In other words, the algorithm proceeds as follows. First of all, we pick uniformly at random two isogeny classes $\mathfrak{t}, \mathfrak{u} \in cl(\mathcal{O})$: they are defined as $\mathfrak{t} = \mathfrak{l}_1^{t_1} \mathfrak{l}_2^{t_2} \ldots \mathfrak{l}_n^{t_n} \in cl(\mathcal{O})$ and $\mathfrak{u} = \mathfrak{l}_1^{u_1} \mathfrak{l}_2^{u_2} \ldots \mathfrak{l}_n^{u_n} \in cl(\mathcal{O})$ where each exponent t_i, u_j is picked uniformly at random from the set $\{-m, \ldots, m\}$. Then we evaluate the action of $\mathfrak{t}$ on E_A and the action $\mathfrak{u}$ on E_B, obtaining two random elliptic curves $E_T, E_U \in \mathbb{G}$. Finally, we submit the new random instance to the algorithm $\mathcal{B}$, which outputs Z', the Montgomery coefficient of the elliptic curve $E_{Z'}$. Since

$$
\begin{aligned}
E_{Z'} &= \mathfrak{t}'\mathfrak{u}' * E_0 \\
&= (\mathfrak{t}\mathfrak{a})(\mathfrak{u}\mathfrak{b}) * E_0 \\
&= (\mathfrak{t}\mathfrak{u})(\mathfrak{a}\mathfrak{b}) * E_0 \\
&= (\mathfrak{t}\mathfrak{u}) * E_{A,B},
\end{aligned}
$$

we can easily retrieve the Montgomery coefficient Z of the elliptic curve $E_{A,B} = \mathfrak{t}^{-1}\mathfrak{u}^{-1} * E_{Z'}$. The advantage of the algorithm $\mathcal{A}^{\mathcal{B}}$ can be calculated as follows:

$$
\mathrm{Prob}[\mathcal{A}^{\mathcal{B}}(E_A, E_B) = Z] = \mathrm{Prob}\left[\mathfrak{t}, \mathfrak{u} \xleftarrow{\$} cl(\mathcal{O}) : \mathcal{B}(\mathfrak{t}*E_A, \mathfrak{u}*E_B) = (\mathfrak{t}\mathfrak{a})(\mathfrak{u}\mathfrak{b})*E_0\right].
$$

By construction, the ideal classes $\mathfrak{t}$ and $\mathfrak{u}$ can be considered as sampled uniformly at random from $cl(\mathcal{O})$ (for the heuristics assumed in CSIDH), and therefore the elliptic curves $E_T = \mathfrak{t} * E_A$ and $E_U = \mathfrak{u} * E_B$ are independent and uniformly distributed on $\mathbb{G}$. Therefore, the oracle consulted by $\mathcal{A}^{\mathcal{B}}$ receives a well formed instance, so we can conclude that

$$
\begin{aligned}
\mathrm{Prob}[\mathcal{A}^{\mathcal{B}}(E_A, E_B) = Z] &= \mathrm{Prob}\left[\mathcal{B}(E_T, E_U) = \mathfrak{t}\mathfrak{a}\mathfrak{u}\mathfrak{b} * E_0 \mid \mathfrak{t}, \mathfrak{u} \xleftarrow{\$} cl(\mathcal{O})\right] \\
&= \mathrm{Adv}_{\mathbb{G}}^{\mathrm{Comp-CSIDH}}(\mathcal{B}).
\end{aligned}
$$

As pointed out in Sect. 2.3, we can efficiently compute the action of the ideal classes $\mathfrak{l}$ and $\mathfrak{l}^{-1}$ by using Vélu-type formulae. Therefore we can conclude that, if $\mathcal{B}$ runs in t-time, then the algorithm $\mathcal{A}^{\mathcal{B}}$ runs in $(t + \delta)$-time, where δ is the small running time required to sample elements and evaluate the action of ideal classes. $\qquad\square$

5 Security of Π-SIDE

In this section, we define some allegedly hard problems in the CSIDH setting. The definition of our security model and the full proof can be found in Appendix B. The structure of the proof is similar to the one for protocol Π [CCG+19], but we have made a number of changes, mostly related to the new re-randomization technique. A straightforward adaption would have not been possible by simply substituting exponentiations with class group evaluations.

5.1 Hard Problems

In Sect. 4.1, we have seen that the Comp-CSIDH problem consists in finding the Montgomery coefficient $Z \in \mathbb{F}_p$ of the elliptic curve $\mathfrak{a}\mathfrak{b} * E_0$ given the Montgomery coefficients of the curves $E_A = \mathfrak{a} * E_0$ and $E_B = \mathfrak{b} * E_0$. In order to keep the notation as simple as possible, we will formulate the next problems referring to the elliptic curve itself, instead of its Montgomery coefficient. The reader should always keep in mind that, when it comes to the implementation, each elliptic curve will be represented by its Montgomery coefficient, which lies in $\mathbb{F}_p$. We start with defining a decisional problem:

Problem 2 (Decisional-CSIDH problem). *In the CSIDH setting, let* $\mathfrak{a}, \mathfrak{b}, \mathfrak{r} \xleftarrow{\$}$ $cl(\mathcal{O})$ *be elements randomly sampled from* $cl(\mathcal{O})$ *and let* $b \xleftarrow{\$} \{0,1\}$ *be the result of a fairly tossed coin. If* $b = 0$ *set* $E_Z = \mathfrak{r} * E_0$, *otherwise set* $E_Z = \mathfrak{a}\mathfrak{b} * E_0$ *and run the adversary on input* $(E_A = \mathfrak{a} * E_0, E_B = \mathfrak{b} * E_0, E_Z)$. *We define the advantage of* $\mathcal{A}$ *in solving the decisional CSIDH problem over* $cl(\mathcal{O})$ *as*

$$Adv_{cl(\mathcal{O})}^{Dec-CSIDH}(\mathcal{A}) := \left| Prob\left[\mathcal{A}(E_A, E_B, E_Z) = b \right] - \frac{1}{2} \right|.$$

In other words, the decisional problem is hard if the adversary succeeds with a negligible probability in distinguishing among a properly computed session key and a random key. Trivially, if we can solve the computational variant of problem then we can also solve its decisional variant. But does the opposite hold?

Problem 3 (Gap-CSIDH problem). *In the CSIDH setting, let* $\mathfrak{a}, \mathfrak{b} \xleftarrow{\$} cl(\mathcal{O})$ *be two elements randomly sampled from* $cl(\mathcal{O})$, *corresponding to the curves* $E_A = \mathfrak{a} * E_0$ *and* $E_B = \mathfrak{b} * E_0$. *Suppose that the adversary* $\mathcal{A}$ *is given access to a Dec-CSIDH oracle* $\mathcal{D}(\cdot, \cdot, \cdot)$, *which outputs 1 if queried on a valid CSIDH triplet* (E_A, E_B, E_{AB}) *and 0 otherwise. We define the advantage of* $\mathcal{A}$ *in solving the Gap-CSIDH problem over* $cl(\mathcal{O})$ *as*

$$Adv_{cl(\mathcal{O})}^{Gap-CSIDH}(\mathcal{A}) := Prob\left[\mathcal{A}(E_A, E_B) = E_{A,B}, providing\ \mathcal{A}\ access\ to\ \mathcal{D}(\cdot, \cdot, \cdot) \right]$$

The security of protocol Π [CCG+19] relies on the Strong-DH problem [ABR01], a variant of the Gap problem in which the adversary is granted access to a more limited decisional oracle.

Problem 4 (Strong-CSIDH problem). *In the CSIDH setting, let* $\mathfrak{a}, \mathfrak{b} \xleftarrow{\$} cl(\mathcal{O})$ *be two elements randomly sampled from* $cl(\mathcal{O})$, *corresponding to the curves* $E_A = \mathfrak{a} * E_0$ *and* $E_B = \mathfrak{b} * E_0$. *Let* $\mathcal{D}$ *be an oracle for the decisional CSIDH problem. Suppose that the adversary* $\mathcal{A}$ *is given access to a decisional oracle with fixed first input* $\mathcal{D}_X(\cdot, \cdot) := \mathcal{D}(E_X, \cdot, \cdot)$, *which outputs 1 if queried on a valid CSIDH triplet* (E_X, E_Y, E_{XY}) *and 0 otherwise. We define the advantage of* $\mathcal{A}$ *in solving the Strong-CSIDH problem over* $cl(\mathcal{O})$ *as*

$$Adv_{cl(\mathcal{O})}^{St-CSIDH}(\mathcal{A}) := Prob\left[\mathcal{A}(E_A, E_B) = E_{A,B},\ providing\ \mathcal{A}\ access\ to\ \mathcal{D}_X(\cdot, \cdot) \right]$$

Rerandomizability of the Gap-CSIDH and the Strong-CSIDH problems follows directly from Theorem 4.1. The full security proof, which strongly relies on these problems, is provided in Appendix B. Based on the current state of the art, there is no reason to believe that the above problems can be easily solved.

6   Comparison

Comparing the efficiency of our scheme with other post-quantum schemes is hard. First of all, many schemes do not have a security proof [Ber19] (and thus we cannot define theoretically-sound parameters); secondly, it is highly non-trivial to convert the concrete analysis into security parameters for many schemes.

Castryck et al. [CLM+18] describe an implementation for a 128-bit security level that requires about $106 \cdot 10^6$ clock cycles to compute the group action. Since our protocol Π-SIDE requires four group action computations, we have a total cost of about $400 \cdot 10^6$ clock cycles, ignoring hashing and other cheap operations.

The most natural target for comparison is SIKE [JAC+19], which the original Π-protocol can also be generalized to. One would probably not attempt to build it on top of the defined KEM, but use the underlying isogeny instead. Table 2.1 from SIKE [JAC+19] suggests that an isogeny computation using the optimized implementation (which probably matches the CSIDH implementation best) requires roughly $50 \cdot 10^6$ clock cycles for the 128 bit security level (SIKEp434), which becomes roughly $200 \cdot 10^6$ clock cycles for the generalized Π-protocol, significantly faster than the CSIDH-based version.

Now suppose we instantiate the protocol with 2^{16} users and 2^{16} sessions per user. In this case, the apparent security level of our protocol falls to about 110 bits. The SIKE-based protocol with the standard security proof will have a quadratic security loss. This means that in order to get a similar theoretically-sound security level from the SIKE-based protocol, we need to switch to SIKEp610. Again, Table 2.1 from SIKE [JAC+19] suggests that an isogeny computation using the optimized implementation requires roughly $160 \cdot 10^6$ clock cycles. The generalized Π-protocol then requires roughly $640 \cdot 10^6$ clock cycles, which is significantly slower than the CSIDH-based version. According to this approximate analysis, the CSIDH-based version is faster than the corresponding SIKE-based protocol when instantiated with theoretically-sound parameters. However, to properly determine which is faster, comparable optimized implementations would be needed.

Another natural comparison target is the Strongly secure AKE from Supersingular Isogenies by Xu et al. [XXW+19] referred to in Sect. 1.2. For their two-pass protocol SIAKE$_2$ and their three-pass protocol SIAKE$_3$, the numbers of cycles are approximately $7 \cdot 10^9$ and $6 \cdot 10^9$, respectively [XXW+19, Table 6]. Our protocol is significantly faster, by about an order of magnitude.

7   Conclusions and Open Problems

In this paper we have shown that it is possible to construct post-quantum isogeny-based key-exchange protocols with optimal tightness, without compromising efficiency and key-size. The protocol is an easy adaptation of protocol Π [CCG+19], where we substitute exponentiations in cyclic groups with actions of ideal classes on elliptic curves. The adaptation of the proof, which requires random self-reducibility of the computational-CSIDH problem, could not be done trivially. Indeed, we have had to exploit a different re-randomization technique for the computational challenge, since we only have one group operation on ideal classes against two operations (addition and multiplication) on exponents. We have shown that the resulting scheme is competitive with other isogeny-based protocols, which lack a security proof or have a larger tightness loss.

Our protocol is proven secure in the Random Oracle Model. In a crucial step we use the Strong-CSIDH oracle to detect if the adversary queries the hashing oracle on an input which contains the solution to a given computational-CSIDH challenge. If we allow the adversary to make quantum queries, the target solution might be hidden in the superposition of states. We believe that collapsing the input state after the oracle's answer is not invalidating our security proof, since we do not need to reprogram the oracle. We leave the proof of security in the QROM as future work.

A stronger security notion can be achieved by adding the static-static term in the session-key computation, or by applying the NAXOS trick [LLM07]. But security against state compromise (ephemeral key reveal) increases the tightness loss, since we cannot tightly deal with state reveal queries. How to move to a stronger security model without losing in tightness is still an open problem.

We have seen how the flexible algebraic structure at the basis of CSIDH can be exploited to remodel protocol Π in the isogeny setting. Nevertheless, the simplicity of this scheme might be further exploited. Other quantum-hard problems might be used to translate the scheme in other algebraic contexts. Adaptions in this direction are left for further research.

As a last remark, we would like to clarify that our scheme is not affected by the algorithm recently published by Castryck et al. [CSV20]. This attack, which breaks some instances of the Decisional CSIDH problem, does not work when $p \equiv 3 \pmod 4$, as per our protocol.

Appendix

A   Security Model

Suppose that we have a certificate authority $\mathcal{CA}$, a set of parties $\mathcal{P} := \{\mathcal{P}_i\}_{i=1}^{\mu}$ and an adversary $\mathcal{M}$. The parties can communicate with each other and with $\mathcal{CA}$ by using an unauthenticated network. $\mathcal{CA}$ can be seen as a globally trusted party, or register, who holds and distributes the static public keys of the parties in $\mathcal{P}$. At any time, a new player can join in $\mathcal{P}$ by communicating his static public key to the $\mathcal{CA}$, and the register can grow indefinitely. As we mentioned before, we do not require different parties to hold different public keys, and neither we demand any proof of knowledge of the related secret key. Our protocol is implicitly authenticated and, as such, no identification or proof of knowledge of any secret information is required. The only constraint we impose is that each member can commit to only one static public key at a time.

Each $\mathcal{P}_i$ is represented as a set of oracles $\{\pi_i^1, \pi_i^2, \ldots, \pi_i^k\}$, one for each of the k sessions the user can participate to. Each oracle $\pi_i^s = (P_i^s, \psi_i^s, K_i^s, \mathsf{sent}_i^s, \mathsf{recv}_i^s, role_i^s)$ maintains an internal state consisting of:

- the identity of the intended peer P_i^s which is supposedly taking part to the key-exchange session;
- $\psi_i^s \in \{\emptyset, accept, reject\}$, which indicates whether the session key has not been computed yet, or if it has been accepted or rejected;
- the session key K_i^s, which is not empty if and only if $\psi_i^s = accept$;
- sent_i^s, the collection of all the messages sent by the oracle;
- recv_i^s, the collection of all the messages received by the oracle;
- the role $role_i^s$ of the oracle (`init` or `resp`).

sent_i^s and recv_i^s together form the view view_i^s of $\mathcal{P}_i$ of the session s.

We now define the attribute for indicating two oracles that allegedly participated to the same key-exchange session. Two oracles π_i^s and π_j^t are called *partner oracles* if

1. $P_i^s = P_j$ and $P_j^t = P_i$, i.e. if they are the intended peer of each other;
2. $\psi_i^s = \psi_j^t = accept$, i.e. they both accepted the session key;
3. $\mathsf{view}_i^s = \mathsf{view}_j^t$, i.e. the messages sent and received by P_i match with the ones respectively received and sent by P_j during the key-exchange session;
4. they have specular roles.

Slightly simplifying the definition, an oracle is *fresh* if and only if its session key has not been revealed, its partner oracle has not been corrupted or tested and the partner's session key has not been revealed. We will later constrain the adversary to test only fresh oracles. A party is *honest* if all its oracles are fresh, i.e. if it has not been corrupted yet.

In this model, the adversary $\mathcal{A}$ has full control over the network and interacts with the oracles through queries that allow it to

- *activate* an oracle π_i^s and assign a role by sending it a message on behalf of a peer P_j;
- *reveal the long-term secret key* of a user P_i. This query provides the target user with the attribute of *corrupted* and all its oracles will answer $\perp$ to each later query;
- *register the long-term public key* for a new user. No knowledge of the corresponding secret key is required and the public key is distributed to all other users;
- *reveal the session key* k_i^s stored in the internal state of any oracle π_i^s. The target oracle is now said to be *revealed*.
- *test* an oracle π_i^s, which outputs $\perp$ if $\psi_i^s \neq accept$. If $\psi_i^s = accept$ it then outputs a key, which is either the session-key or one picked at random, according to a previously defined random bit. The key, may it be real or the random, is consistently issued in case of further tests.

Note that the adversary cannot query on the ephemeral key of any session.

We work in the *Real-or-Random* model: when tested, each oracle will output a real session key or a random key, according to a bit sampled at the beginning of the security game. If $b = 0$ each oracle tested during the game will output a random key, while if $b = 1$ each tested oracle will output the real session key.

Once the environment has been set up, we run the following *AKE security game* $G_\Pi(\mu, k)$, with μ honest parties and at most k sessions per user:

1. at first we toss a coin $b \xleftarrow{\$} \{0,1\}$. We also set up μ parties, providing each of them with a long-term key pair (sk_i, pk_i) and with k oracles;
2. we then run the adversary $\mathcal{A}$, which knows all the public keys and can make any number of the previously defined queries. The only restriction is that an oracle must be fresh when it is tested;
3. at some point, $\mathcal{A}$ will eventually output b', its guess on the initial bit b. If the tested oracles are fresh and $b' = b$, then $\mathcal{A}$ wins the security game.

An adversary can try to break the system in three different ways: it can trick two oracles into computing different session keys (event $\mathsf{break_{Sound}}$), break the unicity of the partnership relation between two oracles (event $\mathsf{break_{Unique}}$) or successfully guess $b' = b$ (event $\mathsf{break_{KE}}$). We formalise these ideas in the following definition.

Definition 5. *In this security model, a protocol Π fails if at least one of* $\mathsf{break_{Sound}}$, $\mathsf{break_{Unique}}$ *and* $\mathsf{break_{KE}}$ *occurs while running game $G(\mu, k)$. Given an adversary $\mathcal{A}$, we define its advantage against the AKE security of protocol Π as*

$$Adv_\Pi^{AKE}(\mathcal{A}) := \max\left\{ Prob[\mathsf{break_{Sound}}], Prob[\mathsf{break_{Unique}}], Prob[\mathsf{break_{KE}}] - \frac{1}{2}\right\}$$

and we say that it $(t, \epsilon_\mathcal{A}, \mu, k)$-breaks the AKE security of Π if it runs in time t and has advantage $Adv_{\Pi-SIDE}^{AKE}(\mathcal{A}) \geq \epsilon_\mathcal{A}$.

B   The Security Proof

As in the proof by Cohn-Gordon et al. [CCG+19], we prove the following:

Theorem 3. *Consider an environment running Π-SIDE together with an adversary $\mathcal{A}$ against AKE security of Π-SIDE. Then there exist 3 Strong-CSIDH adversaries $\mathcal{B}_1, \mathcal{B}_2, \mathcal{B}_3$ such that $\mathcal{A}$'s advantage $Adv_{\Pi-SIDE}^{AKE}(\mathcal{A})$ is at most*

$$\mu \cdot Adv_{cl(\mathcal{O})}^{St-CSIDH}(\mathcal{B}_1) + Adv_{cl(\mathcal{O})}^{St-CSIDH}(\mathcal{B}_2) + \mu \cdot Adv_{cl(\mathcal{O})}^{St-CSIDH}(\mathcal{B}_3) + \frac{\mu k^2}{N}$$

where $\mu = |\mathcal{P}|$ is the number of parties, k is the maximal number of AKE-sessions per party and N is the order of $cl(\mathcal{O})$. The run-time of adversaries $\mathcal{B}_1, \mathcal{B}_2, \mathcal{B}_3$ is almost the same as $\mathcal{A}$ and they make at most as many queries to the Strong-CSIDH oracle as $\mathcal{A}$ does to the hash oracle H.

The proof structure is analogous to the one of Π, rephrased and adapted to our setting. It consists of six different games: Game 0 is the AKE experiment, while the other five games involve the following oracle types:

- type I: an initiator oracle which has received the response from a responder oracle (honest when the response is received) and with which it agrees on the transcript ctxt;
- type II: an initiator oracle whose intended peer is honest until the oracle accepts;
- type III: a responder oracle triggered by an honest initiator, with which it agrees on ctxt and which is still honest when it receives the response;
- type IV: a responder oracle whose intended peer is honest until the oracle accepts;
- type V: an oracle (whether initiator or responder) whose intended peer is corrupted.

Table 1. Oracle types, defined by role, partner's honesty and agreement on ctxt.

Oracle	Init.	Resp.	Honest partner (before acceptance)	Honest partner (after acceptance)	Corrupted partner	Agreement on ctxt
Type I	✓		✓	✓		✓
Type II	✓		✓			
Type III		✓	✓	✓		✓
Type IV		✓	✓			
Type V	✓	✓			✓	

At the time of starting an AKE session, an initiator oracle cannot be entirely sure about the intended peer's honesty: we cannot tell if it is of type I or type II. This uncertainty vanishes when it receives the response and it comes the time to compute the session key. This aspect will be taken in account during the definition of the security games.

We now define six different security games, which will lead to the definition of the three adversaries $\mathcal{B}_1, \mathcal{B}_2, \mathcal{B}_3$ in Theorem 3. In each game we will have to look at the input to the hash function; for future references, we indicate the general form of the input to the hash oracle involving a key-exchange session between parties $\mathcal{P}_A, \mathcal{P}_B$ as

$$\mathcal{P}_A \parallel \mathcal{P}_B \parallel E_A \parallel E_B \parallel E_F \parallel E_G \parallel W_1 \parallel W_2 \parallel W_3 \qquad (2)$$

For $i = 0, 1, \ldots, 5$ we denote with S_j the event "Game i outputs 1", which will indicate a success for the adversary in breaking protocol Π-SIDE (i.e. at least one of the events $\text{break}_{\text{Sound}}$, $\text{break}_{\text{Unique}}$ and break_{KE} happens during Game i).

Game 0. In this game, we simply run the usual AKE security game: the adversary can corrupt some players, reveal some session keys (but not any ephemeral secret key) and delay/redirect messages. When it will be ready, it will pick a fresh oracle and make a query test on its session key. Game 0 will output 1 whenever the adversary breaks the AKE security of protocol Π-SIDE:

$$Prob[S_0] = Prob[\text{break}_{\text{KE}}].$$

Game 1. In this game we abort if the same `ctxt` is computed by two non-partnered oracles. We can upper-bound the probability of this event with the probability that the following conditions are simultaneously verified:

1. two oracles π_i^s, π_i^t belong to the same user P_i;
2. they pick the same ephemeral secret key during their respective sessions;
3. they are involved in two key-exchange sessions with the same user P_j (since the identity of the intended peer is part of the `ctxt`).

Recalling that we have μ users engaging in at most k sessions, we get that

$$|Prob[S_1] - Prob[S_0]| \leq \frac{\mu k^2}{N}$$

and thus, since in this game the unicity of the partner oracle cannot be broken, we can conclude that

$$Prob[\text{break}_{\text{Unique}}] \leq \frac{\mu k^2}{N}.$$

Game 2. In this game we modify how each oracle computes the session key: instead of computing the input to the hash oracle H, it checks if the adversary has queried the oracle on that same input, and behaves consequently: if the answer is yes, then it stores that hash value as the session key (i.e. it properly computes the key), otherwise it picks a key at random and stores that one instead. Note that, when it comes the time for an initiator oracle to compute the session key, the oracle type is fully determined.

A type I oracle (an initiator oracle with a definitely honest partner oracle with which it agrees on the `ctxt`) will store the key computed by the corresponding responder oracle.

Each type II or type V initiator oracles of party $\mathcal{P}_A$ has to check if the input

$$\mathcal{P}_A \parallel \mathcal{P}_B \parallel E_A \parallel E_B \parallel E_F \parallel E_G \parallel \mathfrak{a} * E_G \parallel \mathfrak{f} * E_B \parallel \mathfrak{f} * E_G$$

has been object of any oracle query. If so, it sets its session key to the corresponding hash value (previously stored by the responder oracle), otherwise it picks a session key at random (answering consistently to any following hash query on that same input).

Each type III, IV or V responder oracle of a party $\mathcal{P}_B$ in a session with $\mathcal{P}_A$ will check if any queries have been made on input

$$\mathcal{P}_A \parallel \mathcal{P}_B \parallel E_A \parallel E_B \parallel E_F \parallel E_G \parallel \mathfrak{g} * E_A \parallel \mathfrak{b} * E_F \parallel \mathfrak{g} * E_F.$$

If so, it stores the same result; otherwise, it stores a random key. In any case, each later hash query is consistently answered with the stored session key.

We cannot observe the exact time in which the key derivation oracle is queried for the first time, thus Game 2 outputs 1 whenever Game 1 outputs 1, and vice versa. We can therefore conclude that

$$Prob[S_2] = Prob[S_1].$$

Game 3. In this game (which is a variant of Game 2) we modify how a type IV oracle (a responder oracle whose intended peer is honest until the oracle accepts) chooses the session key. What it does is 1) to pick a random key; 2) to wait for the adversary to possibly corrupt the intended peer $\mathcal{P}_A$; 3) only then modify the hash oracle with the random key k.

We can now define the following events:

- L (for Long-term key), in which the adversary queries the hash oracle on input

$$\mathcal{P}_A \parallel \mathcal{P}_B \parallel E_A \parallel E_B \parallel E_F \parallel E_G \parallel \mathfrak{g} * E_A \parallel \mathfrak{b} * E_F \parallel \mathfrak{g} * E_F$$

  before the long-term secret key of any initiator oracle is revealed;
- L_A is the same event as L, but for a specific intended peer $\mathcal{P}_A$. Trivially $Prob[L] = \sum_i Prob[L_i]$;
- C_A (for Corruption), in which the adversary queries the hash oracle on input

$$\mathcal{P}_A \parallel \mathcal{P}_B \parallel E_A \parallel E_B \parallel E_F \parallel E_G \parallel \mathfrak{g} * E_A \parallel W_2 \parallel W_3$$

before peer $\mathcal{P}_A$ is corrupted; therefore we have $Prob[L_A] \leq Prob[C_A]$.

In order to obtain a bound on $Prob[C_A]$ (and thus a bound on $Prob[L]$), we construct an adversary $\mathcal{B}_1$ against the Strong-CSIDH problem.

Definition 6. [_Adversary $\mathcal{B}_1$_] Consider now an adversary $\mathcal{B}_1$ which is given a Comp-CSIDH challenge (E_S, E_T) and is given access to a $\mathcal{D}_S(\cdot, \cdot)$ oracle. First of all, it chooses a user $\mathcal{P}_A$ uniformly at random and sets its long-term public key to $E_A = E_S$. Then it sets the ephemeral public key of a type IV oracle to be $\mathfrak{r} * E_T$, for a random $\mathfrak{r} \xleftarrow{\$} cl(\mathcal{O})$. Finally, it runs Game 2. If $\mathcal{B}_1$ corrupts $\mathcal{P}_A$, the experiment aborts.

We need to recognise the hash queries that involve the user $\mathcal{P}_A$ (happening in Game 2) and those involving the type IV oracle of any party $\mathcal{P}_B$. In particular,

1. consider hash queries of the form

$$\mathcal{P}_A \parallel \mathcal{P}_B \parallel E_A \parallel E_B \parallel E_F \parallel E_G \parallel W_1 \parallel \mathfrak{b} * E_F \parallel \mathfrak{f} * E_G$$

   involving user $\mathcal{P}_A$ as initiator. We do not know $\mathcal{P}_A$'s secret key $\mathfrak{a} = \mathfrak{s}$, so we have to recognise if W_1 is actually $E_{AG} = \mathfrak{s} * E_G$. This can be done by checking if $\mathcal{D}_S(E_G, W_1) = 1$;
2. consider hash queries of the form

$$\mathcal{P}_B \parallel \mathcal{P}_A \parallel E_B \parallel E_A \parallel E_F \parallel E_G \parallel \mathfrak{b} * E_G \parallel W_2 \parallel \mathfrak{f} * E_G$$

   involving user $\mathcal{P}_A$ as responder. Again, we do not know $\mathcal{P}_A$'s secret key $\mathfrak{a} = \mathfrak{s}$, but this time it is $W_2 = \mathfrak{a} * E_F$ that we cannot compute; thus we have to recognise if W_2 is actually $\mathfrak{s} * E_F$. This can be done by checking if $\mathcal{D}_S(E_F, W_2) = 1$;

3. consider hash queries of the form

$$\mathcal{P}_A \parallel \mathcal{P}_B \parallel E_A \parallel E_B \parallel E_F \parallel E_G \parallel \mathfrak{g}*E_A \parallel W_2 \parallel W_3$$

involving the type IV oracle and user $\mathcal{P}_A$. We have to recognise if W_1 is actually $\mathfrak{rt}*E_A = \mathfrak{g}*E_S$. This can be done by checking if $\mathcal{D}_S(E_G, W_1) = 1$. Whenever we succeed and we find that $W_1 = E_{SG} = \mathfrak{s}*E_G$, since we computed $E_G = \mathfrak{r}*E_T$, we output

$$E_Z = \bar{\mathfrak{r}}*W_1 = \bar{\mathfrak{r}}\mathfrak{s}*E_G = \bar{\mathfrak{r}}\mathfrak{s}\mathfrak{r}*E_T = \bar{\mathfrak{r}}\mathfrak{r}\mathfrak{s}E_T = \mathfrak{s}*E_T = E_{ST}.$$

We have just described an adversary $\mathcal{B}_1$ which succeeds whenever event L_A occurs in Game 2. L_A can occur only before $\mathcal{P}_A$ is corrupt, and thus $\mathcal{B}_1$'s game would have gone through. We can therefore define the upper bound

$$Adv_{cl(\mathcal{O})}^{St-CSIDH}(\mathcal{B}_1) \geq \frac{1}{\mu}\sum_{i=1}^{\mu} Prob[C_I] \geq \frac{1}{\mu}\sum_{i=1}^{\mu} Prob[L_I] = \frac{1}{\mu}Prob[L]$$

from which we get that

$$\left|Prob[S_3] - Prob[S_2]\right| \leq Prob[L] \leq \mu \cdot Adv_{cl(\mathcal{O})}^{St-CSIDH}(\mathcal{B}_1)$$

the first element at the right-hand side of the inequality in Theorem 3.

Game 4. In this game a type III oracle (a responder oracle triggered by an honest initiator, with which it agrees on the ctxt and which is still honest when it receives the response) chooses the session key at random without modifying the key derivation hash oracle. Consider an oracle belonging to user $\mathcal{P}_B$ with static secret key $\mathfrak{b}$ and ephemeral secret key $\mathfrak{g}$ whose intended honest peer $\mathcal{P}_A$ has static secret key $\mathfrak{a}$. The adversary can find out this change only if (call this event L) it makes a query of the form

$$\mathcal{P}_A \parallel \mathcal{P}_B \parallel E_A \parallel E_B \parallel E_F \parallel E_G \parallel W_1 \parallel W_2 \parallel \mathfrak{g}*E_F.$$

This leads us to the following inequality:

$$\left|Prob[S_4] - Prob[S_3]\right| \leq Prob[L].$$

Similarly to what we did in the previous game, we want to bound $Prob[L]$ by constructing an adversary $\mathcal{B}_2$ against the Strong-CSIDH problem.

Definition 7. [*Adversary $\mathcal{B}_2$*] Consider now an adversary $\mathcal{B}_2$ which is given a Comp-CSIDH challenge (E_S, E_T) and is given access to a $\mathcal{D}_S(\cdot, \cdot)$ oracle. It runs Game 3., re-randomizing the challenge as follows: 1) it sets the ephemeral public key of type I and II oracles to $E_F = \mathfrak{r}*E_S$ for a random $\mathfrak{r} \xleftarrow{\$} cl(\mathcal{O})$; 2) it sets the ephemeral public key of type III oracles to $E_G = \mathfrak{r}'*E_T$ for a random $\mathfrak{r}' \xleftarrow{\$} cl(\mathcal{O})$.

In this game, since we embed the challenge in two ephemeral keys, all the static secret keys are known to the adversary. We need therefore to recognise two types of hash oracle queries:

1. hash queries for type II oracles of the form

$$\mathcal{P}_A \parallel \mathcal{P}_B \parallel E_A \parallel E_B \parallel E_F \parallel E_G \parallel \mathfrak{a} * E_G \parallel \mathfrak{f} * E_B \parallel \mathfrak{f} * E_G$$

given the knowledge of the static secret keys, the only information to be detected is whether $W_3 = \mathfrak{f} * E_G = \mathfrak{r}\mathfrak{s} * E_G$ or not. The answer can be obtained by performing the oracle query $\mathcal{D}_S(E_G, \bar{\mathfrak{r}}W_3)$;

2. hash queries for type III oracles of the form

$$\mathcal{P}_A \parallel \mathcal{P}_B \parallel E_A \parallel E_B \parallel E_F \parallel E_G \parallel W_1 \parallel W_2 \parallel \mathfrak{g} * E_F$$

given the knowledge of the static secret keys, the only information to be detected is whether $W_3 = \mathfrak{g} * E_F = \mathfrak{r}'t * E_F$ or not. The answer can again be obtained by performing the oracle query $\mathcal{D}_S(E_G, [\bar{\mathfrak{r}}W_3)$.

If the Strong-CSIDH oracle outputs 1, then we output

$$E_Z = \mathfrak{r}^{-1}\mathfrak{r}'^{-1}W_3 = \overline{\mathfrak{r}\mathfrak{r}'}\mathfrak{f}\mathfrak{g} * E_0 = \overline{\mathfrak{r}\mathfrak{r}'}\mathfrak{r}\mathfrak{s}\mathfrak{r}'t * E_0 = \overline{\mathfrak{r}\mathfrak{r}'}\mathfrak{r}'\mathfrak{s}t * E_0 = E_{ST}.$$

We have just described an adversary $\mathcal{B}_2$ which succeeds whenever event L occurs in Game 2. From this fact we get that

$$\left| Prob[S_4] - Prob[S_3] \right| \leq Prob[L] \leq Adv_{cl(\mathcal{O})}^{St-CSIDH}(\mathcal{B}_2)$$

the second element at the right-hand side of the inequality in Theorem 3.

Game 5. In this game a type II oracle (an initiator oracle whose intended peer is honest until the oracle accepts) chooses a random key E_K and modifies the key derivation hash oracle only if the intended peer is corrupted. Consider an oracle belonging to user $\mathcal{P}_A$ with static secret key $\mathfrak{a}$ and ephemeral secret key $\mathfrak{f}$: if the adversary corrupts the intended peer $\mathcal{P}_B$, the hash oracle will output $E : k$ whenever it is queried on input

$$\mathcal{P}_A \parallel \mathcal{P}_B \parallel E_A \parallel E_B \parallel E_F \parallel E_G \parallel \mathfrak{a} * E_G \parallel \mathfrak{f} * E_B \parallel \mathfrak{f} * E_G.$$

Analogously to what we did in Game 3, we define the following events:

- L: a query on the above input happens before the long-term secret key of any responder oracle is revealed. It follows that

$$\left| Prob[S_5] - Prob[S_4] \right| \leq Prob[L];$$

- L_B: same as L, but for a specific intended peer $\mathcal{P}_B$. Trivially, $Prob[L] = \sum_i Prob[L_i]$;
- C_B: a query on input

$$\mathcal{P}_A \parallel \mathcal{P}_B \parallel E_A \parallel E_B \parallel E_F \parallel E_G \parallel W_1 \parallel W_2 \parallel W_3 \qquad W_2 = \mathfrak{f} * E_B = \mathfrak{b} * E_F$$

happens before user $\mathcal{P}_B$ is corrupted; therefore we have $Prob[L_B] \leq Prob[C_B]$.

As we did in the previous games, we want to find an upper bound on $Prob[L]$.

Definition 8. [*Adversary $\mathcal{B}_3$*] Consider now an adversary $\mathcal{B}_3$ which is given a Comp-CSIDH challenge (E_S, E_T) and is given access to a $\mathcal{D}_S(\cdot, \cdot)$ oracle. It runs Game 4., it embeds the challenge as follows: 1) it sets the static public key of a uniformly-at-random user $\mathcal{P}_B$ to $E_B = E_S$; 2) it sets the ephemeral public key of type I and II oracles whose intended peer is $\mathcal{P}_B$ to $E_F = \mathfrak{r} * E_T$ for a random $\mathfrak{r} \xleftarrow{\$} cl(\mathcal{O})$.

If the adversary corrupts party $\mathcal{P}_B$, the game aborts, since the corresponding static secret key is unknown. We need therefore to recognise three types of queries made to the hash oracle:

1. hash queries for which $\mathcal{P}_B$ acts as responder

$$\mathcal{P}_A \,\|\, \mathcal{P}_B \,\|\, E_A \,\|\, E_B \,\|\, E_F \,\|\, E_G \,\|\, \mathfrak{g} * E_A \,\|\, \mathfrak{b} * E_F \,\|\, \mathfrak{g} * E_F.$$

Given that both $\mathfrak{b} = \mathfrak{s}$ and $\mathfrak{t}$ are unknown, the only information we cannot compute and that has to be detected is whether $W_2 = \mathfrak{b} * E_F = \mathfrak{b} * E_S$. The answer can be obtained by performing the oracle query $\mathcal{D}_S(E_F, W_2)$;

2. hash queries for which $\mathcal{P}_B$ acts as initiator:

$$\mathcal{P}_B \,\|\, \mathcal{P}_A \,\|\, E_B \,\|\, E_A \,\|\, E_F \,\|\, E_G \,\|\, \mathfrak{b} * E_G \,\|\, \mathfrak{f} * E_A \,\|\, \mathfrak{f} * E_G$$

(note that, in this case, the second part of the challenge has not been embedded in E_F). The only information to be detected is whether $W_1 = \mathfrak{b} * E_F = \mathfrak{b} * E_S$, and the answer can be obtained by performing the oracle query $\mathcal{D}_S(E_G, W_1)$;

3. hash queries defining event C_B, i.e. made before the user $\mathcal{P}_B$ is corrupted:

$$\mathcal{P}_A \,\|\, \mathcal{P}_B \,\|\, E_A \,\|\, E_B \,\|\, E_F \,\|\, E_G \,\|\, W_1 \,\|\, W_2 \,\|\, W_3 \qquad W_2 = \mathfrak{f} * E_B = \mathfrak{b} * E_F$$

We have to recognise if W_2 is actually $\mathfrak{f} * E_B = \mathfrak{r}\mathfrak{t} * E_B$, and this can be done by checking if $\mathcal{D}_S(E_F, W_2) = 1$.

If the Strong-CSIDH oracle outputs 1 and realise that $W_2 = \mathfrak{s} * E_F = \mathfrak{s}\mathfrak{r}\mathfrak{t} * E_0$, then we output

$$E_Z = \mathfrak{r}^{-1} W_2 = \overline{\mathfrak{r}}\mathfrak{s}\mathfrak{r}\mathfrak{t} * E_0 = \overline{\mathfrak{r}}\mathfrak{r}\mathfrak{s}\mathfrak{t} * E_0 = E_{ST}.$$

We have just described an adversary $\mathcal{B}_3$ which succeeds whenever event L_B occurs in Game 5. L_B can occur only before $\mathcal{P}_B$ is corrupt, and thus $\mathcal{B}_3$'s game would have gone through. We can therefore upper bound

$$Adv_{cl(\mathcal{O})}^{St-CSIDH}(\mathcal{B}_3) \geq \frac{1}{\mu} \sum_{i=1}^{\mu} Prob[C_I] \geq \frac{1}{\mu} \sum_{i=1}^{\mu} Prob[L_I] = \frac{1}{\mu} Prob[L].$$

from which we get that

$$\left|Prob[S_5] - Prob[S_4]\right| \leq Prob[L] \leq \mu \cdot Adv_{cl(\mathcal{O})}^{St-CSIDH}(\mathcal{B}_3)$$

the third and last element at the right-hand side of the inequality in Theorem 3. *Concluding the Proof.* Following from how we constructed each game in the proof, whenever the games do not abort because of adversarial corruption, the adversary is provided with a random session key, completely independent of every key and sent message. Therefore

$$Pr[S_5] = \frac{1}{2}.$$

We have seen in Game 1. that

$$Prob[\text{break}_{\text{Unique}}] \leq \frac{\mu k^2}{N}$$

and, due to the perfect correctness of the scheme,

$$Prob[\text{break}_{\text{Sound}}] = 0.$$

We can therefore exploit the bounds on adversarial winning probabilities to prove Theorem 3: given an adversary $\mathcal{A}$ against protocol Π-SIDE, we have built three adversaries $\mathcal{B}_1, \mathcal{B}_2, \mathcal{B}_3$ against Strong-CSIDH such that $\mathcal{A}$ wins with advantage $Adv_{\Pi-SIDE}^{AKE}(\mathcal{A})$ at most

$$\mu \cdot Adv_{cl(\mathcal{O})}^{St-CSIDH}(\mathcal{B}_1) + Adv_{cl(\mathcal{O})}^{St-CSIDH}(\mathcal{B}_2) + \mu \cdot Adv_{cl(\mathcal{O})}^{St-CSIDH}(\mathcal{B}_3) + \frac{\mu k^2}{N}$$

where μ is the number of participants to the protocol.

The tightness loss $L = \mathcal{O}(\mu)$ that we achieve in this security proof is optimal for simple protocols such as ours. The arguments adopted by Cohn-Gordon et al. [CCG+19] still hold in our setting and the adaptation is straightforward.

References

AASA+. Alagic, G., et al.: Nistir 8309. https://doi.org/10.6028/NIST.IR.8309

ABR01. Abdalla, M., Bellare, M., Rogaway, P.: The Oracle Diffie-Hellman assumptions and an analysis of DHIES. In: Naccache, D. (ed.) CT-RSA 2001. LNCS, vol. 2020, pp. 143–158. Springer, Heidelberg (2001). https://doi.org/10.1007/3-540-45353-9_12

Ber19. Bernstein, D.J.: Comparing proofs of security for lattice-based encryption. IACR Cryptology ePrint Archive, 2019:691 (2019)

BFG+19. Brendel, J., Fischlin, M., Günther, F., Janson, C., Stebila, D.: Towards post-quantum security for signal's X3DH handshake. Cryptology ePrint Archive, Report 2019/1356 (2019). https://eprint.iacr.org/2019/1356

BFK+14. Bhargavan, K., Fournet, C., Kohlweiss, M., Pironti, A., Strub, P.-Y., Zanella-Béguelin, S.: Proving the TLS handshake secure (as it is). In: Garay, J.A., Gennaro, R. (eds.) CRYPTO 2014, Part II. LNCS, vol. 8617, pp. 235–255. Springer, Heidelberg (2014). https://doi.org/10.1007/978-3-662-44381-1_14

BJLS16. Bader, C., Jager, T., Li, Y., Schäge, S.: On the impossibility of tight cryptographic reductions. In: Fischlin, M., Coron, J.-S. (eds.) EUROCRYPT 2016, Part II. LNCS, vol. 9666, pp. 273–304. Springer, Heidelberg (2016). https://doi.org/10.1007/978-3-662-49896-5_10

BM82. Blum, M., Micali, S.: How to generate cryptographically strong sequences of pseudo random bits. In: 23rd FOCS, pp. 112–117, Chicago, Illinois, 3–5 November 1982. IEEE Computer Society Press (1982)

CCG+19. Cohn-Gordon, K., Cremers, C., Gjøsteen, K., Jacobsen, H., Jager, T.: Highly efficient key exchange protocols with optimal tightness. In: Boldyreva, A., Micciancio, D. (eds.) CRYPTO 2019, Part III. LNCS, vol. 11694, pp. 767–797. Springer, Cham (2019). https://doi.org/10.1007/978-3-030-26954-8_25

CLM+18. Castryck, W., Lange, T., Martindale, C., Panny, L., Renes, J.: CSIDH: an efficient post-quantum commutative group action. In: Peyrin, T., Galbraith, S. (eds.) ASIACRYPT 2018, Part III. LNCS, vol. 11274, pp. 395–427. Springer, Cham (2018). https://doi.org/10.1007/978-3-030-03332-3_15

CSV20. Castryck, W., Sotáková, J., Vercauteren, F.: Breaking the decisional Diffie-Hellman problem for class group actions using genus theory. Cryptology ePrint Archive, Report 2020/151 (2020). https://eprint.iacr.org/2020/151

Deu41. Deuring, M.: Die Typen der Multiplikatorenringe elliptischer Funktionenkörper. Abhandlungen aus dem Mathematischen Seminar der Universität Hamburg 14, 197–272 (1941)

DG19. De Feo, L., Galbraith, S.D.: SeaSign: compact isogeny signatures from class group actions. In: Ishai, Y., Rijmen, V. (eds.) EUROCRYPT 2019, Part III. LNCS, vol. 11478, pp. 759–789. Springer, Cham (2019). https://doi.org/10.1007/978-3-030-17659-4_26

Feo17. De Feo, L.: Mathematics of isogeny based cryptography. CoRR, abs/1711.04062 (2017). http://arxiv.org/abs/1711.04062

Gal18. Galbraith, S.D.: Authenticated key exchange for SIDH. Cryptology ePrint Archive, Report 2018/266 (2018). https://eprint.iacr.org/2018/266

GM82. Goldwasser, S., Micali, S.: Probabilistic encryption and how to play mental poker keeping secret all partial information. In: 14th ACM STOC, San Francisco, CA, USA, 5–7 May 1982, pp. 365–377. ACM Press (1982)

HM89. Hafner, J.L., McCurley, K.S.: A rigorous subexponential algorithm for computation of class groups. J. Am. Math. Soc. 2, 837–850 (1989)

HS09. Silverman, J.H.: The Arithmetic of Elliptic Curves. GTM, vol. 106. Springer, New York (2009). https://doi.org/10.1007/978-0-387-09494-6

JAC+19. Jao, D., et al.: SIKE. Technical report, National Institute of Standards and Technology (2019). https://csrc.nist.gov/projects/post-quantum-cryptography/round-2-submissions

JD11.   Jao, D., De Feo, L.: Towards quantum-resistant cryptosystems from supersingular elliptic curve isogenies. In: Yang, B.-Y. (ed.) PQCrypto 2011. LNCS, vol. 7071, pp. 19–34. Springer, Heidelberg (2011). https://doi.org/10.1007/978-3-642-25405-5_2

JKSS12.   Jager, T., Kohlar, F., Schäge, S., Schwenk, J.: On the security of TLS-DHE in the standard model. In: Safavi-Naini, R., Canetti, R. (eds.) CRYPTO 2012. LNCS, vol. 7417, pp. 273–293. Springer, Heidelberg (2012). https://doi.org/10.1007/978-3-642-32009-5_17

KPW13.   Krawczyk, H., Paterson, K.G., Wee, H.: On the security of the TLS protocol: a systematic analysis. In: Canetti, R., Garay, J.A. (eds.) CRYPTO 2013, Part I. LNCS, vol. 8042, pp. 429–448. Springer, Heidelberg (2013). https://doi.org/10.1007/978-3-642-40041-4_24

Kra05.   Krawczyk, H.: HMQV: a high-performance secure Diffie-Hellman protocol. In: Shoup, V. (ed.) CRYPTO 2005. LNCS, vol. 3621, pp. 546–566. Springer, Heidelberg (2005). https://doi.org/10.1007/11535218_33

KTAT20.   Kawashima, T., Takashima, K., Aikawa, Y., Takagi, T.: An efficient authenticated key exchange from random self-reducibility on CSIDH. Cryptology ePrint Archive, Report 2020/1178 (2020). https://eprint.iacr.org/2020/1178

LLM07.   LaMacchia, B., Lauter, K., Mityagin, A.: Stronger security of authenticated key exchange. In: Susilo, W., Liu, J.K., Mu, Y. (eds.) ProvSec 2007. LNCS, vol. 4784, pp. 1–16. Springer, Heidelberg (2007). https://doi.org/10.1007/978-3-540-75670-5_1

LM06.   Lauter, K., Mityagin, A.: Security analysis of KEA authenticated key exchange protocol. In: Yung, M., Dodis, Y., Kiayias, A., Malkin, T. (eds.) PKC 2006. LNCS, vol. 3958, pp. 378–394. Springer, Heidelberg (2006). https://doi.org/10.1007/11745853_25

Lon18.   Longa, P.: A note on post-quantum authenticated key exchange from supersingular isogenies. Cryptology ePrint Archive, Report 2018/267 (2018). https://eprint.iacr.org/2018/267

NR97.   Naor, M., Reingold, O.: Number-theoretic constructions of efficient pseudo-random functions. In: 38th FOCS, Miami Beach, Florida, 19–22 October 1997, pp. 458–467. IEEE Computer Society Press (1997)

Sho97.   Shor, P.W.: Polynomial-time algorithms for prime factorization and discrete logarithms on a quantum computer. SIAM J. Comput. **26**(5), 1484–1509 (1997)

Sut13.   Sutherland, A.V.: On the evaluation of modular polynomials. In: Tenth Algorithmic Number Theory Symposium (ANTS X), MSP Open Book Series 1, pp. 531–555 (2013)

Vél71.   Vélu, J.: Isogénies entre courbes elliptiques. Comptes-Rendus de l'Académie des Sciences, Série I(273), 238–241 (1971)

Was08.   Washington, L.C.: Elliptic Curves: Number Theory and Cryptography, 2nd edn. Chapman & Hall/CRC, London (2008)

XXW+19.   Xu, X., Xue, H., Wang, K., Au, M.H., Tian, S.: Strongly secure authenticated key exchange from supersingular isogenies. In: Galbraith, S.D., Moriai, S. (eds.) ASIACRYPT 2019, Part I. LNCS, vol. 11921, pp. 278–308. Springer, Cham (2019). https://doi.org/10.1007/978-3-030-34578-5_11

Symmetric-Key Design

Symmetric-Key Design

PRINCEv2

More Security for (Almost) No Overhead

Dušan Božilov[1,2]([⊠]), Maria Eichlseder[3,4]([⊠]), Miroslav Knežević[7]([⊠]),
Baptiste Lambin[4]([⊠]), Gregor Leander[4,5]([⊠]), Thorben Moos[4]([⊠]),
Ventzislav Nikov[1]([⊠]), Shahram Rasoolzadeh[4]([⊠]), Yosuke Todo[4,6]([⊠]),
and Friedrich Wiemer[4,5]([⊠])

[1] NXP Semiconductors, Leuven, Belgium
{dusan.bozilov,ventzislav.nikov}@nxp.com
[2] COSIC KU Leuven and imec, Leuven, Belgium
dusan.bozilov@esat.kuleuven.be
[3] Graz University of Technology, Graz, Austria
maria.eichlseder@iaik.tugraz.at
[4] Ruhr-Universität Bochum, Bochum, Germany
{gregor.leander,thorben.moos,
shahram.rasoolzadeh,yosuke.todo}@rub.de, baptiste.lambin@protonmail.com
[5] cryptosolutions, Essen, Germany
gregor@cryptosolutions.de, friedrich.wiemer@mailbox.org
[6] NTT Secure Platform Laboratories, Tokyo 180-8585, Japan
yosuke.todo.xt@hco.ntt.co.jp
[7] NXP Semiconductors, Austin, USA
miroslav.knezevic@nxp.com

Abstract. In this work, we propose tweaks to the PRINCE block cipher that help us to increase its security without changing the number of rounds or round operations. We get substantially higher security for the same complexity. From an implementation perspective, PRINCEv2 comes at an extremely low overhead compared to PRINCE in all key categories, such as area, latency and energy. We expect, as it is already the case for PRINCE, that the new cipher PRINCEv2 will be deployed in various settings.

Keywords: PRINCE · Low latency · Lightweight · Block cipher

1 Introduction

During the last several years we have been witnessing a very rapid deployment of secure microcontrollers in IoT, automotive and cloud infrastructures. Various technology fields, including industrial automation, robotics as well as the 5th generation mobile network urge for real-time operation and require low-latency execution while preserving the highest levels of security. Low-power and low-energy requirements are of equal importance, especially when considering the IoT market where the majority of devices are in a low-power mode during most of their lifetime. Those devices occasionally wake up, carry out a quick

© Springer Nature Switzerland AG 2021
O. Dunkelman et al. (Eds.): SAC 2020, LNCS 12804, pp. 483–511, 2021.
https://doi.org/10.1007/978-3-030-81652-0_19

computation, the result of which they store or communicate securely and then go back to sleep. A life most humans are craving to have.

Securing a microcontroller involves securing the following three groups of assets:

- End-user data, including dynamic data such as personal information.
- Original equipment manufacturer (OEM) intellectual property, including firmware and software.
- Silicon manufacturer intellectual property, including hardware, ROM code, crypto libraries and various drivers.

Securing each of these assets is a complex problem and requires a multi-layered approach. Starting with trust provisioning and then enabling secure boot, secure debug access, secure firmware update, secure test and life-cycle management is essential for creating a secure execution environment. One of the crucial aspects of a secure execution environment is secure storage, a security mechanism used for keeping confidentiality and integrity of valuable code and data stored on the device. Our paper focuses on memory encryption, which is a fundamental building block of secure storage.

Memory encryption has been used in the PC world for a long time already. Some examples include IBM's SecureBlue++, Intel's SGX and AMD's SEV encryption and integrity mechanisms. Those mechanisms are used to protect valuable assets against an attacker capable of monitoring and/or manipulating the memory content. The attacker is assumed to be employing various software tools running on the targeted platform as well as being able to manipulate the integrity of any underlying hardware by using invasive methods such as probing, voltage glitching, electromagnetic fault injection (EMFI), etc. While the device must remain secure in the hands of such adversary, the level of protection differs depending on whether the memory is volatile or non-volatile or whether it is internal or external to the system on chip (SoC). Securing the SoC-external memory is especially challenging while, at the same time, the advances of CMOS technology lead to increased production of FLASH-less microcontrollers. Add to this the everlasting requirement to minimize power and energy consumption as well as the never-ending race for higher performance and it will become clear why designing an efficient memory encryption scheme is a serious challenge. We are looking for a solution where a single clock cycle encryption is one cycle too many.

PRINCE [BCG+12] is the first publicly known low-latency family of block ciphers that got scrutinized by the cryptographic community.[1] As a result, PRINCE has been deployed in a number of products including LPC55S of NXP Semiconductors [NXP20], which is a family of highly constrained general purpose IoT microcontrollers.

As pointed out in [KNR12, BCG+12], the ultimate goal of low-latency block cipher design is to encrypt a block of data in a single clock cycle. The best illustration of the importance of meeting this goal is to look at the comparison of PRINCE and AES in the low-latency setting. When implemented fully unrolled,

---

[1] see https://www.emsec.ruhr-uni-bochum.de/research/research_startseite/prince-challenge/.

PRINCE occupies 4 times less silicon area while, at the same time, reaching an 8 times higher clock frequency.

Although some design principles have been explored during the design of PRINCE, there has been little work going on to determine the design choices that lead to the lowest-latency and most energy-efficient cipher architecture. Several parameters contribute to the efficiency of a given cipher design: area, latency, throughput, power, and energy. Several other designs, including Midori [BBI+15], MANTIS [BJK+16] and QARMA [Ava17] have been particularly optimized for one or more of these parameters.

This document describes the result of our efforts to increase the security margins of PRINCE without significantly increasing the latency, area, power or energy consumption. We recall the PRINCE security claims as follows: an adversary who has 2^n chosen plaintext-ciphertext pairs (obtained under the same key) needs at least 2^{126-n} calls to the encryption function to recover the secret key. This security level is sufficient for most of the aforementioned applications, yet we set ourselves to explore design opportunities when facing the security requirements NIST put forward in its lightweight crypto competition [NIS]. Therefore, the targeted security level for PRINCEv2 is 112 bits [NIS18]; precisely, we claim that there is no attack against PRINCEv2 with data complexity below 2^{47} (chosen) plaintext-ciphertext pairs (obtained under the same key) and time-complexity below 2^{112}. It has to be noted that the NIST lightweight crypto competition does not focus on the design of low-latency block ciphers. Instead, it focuses on Authenticated Encryption with Associated Data (AEAD) schemes which are, in general, too slow or too big compared to dedicated block ciphers, thus failing to meet the aforementioned design challenges.

One last design constraint we put in front of ourselves is to be able to implement PRINCEv2 on top of the existing PRINCE architecture without adding a significant area overhead nor increasing the latency.

Our Contribution

Starting with the last design constraint mentioned, we tried to minimize the difference from PRINCEv2 to PRINCE. Besides minimizing the overhead of implementing one on top of the other, this has the convenient benefit that a lot of the security analysis that PRINCE received can then either directly be transferred to PRINCEv2 or transferred with small modifications.

To achieve the requested higher security level, a different key schedule is strictly necessary, as without a change there the generic bound of the FX construction applies. Through a carefully crafted and analyzed key schedule we can get a secure cipher meeting the NIST security requirements. Besides the change in the key schedule, we only add a single XOR in the middle rounds. This middle round was unkeyed in PRINCE. From an aesthetic point of view, the new key schedule has the drawback that the α-reflection property is slightly weakened. That is, decryption is not simply encryption with a modified key as in PRINCE, but requires slightly more effort.

Besides being beneficial from a security point of view, our minimal changes result in only minimal performance changes in all the aforementioned dimensions.

This makes PRINCEv2, in the unrolled setting we aim at, nearly as efficient as PRINCE, while achieving a higher security level, echoing the title of our work.

We want to emphasize that the problem we are trying to solve is quite general, yet not an easy task. It touches the least understood part of block cipher design, namely the design of the key-scheduling. For an existing cipher with a potentially non-optimal key-scheduling (here PRINCE), this translates to the question on how to increase security while minimizing the resulting overhead. For the interesting – being deployed in several products – case of PRINCE, we came up with an elegant yet simple and efficient solution to this problem. This simplicity is an advantage concerning our objective. We venture to say that the smaller the change to the original PRINCE design, the higher the value of our contribution.

Outline of the Paper
We specify the design of PRINCEv2 in Sect. 2, highlighting the differences to PRINCE and explaining our choices in Sect. 3. As noted above, the main changes are in the key schedule. By not using the FX construction for this new design, we also follow the advice in [Din15].

In Sect. 4 we report on our findings when implementing PRINCEv2 and compare with PRINCE, Midori, MANTIS and QARMA. As we will explain there, those comparisons are naturally difficult as, for example, MANTIS and QARMA provide a tweak, which PRINCEv2 does not.

We discuss the security analysis in Sect. 5. As PRINCE has attracted quite some third party analysis, e.g. [CFG+14a, DZLY17, Mor17, RR16b], we can build on significant previous work. Besides confirming our belief that PRINCEv2 indeed provides the requested security level, as a side result, we derive some new insights in PRINCE as well.

2   Specification

As discussed above, we aim to keep the changes to PRINCE minimal. To achieve this, we use the same round function and only change the middle layer, key schedule and the round constants compared to PRINCE. To be self-contained, we quickly recall PRINCE's general structure and the round function, before giving the updated parts for PRINCEv2.

2.1   PRINCE

PRINCE is a family of block ciphers with block size of 64 and key size of 128 bits. The encryption function iterates the round function R five times, then applies the middle layer R', followed by five applications of the inverse round function R^{-1}. The round function itself applies an S-box layer SB, followed by a linear layer consisting of a MixColumns operation MC and a ShiftRows SR. The S-box in PRINCE family, can be chosen from one of the 8 Affine equivalent classes given in the proposal paper [BCG+12, Tab. 3]. The S-box used in the PRINCE proposal that is given in Table 1(a), the ShiftRows permutation applied

Table 1. The S-box and ShiftRows permutation used in PRINCE and PRINCEv2. Note that the S-box for PRINCE family can be chosen from 8 Affine equivalent classes and the one given here is the one suggested in the PRINCE proposal paper.

(a) 4-bit S-box of SB																(b) Permutation of SR															
x	0	1	2	3	4	5	6	7	8	9	A	B	C	D	E	F	0	1	2	3	4	5	6	7	8	9	10	11	12	13	14	15
$S(x)$	B	F	3	2	A	C	9	1	6	7	8	0	E	5	D	4	0	5	10	15	4	9	14	3	8	13	2	7	12	1	6	11

in SR in Table 1(b). While the ShiftRows permutation is the same used in the AES, the MixColumns operation is built from the following four 4×4 matrices:

$$M_1 = \begin{pmatrix} 0&0&0&0 \\ 0&1&0&0 \\ 0&0&1&0 \\ 0&0&0&1 \end{pmatrix}, \quad M_2 = \begin{pmatrix} 1&0&0&0 \\ 0&0&0&0 \\ 0&0&1&0 \\ 0&0&0&1 \end{pmatrix}, \quad M_3 = \begin{pmatrix} 1&0&0&0 \\ 0&1&0&0 \\ 0&0&0&0 \\ 0&0&0&1 \end{pmatrix}, \quad M_4 = \begin{pmatrix} 1&0&0&0 \\ 0&1&0&0 \\ 0&0&1&0 \\ 0&0&0&0 \end{pmatrix},$$

or in other words M_i is the 4×4 identity matrix where the ith row is replaced by the zero vector. From these M_i we build the matrices $\widehat{M}^{(0)}$, $\widehat{M}^{(1)}$ and M':

$$\widehat{M}^{(0)} = \begin{pmatrix} M_1 & M_2 & M_3 & M_4 \\ M_2 & M_3 & M_4 & M_1 \\ M_3 & M_4 & M_1 & M_2 \\ M_4 & M_1 & M_2 & M_3 \end{pmatrix}, \widehat{M}^{(1)} = \begin{pmatrix} M_2 & M_3 & M_4 & M_1 \\ M_3 & M_4 & M_1 & M_2 \\ M_4 & M_1 & M_2 & M_3 \\ M_1 & M_2 & M_3 & M_4 \end{pmatrix}, M' = \begin{pmatrix} \widehat{M}^{(0)} & 0 & 0 & 0 \\ 0 & \widehat{M}^{(1)} & 0 & 0 \\ 0 & 0 & \widehat{M}^{(1)} & 0 \\ 0 & 0 & 0 & \widehat{M}^{(0)} \end{pmatrix},$$

i.e., M' is the 64×64 block diagonal matrix with blocks $(\widehat{M}^{(0)}, \widehat{M}^{(1)}, \widehat{M}^{(1)}, \widehat{M}^{(0)})$. Finally, the MC-layer multiplies the state with M' and is an involution.

The round function application is interleaved with additions of the round key $\oplus_{k_i}$ and constant $\oplus_{RC_i}$, where

$$\oplus_{k_i}(x) := x + k_i \qquad \text{and} \qquad \oplus_{RC_i}(x) = x + RC_i.$$

Overall for PRINCE we thus have the structure shown in Fig. 1 (top), where

$$R = \text{SR} \circ \text{MC} \circ \text{SB}, \quad R'_{\text{PRINCE}} = \text{SB}^{-1} \circ \text{MC} \circ \text{SB} \quad \text{and} \quad R^{-1} = \text{SB}^{-1} \circ \text{MC} \circ \text{SR}^{-1}.$$

As we modify the PRINCE key schedule and round constants, we do not give more details about them.

2.2   PRINCEv2

PRINCEv2 is also a family of block ciphers in the same way as PRINCE that the applied S-box can be chosen from 8 Affine equivalent classes. For PRINCEv2, we keep the forward round R and backward round R^{-1} with their operations SB, MC, and SR. The structure for one full encryption is shown in Fig. 1 (bottom) and in full detail in Figs. 9 and 10 in the appendix.

Middle Layer. We change R', which was a key-less operation, to

$$R' = \text{SB}^{-1} \circ \oplus_{RC_{11}+k_1} \circ \text{MC} \circ \oplus_{k_0} \circ \text{SB}.$$

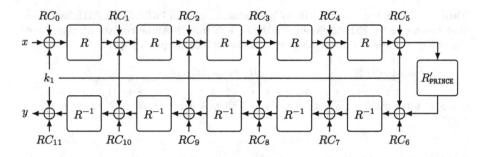

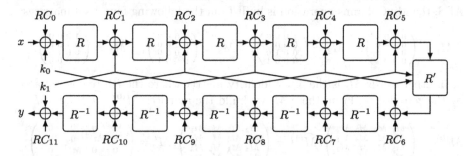

Fig. 1. (Top) PRINCE core structure, leaving out the FX construction; (bottom) PRINCEv2 structure. Note that values of RC_7, RC_9 and RC_{11} in PRINCEv2 are different than the ones in PRINCE.

Key Schedule. Given the 128-bit master key $k = (k_0 \parallel k_1)$, we define the ith round key as

$$k_i := \begin{cases} k_0 & i \in \{0, 2, 4, 6, 8, 10\} \\ k_1 & i \in \{1, 3, 5, 7, 9, 11\} \end{cases},$$

that is, we alternate between the two parts of the master key k_0 and k_1.

Round Constants. The round constants are derived as for PRINCE, but instead of adding the same α for every round constant in the second half of the encryption process ($i \geqslant 6$), we alternate adding α and β as defined in Table 2.

2.3   Encryption vs. Decryption

While PRINCEv2 does not fulfil the α reflection property anymore, the choice of round keys and constants allows to implement both encryption and decryption with only a small area and delay overhead. This is shown in Fig. 10. In this figure the extra control signal **dec** switches between encryption and decryption. In particular, the Swap function is defined as

Table 2. Round constants used in PRINCEv2.

	Constants		
$RC_0 =$ 0000000000000000	$RC_6 =$ 7ef84f78fd955cb1	$= RC_5 \oplus \alpha$
$RC_1 =$ 13198a2e03707344	$RC_7 =$ 7aacf4538d971a60	$= RC_4 \oplus \beta$
$RC_2 =$ a4093822299f31d0	$RC_8 =$ c882d32f25323c54	$= RC_3 \oplus \alpha$
$RC_3 =$ 082efa98ec4e6c89	$RC_9 =$ 9b8ded979cd838c7	$= RC_2 \oplus \beta$
$RC_4 =$ 452821e638d01377	$RC_{10} =$ d3b5a399ca0c2399	$= RC_1 \oplus \alpha$
$RC_5 =$ be5466cf34e90c6c	$RC_{11} =$ 3f84d5b5b5470917	$= RC_0 \oplus \beta$
$\alpha =$ c0ac29b7c97c50dd	$\beta =$ 3f84d5b5b5470917	

$$\texttt{Swap}(k_0, k_1, \text{dec}) = \begin{cases} k_0, k_1 & \text{if dec} = 0 \\ k_1 \oplus \beta, k_0 \oplus \alpha & \text{if dec} = 1 \end{cases}.$$

3 Design Rationale

The main objectives almost immediately results in clear design rationales. The first design rationale is to leave the round function, and not less important the number of rounds, (almost) unchanged, and only change the key-scheduling. Note that the main reason for wanting to keep the number of round unchanged is mainly because having more rounds will necessarily increase latency and cause an overall loss in performances. As we are able to improve the security margin as in PRINCE (see Sect. 5), we believe that this is the correct choice to make. Here, the round-constants are thought of as part of the key-scheduling, even if it is not presented this way in the original PRINCE paper. This rationale (leaving the round function as is) both drastically simplified the design process and made it much more challenging. The simplification is due to the choices being narrowed down to a key-scheduling that has to be picked. More challenging, the analysis has to be much more precise and careful, as clearly the security margin would decrease. It is important to highlight that the security margin is relative to the claimed security level, not in absolute terms.

The only compromise from the goal of leaving the round function unchanged is the middle round. Some attacks that have been developed since the publication of PRINCE take explicit advantage of the symmetry and the key-less middle rounds. To make those attacks, particularly meet-in-the-middle attacks and accelerated exhaustive search procedures, less of a concern, it seems to be a good trade-off to spend two (actually one as will be explained in the implementation section) additional XOR on the critical path. It is noteworthy to mention that the idea of the keyed middle round is previously used in the design of QARMA block cipher.

For the key-scheduling, we were again highly restricted by the requirement of limiting the overhead of implementing decryption on top of encryption. This implies, as it did in PRINCE, that a complicated key-update is not a proper choice but a simple, up to the constants, periodic key-scheduling is best.

We opted for one of the simplest possible options: iterated round-keys.

Originally, in PRINCE, the round keys derived from the 128-bit key $(k_0 \parallel k_1)$ correspond to

$$k_0 \oplus k_1, k_1, k_1, k_1, k_1, k_1, k_1 \oplus \alpha, k_1 \oplus \alpha, k_1 \oplus \alpha, k_1 \oplus \alpha, k_1 \oplus \alpha, k_0' \oplus k_1 \oplus \alpha \,,$$

where k_0' is the result of a simple and efficient bijective linear mapping from k_0, and α is a constant value.

In particular, the value of k_0 is used only in the whitening keys, limiting the security generically. The α-reflection property, that is the fact that decryption is encryption with a modified key, follows as replacing k_1 by $k_1 \oplus \alpha$ reverts the order of the round keys (except for the outer whitening keys).

In PRINCEv2, using a master key $(k_0 \parallel k_1)$, we decide to choose

$$k_0, k_1, k_0, k_1, k_0, k_1, k_0, k_1 \oplus \beta, k_0 \oplus \alpha, k_1 \oplus \beta, k_0 \oplus \alpha, k_1 \oplus \beta, k_0 \oplus \alpha, k_1 \oplus \beta \,,$$

as the round keys where α and β are constant values. The constants are chosen as digits of $\pi = 3.1415\ldots$, as they were done in PRINCE. The new constant β is simply the next in line looking at the binary digits of π, see the appendix for a sage code to reproduce the constants used. Besides, it is noteworthy to mention that due to the key additions in the middle round of PRINCEv2, it has two more round keys than the one for PRINCE.

Here, replacing k_0 by $k_1 \oplus \beta$ and k_1 by $k_0 \oplus \alpha$ does ensure that the first rounds (the first seven round keys) of the encryption circuit perform decryption as required. However, when reaching the middle round (second key addition of the middle round), an additional modification is required to ensure the second half (the second seven round keys) works as well. For the second half of the round keys, we need to XOR all of these round keys with the constant value $\alpha \oplus \beta$. While replacing k_0 by $k_1 \oplus \beta$ and k_1 by $k_0 \oplus \alpha$, needs to implement 64 multiplexers in the critical path, modifying round keys of the second half does not affect the latency. As we will show in Sect. 4, combining decryption together with the encryption circuit does not significantly harm performance.

The only case where this would not be necessary is when α equals β. However, this would introduce a set of weak-keys. Namely, if $k_1 \oplus k_2 = \alpha$, then encryption would equal decryption, that is, the whole cipher would be an involution.

Finally, let us explicitly state the claim we want our design to be tested against:

Security Claim: We claim that there is no attack against PRINCEv2 with data complexity below 2^{50} bytes – 2^{47} (chosen) plaintext-ciphertext pairs obtained under the same key – and time-complexity below 2^{112}. We do not claim any security in the related-key setting and related-keys have to be avoided at the protocol level.

This claim is backed up by the extensive security analysis. It is interesting to see how the advance in the state of the art has made the analysis more precise (e.g., for Boomerang-attacks using connectivity tables and for integral attacks using the division property) and simpler (using mainly MILP-based tools). Those improvements are an important tool to enable a cipher design with a very tight security claim: For a cipher optimized for low-latency, a large security margin is nothing but wasted performance.

Note that as PRINCE did not have any claim regarding security against side-channel and fault attacks, we chose to not make such claims either. Moreover to our knowledge, protecting a fully unrolled primitive against such attacks is not a well-researched area so far.

4   Implementation

The primary objective of PRINCE and PRINCEv2 is to offer low-latency single-cycle encryption and decryption. This objective requires a short critical path in round-unrolled non-pipelined hardware implementations. In other words, the ciphers aim for a small logic depth in circuit representation. Furthermore, adding decryption functionality to an encryption circuit should induce minimal area and latency overhead. PRINCE achieves this goal in part due to the so-called α-reflection property [BCG+12]. This property has been imitated by several other low-latency constructions (e.g. MANTIS [BJK+16] and QARMA [Ava17]) and mandates that decryption with one key corresponds to encryption with a related key. Due to the modified key schedule, PRINCEv2 does not fulfil the α-reflection behaviour of PRINCE. Yet, it implements a modified version that keeps the decryption overhead in hardware fairly small.

A secondary design goal is keeping its unrolled implementation cost-efficient, including a small hardware footprint (little occupied chip area) and a low energy consumption. In fact, the costs should be lower compared to unrolled implementations of other lightweight block ciphers. According to the original proposal, unrolled PRINCE with decryption and encryption capability can be clocked at frequencies up to 212.8 MHz when synthesized in NanGate 45 nm, an open-source standard cell library, and requires as little as 8260 Gate Equivalents (GE) of area [BCG+12]. PRINCEv2 aims to achieve similar performance figures while providing stronger security guarantees overall. Staying close to the initial design of PRINCE enables us to recycle and build upon the extensive security analysis it has already received. Furthermore, it allows us to construct circuits that can perform encryption and decryption in both the new PRINCEv2 *and* original PRINCE at low overhead. This provides needed legacy support and backward compatibility for a variety of applications and environments where PRINCE is already deployed.

In the following, we compare our novel PRINCEv2 design to the original PRINCE concerning the minimum latency and minimum area achieved by unrolled implementations. Since gate count and delay numbers depend on the particular technology used, we provide synthesis results from 4 different commercial standard cell libraries of feature sizes between 90 nm and 28 nm. This redundancy minimizes the influence of a single technology on the comparison's interpretation. All 4 standard cell libraries contain multiple classes of gates, namely a high

Table 3. Area, latency and energy characteristics of unrolled `PRINCE` and `PRINCEv2` when constrained for minimum latency.

Techn.	Mode	Cipher	Area [GE]	Latency [ns]	Energy [pJ]
90 nm LP*	ENC	PRINCE	16244.25	4.101177	1.993172
		PRINCEv2	17661.25	4.047311	2.230068
	ENC/DEC	PRINCE	17808.00	4.106262	2.213275
		PRINCEv2	18888.75	4.151113	2.424250
65 nm LP*	ENC	PRINCE	19877.75	2.866749	1.602513
		PRINCEv2	18798.25	2.944367	1.492794
	ENC/DEC	PRINCE	19966.00	2.946442	1.594025
		PRINCEv2	21171.25	2.930153	1.696559
40 nm LP*	ENC	PRINCE	17177.00	2.521302	0.617719
		PRINCEv2	16556.50	2.509131	0.592155
	ENC/DEC	PRINCE	17377.50	2.541220	0.630223
		PRINCEv2	17799.50	2.583466	0.648450
28 nm HPC**	ENC	PRINCE	38145.33	1.108886	1.258586
		PRINCEv2	33470.33	1.103273	1.108789
	ENC/DEC	PRINCE	35297.67	1.119593	1.181171
		PRINCEv2	38962.33	1.148693	1.299172

* LP = Low Power
** HPC = High Performance Computing

threshold voltage (*hvt*) class, a standard threshold voltage (*std*) class and a low threshold voltage (*lvt*) class. These distinct classes allow to fully explore the latency-vs-leakage tradeoff. More specifically, when placing a tight constraint on the latency of a circuit, primarily *lvt* cells are chosen due to their high speed. On the other hand, when synthesizing without tight timing constraints, *hvt* cells will be chosen due to the lower energy loss through leakage currents. Using manufacturable standard cell libraries from a commercial foundry instead of open-source libraries for a design comparison is often preferable since the reported numbers are more accurate in all key categories, such as area, latency and energy. They are especially superior in power and energy estimation, as common open-source libraries fail to provide industry quality characterization in that regard. However, to keep our results reproducible and make comparisons to existing works easy we provide a comparison of all our unrolled `PRINCE` and `PRINCEv2` circuits to several other low-latency and low-energy constructions in NanGate 45 nm and 15 nm Open Cell Libraries (OCL) later in this section.

We consider the typical process and operating conditions in all our synthesis results, i.e., the typical PVT (process, voltage, temperature) corner case, with a nominal supply voltage and a working temperature of 25 °C. For synthesis, we have used *Synopsys Design Compiler Version O-2018.06-SP4* with three stages of the `compile_ultra` command (two incremental). As a first step, we have

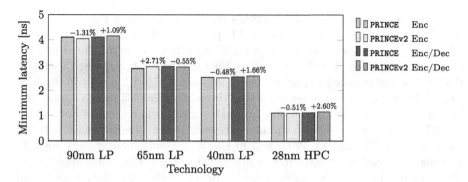

Fig. 2. Minimum achievable latency of unrolled PRINCE and PRINCEv2 across different technologies.

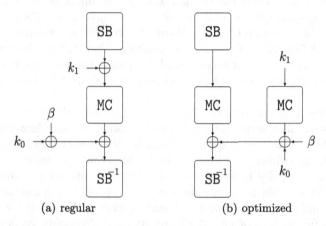

(a) regular   (b) optimized

Fig. 3. Simple latency optimization strategy in the middle round of PRINCEv2 that removes one key addition from the critical path.

constrained our circuits for minimum latency. The results are given in Table 3 and visualized in Fig. 2. We distinguish between circuits that can only encrypt (ENC) and circuits that can decrypt as well (ENC/DEC).

Several interesting observations can be made. Firstly, all four distinct circuits perform decidedly similar in terms of minimum latency. The difference falls in the range of single-digit picoseconds in several cases. To gain a better overview, Fig. 2 provides the differences between corresponding PRINCE and PRINCEv2 circuits as percentages on top of the bar graphs. Interestingly, the encryption-only version of PRINCEv2 outperforms PRINCE in terms of minimum latency in three of four technologies. This may be counter-intuitive, as PRINCEv2 adds two key additions to the middle round. However, as shown in Fig. 3, those two key additions can be merged into a single one regarding the critical path by calculating and adding $MC(K_1)$ in parallel.

This optimization not only improves the minimum latency but also saves area.[2] One may expect the synthesis tool to perform such an optimization implicitly by itself, as two key additions and a MC operation in the middle essentially result in a sequence of four consecutive XORs per bit. Yet, our results suggest that it is indeed required to perform the optimization algorithmically in the RTL code. Additionally, it has to be noted that the original PRINCE design applies two key additions (whitening and round key) to the input before the first Sbox stage. PRINCEv2, on the other hand, applies only one. Hence, the difference between the latency of PRINCE and PRINCEv2 in encryption-only mode comes down to whether the synthesizer implements the additional key XOR at the input more efficiently or the one in the middle round. More often than not, the middle round key addition is more efficient latency-wise since the synthesizer has more freedom to move that XOR stage around (e.g., to the input, output or intermediate signals of the MC operation), while the two key XORs at the input have a fixed location and cannot be optimized beyond instantiating a three-input XOR per bit, since all inputs to the operation (key and plaintext) arrive at approximately the same time. Original PRINCE also requires an additional key XOR at the output. Yet, since the last round's output arrives much later than the keys, the key parts will be added to each other beforehand and only one of the XOR stages affects the critical path.

At this point, we should stress that differences in synthesis results of such a small magnitude may sometimes go beyond algorithmic considerations and can not always be understood in detail without having insight into the proprietary optimization algorithms used by EDA tools. Sometimes a latency optimization with a big area penalty is deemed worth it by the synthesizer, sometimes not. Thresholds for such decisions are unknown and therefore the outcome can not always be predicted. One example for such a case in Table 3 is the difference between the full variant of PRINCEv2 and its encryption-only version in 65 nm LP technology. For unknown reasons, the full variant achieves a lower latency than the encryption-only one, but at the price of a significantly increased area, indicating costly latency optimizations. However, the majority of our reported figures directly corresponds to the algorithmic differences in the analyzed ciphers and modes.

Regarding the cipher variants with decryption capability, the situation is slightly different compared to the encryption-only versions. The more complex key-multiplexing in PRINCEv2 required to choose between encryption and decryption, as apparent in Fig. 10, induces additional delay. In the worst case, this results in an overhead of 2.6%, but on average the overhead is about 1.2%. Table 3 also reports area and energy numbers for the highly constrained circuits. The energy values correspond to the average energy consumed by one evaluation of the unrolled circuits at maximum clock frequency (corresponding to minimum latency). While PRINCEv2 is often more area and energy-efficient than PRINCE in encryption-only mode, PRINCEv2 with decryption capability consistently requires

---

[2] Area is saved by this optimization since slower cells with a lower drive strength can be selected for the parallel calculations. Those cells have a smaller area footprint.

Table 4. Area, latency and energy characteristics of unrolled PRINCE and PRINCEv2 when constrained for minimum area.

Techn.	Mode	Cipher	Area [GE]	Latency [ns]	Energy [pJ]
90 nm LP*	ENC	PRINCE	7937.50	12.859908	0.569694
		PRINCEv2	8111.25	12.856450	0.574683
	ENC/DEC	PRINCE	8183.00	14.015245	0.616671
		PRINCEv2	8440.75	15.513536	0.628298
65 nm LP*	ENC	PRINCE	8316.00	11.434771	0.433378
		PRINCEv2	8385.25	11.504968	0.430286
	ENC/DEC	PRINCE	8547.75	12.349355	0.440872
		PRINCEv2	8792.75	13.376949	0.456154
40 nm LP*	ENC	PRINCE	8563.75	10.144847	0.212027
		PRINCEv2	8608.50	10.063908	0.207317
	ENC/DEC	PRINCE	8780.00	10.886960	0.217739
		PRINCEv2	9039.75	11.798657	0.226534
28 nm HPC**	ENC	PRINCE	8197.00	3.599936	0.127798
		PRINCEv2	8292.00	3.682593	0.127786
	ENC/DEC	PRINCE	8426.33	4.260999	0.131239
		PRINCEv2	8844.67	4.323993	0.134909

* LP = Low Power
** HPC = High Performance Computing

the largest area and consumes the most energy. Yet, the margins are still very thin. In summary, PRINCE's most important property and main selling point, namely high-speed single-cycle encryption, is well preserved by PRINCEv2. For scenarios that require no decryption but only encryption, it may even be slightly improved.

As a second step, we evaluate the minimum area that can be achieved by the unrolled circuits. In this regard, we have executed the same synthesis scripts as before, but without the tight timing constraints. Our results are reported in Table 4 and depicted as a bar graph in Fig. 4.

In contrast to the latency results, a consistent overhead for minimum area can be observed for the PRINCEv2 circuits. This is expected, due to the additional operations in the middle round and the more complex key-multiplexing to decide between encryption and decryption. Yet, the average overhead is less than 1.2% for the encryption-only and less than 3.5% for the full versions. This is a rather small price to pay for the additional security PRINCEv2 provides. When comparing the low-latency and low-area implementations in Tables 3 and 4 respectively, it can be seen that area increases 2 to 4 times from low-area to low-latency constraint. Latency scales down 3 to 4 times. Energy consumption increases between 4 and 10 times, due to a dependency on both factors (caused by leakage currents). These metrics should be carefully considered when choosing operating frequency and target technology for a given application.

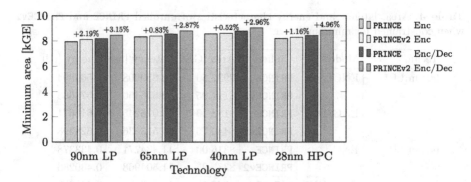

Fig. 4. Minimum achievable area of unrolled PRINCE and PRINCEv2 across different technologies.

Finally, we compare PRINCE and PRINCEv2 to other lightweight block ciphers proposed in the literature. Only a few cryptographic primitives have made low latency a primary design objective. To the best of our knowledge, none of those who have share all design goals and security claims with PRINCE or PRINCEv2. Hence, the following comparison involves ciphers with different security and performance claims and is only supposed to put their hardware efficiency in relation to each other, without concluding the superiority of one or the other. In particular, we compare PRINCE and PRINCEv2 to the low-latency tweakable block ciphers MANTIS [BJK+16] and QARMA [Ava17]. Yet, since both of those constructions are tweakable, unlike all PRINCE versions, they can not easily achieve the same latency and area as PRINCE and PRINCEv2. We also include Midori [BBI+15] in the comparison, as the authors have partially aimed for a low logic depth as well. However, Midori primarily targets energy efficiency in round-based implementations and has no claim to provide low latency in unrolled representation. Additionally, we have developed a combination of PRINCE and PRINCEv2, which we call PRINCE+v2. This combined cipher offers a control signal to select whether the input should be processed according to the PRINCE or the PRINCEv2 specification. In environments where PRINCE is already deployed, this can be useful for backward compatibility and legacy support. We have analyzed all 6 ciphers in two modes each (ENC and ENC/DEC) in NanGate 45 nm and 15 nm Open Cell Libraries and evaluate their area-vs-latency tradeoff. The result is depicted in Fig. 5 for NanGate 45 nm and in Fig. 6 for 15 nm technology. The exact performance figures used to create these graphs can be found in the Appendix in Tables 5 and 6. The results in these two libraries demonstrate that PRINCE and PRINCEv2 are the most suitable choices for high-speed encryption, as long as a tweak input is not required. All PRINCE and PRINCEv2 variants outperform the other ciphers both in terms of minimum latency and minimum area. PRINCEv2 in encryption-only mode is roughly 20% faster than Midori and MANTIS, and 40% faster than QARMA. At the same time, its minimum area is about 15% smaller than Midori, 30% smaller than MANTIS and 40% smaller than QARMA. The results are similar when comparing both encryption and decryption implementations, except for Midori being significantly larger and slower. This outcome is unsurprising since all compared ciphers except Midori are reflection ciphers, i.e., they use a variant of the α-reflection property introduced by PRINCE. Please note that for this reason the full version of Midori64, including decryption, is barely visible in Figs. 5 and 6 as it simply does not fit in the frame due to its much higher latency and area caused by the extra multiplexers required in each round. Yet the full figures for that implementation can be found in Tables 5 and 6 in the Appendix. We chose the particular instances MANTIS$_7$ and QARMA$_7$-64-σ_1 for the comparison as they are supposed to offer a similar security level as PRINCE and PRINCEv2, while being tweakable.

In the original proposal, the maximum achievable frequency in NanGate 45 nm of unrolled PRINCE was given as 212.8 MHz [BCG+12]. Our unrolled PRINCE can be clocked at 242.8 MHz for the full variant and 246.3 MHz for the encryption-only version in the same technology, which corresponds to a 12.4% or 15.7% higher performance respectively. The minimum area was given as 8260 GE in the original proposal, while our implementations are as small as 7868.67 GE for the full variant and 7620.00 GE for the encryption-only version. That corresponds to a 5.0% or 8.4% higher area efficiency respectively. We conclude that our base-implementation used for the construction of PRINCEv2 and PRINCE+v2 (and partially for MANTIS$_7$) is well optimized.

Finally, we compare the energy consumption of the 6 ciphers. As detailed before, open-source libraries are not suitable for power and energy estimation. Thus, we have performed the energy comparison in the commercial 40 nm Low Power CMOS technology. This particular technology proved to be the most energy efficient, as apparent from Tables 3 and 4. The results have been estimated at 50 MHz and are depicted in Fig. 7. Please note the y-axis limits on the bar graph. The differences between the circuits are not as large as they may appear at first sight. Yet, the results confirm once again that PRINCE and PRINCEv2 are the most cost-efficient unrolled circuits.

5 Security Analysis

We analyzed the security of PRINCEv2 building on the previously published analysis of PRINCE. Most dedicated attacks on PRINCEv2 are comparable to PRINCE, while PRINCEv2 offers significantly better resistance to generic attacks. We show that several attacks successful against PRINCE, such as certain accelerated exhaustive search and meet-in-the-middle attacks, do not apply to PRINCEv2. Note that we do not consider analyses of variants with modified operations or related-key attacks, but we provide a discussion of the latter at the end of this section.

Since PRINCEv2 is designed to provide a higher security level, we also need to consider attacks with higher complexity than for PRINCE. For several dedicated attack strategies, we find attacks that cover 1 or 2 more rounds with significantly higher time complexity T or data complexity D. This higher complexity is above

Table 5. Full comparison of unrolled block ciphers in NanGate 45 nm Open Cell Library.

PRINCE				PRINCEv2			
ENC		ENC/DEC		ENC		ENC/DEC	
Lat. [ns]	Area [GE]	Lat. [ns]	Area [GE]	Lat. [ns]	Area [GE]	Lat. [ns]	Area [GE]
4.059997	9873.33	4.119023	10486.33	4.077636	10332.00	4.245165	10780.67
4.500000	8421.67	4.500000	8807.00	4.500000	8526.67	4.500000	9488.00
5.000000	7837.00	5.000000	8213.33	5.000000	8013.00	5.000000	8659.67
5.500000	7684.33	5.500000	7959.33	5.500000	7865.67	5.500000	8328.67
6.000000	7620.00	6.000000	7874.00	6.000000	7812.33	6.000000	8196.00
6.500000	7620.00	6.500000	7868.67	6.500000	7812.33	6.500000	8144.00
7.000000	7620.00	7.000000	7868.67	7.000000	7812.33	7.000000	8141.67

PRINCE+v2				Midori64			
ENC		ENC/DEC		ENC		ENC/DEC	
Lat. [ns]	Area [GE]	Lat. [ns]	Area [GE]	Lat. [ns]	Area [GE]	Lat. [ns]	Area [GE]
4.353092	11258.33	4.469554	12395.67	4.934847	10755.67	7.111567	25058.33
4.500000	9588.33	4.500000	10709.00	4.500000	-	4.500000	-
5.000000	8622.67	5.000000	9870.33	5.000000	10353.67	5.000000	-
5.500000	8276.00	5.500000	9356.00	5.500000	9223.67	5.500000	-
6.000000	8169.67	6.000000	9091.67	6.000000	8858.00	6.000000	-
6.500000	8156.33	6.500000	8990.33	6.500000	8792.33	6.500000	-
7.000000	8155.33	7.000000	8982.00	7.000000	8748.33	7.000000	-
7.500000	8155.33	7.500000	8969.33	7.500000	8748.33	7.500000	19733.00
8.000000	8155.33	8.000000	8969.33	8.000000	8748.33	8.000000	18381.00
9.000000	8155.33	9.000000	8969.33	9.000000	8748.33	9.000000	16241.67
10.000000	8155.33	10.000000	8969.33	10.000000	8748.33	10.000000	14877.67
11.000000	8155.33	11.000000	8969.33	11.000000	8748.33	11.000000	14476.33

MANTIS$_7$				QARMA$_7$-64-σ_1			
ENC		ENC/DEC		ENC		ENC/DEC	
Lat. [ns]	Area [GE]	Lat. [ns]	Area [GE]	Lat. [ns]	Area [GE]	Lat. [ns]	Area [GE]
5.036228	14481.67	5.235198	14810.67	5.756122	17096.67	5.794558	18085.67
5.500000	12445.33	5.500000	12931.67	5.500000	-	5.500000	-
6.000000	11613.33	6.000000	12082.67	6.000000	14821.33	6.000000	15449.67
6.500000	11246.67	6.500000	11786.67	6.500000	13886.00	6.500000	14866.33
7.000000	11134.33	7.000000	11529.00	7.000000	13139.67	7.000000	14019.33
7.500000	11064.67	7.500000	11397.67	7.500000	12698.33	7.500000	13467.33
8.000000	11019.33	8.000000	11322.67	8.000000	12326.67	8.000000	13012.33
8.500000	11019.33	8.500000	11305.33	8.500000	12106.33	8.500000	12801.67
9.000000	11019.33	9.000000	11305.33	9.000000	12039.33	9.000000	12677.00
9.500000	11019.33	9.500000	11305.33	9.500000	12039.33	9.500000	12614.67
10.000000	11019.33	10.000000	11305.33	10.000000	12039.33	10.000000	12610.33
10.500000	11019.33	10.500000	11305.33	10.500000	12039.33	10.500000	12609.00

the bound $D \cdot T < 2^{126}$ claimed for PRINCE, but below the generic bounds of $D < 2^{64}$, $T < 2^{128}$ for PRINCEv2, and thus relevant to judge the security margin of PRINCEv2. We note that the security claim for PRINCEv2 limits the attacker to $D < 2^{47}$ and $T < 2^{112}$, while most of the results we propose for round-reduced PRINCEv2 require more data than permitted by this bound.

Table 6. Full comparison of unrolled block ciphers in NanGate 15 nm Open Cell Library.

PRINCE				PRINCEv2			
ENC		ENC/DEC		ENC		ENC/DEC	
Lat. [ns]	Area [GE]	Lat. [ns]	Area [GE]	Lat. [ns]	Area [GE]	Lat. [ns]	Area [GE]
0.389144	13291.00	0.400530	13468.00	0.387146	13069.50	0.404112	14181.25
0.400000	12380.75	0.400000	-	0.400000	12331.75	0.400000	-
0.450000	9618.50	0.450000	10275.50	0.450000	9859.00	0.450000	11185.25
0.500000	8811.00	0.500000	9115.50	0.500000	8940.75	0.500000	9822.25
0.550000	8621.50	0.550000	8935.50	0.550000	8820.00	0.550000	9272.25
0.600000	8610.50	0.600000	8828.75	0.600000	8787.25	0.600000	9134.50
0.650000	8610.50	0.650000	8828.75	0.650000	8787.25	0.650000	9108.00
0.700000	8610.50	0.700000	8828.75	0.700000	8787.25	0.700000	9105.50
0.750000	8610.50	0.750000	8828.75	0.750000	8787.25	0.750000	9104.00

PRINCE+v2				Midori64			
ENC		ENC/DEC		ENC		ENC/DEC	
Lat. [ns]	Area [GE]	Lat. [ns]	Area [GE]	Lat. [ns]	Area [GE]	Lat. [ns]	Area [GE]
0.415065	14422.75	0.426661	16016.00	0.481522	13775.00	0.657338	30563.50
0.450000	11701.25	0.450000	14280.50	0.450000	-	0.450000	-
0.500000	9698.00	0.500000	11253.50	0.500000	11581.25	0.500000	-
0.550000	9234.00	0.550000	10193.00	0.550000	10427.00	0.550000	-
0.600000	9147.75	0.600000	9991.75	0.600000	9896.25	0.600000	-
0.650000	9163.00	0.650000	9967.25	0.650000	9831.00	0.650000	-
0.700000	9144.00	0.700000	9931.75	0.700000	9806.50	0.700000	28135.25
0.750000	9143.50	0.750000	9931.25	0.750000	9806.50	0.750000	22886.75
0.800000	9143.50	0.800000	9929.75	0.800000	9806.50	0.800000	20793.75
0.850000	9143.50	0.850000	9929.00	0.850000	9806.50	0.850000	18871.75
0.900000	9143.50	0.900000	9929.00	0.900000	9806.50	0.900000	17772.00
1.000000	9143.50	1.000000	9929.00	1.000000	9806.50	1.000000	16423.00
1.100000	9143.50	1.100000	9929.00	1.100000	9806.50	1.100000	15420.75
1.200000	9143.50	1.200000	9929.00	1.200000	9806.50	1.200000	15380.00
1.300000	9143.50	1.300000	9929.00	1.300000	9806.50	1.300000	15318.00

MANTIS$_7$				QARMA$_7$-64-σ_1			
ENC		ENC/DEC		ENC		ENC/DEC	
Lat. [ns]	Area [GE]	Lat. [ns]	Area [GE]	Lat. [ns]	Area [GE]	Lat. [ns]	Area [GE]
0.492660	17542.75	0.504465	18193.75	0.542777	20736.25	0.552887	22130.75
0.500000	17142.75	0.500000	-	0.500000	-	0.500000	-
0.550000	14404.00	0.550000	15159.25	0.550000	20736.25	0.550000	-
0.600000	13650.00	0.600000	14464.50	0.600000	16413.25	0.600000	18195.25
0.650000	12469.00	0.650000	12804.75	0.650000	14864.25	0.650000	16299.75
0.700000	12378.25	0.700000	12681.50	0.700000	13862.00	0.700000	15111.25
0.750000	12285.75	0.750000	12626.75	0.750000	13794.00	0.750000	14542.25
0.800000	12275.00	0.800000	12580.00	0.800000	13531.25	0.800000	14292.25
0.850000	12275.00	0.850000	12565.00	0.850000	13359.00	0.850000	14130.25
0.900000	12275.00	0.900000	12561.25	0.900000	13304.00	0.900000	14009.75
0.950000	12275.00	0.950000	12561.25	0.950000	13304.00	0.950000	13988.75

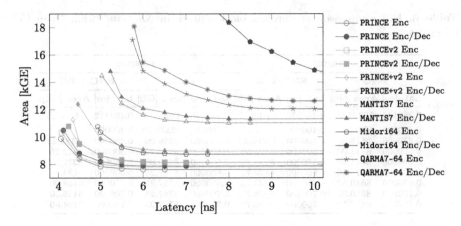

Fig. 5. Comparison of unrolled block ciphers in NanGate 45 nm Open Cell Library.

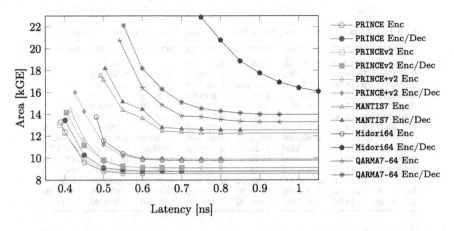

Fig. 6. Comparison of unrolled block ciphers in NanGate 15 nm Open Cell Library.

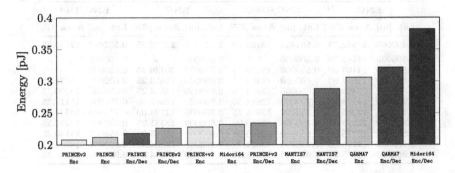

Fig. 7. Average energy consumption of unrolled block ciphers clocked at 50 MHz in a commercial 40 nm Low Power CMOS technology.

Table 7. Overview of the main analysis results on round-reduced PRINCEv2, where 12 is the full number of rounds. Time complexity is given in computation equivalents, data complexity in known plaintexts (KP) or chosen plaintexts (CP). For most attacks in this table except meet-in-the-middle (†), the attacks on PRINCE apply to PRINCEv2 with similar complexity and vice-versa; however, the complexity of the attacks listed for PRINCEv2 is higher than permitted by the PRINCE security claim. For other results, refer to details in Sect. 5.

Attack	Target		Complexity		Reference
	Version	Rounds	Time	Data	
Differential	PRINCE	10	2^{61}	2^{58} CP	[CFG+14a]
	PRINCEv2	11	2^{92}	2^{59} CP	New
Impossible differential	PRINCE	7	2^{54}	2^{56} CP	[DZLY17]
	PRINCEv2	9	$e^{-\alpha} \cdot 2^{128}$	$\alpha \cdot 2^{65}$ CP	New
Integral	PRINCE	7	2^{57}	2^{60} CP	[Mor17]
	PRINCEv2	8	$2^{107.4}$	2^{36} CP	New
Meet-in-the-middle	PRINCE †	10	2^{122}	2 KP	[RR16b]
	PRINCEv2 †	10	2^{112}	2^{48} CP	New

Additionally, we provide several new results, including a linear attack, a 6-round integral distinguisher based on the division property, a more precise evaluation of boomerang attacks using recently published techniques, and a new 10-round Demirci-Selçuk meet-in-the-middle attack.

Table 7 provides an overview of the highlights of this section, including the best attacks on PRINCEv2 and noteworthy new results. In summary, PRINCEv2 is at least as secure as PRINCE against various dedicated attacks and provides better generic security.

Differential [ALL12, CFG+14a, CFG+14b, DP15a, DP15b, GR16a, GR16b]: The truncated differential used in [GR16a, GR16b] applies the subspace trail technique and attacks at most 6 rounds of PRINCE, which is the same for PRINCEv2.

The inside-out differential in [ALL12] took advantage of the key-less middle round to attack at most 6 rounds of PRINCE and is thus not applicable to PRINCEv2.

The most powerful differential attack against PRINCE was the one introduced in [CFG+14a, CFG+14b] that covers 10 rounds using $2^{57.94}$ chosen plaintexts, $2^{60.62}$ computations and $2^{61.52}$ blocks of memory. The distinguisher of this attack covers 6-round and it appends 2 rounds before and 2 rounds after which needs to guess 66 key bits. Using the same distinguisher and attack for PRINCEv2, we need to guess 64 key bits. The complexities of both attacks are roughly the same. The probability of the corresponding differentials are summarized in Table 8.

This attack can be extended by one round with the new key schedule at the cost of significantly higher time complexity, as illustrated in Fig. 8.

1. Query N_s structures of 2^{32} chosen plaintexts P with columns P_1, P_3 fixed within each structure. This yields $N_s \cdot 2^{31} \cdot (2^{32} - 1) \approx N_s \cdot 2^{63}$ candidate pairs as in Fig. 8.

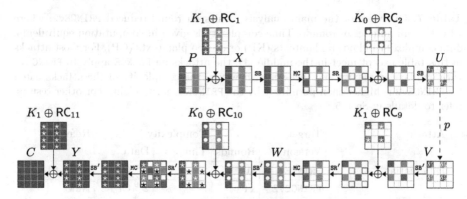

Fig. 8. Differential attack on 11-round PRINCEv2 extending [CFG+14a] by one round.

2. For each of the $N_s \cdot 2^{63}$ candidate pairs (P, P'), we expect 1 candidate for the 96-bit key $(K_1, K_{0,0}, K_{0,2})$, which can be determined by a small number of table lookups:
   (a) We expect 1 key candidate for the key columns $K_{1,0}, K_{1,2}$ ($\star$) that satisfies the pattern through SB, MC in rounds 1 and 11. This costs one lookup in a precomputed table $(\Delta X_0, \Delta Y_0, X_0 \oplus Y_0) \to X_0$ per pair.
   (b) For any fixed difference ΔU, we also get 1 key candidate for the 4 nibbles of K_0 involved in round 2, which determines 4 nibbles of W in round 10 ($\bullet$).
   (c) Due to the pattern for MC in round 10, there are only $2^8 \times 2^8$ possible differences ΔW. The key bits found so far determine 16 bits of this difference and thus on average fully determine ΔW.
   (d) For any fixed difference ΔV, knowing $K_{1,0}, K_{1,2}$, we get on average 1 candidate for the value of the two active columns W_0, W_2. This determines the difference ΔZ and thus the key columns $K_{1,1}, K_{1,3}$ as well as the rest of $K_{0,0}, K_{0,2}$.
3. Rank the obtained $N_s \cdot 2^{63}$ candidates for the 96-bit key $(K_1, K_{0,0}, K_{0,2})$.

Using $N_s = 5/p/2^{31} = 2^{29}$ structures for the best differential $(\delta_0, \delta_1, \delta_0', \delta_1') = (1, 2, 1, 2)$ from Table 8, we expect about 5 right pairs, which should be easily sufficient for distinguishing. The remaining 32 key bits $(K_{0,1}, K_{0,3})$ can be recovered by brute-force search. The overall complexity is $N_s \cdot 2^{32} = 2^{61}$ chosen plaintexts and the time corresponding to $N_s \cdot 2^{63} = 2^{92}$ repetitions of a few table lookups and arithmetic operations, which can be roughly approximated by one encryption equivalent.

The attack can be slightly improved using multiple differentials from Table 8, but fewer structures. For example, we can use the 2^2 permutations of the best differential with the same p and decrease N_s by a factor of 2^2, obtaining an attack with the same expected number of valid pairs and key candidates, while the data complexity is reduced to 2^{59} and the time complexity is slightly lower than before.

Table 8. Differentials and linear hulls fitting to the 6-round activity patterns given in [CFG+14a] for both PRINCE and PRINCEv2.

differential probability (divided by $2^{-72} \times 2^3$)				average square linear correlation (divided by $2^{-91} \times 2^3$)			
(δ_0, δ_1)	(δ_0', δ_1')	PRINCE	PRINCEv2	(δ_0, δ_1)	(δ_0', δ_1')	PRINCE	PRINCEv2
(1,2)	(1,2)	6144	2560	(4,2)	(4,2)	3563313280	2701826048
(1,2)	(1,8)	3328	1344	(4,2)	(4,8)	243931552	177559040
(1,2)	(1,a)	1664	672	(4,2)	(4,a)	215632256	165965824
(1,2)	(4,2)	1536	640	(4,2)	(5,2)	44716840	22956032
(1,2)	(4,8)	1664	928	(4,2)	(5,8)	23525008	14792960
(1,2)	(4,a)	832	336	(4,2)	(5,a)	3662080	2491520
(1,8)	(1,8)	2112	784	(4,8)	(4,8)	16864144	11669888
(1,8)	(1,a)	1056	392	(4,8)	(4,a)	14706248	10906624
(1,8)	(4,2)	832	336	(4,8)	(5,2)	3338620	1510400
(1,8)	(4,8)	1056	520	(4,8)	(5,8)	1723948	972992
(1,8)	(4,a)	528	196	(4,8)	(5,a)	256192	163616
(1,a)	(1,a)	528	196	(4,a)	(4,a)	13067272	10194944
(1,a)	(4,2)	416	168	(4,a)	(5,2)	2613530	1409536
(1,a)	(4,8)	528	260	(4,a)	(5,8)	1385768	908416
(1,a)	(4,a)	264	98	(4,a)	(5,a)	219776	153088
(4,2)	(4,2)	384	160	(5,2)	(5,2)	1221068	203976
(4,2)	(4,8)	416	232	(5,2)	(5,8)	698555	133008
(4,2)	(4,a)	208	84	(5,2)	(5,a)	54472	20960
(4,8)	(4,8)	656	388	(5,8)	(5,8)	466562	87600
(4,8)	(4,a)	264	130	(5,8)	(5,a)	27160	13544
(4,a)	(4,a)	132	49	(5,a)	(5,a)	4024	2312

Linear: Even though there is no published linear analysis for PRINCE, we find out that the activity patterns used in [CFG+14a] for differential analysis are also useful for the linear one. This is because of the MC operation that uses an involutive and self-transpose matrix, i.e. $M'^T = M'^{-1} = M'$. We compute the average square correlation of all 6-round linear hulls which follow the given activity patterns similarly as in [CFG+14a] for both PRINCE and PRINCEv2. These values are summarized in Table 8.

One can use these linear hulls to analyze 10-round PRINCE by guessing 66 key bits and on PRINCEv2 with 64 key bits guesses (similar to differential attack). Data complexity for both of these attacks are factor of 2^{57} known plaintexts.

Impossible Differential [DZLY17]: The best previously known impossible differential attack was discovered by Ding *et al.* [DZLY17], based on a 4-round distinguisher and extended to an attack up to 7 rounds with 2^{56} data, $2^{53.8}$ time and 2^{43} bytes of memory. At Eurocrypt'17, Sasaki and Todo proposed a new way to search for impossible differentials [ST17] based on MILP, leading to

Table 9. Impossible differential distinguishers for 5 rounds.

2 + 2 + 1 rounds	1 + 2 + 2 rounds
0010000000000000 $\nrightarrow$ 0000000040000000	0400000000000000 $\nrightarrow$ 0000000000004000
0000000000100000 $\nrightarrow$ 0000000001000000	0010000000000000 $\nrightarrow$ 0000000000000010
0000000000004000 $\nrightarrow$ 0400000000000000	0000000040000000 $\nrightarrow$ 0010000000000000
0000000000000010 $\nrightarrow$ 0010000000000000	0000000001000000 $\nrightarrow$ 0000000000100000

much more sophisticated distinguishers than previously known. We implemented this algorithm and were able to find new impossible distinguishers over 5 rounds which are given in Table 9. Note that there are two different configurations for our distinguishers: either $1 + 2 + 2$ which means one forward round, the two middles rounds and 2 backward rounds, or $2 + 2 + 1$, *i.e.*, two forward rounds, two middle rounds and one backward round.

Due to the specific shape of these impossible differentials (only one active bit in the input and output), we can take any one of them and use it to mount an attack up to 9 rounds. Using [BNPS14], we were able to estimate that the resulting attack would need $\alpha \cdot 2^{65}$ data and memory, and $2^{128} \cdot e^{-\alpha}$ time, where α is a parameter allowing for a trade-off between data/memory and time complexities (the higher is α, the higher is the data/memory complexity and the lower is the time complexity).

Integral and Higher-Order Differential [JNP+13, Mor17, PN15, RR16c]: The [BCG+12] longest known distinguisher of these types is a higher-order differential that is introduced in [Mor17]. This distinguisher includes 5 nonlinear layers and needs a data set of size 2^{32}. For key recovery, it is possible to append at most 3 rounds to the end of distinguisher and attack 8 round PRINCEv2 by guessing 80 key bits. The complexity of this attack is 2^{112} computations (equivalent to $2^{107.4}$ 8-round PRINCEv2 encryption), 2^{36} chosen plaintexts and 2^{36} blocks of memory.

A more recent technique to build integral distinguisher is to use the so-called *division property* introduced by Todo at Eurocrypt'15 [Tod15]. This technique was later refined into *bit-based division property* at FSE'16 by Todo and Morii [TM16] and some work was done to efficiently search for division property using *e.g.* Mixed Integer Linear Programming (MILP) [XZBL16, ZR19]. We implemented this algorithm to search for division property based distinguishers and we ended up finding such a distinguisher over 6 rounds. This distinguisher requires 2^{62} chosen plaintexts and due to this high data complexity, we do not expect it to be used to mount an attack over more than 8 rounds while also having better complexities than the above-mentioned attack.

Boomerang [PDN15]: The boomerang attack is applied to PRINCE in [PDN15], but there are some flaws on the estimation of the probability, e.g., the effect of the boomerang switching [BK09] is not taken in consideration. The so-called sandwich attack [DKS10, DKS14] is an experimental approach to estimate more rigorously this probability. We estimated the probability for a boomerang distinguisher with 4-round plus the middle layer. The probability of this 6-round distinguisher is about 2^{-34}, but the 7-round distinguisher is clearly worse than the classical differential attack because it involves 9 additional active S-boxes.

Accelerated Exhaustive Search [JNP+13, PDN15, RR16a, RR16b]: These attacks on PRINCE either used the α-reflection and FX-construction property or the key-less middle rounds of the cipher to accelerate the exhaustive search. For PRINCEv2, these properties do not hold anymore and the only possible attack of this type is the one used in [RR16b]. Using the technique of [RR16b] and by starting from the middle of the cipher, attacking 4 round or more requires to guess all the key bits. By starting from the plaintext/ciphertext side, attacking 6 rounds or more requires to guess all the key bits.

Meet-in-the-Middle   [CNPV13a, CNPV13b, DP15a, DP15b, LJW13, RR16b]: Meet-in-the-Middle attacks used in [LJW13, RR16b] took advantage of key-less middle rounds and use super-sboxes in the middle of the cipher to attack at most 10 rounds. These attacks do not work on PRINCEv2 as effective as on PRINCE.

The sieve-in-the-middle attack, introduced in [CNPV13a, CNPV13b], is applicable to 8 rounds of PRINCE which includes 6 rounds for the sieve-in-the-middle and 2 rounds for the biclique part. Applying it to PRINCEv2, the sieve-in-the-middle part will be more complicated. The super-sbox used there will be key-dependent, which increases the time and memory complexity.

The meet-in-the-middle attack used in [DP15a, DP15b] reaches 10 rounds of PRINCE. Applying the tool given in [Der19] by Patrick Derbez which uses the same technique, we find out that it is possible to attack at most 6 rounds of PRINCEv2 with the complexity of either 2^{96} computations and 2^{26} memory blocks or 2^{112} computations and 2^6 memory blocks.

We also analyzed the security of PRINCEv2 against Demirci-Selçuk meet-in-the-middle attacks using the same tool by Derbez. This attack can reach at most 10 rounds using 2^{48} chosen plaintexts, 2^{112} computations and 2^{70} memory blocks.

Time-Data-Memory Trade-Offs [Din15, JNP+13]: Excluding trivial Diffie-Hellman time-data-memory trade-offs, all of these attacks used FX-construction property of the PRINCE and do not work on the PRINCEv2.

Biclique [ALL12, YPO15]: These attacks could accelerate an exhaustive search maximally by a factor of 2, exploiting the FX-construction in PRINCE. Since PRINCEv2 is not an FX-construction anymore and this attack does not improve the exhaustive search generally, we expect this attack to be not applicable.

Collisions [FJM14]: The FX-construction of PRINCE allows a collision-based attack, using 2^{32} data, 2^{96} off-line and 2^{32} on-line computations, to recover the key. But again, it does not apply to PRINCEv2.

Remarks About Related-Key Attacks: We emphasize that we never claim any security under related-key attacks, but it is also important to understand the impact on PRINCEv2 when attackers can use related-key attacks.

First of all, when both rotational and XOR-difference relations are allowed, the trivial related-key distinguishing attack is possible by exploiting the convertible property from encryption to decryption. Even if the relationship is restricted to XOR-difference, attackers can still attack PRINCEv2 by using related-key boomerang attacks. The related-key boomerang attack is applied to PRINCE without whitening keys in [JNP+13]. Inducing differences with the key allows attackers to construct iterative related-key differential characteristics whose number of active S-boxes is only one in each round. This iterative property is lost in the middle round R', but attackers can overcome R' by using related-key boomerang attack, where two iterative related-key differential characteristics are connected. The new key schedule for PRINCEv2 is not designed to avoid this related-key boomerang attack, and there are related-key boomerang characteristics with 12 active S-boxes. Similarly to the single-key boomerang attack, evaluating the probability in detail requires to analyze the effect of the boomerang switching. However, we can estimate the probability is roughly $2^{-12 \times 2 \times 2} = 2^{-48}$ from the number of active S-boxes, and it implies that PRINCEv2 is not secure against the related-key attack.

Again, we never claim any security under related-key attacks, and we believe that a related-key attack never happens in the environment that PRINCEv2 is demanded.

6   Conclusion

The need for a secure and efficient low-latency block cipher which also has low-power and low-energy requirements is ever increasing with the widespread of multiple technologies using microcontrollers. While PRINCE family of block ciphers were specifically designed to tackle this problem, the recent lightweight crypto competition for AEAD from the NIST set a specific security level that PRINCE cannot reach. As a low-latency cipher would probably be deployed in a larger environment using such an AEAD primitive, it makes sense to want this low-latency cipher to reach the same security level. We show how to modify PRINCE to reach the required security level set by the NIST while minimizing the induced overhead, especially in a situation where PRINCE is already deployed.

We solve this problem by showing that a carefully built key-schedule is sufficient to provide the required security goal while keeping (almost) all of the remaining design untouched and propose PRINCEv2 family of block ciphers. As proven by our various experiments, PRINCEv2 only has a very small overhead compared to PRINCE, while still reaching the required higher security level. Moreover, the fact that the PRINCE and PRINCEv2 designs are very similar allows one to implement both PRINCE and PRINCEv2 in the same environment (e.g., for backward compatibility) with a very small overhead.

Finally, the similarities between PRINCE and PRINCEv2 allow us to reuse a majority of the security analysis done by the community over the last 8 years since PRINCE's publication. By doing so and carefully analyzing how the modifications made influenced the previously known attacks on PRINCE, as well as providing new cryptanalysis insights for both versions, we showed that PRINCEv2 meets its security requirements.

We thus believe that PRINCEv2 is a major improvement over PRINCE and we expect it to be widely adopted in the near future. Moreover, our work shows that one can improve the security level of some lightweight primitives with minimal downsides. An open question is thus to see if similar improvements could be made for other microcontroller-targeted ciphers such as Midori, MANTIS and QARMA, which could lead to interesting future work.

We made the reference implementation publicly available on GITHUB in:

https://github.com/rub-hgi/princev2

Acknowledgments. The work described in this paper has been partially supported by the Deutsche Forschungsgemeinschaft (DFG, German Research Foundation) under Germany's Excellence Strategy - EXC 2092 CASA - 390781972 and through the project 271752544 and partially by the German Federal Ministry of Education and Research (BMBF, project iBlockchain – 16KIS0901K).

A   Code

SAGEMATH code to generate the round constants:

```
1   a = RealField(prec=2000)(pi)-3
2   for i in range(1, 9):
3       b = (floor(a*2^(64*i)) + 2^64) % 2^64
4   print("0x%016x" % (b))
```

The output is:

```
0   0x243f6a8885a308d3
1   0x13198a2e03707344
2   0xa4093822299f31d0
3   0x082efa98ec4e6c89
4   0x452821e638d01377
5   0xbe5466cf34e90c6c
6   0xc0ac29b7c97c50dd
7   0x3f84d5b5b5470917
```

The 0th constant is not used in PRINCE, so we skip it, too. The second last constant (line 6) is α and thus we use the last one (line 7) as β.

B   Test Vectors

Plaintext	k_0	k_1	Ciphertext
0000000000000000	0000000000000000	0000000000000000	0125fc7359441690
ffffffffffffffff	0000000000000000	0000000000000000	832bd46f108e7857
0000000000000000	ffffffffffffffff	0000000000000000	ee873b2ec447944d
0000000000000000	0000000000000000	ffffffffffffffff	0ac6f9cd6e6f275d
0123456789abcdef	0123456789abcdef	fedcba9876543210	603cd95fa72a8704

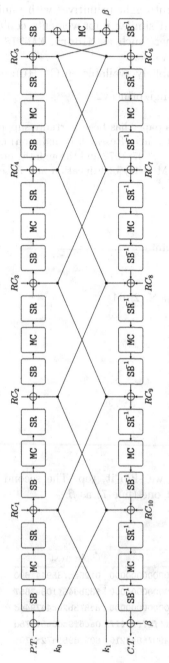

Fig. 9. PRINCEv2 structure for encryption.

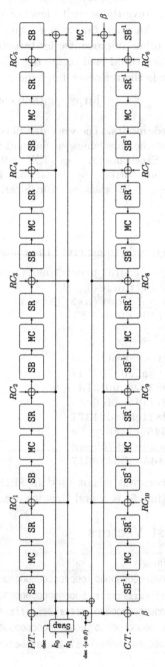

Fig. 10. PRINCEv2 structure for encryption and decryption.

References

[ALL12] Abed, F., List, E., Lucks, S.: On the security of the core of PRINCE against biclique and differential cryptanalysis. IACR Cryptology ePrint Archive 2012/712 (2012)

[Ava17] Avanzi, R.: The QARMA block cipher family. IACR Trans. Symmetric Cryptol. **2017**(1), 4–44 (2017)

[BBI+15] Banik, S., et al.: Midori: a block cipher for low energy. In: Iwata, T., Cheon, J.H. (eds.) ASIACRYPT 2015. LNCS, vol. 9453, pp. 411–436. Springer, Heidelberg (2015). https://doi.org/10.1007/978-3-662-48800-3_17

[BCG+12] Borghoff, J., et al.: PRINCE – a low-latency block cipher for pervasive computing applications. In: Wang, X., Sako, K. (eds.) ASIACRYPT 2012. LNCS, vol. 7658, pp. 208–225. Springer, Heidelberg (2012). https://doi.org/10.1007/978-3-642-34961-4_14

[BJK+16] Beierle, C., et al.: The SKINNY family of block ciphers and its low-latency variant MANTIS. In: Robshaw, M., Katz, J. (eds.) CRYPTO 2016. LNCS, vol. 9815, pp. 123–153. Springer, Heidelberg (2016). https://doi.org/10.1007/978-3-662-53008-5_5

[BK09] Biryukov, A., Khovratovich, D.: Related-key cryptanalysis of the full AES-192 and AES-256. In: Matsui, M. (ed.) ASIACRYPT 2009. LNCS, vol. 5912, pp. 1–18. Springer, Heidelberg (2009). https://doi.org/10.1007/978-3-642-10366-7_1

[BNPS14] Boura, C., Naya-Plasencia, M., Suder, V.: Scrutinizing and improving impossible differential attacks: applications to CLEFIA, Camellia, LBlock and SIMON. In: Sarkar, P., Iwata, T. (eds.) ASIACRYPT 2014. LNCS, vol. 8873, pp. 179–199. Springer, Heidelberg (2014). https://doi.org/10.1007/978-3-662-45611-8_10

[CFG+14a] Canteaut, A., Fuhr, T., Gilbert, H., Naya-Plasencia, M., Reinhard, J.-R.: Multiple differential cryptanalysis of round-reduced PRINCE. In: Cid, C., Rechberger, C. (eds.) FSE 2014. LNCS, vol. 8540, pp. 591–610. Springer, Heidelberg (2015). https://doi.org/10.1007/978-3-662-46706-0_30

[CFG+14b] Canteaut, A., Fuhr, T., Gilbert, H., Naya-Plasencia, M., Reinhard, J.-R.: Multiple differential cryptanalysis of round-reduced PRINCE (full version). IACR Cryptology ePrint Archive 2014/89 (2014)

[CNPV13a] Canteaut, A., Naya-Plasencia, M., Vayssière, B.: Sieve-in-the-middle: improved MITM attacks. In: Canetti, R., Garay, J.A. (eds.) CRYPTO 2013. LNCS, vol. 8042, pp. 222–240. Springer, Heidelberg (2013). https://doi.org/10.1007/978-3-642-40041-4_13

[CNPV13b] Canteaut, A., Naya-Plasencia, M., Vayssière, B.: Sieve-in-the-middle: improved MITM attacks (full version). IACR Cryptology ePrint Archive 2013/324 (2013)

[Der19] Derbez, P.: AES automatic tool (2019). https://seafile.cifex-dedibox.ovh/f/72be1bc96bf740d3a854/

[Din15] Dinur, I.: Cryptanalytic time-memory-data tradeoffs for FX-constructions with applications to PRINCE and PRIDE. In: Oswald, E., Fischlin, M. (eds.) EUROCRYPT 2015. LNCS, vol. 9056, pp. 231–253. Springer, Heidelberg (2015). https://doi.org/10.1007/978-3-662-46800-5_10

[DKS10] Dunkelman, O., Keller, N., Shamir, A.: A practical-time related-key attack on the KASUMI cryptosystem used in GSM and 3G telephony. In: Rabin, T. (ed.) CRYPTO 2010. LNCS, vol. 6223, pp. 393–410. Springer, Heidelberg (2010). https://doi.org/10.1007/978-3-642-14623-7_21

[DKS14] Dunkelman, O., Keller, N., Shamir, A.: A practical-time related-key attack on the KASUMI cryptosystem used in GSM and 3G telephony. J. Cryptol. **27**(4), 824–849 (2014). https://doi.org/10.1007/s00145-013-9154-9

[DP15a] Derbez, P., Perrin, L.: Meet-in-the-middle attacks and structural analysis of round-reduced PRINCE. In: Leander, G. (ed.) FSE 2015. LNCS, vol. 9054, pp. 190–216. Springer, Heidelberg (2015). https://doi.org/10.1007/978-3-662-48116-5_10

[DP15b] Derbez, P., Perrin, L.: Meet-in-the-middle attacks and structural analysis of round-reduced PRINCE. IACR Cryptology ePrint Archive 2015/239 (2015)

[DZLY17] Ding, Y.-L., Zhao, J.-Y., Li, L.-B., Yu, H.-B.: Impossible differential analysis on round-reduced PRINCE. J. Inf. Sci. Eng. **33**(4), 1041–1053 (2017)

[FJM14] Fouque, P.-A., Joux, A., Mavromati, C.: Multi-user collisions: applications to discrete logarithm, Even-Mansour and PRINCE. In: Sarkar, P., Iwata, T. (eds.) ASIACRYPT 2014. LNCS, vol. 8873, pp. 420–438. Springer, Heidelberg (2014). https://doi.org/10.1007/978-3-662-45611-8_22

[GR16a] Grassi, L., Rechberger, C.: Practical low data-complexity subspace-trail cryptanalysis of round-reduced PRINCE. In: Dunkelman, O., Sanadhya, S.K. (eds.) INDOCRYPT 2016. LNCS, vol. 10095, pp. 322–342. Springer, Cham (2016). https://doi.org/10.1007/978-3-319-49890-4_18

[GR16b] Grassi, L., Rechberger, C.: Practical low data-complexity subspace-trail cryptanalysis of round-reduced PRINCE. IACR Cryptology ePrint Archive 2016/964 (2016)

[JNP+13] Jean, J., Nikolić, I., Peyrin, T., Wang, L., Wu, S.: Security analysis of PRINCE. In: Moriai, S. (ed.) FSE 2013. LNCS, vol. 8424, pp. 92–111. Springer, Heidelberg (2014). https://doi.org/10.1007/978-3-662-43933-3_6

[KNR12] Knežević, M., Nikov, V., Rombouts, P.: Low-latency encryption – is "lightweight = light + wait"? In: Prouff, E., Schaumont, P. (eds.) CHES 2012. LNCS, vol. 7428, pp. 426–446. Springer, Heidelberg (2012). https://doi.org/10.1007/978-3-642-33027-8_25

[LJW13] Li, L., Jia, K., Wang, X.: Improved meet-in-the-middle attacks on AES-192 and PRINCE. IACR Cryptology ePrint Archive 2013/573 (2013)

[Mor17] Morawiecki, P.: Practical attacks on the round-reduced PRINCE. IET Inf. Secur. **11**(3), 146–151 (2017)

[NIS] NIST: Lightweight cryptography. https://csrc.nist.gov/projects/lightweight-cryptography

[NIS18] NIST: Submission requirements and evaluation criteria for the lightweight cryptography standardization process (2018). https://csrc.nist.gov/CSRC/media/Projects/Lightweight-Cryptography/documents/final-lwc-submission-requirements-august2018.pdf

[NXP20] NXP: AN12278 LPC55S00 Security Solutions for IoT (2020). https://www.nxp.com/docs/en/application-note/AN12278.pdf

[PDN15] Posteuca, R., Duta, C.-L., Negara, G.: New approaches for round-reduced PRINCE cipher cryptanalysis. Proc. Rom. Acad. Ser. A **16**, 253–264 (2015)

[PN15] Posteuca, R., Negara, G.: Integral cryptanalysis of round-reduced PRINCE cipher. Proc. Rom. Acad. Ser. A **16**, 265–270 (2015)

[RR16a] Rasoolzadeh, S., Raddum, H.: Cryptanalysis of 6-round PRINCE using 2 known plaintexts. IACR Cryptology ePrint Archive 2016/132 (2016)

[RR16b] Rasoolzadeh, S., Raddum, H.: Cryptanalysis of PRINCE with minimal data. In: Pointcheval, D., Nitaj, A., Rachidi, T. (eds.) AFRICACRYPT 2016. LNCS, vol. 9646, pp. 109–126. Springer, Cham (2016). https://doi.org/10.1007/978-3-319-31517-1_6

[RR16c] Rasoolzadeh, S., Raddum, H.: Faster key recovery attack on round-reduced PRINCE. In: Bogdanov, A. (ed.) LightSec 2016. LNCS, vol. 10098, pp. 3–17. Springer, Cham (2017). https://doi.org/10.1007/978-3-319-55714-4_1

[ST17] Sasaki, Y., Todo, Y.: New impossible differential search tool from design and cryptanalysis aspects. In: Coron, J.-S., Nielsen, J.B. (eds.) EURO-CRYPT 2017. LNCS, vol. 10212, pp. 185–215. Springer, Cham (2017). https://doi.org/10.1007/978-3-319-56617-7_7

[TM16] Todo, Y., Morii, M.: Bit-based division property and application to SIMON family. In: Peyrin, T. (ed.) FSE 2016. LNCS, vol. 9783, pp. 357–377. Springer, Heidelberg (2016). https://doi.org/10.1007/978-3-662-52993-5_18

[Tod15] Todo, Y.: Structural evaluation by generalized integral property. In: Oswald, E., Fischlin, M. (eds.) EUROCRYPT 2015. LNCS, vol. 9056, pp. 287–314. Springer, Heidelberg (2015). https://doi.org/10.1007/978-3-662-46800-5_12

[XZBL16] Xiang, Z., Zhang, W., Bao, Z., Lin, D.: Applying MILP method to searching integral distinguishers based on division property for 6 lightweight block ciphers. In: Cheon, J.H., Takagi, T. (eds.) ASIACRYPT 2016. LNCS, vol. 10031, pp. 648–678. Springer, Heidelberg (2016). https://doi.org/10.1007/978-3-662-53887-6_24

[YPO15] Yuan, Z., Peng, Z., Haiwen, O.: Two kinds of biclique attacks on lightweight block cipher PRINCE. IACR Cryptology ePrint Archive 2015/1208 (2015)

[ZR19] Zhang, W., Rijmen, V.: Division cryptanalysis of block ciphers with a binary diffusion layer. IET Inf. Secur. **13**(2), 87–95 (2019)

Nonce-Misuse Security of the SAEF Authenticated Encryption Mode

Elena Andreeva[1]([✉]), Amit Singh Bhati[2]([✉]), and Damian Vizár[3]([✉])

[1] TU Wien, Vienna, Austria
elena.andreeva@tuwien.ac.at
[2] imec-COSIC, KU Leuven, Leuven, Belgium
amitsingh.bhati@esat.kuleuven.be
[3] CSEM, Neuchâtel, Switzerland
damian.vizar@csem.ch

Abstract. ForkAE is a NIST lightweight cryptography candidate that uses the forkcipher primitive in two modes of operation – SAEF and PAEF – optimized for authenticated encryption of the shortest messages. SAEF is a sequential and *online* AEAD that minimizes the memory footprint compared to its alternative parallel mode PAEF, catering to the most constrained devices. SAEF was proven AE secure against nonce-respecting adversaries.

Due to their more acute and direct exposure to device misuse and mishandling, in most use cases of lightweight cryptography, nonce reuse presents a very realistic attack vector. Furthermore, many lightweight applications mandate security for their online AEAD schemes against block-wise adversaries. Surprisingly, a very few NIST lightweight AEAD candidates come with provable guarantees against these security threats.

In this work we investigate the provable security guarantees of SAEF when nonces are repeated under a refined version of the notion of online authenticated encryption OAE given by Fleischmann et al. in 2012. Using the coefficient H technique we show that, with no modifications, SAEF is OAE secure up to the birthday security bound, i.e., up to $2^{n/2}$ processed blocks of data, where n is the block size of the forkcipher. The implications of our work is that SAEF is safe to use in a block-wise fashion, and that if nonces get repeated, this has no impact on ciphertext integrity and confidentiality only degrades by a limited extent up to repetitions of common message prefixes.

Keywords: Authenticated encryption · Forkcipher · Lightweight cryptography · Short messages · Online · Provable security · Nonce misuse

1 Introduction

An authenticated encryption (AE) algorithm aims to achieve message confidentiality and integrity (authentication). The majority of AE schemes nowadays

© Springer Nature Switzerland AG 2021
O. Dunkelman et al. (Eds.): SAC 2020, LNCS 12804, pp. 512–534, 2021.
https://doi.org/10.1007/978-3-030-81652-0_20

process two additional inputs: associated data AD and a nonce. The associated data is a piece of information, such as a network packet header, that does not require the provision of confidentiality but it does require authentication. The nonce input to an AE (AD) scheme is also practically motivated. A nonce is a unique value that enables the simplification of randomized or stateful AE algorithm to a deterministic one. This removes the need for random values generation or storing a state across distinct encryptions. The formalisation of nonce-based authenticated encryption was introduced in 2002 by Rogaway [24].

Two of the most prominent AEAD schemes research, development and standardization efforts in recent years have been the CAESAR competition (2014–2018) [7] and the ongoing NIST lightweight cryptography standardization process (2018–). The CAESAR competition produced a portfolio of algorithms for recommended use in three categories: 1. Lightweight (resource constrained environments): Ascon [9] and ACORN [28]; 2. High-performance: AEGIS-128 [30] and OCB [19]; 3. Defense in depth (stronger security guarantees): COLM [1], Deoxys II [18], and MORUS [29]. The CAESAR winners come with various advantages over the present standards GCM (NIST SP 800-38D) and CCM (IEEE 802.11i, IPsec ESP and IKEv2) and are expected to be adopted by new applications and standards.

The main focus of the defense in depth CAESAR category is nonce misuse resistance (NMR), a security target motivated by attacks which exploit implementation flaws leading to a repeated use of the same nonce by an application. More precisely, authenticity preservation despite nonce misuse is stated as *critical* and a limited privacy damage from nonce misuse as desirable. Nonce-misuse resistant AE (MRAE) was introduced by Rogaway and Shrimpton [26]. Later works dealt with online nonce misuse-resistant AE (OAE) [11] and online AE(OAE2) [15]. Nonce misuse purportedly presents a greater risk for small devices, such as IoT, where nonces could repeat due to various memory or space constraints, or remote usage. Maintaining the correct use of nonces is also especially challenging in distributed systems where nodes and connections can fail at any time. Recent attacks have illustrated the severity of nonce misuse in practice. In 2016 Böck et al. [8] investigated the nonce misuse security of the AES-GCM [10] AE mode and managed to completely break the authenticity of those connections where servers repeated the nonce. Their Internet-wide survey identified 184 such HTTPS servers. They showed how this vulnerability can be utilized to inject seemingly valid content into encrypted sessions. The next year Vanhoef and Piesens [27] introduced the key reinstallation attack which forces nonce repetitions and breaks the WPA2 wireless protocol.

The MRAE [25] and the RAE [14] security notions capture the "best possible" security of nonce based AEAD (the latter for an extended syntax) in face of nonce repetitions but unfortunately can not be satisfied by any online AEAD scheme. These are AE schemes which parse the plaintext as a sequence of smaller, usually fixed-size blocks during encryption, and produce the ciphertext as a sequence of such blocks, such that i^{th} ciphertext block can be immediately computed after having seen the first i plaintext blocks. Importantly, online encryption is better fitted for lightweight applications, where it is often critical to compute the ciphertext blocks on the fly with constant latency (e.g. streaming), or where a constant memory implementation is required. Such constraints can be found most recently in the consumer grade IoT applications, which come with stringent cost constraints and often get inadequate security as a consequence [20,21], and which would greatly benefit from a lightweight AEAD scheme with robust security.

In 2012 Fleischmann et al. [11] proposed a weaker NMR security notion called OAE for online schemes that retains the same level of integrity and a well-defined, albeit lower level of confidentiality in face of nonce misuse. Hoang et al. [15] pointed out inconsistencies in this definition, reformulated it, demonstrated that in certain situations the confidentiality afforded by OAE secure schemes is not sufficient, and critiqued several aspects of the OAE definition. Addressing the latter, Hoang et al. proposed an alternative to OAE dubbed OAE2 which is a stronger security with more versatile syntax. However, the change in syntax also means that the notion is inapplicable to designs adhering to the most common nonce-based AEAD syntax, and as shown by Hoang et al., the possible exploits of the decay in confidentiality are unavoidable in any kind of online schemes, OAE2-secure ones included. Despite this controversy, OAE can afford pragmatic protection against nonce-reuse with a sufficiently large block size and an appropriate use by the higher-level protocol/security primitive/etc.

In 2016 Endignoux and Vizár [13] showed that the notion of OAE is also meaningful in the context of block-wise adaptive attacks. The authors proved that OAE is equivalent with an adapted version of the blockwise-adaptive AE notions from [12]. The equivalence result shows that OAE-secure schemes are safe to use in settings where block-wise adaptive attackers exist. The main observation in [12] was that if an application, such as a smart card, outputs a ciphertext block each time it is fed a plaintext block, then a potential attacker gets more power by allowing him to adaptively construct the queries block-by-block. Such attacks pose a genuine risk in the lightweight setting where small devices are for example not equipped with sufficient memory and work block-wise. The OAE notion has been adopted by several AEAD designs, amongst which the COLM CAESAR winner in the defense in depth category (satisfying the authenticity and limited privacy damage against nonce misuse).

Surprisingly, among the 32 s round candidates, only a handful come with a provable form of nonce misuse security. The SP1 mode in the Spook [6] submission achieves the nonce misuse resilience notion proposed by Ashur et al. [3]. Tiny JAMBU [16] provides authentication security when nonce is misused by adjusting the associated data to also play the role of nonce. When the nonce is repeated but AD is different, the security of the cipher would not be affected by the repeated nonce, yet when both nonce and AD repeat, the scheme does not offer strong security guarantees in the sense of OAE. Romulus-M [17] is an MRAE [25] mode which is secure against misuse (repetition) of nonces in encryption queries but prevents the scheme from being implemented in an online fashion.

Our Contributions. In this work we investigate the OAE security of the ForkAE [2] second round NIST candidate which is optimized to be efficient for short messages. We focus on ForkAE and more precisely on its SAEF mode for three reasons. First, SAEF comes with existing provable security guarantees in the nonce-respecting setting, hence its (in)security in presence of nonce misuse is an interesting open question. Secondly, SAEF is an online scheme and the OAE security as refined by Hoang et al. [15] is a natural target for the analysis of its nonce-reuse security. Finally, an analysis of SAEF sheds more light on the potential of its relatively novel and less researched underlying forkcipher primitive [2] Our results show that the SAEF mode of the ForkAE NIST second round submission is provably OAE secure without the need of applying any design modifications.

The corrected variant of the OAE definition by Hoang et al. [15] (labeled as OAE1 in the publication) was defined to handle plaintext whose length is a multiple of the underlying blocksize n. Hence we extended the formalism to deal with messages that are not n-bits aligned and target the resulting notion in our analysis. Additionally, we opt to use two separate requirements for confidentiality and authenticity of OAE schemes because this allows us to take slightly different approach for analysis for each property in favor of brevity and simplicity of the proofs. We use Coefficient H technique [22] as the main vehicle for the analysis and prove that SAEF is OAE-secure up to $2^{n/2}$ blocks of processed data in total, where n is the block size of the underling forkcipher.

2 Preliminaries

Strings. All strings are binary strings. The set of all strings of length n (for a positive integer n) is denoted $\{0,1\}^n$ and the set of all strings of all possible lengths is denoted $\{0,1\}^*$. We let $\{0,1\}^{\leq n} = \bigcup_{i=0}^{n}\{0,1\}^n$. We denote by $\mathrm{Perm}(n)$ the set of all permutations of $\{0,1\}^n$. We denote by $\mathrm{Func}(m,n)$ the set of all functions with domain $\{0,1\}^m$ and range $\{0,1\}^n$, and we let $\mathrm{Inj}(m,n) \subset \mathrm{Func}(m,n)$ denote the set of all injective functions with the same signature.

For a string X of ℓ bits, we let $X[i]$ denote the ith bit of X for $i = 0, \ldots, \ell-1$ (starting from the left) and $X[i \ldots j] = X[i]\|X[i+1]\| \ldots \|X[j]$ for $0 \leq i < j < \ell$. We let $\mathsf{left}_\ell(X) = X[0 \ldots (\ell-1)]$ denote the ℓ leftmost bits of X and $\mathsf{right}_r(X) = X[((|X|-r) \ldots (|X|-1)]$ the r rightmost bits of X, such that $X = \mathsf{left}_\chi(X)\|\mathsf{right}_{|X|-\chi}(X)$ for any $0 \leq \chi \leq |X|$. Given a (possibly implicit) positive integer n and an $X \in \{0,1\}^*$, we let $X\|10^*$ denote $X\|10^{n-(|X| \bmod n)-1}$ for simplicity. Given an implicit block length n, we let $\mathsf{pad10}(X) = X\|10^*$ return X if $|X| \equiv 0 \pmod{n}$ and $X\|10^*$ otherwise.

String Partitioning. For the rest of the section, we fix an arbitrary integer n and call it the block size. Given a string X, we let $X_1, \ldots, X_x, X_* \xleftarrow{n} X$ denote partitioning X into n-bit blocks, such that $|X_i| = n$ for $i = 1, \ldots, x$, $0 \leq |X_*| \leq n$ and $X = X_1\| \ldots \|X_x\|X_*$, so $x = \max(0, \lceil X/n \rceil - 1)$. We let $|X|_n = \lceil X/n \rceil$. We let $(M', M_*) = \mathsf{msplit}_n(M)$ (as in message split) denote a splitting of a string $M \in \{0,1\}^*$ into two parts $M'\|M_* = M$, such that $|M_*| \equiv |M| \pmod{n}$ and $0 \le |M_*| \le n$, where $|M_*| = 0$ if and only if $|M| = 0$. We let $(C', C_*, T) = \mathsf{csplit}_n(C)$ (as in ciphertext split) denote splitting a string C of at least n bits into three parts $C'\|C_*\|T = C$, such that $|C_*| = n$, $|T| \equiv |C|$ $\pmod{n}$, and $0 \le |T| \le n$, where $|T| = 0$ if and only if $|C| = n$. Finally, we let $C'_1, \ldots, C'_m, C_*, T \leftarrow \mathsf{csplit\text{-}b}_n(C)$ (as in csplit to blocks) denote the result of $\mathsf{csplit}_n(C)$ followed by partitioning of C' into $|C'|_n$ blocks of n bits, such that $C' = C'_1\| \ldots \|C'_m$.

Blocks. We let $\mathsf{B}_n = \{0,1\}^n$ denote the set of all n-bit strings (or else n-bit blocks), and define $\mathsf{B}_n^* = \{\varepsilon\} \cup \bigcup_{i=1}^{\infty} \mathsf{B}_n^i$ with ε denoting the empty string of length 0. We call a string $X \in \mathsf{B}_n^*$ "n-aligned". For an n-aligned string X, X_i denotes its ith n-bit block. For two distinct n-aligned strings $X, Y \in \mathsf{B}_n^*$ such that $|X|_n \le |Y|_n$ w.l.o.g, we let $\mathsf{llcp}_n(X, Y) = \max\{1 \le i \le |X|_n | X_j = Y_j$ for $1 \le j \le i\}$ denote the length of the longest common prefix of X and Y in n-bit blocks.

Miscellaneous. The symbol $\perp$ denotes an error signal, or an undefined value. We denote by $X \leftarrow^\$ \mathcal{X}$ sampling an element X from a finite set $\mathcal{X}$ following the uniform distribution. We let $(n)_q$ denote the falling factorial $n \cdot (n-1) \cdot (n-2) \cdot \ldots \cdot (n-q+1)$ with $(n)_0 = 1$. For a predicate $\mathsf{P}(x)$, we equate $\mathsf{P}(x) = \text{true}$ with $\mathsf{P}(x) = 1$ and $\mathsf{P}(x) = \text{false}$ with $\mathsf{P}(x) = 0$. We use lexicographic comparison of tuples of integers; i.e. $(i', j') < (i, j)$ iff $i' < i$ or $i' = i$ and $j' < j$.

2.1   Coefficient H Technique

The coefficient H technique is a simple but powerful proof technique provided by Patarin in [22]. The coefficient H technique is used to prove indistinguishability of a construction from an idealized object in face of an information-theoretic adversary using the concept of "transcripts". A transcript here is defined as complete record of the interaction of an adversary $\mathcal{A}$ with its oracles in the indistinguishability experiment. To exemplify, if (M_i, C_i) denotes the input and output of the i-th query of $\mathcal{A}$ to its oracle over q queries then the corresponding transcript (denote it τ) is $\tau = \langle (M_1, C_1), \ldots, (M_q, C_q) \rangle$. The task given to $\mathcal{A}$ is to distinguish the real world $\mathcal{O}_{\mathsf{real}}$ from the ideal world $\mathcal{O}_{\mathsf{ideal}}$. Let us denote the distribution of transcripts in the real and the ideal world by Θ_{real} and Θ_{ideal}, respectively. We say a transcript τ is *attainable* if the probability of achieving τ in the ideal world is non-zero. We also assume w.l.o.g. that $\mathcal{A}$ does not make duplicate or prohibited queries. The fundamental Lemma of coefficient H technique can now be stated.

Lemma 1 (Fundamental Lemma of the Coefficient H Technique [22]). *Consider that the set of attainable transcripts is partitioned into two disjoint sets $\mathcal{T}_{good}$ and $\mathcal{T}_{bad}$. Also, assume there exist $\epsilon_1, \epsilon_2 \ge 0$ such that for any transcript $\tau \in \mathcal{T}_{good}$, we have $\frac{\Pr[\Theta_{real} = \tau]}{\Pr[\Theta_{ideal} = \tau]} \ge 1 - \epsilon_1$, and $\Pr[\Theta_{ideal} \in \mathcal{T}_{bad}] \le \epsilon_2$. Then, for all adversaries $\mathcal{A}$, it holds that $|\Pr[\mathcal{A}^{\mathcal{O}_{real}}] - \Pr[\mathcal{A}^{\mathcal{O}_{ideal}}]| \le \epsilon_1 + \epsilon_2$.*

2.2 Syntax of AEAD

Our targeted mode SAEF follows the AEAD syntax by Rogaway [24]. A nonce-based AEAD scheme is a triplet $\Pi = (\mathcal{K}, \mathcal{E}, \mathcal{D})$. The key space $\mathcal{K}$ is a finite set. The deterministic encryption algorithm $\mathcal{E} : \mathcal{K} \times \mathcal{N} \times \mathcal{A} \times \mathcal{M} \to \mathcal{C}$ maps a secret key K, a nonce N, an associated data A and a message M to a ciphertext $C = \mathcal{E}(K, N, A, M)$. The nonce, AD and message domains are all subsets of $\{0, 1\}^*$. The deterministic decryption algorithm $\mathcal{D} : \mathcal{K} \times \mathcal{N} \times \mathcal{A} \times \mathcal{C} \to \mathcal{M} \cup \{\bot\}$ takes a tuple (K, N, A, C) and either returns a message $M \in \mathcal{M}$, or a distinguished symbol $\bot$ to indicate an authentication error.

We require that for every $M \in \mathcal{M}$, we have $\{0, 1\}^{|M|} \subseteq \mathcal{M}$ (i.e. for any integer m, either all or no strings of length m belong to $\mathcal{M}$) and that for all $K, N, A, M \in \mathcal{K} \times \mathcal{N} \times \mathcal{A} \times \mathcal{M}$ we have $|\mathcal{E}(K, N, A, M)| = |M| + \theta$ for some non-negative integer θ called the stretch of Π. For correctness of Π, we require that for all $K, N, A, M \in \mathcal{K} \times \mathcal{N} \times \mathcal{A} \times \mathcal{M}$ we have $M = \mathcal{D}(K, N, A, \mathcal{E}(K, N, A, M))$. We let $\mathcal{E}_K(N, A, M) = \mathcal{E}(K, N, A, M)$ and $\mathcal{D}_K(N, A, C) = \mathcal{D}(K, N, A, C)$.

2.3 OAE Security

Our targeted notion of security is the definition of online AE (OAE) by Fleischmann et al. [11]. We use the variant of the notion described by Hoang et al. [15], extended as necessary to deal with messages that are not n-aligned. We opt for the two-requirement flavor of the notion, separating confidentiality and authenticity.

OAE Confidentiality. An online permutation [5] is a function $\pi : \mathsf{B}_n^* \to \mathsf{B}_n^*$ such that (i) π is a length preserving permutation; i.e., for any integer $m \geq 0$, the function π restricted to mn-bit inputs $\pi(K, T, \cdot) : \mathsf{B}_n^m \to \mathsf{B}_n^m$ is a permutation (with a slight notation abuse); (ii) π preserves the length of blockwise prefix; i.e., for each $M, M' \in \mathsf{B}_n^*$, we have that $\mathsf{llcp}_n(M, M') = \mathsf{llcp}_n(\pi(M), \pi(M'))$.

We denote the set of all such permutations $\mathrm{OPerm}(n)$. We can define the distribution of a "random" online permutation[1] that is useful for experiments with a finite number of queries. We observe that each $\pi \in \mathrm{OPerm}(n)$ can be equivalently defined as a collection $(\pi_M)_{M \in \mathsf{B}_n^*}$, such that for any $M_1 \| M_2 \| \ldots \| M_r \in \mathsf{B}_n^r$ we define $\pi(M_1 \| M_2 \| \ldots \| M_r)$ as $\pi_\varepsilon(M_1) \| \pi_{M_1}(M_2) \| \ldots \| \pi_{M_1 \| \ldots \| M_{r-1}}(M_r)$, and that there is in fact a bijection between $\mathrm{OPerm}(n)$ and the set of all such permutation collections [5]. The expression $\pi \twoheadleftarrow\$ \mathrm{OPerm}(n)$ should thus be understood as lazy sampling of those permutations in the collection $(\pi_M)_{M \in \mathsf{B}_n^*}$ that are necessary to process adversarial queries.

We define OAE confidentiality of an AEAD scheme Π with two games, **oprpf-real**$_\Pi$ and **oprpf-ideal**$_\Pi$. In both games $\mathcal{A}$ can make arbitrary chosen plaintext queries to a black box encryption oracle, in particular $\mathcal{A}$ is allowed to repeat the nonces. In the game **oprpf-real**$_\Pi$, the encryption oracle faithfully implements the encryption algorithm of Π using a randomly sampled

---

[1] $\mathrm{OPerm}(n)$ is a countably infinite set, so the notion of a uniform online permutation is not defined.

secret key. In the game **oprpf-ideal**$_{\Pi}$, upon an encryption query N, A, M the oracle returns $\pi_{N,A}(M_L) \| f_{N,A,M}$ where $M_L \leftarrow \mathsf{left}_{\lfloor M/n \rfloor}(M)$ is the longest n-aligned prefix of M, $\pi_{N,A} \leftarrow_\$ \mathsf{OPerm}(n)$ is a random online permutation for each $N, A \in \mathcal{N} \times \mathcal{A}$, and $f_{N,A,M} \leftarrow_\$ \{0,1\}^{n+(|M| \bmod n)}$ is a random string for each $N, A, M \in \mathcal{N} \times \mathcal{A} \times \mathcal{M}$ (with a length corresponding to the n-bit authentication tag and no more than $n-1$ bit suffix of M remaining after the maximal n-aligned prefix M_L). The **oprpf** advantage of an adversary $\mathcal{A}$ against $\Pi = \mathrm{SAEF}[\mathsf{F}, \nu]$ can now be defined as $\mathbf{Adv}_{\Pi}^{\mathrm{oprpf}}(\mathcal{A}) = \Pr[\mathcal{A}^{\mathrm{oprpf\text{-}real}_{\Pi}}] - \Pr[\mathcal{A}^{\mathrm{oprpf\text{-}ideal}_{\Pi}}]$.

OAE Authenticity. The OAE authenticity notion coincides with the definition of ciphertext integrity where the adversary is allowed to repeat nonces, as first defined by Rogaway and Shrimpton [25]. A nonce-misusing chosen ciphertext attack of an adversary $\mathcal{A}$ against the integrity of a nonce-based AE scheme Π is modeled through the security game **auth**. The adversary is given access to a pair of blackbox oracles. It can make arbitrary chosen plaintext queries to the encryption oracle, including queries with repeated nonces. $\mathcal{A}$ can further make arbitrary chosen ciphertext queries to the decryption oracle with the goal of finding a forgery: a tuple that decrypts correctly but is not trivially known to be correct from the encryption queries. We define the advantage of $\mathcal{A}$ in breaking the authenticity of Π as $\mathbf{Adv}_{\Pi}^{\mathrm{auth}}(\mathcal{A}) = \Pr[\mathcal{A}^{\mathrm{auth}_{\Pi}} \text{ forges}]$ where "$\mathcal{A}$ forges" denotes a decryption query that returns a value $\neq \perp$. We assume w.l.o.g. that $\mathcal{A}$ does not make duplicate queries.

2.4   Forkcipher

We follow the formalism by Andreeva et al. [23]. Informally, a forkcipher F is a tweakable symmetric-key primitive which maps a secret key K, a tweak T and an input block M of n bits to *two* ciphertext blocks C_0 and C_1, such that C_0 and C_1 are each an (independent) permutation of M.

Syntax. Formally, a forkcipher is a pair of deterministic algorithms, the encryption algorithm: $\mathsf{F} : \{0,1\}^k \times \mathcal{T} \times \{0,1\}^n \times \{0,1,\mathsf{b}\} \rightarrow \{0,1\}^n \cup \{0,1\}^n \times \{0,1\}^n$ and the inversion algorithm: $\mathsf{F}^{-1}\{0,1\}^k \times \mathcal{T} \times \{0,1\}^n \times \{0,1\} \times \{\mathsf{i},\mathsf{o},\mathsf{b}\} \rightarrow \{0,1\}^n \cup \{0,1\}^n \times \{0,1\}^n$. The encryption algorithm takes a key K, a tweak $\mathsf{T} \in \mathcal{T}$, a plaintext block M and an output selector s, and outputs the (left) n-bit ciphertext block C_0 if $s = 0$, the (right) n-bit ciphertext block C_1 if $s = 1$, and both the blocks C_0, C_1 if $s = \mathsf{b}$. We write $\mathsf{F}(K, \mathsf{T}, M, s) = \mathsf{F}_K(\mathsf{T}, M, s) = \mathsf{F}_K^{\mathsf{T}}(M, s) = \mathsf{F}_K^{\mathsf{T},s}(M)$ interchangeably. The inversion algorithm takes a key K, a tweak T, a ciphertext block C (left/right half of output block), an indicator b of whether this should be treated as the left or the right ciphertext block and an output selector s, and outputs the plaintext block M if $s = \mathsf{i}$, the other ciphertext block C' if $s = \mathsf{o}$, and both blocks M, C' if $s = \mathsf{b}$. We write $\mathsf{F}^{-1}(K, \mathsf{T}, M, b, s) = \mathsf{F}^{-1}_K(\mathsf{T}, M, b, s) = \mathsf{F}^{-1}{}_K^{\mathsf{T}}(M, b, s) = \mathsf{F}^{-1}{}_K^{\mathsf{T},b,s}(M)$ interchangeably. We call k, n and $\mathcal{T}$ the keysize, blocksize and tweak space of F, respectively.

A tweakable forkcipher F is correct if for each pair of key and tweak, the forkcipher applies two independent permutations to the input to produce the two output blocks. Formally, for each $K \in \{0,1\}^k, \mathsf{T} \in \mathcal{T}, M \in \{0,1\}^n$ and $\beta \in \{0,1\}$ the following conditions must be met: (i) $\mathsf{F}^{-1}(K, \mathsf{T}, \mathsf{F}(K, \mathsf{T}, M, \beta), \beta, \mathsf{i}) = M$, and (ii) $\mathsf{F}^{-1}(K, \mathsf{T}, \mathsf{F}(K, \mathsf{T}, M, \beta), \beta, \mathsf{o}) = \mathsf{F}(K, \mathsf{T}, M, \beta \oplus 1)$, and (iii) $(\mathsf{F}(K, \mathsf{T}, M, 0), \mathsf{F}(K, \mathsf{T}, M, 1)) = \mathsf{F}(K, \mathsf{T}, M, \mathsf{b})$, and (iv) $(\mathsf{F}^{-1}(K, \mathsf{T}, C, \beta, \mathsf{i}), \mathsf{F}^{-1}(K, \mathsf{T}, C, \beta, \mathsf{o})) = \mathsf{F}^{-1}(K, \mathsf{T}, C, \beta, \mathsf{b})$. In the rest of the paper, we assume that $\mathcal{T} = \{0,1\}^t$ for some positive t.

Security. The security of a correct forkcipher F is defined through indistinguishability of the games **prtfp-real$_\mathsf{F}$** (implementing F algorithms faithfully) and **prtfp-ideal$_\mathsf{F}$** which replaces F by two tweakable random permutations $\pi_{\mathsf{T},0}, \pi_{\mathsf{T},1} \leftarrow\!\!{}^\$ \mathrm{Perm}(n)$ for $\mathsf{T} \in \mathcal{T}$ in a natural way, in a chosen ciphertext attack. We define the advantage of $\mathcal{A}$ as $\mathbf{Adv}_\mathsf{F}^{\mathrm{prtfp}}(\mathcal{A}) = \Pr[\mathcal{A}^{\mathbf{prtfp\text{-}real}_\mathsf{F}} \Rightarrow 1] - \Pr[\mathcal{A}^{\mathbf{prtfp\text{-}ideal}_\mathsf{F}} \Rightarrow 1]$ with the games defined in.

3 SAEF and Its OAE Security

SAEF (short for Sequential AE from a Forkcipher) is a nonce-based AEAD scheme. It takes as a parameter a tweakable forkcipher F (as defined in Sect. 2.4) with $\mathcal{T} = \{0,1\}^t$ for a positive $t \le n$. SAEF[F] $= (\mathcal{K}, \mathcal{E}, \mathcal{D})$ has a key space $\mathcal{K} = \{0,1\}^k$, nonce space $\mathcal{N} = \{0,1\}^{t-4}$, and the AD and message spaces are both $\{0,1\}^*$. The ciphertext expansion of SAEF[F] is n bits. The encryption and decryption algorithms are given in Fig. 2 and the encryption algorithm is depicted in Fig. 1.

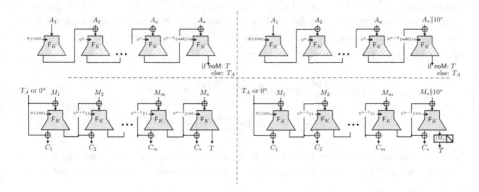

Fig. 1. The encryption algorithm of SAEF[F] mode. The bit $\mathsf{noM} = 1$ iff $|M| = 0$. The picture illustrates the processing of AD when length of AD is a multiple of n (**top left**) and when the length of AD is not a multiple of n (**top right**), and the processing of the message when length of the message is a multiple of n (**bottom left**) and when the length of message is not a multiple of n (**bottom right**). The white hatching denotes that an output block is not computed.

An encryption query is processed in blocks of n bits, first AD and then the message, using a single call to the forkcipher per block. The calls are tweaked by composing: (1) the nonce followed by a 1-bit *in the initial* F *call of the query*, and the string 0^{t-3} otherwise, (2) three-bit flag f. The flag f is used to ensure proper domain separation for different "types" of blocks in the encryption algorithm. The values $f \in \{000, 010, 011, 110, 111, 001, 100, 101\}$ are used, respectively, when processing non-final AD block, the last n-bit long AD block, the last AD block of $< n$ bits, the last AD block of n bits to produce tag, the last AD block of $< n$ bits to produce tag, non-final message block, the last n-bit message block and the last message block of $< n$ bits.

One output block of every F call is used as a chaining value, masking either the input (in AD processing) or both the input and the output (in message processing) of the following F call. The very first F call in each query is unmasked (but has the nonce in the tweak). The tag is the, possibly truncated, last "right" output of F produced in the query (in case of truncation message padding is used for partial integrity check). In a decryption query, the processing is similar to the encryption, with the plaintext blocks and the chaining values in the message processing part being computed with the inverse F algorithm.

3.1 Security of SAEF

Andreeva et al. proved that if nonce-uniqueness is guaranteed, SAEF achieves the standard AEAD confidentiality and integrity up to the birthday bound. There have been no investigations into the security of SAEF under nonce misuse (i.e., if nonces accidentally repeat). We state the formal claim about confidentiality and integrity of SAEF under nonce-misuse in Theorem 1.

Theorem 1. *Let* F *be a tweakable forkcipher with* $\mathcal{T} = \{0,1\}^t$. *Then for any nonce-misuse adversary* $\mathcal{A}$ *who makes at most* $q_e \leq 2^{n-1}$ *encryption queries, at most* q_v *decryption queries such that the total number of forkcipher calls induced by all the queries is at most* σ, *we have*

$$\mathbf{Adv}_{\mathsf{SAEF[F]}}^{\mathrm{oprpf}}(\mathcal{A}) \leq \mathbf{Adv}_{\mathsf{F}}^{\mathrm{prtfp}}(\mathcal{B}) + \frac{3 \cdot \sigma^2}{2^{n+1}}$$

$$\mathbf{Adv}_{\mathsf{SAEF[F]}}^{\mathrm{auth}}(\mathcal{A}) \leq \mathbf{Adv}_{\mathsf{F}}^{\mathrm{prtfp}}(\mathcal{C}) + \frac{\sigma^2 + 4 \cdot q_v}{2^n}$$

for some adversaries $\mathcal{B}$ *and* $\mathcal{C}$, *each making at most* 2σ *queries, and running in time given by the running time of* $\mathcal{A}$ *plus* $\gamma \cdot \sigma$ *for some "small" constant* γ.

The proof of Theorem 1 follows in Sects. 3.2 and 3.3.

Main Ingredients. The crux of the proof lies in adapting the analysis approach to the properties of SAEF arising from its sequential structure. These properties are best illustrated by an example. In two queries using the same nonce N, the same associated data $A_1 \| A_2$ of two blocks and two messages $M_1^1 \| M_2^1 \| M_3^1$ and $M_1^2 \| M_2^2 \| M_3^2$ of three blocks each and *differing in the first message block*, following the encryption algorithm in Fig. 2, the values of the F tweak string and of Δ mask used to process each block of A would be identical between the two queries, as would be the tweak (equal to $0^{n-1}1$) and the Δ mask used to process the first message block M_1^1 and M_1^2 respectively. However, this equality of tweaks and Δ masks together with the non-equality $M_1^1 \neq M_1^2$ imply that the F input blocks $\Delta \oplus M_1^1$ and $\Delta \oplus M_1^2$ will necessarily differ, which will randomize the Δ masks used to process the next of each message.

Similarly, in another case with executing two same queries but with extending the AD used in the first query to $A_1 \| A_2 \| 110^{n-2}$ and for the second query to $A_1 \| A_2 \| 1$, the processing will again be identical for A_1 and A_2 and for the third block, the Δ masks and the F inputs $\Delta \oplus 110^{n-2} = \Delta \oplus \mathsf{pad10}(1)$ will be identical but the tweaks will differ. What emerges is that the internal variables of SAEF's encryption algorithm preserve a certain "common prefix length" between the queries, and get randomized just past it. This observation is at the center of our proofs. Giving a formal definition of a common prefix between AE queries is also concise but is not straightforward, and requires a different representation of queries, which is the second main ingredient of our proofs.

3.2 Integrity

We switch to an alternative definition of AEAD integrity through indistinguishability, which is equivalent with the notion introduced in Sect. 3. We define two games, $\mathbf{auth\text{-}real}_\Pi$ and $\mathbf{auth\text{-}ideal}_\Pi$. In both games $\mathcal{A}$ is given access to an encryption and a decryption oracle. In the game $\mathbf{auth\text{-}real}_\Pi$, both oracles faithfully implement the respective algorithms of SAEF using the same randomly sampled secret key, except that the decryption oracle returns $\top$ in case of a successful forgery, and $\perp$ otherwise. In the game $\mathbf{auth\text{-}ideal}_\Pi$, the encryption oracle is the same as in $\mathbf{auth\text{-}real}_\Pi$ but the decryption oracle always returns $\perp$. We claim that $\mathbf{Adv}_\Pi^{\mathbf{auth}}(\mathcal{A}) = \Pr[\mathcal{A}^{\mathbf{auth\text{-}real}_\Pi}] - \Pr[\mathcal{A}^{\mathbf{auth\text{-}ideal}_\Pi}]$.

It is easy to see that the equality holds, by establishing inequalities in both directions. An adversary $\mathcal{A}$ playing the game $\mathbf{auth}_\Pi$ can be used to construct a distinguishing adversary $\mathcal{B}$ which forwards $\mathcal{A}$'s queries and outputs 1 iff $\mathcal{A}$ forges, achieving the same advantage as $\mathcal{A}$. In the other direction, we can construct an adversary $\mathcal{A}$ for game $\mathbf{auth}_\Pi$ from an indistinguishability adversary $\mathcal{B}$, which forwards $\mathcal{B}$'s queries and automatically wins if $\mathcal{B}$ produces a valid forgery. $\mathcal{A}$ achieves the same advantage as $\mathcal{B}$, because if no forgery occurs, the games $\mathbf{auth\text{-}real}_\Pi$ and $\mathbf{auth\text{-}ideal}_\Pi$ are indistinguishable.

Replacing F. We first replace F with a pair of independent random tweakable permutations $\pi_0 = (\pi_{\mathsf{T},0} \leftarrow\!\!\$ \ \mathrm{Perm}(n))_{\mathsf{T} \in \{0,1\}^t}$ and $\pi_1 = (\pi_{\mathsf{T},1} \leftarrow\!\!\$$ $\mathrm{Perm}(n))_{\mathsf{T} \in \{0,1\}^t}$ and let $\mathrm{SAEF}[(\pi_0, \pi_1)]$ denote the SAEF mode that uses π_0, π_1 instead of F, which yields $\mathbf{Adv}_{\mathrm{SAEF}[\mathsf{F}]}^{\mathbf{auth}}(\mathcal{A}) \leq \mathbf{Adv}_{\mathsf{F}}^{\mathbf{prtfp}}(\mathcal{B}) + \mathbf{Adv}_{\mathrm{SAEF}[(\pi_0,\pi_1)]}^{\mathbf{auth}}(\mathcal{A})$.

The adversary is thus left with the goal of distinguishing between the games $\mathbf{auth\text{-}real}_{\mathrm{SAEF}[(\pi_0,\pi_1)]}$ (called the "real-int world") and $\mathbf{auth\text{-}ideal}_{\mathrm{SAEF}[(\pi_0,\pi_1)]}$ (called the "ideal-int world"). Hence, we want to bound $\mathbf{Adv}_{\mathrm{SAEF}[(\pi_0,\pi_1)]}^{\mathbf{auth}}(\mathcal{A}) = \Pr[\mathcal{A}^{\mathbf{auth\text{-}real}_{\mathrm{SAEF}[(\pi_0,\pi_1)]}}] - \Pr[\mathcal{A}^{\mathbf{auth\text{-}ideal}_{\mathrm{SAEF}[(\pi_0,\pi_1)]}}]$.

Transcripts. Following the coefficients H technique [22], we characterize the interactions of $\mathcal{A}$ with its oracles in a *transcript*:

$$\tau = \langle (N^i, A^i, M^i, C^i)_{i=1}^{q_e}, (\bar{N}^i, \bar{A}^i, \bar{C}^i, b^i)_{i=1}^{q_v} \rangle$$

In the ith query to the encryption oracle (N^i, A^i, M^i), returning the ciphertext C^i, SAEF internally processes A^i, M^i and C^i in blocks $A_1^i, \ldots, A_{a^i}^i, A_*^i$, and $M_1^i, \ldots, M_{m^i}^i, M_*^i$, and $C_1^i, \ldots, C_{m^i}^i, C_*^i, T^i$ respectively (defined according to the encryption algorithm in Fig. 2). We have a^i and m^i equal to, respectively, the length of A^i and M^i in n-bit. SAEF additionally uses whitening masks, denoted here $\Delta_1^i, \ldots, \Delta_{a^i+1}^i$ for the whitening masks used to process $A_1^i, \ldots, A_{a^i}^i, A_*^i$ respectively, and $\Delta_{a^i+2}^i, \ldots, \Delta_{a^i+m^i+2}^i$ for the whitening masks used to process the blocks $M_1^i, \ldots, M_{m^i}^i, M_*^i$ respectively.

Similarly, in the ith decryption query $(\bar{N}^i, \bar{A}^i, \bar{C}^i)$, returning $b^i \in \{\top, \bot\}$ SAEF internally processes $\bar{A}^i$ and $\bar{C}^i$ in blocks, denoted as $\bar{A}_1^i, \ldots, \bar{A}_{\bar{a}^i}^i, \bar{A}_*^i$ and $\bar{C}_1^i, \ldots, \bar{C}_{\bar{m}^i}^i, \bar{C}_*^i, \bar{T}^i$, where $\bar{a}^i$ and $\bar{m}^i$ are respectively equal to the length of $\bar{A}^i$ and the length of $\bar{C}^i$ in n-bit blocks (excluding the tag from the count). Additionally, SAEF internally computes the plaintext blocks $\bar{M}_1^i, \ldots, \bar{M}_{\bar{m}^i}^i, \bar{M}_*^i$ as well as $\bar{\Delta}_1^i, \ldots, \bar{\Delta}_{\bar{a}^i+1}^i$, the whitening masks used to process $\bar{A}_1^i, \ldots, \bar{A}_{\bar{a}^i}^i, \bar{A}_*^i$ respectively, and $\bar{\Delta}_{\bar{a}^i+2}^i, \ldots, \bar{\Delta}_{\bar{a}^i+\bar{m}^i+2}^i$, the whitening masks used to process the blocks $\bar{C}_1^i, \ldots, \bar{C}_{\bar{m}^i}^i, \bar{C}_*^i$ respectively.

Additional Information. To simplify the proofs, we additionally provide the adversary with all the encryption masks Δ_j^i, all the decryption masks $\bar{\Delta}_j^i$ and internally computed plaintexts $\bar{M}_j^i$ when it has made all its queries and only the final response is pending.

In the real-int world, all these variables are internally computed by the oracles faithfully evaluating SAEF. In the ideal-int world, the encryption also evaluates SAEF, so Δ_j^i masks are defined, but the decryption oracle does not make any computations, hence $\bar{\Delta}_j^i$ and $\bar{M}_j^i$ are not defined. We therefore have to define their sampling, to be done *at the end of the experiment* (thus having no influence of adversarial queries).

For $j = 1$, we have $\bar{\Delta}_1^i = 0^n$ for $1 \leq i \leq q_v$. We sample each of the remaining $\bar{\Delta}_j^i$ mask uniformly, except when its value is trivially determined due to a "common prefix" with an encryption, or decryption query (defined shortly). Once the masks are sampled, we run the SAEF decryption algorithm using π_0 and these masks to compute $\bar{M}_j^i$. Clearly, this give away of additional information can only increase the adversary's advantage and thus can be considered here for upper bounding the above mentioned adversarial advantage.

Block-Tuple Representation. The ith encryption query can be equivalently represented as $(\mathsf{T}_j^i, \Delta_j^i, X_j^i, Y_j^i)_{j=1}^{\ell^i}, T^i$, such that $\ell^i = a^i + m^i + 2$ and each of the ℓ^i quadruples represents the processing done in j^{th} call to the forkcipher in the query, consisting of the string T_j^i used as forkcipher tweak, the current whitening mask Δ_j^i, the (possibly padded) associated data/plaintext block X_j^i and the empty/ciphertex block Y_j^i. In more detail:

– In the first block, we always have $\mathsf{T}_1^i = N\|1\|F$ for a flag $F \in \{0,1\}^3$ and $\Delta_1^i = 0^n$. For blocks with $j > 1$ we have $\mathsf{T}_j^i = 0^{t-3}\|F$ for an $F \in \{0,1\}^3$.

- If $|A| > 0$, for $1 \leq j \leq a^i$ we have $X_j^i = A_j^i$, $Y_j^i = \varepsilon$ and $F = 000$. For $j = a^i + 1$ we have $X_j^i = \mathsf{pad10}(A_*^i)$, $Y_j^i = \varepsilon$ and $F \in \{0,1\}^3$ as defined in Fig. 2.
- If $|M| > 0$, for $a^i + 2 \leq j < \ell^i$ we have $X_j^i = M_j^i$, $Y_j^i = C_j^i$ and $F = 001$. For $j = \ell^i$ we have $X_j^i = \mathsf{pad10}(M_*^i)$, $Y_j^i = C_*^i$ and $F \in \{0,1\}^3$ as defined in Fig. 2.
- If $A = M = \varepsilon$, we have $j = \ell^i = 1$, $X_j^i = \mathsf{pad10}(\varepsilon)$, $Y_j^i = \varepsilon$ and $F = 111$.

We call this the *block-tuple* representation.

We similarly define the block-tuple representation $(\bar{T}_j^i, \bar{\Delta}_j^i, \bar{X}_j^i, \bar{Y}_j^i)_{j=1}^{\bar{\ell}^i}, \bar{T}^i, b^i$ for decryption queries with $\bar{\ell}^i = \bar{m}^i + \bar{a}^i + 2$. We further streamline the notation by re-indexing the decryption queries from $q_e + 1$ to $q_e + q_v$, and dispensing of the bar above the variables. The decryption queries are thus denoted as $(T_j^i, \Delta_j^i, X_j^i, Y_j^i)_{j=1}^{\ell^i}, T^i, b^i$ for $q_e + 1 \leq i \leq q_e + q_v$.

Proposition 1. *The transformation of an extended transcript from the default to the block-tuple representation is injective.*

The proof of Proposition 1 is given in Appendix A.

Blockwise Common Prefix of Queries. This notation allows for the following natural definition of longest common blockwise prefix between two *queries*. We define the longest common prefix of the ith and i'^{th} query (in the block-tuple notation) with $\ell^i \leq \ell^{i'}$ w.l.o.g. as

$$\mathsf{llcp}_n(i, i') = \max\{1 \leq u \leq \ell^i | (T_j^i, \Delta_j^i, X_j^i, Y_j^i) = (T_j^{i'}, \Delta_j^{i'}, X_j^{i'}, Y_j^{i'}) \text{ for } 1 \leq j \leq u\}.$$

Note that this definition covers common blockwise prefix between two encryption queries (with $i, i' \leq q_e$), two decryption queries (with $i, i' > q_e$)) and between an encryption and a decryption query (with $1 \leq i' \leq q_e < i \leq q_e + q_v$ w.l.o.g.). Informally, $\mathsf{llcp}_n(i, i')$ counts how many internal chaining values (the Δ masks) are trivially equal between the ith and i'^{th} encryption query. For example, if the nonces N^i and $N^{i'}$ are distinct we have $\mathsf{llcp}_n(i, i') = 0$. If we have two queries with $N^i = N^{i'}$ and one having AD $A^{i'} = A^i \| M_1^i$ equal to the AD of the other appended with its first message block, we will still have $\mathsf{llcp}_n(i, i') = a^i + 1$, thanks to including the tweak string in the block tuples. We finally define the length of the longest common blockwise prefix of a query *with all previous queries* as $\mathsf{llcp}_n(i) = \max_{1 < i' < i} \mathsf{llcp}_n(i, i')$. Note that for a decryption query, all the encryption queries are always taken into account (due to our convention about query indexing).

Sampling of Δ Masks. Using this notation, we now precisely define the sampling of Δ_j^i masks in decryption queries (i.e., for $q_e < i \leq q_e + q_v$) of the ideal-int world. In the ith decryption query, for $1 \leq j \leq \mathsf{llcp}_n(i) + 1$, we let $\Delta_j^i = \Delta_j^{i'}$ for the smallest $i' < i$ such that i'^{th} query has $\mathsf{llcp}_n(i) = \mathsf{llcp}_n(i, i')$. For $\mathsf{llcp}_n(i) + 1 < j \leq \ell^i$, Δ_j^i is sampled uniformly at random. In other words, Δ masks that are trivially known to be equal to some previous mask due to the iterative nature of SAEF are simply set to that value, and the rest is sampled uniformly.

Extended Transcripts. With the new notation in mind, the extended transcripts can be re-defined as

$$\tau = \left\langle \left((\mathsf{T}_j^i, \Delta_j^i, X_j^i, Y_j^i)_{j=1}^{\ell^i}, T^i \right)_{i=1}^{q_e}, \left((\mathsf{T}_j^i, \Delta_j^i, X_j^i, Y_j^i)_{j=1}^{\ell^i}, T^i, b^i \right)_{i=q_e+1}^{q_e+q_v} \right\rangle.$$

Note that q_e, q_v, a and m here are themselves random variables and thus can vary for distinct *attainable* transcripts. However, due to the assumption that the adversary can make at most σ block queries, we always have $\sum_{i=1}^{q_e+q_v}(a^i + m^i + 2) = \sigma$.

The following corollary shows that switching to block-tuple representation does not have an impact of the result of the analysis and in particular on the bounds derived using the block-tuple representation.

Corollary 1. *Due to Proposition 1, it is impossible for two distinct transcripts* $\tau = \langle (N^i, A^i, M^i, C^i)_{i=1}^{q_e}, (\bar{N}^i, \bar{A}^i, \bar{C}^i, b^i)_{i=1}^{q_v} \rangle$ *and* $\tau' = \langle (N'^i, A'^i, M'^i, C'^i)_{i=1}^{q'_e},$ $(\bar{N}'^i, \bar{A}'^i, \bar{C}'^i, b'^i)_{i=1}^{q'_v} \rangle$ *to have the same block-tuple representation.*

Coefficient-H. Let Θ_{rein} and Θ_{idin} represent the distribution of the transcript in the real-int world and the ideal-int world, respectively.

The proof relies on the fundamental lemma of the coefficient H technique defined as Lemma 1 above. We say an attainable transcript τ is bad if one of the following conditions occurs:

BadT_1 a.k.a. "Input Collision": There exists $(i', j') < (i, j)$ (the block indexed by (i', j') precedes (i, j)) such that $1 \leq i \leq q_e + q_v$, $\mathsf{llcp}_n(i) < j \leq \ell^i$ is not in the longest common prefix of the ith query, , and the (i, j) block call has tweak-input collision with the (i', j') block call, i.e., $\mathsf{T}_j^i = \mathsf{T}_{j'}^{i'}$ and $X_j^i \oplus \Delta_j^i = X_{j'}^{i'} \oplus \Delta_{j'}^{i'}$.

BadT_2 a.k.a. "Mask Collision": There exists $(i', j') < (i, j)$ such that $1 \leq i \leq q_e + q_v$, $\mathsf{llcp}_n(i) < j < \ell^i$ (not in the longest common prefix), and both the block calls have the same tweaks $\mathsf{T}_j^i = \mathsf{T}_{j'}^{i'}$ and different inputs $X_j^i \oplus \Delta_j^i \neq X_{j'}^{i'} \oplus \Delta_{j'}^{i'}$, however, the following masks $\Delta_{j+1}^i = \Delta_{j'+1}^{i'}$ collide. (Note that such a collision cannot occur in the real-int world where the masks are generated with permutation).

BadT_3 a.k.a. "Forgery": There exists $q_e + 1 \leq i \leq q_e + q_v$ such that for $j = \ell^i$ we have any of the following:

Case 1. The last bit of T_j^i is 0 and $\pi_{\mathsf{T}_j^i, 1}(X_j^i \oplus \Delta_j^i) = T^i$.

Case 2. The last bit of T_j^i is 1, $\mathsf{right}_{n-|T^i|}(X_j^i) = 10^{n-|T^i|-1}$ and $\mathsf{left}_{|T^i|}(\pi_{\mathsf{T}_j^i, 1}(X_j^i \oplus \Delta_j^i)) = T^i$.

We let $\mathcal{T}_{bad}$ be the set of "bad" transcripts defined as the subset of attainable transcripts for which the transcript predicate $\mathsf{BadT}(\tau) = (\mathsf{BadT}_1(\tau) \vee \mathsf{BadT}_2(\tau) \vee \mathsf{BadT}_3(\tau))$ evaluates true. We define $\mathcal{T}_{good}$ as the set of attainable transcripts which are not in the set $\mathcal{T}_{bad}$ (and therefore from now on called as good transcripts).

Lemma 2. *For $\mathcal{T}_{bad}$ above and $q_e \leq 2^{n-1}$, we have* $\Pr[\Theta_{idin} \in \mathcal{T}_{bad}] \leq \frac{\sigma^2}{2^n} + \frac{4 \cdot q_v}{2^n}$.

Proof. BadT_1. For any transcript in $\mathcal{T}_{bad}$ with BadT_1 set to 1, we know that there exists at least one pair of block indices $(i', j') < (i, j)$ such that $\mathsf{llcp}_n(i) < j \leq \ell^i$ and $\Delta_j^i \oplus \Delta_{j'}^{i'} = X_j^i \oplus X_{j'}^{i'}$.

Note that for all $i' < i$ and $j = j' = \mathsf{llcp}_n(i) + 1$, we have $\Delta_j^i = \Delta_{j'}^{i'}$ but $X_j^i \neq X_{j'}^{i'}$ and thus for such cases the probability that the above equality occurs is 0. On the other hand, for all $i' < i$ and $j' \neq j$ or $j \neq \mathsf{llcp}_n(i) + 1$, the two masks are sampled uniformly and independently in Θ_{idin}. Since there are total σ possible values of (i, j) in a transcript, each having no more than σ possible values of (i', j'), we get $\Pr[\mathsf{BadT}_1(\Theta_{idin}) = 1] \leq \frac{\sigma^2}{2} \cdot \max\left\{0, \frac{1}{2^n}\right\} = \frac{\sigma^2}{2^{n+1}}$.

BadT_2. Similarly, for any transcript in $\mathcal{T}_{bad}$ with BadT_2 set to 1, we know that there exists at least one pair $(i', j') < (i, j)$ such that $\mathsf{llcp}_n(i) < j < \ell^i$ and $\Delta_{j+1}^i \oplus \Delta_{j'+1}^{i'} = 0$.

Note that from the definition of the predicate BadT_2 we have $j+1 \neq \mathsf{llcp}_n(i) + 1$. This means that Δ_{j+1}^i is distributed uniformly and independently of $\Delta_{j'+1}^{i'}$. Since there are total σ possible values of (i, j) in a transcript, each with no more than σ possible values of (i', j'), we get $\Pr[\mathsf{BadT}_2(\Theta_{idin}) = 1] \leq \frac{\sigma^2}{2^{n+1}}$.

BadT_3. Now, for any transcript in $\mathcal{T}_{bad}$ with BadT_3 set to 1 and BadT_1 set to 0, we know for Θ_{idin} one of the following can happen:

For some $i' \leq q_e$, $j = \ell^i$ and $j' = \ell^{i'}$, we have $j = j' = \mathsf{llcp}_n(i)$. Clearly, in such a case $\Delta_j^i = \Delta_{j'}^{i'}$, $X_j^i = X_{j'}^{i'}$ but $T^i \neq T^{i'}$. $T^{i'}$ being the correct tag for the given ciphertext, $T^i \neq T^{i'}$ cannot trigger BadT_3, yielding 0 probability.

For some $i' \leq q_e$, $j = \ell^i$ and $j' = \ell^{i'}$, we have $j = j' = \mathsf{llcp}_n(i) + 1$. We have $\Delta_j^i = \Delta_{j'}^{i'}$ but $X_j^i \neq X_{j'}^{i'}$ and thus the probability of any of the two conditions of BadT_3 occurring for a given query is at most $4/2^n$ assuming $q_e \leq 2^{n-1}$. For the first condition, this holds as every tag there is produced with a tweak used at most once per query, corresponding to a probability $1/(2^n - q_e) \leq 2/2^n$. For the second condition, we upper bound the product of the probabilities of having the correct padding in the block X_j^i (at most $2^{|T^i|}/(2^n - q_e)$), and of having correct truncated tag (at most $2^{n-|T^i|}/(2^n - q_e)$).

For all $i' \leq q_e$, we have $j > \mathsf{llcp}_n(i, i') + 1$. We know that the Δ_j^i is not inherited from an encryption query and is therefore sampled uniformly in Θ_{idin}. The first condition of BadT_3 thus occurs with a probability $1/2^n$. For the second condition, the correct padding is found with probability $1/2^{n-|T^i|}$ (using the randomness of Δ_j^i), and the correct tag is found with probability at most $2^{n-|T^i|}/(2^n - q_e)$, thanks to freshness of $X_j^i \oplus \Delta_j^i$, relying on $\mathsf{BadT}_1(\Theta_{idin}) = 0$ w.l.o.g., yielding a probability of at most $2/2^n$.

Since there are total q_v possible decryption queries, we get $\Pr[\mathsf{BadT}_3(\Theta_{idin}) = 1 | \mathsf{BadT}_1(\Theta_{idin}) = 0] \leq q_v \cdot \max\left\{0, \frac{4}{2^n}, \frac{2}{2^n}\right\} = \frac{4 \cdot q_v}{2^n}$. Hence, we obtain by the union bound that $\Pr[\Theta_{idin} \in \mathcal{T}_{\mathsf{bad}}] \leq \frac{\sigma^2}{2^n} + \frac{4 \cdot q_v}{2^n}$.

Lemma 3. *Let* $\tau \in \mathcal{T}_{good}$ *i.e.* τ *is a good transcript. Then* $\frac{\Pr[\Theta_{rein} = \tau]}{\Pr[\Theta_{idin} = \tau]} \geq 1$.

Proof. Note that a good transcript has the following two properties **(i)** For each $(i', j') < (i, j)$ if (i, j) is not in the longest common prefix of the two queries i.e. $\mathsf{llcp}_n(i, i') < j < \ell^i$ and both π_0 calls have same tweaks (i.e. $\mathsf{T}_j^i = \mathsf{T}_{j'}^{i'}$) then both calls will always have different inputs and different outputs. **(ii)** For each query to the decryption oracle i.e. $1 \leq i \leq q_v$, the transcript contains $b^i = \bot$ in the decryption result i.e. the conditions for a successful verification are not met.

The probability to obtain a good transcript τ in the real-int and the ideal-int worlds can now be computed. Let τ_e and τ_d denote the two parts of a transcript τ consisting respectively encryption and decryption queries, so that $\tau = \langle \tau_e, \tau_d \rangle$. With a slight abuse of notation, we have $\Pr[\Theta_{rein} = \tau] = \Pr[\Theta_{rein,e} = \tau_e] \cdot \Pr[\Theta_{rein,d} = \tau_d | \Theta_{rein,e} = \tau_e]$ and $\Pr[\Theta_{idin} = \tau] = \Pr[\Theta_{idin,e} = \tau_e] \cdot \Pr[\Theta_{idin,d} = \tau_d | \Theta_{idin,e} = \tau_e]$ and consequently

$$\frac{\Pr[\Theta_{rein,e} = \tau_e] \cdot \Pr[\Theta_{rein,d} = \tau_d | \Theta_{rein,e} = \tau_e]}{\Pr[\Theta_{idin,e} = \tau_e] \cdot \Pr[\Theta_{idin,d} = \tau_d | \Theta_{idin,e} = \tau_e]} = \frac{\Pr[\Theta_{rein,d} = \tau_d | \Theta_{rein,e} = \tau_e]}{\Pr[\Theta_{idin,d} = \tau_d | \Theta_{idin,e} = \tau_e]} .$$

This is because the encryption oracles in the real-int world and in the ideal-int world are identical, and so $\Pr[\Theta_{rein,e} = \tau_e] = \Pr[\Theta_{idin,e} = \tau_e]$. Further abusing notation, we let $\tau_{d,\Delta}$ denote the marginal event of all Δ masks in the decryption queries (as variables) being equal to the values in the transcript. We have $\Pr[\Theta_{rein,d} = \tau_d | \Theta_{rein,e} = \tau_e, \Theta_{rein,d,\Delta} = \tau_{d,\Delta}] = \Pr[\Theta_{idin,d} = \tau_d | \Theta_{idin,e} = \tau_e, \Theta_{idin,d,\Delta} = \tau_{d,\Delta}]$ because both sides of this equality correspond to mappings defined with random permutations with the input-output pairs fixed from the encryption part in both worlds. Further, using this equality, we get

$$\frac{\Pr[\Theta_{rein,d} = \tau_d | \Theta_{rein,e} = \tau_e]}{\Pr[\Theta_{idin,d} = \tau_d | \Theta_{idin,e} = \tau_e]} = \frac{\Pr[\Theta_{rein,d,\Delta} = \tau_{d,\Delta} | \Theta_{rein,e} = \tau_e]}{\Pr[\Theta_{idin,d,\Delta} = \tau_{d,\Delta} | \Theta_{idin,e} = \tau_e]} .$$

Let us now consider that τ has in total δ many Δs that are fixed/predefined due to all internal common prefixes. Clearly, one can write that $\delta = \sum_{i=1}^{q_e + q_v} (\mathsf{llcp}_n(i) + 1)$ (the extra 1 here stands for the Δ_1^i which is always fixed to 0). In the ideal-int world, since the Δs corresponding to these $(\sigma - \delta)$ unique block calls are sampled uniformly and independently and all decryption oracle results are $\bot$, one has $\Pr[\Theta_{idin,d,\Delta} = \tau_{d,\Delta} | \Theta_{idin,e} = \tau_e] = \frac{1}{(2^n)^{\sigma - \delta}}$. In the real-int world, these $(\sigma - \delta)$ Δs are no longer uniformly distributed but are defined using the random tweakable permutation (π_0, π_1) with at least $g_1 = \sum_{i=1}^{q_e + q_v} (a^i - 1)$ block calls with the tweak 0^n and at least $g_2 = \sum_{i=1}^{q_e + q_v} (m^i - 1)$ block calls with the tweak $0^{n-1} \| 1$. Thus, one has $\Pr[\Theta_{rein,d,\Delta} = \tau_{d,\Delta} | \Theta_{rein,e} = \tau_e] \geq \frac{1}{(2^n)_{g_1} (2^n)_{g_2} (2^n)^{\sigma - \delta - g_1 - g_2}}$.
Note that the above expression is not an equality and only gives an upper bound on the targeted probability as there are more permutation calls which can have

tweak collisions (To exemplify, the first block calls of any set of queries will have same tweaks if they all have same nonce). Now, from the above expressions, we get

$$\frac{\Pr[\Theta_{rein} = \tau]}{\Pr[\Theta_{idin} = \tau]} \geq \frac{(2^n)^{\sigma-\delta}}{(2^n)_{g_1}(2^n)_{g_2}(2^n)^{\sigma-\delta-g_1-g_2}} = \frac{(2^n)^{g_1}(2^n)^{g_2}}{(2^n)_{g_1}(2^n)_{g_2}} \geq 1 \ .$$

Combining the results of Lemma 2 and 3 (taking $\epsilon_1 = 0$) into Lemma 1, we obtain the upper bound $\mathbf{Adv}^{\mathbf{auth}}_{\mathrm{SAEF}[(\pi_0,\pi_1)]}(\mathcal{A}) \leq \frac{\sigma^2}{2^n} + \frac{4 \cdot q_v}{2^n}$ and thus the integrity result of the Theorem 1.

3.3   Confidentiality

Replacing F. We replace F with a pair of independent random tweakable permutations $\pi_0 = (\pi_{\mathsf{T},0} \leftarrow\!\!\$ \, \mathrm{Perm}(n))_{\mathsf{T} \in \{0,1\}^t}$ and $\pi_1 = (\pi_{\mathsf{T},1} \leftarrow\!\!\$ \, \mathrm{Perm}(n))_{\mathsf{T} \in \{0,1\}^t}$ and let $\mathrm{SAEF}[(\pi_0,\pi_1)]$ denote the SAEF mode that uses π_0, π_1 instead of F, which yields $\mathbf{Adv}^{\mathbf{oprpf}}_{\mathrm{SAEF}[\mathsf{F}]}(\mathcal{A}) \leq \mathbf{Adv}^{\mathbf{prtfp}}_{\mathsf{F}}(\mathcal{B}) + \mathbf{Adv}^{\mathbf{oprpf}}_{\mathrm{SAEF}[(\pi_0,\pi_1)]}(\mathcal{A})$.

With this replaced "F" scenario, the adversary is left with the goal of distinguishing between $\mathbf{oprpf\text{-}real}_{\mathrm{SAEF}[(\pi_0,\pi_1)]}$ (called the "real-conf world") and $\mathbf{oprpf\text{-}ideal}_{\mathrm{SAEF}[(\pi_0,\pi_1)]}$ (called the "ideal-conf world"). We now need to bound

$$\mathbf{Adv}^{\mathbf{oprpf}}_{\mathrm{SAEF}[(\pi_0,\pi_1)]}(\mathcal{A}) = \Pr[\mathcal{A}^{\mathbf{oprpf\text{-}real}_{\mathrm{SAEF}[(\pi_0,\pi_1)]}}] - \Pr[\mathcal{A}^{\mathbf{oprpf\text{-}ideal}_{\mathrm{SAEF}[(\pi_0,\pi_1)]}}] \ .$$

Transcripts and Additional Information. As before, we record the interaction of $\mathcal{A}$ with its oracle in a transcript containing the encryption queries and their responses as $\tau = \langle (N^i, A^i, M^i, C^i)^{q_e}_{i=1} \rangle$ such that the AD A, message M and ciphertext C are further partitioned in blocks as described in the integrity proof. Note that as before, q_e, a and m here are themselves random variables and thus can vary for distinct *attainable* transcripts. We also assume that the adversary can make at most $\sigma' \leq \sigma$ block queries. Thus, we always have $\sum^{q_e}_{i=1}(a^i + m^i + 2) \leq \sigma$.

To simplify the proofs, we again provide the adversary with additional information: **(i)** Δ^i_j masks for $1 \leq i \leq q_e$ and for $1 \leq j \leq \ell^i = a^i + m^i + 2$ that are internally computed by the encryption algorithm of SAEF. **(ii)** Tag bits that would normally be discarded by truncation (if any), i.e., we now have $|T^i| = n$ for $1 \leq i \leq q_e$.

This information is given to the adversary after it has made all its queries. These masks, as well the bits extending the tags to n bits, are well-defined in real-conf world, which faithfully implements SAEF encryption algorithm. In the ideal-conf world, however, they are not defined (as ciphertexts are directly computed by an online permutation and a random function, and the tags are directly sampled with the desired length) and thus the masks are sampled uniformly at random while maintaining the consistency with SAEF's prefix preservation (defined in detail below), and each authentication tag is simply extended by 0 to $n-1$ uniform bits as necessary.

Block-Tuple Representation. As before, we use the block-tuple representation. We represent the ith encryption query as $(\mathsf{T}^i_j, \Delta^i_j, X^i_j, Y^i_j)^{\ell^i}_{j=1}, T^i$, with

$\ell^i = a^i + m^i + 2$ and each of the ℓ^i quadruples consisting of the string T^i_j used as forkcipher tweak, the jth whitening mask Δ^i_j, the (possibly padded) associated data/plaintext block X^i_j and the empty/ciphertext block Y^i_j.

We reuse the same definition of the length of longest common blockwise prefix between the ith and the i'^{th} query $\mathsf{llcp}_n(i, i')$ and between the ith query and all preceding queries $\mathsf{llcp}_n(i)$.

Sampling of Δ Masks. Using the block-tuple representation, we now detail the sampling of Δ masks in the ideal world. For each $1 \le i \le q_e$, we let $\Delta^i_j = \Delta^{i'}_j$ for $1 \le j \le \mathsf{llcp}_n(i) + 1$ with the smallest $i' < i$ such that i'^{th} query has $\mathsf{llcp}_n(i) = \mathsf{llcp}_n(i, i')$. For $\mathsf{llcp}_n(i) + 1 < j \le \ell^i$ we sample the mask Δ^i_j uniformly at random.

Extended Transcripts. The extended transcripts available to the adversary at the decision-making time are denoted as $\tau = \langle ((\mathsf{T}^i_j, \Delta^i_j, X^i_j, Y^i_j)^{\ell^i}_{j=1}, T^i)^{q_e}_{i=1} \rangle$.

Coefficient H. Let Θ_{reco} and Θ_{idco} represent the distribution of the transcripts in the real-conf world and the ideal-conf world, respectively.

The proof relies on the fundamental lemma of the coefficient H technique defined as Lemma 1 above. We represent the jth block call of the ith query in a transcript by the index tuple (i, j). We say an attainable transcript τ is bad if one of the following conditions occur:

BadT$'_1$ a.k.a. "Input Collision": There exists $(i', j') < (i, j)$ (the block indexed by (i', j') precedes (i, j)) such that $1 \le i \le q_e$, $\mathsf{llcp}_n(i) < j \le \ell^i$ is not in the longest common prefix of the ith query, and the (i, j) block call has tweak-input collision with the (i', j') block call, i.e., $\mathsf{T}^i_j = \mathsf{T}^{i'}_{j'}$ and $X^i_j \oplus \Delta^i_j = X^{i'}_{j'} \oplus \Delta^{i'}_{j'}$.

BadT$'_2$ a.k.a. "Output Collision": There exists $(i', j') < (i, j)$ such that $1 \le i \le q_e$, $\mathsf{llcp}_n(i) < j < \ell^i$ (not in the longest common prefix), and both the block calls have the same tweaks $\mathsf{T}^i_j = \mathsf{T}^{i'}_{j'}$ and different inputs $X^i_j \oplus \Delta^i_j \ne X^{i'}_{j'} \oplus \Delta^{i'}_{j'}$, however, one of the outputs collide i.e. one of the followings are true

    I. $j = \mathsf{llcp}_n(i) + 1$ and **(i)** $\Delta^i_{j+1} = \Delta^{i'}_{j'+1}$ if $j < \ell^i$ and $j' < \ell^{i'}$, or **(ii)** $T^i = T^{i'}$ if $j = \ell^i$ and $j' = \ell^{i'}$.

    II. $j > \mathsf{llcp}_n(i) + 1$ and **(i)** $Y^i_j \oplus \Delta^i_j = Y^{i'}_{j'} \oplus \Delta^{i'}_{j'}$ if $j > a^i + 1$, or **(ii)** $\Delta^i_{j+1} = \Delta^{i'}_{j'+1}$ if $j < \ell^i$ and $j' < \ell^{i'}$, or **(iii)** $T^i = T^{i'}$ if $j = \ell^i$ and $j' = \ell^{i'}$.

    (Note that such a collision cannot occur in the real-conf world where the masks and the tags are generated with a permutation).

We let $\mathcal{T}'_{\text{bad}}$ be the set of "bad" transcripts defined as the subset of attainable transcripts for which the transcript predicate $\mathsf{BadT}'(\tau) = (\mathsf{BadT}'_1(\tau) \vee \mathsf{BadT}'_2(\tau))$ evaluates true. We define $\mathcal{T}'_{\text{good}}$ as the set of attainable transcripts which are not in the set $\mathcal{T}'_{\text{bad}}$ (and therefore from now on called as good transcripts).

Lemma 4. *For $\mathcal{T}'_{\text{bad}}$ as defined above, we have $\Pr[\Theta_{idco} \in \mathcal{T}'_{\text{bad}}] \le \frac{3 \cdot \sigma^2}{2^{n+1}}$.*

Proof. **BadT′₁**. For any transcript in T'_{bad} with BadT′₁ set to 1, we know that there exists at least one pair of (i,j) and (i',j') such that $\mathsf{llcp}_n(i) < j \le \ell^i$, $(i',j') < (i,j)$ and $\Delta^i_j \oplus \Delta^{i'}_{j'} = X^i_j \oplus X^{i'}_{j'}$.

Note that for all $i' < i$ and $j = j' = \mathsf{llcp}_n(i) + 1$, we have $\Delta^i_j = \Delta^{i'}_{j'}$ but $X^i_j \ne X^{i'}_{j'}$ and thus for such cases the probability that the above equality occurs is 0 (one should notice that the case when we have only the nonce collision is also covered in here. This is because for all $i' < i$ if $N^i = N^{i'}$ then we have $j = j' = 1$ and $\mathsf{llcp}_n(i) = 0$ which implies that $\Delta^i_1 = \Delta^{i'}_1 = 0$ and $X^i_1 \ne X^{i'}_1$). On the other hand, for all $i' < i$ and $j' \ne j$ or $j \ne \mathsf{llcp}_n(i) + 1$, the two masks are sampled uniformly and independently in Θ_{idco}. Since there are total $\sigma' \le \sigma$ possible values of (i,j) in a transcript, each having no more than $\sigma' \le \sigma$ possible values of (i',j'), we get $\Pr[\mathsf{BadT}'_1(\Theta_{idco}) = 1] \le \frac{\sigma^2}{2} \cdot \max\left\{0, \frac{1}{2^n}\right\} = \frac{\sigma^2}{2^{n+1}}$.

BadT′₂. Similarly, for any transcript in T'_{bad} with BadT′₂ set to 1, we know that there exists at least one pair of blocks $(i',j') < (i,j)$ such that $\mathsf{llcp}_n(i) < j < \ell^i$ and one of the followings is true (with appropriate values of j)

I. $j = \mathsf{llcp}_n(i) + 1$ and ($\Delta^i_{j+1} = \Delta^{i'}_{j'+1}$ or $T^i = T^{i'}$) (in this case, we can't have $Y^i_j + \Delta^i_j = Y^{i'}_{j'} + \Delta^{i'}_{j'}$ as by the definition of $\mathsf{llcp}_n(i)$, $X^i_j \ne X^{i'}_{j'}$ implies that $Y^i_j \ne Y^{i'}_{j'}$)

II. $j > \mathsf{llcp}_n(i) + 1$ and ($Y^i_j + \Delta^i_j = Y^{i'}_{j'} + \Delta^{i'}_{j'}$ or $\Delta^i_{j+1} = \Delta^{i'}_{j'+1}$ or $T^i = T^{i'}$).

Note that from the definition of the predicate BadT′₂ we have for any j, $j + 1 \ne \mathsf{llcp}_n(i) + 1$. This means that Δ^i_{j+1} is distributed uniformly and independently of $\Delta^{i'}_{j'+1}$, with a collision probability $1/2^n$. Each tag is generated as n uniform bits, independent of all other tags, making them collide with probability $1/2^n$. On the other hand, for each $j > \mathsf{llcp}_n(i)$, Δ^i_j is distributed uniformly and independently of $\Delta^{i'}_{j'}$, so the masked ciphertexts also collide with probability $1/2^n$.

There are no more than σ possible values of (i,j) in a transcript to cause a collision of masked ciphertext, each with no more than σ possible values of (i',j'), making for no more than $\sigma^2/2$ pairs. In addition, there are no more than $\sigma - q_e$ valid values of (i,j) for a Δ collision, each with no more that $\sigma - q_e$ possible values of (i',j'), yielding no more than $(\sigma - q_e)^2/2$ pairs. Finally, there are q_e tags that can cause a collision with one another, yielding no more than $q_e^2/2$ pairs. Thus we get $\Pr[\mathsf{BadT}'_2(\Theta_{idco}) = 1] \le \frac{2 \cdot \sigma^2}{2^{n+1}}$.

Hence, we obtain by the union bound that $\Pr[\Theta_{idco} \in T'_{bad}] \le \frac{3 \cdot \sigma^2}{2^{n+1}}$.

Lemma 5. *Let $\tau \in T'_{good}$ i.e. τ is a good transcript. Then $\frac{\Pr[\Theta_{reco} = \tau]}{\Pr[\Theta_{idco} = \tau]} \ge 1$.*

Proof. Note that a good transcript has the following property. For each $(i',j') < (i,j)$ if (i,j) is not in the longest common prefix of the two queries i.e. $\mathsf{llcp}_n(i,i') < j < \ell^i$ and both π_0 (resp. π_1) calls have same tweaks (i.e. $T^i_j = T^{i'}_{j'}$) then both blocks will always have different inputs (i.e., $X^i_j \oplus \Delta^i_j \ne X^{i'}_{j'} \oplus \Delta^{i'}_{j'}$) and different outputs (i.e., $Y^i_j \oplus \Delta^i_j \ne Y^{i'}_{j'} \oplus \Delta^{i'}_{j'}$ and $\Delta^i_{j+1} \ne \Delta^{i'}_{j'+1}$ respectively $T^i \ne T^{i'}$).

The probability to obtain a good transcript τ in the real-conf and the ideal-conf worlds can now be computed. With a slight abuse of notation, we let τ_Δ denote the marginal event of all Δ masks in the queries (as variables) being equal to the values in the transcript. With these notations, we have $\Pr[\Theta_{reco} = \tau | \Theta_{reco,\Delta} = \tau_\Delta] \geq \Pr[\Theta_{idco} = \tau | \Theta_{idco,\Delta} = \tau_\Delta]$. This is true because for fixed and unique (upto common prefix) input-output pairs (excluding the tags), the left side of this inequality corresponds to mappings of a random permutation with input size of n bits whereas the right side of this inequality corresponds to mappings of a random online permutation with input size of $\geq n$-bits. Similarly for the tags (fixed and unique), the left side of this inequality corresponds to a random permutation whereas the right side of this inequality corresponds to a random function both with same input size (n-bits).

Let us now consider that τ has in total δ' Δs that are fixed/predefined due to all internal common prefixes. Clearly, one can write that $\delta' = \sum_{i=1}^{q_e}(\text{llcp}_n(i)+1)$ (the extra 1 here stands for the Δ_1^i which is always fixed to 0). In the ideal-conf world, since the Δs corresponding to these $\sigma' - \delta'$ unique block calls are sampled uniformly and independently, one has $\Pr[\Theta_{idco,\Delta} = \tau_\Delta] = \frac{1}{(2^n)^{\sigma'-\delta'}}$ (Note that the sampling of the tags is already covered with the inequality defined above and is independent of the sampling of Δs here).

In the real-conf world, these $\sigma' - \delta'$ Δs are no longer uniformly distributed but are defined using the random tweakable permutation (π_0, π_1) with at least $g_1' = \sum_{i=1}^{q_e}(a^i - 1)$ block calls with the tweak 0^n and at least $g_2' = \sum_{i=1}^{q_e}(m^i - 1)$ block calls with the tweak $0^{n-1}\|1$. Thus, one has

$$\Pr[\Theta_{reco,\Delta} = \tau_\Delta] \geq \frac{1}{(2^n)_{g_1'}(2^n)_{g_2'}(2^n)^{\sigma'-\delta'-g_1'-g_2'}}.$$

Now, from the above three expressions, we get

$$\frac{\Pr[\Theta_{reco} = \tau]}{\Pr[\Theta_{idco} = \tau]} \geq \frac{(2^n)^{\sigma'-\delta'}}{(2^n)_{g_1'}(2^n)_{g_2'}(2^n)^{\sigma'-\delta'-g_1'-g_2'}} = \frac{(2^n)^{g_1'}(2^n)^{g_2'}}{(2^n)_{g_1'}(2^n)_{g_2'}} \geq 1.$$

Combining the results of Lemma 4 and 5 (taking $\epsilon_1 = 0$) into Lemma 1, we obtain the upper bound $\mathbf{Adv}_{\text{SAEF}[(\pi_0,\pi_1)]}^{\text{oprpf}}(\mathcal{A}) \leq \frac{3 \cdot \sigma^2}{2^{n+1}}$ and thus the confidentiality result of the Theorem 1.

4   Conclusion

We prove that SAEF is OAE-secure w.r.t. both confidentiality and integrity as long as the total amount of data processed with a single key is $\ll 2^{n/2}$ blocks, with n the blocksize of the underling forkcipher. This means that SAEF offers qualitatively stronger guarantees than what has been advertised in the original submission at the same quantitative security levels. Moreover, the newly discovered security properties of SAEF are highly relevant to many resource-constrained applications of lightweight cryptography, as discussed in Sect. 1. At the same time, SAEF can be implemented very efficiently with an efficient forkcipher instance such as ForkSKINNY [23], likely outperforming COLM (the de facto state of the art OAE-secure scheme) instantiated with SKINNY [4] tweakable blockcipher (which gives the most accurate comparison due to similarities with ForkSKINNY).[2] This makes SAEF a much more attractive implementation target than indicated by the previous results, especially for the most constrained devices.

An interesting avenue for future work is investigating the security of SAEF under the release of unverified plaintext (RUP). RUP security is also a natural target in the uses cases for lightweight cryptography, where the same constraints as discussed in Sect. 1 imply that constrained devices may be forced to leak portions of yet-unverified plaintext when decrypting long messages, complementing the blockcwise security of encryption implied by OAE. Our conjecture is that SAEF is INT-RUP secure without any modification.

A   Appendix: Proof of Proposition 1

We prove the proposition by describing the transformation in the backward direction, i.e. reconstructing SAEF input and output arguments from a block-tuple represented query. This is possible thanks to the sequence of tweak strings $\mathsf{T}_1^i, \ldots, \mathsf{T}_{\ell^i}^i$, which allows to unambiguously determine the boundary between the AD and message blocks, as well as whether the final block of AD and message respectively were n-bit long or not. Given a block-tuple represented query $((\mathsf{T}_j, \Delta_j, X_j, Y_j)_{j=1}^{\ell}, T)$, we can reconstruct N, A, M, C as follows (where unpad10(X) removes 10^* from the end of string X) by iterating over the block tuples with current tuple denoted as $(\mathsf{T}, \Delta, X, Y)$:

1. Parse T as $N\|1\|F$. If $F \in \{110, 111, 100, 101\}$ then necessarily $\ell = 1$, and if
   $F = 110$: Set $A = X, M = \varepsilon$ and $C = T$ and stop.
   $F = 111$: Set $A = \mathsf{unpad10}(X), M = \varepsilon$ and $C = T$ and stop.
   $F = 100$: Set $A = \varepsilon, M = X$ and $C = Y\|T$ and stop.
   $F = 101$: Set $A = \varepsilon, M = \mathsf{unpad10}(X)$ and $C = Y\|T$ and stop.
   If $F \in \{010, 011\}$ then set $A = X_1$ respectively $A = \mathsf{unpad10}(X_1)$ and $M = C = \varepsilon$ (no more AD blocks are expected). If $F = 001$ set $A = \varepsilon$, $M = X_1$ and $C = Y_1$ (no more AD blocks are expected). Finally, if $F = 000$ set $A = X_1$ and $M = C = \varepsilon$ (more AD blocks are expected). Set $F_{last} \leftarrow F$ and go to next tuple.
2. Parse T as $S\|F$. If $S \neq 0^{n-3}$ abort. If $F \neq 000$ go to next step. If $F_{last} \neq 000$ abort. Set $A = A\|X$ and $F_{last} = 000$. Go to next tuple and repeat this step.
3. Parse T as $S\|F$. If $S \neq 0^{n-3}$ abort. If $F \notin \{010, 011, 110, 111\}$ go to next step. If $F_{last} \neq 000$ abort. If
   $F = 110$: Set $A = A\|X, M = \varepsilon$ and $C = T$ and stop.
   $F = 111$: Set $A = A\|\mathsf{unpad10}(X), M = \varepsilon$ and $C = T$ and stop.

---

[2] We acknowledge that the performance gain of ForkSKINNY comes with a more ambitious security goal for the construction. However the investigation of this trade-off is out of scope of this work.

$F = 010$: Set $A = A\|X$.

$F = 011$: Set $A\|\text{unpad10}(X)$ and stop.

Set $F_{last} = F$. Go to next tuple.

4. Parse T as $S\|F$. If $S \neq 0^{n-3}$ abort. If $F \neq 001$ go to next step. If $F_{last} \notin \{010, 011, 110, 111\}$ abort. Set $M = M\|X$, $C = C\|Y$ and $F_{last} = 001$. Go to next tuple and repeat this step.

5. Parse T as $S\|F$. If $S \neq 0^{n-3}$ abort. If $F \notin \{100, 101\}$ or if $F_{last} \notin \{010, 011, 001\}$ abort. If

$F = 100$: Set $M = M\|X$.

$F = 101$: Set $M = M\|\text{unpad10}(X)$.

Set $C = C\|Y\|T$ and stop.

```
 1: function  ℰ(K, N, A, M)
 2:     A₁,…,Aₐ, A∗ ←ⁿ A
 3:     M₁,…,Mₘ, M∗ ←ⁿ M
 4:     noM ← 0
 5:     if |M| = 0 then noM ← 1
 6:     Δ ← 0ⁿ; T ← N‖0^{t-4}‖1
 7:     for i ← 1 to a do
 8:         T ← T‖000
 9:         Δ ← F_K^{T,0}(Aᵢ ⊕ Δ)
10:         T ← 0^{t-3}
11:     end for
12:     if |A∗| = n then
13:         T ← T‖noM‖10
14:         Δ ← F_K^{T,0}(A∗ ⊕ Δ)
15:         T ← 0^{t-3}
16:     else if |A∗| > 0 or |M| = 0 then
17:         T ← T‖noM‖11
18:         Δ ← F_K^{T,0}((A∗‖10*) ⊕ Δ)
19:         T ← 0^{t-3}
20:     end if       ▷ Do nothing if A = ε, M ≠ ε
21:     for i ← 1 to m do
22:         T ← T‖001
23:         Cᵢ, Δ ← F_K^{T,b}(Mᵢ ⊕ Δ) ⊕ (Δ, 0ⁿ)
24:         T ← 0^{t-3}
25:     end for
26:     if |M∗| = n then
27:         T ← T‖100
28:     else if |M∗| > 0 then
29:         T ← T‖101
30:     else
31:         return Δ
32:     end if
33:     C∗, T ← F_K^{T,b}(pad10(M∗) ⊕ Δ) ⊕ (Δ‖0ⁿ)
34:     return C₁‖…‖Cₘ‖C∗‖left_{|M∗|}(T)
35: end function
```

```
 1: function  𝒟(K, N, A, C)
 2:     A₁,…,Aₐ, A∗ ←ⁿ A
 3:     C₁,…,Cₘ, C∗, T ← csplit-bₙ C
 4:     noM ← 0
 5:     if |C| = n then noM ← 1
 6:     Δ ← 0ⁿ; T ← N‖0^{t-4}‖1
 7:     for i ← 1 to a do
 8:         T ← T‖000
 9:         Δ ← F_K^{T,0}(Aᵢ ⊕ Δ)
10:         T ← 0^{t-3}
11:     end for
12:     if |A∗| = n then
13:         T ← T‖noM‖10
14:         Δ ← F_K^{T,0}(A∗ ⊕ Δ)
15:         T ← 0^{t-3}
16:     else if |A∗| > 0 or |T| = 0 then
17:         T ← T‖noM‖11
18:         Δ ← F_K^{T,0}((A∗‖10*) ⊕ Δ)
19:         T ← 0^{t-3}
20:     end if       ▷ Do nothing if A = ε, M ≠ ε
21:     for i ← 1 to m do
22:         T ← T‖001
23:         Mᵢ, Δ ← F⁻¹_K^{T,0,b}(Cᵢ ⊕ Δ) ⊕ (Δ, 0ⁿ)
24:         T ← 0^{t-3}
25:     end for
26:     if |T| = n then
27:         T ← T‖100
28:     else if |T| > 0 then
29:         T ← T‖101
30:     else
31:         if C∗ ≠ Δ then return ⊥
32:         return ε
33:     end if
34:     M∗, T' ← F⁻¹_K^{T,0,b}(C∗ ⊕ Δ) ⊕ (Δ, 0ⁿ)
35:     T' ← left_{|T|}(T'); P ← right_{n-|T|}(M∗)
36:     if T' ≠ T return ⊥
37:     if P ≠ left_{n-|T|}(10^{n-1}) return ⊥
38:     return M₁‖…‖Mₘ‖left_{|T|}(M∗)
39: end function
```

Fig. 2. The SAEF[F] AEAD scheme.

References

1. Andreeva, E., et al.: COLM v1 (2014). https://competitions.cr.yp.to/round3/colmv1.pdf
2. Andreeva, E., Lallemand, V., Purnal, A., Reyhanitabar, R., Roy, A., Vizár, D.: Forkcipher: a new primitive for authenticated encryption of very short messages. In: Galbraith, S.D., Moriai, S. (eds.) ASIACRYPT 2019. LNCS, vol. 11922, pp. 153–182. Springer, Cham (2019). https://doi.org/10.1007/978-3-030-34621-8_6
3. Ashur, T., Dunkelman, O., Luykx, A.: Boosting authenticated encryption robustness with minimal modifications. In: Katz, J., Shacham, H. (eds.) CRYPTO 2017. LNCS, vol. 10403, pp. 3–33. Springer, Cham (2017). https://doi.org/10.1007/978-3-319-63697-9_1
4. Beierle, C., et al.: The SKINNY family of block ciphers and its low-latency variant MANTIS. In: Robshaw, M., Katz, J. (eds.) CRYPTO 2016. LNCS, vol. 9815, pp. 123–153. Springer, Heidelberg (2016). https://doi.org/10.1007/978-3-662-53008-5_5
5. Bellare, M., Boldyreva, A., Knudsen, L., Namprempre, C.: Online ciphers and the hash-CBC construction. In: Kilian, J. (ed.) CRYPTO 2001. LNCS, vol. 2139, pp. 292–309. Springer, Heidelberg (2001). https://doi.org/10.1007/3-540-44647-8_18
6. Bellizia, D., et al.: Spook: sponge-based leakage-resistant authenticated encryption with a masked tweakable block cipher. IACR Tran. Symmetric Cryptol. 2020(S1), 295–349 (2020). https://doi.org/10.13154/tosc.v2020.iS1.295-349. https://tosc.iacr.org/index.php/ToSC/article/view/8623
7. Bernstein, D.J.: Cryptographic competitions: CAESAR. http://competitions.cr.yp.to
8. Böck, H., Zauner, A., Devlin, S., Somorovsky, J., Jovanovic, P.: Nonce-disrespecting adversaries: practical forgery attacks on GCM in TLS. In: 10th USENIX Workshop on Offensive Technologies (2016)
9. Dobraunig, C., Eichlseder, M., Mendel, F., Schläffer, M.: ASCON v1.2 (2014). https://competitions.cr.yp.to/round3/asconv12.pdf
10. Dworkin, M.J.: SP 800-38D. Recommendation for Block Cipher Modes of Operation: Galois/Counter Mode (GCM) and GMAC (2007)
11. Fleischmann, E., Forler, C., Lucks, S.: McOE: a family of almost foolproof online authenticated encryption schemes. In: Canteaut, A. (ed.) FSE 2012. LNCS, vol. 7549, pp. 196–215. Springer, Heidelberg (2012). https://doi.org/10.1007/978-3-642-34047-5_12
12. Fouque, P.-A., Joux, A., Martinet, G., Valette, F.: Authenticated on-line encryption. In: Matsui, M., Zuccherato, R.J. (eds.) SAC 2003. LNCS, vol. 3006, pp. 145–159. Springer, Heidelberg (2004). https://doi.org/10.1007/978-3-540-24654-1_11
13. Guillaume Endignoux, D.V.: Linking Online Misuse-Resistant Authenticated Encryption and Blockwise Attack Models. Cryptology ePrint Archive, Report 2017/184 (2017). https://eprint.iacr.org/2017/184
14. Hoang, V.T., Krovetz, T., Rogaway, P.: Robust authenticated-encryption AEZ and the problem that it solves. In: Oswald, E., Fischlin, M. (eds.) EUROCRYPT 2015. LNCS, vol. 9056, pp. 15–44. Springer, Heidelberg (2015). https://doi.org/10.1007/978-3-662-46800-5_2
15. Hoang, V.T., Reyhanitabar, R., Rogaway, P., Vizár, D.: Online authenticated-encryption and its nonce-reuse misuse-resistance. In: Gennaro, R., Robshaw, M. (eds.) CRYPTO 2015. LNCS, vol. 9215, pp. 493–517. Springer, Heidelberg (2015). https://doi.org/10.1007/978-3-662-47989-6_24

16. Hongjun, W., Tao, H.: TinyJAMBU: A Family of Lightweight Authenticated Encryption Algorithms (2019). https://csrc.nist.gov/CSRC/media/Projects/Lightweight-Cryptography/documents/round-1/spec-doc/TinyJAMBU-spec.pdf

17. Iwata, T., Khairallah, M., Minematsu, K., Peyrin, T.: Duel of the titans: the romulus and remus families of lightweight AEAD algorithms. IACR Trans. Symmetric Cryptol. **2020**(1), 43–120 (2020). https://doi.org/10.13154/tosc.v2020.i1.43-120. https://tosc.iacr.org/index.php/ToSC/article/view/8560

18. Jean, J., Nikolić, I., Peyrin, T., Seurin, Y.: Deoxys v1.41 v1 (2016). https://competitions.cr.yp.to/round3/deoxysv141.pdf

19. Krovetz, T., Rogaway, P.: OCB v1.1 (2014). https://competitions.cr.yp.to/round3/ocbv11.pdf

20. O'Donnell, L.: 2 Million IoT Devices Vulnerable to Complete Takeover. Threatpost (2019). https://threatpost.com/iot-devices-vulnerable-takeover/144167/

21. O'Donnell, L.: Serious Security Flaws Found in Children's Connected Toys. Threatpost (2019). https://threatpost.com/serious-security-flaws-found-in-childrens-connected-toys/151020/

22. Patarin, J.: The "Coefficients H" technique. In: Avanzi, R.M., Keliher, L., Sica, F. (eds.) SAC 2008. LNCS, vol. 5381, pp. 328–345. Springer, Heidelberg (2009). https://doi.org/10.1007/978-3-642-04159-4_21

23. Purnal, A., Andreeva, E., Roy, A., Vizár, D.: What the fork: implementation aspects of a forkcipher. In: NIST Lightweight Cryptography Workshop 2019 (2019)

24. Rogaway, P.: Authenticated-encryption with associated-data. In: Proceedings of the 9th ACM Conference on Computer and Communications Security, pp. 98–107 (2002)

25. Rogaway, P., Shrimpton, T.: A provable-security treatment of the key-wrap problem. In: Vaudenay, S. (ed.) EUROCRYPT 2006. LNCS, vol. 4004, pp. 373–390. Springer, Heidelberg (2006). https://doi.org/10.1007/11761679_23

26. Rogaway, P., Shrimpton, T.: Deterministic authenticated-encryption: a provable-security treatment of the key-wrap problem. IACR Cryptology ePrint Archive 2006, 221 (2006)

27. Vanhoef, M., Piessens, F.: Key reinstallation attacks: forcing nonce reuse in WPA2. In: Proceedings of the 2017 ACM SIGSAC Conference on Computer and Communications Security, pp. 1313–1328. ACM (2017)

28. Wu, H.: ACORN v3 (2014). https://competitions.cr.yp.to/round3/acornv3.pdf

29. Wu, H., Huang, T.: MORUS v2 (2014). https://competitions.cr.yp.to/round3/morusv2.pdf

30. Wu, H., Preneel, B.: AEGIS v1.1 (2014). https://competitions.cr.yp.to/round3/aegisv11.pdf

WARP : Revisiting GFN for Lightweight 128-Bit Block Cipher

Subhadeep Banik[1], Zhenzhen Bao[2], Takanori Isobe[3,4]($\boxtimes$), Hiroyasu Kubo[6],
Fukang Liu[3,7], Kazuhiko Minematsu[5]($\boxtimes$), Kosei Sakamoto[3]($\boxtimes$), Nao Shibata[6],
and Maki Shigeri[6]

[1] EPFL, Lausanne, Switzerland
subhadeep.banik@epfl.ch
[2] Nanyang Technological University, Singapore, Singapore
zzbao@ntu.edu.sg
[3] University of Hyogo, Kobe, Japan
takanori.isobe@ai.u-hyogo.ac.jp
[4] NICT, Tokyo, Japan
[5] NEC Corporation, Tokyo, Japan
k-minematsu@ah.jp.nec.com
[6] NEC Solution Innovator, Tokyo, Japan
[7] Shanghai Key Laboratory of Trustworthy Computing,
East China Normal University, Shanghai, China

Abstract. In this article, we present WARP, a lightweight 128-bit block cipher with a 128-bit key. It aims at small-footprint circuit in the field of 128-bit block ciphers, possibly for a unified encryption and decryption functionality. The overall structure of WARP is a variant of 32-nibble Type-2 Generalized Feistel Network (GFN), with a permutation over nibbles designed to optimize the security and efficiency. We conduct a thorough security analysis and report comprehensive hardware and software implementation results. Our hardware results show that WARP is the smallest 128-bit block cipher for most of typical hardware implementation strategies. A serialized circuit of WARP achieves around 800 Gate Equivalents (GEs), which is much smaller than previous state-of-the-art implementations of lightweight 128-bit ciphers (they need more than $1,000$ GEs). While our primary metric is hardware size, WARP also enjoys several other features, most notably low energy consumption. This is somewhat surprising, since GFN generally needs more rounds than substitution permutation network (SPN), and thus GFN has been considered to be less advantageous in this regard. We show a multi-round implementation of WARP is quite low-energy. Moreover, WARP also performs well on software: our SIMD implementation is quite competitive to known hardware-oriented 128-bit lightweight ciphers for long input, and even much better for small inputs due to the small number of parallel blocks. On 8-bit microcontrollers, the results of our assembly implementations show that WARP is flexible to achieve various performance characteristics.

Keywords: Lightweight block cipher · 128-bit block cipher · Generalized feistel network · Unified encryption and decryption

© Springer Nature Switzerland AG 2021
O. Dunkelman et al. (Eds.): SAC 2020, LNCS 12804, pp. 535–564, 2021.
https://doi.org/10.1007/978-3-030-81652-0_21

1   Introduction

Lightweight Block Cipher. Due to the increasing need for encryption and authentication on constrained devices, lightweight cryptography has grown to be one of the central topics in symmetric-key cryptography. Among various symmetric-key primitives, the development of lightweight block cipher probably has the longest history. As demonstrated by PRESENT [25], the first generation of lightweight block ciphers, such as KATAN [32], PRINTCIPHER [44] or LED [37], mainly focused on hardware footprint in the standard, round-based constructions. The block size is typically 64 bits or even smaller to reduce the size. Combined with hardware-oriented components (such as a 4-bit S-box and a bit permutation), they achieved a very small hardware footprint compared to the standard AES. Although small-footprint serial AES implementations are possible [7,50], there is still a gap between what can be done with lightweight block ciphers.

The second generation ciphers aimed at various goals, such as low-latency (Prince [26] and QARMA [2]) or low-energy consumption (MIDORI [3]) or side-channel/fault attack resistance (LS-designs [36], CRAFT [15]), while mostly trying to achieve an equivalent hardware footprint of the first generation ciphers.

Importance of 128-Bit Cipher. In this paper, we focus on lightweight block ciphers with 128-bit block size and 128-bit key. The usefulness of such a primitive is obvious as it can be used as a direct replacement of AES (more precisely AES-128), *without changing the mode of operation*. Most of the popular block cipher modes currently used with AES, such as GCM, have birthday bound security, meaning that $O(2^{64})$ input blocks are sufficient to break the scheme. This also implies a certain limitation on 64-bit block ciphers. It is clear that 64-bit block ciphers have been playing the central role in the development of lightweight cryptography. Having said that, birthday attacks with $O(2^{32})$ data complexity can be a real threat[1]. To thwart them, keys must be renewed very frequently, however this is not trivial in practice (e.g., Sweet32 [19]).

Tweakable block cipher (TBC) of 64-bit block size, such as SKINNY, is another promising way to prevent the birthday attacks of $O(2^{32})$ complexity. It still requires a change of outer modes (though BBB secure modes for TBCs are typically simpler than those for block ciphers) and hence, it generally does not realize a direct replacement of AES.

Consequently, we think lightweight 128-bit block ciphers have their own value. In fact, replacements of AES by lightweight 128-bit ciphers often occur in the development of lightweight authenticated encryption (AE) schemes. For example, COFB [29] and SUNDAE [4] are modern block cipher-based AE modes that were initially specified with AES. Later they were submitted [5,8] to the ongoing NIST lightweight cryptography project[2] with a 128-bit-block version of GIFT, a family

---

[1] Alternatively, we could use beyond-birthday-bound (BBB) secure modes, however they are generally more complex than the birthday-secure ones, and using complex modes may nullify the merit of using lightweight primitive.

[2] https://csrc.nist.gov/Projects/lightweight-cryptography.

of lightweight block ciphers proposed by Banik et al. [10]. Both submissions [5,8] are included in the second-round candidates.

As a lightweight replacement of AES, the size of unified encryption and decryption (ED) circuit is important, since some standard/popular block cipher modes, e.g. CBC, OCB [47] and XTS [40], need a block cipher decryption (inverse) circuit as well as an encryption circuit. Besides, when a block cipher is implemented as a co-processor of general-purpose CPUs, we naturally expect the support of both encryption and decryption, as the co-processor is agnostic to the operating modes. Needless to say, an encryption-only circuit is generally smaller and enough for implementing "inverse-free" modes such as CTR or GCM. From these observations, we set our primary goal to build a lightweight 128-bit block cipher that is significantly smaller than prior arts for both encryption-only and unified ED circuits.

Our Design. When we look at the current list of lightweight block ciphers, the majorities are Substitution-Permutation Network (SPN) ciphers, such as [13, 25,26,37]. However, an SPN is inherently not perfect to our goal, because the decryption circuit generally needs to invert the confusion and diffusion layers. Despite the great research effort on concrete SPN designs using involutory S-boxes and MDS matrices, such as NOEKEON [31], MIDORI, and QARMA, designing an ultimately lightweight SPN cipher with fully involutory components still seems challenging, when unified ED circuit is a primary target. In particular, if we adopt a serialized datapath, we need recursively defined MDS matrices to be efficient with respect to area [37]. However, it is well known that in fields of characteristic 2, such an MDS matrix can never be involutory [38].

A potential alternative is Generalized Feistel Network (GFN) [53,66], because it is involutory in nature. The classical Type-2 GFN [66] has been adapted by many ciphers, such as HIGHT [39], Clefia [58], and Piccolo [57]. However it has a slow diffusion, which is problematic when the number of sub-blocks (branches) is large. Suzaki and Minematsu [60] (hereafter SM10) proposed a way to greatly improve the diffusion of GFN by just changing the permutation of branches from the rotation originally used by Type-2 GFN. They also showed r-branch permutations achieving the fastest diffusion up to $r = 16$. Indeed, TWINE [61] and LBlock [64] are 64-bit block, 16-branch GFN ciphers that can be seen as concrete instantiations of SM10. It is interesting to note that, GFN ciphers of larger-than-16 branches have been actively studied from the viewpoint of permutation design (see below), however no concrete, purely GFN-based block ciphers have been proposed, to the best of our knowledge[3]. In this paper, we revisit GFN to investigate if it fulfills our needs. Specifically, we extend the idea of SM10 to build a 128-bit, 32-branch (nibble) GFN cipher with 128-bit key, named WARP[4]. As observed by SM10, one can achieve the diffusion round (the number of rounds needed for diffusing any input difference to the whole output) as low as $2 \log_2 r$, which implies

---

[3] Liliput [17] is a 128-bit TBC built on a variant of GFN (EGFN [18]). It has a different linear layer structure from GFN and has 16 branches.

[4] The name comes from the resemblance of the cipher structure to strings in a loom.

that a good 128-bit, 32-nibble GFN cipher may only need two more rounds from the case of 64-bit, 16-nibble GFN ciphers. The big challenge is to determine a 32-branch permutation. The diffusion property of r-branch permutations for $r > 16$ has been recently studied, and made a significant progress since SM10 [28,34]. However, these studies do not give a direct answer to us, as we need a permutation having not only a fast full diffusion but also a high immunity against known attacks (differential/linear/impossible differential/integral/division etc.). Because an exhaustive search over all 32-branch permutations is computationally infeasible, we define a subset of permutations that are suitable to serial circuits and search over it with an Mixed Integer Linear Programming (MILP) solver, based on the development of MILP-aided security evaluation initiated by Mouha et al. [51]. Notably, we found that the 32-branch permutations with 9-round full diffusion (which is 1 round smaller than what SM10 showed) by Derbez et al. [34] are not suitable because the number of active S-box grows very slowly. Our permutation has 10-round full diffusion, however performs much better in terms of the number of active S-boxes (see Appendix C).

We adopt an S-box of MIDORI for its small delay and area. It is also very efficient for threshold implementations which is very important when side-channel attacks are possible.

The key schedule of WARP is ultimately simple: the 128-bit key is divided into two 64-bit halves and they are alternately used, i.e. the parity of the round number determines which half is used. This removes a need of additional register. Such permutation-based key scheduling schemes have been employed by a number of recent block ciphers, e.g., LED [37], Piccolo [57] and CRAFT [15] as well as stream ciphers [9,49]. In addition, every sub-key is XORed after S-box is applied to avoid the complement property of Feistel-Type Structures [24], following the idea of Piccolo [57].

Implementation Results. Combining these components, we achieved 763 GE for the bit-serial encryption-only circuit, which is, to our knowledge, the lowest number of 128-bit block cipher hardware implementation to date. Moreover, due to the low-energy and low-delay S-box, the 2-round unrolled implementation of WARP achieved significantly better energy consumption as compared to MIDORI, which is the current state-of-the-art design as a 128-bit low-energy cipher. For the unrolled (Enc-only) implementations, WARP is smaller than QARMA, while keeping relatively small delay, around 1.6 of QARMA-128$_{11}$. We also conducted threshold implementations of WARP for protection against first-order side-channel attacks. The results are quite impressive (Table 10 at Appendix D). All in all, WARP has pretty good performance for multiple hardware metrics not only in size.

For software metrics on microcontrollers, the design of WARP makes it flexible to make different trade-offs. We report performance characteristics of our assembly implementations on 8-bit AVR following various methods. The results show that, for WARP, it is possible to achieve competitively small code size and extremely low RAM consumption, with acceptable execution time.

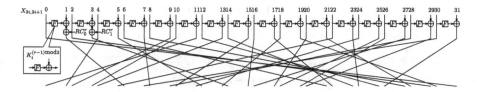

Fig. 1. Round function of WARP.

Finally, thanks to the software-friendly structure of GFN, we report a very efficient software implementation of WARP on modern high-end CPUs equipped with SIMD instructions. Unlike known bitslice implementation of recent lightweight ciphers, which need many block to be processed in parallel, we use a vector permutation (vperm) instruction, in a similar manner to TWINE [16]. This allows us to work with small (or no) parallelism. Surprisingly, the results on modern Intel processors are very competitive to the bitslice implementations of several state-of-the-art lightweight ciphers (GIFT, SKINNY and SIMON [11]). This gives another advantage to WARP when the operating mode is serial, say CBC-MAC or lightweight, serial authenticated encryption mode such as CLOC [42], SAEB [52], or COFB [29].

Organization. This paper is organized as follows. We first present the specification of our cipher at Sect. 2. We provide our design rationale, such as 32-branch permutation and S-box, at Sect. 3. Section 4 describes the details of security evaluations against major cryptanalysis methods. Section 5 and Sect. 6 provide our hardware and software implementations. Finally, we conclude at Sect. 7.

2 Specification

WARP is a 128-bit block cipher with a 128-bit key. The general structure of WARP is a variant of the 32-branch Type-2 GFN. A 128-bit plaintext M and a ciphertext C are loaded into a 128-bit internal state in encryption and decryption processes, respectively. The internal state is expressed as 32 nibbles, $X = X_0 \| X_1 \| \ldots \| X_{31}$, where $X_i \in \{0,1\}^4$. A 128-bit secret key K is denoted as two 64-bit keys K^0 and K^1, i.e. $K = K^0 \| K^1$, where $K^i \in \{0,1\}^{64}$. K^0 and K^1 are also expressed as 16 nibbles, $K^0 = K_0^0 \| K_1^0 \| \ldots \| K_{15}^0$, where $K_i^0 \in \{0,1\}^4$, and $K^1 = K_0^1 \| K_1^1 \| \ldots \| K_{15}^1$, where $K_i^1 \in \{0,1\}^4$, respectively.

Round Function. The round function of WARP consists of a 4-bit S-box $S : \{0,1\}^4 \to \{0,1\}^4$, a nibble XOR : $\{0,1\}^4 \times \{0,1\}^4 \to \{0,1\}^4$, and a shuffle operation $\pi : \{0,\ldots,31\} \to \{0,\ldots,31\}$ applied to 32 nibbles. The round function applies a non-linear unit transformation involving a single S evaluation and round-key addition for each of two consecutive nibbles, adds a round constant, and applies π to all 32 nibbles. See Fig. 1. The S-box S is described in Table 1. The shuffle π and its inverse π^{-1} are described in Table 2.

Table 1. 4-bit S-box S.

x	0	1	2	3	4	5	6	7	8	9	a	b	c	d	e	f
$S(x)$	c	a	d	3	e	b	f	7	8	9	1	5	0	2	4	6

Table 2. Shuffle π on 32 nibbles.

x	0	1	2	3	4	5	6	7	8	9	10	11	12	13	14	15
$\pi(x)$	31	6	29	14	1	12	21	8	27	2	3	0	25	4	23	10
$\pi^{-1}(x)$	11	4	9	10	13	22	1	30	7	28	15	24	5	18	3	16
x	16	17	18	19	20	21	22	23	24	25	26	27	28	29	30	31
$\pi(x)$	15	22	13	30	17	28	5	24	11	18	19	16	9	20	7	26
$\pi^{-1}(x)$	27	20	25	26	29	6	17	14	23	12	31	8	21	2	19	0

Encryption and Decryption. The number of rounds of WARP is 41, where the nibble shuffle operation π in the last round is omitted. For $i = 1, \ldots, 41$, the i-th round uses a 64-bit (16 nibbles) round key RK^i. Then, an i-th round key RK^i is given as $RK^i = K^{(i-1) \bmod 2}$.

The encryption algorithm of WARP is given in Fig. 2. The decryption algorithm is omitted here. It is obtained by just changing π to its inverse π^{-1}.

WARP uses LFSR-based round constants. A state of 6-bit LFSR is written as $(\ell_5, \ell_4, \ell_3, \ell_2, \ell_1, \ell_0)$ and is initialized to 000001. It is updated in each round as

$$(\ell_5, \ell_4, \ell_3, \ell_2, \ell_1, \ell_0) \leftarrow (\ell_4, \ell_3, \ell_2, \ell_1, \ell_0, \ell_0 \oplus \ell_5).$$

Using this LFSR, we define two nibbles $RC_0 = (\ell_5, \ell_4, \ell_3, \ell_2)$ and $RC_1 = (\ell_1, \ell_0, 0, 0)$. RC_0 and RC_1 are xored to the first and third nibbles of the state (note that the numbering of the nibbles is from 0 to 31) after the $X_{2i+1} \leftarrow S(X_{2i}) \oplus K_i^{(r-1) \bmod 2} \oplus X_{2i+1}$ operation. Let RC_0^r and RC_1^r be the r-th round constants. For completeness, we list (RC_0^r, RC_1^r) for all $r = 1, \ldots, 41$ in Table 3.

Claimed Security. WARP claims single-key security, and does not claim any security in related-key and known/chosen-key settings.

Table 3. Round constants (listed in hexadecimal).

r		1	2	3	4	5	6	7	8	9	10	11	12	13	14	15	16	17	18	19	20
RC_0^r		0	0	1	3	7	f	f	f	e	d	a	5	a	5	b	6	c	9	3	6
RC_1^r		4	c	c	c	c	c	8	4	8	4	8	4	c	8	0	4	c	8	4	c
r	21	22	23	24	25	26	27	28	29	30	31	32	33	34	35	36	37	38	39	40	41
RC_0^r	d	b	7	e	d	b	6	d	a	4	9	2	4	9	3	7	e	c	8	1	2
RC_1^r	c	8	4	c	8	4	8	0	4	8	0	4	c	c	8	0	0	4	8	4	c

Algorithm Encryption(K, M)

1. $(K_0^0 \| K_1^0 \| \ldots \| K_{15}^0, K_0^1 \| K_1^1 \| \ldots \| K_{15}^1) \leftarrow K$
2. $X_0 \| X_1 \| \ldots \| X_{31} \leftarrow M$
3. **for** $r = 1$ **to** 40 **do**
4.   **for** $i = 0$ **to** 15 **do**
5. $X_{2i+1} \leftarrow S(X_{2i}) \oplus K_i^{(r-1) \bmod 2} \oplus X_{2i+1}$
6.   **end for**
7. $X_1 \leftarrow X_1 \oplus RC_0^r, X_3 \leftarrow X_3 \oplus RC_1^r$
8. $X_0' \| X_1' \| \ldots \| X_{31}' \leftarrow X_0 \| X_1 \| \ldots \| X_{31}$
9.   **for** $i = 0$ **to** 31 **do**
10. $X_{\pi[j]} \leftarrow X_j'$
11.   **end for**
12. **end for**
13. **for** $i = 0$ **to** 15 **do**
14. $X_{2i+1} \leftarrow S(X_{2i}) \oplus K_i^0 \oplus X_{2i+1}$
15. **end for**
16. $X_1 \leftarrow X_1 \oplus RC_0^{41}, X_3 \leftarrow X_3 \oplus RC_1^{41}$
17. $C \leftarrow X_0 \| X_1 \| \ldots \| X_{31}$
18. **return** C

Fig. 2. Encryption algorithm of WARP.

3 Design Rationale

As described, the goal of WARP is a 128-bit block cipher enabling small hardware implementation, both for encryption-only and unified ED circuits, and both for round-based and serial architectures. We detail the rational of our design choice for each component of GFN below.

3.1 Branch Size and Permutation

We choose to use 32-nibble GFN with a 4-bit S-box, instead of 16-byte GFN with an 8-bit S-box. Although the latter option allows to reuse most of the known design/cryptanalytic results on 16-branch GFN (SM10, TWINE or LBlock and their cryptanalysis such as [23]), 8-bit S-box is much inferior to 4-bit S-box in terms of size/delay/energy.

We need a $r = 32$-branch permutation that is good in terms of diffusion round and resistance to the major attacks, such as differential and linear attacks. Despite the recent research on many-branch GFN [18,28,60], this remains a hard problem, simply because the number of permutation quickly grows ($r!$). When $r = 2^s$, SM10 shows an r-branch permutation of diffusion round being $2s$ based on de Bruijin graph, however, according to our random search, there is a huge number of 32-branch permutations having diffusion round of $2 \log_2 32 = 10$. Besides, the differential/linear Active S-box (AS-box) counts are very different among them, which suggests that we need another criteria before searching.

After some experiments, we limit ourselves to permutations allowing efficient serial hardware implementations, which is our main focus (See Sect. 5 for hardware implementation). In more detail, we searched all permutations of LBlock-like structure that consists of one 16-branch permutation composed of two identical 8-branch permutations, and one rotation on 16 branches with an amount of rotation from 0 to 15 nibbles as shown in Fig. 3. The resulting search space has size $8! \times 16 \approx 2^{19.3}$. The search over this space found 152 candidates of diffusion round 10. We conducted MILP-based differential AS-box counting for them. This evaluation requires about 2 days on computer equipped with 44 cores and 64 GB RAMs. Among them, 21 candidates achieved AS-box of ≥ 64 (which is needed for security) at 19 rounds (and no candidates achieved it at 18 rounds), and 8 out of 21 achieved AS-box of 66, which was the largest among them. These 8 permutations are not isomorphic, however as far as we investigated, the attack characteristics for other attacks (linear AS-box, impossible differential characteristics etc.) are identical for all of them.

Our investigation implies that they are equivalently secure in practice. Moreover, there is no difference from the implementation aspects too. Thus, we arbitrarily chose one among them. A LBlock-like equivalent round function of WARP is shown in Fig. 4.

Recently, Derbez et al. [34] showed four equivalent classes of 32-branch permutations achieving full diffusion after 9 rounds, while WARP requires 10 rounds. However, our MILP-based evaluation revealed that the number of active S-boxes of these grows much slower than ours. Indeed, these require at least 32 rounds for achieving AS-box of ≥ 64. Since WARP achieves it with only 19 rounds, the permutation of WARP is better than them as a 32-branch permutation.

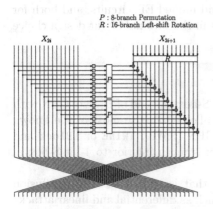

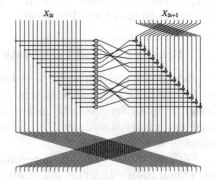

Fig. 3. General LBlock-like round function.

Fig. 4. Equivalent round function of WARP in LBlock-like structure.

3.2 S-Box

According to [3], the small path delay and the small gate area lead to low-energy implementation. We searched a small-delay and lightweight 4-bit S-box which fulfills the following requirements: (1) the maximal probability of a differential is 2^{-2}, (2) the maximal absolute bias of a linear approximation is 2^{-2} and (3) preferably belonging one of the 30 cubic classes (as given in [22]) that allows decomposition into two quadratic s-boxes, so that it can be used to implement a 1st order threshold implementation with 3 shares. This helps us have a very lightweight threshold circuit as well. As a result, we decide to use S-box of MIDORI (Sb_0). Note that other S-boxes used in low-latency ciphers such as Prince and QARMA do not satisfy the requirement (3).

3.3 Key Schedule

The key schedule uses alternately the upper and lower half of the 128-bit key in alternate rounds. This requires only a multiplexer to filter appropriate portions of the round key in each round. As already outlined in [3,15], an elaborate key schedule function requires a register element to store and update the key, which is costly in terms of area and energy consumption. Moreover, a simple key schedule is particularly beneficial to unified ED circuits, because additional hardware is not required to construct an inverse key schedule function. A key alternating cipher like WARP with odd number of rounds, uses the same upper half of the key in the first and the last encryption round (and indeed in all odd rounds) which implies that the decryption routine would also use the upper half of the key in the first, last and all odd rounds. Thus, the order of upper/lower half of keys used in successive rounds is exactly the same for encryption and decryption, thus no additional overhead is imposed to implement decryption alongside the encryption in hardware. In addition, the key XOR operation is applied after the S-box to avoid the complement property of Feistel-Type Structures [24], following the idea of Piccolo [57].

3.4 Round Constants

We use LFSR-based round constants as it is simple and efficient to implement in hardware. We use 6-bit LFSR with a primitive connection polynomial, which has a period of 63, and hence sufficient to cover 41 rounds used in WARP.

4 Security Evaluation

We evaluate the security of WARP against differential, linear, integral, impossible differential, invariant and meet-in-the-middle attacks. Among them, the 21-round impossible differential attack is considered to be the most efficient for WARP. In our evaluation, we do not expect an effective key-recovery attack on up to 32 rounds of WARP by using this 21-round impossible differential distinguisher or even using other ones. Consequently, we conclude that the full-round of WARP is expected to be resistant to those attacks. The details are given in Appendix B.

5   Hardware Performance

One of the principal objectives for our design was efficiency in constrained platforms with respect to multiple metrics of lightweight cryptography. Hence we looked at area, energy and latency which are widely acknowledged to be factors that determine the quality of a design. We first convert the round function to an LBlock-type architecture that helps us construct an efficient serial hardware architecture for WARP. Consider a 2-branch Feistel network, with a 128-bit block composed of $X_a \| X_b$ (each of 64 bits). Further let $X_a[i], X_b[i], K[i], \forall i \in [0, 15]$ denote the individual nibbles of the branches, and the roundkey respectively. Then the LBlock-type function defined below in Fig. 5, can also be used to define the specifications of WARP.

Round Function(X_a, X_b, K)
    for $i = 0$ to 15 **do**
        $T[\pi[i]] \leftarrow S(X_a[i]) \oplus K[\pi[i]],$ -- Sbox, shuffle left branch,addkey
        $U[i] \leftarrow X_b[6 + i \bmod 16],$ -- Rotate 6 nibbles (right branch)
    end for
    for $i = 0$ to 15 **do**
        $U[i] \leftarrow U[i] \oplus T[i],$ -- Add left, right branches
    end for
    $U[0] \leftarrow U[0] \oplus RC_0, U[1] \leftarrow U[1] \oplus RC_1$ -- Round const add

    for $i = 0$ to 15 **do**
        $X_b[i] \leftarrow X_a[i], X_a[i] \leftarrow U[i]$ -- Swap left, right branches
    end for

Fig. 5. Alternative definition of round function

In this definition, π is a permutation which maps i to the i-th element of the following set: $\{3, 7, 6, 4, 1, 0, 2, 5, 11, 15, 14, 12, 9, 8, 10, 13\}$. It is elementary to show that the encryption routine defined by 41 iterations of the round function in Fig. 5 (with the left-right swap omitted in the last round) is equivalent to the definition of the encryption algorithm of WARP up to a shuffle of nibbles.

5.1   Nibble Serial Architecture

Figure 6 shows the architecture for WARP. Each storage element colored yellow/white in the figure is a 4-bit scan/normal flip-flop respectively. Apart from 4-bit xor gates required for round key addition, left-right branch addition, and round-constant addition, we have used a few multiplexers to manoeuvre data

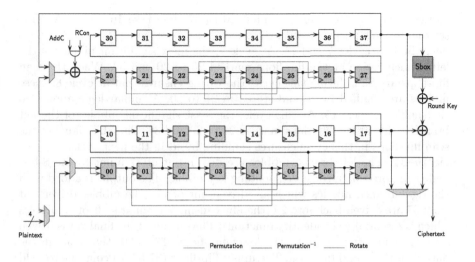

Fig. 6. Nibble serial architecture for WARP. The filter that feeds the permuted roundkey is omitted in the diagram.

through the circuit. The circuit uses only one S-box, and in addition we have a key-multiplexer that filters roundkey nibbles from the 128-bit master key (which is not shown in the figure for space constraints). The circuit computes one round function of WARP in 48 cycles. Following is the cycle-by-cycle description of the circuit operations.

Cycle 0–31: In the first 32 cycles, the plaintext nibbles are loaded on to the state register. After this, the round counter resets to 0, and the following operations are repeated 41 times.

Cycle 0–15: Before this set of cycles start, the left branch of the state, resides in the storage elements marked 37 to 20, and the right branch in those marked 17 to 00, as shown in Fig. 6. In 17 to 00, we need to rotate the right branch by 6 nibbles. This is done as follows: a circular shift is performed for 16 cycles, which is somehow arrested for 10 cycles, to achieve the equivalent functionality of 6 nibble rotation. The 16 nibble flip-flops are divided into 3 groups of 10, 1, 5 (00 to 11, 12 and 13 to 17). An internal circular rotation of nibbles takes place for 10 cycles within each group. Since 10, 1 and 5 are divisors of 10, this rotation effectively executes the identity transformation on the right branch. Thereafter, a normal circular rotation over the entire set of 16 nibbles (00 to 17) occurs for the next 6 cycles, thus achieving the required functionality.

In the upper half, the shuffling denoted by the permutation π is performed on the left branch (note that the order of shuffle and addkey/sbox is interchangeable). We further take advantage of the fact that π can be defined in terms of the 8-element permutation function $\pi' = \{3, 7, 6, 4, 1, 0, 2, 5\}$ over $[0, 7]$ and $[8, 15]$ (i.e. $\pi[i] = \pi'[i]$ if $i < 8$ and $8 + \pi'[i - 8]$ otherwise). This being so, only the nibbles marked 20–27 need to be scan flip-flops. We perform a circular motion over the left branch nibbles (20 to 37) for these 16 cycles (AddC is set to 0 for this purpose), with the select signal controlling the scan flip-flops being SET at cycles 7 and 15. At cycle 7, the most significant nibbles of the left branch reside at the flip-flops marked 26 to 20 and 37. When the scan flip-flops are SET during this cycle, the wiring ensures that at cycle 8, these nibbles are shuffled by π' and stored in 27 to 20. A similar logic applies to the shuffle in cycle 15. At this cycle, the least significant nibbles of the left branch reside at the flip-flops marked 26 to 20 and 37. The SET signal of the scan flip-flops in this cycle ensures shuffling by π' in the next cycle.

Cycle 16–31: The left branch nibbles are driven out of 37 input to the S-box and then xored with the corresponding key nibble. The output is added with the right branch nibbles which are driven out of 17. The nibbles driven out from 37 are driven back into 20 (thereby causing a circular shift of 16 nibbles which is essentially the identity function). The output of the final xor is driven into 00. Thus after cycle 31, the lower flip-flops (17 to 00) thus contain the output of the round function. The upper flip-flops (37 to 20) continue to hold the left branch of the current round (however the nibbles are shuffled with the permutation π executed in cycles 0 to 15).

Cycle 32–47: We need to undo the shuffling of the left branch and then swap the 2 branches. This is done serially over 16 cycles, by a circular rotation over the 32 flip-flop nibbles (37 to 00). The nibbles driven out of 17 are driven into 20, and thus after this set of 16 cycles, the flip-flops in the upper half (37 to 20) will contain the round function output. The nibbles out of 37 are driven into 00 and it is here that the π^{-1} is performed to undo the shuffle. Note that in the bottommost row, the scan flip-flops are wired to perform π^{-1}. The select signals are SET in cycles 40 and 47 to perform π'^{-1} over the lower and upper set of 8 nibbles exactly as in cycles 16–31. This not only moves the left branch nibbles to the lower flip-flops but also undoes the shuffle performed in cycles 0–15, and so we are ready to perform the next round computations. Note that the round constants are added to the register 17 in cycles 32 and 33. This completes the round function. Note that since the left-right swap is omitted in the last round, the ciphertext is output from the flip-flop marked 17 rather than 37.

More circuit details of bit-serial and unified architecture for encryption and decryption are presented in Appendix D.

5.2 Performance Results

In Table 4, we compare the hardware performances of the serial implementations of WARP with other lightweight ciphers, with 128-bit block size and providing 128-bit security. Unless otherwise specified, for all the designs in the table, the following design flow was adhered to. The ciphers were first implemented in VHDL and a functional simulation was done using the *Mentorgraphics Modelsim* software. Thereafter the design was synthesized using the Standard cell library of the STM 90 nm CMOS logic process (CORE90GPHVT v 2.1.a) with the Synopsys Design

Compiler, with the compiler flag set to `compile_ultra`. A timing simulation was done on the synthesized netlist with 1000 test vectors. The switching activity of each gate of the circuit was collected while running post-synthesis simulation. The average power was obtained using Synopsys Power Compiler, using the back annotated switching activity.

Serial implementations are deployed when area is one of the primary metrics to be optimized. As can be seen from Table 4, WARP performs well as far as area is concerned, when compared with other ciphers with similar security level. As in [3,15], we used multiplexers to filter round keys, instead of a register, which saves us 100 to 150 GE of silicon area. The encrypt-only (E) bit-serial version of WARP occupies only 763 GE which is the lowest reported at this security level. Note that for a fair comparison, all the designs in Tables 4, 5 were implemented from scratch except the ones marked by an asterisk.

Table 4. Comparison of performance metrics for serial implementations synthesized with STM 90 nm Standard cell library. Figures separated by / indicate corresponding metrics for encryption/decryption. *Synthesized with the IBM 130 nm process/Power at 100 KHz

	Degree of serial- ization	Area (GE)	Delay (ns)	Cycles	TP$_{MAX}$ (MBit/s)	Power (µW) (@10 MHz)	Energy (nJ)
GIFT-128-128	4/32	1455	2.25	714	76.0	61.7	4.40
GIFT-128-128	1	1213	2.46	6528	7.6	40.3	26.30
SKINNY-128-128	8	1638	1.95	840	74.5	79.1	6.64
SKINNY-128-128	1	1110	0.81	6976	21.6	53.8	37.53
SIMON 128/128	1	1077	1.17	4480	23.3	60.5	27.10
MIDORI 128 (E)	8	1308	4.94	415	62.4	54.4	2.26
MIDORI 128 (ED)	8	1401	6.08	415/463	50.7/45.5	54.6	2.27/2.53
AES 128 (ED)	8	2060	5.79	246/326	85.7/64.7	129.7	3.19/4.23
AES 128 (E) [43]*	1	1560	–	1776	–	0.823	14.61
AES 128 (ED) [43]*	1	1738	–	1776/2512	–	0.852	14.61/15.13
WARP (E)	4	**871**	2.97	2032	20.2	33.2	6.76
WARP (E)	1	**763**	2.01	8128	7.5	28.4	23.04
WARP (ED)	4	**925**	2.58	2032	23.3	34.6	7.03
WARP (ED)	1	**806**	2.13	8128	7.1	29.0	23.59

5.3   Round Based and Round Unrolled Designs

While serial implementations are useful to construct low area architectures, round based and round unrolled architectures offer a lot of benefits such as good energy performances, in addition with reasonably good area and through-put performances. In [6], the authors studied a number of block ciphers and came to the conclusion that round based or 2-round unrolled implementations tend to be the most energy efficient configurations for block ciphers.

For WARP, the round based configuration would need to filter the upper or the lower key half in successive rounds. Thus a multiplexer is necessary for this filtering. In contrast a 2-round unrolled configuration performs 2 round function computations in a single clock cycle. Such a configuration would have circuits for 2 round functions placed serially one after the other. This obviates the use of a multiplexer to filter any round keys, as it is clear that the first round function block can simply use the upper key half and the second block can similarly use the lower half. Thus a 2-round unrolled circuit would consume proportionately lesser resources than a round based circuit both in terms of area and energy. Similar arguments can be made about odd and even round unrolled circuits for WARP. We experimented with 3 configurations for WARP: the round based, the 2 round and the 4 round unrolled circuits. The simulation results along with a comparison with other lightweight block ciphers is presented in Table 5. Indeed, in terms of energy, the 2-round unrolled configuration is the best and is around 30% better with respect to the one round configuration of MIDORI 128, a block cipher, which is the most energy efficient block cipher reported in literature. Note that WARP has odd number of rounds: this means that any even round unrolled implementation will do some redundant computation in the final cycle. For example, a 2-round unrolled implementation will need to operate 21 cycles, to execute 41 round functions: the final cycle performs one additional round function. This amounts to wastage of energy in the final cycle: however this is a small fraction of the total energy consumed (for WARP it is less than 1% of the total energy consumed). Figure 7 further shows a breakdown of area occupied by the corresponding components of the circuit. Appendix D also describes a 1st order threshold implementation of the WARP circuit.

Table 5. Comparison of performance metrics for round based implementations synthesized with STM 90 nm Standard cell library (1R, 2R, 4R refer to 1, 2, and 4 round unrolled circuits).

	Area (GE)	Delay (ns)	Cycles	TP_{MAX} (GBit/s)	TP_{MAX}/area MBit/(s·GE)	Power (μW) (@10 MHz)	Energy (pJ)
GIFT-128-128	1997	1.85	41	1.611	0.826	116.6	478.1
SKINNY-128-128	2104	1.85	41	1.611	0.784	132.5	543.3
SIMON 128/128	2064	1.87	69	0.937	0.465	105.6	728.6
MIDORI 128 (E)	2522	2.25	21	2.649	1.076	89.2	187.3
MIDORI 128 (ED)	3661	2.44	21	2.443	0.683	108.7	228.3
AES 128	7215	3.83	11	3.113	0.442	730.3	803.3
WARP (1R) (E)	1187	2.05	42	1.418	1.223	55.5	233.2
WARP (1R) (ED)	1390	1.74	42	1.671	1.231	59.5	250.0
WARP (2R) (E)	1456	1.95	22	2.911	2.047	58.4	**128.5**
WARP (2R) (ED)	1824	2.67	22	2.126	1.193	69.9	**153.7**
WARP (4R) (E)	2223	3.25	12	3.334	1.536	117.5	141.0
WARP (4R) (ED)	3075	3.93	12	2.758	0.918	177.4	212.9

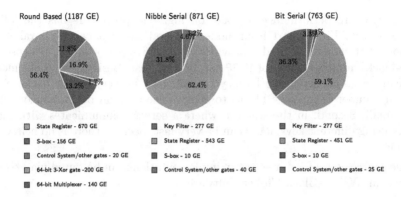

Fig. 7. Breakdown of component-wise area figures for 3 versions of WARP. Nibble and Bit-serial circuits require lesser scan flip-flops which require more area

6 Software Performance

6.1 On 8-Bit AVR Microcontrollers

The design of WARP makes it flexible to make trade-offs to achieve various performance characteristics on 8-bit AVR. Applying different implementation choices results in different trade-offs between ROM, RAM, and execution time. Appendix E.1 presents the details of our implementations. Table 11 summarizes the results and comparison with available results of existing designs with same parameters. It can be seen, on one end of the spectrum, WARP consumes minimized RAM and competitively low ROM; On the other end, it achieves relatively good performance regarding CPU cycles without consuming too much ROM.

6.2 On High-End Processors

The nibble-orientate character of WARP enables implementations of it fit neatly with a Single Instruction Multiple Data (SIMD) instruction commonly seen on modern CPUs. This SIMD instruction performs a vector permutation providing a look up table representation of the permutation offsets, which are called Vector Permutation Instruction (VPI) [61]. For Intel and AMD x86-64 CPUs, the concrete VPI is named (v)pshufb (which were used in our implementations). Both the parallel 4-bit S-box and the nibble shuffle operation can be implemented using (v)pshufb. Thus, the round function of WARP can be fully implemented using a few (v)pxor and (v)pshufb. In Appendix E.2, we present the details of our implementations of WARP using SIMD instructions on x64 CPUs. Our benchmark results of WARP, together with that of two ciphers that are also designed targeted at hardware, i.e., SIMON and SKINNY, are reported in Fig. 10.

The software performance of WARP on high-end processors has the following advantages. First, apart from mode of operations that can be parallelized, for those that cannot, WARP also provides competitive performance, because the single-block implementation of WARP can be very fast. Besides, for those modes that can be parallelized, the latency of WARP can be very small, because the required number of message blocks to achieve the optimal performance is relatively small. Second, in the scenario where a server communicates with many sensors using different keys, WARP can be very fast, because there is no heavy key schedule.

The source codes for our software implementations can be found via https://github.com/WARP-Block-Cipher/Software.

7   Conclusion

We have presented a 128-bit lightweight block cipher WARP. The design of WARP is based on a variant of Type-2 GFN, combined with an improved shuffle over 32 nibbles to boost the diffusion. The primary goal is to achieve a small-footprint 128-bit block cipher, both for encryption-only and unified ED circuits. This has been achieved by carefully choosing the components of GFN. We provided a comprehensive hardware implementation results. They show that WARP is the smallest 128-bit block cipher in the most of typical implementation strategies. Moreover, WARP is very competitive in energy-efficient implementation. Besides, the software of WARP on 8-bit microcontrollers can achieve competitively small code size and extremely low RAM consumption, with acceptable execution time. Finally, WARP is very efficient on software implementation using SIMD on high-end processors. Indeed, our experimental results suggest that, for relatively short inputs, WARP is faster than other hardware-oriented lightweight ciphers, which is a desirable feature when the block cipher is operated in a serial mode.

Acknowledgement. Subhadeep Banik is supported by the Swiss National Science Foundation (SNSF) through the Ambizione Grant PZ00P2_179921. Zhenzhen Bao is partially supported by Nanyang Technological University in Singapore under Grant 04INS000397C230, and Singapore's Ministry of Education under Grants RG18/19 and MOE2019-T2-1-060. Takanori Isobe is supported by Grant-in-Aid for Scientific Research (B) (KAKENHI 19H02141) for Japan Society for the Promotion of Science, Support Center for Advanced Telecommunications Technology Research (SCAT), and SECOM science and technology foundation. Kosei Sakamoto is supported by Grant-in-Aid for JSPS Fellows (KAKENHI 20J23526) for Japan Society for the Promotion of Science.

A   Test Vector

Table 6 shows the test vectors of WARP.

Table 6. Test vectors.

B	0	1	2	3	4	5	6	7	8	9	10	11	12	13	14	15	16	17	18	19	20	21	22	23	24	25	26	27	28	29	30	31
K	0	1	2	3	4	5	6	7	8	9	A	B	C	D	E	F	F	E	D	C	B	A	9	8	7	6	5	4	3	2	1	0
M	0	1	2	3	4	5	6	7	8	9	A	B	C	D	E	F	F	E	D	C	B	A	9	8	7	6	5	4	3	2	1	0
C	2	4	C	E	0	A	8	E	F	D	9	F	3	2	D	E	5	2	9	D	5	F	D	F	4	5	7	0	3	A	8	D
K	0	1	2	3	4	5	6	7	8	9	A	B	C	D	E	F	F	E	D	C	B	A	9	8	7	6	5	4	3	2	1	0
M	0	0	1	1	2	2	3	3	4	4	5	5	6	6	7	7	8	8	9	9	A	A	B	B	C	C	D	D	E	E	F	F
C	9	2	3	C	6	4	F	9	2	8	2	7	E	E	6	2	B	9	6	6	7	D	D	2	5	4	8	F	B	1	2	C
K	0	A	C	D	0	2	2	F	6	8	0	A	5	4	7	F	E	E	0	3	C	0	8	6	7	B	0	9	E	3	D	7
M	A	F	6	C	D	D	9	0	F	C	5	A	6	E	A	A	8	9	7	B	C	D	1	2	0	8	D	3	9	1	E	1
C	6	1	2	3	9	9	5	F	1	9	2	4	D	3	1	4	2	5	6	4	1	A	C	D	D	0	5	8	D	D	4	6

B: Branch Index K: Master key M: Plaintext C: Ciphertext

B   Security Evaluation

In this section, we provide the security evaluations of WARP against differential, linear, integral, impossible differential, invariant and meet-in-the-middle attacks.

B.1   Differential/Linear Attack

Differential cryptanalsis [21] and linear cryptanalsis [48] are among the most powerful techniques available for block ciphers. To evaluate the security against differential and linear attacks, we compute the lower bound for the number of differentially and linearly active S-boxes with a MILP-aided automatic search method, which was proposed by Mouha et al. [51]. We use Gurobi [41] as the solver and search for all nibble-wise truncated differential and linear characteristics.

Table 7 shows the minimum number of differentially and linearly active S-boxes for up to 19 rounds in the single-key setting, where AS_D and AS_L denote the number of differentially and linearly active S-boxes, respectively. It can be observed from Table 7 that WARP has more than 64 active S-boxes after 19 rounds. Since the maximum differential probability and absolute linear bias of the S-box of WARP are both 2^{-2} and the nibble-wise full diffusion requires 10 rounds, even with a 19-round differential distinguisher, we expect that an effective key-recovery attack cannot reach up to $19 + 12 = 31$ rounds. In a word, the full-round WARP is secure against differential and linear attacks.

B.2   Impossible Differential Attack

Generally, an impossible differential attack [20] is one of the most powerful attacks against Feistel-type ciphers. The impossible differential attack exploits

552   S. Banik et al.

Table 7. The lower bound for the number of differentially and linearly active S-boxes in the single-key setting.

#Rounds	1	2	3	4	5	6	7	8	9	10	11	12	13	14	15	16	17	18	19
AS_D/AS_L	0	1	2	3	4	6	8	11	14	17	22	28	34	40	47	52	57	61	**66**

a pair of input-output difference denoted by Δ_{in} and Δ_{out} such that Δ_{in} will never reach Δ_{out} after several rounds.

As mentioned in Sect. 3, WARP achieves the full diffusion after 10 rounds at both the encryption and decryption sides in nibble-wise. Based on a more detailed investigation, we found that the full diffusion requires 12 rounds at both the encryption and decryption sides in bit-wise. Hence, there should be no probability-1 bit-wise impossible differential over 24 rounds.

In order to obtain the longest impossible differential distinguisher, we utilize an impossible differential search tool based on MILP designed by Sasaki and Todo [56]. Specifically, we evaluate the search space such that the plaintext difference and ciphertext difference activate only one bit, respectively. To model the propagation of differences through the 4-bit S-box, we take into account the differential distribution table for the 4-bit S-box. Based on the method as proposed in [59], it can be modeled with the linear inequalities.

As a result, we find the following 21-round impossible differential distinguisher.

$$(00000000000010000000000000000000000000000000000000000000000000000\\0000000000000000000000000000000000000000000000000000000000000000)$$
$$\xrightarrow{21\ rounds} (000000000000000000000000000000000000000000000010000000000000000000\\0000000000000000000000000000000000000000000000000000000000000000)$$

According to Boura et al.'s work [27] in ASIACRYPT 2014 and the corresponding interpretation [33] by Derbez in FSE 2016, when extending the 21-round impossible differential distinguisher for 10 rounds, the required time complexity of the key-recovery attack is almost close to a pure exhaustive key search. Therefore, we do not expect an effective key-recovery attack on up to 32 rounds of WARP by using this 21-round impossible differential distinguisher. In a word, we expect that the full-round WARP is secure against the impossible differential attack.

B.3 Integral Attack

The integral attack was first proposed by Daemen et al. [30] and it was later formalized to the integral property by Knudsen and Wagner [45]. We define the four states for a set of 2^n n-bit cell: **A**: if $\forall i, j\ i \neq j \Leftrightarrow x_i \neq x_j$, **C**: if $\forall i, j$ $i \neq j \Leftrightarrow x_i = x_j$, **B**: $\bigoplus_i^{2^n-1} x_i$, and **U**: Other. The integral attack was further generalized to the division property by Todo [62], which can exploit the hidden feature between **A** and **B** states.

To evaluate the nibble-based division property, we use a MILP-aided automatic search method proposed by Xiang et al. [65], which enables us to efficiently explore the propagation of the division property. Specifically, we evaluate all the cases where 1, 2, 3 nibbles out of 32 nibbles are **C** and the others are all **A** in plaintexts. Thus, we need to evaluate $2^{23.2} (= \binom{32}{1} + \binom{32}{2} + \binom{32}{3})$ nibble-wise patterns.

In this way, we find the following 20-round integral distinguisher.

$$(\mathbf{AAAAAACAAAAAAAAAAAAAAAAAAAAAAAAA})$$
$$\xrightarrow{20 \text{ rounds}} (\mathbf{UUUBUBUUUUUUUUBUUUUUUUUUUUUUBUU})$$

However, due to the high data complexity of this integral distinguisher, one can extend only 1 round to achieve a key-recovery attack and its time complexity is almost close to an exhaustive key search. One may find an integral distinguisher by using a lower data complexity, but the number of rounds will be reduced. Considering that the nibble-wise full diffusion requires 10 rounds and that a common integral distinguisher covering larger rounds always requires a higher data complexity, we expect that the full-round WARP is secure against integral attacks.

B.4   Meet-in-the Middle Attack

We evaluate the security against the meet-in-the-middle attack following the method appeared in the self-evaluation of MIDORI [3] and CRAFT [15]. The 10-round full diffusion property guarantees that any inserted key-bit non-linearly affects all branches after the 10 rounds in the forward and the backward directions, respectively. Thus, the possible number of rounds used for the partial matching (PM) [55] is estimated as 19 $(= (10-1) + (10-1) + 1)$. The condition for the initial structure (IS) [55] is that key differential trails in the forward direction and those in the backward direction do not share active non-linear components. For WARP, since any key differential affects all 16 S-boxes after at least 10 rounds in the forward and the backward directions, there is no such differential which shares active S-box in more than 10 rounds. Thus, the number of rounds used for IS is upper bounded by 9. Assuming that the splice-and-cut technique allows an attacker to add more 3 rounds in the worst case, at most 32-round $(19 + 10 + 3)$ MitM attack may be feasible. However, because of the iterated key insertions of K_0 and K_1 for every two round, we consider that it is difficult to mount a 32-round attack on WARP.

B.5   Invariant Subspace Attack

We use LFSR-based round constants in each round. Following the notions presented in [12], we first tried to find the smallest L-invariant subspace that contains all roundkey differences. Here, L denotes the transformation that describes the linear layer in WARP. Since WARP adds two key halves in an alternating fashion, the master keys repeat every other round, the set of roundkey differences in the even/odd rounds are given by

$$D_{even} = \{\mathbf{RC}^r \oplus \mathbf{RC}^{r+2} : i \in \{0, 2, \ldots\}\}, \quad D_{odd} = \{\mathbf{RC}^r \oplus \mathbf{RC}^{r+2} : i \in \{1, 3, \ldots\}\},$$

where $\mathbf{RC}^r$ is the 128-bit vector defined as $(0^4 \,\|\, RC_0^r \,\|\, 0^4 \,\|\, RC_1^r \,\|\, 0^{112})$. Denoting $D = D_{even} \cup D_{odd}$, we try to find $W_L(D)$, which denotes the smallest L-invariant subspace containing D. We found that $W_L(D)$ is a subspace of dimension 124, which does not automatically guarantee resistance to subspace attacks. As the invariant attack applies only if there is a non-trivial invariant g for the S-box layer such that $W_L(D) \subset LS(g)$, where $LS(g)$ is the subspace of all linear structures of the function g. We ran Algorithm 1 of [12] on $Z = W_L(D)$ first to see if $S(Z)$ hits all the cosets of Z. Experimentally we found that it does indeed, leading us to conclude that g is the constant function which guarantees security against subspace attacks.

C   32-Branch Permutations with 9-Round Full Diffusion [34]

Table 8 shows four equivalent classes of 32-branch permutations of $\pi_0'(x)$, $\pi_1'(x)$, $\pi_2'(x)$, and $\pi_3'(x)$ achieving 9-round full diffusion found by Derbez et al. [34].

Table 9 is a comparison of lower bounds on the number of active S-boxes for WARP and four permutations by our MILP-based Active S-boxes counting. As shown in Table 9, the number of active S-boxes of $\pi_0'(x)$, $\pi_1'(x)$, $\pi_2'(x)$, and $\pi_3'(x)$ grows much slower than WARP. Specifically, $\pi_0'(x)$, $\pi_1'(x)$ and $\pi_2'(x)$, $\pi_3'(x)$ require at least 32 and 48 rounds for achieving AS-box of ≥ 64, respectively.

Table 8. Four equivalent classes of 32-branch permutations with 9-round full diffusion [34].

x	0	1	2	3	4	5	6	7	8	9	10	11	12	13	14	15
$\pi_0'(x)$	3	4	5	12	7	24	9	20	11	2	1	26	15	8	17	30
$\pi_1'(x)$	3	10	5	12	7	26	9	20	11	8	1	24	15	18	17	30
$\pi_2'(x)$	3	4	5	2	7	24	9	16	11	14	1	28	15	10	17	8
$\pi_3'(x)$	3	14	5	12	7	28	9	18	11	22	1	30	15	2	17	24
x	16	17	18	19	20	21	22	23	24	25	26	27	28	29	30	31
$\pi_0'(x)$	19	14	21	18	23	28	13	10	27	16	29	6	25	22	31	0
$\pi_1'(x)$	19	4	21	2	23	28	13	14	27	22	29	6	25	16	31	0
$\pi_2'(x)$	19	26	21	22	23	20	13	30	27	18	25	6	31	12	29	0
$\pi_3'(x)$	13	4	21	26	23	10	19	8	27	20	25	16	29	6	31	0

Table 9. Lower bounds on the number of Active S-boxes for WARP and four permutations of $\pi_0'(x)$, $\pi_1'(x)$, $\pi_2'(x)$, and $\pi_3'(x)$

# of rounds	1	2	3	4	5	6	7	8	9	10	11	12	13	14	15	16	17	18	19
WARP	0	1	2	3	4	6	8	11	14	17	22	28	34	40	47	52	57	61	**66**
$\pi_0'(x)$ [34]	0	1	2	3	4	6	8	11	14	19	22	24	26	28	30	32	34	36	38
$\pi_1'(x)$ [34]	0	1	2	3	4	6	8	11	14	19	22	24	26	28	30	32	34	36	38
$\pi_2'(x)$ [34]	0	1	2	3	4	6	8	10	12	12	14	16	16	18	20	20	22	24	24
$\pi_3'(x)$ [34]	0	1	2	3	4	6	8	10	12	12	14	16	16	18	20	20	22	24	24

D   More Details About Hardware Implementations

D.1   Bit Serial Architecture

The nibble serial architecture can be converted to a bit serial architecture, with some simple circuit-level transformations. The first is explained in Fig. 8. Any nibblewise scan flip-flop can be serialized as shown in Fig. 8, so that only one scan flip-flop per nibble is utilized. Whereas in the nibble serial architecture, the circuit can transfer one of the 2 nibble signals in one clock cycle, the same can be done over 4 cycles in the bit-serial architecture. Thus the bit-serial circuit can perform the same set of round operations in $48 \times 4 = 192$ cycles, in 3 sets of 64 cycle operations as in the nibble serial circuit. We save $18 \times 3 = 54$ scan flip-flops in the bit-serial architecture, and also 4-bit xor gates and multiplexers can be replaced with corresponding single bit gates.

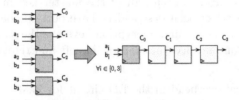

Fig. 8. Nibble to bit serial transformations

D.2   Unified Circuit for Encryption and Decryption

Implementing the functionalities of encryption and decryption (ED) on the same circuit can be beneficial in some instances. Various modes of operations like CBC, XTS, OCB and COLM [1], that use block ciphers as the underlying primitive, require access to both its encryption and decryption functionalities. Thus it is useful to have an implementation that achieves both functionalities of a block cipher with minimal overhead. There are several features in the Feistel network structure, that make it easier to construct the ED architecture. Some of them are as follows:

1. SPN structures generally require involutive S-boxes to ensure efficient ED implementation [3,15]. If not, they require the circuits for the forward and inverse S-box to be implemented together, which increases area [7]. However the inverse round function in Feistel networks can be described with the forward S-box only. This gives us more freedom to search for S-boxes with lightweight characteristics.

2. Some SPN block ciphers, e.g., [15] require the decryption key to be equal to $L \cdot K$, where L denotes the matrix that forms the linear layer of the cipher. Thus additional circuit for matrix multiplication is required. Also a multiplexer is required to filter these keys for encryption/decryption. In the architecture for WARP, this is not necessary.

3. Let F_K denote the function that performs S-box function and the roundkey addition on the left branch. Then by slight abuse of notation we can write the round function as

$$Y_a = P(F_K(X_a)) \oplus (X_b \lll 6), Y_b = X_a \tag{1}$$

where P is the function that performs the nibblewise shuffle of the left branch by moving the i-th nibble to $\pi[i]$. Then it is easy to see that the inverse round function is $X_a = Y_b, X_b = (P(F_K(Y_b)) \oplus (Y_a)) \ggg 6$. However we do omit the left-right swap in the last round, and as a result, decryption can be computed by iterating the following round function 40 times, followed by a "swapless" final round:

$$X_a = (P(F_K(Y_a)) \oplus (Y_b)) \ggg 6, X_b = Y_a. \tag{2}$$

Equations (1) and (2) are similar except that in encryption, the right branch is left rotated by 6 nibbles before addition, whereas in decryption, rotation done is after xoring left and right branches, this time by 6 nibbles towards the right. Since WARP uses each half of the master key in alternate rounds for key addition, it has been designed to have odd number of rounds. This means the first and last round encryption keys are the same, which implies that the encryption and decryption uses the left and right halves of the key in the same order.

Thus the only real overhead in the ED circuit for WARP is to accommodate left and right rotation by six nibbles in different times of the decryption cycle, and arrange for round constants to be generated in the reverse direction, which only requires some strategically placed multiplexers to accommodate the timing of these operations in the decryption cycle.

In essence, one approach would be to not rotate the right branch during cycles 0 to 15, and do rotation only during cycles 31 to 47 when the xoring of right and left branches has been completed. However, this approach is slightly problematic to adopt, as cycles 31 to 47 are used to not only swap left and right branches but also to apply π^{-1} to the left branch as it is being moved to bottom rows of flip-flops. In such a situation the bottom rows cannot accommodate two different types of permutation operations at the same time.

As a result, we need to exercise some fine-grained control over the ED circuit. For decryption, we rotate the right branch by 10 nibbles left in cycles 0–15 (same as 6 nibbles right rotation), although this rotation is not required as per Eq. (2). Thus to maintain functionality, in cycles 16–31, we drive nibbles out through register 11 to do xor between left and right branches (this was done through flip-flop 17 during encryption). After xor, the incoming nibbles are driven in through flip-flop 12 (this was done through 00 during encryption). This method has the added advantage that after round 31, the flip-flops $17-00$ already contain $(P(F_K(Y_a)) \oplus (Y_b)) \ggg 6$. This allows us to have the decryption operations in cycles 32–47 exactly the same in encryption.

For completeness, we discuss two more issues. First, for decryption we choose, cycles 0 and 1 for round constant addition, as this operation has to precede the non-linear operations. To rotate left by 10 nibbles, we need to freeze rotation for 6 cycles. Like in encryption, we divide the bottom row into groups of 6, 6, 2, 2 flip-flops and do internal rotation in these for 6 cycles. To accommodate this operation we need to replace 3 normal flip-flop nibbles with scan flip-flop nibbles.

D.3   Threshold Implementations

The s-box belongs to the cubic class $\mathcal{C}_{266}$ as per the classification in [22] and as such it can be decomposed into 2 quadratic s-boxes $F \circ G$, where

$$G = [0, \text{ f}, 6, 1, 3, 8, \text{ d}, \text{ e}, 4, \text{ b}, 2, 5, 7, \text{ c}, 9, \text{ a}],$$
$$F = [\text{c}, 3, 1, \text{ e}, 8, 5, \text{ d}, 0, \text{ b}, 4, 6, 9, 2, \text{ f}, 7, \text{ a}]$$

Since a minimum of $d+1$ shares are required to implement the 1st order threshold implementation (TI) of a degree d s-box, we can thus implement a 3 share 1st-order TI in the manner shown in [54]. The idea is to implement the TI of G and F separated by a register bank in between, which suppresses the glitches produced by the TI of G.

Since the s-box has degree 3, a straightforward 4-share TI can also be implemented using a direct sharing approach. With regards to circuit architecture, the 4 share versions would only consist of 4 copies of the unshared circuit combined through a shared s-box. The 3-share circuit is slightly complicated owing to the fact that the shared G, F functions have to be executed one after the other. We implemented it in the manner shown in Fig. 9. In the unprotected circuit described earlier, the S-box layer is computed in cycles 16 to 31. And so in the shared circuit, we implement the shared function G in cycles 15 to 30 and the shared function F in cycles 16 to 31. However this creates another problem, as the entire left branch is overwritten by the output of the shared G layer before being fed back into register 20. Since the current left branch is required to serve the role of the right branch in the subsequent round, we need to invert the G layer before we proceed to the next round. This is done by implementing a shared implementation of the quadratic s-box G^{-1} between registers 20 and 21, which is operated from cycles 17 to 32.

Table 10 shows the performance results for the 3-share and 4-share implementations of WARP. The smallest 3-share implementation stands at 1964 GE which

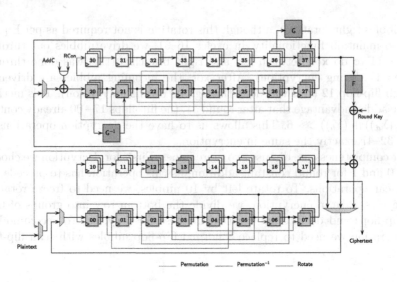

Fig. 9. Sketch of the 3 share nibble serial architecture for WARP

is smaller than known implementations of SKINNY and PRESENT (although these are computed at different level of serialization).

E   More Details of Software Implementations

E.1   Details of Software Implementations on 8-Bit AVR

Our implementations of WARP on 8-bit AVR are in assembly and compiled using AVR macro assembler 2.2.7 in Atmel Studio 7.0. All implementations use the LBlock-type structure (see Fig. 4). Detailed implementation choices are: 1) One-round or two-round unrolling: combining two rounds save the shuffle operation

Table 10. Comparison of performance metrics for serial implementations synthesized with STM 90 nm Standard cell library. (RB denotes round based circuit, 3s, 4s denotes circuits with 3, 4 shares respectively) *Synthesized with the UMC 180 nm process/Power at 100 KHz. **Synthesized with the IBM 130 nm process/power at 100 KHz

	Degree of serial-ization	Area (GE)	Delay (ns)	Cycles	TP$_{MAX}$ (MBit/s)	Power (µW) (@10 MHz)	Energy (nJ)
PRESENT-80 (3s)* [54]	4	2282	–	547	–	5.1	28.16
SKINNY-128-128** (3s) [14]	8	3780	1.63	872	90.0	–	–
WARP (3s)	4	**2288**	3.11	2032	19.3	99.9	20.29
WARP (3s)	1	**1964**	2.54	8128	5.9	87.0	70.72
WARP (3s)	RB	**6033**	2.73	83	545.3	232.5	1.93
WARP (4s)	4	**3363**	3.12	2032	19.3	145.7	29.61
WARP (4s)	1	**3060**	3.26	8128	4.6	136.6	111.03
WARP (4s)	RB	**15761**	3.38	42	880.9	703.3	2.95

between left and right branches, trading ROM for CPU cycles; 2) One-S-box or two-S-box: combining two S-boxes can reduce times of memory accesses, trading ROM or RAM for CPU cycles; 3) Storing the LUT of the S-box in RAM or ROM. Table 11 presents the results and comparisons.

Table 11. Software performance of WARP on 8-bit AVR.

(a) Different performance characteristics of WARP on 8-bit AVR

Unroll	Features	Function	ROM [B]	RAM [B]	Time [cyc.]	Speed [cpB]
One-Round	One-Sbox RAM	ENC	(956 - 46) 910	(176 - 160) 16	50554	394.95
		DEC	(962 - 46) 916	(176 - 160) 16	50908	397.72
		ENC+DEC	(1044 - 46) 998	(176 - 160) 16	101462	792.67
	Two-Sbox ROM	ENC	(1084 - 46) 1038	(160 - 160) 0	40664	317.69
		DEC	(1090 - 46) 1044	(160 - 160) 0	41018	320.45
		ENC+DEC	(1172 - 46) 1126	(160 - 160) 0	81682	638.14
Two-Round	Two-Sbox ROM	ENC	(1404 - 46) 1358	(160 - 160) 0	36504	285.19
		DEC	(1406 - 46) 1360	(160 - 160) 0	36506	285.20
		ENC+DEC	(1516 - 46) 1470	(160 - 160) 0	73010	570.39
	Two-Sbox RAM	ENC	(1264 - 46) 1218	(416 - 160) 256	34348	268.34
		DEC	(1266 - 46) 1220	(416 - 160) 256	34350	268.36
		ENC+DEC	(1376 - 46) 1330	(416 - 160) 256	68698	536.70

(b) Performance of block ciphers (128-bit block and 128-bit key) on 8-bit AVR

Cipher	Block [b]	Key [b]	ROM [B]	RAM [B]	Time [cyc.]
AES	128	128	3000	(406 - 160) 246	58973
LEA	128	128	1650	(629 - 160) 469	61755
SKINNY	128	128	1124	(545 - 160) 385	77451
SPARX	128	128	1726	(751 - 160) 591	84390
WARP [1R]	128	128	1126	(160 - 160) 0	81682
WARP [2R]	128	128	1330	(416 - 160) 256	68698

The target device is ATmega128; The scenario is encryption/decryption of 128 bytes of data in CBC mode [35]. For ROM, that consumed by the main function for initializing data and calling the enc/dec functions are subtracted. For RAM, that required for storing the data to be processed, the master key, and the initialization vector are subtracted. WARP [1R] is for the one-round-based implementation storing the LUT of two-S-box in ROM. WARP [2R] is for the two-round-unrolled implementation storing the LUT of two-S-box in RAM. Results of other ciphers are from https://www.cryptolux. org/index.php/FELICS_Block_Ciphers_Brief_Results.

E.2   Details of Software Implementations on x64 CPUs

Similar to TWINE [61], WARP can be transformed into an equivalent form, in which only half branches go through a nibble shuffle per round. Accordingly, our SIMD implementations use this equivalent form. Besides, to take advantage of the pipelined execution unit on modern CPUs, we provide additional options on parallelism besides the double-block using 256-bit registers – compute each atomic step on quadruple/octuple data blocks. Our benchmark results of WARP, together with that of SIMON and SKINNY, are reported in Fig. 10.

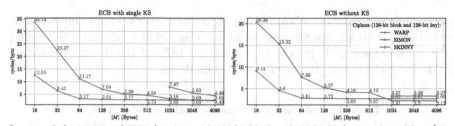

Source code for SKINNY and SIMON (versions with 128-bit block and 128-bit key) were adapted from [48, 65]. Because that of SKINNY only support 64-block parallel processing, results for short message are not available. We used GNU g++ 5.5.0 with -O3 -mavx2 options to compile. The processor is Intel(R) Core(TM) i7-6700 (Skylake). We turned off hyper-threading and disabled Turbo Boost. The timing method used was that in http://github.com/BrianGladman/AES. The instruction is rdtsc. We used time_enc16() evaluating the average time using 10000 samples of messages of a particular length.

Fig. 10. Software performance of WARP, SIMON and SKINNY on the same processor.

References

1. Andreeva, E., et al.: COLM v1. a CAESAR portfolio (2016)
2. Avanzi, R.: The QARMA block cipher family. IACR Trans. Symmetric Cryptol. **2017**(1), 4–44 (2017)
3. Banik, S., et al.: Midori: a block cipher for low energy. In: Iwata, T., Cheon, J.H. (eds.) ASIACRYPT 2015. Part II. LNCS, vol. 9453, pp. 411–436. Springer, Heidelberg (2015). https://doi.org/10.1007/978-3-662-48800-3_17
4. Banik, S., Bogdanov, A., Luykx, A., Tischhauser, E.: SUNDAE: small universal deterministic authenticated encryption for the internet of things. IACR Trans. Symmetric Cryptol. **2018**(3), 1–35 (2018)
5. Banik, S., et al.: SUNDAE-GIFT. A Submission to NIST Lightweight Cryptography Project (2019)
6. Banik, S., Bogdanov, A., Regazzoni, F.: Exploring energy efficiency of lightweight block ciphers. In: Dunkelman, O., Keliher, L. (eds.) SAC 2015. LNCS, vol. 9566, pp. 178–194. Springer, Cham (2016). https://doi.org/10.1007/978-3-319-31301-6_10
7. Banik, S., Bogdanov, A., Regazzoni, F.: Atomic-AES: a compact implementation of the AES encryption/decryption core. In: Dunkelman, O., Sanadhya, S.K. (eds.) INDOCRYPT 2016. LNCS, vol. 10095, pp. 173–190. Springer, Cham (2016). https://doi.org/10.1007/978-3-319-49890-4_10
8. Banik, S., et al.: GIFT-COFB. A Submission to NIST Lightweight Cryptography Project (2019)
9. Banik, S., et al.: Towards low energy stream ciphers. IACR Trans. Symmetric Cryptol. **2018**(2), 1–19 (2018)
10. Banik, S., Pandey, S.K., Peyrin, T., Sasaki, Y., Sim, S.M., Todo, Y.: GIFT: a small present. In: Fischer, W., Homma, N. (eds.) CHES 2017. LNCS, vol. 10529, pp. 321–345. Springer, Cham (2017). https://doi.org/10.1007/978-3-319-66787-4_16
11. Beaulieu, R., Shors, D., Smith, J., Treatman-Clark, S., Weeks, B., Wingers, L.: The SIMON and SPECK families of lightweight block ciphers. Cryptology ePrint Archive, report 2013/404 (2013). http://eprint.iacr.org/2013/404
12. Beierle, C., Canteaut, A., Leander, G., Rotella, Y.: Proving resistance against invariant attacks: how to choose the round constants. In: Katz, J., Shacham, H. (eds.) CRYPTO 2017. LNCS, vol. 10402, pp. 647–678. Springer, Cham (2017). https://doi.org/10.1007/978-3-319-63715-0_22

13. Beierle, C., et al.: The SKINNY family of block ciphers and its low-latency variant MANTIS. In: Robshaw, M., Katz, J. (eds.) CRYPTO 2016. Part II. LNCS, vol. 9815, pp. 123–153. Springer, Heidelberg (2016). https://doi.org/10.1007/978-3-662-53008-5_5

14. Beierle, C., et al.: The SKINNY family of block ciphers and its low-latency variant MANTIS. Cryptology ePrint Archive, report 2016/660 (2016). http://eprint.iacr.org/2016/660

15. Beierle, C., Leander, G., Moradi, A., Rasoolzadeh, S.: CRAFT: lightweight tweakable block cipher with efficient protection against DFA attacks. IACR Trans. Symmetric Cryptol. **2019**(1), 5–45 (2019)

16. Benadjila, R., Guo, J., Lomné, V., Peyrin, T.: Implementing lightweight block ciphers on x86 architectures. In: Lange, T., Lauter, K., Lisoněk, P. (eds.) SAC 2013. LNCS, vol. 8282, pp. 324–351. Springer, Heidelberg (2014). https://doi.org/10.1007/978-3-662-43414-7_17

17. Berger, T.P., Francq, J., Minier, M., Thomas, G.: Extended generalized Feistel networks using matrix representation to propose a new lightweight block cipher: Lilliput. IEEE Trans. Comput. **65**(7), 2074–2089 (2016)

18. Berger, T.P., Minier, M., Thomas, G.: Extended generalized Feistel networks using matrix representation. In: Lange, T., Lauter, K., Lisoněk, P. (eds.) SAC 2013. LNCS, vol. 8282, pp. 289–305. Springer, Heidelberg (2014). https://doi.org/10.1007/978-3-662-43414-7_15

19. Bhargavan, K., Leurent, G.: On the practical (in-)security of 64-bit block ciphers: collision attacks on HTTP over TLS and OpenVPN. In: Weippl, E.R., Katzenbeisser, S., Kruegel, C., Myers, A.C., Halevi, S. (eds.) ACM CCS 2016, pp. 456–467. ACM Press, October 2016

20. Biham, E., Biryukov, A., Shamir, A.: Cryptanalysis of Skipjack reduced to 31 rounds using impossible differentials. In: Stern, J. (ed.) EUROCRYPT 1999. LNCS, vol. 1592, pp. 12–23. Springer, Heidelberg (1999). https://doi.org/10.1007/3-540-48910-X_2

21. Biham, E., Shamir, A.: Differential cryptanalysis of the full 16-round DES. In: Brickell, E.F. (ed.) CRYPTO 1992. LNCS, vol. 740, pp. 487–496. Springer, Heidelberg (1993). https://doi.org/10.1007/3-540-48071-4_34

22. Bilgin, B., Nikova, S., Nikov, V., Rijmen, V., Stütz, G.: Threshold implementations of all 3×3 and 4×4 S-boxes. In: Prouff, E., Schaumont, P. (eds.) CHES 2012. LNCS, vol. 7428, pp. 76–91. Springer, Heidelberg (2012). https://doi.org/10.1007/978-3-642-33027-8_5

23. Biryukov, A., Derbez, P., Perrin, L.: Differential analysis and meet-in-the-middle attack against round-reduced TWINE. In: Leander, G. (ed.) FSE 2015. LNCS, vol. 9054, pp. 3–27. Springer, Heidelberg (2015). https://doi.org/10.1007/978-3-662-48116-5_1

24. Biryukov, A., Nikolić, I.: Complementing Feistel ciphers. In: Moriai, S. (ed.) FSE 2013. LNCS, vol. 8424, pp. 3–18. Springer, Heidelberg (2014). https://doi.org/10.1007/978-3-662-43933-3_1

25. Bogdanov, A., et al.: PRESENT: an ultra-lightweight block cipher. In: Paillier, P., Verbauwhede, I. (eds.) CHES 2007. LNCS, vol. 4727, pp. 450–466. Springer, Heidelberg (2007). https://doi.org/10.1007/978-3-540-74735-2_31

26. Borghoff, J., et al.: PRINCE – a low-latency block cipher for pervasive computing applications. In: Wang, X., Sako, K. (eds.) ASIACRYPT 2012. LNCS, vol. 7658, pp. 208–225. Springer, Heidelberg (2012). https://doi.org/10.1007/978-3-642-34961-4_14

27. Boura, C., Naya-Plasencia, M., Suder, V.: Scrutinizing and improving impossible differential attacks: applications to CLEFIA, Camellia, LBlock and SIMON. In: Sarkar, P., Iwata, T. (eds.) ASIACRYPT 2014. LNCS, vol. 8873, pp. 179–199. Springer, Heidelberg (2014). https://doi.org/10.1007/978-3-662-45611-8_10

28. Cauchois, V., Gomez, C., Thomas, G.: General diffusion analysis: how to find optimal permutations for generalized type-II Feistel schemes. IACR Trans. Symmetric Cryptol. **2019**(1), 264–301 (2019)

29. Chakraborti, A., Iwata, T., Minematsu, K., Nandi, M.: Blockcipher-based authenticated encryption: how small can we go? In: Fischer, W., Homma, N. (eds.) CHES 2017. LNCS, vol. 10529, pp. 277–298. Springer, Cham (2017). https://doi.org/10.1007/978-3-319-66787-4_14

30. Daemen, J., Knudsen, L., Rijmen, V.: The block cipher Square. In: Biham, E. (ed.) FSE 1997. LNCS, vol. 1267, pp. 149–165. Springer, Heidelberg (1997). https://doi.org/10.1007/BFb0052343

31. Daemen, J., Peeters, M., Van Assche, G., Rijmen, V.: Nessie proposal: NOEKEON (2000). http://gro.noekeon.org/Noekeon-spec.pdf

32. De Cannière, C., Dunkelman, O., Knežević, M.: KATAN and KTANTAN—a family of small and efficient hardware-oriented block ciphers. In: Clavier, C., Gaj, K. (eds.) CHES 2009. LNCS, vol. 5747, pp. 272–288. Springer, Heidelberg (2009). https://doi.org/10.1007/978-3-642-04138-9_20

33. Derbez, P.: Note on impossible differential attacks. In: Peyrin, T. (ed.) FSE 2016. LNCS, vol. 9783, pp. 416–427. Springer, Heidelberg (2016). https://doi.org/10.1007/978-3-662-52993-5_21

34. Derbez, P., Fouque, P.-A., Lambin, B., Mollimard, V.: Efficient search for optimal diffusion layers of generalized Feistel networks. IACR Trans. Symmetric Cryptol. **2019**(1), 218–240 (2019)

35. Dinu, D., Le Corre, Y., Khovratovich, D., Perrin, L., Großschädl, J., Biryukov, A.: Triathlon of lightweight block ciphers for the internet of things. J. Cryptogr. Eng. **9**(3), 283–302 (2019). https://doi.org/10.1007/s13389-018-0193-x

36. Grosso, V., Leurent, G., Standaert, F.-X., Varıcı, K.: LS-designs: bitslice encryption for efficient masked software implementations. In: Cid, C., Rechberger, C. (eds.) FSE 2014. LNCS, vol. 8540, pp. 18–37. Springer, Heidelberg (2015). https://doi.org/10.1007/978-3-662-46706-0_2

37. Guo, J., Peyrin, T., Poschmann, A., Robshaw, M.: The LED block cipher. In: Preneel, B., Takagi, T. (eds.) CHES 2011. LNCS, vol. 6917, pp. 326–341. Springer, Heidelberg (2011). https://doi.org/10.1007/978-3-642-23951-9_22

38. Gupta, K.C., Pandey, S.K., Venkateswarlu, A.: Almost involutory recursive MDS diffusion layers. Des. Codes Cryptogr. **87**(2), 609–626 (2018). https://doi.org/10.1007/s10623-018-0582-2

39. Hong, D., et al.: HIGHT: a new block cipher suitable for low-resource device. In: Goubin, L., Matsui, M. (eds.) CHES 2006. LNCS, vol. 4249, pp. 46–59. Springer, Heidelberg (2006). https://doi.org/10.1007/11894063_4

40. Standard for cryptographic protection of data on block-oriented storage devices

41. Gurobi Optimization Inc.: Gurobi optimizer 6.5 (2015). http://www.gurobi.com/

42. Iwata, T., Minematsu, K., Guo, J., Morioka, S.: CLOC: authenticated encryption for short input. In: Cid, C., Rechberger, C. (eds.) FSE 2014. LNCS, vol. 8540, pp. 149–167. Springer, Heidelberg (2015). https://doi.org/10.1007/978-3-662-46706-0_8

43. Jean, J., Moradi, A., Peyrin, T., Sasdrich, P.: Bit-sliding: a generic technique for bit-serial implementations of SPN-based primitives. In: Fischer, W., Homma, N. (eds.) CHES 2017. LNCS, vol. 10529, pp. 687–707. Springer, Cham (2017). https://doi.org/10.1007/978-3-319-66787-4_33

44. Knudsen, L., Leander, G., Poschmann, A., Robshaw, M.J.B.: PRINTCIPHER: a block cipher for IC-printing. In: Mangard, S., Standaert, F.-X. (eds.) CHES 2010. LNCS, vol. 6225, pp. 16–32. Springer, Heidelberg (2010). https://doi.org/10.1007/978-3-642-15031-9_2

45. Knudsen, L., Wagner, D.: Integral cryptanalysis. In: Daemen, J., Rijmen, V. (eds.) FSE 2002. LNCS, vol. 2365, pp. 112–127. Springer, Heidelberg (2002). https://doi.org/10.1007/3-540-45661-9_9

46. Kölbl, S.: AVX implementation of the Skinny block cipher (2019). https://github.com/kste/skinny_avx

47. Krovetz, T., Rogaway, P.: The software performance of authenticated-encryption modes. In: Joux, A. (ed.) FSE 2011. LNCS, vol. 6733, pp. 306–327. Springer, Heidelberg (2011). https://doi.org/10.1007/978-3-642-21702-9_18

48. Matsui, M.: Linear cryptanalysis method for DES cipher. In: Helleseth, T. (ed.) EUROCRYPT 1993. LNCS, vol. 765, pp. 386–397. Springer, Heidelberg (1994). https://doi.org/10.1007/3-540-48285-7_33

49. Mikhalev, V., Armknecht, F., Müller, C.: On ciphers that continuously access the non-volatile key. IACR Trans. Symmetric Cryptol. 2016(2), 52–79 (2016). http://tosc.iacr.org/index.php/ToSC/article/view/565

50. Moradi, A., Poschmann, A., Ling, S., Paar, C., Wang, H.: Pushing the limits: a very compact and a threshold implementation of AES. In: Paterson, K.G. (ed.) EUROCRYPT 2011. LNCS, vol. 6632, pp. 69–88. Springer, Heidelberg (2011). https://doi.org/10.1007/978-3-642-20465-4_6

51. Mouha, N., Wang, Q., Gu, D., Preneel, B.: Differential and linear cryptanalysis using mixed-integer linear programming. In: Wu, C.-K., Yung, M., Lin, D. (eds.) Inscrypt 2011. LNCS, vol. 7537, pp. 57–76. Springer, Heidelberg (2012). https://doi.org/10.1007/978-3-642-34704-7_5

52. Naito, Y., Matsui, M., Sugawara, T., Suzuki, D.: SAEB: a lightweight blockcipher-based AEAD mode of operation. IACR TCHES 2018(2), 192–217 (2018). https://tches.iacr.org/index.php/TCHES/article/view/885

53. Nyberg, K.: Generalized Feistel networks. In: Kim, K., Matsumoto, T. (eds.) ASIACRYPT 1996. LNCS, vol. 1163, pp. 91–104. Springer, Heidelberg (1996). https://doi.org/10.1007/BFb0034838

54. Poschmann, A., Moradi, A., Khoo, K., Lim, C.-W., Wang, H., Ling, S.: Side-channel resistant crypto for less than 2,300 GE. J. Cryptol. 24(2), 322–345 (2011). https://doi.org/10.1007/s00145-010-9086-6

55. Sasaki, Yu., Aoki, K.: Finding preimages in full MD5 faster than exhaustive search. In: Joux, A. (ed.) EUROCRYPT 2009. LNCS, vol. 5479, pp. 134–152. Springer, Heidelberg (2009). https://doi.org/10.1007/978-3-642-01001-9_8

56. Sasaki, Y., Todo, Y.: New impossible differential search tool from design and crypt-analysis aspects. In: Coron, J.-S., Nielsen, J.B. (eds.) EUROCRYPT 2017. Part III. LNCS, vol. 10212, pp. 185–215. Springer, Cham (2017). https://doi.org/10.1007/978-3-319-56617-7_7

57. Shibutani, K., Isobe, T., Hiwatari, H., Mitsuda, A., Akishita, T., Shirai, T.: Piccolo: an ultra-lightweight blockcipher. In: Preneel, B., Takagi, T. (eds.) CHES 2011. LNCS, vol. 6917, pp. 342–357. Springer, Heidelberg (2011). https://doi.org/10.1007/978-3-642-23951-9_23

564   S. Banik et al.

58. Shirai, T., Shibutani, K., Akishita, T., Moriai, S., Iwata, T.: The 128-bit block-cipher CLEFIA (extended abstract). In: Biryukov, A. (ed.) FSE 2007. LNCS, vol. 4593, pp. 181–195. Springer, Heidelberg (2007). https://doi.org/10.1007/978-3-540-74619-5_12

59. Sun, S., Hu, L., Wang, P., Qiao, K., Ma, X., Song, L.: Automatic security evaluation and (related-key) differential characteristic search: application to SIMON, PRESENT, LBlock, DES(L) and other bit-oriented block ciphers. In: Sarkar, P., Iwata, T. (eds.) ASIACRYPT 2014. Part I. LNCS, vol. 8873, pp. 158–178. Springer, Heidelberg (2014). https://doi.org/10.1007/978-3-662-45611-8_9

60. Suzaki, T., Minematsu, K.: Improving the generalized Feistel. In: Hong, S., Iwata, T. (eds.) FSE 2010. LNCS, vol. 6147, pp. 19–39. Springer, Heidelberg (2010). https://doi.org/10.1007/978-3-642-13858-4_2

61. Suzaki, T., Minematsu, K., Morioka, S., Kobayashi, E.: TWINE: a lightweight block cipher for multiple platforms. In: Knudsen, L.R., Wu, H. (eds.) SAC 2012. LNCS, vol. 7707, pp. 339–354. Springer, Heidelberg (2013). https://doi.org/10.1007/978-3-642-35999-6_22

62. Todo, Y.: Structural evaluation by generalized integral property. In: Oswald, E., Fischlin, M. (eds.) EUROCRYPT 2015. Part I. LNCS, vol. 9056, pp. 287–314. Springer, Heidelberg (2015). https://doi.org/10.1007/978-3-662-46800-5_12

63. Wingers, L.: SUPERCOP: SUPERCOP-20190110/crypto_stream/simon128128ctr/avx2 (2019). https://bench.cr.yp.to/supercop/supercop-20190110.tar.xz

64. Wu, W., Zhang, L.: LBlock: a lightweight block cipher. In: Lopez, J., Tsudik, G. (eds.) ACNS 2011. LNCS, vol. 6715, pp. 327–344. Springer, Heidelberg (2011). https://doi.org/10.1007/978-3-642-21554-4_19

65. Xiang, Z., Zhang, W., Bao, Z., Lin, D.: Applying MILP method to searching integral distinguishers based on division property for 6 lightweight block ciphers. In: Cheon, J.H., Takagi, T. (eds.) ASIACRYPT 2016. Part I. LNCS, vol. 10031, pp. 648–678. Springer, Heidelberg (2016). https://doi.org/10.1007/978-3-662-53887-6_24

66. Zheng, Y., Matsumoto, T., Imai, H.: On the construction of block ciphers provably secure and not relying on any unproved hypotheses. In: Brassard, G. (ed.) CRYPTO 1989. LNCS, vol. 435, pp. 461–480. Springer, New York (1990). https://doi.org/10.1007/0-387-34805-0_42

Side Channel Attacks

Subsampling and Knowledge Distillation on Adversarial Examples: New Techniques for Deep Learning Based Side Channel Evaluations

Aron Gohr[✉], Sven Jacob, and Werner Schindler

Bundesamt für Sicherheit in der Informationstechnik (BSI),
Godesberger Allee 185-189, 53175 Bonn, Germany
{Aron.Gohr,Sven.Jacob,Werner.Schindler}@bsi.bund.de

Abstract. This paper has four main goals. First, we show how we solved the CHES 2018 AES challenge in the contest using essentially a linear classifier combined with a SAT solver and a custom error correction method. This part of the paper has previously appeared in a preprint by the current authors (e-print report 2019/094) and later as a contribution to a preprint write-up of the solutions by the winning teams (e-print report 2019/860).

Second, we develop a novel deep neural network architecture for side-channel analysis that *completely breaks* the AES challenge, allowing for fairly reliable key recovery with just a single trace on the unknown-device part of the CHES challenge (with an expected success rate of roughly 70% if about 100 CPU hours are allowed for the equation solving stage of the attack). This solution significantly improves upon all previously published solutions of the AES challenge, including our baseline linear solution.

Third, we consider the question of leakage attribution for both the classifier we used in the challenge and for our deep neural network. Direct inspection of the weight vector of our machine learning model yields a lot of information on the implementation for our linear classifier. For the deep neural network, we test three other strategies (occlusion of traces; inspection of adversarial changes; knowledge distillation) and find that these can yield information on the leakage essentially equivalent to that gained by inspecting the weights of the simpler model.

Fourth, we study the properties of adversarially generated side-channel traces for our model. Partly reproducing recent computer vision work by Ilyas et al. in our application domain, we find that a linear classifier that generalizes to an unseen device *much better than our linear baseline* can be trained using only adversarial examples (*fresh random keys, adversarially perturbed traces*) for our deep neural network. This gives a new way of extracting human-usable knowledge from a deep side channel model while also yielding insights on adversarial examples in an application domain where relatively few sources of spurious correlations between data and labels exist.

The experiments described in this paper can be reproduced using code available at https://github.com/agohr/ches2018.

© Springer Nature Switzerland AG 2021
O. Dunkelman et al. (Eds.): SAC 2020, LNCS 12804, pp. 567–592, 2021.
https://doi.org/10.1007/978-3-030-81652-0_22

Keywords: Power analysis · Machine learning · Deep learning · SAT solver

1 Introduction, Related Work and Contributions

1.1 Introduction

As an additional event to CHES 2018, Riscure ran a side-channel contest that was designed to pit *Deep Learning* against *Classical Profiling*. The goal of the competition was to break implementations of DES, AES and RSA based only on published examples of power traces and corresponding secret keys while implementation details were kept secret. In total, six challenges were published: two sets of attack traces were published for each primitive, one featuring traces from a physical device already represented in the training data set (*known device* setting)[1] and one consisting of traces captured from a device *not* known to the participants (*unknown device*). For each sub-challenge, winners were determined by being the first to submit a solution to sets of challenge traces posted a few days prior to CHES 2018. A recent preprint by Hu et al. [4] describes the winning solutions and gives some context to the challenge.

1.2 Related Work

Previous Solutions of the CHES Challenges. Of the solutions reported so far, most used classical side-channel analysis and none used deep learning:

- The DES challenges were won by team *hut8* (Yongbo Hu, Yeyang Zheng, Pengwei Feng, Lirui Liu and Chen Zhang) using a non-profiled technique, essentially CPA [4] followed by brute-force search for the remaining key bits.
- The AES challenges were won by team *AGSJWS* by a machine learning approach using ridge regression – a form of linear regression with l_2-regularization – to derive the hamming weights of all subkeys during key expansion combined with a SAT-based strategy to solve for the exact key value and correct some remaining errors in the subkey guesses [4]. Later on, Damm, Freud and Klein combined classical profiling techniques (template attacks) with custom code to solve for the key [3] to arrive at a solution with similar performance characteristics.
- The RSA challenges were won by team *hut8*. Their solution is essentially a template attack combined with some brute-force error correction.

In all of the challenges, the number of traces available for training was fairly low: in total 30000 training and 10000 test traces each were supplied for the DES and AES implementations, while the RSA training dataset consisted of only 30 training and 10 test traces (however, these were captured at a very high resolution, so a lot of data was available). Together with the strong linear

---

[1] To be precise, it was known which traces in the training dataset correspond to the challenge device, but no further details about this device were revealed.

leakage already shown in [3,4], this led Damm et al. to conjecture that it would be difficult to showcase a benefit of deep learning based methods on the AES challenge [3].

Artificial Neural Networks. A proper introduction to the machine learning techniques used in this work is beyond the scope of the present work; we refer the interested reader to current textbooks, for instance [1,19]. We will, however, try to qualitatively introduce some of the intuitions and concepts relevant to this paper in Appendix A.

Deep Neural Networks for Side-Channel Analysis. Several prior works have used deep convolutional neural networks for side channel analysis [8–10,18,25]. The neural architectures used have mostly been inspired by deep convolutional networks used in other one-dimensional signal processing tasks such as audio analysis. This is also true for [25], who were the first to successfully apply deep residual networks to side-channel analysis.

The present work departs from this by using a network architecture that is guided by the idea that an approximate extraction of the target variables should (especially in the case of large traces, i.e. traces with high temporal resolution) often be possible already from a downsampled version of the side-channel signal and that a classifier that tries to extract the sensitive variables from all of the data given should treat different downsampled versions of the original signal quite similarly.

Intuitively, this can be viewed as a very natural symmetry property of the side channel prediction task (akin to e.g. translation invariance of the classification target in the image or speech recognition domains). Incorporating known symmetry properties into the design of a machine learning model is regularly very useful for finding a high-performing predictor, because it drastically lowers the number of weights in the model and the ability of the model to memorize training data without (provided that the symmetry property actually holds) excluding models with high predictive power from the search space over which model optimization is being performed.

Leakage Attribution Using Deep Neural Networks. Leakage attribution for deep neural networks was recently studied by Hettwer, Gehrer and Güneysu [18]. They explored three different strategies for attributing leakage using deep neural networks and discovered ways to use leakage attribution techniques for improved side-channel key recovery. Our work adds more data on one attribution method they tried (occlusion of parts of the trace) and suggests two new strategies for leakage analysis (generation of adversarial examples and knowledge distillation on adversarial examples).

1.3 Main Contributions

We show in this work that deep neural networks can significantly outperform the solutions of the AES challenge so far presented. We propose a simple, scalable neural network design that allows us to directly recover the Hamming weights of the subkey bytes of all AES round keys of the attacked implementation from a single power trace with high success rate. The main idea behind our design is that subsampled parts at small offsets to each other of a trace acquired at a high resolution should be treated approximately alike. We show that our design gains considerable power especially if very deep networks are used. Appendix A contains further information on the intuitions behind our network architecture.

As in previous solutions to the AES challenge, a large equation system with a small number of erroneous equations is solved to derive the key. This is done by dropping some equations at random.

We then turn to the problem of leakage attribution and find that *generation of adversarial examples* seems to be a very useful strategy for attributing leakage in our example. Studying adversarial examples on our problem further, we show that a linear classifier that mimics the behaviour of our main network on an adversarially generated dataset generalizes much better to the unknown device challenge of the CHES contest than training on the original data. This partly reproduces work that has been previously done in the image domain [16] in a setting where data acquisition and labelling is much less likely to introduce spurious correlations between data and labels than for images.

2   Our Attack on the AES Implementation

2.1   Data

The organizers provided four sets of power traces of a masked AES-128 implementation together with key, input and output data. Following the notations and conventions of [2,4], we will in the sequel denote these sets of power traces as Set 1 to Set 4. Set 1 to Set 3 used fresh random keys for each trace and we denote the corresponding lists of keys as Keys 1 to Keys 3. The power traces of Set 4 were traces for a single shared key. We denote this single key as Key 4. Each of these sets contained 10000 power traces and keys, and all of these power traces came from three devices A, B, C (Set 1: A, Set 2: B, Set 3: B, Set 4: C).

In the competition, two additional sets of power traces were released, which we will call Set 5 and Set 6. Set 5 contained power traces from the known device C, while Set 6 was obtained from an unknown device D. Both of these additional sets of traces used a single key each, which we will denote by Key 5 and Key 6.

For the purposes of training, we generated a training data set (T, K) consisting of a randomly shuffled union of Set 1, Set 2 and Set 3[2]. Here, T denotes the set of training traces and K denotes the set of corresponding Hamming weight vectors of expanded AES keys. The i-th trace in T is denoted by t_i and the i-th key (or more precisely, the vector of Hamming weights of the corresponding AES key) in K is denoted by $k_i \in \{0, \ldots, 8\}^{176}$.

---

[2] Shuffling of the training set is important here, since we will use the *last* 3000 traces of T as our validation set to monitor training progress and control learning rate drops.

In Sect. 3 we will also introduce a training dataset where the keys k_i have been exchanged for (expanded Hamming weight vectors of) freshly generated keys k_i' and the traces t_i have been replaced by subtly altered traces t_i' to make our deep neural network predict the new keys. This *adversarially perturbed training set* will be denoted by (T', K') in the sequel.

In the sequel, hw(x) will for any 8-bit value x denote the *Hamming weight* of x, $\oplus$ will denote binary addition and S will be the AES S-box.

2.2 Attack Overview

Most side-channel attacks against AES implementations target the round function. Particularly the first and last round are attractive targets, since they may allow the adversary to see the results of combining the key with known plaintext or ciphertext. In the setting where the Hamming weights of these operations are leaking, this gives the adversary fairly straightforward ways of combining the results of many measurements to efficiently recover the actual key values even in the presence of significant noise.

After some preliminary studies, we came to the conclusion that the CHES challenge datasets have a masked round function but that the key schedule is not masked [2]. Basically, this conclusion is based on a comparison between Set 3 and Set 4 since both sets of power traces were generated by the same device, but Set 4 uses only one key. If the key expansion is non-randomized – as is the case here – in Set 4 the key expansion processes the same data for all traces. Indeed, calculating the empirical variance of measured current at each time step in both the Set 3 and Set 4 data, we found a pattern of dips in the Set 4 variance that was consistent with leakage from a non-randomized key expansion where the subkeys for round i are derived just in time for round i. This naturally leads to the idea of attacking the key schedule instead of the round function.

Our attack then follows a simple general plan: given a trace t, we try to guess the Hamming weights of all 176 AES subkey bytes (16 bytes for each of the 11 round keys). For each subkey, two plausible values of its Hamming weight are guessed.

Using these weight guesses and a set of equations describing the AES key schedule, we then solve for the key using a SAT solver[6]. This of course works only if the SAT solver gets a consistent system of equations to solve. In order to be able to tolerate a few wrong constraints, we randomly drop all constraints on the Hamming weight of 20 subkey bytes at each attempt of solving the system.

2.3 Predicting the Hamming Weight

Overall Prediction Strategy. We first decimate the traces by a factor of ten, i.e. of the 650000 data points in each trace, we keep only every tenth, thereby obtaining traces of 65000 points each. We did this mainly to save memory and computation time during training. For the linear models discussed in this article, this step also reduces the number of parameters to fit, thereby reducing the potential for overfitting somewhat.

For each reduced trace t we then calculate $\theta(t) \in \mathbb{R}^{176}$. Here, θ can be any suitable mathematical function; in the competition, we used an affine θ, determining the relevant matrix weights and offsets by *ridge regression*. In this contribution, our main predictor uses a deep neural network trained to minimize *mean squared error* (MSE) loss against the real Hamming weights on the training dataset. We interpret θ_i as a guess of the Hamming weight of b_i, where b_i is the i-th subkey byte produced by the AES key schedule.

If we have multiple traces, we run the predictor on each trace and average the predictions. This gives a vector of real-valued subkey predictions $\beta \in \mathbb{R}^{176}$, which is the final output of the Hamming weight guessing phase.

Baseline Model. As a baseline model, we fitted an affine function

$$\lambda : \mathbb{R}^{65000} \to \mathbb{R}^{176}, x \mapsto Ax + b$$

using ridge regression with regularization parameter $\alpha = 2^{14}$ to the 30000 traces and keys contained in Set 1, Set 2 and Set 3.

The regularization parameter was chosen using grid-search among small positive and negative powers of two, with generalized cross-validation being used to pick the best value. Before performing our final training run, we tested this training strategy on the union of Set 1 and Set 2, holding out Set 3 as a validation set coming from a different device; performance was sufficient that we were confident that we would be able to master the challenge on Set 6 given our overall solving strategy. The baseline model is the model we used to solve the AES challenges in the competition. For details we refer the interested reader to [2].

Deep Neural Network
Overview. In order to guess the 176 Hamming weights of interest, we first create 100 sub-sampled traces with 100-fold decimation at offsets $0, 1, \ldots, 99$ from each reduced power trace (consisting of $65,000$ data points) given and perform a batch-normalization. For each of these subsampled and batch-normalized traces, we then produce a first approximation to the weight prediction by applying a small neural network very similar in design to the baseline model. Subsequent layers of our neural network then refine this prediction, taking into account more non-linear features as well as information from neighbouring sub-traces. Finally, a joint prediction is produced by averaging the prediction vectors coming from all 100 sub-samplings of the given trace.

Preprocessing. Given a trace $t \in \mathbb{R}^{65000}$, we first map it into $\mathbb{R}^{100 \times 650}$, keeping the rows of this matrix contiguous in the original trace.

Overall Network Structure. Our neural network follows the structure of a *deep residual neural network*. Basically, it consists of a chain of *residual blocks*, wherein each *block* is a shallow neural network (in our case, a batch normalization layer followed by a convolutional layer) that takes as input the sum of the outputs of the two preceding blocks and produces an output of its own which is likewise passed to the next block. This network structure has been originally introduced for image recognition tasks in [11], but has since been successfully applied in a number of other domains.

The final residual block of our network outputs a real-valued matrix of size 100×176. This matrix is then sent through an average pooling layer which simply calculates the average of the row-vectors of the matrix. The resulting vector $\beta \in \mathbb{R}^{176}$ is the output vector of our neural network. A version of our network with two residual blocks is illustrated in Fig. 1.

To the best of our knowledge, the only previous uses of deep *residual* neural network architectures for side-channel analysis are given in [12,25]. While in particular Zhou and Standaert [25] showed a quite successful application of a residual network architecture (albeit with only three residual blocks) on a side channel task, both networks are quite different from ours. Deep residual neural networks have also been used quite recently in block cipher cryptanalysis [13].

Networks very similar to those described in the current paper have been used with good results in the submissions to the CHES Challenge 2020 as well [23].

Convolutional Layers. The initial convolutional layer is of width one, i.e. each convolutional layer processes one length-650 slice of the original trace independently of all the others. The convolutional layers in the subsequent residual blocks are all of width 3. Accordingly, each filter sees three output slices of the previous layer. All convolutional layers use the *same* padding, meaning that the number of slices is preserved by the convolutions. In the main residual blocks, each convolution has 176 channels, with each channel corresponding to one subkey byte. All convolutional layers use rectifier activations.

Source Code. A full implementation, including a fully trained version of our largest network, can be found in the supplementary data to this paper at https:// github.com/agohr/ches2018.

Network Size. In our final model, we use 19 residual blocks following the initial convolution layer; in our testing, both network loss on validation data and number of top-2 errors on the Set 6 challenge data decreased with number of residual blocks, indicating good scaling with network size. Table 1 gives relevant data for exploratory training runs of 1000 epochs each. We did not test if this trend continues further past the largest tested size. Our final model has $\approx 1.9 \cdot 10^6$ parameters and a total of 62 layers after the input layer (including reformatting, batch normalization, addition and pooling layers). The difference between the performance of shallower and deeper models of this type is in our tests crucial for solving the challenge in the single-trace setting with high success rate.

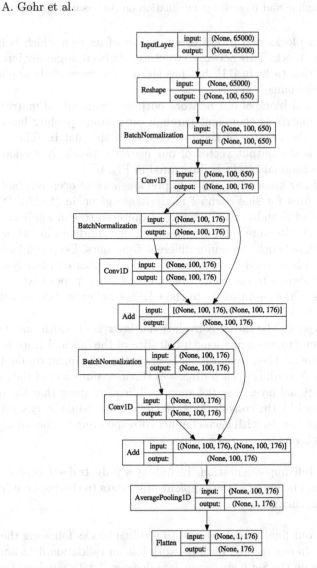

Fig. 1. An instance of our main neural network architecture with two residual blocks. The main network used in our attack on the CHES challenge has the same structure, but 19 residual blocks.

Training the Network. Training was performed on the shuffled concatenation of all training datasets, i.e. on (T, K). For this purpose, power traces and keys were extracted from the files published by Riscure. The keys were then expanded according to the AES key schedule and the Hamming weights of all subkeys

Table 1. Network performance as a function of network size. All networks here given follow the architecture and training regime of our main deep neural network predictor. However, the length of these test runs was only 1000 epochs instead of the full 5000 used in the final training run. The final training run produced a slightly better network, with an average of 3.144 top-2 errors on Set 6. Validation loss is computed on a subset of the union of Set 1, Set 2 and Set 3. Training took roughly 25 s per epoch for our largest network on a computer equipped with a GTX 1080 Ti graphics card, so a full training run with 5000 epochs can be completed in under two days.

Number of residual blocks						
	1	2	5	10	15	19
Validation loss	0.153	0.0934	0.0792	0.0787	0.0769	0.0749
Mean top-2 errors, Set 6	8.334	4.913	4.069	4.195	3.41	3.374
Median top-2 errors, Set 6	8	5	4	4	3	3

were stored in an array of size 30000×176. The traces were preprocessed by ten-fold decimation and the resulting input matrix of size 30000×65000 was reformatted to fit the input layer of our neural network. The data (preprocessed traces and expanded AES keys) was then randomly shuffled and the last 3000 traces and keys after shuffling out of the total 30000 were withheld as validation data. Training on the remaining 27000 traces was performed for 5000 epochs using the Adam optimizer [14] with a batch size of 100 against MSE loss with l_2-regularization (with regularization parameter $\alpha = 10^{-5}$). Initially, Adam was run with default parameters in Keras [15]. Subsequently, validation loss was used to monitor the progress of training, and the learning rate was halved whenever 50 epochs had passed without improvement. The best model by validation loss was saved to disk.

Testing Network Performance. Challenge dataset 6 was used as our primary test of network performance. On the positive side, this is data gathered on a device not seen in training. On the negative side, the test set *only covers one key*. However, testing on Device C would have meant training on only two different devices and at most 20000 traces. Our validation performance and our Set 4 performance both are much better than our test performance, indicating that the model will work for a wide range of key values.

2.4 Combining and Post-processing Trace Predictions

If multiple traces for the same key are given, we predict hamming weight values individually based on each trace and average the results[3]. For the baseline classifier, one could equivalently average the traces and then predict. For our deep neural network, averaging five traces actually leads to a drop in the rate of

---

[3] We tried other ways to combine outputs, such as taking the median of predictions. This did not yield significantly different results.

error-free prediction and only to modest improvements in the success rates with one to four errors. This is natural, since averaging *traces* may destroy features useful to a nonlinear classifier. Averaging of *predictions* works very well, as can be seen from Table 3.

In order to turn our predictions into constraints on an equation system for the AES key schedule, we truncate neural network outputs to the range $[0.01, 7.99]$ because byte Hamming weights are between 0 and 8. Then we set as constraint C_i that the Hamming weight of the i-th subkey k_i is one of $\lfloor \theta_i \rfloor, \lceil \theta_i \rceil$.

2.5   Full Key Recovery

Key Recovery. To recover the key given the information extracted by our neural network, we follow the exact same strategy as [2]. The neural network phase of our attack provides as output a list of constraints of the form $k_i \in \{x_i, x_i + 1\}$ for some $x_i \in \{0, 1, \ldots, 6, 7\}$. We transform these constraints as well as the AES key expansion into CNF clauses and use a SAT solver to find a solution. As some of our constraints may be wrong, each solving run randomly drops 20 of the Hamming weight constraints, in the hopes that this will yield a consistent system of clauses.

Heuristic Motivation. The probability that a uniformly distributed byte has Hamming weight m or $m+1$ is $\leq 126/256 < 0.5$ (with the probability of $126/256$ being reached for $m \in \{3, 4\}$). Hence each top-2 guess provides more than 1 bit information. A straight-forward (admittedly heuristic) argumentation suggests that 156 top-2 guesses from attack Phase I should determine the AES-128 key uniquely. This conclusion matches with our experiments.

Implementation Choices. The Pseudoalgorithm below sketches our attack.

Pseudoalgorithm

```
        Determine 176 top-2 guesses (Attack Phase I)
        Repeat (Attack Phase II)
        - select randomly 20 top-2 guesses ('drop-out')
        - input the remaining 156 top-2 guesses into the SAT
          solver
        - terminate the SAT solver if it is unlikely that a
          solution exists
        until the SAT solver finds the key
```

As SAT solver, we used CryptoMinisat 5.0.1 [6] via the python interface given by the pycryptosat package (version 0.1.4) [7]. Search on a particular SAT instance was terminated if the number of conflicts encountered during search exceeded 300000 (thus limiting the size of the search tree explored by the SAT solver). This took on average 20 s on our machine (using a single logical core of a machine with six physical i7-6850K cores and 128 GB of RAM). The neural network was run on a GTX-1080 Ti graphics card on the same machine, but would not have added significant wall time to the overall computation even on a single CPU[4].

Building the CNF. To obtain a CNF of the AES key schedule, we followed a very simple strategy. First, we created a function that takes as input the truth table of any boolean function and outputs its CNF. We then decomposed the AES key expansion into a sequence of S-box applications, shifts and bitwise additions; each of these operations was then defined as a concatenation of boolean functions. All of the boolean functions appearing in this representation have at most 8 input bits, so their conversion to CNF is easy. The final equation system holds all the subkey bytes and some helper variables that contain the result of applying the AES S-box to some subkey bytes.

The constraints on the hamming weights of subkey bytes are likewise treated just as arbitrary boolean functions and automatically converted to CNF via their truth table.

The exact number of clauses produced by this simple CNF strategy varies depending on the values of the subkey guesses and on dropout, but was generally around 120000 for Set 6 traces with our deep neural network as classifier and a dropout of 20 constraints. On a single thread of a single machine, consistent systems were frequently solved within about 20 s.

It is clear that a much smaller CNF could have been obtained, primarily by choosing a smarter strategy to encode the S-box and the weight constraints. We conjecture that a more compact representation of the equation system would reduce the amount of computation required by the SAT solver.

2.6 Results

Attack Complexity Estimate. The complexity analysis of our attack as a function of the number of errors within the top-2 guesses given by the network is basically the same as in [2]. Given m errors in the Hamming weight top-2 guesses, at each attempt at solving we eliminate all errors with probability $p_{good} = \frac{\binom{20}{m}}{\binom{176}{m}}$. Depending on the settings of the SAT solver, there is then a constant probability p_{solve} that the SAT solver will solve the equation system obtained within the search limits given. In total, at each try, we obtain the solution with probability $p_{win} = p_{solve} \cdot p_{good}$. The expected number of solving attempts is the reciprocal of this value.

Known Device Setting. The known device challenge (attack traces from device C) was easily solved even in the single-trace setting already by our baseline solution as well as the template attack developed in [3]. Our neural network still improves on these solutions: it yields error-free top2-guesses for the 176 subkey

---

[4] Note that in order to solve the Set 6 challenge, the neural network will need to be invoked for at most two or three traces.

byte hamming weights for 916 of the 1000 traces in Set 5. A detailed comparison of the performance of different solutions may be found in Table 2.

Table 2. Set 5 (known device challenge): cumulative distribution of the number of top-2 errors on Set 5 when guessing all 176 Hamming weights based on N traces using the deep neural network of this paper (CNN), the single-layer perceptron baseline (base), the template attack of [3], and the base solution trained on adversarially perturbed samples (Adv). Numbers given reflect the measured percentage of traces (trace-pairs in the case of two-trace prediction) within Set 5 for which the methods compared yield at most the given number of errors.

Number of false top-2 guesses					
	0	≤ 1	≤ 2	≤ 3	≤ 4
This paper, $N = 1$, CNN	91.6%	98.2%	99.8%	100%	100%
This paper, $N = 1$, base	50.7%	79.5%	92.0%	97.5%	99.4%
Template [3], $N = 1$	2.4%	8.7%	24.1%	40.1%	60.8%
Adv, $N = 1$	25.9%	58.8%	79.0%	92.6%	97.5%

Unknown Device Performance. In the sequel, we focus solely on the unknown device challenge (Set 6).

We divided the 1,000 attack traces from Set 6 into non-overlapping subsets of $N \in \{1, 2\}$ power traces. Table 3 shows the empirical cumulative distribution of false top-2 guesses for these sample sizes and compares them to our baseline solution, a solution similar to our baseline solution that was trained on synthetic data (see the next section for details), and the template attack in [3].

Cost of the SAT Solving Stage. For the baseline model, running Cryptominisat with a conflict limit of 300000 does not lose a significant number of error-free problem instances (i.e., $p_{solve} \approx 1$). Unfortunately, however, this finding cannot be reproduced with the constraint systems guessed by our deep neural network. We find that solvable instances very frequently exceed the conflict limit, but that it is not difficult to find a solvable instance within the limit by trying again with fresh drop-out and that a modest upwards adjustment of the conflict limit would mostly fix this. However, this means that the average time to solve a satisfiable SAT instance of roughly 20 s [2] cannot be upheld in our deep neural network based solution. The smaller number of guessing errors has to be 'paid' for by longer execution times of the SAT solver. In order to estimate p_{solve}, we ran the SAT solver on the Hamming weight guesses corresponding to the first 100 traces of Set 6. In order to produce satisfiable instances, we dropped out a random selection of 20 guesses in each instance but made sure that all wrong guesses were included in the dropout. This resulted in 34 solutions, leading to a rough estimate of $p_{solve} \approx 1/3$ with our settings. Computing wall time on a single core of our machine ranged from 5.3 s to 27.6 s, with a median of

Table 3. Set 6 (unknown device challenge): Cumulative distribution of the number of top-2 errors on Set 6 when guessing all 176 Hamming weights based on N traces using the deep neural network of this paper (CNN), the single-layer perceptron baseline (base), the template attack of [3], and the base solution trained on adversarially perturbed samples designed to make the deep neural network predict fresh random keys (Adv). Numbers given reflect the measured percentage of traces (trace-pairs in the case of two-trace prediction) within Set 6 for which the methods compared yield less than the given number of errors.

Number of false top-2 guesses					
	0	≤ 1	≤ 2	≤ 3	≤ 4
This paper, $N = 1$, CNN	7.4%	24.3%	43.0%	61.9%	76.0%
This paper, $N = 1$, base	0%	0%	0.6%	1.9%	5.6%
Template [3], $N = 1$	0%	0.1%	0.6%	2.1%	4.7%
Adv, $N = 1$	0.2%	0.5%	2.6%	7.1%	15.3%
CNN, $N = 2$	52,4%	83.8%	95.4%	98.8%	100%
Base, $N = 2$	1%	8%	24%	41%	57%
Template [3], $N = 2$	1.4%	9.8%	25%	44.8%	62.6%
Adv, $N = 2$	5.8%	23.4%	48.8%	65.6%	80.6%

11.6 s for solved instances and 16.6 s for unsolved instances. Each of the first ten traces was solved within at most five attempts of solving a consistent system of constraints, which is in agreement with the claim of our complexity analysis that varying the randomness in the dropout is sufficient to obtain constraint systems that are solved within the conflict limit. The mean computational effort spent on *inconsistent* systems was in our trials slightly lower than the time used for consistent unsolved instances, since some inconsistent instances are solved very quickly. It seems reasonable to overestimate the time per constraint system with one minute. Under this assumption, solving an instance with up to 4 top-2 errors will take about 100 core-hours on our machine.

The finding that our neural model produces constraints that are harder to solve than the ones returned by the baseline model is likely due to the deep neural network making on average more cautious guesses (closer to the median 4). For instance, on Set 6, the top-2 guesses produced by the deep model contain on average 1.6 bits of information per subkey byte, whereas the baseline model produces slightly more specific guesses, at 1.7 bits of information per subkey byte (empirical results).

When 156 subkey bytes are guessed, this means that the constraints upon the key schedule provided by our network in expectation contain about 15.6 bits less information than the baseline model. It is logical that this will result in a higher workload on the SAT solving stage.

Overall Attack Cost. On the whole, we can solve most of the traces in Set 6 within less than a day of computing time on a single i7-6850 core. Table 4 gives further details.

Table 4. Expected number of trials in Attack Phase II until a consistent system of constraints is found and the expected execution time depending on the number of false top-2 guesses (among all 176 top-2 guesses). Note that roughly two out of three consistent systems are not solved within the conflict limit. The expected time to solution already takes this into account.

Number of false top-2 guesses					
	0	1	2	3	4
$E(\#$ systems of eq.$)$	1	8.8	78	682	5997
$E($exec. time$)$	1 min	9 min	78 min	11 h	100 h

We mention that further improvements might be possible by optimizing the size of the dropout and, as already pointed out, by a smarter way to derive a CNF.

3   Adversarial Examples

Fooling Neural Networks. The study of *adversarial examples* for neural networks was initiated by Szegedy et al. in 2014 [24]. They found that state of the art image recognition models could be made to output misclassifications by small, highly targeted perturbations of the input data and that these adversarial examples generalize to a surprising degree across model architectures. Since then, a large number of followup works have appeared examining this phenomenon; the original and the manipulated input data can often hardly be distinguished by human eyes [20]. Adversarial examples pose a real-world threat to the security of some machine-learning applications. In [22], for example, a face recognition system is fooled by glasses with coloured frames.

It may be surprising that we consider adversarial examples in the context of side-channel analysis. We did it for several reasons. First of all, it is interesting by itself. Unlike e.g. images, side-channel data is complex to interpret, but is captured, produced and labelled by a completely mechanized process. This makes side-channel tasks in some ways a very complex toy domain for supervised machine learning and allows us to study adversarial examples in a setting where some potential confounding factors present in many other application domains have been removed.

Secondly, as a byproduct we obtain a new model that differs from our baseline solution only in the model weights. Interestingly, although trained on completely invented data it is *more efficient* than the baseline classifier on Set 6.

Thirdly, studying the adversarial examples provides an additional technique to probe the neural network for information on the design of the targeted implementation and the nature of its leakage (c.f. Sect. 4). Understanding the leakage model or simply distilling the leakage model into a simpler form might lead to better conventional attacks (e.g. more efficient templates or more suitable vector subspaces for the stochastic approach).

Overall Results. We found that our neural network is very sensitive to generation of adversarial examples. Using projected gradient descent in a small l_2 ball (radius 150) around a given trace, we can easily make the neural network output the Hamming weight vector of any desired AES key; distances between traces e.g. in Set 4 are on average around 600, so the radius in which adversarial examples can be found is very small compared to the distance between real traces[5]. Much smaller adversarial perturbations suffice if we want to only cause a small change in the output, e.g. change just a single Hamming weight. However, we were unsuccessful in generating adversarial examples that change some target output byte by only changing parts of the trace that cannot plausibly affect the target byte. For instance, we could not change the Hamming weights of the very first subkey byte by altering (within a small l_2 ball around the original trace) exclusively trace points after step 15000.

Specifically, we generated an adversarial version T' of the training database T by executing the following steps:

1. We generated 30000 fresh random AES keys k_i' (independent from the correct keys that belong to the traces), expanded them, and determined the Hamming weights of all subkeys. In the sequel, we identify the keys with their Hamming weight vectors.
2. We performed 50 iterations of projected gradient descent on the input data with normalised gradients and step size 0.01 within an l_2 ball of size 150 on each trace of the input database, minimizing the mean square error of the network output with respect to the desired new set of keys. In other words, here the power traces (instead of the weights) are adapted step by step.
3. We rounded the resulting trace values to the nearest 8-bit signed integer in order to make sure that the synthetic traces so obtained had the same format as the original traces. We denote the i-th trace in T' with t_i'.

In this *adversarial training database*, in about 85% of the traces our neural network predicts the target Hamming weights (i.e., of the randomly assigned key bytes) without top-2 errors.

The examples do somewhat transfer to our baseline classifier, which produces 32 top-2 errors on the adversarial examples in the median, far less than the 86.625 top-2 errors expected under optimal blind guessing (for constant top-2 guesses $\{3, 4\}$ or $\{4, 5\}$), standard deviation ≈ 6.6 top-2 errors. Nonetheless, some

---

[5] Note that the traces in Set 4 all share the same key, and that a ball of radius 150 units in $\mathbb{R}^{65000}$ covers a volume a factor of 2^{130000} smaller than a ball of radius 600 units.

of the adversarial examples retain a fair part of the original leakage signal: in 627 out of the 30000 cases, the baseline classifier produces less than 66 errors in predicting the keys k_i (3σ below expectation). In 127 of these cases, the deep neural network reconstructs k_i' with four top-2 errors or less, sufficient to allow full recovery. This shows that there is significant disagreement on the adversarial examples between the baseline classifier and the deep neural network and that in some cases, the baseline finds nontrivial leakage pointing towards the original keys in the adversarial examples even though the deep neural network is able to recover the adversarial target key.

Training a Side-Channel Attack Exclusively on Adversarial Examples. Recent research by Ilyas et al. suggests that adversarial perturbations sometimes change some meaningful information occurring in natural data that is imperceptible to people [16]. With side-channel data, we reasoned that the very strongly localized nature of features should make the direct inspection of adversarial perturbations for meaning easier than in more standard domains. We therefore tested whether one of the experiments in [16] can be reproduced on the CHES challenge side-channel data.

Concretely, we trained a copy *Adv* of the baseline predictor on the adversarial training database (T', K') as constructed above[6]. We then tested the *Adv* predictor on the unchanged Set 6 as well as on Set 4. On Set 6, its performance in terms of top-2 accuracy is *much better than baseline* but on Set 4 (predictably) it did not reach the level of the baseline predictor. The *Adv* predictor outperformed the template attack from [3] for both the non-portability challenge and the portability challenge. The baseline solution is superior to the template attack only for the non-portability challenge. This shows that even a very simple classifier can extract a lot of useful information from the adversarial training dataset. For details, see Tables 2 and 3.

We also checked that there is a part of the leakage signal that is robust to adversarial perturbation[7]. To this end, we trained a version of the baseline classifier to predict the original keys K from the adversarially perturbed traces T'. This worked well enough that the resulting system could solve Set 6 challenge given all 1000 traces, although our other predictors were much better.

Explaining the Performance of the Adversarial Examples Predictor. It might at first sight seem surprising that a linear predictor trained to predict *random keys* on an adversarially changed version of the original training dataset can quite drastically *outperform* both our baseline solution and a dedicated template attack in terms of generalizing to unseen devices. One attempt to explain this finding is to regard the process of training the Adv predictor as a form of knowledge distillation from our deep neural network to a linear classifier, with

---

[6] This means that we performed Ridge regression with the same hyperparameters as for the baseline predictor to predict K' given T'.

[7] This is not obvious for side-channel data, as useful features come from small parts of the trace.

the linear predictor then inheriting some of the generalizing ability of the deep neural network.

To test this idea, we trained a linear predictor using the same settings as the baseline to predict deep neural network outputs given the training traces T, with and without adding a small amount of normally distributed noise. These experiments resulted in classifiers with a similar performance profile to baseline. A second run of the construction of (T', K') with a different set K' of random keys, on the other hand, resulted in a version of the *Adv* predictor that was even stronger than the run reported here. Hence, training on the adversarially generated data reproducibly led to better unknown device performance than simple knowledge distillation.

We consider this partial reproduction of the results of [16] interesting because the side-channel analysis setting eliminates some sources of not adversarially robust features that may be present e.g. in the image domain. Basically, it could be that the fairly complicated process in which images are acquired and labelled introduces subtle hints as to the contents of an image into the image itself that e.g. a robot exploring the world naturally would not have access to. For instance, if images of aquatic animals in ImageNet have a tendency to having been captured by underwater photographic equipment while images of cats do not, this could conceivably be a source of non-robust predictive features in the ImageNet data[8]. In contrast, in the side-channel analysis problem considered in the present paper, all the available data has been produced by the same, fully mechanized process and all available evidence points at the data being very well aligned[9]. In our setting, the data should not contain significant spurious features, i.e. features that have predictive value but are in the wild unrelated to the phenomenon being studied.

Ilyas et al. suggested in [16] that modern image recognition systems successfully use features in images that are not robust to adversarial perturbation and virtually imperceptible to humans, but nonetheless useful for image classification. It is natural to ask whether these features can be explained away as artefacts induced by the image acquisition process. Our work shows similar highly useful non-robust features in an application domain that has comparatively simple and highly mechanized data acquisition and which should therefore be free of such problems. Similar to the case in our domain, it is, however, for instance possible that some non-robust signal in the image domain may be explained by other 'simple' reasons such as detection of very small structures.

---

[8] This idea regarding the source of non-robust features in images is not ours; it is taken from [17] with minor changes.

[9] Sampling is easier and sample collection is even better defined e.g. in cryptanalytic problems, but these have a discrete sample space and it is less clear what adversarial perturbation would mean in this case.

4   Anatomy of Our Classifiers

In order to learn something about the AES implementation used in the contest, we performed several experiments using our baseline, Adv and deep neural network classifiers. First, we examined the weights of our baseline model to see whether anything can be learned from them. Then, we tried to extract similar information from the deep neural network using occlusion and examination of adversarial changes.

Examining the Weights of the Baseline Model. We find that the sixteen bytes of the original key cause a strong power signal in three active regions of the trace, while the remaining bytes of the expanded key have one active region of the trace each. The three active regions for bytes 0 and 1 are shown in Fig. 2.

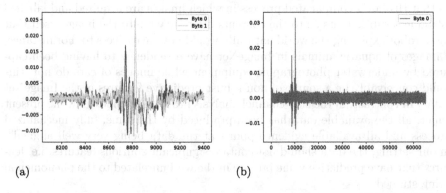

(a)   (b)

Fig. 2. (corresponds to Fig. 2(b), (d) in [2]) Leakage attribution using the baseline model. The horizontal axis denotes the index within a reduced trace. Traces are reduced by using only every tenth data point. The vertical axis gives the numerical weights of our predictor. (a) Weights for the Hamming weight prediction of byte 0 (green) and byte 1 (red) of the AES key in our best classifier. Only the second active region of the trace is shown. (b) All weights for byte 0. The first active region is at the very beginning of the trace. Subkey bytes outside the first round key only have one active region in the trace. (Color figure online)

We see that the active regions for byte 0 and byte 1 have significant overlap. Further, we see that the classifier assumes a negative relationship between the power consumption in some parts of the trace and the Hamming weight of both byte 0 and byte 1.

For some of the relevant points, single-point regression also shows a negative correlation. In other points of the trace, negative coefficients for the prediction of byte 0 seem to coincide with positive values for byte 1. A possible explanation might be that the negative coefficients are an adaptation minimizing crosstalk between the power signatures of consecutive bytes. In general, the curves for single-point regression and the coefficients of our classifier have a similar shape, but do not follow each other entirely.

A more thorough study of the baseline classifier can be found in [2].

Testing the Neural Network Via Partial Occlusion of Traces. In a first attempt to find the sources of leakage picked up by the neural network, we took 1000 traces from T, calculated Hamming weight predictions $h_i \in \mathbb{R}^{176}$ for them using our deep neural network, and then modified the traces by zeroizing the time steps a to $a+100$ in each trace where a was run from 0 to 64900 in steps of size 100. This causes exactly one zeroed time instant in each downsampled slice. We ran our neural network on these modified traces to get new Hamming weight predictions $\tilde{h}_i \in \mathbb{R}^{176}$. We then calculated the average l_2 distance between h_i and $\tilde{h}_i$ and plotted the result. This yielded a rough global map of the leakage (see Fig. 3(d)). By restricting the prediction vector to some chosen subkey bytes before taking the l_2 norm, it is also possible to find out where particular subkey bytes are leaking. This corroborates recent findings of Hettwer, Gehrer and Güneysu [18], who find that occlusion is one viable strategy for using deep neural networks for leakage attribution.

Leakage Attribution by Adversarial Examples. In order to leverage adversarial examples for leakage attribution, we followed two strategies: on the one hand, we examined the weights (affecting the Hamming weight guess for byte 0) of the Adv model in the same way we did with baseline (c.f. Fig. 3(b),(c)). This yielded generally similar information. Upon visual inspection, the weights of the Adv classifier seemed much less smooth than the weights of the baseline classifier. This suggested that the Adv classifier and by extension the deep neural network may use a high-frequency component of the trace signal that is ignored by baseline. We therefore processed the Set 6 traces by a hard low-pass filter, moving the angular cutoff frequency of the low-pass filter in 30 equidistant steps from $\frac{2}{65}\pi$ to $\frac{12}{13}\pi$[10]. We found that baseline and the CNN simply plateaued towards their final performance as the smoothing of the signal was reduced, whereas Adv performance peaked around $\frac{14}{65}\pi$ and then slowly declined towards its level on the original data. Hence, the high-frequency signal components used by Adv are not useful.

We also averaged adversarial perturbations for the first 1000 traces of Set 4, where the target of adversarial optimization was to only increase the predicted Hamming weight of the first subkey byte. Results were qualitatively similar to examining the Adv model.

For details, see Fig. 3.

---

[10] Our low-pass filter for angular frequency $2\pi f$ keeps only the $\lceil N \cdot f \rceil$ lowest-index coefficients of the DFT of the trace signal and their complex conjugates, where N is the size of the reduced traces.

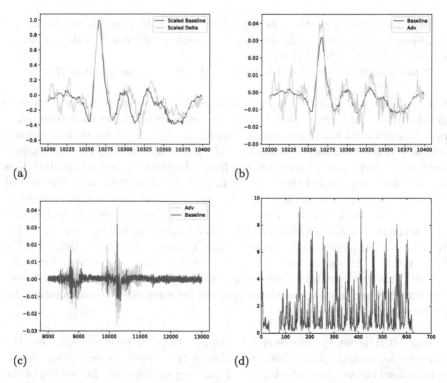

Fig. 3. (All) Leakage Attribution Using the Deep Neural Network. All weights refer to the Hamming weight guess for byte 0 (Figs. (a) to (c)). (a) Average adversarial perturbation Δ for the first 1000 traces of Set 4. The target of the adversary is to increase the Hamming weight prediction of the first subkey byte (byte 0) and leave everything else unchanged. The weights of the baseline classifier and the averaged Δ vector have been rescaled so that their largest absolute value is one. (b) Comparison of the byte 0 coefficients (third active region) of the Adv and baseline predictors. (c) More context for the weights shown in (b). (d) Average l_2 distance between deep neural network output vectors for partially occluded input and original input. The average is taken over all training traces. For each reduced trace, occlusion at window i means zeroisation of trace points $100i$ to $100(i + 1) - 1$. The x-axis gives the index of the occlusion windows. (Color figure online)

5   Stability Against Non-adversarial Changes in the Trace

We tested whether the Hamming weight guesses produced by our neural network are stable against various forms of non-adversarial manipulation of the input data. This is a natural question, as various possible side-channel defenses (such as introduction of intentional jitter) can be viewed as such (they change traces in systematic ways, but cannot be adversarial, since they cannot anticipate the capabilities of an attacker). In particular, we considered misalignment, hybridization of traces, and occlusion of trace data. Stability against occlusion of small parts of the traces was good, as has already been described in the previous section.

Misalignment. We found that our neural network can only tolerate extremely small left-or-right shifts of the input trace; even a shift by just a few positions leads to a marked deterioration of network performance (see Table 5). This suggests that the original trace data has very good alignment and is somewhat surprising given the architecture of our neural network, as the initial layers of the network explicitly treat subsampled slices at varying offsets of the original (decimated) trace alike. We mention that in [9] the problem of misaligned traces was successfully tackled by 'stretching and compressing' the input data, followed by a convolutional network. In principle, such data augmentation techniques should also help our network become more resilient to misalignment.

Table 5. Average number of top-2 errors for our deep neural network on shifted versions of the Set 6 data (single traces). The challenge traces published by Riscure were first shifted to the right by k steps, leaving the first k trace points constant, and then decimated by a factor of ten. The resulting 1000 decimated challenge traces were sent to the neural network for prediction and the number of top-2 errors in the predictions was counted and averaged. Performance deteriorated rapidly for higher shift amounts than here shown.

Shift amount k							
	0	1	2	5	10	15	20
$E(\#$ top-2 errors)	3.144	3.108	3.07	3.116	3.821	5.755	11.387

Hybridization. In order to test whether our classifiers rely on *non-local features*, we decided to see how they respond to synthetic traces spliced together from two power traces corresponding to the same key. To this end, we created random pairs of decimated traces in Set 6 and created out of each pair a new trace consisting of the first 30000 steps of the first trace in the pair and the last 35000 steps of the second trace. On these artificial traces, our baseline classifier shows a clear decline in precision across the whole key. This suggests that the baseline model implicitly uses some global properties of the input traces for its prediction task: if it used only local features, hybridization should affect prediction only around the chosen splice point[11]. For the deep neural network, similar effects were not evident. See Fig. 4 for an overview of the effects of hybridization on different classifiers considered in this paper.

---

[11] Note however that this does not imply that those global features are *useful*: for instance, overfitting by memorizing particular data-label pairs is *using global features*.

Predicting Hybridized Set 6

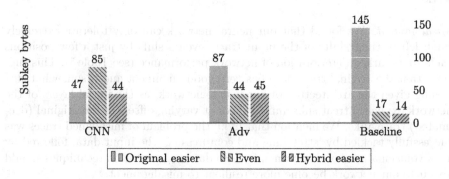

Fig. 4. Classification on Hybridized Traces. Reduced traces in Set 6 were randomly spliced together at time step 30000. For each subkey byte, the number of top-2 prediction errors was counted for the baseline, CNN and Adv models (c.f. Sect. 3) on both hybridized Set 6 and original Set 6. The numbers given show for how many subkey bytes each predictor found the original or the hybridized dataset easier: for instance, the numbers given for the baseline predictor mean that for 145 of the 176 subkey bytes more top-2 errors were made on the hybridized than on the original dataset, for 17 subkey bytes the numbers were equal, and top-2 error was worse for 14 subkey bytes on the original dataset.

Discussion. These experiments show that the neural network uses clearly localized features within the trace, with little or no need to take into account global properties. Our neural network also appears to be very dependent on near-perfect alignment of traces. We suspect that adding local convolution and pooling layers and/or not perfectly aligned training data would fix this.

6   Conclusions

We have shown in this contribution that the AES CHES challenge can be solved using a single trace by an attack that combines a deep neural network for trace exploitation with a SAT-solver based key recovery. This is significantly more efficient than all previous solutions of the same dataset that have been discussed in the open literature. We have also shown that various techniques can extract a lot of information about the implementation from such an attack.

Finally, we show that knowledge distillation from the deep neural network to a linear classifier aimed at exploiting only non-robust features yields a solution that generalizes to unseen devices *better* than training on the original data, i.e. better than the baseline solution.

This is a surprising finding and it suggests that one might be able to obtain traditional side-channel attacks better than the current state of the art by first aiming to optimally exploit the available leakage using deep learning methods and then building a profiling attack using primarily synthetic traces designed to evoke a chosen response from the neural network. In that case, deep learning may well turn out to be a tool for side channel analysis that *supports* classical profiling, instead of one that *replaces* it.

As regards machine learning, we have shown that non-robust features and susceptibility to adversarial examples appear in a natural application domain where sample generation is totally mechanized, in principle reproducible and where alignment of input features is near-perfect. This is interesting because such a setting eliminates some natural sources of non-robust features that are related to data collection complexity. The perfect alignment also makes it easier than in more standard domains to find meaning in adversarial perturbations.

Acknowledgements. We thank Friederike Laus for her careful reading of an earlier iteration of this document. In the same vein, we also thank the anonymous reviewers of SAC 2020 for their thoughtful comments on the submitted version. Both helped us a lot to improve the paper.

Appendix A   Choice of Network Topology: Background and Intuitions

Motivation. Artificial neural networks are machine learning systems which are very loosely inspired by animal brains. Like brains, they consist of a large number of relatively simple computing units (neurons) that are linked together in a directed graph which organizes the information flow within the network. Also like brains, artificial neural networks can be *taught* to perform complex tasks, sometimes at a very high level. However, for typical neural networks, many core elements, e.g. the functioning of individual neurons or the learning algorithms employed, have no resemblance to biology.

Artificial Neural Networks. An artificial neural network is a function family $f_w : \mathbb{R}^n \to \mathbb{R}^m$ defined by a directed graph G that connects n *input nodes* to m output nodes via a (possibly large) number of *hidden nodes*, where each node $g \in G$ has associated to it an *activation function* φ_g. A specific member of the function family is selected by specifying a *weight vector* $w \in \mathbb{R}^k$. Essentially, each neuron sums up input values from nodes in the network that it has incoming connections to, applies its activation function, multiplies the result by the weights of its outgoing connections, and sends the results onwards[12]. Neurons are usually organized in *layers*.

Training Neural Networks. Learning a task using an artificial neural network means finding a weight vector that results in the network being able to solve the task successfully. This is usually done by optimizing the weight vector using

---

[12] Note, however, that modern neural network architectures regularly contain processing layers that cannot be naturally described in this framework, for instance layers that normalize data, reshape it, apply fixed transformations, drop some data during training, or add noise.

stochastic gradient descent (or variants thereof) on some training data with respect to a suitable *loss function* that is (piecewise) differentiable with respect to network weights.

A range of problems can prevent training from being successful, for instance:

- learning rates in stochastic gradient descent may be too low or too high to allow for meaningful convergence,
- the chosen network structure might define a function family that does not contain a good solution (e.g. the network is too shallow, too small or the range of output activations does not fit the problem),
- especially for deep networks, gradients may provide insufficient guidance towards a good solution,
- the network might get stuck in some local optimum of the loss function, far away from any good solutions,
- the network may choose to memorize the training set instead of learning anything useful.

Various responses to these problems have been put forward in the literature. This paper uses quite a few of them. Concretely:

- We use a convolutional network architecture to enforce weight sharing among different parts of the network, thereby limiting the number of parameters to be optimized and the ability of the network to memorize training examples.
- We predict a large number of sensitive variables simultaneously. This should make it hard for the network to memorize desired response vectors.
- We use deep residual networks [11] in order to counteract problems with the convergence of very deep network architectures. Intuitively, in deep residual networks each subsequent layer of the network only computes a correction term on the output of the previous layer. This means that all network layers contribute to the final output in a relatively direct way, making meaningful gradient-based weight updates somewhat easier.
- We use batch normalization to stabilize the statistical properties of hidden network layer inputs between weight updates. This is expected to improve convergence significantly on a wide range of tasks [21].
- We monitor the progress of our network during training by keeping track of its performance on a set of validation examples and use this information to control reductions of a global learning rate parameter.
- We reduce dependency on the choice of a fixed learning rate by using a variant of gradient descent (namely Adam, [14]) that keeps track of past weight updates to adapt learning speed on a per-parameter basis.

Architecture of Our Main Neural Network: Motivations. The main idea behind our network architecture is that the design of a convolutional neural network should reflect symmetries known to exist in the data; previous neural network based approaches to side channel analysis have taken this to mean that low-width convolutions should pick up local features irrespective of their location and that higher network layers should combine these lower-level features to eventually predict the leakage target.

In an attack that is trying to recover all AES subkey bytes, this approach encounters the problem that subkey bytes involved in similar processing steps (e.g. subkey bytes 16 and 32) will cause similar local features, meaning that the convolutional network layers cannot distinguish between them very well; also, the convolutional layers will have trouble picking up global features of the entire trace and may fail to combine leakage on the same subkey byte coming from disparate parts of the trace. The standard way for convolutional networks to overcome these problems is to intersperse convolutional and pooling layers, followed by densely connected layers finally predicting the leakage target. In such a network, roughly speaking, local convolutions are used to detect local features and pooling layers drastically reduce the amount of data that filters through to the prediction layers; finally, a densely connected prediction head draws on the output of these layers to predict the target.

In our design, on the other hand, we assume only that *prediction based on a downsampled version of the power signal should - within reason - be independent of the offset of the downsampling.* Hence, we take the full trace signal, decompose it into downsampled slices according to a fixed decimation factor n, and treat each slice *approximately* as if predicting the target using a fully-connected deep feed-forward network operating on each slice in isolation. Therefore, in our design, each neuron sees information from the entire trace, but the information seen by each neuron differs from that seen by any other. In this architecture, the network is completely free to decide which parts of the trace are important for each feature to be predicted, while at the same time, internal weights are shared between all the subnetworks, thus greatly reducing the problem of overfitting.

References

1. Bishop, C.M.: Pattern Recognition and Machine Learning. Springer (2006). ISBN 978-0387-31073-2
2. Gohr, A., Jacob, S., Schindler, W.: CHES 2018 Side Channel Contest CTF - Solution of the AES Challenges. IACR eprint archive report 2019/094. https://eprint.iacr.org/2019/094
3. Damm, T., Freud, S., Klein, D.: Dissecting the CHES 2018 AES Challenge. IACR eprint archive report 2019/783. https://eprint.iacr.org/2019/783
4. Hu, Y., et al.: Machine Learning and Side-Channel Analysis in a CTF Competition. IACR eprint archive report 2019/860. https://eprint.iacr.org/2019/860
5. Pedregosa, F., et al.: Scikit-learn: machine learning in Python. J. Mach. Learn. Res. **12**, 2825–2830 (2011)
6. Soos, M., Nohl, K., Castelluccia, C.: Extending SAT solvers to cryptographic problems. In: 12th International Conference on Theory and Applications of Satisfiability Testing - SAT 2009 (2009)
7. Pycryptosat homepage. https://pypi.org/project/pycryptosat/. Accessed 08 Oct 2018

8. Picek, S., Samiotis, I.P., Kim, J., Heuser, A., Bhasin, S., Legay, A.: On the performance of convolutional neural networks for side-channel analysis. In: Chattopadhyay, A., Rebeiro, C., Yarom, Y. (eds.) SPACE 2018. LNCS, vol. 11348, pp. 157–176. Springer, Cham (2018). https://doi.org/10.1007/978-3-030-05072-6_10

9. Cagli, E., Dumas, C., Prouff, E.: Convolutional neural networks with data augmentation against Jitter-based countermeasures. In: Fischer, W., Homma, N. (eds.) CHES 2017. LNCS, vol. 10529, pp. 45–68. Springer, Cham (2017). https://doi.org/10.1007/978-3-319-66787-4_3

10. Kim, J., Picek, S., Heuser, A., Bhasin, S., Hanjalic, A.: Make some noise. Unleashing the power of convolutional neural networks for profiled side-channel analysis. IACR Trans. Cryptograph. Hardw. Embedded Syst. **2019**(3), 148–179. https://doi.org/10.13154/tches.v2019.i3.148-179

11. He, K., Xang, X., Ren, S., Sun, J.: Deep residual learning for image recognition. In: Proceedings of the IEEE Conference on Computer Vision and Pattern Recognition (2016). https://www.cv-foundation.org/openaccess/content_cvpr_2016/papers/He_Deep_Residual_Learning_CVPR_2016_paper.pdf

12. Emadjila, R., Prouff, E., Strullu, R., Cagli, E., Dumas, C.: Study of Deep Learning Techniques for Side-Channel Analysis and Introduction to the ASCAD Database. IACR eprint report 2018/053. https://eprint.iacr.org/2018/053

13. Gohr, A.: Improving attacks on round-reduced Speck32/64 using deep learning. In: Boldyreva, A., Micciancio, D. (eds.) CRYPTO 2019. LNCS, vol. 11693, pp. 150–179. Springer, Cham (2019). https://doi.org/10.1007/978-3-030-26951-7_6

14. Kingma, D.P., Ba, J.L.: ADAM: A Method for Stochastic Optimization. ICLR 2015. arXiv:1412.6980 (2015)

15. Chollet, F.: keras, GitHub (2015). https://github.com/fchollet/keras

16. Ilyas, A., Santurkar, S., Tsipras, D., Engstrom, L., Tran, B., Madry, A.: Adversarial Examples Are Not Bugs, They Are Features. NeurIPS 2019. https://arxiv.org/pdf/1905.02175.pdf

17. Barak, B.: Puzzles of Modern Machine Learning, Windows On Theory Research Blog. https://windowsontheory.org/2019/11/15/puzzles-of-modern-machine-learning/. Accessed 19 Nov 2019

18. Hettwer, B., Gehrer, S., Güneysu, T.: Deep neural network attribution methods for leakage analysis and symmetric key recovery. In: Paterson, K.G., Stebila, D. (eds.) SAC 2019. LNCS, vol. 11959, pp. 645–666. Springer, Cham (2020). https://doi.org/10.1007/978-3-030-38471-5_26

19. Goodfellow, I., Bengio, Y., Courville, A.: Deep Learning. MIT Press (2016). https://www.deeplearningbook.org

20. Goodfellow, I., Shlens, J., Szegedy, C.: Explaining and harnessing adversarial examples. arXiv preprint arXiv:1412.6572 (2014)

21. Ioffe, S., Szegedy, C.: Batch normalization: accelerating deep network training by reducing internal covariate shift. In: International Conference on Machine Learning (2015)

22. Sharif, M., Bhagavatula, S., Bauer, L., Reiter, M.K.: Accessorize to a crime: real and stealthy attacks on state-of-the-art face recognition. In: ACM Conference on Computer and Communications Security 2016, New York, pp. 1528–1540 (2016)

23. Belliza, D., Bronchain, O., Cassiers, G., Momin, C., Standaert, F.-X., Udvarhelyi, B.(organizers): CHES CTF 2020 Hall of Fame. Submissions. Accessed 05 July 2021

24. Szegedy, C.: Intriguing Properties of Neural Networks. arXiv:1312.6199

25. Zhou, Y., Standaert, F.-X.: Deep learning mitigates but does not annihilate the need of aligned traces and a generalized ResNet model for side-channel attacks. J. Cryptograph. Eng. **10**(1), 1–11 (2019)

Correlation Power Analysis and Higher-Order Masking Implementation of WAGE

Yunsi Fei[1], Guang Gong[2], Cheng Gongye[1], Kalikinkar Mandal[3(✉)], Raghvendra Rohit[2], Tianhong Xu[1], Yunjie Yi[2], and Nusa Zidaric[2]

[1] Department of Electrical and Computer Engineering, Northeastern University, 360 Huntington Avenue, Boston, MA 02115, USA
yfei@ece.neu.edu, {gongye.c,xu.tianh}@northeastern.edu

[2] Department of Electrical and Computer Engineering, University of Waterloo, Waterloo, ON N2L 3G1, Canada
{ggong,rsrohit,yunjie.yi,nzidaric}@uwaterloo.ca

[3] Faculty of Computer Science, University of New Brunswick, Fredericton E3B 5A3, Canada
kmandal@unb.ca

Abstract. WAGE is a hardware-oriented authenticated cipher, which has the smallest (unprotected) hardware cost (for 128-bit security level) among the round 2 candidates of the NIST lightweight cryptography (LWC) competition. In this work, we analyze the security of WAGE against the correlation power analysis (CPA) on ARM Cortex-M4F microcontroller. Our attack detects the secret key leakage from power consumption for up to 12 (out of 111) rounds of the WAGE permutation and requires 10,000 power traces to recover the 128-bit secret key. Motivated by the CPA attack and the low hardware cost of WAGE, we propose the first optimized masking scheme of WAGE in the t-strong non-interference (SNI) security model. We investigate different masking schemes for S-boxes by exploiting their internal structures and leveraging the state-of-the-art masking techniques. To practically demonstrate the effectiveness of masking, we perform the test vector leakage assessment on the 1-order masked WAGE. We evaluate the hardware performance of WAGE for 1, 2, and 3-order security and provide a comparison with other NIST LWC round 2 candidates.

Keywords: Authenticated encryption · WAGE · Side-channel attack · Correlation power analysis · Masking scheme

1 Introduction

Side-channel analysis is a class of attacks that exploit the implementation and physical execution of a cryptographic algorithm to extract secret information through the power consumption [30] or electro-magnetic emanations [3,24].

© Springer Nature Switzerland AG 2021
O. Dunkelman et al. (Eds.): SAC 2020, LNCS 12804, pp. 593–614, 2021.
https://doi.org/10.1007/978-3-030-81652-0_23

Starting from the seminal work of Kocher *et al.* [30], there has been an active research on evaluating the security of ciphers against differential power analysis (DPA) and its variant correlation power analysis (CPA) [14]. In general, a DPA attack aims to recover the secret information by analyzing the differences in power consumption for varying input data, while a CPA attack focuses on the correlation factor between the hamming weight of handled (unknown) data and power samples. Several standardized encryption algorithms and hash functions such as DES, AES, KECCAK and ASCON have been analyzed against such attacks and countermeasures of side-channel attacks have been proposed [4,5,13,25,26,28,31,38].

An effective countermeasure against side-channel attacks exploiting the power consumption is *masking*. In a masked implementation, each input variable x is secret-shared into n shares such that $x = x^1 \oplus \cdots \oplus x^n$. Each share x^i is processed independently via a sequence of linear and nonlinear operations to produce n output shares $y^1, \cdots, y^n$ satisfying $y = y^1 \oplus \cdots \oplus y^n$ where y is the actual output corresponding to the input x. Any linear operation over the shares can be masked linearly, however processing nonlinear operations such as AND and/or S-box is complex. The design of efficient secure masking schemes for nonlinear operations is a challenging task. Ishai, Sahai and Wagner (ISW) [29] have initiated the study of securely computing a circuit consisting of XOR, AND and NOT gates where the AND gates are replaced by secure AND gadgets. From the security point of view, the ISW construction is resistant to the t-order probing attack when the number of shares $n \geq 2t + 1$, i.e., evaluating the leakage on a set of at most t out of n points does not reveal information about a sensitive variable x. Barthe *et al.* [8] redefined the ISW security and introduced a stronger security notion, called t-strong non interference (t-SNI) security under the ISW probing model, which minimizes the number of shares to $n = t + 1$ (i.e., almost half) and its compositional security definition guarantees the t-SNI security in a large construction by securely composing t-SNI secure gadgets. Several other techniques for side-channel attacks have been proposed, including Threshold implementation [32], Consolidated Masking Scheme [33], Domain Oriented Masking (DOM) [27] and Unified Masking Approach [26]. In [23], De Cnudde *et al.* presented an AES hardware implementation using $t + 1$ shares in the presence of glitches. The countermeasures on the secure evaluation of the AES S-box have been investigated in the literature extensively, e.g., [16,17,19,20,22,34–36] based on finite field computations, randomized lookup table, and customized gate-level implementations. In particular, for the randomized lookup table, a first-order countermeasure for S-boxes was first proposed by Chari *et al.* [17], and later on [19], Coron generalized the randomized lookup table countermeasure [19]. In the follow-up work [22], Coron *et al.* proposed a construction of a randomized lookup table countermeasure that is t-SNI secure.

The aforementioned masking techniques typically introduce an overhead due to performing additional operations on shares, complex nonlinear masking (gadget) operations, and processing randomnesses. However, in actual hardware implementations, they offer varying trade-offs due to the availability of varying gates and memory modules in specific libraries. For resource constrained devices such as Internet of Things (IoT) and sensor networks where the implementation cost is critical, the actual implementation numbers bring more confidence in a cipher's design and in turn provides a fair comparison with other ciphers. The NIST lightweight cryptographic (LWC) competition [11] for standardizing lightweight cryptographic algorithm(s) is currently in the second phase where 32 candidates are being analyzed. The performance of the protected implementations of these ciphers is an important criterion for the selection of next round candidates. WAGE [1,6] is one of the round 2 candidates in this competition. It is a permutation-based authenticated encryption where the construction of the underlying permutation is based on a Galois nonlinear feedback shift register (NLFSR) with two 7-bit S-boxes (WGP and SB) as the nonlinear components. The design offers an efficient performance in hardware with an area of 2540 GE in STMicro 90 nm, the smallest among the round 2 candidates for a security level of 128 bits [1,2]. Further, it can be additionally tweaked to a WG-based pseudo-random bit generator with a low hardware overhead and theoretical randomness properties [6].

Motivated by the smallest hardware footprint and features of WAGE, in this work, we analyze the security of WAGE against the CPA attack and propose the first masking implementations to evaluate its performance in hardware. In what follows, we list our contributions.

- **Correlation power analysis:** We present the first analysis of WAGE against correlation power analysis on ARM Cortex-M4F microcontroller. We use the hamming weight (HW) model on 7-bit state words to detect the leakage. Our experiments show that the power traces for up to 12 out of 111 rounds of the WAGE permutation reveals the secret key information. We use the Pearson correlation coefficient between the HW of the state word value and the power value of the leakage point to recover the entire 128-bit key in a word-wise fashion. In our attack, the key words are recovered in 13 batches and requires 10,000 power traces to recover the entire key.
- **Higher-order masking scheme of WAGE:** To provide resistance against such side-channel attacks, we propose a higher-order masking scheme for WAGE adopting both the gate-level and randomized-lookup table based approaches. To achieve the area optimized masked S-boxes, we exploit the internal structures of the SB and WGP S-boxes. For SB S-box, we exploit its iterative construction and apply the common share multiplication technique to optimize the area while for WGP S-box, we generate an optimized Boolean circuit consisting of 313 XOR, 172 AND and 66 NOT gates. We provide the security analysis of the masked WAGE permutation in the t-SNI security model along with its complexity analysis. We further analyze the first-order masked WAGE (implemented with randomized-lookup table approach) using the standard test vector leakage assessment method [18,37], however the power traces do not reveal any secret key information (see Appendix A).
- **Hardware implementation:** Our hardware architecture for the masked WAGE is parallel. We implement the round function for the t-order ($t = 1, 2, 3$)

masked WAGE in STMicro 65 nm and TSMC 65 nm technologies and provide area results for WGP and SB S-boxes and the WAGE authenticated encryption (AE) scheme in Table 4. For instance, our smallest implementation of WAGE AE has a cost of 11.2 kGE for the 1-order protection in STMicro 65 nm technology. We provide a comparison[1] of WAGE AE with the currently known available first-order protected implementations of the NIST LWC round 2 candidates in Table 1.

Table 1. Comparison of WAGE with NIST LWC round 2 candidates for the 1-order protection. Only the results for the round based implementation of primary members is listed.

Algorithm	Ref.	Impl. type	Technology	Synthesis	Area [GE]
WAGE AE	**Section 5**	Masking	STMicro 65 nm	Physical	**11177**
			TSMC 65 nm		**12711**
ASCON	[28]	Threshold	UMC 90 nm	Physical	28610
SKINNY-AEAD	[12]	DOM	UMC 90 nm	-	20534
			IBM 130 nm	-	18817
GIFT-COFB	[7]	Threshold	STMicro 90 nm	Logic	13131
SUNDAE-GIFT	[15]	Threshold	TSMC 90 nm	Logic	13297

Organization. The rest of the article is organized as follows. Section 2 gives a brief overview of the WAGE and masking schemes for side channel countermeasures. In Sect. 3, we present the correlation power analyis of WAGE on ARM Cortex-M4F. Section 4 explains our construction of the gate-level and randomized-look up table based masking schemes of WAGE. The details of our hardware implementations and a discussion on performance results are provided in Sect. 5. Finally, the paper is concluded in Sect. 6.

2   Preliminaries

In this section, we provide a background on the WAGE authenticated encryption, the adversarial model and basic techniques on the side-channel protection.

Notations. Let $\mathbb{F}_2 = \{0, 1\}$ be the Galois field, and $\mathbb{F}_{2^7}$ be an extension field where each element is a tuple of 7 bits. $\mathbb{F}_2^m$ is a vector space of dimension m. $\oplus$ and $\odot$ denote the bitwise XOR and bitwise AND operations, respectively. Double square brackets $[[x]] = (x^1, x^2, \cdots, x^n)$ denotes the additive shares of $x = \oplus_{i=1}^n x^i$. $r \xleftarrow{\$} \mathbb{F}_p$ denotes the element r is chosen from $\mathbb{F}_p$ uniformly at random.

---

[1] A fair comparison is difficult due to different types of side-channel implementations and ASIC libraries.

2.1 Description of WAGE

We provide a description of WAGE, following the same notations from [1,6]. The WAGE authenticated encryption is built upon the WAGE permutation in the unified sponge duplex mode where the WAGE permutation is a 111-round of an iterative permutation with a state width of 259 bits over an extension field $\mathbb{F}_{2^7}$. The core components of the permutation, described in detail below, include two different S-boxes (WGP and SB), a linear feedback function defined over $\mathbb{F}_{2^7}$, five word-wise XORs, and 111 pairs of 7-bit round constant (rc_1, rc_0). Figure 1 provides an overview of the round function of the WAGE permutation.

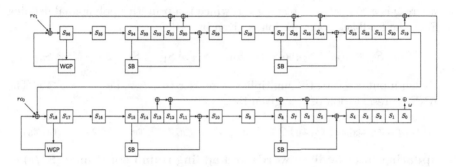

Fig. 1. An overview of the state update function of WAGE [6].

Nonlinear Components of WAGE. WAGE uses two distinct 7-bit S-boxes, namely WGP and SB where WGP is defined over a finite field $\mathbb{F}_{2^7}$ and SB is constructed iteratively at the bit-level from quadratic functions. We now provide a brief description of WGP and SB.

Welch-Gong Permutation (WGP). The WGPerm, denoted by WGP7, is defined over $\mathbb{F}_{2^7}$ which is given by

$$\text{WGP7}(x) = x + (x+1)^{33} + (x+1)^{39} + (x+1)^{41} + (x+1)^{104}, \ x \in \mathbb{F}_{2^7}$$

where $\mathbb{F}_{2^7}$ is defined by the primitive polynomial $x^7 + x^3 + x^2 + x + 1$. WGP is constructed from WGP7 by applying decimation $d = 13$ as $\text{WGP}(x) = \text{WGP7}(x^{13})$.

SB S-box. The 7-bit S-box SB is constructed in an iterative way using the nonlinear transformation Q and the bit permutation P which are given by

$$Q(x_0, x_1, \cdots, x_5, x_6) = (x_0 \oplus (x_2 \odot x_3), x_1, x_2, \overline{x}_3 \oplus (x_5 \odot x_6), x_4, \overline{x}_5 \oplus (x_2 \odot x_4), x_6)$$
$$P(x_0, x_1, x_2, x_3, x_4, x_5, x_6) = (x_6, x_3, x_0, x_4, x_2, x_5, x_1).$$

The construction of SB is given by

$$(x_0, x_1, x_2, x_3, x_4, x_5, x_6) \leftarrow R^5(x_0, x_1, x_2, x_3, x_4, x_5, x_6)$$
$$(x_0, x_1, x_2, x_3, x_4, x_5, x_6) \leftarrow Q(x_0, x_1, x_2, x_3, x_4, x_5, x_6)$$
$$x_0 \leftarrow x_0 \oplus 1; x_2 \leftarrow x_2 \oplus 1$$

where the round R is a composition of Q and P, i.e., $R = P \circ Q$.

State Update Function of WAGE. The 259-bit state of WAGE consists of 37 7-bit words and is denoted by $\mathbf{S} = (S_{36}, \cdots, S_0)$ where each S_i is of 7 bits. The state update function of WAGE, denoted by WAGE_STATEUPDATE, takes as inputs the current state S and a pair of round constants (rc_1, rc_0), and updates the state with the following three steps:

1. **Computing linear feedback:** $fb \leftarrow \mathbf{FB(S)}$. The following primitive polynomial of degree 37 over $\mathbb{F}_{2^7}$ is used as a feedback function

$$\ell(y) = y^{37} + y^{31} + y^{30} + y^{26} + y^{24} + y^{19} + y^{13} + y^{12} + y^8 + y^6 + \omega$$

where ω is a root $x^7 + x^3 + x^2 + x + 1$, which is a primitive polynomial defining $\mathbb{F}_{2^7}$. The feedback computation is given by

$$fb = S_{31} \oplus S_{30} \oplus S_{26} \oplus S_{24} \oplus S_{19} \oplus S_{13} \oplus S_{12} \oplus S_8 \oplus S_6 \oplus (\omega \otimes S_0).$$

For an input $x \in \mathbb{F}_{2^7}$, the multiplier ω maps x to $\omega \otimes x$, i.e., $x \mapsto \omega \otimes x$. The ANF representation of it is given by

$$(x_0, x_1, x_2, x_3, x_4, x_5, x_6) \otimes \omega \rightarrow (x_6, x_0 \oplus x_6, x_1 \oplus x_6, x_2 \oplus x_6, x_3, x_4, x_5).$$

2. **Updating intermediate words and adding round constants:** $(\mathbf{S}, fb) \leftarrow$ **IWRC**$(\mathbf{S}, fb, rc_0, rc_1)$.

$$S_5 \leftarrow S_5 \oplus \mathsf{SB}(S_8)$$
$$S_{11} \leftarrow S_{11} \oplus \mathsf{SB}(S_{15})$$
$$S_{19} \leftarrow S_{19} \oplus \mathsf{WGP}(S_{18}) \oplus rc_0$$
$$S_{24} \leftarrow S_{24} \oplus \mathsf{SB}(S_{27})$$
$$S_{30} \leftarrow S_{30} \oplus \mathsf{SB}(S_{34})$$
$$fb \leftarrow fb \oplus \mathsf{WGP}(S_{36}) \oplus rc_1.$$

3. **Shifting register contents and update the last word: S** $\leftarrow$ **Shift**$(\mathbf{S}, fb)$.

$$S_j \leftarrow S_{j+1}, 0 \leq j \leq 35$$
$$S_{36} \leftarrow fb.$$

On an input state $\mathbf{S}$, the output of the WAGE permutation is obtained by applying the state update function 111 times. Note that only the IWRC transformation performs the nonlinear operations and the others are linear operations.

2.2   Adversarial Model

We consider an adversarial model in which an attacker can probe up to t intermediate variables in the circuit, known as the t-probing (ISW) model [29] or t-non interference (NI) model [9] where the number of shares for each secret variable is $n \geq 2t + 1$. The t-probing security is provided in Definition 1. The security of t-strong non interference (t-SNI) was introduced in [8] (see Definition 3). Intuitively, a t-SNI gadget information-theoretically hides dependencies between each of its inputs and its outputs, even in the presence of internal probes [8]. Note that combining t-probing (or t-NI) secure gadgets does not necessarily results in a t-probing secure algorithm [21]. We consider the standard t-SNI security for WAGE as the number of shares is only $n = t+1$, instead of $n = 2t+1$ in the t-NI security and it provides an assurance on the t-SNI security of the entire scheme when t-SNI secure gadgets are composed securely.

Definition 1 (t-probing Security) [29]. *An algorithm C is t-probing secure if the values taken by at most t intermediate variables of C during its execution do not leak any information about secrets.*

Definition 2 (t-NI Security) [8]. *Let G be a gadget accepting $(x_i)_{1 \leq i \leq n}$ as input and outputting $(y_i)_{1 \leq i \leq n}$. We call the gadget G is t-non interference (t-NI) (also known as t-threshold probing) secure if for any set of $\ell \leq t$ intermediate variables, there exists a subset I of input indices with $|I| \leq \ell$ such that ℓ intermediate variables can be perfectly simulated from $x_{|I} = (x_i)_{i \in I}$.*

Definition 3 (t-SNI Security) [8]. *Let G be a gadget accepting $(x_i)_{1 \leq i \leq n}$ as input and outputting $(y_i)_{1 \leq i \leq n}$. We call the gadget G is t-strongly non-interference (t-SNI) secure if for any set of $\ell \leq t$ intermediate variables and any subset of output indices O such that $\ell + |O| \leq t$, there exists a subset I of input indices with $|I| \leq \ell$ such that the ℓ intermediate variables and output variables $y_{|O}$ can be perfectly simulated from $x_{|I}$.*

2.3 Masking Schemes for Side-Channel Countermeasures

Masking is an effective countermeasure against side-channel attacks such as power analysis on cryptographic algorithms. In a masking scheme, a variable x containing sensitive information is protected by masking it with a random value r as $x' = x \oplus r$, i.e., $x = x' \oplus r$, meaning the sensitive variable x is shared between variables r and x'. In an n-order masking, each sensitive variable x is shared among n variables x^i as $x = x^1 \oplus x^2 \oplus \cdots \oplus x^n$. We denote the n shares of x by $[[x]] = (x^1, x^2, \cdots, x^n)$ such that $x = \oplus_{i=1}^{n} x^i$. For $[[x]] = (x^1, x^2, \cdots, x^n)$ and $[[y]] = (y^1, y^2, \cdots, y^n)$, $[[x]] \oplus [[y]] = (x^1 \oplus y^1, x^2 \oplus y^2, \cdots, x^n \oplus y^n) = [[x \oplus y]]$. For a binary variable x with shares $[[x]]$, it is easy to compute $[[\bar{x}]]$ from $[[x]]$ as $\bar{x} = \bar{x}^1 \oplus x^2 \oplus \cdots \oplus x^n$. Computing the nonlinear operations such as AND and S-box introduce a large overhead when sensitive variables are additively shared. Below we describe the techniques for securely computing an AND gate and an S-box.

Private AND Computation. Ishai, Sahai and Wagner (ISW) [29] have initiated the study of securely computing a circuit where an adversary can probe a certain number of wires in the circuit to extract sensitive information. The construction of ISW is generic and based on secret-sharing each wire in the circuit. Their technique transforms the original circuit into another circuit that is secure in the t-probing model when the number of shares $n \geq 2t + 1$, with an addition overhead. For each AND gate, a gadget taking a $2n$-bit input and producing an n-bit output that securely computes the AND gate is introduced. The multiplication of $x = \oplus_{i=1}^{n} x^i$ and $y = \oplus_{i=1}^{n} y^i$ outputting n shares $[[z]]$ is computed as

$$z = xy = \bigoplus_{0 \leq i,j \leq n} x^i y^j$$

where $z = z^1 \oplus z^2 \oplus \cdots \oplus z^n$ and $z^i = x^i y^i + \bigoplus_{j \neq i} z^{i,j}$ and for each pair (i, j) with $i < j$, a random bit $z^{i,j}$ is generated and $z^{j,i} = z^{i,j} \oplus x^i y^j \oplus x^j y^i$. Each AND gate introduces $O(n^2)$ gates, thus increasing the size of the circuit. In [8], Barthe et $al.$ proposed the construction of the t-SNI secure AND gadgets relying on the ISW construction.

High-Order Randomized Lookup Table. The countermeasures on the (AES) S-box evaluation was studied from various approaches, notably finite field based masking computations, e.g., [16,20,34,35], and the randomized lookup table, e.g., [17,19,22]. A first-order randomized table countermeasure for S-boxes was first proposed by Chari et $al.$ [17] where the countermeasure consists of recomputing the S-box in the RAM with input shifted by some random value r and the output is masked by another random value s, i.e., $T(x) = S(x \oplus r) \oplus s$ where S is the S-box. In [19], Coron generalized the randomized lookup table countermeasure to an n-th order masking as output $y = y^1 \oplus y^2 \oplus \cdots \oplus y^n = S(x \oplus x^1 \oplus \cdots \oplus x^{n-1})$ where $x = \bigoplus_{i=1}^{n} x^i$. This countermeasure is secure against a t-order attack in the ISW probing model (t-NI secure) for $n \geq 2t + 1$. Coron et $al.$ [22] proposed a randomized lookup table scheme that is secure against t-SNI. For the details of the randomized lookup table, the reader is referred to [19,22].

3   Correlation Power Analysis of WAGE

In this section, we present a correlation power analysis (CPA) attack on the unprotected WAGE. The CPA attack is conducted in the microcontroller environment. For simplicity, we consider the first execution of the WAGE permutation in the initialization phase where the key and nonce are loaded and processed.

3.1   Experimental Setup

Figure 2 shows a high-level overview of our experimental setup. The Device Under Test (DUT) is a Pinata[2] board with an ARM Cortex-M4F core running at a 168 MHz clock speed. We measured the voltage of the 3.3 V power supply that powers the entire DUT. The power traces are collected using a LeCroy oscilloscope. We use the reference C implementation code of WAGE from the NIST website [11] and modify it to add a trigger to synchronize the power traces, which is the standard procedure for the power trace acquisition.

---

[2] https://www.riscure.com/product/pinata-training-target/.

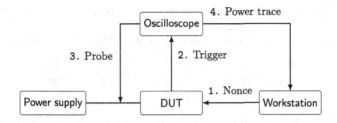

Fig. 2. An overview of our experimental setup. The workstation is used to control the microcontroller and record the nonce and the power traces. Oscilloscope measures the main's voltage.

3.2   The CPA Attack

Leakage Model. We consider the hamming weight (HW) of the state register as a leakage model. We tested both the HW and the hamming distance of WGP and SB output tables, but did not find any leakage for the DUT. We then use the Pearson correlation coefficient (PCC) between the HW of the state value and the power value of the leakage point to detect leakage. The PCC describes a linear correlation between two variables and its value lies in the range of -1 and 1, where higher the absolute value indicates a stronger linear correlation.

Attack Overview. Our attack targets the first 12 rounds of the WAGE permutation after loading the 128-bit key and 128-bit nonce in the initialization phase. The 16-byte nonce and 16-byte key are arranged into 37 state words, 19 key words K_0–K_{18}, and 19 nonce words N_0–N_{18} where K_0–K_{17} contain seven bits, and K_{18} contains only two bits. In our attack, we run the initialization phase 10,000 times with randomly generated nonces for a fixed key where the nonce is assumed as known, and the key is unknown. We run a data flow analysis of the 12-round computations and identify the dependency of state registers[3] in each round on the key words. We identify an initial batch of seven state registers, each of which is only dependent on a single key word (see Table 2). Our attack recovers the key words in two steps, namely the *initial batch* that recovers seven key words and the *final batch* which recovers the rest of the key words sequentially based on the prior recovered key words. The detailed steps are elaborated below.

Recovering the Initial Batch of Key Words. To recover a key word in the initial batch, we need a value of the state word such that it depends on only 1 key word and at least 7 nonce bits at a specific round. Table 2 shows the targeted round and state register positions satisfying this criterion and are utilized to recover a single key word.

We follow the standard CPA procedure to retrieve these seven key words one-by-one. For each key word, the select function is the HW power model of the state register which is dependent on a key word and a nonce. We run the initialization

---

[3] We use "word" and "register" interchangeably throughout this section.

Table 2. Targeted round and state register positions in the initial batch.

Key word	Round	State register	Key word	Round	State register
K_{12}	5	0	K_{15}	3	22
K_{13}	3	21	K_{16}	5	2
K_{14}	5	1	K_{17}	3	23
K_{18}	10	0			

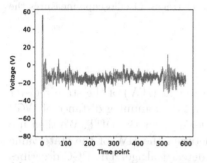 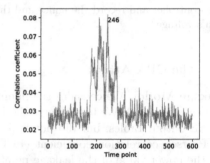

(a) A power trace of round 10 of first call of the WAGE permutation.

(b) Leakage of K_{18} on time axis at round 10 where the maximum leakage is observed at the time point 246.

Fig. 3. Example of a power trace and leakage of a fixed key word.

phase several times where each time, a random, but known nonce is used and the power trace is collected. We collect 10,000 such power traces. Figure 3a shows a sample power trace. We perform the CPA on all the time points in these traces, i.e., enumerate the 128 possible key values and calculate the Pearson correlation between the predicted and measured power values. Figure 3a shows the correlation values along the time points (under the correct key guess), which indicate the leakiest time point is 246. Figure 4 shows the key distinguishing result at this time point, where the correct key guess, 96 (in integer notation), gives the highest correlation coefficient value.

Recovering the Remaining Batch of Key Words. Similar to the initial batch, to recover the rest of key words, we need a value of the state register such that it is associated with only one unknown key word and at least seven nonce bits, at a specific round. Table 5 in Appendix A depicts the targeted round and state register positions to recover the key words of final batch. Due to dependency among key words, the key bytes are recovered in a specific order. Unlike the initial batch recovery, these key words cannot find a state that meets the two conditions in the initial batch, hence few other key words have to be

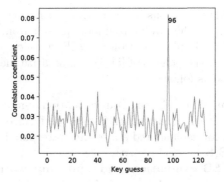

Fig. 4. Highest correlation among all the time points at round 10 for 128 guessed key values of K_{18}.

known first so that there is only one unknown key word associated with the targeted state word. The recovery technique is the same as the initial batch one. The only difference is while calculating the value of a targeted state register using the guessed key value, we use the value of known key words.

Our analysis reveals that the unprotected implementation of WAGE suffers side-channel power analysis attacks, i.e., correlation power analysis attack. Hence, similar to other symmetric-key ciphers, like DES, AES, KECCAK and ASCON [4,5,13,25,26,28,31,38], a protected implementation of WAGE is needed for applications in constrained environments such as chip card technologies. In the following section, we present our masking scheme for WAGE to resist power analysis based side-channel attacks.

4   The Masking Scheme for WAGE

In this section, we present our construction for the masked WAGE permutation, featured for hardware, along with its complexity analysis. We first provide two optimized constructions of masked WGP and SB S-boxes that are t-SNI secure. We start by providing a high-level overview of the masked WAGE permutation.

High-Level Description. We construct a t-SNI secure masking scheme of WAGE where the number of shares $n = t + 1$. In doing so, the state of WAGE, denoted by $\mathbf{S}$, is split into n state shares such that $\mathbf{S} = \mathbf{S}^1 \oplus \mathbf{S}^2 \oplus \cdots \oplus \mathbf{S}^n$ where $\mathbf{S}^i = (S^i_{36}, \cdots, S^i_0)$ is the i-th share of the state $\mathbf{S}$. In our masked WAGE, we update the shared states according to the round function so that at the end of 111 rounds, the state of the WAGE permutation can be constructed from the n state shares. The operations involved in the round function of WAGE are the computation of the linear feedback function, computing WGP and SB and updating intermediate words, and shifting operation where all the operations in the round function on the shared states are performed independently and parallelly, except WGP and SB. To optimized the hardware area for SB with the SNI security, we exploit the iterative construction of SB and apply the common share technique for two AND operations in the Q transformation (see Fig. 5). For the t-SNI secure WGP, we use the randomized lookup table from [22], and develop a new optimized gate-level implementation of WGP in which we replace the AND gates by t-SNI secure AND gadgets of [8]. We summarize the computation steps of the masking scheme as follows:

- **Feedback computation:** As the transformation ω-multiplier is linear, the feedback computation is linear which can be performed parallelly on the n shared states, i.e., for each shared state, the corresponding feedback is computed as $fb^i \leftarrow \mathsf{FB}(\mathbf{S}^i), i \in \{1, \cdots, n\}$.
- **Secure WGP & SB evaluation and updating words:** The evaluation of the masked SB, denoted by SecSB, is performed in a single clock cycle although our technique of the masked SB is iterative. The gate-level implementation of the masked WGP, denoted by SecWGP, is also computed in one clock cycle. On the other hand, the randomized lookup table approach for secure WGP and SB S-boxes takes at least 128 cycles, and was used for the software implementation. The masked S-boxes are computed as $[[S_j]] \leftarrow \mathsf{SecSB}([[S_j]]), j \in \{8, 15, 27, 34\}$ and $[[S_j]] \leftarrow \mathsf{SecWGP}([[S_j]]), j \in \{18, 36\}$ where $S_j = \oplus_{i=1}^{n} S_j^i$.
- **Shifting and updating last word operation:** This operation can be performed parallelly on the shared states, i.e., $\mathbf{S}^i \leftarrow \mathsf{Shift}(\mathbf{S}^i), i \in \{1, \cdots, n\}$.

We are now ready to describe the masking techniques for SB and WGP.

4.1   Construction of an SNI-Secure SB

We present a construction of an area optimized masked SB guaranteeing the t-SNI security. Note that the SB can be decomposed into six elementary transformations where only the Q transformation has AND gates. Our idea is to iteratively compute the SB where in the Q transformation consisting of three AND, three XOR and two NOT gates, we adopt a t-SNI secure AND gadget of [8] to replace each AND gate and apply a t-SNI RefreshMask operation of [8] after the Q transformation to ensure the SNI security. Let $x = (x_0, x_1, x_2, x_3, x_4, x_5, x_6)$ be an input to the S-box SB. The nonlinear Q transformation is given by $Q(x) = (x_0 \oplus x_2 x_3, x_1, x_2, \overline{x}_3 \oplus x_5 x_6, x_4, \overline{x}_5 \oplus x_2 x_4, x_6)$. The input x is shared among n variables as $x = x^1 \oplus x^2 \oplus \cdots \oplus x^n$ where $x^i = (x_0^i, x_1^i, x_2^i, x_3^i, x_4^i, x_5^i, x_6^i), x_j^i \in \mathbb{F}_2$ is the i-th share, and each component x_i is shared as $x_i = x_i^1 \oplus x_i^2 \oplus \cdots \oplus x_i^n$. Note that the multiplications $x_2 x_3$ and $x_2 x_4$ have a common term x_2. We exploit this property to optimize the area. Thus, we apply a common input multiplication, denoted by CommonMult, introduced in [20], for efficiently computing $x_2 x_3$ and $x_2 x_4$. Figure 5 depicts the masked implementation of Q. Algorithm 1 provides the detailed steps of the masked SB where SecMult denotes an SNI-secure AND gadget of [8]. Note the masked SB is evaluated in a single clock cycle in hardware. For instance, our masked implementation of SB for $n = 2$ has an overhead of 4.5× the unprotected SB implementation (see Table 4).

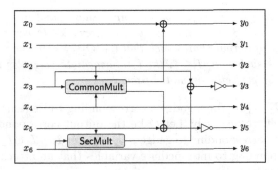

Fig. 5. Schematic of one-round gadget of SB with common multiplication.

Algorithm 1. New Masked SB Computation

1: **Input:** n shares $(x^1, x^2, \cdots, x^n)$ s.t. $x = x^1 \oplus x^2 \oplus \cdots \oplus x^n$.
2: **Output:** n output shares $\{y^1, y^2, \cdots, y^n\}$ s.t. $y = \mathsf{SB}(x) = y^1 \oplus y^2 \oplus \cdots \oplus y^n$.
3: **procedure** SecSB($x^1, x^2, \cdots, x^n$)
4:     **for** $i = 0$ to 4 **do** $\triangleright$ Computing R^5
5:         $(u, w) \leftarrow \mathsf{CommonMult}\Big((x_2^1, x_2^2, \cdots, x_2^n), (x_3^1, x_3^2, \cdots, x_3^n), (x_4^1, x_4^2, \cdots, x_4^n)\Big)$
6:                         $\triangleright\ u = (u^1, u^2, \cdots, u^n)$, $\triangleright\ w = (w^1, w^2, \cdots, w^n)$
7:         $v \leftarrow \mathsf{SecMult}\Big((x_5^1, x_5^2, \cdots, x_5^n), (x_6^1, x_6^2, \cdots, x_6^n)\Big)$ $\triangleright\ v = (v^1, v^2, \cdots, v^n)$
8:         $x^1 \leftarrow (x_0^1 \oplus u^1, x_1^1, x_2^1, 1 \oplus x_3^1 \oplus v^1, x_4^1, 1 \oplus x_5^1 \oplus w^1, x_6^1)$
9:         $x^1 \leftarrow P(x^1)$
10:        **for** $j = 2$ to n **do**
11:            $x^j \leftarrow (x_0^j \oplus u^j, x_1^j, x_2^j, x_3^j \oplus v^j, x_4^j, x_5^j \oplus w^j, x_6^j)$
12:            $x^j \leftarrow P(x^j)$
13:        **end for**
14:        $(x^1, x^2, \cdots, x^n) \leftarrow \mathsf{RefreshMask}(x^1, x^2, \cdots, x^n)$
15:     **end for**
16:     $(u, w) \leftarrow \mathsf{CommonMult}\Big((x_2^1, x_2^2, \cdots, x_2^n), (x_3^1, x_3^2, \cdots, x_3^n), (x_4^1, x_4^2, \cdots, x_4^n)\Big)$
17:     $v \leftarrow \mathsf{SecMult}\Big((x_5^1, x_5^2, \cdots, x_5^n), (x_6^1, x_6^2, \cdots, x_6^n)\Big)$
18:     $y^1 \leftarrow (x_0^1 \oplus u^1, x_1^1, x_2^1, 1 \oplus x_3^1 \oplus v^1, x_4^1, 1 \oplus x_5^1 \oplus w^1, x_6^1)$
19:     $y^1 \leftarrow P(x^1)$
20:     $y^1 \leftarrow (x_0^1 \oplus 1, x_1^1, x_2^1 \oplus 1, x_3^1, x_4^1, x_5^1, x_6^1)$
21:     **for** $j = 2$ to n **do**
22:         $y^j \leftarrow (x_0^j \oplus u^j, x_1^j, x_2^j, x_3^j \oplus v^j, x_4^j, x_5^j \oplus w^j, x_6^j)$
23:         $y^j \leftarrow P(x^j)$
24:     **end for**
25:     $(y^1, y^2, \cdots, y^n) \leftarrow \mathsf{RefreshMask}(y^1, y^2, \cdots, y^n)$
26: **end procedure**

Security. Lemma 1 states that Algorithm 1 is t-SNI secure in the ISW probing model with $n = t + 1$. The proof is straightforward, follows from the security of the composition of the gadgets for each round as proved in [10]. We only show that the security of the gadget CommonMult in [20], and the gadgets SecMult and RefreshMask in [8] ensures the t-SNI security of each round of SB.

Lemma 1. *Let $[[x]] = (x^i)_{1 \leq i \leq n}$ be the input shares and $[[y]] = (y^i)_{1 \leq i \leq n}$ be the output shares of SB. For any subset of ℓ intermediate variables with $\ell \leq t$ and any subset O of output shares such that $\ell + |O| \leq t < n$, there exists a subset I of input indices such that $|I| \leq \ell$, the ℓ intermediate variables and the output shares in O can be perfectly simulated from $x_{|I}$.*

Proof. Let $\mathcal{G}_1$, $\mathcal{G}_2$, $\mathcal{G}_3$ be three gadgets corresponding to RefreshMask and CommonMult, SecMult, respectively. Let O be the output corresponding to $\mathcal{G}_1$ and O_1 be the output corresponding to gadgets $\mathcal{G}_2$, $\mathcal{G}_3$. Let $\mathcal{I} = \mathcal{I}_1 \cup \mathcal{I}_2 \cup \mathcal{I}_3$ be the set of indices corresponding to intermediate variables that an attacker can observe in three gadgets where $|\mathcal{I}| \leq \ell$.

Since RefreshMask is t-SNI secure, there exists a set of indices $\mathcal{S}_1$ such that $|\mathcal{S}_1| \leq |\mathcal{I}_1|$, and the gadget can be perfectly simulated from its input share indices in $\mathcal{S}_1$. Similarly, as CommonMult and SecMult are t-SNI secure, any probe within these two gadgets can generate indices in $\mathcal{I}_2$ or $\mathcal{I}_3$, such that $|\mathcal{S}_2| \leq |\mathcal{I}_2| + |\mathcal{I}_3| + |\mathcal{S}_1|$, and the gadget can be perfectly simulated from its input share indices in $\mathcal{S}_2$. Therefore, $|\mathcal{S}_2| \leq |\mathcal{I}_2| + |\mathcal{I}_3| + |\mathcal{I}_1|$ as $|\mathcal{S}_1| \leq |\mathcal{I}_1|$ from $\mathcal{G}_1$. As the SNI security of each gadget ensures the existence of a simulator, thus the simulator for one round can be constructed by composing these simulators to perfectly simulate from $x_{|I}$ where $I = \mathcal{S}_2$ and $|I| = |\mathcal{S}_2| \leq \ell$. Hence the proof.

4.2   Construction of an SNI-Secure WGP

The input to the WGP is shared as $x = x^1 \oplus x^2 \oplus \cdots \oplus x^n$ and the output $y = \mathsf{WGP}(x)$ is shared as $y = \mathsf{WGP}(x) = y^1 \oplus y^2 \oplus \cdots \oplus y^n$. We explore two approaches, namely randomized lookup table of [22] and the Boolean circuit implementation, for secure evaluation of WGP. We implement the higher-order randomized lookup table of WGP using the technique of [22], in software. We generated an optimized Boolean circuit of WGP, in hardware, consisting of 313 XOR and 172 AND gates (2-input) and 66 NOT gates. We construct a masked WGP using the Boolean circuit by substituting each AND gate by an SNI-secure AND gadget (i.e., SecMult) and composing the gadgets securely, which results in a t-SNI secure masked WGP. For instance, our masked implementation of WGP using ANF for $n = 2$ has an overhead of 3.7× compared to the unprotected (ANF) WGP implementation (see Table 4). The security of the masked WGP implemented using the ANF is straightforward. We omit it here.

4.3   Putting All Together

Our masked WAGE is designed to provide a t-order protection against side-channel attacks such as power analysis. Our hardware architecture for the masked WAGE is parallel and designed to be low-latency. Algorithm 2 describes the pseudocode of the masked WAGE permutation. In each round of the masked WAGE, the state is shared among n state shares ($\mathbf{S}^i$) where the feedback computations in Lines 5–7, updating intermediate words in Lines 10–14 and shift operations in Lines 20–22 that are linear are computed in parallel. Our architecture uses corresponding masked WGP and SB in Lines 8–9 for the S-box operations, which are evaluated in parallel. Note that the pair of round constants at each round are added to only one share (say $\mathbf{S}^1$) in Lines 15–16. A high-level overview of the architecture of the masked WAGE permutation for the first-order protection is shown in Fig. 6. For a low-latency implementation of the masked WAGE, the circuit level implementation of the masked WGP is used as it can be computed in one clock cycle. For software implementations, to avoid bit level operations, we use the randomized lookup table for the secure evaluation of both WGP and SB.

Algorithm 2. The Masked WAGE

1: **Input:** $[[\mathbf{S}]] = (\mathbf{S}^1, \mathbf{S}^2, \cdots, \mathbf{S}^n)$
2: **Output:** $[[\mathbf{S}]]$ where $\mathbf{S} \leftarrow \text{WAGE\_STATEUPDATE}^{111}(\mathbf{S})$
3: **procedure** MASKED_WAGE( )
4:     **for** $i = 0$ to 110 **do**
5:         **for** $j = 1$ to n **do**
6:             $fb^j \leftarrow \text{FB}(\mathbf{S}^j)$
7:         **end for**
8:         $[[S_j]] \leftarrow \text{SecSB}([[S_j]]), j \in \{8, 15, 27, 34\}$
9:         $[[S_{18}]] \leftarrow \text{SecWGP}([[S_{18}]])$
10:        $[[tmp]] \leftarrow \text{SecWGP}([[S_{36}]])$
11:        $[[S_5]] \leftarrow [[S_5]] \oplus [[S_8]]$
12:        $[[S_{11}]] \leftarrow [[S_{11}]] \oplus [[S_{15}]]$
13:        $[[S_{19}]] \leftarrow [[S_{19}]] \oplus [[S_{18})]]$
14:        $[[S_{24}]] \leftarrow [[S_{24}]] \oplus [[S_{27}]]$
15:        $[[S_{30}]] \leftarrow [[S_{30}]] \oplus [[S_{34}]]$
16:        $S_{19}^1 \leftarrow S_{19}^1 \oplus rc_0$
17:        $fb^1 \leftarrow fb^1 \oplus tmp^1 \oplus rc_1$
18:        **for** $j = 2$ to n **do**
19:            $fb^j \leftarrow fb^j \oplus tmp^j$
20:        **end for**
21:        **for** $j = 1$ to n **do**
22:            $\mathbf{S}^j \leftarrow \text{Shift}(\mathbf{S}^j, fb^j)$
23:        **end for**
24:    **end for**
25:    **return** $[[\mathbf{S}]] = (\mathbf{S}^1, \mathbf{S}^2, \cdots, \mathbf{S}^n)$ s.t. $\mathbf{S} = \bigoplus_{i=1}^n \mathbf{S}^i$
26: **end procedure**

Security. The masked WAGE permutation is constructed by composing 111 round function gadgets. Intuitively, according to the compositional security proof of t-SNI security in [8], the masked WAGE permutation is t-SNI secure. We summarize the security of the masked WAGE permutation in the ISW probing model in Theorem 1.

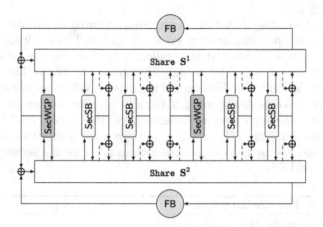

Fig. 6. Schematic of the masked WAGE permutation for 1-order protection.

Theorem 1. *The protected WAGE described in Algorithm 2 is t-SNI secure where $t = n + 1$.*

Complexity. We now provide the amount of random bits required for the masked WAGE permutation in terms of the number of shares n. The randomness amount can be computed by calculating the unit operations of different gadgets. The RefreshMask, CommonMult and SecMult gadgets consume $\frac{7n(n-1)}{2}$, $\frac{3n(n-1)}{2}$ and $\frac{n(n-1)}{2}$ bits, respectively. Thus, the total number of random bits for SecSB is $33n(n-1)$ bits (asymptotically $O(n^2)$). According to [22], the number of random bits for SecWGP with the randomized lookup table is $\frac{64n(n-1)(2n-1)}{3}$ (asymptotically $O(n^3)$). On the other hand, the number of random bits for the gate-level implementation of SecWGP is $87n(n-1)$ bits. For each round of WAGE with masked WGP implemented using gate-level, the amount of bits is $(33n(n-1) \times 4 + 87n(n-1) \times 2) = 255n(n-1)$, thus for evaluating the WAGE permutation the total number of random bits is $255 \times 111 \times n(n-1)$. The (asymptotic) time complexity of the masked WAGE is $O(n^2)$ when SecWGP is implemented using a Boolean circuit.

CPA on the First-Order Masked WAGE. We use the randomized lookup table approach and implemented the Algorithm 2 in C. For the analysis, we first converted the C code to the ARM Cortex-M4F (see Sect. 3.1) environment. We then perform the standard test vector leakage assessment (TVLA) [18,37] to validate that our masked implementation is free of the first-order leakage. We observed that power traces do not detect leakage till 60,000 time points for the protected implementation while only 600 time points are sufficient to detect leakage in case of the unprotected implementation. Note that the protected version has more time points than the unprotected version is due to the slowdown of the masking algorithm. Both traces are the entire execution of one round of the WAGE permutation. Trying to find the leakage with 10,000 traces may not be convincing or visible. Thus, we provided the result for more traces (see Appendix A).

5   Hardware Implementation Results

In this section, we provide the implementation results of the protected WAGE for different masking orders in hardware. Our simulations were done in Mentor Graphics ModelSim SE v10.7c and logic synthesis was performed with Synopsys Design Compiler version P-2019.03 (using the `compile_ultra` command). For the physical synthesis Cadence Encounter v14.13 was used. We used two 65 nm ASIC cell libraries: ST Microelectronics 65 nm and TSMC 65 nm.

Implementation Results. Our preliminary implementation results are provided in Tables 3 and 4. Table 3 shows the comparison of two SecMult multiplication gadgets of [8] with a common share CS_SecMult multiplication gadget of [20]. The two multiplication gadgets in 2x SecMult were implemented with a common input. In Table 4, we include a detailed break down of area and combinational delay (resp. clock period) for $n = 2, 3, 4$ shares (resp. $t = 1, 2, 3$-order protection). For both technologies, the middle column indicates the area overhead compared to the unprotected module. To accurately show the scaling with n, all implementations assume an environment capable of providing random bits. Further details are omitted for brevity.

Table 3. Area comparison [GE] of two SecMult multiplication gadgets with a common share CS_SecMult multiplication gadget.

	STMicro 65 nm			TSMC 65 nm		
	$n = 2$	$n = 3$	$n = 4$	$n = 2$	$n = 3$	$n = 4$
2x SecMult	24	59	119	24	59	130
CS_SecMult	12	69	98	13	69	105

Brief Discussion on Results. Our theoretical and implementation results of the stand-alone modules of SecMult (Table 3) show comparable or smaller area of the common share multiplication gadget. However, the implementation results of the protected SB modules in Table 4 show that this advantage is lost, most likely due to the additional random inputs needed for the common share multiplication gadget and their routing.

Table 4. Implementation results of S-boxes (WGP and SB) and the WAGE AE in ASIC. Italic denotes the use of the common share multiplication gadget.

Algorithm	STMicro 65 nm			TSMC 65 nm		
	Area [GE]	Area overhead	Delay [ns]	Area [GE]	Area overhead	Delay [ns]
WGP						
Constant array [1,2]	258	-	1.4	270	-	0.9
Unprotected ANF	759	-	1.9	804	-	1.3
$n = 2$	2830	3.7	2.3	3090	3.8	1.9
$n = 3$	6030	2.1	3.1	6580	8.1	2.1
$n = 4$	10200	1.7	3.7	11400	14.1	2.4
SB						
Unprotected ANF	63	-	0.9	70	-	0.8
$n = 2$	285	4.5	1.7	307	4.3	1.4
	285	*4.5*	*1.9*	*323*	*4.6*	*1.4*
$n = 3$	626	9.9	2.2	677	9.6	1.5
	715	*11.3*	*2.3*	*829*	*11.8*	*1.5*
$n = 4$	1140	18.1	2.3	1200	17.1	1.9
	1275	*20.2*	*2.2*	*1280*	*18.2*	*2.1*
	Area [GE]	Area overhead	Clk. period [ns]	Area [GE]	Area overhead	Clk. period [ns]
WAGE AE						
Constant array [1,2]	2900	-	1.1	3290	-	0.9
Unprotected ANF	3830	-	1.9	4430	-	1.8
$n = 2$	11177	2.9	3.6	12714	2.9	2.9
	11177	*2.9*	*2.9*	*12711*	*2.9*	*2.9*
$n = 3$	21566	5.6	5.0	23912	5.4	4.9
	21953	*5.7*	*3.9*	*24174*	*5.5*	*3.4*
$n = 4$	33985	8.9	5.2	38818	8.7	4.9
	34238	*8.9*	*4.6*	*39067*	*8.8*	*4.4*

6   Conclusion and Future Work

In this paper, we practically demonstrated that the 128-bit key of WAGE can be recovered using the correlation power analysis, requiring 10,000 power traces. To resist against side-channel attacks, we presented the first high-order masking scheme of WAGE and proved its t-SNI security in the ISW probing model. We designed the hardware of the masked WAGE in ASIC using STMicro 65 nm and TSMC 65 nm technologies for the first, second, and third-order security and reported the detailed performance results along with a comparison with the other NIST LWC round 2 candidates.

As a future work, we will perform side-channel attack experiments and analyze the higher-order masked implementations of WAGE. Furthermore, we will extend our work and incorporate other types of side-channel implementations such as threshold, unified masked multiplication, and domain oriented masking to investigate trade-offs among performance parameters of WAGE.

Acknowledgement. Hardware implementation in this work are based on the original WAGE hardware implementation from [1]. The authors would like to thank Dr. Mark Aagaard for his great help with synthesis tools and valuable suggestions for this work. The work of Yunsi Fei, Cheng Gongye and Tianhong Xu was supported in part by US National Science Foundation under grant SaTC-1563697. The work of Guang Gong, Raghvendra Rohit, Yunjie Yi, and Nusa Zidaric was supported by the NSERC SPG grant, and the work of Kalikinkar Mandal was partially supported by the NSERC SPG grant when he was at University of Waterloo.

A   Details on Correlation Power Analysis of **WAGE**

CPA Attack Final Phase. In Table 5, we provide the details of key words recovery information at different batches in the final phase of the CPA attack.

Table 5. Key word recovery information at different batches in the final phase of attack. The corresponding round number, state register, and previously known key words used for the attack.

Batch	Key word	Round	State register	Known required key word
2	K_1	10	0	K_{18}
3	K_3	10	1	K_{18}, K_1
4	K_5	10	2	K_{18}, K_1, K_3
5	K_7	10	3	K_{18}, K_1, K_3, K_5
6	K_9	12	2	$K_{18}, K_1, K_3, K_5, K_7$
7	K_{11}	12	3	$K_{18}, K_1, K_3, K_5, K_7, K_9, K_{17}$
8	K_0	0	36	$K_{12}, K_{16}, K_1, K_{11}, K_{15}$
9	K_2	1	36	$K_0, K_1, K_3, K_{11}, K_{12}, K_{14}, K_{15}, K_{16}, K_{17}$
10	K_4	2	36	$K_0, K_1, K_2, K_3, K_5, K_{11}, K_{12}, K_{14}, K_{15}, K_{16}, K_{17}$
11	K_6	3	36	$K_0, K_1, K_2, K_3, K_4, K_5, K_7, K_{11}, K_{12}, K_{14}, K_{15}, K_{16}, K_{17}$
12	K_8	4	36	$K_0, K_1, K_2, K_3, K_4, K_5, K_6, K_7, K_9, K_{11}, K_{12}, K_{13}, K_{14}, K_{15}, K_{16}, K_{17}$
13	K_{10}	5	36	$K_0, K_1, K_2, K_3, K_4, K_5, K_6, K_7, K_8, K_9, K_{11}, K_{12}, K_{13}, K_{14}, K_{15}, K_{16}, K_{17}$

Test Vector Leakage Assessment of First-Order Masked WAGE. We use the standard test vector leakage assessment (TVLA) to test the resistance of the first-order masked implementation of WAGE against the CPA attack. We collected same number of traces (nearly 10,000) and applied the TVLA on both the unprotected and first-order masked implementations. An example of TVLA for both implementations for the least significant bit (LSB) of K_{18} is shown in Fig. 7. It can be seen that the t-values are larger than 5 for the unprotected version (Fig. 7a) which indicates the leakage. For the masked WAGE, t-values are uniform for up to 60,000 time points (Fig. 7b) and as such no leakage is detected.

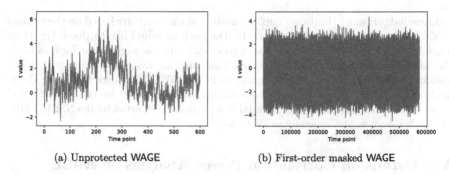

(a) Unprotected WAGE   (b) First-order masked WAGE

Fig. 7. TVLA of LSB of K_{18} at round 10: a) unprotected WAGE and b) first-order masked WAGE.

References

1. Aagaard, M., AlTawy, R., Gong, G., Mandal, K., Rohit, R., Zidaric, N.: WAGE: an authenticated cipher (2019). https://csrc.nist.gov/CSRC/media/Projects/lightweight-cryptography/documents/round-2/spec-doc-rnd2/wage-spec-round2.pdf

2. Aagaard, M., Sattarov, M., Zidarič, N.: Hardware design and analysis of the ACE and WAGE ciphers. In: NIST LWC Workshop (2019). https://arxiv.org/abs/1909.12338

3. Agrawal, D., Archambeault, B., Rao, J.R., Rohatgi, P.: The EM side—channel(s). In: Kaliski, B.S., Koç, K., Paar, C. (eds.) CHES 2002. LNCS, vol. 2523, pp. 29–45. Springer, Heidelberg (2003). https://doi.org/10.1007/3-540-36400-5_4

4. Akkar, M.-L., Bévan, R., Goubin, L.: Two power analysis attacks against one-mask methods. In: Roy, B., Meier, W. (eds.) FSE 2004. LNCS, vol. 3017, pp. 332–347. Springer, Heidelberg (2004). https://doi.org/10.1007/978-3-540-25937-4_21

5. Akkar, M.-L., Giraud, C.: An implementation of DES and AES, secure against some attacks. In: Koç, Ç.K., Naccache, D., Paar, C. (eds.) CHES 2001. LNCS, vol. 2162, pp. 309–318. Springer, Heidelberg (2001). https://doi.org/10.1007/3-540-44709-1_26

6. AlTawy, R., Gong, G., Mandal, K., Rohit, R.: WAGE: an authenticated encryption with a twist. IACR Trans. Sym. Cryptol. **2020**(S1), 132–159 (2020)

7. Banik, S., et al.: GIFT-COFB. Cryptology ePrint Archive, Report 2020/738 (2020). https://eprint.iacr.org/2020/738

8. Barthe, G., et al.: Strong non-interference and type-directed higher-order masking. In: Proceedings of the 2016 ACM SIGSAC Conference on Computer and Communications Security (CCS 2016), pp. 116–129. ACM, New York (2016)

9. Barthe, G., Belaïd, S., Dupressoir, F., Fouque, P.-A., Grégoire, B., Strub, P.-Y.: Verified proofs of higher-order masking. In: Oswald, E., Fischlin, M. (eds.) EUROCRYPT 2015. LNCS, vol. 9056, pp. 457–485. Springer, Heidelberg (2015). https://doi.org/10.1007/978-3-662-46800-5_18

10. Barthe, G., et al.: Strong non-interference and type-directed higher-order masking. Cryptology ePrint Archive, Report 2015/506 (2015). https://eprint.iacr.org/2015/506

11. Bassham, L., Calik, C., Chang, D., Kang, J., McKay, K., Turan, M.S.: Lightweight cryptography: round 2 candidates (2019). https://csrc.nist.gov/Projects/lightweight-cryptography/round-2-candidates

12. Beierle, C., et al.: SKINNY-AEAD and SKINNY-hash. IACR Trans. Sym. Cryptol. **2020**(S1), 88–131 (2020). https://doi.org/10.13154/tosc.v2020.iS1.88-131

13. Benoît, O., Peyrin, T.: Side-channel analysis of six SHA-3 candidates. In: Mangard, S., Standaert, F.-X. (eds.) CHES 2010. LNCS, vol. 6225, pp. 140–157. Springer, Heidelberg (2010). https://doi.org/10.1007/978-3-642-15031-9_10

14. Brier, E., Clavier, C., Olivier, F.: Correlation power analysis with a leakage model. In: Joye, M., Quisquater, J.-J. (eds.) CHES 2004. LNCS, vol. 3156, pp. 16–29. Springer, Heidelberg (2004). https://doi.org/10.1007/978-3-540-28632-5_2

15. Caforio, A., Balli, F., Banik, S.: Energy analysis of lightweight AEAD circuits. Cryptology ePrint Archive, Report 2020/607 (2020). https://eprint.iacr.org/2020/607

16. Carlet, C., Goubin, L., Prouff, E., Quisquater, M., Rivain, M.: Higher-order masking schemes for S-boxes. In: Canteaut, A. (ed.) FSE 2012. LNCS, vol. 7549, pp. 366–384. Springer, Heidelberg (2012). https://doi.org/10.1007/978-3-642-34047-5_21

17. Chari, S., Jutla, C.S., Rao, J.R., Rohatgi, P.: Towards sound approaches to counteract power-analysis attacks. In: Wiener, M. (ed.) CRYPTO 1999. LNCS, vol. 1666, pp. 398–412. Springer, Heidelberg (1999). https://doi.org/10.1007/3-540-48405-1_26

18. Cooper, J., DeMulder, E., Goodwill, G., Jaffe, J., Kenworthy, G.: Test vector leakage assessment (TVLA) methodology in practice. In: International Cryptographic Module Conference, vol. 20 (2013)

19. Coron, J.-S.: Higher order masking of look-up tables. In: Nguyen, P.Q., Oswald, E. (eds.) EUROCRYPT 2014. LNCS, vol. 8441, pp. 441–458. Springer, Heidelberg (2014). https://doi.org/10.1007/978-3-642-55220-5_25

20. Coron, J.-S., Greuet, A., Prouff, E., Zeitoun, R.: Faster evaluation of SBoxes via common shares. In: Gierlichs, B., Poschmann, A.Y. (eds.) CHES 2016. LNCS, vol. 9813, pp. 498–514. Springer, Heidelberg (2016). https://doi.org/10.1007/978-3-662-53140-2_24

21. Coron, J.-S., Prouff, E., Rivain, M., Roche, T.: Higher-order side channel security and mask refreshing. In: Moriai, S. (ed.) FSE 2013. LNCS, vol. 8424, pp. 410–424. Springer, Heidelberg (2014). https://doi.org/10.1007/978-3-662-43933-3_21

22. Coron, J.-S., Rondepierre, F., Zeitoun, R.: High order masking of look-up tables with common shares. IACR Trans. Cryptograp. Hardw. Embed. Syst. (CHES 2018), **2018**(1), 40–72 (2018). https://doi.org/10.13154/tches.v2018.i1.40-72

23. De Cnudde, T., Reparaz, O., Bilgin, B., Nikova, S., Nikov, V., Rijmen, V.: Masking AES with $d+1$ shares in hardware. In: Gierlichs, B., Poschmann, A.Y. (eds.) CHES 2016. LNCS, vol. 9813, pp. 194–212. Springer, Heidelberg (2016). https://doi.org/10.1007/978-3-662-53140-2_10

24. Gandolfi, K., Mourtel, C., Olivier, F.: Electromagnetic analysis: concrete results. In: Koç, Ç.K., Naccache, D., Paar, C. (eds.) CHES 2001. LNCS, vol. 2162, pp. 251–261. Springer, Heidelberg (2001). https://doi.org/10.1007/3-540-44709-1_21

25. Gross, H., Mangard, S.: Reconciling $d + 1$ masking in hardware and software. In: Fischer, W., Homma, N. (eds.) CHES 2017. LNCS, vol. 10529, pp. 115–136. Springer, Cham (2017). https://doi.org/10.1007/978-3-319-66787-4_6

26. Groß, H., Mangard, S.: A unified masking approach. J. Cryptogr. Eng. **8**(2), 109–124 (2018)

27. Groß, H., Mangard, S., Korak, T.: Domain-oriented masking: ccompact masked hardware implementations with arbitrary protection order. In: Proceedings of the 2016 ACM Workshop on Theory of Implementation Security (TIS 2016). p. 3. ACM, New York (2016)

28. Groß, H., Wenger, E., Dobraunig, C., Ehrenhöfer, C.: Suit up! - made-to-measure hardware implementations of ASCON. In: 2015 Euromicro Conference on Digital System Design, pp. 645–652 (2015)

29. Ishai, Y., Sahai, A., Wagner, D.: Private circuits: securing hardware against probing attacks. In: Boneh, D. (ed.) CRYPTO 2003. LNCS, vol. 2729, pp. 463–481. Springer, Heidelberg (2003). https://doi.org/10.1007/978-3-540-45146-4_27

30. Kocher, P., Jaffe, J., Jun, B.: Differential power analysis. In: Wiener, M. (ed.) CRYPTO 1999. LNCS, vol. 1666, pp. 388–397. Springer, Heidelberg (1999). https://doi.org/10.1007/3-540-48405-1_25

31. Mangard, S., Oswald, E., Popp, T.: Power Aanalysis Attacks: Revealing the Secrets of Smart Cards, vol. 31, Springer Science & Business Media, Cham (2008). https://doi.org/10.1007/978-0-387-38162-6

32. Nikova, S., Rechberger, C., Rijmen, V.: Threshold Implementations against side-channel attacks and glitches. In: Ning, P., Qing, S., Li, N. (eds.) ICICS 2006. LNCS, vol. 4307, pp. 529–545. Springer, Heidelberg (2006). https://doi.org/10.1007/11935308_38

33. Reparaz, O., Bilgin, B., Nikova, S., Gierlichs, B., Verbauwhede, I.: Consolidating masking schemes. In: Gennaro, R., Robshaw, M. (eds.) CRYPTO 2015. LNCS, vol. 9215, pp. 764–783. Springer, Heidelberg (2015). https://doi.org/10.1007/978-3-662-47989-6_37

34. Rivain, M., Prouff, E.: Provably secure higher-order masking of AES. In: Mangard, S., Standaert, F.-X. (eds.) CHES 2010. LNCS, vol. 6225, pp. 413–427. Springer, Heidelberg (2010). https://doi.org/10.1007/978-3-642-15031-9_28

35. Roy, A., Vivek, S.: Analysis and improvement of the generic higher-order masking scheme of FSE 2012. In: Bertoni, G., Coron, J.-S. (eds.) CHES 2013. LNCS, vol. 8086, pp. 417–434. Springer, Heidelberg (2013). https://doi.org/10.1007/978-3-642-40349-1_24

36. Sasdrich, P., Bilgin, P., Hutter, M., Marson, M.E.: Low-latency hardware masking with application to AES. IACR Trans. Cryptogr. Hardw. Embed. Syst. **2020**(2), 300–326 (2020). https://doi.org/10.13154/tches.v2020.i2.300-326

37. Standaert, F.-X.: How (not) to use welch's t-test in side-channel security evaluations. In: International Conference on Smart Card Research and Advanced Applications, pp. 65–79. Springer, Heidelberg (2018). https://doi.org/10.1007/978-3-030-68487-7

38. Veyrat-Charvillon, N., Gérard, B., Standaert, F.-X.: Soft analytical side-channel attacks. In: Sarkar, P., Iwata, T. (eds.) ASIACRYPT 2014. LNCS, vol. 8873, pp. 282–296. Springer, Heidelberg (2014). https://doi.org/10.1007/978-3-662-45611-8_15

On the Influence of Optimizers in Deep Learning-Based Side-Channel Analysis

Guilherme Perin$^{(\boxtimes)}$ and Stjepan Picek

Delft University of Technology, Delft, The Netherlands
`s.picek@tudelft.nl`

Abstract. The deep learning-based side-channel analysis represents a powerful and easy to deploy option for profiling side-channel attacks. A detailed tuning phase is often required to reach a good performance where one first needs to select relevant hyperparameters and then tune them. A common selection for the tuning phase are hyperparameters connected with the neural network architecture, while those influencing the training process are less explored.

In this work, we concentrate on the optimizer hyperparameter, and we show that this hyperparameter has a significant role in the attack performance. Our results show that common choices of optimizers (Adam and RMSprop) indeed work well, but they easily overfit, which means that we must use short training phases, small profiling models, and explicit regularization. On the other hand, SGD type of optimizers works well on average (slower convergence and less overfit), but only if momentum is used. Finally, our results show that Adagrad represents a strong option to use in scenarios with longer training phases or larger profiling models.

Keywords: Side-channel analysis · Profiling attacks · Neural networks · Optimizers

1 Introduction

Side-channel attacks (SCA) are non-invasive attacks against security-sensitive implementations [16]. When running on embedded devices, cryptographic implementations need to be protected against such attacks by implementing countermeasures at software and hardware levels. If not sufficiently SCA-resistant, an adversary can measure side-channel leakages like power consumption [12] or electromagnetic emanation [25]. The attacker can then apply statistical analysis to recover secrets, including cryptographic keys, and compromise the product. Side-channel attacks can be mainly divided into unsupervised (or non-profiling) and supervised (or profiling) attacks. Unsupervised methods include simple analysis, differential analysis [12], correlation analysis [1], and mutual information analysis [6]. Supervised attacks are mainly template attacks [3], stochastic attacks [27], and machine learning-based attacks [10,22]. The profiling or training phase in supervised attacks assumes that the adversary has a device under control that is

© Springer Nature Switzerland AG 2021
O. Dunkelman et al. (Eds.): SAC 2020, LNCS 12804, pp. 615–636, 2021.
https://doi.org/10.1007/978-3-030-81652-0_24

identical (or close to identical) to the target device. This way, he can query multiple cryptographic executions with different keys and inputs to create a training set and learn a statistical model from side-channel leakages. The test or attack phase is then applied to a new device identical to the profiling device. If the profiling model provides satisfactory generalization, the adversary can recover secrets from the target device.

Recently, deep learning methods have been applied to side-channel analysis [2,11,15]. The main deep learning algorithms used in profiling SCA are multilayer perceptron (MLP) and convolutional neural networks (CNNs). The application of these techniques opened new perspectives for SCA-based security evaluations mainly due to the following advantages: 1) CNNs demonstrated to be more robust against desynchronized side-channel measurements [2], 2) CNNs and MLPs show the capacity of learning high-order leakages from protected targets [11], 3) preprocessing phases for feature extraction (points of interest) are done implicitly by the deep neural network [2,11], and 4) techniques like visualization [8,17] can help to identify where a complex learning algorithm detects leakages from side-channel measurements.

Despite all the success, the research in the field of deep learning-based SCA continuously seeks for improvements. There, a common option is to optimize the behavior of neural networks by tuning their hyperparameters. Some of those hyperparameters are commonly explored, like the number of layers/neurons and activation functions [24,29]. Some other hyperparameters receive much less attention. Unfortunately, it is not easy to select all the hyperparameters relevant to a specific problem or decide how to tune them. Indeed, the selection of optimal hyperparameters for deep neural networks in SCA requires understanding each of them in the learning phase. The modification of one hyperparameter may have a strong influence on other hyperparameters, making deep neural networks extremely difficult to be tuned.

We can informally divide the hyperparameters into those that influence the architecture (e.g., number of neurons and layers, activation functions) and those that influence the training process (e.g., optimizer, loss function, learning rate). Interestingly, the first category is well-explored in SCA with papers discussing methodologies or providing extensive experimental results [24,31]. The second category is much less explored, see, e.g., [13]. One of those less explored (or not explored) hyperparameters is the optimizer. With the learning rate, the optimizer minimizes the loss function and, thus, improves neural networks' performance. Despite its importance, this hyperparameter is commonly overlooked in SCA, and researchers usually either do not tune it at all or provide only a limited set of options to investigate.

There are several reasons why to explore the influence of optimizers on the performance of deep learning-based SCA:

1. As already stated, the optimizer is an important hyperparameter for tuning neural networks, but up to now, it did not receive much attention. More precisely, the researchers investigated its significance in the context of SCA only marginally.

2. Recent works showed that even relatively shallow deep learning architectures could reach top performance in SCA [11,31]. This means that we do not have issues with the network capacity (i.e., the network's ability to find a good mapping between inputs and outputs and generalize to the new measurements). This makes the search for a good neural network architecture easier as it limits the number of hyperparameter tuning experiments one needs to conduct. Simultaneously, we need to be careful to train the neural networks well, which means finding good weight parameter values that will not cause getting stuck in local optima.
3. Finally, there is a well-known discrepancy between machine learning and side-channel analysis metrics [21]. It is far from trivial to decide when to stop the training process to avoid overfitting. Different optimizers show different behavior where overfitting does not occur equally easy. Instead of finding new ways to indicate when to stop the training [19], we can also explore whether there is a more suitable choice of optimizers that are more aligned with the SCA goals.

To provide detailed results, we run experiments on two datasets and numerous scenarios, which resulted in more than 700 h of continuous GPU runtime. We analyze two categories of optimizers: stochastic gradient descent (SGD) and adaptive gradient methods (Adam, RMSprop, Adagrad, and Adadelta). Our results show that when using SGD optimizers, momentum should always be used. What is more, with *Nesterov*, it additionally reduces the chances to overfit. At the same time, these optimizers require a relatively long training process to converge. While less pronounced, such optimizers can also overfit, especially for long training phases.

From adaptive optimizers, Adam and RMSprop work the best if one uses short training phases. Unfortunately, these optimizers also easily overfit, which means extra care needs to be taken (for instance, to develop an appropriate early stopping mechanism). Since those two optimizers overfit for longer training phases, they also work better for smaller profiling models. Finally, if one requires longer training phases or larger profiling models, Adagrad behaves the best. We consider this to be very interesting as Adagrad is not commonly used in profiling SCA. This finding could be especially relevant in future research when more complex datasets are considered, and we are forced to use profiling models that have a larger capacity. Interestingly, in some of our results, we also observe a deep double descent phenomenon [18], which indicates that longer training is not always better. This is the first time this phenomenon is observed in the SCA domain to the best of our knowledge.

2   Background

2.1   Profiling SCA and Deep Learning

We consider a typical profiling side-channel analysis setting. A powerful attacker has a device (clone device) with knowledge about the secret key implemented.

The attacker can obtain a set of N profiling traces $X_1, \ldots, X_N$ (where each trace corresponds to the processing or plaintext or ciphertext T_p). With this information, he calculates a leakage model $Y(T_p, k^*)$. Then, the attacker uses that information to build a profiling model f (thus, this phase is commonly known as the profiling phase). The attack is carried out on another device by using the mapping f. The attacker measures an additional Q traces $X_1, \ldots, X_Q$ from the device under attack to guess the unknown secret key k_a^* (this is known as the attack phase).

To evaluate the performance of an attack, we need evaluation metrics. The most common evaluation metrics in SCA are success rate (SR) and guessing entropy (GE) [28]. GE states the average number of key candidates an adversary needs to test to reveal the secret key after conducting a side-channel analysis. More precisely, let Q be the number of measurements in the attack phase and that the attack outputs a key guessing vector $g = [g_1, g_2, \ldots, g_{|\mathcal{K}|}]$ in decreasing order of probability with $|\mathcal{K}|$ being the size of the keyspace. The guessing entropy is the average position of k_a^* in g over multiple experiments. We average guessing entropy over 100 experiments. Note, we calculate guessing entropy for a single key byte, so the proper term is partial guessing entropy. Nevertheless, we use both terms interchangeably.

One can observe that the same process is followed in the supervised learning paradigm, enabling us to use supervised machine learning for SCA. More precisely, the profiling phase is the same as the training, while the attack phase represents the testing. There are three essential components of machine learning algorithms: 1) model, 2) loss function (by convention, most objective functions in machine learning are intended to be minimized), and 3) optimization procedure to minimize the loss. To build a good profiling model (i.e., one that generalizes well to unseen data), we train a set of its parameters θ such that the loss is minimal[1]. Finally, to define the learning model, we use a set of hyperparameters λ[2]. In our experiments, we consider two neural network types: multilayer perceptron and convolutional neural networks. As evident from related works (Sect. 3), these methods represent common choices in SCA. Note that we provide additional info on those methods in Appendix A.

2.2   Optimizers

There are multiple ways how to minimize the objective function, i.e., to minimize the loss function. A common assumption in machine learning is to assume that the objective function is differentiable, and thus, we can calculate the gradient at each point to find the optimum. More precisely, gradients point toward higher values, so we need to consider the gradient's opposite to find the minimal value. In the context of unconstrained optimization, we can apply gradient descent as

---

[1] The parameters are the configuration variables internal to the model and whose values can be estimated from data.

[2] The hyperparameters are all those configuration variables that are external to the model.

the first-order optimization algorithm. To find a local minimum, we take steps proportional to the negative of the gradient of the function at the current point. In gradient descent, one conducts a "batch" optimization. More precisely, using the full training set N to update θ (i.e., one update for the whole training set). When the model training dataset is large, the cost of gradient descent for each iteration will be high. For additional information about optimizers, we refer interested readers to [4].

SGD. Stochastic gradient descent is a stochastic approximation of the gradient descent algorithm that minimizes the objective function written as a sum of differentiable functions. SGD reduces computational cost at each iteration as it uniformly samples an index $i \in 1, \ldots, N$ at random and computes the gradient to update θ (one update of parameters for each training example). Due to the frequent updates with a high variance for SGD, this can cause large fluctuations of the loss function. Instead of taking only a single example to update the parameters, we can also take a fixed number of them: a mini-batch. In that case, we talk about mini-batch SGD.

Momentum. SGD can have problems converging around the local optima due to the shape of the surface curves. Momentum (also called classical momentum) is a technique that can help alleviate this and accelerate SGD in the relevant direction. It does this by adding a fraction γ (momentum term) of the update vector of the past time step to the current update vector. The momentum term increases for dimensions whose gradients point in the same directions and reduces updates for dimensions whose gradients change directions.

Nesterov. Nesterov (Nesterov accelerated gradient) improves upon momentum by approximating the next position of the parameters. More precisely, we can calculate the gradient for the approximate future position of parameters. This anticipatory step prevents momentum from going too fast, increasing the performance of the neural network.

Adagrad. Adagrad adapts the learning rate to the parameters, performing smaller updates (small learning rates) for parameters associated with frequently occurring features, and larger updates (high learning rates) for parameters associated with less frequent features. One of Adagrad's main benefits is that it eliminates the need to tune the learning rate manually. On the other hand, during the training process, the learning rates shrink (due to the accumulation of the squared gradients), up to the point where the algorithm cannot obtain further knowledge.

Adadelta. Adadelta represents an extension of the Adagrad method. In Adadelta, we aim to reduce its monotonically decreasing learning rate. More precisely, instead of accumulating all past squared gradients, Adadelta restricts the window of accumulated past gradients to some fixed size. The sum of gradients is recursively defined as a decaying average of all past squared gradients to avoid storing those squared gradients.

RMSprop. RMSprop is an adaptive learning rate method that aims to resolve Adagrad's aggressively decreasing learning rates (like Adadelta). RMSprop divides the learning rate by an exponentially decaying average of squared gradients.

Adam. Adam (Adaptive Moment Estimation) is one more method that computes adaptive learning rates for each parameter. This method combines the benefits of Adagrad and RMSprop methods. This way, it stores an exponentially decaying average of past squared gradients, but it also keeps an exponentially decaying average of past gradients, similar to the momentum method.

2.3   Datasets

We consider two publicly available datasets, representing software AES implementations protected with the first-order Boolean masking - the ASCAD database [24]. The traces were measured from an implementation consisting of a software AES implementation running on an 8-bit microcontroller. The AES is protected with the first-order masking, where the two first key bytes (index 1 and 2) are not protected with masking (e.g., masks set to zeros) and the key bytes 3 to 16 are masked.

The first dataset is the ASCAD dataset with the fixed key. For the data with fixed key encryption, we use a time-aligned dataset in a prepossessing step. There are 60 000 EM traces (50 000 training/cross-validation traces and 10 000 test traces), and each trace consists of 700 points of interest (POI).

For the second dataset, we use ASCAD with random keys, where there are 200 000 traces in the profiling dataset and 100 000 traces in the attack dataset. A window of 1 400 points of interest is extracted around the leaking spot. We use the raw traces and the pre-selected window of relevant samples per trace corresponding to masked S-box for $i = 3$.

The first dataset can be considered as a small dataset, while the second one is large. This difference is important for the performance of the optimizers, as seen in the next sections. Since the ASCAD dataset leaks mostly in the Hamming weight leakage model, we consider that leakage model in our experiments. The ASCAD dataset is available at https://github.com/ANSSI-FR/ASCAD.

3   Related Works

The number of works considering machine learning (and especially deep learning) in SCA has grown rapidly in recent years. This is not surprising as most of those works report excellent attack performance and breaking targets protected with countermeasures [2,11]. From a wide plethora of available deep learning techniques, multilayer perceptron and convolutional neural networks are commonly used and achieve top performance. To achieve such top results, one needs to (carefully) tune the neural network architecture. We can informally divide research works based on the amount of attention that the tuning takes. Indeed, the first works do not discuss how detailed tuning is done, or the final hyperparameters selected [7,9].

More recently, researchers give more attention to the tuning process, and they report the best settings selected from a wide pool of tested options. To find such good hyperparameters, common choices are random search, grid search, or grid search within specific ranges [20,23,24]. A more careful look at those works reveals that most of the attention goes toward the architecture hyperparameters [24], and only rarely toward the training process hyperparameters [13]. What is more, those works commonly conduct hyperparameter tuning as the necessary but less "interesting" step, which means there are no details about performance for various settings nor how difficult it was to find good hyperparameters. Still, we note works are investigating how to find a good performing neural network [31], but even then, the training process hyperparameters receive less attention. Differing from those works, we 1) concentrate on the hyperparameter tuning process, and 2) investigate the optimizer hyperparameter as one of the essential settings of the training process. First, in Sect. 4, we concentrate on the influence of optimizers regardless of the selection of other hyperparameters (thus, we present averaged results over numerous profiling models). In Sect. 5, we investigate the influence of optimizers on specific neural network architectures.

4   The General Behavior of Optimizers in Profiling SCA

To understand the influence of optimizers, we analyze the results based on GE's evolution concerning the number of epochs. Note that such an analysis is computationally very expensive, as it requires to calculate GE for every epoch. Additionally, to explore the influence of optimizers in combination with the architecture size, we divide the architectures into small (less than 400 000 trainable parameters) and large (more than 1 000 000 trainable parameters).

As shown next, the selection of an optimizer in SCA mostly depends on the model size and the regularization (implicit or explicit). What is more, most related works use Adam or RMSprop in MLP or CNN architectures. This choice is possibly related to the nature of the attacked dataset and the fast convergence provided by these two optimizers. Moreover, we also demonstrate that a model's capacity to generalize (here, generalization is measured with GE of correct key byte candidate) or overfit is directly related to implicit and explicit regularization. Implicit regularization can be provided by the optimization algorithm itself or by the model size concerning the number of profiling traces. Smaller models trained on larger datasets show implicit regularization, and the models tend to generalize better. On the other hand, larger models, even on larger datasets, tend to provide less implicit regularization, allowing the model to overfit very fast. The results in this section are obtained from a random hyperparameter search, both for MLPs and CNNs. Tables 1 and 2 in Appendix B specify the range of hyperparameters we investigated. To calculate the average GE, we run the experiments for 1 000 independent profiling models, and then we average those results.

All results show the ASCAD dataset results for fixed key or random keys. In the first case, there are 50 000 traces in the profiling phase. The guessing entropy is computed from a separate test set of 1 000 traces, having a fixed key. The ASCAD random key dataset consists of 200 000 training traces with random keys, while the attack phase uses 2 000 traces with a fixed key.

4.1 Stochastic Gradient Descent Optimizers

We tested SGD optimizer in four different configurations: SGD, SGD with *Nesterov*, SGD with momentum (0.9), and SGD with both momentum (0.9) and *Nesterov*. Note that we take the default value for the momentum.

Figures 1a and 1b show results for guessing entropy for the ASCAD fixed key for small and large models, respectively. Figures 2a and 2b provide results for the guessing entropy evolution for the ASCAD random keys datasets, for small and large models, respectively.

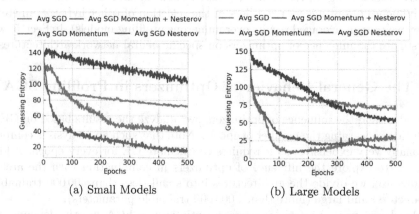

(a) Small Models   (b) Large Models

Fig. 1. SGD optimizers and model size for the ASCAD fixed key dataset.

Results for both datasets for SGD optimizers indicate that SGD performs better on small and large datasets when momentum is considered. Without momentum, we verified that SGD performs relatively better for large models, especially when *Nesterov* is applied. Moreover, we observe that SGD with momentum tends to perform better for large datasets and large models, as seen in Fig. 2b. Additionally, for ASCAD with a fixed key, we observe a slower convergence for small models but no overfitting. On the other hand, for large models, SGD with momentum reaches top performance around epoch 150, and afterward, GE increases, indicating model overfit. For ASCAD with random keys, we do not observe overfitting even if using large models, which is a clear indication that random keys make the classification problem more difficult, and the model needs more capacity to fit the data. Interestingly, small models show a similar trend for the ASCAD fixed key dataset, demonstrating that such models already reach the top of their capacity for the simpler dataset.

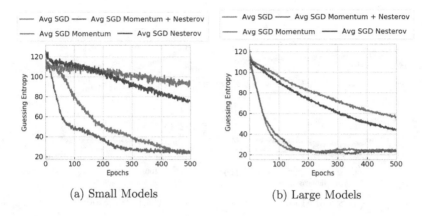

(a) Small Models   (b) Large Models

Fig. 2. SGD optimizers and model size for the ASCAD random keys dataset.

4.2   Adaptive Gradient Descent Methods

In [30], the authors analyze the empirical generalization capability of adaptive methods. They conclude that overparameterized models can easily overfit with adaptive optimizers. As demonstrated in [14], adaptive optimizers such as Adam and RMSprop display faster progress in the initial portion of training, and the performance usually degrades if the number of training epochs is too large. As a consequence, the model overfits. This leaves the need for additional (explicit) regularization in order to overcome the overfitting.

We analyze the behavior of adaptive optimizers for profiling SCA, and we show that the easy overfitting of adaptive methods reported in [30] happens for Adam and RMSprop, but not for Adagrad and Adadelta. In particular, we show that Adagrad and Adadelta tend to work better for larger models and longer training times.

Figures 3a and 3b show the averaged guessing entropy results for the ASCAD with fixed key for small and large models, respectively. Figures 4a and 4b show GE evolution during training for small and large models for ASCAD with random keys.

The general behavior of guessing entropy evolution during training with adaptive optimizers is similar for both datasets, indicating that this could be a typical optimizer behavior regardless of the attacked dataset. Adam and RMSprop usually converge very fast. In these cases, guessing entropy for correct key candidates tends to drop to a low value (under 20) when the model can provide some level of generalization. However, after the guessing entropy reaches its minimum value (i.e., maximum generalization), the processing of more epochs does not benefit and only degrades the model generalization. This means that Adam optimizer tends to overfit very fast, and *early stopping* would be highly beneficial to deal with this problem. A long training process is not beneficial when Adam optimizer is considered for profiling SCA. RMSprop tends to work less efficiently than Adam for larger models and larger datasets.

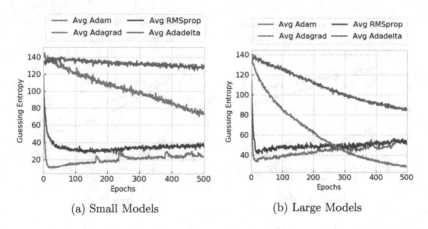

(a) Small Models   (b) Large Models

Fig. 3. Adaptive optimizers and model size for the ASCAD fixed key dataset.

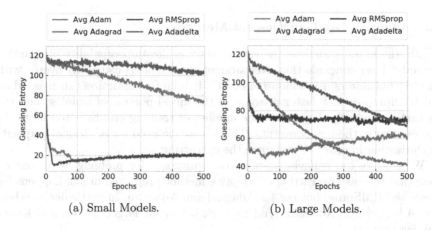

(a) Small Models.   (b) Large Models.

Fig. 4. Adaptive optimizers and model size for the ASCAD random keys dataset.

Adagrad provides a slighter decrease in guessing entropy if the model can provide some generalization. Unlike Adam and RMSprop, it does not degrade the guessing entropy with the processing of more epochs, which indicates that a long training process is beneficial when Adagrad is selected as an optimization algorithm. Normally, generalization can happen very late in the training process [20], which means that a larger number of epochs might be necessary for Adagrad. Adadelta shows less capacity to generalize in different deep neural network configurations. Like Adagrad, once the generalization starts to occur, it does not degrade with the processing of more epochs. Generalization can start very late in the training process. Our results indicate that Adagrad should be the optimizer of choice, especially if using larger models (thus, if expecting that the dataset is difficult, and we require large profiling model capacity) and uncertain how to tune other hyperparameters. Besides the above observations, we also verified that, on average, MLPs tend to provide a faster convergence (faster dropping in guessing entropy) for Adam and RMSprop in comparison to CNNs for the ASCAD random keys dataset. On the other hand, for Adagrad and Adadelta, we did not observe a significant difference in performance for MLPs and CNNs.

5   Optimizers and Specific Profiling Models

In the previous section, we provided averaged different optimizers behaviors if other hyperparameters are randomly selected. This type of analysis can indicate the optimizers' typical behavior independently of the rest of the hyperparameters. We aim to confirm if a fixed neural network architecture can show specific behavior for different optimizers, i.e., whether the selection of optimizer influences another hyperparameter. For that, we define small and large MLPs as well as small and large CNNs. All neural network models (MLP or CNN) are trained with a batch size of 400, a learning rate of 0.001, and default *Keras* library initialization for weight and biases.

The small MLP and CNN models are defined as follows:

- A **small MLP**: four hidden layers, each having 200 neurons.
- A **small CNN**: one convolutional layer (10 filters, kernel size 10, and stride 10) and two fully-connected layers with 200 neurons.
- A **large MLP**: ten hidden layers, each having 1000 neurons.
- A **large CNN**: four convolutional layers (10, 20, 40, and 80 filters, kernel size 4, and stride 2 in all the four convolutional layers) and four fully-connected layers with 1 000 neurons each.

The output layers for MLP and CNN contain nine neurons (the Hamming Weight leakage model) with the *Softmax* activation function. Unless specified otherwise, all neural networks have the *RelU* activation function in all the layers. For adaptive optimizers and large profiling models, we also provide results for the *ELU* activation function. We train these neural networks on both ASCAD datasets, with fixed and random keys in the training data. For every neural network and dataset, we run the analysis *ten* times (10 experiments with the same architecture) and then average GE results from these ten executions.

5.1   SGD Optimizers on Small MLP and CNN

Shallow neural networks with only a few hidden layers implement learning models with a relatively small number of trainable parameters. As a result, a large amount of training data would hardly overfit these models. Thus, a small model implements an implicit regularization given by its reduced capacity to fit the training data completely. Empirical results observed in this work lead us to conclude that some optimizers pose no additional regularization effect on the learning process, while some other optimizers present a more significant implicit regularization.

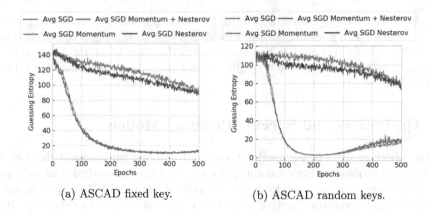

(a) ASCAD fixed key.   (b) ASCAD random keys.

Fig. 5. SGD optimizers on small MLP models.

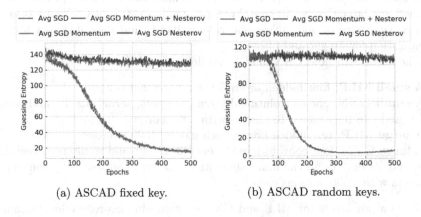

(a) ASCAD fixed key.   (b) ASCAD random keys.

Fig. 6. SGD optimizers on small CNN models.

The behaviors of SGD optimizers on a small MLP and a small CNN are shown in Figs. 5 and 6. Without *momentum*, SGD shows limited capacity to learn side-channel leakages. For CNN, GE for the scenario without momentum remains at the same level during the processing of 500 epochs. For MLP, we see a small convergence, indicating that the model can learn without momentum. However, it takes a large number of epochs. When momentum, with or without Nesterov, is considered, we observe a smooth convergence of the guessing entropy during training for small MLP and small CNN. When the training set is larger, as is the case of the ASCAD random keys dataset, the convergence is slightly faster. To conclude, we can assume that small MLP and CNN models with SGD as the optimizer requires momentum to improve model learnability. What is more, we see that we generally require a large number of epochs to converge to small GE (observing related works, most of them do not consider such long training processes).

5.2   SGD Optimizers on Large MLP and CNN

Again, SGD optimizers on large models present better performance when momentum is used, either with or without *Nesterov*. As for CNN models, without momentum, GE stays around the same level during the whole training. Although large MLP models show better capacity to fit side-channel leakage for SGD without momentum, the results from Figs. 7 and 8 show once more that SGD works much better with momentum in the side-channel context.

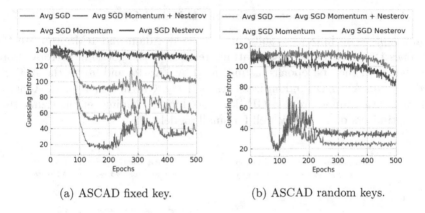

(a) ASCAD fixed key.   (b) ASCAD random keys.

Fig. 7. SGD optimizers on large MLP models.

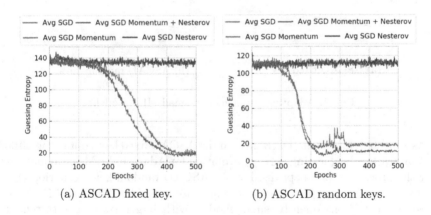

(a) ASCAD fixed key.   (b) ASCAD random keys.

Fig. 8. SGD optimizers on large CNN models.

Note, that the results observed in Figs. 7 and 8 for the SGD optimizers with momentum are representative of the recently described behavior of neural networks called the *deep double descent* [18]. Interestingly, these results indicate that longer training phases, larger profiling models, or more training examples do not necessarily improve the classification process. The results first show convergence (decrease of GE), after which there is a GE increase, and then, again, GE decreases (thus, double descent). We believe this phenomenon was not observed before in the SCA context as commonly, the training phase was too short. Comparing the results for small and large models shows that the final GE values are very similar. This means that it makes more sense to invest extra computational time into longer training phases than larger models.

5.3   Adaptive Optimizers on Small MLP and CNN

From adaptive optimizers, results indicate that Adam and RMSprop are the only ones that provide successful attack results, as the guessing entropy drops consistently in the first epochs, as indicated by Figs. 9a and 9b on the ASCAD fixed key and ASCAD random keys, respectively. On the other hand, Adagrad and Adadelta cannot provide GE decrease during training, emphasizing that these optimizers do not work well for small models.

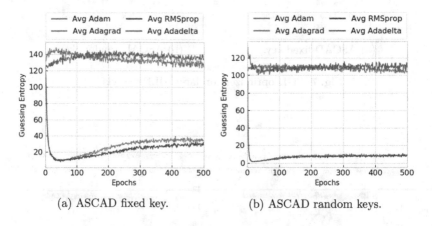

(a) ASCAD fixed key.   (b) ASCAD random keys.

Fig. 9. Adaptive optimizers on small MLP model.

As expected, for the model trained on the ASCAD fixed key, containing 50 000 training traces, the guessing entropy evolution for Adam and RMSprop increases after the processing of 50 epochs. For the ASCAD random keys scenario, where 200 000 traces are used for training, the increase in GE for Adam and RMSprop is less distinct. Consequently, small models with larger training sets tend to work well for Adam and RMSprop optimizers. However, these two optimizers require additional regularization mechanisms to ensure that the model is not over-trained. In the results provided in Figs. 9a and 9b, early stopping would be a good alternative, as already discussed [19, 26].

As shown in Figs. 10a and 10b, Adam and RMSprop also provided faster guessing entropy convergence for a small CNN model. Adagrad shows slightly better results for a small CNN than a small MLP, indicating that this type of adaptive optimizer may provide successful attack results if the number of epochs is very large (guessing entropy decreases up to epoch 500). For the Adadelta optimizer, a small CNN model shows no convergence at all.

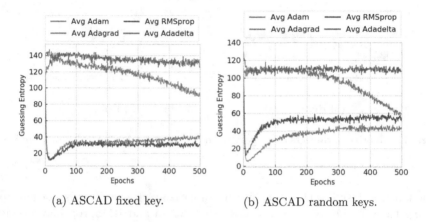

(a) ASCAD fixed key.   (b) ASCAD random keys.

Fig. 10. Adaptive optimizers on small CNN model.

5.4   Adaptive Optimizers on Large MLP and CNN

Here, we observe different behavior for adaptive optimizers and different activation functions. Adam and RMSprop tend to show poor performance in comparison to small MLP models, especially when ELU is selected as the activation function, as shown in Fig. 11b. For the ReLU activation function (see Fig. 11a), which is commonly employed in state-of-art neural network architectures, these two optimizers tend to perform relatively better, even though they are very sensitive to overfitting, as GE increases if the amount of training epochs is too large.

For Adagrad and Adadelta, we observed that a large MLP performs relatively well if ELU activation function is selected for hidden layers, as shown in Fig. 11b. In this case, the network requires more training epochs to converge to a low guessing entropy (approx. 400 epochs in Fig. 11b). The advantage of Adagrad and Adadelta with large MLP models and ELU is that guessing entropy stays low even if the number of epochs is very large (e.g., 500 epochs). Results for the four studied adaptive optimizers for large MLP on ReLU and ELU activation functions are shown in Figs. 11a and 11b, respectively.

Similar behavior is observed for the ASCAD fixed key dataset. Figures 12a and 12b show results for a large MLP model with ReLU and ELU activation functions, respectively. As the analysis in this section suggests, large MLP models work better with Adagrad and Adadelta as optimizers and ELU activation function. For Adam and RMSprop cases, even carefully selecting the activation

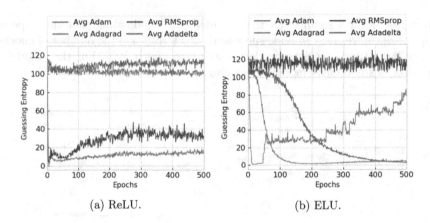

(a) ReLU.   (b) ELU.

Fig. 11. Adaptive optimizers on large MLP models for the ASCAD with random keys.

function was insufficient to achieve a stable convergence of guessing entropy during training. Once more, we verify that Adam and RMSprop may provide better performance by adding extra regularization artifacts, such as early stopping. When the training set consists of a small number of measurements, as is the case of the ASCAD fixed key dataset, Adam and RMSprop tend to provide a narrow generalization interval. As Fig. 12a shows, low guessing entropy for Adam and RMSprop last for less than 10 epochs and after that, guessing entropy only increases. For larger training sets, as provided by the ASCAD random keys dataset, the interval in which guessing entropy is low is wider, as seen in the example of Fig. 11b. In this case, the guessing entropy remains low until at least the processing of 50 epochs.

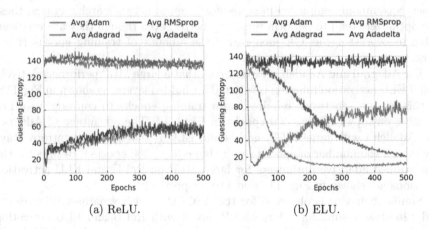

(a) ReLU.   (b) ELU.

Fig. 12. Adaptive optimizers on large MLP models for the ASCAD fixed key dataset.

As shown in Figs. 13 and 14, Adagrad shows superior performance for large CNN models with ELU activation function in a long training process. This is even more clear in Fig. 13b where large CNN is trained on a large dataset. Although Figs. 13b and 14b show guessing entropy convergence for Adam and RMSprop in the first epochs, a large CNN model seems to provide worse performance than a large MLP for these two adaptive optimizers. One possible explanation for this behavior could be that large CNNs simply have too large capacity and cannot conduct sufficient feature selection for a good attack. For Adadelta, we observed a slow GE convergence after 400 epochs in the scenario illustrated in Fig. 13b. Besides that, Adadelta provided no promising results in the evaluated large CNN.

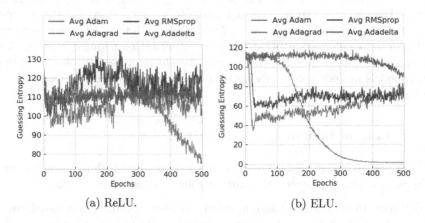

(a) ReLU.   (b) ELU.

Fig. 13. Adaptive optimizers on large CNN models for the ASCAD random keys dataset.

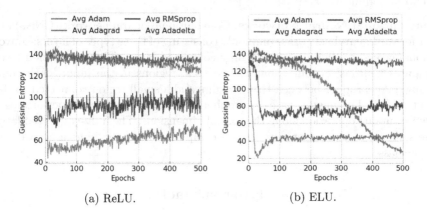

(a) ReLU.   (b) ELU.

Fig. 14. Adaptive optimizers on large CNN models for the ASCAD fixed key dataset.

6   Conclusions

The selection of an optimizer algorithm for the training process during the profiling SCA has a significant influence on the attack results. In this work, we provide results for eight different optimizers, separated into adaptive and SGD groups. We verified that Adam and RMSprop optimizers show better performance when the neural network is small, and the training process is short. The adaptive Adagrad and Adadelta show good performance when large models are considered. Additionally, we confirmed that the adaptive optimizer selection strictly depends on the activation function for hidden layers.

In future work, we plan to investigate the behavior of different optimizers and identity value leakage model. Besides that, in this work, we concentrate on two datasets only. To confirm our findings, we aim to extend the analysis with more publicly available datasets. Finally, we are interested in exploring the double descent behavior in SCA. While we observed that longer training does not necessarily mean better performance, we are interested in observing that larger models are not necessarily better or that larger profiling phases improve the behavior.

A   Machine Learning Classifiers

We consider two neural network types that are standard techniques in the profiling SCA: multilayer perceptron and convolutional neural networks.

Multilayer Perceptron. The multilayer perceptron (MLP) is a feed-forward neural network that maps sets of inputs onto sets of appropriate outputs. MLP consists of multiple layers of nodes in a directed graph, where each layer is fully connected to the next one (thus, layers are called fully-connected or dense layers). An MLP consists of three or more layers (since input and output represent two layers) of nonlinearly-activating nodes [5].

Convolutional Neural Networks. Convolutional neural networks(CNNs) are feed-forward neural networks commonly consisting of three types of layers: convolutional layers, pooling layers, and fully-connected layers. The convolution layer computes neurons' output connected to local regions in the input, each computing a dot product between their weights and a small region connected to the input volume. Pooling decrease the number of extracted features by performing a down-sampling operation along the spatial dimensions. The fully-connected layer (the same as in multilayer perceptron) computes either the hidden activations or the class scores.

B   Neural Networks Hyperparameter Ranges

In Table 1, we show the hyperparameter ranges we explore for the MLP architectures, while in Table 2, we show the hyperparameter ranges for CNNs.

Table 1. Hyperparameter search space for multilayer perceptron.

Hyperparameter	Min	Max	Step
Learning rate	0.0001	0.01	0.0001
Mini-batch	400	1 000	100
Dense (fully-connected) layers	1	10	1
Neurons (for dense layers)	100	1 000	10
Activation function (all layers)	ReLU, Tanh, ELU, or SELU		

Table 2. Hyperparameters search space for convolutional neural network (l = convolution layer index).

Hyperparameter	Min	Max	Step
Learning rate	0.0001	0.01	0.0001
Mini-batch	400	1 000	100
Convolution layers	1	4	1
Convolution filters	4*l	8*l	1
Convolution kernel size	1	40	1
Convolution stride	1	4	1
Dense (fully-connected) layers	1	10	1
Neurons (for dense layers)	100	1 000	10
Activation function (all layers)	ReLU, Tanh, ELU, or SELU		

In our experiments, training, validation, and test side-channel traces are normalized using *z-score* normalization:

$$t_i = \frac{t_i - \mu_{T_{train}}}{\sigma_{T_{train}}}, \qquad (1)$$

where T_{train} is the set of training traces and t_i is a single trace from training, validation, or test sets. Note that all traces are normalized according to the training set. For all configured neural networks, there are no *batch normalization* layers.

References

1. Brier, E., Clavier, C., Olivier, F.: Correlation power analysis with a leakage model. In: Joye, M., Quisquater, J.-J. (eds.) CHES 2004. LNCS, vol. 3156, pp. 16–29. Springer, Heidelberg (2004). https://doi.org/10.1007/978-3-540-28632-5_2
2. Cagli, E., Dumas, C., Prouff, E.: Convolutional neural networks with data augmentation against jitter-based countermeasures. In: Fischer, W., Homma, N. (eds.) CHES 2017. LNCS, vol. 10529, pp. 45–68. Springer, Cham (2017). https://doi.org/10.1007/978-3-319-66787-4_3

3. Chari, S., Rao, J.R., Rohatgi, P.: Template attacks. In: Kaliski, B.S., Koç, K., Paar, C. (eds.) CHES 2002. LNCS, vol. 2523, pp. 13–28. Springer, Heidelberg (2003). https://doi.org/10.1007/3-540-36400-5_3

4. Choi, D., Shallue, C.J., Nado, Z., Lee, J., Maddison, C.J., Dahl, G.E.: On empirical comparisons of optimizers for deep learning (2019)

5. Collobert, R., Bengio, S.: Links between perceptrons, MLPs and SVMs. In: Proceedings of the Twenty-First International Conference on Machine Learning, ICML 2004, p. 23. ACM, New York (2004). https://doi.org/10.1145/1015330.1015415

6. Gierlichs, B., Batina, L., Tuyls, P., Preneel, B.: Mutual information analysis. In: Oswald, E., Rohatgi, P. (eds.) CHES 2008. LNCS, vol. 5154, pp. 426–442. Springer, Heidelberg (2008). https://doi.org/10.1007/978-3-540-85053-3_27

7. Gilmore, R., Hanley, N., O'Neill, M.: Neural network based attack on a masked implementation of AES. In: 2015 IEEE International Symposium on Hardware Oriented Security and Trust (HOST), pp. 106–111, May 2015. https://doi.org/10.1109/HST.2015.7140247

8. Hettwer, B., Gehrer, S., Güneysu, T.: Deep neural network attribution methods for leakage analysis and symmetric key recovery. In: Paterson, K.G., Stebila, D. (eds.) SAC 2019. LNCS, vol. 11959, pp. 645–666. Springer, Cham (2020). https://doi.org/10.1007/978-3-030-38471-5_26

9. Heuser, A., Picek, S., Guilley, S., Mentens, N.: Side-channel analysis of lightweight ciphers: does lightweight equal easy? In: Hancke, G.P., Markantonakis, K. (eds.) RFIDSec 2016. LNCS, vol. 10155, pp. 91–104. Springer, Cham (2017). https://doi.org/10.1007/978-3-319-62024-4_7

10. Heuser, A., Zohner, M.: Intelligent machine homicide. In: Schindler, W., Huss, S.A. (eds.) COSADE 2012. LNCS, vol. 7275, pp. 249–264. Springer, Heidelberg (2012). https://doi.org/10.1007/978-3-642-29912-4_18

11. Kim, J., Picek, S., Heuser, A., Bhasin, S., Hanjalic, A.: Make some noise. Unleashing the power of convolutional neural networks for profiled side-channel analysis. IACR Trans. Cryptogr. Hardw. Embed. Syst. 2019(3), 148–179 (2019). https://doi.org/10.13154/tches.v2019.i3.148-179. https://tches.iacr.org/index.php/TCHES/article/view/8292

12. Kocher, P., Jaffe, J., Jun, B.: Differential power analysis. In: Wiener, M. (ed.) CRYPTO 1999. LNCS, vol. 1666, pp. 388–397. Springer, Heidelberg (1999). https://doi.org/10.1007/3-540-48405-1_25. http://dl.acm.org/citation.cfm?id=646764.703989

13. Li, H., Krcek, M., Perin, G.: A comparison of weight initializers in deep learning-based side-channel analysis. IACR Cryptology ePrint Archive 2020/904 (2020). https://eprint.iacr.org/2020/904

14. Luo, L., Xiong, Y., Liu, Y., Sun, X.: Adaptive gradient methods with dynamic bound of learning rate. In: 7th International Conference on Learning Representations, ICLR 2019, New Orleans, LA, USA, 6–9 May 2019. OpenReview.net (2019). https://openreview.net/forum?id=Bkg3g2R9FX

15. Maghrebi, H., Portigliatti, T., Prouff, E.: Breaking cryptographic implementations using deep learning techniques. In: Carlet, C., Hasan, M.A., Saraswat, V. (eds.) SPACE 2016. LNCS, vol. 10076, pp. 3–26. Springer, Cham (2016). https://doi.org/10.1007/978-3-319-49445-6_1

16. Mangard, S., Oswald, E., Popp, T.: Power Analysis Attacks: Revealing the Secrets of Smart Cards. Springer, Heidelberg (2007). https://doi.org/10.1007/978-0-387-38162-6. http://www.dpabook.org/. ISBN: 978-0-387-30857-9

17. Masure, L., Dumas, C., Prouff, E.: Gradient visualization for general characterization in profiling attacks. In: Polian, I., Stöttinger, M. (eds.) COSADE 2019. LNCS, vol. 11421, pp. 145–167. Springer, Cham (2019). https://doi.org/10.1007/978-3-030-16350-1_9

18. Nakkiran, P., Kaplun, G., Bansal, Y., Yang, T., Barak, B., Sutskever, I.: Deep double descent: where bigger models and more data hurt. In: 8th International Conference on Learning Representations, ICLR 2020, Addis Ababa, Ethiopia, 26–30 April 2020. OpenReview.net (2020). https://openreview.net/forum?id=B1g5sA4twr

19. Perin, G., Buhan, I., Picek, S.: Learning when to stop: a mutual information approach to fight overfitting in profiled side-channel analysis. Cryptology ePrint Archive, report 2020/058 (2020). https://eprint.iacr.org/2020/058

20. Perin, G., Chmielewski, L., Picek, S.: Strength in numbers: improving generalization with ensembles in machine learning-based profiled side-channel analysis. IACR Trans. Cryptogr. Hardw. Embed. Syst. **2020**(4), 337–364 (2020). https://doi.org/10.13154/tches.v2020.i4.337-364. https://tches.iacr.org/index.php/TCHES/article/view/8686

21. Picek, S., Heuser, A., Jovic, A., Bhasin, S., Regazzoni, F.: The curse of class imbalance and conflicting metrics with machine learning for side-channel evaluations. IACR Trans. Cryptogr. Hardw. Embed. Syst. **2019**(1), 209–237 (2019). https://doi.org/10.13154/tches.v2019.i1.209-237

22. Picek, S., et al.: Side-channel analysis and machine learning: a practical perspective. In: 2017 International Joint Conference on Neural Networks, IJCNN 2017, Anchorage, AK, USA, 14–19 May 2017, pp. 4095–4102 (2017)

23. Picek, S., Samiotis, I.P., Kim, J., Heuser, A., Bhasin, S., Legay, A.: On the performance of convolutional neural networks for side-channel analysis. In: Chattopadhyay, A., Rebeiro, C., Yarom, Y. (eds.) SPACE 2018. LNCS, vol. 11348, pp. 157–176. Springer, Cham (2018). https://doi.org/10.1007/978-3-030-05072-6_10

24. Prouff, E., Strullu, R., Benadjila, R., Cagli, E., Dumas, C.: Study of deep learning techniques for side-channel analysis and introduction to ASCAD database. Cryptology ePrint Archive, report 2018/053 (2018). https://eprint.iacr.org/2018/053

25. Quisquater, J.-J., Samyde, D.: Electro magnetic analysis (EMA): measures and counter-measures for smart cards. In: Attali, I., Jensen, T. (eds.) E-smart 2001. LNCS, vol. 2140, pp. 200–210. Springer, Heidelberg (2001). https://doi.org/10.1007/3-540-45418-7_17

26. Robissout, D., Zaid, G., Colombier, B., Bossuet, L., Habrard, A.: Online performance evaluation of deep learning networks for side-channel analysis. Cryptology ePrint Archive, report 2020/039 (2020). https://eprint.iacr.org/2020/039

27. Schindler, W., Lemke, K., Paar, C.: A stochastic model for differential side channel cryptanalysis. In: Rao, J.R., Sunar, B. (eds.) CHES 2005. LNCS, vol. 3659, pp. 30–46. Springer, Heidelberg (2005). https://doi.org/10.1007/11545262_3

28. Standaert, F.-X., Malkin, T.G., Yung, M.: A unified framework for the analysis of side-channel key recovery attacks. In: Joux, A. (ed.) EUROCRYPT 2009. LNCS, vol. 5479, pp. 443–461. Springer, Heidelberg (2009). https://doi.org/10.1007/978-3-642-01001-9_26

29. Weissbart, L.: On the performance of multilayer perceptron in profiling side-channel analysis. Cryptology ePrint Archive, report 2019/1476 (2019). https://eprint.iacr.org/2019/1476

30. Wilson, A.C., Roelofs, R., Stern, M., Srebro, N., Recht, B.: The marginal value of adaptive gradient methods in machine learning. In: Guyon, I., et al. (eds.) Advances in Neural Information Processing Systems 30: Annual Conference on Neural Information Processing Systems 2017, 4–9 December 2017, Long Beach, CA, USA, pp. 4148–4158 (2017). http://papers.nips.cc/paper/7003-the-marginal-value-of-adaptive-gradient-methods-in-machine-learning
31. Zaid, G., Bossuet, L., Habrard, A., Venelli, A.: Methodology for efficient CNN architectures in profiling attacks. IACR Trans. Cryptogr. Hardw. Embed. Syst. **2020**(1), 1–36 (2019). https://doi.org/10.13154/tches.v2020.i1.1-36. https://tches.iacr.org/index.php/TCHES/article/view/8391

Cryptographic Applications

On Self-equivalence Encodings
in White-Box Implementations

Adrián Ranea$^{(\boxtimes)}$ and Bart Preneel

imec-COSIC, KU Leuven, Leuven, Belgium
{adrian.ranea,bart.preneel}@esat.kuleuven.be

Abstract. All academic methods to secure software implementations of block ciphers against adversaries with full control of the device have been broken. Despite the huge progress in the cryptanalysis of these white-box implementations, no recent progress has been made on the design side. Most of the white-box designs follow the CEJO framework, where each round is encoded by composing it with small random permutations. While several generic attacks have been proposed on the CEJO framework, no generic analysis has been performed on self-equivalence encodings, a different design where only the affine layer of each round is encoded with random self-equivalences of the S-box layer, that is, affine permutations commuting with the non-linear layer.

In this work, we analyse the security of white-box implementations based on self-equivalence encodings for a broad class of SPN ciphers. First, we characterize the self-equivalence groups of S-box layers, and we prove that all the self-equivalences of a cryptographically strong S-box layer have a diagonal shape. Then, we propose the first generic attack on self-equivalence encodings. Our attack, based on affine equivalence problems, identifies the connection between the security of self-equivalence encodings and the self-equivalence structure of the cipher components. While we show that traditional SPN ciphers with cryptographically strong S-box layers cannot be secured with self-equivalence encodings, our analysis shows that self-equivalence encodings resist the generic attack if the cipher components satisfy several conditions, revealing the potential of self-equivalence encodings to secure other types of ciphers.

Keywords: White-box cryptography · Self-equivalence · SPN

1 Introduction

Traditional black-box cryptography assumes that the endpoints of the communication are secured. However, in some real-word scenarios, the adversaries can access the endpoints and tamper with the cryptographic device. While several hardware-based countermeasures have been proposed to preclude grey-box attacks, such as side-channel and fault attacks, some applications (e.g., DRM

© Springer Nature Switzerland AG 2021
O. Dunkelman et al. (Eds.): SAC 2020, LNCS 12804, pp. 639–669, 2021.
https://doi.org/10.1007/978-3-030-81652-0_25

or mobile banking) demand software-only solutions against adversaries with full control of the cryptographic device.

To model this powerful adversary from a cryptographic point of view, Chow et al. proposed the white-box model [13], where the adversary has full control of the cryptographic device. In particular, the adversary can observe and modify at will the intermediate values in the execution of the cryptographic algorithm.

In the same seminal work, Chow et al. proposed the first white-box implementation of a block cipher, a software implementation of AES designed to resist key-extraction attacks in the white-box model. Although their method only focused on key-extraction resistance, omitting other white-box threats such as code lifting orattacks inverting the functionality, it was the first practical approach considering a cryptographic adversary, as opposed to other heuristic countermeasures such as software obfuscation or software tamper-resistance.

The method by Chow et al., also called the CEJO framework, represents the cryptographic computation as a network of look-up tables and randomizes each look-up table by composing it with random encodings. To preserve the functionality, the output encoding of one step cancels the input encoding of the next step. Thus, the resulting white-box implementation is functionally equivalent to the original cipher up to the first and last encodings, which are not cancelled. Without these external encodings, the method is trivially insecure.

The white-box implementation by Chow et al. was broken by the BGE attack, and all the subsequent CEJO implementations [3,14,25,30,31,35,38] have also been broken [3,12,16,17,22,24,27,29,33,37]. Lastly, McMillion et al. considered a white-box implementation of AES based on self-equivalences encodings and showed it was insecure [32]. As opposed to CEJO implementations, self-equivalence encodings randomize only the affine part of each round, by composing with random self-equivalences of the S-box layer SL, that is, affine permutations (A, B) such that $SL = B \circ SL \circ A$.

Due to the complexity of designing secure white-box implementations and the practical limitations introduced by external encodings, several commercial white-box implementations have been designed without external encodings but whose security relies on the secrecy of their design. Apart from the drawbacks of security by obscurity, several white-box attacks based on grey-box techniques have been proposed that do not require knowledge of the design, such as [5,10,34]. The effectiveness of these attacks was shown in the WhibOx Contest [36], a competition where participants submitted white-box implementations of AES and broke other participants' submissions. In the first edition all the submissions were broken, and in the second edition 3 implementations stayed unbroken during the attack period of the competition, but they were broken afterwards [23].

Apart from white-box implementations of existing block ciphers, other white-box constructions have been published, such as white-box implementations of ciphers with secret S-boxes [4,11] or incompressible white-box ciphers [7,9]. The latter constructions are dedicated ciphers designed to preclude code lifting attacks by relying on a huge implementation such that an adversary with partial access cannot find an equivalent implementation with significantly less size.

In this work we address the challenging problem of designing white-box implementations of block ciphers in the white-box model proposed by Chow et al., that is, where the specifications of the design are public and the security relies on the secrecy of the internal and external encodings. While there has been outstanding progress in adapting grey-box techniques to attack white-box implementations relying on secret designs, these techniques do not pose a threat to white-box implementations relying on external encodings yet, as long as the external encodings are chosen carefully [2]. Thus, grey-box techniques are outside the scope of this paper, and we focus instead on the design side of white-box implementations, for which no significant progress has been made recently.

Apart from the CEJO implementations and the white-box AES implementation based on self-equivalence encodings, no more white-box implementations following this model have been published. Some generic attacks have been proposed on the CEJO framework [3,17,33], showing that CEJO implementations are not suitable for a broad class of SPN ciphers. However, self-equivalence encodings have only been considered for AES, and the security of this type of encodings has not been analysed for other ciphers.

Contributions. In this paper, we analyse the security of self-equivalence encodings in white-box implementations of SPN ciphers. We first formalize self-equivalence implementations, a class of white-box implementations that hide the round key material in random-looking affine permutations built from self-equivalences of the S-box layer. We also illustrate how CEJO implementations can be efficiently transformed into self-equivalence implementations.

Then, we study the self-equivalence group of an S-box layer, on which the security of self-equivalence encodings is based. To this end, we introduce diagonal self-equivalences; given a permutation F built from the concatenation of smaller permutations, a diagonal self-equivalence of F is a self-equivalence that can also be decomposed as the concatenation of smaller permutations. We prove that in order to have non-diagonal self-equivalences, F needs to have additive self-equivalences, linear components and several linear structures, or equivalently, differential and linear approximations of probability one. As a result, S-box layers of SPN ciphers employing cryptographically strong S-boxes have only diagonal self-equivalences. Our characterization of diagonal self-equivalences can be of independent interest. For example, it can be applied to count the number of solutions (A, B) of an affine equivalence problem $G = B \circ F \circ A$ where the central map F is given as the concatenation of smaller permutations.

Finally, we propose the first generic attack on self-equivalence implementations of SPN ciphers with cryptographically strong S-boxes. Our attack partially recovers the self-equivalence encodings up to some unknown affine permutations belonging to a small subgroup of the self-equivalence group; the key is then recovered by a brute force search over the small subgroup. The attack is based on affine and linear equivalence problems and its complexity depends on the self-equivalence groups of the linear layer blocks and the S-boxes.

Our analysis shows that if these self-equivalence groups satisfy some properties, a self-equivalence implementation is secure against the generic attack. While traditional SPN ciphers such as AES do not satisfy these properties, our analysis provides the foundations to secure a different class of ciphers with self-equivalence encodings.

Outline. In Sect. 2, the notation and the preliminaries are introduced. The CEJO framework is described Sect. 3 and self-equivalence implementations are introduced in Sect. 4. Diagonal self-equivalences are characterized in Sect. 5, and the generic attack on self-equivalence encodings is described in Sect. 6. Section 7 presents the conclusions and the future work.

2 Preliminaries

2.1 Basics

In this document, capital letters are used for functions (e.g., F, G), lower letters for values (e.g., x, y), and calligraphic letters for sets of functions (e.g., $\mathcal{F}, \mathcal{G}$).

Let $\mathbb{F}_q$ be the finite field with q elements. The vector space of n-bit values is denoted by $\mathbb{F}_2^n$, and the addition in $\mathbb{F}_2^n$ by $\oplus$. A function $F : \mathbb{F}_2^n \mapsto \mathbb{F}_2^m$ is called an (n, m)-bit function, or just n-bit function if $n = m$. Given two functions F and G, their composition is denoted by $F \circ G$ and their concatenation by $F \parallel G$, that is, $(F \parallel G)(x, y) = (F(x), G(y))$. The n-bit identity function is denoted by $\mathrm{Id}_n(x) = x$, and the addition by a constant is denoted by $\oplus_a(x) = x \oplus a$.

Given an affine function A, we denote its linear part by $\mathrm{Lin}(A)$, that is, $A = \oplus_a \circ \mathrm{Lin}(A)$ for some constant a. If $L : (\mathbb{F}_2^n)^m \to (\mathbb{F}_2^n)^m$ is a linear function, we denote by $\{L_{i,j} : 1 \leq i, j \leq m\}$ the n-bit linear functions associated with the blocks of L seen as a block matrix, that is, in matrix notation

$$
L \times \begin{pmatrix} x_1 \\ \vdots \\ x_m \end{pmatrix} = \begin{pmatrix} L_{1,1} & \cdots & L_{1,m} \\ \vdots & \ddots & \\ L_{m,1} & & L_{m,m} \end{pmatrix} \times \begin{pmatrix} x_1 \\ \vdots \\ x_m \end{pmatrix}.
$$

The general linear group consisting of all n-bit linear permutations is denoted by GL_n, and the affine general linear group of $\mathbb{F}_2^n$ is denoted by AGL_n.

The cardinality of a set $\mathcal{F}$ is denoted by $|\mathcal{F}|$ and the Cartesian product of sets $\mathcal{F}$ and $\mathcal{G}$ is denoted by $\mathcal{F} \times \mathcal{G}$. We translate the inversion, concatenation and composition of functions to set operations as follows:

$$
\mathcal{F}^{-1} = \{F^{-1} : F \in \mathcal{F}\},
$$
$$
\mathcal{F} \parallel \mathcal{G} = \{F \parallel G : F \in \mathcal{F}, G \in \mathcal{G}\},
$$
$$
\mathcal{F} \circ \mathcal{G} = \{F \circ G : F \in \mathcal{F}, G \in \mathcal{G}\}.
$$

Moreover, given a set of affine permutations $\mathcal{A}$, we denote its linear part by $\mathrm{Lin}(\mathcal{A}) = \{\mathrm{Lin}(A) : A \in \mathcal{A}\}$. When a set contains a single element $\{F\}$, we denote $F \circ \mathcal{G} = \{F\} \circ \mathcal{G}$ and $F \parallel \mathcal{G} = \{F\} \parallel \mathcal{G}$ with a slight abuse of notation.

SPN Ciphers. Given an n-bit iterated block cipher, we denote the encryption function for a fixed key k by $E_k = E_{k^{(n_r)}}^{(n_r)} \circ \cdots \circ E_{k^{(1)}}^{(1)}$, where $E_{k^{(r)}}^{(r)}$ denotes the rth round function and $k^{(r)}$ denotes the rth round key. For ease of notation, we omit the round-key subscript of the round functions. An SPN (Substitution-Permutation Network) cipher is an iterated block cipher where the rth round function is defined by

$$E^{(r)} = LL \circ SL \circ \oplus_{k^{(r)}},$$

where LL is the n-bit linear layer, $SL = S_1 \parallel \cdots \parallel S_\rho$ is the S-box layer composed of m-bit S-boxes S_i, and $k^{(r)}$ is the rth round key. In some cases, the first and last rounds are defined in a different way. Figure 1 depicts the round function of an SPN cipher.

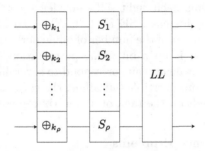

Fig. 1. The round function of an SPN cipher.

2.2 Self-equivalences

In this section, we introduce the notion of self-equivalence [8] and some of its properties for n-bit functions.

Definition 1. *Let F be an n-bit function. A pair of n-bit affine permutations (A, B) such that $F = B \circ F \circ A$ is called an (affine) self-equivalence of F.*

We also say A (resp. B) is a right (resp. left) self-equivalence of F. If A and B are linear, (A, B) is called a linear self-equivalence, and if $(A, B) = (\oplus_a, \oplus_b)$ are constants, (A, B) is called an additive self-equivalence.

Definition 2. *Two n-bit functions F and G are said to be affine (resp. linear) equivalent if there exists a pair of n-bit affine (resp. linear) permutations (A, B) such that $G = B \circ F \circ A$.*

The notion of (affine) self-equivalence arises from the affine equivalence relation. This equivalence relation induces a partition on the set of n-bit functions, where a function belongs to the affine class containing all its affine equivalent functions.

We denote the set of self-equivalences of F by $SE(F)$, the set of left self-equivalences by $LSE(F)$, and the set of right self-equivalences by $RSE(F)$, i.e.,

$$\mathrm{SE}(F) = \{(A, B) \in \mathrm{AGL}_n \times \mathrm{AGL}_n : F = B \circ F \circ A\},$$
$$\mathrm{RSE}(F) = \{A : \exists B \text{ s.t. } (A, B) \in \mathrm{SE}(F)\},$$
$$\mathrm{LSE}(F) = \{B : \exists A \text{ s.t. } (A, B) \in \mathrm{SE}(F)\}.$$

The next lemma recalls the well-known fact that the self-equivalences form a group, which can be easily proved by noticing that $\mathrm{SE}(F)$ is the stabilizer of a group action where $\mathrm{AGL}_n \times \mathrm{AGL}_n$ acts over the set of n-bit functions [20, 28].

Lemma 1. $\mathrm{SE}(F)$ *is a subgroup of* $\mathrm{AGL}_n \times \mathrm{AGL}_n$, *and* $\mathrm{LSE}(F)$ *and* $\mathrm{RSE}(F)$ *are subgroups of* AGL_n. *Moreover, if* G *is a function affine equivalent to* F, *i.e.,* $G = B \circ F \circ A$, *then the self-equivalence groups of* F *and* G *are conjugates, that is,* $\mathrm{RSE}(G) = A^{-1} \circ \mathrm{RSE}(F) \circ A$ *and* $\mathrm{LSE}(G) = B \circ \mathrm{LSE}(F) \circ B^{-1}$.

If F is a permutation, each right self-equivalence corresponds to a unique left self-equivalence. In this case, $\mathrm{SE}(F), \mathrm{LSE}(F)$ and $\mathrm{RSE}(F)$ have the same cardinality, which is a divisor of the number of affine permutations. In particular, $|\mathrm{SE}(F)| = |\mathrm{AGL}_n|$ if F is an n-bit affine permutation. For a non-invertible function, a right self-equivalence can correspond to several left self-equivalences, and vice-versa. If F is non-invertible but affine, the cardinality of $\mathrm{SE}(F)$ can be computed, which depends on the rank of its matrix representation over $\mathbb{F}_2$ [28].

2.3   Affine Equivalence Problems

Self-equivalences are strongly related to the solutions of affine and linear equivalence problems, on which many white-box implementations are based.

Definition 3. *An affine (resp. linear) equivalence problem is a functional equation of the form* $G = Y \circ F \circ X$ *where* F *and* G *are known n-bit functions and* (X, Y) *are unknown affine (resp. linear) permutations.*

Given any solution (X_0, Y_0) of the affine equivalence problem $G = Y \circ F \circ X$, the solution set can be seen as the subgroup $\mathcal{S} = \{(A \circ X_0, Y_0 \circ B) : (A, B) \in \mathrm{SE}(F)\}$ of $\mathrm{AGL}_n \times \mathrm{AGL}_n$. Thus, the number of solutions is equal to the number of self-equivalences of F. If the unknowns (X, Y) are restricted to given subgroups $(\mathcal{A}, \mathcal{B})$, then the solution set can be seen as the subgroup

$$\mathcal{S} = \{(A \circ X_0, Y_0 \circ B) : (A, B) \in \mathrm{SE}(F) \cap (\mathcal{A} \times \mathcal{B})\}.$$

Several algorithms have been published for finding a solution of an equivalence problem. For n-bit permutations, Biryukov et al. proposed an $\mathcal{O}(n^3 2^n)$ algorithm to solve the linear case and an $\mathcal{O}(n^3 2^{2n})$ algorithm to solve the affine case [8], whereas Dinur recently proposed an $\mathcal{O}(n^3 2^n)$ algorithm to solve the affine case for random permutations [18]. Since we will mostly consider affine equivalence problems involving permutations with several self-equivalences, which is fairly rare in the random case, in this document we will assume $O(n^3 2^{2n})$ to be the complexity of solving an affine equivalence problem with n-bit permutations.

For n-bit functions $F = F_1 \parallel \cdots \parallel F_\rho$ composed of m-bit cryptographic S-boxes[1] F_i, Derbez et al. obtained an algorithm to solve the affine equivalence problem with time complexity $O(2^m n^3 + n^4/m + 2^{2m} m n^2)$ [17]. For n-bit affine functions F, the affine equivalence problem can be represented as a linear system of $n + 1$ equations and solved with Gaussian elimination in time $\mathcal{O}((n + 1)^\omega)$, where $2 < \omega < 3$ is the matrix multiplication constant.

While several efficient algorithms have been proposed for finding a solution of an equivalence problem, no efficient techniques have been proposed to count its number of solutions. In general, the algorithm by Biryukov et al. can be applied to find all the solutions by repeating the algorithm for each possible initial guess. The work factor of this approach is at least 2^{2n} for the linear case and 2^{3n} for the affine case, and it is also lower bounded by the number of solutions.

A particular class of problems for which we can characterize the solution set is the class of univariate linear equivalence problem $G = X^{-1} \circ M_\alpha \circ X$ where M_α is the n-bit linear permutation corresponding to the multiplication by the finite field element $\alpha \in \mathbb{F}_{2^n}$. For an n-bit function F, let $\mathrm{C}(F) = \{A \in \mathrm{GL}_n : A \circ F = F \circ A\}$ be the centralizer of F, that is, the subgroup of linear permutations commuting with F. Then, the solution set of $G = X^{-1} \circ M_\alpha \circ X$ is $\mathcal{S} = \mathrm{C}(M_\alpha) \circ X_0$, for any particular solution X_0. If α has multiplicative order d (i.e., the minimum exponent such that $\alpha^d = 1$), then $\mathrm{C}(M_\alpha)$ is isomorphic to the set of invertible $\frac{n}{d} \times \frac{n}{d}$ matrices over $\mathbb{F}_{2^d}$ [21]. In particular, $\mathrm{C}(M_\alpha) = \{M_\gamma : 0 \neq \gamma \in \mathbb{F}_{2^n}\}$ if α is a primitive element.

3   CEJO Implementations

In this section we introduce CEJO implementations and the generic cryptanalysis of the CEJO framework. CEJO implementations are a particular class of white-box implementations based on encoded round functions.

Definition 4 [13]. *Let F be an (n, m)-bit function and let (I, O) be a pair of n-bit and m-bit permutations, respectively. The function $\overline{F} = O \circ F \circ I$ is called an encoded F, and I and O are called the input and output encoding, respectively.*

Definition 5. *Let $E_k = E^{(n_r)} \circ \cdots E^{(1)}$ be the encryption[2] function of an iterated n-bit cipher with fixed key k. An encoded implementation of E_k is an encoded E_k composed of encoded round functions, that is,*

$$\overline{E_k} = \overline{E^{(n_r)}} \circ \cdots \circ \overline{E^{(1)}} = (O^{(n_r)} \circ E^{(r)} \circ I^{(n_r)}) \circ \cdots \circ (O^{(1)} \circ E^{(1)} \circ I^{(1)}),$$

for some n-bit permutations $(I^{(r)}, O^{(r)})$ satisfying $I^{(r+1)} = \left(O^{(r)}\right)^{-1}$.

---

[1] The algorithm by Derbez et al. assumes that the S-boxes do not have non-trivial linear components, i.e., there does not exist a non-zero $(m, 1)$-bit linear function B such that $(B \circ S)(x) = \sum b_i S(x)_i$ is a linear function. Most SPN ciphers employ cryptographically strong S-boxes satisfying this requirement.

[2] In this paper we focus on white-box implementations of encryption functions; the definitions for decryption functions are similar.

In other words, an encoded implementation is the composition of encoded round functions where the intermediate encodings are cancelled out, that is, $\overline{E_k} = O^{(n_r)} \circ E_k \circ I^{(1)}$. The intermediate encodings are also called the round encodings, and the encodings $(I^{(1)}, O^{(n_r)})$ are called the external encodings. The round encodings are sampled at random from a group $\mathcal{E}$ herein called the round encoding space, which varies from implementation to implementation.

All the white-box implementations of block ciphers published in the literature are encoded implementations following the so-called CEJO framework [14]. CEJO implementations employ round encoding spaces composed of small non-linear permutations and wider linear functions.

Definition 6. *Let $\mathcal{N}_{m_n}$ be the set of m_n-bit non-linear permutations. A CEJO implementation with m_n-bit non-linear encodings and m_l-bit linear encodings is an encoded implementation of an SPN cipher with round encoding space*

$$\mathcal{E} = (\mathcal{N}_{m_n} \| \cdots \| \mathcal{N}_{m_n}) \circ (\mathrm{GL}_{m_l} \| \cdots \| \mathrm{GL}_{m_l}).$$

Figure 2 depicts an CEJO encoded round function with the usual parameters $2m_n = m_l = m$, where m is the bit-size of the S-box. For example, the encoded AES implementation proposed by Chow et al. employs 4-bit non-linear encodings and 8-bit linear encodings.

Internally, a CEJO encoded round function is implemented in software as a network of look-up tables, requiring roughly $\mathcal{O}(2^{\max(2m_n, m_l, m)})$ bits of memory. Since white-box attacks to CEJO implementations only require black-box access to the encoded round functions, we will omit the internal description of a CEJO encoded round function and refer to [3,14] for more details.

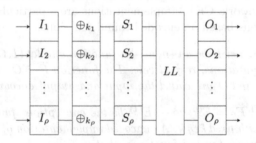

Fig. 2. A CEJO encoded round function with $\frac{m}{2}$-bit non-linear encodings and m-bit linear encodings. Each m-bit function I_i and O_i consists of the concatenation of two $\frac{m}{2}$-bit non-linear permutations composed with an m-bit linear permutation.

3.1 Security of CEJO Implementations

The white-box implementation by Chow et al. and the subsequent CEJO implementations were designed to prevent key-extraction attacks in the white-box model, that is, an attacker with full control on the implementation should not be able to recover the key; the specifications of the cipher and the implementation are public, but the key and the encodings are unknown to the adversary.

CEJO implementations do not aim to prevent attacks inverting the implementation. In some scenarios (e.g., DRM), inverting the functionality is not a threat. Note that designing a white-box implementation preventing both key-extraction and inversion attacks is a much harder problem, since it would turn a symmetric cipher into a public-key encryption scheme.

Informally, the security of CEJO implementations relies on a disambiguation problem; for a given encoded round function, many pairs of round keys and round encodings result in the same encoded round function. While encoded round functions are individually secure, all CEJO implementations have been broken by analysing few consecutive rounds.

Key-extraction attacks on CEJO implementations typically consists of two main steps: reducing the round encoding space and guessing the round keys. First, the adversary obtains new encoded round functions with the same underlying round keys but with round encodings restricted to a smaller encoding space. Then, the adversary performs an exhaustive search over the reduced round encoding space to recover the round keys. For most SPN ciphers, the key schedule can be inverted and few round keys can uniquely determine the master key.

The crucial step is the reduction of the round encoding space. While several reduction attacks to CEJO implementations have been published, only three generic reduction attacks (i.e., considering a broad class of ciphers) have been proposed. Michiels et al. proposed the first reduction attack [33], composed of one algorithm to remove the non-linear part of the encodings and another algorithm to partially recover the remaining affine encodings. Baek et al. generalized the algorithm to remove the non-linear part of the encodings [3] and Derbez et al. improved the recovering of the affine encodings by an efficient algorithm to solve affine equivalence problems of S-box layers [17]. The following proposition illustrates the reach of current generic reduction attacks, proved in Appendix A.

Proposition 1. *Let E_k be the encryption function of an n-bit SPN cipher with linear layer LL and S-box layer SL consisting of m-bit cryptographic S-boxes, and let $\overline{E_k}$ be a CEJO implementation of E_k with m_n-bit non-linear encodings and m_l-bit linear encodings. Given black-box access to three consecutive encoded round functions $\overline{E^{(r-2)}}, \overline{E^{(r-1)}}$ and $\overline{E^{(r)}}$, one can find another encoded $E^{(r)}$ with round encoding space $LL \circ \mathrm{LSE}(SL)$, i.e.,*

$$\widehat{E^{(r)}} = \widehat{O} \circ E^{(r)} \circ \widehat{I}, \quad \widehat{I}, \widehat{O^{-1}} \in LL \circ \mathrm{LSE}(SL),$$

in time $\mathcal{O}\left((n/m_n)2^{3m_n} + 2^m n^3 + n^4/m + 2^{2m}mn^2\right)$.

As a result, given a CEJO implementation of an SPN cipher, we can find another encoded implementation where the round encoding space has been reduced to $LL \circ \mathrm{LSE}(SL)$. This reduction attack is efficient for practical CEJO implementations, since the complexity of Proposition 1 is similar to the memory complexity of a CEJO implementation.

For white-box implementations of AES, several reduction attacks have been proposed that reduced the round encoding space to a single element [6,17,27]. However, no generic attack has been proposed reducing the round encoding space further than Proposition 1. This round encoding space is strongly related to the self-equivalence set of the S-box layer. In the next section, we introduce a class of white-box implementations where the round encodings are sampled at random from the self-equivalences set of the S-box layer and analyse their security.

4   Self-equivalence Implementations

In [32], McMillion et al. considered a white-box implementation of AES where the round encodings were self-equivalences of the S-box layer and showed it was insecure. However, this type of encodings has not been considered for other ciphers, nor their generic security have been addressed. In this section, we introduce and analyse self-equivalence implementations, a particular class of white-box implementations based on self-equivalence encodings.

As opposed to encoded implementations, self-equivalence implementations only encode the affine part of the round function. Given an encryption function $E_k = E^{(n_r)} \circ \cdots E^{(1)}$ of an SPN cipher with round function $E^{(r)} = LL \circ SL \circ \oplus_{k^{(r)}}$, we define the intermediate affine layers by

$$AL^{(r)} = \oplus_{k^{(r)}} \circ LL, \quad r = 2, \ldots, n_r$$

and the first and last layer affine layers by $AL^{(1)} = \oplus_{k^{(1)}}$ and $AL^{(n_r+1)} = LL$. Although affine layers depends on the round keys, we omit the round-key subscript for ease of notation. Note that the rth affine layer includes the round key of the rth round but the linear layer of the previous round. The first and last affine layers might be defined differently if the SPN cipher defines the first and last round in a different way.

Definition 7. *Let E_k be the encryption function of an SPN cipher. A self-equivalence implementation is an encoded E_k given by*

$$\overline{E_k} = AL^{(n_r+1)} \circ SL \circ \overline{AL^{(n_r)}} \circ SL \circ \overline{AL^{(n_r-1)}} \circ \cdots \circ \overline{AL^{(2)}} \circ SL \circ \overline{AL^{(1)}},$$

where the intermediate encodings of the affine layers are self-equivalences of the S-box layer, i.e.,

$$\overline{AL^{(r)}} = O^{(r)} \circ AL^{(r)} \circ I^{(r)}, \quad (O^{(r)}, I^{(r+1)}) \in SE(SL),$$

and the external encodings $(I^{(1)}, O^{(n_r)})$ are affine permutations.

The last affine layer is not encoded since it is not key-dependent. The intermediate encodings are cancelled due to the self-equivalence property, i.e.,

$$\overline{AL^{(r+1)}} \circ SL \circ \overline{AL^{(r)}} = O^{(r+1)} \circ AL^{(r+1)} \circ (I^{(r+1)} \circ SL \circ O^{(r)}) \circ AL^{(r)} \circ I^{(r)}$$
$$= O^{(r+1)} \circ AL^{(r+1)} \circ SL \circ AL^{(r)} \circ I^{(r)}.$$

Similar to encoded implementations, the intermediate encodings are called the round encodings, and the subgroup of self-equivalences from which the round encodings are sampled at random is called the round encoding space $\mathcal{E} \leq \mathrm{SE}(SL)$.

Self-equivalence implementations can be implemented in software in a simple and efficient way. An encoded affine layer can be implemented by a single $n \times n$ binary matrix and an n-bit constant, requiring $\mathcal{O}(n^2 + n)$ bits of memory and $\mathcal{O}(n^2/\log_2 n)$ bit operations to evaluate [1]. In addition, the S-box layer does not need to be protected, and there are no restrictions on the bit-size of the S-boxes.

A CEJO implementation can be efficiently transformed into a self-equivalence implementation following Proposition 1, and a self-equivalence implementation can be considered as a CEJO implementation with n-bit linear encodings by defining the encoded round function as

$$\overline{E^{(r)}} = SL \circ \overline{AL^{(r)}} = \left(LL \circ I^{(r+1)} \right)^{-1} \circ E^{(r)} \circ \left(LL \circ I^{(r)} \right)$$

While the memory complexity of a CEJO implementation is exponential in terms of the bit-size of the encodings, self-equivalence implementations can be efficiently implemented in all cases. Therefore, practical CEJO implementations can be efficiently translated to self-equivalence implementations, but the latter ones cannot be efficiently transformed to practical CEJO implementations if the self-equivalences of the S-box layer are not composed of smaller affine permutations. In the next section, we study the self-equivalences of S-box layers and analyse the case when all the self-equivalences are composed of smaller permutations.

5   Diagonal Self-equivalences

Let $F = F_1 \parallel \cdots \parallel F_\rho$ be an arbitrary n-bit permutation composed of smaller m-bit permutations F_i. If (A_i, B_i) is a self-equivalence of F_i for $i = 1, \ldots, \rho$, then $(A_1 \parallel \cdots \parallel A_\rho, B_1 \parallel \cdots \parallel B_\rho)$ is a self-equivalence of F. In addition, if two of the smaller permutations (F_i, F_j) are the same, then the transposition (i, j) is also a self-equivalence of the S-box layer.

Definition 8. *A $(m \times \rho)$-bit linear permutation P is called an $[m, \rho]$-block permutation if $P(x_1, \ldots, x_\rho) = (x_{\pi(1)}, \ldots, x_{\pi(\rho)})$ for some permutation π of $\{1, \ldots, \rho\}$. We denote the set of block permutations by $\mathcal{P}_{m,\rho}$.*

In particular, if all the small permutations F_i are the same, then the set

$$\mathcal{D} = \left\{ \left((A_1 \parallel \cdots \parallel A_\rho) \circ P, P^{-1} \circ (B_1 \parallel \cdots \parallel B_\rho) \right) : \begin{array}{l} (A_i, B_i) \in \mathrm{SE}(F_i) \\ P \in \mathcal{P}_{m,\rho} \end{array} \right\}$$

is a subgroup of $\mathrm{SE}(F)$. In some cases, the set $\mathcal{D}$ contains all the self-equivalences of F. For example, De Mulder et al. [16] computed all the linear self-equivalences of $S \parallel S$, where S is the AES S-box, and found that all the right (resp. left) linear self-equivalences have a diagonal shape of the form

$$\begin{pmatrix} A_1 & 0 \\ 0 & A_2 \end{pmatrix}, \quad \begin{pmatrix} 0 & A_1 \\ A_2 & 0 \end{pmatrix},$$

where A_1 and A_2 are right (resp. left) linear self-equivalence of S.

Unfortunately, it is not known in which cases the subgroup $\mathcal{D}$ is the total self-equivalence group $\mathrm{SE}(F)$. To consider also functions $F = F_1 \circ \cdots \circ F_\rho$ with different permutations F_i, we define diagonal self-equivalences as follows.

Definition 9. *Let* $F = F_1 \parallel \cdots \parallel F_\rho$ *be an n-bit permutation composed of m-bit permutations* F_i. *An (affine) diagonal self-equivalence* (A, B) *of* F *is a pair of n-bit affine permutations* $(A, B) \in \mathrm{SE}(F)$ *such that*

$$A = (A_1 \parallel \cdots \parallel A_\rho) \circ P, \qquad B = P^{-1} \circ (B_1 \parallel \cdots \parallel B_\rho),$$

for some m-bit functions A_i *and* B_i *and some* $[m, \rho]$-*block permutation* P.

The set of diagonal self-equivalences is a subgroup of $\mathrm{SE}(F)$, and it includes $\mathcal{D}$ when all F_i are the same. Moreover, if (A, B) is a diagonal self-equivalence, then A_i and B_i are permutations and the matrices corresponding to $\mathrm{Lin}(A)$ and $\mathrm{Lin}(B)$ are diagonal block matrices up to some permutation of the blocks, i.e.,

$$\mathrm{Lin}(A) = \begin{pmatrix} \mathrm{Lin}(A_1) & & \\ & \ddots & \\ & & \mathrm{Lin}(A_\rho) \end{pmatrix} \times P.$$

The property of having non-diagonal self-equivalences is not invariant in the affine class. However, if we consider the subgroup of affine permutations $\mathcal{Q} = \{Q_1 \parallel \cdots \parallel Q_\rho : Q_i \in \mathrm{AGL}_m\}$, then F has non-diagonal self-equivalences if and only if $Q' \circ F \circ Q$ has non-diagonal self-equivalences, for all $Q, Q' \in \mathcal{Q}$.

The main result of this section is Theorem 1, which shows that in order to have non-diagonal self-equivalences a function F must have additive self-equivalences, linear components and several linear structures. We first introduce these concepts before stating the theorem.

Given an (n, m)-bit function G, we denote by $(G_1, \ldots, G_m)$ the canonical or coordinate components of G, that is, $G(x) = (G_1(x), \ldots, G_m(x))$. The set of (Boolean) components of G can be defined as the set of n-bit Boolean functions given by the linear combinations of the canonical components of G, i.e.,

$$\left\{ \sum_{i=1}^m a_i G_i \mid (a_1, \ldots, a_m) \in \mathbb{F}_2^m \right\}.$$

Excluding the trivial component defined by $(a_1, \ldots, a_m) = (0, \ldots, 0)$, we say that r components $\sum_i a_i^{(1)} G_i, \ldots, \sum_i a_i^{(r)} G_i$ are linear independent if the $\mathbb{F}_2$-vectors $(a^{(1)}, \ldots, a^{(r)})$ are linear independent.

An additive self-equivalence of an (n, m)-bit function G is a pair of functions $(\oplus_a, \oplus_b)$, where a is an n-bit constant and b is an m-bit constant, such that $G = \oplus_b \circ G \circ \oplus_a$. For Boolean functions, this notation coincides with the notion of linear structure [19], while for vectorial Boolean functions the notion of linear structure is weaker.

Definition 10. *Let* $G : \mathbb{F}_2^n \to \mathbb{F}_2$ *be a Boolean function. An n-bit vector a is called a linear structure of G if there exists a bit b such that* $\oplus_b \circ G = G \circ \oplus_a$.

Definition 11. *Let* G *be an (n, m)-bit function. An n-bit vector a is a linear structure of G if a is a linear structure of some canonical component of G.*

Any (vectorial) Boolean function has the trivial linear structure $a = 0$ and the trivial additive self-equivalence $(\oplus_0, \oplus_0)$. We are now ready to state the main result of this section.

Theorem 1. *Let* $F = F_1 \| \cdots \| F_\rho$ *be an n-bit permutation, where each F_i is an m-bit permutation. If F has a non-diagonal self-equivalence, then F contains three permutations* (F_i, F_j, F_h), $j \neq h$, *such that*

(a) F_i *has a non-trivial additive self-equivalence.*
(b) F_j *has a non-trivial linear component.*
(c) F_h *has 2^{m-r} linear structures that are common to r linear independent components, for some $0 < r < m$.*

The proof of Theorem 1 is presented in Appendix B. Note that if $F_i = F_h$, then the condition (c) is redundant since (a) would imply (c). However, if $F_i = F_j$ neither (a) implies (b) nor vice-versa.

We checked for each 4-bit affine class $\mathcal{C}_i$ whether $\mathcal{C}_i \| \mathcal{C}_i$ has a non-diagonal self-equivalence. Using the list of 4-bit affine classes by De Cannière [15], we found that only the last 8 classes $\mathcal{C}_{293}, \mathcal{C}_{294}, \ldots, \mathcal{C}_{301}$ have non-diagonal self-equivalences when concatenated with themselves. These classes are actually the only ones that have both additive self-equivalences and linear components, showing that the necessary conditions of Theorem 1 are also sufficient for this case.

Cryptographically strong S-boxes do not have non-trivial linear components or additive self-equivalences, since they correspond to linear approximations and differentials with probability one, respectively. Most SPN ciphers employ S-box layers SL given by the concatenation of a single cryptographically strong S-box S, and for this case we can characterize the self-equivalence group of SL as follows.

Corollary 1. *Let* S *be an m-bit permutation without non-trivial additive self-equivalences or linear components, and consider the $(m \times \rho)$-bit permutation* $SL = S \circ \cdots \circ S$. *Then, the self-equivalence group of SL is given by*

$$\mathrm{SE}(SL) = \left\{ ((A_1 \| \cdots \| A_\rho) \circ P, P^{-1} \circ (B_1 \| \cdots \| B_\rho)) : \begin{array}{c} (A_i, B_i) \in \mathrm{SE}(S) \\ P \in \mathcal{P}_{m, \rho} \end{array} \right\}.$$

In addition, $|\mathrm{SE}(SL)| = \rho! \times |\mathrm{SE}(S)|^\rho$.

While we apply the study of diagonal self-equivalences and Theorem 1 for the security analysis of self-equivalence implementations, they can also be of independent interest. For example, Theorem 1 can be used to characterize and count the number of solutions of affine equivalence problems $G = Y \circ F \circ X$ where F is given by the concatenation of cryptographically strong S-boxes.

6   Security of Self-equivalence Implementations

In this section, we analyse the security of self-equivalence implementations against key-extraction attacks in the white-box model. Similar to CEJO implementations, self-equivalence implementations do not aim to prevent attacks inverting the implementation. Moreover, it is assumed that the specifications of the block cipher and the self-equivalence implementation are public, but the key and the encodings are unknown to the adversary.

In a self-equivalence implementation the round key material is hidden in the encoded affine layer, given as a binary constant and a binary matrix; the binary constant masks the round key with the round encodings and the binary matrix masks the linear part of the input and output encodings with each other. If many pairs of round keys and self-equivalences lead to the same encoded affine layer, each encoded affine layer is individually secure and the adversary is forced to solve a disambiguation problem involving several rounds.

Since CEJO encodings can be reduced to self-equivalence encodings, several white-box attacks [6,17,27] on CEJO implementations of AES contain steps to disambiguate diagonal self-equivalence encodings. However, they exploit specific properties of AES, and no generic attack on self-equivalence encodings, or even diagonal encodings, have been proposed this far.

To analyse the security of self-equivalence encodings, we describe the first generic attack on self-equivalence implementations. Since this is the first generic analysis, we focus on the class of SPN ciphers where the S-box layer does not have both a non-trivial additive self-equivalence and a linear component. Otherwise, the S-box layer will have a differential and a linear approximation with probability one, which are usually avoided in most SPN designs.

As most white-box attacks, our generic attack is a reduction attack. In other words, we describe a method to obtain new encoded affine layers for which the round encodings are restricted to a smaller encoding space. Afterwards, the key can be recovered by performing an exhaustive search over the reduced encoding space and filtering wrong candidates using the key schedule. Thus, the complexity of the key-recovery attack is given by the complexity to reduce the round encoding space and the complexity to brute force the reduced encoding space, where the latter step is lower bounded by the cardinality of the reduced encoding space.

The reduction step is based on equivalence problems involving the linear part of the round encodings with small solution sets, inspired from the white-box attacks on AES [6,17,27]. These equivalence problems consider unknowns restricted to some self-equivalence subgroup of the S-boxes, and estimating the complexity of these problems highly depends on the structure of the subgroup. Thus, our complexity metric is the cardinality of the reduced round encoding space, which provides a lower bound of the complexity of the whole attack.

Before we describe the attack, we recall the notation and the components of a self-equivalence implementation. Let E_k be the encryption function for a fixed key k of an arbitrary SPN cipher whose S-box layer SL does not have a non-trivial additive self-equivalence or a linear component. Let $\overline{E_k}$ be a self-equivalence implementation of E_k with encoded affine layers $\overline{AL^{(1)}}, \ldots, \overline{AL^{(n_r)}}$. Recall the rth intermediate encoded affine layer is defined by $\overline{AL^{(r)}} = O^{(r)} \circ (\oplus_{k^{(r)}} \circ LL) \circ I^{(r)}$, where $k^{(r)}$ is the rth round key, LL is the linear layer and $(I^{(r)}, O^{(r)})$ are the round encodings satisfying $(O^{(r)}, I^{(r+1)}) \in \mathrm{SE}(SL)$.

For this class of SPN ciphers all the self-equivalences of the S-box layer are diagonal, following Theorem 1. For ease of explanation, we will consider diagonal self-equivalences without block permutations, since they do not significantly impact the reduction step. In this case, the round encoding space of the self-equivalence implementation is $\mathrm{SE}(S_1) \, \| \, \cdots \, \| \, \mathrm{SE}(S_\rho)$. Figure 3 depicts an intermediate encoded affine layer with this type of round encoding space.

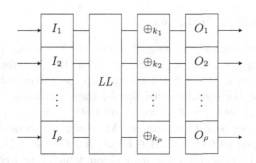

Fig. 3. An encoded affine layer with diagonal self-equivalence encodings.

Given an intermediate[3] encoded affine layer $\overline{AL^{(r)}}$, the core step in the reduction attack is to obtain another encoded affine layer differing only in the ith block of the output encoding, i.e.,

$$\widehat{AL^{(r)}} = O'^{(r)} \circ AL^{(r)} \circ I^{(r)}, \quad O_h'^{(r)} = O_h^{(r)} \; \forall h \neq i,$$

such that $\mathrm{Lin}(O_i'^{(r)})$ belongs to a proper subgroup of $\mathrm{Lin}(\mathrm{RSE}(S_i))$. The encoding space of the whole round encoding $(I^{(r)}, O^{(r)})$ can be then reduced by applying this step for all output encoding blocks of $\overline{AL^{(r)}}$ and $\overline{AL^{(r-1)}}$ and using the self-equivalence property $SL = I^{(r)} \circ SL \circ O^{(r-1)}$.

---

[3] The attack does not target the external encodings, which are assumed to be random affine permutations. Note that a self-equivalence implementation without external encodings is trivially insecure.

The reduction of the linear part of the output encoding is based on equivalence problems, and we do not reduce the constant part of the round encodings to avoid equivalence problems dependent on the round key. Recall an affine (resp. linear) equivalence problem is a functional equation $G = Y \circ F \circ X$ where F and G are given n-bit functions and (X, Y) are unknown n-bit affine (resp. linear) permutations. In our case, the unknowns (X, Y) are restricted to some given subgroup $\mathcal{A} \times \mathcal{B}$; given any solution (X_0, Y_0) the solution set is the group

$$\mathcal{S} = \{(A \circ X_0, Y_0 \circ B) : (A, B) \in \mathrm{SE}(F) \cap (\mathcal{A} \times \mathcal{B})\}.$$

We will describe two generic classes of equivalence problems that contain the output round encoding as a particular solution, and we will reduce the round encoding space to their solution sets. These two classes of equivalence problems, the centralizer and the asymmetric problems, can be combined and do not assume any particular structure in the self-equivalences groups of the S-boxes. However, other equivalence problems can be considered by exploiting specific properties of the self-equivalence groups. As an example, we will also describe a class of linear equivalence problems for S-boxes with only linear self-equivalences.

6.1   The Centralizer Problems

The centralizer problems are a class of univariate linear equivalence problems that allow reducing the round encoding space to the centralizer of linear layer blocks. Since these equivalence problems only involve the encoded affine layer of one round, we omit the round superscript for these problems.

Given an $(m \times \rho)$-bit linear function A, recall that we denote by $A_{i,j}$ the (i, j) m-bit block of A seen as a block matrix. Moreover, the centralizer of an n-bit function F is defined as $\mathrm{C}(F) = \{A \in \mathrm{GL}_n : A \circ F = F \circ A\}$. The centralizer problems are based on the following proposition, which is proved in Appendix C.

Proposition 2. *Let* $\overline{AL} = O \circ AL \circ I$ *be the encoded affine layer of an intermediate round and consider the linear layer block* $L = LL_{i,j} \circ \left(LL^{-1}\right)_{j,i}$. *Then, the univariate linear equivalence problem,*

$$\mathrm{Lin}\left(\overline{AL}\right)_{i,j} \circ \mathrm{Lin}\left(\overline{AL}^{-1}\right)_{j,i} = X \circ L \circ X^{-1}, \quad X \in \mathrm{Lin}(\mathrm{RSE}(S_i)), \qquad (1)$$

contains $X_0 = \mathrm{Lin}(O_i)$ *as a solution. In particular, its solution set is given by*

$$\mathcal{S} = \mathrm{Lin}(O_i) \circ \left(\mathrm{C}(L) \cap \mathrm{Lin}(\mathrm{RSE}(S_i))\right).$$

Without the restriction $X \in \mathrm{Lin}(\mathrm{RSE}(S_i))$, a solution of Eq. 1 could be easily obtained with complexity $\mathcal{O}(m^w)$, for $2 < w < 3$. However, the restriction makes the complexity harder to estimate, which strongly depends on the structure of $\mathrm{Lin}(\mathrm{RSE}(S_i))$. In general, one can perform an exhaustive search over $\mathrm{Lin}(\mathrm{RSE}(S_i))$ using the algorithm of Biryukov et al. [8]; the complexity of this approach is at least 2^{3m} and is also lower bounded by $|\mathrm{Lin}(\mathrm{RSE}(S_i))|$.

Let $X_0 = \text{Lin}(O_i) \circ H$ be an arbitrary solution of Eq. 1, for some unknown $H \in C(L) \cap \text{Lin}(\text{RSE}(S_i))$. Since $X_0 \in \text{Lin}(\text{RSE}(S_i))$, there exists an m-bit constant x_0 such that $\oplus_{x_0} \circ X_0 \in \text{RSE}(S_i)$. Let $C = (C_1 \parallel \cdots \parallel C_\rho)$ be the right self-equivalence of SL where $C_i = (\oplus_{x_0} \circ X_0)^{-1}$ and $C_h = \text{Id} \ \forall h \neq i$. Then, we can obtain another encoded affine layer

$$\widehat{AL} = C \circ \overline{AL} = O' \circ AL \circ I, \quad O'_h = O_h \ \forall h \neq i,$$

with (unknown) self-equivalences as round encodings and that only differs in the ith block of the output encoding. In addition, the linear part of O'_i is restricted to the subgroup $\text{Lin}(\text{RSE}(S_i)) \cap C(L)$.

In other words, the centralizer problem given by Eq. 1 allows reducing the encoding space associated to the linear part of the ith output encoding block, $\text{Lin}(\text{RSE}(S_i))$, to the subgroup $\text{Lin}(\text{RSE}(S_i)) \cap C(L)$. Note that this subgroup is related to the self-equivalences of the linear layer blocks, showing that the security of self-equivalence implementations not only depends on the self-equivalences of the S-box layer but also on the self-equivalence structure of the linear layer.

If L is the identity or its matrix representation over $\mathbb{F}_2$ has low rank, its centralizer contains too many elements and the reduction is not significant. Nevertheless, we can consider similar equivalence problems involving other blocks of $\overline{AL}$ and LL. In general, any sequence of the form

$$A = A_{i_1, j_1} A_{j_1, i_2} \cdots A_{i_s, j_s} A_{j_s, i_{s+1}}, \quad i_1 = i_{s+1}$$

$$A_{i_h, j_h} \in \left\{ \text{Lin}(AL)_{i_h, j_h}, \left(\text{Lin}\left(AL^{-1}\right)_{i_h, j_h} \right)^{-1} \right\}$$

$$A_{j_h, i_{h+1}} \in \left\{ \text{Lin}\left(AL^{-1}\right)_{j_h, i_{h+1}}, \left(\text{Lin}(AL)_{i_{h+1}, j_h} \right)^{-1} \right\}$$

leads to a centralizer problem of the form $A = \text{Lin}(O_{i_1}) \circ L \circ \text{Lin}(O_{i_1})^{-1}$, for some L composed of blocks of LL. In Appendix E we provide an example of a centralizer problem to reduce the round encoding space of a self-equivalence implementation of AES.

6.2   The Asymmetric Problems

The asymmetric problems are a class of affine equivalence problems that allow reducing the round encoding space to the intersection between the right and left self-equivalence groups of the S-boxes. As in the centralizer problems, we omit the round superscript for ease of notation. The asymmetric problems are based on the following proposition, whose proof is given in Appendix D.

Proposition 3. *Let $\overline{AL} = O \circ AL \circ I$ be the encoded affine layer of an intermediate round. Then, the affine[4] equivalence problem*

$$\text{Lin}\left(\overline{AL}\right)_{i,j} \circ S_j = X \circ LL_{i,j} \circ S_j \circ Y, \quad \text{Lin}(X) \in \text{Lin}(\text{RSE}(S_i)) \quad (2)$$

---

[4] If I_j is linear and $S_j(0) = 0$, then Eq. 2 is a linear equivalence problem.

contains a solution (X_0, Y_0) such that $\mathrm{Lin}(X_0) = \mathrm{Lin}(O_i)$. In particular, the linear part of the set of X-solutions $\mathcal{S}_X$ is given by the GL_n-subgroup

$$\mathrm{Lin}\,(\mathcal{S}_X) = \mathrm{Lin}\,(O_i) \circ \big(\,\mathrm{Lin}(\mathrm{LSE}(LL_{i,j} \circ S_j)) \cap \mathrm{Lin}(\mathrm{RSE}(S_i))\big).$$

As in the previous case, the complexity to obtain a solution of Eq. 2 is harder to estimate and strongly depends on $\mathrm{Lin}(\mathrm{RSE}(S_i))$. In general, the algorithm by Biryukov et al. can be used to perform an exhaustive search over $\mathrm{Lin}(\mathrm{RSE}(S_i))$ with complexity lower bounded by $\max(2^{3m}, |\,\mathrm{Lin}(\mathrm{RSE}(S_i))|)$.

Let (X_0, Y_0) be an arbitrary solution of Eq. 2. Then, there exists an $H \in \mathrm{Lin}(\mathrm{LSE}(LL_{i,j} \circ S_j)) \cap \mathrm{Lin}(\mathrm{RSE}(S_i)$ satisfying $\mathrm{Lin}(X_0) = \mathrm{Lin}\,(O_i) \circ H$. Let x_0 be an m-bit constant such that $\oplus_{x_0} \circ \mathrm{Lin}(X_0) \in \mathrm{RSE}(S_i)$ and consider $C = (C_1 \,\|\, \cdots \,\|\, C_p) \in \mathrm{SE}(SL)$ such that $C_i = (\oplus_{x_0} \circ \mathrm{Lin}(X_0))^{-1}$ and $C_h = \mathrm{Id}, \forall h \neq i$. Then, we can obtain another encoded affine layer with self-equivalence encodings,

$$\widehat{AL} = C \circ \overline{AL} = O' \circ AL \circ I, \quad O'_h = O_h\ \forall h \neq i,$$

that only differs in the ith block of the output encoding. Moreover, while $\mathrm{Lin}(\mathrm{RSE}(S_i))$ was the encoding space of $\mathrm{Lin}(O_i)$, the encoding space of $\mathrm{Lin}(O'_i)$ has been reduced to $\mathrm{Lin}(\mathrm{LSE}(LL_{i,j} \circ S_j)) \cap \mathrm{Lin}(\mathrm{RSE}(S_i))$.

If $LL_{i,j}$ is invertible, note that $\mathrm{Lin}(\mathrm{LSE}(LL_{i,j} \circ S_j))$ is the conjugate of $\mathrm{Lin}(\mathrm{LSE}(S_j))$ by $LL_{i,j}$, i.e., $\mathrm{Lin}(\mathrm{LSE}(LL_{i,j} \circ S_j)) = LL_{i,j} \circ \mathrm{Lin}(\mathrm{LSE}(S_j)) \circ LL_{i,j}^{-1}$. Thus, this equivalence problem allows reducing the encoding space of the linear part of the ith output encoding block to the intersection between $\mathrm{Lin}(\mathrm{RSE}(S_i))$ and a conjugate group of $\mathrm{LSE}(S_j)$ by a linear layer block. In Appendix F we show how an asymmetric problem can completely break a self-equivalence implementation of AES by reducing the encoding space to a set of one element.

Other Equivalence Problems. The centralizer and the asymmetric problems are generic equivalence problems that can be considered for any self-equivalence implementation. However, other equivalence problems can be considered, either by combining these two or by exploiting specific properties of the self-equivalence structure of the cipher components.

For example, if all the self-equivalences of the S-box layer are linear, we can combine the centralizer and the asymmetric problems to obtain

$$A_{i,i}^{(r)} \circ S_i \circ A_{i,j}^{(r-1)} \circ B_{j,i}^{(r-1)} \circ S_i^{-1} \circ B_{i,i}^{(r)} =$$
$$O_i^{(r)} \circ LL_{i,i} \circ S_i \circ LL_{i,j} \circ \big(LL^{-1}\big)_{j,i} \circ S_i^{-1} \circ \big(LL^{-1}\big)_{i,i} \circ \Big(O_i^{(r)}\Big)^{-1},$$

where $A^{(r)} = \mathrm{Lin}\left(\widehat{AL^{(r)}}\right)$ and $B^{(r)} = \mathrm{Lin}\left(\widehat{AL^{(r)}}\right)^{-1}$. By considering $X = O_i^{(r)}$ as the unknown, we obtain an univariate linear equivalence problem that reduces the encoding space associated to $O_i^{(r)}$ to

$$\mathrm{RSE}(S_i) \cap \mathrm{C}(LL_{i,i} \circ S_i \circ LL_{i,j} \circ \big(LL^{-1}\big)_{j,i} \circ S_i^{-1} \circ \big(LL^{-1}\big)_{i,i}).$$

This class of linear equivalence problems can be extended to any number of rounds, leading to many potential significant reductions.

7   Conclusion

In this document, we analysed the security of self-equivalence encodings. We described how a CEJO implementation can be transformed into a self-equivalence implementation, we characterized the self-equivalences of an S-box layer, and we propose a generic attack on a self-equivalence implementation of an SPN cipher with a cryptographically strong S-box layer.

Our generic attack shows that if the cipher components satisfy some properties, namely linear layer blocks with low rank or with big centralizers and S-boxes with plenty of affine self-equivalences and with similar left and right self-equivalences, a self-equivalence implementation resists the generic attack.

While traditional SPN ciphers with cryptographically strong S-box layers, such as AES, do not satisfy these strong requirements, our analysis reveals the potential of self-equivalence encodings to secure other types of ciphers. In particular, our analysis identifies future research directions that can lead to secure white-box implementations, namely non-diagonal self-equivalence encodings and self-equivalences implementations of ciphers with weaker round functions.

Acknowledgements. Adrián Ranea is supported by a PhD Fellowship from the Research Foundation – Flanders (FWO). The authors would like to thank the anonymous reviewers for their comments and suggestions.

A   Proof of Proposition 1

Proposition 1. *Let E_k be the encryption function of an n-bit SPN cipher with linear layer LL and S-box layer SL consisting of m-bit cryptographic S-boxes, and let $\overline{E_k}$ be a CEJO implementation of E_k with m_n-bit non-linear encodings and m_l-bit linear encodings. Given black-box access to three consecutive encoded round functions $\overline{E^{(r-2)}}, \overline{E^{(r-1)}}$ and $\overline{E^{(r)}}$, one can find another encoded $E^{(r)}$ with round encoding space $LL \circ \mathrm{LSE}(SL)$, i.e.,*

$$\widehat{E^{(r)}} = \widehat{O} \circ E^{(r)} \circ \widehat{I}, \quad \widehat{I}, \widehat{O^{-1}} \in LL \circ \mathrm{LSE}(SL),$$

in time $\mathcal{O}\left((n/m_n)2^{3m_n} + 2^m n^3 + n^4/m + 2^{2m}mn^2\right)$.

Proof. We apply first the algorithm by Baek et al. [3, Theorem 1 and 2] to recover the non-linear part of the output encodings of $\overline{E^{(i)}}$, for $i \in \{r-2, r-1, r\}$. Each m_n-bit non-linear function is recovered up to an affine transformation in time $\mathcal{O}\left((n/m_n)2^{3m_n}\right)$. As a result, new encoded round functions are obtained,

$$\widetilde{E^{(i)}} = \widetilde{O^{(i)}} \circ E^{(i)} \circ \widetilde{I^{(i)}}, \quad i \in \{r-1, r\}, \tag{3}$$

where the input and output round encodings are unknown affine permutations.

Since $\widetilde{E^{(r-1)}}$ and $\widetilde{E^{(r)}}$ are affine equivalent to the S-box layer SL, the corresponding affine equivalence problems can be solved with the algorithm by Derbez et al. in time $O(2^m n^3 + n^4/m + 2^{2m} mn^2)$ [17, Algorithm 1]. Thus, two pairs of affine permutations, $(A^{(r-1)}, B^{(r-1)})$ and $(A^{(r)}, B^{(r)})$, are obtained such that

$$\widetilde{E^{(i)}} = B^{(i)} \circ SL \circ A^{(i)}, \quad i \in \{r-1, r\}. \tag{4}$$

Combining Eqs. 3 and 4 leads to the functional equation

$$B^{(i)} \circ SL \circ A^{(i)} = (\widetilde{O^{(i)}} \circ LL) \circ SL \circ (\oplus_{k^{(i)}} \circ \widetilde{I^{(i)}}).$$

Note that $(A^{(i)}, B^{(i)})$ is not necessarily equal to $(\oplus_{k^{(i)}} \circ \widetilde{I^{(i)}}, \widetilde{O^{(i)}} \circ LL)$. Nevertheless, there exists a self-equivalence $(C^{(i)}, D^{(i)}) \in SE(SL)$ such that

$$A^{(i)} = C^{(i)} \circ \oplus_{k^{(i)}} \circ \widetilde{I^{(i)}},$$
$$B^{(i)} = \widetilde{O^{(i)}} \circ LL \circ D^{(i)}.$$

Finally, by composing $\widetilde{E^{(r)}}$ with the key-independent permutations $B^{(r-1)}$ and $B^{(r)}$, we can obtain an encoded $E^{(r)}$ with round encoding space $LL \circ LSE(SL)$,

$$\widehat{E^{(r)}} = \left(B^{(r)}\right)^{-1} \circ \widetilde{E^{(r)}} \circ B^{(r-1)} = (LL \circ D^{(r)})^{-1} \circ E^{(r)} \circ (LL \circ D^{(r-1)}).$$

$\square$

B   Proof of Theorem 1

First, we will introduce some concepts and lemmas connecting the notions of additive self-equivalences, linear structures and linear components.

Lemma 2. *Let G be an n-bit function. Then $(\oplus_a, \oplus_b)$ is an additive self-equivalence of G if and only if a is a linear structure of all canonical components of G.*

Proof. The lemma immediately follows from the definition of additive self-equivalence and linear structure. If $(\oplus_a, \oplus_b) \in SE(G)$, then $\oplus_b \circ G = G \circ \oplus_a$, which is equivalent to $\oplus_{b_i} \circ G_i = G_i \circ \oplus_a$ for $i = 1, \ldots, n$. $\square$

Given an n-bit Boolean function G, we say that G is independent of the jth input x_j if x_j does not appear in the Algebraic Normal Form (ANF) of G, i.e., the unique representation of G as an n-variable polynomial over $\mathbb{F}_2$. Similarly, we say that G is linear in x_j if all the ANF terms that contains x_j are of degree one. The next lemma shows the connection between independent variables and additive self-equivalences, previous analysed in [26].

Lemma 3. *Let G be an n-bit function and consider the jth canonical n-bit vector $e^{(j)}$, where $e_i^{(j)} = 0$ if and only if $i \neq j$. If each canonical component of G is linear in the jth input x_j or independent of x_j, then there exists an n-bit value b such that $(\oplus_{e^{(j)}}, \oplus_b)$ is an additive self-equivalence of G.*

Proof. Let G_i be a canonical component of G. If G_i is linear in x_j, note that $G_i(x + e^{(j)}) = G_i(x) \oplus G_i(e^{(j)})$, that is, $\oplus_{G_i(e^{(j)})} \circ G_i = G_i \circ \oplus_{e^{(j)}}$ and $e^{(j)}$ is a linear structure of G_i. Similarly, if G_i is independent of x_j, $G_i(x + e^{(j)}) = G_i(x)$ and $e^{(j)}$ is also a linear structure of G_i. Therefore, $e^{(j)}$ is a linear structure of all canonical components, and by Lemma 2 G has an additive self-equivalence with $e^{(j)}$ as the right equivalence. $\qquad\square$

The last lemma required by the proof of Theorem 1 is the following technical lemma to obtain a "normal form" of block matrices.

Lemma 4. *Let A_1 and A_2 be two m-bit matrices where $0 < \mathrm{rank}(A_1) \le \mathrm{rank}(A_2)$. Let $A = (A_1 | A_2)$ be the block matrix composed of one block row and two block columns. Then, there exists an invertible (m, m)-bit matrix D_A and a block matrix*

$$C_A = \begin{pmatrix} C_{A,1} & 0 \\ 0 & C_{A,2} \end{pmatrix},$$

where $C_{A,1}$ and $C_{A,2}$ are invertible (m, m)-bit matrices, such that $A' = D_A \times A \times C_A$ is of the form

$$A' = \left(\begin{array}{c|ccc} \mathrm{Id}_{\mathrm{rank}(A_1)} & & M_A & \\ 0 & 0 & \mathrm{Id}_r & 0 & 0 \\ 0 & & 0 & \end{array} \right)$$

where $r = \mathrm{rank}(A) - \mathrm{rank}(A_1)$ and M_A is a $(\mathrm{rank}(A_1), \mathrm{rank}(A_2))$-bit matrix with full rank, i.e., $\mathrm{rank}(M_A) = \mathrm{rank}(A_1)$.

Proof. We will show that we can obtain A' by doing elementary row operations (represented by D_A) and elementary column operations (represented by C_A). Due to the block diagonal shape of C_A, column operations involving both left columns and right columns are not allowed. Thus, we will employ left (resp. right) column operations, i.e., elementary column operations only involving the first (resp. last) m columns. The sequence of elementary operations is the following.

1. With left column operations we can make the last $m - \mathrm{rank}(A_1)$ columns on the left side zero. Similarly, on the right side we can make the last $m - \mathrm{rank}(A_2)$ columns zero with right column operations,

$$\left(\begin{array}{cc|cc} * & 0 & * & 0 \\ * & 0 & * & 0 \\ * & 0 & * & 0 \end{array} \right).$$

2. With row operations we can make the last $m - \mathrm{rank}(A)$ rows zero,

$$\left(\begin{array}{cc|cc} * & 0 & * & 0 \\ * & 0 & * & 0 \\ 0 & 0 & 0 & 0 \end{array} \right).$$

3. With row operations we can make the rows $(\operatorname{rank}(A_1) + 1, \operatorname{rank}(A))$ in the left part zero, obtaining

$$\begin{pmatrix} A'_1 & 0 & * & 0 \\ 0 & 0 & * & 0 \\ 0 & 0 & 0 & 0 \end{pmatrix}$$

where A'_1 is an invertible $\operatorname{rank}(A_1)$-bit matrix.

4. With row operations and left column operations, we can replace A'_1 by $\operatorname{Id}_{\operatorname{rank}(A_1)}$ and obtain

$$\begin{pmatrix} \operatorname{Id}_{\operatorname{rank}(A_1)} & 0 & * & 0 \\ 0 & 0 & A'_2 & 0 \\ 0 & 0 & 0 & 0 \end{pmatrix}$$

where A'_2 is a $(r, \operatorname{rank}(A_2))$-bit matrix with rank $r = \operatorname{rank}(A) - \operatorname{rank}(A_1)$.

5. With right column operations and row operations involving only the middle rows, we can replace A'_2 by $(\operatorname{Id}_r | 0)$,

$$\begin{pmatrix} \operatorname{Id}_{\operatorname{rank}(A_1)} & 0 & * & 0 \\ 0 & 0 & \operatorname{Id}_r & 0 & 0 \\ 0 & 0 & 0 & 0 \end{pmatrix}.$$

6. Finally, with right column operations and by adding middle rows to the first rows, we can obtain

$$\begin{pmatrix} \operatorname{Id}_{\operatorname{rank}(A_1)} & 0 & M_A & 0 \\ 0 & 0 & \operatorname{Id}_r & 0 & 0 \\ 0 & 0 & 0 & 0 \end{pmatrix}$$

where M_A is a $(\operatorname{rank}(A_1), \operatorname{rank}(A_2))$-bit matrix with full rank.   □

We are now ready to start with the proof of Theorem 1. The conducting idea of the proof is that F has a non-diagonal self-equivalence (A, B) if and only if there is a function F', Q-affine equivalent to F, such that F' has a simpler non-diagonal self-equivalence (A', B'), where many blocks of A' and B' are the identity. We will extract some Q-invariant necessary conditions to have a non-diagonal self-equivalence from F', and we will translate them to F.

Theorem 1. *Let $F = F_1 \| \cdots \| F_\rho$ be an n-bit permutation, where each F_i is an m-bit permutation. If F has a non-diagonal self-equivalence, then F contains three permutations (F_i, F_j, F_h), $j \neq h$, such that*

(a) F_i has a non-trivial additive self-equivalence.
(b) F_j has a non-trivial linear component.
(c) F_h has 2^{m-r} linear structures that are common to r linear independent components, for some $0 < r < m$.

Proof. Let (A, B^{-1}) be an arbitrary non-diagonal self-equivalence of F. Then, $B \circ F = F \circ A$ and $\mathrm{Lin}(A)$ contains two non-zero blocks in the same row, i.e., $\mathrm{Lin}(A)_{i,j}$ and $\mathrm{Lin}(A)_{i,h}$ for some i, j, h. Note that i could be equal to j or h but $j \neq h$.

By evaluating $B \circ F = F \circ A$ at $(x_1, \ldots, x_\rho)$, where $x_k = 0$, $\forall k \neq j, h$, we obtain the following equations for the ith row:

$$c' \oplus \mathrm{Lin}(B)_{i,j}(F_j(x_j)) = F_i(\mathrm{Lin}(A)_{i,j}(x_j) \oplus c), \quad \forall x_j \in \mathbb{F}_2^m,$$
$$c''' \oplus \mathrm{Lin}(B)_{i,h}(F_j(x_h)) = F_i(\mathrm{Lin}(A)_{i,h}(x_h) \oplus c''), \quad \forall x_h \in \mathbb{F}_2^m,$$

for some constants c, c', c'', c'''. Thus, it is easy to see that $\mathrm{Lin}(B)_{i,j}$ and $\mathrm{Lin}(B)_{i,h}$ have the same rank as $\mathrm{Lin}(A)_{i,j}$ and $\mathrm{Lin}(A)_{i,h}$, respectively.

We will consider two cases depending on whether the blocks $\mathrm{Lin}(A)_{i,j}$ and $\mathrm{Lin}(A)_{i,h}$ have full rank.

Case 1: $\mathrm{Lin}(A)_{i,j}$ *and* $\mathrm{Lin}(A)_{i,h}$ *are invertible.* In this case, consider a diagonal self-equivalence $(C, D^{-1}) = (C_1 \| \cdots \| C_\rho, D_1^{-1} \| \cdots \| D_\rho^{-1}) \in \mathrm{SE}(F)$ satisfying

$$(\mathrm{Lin}(C_j), \mathrm{Lin}(D_j)) = (\mathrm{Lin}(A)_{i,j}^{-1}, \mathrm{Lin}(B)_{i,j}^{-1}),$$
$$(\mathrm{Lin}(C_h), \mathrm{Lin}(D_h)) = (\mathrm{Lin}(A)_{i,h}^{-1}, \mathrm{Lin}(B)_{i,h}^{-1}),$$
$$C_k = D_k = \mathrm{Id}, \quad \forall k \neq j, h.$$

Thus, $(A \circ C, D^{-1} \circ B^{-1})$ is a non-diagonal self-equivalence which satisfies

$$\mathrm{Lin}(A \circ C)_{i,j} = \mathrm{Lin}(A \circ C)_{i,h} = \mathrm{Lin}(B \circ D)_{i,j} = \mathrm{Lin}(B \circ D)_{i,h} = \mathrm{Id}.$$

By evaluating $(B \circ D) \circ F = F \circ (A \circ C)$ at $(x_1, \ldots, x_\rho)$, where $x_k = 0$, $\forall k \neq j, h$, we obtain the following equation for the ith row:

$$c' + F_j(x_j) \oplus F_h(x_h) = F_i(x_j + x_h + c), \quad \forall x_j, x_h \in \mathbb{F}_2^m, \tag{5}$$

for some constants c, c'. Equation 5 implies that F_i is linear, since the left-hand side of the equation does not contain ANF terms multiplying x_j and x_h bits. But then F_j and F_h are also linear, and the conditions (a), (b), and (c) hold for Case 1.

Case 2: $\mathrm{Lin}(A)_{i,j}$ *or* $\mathrm{Lin}(A)_{i,h}$ *is non-invertible.* Consider the block matrices

$$A^\dagger = (\mathrm{Lin}(A_{i,j}) | \mathrm{Lin}(A_{i,h})),$$
$$B^\dagger = (\mathrm{Lin}(B_{i,j}) | \mathrm{Lin}(B_{i,h})).$$

Without loss of generality, we assume $0 < \mathrm{rank}(\mathrm{Lin}(A)_{i,j}) \leq \mathrm{rank}(\mathrm{Lin}(A)_{i,h})$ and $\mathrm{rank}(A^\dagger) - \mathrm{Lin}(A)_{i,j} > 0$. Let r_j and r_h be the rank of $A_{i,j}$ and $A_{i,h}$, respectively, and let $r = \mathrm{rank}(A^\dagger) - r_j$.

According to Lemma 4 there exist invertible m-bit matrices D_A and D_B and $2m$-bit block matrices C_A and C_B such that

$$A' = D_A \times A^\dagger \times C_A = \left(\begin{array}{cc|ccc} \mathrm{Id}_{r_j} & & M_A & & \\ 0 & 0 & \mathrm{Id}_r & 0 & 0 \\ \hline 0 & & 0 & & \end{array} \right)$$

$$B' = D_B \times B^\dagger \times C_B = \left(\begin{array}{cc|ccc} \mathrm{Id}_{r_j} & & M_B & & \\ 0 & 0 & \mathrm{Id}_r & 0 & 0 \\ \hline 0 & & 0 & & \end{array} \right)$$

where M_A and M_B are (r_j, r_h)-bit matrices with full rank.

By evaluating $B \circ F = F \circ A$ at $(x_1, \ldots, x_\rho)$, where $x_k = 0$, $\forall k \neq j, h$, we obtain the following equation for the ith row:

$$c' + B^\dagger(F_j(x_j), F_h(x_h)) = F_i(A^\dagger(x_j, x_h) + c), \quad \forall x_j, x_h \in \mathbb{F}_2^m,$$

for some constants c and c'. For ease of notation, we will consider the constants c and c' to be zero; the generalization of the proof for arbitrary values of c and c') is straightforward.

By substituting $A^\dagger = D_A^{-1} \times A' \times C_A^{-1}$, $B^\dagger = D_B^{-1} \times B' \times C_B^{-1}$ and $(x_j, x_h) = C_A(x^{(j)}, x^{(h)})$, we obtain

$$B'((C_{B,1}^{-1} \circ F_j \circ C_{A,1})(x^{(j)}), (C_{B,2}^{-1} \circ F_h \circ C_{A,2})(x^{(h)}))$$
$$= (D_B \circ F_i \circ D_A^{-1})(A'(x^{(j)}, x^{(h)})) \qquad \forall x^{(j)}, x^{(h)} \in \mathbb{F}_2^m.$$

Let $F^{(i)}$, $F^{(j)}$ and $F^{(h)}$ be the m-bit permutations affine equivalent to F_i, F_j and F_j, respectively, given by

$$F^{(i)} = D_B \circ F_i \circ D_A^{-1}$$
$$F^{(j)} = C_{B,1}^{-1} \circ F_j \circ C_{A,1}$$
$$F^{(h)} = C_{B,2}^{-1} \circ F_h \circ C_{A,2}.$$

Then, we can rewrite the previous equation as follows,

$$B'(F^{(j)}(x^{(j)}), F^{(h)}(x^{(h)})) = F^{(i)}(A'(x^{(j)}, x^{(h)})), \quad \forall x^{(j)}, x^{(h)} \in \mathbb{F}_2^m. \quad (6)$$

Given an m-bit function G with canonical components $(G_1, G_2, \ldots, G_m)$, let $G_{a,b}$ be the $(m, b - a + 1)$-bit function given by $G_{a,b} = (G_a, G_{a+1}, \ldots, G_b)$. Similarly, given an m-bit variable $x = (x_1, \ldots, x_m)$ we denote $x_{a,b} = (x_a, x_{a+1}, \ldots, x_b)$. Then, Eq. 6 can be decomposed into the following three equations:

$$F_{1,r_j}^{(j)}(x^{(j)}) + M_B(F_{1,r_h}^{(h)}(x^{(h)})) = F_{1,r_j}^{(i)}(y), \qquad (7a)$$

$$0 + F_{1,r}^{(h)}(x^{(h)}) = F_{r_j+1,r_j+r}^{(i)}(y), \qquad (7b)$$

$$0 + 0 = F_{r_j+r+1,m}^{(i)}(y). \qquad (7c)$$

where $y = A'(x^{(j)}, x^{(h)}) = (x_{1,r_j}^{(j)} + M_A(x_{1,r_h}^{(h)}), x_{1,r}^{(h)}, 0)$. Note that $M_A(x_{1,r_h}^{(h)})$ fully spans $\mathbb{F}_2^{r_j}$ and that the first r_j bits of y contain bits from both $x^{(j)}$ and $x^{(h)}$.

In Eq. 7a the left-hand side does not contain ANF terms multiplying $x^{(j)}$ and $x^{(h)}$ bits. Therefore, $F_{1,r_j}^{(i)}$ is linear in the first r_j inputs, which implies that $F_{1,r_j}^{(j)}$ is linear.

From Eq. 7b and Eq. 7c we can deduce that $F_{r_j+1,m}^{(i)}$ is independent of the first r_j input bits. Therefore, $F^{(i)}$ has at least 2^{r_j} additive self-equivalences by Lemma 3.

Finally, Eq. 7b also implies that $F_{1,r}^{(h)}$ is independent of the last $m - r$ inputs. Equivalently, $F^{(h)}$ has at least 2^{m-r} linear structures that are common to r independent components following Lemmas 2 and 3.

As a result, if F has a non-diagonal self-equivalence, we have obtained the following necessary conditions, for $1 \leq r_j, r < m$.

- $F^{(i)}$ has at least 2^{r_j} additive self-equivalences.
- $F^{(j)}$ has at least r_j linear independent components that are linear.
- $F^{(h)}$ has at least 2^{m-r} linear structures that are common to r independent components.

It is easy to see that these three properties are invariant in the class $\mathcal{Q} \circ F \circ \mathcal{Q}$. Therefore, F_i, F_j and F_h verify the same properties, which concludes the proof. $\square$

C   Proof of Proposition 2

Proposition 2. *Let $\overline{AL} = O \circ AL \circ I$ be the encoded affine layer of an intermediate round and consider the linear layer block $L = LL_{i,j} \circ (LL^{-1})_{j,i}$. Then, the univariate linear equivalence problem,*

$$\mathrm{Lin}\left(\overline{AL}\right)_{i,j} \circ \mathrm{Lin}\left(\overline{AL}^{-1}\right)_{j,i} = X \circ L \circ X^{-1}, \quad X \in \mathrm{Lin}(\mathrm{RSE}(S_i)),$$

contains $X_0 = \mathrm{Lin}(O_i)$ as a solution. In particular, its solution set is given by

$$S = \mathrm{Lin}(O_i) \circ \left(C(L) \cap \mathrm{Lin}(\mathrm{RSE}(S_i))\right).$$

Proof. Note that the linear blocks of the encoded affine layer are defined as

$$\mathrm{Lin}\left(\overline{AL}\right)_{i,j} = \mathrm{Lin}(O_i) \circ LL_{i,j} \circ \mathrm{Lin}(I_j).$$

The input encoding can be removed by composing with the inverse of the encoded affine layer, obtaining the equation

$$\mathrm{Lin}\left(\overline{AL}\right)_{i,j} \circ \mathrm{Lin}\left(\overline{AL}^{-1}\right)_{j,i} = \mathrm{Lin}(O_i) \circ LL_{i,j} \circ (LL^{-1})_{j,i} \circ \mathrm{Lin}(O_i)^{-1}$$

where the only secret information is $\mathrm{Lin}(O_i)$. Thus, the univariate linear equivalence problem

$$\mathrm{Lin}\left(\overline{AL}\right)_{i,j} \circ \mathrm{Lin}\left(\overline{AL}^{-1}\right)_{j,i} = X \circ LL_{i,j} \circ (LL^{-1})_{j,i} \circ X^{-1}$$

with unknown $X \in \mathrm{Lin}(\mathrm{RSE}(S_i))$ has $\mathrm{Lin}(O_i)$ as particular solution. $\square$

D   Proof of Proposition 3

Proposition 3. *Let $\overline{AL} = O \circ AL \circ I$ be the encoded affine layer of an interme-diate round. Then, the affine equivalence problem*

$$\mathrm{Lin}\left(\overline{AL}\right)_{i,j} \circ S_j = X \circ LL_{i,j} \circ S_j \circ Y, \quad \mathrm{Lin}(X) \in \mathrm{Lin}(\mathrm{RSE}(S_i))$$

contains a solution (X_0, Y_0) such that $\mathrm{Lin}(X_0) = \mathrm{Lin}(O_i)$. In particular, the linear part of the set of X-solutions S_X is given by the GL_n-subgroup

$$\mathrm{Lin}\left(S_X\right) = \mathrm{Lin}\left(O_i\right) \circ \left(\mathrm{Lin}(\mathrm{LSE}(LL_{i,j} \circ S_j)) \cap \mathrm{Lin}(\mathrm{RSE}(S_i))\right).$$

Proof. Let $\overline{AL} = \overline{AL^{(r)}}$ be the encoded affine layer of the rth round. From the definition of encoded affine layer and the self-equivalence property

$$I_j^{(r)} \circ S_j = S_j \circ \left(O_j^{(r-1)}\right)^{-1},$$

it is easy to show that there exists a constant c such that

$$\mathrm{Lin}\left(\overline{AL^{(r)}}\right)_{i,j} \circ S_j = \oplus_c \circ \mathrm{Lin}\left(O_i^{(r)}\right) \circ LL_{i,j} \circ S_j \circ \left(O_j^{(r-1)}\right)^{-1}.$$

Thus, we can consider the affine equivalence problem

$$\mathrm{Lin}\left(\overline{AL^{(r)}}\right)_{i,j} \circ S_j = X \circ LL_{i,j} \circ S_j \circ Y.$$

where X and Y are unknown affine permutations such that $\mathrm{Lin}(X) \in \mathrm{Lin}(\mathrm{RSE}(S_i))$. If (X_0, Y_0) is an arbitrary solution, then the solution set S is given by

$$S = \{(X_0 \circ B, A \circ Y_0) : (A, B) \in \mathrm{SE}(LL_{i,j} \circ S_j), \ \mathrm{Lin}(B) \in \mathrm{Lin}(\mathrm{RSE}(S_i))\}.$$

Since $\oplus_c \circ \mathrm{Lin}(O_i^{(r)})$ is a particular X-solution, the linear part of the set of X-solutions is given by the GL_n-subgroup

$$\mathrm{Lin}\left(S_X\right) = \mathrm{Lin}\left(O_i^{(r)}\right) \circ \left(\mathrm{Lin}(\mathrm{LSE}(LL_{i,j} \circ S_j)) \cap \mathrm{Lin}(\mathrm{RSE}(S_i))\right).$$

$\square$

E   Example of the Centralizer Problem

We will show the application of a centralizer problem to reduce the round encoding space of a self-equivalence implementation of AES.

Let $\mathbb{F}_{2^8}$ be the finite field used in AES and let P_d be the 8-bit function corresponding to the power function $x \mapsto x^d$ in $\mathbb{F}_{2^8}$ and M_α be the 8-bit function corresponding to the multiplication $x \mapsto \alpha \times x$ by an $\mathbb{F}_{2^8}$-constant α. The AES

S-box is an 8-bit function given by $S(x) = L(P_{254}(x)) + c$, for some linear permutation L and constant c. Since we can push the S-box constant to the round key, we can redefine the S-box as $S = L \circ P_{254}$, whose self-equivalences are given by [8]

$$\mathrm{RSE}(S) = \{M_\alpha \circ P_{2^i} : 0 \neq \alpha \in \mathbb{F}_{2^8}, \ i \in \{0, \dots, 7\}\},$$
$$\mathrm{LSE}(S) = \{L \circ (M_{\alpha^{254}} \circ P_{2^i})^{-1} \circ L^{-1} : 0 \neq \alpha \in \mathbb{F}_{2^8}, \ i \in \{0, \dots, 7\}\}.$$

Note that $\mathrm{RSE}(S)$ and $\mathrm{LSE}(S)$ only consist of linear permutations.

For ease of explanation, we consider the round function restricted to a column state and omit the action of ShiftRows. Thus, the linear layer LL corresponds to the action of MixColumns on a column, and its block matrix representation with 8-bit blocks is given by

$$LL = \begin{pmatrix} M_2 & M_3 & M_1 & M_1 \\ M_1 & M_2 & M_3 & M_1 \\ M_1 & M_1 & M_2 & M_3 \\ M_3 & M_1 & M_1 & M_2 \end{pmatrix},$$

where M_1 denotes the 8-bit identity, and M_2 and M_3 corresponds to the multiplication by 2 and 3 in $\mathbb{F}_{2^8}$, respectively.

Let $\overline{AL} = O \circ \oplus_k \circ LL \circ I$ be an intermediate encoded affine layer, where $O = O_1 \| O_2 \| O_3 \| O_4 \in \mathrm{RSE}(S)^4$. To reduce the encoding space of O_1, we can consider the centralizer problem

$$\mathrm{Lin}\left(\overline{AL}\right)_{1,2} \circ \left(\mathrm{Lin}\left(\overline{AL}\right)_{2,1}\right)^{-1} = X \circ M_3 \circ M_1^{-1} \circ X^{-1}, \quad X \in \mathrm{RSE}(S)$$

with solution set $\mathcal{S} = O_1 \circ (\mathrm{C}(M_3) \cap \mathrm{RSE}(S))$ following Proposition 2. Since 3 is a primitive element in $\mathbb{F}_{2^8}$, the centralizer of M_3 is the set of functions corresponding to the multiplication by non-zero $\mathbb{F}_{2^8}$-elements, i.e.,

$$\mathrm{C}(M_3) = \{M_\alpha : 0 \neq \alpha \in \mathbb{F}_{2^8}\} < \mathrm{RSE}(S).$$

The set $\mathrm{RSE}(S)$ only contains 2040 elements, and we can simply brute force $\mathrm{RSE}(S)$ to obtain an arbitrary solution $X_0 = O_1 \circ M_\gamma$, for some unknown M_γ. Composing $C = (X_0^{-1} \| \mathrm{Id} \| \mathrm{Id} \| \mathrm{Id})$ with $\overline{AL}$ leads to a new encoded AL,

$$\widehat{AL} = C \circ \overline{AL} = (M_\alpha \| O_2 \| O_3 \| O_4) \circ AL \circ I,$$

where the encoding space of the first block of the output encoding has been reduced to $\{M_\alpha : 0 \neq \alpha \in \mathbb{F}_{2^8}\}$.

While the centralizer problem does not provide a drastic reduction in this case, it shows how the self-equivalence structure of the linear layer also influences the success of the reduction. Thus, even if the AES S-box is replaced with another S-box with more self-equivalences, we can still reduce the encoding space of each block to $\{M_\alpha : 0 \neq \alpha \in \mathbb{F}_{2^8}\}$ thanks to the centralizers of the MixColumns blocks.

F   Example of the Asymmetric Problem

We will show how the asymmetric problem can completely break a self-equivalence implementation of AES by reducing the encoding space to a set of one element. For ease of explanation, we will apply the asymmetric problem to the reduced self-equivalence implementation obtained in the previous example, where we applied the centralizer problem to reduce the encoding space corresponding to the first block of the output encoding to $\{M_\alpha : 0 \neq \alpha \in \mathbb{F}_{2^8}\}$.

Let $\overline{AL}$ be an intermediate encoded affine layer restricted to a column,

$$\overline{AL} = (O_1 \parallel O_2 \parallel O_3 \parallel O_4) \circ \oplus_k \circ LL \circ (I_1 \parallel I_2 \parallel I_3 \parallel I_4),$$

such that $O_1 \in \{M_\alpha : 0 \neq \alpha \in \mathbb{F}_{2^8}\} < \mathrm{RSE}(S)$. To reduce the encoding space of O_1, we consider the asymmetric problem

$$\mathrm{Lin}\left(\overline{AL}\right)_{1,3} \circ S = X \circ M_1 \circ S \circ Y, \quad X \in \{M_\alpha : 0 \neq \alpha \in \mathbb{F}_{2^8}\}$$

that contains the particular X-solution O_1 according to Lemmas 3. It is easy to see that this asymmetric problem is a linear equivalence problem, since $S(0) = 0$ and all the right self-equivalences of S are linear. Thus, the X-solution set is given by

$$\mathcal{S}_X = O_1 \circ (\mathrm{LSE}(S) \cap \{M_\alpha : 0 \neq \alpha \in \mathbb{F}_{2^8}\}).$$

Since this intersection is trivial, i.e., $\mathrm{LSE}(S) \cap \{M_\alpha : 0 \neq \alpha \in \mathbb{F}_{2^8}\} = \{\mathrm{Id}\}$, the asymmetric problem only has one solution.

We can simply perform an exhaustive search over the set $\{M_\alpha : 0 \neq \alpha \in \mathbb{F}_{2^8}\}$ containing 255 elements to obtain the unique solution $X_0 = O_1$, fully recovering the first block of the output encoding. Proceeding similarly with the rest of the output encoding blocks, we can reduce the round encoding space of $\overline{AL}$ to a set of one element. Afterwards, the round encodings and the master key can be recovered easily.

References

1. Albrecht, M.R., Bard, G.V., Hart, W.: Algorithm 898: efficient multiplication of dense matrices over GF(2). ACM Trans. Math. Softw. **37**(1), 9:1–9:14 (2010)
2. Amadori, A., Michiels, W., Roelse, P.: A DFA attack on white-box implementations of AES with external encodings. In: Paterson, K.G., Stebila, D. (eds.) SAC 2019. LNCS, vol. 11959, pp. 591–617. Springer, Cham (2020). https://doi.org/10.1007/978-3-030-38471-5_24
3. Baek, C.H., Cheon, J.H., Hong, H.: White-box AES implementation revisited. J. Commun. Networks **18**(3), 273–287 (2016)
4. Bai, K., Wu, C.: An AES-like cipher and its white-box implementation. Comput. J. **59**(7), 1054–1065 (2016)
5. Banik, S., Bogdanov, A., Isobe, T., Jepsen, M.B.: Analysis of software countermeasures for whitebox encryption. IACR Trans. Symmetric Cryptol. **2017**(1), 307–328 (2017)

6. Billet, O., Gilbert, H., Ech-Chatbi, C.: Cryptanalysis of a white box AES implementation. In: Handschuh, H., Hasan, M.A. (eds.) SAC 2004. LNCS, vol. 3357, pp. 227–240. Springer, Heidelberg (2004). https://doi.org/10.1007/978-3-540-30564-4_16

7. Biryukov, A., Bouillaguet, C., Khovratovich, D.: Cryptographic schemes based on the ASASA structure: black-box, white-box, and public-key (extended abstract). In: Sarkar, P., Iwata, T. (eds.) ASIACRYPT 2014. LNCS, vol. 8873, pp. 63–84. Springer, Heidelberg (2014). https://doi.org/10.1007/978-3-662-45611-8_4

8. Biryukov, A., De Cannière, C., Braeken, A., Preneel, B.: A toolbox for cryptanalysis: linear and affine equivalence algorithms. In: Biham, E. (ed.) EUROCRYPT 2003. LNCS, vol. 2656, pp. 33–50. Springer, Heidelberg (2003). https://doi.org/10.1007/3-540-39200-9_3

9. Bogdanov, A., Isobe, T.: White-box cryptography revisited: space-hard ciphers. In: ACM Conference on Computer and Communications Security, pp. 1058–1069. ACM (2015)

10. Bos, J.W., Hubain, C., Michiels, W., Teuwen, P.: Differential computation analysis: hiding your white-box designs is not enough. In: Gierlichs, B., Poschmann, A.Y. (eds.) CHES 2016. LNCS, vol. 9813, pp. 215–236. Springer, Heidelberg (2016). https://doi.org/10.1007/978-3-662-53140-2_11

11. Bringer, J., Chabanne, H., Dottax, E.: White box cryptography: another attempt. IACR Cryptol. ePrint Arch. **2006**, 468 (2006)

12. Cheon, J.H., Hong, H., Lee, J., Lee, J.: An efficient affine equivalence algorithm for multiple S-boxes and a structured affine layer. In: Avanzi, R., Heys, H. (eds.) SAC 2016. LNCS, vol. 10532, pp. 299–316. Springer, Cham (2017). https://doi.org/10.1007/978-3-319-69453-5_17

13. Chow, S., Eisen, P., Johnson, H., Van Oorschot, P.C.: White-box cryptography and an AES implementation. In: Nyberg, K., Heys, H. (eds.) SAC 2002. LNCS, vol. 2595, pp. 250–270. Springer, Heidelberg (2003). https://doi.org/10.1007/3-540-36492-7_17

14. Chow, S., Eisen, P., Johnson, H., van Oorschot, P.C.: A White-box DES implementation for DRM applications. In: Feigenbaum, J. (ed.) DRM 2002. LNCS, vol. 2696, pp. 1–15. Springer, Heidelberg (2003). https://doi.org/10.1007/978-3-540-44993-5_1

15. De Cannière, C.: Analysis and design of symmetric encryption algorithms. Doctoral Dissertaion, KU Leuven (2007)

16. De Mulder, Y., Roelse, P., Preneel, B.: Cryptanalysis of the Xiao – Lai Whitebox AES implementation. In: Knudsen, L.R., Wu, H. (eds.) SAC 2012. LNCS, vol. 7707, pp. 34–49. Springer, Heidelberg (2013). https://doi.org/10.1007/978-3-642-35999-6_3

17. Derbez, P., Fouque, P., Lambin, B., Minaud, B.: On recovering affine encodings in white-box implementations. IACR Trans. Cryptogr. Hardw. Embed. Syst. **2018**(3), 121–149 (2018)

18. Dinur, I.: An improved affine equivalence algorithm for random permutations. In: Nielsen, J.B., Rijmen, V. (eds.) EUROCRYPT 2018. LNCS, vol. 10820, pp. 413–442. Springer, Cham (2018). https://doi.org/10.1007/978-3-319-78381-9_16

19. Evertse, J.-H.: Linear structures in blockciphers. In: Chaum, D., Price, W.L. (eds.) EUROCRYPT 1987. LNCS, vol. 304, pp. 249–266. Springer, Heidelberg (1988). https://doi.org/10.1007/3-540-39118-5_23

20. Faugère, J.-C., Perret, L.: Polynomial equivalence problems: algorithmic and theoretical aspects. In: Vaudenay, S. (ed.) EUROCRYPT 2006. LNCS, vol. 4004, pp. 30–47. Springer, Heidelberg (2006). https://doi.org/10.1007/11761679_3

21. Gordon, N.A., Jarvis, T.M., Shaw, R.: Some aspects of the linear groups gl (n, q) (2003)
22. Goubin, L., Masereel, J.-M., Quisquater, M.: Cryptanalysis of white box DES implementations. In: Adams, C., Miri, A., Wiener, M. (eds.) SAC 2007. LNCS, vol. 4876, pp. 278–295. Springer, Heidelberg (2007). https://doi.org/10.1007/978-3-540-77360-3_18
23. Goubin, L., Rivain, M., Wang, J.: Defeating state-of-the-art white-box countermeasures with advanced gray-box attacks. IACR Trans. Cryptogr. Hardw. Embed. Syst. **2020**(3), 454–482 (2020)
24. Jacob, M., Boneh, D., Felten, E.: Attacking an obfuscated cipher by injecting faults. In: Feigenbaum, J. (ed.) DRM 2002. LNCS, vol. 2696, pp. 16–31. Springer, Heidelberg (2003). https://doi.org/10.1007/978-3-540-44993-5_2
25. Karroumi, M.: Protecting white-box AES with dual ciphers. In: Rhee, K.-H., Nyang, D.H. (eds.) ICISC 2010. LNCS, vol. 6829, pp. 278–291. Springer, Heidelberg (2011). https://doi.org/10.1007/978-3-642-24209-0_19
26. Lai, X.: Additive and linear structures of cryptographic functions. In: Preneel, B. (ed.) FSE 1994. LNCS, vol. 1008, pp. 75–85. Springer, Heidelberg (1995). https://doi.org/10.1007/3-540-60590-8_6
27. Lepoint, T., Rivain, M., De Mulder, Y., Roelse, P., Preneel, B.: Two attacks on a white-box AES implementation. In: Lange, T., Lauter, K., Lisoněk, P. (eds.) SAC 2013. LNCS, vol. 8282, pp. 265–285. Springer, Heidelberg (2014). https://doi.org/10.1007/978-3-662-43414-7_14
28. Lin, D., Faugère, J., Perret, L., Wang, T.: On enumeration of polynomial equivalence classes and their application to MPKC. Finite Fields Appl. **18**(2), 283–302 (2012)
29. Lin, T., Yan, H., Lai, X., Zhong, Y., Jia, Y.: Security evaluation and improvement of a white-box SMS4 implementation based on affine equivalence algorithm. Comput. J. **61**(12), 1783–1790 (2018)
30. Link, H.E., Neumann, W.D.: Clarifying obfuscation: improving the security of white-box DES. In: ITCC (1), pp. 679–684. IEEE Computer Society (2005)
31. Luo, R., Lai, X., You, R.: A new attempt of white-box AES implementation. In: SPAC, pp. 423–429. IEEE (2014)
32. McMillion, B., Sullivan, N.: Attacking white-box AES constructions. In: SPRO@CCS, pp. 85–90. ACM (2016)
33. Michiels, W., Gorissen, P., Hollmann, H.D.L.: Cryptanalysis of a generic class of white-box implementations. In: Avanzi, R.M., Keliher, L., Sica, F. (eds.) SAC 2008. LNCS, vol. 5381, pp. 414–428. Springer, Heidelberg (2009). https://doi.org/10.1007/978-3-642-04159-4_27
34. Rivain, M., Wang, J.: Analysis and improvement of differential computation attacks against internally-encoded white-box implementations. IACR Trans. Cryptogr. Hardw. Embedded Syst. **2019**(2), 225–255 (2019)
35. Shi, Y., Wei, W., He, Z.: A lightweight white-box symmetric encryption algorithm against node capture for WSNS. Sensors **15**(5), 11928–11952 (2015)
36. Capture the Flag Challenge - The WhibOx Contest. https://whibox-contest.github.io/

37. Wyseur, B., Michiels, W., Gorissen, P., Preneel, B.: Cryptanalysis of white-box DES implementations with arbitrary external encodings. In: Adams, C., Miri, A., Wiener, M. (eds.) SAC 2007. LNCS, vol. 4876, pp. 264–277. Springer, Heidelberg (2007). https://doi.org/10.1007/978-3-540-77360-3_17
38. Xiao, Y., Lai, X.: A secure implementation of white-box AES. In: 2009 2nd International Conference on Computer Science and its Applications, pp. 1–6. IEEE (2009)

Protecting the Privacy of Voters: New Definitions of Ballot Secrecy for E-Voting

Ashley Fraser[✉] and Elizabeth A. Quaglia

Information Security Group, Royal Holloway, University of London, London, UK
{Ashley.Fraser.2016,Elizabeth.Quaglia}@rhul.ac.uk

Abstract. Protecting the privacy of voters is a basic requirement of any electronic voting scheme, and formal definitions can be used to prove that a scheme satisfies privacy. In this work, we provide new game-based definitions of ballot secrecy for electronic voting schemes. First, we propose an intuitive definition in the honest model, i.e., a model in which all election officials are honest. Then, we show that this definition can be easily extended to the malicious ballot box setting and a setting that allows for a distributed tallier. In fact, to the best of our knowledge, we provide the first game-based definition of ballot secrecy that models both a malicious ballot box *and* a malicious subset of talliers. We demonstrate that our definitions of ballot secrecy are satisfiable, defining electronic voting scheme constructions which we prove satisfy our definitions. Finally, we revisit existing definitions, exploring their limitations and contextualising our contributions to the field.

Keywords: E-voting · Ballot secrecy · Game-based definitions

1 Introduction

Voter privacy ensures that a voter can participate in democratic processes without risk of intimidation or blackmail, and is regarded as a basic requirement in many elections.[1] At a fundamental level, voter privacy is defined as *ballot secrecy*, which intuitively states that a voter's vote remains secret throughout the election, except when the result of the election reveals the vote, for example, in the event of a unanimous result. Stronger notions of privacy exist [23], including receipt-freeness and coercion-resistance but, in this work, we restrict discussion to the basic requirement of ballot secrecy.

Rigorous definitions of privacy have been proposed in the literature, the most common of which are game-based definitions. Early game-based definitions [4,5] follow the well-established route of indistinguishability experiments (such as, for

---

[1] Though the focus of this paper is privacy, another basic property of e-voting schemes is *verifiability*, by which any interested party can check that the result of the election is computed correctly. For a full discussion of this notion, including formal definitions, the interested reader can consult [18].

© Springer Nature Switzerland AG 2021
O. Dunkelman et al. (Eds.): SAC 2020, LNCS 12804, pp. 670–697, 2021.
https://doi.org/10.1007/978-3-030-81652-0_26

example, IND-CPA for public key encryption [27]). That is, an adversary must distinguish two different election views, when provided with a result computed with respect to the viewed election. Informally, we refer to this approach as the Benaloh approach, recognising the fact that Benaloh established this approach in early works [4,5].[2] The Benaloh approach is utilised in a number of ballot secrecy definitions [10,11,19,30]. However, to address the fact that the Benaloh approach limits the class of voting result functions that can be considered (see Sect. 5), a separate line of research departed from this approach, focusing instead on definitions that provide an adversary with a view of a 'real' election or a 'fake' election [7–9,16,20]. Here, the adversary is always provided with a tally computed with respect to the 'real' election. In particular, this approach is favoured by BPRIV [7], a highly-regarded definition of ballot secrecy. More generally, the majority of game-based definitions of ballot secrecy position themselves in the so-called *honest* model. That is, they consider all election officials to be trusted. With respect to formal definitions, the consideration of the malicious setting is a young area of research and has focused on a malicious ballot box [11,19,20].

1.1 Our Contributions

New Definitions of Ballot Secrecy. In this work, we revisit the approach taken in [5] and present new definitions of ballot secrecy. We choose this approach due to the well-established, intuitive nature of indistinguishability experiments. Moreover, though we recognise that the Benaloh approach limits the class of result functions considered, an issue that we explore in Sect. 3 and Sect. 5, the Benaloh approach, and our definitions specifically, provides a number of advantages over existing definitions, which we discuss below.

First, we define BS, a definition of ballot secrecy in the honest model (Sect. 3). BS builds upon [5], capturing several additional functionalities. First of all, BS models e-voting schemes with a registration phase. That is, eligible voters are provided with a credential that is required to cast a ballot. Voter registration is not modelled in [5] or subsequent, related, definitions [10,11] and, hence, BS is the first definition that follows this approach to model voter registration. This reflects how advanced e-voting schemes are modelled, for example, Belenios [2, 17] and Civitas [14,15]. Secondly, BS allows for *adaptive* corruption of voters. Previous game-based definitions that model registration of voters are limited to static corruption of voters only [16,19] or allow for voters to cast only a single ballot [30]. Therefore, BS improves upon existing definitions in the honest model by modelling registration of voters and adaptive corruption of voters.

Our second definition, mbbBS, extends BS to the malicious ballot box setting (Sect. 4.1). mbbBS is similar to the definition presented in [11], which also adopts the approach of [5]. However, contrary to [11], and similarly to BS, mbbBS models registration of voters. Our model for mbbBS captures static corruption of voters only, a consequence of using the Benaloh approach, as we will explain in Sect. 4.1.

---

[2] In particular, Benaloh is the sole author of [4] and is a co-author of [5].

We note, however, that *all* ballot secrecy definitions that model voter registration in the malicious ballot box setting only capture static voter corruption [19,20].

Finally, we define dtBS, which, to the best of our knowledge, is the first ballot secrecy definition that models a malicious ballot box and a distributed tallier, in which the adversary corrupts a subset of talliers (Sect. 4.2). dtBS extends mbbBS to model an adversary that corrupts a subset of talliers. Like mbbBS, dtBS considers static corruption of voters. Given that the malicious setting has received significantly less attention than the honest model, and a malicious tallier has not been explored, we believe that definitions in the malicious model, such as dtBS, are valuable and desirable. In particular, Helios [28] distributes the role of the tallier, yet proofs of ballot secrecy for Helios model the tallier as a single entity [7,17]. As such, we see dtBS as an important step towards formal proofs of security under realistic trust assumptions.

Feasibility of Our Definitions. For all of our definitions, we show feasibility, proving that our definitions can be satisfied. Specifically, we define an e-voting scheme Γ_{mini}, and prove it satisfies BS and mbbBS. We then extend Γ_{mini} to a setting with a distributed tallier, in a construction that we call Γ'_{mini}, and prove that it satisfies dtBS. Our scheme Γ_{mini} is a simple construction; specifically, it is not verifiable. However, Γ_{mini} can be used to prove the security of real, verifiable, e-voting schemes, similarly to how minivoting was used to prove ballot secrecy of Helios in [8].[3] Indeed, using the technique of [8], Γ_{mini} can also be extended to a generic, Helios-like, e-voting protocol which can be shown to satisfy our notions of ballot secrecy if Γ_{mini} satisfies ballot secrecy (and the verification process is secure). As such, though we simply demonstrate feasibility, our definitions can be applied to practical e-voting schemes.

Contextualising Our Definitions. Finally, we compare ballot secrecy definitions, with the goal of better understanding the limitations of definitions. In particular, we discuss related work and place our definitions in the context of the existing literature in Sect. 5. It emerges that our definitions provide an advantage with respect to extendibility, when compared to BPRIV. Moreover, our definitions improve upon existing definitions that follow the Benaloh approach, particularly with respect to the attacker model.

2   Preliminaries

Notation. We write $x \leftarrow X$ to denote assignment of X to x. We use standard set notation and write $\{\{x_1, \ldots, x_n\}\}$ to denote a multiset consisting of elements

---

[3] In fact, in [8], Bernhard *et al.* introduce minivoting, a simple e-voting scheme in which voters simply encrypt their vote and a tallier decrypts each ciphertext and computes the result from the resulting plaintext votes. Like Γ_{mini}, mini-voting is not verifiable. However, Bernhard *et al.* prove that mini-voting satisfies a notion of ballot secrecy and subsequently build a generic, verifiable, e-voting scheme with homomorphic tallying that also satisfies ballot secrecy. Helios is an instantiation of this generic e-voting scheme and, therefore, Helios can be shown to satisfy ballot secrecy if the underlying mini-voting construction is ballot secret.

$x_1, \ldots, x_n$, writing $\{\{\}\}$ to denote the empty multiset. Additionally, we write $L = (x_1, \ldots, x_n)$ to denote a list L with entries $x_1, \ldots, x_n$, and write $L \leftarrow L \| y$ to denote appending y to the list L. We let $A(x_1, \ldots, x_n; c)$ denote the output of algorithm A on inputs $x_1, \ldots, x_n$ and coins c. Generally, we omit coins and simply write $A(x_1, \ldots, x_n)$. Moreover, we write $A^{\mathcal{O}}$ to denote algorithm A with oracle access to $\mathcal{O}$.

We provide syntax for a *single-pass* e-voting scheme, which requires a voter to post a single message in order to cast a vote. We consider that an e-voting scheme is defined relative to a result function[4] $f : (\mathcal{V} \times \mathcal{C})^* \rightarrow R$, where $\mathcal{V} = \{id_1, \ldots, id_{n_v}\}$ is the set of n_v eligible voters, $\mathcal{C} = \{1, \ldots, n_c\}$ is the set of n_c candidates, and R is the result space of the election. Informally, our syntax captures an e-voting scheme with the following structure. Firstly, an election administrator publishes public parameters of the scheme. Then, a registrar provides eligible voters with a public and private credential and adds public credentials to a set $\mathcal{L}$. Voters cast ballots that are linked to their public credential, and a ballot box manager processes and posts ballots to a ballot box $\mathcal{BB}$. We assume that the ballot box is private and the ballot box manager publishes a public view of the ballot box, known as the bulletin board, $\mathcal{PBB}$. Finally, the tallier computes and publishes the result of the election with a proof of correct tallying that can be verified by anyone. We formally define the syntax of an e-voting scheme, adapted from the syntax of [7,12], in Definition 1.

Definition 1 (E-voting scheme). *An* e-voting *scheme Γ for a result function f is a tuple of probabilistic polynomial-time (PPT) algorithms* (Setup, Register, Vote, Valid, Append, Publish, Tally, Verify) *such that:*

Setup(1^λ) On input security parameter 1^λ, algorithm Setup initialises set $\mathcal{L}$ and ballot box $\mathcal{BB}$ as empty. Setup outputs an public/private election key pair (pk, sk). We assume that pk includes the sets $\mathcal{V}$ and $\mathcal{C}$.

Register($id, \mathcal{L}, pk$) On input voter identity id, set $\mathcal{L}$ and pk, algorithm Register outputs a public/private credential pair (pk_{id}, sk_{id}) and updates set $\mathcal{L}$ with pk_{id} such that $\mathcal{L} \leftarrow \mathcal{L} \cup \{pk_{id}\}$.

Vote(v, pk_{id}, sk_{id}, pk) On input vote v, pk_{id}, sk_{id} and pk, algorithm Vote outputs a ballot b that includes the voter's public credential.

Valid($b, \mathcal{BB}, \mathcal{L}, pk$) On input ballot b, ballot box $\mathcal{BB}$, set $\mathcal{L}$ and pk, algorithm Valid outputs 1 if ballot b is accepted to ballot box $\mathcal{BB}$, and 0 otherwise.

Append($b, \mathcal{BB}, \mathcal{L}, pk$) On input b, $\mathcal{BB}$, set $\mathcal{L}$ and pk, algorithm Append outputs the updated ballot box to include ballot b.

Publish($\mathcal{BB}$) On input $\mathcal{BB}$, algorithm Publish outputs bulletin board $\mathcal{PBB}$.

Tally($\mathcal{BB}, \mathcal{L}, sk$) On input $\mathcal{BB}$, set $\mathcal{L}$ and sk, algorithm Tally computes and outputs the election result $r \in R$ with a proof π that the result is correct.

Verify($\mathcal{BB}, \mathcal{L}, r, \pi, pk$) On input $\mathcal{BB}$, set $\mathcal{L}$, result r, proof π and pk, algorithm Verify outputs 1 if the election result verifies, and 0 otherwise.

---

[4] Our result function, similar to the result function in [7], determines how the result of the election is computed.

E-voting schemes must satisfy *correctness*, which requires that the result output by algorithm Tally is equivalent to result function f applied to all votes input to algorithm Vote.

Definition 2 (Correctness). *An e-voting scheme Γ defined with respect to a result function f is correct if, for any set of n_v voters $\mathcal{V} = \{id_1, \ldots, id_{n_v}\}$ and votes $v_1, \ldots, v_{n_v} \in \mathcal{C}$, there exists a negligible function* negl *such that*

$$\Pr\left[\begin{array}{c} (pk,sk)\leftarrow\text{Setup}(1^\lambda);\ \text{for } i=1,\ldots n_v: \\ \big\{(pk_{id_i},sk_{id_i})\leftarrow\text{Register}(id_i,\mathcal{L},pk);\ b_i\leftarrow\text{Vote}(v_i,pk_{id_i},sk_{id_i},pk); \\ \text{if } \text{Valid}(b_i,\mathcal{BB},\mathcal{L},pk)=1:\ \mathcal{BB}\leftarrow\text{Append}(b_i,\mathcal{BB},\mathcal{L},pk)\big\}; \\ (r,\pi)\leftarrow\text{Tally}(\mathcal{BB},\mathcal{L},sk):\ r=f((pk_{id_1},v_1),\ldots(pk_{id_{n_v}},v_{n_v})) \end{array}\right] \geq 1 - \text{negl}(\lambda).$$

3   Ballot Secrecy in the Honest Model

We introduce BS, a definition of ballot secrecy in which an adversary can *adaptively* corrupt voters, submitting ballots on their behalf, and can submit two votes (the left and right vote) on behalf of honest voters. Thus, BS describes an experiment in which an adversary is provided with access to a bulletin board, and the corresponding election result, that consists of ballots for the left or right vote submitted on behalf of honest voters, in addition to ballots submitted on behalf of corrupted voters. If the adversary cannot determine whether the bulletin board and result contains the left or right votes submitted by honest voters, a scheme is said to satisfy BS.

BS requires a *balancing condition* to ensure that the adversary cannot trivially distinguish views. For example, an adversary in the BS experiment could submit '0' as the left vote and '1' as the right vote on behalf of *all* honest voters. Then, the election result allows the adversary to trivially distinguish the two possible views. We define our balancing condition to prevent such trivial distinctions, and to model adaptive voter corruption. We first describe BS, followed by details of our balancing condition.

The BS experiment $\text{Exp}_{\Gamma,\mathcal{A}}^{\text{BS}}(\lambda)$ for adversary $\mathcal{A} = (\mathcal{A}_1, \mathcal{A}_2)$, formally defined in Fig. 1, proceeds as follows. A challenger initialises sets V_0 and V_1, required to model the balancing condition, as empty, generates the election key pair (pk, sk), and chooses a bit β. Adversary $\mathcal{A}_1$ is given public key pk and proceeds to query a number of oracles, formally defined in Fig. 1 and described as follows. We write $\mathcal{O}\text{x}_{(y_1,\ldots,y_n)}(z_1, \ldots, z_n)$ to denote oracle $\mathcal{O}\text{x}$ parametrised by $y_1, \ldots, y_n$ that takes as input $z_1, \ldots, z_n$.

$\mathcal{O}\text{reg}_{(pk,\mathcal{L}\mathcal{Q}\text{reg})}(id)$ registers an eligible voter. If id is in the set of eligible voters $\mathcal{V}$, oracle $\mathcal{O}\text{reg}$ runs algorithm Register on behalf of id and returns the voter's public credential pk_{id} to $\mathcal{A}_1$. Oracle $\mathcal{O}\text{reg}$ additionally updates a list of queries $\mathcal{Q}\text{reg}$ to include the tuple (id, pk_{id}, sk_{id}).

$\mathcal{O}\text{corrupt}_{(\mathcal{Q}\text{reg},\mathcal{Q}\text{corrupt})}(id)$ corrupts a voter. If id is a registered voter, oracle $\mathcal{O}\text{corrupt}$ returns the voter's private credential sk_{id} to $\mathcal{A}_1$, and updates a list of queries $\mathcal{Q}\text{corrupt}$ to include the tuple (id, pk_{id}, sk_{id}).

$\mathcal{O}\text{vote}_{(pk,\mathcal{L},\mathcal{BB},\mathcal{Q}\text{reg},\mathcal{Q}\text{corrupt},V_0,V_1)}(pk_{id},v_0,v_1)$ produces and submits a ballot for vote v_β on behalf of an uncorrupted voter. If voter pk_{id} is registered but not corrupt, and v_0, v_1 are valid vote choices, oracle $\mathcal{O}\text{vote}$ runs algorithms Vote and Append on behalf of voter pk_{id} and vote v_β. Oracle $\mathcal{O}\text{vote}$ also updates sets V_0 and V_1 to include votes v_0 and v_1 respectively, and removes any previous entries for pk_{id}, modelling an e-voting scheme with a last-vote-counts revote policy.

$\mathcal{O}\text{cast}_{(pk,\mathcal{L},\mathcal{BB},V_0,V_1)}(pk_{id},b)$ submits a ballot on behalf of a voter. If ballot b is valid and created for voter pk_{id}, and ballot b does not exist in $\mathcal{BB}$, oracle $\mathcal{O}\text{cast}$ appends ballot b to ballot box $\mathcal{BB}$. Oracle $\mathcal{O}\text{cast}$ also removes any entries in sets V_0 and V_1 for pk_{id}.

$\mathcal{O}\text{board}_{\mathcal{BB}}()$ returns bulletin board $\mathcal{PBB}$ to $\mathcal{A}_1$.

Adversary $\mathcal{A}_1$ outputs state information st, indicating that the experiment should transition to the tallying phase. Upon receiving the result r and proof of correct tallying π, $\mathcal{A}_2$ outputs a bit β'. The experiment returns 1 if $\beta' = \beta$ and the balancing condition is satisfied.

Definition 3 (BS). *An e-voting scheme Γ satisfies* BS *if, for any PPT adversary $\mathcal{A} = (\mathcal{A}_1, \mathcal{A}_2)$, there exists a negligible function* negl *such that*

$$\Pr\left[\text{Exp}_{\Gamma,\mathcal{A}}^{\text{BS}}(\lambda) = 1\right] \leq \frac{1}{2} + \text{negl}(\lambda)$$

where $\text{Exp}_{\Gamma,\mathcal{A}}^{\text{BS}}(\lambda)$ is the experiment defined in Fig. 1.

3.1 Our Balancing Condition

Following a query to oracle $\mathcal{O}\text{vote}$, sets V_0 and V_1 are updated to contain tuples (pk_{id}, v_0) and (pk_{id}, v_1) respectively. After the result of the election is announced, multisets V_0' and V_1' are defined to contain the votes v_0 and v_1 from sets V_0 and V_1 respectively. Our balancing condition, $V_0' = V_1'$, ensures that, for every left-hand vote of an honest voter, there exists an honest voter for whom the same vote is submitted as their right-hand vote. Thus, we prevent trivial distinctions.

This notion of balance is inspired by Benaloh and Yung's early definition of ballot secrecy [5] and is used by Bernhard and Smyth in their ballot secrecy definition IND $-$ SEC [10]. However, in comparison to BS, neither IND $-$ SEC nor Benaloh and Yung's approach model registration of voters. It transpires that, to capture registration of voters and, in particular, to capture revoting and adaptive corruption of voters for e-voting schemes with voter registration, the balancing condition described above must include more complex features. We describe these subtleties and demonstrate their necessity through examples.

Eliminating Entries from $\mathcal{O}\text{vote}$. We require that, following a query to $\mathcal{O}\text{vote}$ on behalf of a voter pk_{id}, previous entries containing pk_{id} are removed from sets V_0 and V_1. Else, it is possible that an adversary can submit oracle queries

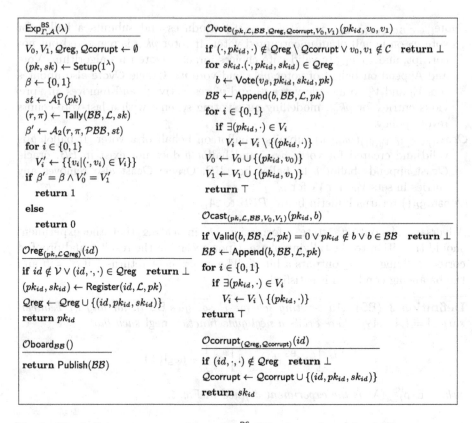

Fig. 1. The ballot secrecy experiment $\mathsf{Exp}^{BS}_{\Gamma,\mathcal{A}}(\lambda)$ where $\mathcal{A} = (\mathcal{A}_1, \mathcal{A}_2)$ has access to oracles $\mathcal{O} = \{\mathcal{O}\mathsf{reg}, \mathcal{O}\mathsf{corrupt}, \mathcal{O}\mathsf{vote}, \mathcal{O}\mathsf{cast}, \mathcal{O}\mathsf{board}\}$.

that allow trivial distinctions, even if a scheme is intuitively ballot secret. Consider an e-voting scheme that employs a last-vote-counts revote policy and allows voters to cast a ballot for '0' or '1'. Let the election result be a vector of size two, indicating the number of votes cast for each candidate. Assume that $\mathcal{O}\mathsf{vote}$ does *not* remove any entries from sets V_0 or V_1. Then an adversary in the BS experiment can query $\mathcal{O}\mathsf{vote}(pk_{id_1}, 0, 1)$, $\mathcal{O}\mathsf{vote}(pk_{id_2}, 1, 0)$, $\mathcal{O}\mathsf{vote}(pk_{id_1}, 1, 0)$ and $\mathcal{O}\mathsf{vote}(pk_{id_3}, 0, 1)$ for pk_{id_1}, pk_{id_2} and pk_{id_3} obtained via queries to $\mathcal{O}\mathsf{reg}$ such that $V_0 = \{(pk_{id_1}, 0), (pk_{id_2}, 1), (pk_{id_1}, 1), (pk_{id_3}, 0)\}$ and $V_1 = \{(pk_{id_1}, 1), (pk_{id_2}, 0), (pk_{id_1}, 0), (pk_{id_3}, 1)\}$. Subsequently, $V_0' = V_1'$ and the balancing condition is satisfied. However, if $\beta = 0$, $r = (1, 2)$ and, if $\beta = 1$, $r = (2, 1)$. Then the adversary trivially distinguishes the two views and succeeds in the BS experiment. Therefore, it is essential that $\mathcal{O}\mathsf{vote}$ removes previous entries that contain pk_{id} from sets V_0 and V_1. Indeed, if the first entry of V_0 and V_1 is removed, the balancing condition is not satisfied and the adversary cannot succeed in the BS experiment.

Eliminating Entries from $\mathcal{O}$cast. Similarly, following a query to $\mathcal{O}$cast on behalf of voter pk_{id}, it is essential that entries containing pk_{id} are removed from sets V_0 and V_1. In fact, rather than the second two queries to $\mathcal{O}$vote in the example above, the adversary can query $\mathcal{O}$cast(pk_{id_1}, b) where b encodes a vote for '1'. Then, if $\mathcal{O}$cast does not remove the previous entry for pk_{id_1}, the balancing condition is satisfied. Yet, the result $r = (0, 2)$ (if $\beta = 0$) or $r = (1, 1)$ (if $\beta = 1$). Under static corruption of voters, removal of entries is not necessary as an adversary cannot make a query to $\mathcal{O}$vote on behalf of a corrupted voter, i.e., voter pk_{id_1} in the example. Thus, removal of previous entries is key to ensure that our balancing condition allows for adaptive corruption of voters.

Voting Policies. Our balancing condition models a last-vote-counts revote policy, a policy applied to implemented e-voting schemes, for example, the Estonian i-Voting scheme [25]. On the other hand, it is common to implement an e-voting scheme with a no revote policy. For instance, Helios [1,28] allows for both a last-vote-counts and a no revote policy. For this reason, we briefly describe how our balancing condition can be modified in a straightforward way to account for a no revote policy as follows. $\mathcal{O}$vote does not remove previous entries containing pk_{id} from sets V_0 and V_1 following a query on behalf of voter pk_{id}. Additionally, $\mathcal{O}$vote adds new entries to sets V_0 and V_1 only if the sets do not contain an entry on behalf of pk_{id}. Finally, $\mathcal{O}$cast does not update sets V_0 and V_1.

3.2 Satisfiability of BS

We demonstrate satisfiability of BS by constructing an e-voting scheme Γ_{mini}, defined formally in Fig. 2. Γ_{mini} relies on a homomorphic public key encryption scheme Π and a signature of knowledge SOK, both of which are formally defined in Appendix A. A voter with credential pair (pk_{id}, sk_{id})[5] casts a ballot for $v \in \{0,1\}^6$ by producing an encryption, denoted c, of v under Π, and generating a signature of knowledge, denoted σ, that the resulting ciphertext encrypts $v \in \{0,1\}$ using their private credential under SOK. The form of a ballot b is (pk_{id}, c, σ). If ciphertext c does not appear in a ballot on the ballot box, and signature of knowledge σ verifies, the ballot is appended to the ballot box. The ballot box and the bulletin board are identical in this scheme. To compute the result, ciphertext c is extracted from the final ballot cast by each voter. The extracted ciphertexts are homomorphically tallied and the homomorphic ciphertext is decrypted, giving the result of the election. As we do not focus on verifiability, we simply define algorithm Tally to output $\bot$ in place of a proof of correct tallying, and algorithm Verify is defined to always return 1.

To satisfy BS, we require that Π satisfies non-malleable-CPA security [3], NM-CPA, and SOK satisfies extractability [13]. We define these security properties in Appendix A. We obtain the result in Theorem 1.

---

[5] We write that credential pairs are generated by a one-way function f.

[6] This can be extended to multi-candidate elections in the style of Helios [1,28].

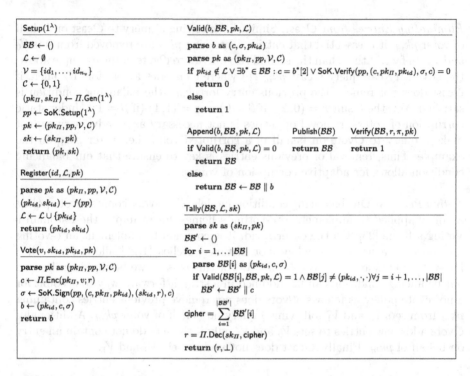

Fig. 2. The e-voting scheme Γ_{mini} constructed from public key encryption scheme Π and signature of knowledge SOK.

Theorem 1. Γ_{mini} *(Fig. 2) satisfies* BS *if public key encryption scheme* Π *satisfies* NM-CPA *and signature of knowledge* SOK *satisfies extractability.*

We formally prove Theorem 1 in Appendix B. Informally, assuming that an adversary queries $\mathcal{O}$vote and $\mathcal{O}$cast such that $V_0' = V_1'$, the result computed over $\mathcal{BB}$ in the BS experiment for $\beta = 0$ is indistinguishable from the result for $\beta = 1$. In fact, with respect to the ballots included in the election result, $\mathcal{BB}$ contains the same number of votes for each candidate, regardless of β. Moreover, an adversary cannot distinguish whether $\mathcal{BB}$ contains ballots for a left- or right-hand vote on behalf of honest voters if Π satisfies NM-CPA. Finally, NM-CPA security of Π and extractability of SOK ensures that an adversary cannot submit ballots on behalf of a corrupt voter that are meaningfully related to the ballots of honest voters, thus skewing the result and allowing the adversary to distinguish views [21].

3.3 Limitation of BS

For transparency, we elaborate on an aspect of BS that limits the class of e-voting schemes that can be captured by BS. We believe that such discussion is essential to understand security definitions for e-voting and ensure that, to prove security of an e-voting scheme, the most relevant definition is chosen based on the nuances of the scheme. In Sect. 5, we elaborate on the complexities and limitations of ballot secrecy definitions in the literature, further casting light on the applicability of definitions.

Our balancing condition limits the class of result functions that can be captured. In particular, consider an e-voting scheme in which a voter can submit a score for a candidate, e.g., $\mathcal{C} = \{0, 1, 2\}$, and the result consists of the sum of all scores submitted. In [7], the authors show that Benaloh and Yung's ballot secrecy definition [5], upon which BS is based, does not capture this result function. Specifically, [5] and BS do not model an attacker that can distinguish different vote assignments that lead to the same result, for example, two voters voting 0 and 2 respectively, and both voters voting 1. Despite this, common result functions, such as plurality voting, are within the scope of our definition.

4   Extending BS to the Malicious Setting

Corrupt election officials can break ballot secrecy. In particular, a malicious *ballot box* can 'stuff' the ballot box with ballots, which can lead to attacks against ballot secrecy [21]. Furthermore, a malicious *tallier* can potentially reveal the votes of all honest voters, for example, if ballots consist of a vote encrypted under the tallier's public key, such as in our construction Γ_{mini}. To overcome this, many e-voting schemes distribute the role of the tallier [29,31] and assume that a proportion of talliers are honest. We define mbbBS, a definition that extends BS to the malicious ballot box setting, and dtBS, an extension of mbbBS in which the adversary can further corrupt a subset of talliers where the role of the tallier is distributed. In doing so, we provide definitions that allow a scheme designer to prove ballot secrecy in the event of an attacker that can corrupt the ballot box *and* a proportion of talliers.

4.1   Malicious Ballot Box Manager

We extend BS to mbbBS, defining an adversary that arbitrarily constructs the ballot box, obtaining ballots for honest voters that correspond to either a left or right vote submitted to an oracle $\mathcal{O}$vote. Hence, mbbBS models a corrupt ballot box, but considers all other election entities to be honest. We note that, in this setting, the adversary can only *statically* corrupt voters, a common restriction [16,20]. This arises as a consequence of the balancing condition, which we elaborate on following the formal definition.

The mbbBS experiment $\text{Exp}_{\Gamma,\mathcal{A}}^{\text{mbbBS}}(\lambda)$ for adversary $\mathcal{A} = (\mathcal{A}_1, \mathcal{A}_2, \mathcal{A}_3)$, formally defined in Fig. 3, registers all n_v eligible voters and provides the adversary $\mathcal{A}_1$ with the set of public credentials $\mathcal{L}$ and the election public key pk. $\mathcal{A}_1$ selects a subset of public credentials $\text{corr}\mathcal{L}$ to corrupt and $\mathcal{A}_2$ receives a list of corresponding private credentials $c\mathcal{L}$. Adversary $\mathcal{A}_2$ is provided with access to an oracle $\mathcal{O}$vote$_{(pk,\mathcal{L},\text{corr}\mathcal{L},V)}(pk_{id}, v_0, v_1)$ that returns ballots for v_β on behalf of honest voters, and constructs a ballot box $\mathcal{BB}$, which may include both honestly and maliciously generated ballots. Upon receiving the result r computed over $\mathcal{BB}$ and a proof of correct tallying π, $\mathcal{A}_3$ outputs a bit β'. If $\beta' = \beta$ and the balancing condition is satisfied, the experiment returns 1. We observe that the adversary does not require access to oracles $\mathcal{O}$reg and $\mathcal{O}$corrupt, as defined for BS, because voters are statically corrupted. Moreover, the adversary does not require access to an oracle $\mathcal{O}$cast because $\mathcal{A}_2$ constructs the ballot box.

Definition 4 (mbbBS). *An e-voting scheme Γ satisfies* mbbBS *if, for any PPT adversary $\mathcal{A} = (\mathcal{A}_1, \mathcal{A}_2, \mathcal{A}_3)$, there exists a negligible function* negl *such that*

$$\Pr\left[\mathsf{Exp}_{\Gamma,\mathcal{A}}^{\mathsf{mbbBS}}(\lambda) = 1\right] \leq \frac{1}{2} + \mathsf{negl}(\lambda)$$

where $\mathsf{Exp}_{\Gamma,\mathcal{A}}^{\mathsf{mbbBS}}(\lambda)$ *is the experiment defined in Fig. 3.*

$\mathsf{Exp}_{\Gamma,\mathcal{A}}^{\mathsf{mbbBS}}(\lambda)$	$\mathcal{O}\mathsf{vote}_{(pk,\mathcal{L},\mathsf{corr}\mathcal{L},L,V)}(pk_{id}, v_0, v_1)$
$V \leftarrow \{\}$	**if** $pk_{id} \notin \mathcal{L} \setminus \mathsf{corr}\mathcal{L} \vee v_0, v_1 \notin \mathcal{C}$ **return** $\perp$
$V_0, V_1 \leftarrow \{\{\}\}$	**for** $sk_{id}.(pk_{id}, sk_{id}) \in L$
$\beta \leftarrow \{0,1\}$	$b \leftarrow \mathsf{Vote}(v_\beta, pk_{id}, sk_{id}, pk)$
$(pk, sk) \leftarrow \mathsf{Setup}(1^\lambda)$	$V \leftarrow V \cup \{(pk_{id}, v_0, v_1, b)\}$
for $i = 1, \ldots, n_v$	**return** b
$\quad (pk_{id_i}, sk_{id_i}) \leftarrow \mathsf{Register}(id_i, \mathcal{L}, pk)$	
$L \leftarrow \{(pk_{id_1}, sk_{id_1}), \ldots, (pk_{id_{n_v}}, sk_{id_{n_v}})\}$	
$(\mathsf{corr}\mathcal{L}, st_1) \leftarrow \mathcal{A}_1(pk, \mathcal{L})$	
$c\mathcal{L} \leftarrow \{(pk_{id}, sk_{id}) \mid pk_{id} \in \mathsf{corr}\mathcal{L} \cap \mathcal{L}\}$	
$(\mathcal{BB}, st_2) \leftarrow \mathcal{A}_2^{\mathcal{O}\mathsf{vote}}(c\mathcal{L}, st_1)$	
$(r, \pi) \leftarrow \mathsf{Tally}(\mathcal{BB}, \mathcal{L}, sk)$	
$\beta' \leftarrow \mathcal{A}_3(r, \pi, \mathcal{BB}, st_2)$	
for $i = 1, \ldots, |\mathcal{BB}|$	
$\quad$ **if** $\exists(pk_{id}, v_0, v_1, \mathcal{BB}[i]) \in V$	
$\qquad$ **for** $j = i+1, \ldots, |\mathcal{BB}|$	
$\qquad\quad$ **if** $\nexists(pk_{id}, *, *, \mathcal{BB}[j]) \in V$	
$\qquad\qquad V_0 \leftarrow V_0 \cup \{\{v_0\}\}$	
$\qquad\qquad V_1 \leftarrow V_1 \cup \{\{v_1\}\}$	
if $\beta' = \beta \wedge V_0 = V_1$	
$\quad$ **return** 1	
else	
$\quad$ **return** 0	

Fig. 3. The malicious ballot box ballot secrecy experiment $\mathsf{Exp}_{\Gamma,\mathcal{A}}^{\mathsf{mbbBS}}(\lambda)$ where $\mathcal{A} = (\mathcal{A}_1, \mathcal{A}_2, \mathcal{A}_3)$ has access to oracle $\mathcal{O}$vote.

Our Balancing Condition. mbbBS maintains a list of queries to $\mathcal{O}$vote in a set V such that each entry in V consists of a tuple (pk_{id}, v_0, v_1, b). Then, if b appears on ballot box $\mathcal{BB}$ and the tuple contains the final ballot that appears on $\mathcal{BB}$ with respect to voter pk_{id}, the experiment adds v_0 (resp., v_1) to a multiset V_0 (resp., V_1). In other words, multisets V_0 and V_1 contain only the final vote for every honest voter such that a corresponding ballot is appended to $\mathcal{BB}$.[7]

As a result of our balancing condition, mbbBS considers *static* corruption of voters. Indeed, if mbbBS allows *adaptive* corruption of voters, a trivial distinguishing attack is possible. To demonstrate this, we recall our construction Γ_{mini} (Fig. 2) and assume that an adversary in the mbbBS experiment can adaptively corrupt voters. That is, the adversary has access to oracles $\mathcal{O}$reg and $\mathcal{O}$corrupt as defined in Fig. 1. Then, the adversary queries $b_1 \leftarrow \mathcal{O}$vote$(pk_{id_1}, 0, 1)$ and $b_2 \leftarrow \mathcal{O}$vote$(pk_{id_2}, 1, 0)$ for pk_{id_1} and pk_{id_2} obtained via queries to $\mathcal{O}$reg. Voter pk_{id_1} is corrupted via a query to $\mathcal{O}$corrupt and the adversary appends b_1, b_2 and b_3, a ballot for '1' on behalf of pk_{id_1}, to $\mathcal{BB}$. The balancing condition is satisfied but, if $\beta = 0$ (resp., $\beta = 1$), $r = (0, 2)$ (resp., $r = (1, 1)$), and the adversary can trivially distinguish the two views. Consequently, we restrict mbbBS to allow only static corruption of voters. Then, if the adversary wishes to corrupt pk_{id_1}, they cannot make queries to $\mathcal{O}$vote on behalf of pk_{id_1} and, in the example above, the balancing condition is not satisfied. Therefore, the adversary does not succeed in the mbbBS experiment.

Satisfiability of mbbBS. We show that our e-voting construction Γ_{mini} (Fig. 2) satisfies mbbBS under the same conditions that Γ_{mini} satisfies BS. Indeed, we design the ballots in Γ_{mini} to be *non-malleable*, which is required to satisfy mbbBS, a fact that we elaborate on following our formal result. In other words, we intentionally design Γ_{mini} to satisfy stronger notions of ballot secrecy than BS. We require a NM-CPA secure public key encryption scheme and a signature of knowledge that satisfies extractability. We obtain the result in Theorem 2.

Theorem 2. Γ_{mini} *(Fig. 2) satisfies* mbbBS *if public key encryption scheme* Π *satisfies* NM-CPA *and signature of knowledge* SOK *satisfies extractability.*

We formally prove Theorem 2 in Appendix B. The proof of Theorem 2 is very similar to the proof that Γ_{mini} satisfies BS (Theorem 1). In particular, an adversary cannot distinguish whether $\mathcal{O}$vote returns a ballot corresponding to v_0 or v_1 as a result of NM-CPA security of Π. Moreover, the ballots returned by $\mathcal{O}$vote cannot be modified by the adversary in a meaningful way due to non-malleability of the ballot, provided by extractability of SOK and NM-CPA security of Π. Thus, any ballot in $\mathcal{BB}$ is either a ballot of a corrupt voter that is independent of any other ballot, or an output of oracle $\mathcal{O}$vote. Then, if the balancing condition is satisfied, the result computed over $\mathcal{BB}$ constructed by the adversary is indistinguishable for $\beta = 0$ or 1.

As noted, ballots must be non-malleable to satisfy mbbBS. Intuitively, if an attacker with control of the ballot box can transform ballots, then they can append ballots to the ballot box that are meaningfully related to the vote of

---

[7] As with BS, our balancing condition can be modified to model a no-revote policy.

an honest voter such that the result reveals the honest voter's vote. We demonstrate this by describing an attack against our e-voting scheme Γ_{mini} where we replace the signature of knowledge with a standard digital signature scheme. An adversary in the mbbBS experiment can query $b_1 \leftarrow \mathcal{O}\text{vote}(pk_{id_1}, 0, 1)$, $b_2 \leftarrow \mathcal{O}\text{vote}(pk_{id_2}, 1, 0)$ and $b_3 \leftarrow \mathcal{O}\text{vote}(pk_{id_3}, 0, 1)$, appending ballots b_1 and b_2 to $\mathcal{BB}$. Let $b_3 = (pk_{id_3}, c_3, \sigma_3)$. The adversary produces a signature σ_4 for ciphertext c_3 for a corrupt voter pk_{id_4} and appends the modified ballot $b^* = (pk_{id_4}, c_3, \sigma_4)$ to $\mathcal{BB}$. The balancing condition is satisfied, yet, if $\beta = 0$, $r = (2, 1)$ and, if $\beta = 1$, $r = (1, 2)$, which allows $\mathcal{A}$ to distinguish the two views. This attack is possible because the ballot is malleable. In contrast, if σ is a signature of knowledge, the adversary requires knowledge of the plaintext encrypted by c_3 in order to construct a signature of knowledge for pk_{id_4}. Therefore, we conclude that e-voting schemes that allow malleable ballots cannot satisfy mbbBS.

We recognise that there exists e-voting schemes for which the ballots are malleable, for example, e-voting schemes that include a timestamp in the ballot. An adversary in the mbbBS experiment can modify the timestamp in a ballot output by $\mathcal{O}\text{vote}$ and append the modified ballot to $\mathcal{BB}$. Then, the result trivially reveals β and the balancing condition holds. However, there may not be a ballot secrecy issue with the scheme in practice. Therefore, if a scheme produces ballots that contain a malleable part, the scheme does not satisfy mbbBS, despite the fact that it is intuitively ballot secret. Despite this, we believe that non-malleable ballots are desirable. For example, if a ballot includes a malleable timestamp, an attacker with control of the ballot box can modify the timestamp, potentially ensuring that a ballot is not included in the result of the election. Furthermore, ballots with malleable elements can be modified to ensure non-malleability. For instance, a ballot can include a signature of knowledge or proof of knowledge that ties the signature or proof to the malleable element, ensuring that the malleable element cannot be modified without detection (which, in turn, ensures that a modified ballot is not valid).

4.2   Distributed and Malicious Tallier

We now consider an extension of mbbBS for e-voting schemes with a distributed tallier, that is, we write tallier $\mathcal{T}$ as $\mathcal{T} = (\mathcal{T}_1, \ldots, \mathcal{T}_n)$. In this case, we consider an election private key that is distributed amongst n talliers such that $sk = (sk_{\mathcal{T}_1}, \ldots, sk_{\mathcal{T}_n})$ and at least t shares are required to reconstruct sk where $t \leq n$.[8] We extend mbbBS to a definition dtBS that models a corrupt ballot box *and* a subset of corrupt talliers. In particular, we model an attacker that obtains the private key share of up to $t-1$ talliers. As with mbbBS, we consider other election entities to be honest and only allow the static corruption of voters.

The corruption strategy captured by dtBS does not model an attacker that generates key shares for corrupt talliers. In fact, we consider that all key shares are generated honestly. In other words, the attacker corrupts talliers *after* key

---

[8] We note that, specifically, $t = n$ is possible. That is, all n shares are required to reconstruct the private key.

generation and, therefore, cannot influence the generation of key shares. As dtBS is a preliminary exploration of ballot secrecy with a malicious ballot box and tallier, we consider the attack strategy captured by dtBS to be appropriate and leave the case of stronger attacker models as an open problem.

We define the dtBS experiment $\mathsf{Exp}_{\Gamma,\mathcal{A}}^{\mathsf{dtBS}}(\lambda, t, n)$, parametrised by the number of talliers n and the number of shares required to reconstruct the election private key t, as the mbbBS experiment, defined in Fig. 3, but with the following modifications. In addition to statically corrupting a subset of voters, adversary $\mathcal{A}$ corrupts $t-1$ talliers. That is, $\mathcal{A}$ submits $t-1$ unique indices $\{i_1, \ldots, i_{t-1}\}$ and obtains the set of private key shares $\{sk_{T_{i_1}}, \ldots, sk_{T_{i_{t-1}}}\}$. Additionally, algorithm Tally takes as input t private key shares that include the $t-1$ shares returned to $\mathcal{A}$. In all other respects, the dtBS experiment is identical to the mbbBS experiment.

Definition 5 (dtBS). *An e-voting scheme Γ for n talliers and threshold t, where election private key $sk = (sk_{T_1}, \ldots, sk_{T_n})$, satisfies dtBS if, for any PPT adversary $\mathcal{A} = (\mathcal{A}_1, \mathcal{A}_2, \mathcal{A}_3)$, there exists a negligible function negl such that*

$$\Pr\left[\mathsf{Exp}_{\Gamma,\mathcal{A}}^{\mathsf{dtBS}}(\lambda, t, n) = 1\right] \leq \frac{1}{2} + \mathsf{negl}(\lambda)$$

where $\mathsf{Exp}_{\Gamma,\mathcal{A}}^{\mathsf{dtBS}}(\lambda, t, n)$ is the mbbBS experiment defined in Fig. 3 for $\mathcal{A}$ provided with $t-1$ private key shares of their choice and where algorithm Tally takes as input the $t-1$ private keys provided to $\mathcal{A}$.

Satisfiability of dtBS. To illustrate satisfiability of dtBS, we consider a modification to Γ_{mini} (Fig. 2) that uses a (t, n)-threshold public key encryption scheme [24], Φ, which we define in Appendix A. We call our modified construction Γ'_{mini}. Formally, Γ'_{mini} is identical to Γ_{mini} with the exceptions of the following modifications to algorithms Setup, Vote and Tally. We write that Setup takes additional input t and n and, rather than running algorithm $\Pi.\mathsf{Gen}$, Setup runs algorithm $\Phi.\mathsf{Gen}$ to generate a public key pk_ϕ and n private keys $sk_{\phi_1}, \ldots, sk_{\phi_n}$. Each tallier is provided with a private key. Algorithm Vote encrypts vote v by running $\Phi.\mathsf{Enc}$, rather than $\Pi.\mathsf{Enc}$. Finally, algorithm Tally requires interaction between t talliers. In detail, any tallier can produce the homomorphic ciphertext cipher, and, then, t talliers each produce a partial decryption of cipher by running algorithm $\Phi.\mathsf{Dec}$. The final result r is computed by running algorithm $\Phi.\mathsf{Combine}$ on input of the t partial decryptions.

As for our previous results, to satisfy dtBS, we require that Φ satisfies t-NM-CPA security and SOK satisfies extractability. We define t-NM-CPA security for a (t, n)-threshold encryption scheme in Appendix A. Briefly, security of a (t, n)-threshold encryption scheme is defined as a natural extension of security for a standard encryption scheme with the exception that the adversary can statically corrupt $t-1$ decryption servers, see, for example [26,32]. Therefore, t-NM-CPA security for Φ is equivalent to NM-CPA security for a standard public key encryption scheme but the adversary obtains the private keys of $t-1$ decryption servers of their choice. We obtain the result in Theorem 3.

Theorem 3. Γ'_{mini} *satisfies* dtBS *if* (t, n)-*threshold public key encryption scheme* Φ *satisfies* t-NM-CPA *and signature of knowledge* SOK *satisfies extractability.*

We formally prove Theorem 3 in Appendix B. The proof of this result follows largely from the fact that Γ_{mini} satisfies mbbBS and, as such, the result and output of $\mathcal{O}$vote is indistinguishable for $\beta = 0$ or 1. Moreover, by t-NM-CPA security of the threshold encryption scheme, access to $t - 1$ private keys does not provide the adversary with any more information about the votes of honest voters.

5   A Comparison of Ballot Secrecy Definitions

In this section, we provide a comparison of existing game-based definitions, grouping them according to their underlying intuition. In particular, we identify two types of definitions: those that tally the 'real' election, and those that rely on a balancing condition and tally the viewed election. We place our definitions (Definitions 3–5) in context, highlighting our contribution to the area.

5.1   Tally the 'Real' Election

Recall from the introduction that definitions in this category provide the adversary with a view of a real or fake election, depending on the value of a coin flip, and always compute the tally for the real election. This approach to defining ballot secrecy was introduced in [8], and refined in [9]. In [7], Cortier *et al.* reviewed ballot secrecy definitions from the literature and defined BPRIV as an alteration of [8,9], avoiding weaknesses found in both previous, related, definitions.[9] Arguably, BPRIV has since become the most well-known and widely used definition of ballot secrecy in the literature. In fact, in [6], it was used to prove the security of Helios and has been extended to capture receipt-freeness [12]. Moreover, it has been extended to model e-voting schemes with registration of voters [16] and to capture a malicious ballot box [20]. As BPRIV is the state-of-the-art definition in this category, we focus on BPRIV and its extensions from [16] and [20]. BPRIV avoids the limitations of existing definitions, including those definitions that follow the 'tally the viewed election' approach (see Sect. 5.2). Moreover, BPRIV is shown to imply a simulation-based notion of ballot secrecy [7], reinforcing the correctness and strength of the BPRIV approach. Despite this, we highlight two drawbacks of this approach.

Need for Additional Properties. BPRIV is strong and well-established, yet, as a stand-alone definition, it is subject to attacks, as highlighted by Cortier *et al.*, the authors of BPRIV [7]. Specifically, BPRIV does not capture an attacker that can cause the rejection of honestly created ballots, which can violate ballot secrecy. Cortier *et al.* define an e-voting scheme such that ballots are appended

---

[9] For full details of the review and weakness found in [8,9], and other ballot secrecy definitions, consult [7].

with a bit, 0 or 1, where algorithm Vote always appends a 0. Then, if there exists a ballot in $\mathcal{BB}$ that is appended with 1, all subsequent ballots are rejected. As BPRIV always computes the result of the 'real' election, such a scheme satisfies BPRIV. Yet, an attacker can ensure that a majority of honestly created ballots are rejected, potentially revealing the votes of a small subset of honest voters. Therefore, Cortier et al. define strong correctness, an additional property required to prevent such attacks. Our definition BS, and other definitions in the same category [4,5,10,11,19,30], on the other hand, capture this attack. In fact, the balancing condition of BS ensures that votes of honest voters are added to multisets V_0' and V_1', even if the ballot is rejected by algorithm Valid, yet the votes contained in these multisets will not necessarily be included in the result. As a consequence, the adversary can output a ballot box such that the balancing condition is satisfied, and determine β from the result computed over $\mathcal{BB}$.

Furthermore, Cortier et al. highlight that BPRIV is subject to another attack in which the ballots of honest voters are not included in the result, potentially revealing the vote of an honest voter, and describe an e-voting scheme for a referendum that rejects the ballot of the first voter if the ballot is for a specified candidate [7]. Then, depending on whether the ballot is included in the result, it is possible to determine how the first voter voted. This scheme satisfies BPRIV despite the fact that, intuitively, it is not ballot secret. Therefore, BPRIV must be accompanied by a second additional property, strong consistency, that prevents this attack. By contrast, BS and [4,5,10,11,19,30] capture this attack. By defining an adversary that submits a query to $\mathcal{O}$vote such that the left-hand vote is for the specified candidate and the right-hand vote is for a second candidate, the balancing condition can be satisfied and the result returned to the adversary in the BS experiment reveals whether the first ballot was removed. We additionally note that definitions derived from BPRIV [12,16,20] also require strong consistency and strong correctness to capture the two attacks outlined above.

Extendibility. For schemes with a registration phase, BPRIV has been extended to *static* voter corruption only [16]. In fact, extending BPRIV to an e-voting scheme with a registration phase is non-trivial and attempting to model adaptive corruption of voters in a logical fashion (e.g., by providing access to a corrupt oracle as in our definition BS) results in a definition that is too strong [16]. By contrast, BS captures adaptive corruption.

BPRIV is also difficult to extend to the malicious ballot box setting, though a recent attempt was made in [20]. There, $\mathcal{BB}_\beta$ is the ballot box created by the adversary in the BPRIV experiment for $\beta \in \{0,1\}$. Briefly, if $\beta = 0$, the result and tallying proof are returned for $\mathcal{BB}_0$. If $\beta = 1$, the experiment returns the tally computed over $\mathcal{BB}_0$ such that $\mathcal{BB}_0$ is transformed according to the ways in which the adversary tampers with the ballots on $\mathcal{BB}_1$. This ensures that the result returned to the adversary corresponds to the actions taken by the adversary when constructing the ballot box. To achieve this, the extension defines an algorithm that detects the ways in which an adversary can tamper with ballots in the ballot box (e.g., the algorithm can be defined to include one or more of the following actions: delete, modify, re-order ballots). In doing so, the definition is flexible, capable of capturing different potential attack scenarios. However, this means that, before applying the definition, it is necessary to first define an algorithm, presenting an opportunity for flawed security proofs if the algorithm is not defined correctly. On the other hand, BS can be easily extended to mbbBS and does not require additional algorithms, providing a simple-to-apply definition in the malicious setting. Further, BPRIV cannot be easily extended to a setting in which the tallier is distributed and a subset of talliers can be corrupted. Indeed, in [22], del Pino *et al.* state that it is difficult to adapt BPRIV to this setting because corrupted talliers must participate in the tallying stage of the election for *both* ballot boxes, yet BPRIV only ever returns the result for the ballot box corresponding to the 'real' election. To overcome this, like our definition dtBS, del Pino *et al.* also rely on a balancing condition, effectively departing from BPRIV's approach.

5.2   Tallying the Viewed Election

Recall that the second type of approach, introduced in [4,5], tallies the ballot box corresponding to the bulletin board viewed by the adversary. The definitions in [4] and [5] have been adopted in subsequent definitions and extended to the malicious ballot box setting. Namely, [4] (respectively, [5]) has been adopted by [30] (respectively, [10]) and extended to the malicious ballot box setting in [19] (respectively, [11]). The definitions that follow this approach require a balancing condition. The approaches defined in [4] and [5] differ with respect to the balancing condition. We choose to follow [5] to avoid the requirement of a *partial tally assumption*, which we describe in this section, and which is required by definitions that follow [4]. As a result, the definitions presented in this paper are close in spirit to [5,10,11]. However, our definitions are distinct. In fact, our definitions extend to e-voting schemes with voter registration, and avoid an incompatibility issue found with [10] and outlined below. We now discuss some of the benefits and limitations of this approach and, in particular, we elaborate on the features that set BS apart from other definitions that follow this approach.

Restricted Result Functions. The balancing condition required in this style of definition restricts the class of result functions that can be captured, a criticism that does not apply to BPRIV. Some definitions [4,19,30] define the balancing condition such that the output of the result function applied to each of the two multisets is equal, i.e., $f(V_0) = f(V_1)$. It is well-known that this approach requires a *partial tally assumption* [7,19]. That is to say, where a set of votes can be written as $V = V' \cup V''$, the partial tally assumption states that $f(V) = f(V') * f(V'')$. We avoid the partial tally assumption by following the approach of [5,10,11], and require that two sets, when viewed as multisets, are equal (we additionally extend this to e-voting schemes with a registration phase). However, this approach does still restrict the class of result functions. In fact, as we discuss in Sect. 3.3, our definitions, and those in [5,10,11], do not capture result functions that allow different vote assignments that lead to the same result. Despite this, we note that common result functions, such as plurality voting, are within the scope of our definitions.

Extendibility. Unlike BPRIV, it has been shown that definitions in this category can be easily extended to the malicious setting. In particular, Bernhard and Smyth [11] and Cortier and Lallemand [19] extend this approach to the malicious ballot box setting in an intuitive way. Our definitions mbbBS and dtBS also demonstrate how this approach can be extended to the malicious ballot box and distributed tallier settings respectively.

On the other hand, extending to model e-voting schemes with a registration phase is not as well understood. Definitions in this category that model voter registration either allow static corruption of voters only [19], or allow adaptive corruption but only allow the adversary to submit a single left- and right-hand vote on behalf of each honest voter [30]. In this paper, we show that it is possible to model adaptive corruption of voters *and* allow the adversary to submit an arbitrary number of votes on behalf of each voter, capturing e-voting schemes with revoting policies. Thus, BS models an attack strategy that has not yet captured been captured by any previous definition.

Compatibility with Verifiability. Though in this paper we focus on *privacy* for e-voting, it is desirable that a ballot secrecy definition is compatible with *verifiability* [18]. In [7] it was discovered that $\mathsf{IND-SEC}$ [10], a ballot secrecy definition that relies on a balancing condition that is very similar to ours, is *not* compatible with verifiability. $\mathsf{IND-SEC}$, like BS, requires that the multisets of left- and right-hand votes submitted on behalf of honest voters are equal. However, if these two multisets are not equal, $\mathsf{IND-SEC}$ returns the result and accompanying tallying proof computed over the ballot box corresponding to the $\mathsf{IND-SEC}$ experiment where $\beta = 0$. In [7], Cortier *et al.* prove that an e-voting scheme cannot simultaneously satisfy $\mathsf{IND-SEC}$ *and* tally uniqueness, a minimal property required to ensure verifiability of an e-voting scheme, as a result of the actions performed when the multisets are not equal. We refer the reader to [7] for full details of this result. A fix to $\mathsf{IND-SEC}$ was put forth in [33] to overcome this weakness, proposing that, if the multisets are not equal, the $\mathsf{IND-SEC}$ experiment still returns the result computed over $\mathcal{BB}$ for $\beta = 0$, but not the tallying proof. However, a definition that does not return a tallying proof does not capture verifiable voting schemes. Instead, our definitions avoid the verifiability compatibility issue of both versions of $\mathsf{IND-SEC}$ [10,33] by restricting the adversary and *requiring* that the two multisets are equal, i.e., the experiment returns 0 otherwise.

5.3 Summarising Our Contributions

Game-based definitions of ballot secrecy in the honest model are well-studied. BPRIV, in particular, has received a lot of attention and is often regarded as the *de facto* definition of ballot secrecy. In contrast, the ballot secrecy definitions introduced in this paper follow the approach of [5]. Consequently, our definitions are not affected by the limitations of BPRIV, namely, the need for additional properties in order to prove security of an e-voting scheme, and the difficulties of extendibility. In fact, our definitions inherit the benefits of the Benaloh approach, that is, our definitions are intuitive, based on long-established techniques for indistinguishability experiments, and are well-suited to extensions into the malicious setting. Moreover, our definitions differ from existing definitions that also follow this approach. In particular, our definitions model e-voting schemes with a registration phase and, in comparison to existing definitions, BS captures *adaptive* voter corruption in an e-voting scheme with a registration phase, whilst also modelling revoting policies. Moreover, though we do restrict the set of result functions that can be considered, we do not require a partial tally assumption. We believe that, to model realistic attack scenarios, the way forward is ballot secrecy definitions that model corrupted election officials. Our definitions mbbBS and dtBS model such attack scenarios and provide a spring-board for future research in this direction. Finally, we comment that, in light of current restrictions on movement caused by global pandemics, and the potential that democratic processes could move on-line as a result, we believe it is an apt time to revisit existing approaches and explore new definitions of ballot secrecy.

Acknowledgement. This work is partly supported by the EPSRC and the UK government as part of the Centre for Doctoral Training in Cyber Security at Royal Holloway, University of London (EP/P009301/1)

A   Building Blocks for our Constructions

A.1   Public-Key Encryption

Definition 6. *(PKE scheme) A public key encryption scheme Π is a tuple of PPT algorithms (Π.Gen, Π.Enc, Π.Dec) such that*

Π.Gen(1^λ) On input security parameter 1^λ, algorithm Π.Gen outputs a key pair (pk_Π, sk_Π).

Π.Enc(pk_Π, m) On input public key pk_Π and message m, algorithm Π.Enc outputs a ciphertext c.

Π.Dec(sk_Π, c) On input private key sk_Π and ciphertext c, algorithm Π.Dec outputs a message m.

Definition 7 (NM-CPA). *A public key encryption scheme Π satisfies NM-CPA if, for any PPT adversary $\mathcal{A} = (\mathcal{A}_1, \mathcal{A}_2)$, there exists a negligible function negl such that*

$$\Pr\left[\mathsf{Exp}^{\mathsf{NM\text{-}CPA}}_{\Pi,\mathcal{A}}(\lambda) = 1\right] \leq \frac{1}{2} + \mathsf{negl}(\lambda)$$

where $\mathsf{Exp}^{\mathsf{NM\text{-}CPA}}_{\Pi,\mathcal{A}}(\lambda)$ is the experiment defined in Fig. 4.

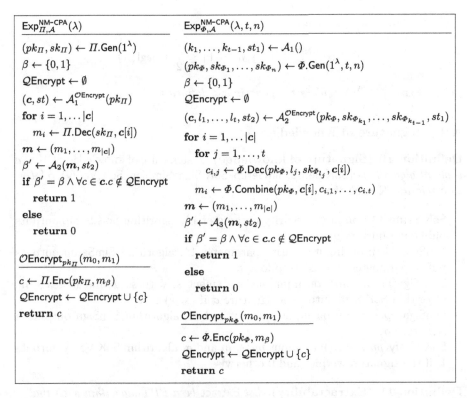

Fig. 4. The NM-CPA experiment $\mathsf{Exp}_{\Pi,\mathcal{A}}^{\mathsf{NM\text{-}CPA}}(\lambda)$ for public key encryption scheme Π and the t-NM-CPA experiment $\mathsf{Exp}_{\Phi,\mathcal{A}}^{t\text{-}\mathsf{NM\text{-}CPA}}(\lambda)$ for (t,n)-threshold public key encryption scheme Φ.

A.2   Threshold Public Key Encryption

Definition 8. *(Threshold PKE scheme) A (t,n)-threshold public key encryption scheme Φ is a tuple of PPT algorithms $(\Phi.\mathsf{Gen}, \Phi.\mathsf{Enc}, \Phi.\mathsf{Dec}, \Phi.\mathsf{Combine})$ such that*

$\Phi.\mathsf{Gen}(1^\lambda, t, n)$ On input security parameter 1^λ, threshold t and n, algorithm $\Phi.\mathsf{Gen}$ outputs a public key pk_Φ and n private keys, $sk_{\Phi_1}, \ldots, sk_{\Phi_n}$.

$\Phi.\mathsf{Enc}(pk_\Phi, m)$ On input public key pk_Φ and message m, algorithm $\Phi.\mathsf{Enc}$ outputs a ciphertext c.

$\Phi.\mathsf{Dec}(pk_\Phi, i, sk_{\Phi_i}, c)$ On input public key pk_Φ, an index $1 \leq i \leq n$, private key sk_{Φ_i} and ciphertext c, algorithm $\Phi.\mathsf{Dec}$ outputs a decryption share c_i.

$\Phi.\mathsf{Combine}(pk_\Phi, c, c_1, \ldots, c_t)$ On input public key pk_Φ, ciphertext c and t decryption shares $c_1, \ldots, c_t$, algorithm $\Phi.\mathsf{Combine}$ outputs a message m.

Definition 9 (t-NM-CPA). *A (t,n)-threshold public key encryption scheme Φ satisfies t-NM-CPA if, for any PPT adversary $\mathcal{A} = (\mathcal{A}_1, \mathcal{A}_2)$, there exists a* *negligible function* negl *such that*

$$\Pr\left[\mathsf{Exp}_{\Phi,\mathcal{A}}^{t\text{-NM-CPA}}(\lambda,t,n)=1\right] \leq \frac{1}{2} + \mathsf{negl}(\lambda)$$

where $\mathsf{Exp}_{\Phi,\mathcal{A}}^{t\text{-NM-CPA}}(\lambda,t,n)$ *is the experiment defined in Fig. 4.*

A.3   Signature of Knowledge

Definition 10 (Signature of knowledge). *A signature of knowledge* SOK *is a tuple of algorithms* (SoK.Setup, SimSetup, SoK.Sign, SimSign, SoK.Verify) *relative to a relation* $\mathcal{R}$ *such that*

– SoK.Setup(1^λ): on input security parameter 1^λ, algorithm SoK.Setup outputs public parameters *pp*.
– SimSetup(1^λ): on input security parameter 1^λ, algorithm SimSetup outputs public parameters *pp* and trapdoor τ.
– SoK.Sign(*pp, s, w, m*): on input *pp*, statement *s*, witness *w* and message *m*, algorithm SoK.Sign outputs a signature σ if $(s,w) \in \mathcal{R}$.
– SimSign(*pp, s, τ, m*): on input *pp*, *s*, τ and *m*, algorithm SimSign outputs a signature σ.
– SoK.Verify(*pp, s, m, σ*): on input *pp*, *s*, *m* and σ, algorithm SoK.Verify outputs 1, if the signature verifies and 0 otherwise.

Definition 11 (Extractability). *Let* Extract *be a PPT algorithm such that*

– Extract(*pp, τ, s, m, σ*): *on input public parameters pp, trapdoor τ, statement s, message m and signature σ, algorithm* Extract *outputs a witness w.*

Then signature of knowledge SOK *satisfies extractability if, for all PPT adversaries* $\mathcal{A}$, *there exists a negligible function* negl *such that*

$$\Pr\left[\mathsf{Exp}_{\mathsf{SOK},\mathcal{A},\mathsf{Extract}}^{\mathsf{Ext}}(\lambda)\right] \leq \mathsf{negl}(\lambda)$$

where $\mathsf{Exp}_{\mathsf{SOK},\mathcal{A},\mathsf{Extract}}^{\mathsf{Ext}}(\lambda)$ *is the experiment defined in Fig. 5.*

B   Ballot Secrecy of our Constructions

B.1   Proof of Theorem 1

Let $\mathcal{A}$ be an adversary in the experiment $\mathsf{Exp}_{\Gamma_{\mathsf{mini}},\mathcal{A}}^{\mathsf{BS}}(\lambda)$ where Γ_{mini} is the construction in Fig. 2. Assume that $\mathcal{A}$ can output a bit β' such that $\beta' = \beta$ and $\mathcal{A}$ queries $\mathcal{O}$vote and $\mathcal{O}$cast such that $V_0' = V_1'$. Then $\mathcal{A}$ succeeds in experiment $\mathsf{Exp}_{\Gamma_{\mathsf{mini}},\mathcal{A}}^{\mathsf{BS}}(\lambda)$ with probability non-negligibly greater than $\frac{1}{2}$. We note that, throughout the experiment, $\mathcal{A}$ can only gain information about β through access to the bulletin board $\mathcal{BB}$ and the election result r.

$$\mathsf{Exp}^{\mathsf{Ext}}_{\mathsf{SOK},\mathcal{A},\mathsf{Extract}}(\lambda)$$

$\mathcal{Q} \leftarrow \emptyset$

$(pp, \tau) \leftarrow \mathsf{SimSetup}(1^\lambda)$

$(s, m, \sigma) \leftarrow \mathcal{A}^{\mathcal{O}}(pp)$

$w \leftarrow \mathsf{Extract}(pp, s, m, \sigma)$

if $(s, w) \notin \mathcal{R} \wedge (s, m, \sigma) \notin \mathcal{Q} \wedge \mathsf{SoK.Verify}(pp, s, m, \sigma) = 1$

    return 1

else

    return 0

$$\mathcal{O}_{pp,\tau}(s, w, m)$$

$\sigma \leftarrow \mathsf{SimSign}(pp, s, \tau, m)$

$\mathcal{Q} \leftarrow \mathcal{Q} \cup (s, m, \sigma)$

return σ

Fig. 5. The extractability experiment $\mathsf{Exp}^{\mathsf{Ext}}_{\mathsf{SOK},\mathcal{A},\mathsf{Extract}}(\lambda)$ for signature of knowledge SOK.

Let Forge denote the event that $\mathcal{A}$ submits a valid ballot $b = (pk_{id}, c, \sigma)$ to $\mathcal{O}\mathsf{cast}$ where $(\cdot, pk_{id}, \cdot) \in \mathcal{Q}\mathsf{reg} \setminus \mathcal{Q}\mathsf{corrupt}$. We write that b is valid if $\mathsf{Valid}(b, \mathcal{BB}, pk, \mathcal{L}) = 1$ which requires, in particular, that $\mathsf{SoK.Verify}(pp, (c, pk_\Pi, pk_{id}), c, \sigma) = 1$. Moreover, let Success denote the event that experiment $\mathsf{Exp}^{\mathsf{BS}}_{\Gamma_{\mathsf{mini}}, \mathcal{A}}(\lambda)$ returns 1. Note that,

$$\Pr\left[\mathsf{Exp}^{\mathsf{BS}}_{\Gamma_{\mathsf{mini}}, \mathcal{A}}(\lambda) = 1\right] \leq \Pr[\mathsf{Success} \wedge \mathsf{Forge}] + \Pr\left[\mathsf{Success} \wedge \overline{\mathsf{Forge}}\right]$$

$$\leq \Pr[\mathsf{Forge}] + \Pr\left[\mathsf{Success} \wedge \overline{\mathsf{Forge}}\right].$$

We show that $\Pr[\mathsf{Forge}] \leq \mathsf{negl}(\lambda)$ and $\Pr\left[\mathsf{Success} \wedge \overline{\mathsf{Forge}}\right] \leq \frac{1}{2} + \mathsf{negl}(\lambda)$. The result of the Theorem then follows.

First, we show that $\Pr[\mathsf{Forge}] \leq \mathsf{negl}(\lambda)$. In fact, we show that, if $\mathcal{A}$ can submit a valid ballot to $\mathcal{O}\mathsf{corrupt}$, then $\mathcal{A}$ can be used to construct an adversary $\mathcal{B}$ in the extractability experiment $\mathsf{Exp}^{\mathsf{Ext}}_{\mathsf{SOK},\mathcal{B},\mathsf{Extract}}(\lambda)$, where $\mathcal{B}$ plays the role of the challenger in the BS experiment and $\mathcal{C}$ is the challenger in the extractability experiment. In detail, we construct adversary $\mathcal{B}$ as follows.

1. $\mathcal{B}$ obtains public parameters pp for signature of knowledge SOK from $\mathcal{C}$ and runs $(pk_\Pi, sk_\Pi) \leftarrow \Pi.\mathsf{Gen}(1^\lambda)$, and performs the setup of Γ_{mini}, providing $\mathcal{A}$ with pk. $\mathcal{B}$ additionally performs the initialisation steps of the BS experiment and selects a bit $\beta \leftarrow \{0, 1\}$.
2. $\mathcal{B}$ answers queries to $\mathcal{O}\mathsf{reg}$, $\mathcal{O}\mathsf{corrupt}$ and $\mathcal{O}\mathsf{board}$ as described in the BS experiment. Moreover, $\mathcal{B}$ computes the election result as described in algorithm Tally.

3. For queries to $\mathcal{O}\mathsf{vote}(pk_{id}, v_0, v_1)$, $\mathcal{B}$ computes $c \leftarrow \Pi.\mathsf{Enc}(pk_\Pi, m_\beta; r)$ and queries $\mathcal{O}_{pp,\tau}((c, pk_\Pi, pk_{id}), (sk_{id}, r), c)$ in the extractability experiment, receiving a signature of knowledge σ. $\mathcal{B}$ constructs ballot $b \leftarrow (pk_{id}, c, \sigma)$ and appends the ballot to $\mathcal{BB}$.

4. $\mathcal{B}$ answers queries to $\mathcal{O}\mathsf{cast}$ as described in the BS experiment. By assumption that event Forge occurs, SoK.Verify returns 1 for at least one tuple (pk_{id}, b) queried to $\mathcal{O}\mathsf{cast}$ such that $pk_{id} \in \mathcal{Q}\mathsf{reg} \setminus \mathcal{Q}\mathsf{corrupt}$. We denote this ballot as $(pk_{id}^*, c^*, \sigma^*)$. Then, $\mathcal{B}$ output $((c^*, pk_\Pi, pk_{id}^*), c^*, \sigma^*)$ in the extractability experiment.

$\mathcal{B}$ perfectly simulates the role of the challenger in the BS experiment to $\mathcal{A}$. In fact, $\mathcal{B}$ trivially simulates oracles $\mathcal{O}\mathsf{reg}$, $\mathcal{O}\mathsf{corrupt}$ and $\mathcal{O}\mathsf{board}$, and trivially computes the result of the election and returns r to $\mathcal{A}$. Moreover, when $\mathcal{A}$ queries $\mathcal{O}\mathsf{vote}$, $\mathcal{B}$ returns a ciphertext consisting of an encryption c that is identical to the encryption viewed by $\mathcal{A}$ in the BS experiment and obtains a signature of knowledge from $\mathcal{O}$ in the extractability experiment that is identical to the signature viewed by $\mathcal{A}$ in the BS experiment. Therefore, $\mathcal{B}$ perfectly simulates $\mathcal{O}\mathsf{vote}$ to $\mathcal{A}$. Furthermore, $\mathcal{B}$ perfectly simulates $\mathcal{O}\mathsf{cast}$ to $\mathcal{A}$ and, if event Forge occurs, $\mathcal{A}$ successfully creates a valid signature of knowledge without witness (sk_{id}, r), and, therefore, $\mathcal{B}$ can output this signature in the extractability experiment and succeeds. By assumption, the signature of knowledge SOK satisfies extractability, and hence, we conclude that $\Pr[\mathsf{Forge}] \leq \mathsf{negl}(\lambda)$.

We now show that $\Pr[\mathsf{Success} \wedge \overline{\mathsf{Forge}}] \leq \frac{1}{2} + \mathsf{negl}(\lambda)$. That is, we show that, if $\mathcal{A}$ succeeds in the BS experiment without event Forge occurring, we can use $\mathcal{A}$ to construct an adversary $\mathcal{B}'$ in the NM-CPA experiment $\mathsf{Exp}_{\Pi,\mathcal{B}'}^{\mathsf{NM\text{-}CPA}}(\lambda)$, where $\mathcal{B}'$ plays the role of the challenger in the BS experiment and $\mathcal{C}$ is the challenger in the NM-CPA experiment against scheme Π. In detail, we construct adversary $\mathcal{B}'$ as follows.

1. $\mathcal{B}'$ obtains a public key pk_Π for public key encryption scheme Π from $\mathcal{C}$, runs $(pp, \tau) \leftarrow \mathsf{SimSetup}(1^\lambda)$, and performs the setup of Γ_{mini}, providing $\mathcal{A}$ with pk. $\mathcal{B}'$ additionally performs the initialisation steps of the BS experiment.

2. $\mathcal{B}'$ answers queries to oracles $\mathcal{O}\mathsf{reg}$, $\mathcal{O}\mathsf{corrupt}$, $\mathcal{O}\mathsf{cast}$ and $\mathcal{O}\mathsf{board}$ as described in the BS experiment.

3. For queries $\mathcal{O}\mathsf{vote}(pk_{id}, v_0, v_1)$, $\mathcal{B}'$ queries $(m_0 = v_0, m_1 = v_1)$ to oracle $\mathcal{O}\mathsf{Encrypt}$ in the NM-CPA experiment and receives a ciphertext c of m_β. $\mathcal{B}'$ then computes $\sigma \leftarrow \mathsf{SimSign}(pp, (c, pk_\Pi, pk_{id}), \tau, c)$ and appends ballot $b = (pk_{id}, c, \sigma)$ to $\mathcal{BB}$.

4. $\mathcal{B}'$ computes the election result. Throughout, $\mathcal{B}'$ keeps track of tuples (pk_{id}, b) queried by $\mathcal{A}$ to $\mathcal{O}\mathsf{cast}$, such that the query results in a ballot that will be included in the result. We denote by B the set of all tuples of the form (pk_{id}, b). $\mathcal{B}'$ constructs a vector $\mathbf{c}$ that consists of the ciphertext element of each ballot in B and submits $\mathbf{c}$ to $\mathcal{C}$. $\mathcal{C}$ returns a vector of plaintexts $\mathbf{m}$ (i.e., the plaintext votes encoded in ballots submitted to $\mathcal{O}\mathsf{cast}$) to $\mathcal{B}'$. For each tuple $(pk_{id}, b) \in B$, $\mathcal{B}'$ replaces ballot b with the corresponding plaintext included in vector $\mathbf{m}$. $\mathcal{B}'$ then computes the result r by computing the result function $f(V_0 \cup B)$.

5. $\mathcal{B}'$ returns the bit β' output by $\mathcal{A}$.

We show that $\mathcal{B}'$ perfectly simulates the role of the challenger in the BS experiment to $\mathcal{A}$. Trivially, $\mathcal{B}'$ simulates oracles $\mathcal{O}$reg, $\mathcal{O}$corrupt, $\mathcal{O}$cast and $\mathcal{O}$board to $\mathcal{A}$. Additionally, $\mathcal{B}'$ answers queries to $\mathcal{O}$vote by obtaining a ciphertext from $\mathcal{O}$Encrypt in the NM-CPA experiment that is identical to the encryption viewed by $\mathcal{A}$ in the BS experiment and constructs a signature of knowledge that is identical to that viewed by $\mathcal{A}$. Consequently, the ballot obtained by $\mathcal{B}'$, and subsequently appended to the ballot box, is identical to the ballot computed by $\mathcal{O}$vote. Therefore, $\mathcal{B}'$ perfectly simulates $\mathcal{O}$vote. Finally, $\mathcal{B}'$ computes the result function for set V_0 (and B). By the assumption that event Forge does not occur, B cannot contain ballots meaningfully related to the votes of honest voters. Moreover, by assumption that $\mathcal{A}$ succeeds in the BS experiment, $V_0 = V_1$ and, as such, $\mathcal{B}'$ perfectly simulates algorithm Tally to $\mathcal{A}$. Moreover, we have that β' output by $\mathcal{B}'$ is equal to the bit β chosen by $\mathcal{C}$ in the NM-CPA experiment. In particular, if $\mathcal{A}$ correctly guesses β' in the BS experiment, $\mathcal{A}$ correctly determines whether $\mathcal{BB}$ contains ballots corresponding to left- or right-hand votes submitted via $\mathcal{O}$vote. As these ballots are created by calling $\mathcal{O}$Encrypt in the NM-CPA experiment where the bit β is chosen by the NM-CPA challenger, $\mathcal{B}'$ succeeds in the NM-CPA experiment. However, by assumption, Π satisfies NM-CPA security and we conclude that $\Pr\left[\text{Success} \wedge \overline{\text{Forge}}\right] \leq \frac{1}{2} + \mathsf{negl}(\lambda)$. $\qquad\square$

B.2   Proof of Theorem 2

The details of this result follow largely from the proof of Theorem 1. We let $\mathcal{A}$ be an adversary in the experiment $\mathsf{Exp}_{\Gamma_{\mathsf{mini}},\mathcal{A}}^{\mathsf{mbbBS}}(\lambda)$ where Γ_{mini} is the construction in Fig. 2. We assume that $\mathcal{A}$ succeeds in experiment $\mathsf{Exp}_{\Gamma_{\mathsf{mini}},\mathcal{A}}^{\mathsf{mbbBS}}(\lambda)$ with probability non-negligibly greater than $\frac{1}{2}$, that is, $\mathcal{A}$ outputs a bit β' such that $\beta' = \beta$ and constructs ballot box $\mathcal{BB}$ such that $V_0 = V_1$. Throughout the experiment, $\mathcal{A}$ obtains information about β through ballots output by $\mathcal{O}$vote and the election result r.

Let Forge denote the event that $\mathcal{A}$ posts a valid ballot $b = (pk_{id}, c, \sigma)$ to $\mathcal{BB}$ where $pk_{id} \in \mathcal{L} \setminus \mathsf{corr}\mathcal{L}$ and b is not the output of $\mathcal{O}$vote. We write that b is valid if $\mathsf{SoK}.\mathsf{Verify}(pp, (c, pk_\Pi, pk_{id}), \sigma, c) = 1$. Moreover, let Success denote the event that experiment $\mathsf{Exp}_{\Gamma_{\mathsf{mini}},\mathcal{A}}^{\mathsf{mbbBS}}(\lambda)$ returns 1. As before,

$$\Pr\left[\mathsf{Exp}_{\Gamma_{\mathsf{mini}},\mathcal{A}}^{\mathsf{mbbBS}}(\lambda) = 1\right] \leq \Pr[\mathsf{Forge}] + \Pr\left[\mathsf{Success} \wedge \overline{\mathsf{Forge}}\right].$$

We show that $\Pr[\mathsf{Forge}] \leq \mathsf{negl}(\lambda)$ and $\Pr\left[\mathsf{Success} \wedge \overline{\mathsf{Forge}}\right] \leq \frac{1}{2} + \mathsf{negl}(\lambda)$. The result of the Theorem then follows.

First, we show that $\Pr[\mathsf{Forge}] \leq \mathsf{negl}(\lambda)$. In fact, we show that, if $\mathcal{A}$ can post a valid ballot to $\mathcal{BB}$ for an honest voter (without calling $\mathcal{O}$vote), then $\mathcal{A}$ can be used to construct an adversary $\mathcal{B}$ in the extractability experiment $\mathsf{Exp}_{\mathsf{SOK},\mathcal{B},\mathsf{Extract}}^{\mathsf{Ext}}(\lambda)$, where $\mathcal{B}$ plays the role of the challenger in the mbbBS experiment and $\mathcal{C}$ is the challenger in the extractability experiment. The detailed construction of $\mathcal{B}$ is very similar to the adversary $\mathcal{B}$ described in the proof of Theorem 1, and we refer the reader to this proof for full details. We describe the following changes to the adversary $\mathcal{B}$:

1. In step 2, $\mathcal{B}$ does not answer queries to oracles $\mathcal{O}$reg, $\mathcal{O}$corrupt or $\mathcal{O}$board as $\mathcal{A}$ does not have access to these oracles in the mbbBS experiment.
2. In step 4, by assumption that event Forge occurs, SoK.Verify returns 1 for at least one ballot, which we denote $b^* = (pk_{id}^*, c^*, \sigma^*)$, that appears on $\mathcal{BB}$ such that $pk_{id} \in \mathcal{L} \setminus \text{corr}\mathcal{L}$ and b is not the output of $\mathcal{O}$vote. Then, $\mathcal{B}$ output $((c^*, pk_\Pi, pk_{id}^*), c^*, \sigma^*)$ in the extractability experiment.

$\mathcal{B}$ perfectly simulates the role of the challenger in the mbbBS experiment to $\mathcal{A}$. As in the proof of Theorem 1, $\mathcal{B}$ perfectly simulates $\mathcal{O}$vote to $\mathcal{A}$. Furthermore, if event Forge occurs, $\mathcal{A}$ successfully creates a valid signature without witness (sk_{id}, r), and, therefore, $\mathcal{B}$ can output this signature in the extractability experiment and succeeds. By assumption, the signature of knowledge SOK satisfies extractability, and hence, we conclude that $\Pr[\text{Forge}] \leq \text{negl}(\lambda)$.

We now show that $\Pr\left[\text{Success} \wedge \overline{\text{Forge}}\right] \leq \frac{1}{2} + \text{negl}(\lambda)$. That is, we show that, if $\mathcal{A}$ succeeds in the NM-CPA experiment without event Forge occurring, we can use $\mathcal{A}$ to construct an adversary $\mathcal{B}'$ in the NM-CPA experiment $\text{Exp}_{\Pi, \mathcal{B}'}^{\text{NM-CPA}}(\lambda)$, where $\mathcal{B}'$ plays the role of the challenger in the mbbBS experiment and $\mathcal{C}$ is the challenger in the NM-CPA experiment. Again, the detailed construction of $\mathcal{B}'$ is very similar to the adversary $\mathcal{B}'$ described in the proof of Theorem 1, and we describe the following changes to $\mathcal{B}'$:

1. Step 2 is no longer required as $\mathcal{A}$ does not have access to oracles $\mathcal{O}$reg, $\mathcal{O}$corrupt or $\mathcal{O}$board in the mbbBS experiment.
2. For queries to $\mathcal{O}$vote(pk_{id}, v_0, v_1), rather than appending ballot b to $\mathcal{BB}$, $\mathcal{B}'$ outputs b to $\mathcal{A}$.
3. To compute the election result, $\mathcal{B}'$ creates a set B that consists of tuples (pk_{id}, b) such that ballot b, submitted on behalf of voter credential pk_{id}, appears on $\mathcal{BB}$, is not an output of $\mathcal{O}$vote, and will be included in the result (i.e., is the last ballot cast for voter pk_{id}). $\mathcal{B}'$ then constructs vector c from set B and proceeds to compute the election result as described in Step 4 in the proof of Theorem 1.

$\mathcal{B}'$ perfectly simulates the role of the challenger in the mbbBS experiment to $\mathcal{A}$. In particular, the ballot output by $\mathcal{B}'$ following a query to $\mathcal{O}$vote is identical to the ballot output by $\mathcal{O}$vote because $\mathcal{B}'$ obtains the ballot by querying $\mathcal{O}$Encrypt in the NM-CPA experiment. Moreover, as in the proof of Theorem 1, $\mathcal{B}'$ perfectly simulates algorithm Tally to $\mathcal{A}$ as we assume that $V_0 = V_1$ and, as such, the results computed for $\beta = 0$ and $\beta = 1$ are identical. $\mathcal{B}'$ outputs $\beta' = \beta$ in the NM-CPA experiment. That is, if $\mathcal{A}$ outputs $\beta' = \beta$ in the mbbBS experiment, $\mathcal{A}$ correctly determines whether $\mathcal{O}$vote returns a ballot corresponding to the left- or right-hand vote. As the ballot is constructed by calling $\mathcal{O}$Encrypt, where β is chosen by the challenger $\mathcal{C}$, $\mathcal{B}'$ succeeds in the NM-CPA experiment. By assumption, Π satisfies NM-CPA security and we conclude that $\Pr\left[\text{Success} \wedge \overline{\text{Forge}}\right] \leq \frac{1}{2} + \text{negl}(\lambda)$. $\qquad \square$

B.3   Proof of Theorem 3

The details of this result follow largely from the proof of Theorem 2. We focus on the changes to the proof of Theorem 2. We let $\mathcal{A}$ be an adversary in the experiment $\mathsf{Exp}^{\mathsf{dtBS}}_{\Gamma'_{\mathsf{mini}}, \mathcal{A}}(\lambda, t, n)$ where Γ'_{mini} is the construction described in Sect. 4.2. We assume that $\mathcal{A}$ succeeds in experiment $\mathsf{Exp}^{\mathsf{dtBS}}_{\Gamma'_{\mathsf{mini}}, \mathcal{A}}(\lambda, t, n)$ with probability non-negligibly greater than $\frac{1}{2}$. We define events Forge and Success as in the proof of Theorem 2 and we show that $\Pr[\mathsf{Forge}] \leq \mathsf{negl}(\lambda)$ and $\Pr\left[\mathsf{Success} \wedge \overline{\mathsf{Forge}}\right] \leq \frac{1}{2} + \mathsf{negl}(\lambda)$. The result of the Theorem then follows.

First, we show that $\Pr[\mathsf{Forge}] \leq \mathsf{negl}(\lambda)$. This part of the proof is identical to the proof of Theorem 2, with the following exceptions. In step 1 of the description of adversary $\mathcal{B}$, $\mathcal{B}$ runs $(pk_\Phi, sk_{\Phi_1}, \ldots, sk_{\Phi_n}) \leftarrow \Phi.\mathsf{Gen}(1^\lambda, t, n)$ and provides $\mathcal{A}$ with $t - 1$ private keys of $\mathcal{A}$'s choice. Additionally, $\mathcal{B}$ computes the result using the $t - 1$ private keys given to $\mathcal{A}$ plus one other private key. As in the proof of Theorem 2, $\mathcal{B}$ perfectly simulates the role of the challenger in the dtBS experiment to $\mathcal{A}$. In particular, $\mathcal{B}$ generates the keys for Φ and provides $\mathcal{A}$ with $t - 1$ private keys as expected. This concludes the first part of the proof.

We now show that $\Pr\left[\mathsf{Success} \wedge \overline{\mathsf{Forge}}\right] \leq \frac{1}{2} + \mathsf{negl}(\lambda)$. We describe the following change to adversary $\mathcal{B}'$. In step 1, $\mathcal{B}'$ requests the $t - 1$ private keys from $\mathcal{C}$ that $\mathcal{A}$ requests, and $\mathcal{B}'$ returns the private keys provided by $\mathcal{C}$ to $\mathcal{A}$. Specific to the proof of this result, $\mathcal{B}'$ returns private keys to $\mathcal{A}$ that are identical to the private keys output to $\mathcal{A}$ in the dtBS experiment. Therefore, the second part of the proof holds.   □

References

1. Adida, B.: Helios: web-based open-audit voting. In: USENIX 2008, vol. 17, pp. 335–348 (2008)
2. Belenios voting system. https://www.belenios.org/index.html
3. Bellare, M., Desai, A., Pointcheval, D., Rogaway, P.: Relations among notions of security for public-key encryption schemes. In: Krawczyk, H. (ed.) CRYPTO 1998. LNCS, vol. 1462, pp. 26–45. Springer, Heidelberg (1998). https://doi.org/10.1007/BFb0055718
4. Benaloh, J.: Verifiable secret-ballot elections. Ph.D. thesis (1987)
5. Benaloh, J., Yung, M.: Distributing the power of a government to enhance the privacy of votes. In: PODC 1986, pp. 52–62 (1986)
6. Bernhard, D., Cortier, V., Galindo, D., Pereira, O., Warinschi, B.: A comprehensive analysis of game-based ballot privacy definitions. ePrint Report 2015/255 (2015)
7. Bernhard, D., Cortier, V., Galindo, D., Pereira, O., Warinschi, B.: SoK: a comprehensive analysis of game-based ballot privacy definitions. In: S&P 2015, pp. 499–516 (2015)
8. Bernhard, D., Cortier, V., Pereira, O., Smyth, B., Warinschi, B.: Adapting helios for provable ballot privacy. In: Atluri, V., Diaz, C. (eds.) ESORICS 2011. LNCS, vol. 6879, pp. 335–354. Springer, Heidelberg (2011). https://doi.org/10.1007/978-3-642-23822-2_19

9. Bernhard, D., Pereira, O., Warinschi, B.: How not to prove yourself: pitfalls of the Fiat-Shamir heuristic and applications to helios. In: Wang, X., Sako, K. (eds.) ASIACRYPT 2012. LNCS, vol. 7658, pp. 626–643. Springer, Heidelberg (2012). https://doi.org/10.1007/978-3-642-34961-4_38

10. Smyth, B., Bernhard, D.: Ballot secrecy and ballot independence coincide. In: Crampton, J., Jajodia, S., Mayes, K. (eds.) ESORICS 2013. LNCS, vol. 8134, pp. 463–480. Springer, Heidelberg (2013). https://doi.org/10.1007/978-3-642-40203-6_26

11. Bernhard, D., Smyth, B.: Ballot secrecy with malicious bulletin boards. ePrint Report 2014/822 (2014)

12. Chaidos, P., Cortier, V., Fuchsbauer, G., Galindo, D.: BeleniosRF: a non-interactive receipt-free electronic voting scheme. In: CCS 2016, pp. 1614–1625, New York (2016)

13. Chase, M., Lysyanskaya, A.: On signatures of knowledge. In: Dwork, C. (ed.) CRYPTO 2006. LNCS, vol. 4117, pp. 78–96. Springer, Heidelberg (2006). https://doi.org/10.1007/11818175_5

14. Civitas voting system. www.cs.cornell.edu/projects/civitas/

15. Clarkson, M.R., Chong, S., Myers, A.C.: Civitas: toward a secure voting system. In: S&P 2008, pp. 354–368. IEEE (2008)

16. Cortier, V., Dragan, C.C., Dupressoir, F., Warinschi, B.: Machine-checked proofs for electronic voting: privacy and verifiability for Belenios. In: CSF 2018, pp. 298–312 (2018)

17. Cortier, V., Galindo, D., Glondu, S., Izabachène, M.: Election verifiability for helios under weaker trust assumptions. In: Kutyłowski, M., Vaidya, J. (eds.) ESORICS 2014. LNCS, vol. 8713, pp. 327–344. Springer, Cham (2014). https://doi.org/10.1007/978-3-319-11212-1_19

18. Cortier, V., Galindo, D., Küsters, R., Müller, J., Truderung, T.: SoK: verifiability notions for e-voting protocols. In: S&P 2016, pp. 779–798 (2016)

19. Cortier, V., Lallemand, J.: Voting: you can't have privacy without individual verifiability. In: CCS 2018, pp. 53–66, New York (2018)

20. Cortier, V., Lallemand, J., Warinschi, B.: Fifty shades of ballot privacy: privacy against a malicious board. ePrint Report 2020/127 (2020)

21. Cortier, V., Smyth, B.: Attacking and fixing helios: an analysis of ballot secrecy. In: CSF 2011, pp. 297–311 (2011)

22. del Pino, R., Lyubashevsky, V., Neven, G., Seiler, G.: Practical quantum-safe voting from lattices. In: CCS 2017, pp. 1565–1581, New York (2017)

23. Delaune, S., Kremer, S., Ryan, M.: Coercion-resistance and receipt-freeness in electronic voting. In: CSFW 2006, pp. 12–42 (2006)

24. Desmedt, Y., Frankel, Y.: Threshold cryptosystems. In: Brassard, G. (ed.) CRYPTO 1989. LNCS, vol. 435, pp. 307–315. Springer, New York (1990). https://doi.org/10.1007/0-387-34805-0_28

25. i-voting. e-estonia.com/solutions/e-governance/i-voting/

26. Fouque, P.-A., Poupard, G., Stern, J.: Sharing decryption in the context of voting or lotteries. In: Frankel, Y. (ed.) FC 2000. LNCS, vol. 1962, pp. 90–104. Springer, Heidelberg (2001). https://doi.org/10.1007/3-540-45472-1_7

27. Goldwasser, S., Micali, S.: Probabilistic encryption. J. Comput. Syst. Sci. 28(2), 270–299 (1984)

28. Helios voting system. heliosvoting.org/

29. Juels, A., Catalano, D., Jakobsson, M.: Coercion-resistant electronic elections. In: Chaum, D., et al. (eds.) Towards Trustworthy Elections. LNCS, vol. 6000, pp. 37–63. Springer, Heidelberg (2010). https://doi.org/10.1007/978-3-642-12980-3_2

30. Kiayias, A., Zacharias, T., Zhang, B.: End-to-end verifiable elections in the standard model. In: Oswald, E., Fischlin, M. (eds.) EUROCRYPT 2015. LNCS, vol. 9057, pp. 468–498. Springer, Heidelberg (2015). https://doi.org/10.1007/978-3-662-46803-6_16
31. Pereira, O.: Internet voting with helios. Real-World Electronic Voting, pp. 277–308 (2016)
32. Shoup, V., Gennaro, R.: Securing threshold cryptosystems against chosen ciphertext attack. In: Nyberg, K. (ed.) EUROCRYPT 1998. LNCS, vol. 1403, pp. 1–16. Springer, Heidelberg (1998). https://doi.org/10.1007/BFb0054113
33. Smyth, B., Bernhard, D.: Ballot secrecy and ballot independence: definitions and relations. ePrint Report 2013/235 (2013)

High-Throughput Elliptic Curve Cryptography Using AVX2 Vector Instructions

Hao Cheng[✉], Johann Großschädl, Jiaqi Tian, Peter B. Rønne,
and Peter Y. A. Ryan

DCS and SnT, University of Luxembourg, 6, Avenue de la Fonte,
L-4364 Esch-sur-Alzette, Luxembourg
{hao.cheng,johann.groszschaedl,peter.roenne,peter.ryan}@uni.lu,
jiaqi.tian.002@student.uni.lu

Abstract. Single Instruction Multiple Data (SIMD) execution engines like Intel's Advanced Vector Extensions 2 (AVX2) offer a great potential to accelerate elliptic curve cryptography compared to implementations using only basic x64 instructions. All existing AVX2 implementations of scalar multiplication on e.g. Curve25519 (and alternative curves) are optimized for low latency. We argue in this paper that many real-world applications, such as server-side SSL/TLS handshake processing, would benefit more from throughput-optimized implementations than latency-optimized ones. To support this argument, we introduce a throughput-optimized AVX2 implementation of variable-base scalar multiplication on Curve25519 and fixed-base scalar multiplication on Ed25519. Both implementations perform four scalar multiplications in parallel, where each uses a 64-bit element of a 256-bit vector. The field arithmetic is based on a radix-2^{29} representation of the field elements, which makes it possible to carry out four parallel multiplications modulo a multiple of $p = 2^{255} - 19$ in just 88 cycles on a Skylake CPU. Four variable-base scalar multiplications on Curve25519 require less than 250,000 Skylake cycles, which translates to a throughput of 32,318 scalar multiplications per second at a clock frequency of 2 GHz. For comparison, the to-date best latency-optimized AVX2 implementation has a throughput of some 21,000 scalar multiplications per second on the same Skylake CPU.

Keywords: Throughput-optimized cryptography · Curve25519 · Single instruction multiple data (SIMD) · Advanced vector extension 2 (AVX2)

1 Introduction

Essentially any modern high-performance processor architecture supports vector instruction set extensions to enable parallel processing based on the Single Instruction Multiple Data (SIMD) paradigm. Typical and well-known examples of vector extensions include MMX, SSE, and AVX developed by Intel, AMD's

© Springer Nature Switzerland AG 2021
O. Dunkelman et al. (Eds.): SAC 2020, LNCS 12804, pp. 698–719, 2021.
https://doi.org/10.1007/978-3-030-81652-0_27

3DNow, and the AltiVec instruction set for the PowerPC. Besides architectures that target the personal computing and server markets, vector extensions have also been integrated into instruction sets aimed at the embedded and mobile domain, e.g. ARM NEON. Taking Intel's x86/x64 platform as a case study, the evolution of vector extensions over the past 25 years can be briefly summarized as follows. In 1997, Intel introduced the MMX extensions for the 32-bit x86 architecture, which initially supported operations on packed integers using the eight 64-bit wide registers of the Floating-Point (FP) unit. Two years later, in 1999, Intel announced SSE, the first of a series of so-called Streaming SIMD Extensions, enriching x86 by eight 128-bit registers (XMM0 to XMM7) and dozens of new instructions to perform packed integer and FP arithmetic. Starting with the Sandy Bridge microarchitecture (released in early 2011), Intel equipped its x64 processors with AVX (Advanced Vector eXtensions), which added packed FP instructions using sixteen 256-bit registers (YMM0 to YMM15). These registers are organized in two 128-bit lanes, whereby the lower lanes are shared with the corresponding 128-bit XMM registers. AVX2 appeared with Haswell in 2013 and enhanced AVX to support new integer instructions that are capable to operate on e.g. eight 32-bit elements, four 64-bit elements, or sixteen 16-bit elements in parallel. The most recent incarnation of AVX is AVX-512, which augments the execution environment of x64 by 32 registers of a length of 512 bits and various new instructions. Consequently, the bitlength of SIMD registers increased from 64 to 512 over a period of just 20 years, and one can expect further expansions in the future. For example, the recently introduced Scalable Vector Extension (SVE) of ARM supports vectors of a length of up to 2048 bits[1] [22], while the RISC-V architecture can have vectors that are even 16,384 bits long [13].

Though originally designed to accelerate audio and video processing, SIMD instruction sets like SSE and AVX turned out to be also beneficial for various kinds of cryptographic algorithms [1,21]. Using prime-field-based Elliptic Curve Cryptography (ECC) as example, an implementer can take advantage of SIMD parallelism to speed up (i) the field arithmetic by adding or multiplying several limbs of field elements in parallel, (ii) the point addition/doubling by executing e.g. two or four field operations in parallel, and (iii) a combination of both. The latency of arithmetic operations in a large prime field can be reduced with the help of SIMD instructions in a similar way as described in e.g. [6,11,12] for the RSA algorithm and other public-key schemes. All these implementations have in common that they employ the product-scanning method [14] in combination with a "reduced-radix" representation (e.g. $w = 28$ bits per limb) to perform multiple-precision multiplication in a 2-way parallel fashion, which means two $(w \times w \to 2w)$-bit multiplications are carried out simultaneously. Also the point arithmetic offers numerous possibilities for parallel execution. For example, the so-called ladder-step of the Montgomery ladder for Montgomery curves [19] can be implemented in a 2-way or 4-way parallel fashion, so that two or four field operations are carried out in parallel, as described in e.g. [9, Algorithm 1] and [15, Fig. 1] for AVX2. Scalar multiplication on twisted Edwards curves [4] can be accelerated through

---

[1] SVE registers can be between 128 and 2048 bits long, in steps of 128 bits.

parallel execution at the layer of the point arithmetic as well. For example, 2-way and 4-way parallel implementations of point addition and doubling were introduced in e.g. [5,7,10] and [8,10,16], respectively; these execute either two or four field-arithmetic operations in parallel. Finally, there are also a few implementations that combine parallelism at the field-arithmetic and point-arithmetic layer, which can be characterized as $(n \times m)$-way parallel implementations: they perform n field operations in parallel, whereby each field operation is executed in an m-way parallel fashion and, thus, uses m elements of a vector. For example, Faz-Hernández et al. developed a (2×2)-way parallel AVX2 implementation of scalar multiplication on Curve25519 and reported an execution time of 121,000 Haswell cycles (or 99,400 Skylake cycles) [10]. Hisil et al. presented very recently an AVX-512 implementation of Curve25519 that is (4×2)-way parallelized (i.e. four field operations in parallel, each of which uses two 64-bit elements) and executes in only 74,368 Skylake cycles [15].

Benchmarking results reported in the recent literature indicate that parallel implementations of Curve25519 do not scale very well when switching from one generation of AVX to the next. While AVX-512 (in theory) doubles the amount of parallelism compared to AVX2 (since it is capable to perform operations on eight 64-bit elements instead of four), the concrete reduction in execution time (i.e. latency) is much smaller, namely around 25% (74,368 vs. 99,400 Skylake cycles [15]). This immediately raises the question of how an implementer can exploit the massive parallelism of future SIMD extensions operating on vectors that may be 2048 bits long, or even longer, given the modest gain achieved in [15]. Going along with this "how" question is the "why" question, i.e. why are fast implementations of e.g. Curve25519 needed, or, put differently, what kinds of application demand a low-latency implementation of Curve25519. Unfortunately, none of the papers mentioned in the previous paragraph identifies a use case or a target application for their latency-optimized implementations. Since many security protocols nowadays support Curve25519 (e.g. TLS 1.3), one can argue that a fast implementation of Curve25519 reduces the overall handshake-latency a TLS client experiences when connecting to a server. The main issue with this reasoning is that transmitting the public keys over the Internet will likely introduce an orders-of-magnitude higher latency than the computation of the shared secret. Furthermore, given clock frequencies of 4 GHz, most users will not recognize an execution-time reduction by a few 10,000 cycles. It could now be argued that variable-base scalar multiplication is not only required on the client side, but has to be performed also by the TLS server[2]. Indeed, TLS servers of corporations like Google or Facebook may be confronted with several 10,000 TLS handshakes per second, and a faster Curve25519 implementation will help them cope with such extreme workloads. However, what

---

[2] The termination of SSL/TLS connections is often off-loaded to a so-called "reverse proxy," which transparently translates SSL/TLS sessions to normal TCP sessions for back-end servers. The cryptographic performance of such reverse proxies can be significantly improved with dedicated hardware accelerators. Jang et al. introduced *SSLShader*, a SSL/TLS reverse proxy that uses a Graphics Processing Unit (GPU) to increase the throughput of public-key cryptosystems like RSA [18].

really counts on the server side is not the latency of a single scalar multiplication, but the throughput, i.e. how many scalar multiplications can be computed in a certain interval. Given this requirement, would it not make sense to optimize software implementations of Curve25519 for maximum throughput instead of minimal latency? What throughput can a throughput-optimized implementation achieve compared to a latency-optimized implementation? Surprisingly, it seems these questions have not yet been answered in the literature[3].

In this paper we make a first step to answer these questions and introduce a throughput-optimized AVX2 implementation of variable-base scalar multiplication on Curve25519 and fixed-base scalar multiplication on Ed25519. Both implementations perform (4×1)-way parallel scalar multiplications; this means they execute four scalar multiplications simultaneously in SIMD fashion, where each can have a different scalar and, in the case of Curve25519, a different base point. The point arithmetic and also the underlying field arithmetic operations of each scalar multiplication use only a single 64-bit element of a 256-bit AVX2 vector. This "coarse-grained" form of parallelism has the advantage that it is fairly easy to implement (by simply vectorizing a reduced-radix implementation for a 32-bit processor), which simplifies the effort for formal verification of the correctness of the software. In addition, we expect this approach to scale well with increasing vector lengths; for example, migrating from AVX2 to AVX-512 should roughly double the throughput. Unlike most previous AVX2 implementations, we employ a radix-2^{29} representation of the field elements (i.e. 29 bits per limb), which turned out to be the best option for our (4×1)-way parallel scalar multiplication when we analyzed different representations, including the classical 25.5 bits-per-limb variant [2]. Our benchmarking results show that, on a Skylake processor, four scalar multiplications can be performed in less than 250,000 clock cycles. For comparison, the to-date best latency-optimized AVX2 implementation needs over 374,000 Skylake cycles to execute four variable-base scalar multiplications on Curve25519, which means our software achieves a 1.5 times higher throughput than the current leader in the low-latency domain.

2   The AVX2 Instruction Set

Intel's Advanced Vector eXtension 2 (AVX2) is an x86 instruction set extension for SIMD processing that supports packed integer operations on 256-bit wide registers. AVX2 was announced in 2011 and first integrated into the Haswell microarchitecture, which appeared in 2013. Besides the increased length of the integer instructions, AVX2 also differs from the older AVX by the instruction format (i.e. three operands instead of two). We performed our experiments on Haswell and Skylake processors since both were used as reference platforms in previous papers, e.g. [10, 20]. On both the Haswell and Skylake microarchitecture,

---

[3] A throughput-optimized implementation of variable-base scalar multiplication on a 251-bit *binary* Edwards curve was presented by Bernstein [3]. This implementation uses bitslicing for the low-level binary-field arithmetic and is able to execute 30,000 scalar multiplications per second on an Intel Core 2 Quad Q6600 CPU.

instructions (including AVX instructions) are fetched from the instruction cache and decoded into micro-operations (micro-ops) by the "front end" of the core. These micro-ops are stored in a buffer and will be assigned to available execution ports by the superscalar execution engine. The execution engine can issue micro-ops in an out-of-order fashion, i.e. the order in which the micro-ops are executed is not (necessarily) the order in which they were decoded. This is because micro-ops can leave the buffer and get issued to a suitable execution port as soon as their input-operands are available, even if there are still some older micro-ops in the buffer, which helps to improve processing efficiency. Both the Haswell and the Skylake microarchitecture have a total of eight execution ports (i.e. port 0 to port 7), whereby micro-ops of vector ALU instructions are issued to execution units through port 0, 1, and 5. Memory accesses (i.e. loads and stores) are issued through port 2, 3, 4, and 7, while port 6 handles various kinds of branches. Haswell and Skylake differ regarding the capabilities of the AVX2-related ports (i.e. port 0, 1, 5) and execution engines. Taking the AVX2 instructions VPMULUDQ, VPADDQ, and VPAND as example, these differences can be summarized as follows:

- VPMULUDQ: port 0 on Haswell; port 0 and 1 on Skylake
- VPADDQ: port 1 and 5 on Haswell; port 0, 1, and 5 on Skylake
- VPAND: port 0, 1, and 5 on Haswell; port 0, 1, and 5 on Skylake

The micro-ops of the AVX2 vector multiply instruction VPMULUDQ can be issued through two ports on a Skylake CPU, but only one port on a Haswell CPU. As a consequence, the throughput of VPMULUDQ differs for these two platforms; it is one instruction/cycle on Haswell, but two instructions/cycle on Skylake.

The operands used by the AVX2 ALU instructions have to be stored in the 256-bit YMM vector registers, whereby, depending on the concrete instruction, the two operands are interpreted as vectors consisting of e.g. four 64-bit elements or eight 32-bit elements. Depending on the microarchitecture, several (or even all) operations on the 32 or 64-bit elements are executed in parallel. Similar to other vector units, AVX2 does not support "widening" multiplication, i.e. when using VPMULUDQ to multiply vectors of four unsigned 64-bit integers, each of the four products has a length of 64 bits. This, in turn, restricts the length of the limbs of a multiple-precision integer to 32 bits, or even less (e.g. 25–30 bits) in the case of a reduced-radix representation.

3   Vectorized Prime-Field Arithmetic

This section describes our (4×1)-way parallel implementation of arithmetic in $\mathbb{F}_p$ where $p = 2^{255} - 19$. We first introduce the notion of a limb vector set and explain the rationale of its radix-2^{29} representation. Afterward, we demonstrate how limb vector sets can be used to implement (4×1)-way field operations.

3.1   Radix-2^{29} Limb Vector Set

The literature contains numerous discussions on how to represent the elements of the 255-bit prime field $\mathbb{F}_p$ used by Curve25519, whereby the bottom line was always that the choice of the number representation radix is determined by the characteristics of the target platform [10, 15, 17]. A well-known and widely-used choice is the radix-$2^{25.5}$ representation originally proposed in [2], which means a 255-bit integer consists of ten limbs; five are 25 bits long, while the other five have a length of 26 bits. More formally, a field element f is given as

$$f = f_0 + 2^{26} f_1 + 2^{51} f_2 + 2^{77} f_3 + 2^{102} f_4 + 2^{128} f_5 + 2^{153} f_6 + 2^{179} f_7 + 2^{204} f_8 + 2^{230} f_9,$$

where $0 \leq f_{2j} < 2^{26}$ and $0 \leq f_{2j+1} < 2^{25}$ for $0 \leq j \leq 4$. This representation is attractive because it allows implementers to efficiently integrate the reduction modulo $p = 2^{255} - 19$ into the multiplication due to the fact that $19f_i$ still fits in a 32-bit integer. In this way, it is possible to delay the propagation of excess bits (often called "carries") from one limb to the next-higher limb until the end of the modular multiplication, which is beneficial since these propagations are highly sequential and, thus, relatively slow on modern CPUs. For example, the (2×2)-way parallel AVX2 implementation for Curve25519 described in [9] uses a radix of $2^{25.5}$ to combine the reduction operation with the multiplication.

A number representation that enables low latency for a (2×2)-way parallel implementation is not necessarily the best choice when high throughout is the main goal. Considering our (4×1)-way strategy and the processing capabilities of the AVX2 engine of Haswell/Skylake, we opted for a radix-2^{29} representation of the field elements, which means any $f \in \mathbb{F}_p$ consists of nine 29-bit limbs:

$$f = f_0 + 2^{29} f_1 + 2^{58} f_2 + 2^{87} f_3 + 2^{116} f_4 + 2^{145} f_5 + 2^{174} f_6 + 2^{203} f_7 + 2^{232} f_8,$$

where $0 \leq f_i < 2^{29}$ for $0 \leq i \leq 8$. Our implementation performs all arithmetic operations modulo $q = 2^6 p = 64(2^{255} - 19) = 2^{261} - 1216$ instead of the prime $p = 2^{255} - 19$. A benefit of this representation is the smaller number of limbs compared to the radix-$2^{25.5}$ approach, which usually[4] implies that fewer limb-multiplications have to be carried out when multiplying two field elements. The main drawback is a higher number of excess-bit (i.e. carry) propagations since the reduction modulo q can only be done *after* the multiplication. However, we found through a number of experiments that, on both Haswell and Skylake, the advantage of fewer limbs outweighs the additional carry propagations.

The main data structure of our (4×1)-way parallel software is what we call a *limb vector set*. Given $e, f, g, h \in \mathbb{F}_p$, a limb vector set $\boldsymbol{V}$ is defined as:

$$\boldsymbol{V} = [e, f, g, h] = \left[\sum_{i=0}^{8} 2^{29i} e_i, \sum_{i=0}^{8} 2^{29i} f_i, \sum_{i=0}^{8} 2^{29i} g_i, \sum_{i=0}^{8} 2^{29i} h_i \right]$$

$$= \sum_{i=0}^{8} 2^{29i} [e_i, f_i, g_i, h_i] = \sum_{i=0}^{8} 2^{29i} \boldsymbol{v}_i \quad \text{with} \quad \boldsymbol{v}_i = [e_i, f_i, g_i, h_i]. \quad (1)$$

---

[4] A (2×2)-way parallel AVX2 implementation (i.e. an implementation executing two field operations in parallel, each using two 64-bit elements of a 256-bit vector) can not profit from a radix-2^{29} representation since the limbs are processed in pairs and the number of limb-pairs is the same as for radix $2^{25.5}$, namely five.

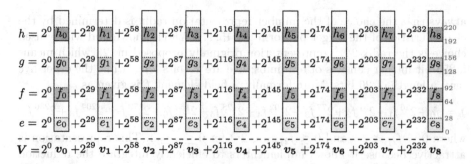

Fig. 1. Limb vector set V representing the four operands $e, f, g, h \in \mathbb{F}_p$ (there are nine limb vectors v_i, each of which contains four 29-bit limbs).

In essence, a limb vector set V consists of nine *limb vectors* v_i, each of which contains four 29-bit limbs. However, it is important to note that the four limbs in v_i come from four *different* field-elements and have the same index i, i.e. the least-significant limb vector v_0 contains the least-significant limbs of $e, f, g, h \in \mathbb{F}_p$, namely e_0, f_0, g_0, and h_0, while v_8 contains the four most-significant limbs of e, f, g, and h. In general, the number of limbs per limb vector is determined by the number of elements in a vector of the underlying SIMD engine (four in our case), whereas the number of limb vectors in a limb vector set depends on the bit-length of the prime and the representation radix. Figure 1 shows the structure of an element vector set V for AVX2, where the 29-bit limbs are in four coloured rows (depicting four field-elements), and each column represents a limb vector v_i. The exact bit position of a 29-bit limb within a 256-bit AVX2 vector is given on the right of the column of v_8; concretely, the four limbs are placed at the bit positions from $64i$ to $64i + 28$ for $0 \leq i \leq 3$. Even though the radix-2^{29} representation does not permit the integration of modular reduction into the multiplication, it provides sufficient "headroom" (namely three bits) to delay the carry propagation of certain operations like the field-addition.

Our representation of operands for high-throughput arithmetic for ECC is similar to the "bit-sliced" and "byte-sliced" representations used in symmetric cryptography (e.g. for DES or AES) to improve the throughput at the expense of latency. Thus, our approach could be referred to as "limb-slicing."

3.2   AVX2 Implementation of Field-Operations

All inputs to the field-operations described in the following are limb vector sets with limbs that are 29 long or slightly longer. As already explained before, the arithmetic operations are performed modulo $q = 64p = 2^{261} - 1216$ and not the actual prime p (except at the very end of a scalar multiplication). An operand can, therefore, be up to 261 bits long. Simplified C source code of some of the

(4×1)-way parallel field-operations can be found in Appendix A (except of the (4×1)-way field-multiplication, which is already given in this subsection).

Addition. The vectorized addition $R = A + B$ is implemented in a straight-forward way, which means nine VPADDQ instructions are executed to obtain the limb-sums $r_i = a_i + b_i$ for $0 \leq i \leq 8$. We neither propagate the carries from less-significant to more-significant limb-vectors, nor do we perform a reduction modulo q. Thus, each limb of the sum vector set R can be one bit longer than the corresponding limbs of the operands A and B.

Subtraction. Computing the subtraction in the usual way as $R = A - B$ can yield negative limbs and also negative final results; therefore, we implemented the subtraction using the equation $R = 2Q + A - B$, whereby the limb-vectors of $2Q$ have the form $2q_i$, i.e. the limbs are 30 bits long. The limbs of the final result R can be up to 31 bits long, which means they may cause an overflow in the subsequent field-operation (e.g. when the result is used as input of a field-squaring). Therefore, we implemented an alternative version of the subtraction that includes both a carry propagation to obtain 29-bit limbs and a reduction modulo q, which is performed in the usual way (taking $2^{261} \equiv 1216 \bmod q$ into account). The baseline version of the subtraction is very similar to the addition (see above) and executes nine VPADDQ and VPSUBQ instructions, respectively. On the other hand, the second version of the subtraction is much more costly due to the sequential carry propagation; thus, we use it only when necessary.

Multiplication. Multiplication is (apart from inversion) the most costly field-operation and has a significant impact on the performance of any elliptic-curve cryptosystem. Our AVX2 implementation aims at maximizing instruction-level parallelism by optimizing the port utilization, such that as many micro-ops as possible can be executed simultaneously. However, achieving optimal utilization of ports (and execution units) is not always possible due to inherent sequential dependencies, e.g. when an instruction uses the result of another instruction as operand, or when an instruction has to wait for an operand to be loaded from RAM. But a smart combination of arithmetic algorithms and implementation options can reduce these dependencies, e.g. reduced-radix product scanning is better suited for AVX2 than full-radix operand scanning. Special attention has to paid to the modular reduction and the carry propagation (i.e. conversion to 29-bit limbs) since some sequential dependencies are unavoidable in these operations. In some cases, the length of a dependency chain can be shortened with the help of additional instructions. All this makes finding a multiplication strategy that schedules the instruction sequence to fully exploit the platform's parallel processing capabilities a highly challenging task.

Taking into account the different latency and throughput properties of the relevant AVX2 instructions, we carried out experiments with a dozen variants of modular multiplication; all of them use product-scanning [14] in combination with a reduced-radix representation, but they differ in the following aspects:

```
1  #include <immintrin.h>
2  #define VADD(X,Y) _mm256_add_epi64(X,Y)   /* VPADDQ */
3  #define VMUL(X,Y) _mm256_mul_epu32(X,Y)   /* VPMULUDQ */
4  #define VAND(X,Y) _mm256_and_si256(X,Y)   /* VPAND */
5  #define VSRL(X,Y) _mm256_srli_epi64(X,Y)  /* VPSRLQ */
6  #define VBCAST(X) _mm256_set1_epi64x(X)    /* VPBROADCASTQ */
7  #define MASK29    0x1fffffff               /* mask of 29 LSBs */
8
9  void gfp_mul(__m256i *r, const __m256i *a, const __m256i *b)
10 {
11    int i, j, k; __m256i t[9], accu;
12
13    /* 1st loop of the product-scanning multiplication */
14    for (i = 0; i < 9; i++) {
15      t[i] = VBCAST(0);
16      for(j = 0, k = i; k >= 0; j++, k--)
17        t[i] = VADD(t[i], VMUL(a[j], b[k]));
18    }
19    accu = VSRL(t[8], 29);
20    t[8] = VAND(t[8], VBCAST(MASK29));
21
22    /* 2nd loop of the product-scanning multiplication */
23    for (i = 9; i < 17; i++) {
24      for (j = i-8, k = 8; j < 9; j++, k--)
25        accu = VADD(accu, VMUL(a[j], b[k]));
26      r[i-9] = VAND(accu, VBCAST(MASK29));
27      accu = VSRL(accu, 29);
28    }
29    r[8] = accu;
30
31    /* modulo reduction and conversion to 29-bit limbs */
32    accu = VBCAST(0);
33    for (i = 0; i < 9; i++) {
34      accu = VADD(accu, VMUL(r[i], VBCAST(64*19))));
35      accu = VADD(accu, t[i]);
36      r[i] = VAND(accu, VBCAST(MASK29));
37      accu = VSRL(accu, 29);
38    }
39
40    /* limbs in r[0] can finally be up to 30 bits long */
41    r[0] = VADD(r[0], VMUL(accu, VBCAST(64*19)));
42 }
```

Listing 1. Simplified C source code for (4×1)-way field-multiplication.

1. Whether the reduction modulo q is separated from or interleaved with the multiplication (and, in the latter case, how it is interleaved).
2. In which way the carry propagation is performed.
3. Whether and how intermediate values are stored in local variables.

We benchmarked all 12 variants (including one based on the radix-$2^{25.5}$ representation from [2]) on Haswell and Skylake, and found that the version shown in Listing 1 is the fastest one. This source code implements a (4×1)-way parallel field-multiplication, whereby the reduction modulo q (third loop) is performed separately after the product-scanning multiplication (first two loops). The local array t serves as storage for the intermediate results (i.e. column sums) of the first loop; these sums must not exceed 64 bits so as to prevent overflow. In the second loop, the carries are propagated to obtain the column sums in the form of 29-bit limbs (stored in array r) since this simplifies the subsequent reduction

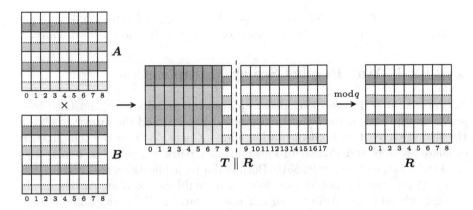

Fig. 2. (4×1)-way field-multiplication (A, B, T, and R are limb vector sets).

operation. The reduction of the product modulo q is done in the conventional way (i.e. by using $2^{261} \equiv 1216 \bmod q$) and combined with a carry propagation to get the final result in 29-bit limbs. Consequently, the modular multiplication involves two carry propagations altogether. Figure 2 illustrates our vectorized modular multiplication and shows the limb-length of all 18 column sums of the product AB; these sums are stored in the limb vector set T (lower half of the product) and R (upper half), which correspond to t and r in Listing 1.

An important aspect when choosing a number-representation radix for the product-scanning method is to ensure that the column sums will never become longer than 64 bits so as to prevent overflows. The impossibility of overflows is fairly easy to show when all limbs of the two operands are 29 bits long. In this case, a limb-product consists of 58 bits, and the maximum length of a column sum is 62 bits. The biggest column sum is t_8, which is computed as follows.

$$t_8 = a_0b_8 + a_1b_7 + a_2b_6 + a_3b_5 + a_4b_4 + a_5b_3 + a_6b_2 + a_7b_1 + a_8b_0$$

During the execution of the reduction loop (line 34 to 37 of Listing 1), the sum of t_7, the product $1216r_7$, and the carry of the previous iteration (in accu) is computed. This sum can not overflow a 64-bit element of an AVX2 vector since the carry can be at most $64 - 29 = 35$ bits long, and r_7 has a length of 29 bits (i.e. the length of $1216r_7$ is at most 40 bits). It is worth noting that overflows are not possible even when the limbs of the operands are slightly longer than 29 bits. To give a concrete example, let us assume operand A and B are the result of a field-addition and a field-subtraction, respectively. In this case, the limbs are bounded by $a_i < 2 \cdot 2^{29} \leq 2^{30}$ and $b_i < 3 \cdot 2^{29} < 2^{30.59}$, which implies $t_8 < 2^{63.76}$ (i.e. t_8 fits in a 64-bit element of an AVX2 vector). Consequently, an overflow is not possible, neither in the multiplication nor in the reduction.

Squaring. Our implementation of squaring $R = A^2 \bmod Q$ exploits the usual "shortcut" of computing limb-products of the form $a_i a_j$ with $i \neq j$ once and doubling them by a left-shift. Apart from that, we applied similar optimization strategies with respect to carry propagation and reduction as outlined above.

4   (4 × 1)-Way Parallel Scalar Multiplication

An ephemeral ECDH key exchange requires both variable-base and fixed-base scalar multiplication; the latter to generate a key pair and the former to obtain the shared secret. Our implementation adopts Curve25519 for the computation of shared secrets and Ed25519 to generate key pairs, whereby the public keys need to be mapped to Curve25519. Both scalar multiplications are vectorized in a (4 × 1)-way parallel fashion, i.e. four scalar multiplications are carried out in parallel, whereby they can use four different scalars (and also four different base points in the variable-base setting).

4.1   Variable-Base Scalar Multiplication

The Montgomery ladder [19] is the standard way to implement a variable-base scalar multiplication kP on Curve25519. For each bit of the scalar k, a so-called *ladder step* is performed, which mainly consists of a differential point addition and a point doubling; both operations can be carried out with the (projective) X and Z coordinate only (i.e. the Y coordinate is not needed). The ladder has constant run-time since each step executes a fixed instruction sequence.

Point Vector Set. A *point vector set* consists of several limb vector sets (one for each coordinate), which represents always four points, corresponding to the number of limbs in a limb vector set. For example, a point vector set in affine coordinates for the four points $A = (x_A, y_A)$, $B = (x_B, y_B)$, $C = (x_C, y_C)$, and $D = (x_D, y_D)$ can be written as

$$\mathcal{P} = [A, B, C, D] = [(x_A, y_A), (x_B, y_B), (x_C, y_C), (x_D, y_D)] =$$
$$= ([x_A, x_B, x_C, x_D], [y_A, y_B, y_C, y_D]) = (\boldsymbol{x}_{\mathcal{P}}, \boldsymbol{y}_{\mathcal{P}}).$$

That is, $\mathcal{P}$ consists of the two limb vector sets $\boldsymbol{x}_{\mathcal{P}}$ and $\boldsymbol{y}_{\mathcal{P}}$; the former contains the four x-coordinates of A, B, C, D, and the latter the four y-coordinates. In the case of projective coordinates, $\mathcal{P}$ has the form $\mathcal{P} = (\boldsymbol{X}_{\mathcal{P}}, \boldsymbol{Y}_{\mathcal{P}}, \boldsymbol{Z}_{\mathcal{P}})$.

(4 × 1)-Way Montgomery Ladder. The normal ladder-step operation gets the (projective) X and Z coordinate of two points P and Q as input, plus the affine x-coordinate x_{QP} of the difference $Q - P$ of the points (which actually is a public key). It outputs two points P' and Q' whose difference $Q' - P'$ has the same affine x-coordinate as $Q - P$. However, our (4 × 1)-way implementation of the ladder step operates on point vector sets instead of ordinary points. To simplify the explanation, we write the conventional Montgomery ladder step as $(P', Q') \leftarrow \text{LStep}(P, Q, x_{QP})$, and, analogously, the (4 × 1)-way ladder step as $(\mathcal{P}', \mathcal{Q}') \leftarrow \text{ParLStep}(\mathcal{P}, \mathcal{Q}, \boldsymbol{x}_{\mathcal{QP}})$. We suppose that the two point vector sets $\mathcal{P}$ and $\mathcal{Q}$ represent the points A, B, C, D and E, F, G, H, respectively, whereas

Op.	ParLStep	Instance 0	Instance 1	Instance 2	Instance 3
1	$T \leftarrow X_\mathcal{P} + Z_\mathcal{P}$	$s \leftarrow X_A + Z_A$	$t \leftarrow X_B + Z_B$	$u \leftarrow X_C + Z_C$	$v \leftarrow X_D + Z_D$
2	$X_\mathcal{P} \leftarrow X_\mathcal{P} - Z_\mathcal{P}$	$X_A \leftarrow X_A - Z_A$	$X_B \leftarrow X_B - Z_B$	$X_C \leftarrow X_C - Z_C$	$X_D \leftarrow X_D - Z_D$
3	$T' \leftarrow X_\mathcal{Q} + Z_\mathcal{Q}$	$s' \leftarrow X_E + Z_E$	$t' \leftarrow X_F + Z_F$	$u' \leftarrow X_G + Z_G$	$v' \leftarrow X_H + Z_H$
4	$X_\mathcal{Q} \leftarrow X_\mathcal{Q} - Z_\mathcal{Q}$	$X_E \leftarrow X_E - Z_E$	$X_F \leftarrow X_F - Z_F$	$X_G \leftarrow X_G - Z_G$	$X_H \leftarrow X_H - Z_H$
5	$Z_\mathcal{P} \leftarrow T^2$	$X_A \leftarrow s^2$	$X_B \leftarrow t^2$	$X_C \leftarrow u^2$	$X_D \leftarrow v^2$
6	$Z_\mathcal{Q} \leftarrow T' \times X_\mathcal{P}$	$Z_E \leftarrow s' \times X_A$	$Z_F \leftarrow t' \times X_B$	$Z_G \leftarrow u' \times X_C$	$Z_H \leftarrow v' \times X_D$
7	$T' \leftarrow X_\mathcal{Q} \times T$	$s' \leftarrow X_E \times s$	$t' \leftarrow X_F \times t$	$u' \leftarrow X_G \times u$	$v' \leftarrow X_H \times v$
8	$T \leftarrow X_\mathcal{P}^2$	$s \leftarrow X_A^2$	$t \leftarrow X_B^2$	$u \leftarrow X_C^2$	$v \leftarrow X_D^2$
9	$X_\mathcal{P} \leftarrow Z_\mathcal{P} \times T$	$X_A \leftarrow Z_A \times s$	$X_B \leftarrow Z_B \times t$	$X_C \leftarrow Z_C \times u$	$X_D \leftarrow Z_D \times v$
10	$T \leftarrow Z_\mathcal{P} - T$	$s \leftarrow Z_A - s$	$t \leftarrow Z_B - t$	$u \leftarrow Z_C - u$	$v \leftarrow Z_D - v$
11	$X_\mathcal{Q} \leftarrow T \times a_{24}$	$X_E \leftarrow s \times a_{24}$	$X_F \leftarrow t \times a_{24}$	$X_G \leftarrow u \times a_{24}$	$X_H \leftarrow v \times a_{24}$
12	$X_\mathcal{Q} \leftarrow X_\mathcal{Q} + Z_\mathcal{P}$	$X_E \leftarrow X_E + Z_A$	$X_F \leftarrow X_F + Z_B$	$X_G \leftarrow X_G + Z_C$	$X_H \leftarrow X_H + Z_D$
13	$Z_\mathcal{P} \leftarrow X_\mathcal{Q} \times T$	$Z_A \leftarrow X_E \times s$	$Z_B \leftarrow X_F \times t$	$Z_C \leftarrow X_G \times u$	$Z_D \leftarrow X_H \times v$
14	$T \leftarrow T' + Z_\mathcal{Q}$	$s \leftarrow s' + Z_E$	$t \leftarrow t' + Z_F$	$u \leftarrow u' + Z_G$	$v \leftarrow v' + Z_H$
15	$X_\mathcal{Q} \leftarrow T^2$	$X_E \leftarrow s^2$	$X_F \leftarrow t^2$	$X_G \leftarrow u^2$	$X_H \leftarrow v^2$
16	$T \leftarrow T' - Z_\mathcal{Q}$	$s \leftarrow s' - Z_E$	$t \leftarrow t' - Z_F$	$u \leftarrow u' - Z_G$	$v \leftarrow v' - Z_H$
17	$T' \leftarrow T^2$	$s' \leftarrow s^2$	$t' \leftarrow t^2$	$u' \leftarrow u^2$	$v' \leftarrow v^2$
18	$Z_\mathcal{Q} \leftarrow T' \times x_{\mathcal{QP}}$	$Z_E \leftarrow s' \times x_{EA}$	$Z_F \leftarrow t' \times x_{FB}$	$Z_G \leftarrow u' \times x_{GC}$	$Z_H \leftarrow v' \times x_{HD}$

Fig. 3. (4×1)-way parallel Montgomery ladder step. This implementation works "in place" and updates the input $\mathcal{P}, \mathcal{Q}$ with the output $\mathcal{P}', \mathcal{Q}'$. The subtractions at step 2 and 16 require a reduction and conversion of the result to 29-bit limbs.

the limb vector set $x_{\mathcal{QP}}$ represents the field-elements $x_{EA}, x_{FB}, x_{GC}, x_{HD}$, all of which are affine x-coordinates of differences of two points (these coordinates are, in fact, public keys). The relation between ParLStep and LStep can be formally described as follows:

$$\text{ParLStep}(\mathcal{P}, \mathcal{Q}, x_{\mathcal{QP}}) =$$
$$\text{ParLStep}([A, B, C, D], [E, F, G, H], [x_{EA}, x_{FB}, x_{GC}, x_{HD}]) =$$
$$[\text{LStep}(A, E, x_{EA}), \text{LStep}(B, F, x_{FB}), \text{LStep}(C, G, x_{GC}), \text{LStep}(D, H, x_{HD})]$$

ParLStep consists of four LStep operations, which are carried out in parallel and execute (besides other operations) five (4×1)-way field-multiplications as well as four (4×1)-way field-squarings. Figure 3 illustrates the exact sequence of field-operations for each of the four parallel LStep instances. There are two temporary limb vector sets $T = [s, t, u, v]$ and $T' = [s', t', u', v']$ involved in the computation, and also the limb vector $a_{24} = [a_{24}, a_{24}, a_{24}, a_{24}]$, which contains four times the curve constant $a_{24} = (A - 2)/4 = 121665$.

4.2   Fixed-Base Scalar Multiplication

The fixed-base scalar multiplication $R = kG$ is performed on Ed25519, which is a twisted Edwards curve that is birationally equivalent to Curve25519 [5]. The generator G has the form $(x, 4/5)$ (corresponding to the generator $G = (9, y)$ on Curve25519) and the scalar k is a 255-bit integer. This scalar can be written as $\sum_{i=0}^{63} 16^i k_i$ where $k_i \in \{-8, -7, \ldots, 6, 7\}$ and $R = kG$ computed via

$$R = \sum_{i=0}^{63} k_i \cdot 16^i G. \tag{2}$$

Since the point G is fixed, it is possible to speed up the scalar multiplication with the help of a pre-computed look-up table as demonstrated in e.g. [5]. The table contains the eight multiples $16^i G$, $2 \cdot 16^i G$, $\ldots$, $8 \cdot 16^i G$ for each of the 64 points of the form $16^i G$, which amounts to 512 points altogether. One can efficiently obtain $k_i \cdot 16^i G$ by first loading the point $|k_i| \cdot 16^i G$ from the table and then negating it when $k_i < 0$. Both the table look-up and the conditional negation can be implemented in such a way that they do not leak information about the secret scalar in a timing attack; see [5] for details. It is also possible to reduce the size of the look-up table by splitting Eq. (2) into two parts:

$$R = \sum_{i=0}^{31} k_{2i} \cdot 16^{2i} G + 16 \cdot \sum_{i=0}^{31} k_{2i+1} \cdot 16^{2i} G. \tag{3}$$

In this way, the size of the look-up table is reduced from $64 \times 8 = 512$ points to $32 \times 8 = 256$ points at the expense of four point doublings. The full cost of the fixed-base scalar multiplication according to Eq. (3) amounts to 64 table look-ups, 64 point additions, and four point doublings. Our AVX2 implementation uses this method and performs four scalar multiplications in parallel via

$$\mathcal{R} = \sum_{i=0}^{31} k_{2i} \cdot 16^{2i} \mathcal{G} + 16 \cdot \sum_{i=0}^{31} k_{2i+1} \cdot 16^{2i} \mathcal{G}, \tag{4}$$

where $\mathcal{G} = [G, G, G, G]$, i.e. each instance uses the same generator. The table in our software does not need to be a vectorized table containing four duplicate entries. Instead, we use a normal table to load the four points corresponding to nibbles of the four scalars and generate a point vector set with them.

Look-Up Table. As mentioned above, the pre-computed look-up table holds 256 points in total, all of which are multiples of the fixed generator G. We use a *full-radix* representation instead of the radix-2^{29} representation for the points in the table, i.e. the limbs of the coordinates are 32 bits long. Furthermore, we store the points in *extended affine coordinates* of the form (u, v, w) where

$$u = (x + y)/2, \quad v = (y - x)/2, \quad w = dxy,$$

and d is a parameter of the twisted Edwards curve [5]. Hence, each coordinate occupies 32 bytes in the table and a point has a size of 96 bytes. The total size of the look-up table is roughly 24 kB. Representing the pre-computed points in extended projective coordinates allows one to use the highly-efficient formulae for mixed point addition presented in [16]. In order to resist timing attacks, all

Table 1. Execution time (in cycles) of (4×1)-way field and point operations.

Domain	Operation	Faz-H. et al. [10]		This work	
		Haswell	Skylake	Haswell	Skylake
Prime field $\mathbb{F}_p$	Addition	12	12	11	11
	Basic subtraction	n/a	n/a	14	12
	Mod. subtraction	n/a	n/a	32	31
	Mod. multiplication	159	105	122	88
	Mod. squaring	114	85	87	65
Twisted Edwards curve	Point addition	1096	833	965	705
	Point doubling	n/a	n/a	830	624
	Table query	208	201	218	205
Montgomery curve	Ladder step	n/a	n/a	1118	818

eight points of each set of the form $\{16^{2i}G, 2 \cdot 16^{2i}G, \ldots, 8 \cdot 16^{2i}G\}$ need to be loaded from the table and the desired point has to obtained through arithmetic (resp. logical) operations as described in [5]. However, our (4×1)-way parallel software actually obtains four points, one for each of the four scalars. Once the four points have been extracted, a point vector set is generated, which includes a conversion of coordinates from full-radix to reduced-radix representation.

(4×1)-**Way Point Operations.** A (4×1)-way parallel scalar multiplication in the fixed-base setting consists of three kinds of operation: table query, mixed point addition, and point doubling. The latter two operate on point vector sets and execute four instances in parallel, using the AVX2 implementations of the field arithmetic. All three operations have in common that they do not perform any secret-dependent memory accesses or branches, which makes our software highly resistant against timing attacks. The C source code of the point addition and point doubling can be found in Appendix B.

5   Performance Evaluation and Comparison

We measured the execution time of our software on two 64-bit Intel processors that come with an AVX2 engine; the first is a Core i7-4710HQ Haswell clocked with a clock frequency of 2.5 GHz, and the second is a Core i5-6360U Skylake clocked at 2.0 GHz. The source codes were compiled with Clang version 10.0.0 on both processors, using optimization level O2. We disabled turbo boost and hyper-threading during the performance measurements.

Table 1 shows the latency of our (4×1)-way parallel arithmetic operations in the prime field and on the two curves, and compares them with the (4×1)-way operations reported by Faz-Hernández et al. in [10]. They implemented the modular multiplication based on a number representation radix of $2^{25.5}$ so as to minimize the carry propagation. However, according to the results given in Table 1, our 29-bits-per-limb multiplication outperforms [10] by 37 clock cycles

Table 2. Latency and throughput of our AVX2 software on a Haswell i7-4710HQ and a Skylake i5-6360U CPU (latency is the execution time of four parallel instances).

Platform	CPU Frequency	Keypair generation		Shared secret	
		Latency	Throughput	Latency	Throughput
Haswell	2.5 GHz	104,579 cycles	95,568 ops/s	329,455 cycles	30,336 ops/s
Skylake	2.0 GHz	80,249 cycles	99,363 ops/s	246,636 cycles	32,318 ops/s

on Haswell and 17 cycles on Skylake, despite the drawback of requiring more carry propagations. Also our squaring is faster than that from [10], and these gains at the field arithmetic translate to faster point arithmetic; e.g. they make point addition on Ed25519 exactly 101 cycles faster on Haswell and 135 cycles faster on Skylake. We also benchmarked point operations on Curve25519; the ladder step takes 1118 cycles on Haswell and 300 cycles less on Skylake.

Table 2 shows the performance of our (4×1)-way parallel implementation of keypair generation (i.e. fixed-base scalar multiplication on Ed25519) and the computation of shared secret keys (i.e. variable-base scalar multiplication on Curve25519). The latency figures represent the execution time of four parallel scalar multiplications; for example, computing four variable-base scalar multiplications takes 246.6 k cycles on Skylake. Thanks to a 24 kB look-up table, the generation of keypairs is (on both platforms) over three times faster than the computation of shared secrets. Regarding throughput, our software is able to compute 95 k keypairs or 30 k shared secrets on a 2.5 GHz Haswell CPU. When clocked with the same frequency, a Skylake CPU running our software reaches a 30% higher throughout than a Haswell CPU.

Table 3. Comparison of AVX2 implementations of Curve25519 on Haswell CPUs (all throughput figures are scaled to a common clock frequency of 2.5 GHz).

Ref.	Impl.	CPU	Compiler	Keypair generation		Shared secret	
				Latency [cycles]	Throughput [ops/s]	Latency [cycles]	Throughput [ops/s]
Faz-H.	(2×2)-way	i7-4770	Clang 5.0.2	43,700	57,208[†]	121,000	20,661[†]
[10]	(2×2)-way	i7-4710HQ	Clang 10.0	41,938	59,575	121,499	20,563
Nath	(4×1)-way	i7-6500U	GCC 7.3.0	100,127	24,968[†]	120,108	20,815[†]
[20]	(4×1)-way	i7-4710HQ	GCC 8.4.0	100,669	24,820	120,847	20,676
This work	(4×1)-way	i7-4710HQ	Clang 10.0	104,579* +60.4%	**95,568**	329,455* +45.7%	**30,336**

[†] Reference [10] and [20] do not give throughput results. Therefore, we list the theoretical throughput obtained by dividing the frequency of 2.5 GHz by the latency (in cycles).

* The latency of our implementation is the execution time of four parallel instances.

Table 3 compares our results with that of two other AVX2 implementations of Curve25519 on the Haswell microarchitecture. In order to reduce (as much as possible) the impact of different compilers and different CPUs, we downloaded and compiled the source code of [10] and [20] in our own experimental environment and measured the corresponding performance data. The results given in Table 3 include both our own measurements and the results which the authors reported in the respective papers. The former are easy to identify in the table because we used more recent versions of the compiler (GCC or Clang) and also a newer Haswell CPU for benchmarking. We tried to compile Nath et al.'s code with Clang version 10.0.0, but the performance was worse than that reported in [20]. A possible explanation might be that Nath et al. "tuned" their source code specifically for the capabilities of GCC, which often comes at the expense of sub-optimal performance when using a different compiler. In order to ensure a fair comparison, we compiled their source code with the most recent version of GCC, namely GCC 8.4.0 (released in March 2020). Since throughput figures depend on the clock frequency of the CPU, we "normalized" the throughputs in Table 3 for a frequency of 2.5 GHz; this makes it also easier to compare the three implementations. Besides measuring the throughput, it is, of course, also possible to obtain theoretical throughput values by simply dividing the CPU's clock frequency by the latency-cycles of a single instance. The implementation introduced in [10] performs (2×2)-way field operations, but it takes advantage of a (4×1)-way table query for fixed-base scalar multiplication. Our software outperforms [10] in terms of throughput of keypair generation by over 60%. On the other hand, the throughput of Nath et al. [20] is much lower since they do not employ a look-up table in the fixed-base scenario. As for the computation of shared secrets, our implementation achieves a 45.7% higher throughput than the currently best latency-optimized software, which is that of [20].

A comparison between our software and other implementations on the Skylake platform can be found in Table 4. Similar as before, we include both the original results reported by the authors and the latency/throughput measured by ourselves. Our implementation is able to generate almost 100,000 key pairs per second on a 2.0 GHz Skylake CPU, which exceeds the throughput achieved in [10] by roughly 71.4%. The currently fastest latency-optimized variable-base scalar multiplication was introduced by Nath et al. [20]; the execution time of their implementation became even slightly better (by 1780 cycles) when we compiled it with the latest version of GCC. Nonetheless, our implementation outperforms throughput-wise the software of Nath et al. by 52.7%. The results in Table 3 and Table 4 indicate that using a newer version of a compiler does not always yield better performance. For example, Hisil et al.'s implementation for Skylake described in [15] became actually slower when the source code was compiled with GCC 8.4.0 instead of GCC 5.4.

Table 4. Comparison of AVX2 implementations of Curve25519 on Skylake CPUs (all throughput figures are scaled to a common clock frequency of 2.0 GHz).

Ref.	Impl.	CPU	Compiler	Keypair generation		Shared secret	
				Latency	Throughput	Latency	Throughput
				[cycles]	[ops/s]	[cycles]	[ops/s]
Faz-H.	(2 × 2)-way	i7-6700K	Clang 5.0.2	34,500	57,971[‡]	99,400	20,150[‡]
[10]	(2 × 2)-way	i5-6360U	Clang 10.0	35,629	55,955	95,129	20,939
Hisil	(4 × 1)-way	i9-7900X	GCC 5.4	n/a	n/a	98,484	20,308[†]
[15]	(4 × 1)-way	i5-6360U	GCC 8.4.0	n/a	n/a	116,595	16,656
Nath	(4 × 1)-way	i7-6500U	GCC 7.3.0	84,047	23,796[†]	95,437	20,956[†]
[20]	(4 × 1)-way	i5-6360U	GCC 8.4.0	82,054	24,406	93,657	21,168
This	(4 × 1)-way	i5-6360U	Clang 10.0	80,249*	**99,363**	246,636*	**32,318**
work					+71.4%		+52.7%

[†]Reference [15] and [20] do not give throughput results. Therefore, we list the theoretical throughput obtained by dividing the frequency of 2.0 GHz by the latency (in cycles).
[‡]Reference [10] provides throughput results for a 3.6 GHz CPU. We list the theoretical throughput obtained by scaling the reported throughput with a factor of $2/3.6 = 1/1.8$ to facilitate an intuitive comparison of the results.
* The latency of our implementation is the execution time of four parallel instances.

6 Conclusions

The length of vectors supported by common vector instruction sets like Intel's AVX has increased steadily over the past ten years, and this trend is expected to continue. For example, future generations of ARM and RISC-V processors can use vectors that are more than 1000 bits long. This makes a strong case to research how such enormous parallel processing capabilities can be exploited in ECC. An analysis of existing AVX implementations of Curve25519, which are all optimized for low latency, indicates that they will most likely not be able to gain much from longer vectors and increased vector parallelism, mainly due to some inherent sequential dependencies in the point arithmetic. We proposed in this paper to use vector engines to maximize throughput rather than minimize latency. In particular, we introduced the "limb-slicing" technique for AVX2 to execute four scalar multiplications with different inputs in parallel, each using a 64-bit element of a 256-bit vector. The parallel processing of four instances of scalar multiplication that are fully independent among each other improves the utilization of the vector engine and increases throughput. Our experiments confirm that limb-sliced AVX2 implementations of fixed-base and variable-base scalar multiplication outperform their latency-optimized counterparts in terms of throughput by up to 71.4%. Furthermore, limb-slicing also scales very well across vector lengths; for example, one can expect that migrating our software from AVX2 to AVX-512 will roughly double the throughput.

We envision that limb-slicing will play a similar role in public-key cryptography as bit-slicing in symmetric cryptography and hope that this paper serves as inspiration for future research activities in high-performance cryptographic software. As part of our future work we plan to develop a limb-sliced software implementation of EdDSA signature verification using AVX-512 instructions. In addition, we will develop high-throughput software for isogeny-based ECC.

Acknowledgements. The source code of the presented software is available online at https://gitlab.uni.lu/APSIA/AVXECC under GPLv3 license. This work was supported by the European Union's Horizon 2020 research and innovation programme under grant agreement No. 779391 (FutureTPM).

A   Source Code of Vectorized Field Operations

Listing 2. Simplified C implementation of (4×1)-way vectorized field operations

```
 1  #include <immintrin.h>
 2  #define VADD(X,Y)  _mm256_add_epi64(X,Y)    /* VPADDQ */
 3  #define VSUB(X,Y)  _mm256_sub_epi64(X,Y)    /* VPSUBQ */
 4  #define VMUL(X,Y)  _mm256_mul_epu32(X,Y)    /* VPMULUDQ */
 5  #define VAND(X,Y)  _mm256_and_si256(X,Y)    /* VPAND */
 6  #define VSRL(X,Y)  _mm256_srli_epi64(X,Y)   /* VPSRLQ */
 7  #define VSLL(X,Y)  _mm256_slli_epi64(X,Y)   /* VPSLLQ */
 8  #define VBCAST(X)  _mm256_set1_epi64x(X)    /* VPBROADCASTQ */
 9  #define MASK29     0x1fffffff               /* mask of 29 LSBs */
10
11  /* field addition */
12  void gfp_add(__m256i *r, const __m256i *a, const __m256i *b)
13  {
14    for (int i = 0; i < 9; i++) r[i] = VADD(a[i], b[i]);
15  }
16
17  /* field subtraction (without a carry propagation) */
18  void gfp_sub(__m256i *r, const __m256i *a, const __m256i *b)
19  {
20    /* subtraction loop */
21    r[0] = VADD(VBCAST(2*0x1ffffb40), VSUB(a[0], b[0]));
22    for (int i = 1; i < 9; i++)
23      r[i] = VADD(VBCAST(2*0x1fffffff), VSUB(a[i], b[i]));
24  }
25
26  /* field subtraction (with a carry propagation) */
27  void gfp_sbc(__m256i *r, const __m256i *a, const __m256i *b)
28  {
29    /* subtraction loop */
30    r[0] = VADD(VBCAST(2*0x1ffffb40), VSUB(a[0], b[0]));
31    for (int i = 1; i < 9; i++)
32      r[i] = VADD(VBCAST(2*0x1fffffff), VSUB(a[i], b[i]));
33
34    /* carry propagation and conversion to 29-bit limbs*/
35    for (int i = 1; i < 9; i++) {
36      r[i] = VADD(r[i], VSRL(r[i-1], 29));
37      r[i-1] = VAND(r[i-1], VBCAST(MASK29));
38    }
39
40    /* limbs in r[0] can finally be 30 bits long */
41    r[0] = VADD(r[0], VMUL(VBCAST(64*19), VSRL(r[8], 29)));
42    r[8] = VAND(r[8], VBCAST(MASK29));
43  }
44
```

```
45  /* field squaring */
46  void gfp_sqr(__m256i *r, const __m256i *a)
47  {
48    int i, j, k; __m256i t[9], accu, temp;
49
50    /* 1st loop of the product-scanning squaring */
51    t[0] = VMUL(a[0],a[0]);
52    for (i = 1; i < 9; i++) {
53      t[i] = VBCAST(0);
54      for (j = 0, k = i; j < k; j++, k--)
55        t[i] = VADD(t[i], VMUL(a[j], a[k]));
56      t[i] = VSLL(t[i], 1);
57      if (!(i&1)) t[i] = VADD(t[i], VMUL(a[j], a[j]));
58    }
59    accu = VSRL(t[8], 29);
60    t[8] = VAND(t[8], VBCAST(MASK29));
61
62    /* 2nd loop of the product-scanning squaring */
63    for (i = 9; i < 16; i++) {
64      temp = VBCAST(0);
65      for (j = i-8, k = 8; j < k; j++, k--)
66        temp = VADD(r[i-9], VMUL(a[j], a[k]));
67      accu = VADD(accu, VSLL(temp, 1));
68      if (!(i&1)) accu = VADD(accu, VMUL(a[j], a[j]));
69      r[i-9] = VAND(accu, VBCAST(MASK29));
70      accu = VSRL(accu, 29);
71    }
72    accu = VADD(accu, VMUL(a[8], a[8]));
73    r[7] = VAND(accu, VBCAST(MASK29));
74    r[8] = VSRL(accu, 29);
75
76    /* modulo reduction and conversion to 29-bit limbs */
77    accu = VBCAST(0);
78    for (i = 0; i < 9; i++){
79      accu = VADD(accu, VMUL(r[i], VBCAST(64*19))));
80      accu = VADD(accu, t[i]);
81      r[i] = VAND(accu, VBCAST(MASK29));
82      accu = VSRL(accu, 29);
83    }
84
85    /* limbs in r[0] can finally be 30 bits long */
86    r[0] = ADD(r[0], VMUL(accu, VBCAST(64*19)));
87  }
```

B   Source Code of (4×1)-Way Point Operations

Listing 3. Simplified C implementation of (4×1)-way point operations

```
1   /**
2    * @brief Point addition.
3    *
4    * @details
5    * Unified mixed addition R = P + Q on a twisted Edwards
6    * curve with a = -1.
7    *
8    * @param R Point in extended projective coordinates
9    *          [x, y, z, e, h], e*h = t = x*y/z
10   * @param P Point in extended projective coordinates
11   *          [x, y, z, e, h], e*h = t = x*y/z
12   * @param Q Point in extended affine coordinates
13   *          [(y+x)/2, (y-x)/2, d*x*y]
14   */
```

```
15 void point_add(ExtPoint *R, ExtPoint *P, ProPoint *Q)
16 {
17   __m256i t[9];
18
19   gfp_mul(t, P->e, P->h);          /*   T = E_P × H_P    */
20   gfp_sub(R->e, P->y, P->x);       /*   E_R = Y_P - X_P  */
21   gfp_add(R->h, P->y, P->x);       /*   H_R = Y_P + X_P  */
22   gfp_mul(R->x, R->e, Q->y);       /*   X_R = E_R × Y_Q  */
23   gfp_mul(R->y, R->h, Q->x);       /*   Y_R = H_R × X_Q  */
24   gfp_sub(R->e, R->y, R->x);       /*   E_R = Y_R - X_R  */
25   gfp_add(R->h, R->y, R->x);       /*   H_R = Y_R + X_R  */
26   gfp_mul(R->x, t, Q->z);          /*   X_R = T × Z_Q    */
27   gfp_sbc(t, P->z, R->x);          /*   T = Z_P - X_R    */
28   gfp_add(R->x, P->z, R->x);       /*   X_R = Z_P + X_R  */
29   gfp_mul(R->z, t, R->x);          /*   Z_R = T × X_R    */
30   gfp_mul(R->y, R->x, R->h);       /*   Y_R = X_R × H_R  */
31   gfp_mul(R->x, R->e, t);          /*   X_R = E_R × T    */
32 }
33
34 /**
35  * @brief Point doubling.
36  *
37  * @details
38  * Doubling R = 2*P on a twisted Edwards curve with a = -1.
39  *
40  * @param R Point in extended projective coordinates
41  *          [x, y, z, e, h], e*h = t = x*y/z
42  * @param P Point in extended projective coordinates
43  *          [x, y, z, e, h], e*h = t = x*y/z
44  */
45 void point_dbl(ExtPoint *R, ExtPoint *P)
46 {
47   __m256i t[9];
48
49   gfp_sqr(R->e, P->x);             /*   E_R = X_P^2      */
50   gfp_sqr(R->h, P->y);             /*   H_R = Y_P^2      */
51   gfp_sbc(t, R->e, R->h);          /*   T = E_R - H_R    */
52   gfp_add(R->h, R->e, R->h);       /*   H_R = E_R + H_R  */
53   gfp_add(R->x, P->x, P->y);       /*   X_R = X_P + Y_P  */
54   gfp_sqr(R->e, R->x);             /*   E_R = X_R^2      */
55   gfp_sub(R->e, R->h, R->e);       /*   E_R = H_R - E_R  */
56   gfp_sqr(R->y, P->z);             /*   Y_R = Z_P^2      */
57   gfp_mul29(R->y, R->y, 2);        /*   Y_R = 2 · Y_R    */
58   gfp_add(R->y, t, R->y);          /*   Y_R = T + Y_R    */
59   gfp_mul(R->x, R->e, R->y);       /*   X_R = E_R × Y_R  */
60   gfp_mul(R->z, R->y, t);          /*   Z_R = Y_R × T    */
61   gfp_mul(R->y, t, R->h);          /*   Y_R = T × H_R    */
62 }
```

References

1. Aoki, K., Hoshino, F., Kobayashi, T., Oguro, H.: Elliptic curve arithmetic using SIMD. In: Davida, G.I., Frankel, Y. (eds.) ISC 2001. LNCS, vol. 2200, pp. 235–247. Springer, Heidelberg (2001). https://doi.org/10.1007/3-540-45439-X_16

2. Bernstein, D.J.: Curve25519: new Diffie-Hellman speed records. In: Yung, M., Dodis, Y., Kiayias, A., Malkin, T. (eds.) PKC 2006. LNCS, vol. 3958, pp. 207–228. Springer, Heidelberg (2006). https://doi.org/10.1007/11745853_14

3. Bernstein, D.J.: Batch binary Edwards. In: Halevi, S. (ed.) CRYPTO 2009. LNCS, vol. 5677, pp. 317–336. Springer, Heidelberg (2009). https://doi.org/10.1007/978-3-642-03356-8_19

4. Bernstein, D.J., Birkner, P., Joye, M., Lange, T., Peters, C.: Twisted Edwards curves. In: Vaudenay, S. (ed.) AFRICACRYPT 2008. LNCS, vol. 5023, pp. 389–405. Springer, Heidelberg (2008). https://doi.org/10.1007/978-3-540-68164-9_26

5. Bernstein, D.J., Duif, N., Lange, T., Schwabe, P., Yang, B.-Y.: High-speed high-security signatures. J. Cryptogr. Eng. **2**(2), 77–89 (2012)

6. Bos, J.W., Montgomery, P.L., Shumow, D., Zaverucha, G.M.: Montgomery multiplication using vector instructions. In: Lange, T., Lauter, K., Lisoněk, P. (eds.) SAC 2013. LNCS, vol. 8282, pp. 471–489. Springer, Heidelberg (2014). https://doi.org/10.1007/978-3-662-43414-7_24

7. Chou, T.: Sandy2x: new curve 25519 speed records. In: Dunkelman, O., Keliher, L. (eds.) SAC 2015. LNCS, vol. 9566, pp. 145–160. Springer, Cham (2016). https://doi.org/10.1007/978-3-319-31301-6_8

8. de Valence. H.: Accelerating Edwards curve arithmetic with parallel formulas. Blog post (2018). https://medium.com/@hdevalence/accelerating-edwards-curve-arithmetic-with-parallel-formulas-ac12cf5015be

9. Faz-Hernández, A., López, J.: Fast implementation of Curve25519 using AVX2. In: Lauter, K., Rodríguez-Henríquez, F. (eds.) LATINCRYPT 2015. LNCS, vol. 9230, pp. 329–345. Springer, Cham (2015). https://doi.org/10.1007/978-3-319-22174-8_18

10. Faz-Hernández, A., López, J., Dahab, R.: High-performance implementation of elliptic curve cryptography using vector instructions. ACM Trans. Math. Softw. **45**(3), 1–35 (2019)

11. Grabher, P., Großschädl, J., Page, D.: On software parallel implementation of cryptographic pairings. In Avanzi, R.M., Keliher, L., Sica, F.: (eds.) Selected Areas in Cryptography – SAC 2008, vol. 5381 of Lecture Notes in Computer Science, pp. 35–50. Springer Verlag (2009)

12. Gueron, S., Krasnov, V.: Software implementation of modular exponentiation, using advanced vector instructions architectures. In: Özbudak, F., Rodríguez-Henríquez, F. (eds.) WAIFI 2012. LNCS, vol. 7369, pp. 119–135. Springer, Heidelberg (2012). https://doi.org/10.1007/978-3-642-31662-3_9

13. Halfhill. T.R.: RISC-V vectors know no limits. Linley Newsletter (2020). https://www.linleygroup.com/newsletters/newsletter_detail.php?num=6154

14. Hankerson, D.R., Menezes, A.J., Vanstone, S.A.: Guide to Elliptic Curve Cryptography. Springer Verlag (2004). https://doi.org/10.1007/b97644

15. Hişil, H., Eğrice, B., Yassi. M.: Fast 4 way vectorized ladder for the complete set of Montgomery curves. Cryptology ePrint Archive, Report 2020/388, 2020. https://eprint.iacr.org

16. Hisil, H., Wong, K.K.-H., Carter, G., Dawson, E.: Twisted Edwards curves revisited. In: Pieprzyk, J. (ed.) ASIACRYPT 2008. LNCS, vol. 5350, pp. 326–343. Springer, Heidelberg (2008). https://doi.org/10.1007/978-3-540-89255-7_20

17. Huang, J., Liu, Z., Hu, Z., Großschädl, J.: Parallel implementation of sm2 elliptic curve cryptography on intel processors with AVX2. In: Liu, J.K., Cui, H. (eds.) ACISP 2020. LNCS, vol. 12248, pp. 204–224. Springer, Cham (2020). https://doi.org/10.1007/978-3-030-55304-3_11

18. Jang, K., Han, S., Han, S., Moon, S.B., Park, K.: SSLShader: cheap SSL acceleration with commodity processors. In: Andersen, D.G. Ratnasamy, S. (eds.) Proceedings of the 8th USENIX Symposium on Networked Systems Design and Implementation (NSDI 2011). USENIX Association (2011)

19. Montgomery, P.L.: Speeding the Pollard and elliptic curve methods of factorization. Math. Comput. **48**(177), 243–264 (1987)

20. Nath, K., Sarkar. P.: Efficient 4-way vectorizations of the Montgomery ladder. Cryptology ePrint Archive, Report 2020/378 (2020). https://eprint.iacr.org
21. Page, D., Smart, N.P.: Parallel cryptographic arithmetic using a redundant Montgomery representation. IEEE Trans. Comput. **53**(11), 1474–1482 (2004)
22. Stephens, N., et al.: The ARM scalable vector extension. IEEE Micro **37**(2), 26–39 (2017)

Author Index

Printed in the United States
by Baker & Taylor Publisher Services